Regiments and Corps of the British Empire and Commonwealth 1758 - 1993

A Critical Bibliography of their Published Histories

Compiled and published by
Roger Perkins

1994

PO Box 29 · Newton Abbot · Devon TQ12 1XU

REGIMENTS

Regiments and Corps of the British Empire and Commonwealth
1758 - 1993
A Critical Bibliography of their Published Histories

ISBN 0 9506429 3 2

British Library Cataloguing-in-Publication Data.
A catalogue record for this book is available from the British Library.

By the same author

(for Kenneth Mason, Havant, Hampshire)

GUNFIRE IN BARBARY (with Capt K J Douglas-Morris RN, 1982)

(for Picton Publishing, Chippenham, Wiltshire)

ANGELS IN BLUE JACKETS (with J W Wilson, 1983)
THE KASHMIR GATE (1983)
THE PUNJAB MAIL MURDER (1986)
OPERATION PARAQUAT - THE BATTLE FOR SOUTH GEORGIA 1982 (1986)
THE AMRITSAR LEGACY (1989)

(privately)

REGIMENTS OF THE EMPIRE - A BIBLIOGRAPHY (1989)
PATHFINDER PILOT (1992)

Typeset by the compiler and published privately.
Printed on Fineblade 115 gsm paper manufactured by Townsend Hook Ltd in compliance with American National Standard code Z 39.48 (Permanence of Paper for Publications and Documents in Libraries and Archives).

Printed and bound by Antony Rowe Ltd, Chippenham, Wiltshire, UK, in compliance with British Standards Institute code 5750 (Quality Control, accreditation FM 22361).

CONTENTS

Note:

In those instances where one or more books describe the services of a particular unit during a specific overseas campaign, and if their narratives deal exclusively with those services, they may be recorded in this bibliography under the heading of the country where the campaign was fought and not under the unit's own national heading. All such entries are cross-referenced in the Indexes.

New owners of REGIMENTS are advised to familiarise themselves at an early stage with the Contents pages and with the Indexes (pages 743 and 783 in particular).

INDEXES
of Specialist Subjects

APPENDIXES

KEY TO COUNTRIES AND TERRITORIES

With Dates of British Responsibility or Significant Influence and with Post-independence Changes of Title

COMPILER'S INTRODUCTION

In the mid-1970s, under the tutelage of my old friend Max Powling, I began to build a collection of regimental history books. The intention was to assemble a bank of reference sources which would assist me with my two hobby activities at that period - writing military history and collecting medals.

It soon became apparent that some of the books which I was beginning to acquire were not simply authoritative sources of information. They were also very fine examples of the traditional skills of the printer, the illustrator, and the binder. They were pleasing objects to handle and to possess. Each was a mirror of the regiment's status and pride in itself, a permanent memorial to generations of old soldiers who have long since faded away. The books carried an aura of their own.

Another early discovery was that I had embarked upon a journey for which there was no map and few signposts. Two pioneer bibliographers - Arthur White and Charles Dornbusch - had each in their own excellent styles shown the way forward for people like myself, but their work was by then out of date and left many of my questions unanswered.

In 1986, with no realistic appreciation of the size of the task, I resolved to compile a bibliography of my own. It would be devoted not to the regiments of the British Army - which were already catalogued in one way or another - but to the largely unrecorded forces of the British Empire and Commonwealth. Further, if the job was worth doing at all, it was worth doing as well as could be. The decision was made, therefore, to break with the usual conventions. Frustrated by catalogues which listed little more than titles, sub-titles, authors, and dates of publication, I wanted to incorporate in the entry for each book a precise description of its technical features and a commentary regarding its narrative content. In short, I hoped to produce a bibliography of the type which I - as a collector and researcher - would have found useful if one had existed.

Such grand ideas could be put into practice only with a great deal of assistance. It was clear that this particular mountain could never be climbed by an individual acting alone. The project would need to be a world-wide effort, with each member of the team contributing information based upon his or her own specialist knowledge and local resources. One of the earliest tasks, therefore, was to make contact with fellow enthusiasts in other countries and to invite their support.

Events soon gathered pace and, by 1989, sufficient material had been assembled to justify the publication of a first edition. I was acutely aware that it would have a great number of shortcomings. I had failed, for example, to promote the project adequately in Canada and Australia. A few sympathetic correspondents in those two countries had done their best to help me but, in practical terms, I had reached a dead end.

Guided by the journalistic principle of 'publish and be damned', I went ahead with REGIMENTS OF THE EMPIRE - A BIBLIOGRAPHY OF THEIR PUBLISHED HISTORIES. To my surprise, it was well received, favourably reviewed, and sold briskly. With the benefit of hindsight, its modest success was probably due more to the fact that it was an innovative work, with no competitor in the market place, than to its merits as a research tool. Reviewers were willing to forgive the faults on the basis that, as a first attempt, it might have been a great deal worse.

Although the initial objective had been to meet the needs of people with my own special interests, it emerged that the book was proving useful to a much wider range of researchers. Many copies were purchased, for example, by genealogists, and by historians who were as interested in the social and political aspects of the Empire as in its purely military ethos. Similarly, professional book dealers and librarians found that they could save time and effort by using the book as a day-to-day working source of reference.

It was the positive response to the first edition which confirmed the need for a bibliography such as this. Much of the correspondence which it generated came from people who had not been involved in its preparation but who, having now discovered its existence and purpose, were keen to be involved in the compilation of a second and much expanded edition. Work began almost immediately on the task of eradicating the previous errors and omissions. There was an obvious need to improve the Canadian, Australian and African sections, but the entire project required a major restructuring. I had mistakenly ignored the value of an 'Index of Authors', and had given insufficient heed to the advantages of listing the regiments and Corps in their correct orders of precendence. This new edition would be the final edition, so it was vital that it should be as accurate and comprehensive as possible in the circumstances of such a large undertaking. It would need to be more thoroughly indexed and cross-referenced, and some sort of chronological framework was required to place the entries in their broader historical context. The new book would benefit also from a more explanatory and concise title and sub-title. In short, and although the objectives upon which it is founded are unaltered, this second version is in all other respects a radically different book.

The new REGIMENTS is the result of the post-1989 impetus and of the unbounded support which I have been privileged to enjoy. Nearly two hundred individuals have contributed in one way or another. Some of them are named on pages 27 to 31. All those who compiled at least one full report are noted on pages 31 to 33.

Of those involved, there are several without whose detective skills and persistence this book would never have seen the light of day. Their initials appear at the foot of a great many of the entries - testimony to the time and effort which they invested. A major contributor to the first edition, Lieut Col Patric Emerson ('PJE') has continued to be a tower of strength during the past four years of work on the second edition. Lieut Col Maxwell Macfarlane ('AMM') has always responded to calls for assistance since the project was conceived in 1986. The same is true of Howard Chamberlain ('HEC'), the project's main gatherer of information in New Zealand.

Amongst the many new (post-1989) contributors, five in particular command not only my own gratitude but also that of everyone who, for many years to come, will be consulting the fruits of their investigations. They are Michael D'Arcy, of Canberra, Australia ('MCND'A', noted at the foot of more than three hundred entries), John Devereau, of Moncton, New Brunswick ('JRD', who provided so much of the Canadian material), Gordon Bickley, of Northcliff, South Africa ('GTB', who has greatly expanded the earlier work done by Bruce Cazell), Henry 'Bud' Shaw, of Alexandria, Virginia ('HIS', who almost single-handedly created the new American Loyalist section), and John 'Ham' Hamilton ('JALH', who, in the space of less than a year, completely transformed the quality and quantity of entries for the continent of Africa).

A key stage in the production of this book has been the painstaking process of double-checking the factual material and proof-reading the compiler's often errant typing. This task has been shared by several members of the team - some of whom are named above, others not - Rick Haller, of Cupertino, California, Col Denis Wood, of the Gurkha Museum Trust, FM Sir John Chapple, Governor of Gibraltar, Richard Humble, of Newton Abbot, Devon, and Cliff Parrett, of La Celle St Cloud, France. Cliff's prodigious knowledge of the Indian Army and its forebears has been of the greatest value.

Several other contributors kindly agreed to assist in various ways during the final stages of compilation. Amongst those not listed elsewhere were David Gray and The Right Revd Michael Mann (private collectors), Tom Ofkansky, Tim Parsons and Rick Meixsel (American post-graduate researchers), David Strong and Harry Kerry (both formerly of Gale & Polden Ltd), Bill Neale (formerly Senior Archivist to the governments of Rhodesia and then Zimbabwe), John Burridge (publisher, of Swanbourne, Western Australia), Geraldene Kenny (of the British Library), Ian Baxter (of the Oriental and India Office Collections, British Library), Nigel Roberts (of Haslemere, Surrey), Brig Michael Biggs (formerly Chief of Staff, East Africa Command), Col Bruce Gilchrist (of the Canadian High Commission, London), and Sir Anthony Parsons (formerly British Ambassador to the United Nations).

Several members of the antiquarian and second-hand book trade were generous with their time and expertise - Gerald Rilling, Bryan Maggs, Nicola Hemingway, and Jack St Aubyn in particular.

Thanks are due also to the Curators and Librarians, and their staffs, of the seventy-eight museums and libraries which have been consulted by members of the team in various parts of the world. The majority are not known to me personally but, referring to those of whom I do have direct knowledge, I wish to record the assistance rendered by Julian Ahearne (Devon County Library Service), Terry Barringer (Royal Commonwealth Society Collection, Cambridge University Library), Mrs J Blacklaw (Ministry of Defence Library, London), Peter Boyden (National Army Museum, London), Elizabeth Drakoulis (Australian War Memorial, Canberra), Chris Dawkins (Australian Defence Force Academy, Canberra), Andrew Orgill (Central Library, Royal Military Academy, Sandhurst), Capt Mark Reid (Canadian War Museum, Ottawa), Shamus Wade (Commonwealth Forces History Trust, London), and Tim Ward (Prince Consort's Library, Aldershot).

I must express my appreciation also to Mike Dando and his colleagues at Antony Rowe Ltd, of Chippenham, who have worked hard to ensure that REGIMENTS is printed and bound in such a way that it will withstand heavy usage over many years.

With such a large number of organisations and individuals having contributed to the whole, it is not practicable to name them all. They know who they are, and I thank them. At the end of the day, however, the name which appears on the title page is mine, and I accept full responsibility for any errors of commission or omission which may have fallen through the safety net.

The REGIMENTS reporting team has striven hard to produce a working reference tool which will assist a great number of people in their professions and in the pursuit of their studies. It is my personal view that we have come very close to meeting our original high ambitions. At the same time, given the complexity and scale of the subject matter, it is entirely possible that mistakes have been made. If this proves to be the case, I would be glad to be advised of them. I have no intention of embarking upon a third edition. Apart from any other consideration, it seems most improbable that a third edition will ever be justified (for the reasons discussed in the section headed 'The Regimental History and its Evolution'). However, if the book is well received, it may be appropriate to arrange for it to be reprinted. It would be a simple matter, at that time, to make whatever textual corrections may be found necessary.

The process of drawing the project to an end has not been easy. It began several months before the typescript was delivered to the printer. During that time, a number of new books of the type qualifying for inclusion appeared on the market for the first time (especially in Australia). Most of these titles were noticed and included before the door was finally closed, but not all of them. This will explain why one or two books published in 1993 or early 1994 are not recorded here. In the circumstances, their exclusion was unavoidable and implies no criticism of their worth. As in all things, it is necessary at a certain point to 'draw the line'.

In a broader sense, I have felt obliged to 'draw the line' on many titles which some users of this bibliography might have wished to see included. More than two thousand books are recorded in the following pages, and virtually all of them are regimental or Corps histories, formally published and available in conventional permanent bindings. They are all accessible - some a great deal more easily than others - to the diligent researcher or collector who wishes to consult them. A small number of general reference books and campaign histories have been included in order to set the scene for the unit histories, or for other reasons which are apparent in the observations with which each entry is accompanied. However, I have in broad terms followed a policy of excluding all items of ephemera, personal memoirs, generalised war stories, books in which fiction and fact are blended into a single narrative, and any other publication which does not satisfy two fundamental criteria - is this the history of a specific formation or unit during a specified period of time, and is it assessed to be authoritative and reliable? It has been necessary - for reasons of space and therefore cost - regretfully to exclude many otherwise excellent items which do not fulfil those parameters.

Finally, I must say something about the military chronologies which precede each geographical section. They have been compiled with the intention of setting the bibliographic entries into a broad historical context. As an example, it seems to me that a report on the history of the Iraq Levies is likely to make more sense if there is already in the reader's mind a general appreciation of events in the Middle East as a whole. This attempt at 'instant history' is fraught with difficulty because it involves a simplification, to basic skeletal form, of matters which were often highly complex and which, to the historian, are open to more than one explanation. Considerations of space have precluded any possibility of descending into detail. However, on the basis that 'something is better than nothing', I hope that these chronologies will prove helpful.

The amount of space given to each chronology is in inverse proportion to the number of related books. For any country which is already well recorded in its bibliography, such as Canada or Australia, the chronology has been kept very brief indeed. For other regions, such as East Africa or the Middle East, which have only limited bibliographies, the chronologies are more detailed (particularly in respect of those periods or events which are otherwise barely known except to a limited number of experts). In other words, they are intended to illuminate the grey areas, to fill the gaps in the published record.

I hope that future users of REGIMENTS will derive the same interest from its pages as I have in compiling them. They may feel, as I do, that the book has evolved into something more than a bibliography. It has become, in effect, a history of the Empire itself, and an epitaph to the men and women who served it and its diverse peoples over a period of two hundred years.

Roger Perkins

Newton Abbot
Devon

USER'S MANUAL

It will assist users of this bibliography if they know how it has been compiled. As a first step, they should familiarise themselves with the 'Glossary' and the 'List of Abbreviations'. Similarly, they should study the layout of the various indexes. The book is intended to be 'user friendly', hence the indexes are heavily cross-referenced so that every researcher, having his or her own special areas of interest, should be able to find quickly the subject matter which interests them.

A major dilemma has been that of deciding how best to arrange the sequence of the bibliographic pages. One solution would be to list the countries in their alphabetical order, but this would create many anomalies. Two or more countries having a close geographical or historical affinity would become widely separated in different parts of the book. Another solution would be to distinguish between the size and status of the Commonwealth countries, listing first the Dominions and then concluding with what were once the small mandated territories and Protectorates. This solution would be unjust, and would create even more anomalies.

The route chosen, for no better reason than that it pleases the compiler, is to cover the globe on a broad west-to-east sweep. It starts with the countries of the South Atlantic and Latin America, proceeds north through the (pre-1783) American Colonies to Canada, then across the North Atlantic to Europe, down to the Middle East and the continent of Africa, then eastwards to India, the Far East and the Pacific Ocean, and finally to Australia and New Zealand. The countries which comprise the larger regions are alphabetically indexed, but their individual bibliographic sections are placed in conjunction with those with which they share a common geographic border.

Each bibliographic entry follows a standard pattern of compilation. The details are presented in three main parts - the technical specification, the narrative description (observations), and the coded information regarding sources and value. Thus:

1. Each entry commences with the book's main title, and this is shown in bold upper case lettering. In those instances where the wording on the dust-jacket, spine, or outer cover does not match that shown on the title page, it is normally the latter which is quoted in this bibliography.

2. The next line, shown in bold lower case lettering, is the book's sub-title. As with (1) above, the wording on the title page normally takes precedence.

3. The name of the author is shown as printed in the book, with explanatory notes if necessary. Military ranks, honours and decorations are shown as appropriate, but not civilian or technical qualifications. In most cases, no distinction has been made between 'authors', 'editors', 'compilers', or 'committee members'.

4. Whenever possible, details are given regarding the printer and publisher (for the reasons discussed later in these pages).

5. Unless otherwise stated, all books are casebound (hardback) in cloth (or pseudo-cloth) covered boards, and are of conventional assembly.

6. The format (measurements) of any book can be described in various ways. The traditional nomenclatures are 'folio', 'quarto', 'royal octavo', 'octavo', and 'sextodecimo'. These terms apply to the number of times an original sheet of paper was folded before being bound into the finished book. Such terms are imprecise because the dimensions of the sheet, and the way in which it was later trimmed, can vary considerably. The compiler has opted for the unit of measurement in use at the time when most of these books were printed - the inch - with the height

shown first, and then the width. The modern practice of showing only the height - expressed in centimetres - has been avoided because it makes no allowance for the fact that some books are 'landscape' (wider than they are high). As a general rule, it will be seen that most of the books recorded in REGIMENTS have one of the following approximate formats - 12.5 x 8.5 inches (quarto), 9.5 x 6.0 inches (royal octavo), 8.5 x 6.0 (octavo), or 5.5 x 4.0 (sextodecimo).

7. To the possible disappointment of the true bibliophile, no reference has been made to the finer aspects of the book-designer's art - the colour of headbands, the presence of marker ribands, the method by which illustrations were prepared and printed, the colour and pattern of end-papers, and so forth. Such matters are without doubt of interest, but to have called for such information would have placed an even greater burden upon the members of the reporting team, and it would have occupied a great deal of (costly) page space.

8. The number of pages in each book is shown in the conventional way. Preliminary pages are indicated in lower case Roman numerals, the narrative and other pages in Arabic numerals. In a few instances, there is a third run of numerals, these being allocated to the appendixes, the Index, or to commercial advertisements.

9. In most cases, the precise number of photographs and maps has been stated with the aim of not only describing the book's features but also assisting a potential purchaser to check if anything is missing.

10. As far as practicable, all appendixes have been described in detail. Nominal rolls of personnel who served, lists of casualties, the recipients of honours and awards, and so forth, are of particular interest to a wide range of researchers.

11. The narrative observations in each entry are intended to tell anyone who has never seen a particular book what it is that he or she is likely to find when eventually a copy does come their way. To a degree, these critiques reflect the judgement of the individual team members who compiled the original reports. It is hoped that they will prove to be objective and helpful.

12. At the foot of each entry there is a symbol (R/-) which indicates rarity, and another (V/-) which indicates value as a research source. Both are on a scale of one to five. An excessively rare publication, containing little useful information, will be graded R/5 V/1. Conversely, a first-class reference work, published in recent years and still easily obtainable, will be graded R/1 V/5. The V/5 rating has not been given to any book which does not contain an Index. These assessments are highly subjective. A book easily found in Canada might be almost unknown in Australia, for example. Similarly, a book which might please one reader might disappoint another. However, the ratings should prove useful as a rough and ready guide.

13. The concluding symbols indicate the known location(s) of a copy of the book in question, and the name of the individual(s) who contributed the original report.

Users of REGIMENTS may be interested to know what facts and assessments were requested on the forms distributed to members of the reporting team during the survey stage of the project. The questions are not exhaustive, but the answers do permit the compilation of a clear 'word picture' of each book examined and recorded. The same procedure may be useful to users wishing to compile records of their own.

Main title (in full, as shown on the title pages)

Sub-title (or title page preamble)

Name of author (with rank, and post-nominals, as appropriate)

Name of printing house (if shown)

Name of publisher (with town or city where located)

Date of publication (as shown, or deduced if not)

Type of binding (casebound, stiff card, soft card, etc)

Colour(s) of the binding (with note of any decorative motif)

Colour(s) of lettering (on the exterior)

Dimensions of the casing (height, then width, in inches)

Number of preliminary and main narrative pages (for example, xv/231)

Frontispiece (stating whether one is present or not)

Number of monochrome photographs (excluding the Frontispiece)

Number of coloured illustrations (excluding the Frontispiece)

Number and type of other illustrations (sketches, cartoons, etc)

Number and types of map or plan (printed directly onto the text pages unless otherwise stated)

Glossary (applied generically to glossaries and lists of abbreviations)

Bibliography (or author's list of sources)

Index, indexes (with details as appropriate if more than one)

Appendixes (with full explanations)

Descriptive observations or critique (with details, especially dates)

Assessment of rarity (from 'easily found' to 'extremely rare')

Assessment of value in research or reference terms (from 'very limited' to 'prime source')

Location (library where a copy has been seen or is known to be held)

Contributor (name of person who provided the details)

Users of this bibliography may wish to know also that, as far as practicable, the book entries have been arranged in a sequence which generally conforms with the Order of Precedence (or Seniority) of the main arms and Corps as designated within the British Army. The principal section headings are:

General reference sources and campaign histories

Divisional and Brigade histories

Mounted & mechanised (or 'Cavalry' in the case of India)

Artillery

Engineers

Signals

Infantry (and Machine Gun Corps)

Special and Irregular forces

Chaplains

Service Corps (Transport)

Medical services

Ordnance

Electrical & Mechanical Engineers

Military Police

Pay Corps

Veterinary Service

Education Corps

Home defence units

Women's services

Police forces

The military elements within the above listing are not necessarily the same as those found in every Commonwealth army. Indeed, South Africa's system is uniquely different (for reasons explained in that section of this bibliography). Further, since the end of WWII, there has been a continuous process of amalgamating or disbanding the supporting services or Corps. Many of the traditional titles have disappeared, some being replaced by entirely new titles which reflect the introduction of new technologies into the military infrastructure. In broad terms, however, the sequence adopted for this book provides continuity and consistency of cataloguing.

NOTES ON BOOK PRESERVATION

In recent years, prices paid for out-of-print regimental histories have risen strongly. With increasing demand, and a finite available stock, the upward trend is likely to continue. For financial and academic reasons in equal measure, it is important that surviving examples of the genre should be treated with respect and carefully preserved for the benefit of future generations.

A book is more than a source of information - it is a complex physical structure. It incorporates several degradable materials in varying combination. Most commonly, these are leather, cloth, cardboard, twine, glue, paper, ink, and colouring agents. When bound into a book and brought into immediate contact, the materials may react chemically with each other. Adding then 'the human element' of careless handling, hard usage, accidental fire and flood, it is evident that a high rate of attrition will occur unless thought is given to minimising the risks.

The recommended environmental parameters for the storage and exhibition of all archival documents - including books - were published by the British Standards Institute in 1989 (BS 5454). They are practical and not excessively complicated. Any owner of a valuable collection who intends to install an air-conditioning system, or who already has such a system, is recommended to consult a copy of BS 5454 to ensure that the levels of humidity, temperature and air flow which it generates are within the guidelines.

For collectors who do not have an artificially controlled environment for their books, certain basic rules can still be observed. The air temperature within the library or book storage area should be constant within the range 13 to 18 degrees Celsius. Outside that range, it is better that the temperature should be too low rather than too high. The air should be able to circulate freely and, ideally, points of ingress should be filtered. The relative humidity should be within the range 50.0% to 65.0%. This may be difficult to achieve in some climates and at certain times of the year. A simple domestic humidifier, or dehumidifier, may provide some degree of control. During a northern hemisphere winter, in any building equipped with central heating, even a dish of water placed on top of each radiator will, by evaporation, prevent the air from becoming excessively dry. A maximum-minimum thermometer and a humidity gauge are a sound and inexpensive investment.

Direct or bright sunlight is the cause of much damage. Apart from creating heat, the sun's ultra-violet rays will cause 'browning' on the outer edges of the text pages and will cause the colour of the casing to fade. It is better to have too little light, natural and artificial, than too much. Windows should be fitted with blinds or curtains, and ultra-violet filters fitted to all windows and flourescent lighting tubes.

Good shelving is important. It should be designed to accomodate the size and weight of books stacked within it so that they are fully supported, with no strain on the casing or binding. Large format books should be stacked flat rather than vertically. No books, of any size, should be packed so tightly that they are damaged when removed, or so loosely that they rest at an angle. If the shelving is made of veneered wood, it must be cleaned and brightened only with acid-free polish. If metal shelving is used, ensure that there are no protruding bolts or screws, and no rust. Good housekeeping (regular cleaning and dusting) is essential.

With books of high value, or those which are in frequent use, it is advisable to cover the outside and the top edge with a simple wrap-around cover. This can be cut to size from any piece of strong paper, but it must be acid-free (ph negative or very nearly so). Alternatively, archival boxes can be purchased from specialist suppliers at modest cost. Apart from protecting the book, a wrapper or box can be marked with the book's catalogue or reference number, thus avoiding the need to deface the spine with an adhesive label or ink. Wrappers and boxes are also an insurance against the minor disasters which occasionally can happen to even the most careful owner (spilled drinks, for example).

If the run of shelving is not sufficient to accomodate all the volumes in the collection, and if they must be stored in boxes, it is important to plan the operation with care. Purpose made archival packaging materials can be purchased from specialist firms, or ordinary cast-off cardboard boxes can be used. With the latter, it is important to reinforce the lower flaps with strong adhesive tape to withstand the weight. Very large boxes should not be used. When full of books, and therefore heavy, they tend to be dropped hard when being moved around.

Some collectors are obliged to store their boxes in places which are particularly hostile to books. If damp is the greatest threat, it may be prudent - prior to filling the boxes - to line them with an opened plastic bin liner. When the box is full, draw the neck of the liner together and tie it with cord so that it is air-tight. This will prevent the ingress of water or humidity. Before sealing, a pack of dessicant gel crystals (of the type supplied by camera manufacturers) can be placed within the liner as an added precaution. It is, of course, vital that the books should not be damp before they are packed in this way. The boxes should then be stored on strong racking, individually and not on top of each other. Each box should be labelled or marked in such a way that any required book can be located easily and retrieved.

Most collectors and librarians do observe commonsense rules, at least as far as they are able, but the degree of damage suffered by the average regimental history over a period of years is usually considerable. Condition is often a large part of the equation when a book is being valued or offered for sale. It is advisable, therefore, that the prospective buyer should follow a set procedure when examining any book which he or she is planning to purchase. The following tips may prove helpful.

The first step is to resist the temptation to open the book and immediately begin looking at or reading the text. The narrative is a permanent feature which can be studied at leisure at a later stage. The primary concern must be the condition of the individual copy. Examining it should be a progressive procedure, starting with the exterior. Assuming that it has a conventional leather or cloth casing, check for the following faults:

1. digs, gouges, or depressions in the surface of the boards and spine (resulting from contact with sharp objects, or from pressure caused by string when the book was once tied in a bundle or postal parcel).

2. 'bumping' of the corners of the boards (caused by the book having fallen onto a hard surface, or being inadequately packed while in postal transit).

3. 'bumping' and/or tearing of the top of the spine - the head cap - and of the foot of the spine - the toe or tail cap (caused by careless handling).

4. weakness in the front and rear hinges (reflecting poor original manufacture, repeated usage, or rough handling).

5. 'sunning' of the colours (fading caused by prolonged exposure to light, both natural and artificial).

6. damage of any kind to the lettering on the spine and boards (from any cause).

7. general wear and tear, stains, 'dulling' caused by abrasion, and traces of old

auctioneers' labels, library labels, or catalogue serial numbers (all suggesting an earlier lack of care).

The next stage is to open the front cover. Look for:

8. 'tenderness' or tearing of the inner hinge, the point at which the main body of the book is attached to the outer casing (damage here results from rough handling or inadequate original assembly).

9. signs of damp or mould (detectable not only by sight but also by a musty smell).

10. disfiguring library stamps or uninteresting superscriptions by previous owners (which may detract from the book's value).

11. well executed 'ex libris' plates and interesting superscriptions by a famous former owner or by the author (which may add to the value of the book).

The third stage is to check the inner end-papers and opening folios:

12. the end-papers (one or more of which may have been torn out).

13. the frontispiece (which, if it was glued, 'tipped in', may have fallen out).

14. the Contents page (which may be missing).

15. the 'index of illustrations' and 'index of maps' (which, if provided, should be checked against the plates and maps which are still in the book. Fine illustrations are sometimes cut out by people wishing to frame them as decorations).

The fourth stage is to repeat the above examination at the rear of the book, i.e. to look for 'damping' or mould, superscriptions, damage to the inner hinge, and to see whether there is a main narrative index.

The fifth stage is to examine the paper upon which the text is printed, and the manner in which the folios have been gathered together and bound. This is a large and complicated subject. Collectors interested in manufacturing methods may wish to broaden their knowledge by talking to people employed in the paper-making, printing, and binding trades, and by reading some basic text books. Knowledge breeds knowledge, and adds to the pleasures of ownership. Check the following:

16. the folio numbers are complete and in their correct sequence (errors are sometimes found in misbound books, or some folios may have been torn out).

17. the book has been correctly trimmed in the guillotine, with no loss of text (this is an infrequent fault, but it can occur).

18. the text is clear and legible (some inks deteriorate in badly stored books, or the text may have been printed poorly at the outset).

19. the gatherings, or quires, or signatures - these being ways of describing the bundles of folios produced by folding the original sheet of paper - are all firmly attached to their neighbours and to the backing (looseness, even separation, will occur in books which have become dry and brittle, deteriorated through old age, been split violently open, or were badly assembled in the first place).

20. none of the pages have stuck together (a common fault with modern coated 'art' papers which have been permitted at some stage to become damp).

21. the paper is flat, and has not buckled or rippled (the result of bad storage, with wide seasonal or day/night fluctuations in temperature and humidity).

22. the paper, or possibly the entire book, has not developed a bow shape (often the result of excessively low humidity and high temperatures, or by incorrect shelving).

23. the paper is not 'foxed' (a common fault, even in well stored books, which consists of unsightly blotches caused by chemical impurities, especially in old-style 'rag' papers.).

24. the outer edges of the folios are not 'browned' (discolouration resulting from excessive light, or tobacco smoke).

25. unwanted superscriptions or annotations (made by children or by previous owners who disagreed with the author. On the other hand, interesting margin notes by a known authority on the subject might add to the book's value).

26. publication date, usually shown on the reverse of the title page (some editions of a particular title may be thought more desirable than others).

27. addenda and corrigenda slips (if it is known that such slips ought to be included in a particular book, check that they are present).

Having completed this initial survey, which need take only a few minutes, the prospective buyer is now free to start reading the narrative and deciding whether the book contains the information which he or she is seeking. In many instances, the need for information overrides the fact that the copy on offer has seen much hard service and is now in a distressed condition. Assuming that the price reflects the condition, and providing that the nature of the damage is such that it can be corrected, it can still be safely purchased. However, it is important to halt the decline by passing the book to an experienced conservator (book restorer) at an early stage. There may be a temptation to instruct the conservator to 'save money' by using the cheapest methods and materials. This is usually counter-productive in the long term. Assuming that a book is basically desirable and collectable, it is better to give the expert a free hand. Modern conservation techniques can involve the removal of the outer covers which are then fixed onto a new strong spine and new pair of boards. Given the opportunity, a skilled professional can refurbish a book in such a way that it looks almost the same as the original, and it will quite possibly have a construction even sturdier than the original. Apart from the casing, the conservator may also be able to breath new life into the interior of a book, repairing torn plates and maps, and so forth. As in most things, initial cost-cutting may prove later to have been the most expensive solution.

For detailed information on book conservation, and for a list of companies which supply all the relevant materials and services, contact may be made with:

The National Preservation Office
The British Library
Great Russell Street
London WC1B 3DG

THE REGIMENTAL HISTORY AND ITS EVOLUTION

The British Army was established in 1660 when Charles II was restored to the throne of England. Ironically, and setting a precedent which was to be repeated time and again in later decades, it began with a series of amalgamations. The Cavaliers and the Roundheads, who had fought each other so bitterly during the Civil War, came together to form the first regular regiments in Royal Service. Through times of war and peace, triumph and disaster, they evolved into an organisation which would be recognisable to a modern observer as being a fully integrated military force. That stage was reached between 1793 and 1814 - the time of 'the first world war', the Revolutionary and Napoleonic Wars with France. By then, Great Britain had already begun to assume responsibilities in many parts of the world which far exceeded her military capabilities to sustain and defend. The greatest of these was India.

The Honourable East India Company was formed not for conquest but for trade. Inevitably, however, it became embroiled in the 17th and 18th Century conflicts between its own national government and that of France. There were no regiments of the British Army in the sub-continent to support the Company. The first such unit - of artillery - did not arrive until 1748. The Company was obliged, therefore, for find its own troops. Mainly men recruited at home, they included East Africans, and Dutch, Portuguese and French mercenaries. Authority for their recruitment was given in 1661, but there was no central control until 1748. In that year, Major John Stringer Lawrence was made Commander-in-Chief with the task of imposing uniformity upon the armed forces of the three Presidencies.

Competition in India, between France and the British, came to the boil during the Seven Years War of 1757-1763. The handful of British Army and Company units was being overwhelmed by the well led French. The solution was to raise more regiments in situ. One of Lawrence's former subordinates, Robert Clive, became the key figure in saving the Company and in laying the foundation of the future British Indian Empire. In 1756, he followed Lawrence's example by recruiting more Europeans and forming them into the Bengal European Regiment. In addition, and more significantly, he recruited men from the local population. In 1758, following the successful example set by the French, he recruited Indians as Regular soldiers and trained them to fight according to the European military tactics of the day. It was a seminal event in the growth of the Empire worldwide. Clive showed that the British could acquire territory, defend it against competitors, and then sustain a presence, without always involving the limited resources of the British Army.

Clive's example would be adopted, in later years, in many other parts of the world. He had shown that regiments raised from indigenous populations were better adapted to local conditions, and sometimes cost far less to maintain. With good leadership and motivation, they fought as well, or better, than their European counterparts. Their battles, however, were often fought in wild and distant places, far from British public gaze. Popular interest was centred upon the campaigns and their outcome rather than the actions of individual regiments. There was, therefore, no widespread demand for regimental history books per se. The majority of the officers were following short-term careers with purchased Commissions and they exchanged frequently between regiments. The rank and file of the British Army was mainly illiterate, and the men of the units recruited overseas usually spoke no English. The decades rolled by, wars were fought and treaties made, but the services of the common trooper and private soldier went largely unrecorded.

There was just one exception to the general rule. In 1637, a book was produced in London which is broadly accepted as having been 'the first regimental history'. Written by Colonel Robert Monro and printed by William Jones of Red-crosse Street, it was entitled MONRO, HIS EXPEDITION WITH THE WORTHY SCOTS REGIMENT (CALLED MAC-EYES REGIMENT), LEVIED IN AUGUST 1626. A two-part work, of 368 pages, it dealt with one of the Scottish mercenary regiments and its services, between 1626 and 1634, in the armies of first the King of Denmark and then the King of Sweden. Monro not only told the story of the regiment's campaign services, he also included a roll of all the officers and some notes on the use of artillery. His book pointed the way forward, but nobody attempted to emulate it until 1803, one hundred and sixty-six years later.

Nine books were published between 1803 and 1833 which qualify for inclusion in any bibliography of unit histories. They were:

HISTORICAL REVIEW OF THE ROYAL MARINES, by Alexander Gillespie (M Swinney, Birmingham, 1803)
HISTORY OF THE HONOURABLE ARTILLERY COMPANY, by Anthony Highmore (R Wilks, Chancery Lane, London, 1804)
LIST OF OFFICERS OF THE ROYAL REGIMENT OF ARTILLERY, by John Kane (Albion Printing Office, Greenwich, 1815)
SOME ACCOUNT OF THE TWENTY-SIXTH OR CAMERONIAN REGIMENT, anon (Gunnell & Shearman, for G Mills, London, 1828)
THE RECORDS OF HIS MAJESTY'S 87th REGIMENT OR THE ROYAL IRISH FUSILIERS, by Gen Sir John Doyle (Mathew Iley, London, 1830)
AN HISTORICAL ACCOUNT OF HIS MAJESTY'S FIRST OR THE ROYAL REGIMENT OF FOOT, by Maj Joseph Wetherall (W Clowes, London, 1832)
HISTORICAL RECORDS OF THE THIRD OR KING'S OWN REGIMENT OF LIGHT DRAGOONS, FROM THE YEAR 1685 TO THE PRESENT TIME, by C Stisted (J Clarke, Glasgow, 1833)
ORIGIN AND SERVICES OF THE COLDSTREAM GUARDS, in two volumes, by Col D MacKinnon (Richard Bentley, London, 1833)

It would seem that these books were printed in modest numbers and were given or sold to serving officers, to friends of the authors, and to persons in authority. As far as is known, none of them were intended for a wide or general readership. Further, they dealt with only a handful of the regiments currently in the Army List.

It was King William IV who is said to have first raised the matter. He pointed out, possibly after some prompting from interested parties, that each of his regiments had acquired a proud tradition and a roll of Battle Honours, that each had its own archives, but that they were accessible only to its own officers. He gave instructions that a series of histories should be produced which could be offered to all categories of potential reader. Army funds would be made available for the production of an historical account of every regiment of the British Army. The Adjutant General, Sir John Mcdonald, would superintend the project and the practical work of compilation was assigned, by Royal Warrant, to Richard Cannon.

Cannon was the Chief Clerk at Horse Guards (or the War Office, as it was to become). Appointed to that post in 1805 at the age of twenty-six, he was to retain it for nearly fifty years. He commenced work immediately and, not surprisingly, the first book to be published under the new arrangement, in 1837, was a history of the Life Guards.

Over the next sixteen years, Cannon produced a total of sixty-eight books. His Warrant expired on the death of the King, but he received a new Warrant upon the ascent to the throne of Victoria. Unfortunately, the official funding was not maintained. By now totally involved in what he was doing, Cannon attempted to continue the project with his own money. When that ran out, his family's finances became so bad that his daughters were reduced to petitioning Earl Russell for a Civil List pension. The last title in what is now known as 'the Richard Cannon series' was published in 1853, but several second or revised editions were produced subsequently under different managements. The series covered all twenty-four regiments of Cavalry and forty-three regiments of Infantry (half of those on the establishment of that period).

Only one (additional) title within the series did not relate to a regiment of the British Army. That was THE HISTORY OF THE CAPE MOUNTED RIFLEMEN, produced on contract for Richard Cannon in 1842 by John W Packer, of London, one of the three printing houses engaged in printing and binding these books. Cannon's son, George Edward, had obtained a Commission in the CMR, a fact which may explain the publication of this book.

The Richard Cannon books set the standards to be expected of all future regimental histories. His modus operandi was to liaise directly with the regiments concerned, relying upon them to consult their own records, and to write and proof-read their own texts. His function was essentially that of coordinator and editor. The resultant work was authoritative and reliable. Based upon a combination of archival sources and the personal knowledge of past and serving officers, it provided accurate information regarding dates, engagements, moves and locations. The books contained helpful illustrations - often executed to a high standard - showing details of uniforms and equipment. There was little if any of the fine detail or human interest which later generations of reader came to expect, but the essential blue-print had been drawn.

There was a long hiatus after Richard Cannon's time. New titles were published occasionally, but not on a large scale. There was a burst of activity in India in the 1890s, there was a similar flurry of publications in Canada at about that same time, and the Anglo-Boer War of 1899-1902 provoked its own spate of unit histories, but it was the Great War of 1914-1918 which opened the golden era for this genre of book. There are several reasons why this should have been so.

Until 1914, the British Empire's wars had been fought largely by professional soldiers. Citizen volunteers, a few years earlier, had fought in South Africa, but that was an exception to the general rule. It was only when Kitchener pointed his famous finger at the British populace, and when a tide of patriotic fervour swept through the Colonies and the Dominions, that millions of men donned for the first time in their lives a military uniform. When, in 1919, they returned home, there was in every household a direct interest in knowing what their menfolk had done to win the war. The veterans who survived wanted to see in print an account of their own services and of their friends who had not come back.

There were other factors which prompted the rush of publications in the 1920s and early 1930s. Mass literacy had for many decades been the norm. Book ownership was no longer restricted to the upper classes. The library network had spread to even the smallest towns. Advances in the printing industry meant that well bound books could be produced at moderate cost. Officers no longer came and went as they had in the old days. They were 'married' to their own regiment and this continuity was reflected in the strength of Regimental Associations which could find the funds to sponsor the compilation and publication of printed records. All of the ingredients were in place, and some of the finest regimental histories are those which deal with the events of 1914-1918.

The same situation arose in the aftermath of the second world war. It had been fought, in the main, by citizen armies. The British Army had expanded enormously by conscription, and the regiments and Corps of Canada, South Africa, Australia, and New Zealand comprised hundreds of thousands of civilian volunteers, fighting for 'the mother country' and for a cause in which they believed. The pride and growing sense of national identity which had taken root in Gallipoli and on the Western Front between 1914 and 1918 was reinforced by the battles of the Western Desert, Dieppe, New Guinea, and Normandy. As a consequence, there was another high tide of books emerging from the presses in the late 1940s and the 1950s. In some Commonwealth countries, the tide has never entirely receded. On the contrary, in Australia, the production of new unit histories relating to the 1939-1945 period has increased rather than diminished (for reasons discussed in that section of this bibliography). In general terms, however, it is reasonable to assume that the regimental history - as a specialised genre of book, connected directly to the British Imperial period - has now run its course. Nearly fifty years have passed since the British left India. Almost all of the former Colonies are now independent States. The great Dominion countries have found their own ways forward in the world. The current political changes in Eastern Europe have led to reductions in military establishments. Regiments which might otherwise have sponsored periodic accounts of their activities have been amalgamated. The prime motivation for such books - the recording of war services - has changed as the role of the military has moved from conventional warfare to counter-terrorism and humanitarian roles. A global conflict would involve the use of weapons of mass destruction which would leave no readership for such material. For the present, the peace-keeping missions in which many Commonwealth countries are engaged are not, sadly, the stuff of vivid history. In sum, and as far as the British Empire and Commonwealth forces are concerned, the books listed in REGIMENTS probably represent ninety-nine percent of those which are likely ever to be published. Future regimental histories will deal, in the main, with future events and with the services of units which (following the examples of India, Pakistan, South Africa, and most of the Colonies) may no longer incorporate the Crown in their cap badge. For the moment, therefore, we may concentrate upon the books which have been written, and consider the ways in which they have been produced.

The quality of any book depends upon three ingredients - the competence of the author, the skills of the printing and binding team, and the level of financial backing. A well researched and fluently written narrative deserves an attractive and durable presentation. Ineptitude or under-funding during the production stage will produce a book which is disappointing to handle, and which will have a limited shelf-life. These factors have particular relevance to the manner in which regimental histories are conceived, compiled, and published. They are required to be hard-working reference tools, to be consulted frequently and over a long period of time.

Quality of authorship rarely causes difficulty. With few exceptions, unit histories are compiled by one of three main categories of writer - professional military historians, or non-professional individuals who at one time served with the unit under review, or by an editor and committee appointed by the regimental association. Whether they undertake the work for financial reward or simply for the satisfaction of recording former services for posterity, they are all very aware of the close scrutiny which will be applied to their labours once they have been committed to print. The need to avoid errors of fact - quickly identifiable by the thousands of men who passed through the unit in years gone by - creates a pressure which concentrates the mind most wonderfully. Some narratives are written more lucidly than others, some are arranged in a more logical sequence than others, but the basic accuracy of the factual content is usually beyond dispute.

There are certain authors whose research and writing abilities have caused them to be commissioned by more than one regiment or Corps to compile their records. They have earned their livings, at least in part, from this exacting work. As the 'Index of Authors' will show, each of the Dominions has produced its own specialist writers, men who have gained fine reputations for sound history. By consulting the Index and then reading some examples of their work, users of REGIMENTS can form their own assessments as to the quality of authorship they are likely to encounter in a previously unseen book.

Quality of production is a subject much more complicated than authorship. Books incorporate a variety of materials which, in the main, derive from organic sources.

With time, they will deteriorate. The process is accelerated if a book is roughly handled or wrongly housed (a subject discussed in detail in the preceding 'Notes on Book Preservation'). The printer has no control over his product once it leaves his premises, but there is much he can do to give the author's work a maximum life expectancy.

It will be seen in this bibliography that, over the decades, regimental histories have flowed from the presses of hundreds of different printing firms located in all parts of the world. The quality of their work has varied greatly. There are several reasons why this should be so. In some countries, at times of economic austerity, neither the materials nor the funds were available to ensure a satisfying end-product. In others, the machinery and the competence of the labour force were limiting factors. In many instances, the printer may have been told to cut corners, to reduce costs by using the cheapest materials and the quickest techniques. In far fewer cases, the printer has been instructed to use only the finest materials and the most painstaking methods. These are the books which bring such pleasure to the bibliophile.

There is a paradox here. The narrative content and reference value of an 'economy' edition can be precisely the same as that of a 'de luxe' edition. Both, in theory, should be equally useful and useable over many years of working life. But an unattractive book commands less respect from the user. It may be shelved and handled with less care. Having been poorly assembled, it will then start to disintegrate. Within a few decades, possibly much sooner, the few surviving intact copies become rarities and their historical reference value is restricted to a handful of fortunate owners. This entirely defeats the original intentions of the author and his sponsors. Conversely, a beautiful book, self-evidently assembled with care, is shelved and handled with the respect which it merits. Its contents therefore continue to be available over a very much longer time.

Care has been taken in REGIMENTS to record in each entry full details of the name and location of the printer and, if he was contracting for a commercial publishing house or regimental association, those particulars also. This information should assist the potential purchaser of a previously unseen book in assessing its probable overall quality before he decides to acquire it.

One name appears time and again in dealers' catalogues or any list of regimental histories - Gale & Polden Limited, of Aldershot, Hampshire. Apart from having been for more than a century the premier supplier of printed materials to the British Army, this firm was prominent in producing the histories of numerous Colonial and Dominions regiments, and in particular, those of the Indian Army. The connections were so strong that the story of Gale & Polden Ltd is, in effect, the story of the evolution of the regimental history as a publishing phenomenon, and of the British Empire itself.

In 1868, the firm's founder, James Gale, opened a bookshop and stationers in Old Brompton, Chatham. The large naval dockyard and military garrison provided the bulk of his trade. He soon began to provide a printing service from a one-man press in his garden shed. In 1873 he produced his first book - CAMPAIGN OF 1870 -1871, THE OPERATIONS OF THE CORPS OF GENERAL v WERDER, by Ludwig Lohlein.

His third apprentice, who joined him in 1875, was Thomas Ernest Polden. Nine years later, such was Thomas's energy and ability, that he became a full partner (and then Managing Director when, in 1892, the firm was incorporated and James Gale retired). The company moved to Aldershot a year later and continued to expand steadily under his guidance until he died in 1916. His place was taken by his brother, Russell Polden, who formerly had managed the company retail shop in Paternoster Row, London.

At this time, Gale & Polden expanded into many areas of printing and publishing. Between 1894 and 1904, it launched three successful weekly newspapers - The Aldershot News, The Camberley News, and The Military Mail. The bulk of its work, however, was connected with printing jobs for the military (at regimental rather than War Office level).

As early as the 1880s, Thomas Polden had identified a gap in the market - there were no text-books or manuals for rank and file soldiers who wanted to study for the Army Certificates of Education, or to generally improve their military skills with a view to promotion. The publication of the 'Military Series' established the company's reputation for well printed and well bound books which exuded an air of authority. Further diversification came with the launch, in 1909, of the 'History and Tradition' series of military postcards, authorised by the War Office. Vast numbers of Christmas cards, die-stamped in full colour, were printed for Crown units in many parts of the world. The range of material included recruiting posters, lantern slides, and illustrated badge and medal wall charts. All of these products have since become collector's items.

By virtue of their connections with serving and retired officers, Gale & Polden was often the automatic choice when, in the 1920s and 1930s, many regimental associations decided to sponsor a record of their services during the recent world conflict. The two decades between the wars witnessed the publication of dozens of such books. The majority carried the hallmarks of Gale & Polden's standards of quality - a good binding, well reproduced illustrations, finely executed maps, clearly arranged appendixes, and, whenever the customer could be persuaded to meet the additional cost, an Index. There were several other firms engaged in the production of equally attractive books - Swiss & Company of Devonport, Butler & Tanner of Frome, Robert Maclehose of Glasgow, as examples - but none could match the number of titles bearing the Gale & Polden imprint.

The end of the second world war brought another rush of orders, but the social and economic climates had changed. There was less money available to pay for 'prestige' books, and the regiments were concerned that their new publications should be priced at a level which all ranks could afford. This had not always been the case after the war of 1914-1918. Faced with increased costs and limited budgets, the company bowed to market pressures. It still had the capability to produce a luxurious book if so requested, but the demand had almost disappeared.

As early as 1946, the management of Gale & Polden foresaw that the military market would eventually decline. It geared itself more for general commercial printing, and obtained the contracts to produce various successful gardening and 'society' periodicals. In the 1950s, it acquired a number of small printing firms (including Foster Groom & Company, established since 1840 as military booksellers and stationers). Financially, the period between 1947 and 1960 was highly profitable.

Gale & Polden remained autonomous until 1963. In that year, its share capital was acquired by the Purnell Group. Two years later, the last members of the Polden family departed the company and the Purnell Group was merged with the Sun Group to form the British Printing Corporation. In 1968, the military printing element in the Gale & Polden business was reduced and all stocks of books and original prints and water-colours were auctioned by Christie, Manson & Woods, of London.

Over the years, more by accident than intent, the firm had accrued an extensive archive of original author's typescripts, correspondence, and original photographs and negatives. This material, sold or donated to a military museum or library, would have provided future researchers with a unique source of reference. The photographic material alone would be worth today a substantial sum. Apparently it was all destroyed.

In 1981, the British Printing Corporation was purchased by Pergamon Press, owned by Robert Maxwell, and restyled as the British Printing & Communications Corporation. In that same year, on Maxwell's orders, Gale & Polden ceased trading. All that remains of the company's contribution to the printed record are the fine books noted in this bibliography and elsewhere.

Much has changed since people such as Richard Cannon pioneered the concept of the regimental history in the 19th Century and since firms such as Gale & Polden developed it in the first half of the 20th Century. The most obvious improvements have been the increased adoption of descriptive narrative (as opposed to verbatim quotations from official documents), and the increased emphasis upon the services of all ranks (rather than those of officers only). The latter is a reflection of the changes in social structures which followed the slaughter of the first world war, and possibly a recognition by historians that, in the final analysis, battles are often decided by the fortitude of the common soldier.

The same influences reveal themselves in the appendixes at the rear of every good regimental history. Unlike Waterloo, where the dead were left where they fell, unburied and forgotten, every regiment has long since embraced the duty of recording the names of all those who died. Many writers, in Canada and Australia in particular, have extended the principle much further by listing not only the personnel who were killed, wounded, or taken prisoner, but also the name of every officer and other rank who was on the strength during a stated period. As a result, one third or even one half of the pages in any given book may be devoted to such appendixes. They are now a primary source for the genealogist, the medal collector, and the social historian.

There have been other improvements, thanks partly to advances in printing technology and paper quality. Computer scanning of photographs, for example, can produce a uniformity and enhanced clarity of reproduction which was impossible in the days of the acid-etched coarse-screen block. Modern high grade papers will accept the imposition of images and texts of a quality far superior to anything known in the past. Sadly, the arrival of the computer and its related systems has also opened the door for the publisher interested only in cutting his costs to the bone. The effect of that policy on the finished product is often all too evident. In general terms, however, the march of technical progress has created possibilities for the book designer and illustrator which were denied to his predecessors.

The one feature which is still too often ignored is the need for indexes. In this regard, little progress has been made. Approximately 80.0% of the book's listed in this bibligraphy do not have an index of any kind. This lamentable statistic begs the question - why does anyone produce any regimental history in the first place? What is its intended purpose? Most end-users will say that they wish to read the book, and then refer to it from time to time when they need to verify or confirm a particular date, name, location, or event. These are not 'read and discard' books. They are not lightweight items of ephemera. On the contrary, they are usually packed with authoritative historical facts of every kind, information which needs to be accessible and retrievable if the book is to fulfil the purpose for which, in theory at least, it was intended. Whenever an author fails to index his work, or is denied that opportunity by his publisher, the end product is severely diminished as a source of reference. It is a treasure chest to which there is no key. Future writers of regimental history might care to keep this need in mind.

GLOSSARY

Army – two alternative connotations. First, generically, describing a nation's military forces. Secondly, a military formation consisting of two or more corps and commanded by a General.

Battalion – a unit consisting of 500–1150 all ranks (depending upon the period in question), comprising between four and eight companies, and commanded by a Lieutenant Colonel.

Battery – a unit of artillery comprising 80–150 all ranks, equating to a company of infantry, and commanded by a Major.

Brigade – a military formation consisting, usually, of three battalions, commanded by a Brigadier. Also, until 1 May 1938, it was the designation given to a regiment of artillery.

Colony – a territory settled, in whole or in part, by people from another country and whose parent government retained some degree of control over local affairs.

Commonwealth (British) – a free association between Great Britain and fifty independent states which acknowledge the British Crown as a symbol of their union. It has no central government and no legislative powers. Some member nations accept the Queen as their head of state (represented by a Governor General), others have evolved as republics (headed by their own Presidents). The Commonwealth, which represents a fifth of the world's total population, was formed in 1931 by the Statute of Westminster. Its first members were Great Britain, Canada, Australia, and New Zealand. They have since been joined by most of the Colonies which subsequently achieved independence, and by India and Pakistan. Apart from maintaining the historical ties formed during the period of Empire, the Commonwealth embodies various principles connected with open trade, human rights, and mutual defence.

Corps – two alternative connotations. First, the title of a branch of the Army (Armoured Corps, Corps of Signals, Medical Corps, and so forth). Secondly, a military formation consisting of two, three, or four Divisions, and commanded by a Lieutenant General.

Crown forces – loosely, every Empire and Commonwealth unit which incorporated the British Crown in its cap badge, its Colours, or its Guidon. In this bibliography, the term 'Imperial forces' has been avoided. Often used in the past to describe units of the British Army, 'Imperial' would cause confusion in view of its use in other contexts (the 'Australian Imperial Forces' of WWI and WWII, for example).

Crown services – a term used in this bibliography to describe the services of any Empire or Commonwealth unit performed (ultimately) on behalf of the Monarch.

Division – a military formation consisting of three brigades, and commanded by a Major General.

Dominion – a title at one time applied to certain self-governing independent countries within the Empire (and then within the Commonwealth, post-1931). The term was abandoned after WWII. Examples were Canada, New Zealand, and Australia.

Mandated territory – any land governed by the authority of an international organisation (the League of Nations and then, later, the United Nations). Examples were Palestine (1920–1948) and Tanganyika (1919–1961).

Perfect bound - a book in which the signatures (gatherings of folios) are not sewn (stitched) but are attached to the spine and outer covers by glue (or by a modern bonding agent). Such books tend to be more vulnerable than conventionally bound volumes to poor storage or rough handling, although great advances have been made in recent years in the quality of the adhesives used.

Protectorate - in the British context, a territory for the which the Crown assumed responsibility in order to establish the rule of law or to prevent occupation by a competitor nation. The land still belonged to the people and their rulers and, normally, could not be purchased or settled by Britons or other outsiders. As an example, Uganda was a British Protectorate from 1896 through to 1962 when it became independent. It never passed through a transitional period of colonisation.

Ranks in the Indian Army - did not in each instance have a precise equivalent in the British Army or in armies modelled upon it. In the 'India' section of this bibliography, the following officer ranks are mentioned frequently. In the cavalry - Risaldar Major, Risaldar, and Jemadar. A Risaldar commanded a squadron, a Jemadar was a troop officer. In the infantry - Subadar Major, Subadar, and Jemadar. A Subadar commanded a company, a Jemadar was a company officer. The Risaldar Major and the Subadar Major were the senior Indian officers in their respective regiments or battalions, directly responsible to the Commanding Officer (Commandant) for all matters relating to discipline and morale. They were the only such channel of communication. They were, therefore, men of immense experience and influence. The rank and file were known as Sowars (troopers, in the cavalry), and Sepoys (private soldiers, or enlisted men, in the infantry).

Regiment - a military unit having its own distinctive designation or title, its own identity as demonstrated in its cap badge, Battle Honours, Colours, or Guidon, and its own unique 'family' or regimental spirit. Traditionally the command of a Colonel, the regiment is a component part of all the main combat arms - cavalry, artillery, engineers, signals, and infantry. A regiment of infantry might have a strength of only one battalion or, in time of war in particular, it might have a great many more.

Roll of Honour - a term used to describe any nominal roll of personnel who died or suffered wounds while in service. Such rolls are to be found in all good regimental histories, either at the rear or inserted within the main text.

Squadron - a sub-unit within a regiment of cavalry, engineers, or signals, with a strength of 60-150 all ranks, and commanded by a Major. A squadron equates to a company of infantry.

Troop - a sub-unit within a squadron, comprising 20-70 all ranks, and commanded by a Lieutenant. A troop equates to a platoon of infantry.

Western Desert - that area of North Africa, between El Alamein (Egypt) and the coast of the Gulf of Sirte (Libya), where in 1940-1942 a series of battles was fought between Axis forces and forces of the British Army and Commonwealth.

Western Front - the decisive battleground of WWI where, for four years, the Allies attempted to destroy the Imperial German Army. The front line stretched over 500 miles from the English Channel to the Swiss-French frontier and, on the Allied side, was manned primarily by the French Army. The northern flank (in Flanders, West Belgium, and in Picardy, NE France) was manned by the British Army and Empire forces. They were joined in the Spring of 1918 by Divisions of the United States Army.

A/A	Anti-aircraft
AIF	Australian Imperial Force
ANCO	African Non-commissioned Officer
Anon	Anonymous
Apps	Appendixes
Armd	Armoured
A/T	Anti-tank
Bde	Brigade
BEM	British Empire Medal
BOR	British Other Rank
Bn	Battalion
BNCO	British Non-commissioned Officer
Cav	Cavalry
CB	Commander of the Order of the Bath
CBE	Commander of the Order of the British Empire
CEF	Canadian Expeditionary Force
Cld	Coloured (for maps and illustrations)
CMG	Commander of the Order of St Michael & St George
CO	Commanding Officer (also, for India, Commandant)
DCM	Distinguished Conduct Medal
Div/Divsl	Division/Divisional
DOD	Died of Disease
DOW	Died of Wounds
DSO	Distinguished Service Order
ERE	Extra-regimentally Employed (detached for other duties)
Et passim	On this and on following pages
Fp	Frontispiece (either coloured or monochrome)
H&A	Honours and Awards
HEIC	Honourable East India Company (or 'John Company')
Idem	The same, or the same as before
Ills	Illustrations
Inf	Infantry
IOM	Indian Order of Merit
IS	Internal Security (usually 'aid to the civil power')
KIA	Killed in Action
LRDG	Long Range Desert Group
LS&GC	Long Service & Good Conduct Medal
MBE	Member of the Order of the British Empire
MC	Military Cross
MIA	Missing in Action
MID	Mentioned in Despatches
MM	Military Medal
Mono phots	Monochrome photographs (black and white, or sepia)
MSM	Meritorious Service Medal
NCO	Non-commissioned Officer
n.d.	No date (date of publication not shown)
NWF	North West Frontier (of India)
OBE	Officer of the Order of the British Empire
OBI	Order of British India
POW	Prisoner of War
Recce	Recconaissance
RPM	Regimental Pipe Major (in Scottish Regiments)
RSM	Regimental Sergeant Major
SNCO	Senior Non-commissioned Officer
Sqn	Squadron
VC	Victoria Cross
VCO	Viceroy's Commissioned Officer (in the Indian Army)
WIA	Wounded in Action
WO	Warrant Officer

INDEX OF CONTRIBUTORS

Compilation of this bibliography would have been impossible without the active support of a large number of individuals and institutions. Nearly two hundred authors, publishers, librarians, historians and former officers have assisted with information of one kind or another. Of these, more than half have been able to contribute detailed reports on books which were known to them. Wherever appropriate, their initials are shown at the foot of each bibliographic entry. The key to those initials appears on the following pages.

Additionally, and apart from wishing to know the name of each contributor, future users of this bibliography may find interest in the personal backgrounds and qualifications of those involved. Limitations of space do not allow the publication of full details for each and every one, but the representative cross-section shown below will serve to demonstrate the wide range of knowledge and experience to which the compiler has been privileged to have access.

John L Arnold
United Kingdom. Military historian, book collector, professional researcher. As a National Service officer, Commissioned into the Royal West Kent Regiment, he was seconded to the Nigeria Regiment, Royal West Africa Frontier Force. From 1954 to 1960, he served in the Colonial Police, in Tanganyika, and then joined the Petrochemicals (Marketing) Division of British Petroleum. Retiring in 1985, he formalised his long-standing interest in naval and military research by becoming a Record Agent. He is the author of 'The African DCM - Awards of the KAR and WAFF DCM'.

Captain Timothy Ash MBE WKhM
United Kingdom. Medal collector, researcher. He served with the Royal Corps of Signals from 1951 until transferred to the General List in 1967. From 1968 to 1971 he was the Desert Intelligence Officer of the Trucial Oman Scouts in Ras al Khaimah. Subsequently he was in the service of His Highness the Ruler of Ras al Khaimah until 1979, and then the Government of the Sultanate of Oman until 1985. During his twenty-one years in the Persian Gulf region, he became interested in its history and, thereby, the history of British India.

Miss Terry Barringer MA Dip Lib ALA
United Kingdom. Bibliographer, book reviewer. She graduated from St Anne's College, Oxford, with a Degree in history, trained as a librarian while working at the Institute of Education Library, University of London, and studied at the Polytechnic of North London. She joined the staff of the Royal Commonwealth Society Library in 1980 and was appointed its Librarian in 1988.

Gordon T Bickley
Republic of South Africa. Researcher, medal collector. A civil engineer by profession, he served in the South African Corps of Signals in WWII as a Sergeant Radar Technician. Now retired, he held at various dates the appointments of Deputy Town Engineer in Spluys, Engineer to the Northern Rhodesia Housing Board, Director of Public Works (Power and Communications) in Swaziland, and Principal Engineer (Services) Electricity Supply Commission in Johannesburg. Since 1977 he has been Secretary and Newsletter Editor of the Military Medal Society of South Africa.

Chris Bilham BA LLB
Hong Kong. Medal and military book collector. A New Zealander, Chris Bilham graduated from Auckland University in 1981 and was admitted to the bar that same year. During his student years, he was a member of the Territorial Force (initially

the Royal New Zealand Infantry Regiment, then the NZ Special Air Service). Later in 1981 he joined the Royal Hong Kong Police and is currently a Detective Chief Inspector with that force. He became a medal collector in 1980 and he is Honorary Secretary of the Hong Kong branch of the Orders & Medals Research Society.

Howard Chamberlain MSM
New Zealand. Researcher, author, medal collector. A former professional soldier, he retired recently after thirty-one years with the Royal New Zealand Engineers. He served in Malaya, North Borneo, the Solomon Islands, Fiji and North Sumatra before being appointed Regimental Sergeant Major at the School of Military Engineering. He was for twelve years on the RNZE Corps Committee and is Curator of the Corps Memorial Collection. His final appointment was Warrant Officer User Representative at the Defence Services Computer Bureau. A holder of the NZ Meritorious Service Medal, he is currently compiling a biographical roll of all 466 recipients.

Field Marshal Sir John Chapple GCB CBE MA FRGS FZS FLS
United Kingdom. Researcher, collector of artefacts relating to the Indian Army and the former Irish regiments. He was a National Service officer between 1950 and 1952 before going up to Trinity College, Cambridge, to read Modern Languages and History. In 1954 he re-entered the Army as a Regular officer with 2nd King Edward's Own Goorkhas (The Sirmoor Rifles), served with them in Malaya, Borneo and Hong Kong, and commanded the 1st Bn in 1970. After various appointments within the Brigade of Gurkhas, he was successively C-in-C UK Land Forces and Chief of the General Staff. In 1993 he became HM's Governor of Gibraltar. He is Deputy Chairman of the National Army Museum, and Chairman of the Society for Army Historical Research. He is also President of the Military Historical Society, and a Trustee of the Gurkha Museum. He started collecting military pictures and insignia while a young man and has since compiled a Gurkha bibliography and has written many of the pamphlets published by the Gurkha Museum.

Major M C N D'Arcy jssc psc
Australia. Researcher, author. Michael D'Arcy served with the Royal Horse Artillery in North West Europe in WWII, and then in India, Egypt and Palestine. He saw service during the Malayan Emergency and later, as a Staff Officer, held various appointments in Cyprus, Kenya and Aden. Retiring from the British Army, he served for twelve years with the Australian Regular Army. He finally retired in 1987 after ten years in the Australian Public Service. He has made a study of armory and is a Fellow of the Heraldry and Genealogy Society of Canberra. He has written many articles on heraldic and genealogical topics, and has acquired a wide knowledge of British and Australian military history.

John Devereau
Canada. Book collector and researcher. A self-educated historian, John Devereau lived all his life in the Maritime Province of New Brunswick. His early ambition to attest for uniformed service was frustrated by chronic poor health. In 1949 he joined the Canadian National Railways as a clerk. He retired, in 1985, as an office supervisor. Isolated from the main reference libraries and centres of learning, he made many friends by correspondence and accumulated a great knowledge of his country's military history. A dedicated book collector, his personal library came to be recognised as one of the best private collections of regimental histories in Canada. That the Canadian section of this bibliography is so extensive and detailed is due in large part to his enthusiasm and experience. Sadly for all those who knew him, he died in 1992 and without seeing his work in print.

Lieutenant Colonel Patric J Emerson
United Kingdom. Researcher. Educated at Beaumont College and the Royal Military College, Sandhurst, he was Commissioned into the 4th Bombay Grenadiers, Indian Army, in 1938. He served throughout the war in India, latterly on attachment to the Corps of Military Police. He was Assistant Provost Marshal, British Commonwealth Occupation Force, Japan, and then (1947-1949) Officer Commanding the

3/14th Punjab Regiment, Pakistan Army. Later he was granted a Commission in the Australian Regular Army and served with it in Korea (initially as a Company Commander and subsequently as a Staff Officer with the Commonwealth Division). In 1969 he became Honorary Secretary of the Indian Army Association. He still occupies that post, and is Editor of the Association's biannual Newsletter.

Lieutenant Colonel C R D Gray psc
United Kingdom. Regimental militaria collector. Educated at Fettes and the RMC Sandhurst, Douglas Gray was Commissioned into the Indian Army in 1930. After initial service in the 1930 Frontier campaign, he joined Skinner's Horse (1st Duke of York's Own Cavalry). His military duties included a term as ADC to HE the Governor of Burma (1935-1938), active service with his Regiment in East Africa (1941), Quetta Staff College (1942), Staff Officer with GHQ New Delhi (1943), Second-in-Command of his Regiment in Italy (1945), and Staff Officer (GSO1) with 7th Indian Division in Burma (1946-1947, when Independence obliged him to retire). A natural horseman, he won the Lucknow Grand National (1933), the Kadir Cup (1934), rode his own horse in the Aintree Grand National (1938), and is today President of the Indian Cavalry Officers Association.

John Hamilton MA
United Kingdom. Researcher, author. Formerly a Williams and Domus Exhibitioner of Balliol College, Oxford, he served in Burma (both Kaladan campaigns) with The Gambia and the Gold Coast Regiments, 81st (West African) Division. After six years' war service, he returned to Oxford to complete his Degree course. He became a classics master and headmaster of grammar schools in Yorkshire and Surrey. He has contributed a chapter on African Colonial Forces to the National Army Museum's publication, 'The Forgotten War, the British Army in the Far East, 1941-1945', and is currently compiling a history of the 81st (West African) Division.

Major Alan Harfield BEM FRHistS FCMH
United Kingdom. Researcher, author, military book collector. In 1980 he completed thirty-six years' service with the British and Indian Armies, a period during which he served throughout the Far East. He established the Royal Brunei Regiment museum and compiled that Regiment's first published history. The author of fifteen books on military history, he has at various dates been Editor of the Military Historical Society Journal, Treasurer of the Society for Army Historical Research, Consultant to the Army Museums Ogilby Trust, and Deputy Director of the Royal Signals Museum.

Lieutenant Colonel A M Macfarlane psc
United Kingdom. Medal collector, researcher, author. He passed out of the RMA Sandhurst in 1950 and was Commissioned into the Royal Artillery. Service in the Korean War, where in 1953 he was wounded, was followed by a number of Regimental appointments in various parts of the world. Between 1974 and 1977 he was Defence Attaché in Lebanon and Syria. He retired from the Army in 1985 and is currently involved in officer recruitment and selection for the Royal Artillery. He is a member of the Orders & Medals Research Society, writes on military and medallic topics, and has published two ornothological books (based upon his observations while serving in Korea, the Levant, and Hong Kong).

Bryan D Maggs
United Kingdom. Rare book dealer, private collector. He performed his National Service with the Royal Air Force and then, in 1953, joined the family antiquarian book-selling firm, Maggs Brothers Limited, London. Over the past thirty years he has maintained a keen interest in the history of the Indian Army and the military campaigns of the Victorian era. He has a particular interest in the books, photographs and paintings which relate to those subjects. Since 1991 he has been the Director of the J Paul Getty Jr Library, at Wormsley, Oxfordshire.

Lieutenant Colonel Tony Mains psc
United Kingdom. Author, historian. He served on the North West Frontier of India in 1939-1940 and 1944-1946 as a Regimental officer of the 9th Gurkha Rifles. Between those dates he was on the Security Intelligence Staff in Iraq, Burma and India. His last Intelligence appointment was Chief Intelligence Officer of Central Command, India, in 1946. Since retirement in 1953 he has held, or holds, many appointments in organisations connected with military history, and is currently President of the 9th Gurkha Rifles Association. Amongst his various published works are 'Retreat from Burma, Field Security', and 'Soldier with Railways'.

Major Edwin Parks
Channel Islands. Historian, military book collector. A former professional soldier, he completed twenty years' service with the Royal Artillery (including a period as a Battery Commander with the Sultan of Oman's Armed Forces) before becoming a journalist in 1987. Apart from his work for the 'Guernsey Evening Press', he is the author of 'Diex Aix - God Help Us', the story of the Guernseymen who volunteered for military service in WWI, and 'The Royal Guernsey Militia', a full history of that Regiment.

Cliff Parrett MA
France. Medal and military book collector. After studying economics and social anthropology at Exeter University, he entered the chemicals industry and, in 1967, became Sales Manager (West Africa) for Colgate Palmolive. This was followed by executive appointments in the Middle and Far East, and currently he is Managing Director (Western Europe Division) of the Yardley Lentheric Group. While living in Teheran, he developed an interest in the British 19th Century interventions in Afghanistan and Persia. This led to frequent visits to local shops and bazaars in search of early British militaria. The discovery of a Swinburn double-barrelled percussion carbine bearing the stamp of the Scinde Irregular Horse inspired an abiding fascination with Irregular Indian Cavalry regiments, a subject on which he is now an acknowledged authority.

Jack St Aubyn
United Kingdom. Medal collector, military book dealer. Commissioned into the East Surrey Regiment in 1940, Jack St Aubyn was sent to West Africa on secondment to The Gambia Regiment, Royal West African Frontier Force. Subequently he served with the Nigeria Regiment, as a Company Commander, with 82nd (West African) Division in Burma. Post-war, he served with the Malay Regiment (1949-1955). Upon leaving the Army, he was employed by the Colonial Office in Nyasaland (1960-1963), and by the War Office in Malaya, Scotland, and at Warminster (1966-1986). He is co-proprietor of Woolcott Books, Dorchester.

Henry I Shaw Jr MA
United States of America. Historian, author, military book collector. In 1944-1946, as a Private First Class in the United States Marine Corps, he took part in the Battle of Okinawa and the occupation of North China. At the outbreak of the Korean War, he was recalled and promoted Sergeant. In 1951 he was appointed a civilian historian to the Corps. In 1962 he was appointed Chief Historian, USMC History and Museums Division. Recently retired after thirty years in that post, he is a Member of a large number of military historical Societies, has been an Editor to several of their Journals, and Secretary of the 1st Marine Division Association. Amongst his subjects of special interest is the bibliography of the American War of Independence.

John Tamplin TD
United Kingdom. Author, researcher, medal collector. He served as a Second Lieutenant, Royal Artillery, in North Africa at the end of WWII and subsequently held various appointments over eighteen years with Territorial Army gunner units in

London. After leaving the Regular Army he worked in the printing industry until 1966. Since that time he has worked with the Army Museums Ogilby Trust. He was for many years Treasurer of the Society for Army Historical Research, is a Past President of the Orders & Medals Research Society, and has just completed twenty years as Editor of that Society's Journal. His major history of the Lambeth and Southwark Volunteers was published in 1965.

Shamus O D Wade FRSAI
United Kingdom. Researcher and historian. As a Lance Corporal, he served with the Royal Engineers in Malaya (1947-1948) before entering the advertising industry. From 1969 to 1988, he was the world's largest dealer in old toy soldiers, and produced the 'Nostalgia Empire' models from 1974 to 1984. At various times he was Councillor of the Royal Borough of Kensington, Member of the Council of the Kipling Society, and President of the Irish Model Soldier Society. He is an Honorary Life Member of the Irish Model Soldier Society, the Gibraltar Model Soldier Society, and the Holger Eriksson Society. In 1988 he founded the Commonwealth Forces History Trust of which he is Secretary.

Colonel Denis Wood
United Kingdom. Researcher and author, collector of militaria. Commissioned in 1946 into 2nd King Edward VII's Own Goorkhas (The Sirmoor Rifles), he saw campaign service in India, Malaya and Borneo before retiring in 1973. His final appointment was within the Ministry of Defence, London. Currently he is Chairman of The Trustees of the Gurkha Museum, Winchester, of The Sirmoor Club (Regimental Association of the 2nd Goorkhas), and of The Military Historical Society. He has been a regular contributor to various military Journals and, in 1988, compiled and published 'The Fifth Fusiliers and Its Badges'.

Lieutenant Colonel Bob Wyatt MBE TD
United Kingdom. Author, researcher, military book collector, historian. He served eighteen years with the Royal Military Police (Volunteers) following eight years as a Regular officer with the Royal Electrical & Mechanical Engineers. In civilian life he was, before retirement, Transport Manager of the Automobile Association. He began collecting military books in 1944 and now has a personal library of 11,000 volumes. He has written extensively on motoring and military history, and is Editor of the Bulletin of the Military Historical Society.

Key to Contributors' Initials

AAM	Lieut Col A A Mains
ACT	Prof A C Thomas
AGB	Maj A G Bond
AGY	A G Young
AH	Maj Alan Harfield
AJW	Lieut Col A J Ward
AM	Ann Melvin
AMcC	Anthony McClenaghan
AMM	Lieut Col Maxwell Macfarlane
AN	Ashok Nath
APR	Alberto Peralta-Ramos
AS	Maj Anthony Sudlow

BCC	Bruce C Cazel
BDM	Bryan Maggs
BWR	Brian Ritchie
CB	Christopher Bryant
CJP	Cliff Parrett
CMF	C M Fagg
CEP	Maj Edwin Parks
CRDG	Lieut Col Douglas Gray
CSM	Colin Message
DAD	Denis A Darmanin
DBP-P	David Picton-Phillips
DCSD	Col D C S David
DH	David Harding
DJB	David Barnes
DKD	David Dorward
DMa	David Mahoney
DMi	Lieut Col David D Milman
DW	Col Denis Wood
ECL	Eric Lanning
EGV	Count E G Vitteti
EDS	Lieut Col E DeSantis
EJA	Eric Alston
ESS	Maj E S Straus
FC	Finola Chamberlain
FRB	Dr Frank Bradlow
FWST	F W S Taylor
GC	Gene Christian
GRB	G R Binns
GTB	Gordon T Bickley
HEC	Howard Chamberlain
HIS	Henry I Shaw Jr
HLL	Henry Lloyd
HRC	Lieut Col H R Carmichael
JA	John Arnold
JALH	John Hamilton
JBC	Joy Cave
JBF	Maj Jeffrey Floyd
JEB	James Bradbury
JFE	Maj John Etienne
JHFPJ	Lieut Col J F H P Johnson
JFS	J F Sutherland
JHG	J H Girling
JLC	Field Marshal Sir John Chapple
JMAT	John Tamplin
JPR	Brig J P Randle
JRD	John Devereau
JRStA	Maj Jack St Aubyn
JRT	John Thyen
JS	Jeremy Seed
JWW	Capt J W Webb

LBR	Leslie Ryan
LD	Lionel Digby
LM	Laurie Manton
MAR	Capt Mark Reid
MCJ	Michael Johnson
MCND'A	Michael D'Arcy
MGHW	M G H Wright
MWB	Brig Michael Biggs
MP	Max Powling
NH	Niçola Hemingway
NO	Col Neil Orpen
OSS	O S Sachdeva
PGM	Maj P G Malins
PJE	Lieut Col Patric Emerson
PRC	Peter Charlton
PS	Paul Street
RBM	Richard Meixsel
RGB	Ronald Baxter
RGH	R G Harris
RH	Richard Haller
RJW	Lieut Col R J Wyatt
RLP	Ron Platt
RP	Roger Perkins
RR	R Rolleg
RS	Lieut Col Robin Stewart
SB	Stuart Barr
SDC	Maj S D Clarke
SJH	Jean Hobson
SODW	Shamus Wade
SS	S Snelling
TA	Capt Timothy Ash
TAB	Terry Barringer
TD	Tom Donovan
TK-C	Trevor Kingsley-Curry
TM	Timothy Mole
TP	Timothy Parsons
VS	Victor Sutcliffe
WEL	Lieut Col W Elliott-Lockhart
WMTM	Brig W M T Magan

INDEX OF SOURCES

The majority of the entries in this bibliography conclude with a symbol which indicates the name of at least one library where a copy of the book in question is known to be lodged. The intention is to assist the researcher in possibly obtaining access through the inter-library loan system, or at least requesting a specific item of information by correspondence with the librarian in charge.

A few entries refer to privately-owned books, other copies of which have not been located in an open or public library. Such entries are annotated 'PC', for personal collection.

Key to Source Abbreviations

ADFA	Australian Defence Force Academy, Canberra (Aust)
AL	Africana Library, Johannesburg (RSA)
AldMM	Aldershot Military Museum, Aldershot (UK)
AMOT	Army Museums Ogilby Trust, London (UK)
ANL	Australian National Library, Canberra (Aust)
ASKBMC	Anne S K Browne Collection, Browne University, Providence, Rhode Island (USA)
ATL	Alexander Turnbull Library, Wellington (NZ)
AWM	Australian War Memorial, Canberra (Aust)
BCPL	British Columbia Provincial Library, Victoria (Can)
BM	British Museum, London (UK)
BSI	Bikaner State Archives, Bikaner, Rajasthan (India)
CFHT	Commonwealth Forces History Trust, London (UK)
CIAL	Central Intelligence Agency Library, Washington (USA)
CPL	Christchurch Public Library, Christchurch (NZ)
CRLC	Center for Research Libraries, Chicago (USA)
CWM	Canadian War Museum, Ottawa (Can)
DCLS	Devon County Library Service, Exeter, Devon (UK)
DND	Department of National Defence Library, Ottawa (Can)
DUL	Denison University Library, Granville, Ohio (USA)
ELJHU	Milton S Eisenhower Library, John Hopkins University, Baltimore, Maryland (USA)
EPL	Enoch Pratt Library, Baltimore, Maryland (USA)
FFL	Fort Frontenac Library, National Defence College, Kingston, Ontario (Can)
GWUL	George Washington Library, Washington DC (USA)
HSCL	Hampden-Sydney College Library, Hampden-Sydney, Virginia (USA)
IOL	Oriental & India Office Collections, British Library, London (UK)
ISL	Illinois State Library, Normal, Illinois (USA)
KHCL	Kenya High Commission Library, London (UK)
LOC	Library of Congress, Washington DC (USA)

MODL	Ministry of Defence Library, London (UK)
MUL	Miami University Library, Oxford, Ohio (USA)
NAM	National Army Museum, London (UK)
NCSL	North Carolina State Library, Raleigh, NC (USA)
NDHQL	National Defence Headquarters Library, Ottawa (Can)
NLC	National Library of Canada, Ottawa (Can)
NLM	National Library of Malta, Valetta (Malta GC)
NLNZ	National Library of New Zealand, Wellington (NZ)
NSWPLS	New South Wales Police Library, Sydney (Aust)
NUL	Northwestern University Library, Evanston, Illinois (USA)
NYPL	New York Public Library
NZECML	New Zealand Engineer Corps Memorial Library, Wellington (NZ)
NZMODL	New Zealand Ministry of Defence Library, Wellington (NZ)
ODUL	Old Dominion University Library, Norfolk, Virginia (USA)
OUL	Ohio University Library, Athens, Ohio (USA)
PALO	Public Archives Library, Ottawa (Can)
PCAL	Prince Consort's Army Library, Aldershot (UK)
PLG	Priaulx Library, Guernsey (CI)
PPL	Porirua Public Library, Porirua (NZ)
RAI	Royal Artillery Institute, London (UK)
RCAM	Royal Canadian Artillery Museum, CFB Shilo (Can)
RCMI	Royal Canadian Military Institute, Toronto (Can)
RCSL	Royal Commonwealth Society Library, London (UK) (now transferred to Cambridge University Library)
RHL	Rhodes House Library, Oxford (UK)
RMAS	Royal Military Academy, Central Library, Sandhurst, Camberley, Surrey (UK)
RMCL	Royal Military College Library, Kingston, Ontario (Can)
RSAEL	Republic of South Africa Embassy Library, London (UK)
SADFA	South African Defence Force Archives, Pretoria (RSA)
SAPLCT	South African Public Library, Cape Town (RSA)
SLT	State Library of Tasmania, Hobart (Aust)
SANMMH	South African National Museum of Military History, Saxonwold (RSA)
SLV	State Library of Victoria, Melbourne (Aust)
SSL	Sherborne School Library, Sherborne, Dorset (UK)
TPL	Toronto Public Library, Toronto (Can)
UAL	University of Alberta Library, Edmonton (Can)
UCL	University College Library, London (UK)
UCSRL	University of California, Southern Regional Library, California (USA)
UM	University of Minnesota, Minneapolis (USA)
UML	University of Maryland Library, College Park, Maryland (USA)
UMiamiL	University of Miami Library, Miami, Florida (USA)
USAMHI	United States Military Institute Library, Carlisle, Pennsylvania (USA)
USRCL	University of Saskatchewan, Regina College Library, Saskatoon (Can)

USII	United Service Institution of India, Delhi (India)
USL	University of Saskatchewan Library, Saskatoon (Can)
UWM	University of Wisconsin Library, Madison, Wisconsin (USA)
UWOL	University of Western Ontario Library, London, Ontario (Can)
VSL	Virginia State Library, Richmond, Virginia (USA)
WAPL	Western Australia Police Library, East Perth (Aust)
W&MCL	William and Mary College Library, Williamsburg, West Virginia (USA)
YUL	Yale University Library, New Haven, Connecticut (USA)

PART 1

NOTES

THE EMPIRE IS MARCHING
A Study of the Military Effort of the British Empire, 1800-1945
Glen St J Barclay * Weidenfeld & Nicholson, London, 1976. Purple, gold, 8.75 x 5.5, -/276. 17 mono phots, 6 maps, Bibliography, Chapter Notes (extensive), no appendixes, Index.
* An important book by a professional Australian historian, based upon original source documents. Despite the jingoistic title, his analysis concludes that Great Britain was never a truly imperialistic power - comparable with Rome - because no British government ever organised the military resources of its overseas Empire to any effective end. The Boer War had shown, not necessarily in the most desirable context, that Empire forces could unite in a common cause. The author argues that this war was unique. On the two later occasions when Dominion and Colonial forces were persuaded to come to Great Britain's aid, they did so because 'the mother country' itself was in direct peril. British policy was, in other words, parochial and euro-centric. By 1945, even the most devoted Empire countries had concluded that their future lay in self-determination. As a result, two new super powers took over the responsibility of policing the globe. For British readers, this is a disturbing but convincing view of the Empire's history. R/2 V/5. DCLS. RP.

THE LAND FORCES OF THE BRITISH COLONIES AND PROTECTORATES
Anon * His Majesty's Stationery Office, London. 'Compiled by the Intelligence Division, War Office, 1902, revised by the War Office General Staff, 1905'. Red, gold, 'For Official Use Only' on front cover, 9.5 x 6.25, viii/424. No ills, no maps, no Index (Contents page only). Apps: tables of establishments and strengths of each Colony and Protectorate.
* This publication contains brief details of the constitution and organisation of every unit (including Armed Police) which received training in the use of firearms. The contents are arranged alphabetically from Australia to the Windward Islands. A superb statistical and factual research source. R/4 V/5. PC. VS.
Note: it is reported that the print run for each of the two editions mentioned above was 1800 copies. It is known that the work was first published in 1889. Other editions were published in 1922, 1925, 1928, 1930 and 1934. There were some slight variations to the title (THE LOCAL LAND FORCES... and THE MILITARY FORCES...), but the basic format and purpose of each edition was the same.

THE ARMIES OF THE COMMONWEALTH
F W Perry * No publisher's details shown. Seen as five matching volumes, dated 1977 and 1978. Red, gold, 11.5 x 8.25, -/1342 (in all). No ills, no maps, no appendixes, no Index.
* A mammoth work of compilation, presented in facsimile typescript. It appears to be a private production, distributed in limited numbers to a few specialist libraries. The author has brought together the unit titles of all former British Army and Empire (Commonwealth) forces to show their place in changing orders of battle at different periods in time. He provides brief details of each unit's ancestry, changes of title, and (when appropriate) the date of its demise. This is not a narrative account but purely a listing for reference purposes. Two of the most fascinating sections are those which deal with the diverse early Colonial Militia and the numerous foreign mercenary regiments which were at one time or another in Crown service. The work is particularly useful to researchers concerned with regimental lineages. R/5 V/5. NAM. RP.
Note: another comprehensive reference source is BATTLE HONOURS OF THE BRITISH AND COMMONWEALTH ARMIES, by Maj A H R Baker (Ian Allan Ltd, London, 1986), this being a detailed listing (398 pages) of every Empire campaign which resulted in the award of a Battle Honour, with the names of the regiments so honoured.

HER MAJESTY'S ARMY

A Descriptive Account of the Various Regiments now Comprising the Queen's Forces in India and the Colonies

Walter Richards * J S Virtue & Co Ltd, London, n.d. (c.1888). Red, gold, 11.25 x 9.0, vi/376. Fp, 14 cld ills (by H Burnett), no maps, no appendixes, no Index.
* This is Vol III of a three volume set, the first two being devoted entirely to the British Army. It consists of floridly written sketches of the history of the Caribbean regiments, the Indian forces, and those of Canada, Australia and New Zealand. The author's main aim is to describe the organisation and condition of each unit as it was in the 1880s, but he includes some useful information regarding their earlier fighting achievements. R/5 V/3. PC. HIS.

THE UNIFORMS AND HISTORY OF THE SCOTTISH REGIMENTS

Britain, Canada, Australia, New Zealand, South Africa, 1625 to the Present Day

Maj R Money Barnes and C Kennedy Allen * Seeley Services Co, London, 1956. Red red, gold on black, 10.0 x 6.0, -/351. Fp, 11 cld ills, 26 line drawings, Index. Apps: 6 in total, incl notes on Scottish regts of the British, Canadian, Australian, New Zealand and South African armies, plus existing (1954) and disbanded Scottish units in India and the Colonies.
* A well written and useful book. Twelve chapters, each covering a stated historical period, describe important events in the lives of all Scottish regts between 1625 and 1954. Three chapters are devoted entirely to Commonwealth regts having Scottish affiliations. Another deals with Scottish weapons, and another with pipe music. Two more chapters deal with uniforms. The appendixes give a good condensed history of each regt, with information regarding their uniforms, Battle Honours, mottoes, and regtl connections. An excellent starting point for research on individual units. R/3 V/4. NAM. PJE.

ORDER OF BATTLE

Second World War, 1939-1945

Lieut Col H F Jolsen * Her Majesty's Stationery Office, London, 1960. Charcoal, gold, 12.0 x 8.0, xii/628. No ills, no maps, one appendix, Glossary, Index.
* A massive but basic source of reference. It lists all of the British and Empire Divs mobilised in WWII and identifies the Bdes, Regts, Bns and sub-units which formed part of those Divs. The entries include limited but useful information regarding the senior commanders, deployments, major engagements, scales of equipment, etc, for each unit. There is mention of various 'foreign' units which, from time to time, came under British command, e.g. American forces and the 'Free Forces' of France, Belgium, Poland, Czechoslovakia, and so forth. For users of REGIMENTS, this work by Jolsen would be helpful in understanding the larger framework within which the smaller units (as listed in the following pages) were operating between 1939 and 1945. R/1 V/4. PC. RP.
Note: the edition recorded above was republished in facsimile in 1990 by London Stamp Exchange and Liverpool Coin & Medal Co.

THE REGIMENTS DEPART

A History of the British Army, 1945-1970

Gregory Blaxland * William Kimber, London, 1971. Red, gold, 9.5 x 6.0, xi/532. No ills, 19 maps, Bibliography, Index. Apps: Orders of Battle of the British Army in 1945 and 1970, succession rolls of senior officers, notes on Battle Honours and campaign awards, roll of recipients of the VC, GC and DSO (1945-1970), statistical summary of casualties.
* This book describes the departure of the British Army from most of the territories which were at one time part of the Empire and which gained their independence during the twenty-five years following the end of WWII. The title also reflects the departure into history of those regiments which were amalgamated and redesignated during the major restructuring of the Army in the 1960s. The lively narrative is packed with incident, many minor actions being described in detail

and based upon eye-witness accounts. The book is a primary source for an understanding of the Army's role in securing (or attempting to secure) an orderly withdrawal from its previous global commitments during the 1940s, 1950s and 1960s. It also deals with operations aimed at sustaining a continued British presence in areas where it was not overwhelmingly acceptable to the local population. These campaigns included Palestine, Malaya, Korea, Suez, Kenya, Cyprus, Borneo, Southern Arabia, the Gulf and Northern Ireland. Integral to the story of the British Army during that period are the histories of many local units - the Aden Protectorate Levies, Arab Legion, Borneo Border Scouts, Cyprus Police, Dyak Trackers, Fijian Regt, Federal Regt of Malaya, Malay Regt, Malayan Home Guard, Kenya Police Reserve, Sarawak Rangers, South Arabian Army, Trans-Jordan Frontier Force, Trucial Oman Scouts, and the West Indies Regt. An excellent background source, with clear helpful maps. R/2 V/5. RMAS. RP.
Note: additional reference may be made to WITHDRAWAL FROM EMPIRE, A MILITARY VIEW, by Gen Sir William Jackson GBE KCB MC (B T Batsford Ltd, London, 1986). This book covers a wider canvas than Blaxford's work because the author explains why the Empire grew before it declined. Further, because Jackson was writing fifteen years later than Blaxford (and post-Falklands War), he could take a longer historical perspective and discuss the merits of maritime versus continental military strategies for the future.

IMPERIAL SUNSET
Frontier Soldiering in the 20th Century
James Lunt * Macdonald Futura Publishers, London, 1981. Beige, gold, 9.5 x 6.0, xvii/422. 41 mono phots, 4 maps, Bibliography, no appendixes, Index.
* A superb book which conveys both the fact and the spirit of Empire soldiering in clear and accurate terms. The narrative is divided into sections, each of which deal with a Regt or Corps of the type mentioned elsewhere in this bibliography, many of which never managed to have themselves recorded in print. Units which otherwise might have passed unnoticed were - The Trucial Oman Scouts, Hadhrami Bedouin Legion, Somaliland Camel Corps, and the Somaliland Scouts. R/2 V/5. PC. RP.

IMPERIAL POLICING
Maj Gen Sir Charles W Gwynn KCB CMG DSO * Macmillan & Co, London, 1939. Rust red, gold, 8.75 x 5.5, xi/417. No ills, 14 maps, no appendixes, no Index.
* This book is widely regarded as a classic source of reference on the subject of 'aid to the civil power', but its reputation is linked to the fact that almost nothing had been written on this difficult subject in earlier years.The narrative consists of little more than a compendium of cautiously worded accounts of several well known episodes when the military came into collision with a civil population - Amritsar 1919, Moplah Rebellion 1921, Chanak Crisis 1922, Shanghai 1927, Palestine 1929, etc. Basically a disappointing book. R/2 V/2. PCAL. RP.

THE COLONIAL POLICE
Sir Charles Jeffries KCMG OBE * Max Parrish, London, 1952. Pale blue, gold, 8.5 x 5.5, -/232. No ills, no maps, Bibliography, Index. Apps: notes regarding the police forces of forty-two different Colonial territories, with details of ranks, etc.
* The narrative covers the period from 1835 to 1951, and is an excellent general account of police and IS work in the Caribbean, Far East, West and East Africa, and all of the minor territories. Many of the smaller units are not recorded elsewhere. R/3 V/4. PC. RP.

MULTI-NATIONAL FORCES

MERCENARIES FOR THE CRIMEA
The German, Swiss and Italian Legions in British Service, 1854-1856
C C Bayley * McGill-Queens University Press, Montreal and London, 1977. Black, gold, 8.75 x 5.5, viii/197. No ills, no maps, Bibliography (extensive), Index. Apps: notes on the numbers of men recruited into each Legion, details of officers' services.
* Due to the British Army's recruitment difficulties prior to the outbreak of the war, it was decided to boost the strength of the Crimean expeditionary force by recruiting foreigners. To this end, after some dissent, the Foreign Enlistment Act came into effect. This book recounts in detail the way in which the Legions were raised and the associated diplomatic wrangles with the governments of Germany, Switzerland and Italy. It covers the way in which the drafts were brought to England for training and what happened to them thereafter. In the event, administrative and political problems prevented these units from ever seeing action. Some got no further than Malta, others reached Scutari but were there smitten by cholera. It was then decided to abandon the entire project. The disbandments caused much ill-feeling on all sides. R/2 V/4. NAM. PJE.

FORGOTTEN AS BECOMES A FRONTIERSMAN
The Early History of the Legion of Frontiersmen
Geoffrey A Pocock * No publication details shown, 1991. Illustrated soft card, 'mounted Frontiersman' picture, buff, sepia, -/19. No ills, no maps, no appendixes, no Index.
* Although nicely written, this rambling 'history' offers only the briefest glimpse into a fascinating story. Founded in 1904 by an English adventurer-cum-soldier-cum-explorer, Roger Pocock, the Legion comprised all manner of men who shared a common enthusiasm for defending the Empire. They fell into two broad groups - former Army officers looking for adventure, and those who, like Pocock himself, had specialist knowledge of the less accessible corners of the globe. The spirit which motivated them seems to have been an amalgam of Boy Scout, Secret Service and SAS. By 1914, the Legion's strength had grown to 17,500, with branches in China, the Dominions, several Colonies and the United Kingdom. Only marginally recognised by the War Office, the Legion despatched a Contingent to France on 2 August 1914, two days ahead of the BEF. It cheerfully attached itself to the Belgian Army and gave sterling service. Other groups joined the Australian Imperial Force and the New Zealand Expeditionary Force en bloc. Full acceptance by the War Office came in February 1915 when it authorised the formation of the 25th (Service) Bn, Royal Fusiliers (Frontiersmen). It fought in the East Africa campaign where one of its members, Lieut W T Dartnell, won the VC. The only other 'named' unit was Canadian. This was the 210th (Frontiersmen) Bn CEF. The frustrating narrative runs out of steam circa 1928, but it implies that the Legion was involved in WWII. Many extraordinary individuals are named here, all of them worthy of further research. R/2 V/3. PC. RJW.

THE HISTORY OF KING EDWARD'S HORSE
The King's Overseas Dominions Regiment
Lieut Col Lionel James * Sifton Praed, London, 1921. Grey, gold, Regtl crest, 8.75 x 5.75, xv/401. Fp, 14 mono phots, 8 maps (bound in), no Index. Apps: Roll of Honour.
* In November 1901, a unit was raised from Colonials resident in South East England. The first Honorary Colonel was Edward, Prince of Wales, and the unit was designated The King's Colonials. It had four mounted elements: A Sqn (British Asian), B Sqn (Canadian), C Sqn (Australasian), and D Sqn (South African). Each wore the Regtl badge and a Sqn badge to distinguish its origins. The latter were discontinued in 1909. Following the accession to the throne of George V, and his appointment as Colonel-in-Chief, the Regt was renamed King Edward's Horse in memory of his father. Mobilised in WWI, it fought in France in 1915, served in Ireland during the

'troubles' of 1916, returned to France in 1918 (suffering great losses at Vieille Chappelle in April), and then moved to Italy (serving as Div Cavalry with the XI Corps). The Regt was disbanded in March 1924. This is one of Sifton Praed's high quality productions, and the narrative is full of interest. To quote from the Preface: 'There was no Dominion, Dependency, Colony, nor portion of the globe where the British tongue is spoken that had not a representative in the uniform of King Edward's Horse'. An Empire classic. R/3 V/4. PC. RP.

HISTORY OF THE ROYAL REGIMENT OF ARTILLERY
The Forgotten Fronts and the Home Base, 1914-1918
Gen Sir Martin Farndale KCB * Royal Artillery Institution, Woolwich, 1988. Dark blue, gold, Regtl crest, 10.0 x 7.0, xv/490. 53 mono phots, 82 maps (bound in), Glossary, Bibliography, Index. Apps: list of senior RA officers who served in WWI other than in France, plus several Orders of Battle.
* The history of the RA and the Empire artilleries, but excluding services on the Western Front. It covers the campaigns in Egypt, the Dardanelles, Aden, Palestine, Macedonia, Italy, Mesopotamia, West Africa, East Africa, and on the NWF of India. It is a massive work which contains mention of all the Btys which originated in Australia, New Zealand, Canada, South Africa, India, West Africa and the Malay States. Few of the Btys are dealt with in detail, but the author sets the scene for, and describes the progress of, all the relevant campaigns. The narrative does include numerous accounts of battles and lesser engagements, but the book's main value is the general framework for further reading of individual unit histories. R/2 V/5. RAI. AMM.

REGISTER OF TUNNELLING COMPANY OFFICERS
Royal Engineers, Canadian Engineers, Australian Engineers, New Zealand Engineers, Roll of Honour, France, Flanders, Gallipoli, 1915-1918
Anon * Diamond Fields Advertiser, Kimberley, South Africa, 1925. Soft card, stapled, pale green, black, 9.5 x 7.25, -/44. Fp, one mono phot, no maps, Bibliography (of military mining), no Index. Apps: Roll of Honour (with nationality, unit and date), register of all officers who served with each Tunnelling Coy (with nationality and address).
* For many researchers, the main value of this little book is to be found in the appendixes. Nearly 1000 names are listed. The introductory paragraphs describe tunnelling operations in Gallipoli and France (especially Messines). A useful 'War Diary' contains details and dates of interest. R/3 V/3. AWM. MCND'A.

SOME TALK OF PRIVATE ARMIES
Len Whittaker * Albanium Publishing, Harpenden, UK, 1984. Green, gold, 8.75 x 6.0, -/91 (plus 10 pages of cld ills), no maps, Bibliography, no Index (and no Contents page). Apps: list of WWII 'private armies' with useful details on dates of formation and disbandment (61 unit designations).
* A good starting point for further research into irregular warfare in WWII. Some of these units have since become famous (SAS, PPA, FANY and Phantom), but others have received little recognition. Amongst those having an 'Empire' or 'foreign' composition were the Greek Sacred Squadron, French Squadron SAS, Belgian Independent Coy SAS, Burma Intelligence Corps, Lushai Scouts, Western Chin Levies, and the Indian Field Broadcasting Units. There is a passing reference to the Chinese Canadians (rejected for service in the Canadian Army) who were recruited in Vancouver to fight as guerillas in Japanese-occupied Malaya. A tantalising summary of a very large subject. R/1 V/3. DCLS. RP.

PROVIDENCE THEIR GUIDE
A Personal Account of the Long Range Desert Group, 1940-1945
Maj Gen D L Lloyd-Owen CB DSO OBE MC * G Harrap & Co Ltd, London, 1980. Pale blue, gold, 9.5 x 6.25, xviii/238. 33 mono phots (indexed), 3 maps (one printed in the text, 2 on the end papers), Bibliography, no appendixes, Index.
* Despite the 'personal account' wording of the sub-title, this is a comprehensive

history by an officer who joined the LRDG in 1941 and rose to command it in 1944. The story falls into two parts: the well-known deep penetration operations in North Africa (June 1940 to April 1943), and the less familiar activities in the Aegean, Greece, Albania and Yugoslavia (May 1943 to May 1945). A truly 'Empire' unit, the LRDG comprised five semi-independent elements: the Indian Long Range Squadron, the New Zealand Patrol, the Rhodesian Patrol (which included some South Africans), and two Patrols of British Army personnel (Guards Patrol and Yeomanry Patrol). By general consent, the New Zealand Patrol was outstanding. The Australians declined an early invitation to participate. This was an unfortunate decision because men accustomed to the self-sufficient life of Australia's outback would have thrived in the LRDG's operational environment. Required reading for all students of Special Forces. R/1 V/4. ANL. MCND'A.

Note: several books have been written about the LRDG, or referring to it. Amongst those available are THE DESERT MY DWELLING PLACE, by the same author (Cassell, 1957). Also LONG RANGE DESERT GROUP, W B Kennedy-Shaw (Collins, 1945), and EASTERN APPROACHES, by Fitzroy Maclean (Jonathan Cape, 1949). Recommended additional reading is POPSKI'S PRIVATE ARMY, by Lieut Col Vladimir Peniakoff DSO MC (various editions, 1950-1991). The PPA was quite separate from the LRDG, but its military ethos was equally unconventional and multi-national, and at times they assisted each other.

THE BLUE BERETS
The Story of the United Nations Peacekeeping Forces
Michael Harbottle * Leo Cooper Ltd, London, 1975. Pale blue, gold, 9.0 x 5.5, -/182. 18 mono phots, 7 maps, Bibliography, Index. Apps: table of eleven major UN operations, with details of dates, costs, etc.

* Although written by an expert, this is a curiously lightweight account of some of the most interesting multi-national deployments since the end of WWII. Troops from several Commonwealth countries have joined in these operations, and the book does provide an overview of the reasons behind their involvement. A frustration for the military historian is that none of them are identified by unit title. However, the Index is good and the Bibliography is extensive. R/1 V/3. PC. RP.

MULTI-NATIONAL FORCES - MIDDLE EAST - WWI

IMPERIAL CAMEL CORPS
Geoffrey Inchbald * Johnson Publications Ltd, London, 1970. Red, black/gold, 8.5 x 5.0, xviii/166. 24 mono phots (incl captioned officers' portraits), 4 maps, no appendixes, Index.

* Effectively an unofficial history of 2nd Bn, ICC, from formation in early 1916 to disbandment in 1919. Raised almost entirely from British Yeomanry regts, it had 30 officers, 800 ORs, and nearly 1000 camels. The author, who served throughout, makes useful references to the Australian and New Zealand Bns which also formed part of the ICC. Many officers are mentioned in the narrative, the descriptions of camel behaviour are informative, and the various battles (Egypt, Palestine and Trans-Jordan, including the support given to Lawrence in 1918) are well covered. R/2 V/3. MODL. AMM.

Note: Inchbald's autobiography, CAMELS AND OTHERS (Johnson Publications Ltd, London, 1968), also contains substantial reference to his services with the ICC.

SAND, SWEAT AND CAMELS
The Australian Companies of the Imperial Camel Corps
George F Langley and Edmee M Langley * Lowden Publishing Co, Kilmore, Victoria, 1976. Umber, gold, 9.25 x 6.25, xv/188. Fp, 32 mono phots, 3 maps, Bibliography, Index. Apps: three devoted to marching orders, scales of rations for men and camels, and rolls of officers (shown as serving with 1st and 3rd Aust Camel Bns, with 4th ANZAC Camel Bn, at Bde HQ, and at the Depot).

* Autobiographical, but readable and generally informative. The narrative covers, in particular, the organisation and role of Australia's contribution to the ICC in the campaign against the Senussi and then against the Turks (Romani Magdala, Rafa, Gaza, the advance to the Jordan and the destruction of the Hejaz railway). By mid-1918 the camel had lost its usefulness. The ten Australian Companies were then remounted on horses as 14th and 15th Light Horse. R/1 V/4. ANL. MCND'A.

THE CAMELIERS

Oliver Hogue * Andrew Melrose Ltd, London, 1919. Blue, gold, 7.5 x 5.0, xiv/279. No ills, no maps, no appendixes, no Index.

* A personal account of the role of the ICC in driving the Turks from Egypt, Sinai and Palestine by a Trooper who served. The actions at Romani and Beersheba are well covered. A useful source when read in conjunction with other books on the same subject. R/3 V/3. ANL. MCND'A.

Note: another and similar source is THE FIGHTING CAMELIERS, by Frank Reid (Angus & Robertson, Sydney, 1934).

WITH THE CAMELIERS IN PALESTINE
History of the New Zealand Companies of the Camel Corps

John Robertson * A H & A W Reed, Dunedin and Wellington, NZ, n.d. (c.1938). Dark blue, black, 8.75 x 6.0, -/244. Fp, 51 mono phots, 4 maps, no appendixes, Index.

* The ICC consisted of officers and men drawn from the Australian Light Horse, New Zealand Mounted Rifles, Indian Army, several British Army Yeomanry regts, and a small contingent of Rhodesian Police. Artillery support was provided by a Mountain Battery of the Hong Kong & Singapore Royal Garrison Artillery. The Corps also had its own Machine-gun Coys. Formed in Egypt in 1915, this special force was required to operate in a highly mobile reconnaissance and raiding role in arid areas where food, water and communications were all lacking. The book deals mainly with the New Zealand contribution, its personnel being former horsemen from various Regts of Mounted Rifles. The NZ Camel Coys fought in several engagements on the Egypt-Palestine border, in both of the Gaza battles, and then in the advance north towards Jerusalem. The author, who served with the Corps, was clearly fascinated by the Biblical and Classical parallels between this campaign and those of former millenia. He makes several such allusions, particularly when describing the raid on Amman and operations in the valley of the Jordan. He concludes with an account of the final breaking of the Turkish forces and the race for Damascus. A book written in easy style, but which could have been much improved by the provision of some basic appendixes. R/4 V/4. PC. HEC.

THE MOUNTED RIFLEMEN IN SINAI AND PALESTINE
The Story of New Zealand's Crusaders

A Briscoe Moore * Whitcombe & Tombs Ltd, Christchurch and Auckland, NZ, 1920. Illustrated soft card, 'Trooper feeding horse' motif, grey brown, green, 7.25 x 4.75, -/175. Fp, 29 mono phots, one line drawing, 3 maps (folding, bound in), no Index. Apps: Roll of Honour (all ranks, for the Auckland Mounted Rifles, the Wellington Mounted Rifles, and the Canterbury Mounted Rifles).

* Covers the work of the NZ Mounted Bde in Egypt and Palestine. Apart from the three MR Regts noted above, there is also mention of the Rarotongan Contingent which aided the Bde significantly as L of C troops. This is a condensed easy-to-read account of operations which were often overshadowed by events in France. The text is printed on low-grade paper, the illustrations on a higher-grade paper and therefore quite well defined. R/3 V/3. NYPL. HEC.

Note: reference should be made also to THE NEW ZEALANDERS IN SINAI AND PALESTINE, by Lieut Col C Guy Powles and Maj A Wilkie (Whitcombe & Tombs, for the NZ Govt, 1922). Having xv/284 pages, this book amplifies the information contained in Moore's account.

THE DESERT MOUNTED CORPS
An Account of the Cavalry Operations in Palestine and Syria, 1917-1918
Lieut Col the Hon R M P Preston DSO * Constable & Co, London, 1921. Red, gold, 'Palm tree' motif, 9.5 x 6.0, xxiv/356. Fp, 33 mono phots, 11 maps (7 printed in the text, 4 folding, bound in), Index. Apps: Organisation of the Desert Corps, Notes on the Arab Movement, Summary of the Terms of the Turkish Armistice.
* After two introductory chapters, the book becomes a chronological account of the activities of the Corps between 27 October 1917 and 31 October 1918. It concludes with useful accounts of the administration of conquered territories in the Levant, the work of the Horse Artillery, and matters relating to transport and supply. R/4 V/4. RSCL. TAB.

HISTORY OF THE M.T. OF THE DESERT MOUNTED CORPS DURING OPERATIONS IN PALESTINE AND SYRIA, 1918
Anon * Palestine News Press, Cairo, 1919. Soft card, yellow, black, 6.75 x 4.75, -/8. No ills, no maps, no appendixes, no Index.
* Despite its brevity, this booklet does explain in useful detail the role of the Desert Mounted Corps's three Motor Transport Lorry Companies (905, 906 and 1009) towards the end of Allenby's campaign. R/5 V/1. AWM. MCND'A.

Note: an additional popular source is THE DESERT COLUMN, by Ion Idriess (Angus Robertson, Sydney, first published in 1932, republished by the same firm in various bindings in 1933, 1934, 1935, 1936, 1937, 1939, 1941, 1944 and 1985). This is an autobiographical account, written in diary form, by a Trooper of Light Horse who served in the Palestine campaign from 1916 onwards.

SPECIAL INTEREST SOURCES

HERALDRY IN WAR
Formation Badges, 1939-1945
Lieut Col Howard N Cole OBE TD * Gale & Polden Ltd, Aldershot, 1950. Tan, red, '1st Army, 21st Army Group, and 14th Army flashes' motif, 8.75 x 5.5, xxx/290. Fp, 15 mono phots, 5 cld plates, 550 sketches (formation badges/flashes), no maps, Glossary, Sources, Index (Appendix IV). Apps: arm of service strips, vehicle arm of service strips.
* This book covers WWII formation badges. It focuses primarily upon British Army formations, but there are many helpful references also to Dominion, Colonial and Allied commands. The author opens with a brief summary of the history of military heraldry. The bulk of his substantial work is then devoted to the individual entries, each of which states the formation's date of initial authorisation, a narrative description of its badge, the heraldic symbolism thereof, and a line drawing. Appendix IV - effectively an Index - is full of interest. It reveals the way in which WWII formation badges/flashes incorporated a wide range of symbols - fish, flowers, fruit, trees, aircraft, stars, buildings, torches, bells, feathers, ships, and much else besides. The animal section alone has thirty-two sub-headings. This is an unusual and stimulating view of the Commonwealth's war effort.
R/4 V/5. PC. RH.

Note: first published in 1946. A second and expanded edition (230 pages) was published in 1947.

ADDITIONAL SOURCES

Many Empire units - Regiments and Corps - have never been recorded in published histories of the type which constitutes the bulk of this bibliography. Researchers seeking information on such units are obliged, therefore, to consult various original archival sources. Amongst the most useful of these are the GAZETTES which were published by most (but not all) former Dominions and Colonies.

The GAZETTES were, in essence, official newspapers. Intended for the information of the authorities and the public alike, they were published every few months (with special Supplements if need arose in the interim). Typically, they carried a mixture of proclamations, ordinances, invitations to tender, statisticial surveys, meteorological reports and commercial advertisements. Their compilation was largely a matter for each local editor's discretion, but frequently they reported matters of a military nature, e.g. the formation or disbandment of Militia or police units, embodiments in time of emergency, officers' promotions and postings, their honours and awards, parades, presentations, and the like. Much of this information would have appeared in a formal unit history if one had ever been written.

Until 1837, most overseas territories were administered by the War Office. Some GAZETTES were published during those early years, but new regulations then placed them on a formal and regular basis. Copies were despatched to London and were lodged with various Government departments, the two most important being the Colonial Office and the India Office. Complete runs of these GAZETTES have survived and are open to public inspection.

India was a special case because it never went through the process of being a Colony before becoming a Dominion. In archival terms, there is the complication that its affairs were managed until 1858 by the Honourable East India Company. However, GAZETTES became a regular feature in the 1830s and complete runs of Government of India and Provincial Government GAZETTES are held at the India Office Library & Records, Orbit House, Blackfriars Road, London. Full details are available in the GENERAL GUIDE TO THE INDIA OFFICE RECORDS, by Martin Moir, published in 1988, which can be purchased by mail.

The GAZETTES published in all the other Colonies and Dominions (including India) are held at the Public Record Office, Kew, Richmond, Surrey. They appear under two separate PRO classifications. They are prefixed 'CO' (Colonial Office) and 'DO' (Dominions Office). The former extends from the 1830s through to the 1920s. The granting of Dominion status to various former Colonies led to a division of responsibilities in London, hence the creation of the Dominions Office in 1925 (replaced by the Commonwealth Relations Office in 1947). Those territories which did not acquire Dominion status continued to be administered by the Colonial Office. The 'CO' and 'DO' prefixes reflect these changes.

The following list specifies the series of GAZETTES held at the PRO, together with their classification numbers and the periods of time which they cover. Researchers needing a more detailed listing of the PRO's holdings can purchase, by mail, the PUBLIC RECORD OFFICE CURRENT GUIDE, 1992. The microfiche edition consists of eighteen 270-frame fiches with an introductory booklet.

CO16	**South Australia,** 1839 to 1925, 135 volumes
CO21	**Western Australia,** 1836 to 1925, 74 volumes
CO32	**Barbados,** 1867 to 1975, 191 volumes
CO46	**Canada Government,** 1825 to 1925, 172 volumes
CO52	**Cape of Good Hope (Cape Colony),** 1823 to 1925, 120 volumes
CO58	**Ceylon,** 1813 to 1946, 314 volumes
CO63	**British Columbia,** 1863 to 1915, 101 volumes
CO70	**Cyprus,** 1878 to 1965, 59 volumes

CO75 **Dominica,** 1865 to 1975, 57 volumes
CO86 **Fiji,** 1874 to 1975, 71 volumes
CO94 **Gibraltar,** 1839 to 1965, 182 volumes and papers
CO99 **Gold Coast,** 1872 to 1957, 103 volumes
CO115 **British Guiana and Guyana,** 1838 to 1975, 322 volumes
CO127 **British Honduras,** 1861 to 1975, 94 volumes
CO132 **Hong Kong,** 1846 to 1990, 178 volumes
CO141 **Jamaica,** 1794 to 1968, 156 volumes
CO150 **Lagos,** 1881 to 1905, 12 volumes
CO156 **Leeward Islands,** 1872 to 1965, 60 volumes
CO162 **Malta,** 1818 to 1975, 199 volumes
CO171 **Mauritius,** 1823 to 1975, 173 volumes
CO182 **Natal,** 1858 to 1925, 59 volumes
CO192 **New Brunswick,** 1842 to 1923, 26 volumes
CO198 **Newfoundland,** 1844 to 1923, 13 volumes
CO205 **New South Wales,** 1832 to 1925, 309 volumes
CO212 **New Zealand,** 1841 to 1925, 115 volumes
CO216 **North-West Territories,** 1883 to 1905, 4 volumes
CO230 **Prince Edward Island,** 1832 to 1925, 20 volumes
CO237 **Queensland,** 1859 to 1925, 125 volumes
CO242 **St Christopher (St Kitts), Nevis and Anguilla,** 1849 to 1989, 53 volumes
CO251 **St Helena,** 1845 to 1965, 11 volumes
CO257 **St Lucia,** 1857 to 1975, 125 volumes
CO264 **St Vincent,** 1831 to 1975, 82 volumes
CO276 **Straits Settlements,** 1867 to 1942, 161 volumes
CO283 **Tasmania,** 1816 to 1925, 143 volumes
CO289 **Tobago,** 1872 to 1898, 30 volumes
CO294 **Transvaal,** 1869 to 1925, 58 volumes
CO299 **Trinidad and Tobago,** 1833 to 1975, 193 volumes
CO308 **Vancouver Island,** 1864 to 1866, 1 volume
CO312 **Victoria,** 1851 to 1925, 183 volumes
CO323 **Colonies, General (Original Correspondence),** 1689 to 1952, 1931 volumes. Between 1801 and 1854, matters relating to War and the Colonies were controlled by the same Secretary of State. These papers are therefore a useful supplement to (or substitute for) the GAZETTES of that period.
CO445 **Niger and West Africa Frontier Force and West African Frontier Force Original Correspondence,** 1898 to 1926, 69 volumes. This also is a collection of original letters, not a run of GAZETTES, but it represents a useful additional source. Vide also CO820.
CO451 **British Bechuanaland,** 1887 to 1895, 1 volume.
CO453 **British New Guinea (Papua),** 1888 to 1921, 4 volumes
CO455 **British South Africa Company,** 1894 to 1923, 8 volumes
CO457 **East Africa and Uganda Protectorates,** 1899 to 1907, 7 volumes
CO463 **Negri Sembilan, Sungei Ujong and Jelebu,** 1896 to 1908, 26 volumes
CO467 **Pahang,** 1897 to 1977, 25 volumes
CO468 **Perak,** 1888 to 1980, 56 volumes
CO469 **Selangor,** 1890 to 1975, 41 volumes
CO470 **Seychelles,** 1889 to 1976, 59 volumes
CO475 **Sungei Ujong,** 1893, 1 volume
CO541 **Nyasaland (Malawi),** 1894 to 1975, 65 volumes
CO542 **Kenya,** 1908 to 1975, 103 volumes
CO548 **South Africa,** 1901 to 1922, 3 volumes
CO552 **Union of South Africa,** 1910 to 1925, 57 volumes
CO556 **Alberta,** 1905 to 1924, 15 volumes
CO559 **Commonwealth of Australia,** 1901 to 1925, 36 volumes
CO564 **Bahamas,** 1894 to 1965, 32 volumes
CO573 **Labuan,** 1890 to 1906, 1 volume

CO574 **Labuan,** 1890 to 1906, 1 volume
CO574 **Federated Malay States,** 1909 to 1948, 96 volumes
CO586 **Northern Nigeria,** 1900 to 1913, 6 volumes
CO591 **Southern Nigeria,** 1900 to 1913, 12 volumes
CO593 **Nova Scotia and Cape Breton,** 1905 to 1925, 17 volumes
CO595 **Ontario,** 1905 to 1925, 34 volumes
CO597 **Orange River Colony,** 1900 to 1910, 13 volumes
CO602 **Quebec,** 1905 to 1925, 41 volumes
CO604 **Sarawak,** 1903 to 1980, 115 volumes
CO605 **Saskatchewan,** 1905 to 1925, 19 volumes
CO612 **Uganda,** 1908 to 1973, 74 volumes
CO616 **Dominions (War of 1914 to 1918), Original Correspondence,** 1914 to 1919, 82 volumes. These are original documents, not GAZETTES, but the in-depth researcher will find much of value in these volumes.
CO647 **Bermuda,** 1902 to 1965, 20 volumes
CO653 **Johore,** 1911 to 1979, 66 volumes
CO658 **Nigeria,** 1914 to 1976, 273 volumes
CO662 **Orange Free State,** 1911 to 1925, 10 volumes
CO667 **New Guinea (Former German Territory),** 1914 to 1925, 2 volumes
CO669 **North-Eastern Rhodesia,** 1903 to 1911, 1 volume
CO670 **Northern Rhodesia and Zambia,** 1911 to 1970, 56 volumes
CO675 **Tonga,** 1905 to 1975, 21 volumes
CO681 **Turks and Caicos Islands,** 1907 to 1965, 13 volumes
CO689 **Zanzibar,** 1913 to 1965, 67 volumes
CO692 **Western Pacific,** 1914 to 1971, 30 volumes and papers
CO696 **Iraq, Sessional Papers,** 1917 to 1931, 7 volumes
These papers are the main archive relating to the period of British administration between 1917 and 1921. Vide also CO813, below.
CO737 **Tanganyika,** 1919 to 1964, 72 volumes
CO738 **South West Africa,** 1915 to 1925, 2 volumes
CO742 **Palestine,** 1919 to 1948, 26 volumes
CO744 **Wei-hai-Wei,** 1908 to 1930, 3 volumes
CO813 **Iraq,** 1921 to 1955, 35 volumes
CO815 **Southern Rhodesia,** 1923 to 1925, 1 volume
CO819 **Kedah and Perlis,** 1925 to 1979, 38 volumes
CO820 **Military Original Correspondence,** 1927 to 1951, 77 volumes and files. These are batches of reports and letters, not GAZETTES, but are a primary source. The contents refer to various Colonial forces. For the period prior to 1927, vide CO445 (West Africa Frontier Force) and CO534 (King's African Rifles).
CO822 **East Africa, Original Correspondence,** 1927 to 1965, 20 volumes.
Again, source documents, not GAZETTES. The file is noted here because it contains useful references to the Mau-Mau emergency of 1952-1956.
CO829 **New Hebrides,** 1927 to 1969, 5 volumes and papers
CO853 **Aden,** 1932 to 1967, 41 volumes
CO855 **British North Borneo and Sabah,** 1883 to 1908, 108 volumes
CO909 **Trengganu,** 1939 to 1975, 20 volumes
CO921 **East Africa High Commission,** 1948 to 1966, 16 volumes
CO922 **Somaliland,** 1941 to 1960, 8 volumes
CO928 **Kelantan,** 1948 to 1979, 21 volumes
CO929 **Malacca,** 1948 to 1979, 18 volumes
CO930 **Federation of Malaya (Malaysia),** 1948 to 1980, 181 volumes
CO931 **Perlis,** 1948 to 1977, 10 volumes
CO932 **Singapore,** 1945 to 1970, 123 volumes
CO933 **Penang,** 1948 to 1977, 27 volumes
CO968 **Defence, Original Correspondence,** 1941 to 1962, 706 boxes of files. Source documents, not GAZETTES. Vide also CO323 and CO974.

CO985 **Brunei,** 1951 to 1975, 25 volumes
CO1019 **Cayman Islands,** 1956 to 1990, 67 volumes
CO1049 **Antigua,** 1967 to 1989, 23 volumes
CO1051 **Gilbert & Ellice Islands,** 1968 to 1974, 5 volumes

The following 'DO' classification relates to records created by, or inherited by, the Dominions Office, the Commonwealth Relations Office, and the Foreign & Commonwealth Office.

DO12 **Union of South Africa,** 1926 to 1978, 343 volumes
DO14 **Alberta,** 1925 to 1980, 144 volumes
DO16 **Commonwealth of Australia,** 1926 to 1987, 282 volumes
DO24 **Western Australia,** 1926 to 1989, 243 volumes
DO29 **Canada,** 1926 to 1978, 272 volumes
DO32 **Cape of Good Hope,** 1926 to 1961, 68 volumes
DO34 **British Columbia,** 1926 to 1975, 167 volumes
DO38 **Manitoba,** 1926 to 1975, 83 volumes
DO40 **Natal,** 1926 to 1961, 48 volumes
DO43 **New Brunswick,** 1924 to 1968, 18 volumes
DO46 **New South Wales,** 1926 to 1980, 206 volumes
DO50 **New Zealand,** 1926 to 1965, 195 volumes
DO52 **Nova Scotia,** 1926 to 1975, 74 volumes
DO54 **Ontario,** 1926 to 1978, 161 volumes
DO56 **Orange Free State,** 1926 to 1961, 47 volumes
DO59 **Quebec,** 1926 to 1973, 186 volumes
DO62 **Queensland,** 1926 to 1980, 269 volumes
DO65 **Southern Rhodesia,** 1926 to 1966, 102 volumes
DO66 **Saskatchewan,** 1926 to 1966, 42 volumes
DO70 **Tasmania,** 1926 to 1980, 118 volumes
DO73 **Transvaal,** 1926 to 1960, 40 volumes
DO76 **Victoria,** 1926 to 1980, 170 volumes
DO78 **South West Africa,** 1926 to 1968, 56 volumes
DO83 **Nauru,** 1926 to 1965, 15 volumes
DO85 **New Guinea and Papua New Guinea,** 1926 to 1948, 7 volumes
For the period prior to 1926, vide CO667.
DO86 **Papua,** 1922 to 1949, 2 volumes
For the period prior to 1922, vide CO453.
DO87 **Prince Edward Island,** 1926 to 1968, 16 volumes
For the period prior to 1926, vide CO230.
DO91 **South Africa High Commission,** 1923 to 1960, 8 volumes
DO104 **Ceylon and Sri Lanka,** 1947 to 1975, 230 volumes
DO105 **India,** 1948 to 1979, 469 volumes
DO106 **Pakistan,** 1948 to 1972, 107 volumes
DO107 **Western Samoa,** 1902 to 1973, 5 volumes
DO108 **Australia, Northern Territory,** 1948 to 1969, 8 volumes
DO125 **Federation of Rhodesia and Nyasaland,** 1953 to 1963, 27 volumes
DO132 **Ghana,** 1957 to 1975, 75 volumes
DO135 **Norfolk Island,** 1956 to 1960, 1 volume
DO136 **Federation of the West Indies,** 1958 to 1961, 6 volumes
DO145 **Basutoland and Lesotho, Bechuanaland Protectorate and Botswana, and Swaziland,** 1961 to 1975, 56 volumes
DO146 **Tanzania,** 1964 and 1975, 29 volumes

Part 2

Southern & Central Americas

NOTES

SOUTH ATLANTIC REGION

TRISTAN DA CUNHA
And the Roaring Forties
Allan Crawford * Charles Skilton Ltd, Edinburgh, 1982. Blue, gold, 8.5 x 6.0, -/255. Fp, approx 150 mono phots, 12 maps, no appendixes, Bibliography, Index.
* This is the history of the island from 1586 to 1981. The bulk of the narrative deals with the author's own time there, from 1937 to the evacuation in 1961. Just three pages are devoted to the military aspect. In WWII, a signals section was established to transmit weather and shipping movement reports. In 1943, with German commerce raiders on the loose in the South Atlantic and Southern Oceans, sixteen local men were recruited to form the Tristan Defence Volunteers. Armed with rifles and Lewis guns, their task would have been to contest any German landing and give the radio operators time in which to send out an alarm and destroy their code books. The TDV was very probably the smallest integral military unit ever to serve the Crown. R/2 V/3. CFHT. PJE.

THE HISTORY OF THE FALKLAND ISLANDS DEFENCE FORCE
Sydney Miller * Unpublished facsimile TS, single-sided, 11.75 x 8.25, -/64, n.d. ('Preface' dated February 1982). No ills, no maps, no appendixes, no Index.
* Completed only a few weeks before the Argentine invasion, this is an excellent summary of part-time soldiering on the Falkland Islands from the mid-19th Century. Sydney Miller, a leading local resident, drew upon many official and unofficial sources and his account is clear, concise and liberally seeded with the names of those who served. In 1854, in response to a perceived invasion threat from Imperial Russia, a Detachment of Pensioners, eighty strong, was formed under the command of Sgt Maj George Felton, formerly of the Life Guards. In 1892, authority was granted for the formation of the Falkland Islands Volunteer Corps (later Defence Corps) to contest any 'actual or apprehended invasion'. Membership was 170 all ranks, of whom 100 were mounted. They went over to a war footing in 1914 when the Imperial German Navy was operating in the South Atlantic and posing a threat to the important coaling facilities and wireless station at Port Stanley. An Artillery section manned the two 6 inch guns guarding the harbour entrance. Some members volunteered for service overseas and amongst their awards were one DSO, two MCs, one DCM, and one MM. The Force was mobilised again in 1939 and service made compulsory for all male islanders ('Kelpers') between 18 and 60 years of age. The Nazi Bund in Argentina, 100,000 strong, posed a powerful threat, so the defence of the islands was sharply increased by the arrival of Force 122, a British Army Brigade Group based upon 11th West Yorkshire Regt. It remained in the Falklands from August 1942 until January 1944. The next mobilisation came in 1966 when a hi-jacked Argentine civil airliner landed on Stanley race-course. A party of extremists made their 'symbolic invasion' but were arrested by the FIDF a few hours later. Local defence gradually devolved in later years to a continuing Royal Marines presence at Moody Brook and FIDF membership had sunk to only thirty-two all ranks by the night of 1/2 April 1982 when Argentina made its full-scale landings. Even so, the Force was called out by the Governor and C-in-C, Mr Rex Hunt, and it provided sentries at various key points until ordered to stand down on the following morning. R/5 V/3. NAM. RP.
Note: a detailed account of events leading up to the Argentine invasion of the Falkland Islands is to be found in OPERATION PARAQUAT - THE BATTLE FOR SOUTH GEORGIA, 1982, by Roger Perkins (Picton Publishing, Chippenham, Wiltshire, 1986). This book incorporates additional information regarding military events on and around other British possessions in the South Atlantic and Southern Oceans - Ascension Island, St Helena, the South Shetlands, and the South Orkneys.

LATIN AMERICA

ACTIVITIES OF THE BRITISH COMMUNITY IN ARGENTINA DURING THE GREAT WAR 1914-1919

To Place on Record the Response of the British Coummunity in Men, Money and Material to the Call of the Motherland

Arthur L Holder * The Buenos Aires Herald, Buenos Aires, for the British Society in the Argentine Republic, 1920. Seen rebound in blue, gold, 10.0 x 8.5, -/485. Fp, more than 400 mono phots (studio portraits), no maps, Index. Apps: H&A (incl biographical notes).

* A valuable source for genealogists, medal collectors and students of social history. Looking specifically at the 'military' content, the Roll of Honour section contains an abundance of biographical information concerning Britons and Anglo-Argentines, living and working in Argentina, who voluntarily left that country to 'join up', and many of whom died on active service. Most of the entries are accompanied by good quality portraits and details of awards. One officer thus recorded is Lieut John Holland. He won his VC while serving in France with the Leinster Regt. R/4 V/4. RMAS. RP.

ACTIVITIES OF THE BRITISH COMMUNITY IN THE ARGENTINE REPUBLIC DURING THE 1939-1945 WAR

Anon * The British Community Council in the Argentine Republic, Buenos Aires, 1953. Soft card, beige, black, 8.5 x 5.5, iv/127. No ills, no maps, Bibliography, Index. Apps: Roll of Honour, H&A, various other rolls.

* Like the publication described above, this is an informative listing of all those Argentine nationals and British ex-patriates who volunteered for Crown service. The rolls give full details of rank, unit and awards. The Roll of Honour lists all those who lost their lives in action and from natural causes. Additionally, the book contains much information concerning the fund-raising work of the British Community Council which paid the cost of equipping No 164 (Argentine-British) Squadron, RAF. R/4 V/4. PC. APR.

A SHORT HISTORY OF THE VOLUNTEER FORCES OF BRITISH HONDURAS (NOW BELIZE)

Lieut Col D N A Fairweather OBE TD * Publication details not shown (probably at Belize, c.1970). Soft card, wire stitch-bound, white, black, 9.75 x 6.75, -/43. Two fps, 6 other mono phots (all formal groups), one map, no Index. Apps: list of former COs (of all the various local forces which existed between 1817 and 1963).

* A brief but readable story which covers the period 1804 to 1963. The narrative describes a complicated chain of events in clear style, and the illustrations are helpful in any study of local uniforms, weaponry and racial composition. Honduras was originally the target for Spanish treasure hunters before becoming a lair for pirates. The arrival of the British in the early 19th Century was prompted by a need for the country's hardwoods (mahogany in particular). Logging activities were resisted by the local tribes. The formation of the Prince Regent's Royal Honduras Militia, in 1814, was intended to protect British commercial interests against such tribal attacks and against possible foreign invasion. This force was later disbanded, reformed, renamed and restructured, but its role throughout the 19th Century remained basically the same - pacification of unruly tribes, aid to the civil power, and resisting border incursions from Guatemala. In 1915 a Contingent of 129 officers and men was despatched to form part of the newly-raised British West Indies Regt. A second Contingent of 400 served in Egypt and Palestine, taking part in the two battles for Gaza. In 1916 a Territorial Force was raised to deal with insurgents from Guatemala. In 1939, members of the British Honduras Defence Force volunteered for aircrew training with the RAF and for work as skilled loggers in Scotland. Many individuals are mentioned throughout (incl lists of those who travelled to London in 1911 and 1936 for the Coronation and Jubilee celebrations). R/3 V/4. AMOT/MODL. RP.

THE HISTORY OF THE BRITISH GUIANA POLICE

Col W A Orrett CBE * The Daily Chronicle Ltd, Georgetown, 1951. Soft card, light blue, dark blue, 7.5 x 5.0, -/74 plus 8 unnumbered. Fp, no other ills, no maps, no Index. Apps: H&A (officers holding decorations or medals for gallantry or meritorious service), roll of officers, WOs and NCOs (those serving at 31.12.1950).

* The author was Commissioner from 1943 to 1952. In this slim volume, he traces the history of the Force from 1839 to the early 1950s. It is an unpretentious book, lacking some of the features which are usually desirable in a unit history, but the narrative is packed with all sorts of useful information. Col Orrett states that his account is based upon considerable research in Guiana and in the UK, but unfortunately he does not quote any of his sources and does not provide a Bibliography. R/4 V/3. RSCL. TAB.

HISTORY OF POLICING IN GUYANA

John Campbell * HQ Guyana Police Force, Georgetown, 1987. Illustrated stiff card, red, blue, white, 9.0 x 6.0, -/244. Numerous small mono phots, no maps, Sources, Bibliography, Index. Apps: Roll of Honour, H&A, 'Regulations for Government of Berbice Police, 1835'.

* A well researched book on the history of the Guyana Police Force from its formation in 1839 to the 1960s, with a chapter on pre-1839 law and order arrangements. The author acknowledges his debt to Col Orrett (vide preceding entry), and draws heavily upon him. The book is strong on statistics, and useful tables and nominal rolls are inserted in the text at various points, but the whole work remains readable throughout. The author served in the force for forty years, rising from Constable to Assistant Commissioner. R/2 V/5. RCSL. TAB.

Note: in his 'Introduction', the author describes this as the first in a planned two-volume series, but no trace of a 'Volume II' has been traced. Presumably it would cover the period of the 1960s, 1970s and 1980s, and for reasons of political sensitivity he may have found it difficult to continue with his project.

OTHER CORPS

TELLING THE TRUTH

The Life and Times of the British Honduran Forestry Unit in Scotland (1941-44)

Amos A Ford * Karia Press, London, 1985. Illustrated paper, green/black, 8.5 x 5.25, x/96. Fp, 16 mono phots, 2 maps, no Index. Apps: nominal roll of the men repatriated from Scotland on 27 December 1943.

* It is not entirely clear whether this 'unit' was subject to military law or whether the personnel were all employed on a civilian contract. In any event, the book is recorded here as reflecting yet another little-known facet of the Honduran voluntary effort to assist the Crown in WWII. The unit comprised skilled loggers who were recruited to work in the woodlands and timber mills of Scotland. The author himself served with the BHFU, but this is much more than a memoir. The narrative is based upon official records held at the Public Record Office, Kew, London, and upon interviews with his former friends and workmates. He covers all phases - from recruitment, the journey to Scotland, the experiences of the men, the work they did, and their return to Honduras and the disbandment of 1943. The book highlights the institutionalised racism encountered by the men while they were in Scotland. A book which is probably of little interest to the military historian, but certainly of value to the social and/or economic historian. R/2 V/4. RCSL. TAB.

CARIBBEAN REGION

SLAVES IN RED COATS
The British West India Regiments, 1795-1815
Roger Norman Buckley * Yale University Press, Battleboro, Vermont, 1979. Red, gold, 9.5 x 6.25, xi/210. Fp, no other ills, 2 maps, Bibliography, Index.
Apps: verbatim text (in French) of the order which created the Corps de Negres in 1795, text of the contract to supply slaves for service in the 1st, 7th and 8th West India Regts.
* In 1795, two Regts of local negroes and creoles were recruited into British service because freshly arrived British Army units were suffering huge losses from diseases to which they had no acquired immunity. The force was expanded to a total strength of thirteen Bns. The book traces the evolution of the BWIR, its deployments, and its political, social and economic status vis-a-vis the Empire (and British attitudes towards the slave trade). Good background reading, albeit with the usual American 'anti-colonialism' undertone. Particularly good for the period 1795-1806. R/1 V/3. PC. RP.

THE HISTORY OF THE FIRST WEST INDIA REGIMENT
Maj A B Ellis * Printed by Charles Dickens & Evans, Crystal Palace Press, for Chapman Hall Ltd, London, 1885. Red, gold, Regtl crest, 9.0 x 5.5, xi/366 (plus 40 pages of advertisements). Fp, no other ills, 14 maps, Index (of persons).
* After the American Revolution (War of Independence), His Majesty's Troop of Black Dragoons, His Majesty's Corps of Black Artificers, and His Majesty's Corps of Black Pioneers, who had all fought for the Crown, were formed into The Black Carolina Corps. In 1795, the Corps was merged with Malcolm's Rangers (which had been raised that year in Martinique) to form the 1st West India Regt. The WIR subsequently fought in the West Indies (Martinique and Guadeloupe, 1809-1810), against the Americans (New Orleans, 1814-1815), and in West Africa (incl Ashantee, 1873-1874). The book is written in a dry but informative style and is accurate after 1795. Pages 26 to 52, which deal with the American Revolution, are unfortunately very unreliable. R/5 V/4. PCAL/MODL. SODW/AMM.

ONE HUNDRED YEARS' HISTORY OF THE 2nd BATTALION, WEST INDIA REGIMENT, FROM DATE OF RAISING 1795 TO 1898
Col J E Caulfield * Publisher not stated, printed by Foster Groom & Co, London, 1899. Blue and red, gold, 8.5 x 5.5, -/221. Fp, 5 mono phots, no maps, no Index. Apps: list of former COs (1795-1892), chronology of movements and stations.
* The narrative covers the period stated in the title in uniform detail. It has good coverage of several little-known operations in the West Indies and in West Africa. The syle is dry and tedious, but the contents appear to be accurate.
R/5 V/3. PCAL/RMAS. RP.

JAMAICA'S PART IN THE GREAT WAR, 1914-1918
Frank Cundall * Hazell, Watson & Viney Ltd, for The Institute of Jamaica, 1925. Rifle green, gold, 10.0 x 7.25, -/155. Fp, 28 mono phots, 3 maps, Bibliography, no Index. Apps: Rolls of Honour (incl one for officers only, with detailed notes of service for each, and another roll for ORs, with Service numbers, dates of death and home addresses), plus notes on fund-raising, recruitment, etc.
* In the autumn of 1914, Volunteer Contingents began to arrive in England from all parts of the Caribbean. They consisted of various races, but the majority were coloured soldiers and British (European) officers and SNCOs. Initially they were split up and drafted into a variety of British Army units and Corps. In October and November 1915, several Contingents were brought together at Seaford, West Sussex, to form the British West Indies Regt. Its initial composition was: 'A' Coy - British Guiana, 'B' Coy - Trinidad, 'C' Coy - Trinidad and St Vincent, 'D' Coy - Grenada and Barbados. Wastage was high. Men died of pneumonia or were sent home medically unfit. A fresh draft of 725 men from Jamaica, British Honduras and Barbados made the Regt viable for further training and eventually it expanded to

four Bns. They served variously in East Africa, Egypt, Palestine, and on the Western Front. This book tells their stories in interesting detail. It recounts also the services of Jamaicans who were assigned to other Empire forces, to the Royal Flying Corps, and so forth. A valuable record of a now almost forgotten contribution to the final Allied victory. R/5 V/4. RCSL. RP.

THE BAHAMAS DURING THE GREAT WAR
Frank Holmes * The Tribune Press, Nassau, 1924. Green, gold, Armorial bearings, 8.0 x 5.75, xii/180. Fp, 5 mono phots, no maps, no Index. Apps: nominal roll of Bahamanians who served in the 2nd and 3rd Contingents and in replacement drafts for the British West Indies Regt.
* The narrative is devoted mainly to the war's economic and governmental impact. It contains little of a military nature. However, the genealogist will find it useful. Apart from the appendixes noted above, the author included in his text a nominal roll for the 1st Contingent and a Roll of Honour of all Bahamanians who died in service (regardless of cause, arm, or unit). R/5 V/3. MU. HIS.

WAR DIARY, 1st BATTALION, BRITISH WEST INDIES REGIMENT, 1915-1918
Anon * Not seen, but noted on one occasion in a dealer's catalogue and there described as 'a presentation volume to the West India Committee from the Regiment', MS and TS, folio, bound in full maroon calf-skin, having 6 maps, 245 pages, and the imprint '1918'. It is possible that this was the original War Diary and therefore the only copy extant. However, copies may have been made and a future researcher might be more successful than this bibliographer in finding one.
Note: the Bn served in Egypt, Sinai, Palestine, and Syria. Its CO, Lieut Col C Wood Hill DSO, subsequently produced a leaflet of eleven pages containing a condensed (and somewhat bitter) account of his Bn's experiences. IWM. SODW.

THE CARIB REGIMENT OF WORLD WAR II
Elvey Watson * Vantage Press, New York, 1964. Mottled green, black, 8.0 x 5.5, -/149. 8 mono phots, no maps, no appendixes, no Index.
* A personal account, based mainly upon diaries and the author's memory. He began his military service in 1942 when he joined the Barbados Bn.
This was merged with the Windward Islands Bn to form The Islands Bn which, in turn, was absorbed into The Caribbean Regt when the latter was formed for overseas service in April 1944. Other elements were Contingents from pre-war local Volunteer Defence units and men recruited in Antigua, the Bahamas, Barbados, Barbuda, Bermuda, British Guiana, British Honduras, Dominica, Grenada, Jamaica, Monserrat, St Lucia, St Vincent, Trinidad and Tobago. The personnel were officers and men of the islands, of all creeds and colours, with a few officers and SNCOs posted in from British Army units. The author refers to 'The Caribbean Regiment' and 'The Carib Regiment' without explanation or comment. The former was the official title, so the latter may have been a shortened version used by those who served with it. After a short training period in Trinidad and the USA, it moved to Italy in July 1944 and was employed on general duties in the rear areas. Next, in October, it sailed for Egypt as escort to 4000 German POW. Subsequently it was engaged in mine-clearance work around Suez and in the Canal area before returning home and being disbanded in January 1946. The fact that it never saw front-line service was due partly to its inadequate training and partly to worries about the political impact in the islands if it had incurred heavy casualties. The narrative is a blend of day-to-day events in the unit combined with comments on the progress of the war in general. The latter element is sometimes inaccurate. It contains several references to individual personnel, mainly officers. The book lacks many of the features expected in a conventional unit history, but it is useful as the only record of this scarcely known contribution to the Allied war effort.
R/4 V/2. MODL. AMM/RH.
Note: researchers fortunate enough to locate a copy of ARMED FORCES OF THE BRITISH WEST INDIES, by Maj G Tylden (unpublished TS), will be able to obtain further information regarding the many units raised from time to time in that

region. As an illustration of the scale of the subject, Trinidad & Tobago alone generated ninety-two different unit titles. Sadly, no formal histories were ever published for any of them. SODW.

DEFENCE NOT DEFIANCE
A History of the Bermuda Volunteer Rifles Corps
Jennifer M Ingham * The Island Press Ltd, Bermuda, 1992. Soft card, green, black, Corps crest, 8.5 x 6.0, ii/105. Fp, 36 mono phots, no maps, Bibliography (very detailed), Chapter Notes, Index. Apps: Roll of Honour (WWII), list of former COs, idem Adjutants, nominal roll of the Overseas Contingent (WWI).
* The group of mid-Atlantic islets known collectively as Bermuda have a land area of less than twenty square miles. They have a long association with the Royal Navy and, for much of the 19th Century, they had a significant British Army garrison. At the same time, Bermuda had its own tradition of military service in the form of the Bermuda Volunteer Rifle Corps. This brief but very readable account of the Colony's own Regiment begins with a description of the founding of Bermuda in 1609, its early Militia forces and, in more detail, the key years of 1894 to 1900. The Corps did not serve overseas as an integral unit, but it provided Contingents or drafts in WWI and WWII for service with other Regiments (and in particular the Lincolnshire Regt). Three chapters are devoted to those world war services. The story ends with disbandment in 1945. R/2 V/4. HLB. JA.
Note: there are TS reports covering the Corps' history in both WWI and WWII housed in the Hamilton Library, Bermuda, but the item described above is the first account to have been formally published.

Police

THE STORY OF A WEST INDIAN POLICEMAN
Or Forty-seven Years of the Jamaica Constabulary
Herbert T Thomas * The Gleaner Co Ltd, Kingston, Jamaica, 1927. Red, black, 8.0 x 5.0, viii/416. Fp (portrait of the author), 17 mono phots, one map (folding, bound in at the rear), no appendixes, no Index.
* A prolix and opinionated account by the author of his service between 1876 and 1924. Thomas was embittered by his failure to win promotion or official recognition. For this he blamed the Governor, Sir Sidney (later Lord) Olivier. Much of the book is devoted to these personal vicissitudes, but he does include some useful references to various unusual police cases and to events such as the Montego Bay riots of 1902. He comments upon the character and capabilities of some of his brother officers and vents his opinions upon a number of subjects which might interest the social or police historian - the granting of Commissions to native-born Jamaicans, race relations, the island and its history, the Maroons, the Obeah (sorcerers), and so forth. R/4 V/3. RCSL. TAB.

PART 3

Colonial North America

NOTES

COLONIAL NORTH AMERICA - A MILITARY CHRONOLOGY

1773: the British Government has been attempting to raise taxes in the Thirteen Colonies to pay for its garrison troops. Despite being under direct threat from the French and their Indian friends, the Colonists protest against the imposition of such taxes because they have been denied the right to elect their own political leaders. A rallying cry is - 'No taxation without representation'. Radical protesters in Boston, acting upon a variety of motives, throw three ship-loads of tea into the harbour.

1775: a Virginian landowner and experienced soldier, George Washington, heads with others a revolutionary movement against the British administration. Fighting breaks out between the rebels and units of the British Army. Not all Americans agree with the Washington faction. Ignoring the absence of a coherent British policy, they begin to form themselves into 'Loyalist' Provincial line regiments to fight their revolutionary compatriots.

1776: the rebels formally declare their independence from the Crown. The fighting intensifies.

1777: a British Army expeditionary force from Canada, commanded by General John Burgoyne, is forced to surrender to the rebels at Saratoga, Upper New York. Having lost five thousand Regular soldiers, the British accelerate the rate of recruitment of Loyalist volunteers. Their terms of service are improved and their numbers rise quickly. They have some success on the Canadian border. With their Indian allies, they mount aggressive raids into New York. For the rest, they are mishandled by the British high command.

1778: France declares war on Great Britain, thereby limiting severely the Royal Navy's ability to sustain the remaining British Army forces in North America. In this same year, British strategy shifts to a pacification of the Southern Colonies. North Carolina, South Carolina and Georgia become a chaotic battleground. The campaign, effectively a civil war with neighbour fighting neighbour, is fought with a ferocity exceeding even that of the later Civil War of 1861-1865.

1780: more than 25,000 Loyalists are bearing arms against their compatriots and, simultaneously, the forces of France and Spain. By war's end, 430 Loyalist units will have been raised. Some Provincial line regiments are well commanded, well equipped, and officially integrated into the British Army's order of battle. Others are brave but poorly armed guerilla bands operating deep inside rebel territory. Many of these appear spontaneously and then as quickly disintegrate. The Crown will have the additional support of fifty-three different Indian tribes during these tumultuous years.

1781: the British, under General Charles Cornwallis, are defeated at Yorktown, Virginia, by the now well-organised American Continental Army (led by General George Washington) and units of the French Army. King George III decides to abandon the Thirteen Colonies, leaving the Loyalists and his Indian allies to their unpleasant fate.

1782: the last British Army units have gone. Fighting between Revolutionary and Loyalist units continues to rage for several months in the south, but the main motives now are loot and revenge. A mass exodus begins as families which backed the wrong side, by supporting the Crown, seek to escape retribution. At least 80,000 men, women and children emigrate to Canada, the West Indies and Great Britain.

1783: the victorious Americans move towards a Federal system of self-government. The Treaty of Paris recognises the autonomy of the United States of America.

1787: a Convention of State Representatives drafts the Constitution of the new nation. George Washington is unanimously elected its first President.

The principal Loyalist units, those which served until the end, maintaining an effective strength throughout, were raised in the following years:

1775
Loyal Nova Scotia Volunteers
Royal Fencible Americans
Royal Highland Emigrant Corps (became 84th Regiment in 1778, disbanded in 1783)
Plus various Militia Companies in Massachusetts, North Carolina, and Virginia (in the area of Norfolk)

1776
New York Volunteers (became 3rd American Regiment in 1779)
DeLancey's Brigade
Skinner's New Jersey Volunteers
King's Royal Regiment of New York
King's American Regiment (became 4th American Regiment in 1781)
Queen's Rangers (became 1st American Regiment in 1779)

1777
Prince of Wales's American Regiment
Loyal American Regiment
Maryland Loyalists
Pennsylvania Loyalists
Volunteers of Ireland (became 2nd American Regiment in 1779, then 105th Regiment in 1782, disbanded in 1783)

1778
British Legion (became 5th American Regiment in 1781)
Butler's Rangers
South Carolina Royalists
Royal Garrison (Royal Bermudian) Regiment

1779
East Florida (King's) Rangers
Georgia Loyalists

1780
Loyal North Carolina Regiment
North Carolina Volunteers

1781
Duke of Cumberland's Regiment
King's American Dragoons

These two dozen Regiments have been recorded, their services well documented. Some have even had books written about them, and these are described in detail on the following pages. The majority of Loyalist units, however, disbanded themselves during the great exodus of 1782-1783 and others had ceased to exist even earlier. Some of their titles can be seen mentioned in the lists of refugees, but many were never recorded in any way. Their only memorials are passing references written by their enemies - 'four hundred insurgents under a Colonel Murphy', 'nearly thirteen hundred poorly armed Loyalists', 'eight hundred Tories gathered on the Yadkin river', 'a group of Scopholites', 'irregulars from the upper country'. These men, and their units, have no known grave.

GENERAL INTRODUCTORY SOURCES

THE HISTORY OF THE INDIAN WARS
Robert M Utley and Wilcomb A Washburn * American Heritage Publishing Co and Michael Beazley Ltd, London, 1977. Olive spine, red boards, 11.25 x 8.5, -/352. More than 350 ills (of excellent quality, many in colour), 4 maps, no appendixes, Index.
* An opulent book, authoritative, and very finely illustrated. From the 1600s to 1776, a period when French settlements stretched thinly through the hinterland from the St Lawrence to the Mississipi, the British were expanding their seaboard Colonies of New England, New York, Virginia and the Carolinas. Reflecting the conflicts in Europe, the two factions were repeatedly at war, groping to find each other in the vast expanse of virgin forest. This was the home of the Iroquois, Chickasaw, Mohawk, Abnaki, Natchez, Shawnee, Cherokee, Seneca and Chippewa. Both imperial powers coerced them to fight at various times on their behalf. It is a story of unremitting betrayal, torture, and killing. After the French had been defeated and when some of the American Colonists began to rebel against London's rule, English commanders in the field became increasingly successful in persuading Indian chiefs to support the forces of the Crown. Four of the Six Nations joined in the murderous campaign against the Revolutionaries and their families. Later, when the British departed, they were to pay a bitter price for that alliance. Part I of this book is an excellent account of the Indian tribes' involvements with the Loyalists and the red coats of the British Army. Part II describes their tragic experiences against the blue coats of the US Army.
R/2 V/4. PC. RP.

ENCYCLOPEDIA OF BRITISH, PROVINCIAL AND GERMAN ARMY UNITS, 1775-1783
Philip R N Katcher * Stackpole Books, Harrisburg, Pennsylvania, 1973. Grey, red, 9.25 x 6.25, xii/147 (numbered 13 to 160). Fp, 25 mono phots, 40 line drawings, no appendixes, Bibliography, Index.
* The author covers a wide range of units, some of which have no connection with America. The book is listed here because the American section lists a number of Loyalist units which had a short life-span before being merged with others and are therefore not widely recorded elsewhere. The entry for each such unit gives brief details of date and place of formation, employment and disbandment, with names of Colonels and other officers. The book is reported to be generally accurate and the illustrations of uniforms and badges are expertly presented. R/4 V/4. PC. HIS.
Note: the same author wrote THE AMERICAN PROVINCIAL CORPS, 1775-1784, in the Men-at-Arms series (Osprey, Reading, UK, 1973). It contains much useful information on Loyalist uniforms (illustrated by Michael Youens) and a condensed account of actions in which Provincial line regiments were engaged. Another useful source is THE JOURNAL OF THE SOCIETY FOR ARMY HISTORICAL RESEARCH, Vol XVI, No 62, pages 119-120, Vol XIX, No 75, pages 163-166, and Vol XX, No 80, pages 190-192 and 443, printed by Gale & Polden Ltd, Aldershot, 1937, 1940 and 1942. Compiled by C T Atkinson from original sources, these articles and addenda contain details of British, German and Provincial units from the outbreak of the Revolution through to Yorktown.

LOYALISTS AND REDCOATS
A Study of British Revolutionary Policy
Paul H Smith * Printed by the University of North Carolina Press for the Institute of Early American History and Culture, Williamsburg, Virginia, 1964. Red, gold, 9.0 x 6.5, xii/199. No ills, no maps, Index. Apps: notes on British plans for erecting a Loyalist haven at Penobscot Bay, Maine.

* This history is the best analysis to date of British official policy towards the Loyalists. It discusses the Crown's initial aversion to raising Provincial units, their second-class status, and their mismanagement by higher command. It was not until 1777, following the capture of New York, that Loyalists were allowed to take a prominent part in the fighting. The author gives little information on individual Regts, but he does provide much useful detail regarding conditions of recruitment and service. R/3 V/4. PC. HIS.
Note: reprinted by W W Norton, New York, 1972. Another prime source for an understanding of the Loyalist cause, particularly at grass-roots level, is THE LOYALISTS IN REVOLUTIONARY AMERICA, 1766-1781, by Robert McClure (Harcourt Brace Janovich Inc, New York, 1973).

ROYAL RAIDERS
The Tories of the American Revolution
North Callahan * The Bobbs-Merrill Company, Indianapolis, 1963. Mottled tan, brown, 9.25 x 6.25, vi/7-288. No ills, no maps, no appendixes, Bibliography, notes, Index.
* A very readable account, by a distinguished historian, of Loyalist participation in the Revolutionary War. Extensively researched, the text is filled with references to the exploits of individual units. Unfortunately, the author pays scant attention to the niceties of military organisation or the accuracy of unit designations, thus rendering the Index unreliable. The book is otherwise a good starting point for further research. R/3 V/3. PC. HIS.

BIOGRAPHICAL SKETCHES OF LOYALISTS OF THE AMERICAN REVOLUTION
With an Historical Essay
Lorenzo Sabine * Little, Brown & Co, Boston, 1864. Two matching volumes, brown, gold, 9.0 x 5.75.
Volume I : vii/608
Volume II : -/600.
No ills, no maps, no appendixes, no Index (in either volume).
* A seminal work. Included in the biographical sketches are extensive quotations from contemporary documents, with much detail on individual officers and the actions of units in which they served. Arranged alphabetically, the book is a basic source for names appearing elsewhere in Muster Rolls, military diaries and Orderly Books. The indicated essay (vide sub-title) is also a primary source.
R/4 V/5. PC. HIS.
Note: an earlier version, entitled THE AMERICAN LOYALISTS, by the same author and published in 1847, is neither as complete nor as reliable.

BIOGRAPHICAL SKETCHES OF LOYALISTS OF THE AMERICAN REVOLUTION
Gregory Palmer * Meckler Publishing, with the American Antiquarian Society, Westport and London, 1984. Red, gold, 9.5 x 6.0, xxxviii/959. No ills, no maps, no appendixes, no Index.
* This revised edition of Sabine's work (vide preceding entry) was compiled to supplement, not replace, that classic work. Written by a staff member of the British Library, it introduces hundreds of additional names and facts garnered from a wide range of sources which were not available to Sabine. It also provides new information on many of the individuals noted in the 1864 edition. A prime source for the genealogist. R/3 V/5. PC. HIS.

A HISTORICAL ACCOUNT OF THE SETTLEMENT OF SCOTCH HIGHLANDERS IN AMERICA PRIOR TO THE PEACE OF 1873
Together with Notices of Highland Regiments and Biographical Sketches
J P MacLean * The Helman-Taylor Company, Cleveland, Ohio, 1900. Seen in brown and white, xvi/459. Fp, 18 engravings, no maps, no Index. Apps: 15 in total, mainly extensive quotations from contemporary sources.
* Although the author displays a personal bias against the losing British side in this war, his narrative is a helpful examination of the Scottish Highland settlers

in North America at the outbreak of the Revolution and their subsequent services under the Crown. He gives particularly good coverage of the recruitment and services of the North Carolina Loyal Highland Volunteers, Johnson's Royal Regiment of New York, and the Royal Highland Emigrants. A good source for researchers who favour the ethnic approach to regimental history. R/4 V/3. UML. HIS.
Note: the book was published simultaneously by John Mackay, Glasgow, and then reprinted in 1968 by the Genealogical Publishing Company of Baltimore.

THE NORTHERN COLONIES

ROLLS OF THE PROVINCIAL (LOYALIST) CORPS, CANADIAN COMMAND, AMERICAN REVOLUTIONARY PERIOD
Mary Beacock Fryer and Lieut Col William A Smy CD * Dundurn Press Ltd, Toronto, 1981. Stiff card, white, red/blue, 8.5 x 5.5, -/104. No ills, no maps, no appendixes, no Index.
* Using a diversity of sources, the authors compiled a representative muster roll for each Corps at a crucial time in its existence. The information is arranged by Company and covers all those which served in the Northern Department (Canada) between 1778 and 1783. Amongst the units so listed are the 1st and 2nd Bns of the Royal Highland Emigrants (84th Foot), the King's (Johnson's) Royal Regiment of New York, Butler's Rangers, the Loyal Rangers, and the King's Rangers. Clearly, a prime source for genealogists. R/3 V/4. PC. HIS.

WINSLOW PAPERS, A.D. 1776-1826
Rev W O Raymond * Printed by Sun Printing Co Ltd for the New Brunswick Historical Society, St John, New Brunswick, 1901. Brown, gold, unidentified crest on spine, 9.75 x 6.75, -/732. 15 mono phots, one page of facsimile autographs of prominent Loyalists, no formal appendixes, Index.
* This collection of correspondence, all concerning Col Edward Winslow Jnr, Muster Master General of Provincial Troops during the Revolution and of the disbanded troops in New Brunswick, is unique. There are numerous references to Provincial officers and units (including the Loyal Associated Refugees, commanded by Winslow himself). While much of the book relates to his role in the foundation of New Brunswick (separated from Nova Scotia in 1784), the early correspondence is certainly useful to military historians and to genealogists. R/4 V/4. PC. HIS.
Note: reprinted at The Gregg Press, Boston, 1972.

JESSUP'S RANGERS AS A FACTOR IN LOYALIST SETTLEMENT
E Rae Stuart * Ontario Dept of Public Records & Archives, Toronto, 1961. Seen casebound, blue, white, 9.0 x 6.75, x/158. No ills, no maps, Bibliography, Index. Apps: nominal rolls (Loyal Rangers, 1783, and King's Loyal Americans, 1777), the Jessup family tree, notes on settled Loyalists (1784).
* Written originally as a thesis, this is an account of the services of the Jessup brothers - Ebenezer, Edward, and Joseph. All three served as COs or as Company commanders in Jessup's Corps (King's Loyal Americans). The Corps was raised from New York Loyalists and served with Burgoyne. It was captured at Saratoga in 1777. Its successor was Jessup's Rangers (Loyal Rangers). This Regt was raised in 1780, served on the Canadian border, and was disbanded in 1783. The narrative describes raids into New York, fortifications around Lake Champlain and border areas, and the later emigrations into Ontario. Half of the text is devoted to recruitment policies, terms of service, uniforms and matters relating to provisioning. R/4 V/3. UV. HIS.

LETTER-BOOK OF CAPTAIN ALEXANDER McDONALD OF THE ROYAL HIGHLAND EMIGRANTS 1775-1779
Contained in Collections (Volume XV) of the New York Historical Society, 1882
Anon * Printed for the Society, New York, 1883. Green, gold, 'Three leaf clover' motif on spine, 10.0 x 6.0, xii/292 (being pages 203-495 of Vol 515 of the Collections). No ills, no maps, no appendixes, Index.

* Capt McDonald was Senior Captain of the 2nd Bn of the Regt and he served at Halifax and Fort Edward throughout 1779. His correspondence with his Commanding Officer, Maj Small, and his Regtl Commander, Col McLean, is replete with details regarding pay, recruiting, officer preference and conditions of service for that part of the Regt which performed garrison duties in Nova Scotia during the period noted in the sub-title. The 2nd Bn was recruited mainly from the Scots resident in the area of New York. Several Companies fought in the southern campaigns.
R/4 V/4. PC. HIS.

THE STORY OF BUTLER'S RANGERS AND THE SETTLEMENT OF NIAGARA
Ernest Cruikshank * Tribune Printing House, Welland, Ontario, for Lundy's Lane Historical Society, 1893. Seen casebound in brown, black, 8.75 x 6.0, iv/114.
No ills, no maps, no appendixes, no Index.
* A detailed account of a Loyalist unit raised to fight alongside friendly Indians, mainly of the Iroquois tribes. Commanded by John Butler (later Colonel), the unit consisted of nearly 500 farmers and woodsmen recruited in 1777 from Tryon County (north west New York). It was constantly engaged in scouting, raids and ambushes, and was greatly feared by rebel Americans who accused Butler and his men of many atrocities. Defeated only by Sullivan's Continentals in 1779, it continued to raise havoc as far south as Kentucky, west to Detroit, and into the Hudson Valley. At war's end, its members settled on the Canadian side of the Niagara and formally disbanded themselves in June 1784. Unusually for this genre of publication, the author concentrates upon the military aspects of the story, leaving the social and political implications to be described elsewhere. R/4 V/4. VSL. HIS.

WAR OUT OF NIAGARA
Walter Butler and the Tory Rangers
Howard Swigget * The Torch Press, Cedar Rapids, Iowa, for the Columbia University Press, 1923. Blue, gold, Columbia University crest, New York State Historical Society logo on spine, 9.25 x 6.25, xxv/309. Fp, 5 mono phots, one map, no appendixes, Index.
* Despite the sub-title, this well-referenced book is focussed less upon Walter Butler himself than it is upon the unit commanded by his father - Butler's Rangers. The son, Walter, was a 'Captain of a Corps of Rangers' who took part in some of the infamous raids of 1778 and gained a reputation as a butcher of rebels and their families. The book is a balanced analysis of the war on the frontier between New York and Canada, and contains much interesting operational detail. It ends with Walter Butler's death in 1781, shortly after the British defeat at Yorktown.
R/4 V/4. HSCL. HIS.

SIMCOE'S MILITARY JOURNAL
A History of the Operations of a Partisan Corps, Called the Queen's Rangers, Commanded by Lieutenant Colonel J G Simcoe during the War of the American Revolution
J G Simcoe * Bartlett & Welford, New York, 1844. Seen rebound in red cloth, blind, 9.5 x 6.0, xvii/328. No ills, 10 maps (folding, bound in), no Index. Apps: extensive quotations from contemporary correspondence, extracts from other historical accounts, and notes which document various references in the main narrative.
* The book was published originally, by the author, in 1787. In 1844 it was republished with the addition of an editorial memoir of Simcoe's life. This is the version recorded here. The narrative describes the services of one of the most active and successful Loyalist units. As a reference source, it is particularly useful with regard to the operations of the Queen's Rangers and its officer personalities between 1777 (Philadelphia) and 1781 (Yorktown), this being the period of Simcoe's command. The Rangers were unusual in that they comprised not only the customary Battalion and Flank Companies but also a Highland Company and a Squadron of Cavalry. R/5 V/4. PC. HIS.
Note: a facsimile reprint was produced by New York Times/Arno Press in 1968, as was another by Genealogical Publishing Co, Baltimore, in 1972.

THE QUEEN'S RANGERS IN THE REVOLUTIONARY WAR

Col C J Ingles VD and Lieut Col H M Jackson MBE ED * The Industrial Shops for the Deaf, Montreal, 1956. Green, black, 9.25 x 6.0, xii/301. Fp, no other ills, 20 maps, no Index. Apps: list of former officers (with detailed biographical notes), nominal roll of all personnel who surrendered at Yorktown.

* The Regt was raised in 1776 from the local population of the Northern Colonies by a famous leader from the French and Indian wars, Maj Robert Rogers. Later commanded by Lieut Col John Simcoe, its exploits during the Revolutionary War were recounted in SIMCOE'S MILITARY JOURNAL (vide preceding entry). After the withdrawal of the British, Simcoe moved to New Brunswick, Canada, where he continued to command the Regt until its disbandment in 1783. It was re-embodied as an Active Militia unit in 1791, again commanded by Simcoe, then disbanded again three years later. During the rebellion of 1837-1838, the title was given to a temporary Canadian Militia unit before discarded for nearly half a century. It was resurrected in 1925 with the formation of The Queen's Rangers, a Canadian Active Militia unit subsequently renamed The Queen's York Rangers (1st American Regt), Royal Canadian Armoured Corps. Reference should be made to the 'Canada' Index of this Bibliography for sources concerning all those later developments. The book recorded here deals only with the period of Simcoe's tenure and is based largely upon his own account (expanded with extensive biographical notes and edited so that it acquires a better historical perspective). R/3 V/4. PCAL. RP.

THE QUEEN'S RANGERS IN UPPER CANADA
1792 and After

Lieut Col H M Jackson MBE ED * Industrial Shops for the Deaf, Montreal, n.d. (c.1948). Green, black, 6.5 x 4.0, v/117. Fp, no other ills, no maps, no Index. Apps: list of former officers (in 1798, 1813, 1821, 1837, etc), notes on grants of land in Upper Canada to members of the Regt.

* The various incarnations of the Queen's Rangers (vide preceding entry) are here described in some detail, as are its experiences from 1792 through to the end of the War of 1812, the rebellion of 1837-1838, and the early settlement of the frontier. The WWI and WWII services of the Regt's Canadian successors are covered in short chapters at the end of the book. The 'Land Grants' appendix may be of value to social historians and to genealogists. R/3 V/3. ASKBC. CB.

THE NARRATIVE OF COLONEL STEPHEN JARVIS
Loyalist Narratives from Upper Canada

James J Talmon * Champlain Society Publication XXVII, Toronto, 1946. Red, gold, 9.5 x 6.25, Lxv/411. No ills, no maps, Index. Apps: ten in total, these being Memorials addressed to the Claims Commissioners by Loyalist officers seeking compensation for their personal losses.

* A quarter of the book is Jarvis's own engaging account of active service with the Queen's Rangers Cavalry in New York and South Carolina. It contains much operational detail and is unique in that he saw service in every rank from private soldier to Colonel. Talmon, as editor, has added an excellent introduction to summarise the Loyalist position, and gives some account of other units involved (including Jessup's King's Loyal Americans). R/3 V/4. USAMRC. HIS.

LOYALISM IN NEW YORK DURING THE AMERICAN REVOLUTION

Alexander Clarence Flick * Arno Press/New York Times, New York, 1969. Blue, white, 8.75 x 5.75, viii/281. No ills, no maps, Bibliography, no Index. Apps: notes on the sale of forfeited estates in the southern and middle districts of New York.

* Flick's researches were confined mainly to original archives and are concerned with the overall story of Loyalists in New York and its surrounding Counties. Chapter VI (pages 101-116) deals specifically with the Loyalist units raised in that area (comprising 23,500 men, the largest recruitment of any comparable area). There is interesting material throughout the book concerning the nature of

Loyalism and the benefits gained by those who supported the Crown, especially in grants of land, and the losses suffered through subsequent exile.
R/4 V/3. CIAL. HIS.
Note: the edition recorded here is a facsimile reprint of the original edition published by Columbia University Press, New York, 1901. It was reprinted also by AMS Press, New York, in 1970.

ORDERLY BOOK OF THE THREE BATTALIONS OF LOYALISTS COMMANDED BY BRIGADIER GENERAL OLIVER DE LANCEY, 1776-1778
To Which is Appended a List of New York Loyalists in the City of New York during the War of Revolution, Compiled by William Kelby
Anon (apart from the reference to Kelby) * The New York Historical Society, New York, 1917. Maroon, gold, crest of the NYHS, 10.0 x 6.5, xi/147. No ills, no maps, no formal appendixes, Index.
* The book covers the activities of the three Bns of de Lancey's Bde which was raised and stationed on Long Island during the period stated in the title. Included is the text of the order which authorised the Bde on 29 September 1776. The narrative has considerable detail of the conditions of service and the fighting role of Provincial forces in the New York area, with interesting information on uniforms, equipment, appointments, promotions and Court Martial proceedings.
R/4 V/4. PC. HIS.
Note: reprinted in facsimile by the Genealogical Publishing Co, Baltimore, 1972.

ORDERLY BOOK OF SIR JOHN JOHNSON DURING THE ORISKANY CAMPAIGN, 1776-1777
William L Stone * Joel Munsell's Sons, Albany, New York, 1882. Cloth with leather spine, black, gold, 8.5 x 6.5, cLxviii/273. Fp, 14 engraved plates (mainly portraits), one map (bound in), Index. Apps: numerous, of little research value.
* The core of this book is the text of the original Orderly Book of the Colonel's Company of Johnson's King's Royal Regiment of New York. The period covered is from 4 November 1776 to 31 July 1777. The text is accompanied by explanatory notes, a long-winded introduction by J Watts de Peyster concerning the Johnson family and the Battle of Oriskany, and a rambling discourse on Loyalists by Theodorus B Meyers. The editor, Stone, writes in a much clearer style and his comments are interesting and helpful. The events covered in the Orderly Book itself are the assembly of St Leger's force near Montreal and its move to Fort Stanwix. The entries include details of camps, guard duties, drills, uniforms and Courts Martial. The Regt was known also as Johnson's Royal Greens. R/4 V/3. NCSL. HIS.

A HISTORY OF THE CAMPAIGNS OF 1780 AND 1781 IN THE SOUTHERN PROVINCES OF NORTH AMERICA
Lieut Col (Banastre) Tarleton * Coles, Exshaw, H Whitehouse, Burton & Byrne, Dublin, Ireland, 1787. Seen rebound in blue, white, 8.0 x 5.0, vii/533. No ills, no maps, no Index. Apps: reproductions of documents concerning the actions at Camden, Ninety-Six and Agusta in 1781.
* Tarleton commanded the British Legion first raised in the north (vide following entry). This is his own account of actions in the south from Charleston in 1780 through to Biggins Bridge, Wacsaws, Camden, Catawba Fords, Blackstock's Hill, Cowpens, Guildford Courthouse and Yorktown. During most of this time, Tarleton commanded not only his own Regt but also the British Cavalry and the mounted infantry. Every chapter is supported by quotations from contemporary documents.
R/4 V/5. WVU. HIS.
Note: the edition recorded above is the commoner Dublin printing. In that same year (1787), a Quarto edition was published in London by T Cadell with leather bindings and five maps. In 1968, a handsome facsimile version of the London edition was produced by Arno Press/New York Times. Reprints dated 1967, by Reprint Co of Spartenberg, South Carolina, and 1972, by T Cassells Jnr, have been noted.

THE GREEN DRAGOON
The Lives of Banastre Tarleton and Mary Robinson
Robert D Bass * Henry Holt & Co, New York, 1957. Black, green and white, 9.5 x 6.25, viii/489. 22 mono phots, 4 maps (photographic plates, bound in), no appendixes, Bibliography & Sources, Index.
* Although this finely written book is a biography of Tarleton and his mistress, it is also a detailed account of the British Legion, its recruitment, active services, and its fearsome reputation. The Legion, matched only by the Queen's Rangers as superior Loyalist soldiers, was raised on 18 July 1778 from three Troops of Pennsylvania Light Dragoons and four Companies of Infantry. The Regt fought with furious spirit in most of the major battles in the Carolinas and Virginia from 1779 to 1781. Tarleton was regarded by the Rebels as the most able of the British officers opposing them. R/3 V/4. PC. HIS.

LOYALIST TROOPS OF NEW ENGLAND
Wilbur H Siebert * Reprinted extract from THE NEW ENGLAND QUARTERLY, Vol IV, No 1, 1931. Soft card, blue, black, 9.0 x 6.0, ii/45. No ills, no maps, no appendixes, no Index.
* Siebert discusses the circumstances leading to the recruitment of resident New Englanders to form several Regts not commonly recorded elsewhere - the Loyal Associated Volunteers, Wentworth's Volunteers, Loyal New Englanders, Loyal Newport Associates, King's American Regt, Prince of Wales's American Regt, and the unit which later absorbed many of the smaller ones - The King's American Dragoons. Apart from some references to New England raids from Long Island, the book contains little in the way of operational detail. R/4 V/2. DU. HIS.

THE MIDDLE COLONIES

THE NEW JERSEY VOLUNTEERS (LOYALISTS) IN THE REVOLUTIONARY WAR
William S Stryker * Printed by Naas, Day & Naas, Trenton, New Jersey, for the author, 1887. Seen in library bindings only, page size 9.0 x 5.5. No ills, no maps, no appendixes, Bibliography, no Index.
* Although the author was not sympathetic to the Loyalist cause, this frequently cited monograph does contain a good general history of the New Jersey Volunteers. It covers the services of the Regt's various Bns on Staten Island, the raids into New Jersey, and operations in South Carolina. More than half of the text is composed of capsule biographies of the officers of the six Bns of Skinner's Brigade. R/5 V/4. ISL. HIS.

ORDERLY BOOK OF THE MARYLAND LOYALIST REGIMENTS, JUNE 18th 1778 TO OCTOBER 12th 1778
Paul Leicester Ford * Historical Printing Club, Brooklyn, New York, 1891. Leather spine, maroon cloth boards, gold, 9.25 x 7.0, -/111. Fp, no other ills, no maps, no appendixes, no Index.
* Based mainly upon Orders issued to British Army units during the stated period, but including some Orders issued directly to the Maryland Loyalists and other Provincial troops, thereby illustrating the daily routine of some of the Regts concerned. The text deals with the garrisoning of New Jersey, the march to New York, the Battle of Monmouth, and guard and foraging activities on Long Island. There is also a brief and not very reliable history of the Regt based upon the compiler's own researches. R/4 V/3. PC. HIS.

THE LOYALISTS OF PENNSYLVANIA
Wilbur Henry Siebert * Gregg Press, Boston, 1972. Blue, gold on red, 9.25 x 6.0, x/117. No ills, no maps, no appendixes, Bibliography, Index.
* Siebert, perhaps the most knowledgeable and prolific of writers on American Loyalism, describes in this book all its aspects as manifested in Colonial Pennsylvania. The narrative contains little operational detail, but is comprehensive

in its account of the raising of local units following the British occupation of Philadelphia (1777). Amongst the units which he describes in detail are the Pennsylvania Loyalists, New Jersey Volunteers, Queen's Rangers, British Legion, and the Guides and Pioneers. Post-war, most of the soldiers from these Regts were settled in New Brunswick. R/4 V/3. USMHI. HIS.
Note: the above is a reprint of the work first published in Columbus, Ohio, by the Ohio State University Press in 1920 as Vol XXIV, No 23, of The Ohio State University Bulletin. Reference may be made also to pages 13-84 of PROCEEDINGS, LEHIGH COUNTY HISTORICAL SOCIETY, Vol XXIV, 1966, in which there is an article entitled REBEL AND TORY COLONEL, LIEUTENANT COLONEL WILLIAM ALLEN Jr, by Scott A Trexter II and Lee A Walck. The narrative concentrates upon Allen's turbulent career but also contains much useful material regarding the raising of the 1st Bn of Pennsylvania Loyalists, the Battle of Monmouth, the move to Pensacola (1779), the fight with the Spanish at Mobile (1780), and the defeat at Pensacola (1781).

THE SOUTHERN COLONIES

LOYALISTS IN THE SOUTHERN CAMPAIGN OF THE REVOLUTIONARY WAR
Murtie June Clark * Genealogical Publishing Co Inc, Baltimore, 1981. Three matching volumes, red, gold, 8.75 x 5.75.
Vol I : Official Rolls of Loyalists Recruited from North and South Carolina, Georgia, Florida and Mississipi, xxiv/635. Four appendixes giving additional information on individual Provincial and Militia soldiers.
Vol II : Official Rolls of Loyalists Recruited from Maryland, Pennsylvania and Virginia, and Those Recruited from Other Colonies for the British Legion, Guides and Pioneers, Loyal Foresters and Queen's Rangers, xx/687.
Vol III : Official Rolls of Loyalists Recruited from the Middle Atlantic Colonies, with lists of Refugees from Other Colonies, xx/484. No ills, no maps, Sources, Index.
* The series is invaluable for its muster rolls and information concerning almost every Loyalist unit which served in the south. The organisational and locational data are well presented, by Company, for the period 1779-1784 and identify many obscure Militia units in addition to the better-known Provincial units such as The British Legion, Queen's Rangers, de Lancey's Brigade, Skinner's Greens, King's Rangers, South Carolina Loyalists, and The Volunteers of Ireland. Vol III contains a unique roll of Loyalist officers serving in New York in November 1783, and a roll of officers seconded from Provincial Line Regts (these rolls including some biographical notes on the officers so listed). R/4 V/5. PC. HIS.

THE LOYALISTS OF NORTH CAROLINA DURING THE REVOLUTION
Robert O DeMond * Printed by Seeman Printery, for Duke University Press, Durham, North Carolina, 1940. Blue, gold, 8.75 x 6.0, -/286. No ills, no maps, Bibliography, Index. Apps: muster roll of North Carolina units, lists of lands confiscated from Loyalists, notes on claims for compensation, British pension rolls for North Carolina Loyalists.
* Only one Regular unit of Loyalists was raised in North Carolina, but there were Militia units in plenty. Skirmishes and battles, ambushes and massacres, all were part of daily life during that dark period. The story is well told here, and it is set against a clearly described social and political background. The author gives good accounts of the most prominent Loyalist leaders and he also covers the main actions between 1775 and 1782 (Moore's Creek Bridge, Ramsaur's Mill, Hanging Rock, King's Mountain, Hillsboro, Drowning Creek and Lindley's Mill). R/4 V/4. PC. HIS.
Note: reproduced without amendment by University Microfilms, University of Michigan, Ann Arbor, Michigan, 1963.

COLONEL DAVID FANNING'S NARRATIVE
Of His Exploits and Adventures as a Loyalist of North Carolina in the American Revolution, Supplying Important Omissions in the Copy Published in the United States
A W Savary (as editor) * Reprinted from The Canadian Magazine, Toronto, 1908. Green, gold, 9.5 x 6.5, -/55. No ills, no maps, no appendixes, reference notes, Index.
* After a series of astonishing adventures as a Loyalist Militiaman in South and North Carolina, Fanning was Commissioned as Colonel of the Militia of Randolph and Chatham Counties (The North Carolina Loyal Militia) in July 1781. His command, consisting of twenty-two Companies, gained a reputation throughout the Middle South for savagery against rebel settlers and their families. Fanning was one of only three men excluded from the Pardon granted at war's end by the North Carolina Legislature to former Loyalists. He moved to East Florida and then removed himself permanently to Canada. This personal memoir concentrates upon his force's operations in the field and is therefore a useful source for the military historian.
R/5 V/4. W&MCL. HIS.
Note: Savary's edited version of Fanning's account, as reported above, is the most complete. Two earlier (attenuated) versions have been recorded - one of 50 copies, published in 1861 in Richmond, Virginia, and a second one of 200 copies, published in New York (hence the otherwise inscrutable sub-title of this work). Savary's version was reprinted in 1981 by Briarpatch Press, of Davidson, North Carolina, with the title NARRATIVE OF COLONEL DAVID FANNING. This book incorporates many informative notes by Lindley S Butler (as additional editor).

THE JOURNAL OF ALEXANDER CHESNEY
A South Carolina Loyalist in the Revolution and After
A Alfred Jones * Ohio State University, Columbus, Ohio, 1921. Maroon and light blue, black, 10.0 x 6.5, xvi/166. No ills, no maps, Bibliography, Index. Apps: eight in total, all relating to Chesney's claims for 'loss of property compensation'.
* Chesney served as an officer of the South Carolina Loyal Militia between 1780 and 1782 and fought at King's Mountain and Cowpens. His original memoir is patchy, but the voluminous notes (62 pages) compiled by this book's editor are a valuable source of reference in their own right. Alfred Jones describes South Carolina's Militia units (six Regts, with thirty Companies, in 1781), and their part in the losing struggle which resulted in most Loyalist forces in the south withdrawing to Charleston in 1782. The Index (15 pages) is exceptionally detailed and helpful. The book pinpoints various scarce research sources for Loyalist claims, a field of enquiry which would be otherwise tedious and time-consuming.
R/4 V/3. GWUL. HIS.

DIARY OF LIEUTENANT ANTHONY ALLAIRE OF FERGUSON'S CORPS
Anthony Allaire * Printed by the New York Times for the Arno Press, New York, 1968. Blue and brown, silver, 'Soldier' motif , 8.75 x 5.75, -/36. No ills, no maps, no appendixes, no Index.
* The diary of an officer who, like many from other Regts, volunteered to leave the Loyal American Regt to serve under Lieut Col Patrick Ferguson. The period covered is 5 March 1789 to 25 November 1780. Written in bold colourful language, the condensed narrative describes numerous small actions in South Carolina when British and Loyalist forces combined to fight against the Revolutionaries.
R/3 V/4. PC. HIS.
Note: the material within this slim volume first appeared as an appendix to KING'S MOUNTAIN AND ITS HEROES, by Draper, 1882, and is recorded here in its bound reprint format.

THE KING'S RANGER

Thomas Brown and the American Revolution on the Southern Frontier

Edward Cashin * University of Georgia Press, Athens, Georgia, 1989. Red, black, 9.25 x 6.25, xii/360. No ills, 6 maps, Bibliography, footnotes, Index. Apps: nominal roll by Company (1779-1782), biographical notes.

* Thomas Brown, a merchant from Yorkshire, arrived in Georgia in 1774. When war broke out, he raised the East Florida Rangers and an irregular force of Cherokee and Cree Indians. One of the leading Loyalist commanders in the fighting in Georgia and South Carolina, he was remarkably successful. His men carried out some of the bloodiest assaults on rebel units and communities, and were deservedly feared. The book is basically a biography, but it includes much useful detail (based upon contemporary documents) concerning the Rangers' active services. The Regt was known also as The King's Rangers and as the Carolina King's Rangers. After the war, Brown returned to civilian life as a planter in the Bahamas, was imprisoned in England for debt, and then finally became a planter on St Vincent.
R/1 V/5. PC. HIS.

LOYALISTS IN EAST FLORIDA, 1774 TO 1785

The Most Important Documents Pertaining Thereto, Edited with an Accompanying Narrative

Wilbur Henry Siebert * The Florida State Historical Society, Deland, Florida, 1929. Two matching volumes, red, gold, Royal arms, 11.5 x 9.0.

Vol I : xiv/263
Vol II : x/431

* The first volume contains the histories of Loyalist units active in East Florida, South Carolina and Georgia - the Carolina King's Rangers, East Florida Rangers, Royal North Carolina Volunteers, and South Carolina Royalists. The second volume deals mainly, and in great detail, with the survivors' post-war claims for compensation. Both volumes are supported by extensive notes and the personal details of prominent Loyalist officers. Many of them, and even complete military units, later emigrated and settled in the Bahamas, Jamaica and Dominica.
R/5 V/3. PC. HIS.
Note: reprinted at the Gregg Press, Boston, in 1972.

PART 4

Canada, with Newfoundland

NOTES

INTRODUCTION

Many Canadian regiments carry titles or designations which mirror to perfection the origins and development of this huge young nation. The cultural roots of the early settlers, particularly the immigrants from France, Scotland and Colonial America, are perpetuated in the names and traditions of individual regiments. The deep feelings of loyalty to the Crown which so characterised the reigns of Queen Victoria and King Edward VII can still be seen today in regimental titles of distinction such as 'Duke of Connaught's', 'Princess Louise's', and 'Princess of Wales's'. Community pride is reflected in regional and place names. All of these diverse influences - French, British and Canadian - have generated some of the most evocative, even romantic, regimental titles to be found anywhere in the Commonwealth.

The researcher is cautioned to have two particular points in mind while studying the following pages. First, some regiments have titles which are confusingly similar to those of other quite different units. The unwary, for example, might at first have difficulty in distinguishing between The Royal Canadian Regiment, The Royal Rifles of Canada, and The Royal Regiment of Canada, or between The Cameron Highlanders of Ottawa and The Queen's Own Cameron Highlanders of Canada, or between Les Fusiliers de Sherbrooke and The Sherbrooke Regiment. Secondly, the title of a regiment may indicate a role quite different to that which it performed at various stages in its history. Some Canadian Militia units began life as infantry, became Mounted Infantry, reverted to fighting on foot, retrained as machine-gun battalions, reverted again to infantry status, then learned to fight in tanks before finally becoming artillerymen. All of this creates a problem for the bibliographer attempting to place their published histories in convenient pigeon-holes.

An added complication is the fact that Canada did not have a permanently established army until 1871 (and that consisted only of artillery batteries at Kingston and Quebec City). Previously, the military forces consisted of part-time Militia units, with a small number of full-time paid Militia and British Army cadres responsible for administration and training. The essentially part-time volunteer army took great pride in its local and cultural connections.

In 1914, there was much resentment when Sir Sam Hughes, Minister for Militia and Defence, decreed that no Militia regiment could proceed overseas as an integral unit. The tens of thousands of Militiamen (and new recruits) who volunteered for service in Europe were re-attested into the newly-formed Canadian Expeditionary Force units. These were designated with colourless numerical cyphers in which it was difficult, at least initially, for the soldiers to take the same pride as they had in their pre-war cap badges. Some units did succeed in having their peacetime titles incorporated in their CEF designations, and four regiments even managed to reach the Western Front without ever adopting the numerical system. In general terms, however, the magnificent Canadian contribution to the Allied cause in WWI was achieved with an ephemeral order of battle which was scrapped in 1919. This factor also can cause difficulty for the bibliographer.

For the purposes of continuity and clarity, books relating to those temporary CEF units have been grouped in this bibliography together with those which refer to peacetime regiments with which they had a known connection, or by which they were officially 'perpetuated' after the war.

For the rest, the 'mounted and mechanised' and 'infantry' sections of REGIMENTS are arranged according to the Order of Precedence authorised in February, 1964. In those cases where the 1964 Order shows a particular regiment as having both Regular and Militia battalions, most of the latter have been grouped with the former for ease of reference.

Canada has generated several fine professional writers of regimental histories, and their work is much admired. It will be seen that the names of Capt Ernest J Chambers, R C Fetherstonhaugh, Lieut Col H M Jackson, and Lieut Col G R Stevens appear in a large number of entries.

The quality of production of Canadian unit histories is generally very good. The Militia system has ensured, since 1855 and even during the difficult years between the two world wars, that there were always sufficient people, able to supply adequate funding, for the compilation and publication of such books. The spirit and continuity of the individual regimental associations has been the main driving force behind most of the publications listed in the following pages. Such organisations possess the knowledge, the connections, and the fund-raising resources, needed to ensure an attractive and authoritative end-product.

One feature of Canadian unit histories which will strike the reader who is not familiar with the material is the great emphasis given to nominal rolls of the personnel who served. While it is customary for any unit history to incorporate some appendixes of former officers, or of men who died, or the recipients of honours and awards, the Canadian convention is to list every single man who was a member of the regiment or battalion during a particular campaign or war. In addition, in some books, the authors provide brief details of each man's service - joining and leaving dates, fatalities, injuries, promotions, appointments, awards, and so forth. These rolls may occupy as much as half the total number of pages in a given history. This means that Canadian histories can be a prodigious source of information for medal collectors and genealogists.

One difficulty encountered by this bibliographer has been that of assessing the rarity of some of these books. For the reasons stated, Canada's regiments have always been strongly rooted in their own local recruiting areas. Whenever a new history has been published, with a print run of probably no more than 1000 or 1500 copies, most of them have been purchased by members of the regiment and by local people. Often they will have been handed down within a family. Therefore, a book which can be seen quite often in, say, Halifax, might be almost unknown in Vancouver. Canada is a large country. Three thousand miles separate the Maritime Provinces from the west coast. A complicating factor is that of language. A unit history which is freely available in the French-speaking regions will be difficult to purchase in the English-speaking Provinces if the publisher, or the book dealers, felt that it was unprofitable to promote it on a nationwide basis.

The assessment of rarity shown at the foot of each entry is based upon the advice received from the contributor, from Canadian book dealers, and from the compiler's own experience in attempting to track down some of the more elusive items. In particular, the assessments have been influenced by the difficulty which a collector or librarian might experience in acquiring a copy if he or she resides in a country other than Canada itself.

Finally, it will be seen that there are no entries of any kind for certain regiments. The reason for these gaps is that, despite prolonged enquiries, no formally published histories for these units could be traced. In some cases, very brief summaries have been produced which give a condensed history of the unit's origins and evolution, but those seen consisted of little more than several pages of cyclostyled foolscap, stapled together. Presumably they were intended for public relations purposes, or for the instruction of new recruits. They have been assessed as unsuitable for inclusion in this bibliography. The lack of full-size printed histories for such units may be explained by the fact that they did not see active service overseas. The Hughes edict restricted them to draft-finding and training roles in WWI, and they may have been retained for home defence duties in Canada during WWII.

ORDER OF PRECEDENCE
of the Regiments and Corps,
as authorised, February 1964

Cadets of the Canadian Services Colleges
Royal Canadian Horse Artillery
Royal Canadian Armoured Corps
Royal Regiment of Canadian Artillery
Corps of Royal Canadian Engineers
Royal Canadian Corps of Signals
Royal Canadian Infantry Corps
Royal Canadian Army Service Corps
Royal Canadian Army Medical Corps
Royal Canadian Dental Corps
Royal Canadian Ordnance Corps
Corps of Royal Canadian Electrical & Mechanical Engineers
Royal Canadian Army Pay Corps
Royal Canadian Postal Corps
Royal Canadian Army Chaplain Corps
Canadian Provost Corps
Canadian Women's Army Corps
Canadian Intelligence Corps

Royal Canadian Armoured Corps

Canadian Army (Regular)

Royal Canadian Dragoons
Lord Strathcona's Horse (Royal Canadians)
8th Canadian Hussars (Princess Louise's)
Fort Garry Horse

Canadian Army (Militia)

Governor General's Horse Guards
4th Princess Louise Dragoon Guards
Halifax Rifles (RCAC)
8th Canadian Hussars (Princess Louise's) (Militia)
Grey and Simcoe Foresters (RCAC)
Elgin Regiment (RCAC)
Ontario Regiment (RCAC)
Queen's York Rangers (1st American Regiment) (RCAC)
Sherbrooke Regiment (RCAC)
7th/11th Hussars
Le Régiment de Trois-Rivières (RCAC)
1st Hussars
Prince Edward Island Regiment (RCAC)
Royal Canadian Hussars (Montreal)
British Columbia Regiment (Duke of Connaught's Own) (RCAC)
Algonquin Regiment (RCAC)
12th Manitoba Dragoons
South Alberta Light Horse
Saskatchewan Dragoons
19th Alberta Dragoons
14th Canadian Hussars
King's Own Calgary Regiment (RCAC)
British Columbia Dragoons
Fort Garry Horse (Militia)
Le Régiment de Hull (RCAC)
Windsor Regiment (RCAC)

Royal Canadian Infantry Corps

Canadian Army (Regular)

1st Bn, Canadian Guards
2nd Bn, Canadian Guards
1st Bn, Royal Canadian Regiment
2nd Bn, Royal Canadian Regiment
1st Bn, Princess Patricia's Canadian Light Infantry
2nd Bn, Princess Patricia's Canadian Light Infantry
1er Bataillon, Royal 22e Régiment
2e Bataillon, Royal 22e Régiment
3e Bataillon, Royal 22e Régiment
1st Bn, Queen's Own Rifles of Canada
2nd Bn, Queen's Own Rifles of Canada
1st Bn, Black Watch (Royal Highland Regiment) of Canada
2nd Bn, Black Watch (Royal Highland Regiment) of Canada

Canadian Army (Militia)

Governor General's Foot Guards (5th Bn, Canadian Guards)
Canadian Grenadier Guards (6th Bn, Canadian Guards)
3rd Bn, Queen's Own Rifles of Canada
Victoria Rifles of Canada
3rd Bn, Black Watch (Royal Highland Regiment) of Canada
Royal Rifles of Canada
Les Voltigeurs de Québec
Royal Regiment of Canada
Royal Hamilton Light Infantry (Wentworth Regiment)
Princess of Wales' Own Regiment
Hastings and Prince Edward Regiment
Lincoln and Welland Regiment
3rd Bn, Royal Canadian Regiment (London and Oxford Fusiliers)
Lorne Scots (Peel, Dufferin and Halton Regiment)
Perth Regiment
Highland Light Infantry of Canada
Brockville Rifles
Lanark and Renfrew Scottish Regiment
Stormont, Dundas and Glengarry Highlanders
Les Fusiliers du St-Laurent (5e Bataillon, Royal 22e Régiment)
Le Régiment de la Chaudière
4e Bataillon, Royal 22e Régiment (Chateauguay)
6e Bataillon, Royal 22e Régiment
Les Fusiliers Mont-Royal
Princess Louise Fusiliers
1st Bn, Royal New Brunswick Regiment (Carleton and York)
2nd Bn, Royal New Brunswick Regiment (North Shore)
West Nova Scotia Regiment
Le Régiment de Joliette
1st Bn, Nova Scotia Highlanders (North)
2nd Bn, Nova Scotia Highlanders (Cape Breton)
Le Régiment de Maisonneuve
Cameron Highlanders of Ottawa
Royal Winnipeg Rifles
1st Bn, Essex and Kent Scottish
2nd Bn, Essex and Kent Scottish
48th Highlanders of Canada
Le Régiment du Saguenay
Argyll and Sutherland Highlanders of Canada (Princess Louise's)

Lake Superior Scottish Regiment
1st Bn, North Saskatchewan Regiment (Prince Albert and Battleford Volunteers)
2nd Bn, North Saskatchewan Regiment (Saskatoon Light Infantry)
Regina Rifle Regiment
South Saskatchewan Regiment
Rocky Mountain Rangers
Loyal Edmonton Regiment (3rd Bn, Princess Patricia's Canadian Light Infantry)
Winnipeg Grenadiers
Queen's Own Cameron Highlanders of Canada
Westminster Regiment
Calgary Highlanders
Les Fusiliers de Sherbrooke
Seaforth Highlanders of Canada
Canadian Scottish Regiment (Princess Mary's)
Irish Fusiliers of Canada (Vancouver Regiment)
Scots Fusiliers of Canada
Royal Montreal Regiment
Irish Regiment of Canada
Toronto Scottish Regiment
Royal Newfoundland Regiment
Yukon Regiment

Note:

Despite a succession of Treasury-inspired 'rationalisations' by both governments over the past thirty years, there are still more than twice as many Scottish regiments in the Canadian Army as there are in the British Army - seventeen, as against just eight.

A Military Chronology

1498: John Cabot, a Venetian navigator, discovers Newfoundland and Labrador. French expeditions begin to explore the valley of the St Lawrence River.
1627: on behalf of King Louis XIII, Cardinal Richelieu grants legal status to the French settlements.
1642: Montreal is founded. The French become widely established in the territory known as Quebec. They name their colony New France.
1665: King Louis XIV sends a Regular force, the Carignan-Salieres Regiment, from France to protect the settlers. Iroquois war parties continue to harass the European intruders.
1713: the Spanish War of Succession ends with the Peace of Utrecht. Under the terms of the various treaties made, Great Britain gains title to Newfoundland and Nova Scotia. The French still dispute ownership of New Brunswick and Prince Edward Island.
1756: France and England fight The Seven Years War. In 1759, General James Wolfe leads the British forces in Canada against the key fortified French settlement at Quebec. The decisive battle on the Heights of Abraham, in which Wolfe is killed, establishes Great Britain as the dominant power in the region.
1775–1783: the American settlers in the Thirteen Colonies are divided in their loyalties to England. In 1775, the revolutionaries commence their War of Independence. Their troops move north and occupy Montreal. General John Burgoyne counter-attacks and advances south towards New York. He is beaten and forced to surrender at Saratoga (1777). The British are beaten again at Yorktown (1781). King George III decides to abandon the Thirteen Colonies and orders the withdrawal of all British Army forces. Loyalist Americans fight on, unaided, but their cause is lost. The Treaty of Paris (1783) acknowledges American independence. Thousands of Loyalist officers and men, with their families and retainers, migrate north and settle in Ontario, Nova Scotia, and Southern Quebec. They and their descendents will have a great impact upon Canada's future economic and military development.
1791: the area settled mainly by the Loyalists and by immigrants from Scotland and Ireland, known as Ontario, is designated Upper Canada, while the traditionally French-speaking region, mainly Quebec, is titled Lower Canada. Both are garrisoned by the British Army.
1793: revolution in France produces the First Republic and another war with Great Britain. The French lack the resources to attempt a repossession of their lost territories in Canada, but English-speaking Militia units are raised to guard against that risk.
1812: war breaks out between America and Great Britain. American forces invade Canadian territory claimed by the British. A counter-invasion by the British Army is supported by many new Militia units recruited from recently immigrated groups (especially the Scots) and from the re-settled American Loyalists and their sons. It is in these units that many modern Canadian Army regiments can claim their roots.
1837: bad central government leads to civil unrest. In Lower Canada it is inspired by Louis Papineau, in Upper Canada by William McKenzie. Disturbances in Montreal and Toronto are suppressed by local Militia forces. The two leaders flee across the border to America.
1840: the Act of Union brings Upper and Lower Canada into a single Province.
1848: the Province, together with the autonomous Maritime Provinces, is granted internal self-government.
1855: a new Militia Act brings coherence to the organisation of the many small local part-time units and starts to establish patterns of training and equipment. Total initial strength of the Militia is 5000 all ranks.
1858: ardent nationalists in Ireland form the Republican Brotherhood and establish branches in the United States of America. They hope to raise a rebellion amongst the Irish community in Canada. Known as Fenians, they will launch a military invasion across the border into Ontario in 1866, and another into Quebec Province

in 1870. Both incursions are defeated by British Army and Canadian Militia forces.
1867: Canada becomes a Dominion. It is a confederation of the Provinces of Ontario, Quebec, New Brunswick, and Nova Scotia. Other Provinces will join the Confederation in later years, the last being Newfoundland in 1949.
1871: the last British Army garrison regiments depart. The Canadian Government orders the recruitment of the first indigenous Regular units (the Permanent Force). The first such are artillery units in Quebec City and Kingston, Ontario.
1873: following the purchase of the wilderness of Rupertsland, owned until 1869 by the Hudson Bay Company, the Dominion recognises the need for an armed constabulary. The North West Mounted Police are raised to control lawless trapping and prospecting communities in the northern forests. Travelling alone or in small detachments, in areas where conventional soldiers could not survive, its men give root to the enduring 'Mounties' legend.
1876: the Royal Military College of Canada is established at Kingston.
1883: a new Militia Act authorises a Troop of 'regular' cavalry and three 'regular' companies of infantry to serve as Cavalry and Infantry School Corps. Later they evolve as The Royal Canadian Dragoons and The Royal Canadian Regiment.
1884: the Nile Voyageurs - 366 Militia, civilian and Indian boatmen - join the campaign in the Sudan against the Mahdists. They are the first Canadians to aid the Crown in a foreign war.
1885: unrest in South Saskatchewan results in a revolt headed by Louis Riel. General Middleton is sent by Ottawa to deal with it. His force consists of elements of Canadian Militia and the North West Mounted Police. After several skirmishes, with casualties on both sides, Riel is captured and hanged. His allies, the Indian leaders Poundmaker and Big Bear, are obliged to submit following the Battle of Cut Knife Hill (Creek).
1899: war breaks out in South Africa. The 2nd Battalion of The Royal Canadian Regiment provides the basis for the first of several Canadian Contingents to join similar Contingents from Ceylon, India, Australia, and New Zealand in support of 'the mother country' in her fight with the Boers.
1904: the authorised establishment of the Permanent Force is 2000 all ranks.
1914: Canada has a well structured and well trained Militia Force. Although its personnel are attested only for home service, they expect to be mobilised and re-attested for service in France. Sir Sam Hughes, Minister for Defence and Militia, instead decrees that no Militia unit shall embark intact for overseas duty. He orders the raising of an entirely new army, the Canadian Expeditionary Force. The first hastily assembled units embark almost immediately, each bearing only a serial number as its title, and each consisting of officers and men who have volunteered from a wide variety of Militia regiments. All the advantages of unified peace-time training and esprit de corps have been cast aside. Worse, the troops are equipped with the Ross rifle, a weapon sponsored by Hughes. Developed from a game hunting weapon, it is almost useless for trench warfare. Less then three months after formation, the first Contingent of the CEF meets the cream of the Imperial German Army at Ypres. Over the next four years, the Canadian Corps will be in action continuously on the Western Front.
1916: Hughes departs from the Canadian Government. The Ross rifle is discarded in favour of the Lee Enfield. Despite Hughes' departure, Canada's citizen soldiers continue to fight under the temporary wartime numerical designations. Only a handful of regiments evade his edict by serving in Europe under their customary titles. Despite its early difficulties, the CEF grows in strength and capability, winning fame and glory at Festubert, on the Somme, on Vimy Ridge, at St Eloi and Hill 70, and elsewhere along the front.
1919: a total of 619,636 men and women have served in the CEF and its various supporting units. Of these, 59,544 have died and 233,494 have been wounded. The Force is now disbanded, but fresh units are despatched to Siberia and North Russia as part of the Allied effort to support the White Armies against the Bolsheviks.
1922-1928: Canada's military strength is much reduced and there is a long period of reorganisation of the Militia forces. There is an abortive attempt to create a Department of National Defence, with all three services subject to the command

of a single Chief of Staff.
1936: several cavalry and infantry regiments convert to the machine-gun role.
1939: the Militia begin to mobilise. Within weeks, several peacetime units have been brought up to full strength, have re-attested for service overseas as part of a new Canadian Active Service Force, and have embarked for England. More will follow them during the winter months.
1940: in May, with the Germans streaming across Northern France, Canadian units in England prepare to cross the Channel to assist the retreating French and British Armies. A few embark, and one even spends several days on French soil, before the orders are cancelled. Canadian troops are saved from direct involvement in the debacle. They concentrate in Sussex and Kent, an important element in the anti-invasion force. Their presence permits the despatch of more experienced British Army units to fight the Italians in the Middle East. More units will arrive from Canada during the next two years, being formed as 1st Canadian Infantry Division and 1st Canadian Armoured Brigade. At home, in June, the National Resources Mobilisation Act is passed. It enables the introduction of a limited form of conscription (for home service duties only). Its terms will be extended later.
1941: the Canadian Government agrees to send troops to Hong Kong to strengthen the Colony's garrison force. Two CASF Militia units are chosen - the Winnipeg Grenadiers (which have been providing local defence on the island of Jamaica), and the Royal Rifles of Canada (which have been guarding Newfoundland and which are now brought up to strength with 400 officers and men of the Sherbrooke Regiment). The two under-trained and under-equipped battalions arrive in Hong Kong in November. Three weeks later, they fight valiantly in the island's hopeless defence.
1942: Operation Jubilee. To appease Stalin, and to test their amphibious warfare theories, the British plan a raid in strength on the French port of Dieppe. Apart from British Commando and American Ranger elements, the attacking force consists exclusively of Canadian forces (4th and 6th Infantry Brigades and 14th Army Tank Battalion). Through no fault of their own, and despite desperate gallantry, the Canadians are almost wiped out.
1943: 1st Canadian Infantry Division and 1st Canadian Armoured Brigade leave England to take part in Operation Husky - the invasion of Sicily. At the same time (August), a Canadian Brigade Group takes part in the American occupation of the Aleutian island of Kiska. In September, 5th Canadian Armoured Division reaches the Mediterranean from England and joins in the invasion of mainland Italy. The Canadians will distinguish themselves in the Italian campaign at Ortona and Cassino, and in the approach battles to the Po Valley in the winter of 1944-1945.
1944: the First Canadian Army, containing powerful armoured and artillery elements, plays a key role in the Normandy landings. After the breakout, it is given the task of destroying the German coastal garrisons in the Pas de Calais and Belgium. In November, the policy of 'voluntary service overseas' is discontinued. The need for battle casualty replacements makes it necessary that conscripted (drafted) men shall be liable for service, at home or overseas, for the remainder of the war.
1945: between January and March, 1st Canadian Corps is transferred from Italy to Holland in preparation for the final assault into the German homeland. It is heavily involved in the Rhine crossings and the bitter fighting on the Dutch/German border before the Germans finally collapse. Plans are made for an all-volunteer Pacific Force, but the Japanese surrender makes its despatch unnecessary. By war's end, 730,625 men and women have served in the Canadian forces. Of these, 22,917 have died, and 52,679 have been wounded.
1946: national defence policy begins to develop three separate but related strands - defence of the North Americas in close cooperation with the United States (from 1946), membership of NATO (from 1949), and a strong commitment to United Nations operations (Korea, Egypt, Indo-China, Gaza, Kashmir, The Congo, Yemen, Lebanon, and West New Guinea). The Commonwealth connection is still strong, but Canada will follow an increasingly independent line in world affairs.

1947: the Defence Research Board is established.
1950: the Canadian Army Special Force, raised by special enlistment, is sent to Korea to join the 27th Commonwealth Brigade (subsequently the Commonwealth Division).
1951–1953: additional Active Force battalions are raised to meet the increased NATO commitment in Germany. The strength of the Active Force rises to nearly 50,000 all ranks.
1959: in response to the Soviet nuclear missile threat, the Militia forces are given a civil defence role under the National Survival programme.
1964: severe reductions in the Militia establishment, resulting from the National Survival policy, cause much discontent. In this same year, it is proposed that the Royal Canadian Navy, the Canadian Army, and the Royal Canadian Air Force, be unified under a single command structure with the title Canadian Armed Forces. It will be controlled by a Chief of Defence Staff. The Army's combat units are restructured into four main groupings - Royal Canadian Armoured Corps (Regular and Militia), and Royal Canadian Infantry Corps (Regular and Militia).
1968: the new Armed Forces Act comes into full effect. The Navy and the Air Force lose their 'Royal' prefixes (even though Canada continues to be a leading member of the Commonwealth). The changes have less effect upon the Army. Regiments and Corps which were distinguished already by the 'Royal' prefix and by royal family titles of distinction are permitted to retain them.
1970: an extremist group, the Front de Liberation de Québec (the FLQ), attempts to achieve political gain by kidnapping the British Trade Commissioner and the Quebec Minister of Labour. The Army is mobilised to guard government buildings and leading public figures. Several mechanised, artillery, and infantry units are deployed throughout 350 miles of the St Lawrence Valley. The kidnappers flee to Cuba. The operation, lasting nearly three months, is an outstanding instance of 'aid to the civil power'.
1990: in addition to naval and aviation units, Canada sends an army medical unit and elements The Royal Canadian Regiment and The Royal 22e Regiment to the Arabian Gulf as part of the Coalition Force.
1991: the total strength of the Armed Forces stands at 55,000 all ranks.
1994: over four decades, members of the Canadian Armed Force have served in every United Nations peacekeeping mission, plus several which did not come under the auspices of the UN. More than 50,000 servicemen and women have worn the blue beret. Currently, there are more than 3000 of them serving in twenty-two different countries.

Reference sources:

The majority of published Canadian unit histories are recorded in the following pages. For additional information regarding certain specific campaigns, reference should be made to other sections of this bibliography. Vide page 746, Index, 'Canadians Abroad'.

GENERAL REFERENCE

THE GOOD REGIMENT
The Carignan-Salieres Regiment in Canada, 1665-1668
Jack Verney * McGill-Queen's University Press, Kingston, Ontario, 1991. White, gold, 9.25 x 6.25, ix/222. No ills, 4 maps (2 printed in the text, 2 on the end-papers), Glossary, Bibliography, Chapter Notes, Index. Apps: extensive information regarding equipment, food supplies, clothing, etc, plus biographical notes on very nearly all of the officers and men who served in Canada (both those who stayed and those who returned to France).
* The Carignan-Salieres was never a Regt of the British Empire, but it is listed here as a matter of record (and because the descendents of some of its members no doubt later served the British Crown). In 1664, King Louis XIV ordered that a 'good regiment' should be despatched to New France (Eastern Canada). The intention was to destroy the Iroquois Nation and thereby aid French settlement. Consisting of twenty-four Companies, it disembarked at Quebec City in June 1665. Forts were established along the line of the Richelieu Valley, from Lake Champlain to the St Lawrence. A column set out to attack the Mohawks in the following January. The result was a disaster. Ill-equipped and untrained in forest warfare, the Regt lost 460 men from starvation and the effects of the winter weather. A second expedition was launched in October 1666 and it managed to burn four Mohawk villages. Thereafter, it settled down for quiet garrison duties. The Regt returned to France in 1668, but 400 men took local discharge and became part of the small French colony. This well researched history is full of interesting detail, and the nominal roll is a prime source for genealogists. R/1 V/5. PC. JRD.

LES COMPAGNIES FRANCHES DE LA MARINE
Canada's First Military Corps
David M Stewart * The Lake St Louis Historical Society, Pointe Claire, QP, 1967. Illustrated stiff card, white, blue/black, 'Marine c.1740' motif, 8.0 x 5.5, -/38. Fp, 6 mono phots, no maps, no appendixes, no Index.
* The work describes, in brief fashion, the 18th Century services in Canada of the Companies of Marines sent to Canada by the French Government in 1683 and withdrawn in 1760. The Corps was recreated as a 're-enactment unit' in 1963. A few verbatim extracts from contemporary documents are included in the text.
R/2 V/2. ASKBMC. CB.

CANADA'S SOLDIERS
The Military History of an Unmilitary People
George F G Stanley * The Macmillan Co of Canada Ltd, Toronto, 1974. Wine red, gold, 9.25 x 6.25, xi/487. Fp, 16 mono phots, 39 maps, Bibliography, 4 Indexes (one General, three of military formations). Apps: 7 in total, mainly lists of senior officers and Ministers.
* A massive narrative account of military activity in Canada from 1604 through to 1974, which in effect is the history of the nation. Everything is covered - early French fights with the Iroquois, the arrival of the British garrisons, the growth of the Fencibles and the Militia, coastal fortifications, the wars of 1914-1918 and 1939-1945, the post-war years, and much more besides. Apart from senior political figures, few individuals are mentioned by name. However, many different Corps and Regiments are referred to directly, and the extensive Indexes are invaluable in this regard. An excellent overall analysis. R/2 V/5. PC. JRD.
Note: first published in 1954. At least two other (updated) versions have been recorded, and there may have been more.

THE ARMED FORCES OF CANADA
A Century of Achievement
Lieut Col D J Goodspeed CD * Department of National Defence, Ottawa, 1967. Green, gold, 11.25 x 8.75, xi/289. Fp, 210 mono phots, 35 cld ills, 11 maps (10 printed in the text, plus one cld double spread), Bibliography, Index. Apps: roll of VC winnners (1900-1945), extensive list of senior officers and politicians.
* A scholarly and complete overview of Canada's transition from being a defenceless cluster of Provinces to leading player on the world stage. The author makes the point that his country's international influence derives solely from its armed forces. His case is persuasive. Never having had any aspirations to invade other countries, the Canadian people were nevertheless obliged to develop a powerful army, navy and air force during the century under review. A truly fascinating analysis. R/1 V/5. PC. JRD.

THE CANADIAN ARMY
Regimental Histories and a Guide to the Regiments
Charles E Dornbusch * Hope Farm Press, Cornwallville, New York, 1959. Soft card, 'Perfect' binding, pale blue, black, 10.25 x 7.0, -/216. Fp, 3 other ills, no maps, no appendixes, Index of Authors, Indexes of Sources.
* As noted elsewhere (vide Index of Authors), Dornbusch was a librarian employed at the New York Public Library and having a special interest in British Empire unit histories. This was the first of three bibliographies which he published privately (the others referring to Australia and New Zealand). Of the three, it is the most useful and the best in terms of internal arrangement. One of its strengths is the 'Guide' element, this being a condensed chronological summary of the lineage of each Regiment. R/4 V/4. PC. RP.
Note: an additional source - covering a wider spread of material - is THE CANADIAN MILITARY EXPERIENCE, 1867-1983, A BIBLIOGRAPHY, by O A Cooke (Directorate of History, Department of National Defence, Ottawa, 1984).

THE REGIMENTS AND CORPS OF THE CANADIAN ARMY
Anon * The Queen's Printer, Ottawa, for The Army Historical Section, Dept of National Defence, Ottawa, 1964. Red, gold, Canadian Infantry Corps crest, 8.75 x 5.75, -/253. No ills, no maps, no Index. Apps: explanatory notes and Order of Precedence (17.2.1964).
* A very handy source of reference. Each Regt is individually described, with full details of its origins, evolution, operational roles, affiliations, Battle Honours, cap badges, motto, Regtl music, Regtl HQ, and so forth. An excellent starting point for any study of the Canadian Army, much more comprehensive and professionally presented than any equivalent official publication produced by any other Commonwealth government. R/3 V/5. PC. JRD.

THE CONCISE LINEAGES OF THE CANADIAN ARMY, 1855 TO DATE
Charles H Stewart * Publication details not shown, Toronto, 1982. Soft card, buff, black, litho offset, 'Perfect' binding, '13th Canadian Militia badge' motif, 11.0 x 8.5, -/193/xv. Numerous ills (helmet plates and cap badges, poorly reproduced), no maps, Bibliography, Index. Apps: notes on British Army affiliations ('Alliances').
* A reference work, to be consulted by researchers wishing to trace the roots and evolution of each Regiment and Corps of the modern Canadian Army (Permanent and Militia). Most of the entries include also a few interesting snippits of information concerning the unit's services and traditions. Under separate headings are each unit's Battle Honours and CEF perpetuations. For the latter, a 'reverse Index' would have been helpful, i.e. a list of all the CEF Bns in numerical order, with the titles of the modern units which perpetuate them. R/2 V/4. PC. RP.
Note: this is an expanded and corrected edition of the author's first attempt at this complex subject which he published in 1969. The first edition's format was - stiff card, spiral binding, grey, black, Militia badge, 8.5 x 7.0, xxxii/132. The 1982 (second) edition extends the coverage provided by the official compilation described in the preceding entry.

CANADIAN BRASS
The Makings of a Professional Army
Stephen J Harris * University of Toronto Press, Toronto, 1988. Pale blue, gold, 9.25 x 6.0, -/271. 23 mono phots, no maps, Bibliography, Sources, no appendixes, Index.
* Essentially an academic's view of the political framework within which the Canadian Army has evolved over the decades. From the time of Confederation to the outbreak of WWII, the Canadian military struggled to establish themselves as a professional armed service. According to the author, attempts by senior officers to convince the politicians that the country needed an army as a permanent element in national life were repeatedly thwarted - partly through the obduracy of the civilians and partly through lack of drive by some top soldiers.
R/1 V/4. RMAS. RP.

FORGOTTEN SOLDIERS
For Canada's Native Peoples Who Served in Both World Wars
Fred Gaffen * Theytus Books Ltd, Penticton, BC, 1985. Illustrated soft card, blue/red, 'Warriors' motif, 11.0 x 8.5, -/152. 49 mono phots, 5 maps, Glossary, Bibliography, Index. Apps: Roll of Honour (with details of the unit with which each man was serving at the time of his death, WWI and WWII), H&A (WWI and WWII), notes on land sales to Veterans.
* The 'native peoples' mentioned in the sub-title were the North American Indians whose tribal areas lay north of the Canadian/US border. Many volunteered during both world wars. In WWI, their natural skills as woodsmen and warriors were put to good use in the Forestry Corps and in CEF fighting units (107th and 114th Inf Bns were composed entirely of Indians, but there were at least a few in almost every other CEF unit). In WWII, their sons fought on foot, in tanks, and in the air. This book has a main narrative which is little more than an anthology of personal stories, but it is a poignant record of service and bravery. The appendixes are invaluable to family historians and to medal collectors. The illustrations - mainly photographs of Indians in uniform - have a compelling quality and would not be seen elsewhere. R/1 V/4. RCSL. RP.

The Militia

THE ROLL OF THE REGIMENTS (THE ACTIVE MILITIA)
Lieut Col H M Jackson MBE TD * Publication details not shown, 1959. Stiff card, red, black, 8.25 x 5.5, x/176. No ills, no maps, no appendixes, Index.
* To quote from the author: 'This volume is an attempt to show the rotation in units, the changes which have taken place in the regiments of infantry and Rifles of the Canadian Militia, from the dates of their organisation to the present time (1959). It indicates amalgamations, disbandments, conversion to other arms, and the organisation of new units with disused numbers'. An immensely detailed source of reference for titles, locations, dates, and the names of original unit COs.
R/4 V/5. MODL. AMM.
Note: in 1960 the same author published a companion work - THE ROLL OF THE REGIMENTS (THE SEDENTARY MILITIA). Having 100 pages and the same purpose and format as his first book, it deals with the cadres from which the Active Militia drew its recruits during the period from 1846 to (circa) 1869.

THE CANADIAN MILITIA
From 1855 - An Historical Summary
David A Morris CD * The Boston Mills Press, Erin, Ontario, 1983. Illustrated covers, 10.25 x 7.75, -/328. Fp, 2 mono phots, 33 line drawings of Regtl crests (some on the front cover, others within the text), no appendixes, no Index.
* This is a book which meets two separate needs. Firstly, it traces the evolution of the early citizen-soldier movement - the defence of Quebec in 1690, the British conquest of Eastern Canada in 1760, the American incursions of 1776, the war

with America in 1812, and the passing of the Militia Act in 1855. Secondly, it lists the Militia units of 1855-1900, the CEF units of WWI, and each individual Artillery, Engineer, and Infantry unit extant in WWII. Considerable detail is given for all arms down to basic unit level. The book complements and updates the work by Jackson (vide preceding entry). R/1 V/4. PC. JRD.

THE GUIDE
A Manual for the Canadian Militia (Infantry)
Maj Gen Sir William D Otter KCB CVO * The Copp Clark Co Ltd, Toronto, 1914. Red, black, 6.5 x 4.5, -/325. No ills, no maps, no appendixes, no Index.
* As explained on its title page, this is 'A Manual ... embracing the interior economy, duties, discipline, drills and parades, dress, books and correspondence of a Battalion, with Regulations for marches, transport and encampment, also forms and bugle calls'. It appears to have been a private venture by the author, but the contents are based directly upon King's Regulations, the Army Act, Militia Regulations and Orders, and the Standing Orders of various Regts of the British Army. An interesting publication containing much sound advice - as relevant to the administration of an Infantry Battalion today as it was in 1914.
R/3 V/3. PC. RP.
Note: the above details apply to the 'Ninth (Revised) Edition' of 1914. Publication dates for other editions are not stated, but the first was produced (and published by the same author) in 1880.

ROOTS OF THE CANADIAN ARMY, MONTREAL DISTRICT, 1846-1870
Elinor Kyte Senior * Society of the Montreal Museum, Montreal, 1981. Illustrated stiff card, white, blue, 8.25 x 7.0, xi/125. Fp, 65 mono phots (incl identified groups and individuals), 2 maps (bound in), explanatory notes, Glossary, Sources, Bibliography, Index.
* This is an important explanation of the early military history of Quebec Province and the evolution of its English- and French-speaking Militia units. Experience had shown that Montreal was the key to Canada's territorial defences. It was always strongly garrisoned by Regts of the British Army. Their departure for the Crimea, in 1854, and the subsequent rebellions amongst the Irish immigrant population, emphasised the need for the Canadian Provinces to build their own integral military resources. An expanding Militia movement was the result. It is in many of those local Volunteer units that the modern Canadian Army has its roots.
R/3 V/5. PC. JRD.

THE GORE DISTRICT MILITIA OF 1821, 1824, 1830 AND 1838, THE MILITIA OF WEST YORK AND WEST LINCOLN OF 1804, WITH LISTS OF OFFICERS
Together with Some Historical and Biographical Notes on the Militia Within the Territory at Present Constituting the County of Wentworth in the Years Named
H H Robertson * Griffin & Kidner Co Ltd, Hamilton, Ontario, 1904. Dark red, gold, 9.0 x 6.0, -/61. Fp, 12 mono phots (portraits), no maps, no appendixes, no Index.
* A poorly presented retrospective of the history of the territory which became the County of Wentworth. It is a compilation of several undoubtedly important and little-known documentary sources, but there is no attempt to analyse them or to link them in a coherent narrative. R/5 V/2. RCSL. TAB.

A THOUSAND YOUNG MEN
The Colonial Volunteer Militia and Prince Edward Island, 1775-1874
David Webber * Prince Edward Island Museum & Heritage Foundation, 1990. Illustrated soft card, 'Figures in uniform' motif, red/black, 8.5 x 11.0, -/140. 18 mono phots, 11 cld ills, 8 maps, Bibliography, Index. Apps: list of COs, notes on the Militia Act, General Orders, Garrison Companies, Regulations, Establishments.
* A detailed but readable account of local Volunteer Militia units, interspersed with quotations from memoirs, letters, and official documents of the period. A book which has obvious value to local historians and those interested in uniforms.
R/1 V/5. CFHT. PJE.

THE NEW BRUNSWICK MILITIA, 1787-1867
David Farcey Crowther * New Ireland Press, Fredericton, for the New Brunswick Historical Society, 1990. Illustrated soft glossy card, 'Shako' motif, full colour, 9.0 x 6.0, x/191. 4 mono phots (unidentified groups), 3 cld ills (uniforms), one map, Bibliography, Chapter Notes, Index. Apps: list of all New Brunswick units (1787-1867, with names of their COs).
* The conclusion of the American War of Independence brought a flood of former Loyalist soldiers and their families as settlers in Southern Quebec and in Nova Scotia. In the St John River valley alone, 10,000 of them came to start a new life. In 1784, Nova Scotia was partitioned, and the Province of New Brunswick was formed. This book is an academic account of the long and complex development of the part-time Volunteer movement in the Province during the following eighty years. Very many Volunteer units were raised, amalgamated, disbanded, reformed and renamed during that time, and they are all described here in somewhat tedious detail. The War of 1812 did not spread to New Brunswick, indeed the Province's economy prospered and expanded greatly as a consequence of that war. The narrative, therefore, has a substantial socio-politico-economic content. It is a sound source of reference for everyone having a particular interest in the history of New Brunswick. R/2 V/5. PC. JRD.
Note: for information regarding the background events preceding the arrival of these people in New Brunswick, reference should be made to the 'Colonial North America' section of this bibliography.

Training Establishments

QUEEN'S MEN, CANADA'S MEN
The Military History of Queen's University, Kingston
Kathryn M Bindon * Published by Queen's University Contingent COTC, Kingston, Ontario, 1978. Stiff card, buff, black, 'Thistle collar badge' motif, 9.0 x 6.0, xii/180. Fp, 17 mono phots, one cartoon, no maps, Glossary, Bibliography, Index. Apps: list of former COs (RCN, Army and RCAF sections).
* An academic treatment of the history (1862-1866 and 1880-1968) of a University Officer Training Corps whose role it was to train potential leaders for Regular and Militia units. The narrative is lacklustre but reliable. R/3 V/5. MODL. AMM.

CANADA'S RMC - A HISTORY OF THE ROYAL MILITARY COLLEGE
Richard Arthur Preston * University of Toronto Press, Toronto, for the RMC Club, 1969. Red, gold, 9.25 x 6.25, xvii/415. Fp, 83 mono phots (incl many captioned groups and individual portraits), no maps, Bibliography, Chapter Notes, Index. Apps: list of former COs (1875-1967, with portraits), idem Adjutants, idem RSMs, idem various other office holders, notes on sport, etc.
* The RMC was founded in 1875 'for the purpose of imparting a complete education in all branches of military tactics, fortifications and engineering'. In 1950, its task was broadened to include Cadets destined for naval and aviation careers. A detailed informative history, with many individuals named.
R/1 V/5. PC. JRD.

Campaigns

A PARTICULAR DUTY
The Canadian Rebellions, 1837-1839
Michael Mann * Michael Russell (Publishing) Ltd, Wilton, Salisbury, UK, 1986. Blue, gold, 8.75 x 5.5, xi/211. 19 mono phots, 5 maps, Bibliography and Sources (specifically the Colborne Papers and the Cathcart Papers), Index. Apps: list of all Volunteer Corps extant or raised in the Lower Province (1837).
* A book prompted by the discovery of the Cathcart papers and the author's interest in the role of the British Army's King's Dragoon Guards in early Canada. The Rebellion emerged from the cultural clashes between the established conserv-

ative Roman Catholic French community and the later-arrived liberal Anglican 'Britons' who had immigrated in part from Great Britain and in part from Loyalist America after 1782. The French-speaking peoples felt threatened by the rapidly growing dominance - political, commercial and agricultural - of the newcomers. Their resentment was voiced in a political movement - Les Patriotes - under its elected leader, Louis-Joseph Papineau. Entering the House of Assembly in 1834, these republican politicians were so frustrated by their lack of progress that a civil war erupted in 1837. It persisted for two years. During that time, the British Army's tiny garrison force needed to be reinforced to the point at which a quarter of its entire effective strength was sent to the Province - two Regts of Cavalry, two Bns of Guards, and twenty-one Regts of the Line. This is a unique account of the affair because it is told largely from the viewpoint of the British high command. Many locally-raised English-speaking Volunteer units are given good coverage in the narrative (and all are listed in the appendix). R/1 V/5. PC. RP.

THE LAST WAR DRUM
The North West Campaign, 1885
Desmond Morton * A M Hakkert Ltd, Toronto, 1972. Dark orange, black, 10.0 x 6.5, x/193. 5 fps, 75 mono phots (incl named individuals), 34 sketches, 5 cartoons, 7 maps, Bibliography, Chapter Notes, Index. Apps: Order of Battle.
* The story opens with the North America Act which created, on 1 July 1867, the Confederation of Nova Scotia, New Brunswick, Quebec and Ontario. It ends with the hanging of Riel, at Regina, on 1 July 1885. The intervening battles (Duck Lake, Fish Creek, Batoche, Cut Knife Hill, Frenchman's Butte) are described well, with useful references to the various NWMP and Militia units engaged. The book paints the large political picture, but with plenty of individual soldiers and police officers being mentioned in the narrative. R/3 V/5. PC. JRD.

WORLD WAR I

OVERSEAS

The Lineages and Insignia of the Canadian Expeditionary Force, 1914-19

Charles H Stewart * Mission Press, Toronto, for Little & Stewart, 1970. Soft card, 'Perfect' binding, buff, black, 8.5 x 5.5, -/167. Fp, 30 pages of small mono phots (mainly cap and lapel badges), no maps, no appendixes, Index (of units).

* This is a condensed but handy listing of the 260 different Bns, Regts and Corps which constituted the CEF. For each unit, the author provides notes on dates of raising and disbandment, unit strengths, movements and active services, affiliations, notes on uniforms and insignia, and much else of value to the military historian. An excellent and unique initial source of reference for further research on individual units. R/2 V/5. PCAL. RP.

Note: a reprint dated 1971 has been noted.

CANADA IN FLANDERS

The Official History of the Canadian Expeditionary Force

Sir Max Aitken and Maj Charles G S Roberts * Hodder & Stoughton, London, various dates (see below). Three matching Volumes, red, gold, 7.5 x 5.0.

Volume I : Sir Max Aitken, xx/247, published in 1916

Volume II : Sir Max Aitken, xx/258, published in 1917

Volume III : Maj C G S Roberts, -/144, published in 1918

All three Volumes having illustrations, but no maps or Indexes.

* This series of books covers the services of the CEF on the Western Front up to 28 November 1916. Many units and individuals receive a specific mention in the narrative, and the battle descriptions are clear, but the reader must wonder how it was possible to produce 'official histories' at such speed and while the conflict was still in progress. Aitken was the Canadian Government's representative on the Western Front and had full access to documents and to senior officers, but good history needs time to mature. The political need to give his country's contribution to the war a high profile may have been the driving force behind these three books. R/1 V/3. PC. RLP/RP.

CANADIAN EXPEDITIONARY FORCE, 1914-1919

Official History of the Canadian Army in the First World War

Col G W L Nicholson * The Queen's Printer, Ottawa, for the Ministry of National Defence, 1962. Red, gold, CEF crest, 10.0 x 6.5, xiv/621. Fp, 48 mono phots, 55 line drawings, 16 maps (cld, 15 bound in, one printed on the end-papers), Glossary, Bibliography, Index. Apps: 7 in total, incl lists of units serving in France and Flanders at November 1918, notes on battles fought, distinguishing flashes of Canadian units in the field (coloured fold-out).

* After WWI, work was commenced on an eight-volume OFFICIAL HISTORY OF THE CANADIAN FORCES IN THE GREAT WAR. Volume I, by Col Duguid, was published (with an accompanying volume of appendixes and maps) in 1938. It dealt with events between August 1914 and September 1915. A volume entitled THE MEDICAL SERVICES had already appeared in 1924. All work ceased during WWII and it was then decided to abandon the entire project. Col Nicholson, an established historian, was then invited to pick up the pieces and to produce a single volume in place of the originally planned eight. The result of his efforts is a first-class history, well written and totally authoritative, with excellent supporting maps. R/2 V/5. PC. SB.

AMID THE GUNS BELOW

The Story of the Canadian Corps

Larry Worthington * McClelland & Stewart Ltd, Toronto, 1965. Beige, brown, 'Canadian soldier' motif, 9.0 x 5.75, xvi/171. 11 mono phots, one map (printed on the end-papers), Bibliography, no appendixes, Index.

* A broad-brush account of a famous Corps. The author pays over-due credit to the leadership qualities of General Sir Arthur Currie, the Corps Commander. The

author also includes little-known information concerning Brig Gen Raymond Brutinel, commander of the Canadian Machine-gun Corps. An easy and fluent narrative which is best read in conjunction with Nicholson (vide preceding entry). R/2 V/3. PC. JBC.

TO SEIZE THE VICTORY
The Canadian Corps in World War I
John Swettenham * The Ryerson Press, Toronto, 1965. Slate grey, gold, 9.5 x 6.0, xvi/265. Fp, 20 mono phots, 16 maps (14 printed in the text, 2 printed on the end -papers), Bibliography and Sources, no appendixes, Index.
* A lucid and wide-ranging account of the political decision to raise a Corps for service in France, its despatch to England, and its subsequent four years of valour and sacrifice on the Western Front. Excellent background reading, particularly with regard to the debates within Canadian Government circles in 1914 and 1915.
R/1 V/4. RMAS. RP.

THE INTELLIGENCE SERVICES WITHIN THE CANADIAN CORPS, 1914-1918
Maj J E Hahn * The McMillan Co, Toronto, 1930. Red, gold, 9.25 x 6.0, xxii/263. 16 mono phots, 6 maps, no appendixes, no Index.
* Doubtless of interest to the specialist researcher, but less so to the general reader. R/2 V/4. PC. JEB.

WITH THE FIRST CANADIAN CONTINGENT
Published on Behalf of the Canadian Field Comforts Association
Anon * Hodder & Stoughton, London, September 1915. Olive, brown, 'Maple leaf' motif, 9.75 x 7.25, -/119. Fp, 100 mono phots, no maps, no appendixes, no Index.
* An assemblage of poems and letters sent home by Canadian soldiers serving in France during the early months of the war. Presumably published to help raise funds for the despatch of 'comfort parcels'. Sadly, the text is not very interesting and the illustrations are exceptionally poor. R/3 V/1. RCSL. RP.

VIMY
Henry Fairlie Wood * Transworld Publishers Ltd, London, 1972. Seen as a Corgi illustrated paperback, but first published by Macdonald in 1967. Paperback version 7.0 x 4.5, -/175. 21 mono phots, 2 maps, Bibliography, Index. Apps: Order of Battle for the Canadian Corps (1917).
* A detailed account of the assault and capture of Vimy Ridge in 1917 by the four Canadian Infantry Divisions. They won four VCs during the battle, but lost 11,297 in dead and wounded. Canada's soldiers fought in many other battles on the Western Front, but it was from the cauldron of Vimy that the nation's modern sense of identity emerged. R/1 V/4. PC. PS.
Note: equally good is a book with the same title - VIMY - by Pierre Berton, first published in hardback in 1986 and in 1987 in soft covers (Penguin Books Canada Ltd, Markham, Ontario).

THE CALL TO ARMS
Montreal's Roll of Honour, European War, 1914
Bernard K Sandwell * Southam Press Ltd, Montreal, 1914. Stapled stiff card and cloth, red, black, 'Bugle and scroll' motif, 9.0 x 6.0, -/209 (plus 19 pages of advertisements). 5 fps, more than 100 mono phots (all studio portraits and group pictures, fully captioned), no maps, no appendixes, no Index.
* Published at the end of 1914, this is a typical example of the public fervour for the war and the wish to show support 'for the boys at the Front'. It is essentially an assemblage of initial muster rolls for every CEF unit raised in and around the city of Montreal. The officers and men who volunteered for service overseas came mainly from the well-established local Militia units - 1st Prince of Wales' Regt, 5th Royal Highlanders of Canada, Le Regiment Royal Canadien, The Westmount Rifles, and The Irish Canadian Rangers. Brief historical summaries of each of these Regts is included, but the main research value of the book would be to the medal collector and genealogist. R/4 V/3. PC. JRD.

CANADA'S THIRD CONTINGENT FROM 1st AND 2nd DIVISIONS, ONTARIO
In Commemoration of the 3rd Contingent Going to the Front, 1915
Anon * No publication details shown, n.d. Illustrated soft card, 'Flags, Maple leaf, ship, troops' motif, green, red/blue, 12.25 x 9.25, -/80 (not numbered, plus 48 pages of advertisements). 152 mono phots, no maps, no Index. Apps: list of former officers, list of 'Companies who have made this publication possible'.
* An entirely pictorial record, with virtually no narrative. It depicts the men who sailed for Europe with 33rd, 34th, 35th and 58th Bns CEF, plus the portraits of some senior officers of the 1st and 2nd Divisions (of Militia). Fully captioned formal group photographs are included for each Bn's HQ personnel, band, Corps of Bugles, signal section, and all ranks of each rifle Platoon. An extraordinary record, of prime interest to family historians and medal collectors. It seems to have been published in 1915 when the Bns were embarking, or shortly thereafter.
R/5 V/3. PC. JRD.

NOVA SCOTIA'S PART IN THE WAR
Capt M Stuart Hunt * The Nova Scotia Veteran Publishing Co, Halifax, NS, 1920. Red, black, Provincial armorial bearings, 9.75 x 5.75, xii/432. Fp, many other mono phots (officers who were KIA and WIA), no maps, no Index. Apps: Roll of Honour, H&A.
* The Province sent drafts to fill the ranks of many different CEF units. This book is a compendium of histories of those units, with many individuals named in the text. A useful secondary source for - 6th Cdn Mounted Rifles, 9th Siege Bty, 10th Siege Bty, 17th Field Bty, 14th Bde CFA, and the following CEF Bns of Infantry - 17th, 25th, 40th, 64th, 85th, 106th, 112th, 185th, 193rd, 219th and 246th. There are condensed histories also of the 1st CGA (Militia), 63rd, 66th and 94th Composite Bns (Militia). Between ten and twenty pages of text are devoted to each of these numerous units. R/4 V/4. MODL. MCJ.

THE BANTAMS
The Untold Story of World War One
Sidney Allison * Mosaic Press, Oakville, Ontario, 1982. Grey, red, 9.0 x 6.0, -/287. 27 mono phots, one line drawing, Bibliography, no appendixes, Index.
* As the casualty lists grew ever longer, and as the Generals demanded more and more men, the War Office gradually relaxed the physical standards to be applied to new recruits. The 'minimum height' requirement was progressively reduced. Under-sized men were allocated to special 'Bantam' units. The same policy was followed in Canada. The author of this book interviewed 300 survivors and made use of unpublished journals and letters to compile this record.
R/1 V/2. SLV. PS.
Note: first published by Howard Baker Press Ltd, Wimbledon, UK, 1981.

WORLD WAR II

THE CANADIAN ARMY, 1939-1945
An Official Historical Summary
Col C P Stacey * Edmond Cloutier (King's Printer), for the Ministry of National Defence, Ottawa, 1948. Red, gold, MND crest, 10.0 x 6.5, xv/354. Fp, 11 other cld ills, 18 maps (13 cld, 3 black/white, all bound in, 2 printed on the end-papers, all drawn by Lieut C C J Bond), Glossary, Index. Apps: list of persons holding principal appointments (1939-1945), composition of 1st Canadian Army (at 5.5.1945), notes on the organisation of Infantry and Armoured Divs (by sub-unit, May 1945).
* An excellent general account, well presented and well indexed. It covers all WWII operations in which Canadian troops were engaged, including detailed accounts of the disasters at Hong Kong and Dieppe. A fine tribute to Canada's citizen army.
R/3 V/5. RMAS. RP.

NEWFOUNDLAND

Newfoundland was Great Britain's oldest Colony until April 1949 when, with Labrador, it became Canada's tenth Province. Each of the following book entries refer to Newfoundland's pre-1949 military history, and it is for this reason that they are recorded here under their own collective heading.

THE FIRST FIVE HUNDRED
A Historical Sketch of the Military Operations of the Royal Newfoundland Regiment in Gallipoli and on the Western Front during the Great War (1914-1918)
Richard Cramm * C F Williams & Sons Inc, Albany, New York, n.d. (c.1922). Black, gold, Regtl crest, 10.5 x 8.0, xviii/297. 370 mono phots, 8 maps (7 printed in the text, one bound in), no appendixes, no Index.
* This is one of the most intimate of Regtl histories. The population of Newfoundland in 1914 was very small (approximately 260,000 souls) and the heavy losses suffered by the Regt had a particularly devastating effect upon local families and the local economy. The title of the book refers to the first draft of volunteers - known as 'the blue puttees' - who crossed over to Europe. The first 109 pages give a fairly accurate description of the Regts' movements and battles, with lists (in the text) of awards for those battles. The second half of the book (193 pages) consists of a biographical entry for each man with, in many cases, a portrait photograph of him. The Regt gained one VC - Pte (later Sgt) Thomas Ricketts. R/5 V/4. PC. JEB/JBC.
Note: given its maritime and fishing tradition, the Colony also provided a large number of experienced seamen for the Royal Navy.

THE TRAIL OF THE CARIBOU
The Royal Newfoundland Regiment, 1914-1918
Maj R H Tait MC * Newfoundland Publishing Co Inc, Boston, Massachusetts, 1933. Red, white, Regtl crest, 7.5 x 5.0, ix/65. 3 mono phots, no maps, no Index. Apps: Roll of Honour (statistics only), H&A (idem), analysis of enlistments (idem).
* At the outbreak of war, Newfoundland had no indigenous Militia forces and almost no local military tradition. The first 500 men to volunteer were totally lacking in soldierly experience. After less than a year of basic instruction, they were fighting on Gallipoli. Their Regt was then virtually annihilated in July 1916 on the Western Front. This is a somewhat patchy history, with few dates or names mentioned, but there are some references to awards in the text. A secondary source, to be read in conjunction with Nicholson (vide following entry).
R/4 V/2. NYPL. JEB/JRD.

THE FIGHTING NEWFOUNDLANDER
The History of the Royal Newfoundland Regiment
Col G W L Nicholson CD * Printed by Thomas Nelson (Printers) Ltd, London, UK, for the Government of Newfoundland, 1964. Ivory, ochre/black, black, 9.75 x 6.25, xix/614. Fp, 78 mono phots, line drawings of badges, 18 maps (11 printed in the text, 5 folding, bound in, 2 printed on the end-papers), Bibliography, Index.
Apps: 7 in total, incl Roll of Honour (WWI, KIA, all ranks, with dates), H&A (all ranks, with dates of the engagements for which awarded), notes on Battle Honours, idem the Newfoundland Volunteers (1780).
* A well written and very detailed narrative account of the Regt from its origins through to 1964. However, the bulk of the book is devoted to the war of 1914-1918 when the Regt gained a fine reputation for courage and endurance, but suffered horrendous losses in the process. It will be forever associated with the first day of the Somme battle (1 July 1916) when, in the space of a few hours at Beaumont Hamel, it lost 710 battle casualties. The photographs are not well reproduced but, in general terms, this is an attractive production. The maps, drawn by E H Ellwand, of the Royal Canadian Engineers, are exceptionally good.
R/3 V/5. PCAL/MODL. SB/RP.

MORE FIGHTING NEWFOUNDLANDERS
A History of Newfoundland's Fighting Forces in the Second World War
Col G W L Nicholson CD * Hazell, Watson & Viney Ltd, Aylesbury, UK, for the Government of Newfoundland and Labrador, 1969. Ivory, with the crests of the three fighting services, 9.75 x 6.25, xiii/621. Fp, 114 mono phots, 16 maps (14 bound in, 2 printed on the end-papers), Bibliography, Index. Apps: Roll of Honour, H&A, note on drafts.
* As the sub-title indicates, this large and very informative book deals with the services of Newfoundlanders who served in WWII in the Army, Navy, and Air Force. Eleven of the sixteen chapters are devoted to the Colony's two gunner units - 59th (Newfoundland) Heavy Regt RA, which served in England and NW Europe, and 166th (Newfoundland) Field Regt RA, which served in North Africa and Italy. Two chapters deal with naval services, and one chapter is dedicated to 125 (Newfoundland) Sqn RAF. The latter was reformed at Colerne (UK) in 1941 as an element of Fighter Command. Many of its early personnel were Newfoundlanders.
R/3 V/5. PC. SB/RH.

WHAT BECAME OF CORPORAL PITTMAN?
Joy B Cave * Breakwater Books Ltd, St John's, Newfoundland, 1976. Blue, white, 8.0 x 5.5, xiv/180/Lxviii. 10 mono phots, 3 maps (bound in at the rear), no Index. Apps: Roll of Honour (KIA and WIA, on 1.7.1916), nominal roll of survivors.
* This is the story of the near total destruction of the Royal Newfoundland Regt in the disastrous attack at Beaumont Hamel on the opening day - 1 July 1916 - of the Somme offensive. Joy Cave has constructed nominal rolls of all the officers and men of the Regt who took part - those killed that day, those wounded that day, those who died subsequently of their wounds, and those who survived. She provides details of the home addresses and locations of burial (or memorial) for each and every casualty. These appendixes occupy the last 68 pages of her book and they represent a great deal of dedicated research. The main narrative (180 pages) is an account of the preparations for the battle (including the raid on 28 June) and the battle itself. A labour of love. R/2 V/4. PC. SB.

THEY ALSO SERVED
The Newfoundland Overseas Forestry Unit, 1939-1946
Tom Curran * Jesperson Press, St John's Newfoundland, 1987. Illustrated soft card, 'Logger' motif, green, white, v/119. 55 mono phots (incl one named group), no maps, no Index. Apps: Roll of Honour (killed in accidents and DOD, with their home addresses, dates, and locations of burial), verbatim extracts from documents regarding the Unit's formation and administration.
* Following an offer of assistance at the outbreak of war, the British Government asked the Colony to immediately provide 625 volunteers for the Royal Navy and 'a labour force to cut pit props in connection with coal production in Britain .. vital to the war economy'. By February 1940, the first of 2150 experienced loggers and sawyers had arrived. Paid $2.00 per day, they worked at thirty-five camps in Scotland and the north of England. A third of them volunteered to join the (part-time) Home Guard and formed the 3rd Inverness (Newfoundland) Bn. This unit was unique in being the only Home Guard Bn composed exclusively of Colonials. Several members received awards, and these are noted in the narrative. Logging work went on until July 1946 when the Unit returned home for disbandment. R/2 V/4. PC. JRD.

Note: apart from its major efforts during WWI and WWII, the Colony had earlier raised a short-lived local defence unit during the Revolutionary War with France. It is recorded in a booklet of vii/81 pages entitled SKINNER'S FENCIBLES - THE ROYAL NEWFOUNDLAND REGIMENT, 1795-1802, by David A Webber. The author was Curator of the Newfoundland Naval & Military Museum. Produced by the Government Printer in 1964, it contains a list of officers and 19 plates of illustrations (some folding).

Newfoundland Police

A HISTORY OF THE NEWFOUNDLAND RANGER FORCE
Harold Horwood * Breakwater Books, St John's, Newfoundland, n.d. (c.1986).
Blue, gold, 9.25 x 6.0, -/183. 54 mono phots, no maps, no Index. Apps: details of duties performed by the Corps, letters of appreciation, nominal roll of all ranks who served.
* The NRF was formed in 1935 and disbanded in 1949 (when it was absorbed by the RCMP). During the short span of its existence, the Corps performed a huge variety of services to the community - wildlife surveys, forestry protection, ice patrols, liaison with the Inuit Indians, Customs control, search and rescue, and so forth. This official history is based upon references to source documents linked to the recollections of former members, and covers both peacetime and wartime events. R/1 V/4. FFL. RP.

THE NEWFOUNDLAND CONSTABULARY
Arthur Fox * Robinson Blackmore Printing & Publishing Co, Newfoundland, 1971.
Dark blue, silver, 8.75 x 5.5, -/147. Fp, 72 mono phots, no maps, Bibliography, no Index. Apps: list of COs (1853-1971), Chronology (1497-1970).
* The Newfoundland Constabulary was established in 1871. There had been a rudimentary police force for some years prior to that date, but responsibility for maintaining law and order had rested mainly with the Imperial garrison units. When they were withdrawn, there was an obvious need for a regular police force. This nicely balanced record celebrates the Force's centenary. The Colony evolved without any civil or communal strife, so the work of the police was geared to the usual gamut of small-scale crime and domestic disputes, but the book pays tribute to the way in which the personnel of the Force responded to the pressures of two world wars. The illustrations are poorly reproduced, but they do include many named individuals. R/4 V/4. MODL. AMM.

BRITISH ARMY REGIMENTS ORIGINATING IN CANADA

Two Regiments have at various periods appeared in the Order of Battle of the British Army and having a common root in Canada. Indeed, one of them, the Leinster Regiment, could properly claim to have originated partly in Canada and partly in India.

THE HISTORY OF THE PRINCE OF WALES'S LEINSTER REGIMENT (ROYAL CANADIANS)
Lieut Col F E Whitton CMG * Gale & Polden Ltd, Aldershot, n.d. (c.1924). Two matching volumes, blue, green, Regtl crest, 8.5 x 5.5.
Volume I : Fp, 3 mono phots, 4 maps, no appendixes, Index, viii/483.
Volume II : Fp, 7 mono phots, 14 maps, no appendixes, Index, vi/570.
* Six Regts of the British Army have at different times, between 1761 and 1881, borne the number 100. The last of these was the 100th (Prince of Wales's Royal Canadian) Regiment. Raised in 1858 in Quebec and Montreal, it was intended to assist in the suppression of the Indian Mutiny. In the event, due to the demise of the Mutiny, the Regt was deployed on garrison duties in Gibraltar, Malta, England and Canada. In 1881 it was amalgamated with the 109th (Bombay Infantry) Regt to form the 1st and 2nd Bns respectively of The Prince of Wales's Leinster Regiment (Royal Canadians). Volume I covers the origins and early services of the two founder Regts, while Volume II deals exclusively with the Leinster's WWI services and the Regt's disbandment in 1922. The narrative is entertaining and full of good reference material. R/3 V/4. PCAL. RP.

REMINISCENCES OF THE NORTH WEST REBELLIONS
With a Record of Her Majesty's 100th Regiment in Canada, and a Chapter on Canadian Social and Political Life
Maj Charles Arkall Boulton * Grip Printing & Publishing Co, for Davis & Henderson, Toronto, 1886. Green, gold, 'Boulton's Scout' motif, 7.0 x 5.5, -/531. Fp, 2 mono phots, one line engraving, one lithograph, 4 maps (3 printed in the text, one bound in), no Index. Apps: nominal roll for the North West Field Force of 1885 (all ranks, with details of casualties listed by unit).
* As described in the preceding entry, the '100th' designation was given to a succession of British Army units. The Regt referred to in the title of this book was The Prince of Wales's Leinster Regiment (Royal Canadians). The origins of the Regt are summarised in Chapter One (thereby covering the same ground as that covered in greater detail by Whitton in his Volume I). The bulk of the narrative then deals with the Rebellion of 1885 and the role of the Regt in suppressing it. The style is interesting and informative, with much anecdotal material woven into the text. The author raised and commanded Boulton's Scouts, and the book may be regarded as a history of that unit also. R/4 V/4. ASKBMC. CB.
Note: to avoid confusion, researchers should keep in mind the existence of The Royal Canadian Regt. This was an entirely unrelated Canadian Militia unit. It too served in the North West Rebellion campaign and is today an element of the Royal Canadian Infantry Corps (Regular).

THE 104th REGIMENT OF FOOT (THE NEW BRUNSWICK REGIMENT), 1803-1817
W Austin Squires * The Brunswick Press, Fredericton, NB, 1962. Red, gold, 8.5 x 5.75, xii/13/246. 11 mono phots (incl ills of uniforms, buttons and badges), 2 maps (printed on the end-papers), Bibliography, no Index. Apps: list of officers (with biographical details), lyrics of Regtl songs.
* The '104th' designation was given to a succession of British Regts between 1761 and 1881. One of these was formerly the HEIC's 2nd Bengal Fusiliers. This book, however, deals solely with the 104th Regt which was raised in 1806 and disbanded in 1816. The men were recruited partly in Great Britain and partly in British America. The dry and rather uninspiring narrative describes their role in the War of 1812 and includes helpful and otherwise rarely recorded information concerning The New Brunswick Provincials. R/2 V/4. PCAL. RP.

MOUNTED & MECHANISED

Former Cavalry

THE STANSTEAD CAVALRY - HISTORY, LEGEND, STORY - 1914
Opportunities and Possibilities
Maj William Melrose * Plimpton Press, Hartford, Connecticut, USA, 1914. Red, gold, 9.25 x 6.0, -/52. Fp, 27 mono phots (mainly groups), no maps, no Index. Apps: list of officers, '26th Standstead Dragoons, the 4th Eastern Townships Cavalry Brigade, 4th Division, at Hatley, Quebec, April 1914'.
* The 26th Stanstead Dragoons had their roots in the volunteer cavalry formed by United Empire Loyalists who arrived from America in 1783. A party of seventy-five Stanstead cavalrymen saw service in the Battle of Chateauguay during the War of 1812. The Regt was again in action in 1866 when it fought the Fenians at St Armond (losing several men there). The narrative traces the many changes of title and organisation at the turn of the century, describes the usual round of annual camps, parades, competitions, etc, and names various officers. A useful insight into part-time soldiering in the Eastern Townships area of Quebec Province.
R/5 V/3. NDL. JRD.
Note: having been renamed The Eastern Townships Mounted Rifles in March 1920, the Regt became an Artillery unit in December 1936.

Armour

4th CANADIAN ARMOURED BRIGADE
A Brief History of the 4th Canadian Armoured Brigade in Action
July 1944 - May 1945
Capt N A Buckingham and Maj G M Alexander * Printed by West Brothers, Mitcham, Surrey (UK), n.d. (c.1945). Green, gold, 8.5 x 6.0, -/48. Fp, no mono phots, 5 line drawings, one map (bound in), no Index. Apps: Roll of Honour (KIA and WIA, listed by constituent Regt), H&A (also by Regt), list of Bde and Regtl COs, notes on tank losses and fuel consumption.
* The Bde formed part of 4th Cdn Armd Div. Its constituent Regts after 1943 were Governor General's Foot Guards, Canadian Grenadier Guards, British Columbia Regt, and Lake Superior Regt. One page is given to a brief history of each of these Regts, but most of the narrative deals with the Bde's time in England, the landings in Normandy, the breakout to Belgium, and the final battles in Holland and Germany. Although brief, the story covers all the main events (the British Columbia Regt lost 44 tanks in action at Hill 195 in August, Brig E L Booth, DSO and bar, was killed in that same month, etc). R/3 V/3. NYPL. JRD.
Note: seen also as a reprint by The News Chronicle, Port Arthur, Ontario, 1946.

THE HISTORY OF THE KANGAROOS
1st Canadian Armoured Carrier Regiment
Anon * SMIT, Hengelo, Holland, n.d. (c.1945). Paper covers, Regtl crest, 8.75 x 6.0, -/11. Fp, 5 line drawings (all of Kangaroo vehicles), one map, no Index. Apps: Roll of Honour (KIA and DOW, with dates), list of every unit of 2nd British Army which the Kangaroos carried into action.
* Heavy losses inflicted by German artillery on Allied infantrymen advancing to contact in Normandy persuaded the British to experiment with an ad hoc armoured personnel carrier. A number of Priest M7(SP) guns were handed to Field Workshops where their 105 mm guns were removed and additional armour welded on. A scratch force of drivers from Artillery units and base depots was hastily assembled in the field and shown how to operate these vehicles. Within days, several of them were sent into action at Rouvre, on the road to Falaise. Their passengers arrived at the start line with minimal casualties. With this success behind it, the force was given Squadron status, attached to 25th Cdn Armd Regt, and equipped with 0.5 inch Brownings and some radios. These vehicles were dubbed 'Kangaroos'. In September 1944, the Priests were replaced by Canadian Ram tanks (with turrets removed and

heavily modified), and their numbers increased. The Regt was formally established in October and assigned to the British 79th Armoured Div. In the following months it carried infantry passengers into almost every major action in NW Europe. This regrettably brief account is a valuable record of the origins and development of the modern tracked AFV (Armoured fighting vehicle). R/5 V/3. DNDC. JLC/JRD.

Royal Canadian Dragoons

A SHORT HISTORY OF THE ROYAL CANADIAN DRAGOONS
R C Fetherstonhaugh * Southam Press Ltd, Toronto, 1932. Stiff card, red, gold, Regtl crest, 8.25 x 5.25, -/52. Fp, 8 mono phots, no maps, no Index. Apps: notes on Battle Honours.
* The Regt was formed in 1883 and fought two years later in Riel's Rebellion. Next mobilised in 1899, it fought in South Africa as the 1st Canadian Mounted Rifles (seeing much action and winning three VCs). The third mobilisation came in October 1914. Reorganised in May 1915 as an infantry unit, the Regt sailed for Europe as an element of the CEF but with permission to operate under its peace-time title with the Canadian Cavalry Bde. Despite the limited opportunities for mounted action on the Western Front, it took part in several charges (the last of these being at Le Cateau on 9 October 1918 when the CO, Lieut Col C T Van Straubenzee, was killed at the head of his Regiment). The short narrative contains many useful references to casualties and awards (thereby partly compensating for the lack of appendixes), and there are references to other elements of the Cdn Cav Bde - Fort Garry Horse, Lord Strathcona's Horse, Royal Canadian Horse Artillery, a RNWMP Sqn, and (briefly) King Edward's Horse. R/4 V/3. MODL. AMM/MAR.

ROYAL CANADIAN DRAGOONS, 1939-1945
Lieut Col K D Landell DSO * Southam Press, Montreal, for the Regt, 1946. Red and blue, gold, Regtl crest, 9.25 x 6.0, xxiii/233. Fp, 38 mono phots, one cartoon, 7 maps (bound in), no Index. Apps: Roll of Honour (KIA, WIA and DOW, with dates), H&A (incl former members decorated while serving with other units), seven separate rolls of officers (at various dates), nominal roll (all ranks who returned home in 1946), idem all ranks who were recruited after 1939, etc. Also notes regarding vehicles on the establishment, German Army Order of Battle (May 1945), and other useful reference material.
* The story opens with a brisk survey of the Regt's early years, service in South Africa, and then on the Western Front. The bulk of the narrative is devoted to WWII. It commences with mobilisation on 7 September 1939, initial training and home defence duties during the next two years, arrival in England in November 1941, designation as 1st Cdn Armoured Regt, and training with Daimler, Humber, and Guy armoured cars. These were replaced in 1943 with Fox, Lynx, and Staghound vehicles prior to embarkation for Italy. The book gives a good account of the following twelve months' fighting advance up the Adriatic coast from Brindisi to the lower Po Valley. By Christmas Eve, 1944, the Regt was on the Senio River. The Germans were very near, and both sides joined in singing 'Silent night' in their respective languages. The Regt was withdrawn from battle a few days later and moved to Holland (where, on 15 April, it liberated the city of Leeuwarden). Many individuals are mentioned in the well written text of this comprehensive history. R/4 V/4. UWOL/NYPL/MODL. JRD.

THE SPUR AND SPROCKET
The Story of the Royal Canadian Dragoons
Larry Worthington * Reeve Press Ltd, Kitchener, Ontario, 1968. Blue, gold, Regtl crest, 8.5 x 5.5, -/170. 39 mono phots, 2 cld ills, 8 maps (bound in), no Index. Apps: Rolls of Honour (South Africa, WWI, WWII, plus UN peace-keeping missions), H&A (South Africa, WWI, WWII), list of Colonels in Chief, idem COs (1895-1967), idem RSMs (1898-1966).
* This is a fairly condensed history of Canada's oldest permanent Cavalry unit. It opens with a short summary of services in South Africa, WWI, and WWII, and then

breaks fresh ground by describing the Regt's work in Korea (mounted on tanks) and subsequent deployments as part of Canada's numerous contributions to UN peace-keeping operations. The final section concludes with events up to 1967.
R/2 V/4. MODL. JEB.

DRAGOON
The Centennial History of the Royal Canadian Dragoons, 1883-1983
Brereton Greenhous * The Guild of the Royal Canadian Dragoons, Belleville, Ontario, 1983. Black, gold, Regtl crest, 9.75 x 7.0, xiii/557. Fp, 300 mono phots, 5 cld ills, one line drawing, 22 maps (16 printed in the text, 6 bound in), Index. Apps: Roll of Honour (KIA and WIA, South Africa, WWI, WWII, UN duties, with locations of graves), H&A (for all campaigns outside Canada, statistical summaries only), list of Colonels in Chief (1921-1936), idem Honorary Colonels (1908-1958), idem COs (1883-1982), idem RSMs (1898-1982), notes on the evolution of the Regt, list of affiliated units, source notes for each chapter, notes on Battle Honours.
* A pleasantly readable narrative which gives a balanced coverage to each phase of the Regt's history. Frustratingly few of the picture captions name the persons who appear in them, but the narrative contains plenty of interesting detail for actions and skirmishes in different times and places. Amongst the Regt's post-WWII services were Korea (where it arrived in 1954, after the fighting had finished), then Egypt (after the Anglo-French withdrawal in 1956), and Cyprus (1964-1967). A fine record, strongly supported by an excellent run of appendixes.
R/1 V/5. MODL. JRD.

Lord Strathcona's Horse

LORD STRATHCONA'S HORSE (ROYAL CANADIANS)
A Record of Achievement
Lieut Col J M McAvity DSO MBE * Brigdens Ltd, Toronto, presumably for the Regt, 1947. Red/green, gold, 'Shoulder patch' motif, 9.0 x 6.25, -/280. 78 mono phots (almost all captioned portraits and groups), 15 small line drawings, 14 maps (12 printed in the text, 2 on the end-papers), no Index. Apps: Roll of Honour (KIA, DOW and WIA), H&A, unit muster roll (with dates of joining and leaving), extensive notes regarding the history of each individual tank used by the Regt during WWII, notes on Standing Orders, notes on Battle Honours (South Africa, WWI and WWII).
* In December 1899, a wealthy Scottish politician and businessman who lived most of his life in Canada concluded that British tactics in South Africa would lead to disaster. He was Donald Alexander Smith, Lord Strathcona and Mount Royal. Having seen the reports coming from the battlefield, he argued that the Boers could be matched only by the hardy independent horsemen of Canada's western plains and hills. His offer to raise a regiment for service in South Africa was accepted, and it was given his name as its title. The nucleus for his recruiting programme were men who had served in the Royal School of Mounted Infantry, Winnipeg, and with the Yukon Field Force of 1898. Equipped and maintained at his lordship's expense, they gained a fine reputation in the Anglo-Boer War and the Regt went on to win many more laurels in WWI (on the Western Front, initially dismounted and than as part of the Cdn Cav Bde) and in WWII (as 2nd Armoured Regt, England, Italy, and NW Europe). The bulk of the narrative is devoted to WWII, with excellent detail of dramatic actions such as the forcing of the Melfa River (24 May 1944).
R/3 V/5. UWOL/MODL. JRD.
Note: reference should be made also to CANADA'S SONS ON KOPJE AND VELDT, by T G Marquis (vide the Index of Authors).

ALWAYS A STRATHCONA

W B Fraser * Comprint Publishing Co, Calgary, Alberta, for the Regt, 1976. Dark brown, gold, 9.25 x 6.25, -/252. 16 mono phots (incl portraits), 8 cld ills (of uniforms, 1886-1939), 6 maps, Index. Apps: Rolls of Honour (KIA and DOW, with dates, for South Africa, WWI and WWII), list of COs (1885-1976), idem former officers, idem RSMs, Regtl music, Battle Honours, uniforms, affiliations.

* This is an updated history which brings the story forward from McAvity's account (vide preceding entry) and which gives slightly more uniform coverage to each of the important periods. The first VC to be won by a Canadian solider serving under British command was won in South Africa by a member of the Regt - Sgt A H L Richardson. Mobilised on 1 August 1914, the Regt was frequently in action during WWI and an entire chapter is given to the Battle of Moreuil Wood. By war's end, the Regt had suffered 809 casualties and had won 147 bravery awards (including two more VCs). The WWI coverage is detailed, with numerous references to individual officers and men. The Regt became part of the Regular Army on 1 April 1919. Services during WWII are described in terms fairly similar to those found in McAvity, but Fraser follows on with useful accounts of the fighting in Korea and peacetime NATO services in Germany (equipped with Centurion tanks). In 1970 the tanks were replaced by Ferret and Lynx armoured cars and the Regt became a Reconnaissance unit. The story concludes with UN deployments in Egypt and Cyprus. A thorough history, best read in conjunction with McAvity. R/3 V/4. MODL. JRD.

Note: reported to have been reprinted without amendment in 1986.

STAND TO YOUR HORSES

Through the First Great World War, 1914-1918, with Lord Strathcona's Horse (Royal Canadians)

Capt S H Williams MC * Printed by D W Friesen & Sons Ltd, Altona, Manitoba, apparently for the author, 1961. Blue, gold, 9.5 x 6.5, xi/308. Fp, 63 mono phots, 6 maps (bound in), no Index. Apps: Roll of Honour (KIA and DOW, with some details) H&A, list of COs (1912-1946), nominal roll of all ranks who served on the Western Front.

* Essentially the autobiography of an officer who served overseas with the Regt throughout the war, this book contains much detail not found in the broader histories by McAvity and by Fraser (vide preceding entries). The book has twenty-six chapters and they cover all aspects of the Regt's adventures from mobilisation through to the Armistice. Descriptions of the Regt's periods out of the line and on leave are helpful to an understanding of a cavalryman's life in that war. Many of the author's brother officers feature in the story, particularly those who were killed, wounded, or decorated. The nominal roll is, of course, a useful source for genealogists and medal collectors. R/3 V/4. FFL. RP.

8th Canadian Hussars

THE 8th HUSSARS

A History of the Regiment

Douglas How * Printed by Maritime Printing Co Ltd, Sussex, New Brunswick, for the Regt, 1964. Blue, gold, Regtl crest, 9.25 x 6.25, xL/449. Fp, 65 mono phots (mainly captioned portraits of officers), 3 line drawings (cap badges), 2 maps (printed on the end-papers), Index. Apps: Roll of Honour, H&A (WWII, with full citations), lists of former officers, notes on Battle Honours, table showing Regtl organisation and changes in title (1848-1960).

* The Regt claims its roots in the American Colony of Virginia where, in 1775, a Loyalist officer by the name of Capt John Saunders raised at his own expense a troop of cavalry to fight the rebels led by George Washington. Saunder's Horse gained a fiercesome reputation during the War of Independence but, after the defeat at Yorktown, the entire Regt and its families emigrated to the British Colony of New Brunswick to start a new life. The narrative traces the local development of the Militia movement, and the ever-changing unit titles, throughout the 19th

Century. The Regt unsuccessfuly offered its services to the Crown for the Crimean War, and later at the time of the North West Rebellion, the Sudan campaign, and the war in South Africa. Some of its members did transfer to the Royal Canadian Regt in South Africa and fought at Paardeburg, but it was not until WWI that the Regt came into its own. It supplied drafts to seven Infantry Bns of the CEF and, in 1915, sent a Squadron to France with the 6th Cdn Mounted Rifles. Peacetime economies brought an end to the horse-mounted era, but mechanised training was possible only by the use of hired motor cars. This enthusiasm was rewarded in September 1939 when, for the first time since 1848 (when they were formally established as the New Brunswick Yeoman Cavalry), the 8th Hussars were mobilised for war service as an integral unit. After two years' training in England, they moved to Italy and fought as 5th Cdn Armoured Regt from Ortona to Lake Commachio. Mounted on Sherman tanks, the Regt then transferred to Holland in April 1945. Ironically, one of its hardest actions in that country was the destruction of 300 fanatical Dutch SS troops at Deelen Barneveld. Disbanded in 1946, the Regt was reactivated for the Korean War and became a Regular Army (RCAC) unit in 1957. The story concludes with the later NATO and UN commitments. A good account, authoritative, and particularly detailed for WWII services.
R/3 V/5. AldMM/MODL. JRD.

A PICTORIAL HISTORY OF THE 8th CANADIAN HUSSARS (PRINCESS LOUISE'S)
Maj E D Crook CD and Maj J K Marteinson CD * Published by the Regt, no other details shown, 1973. Dark blue, gold, Regtl crest and dates on front cover, 11.25 x 8.75, x/343. 5 fps, 657 mono phots, 3 cld ills, 9 line drawings, 16 maps, no appendixes, no Index (but a useful 'Contents' page).
* This is an essential complement to the Douglas How history (vide previous entry). Although it contains a condensed comprehensive narrative history (1775-1973), its pictorial content is exceptional. The material is drawn from a wide variety of sources and extends from the late 1700s (the Revolutionary War) through to the 1960s (Germany, Sinai, Cyprus). Early oil paintings are reproduced to a high standard, but the quality of the monochrome photographs reflects the limitations of camera equipment at certain periods. The coverage of WWI and the inter-war years is patchy, but picture quality starts to improve markedly with the Italian campaign. Standards of reproduction for the post-WWII years are, as might be expected, very good. The subject matter covers all aspects of the Regt's history - personnel, uniforms, horses, vehicles, weaponry, medals, etc. Whenever possible, the authors have named the individuals depicted, and the book is therefore a prime source for family historians. An evocative record of Canadian soldiering.
R/1 V/5. MODL. JRD/RP.
Note: in 1944, at Coriano (Italy), the Regt 'liberated' a horse which, being a mare, was given the name Princess Louise. She accompanied the Regt throughout the Italian campaign, travelled with it to France, Belgium, Holland, and Germany, and then to Canada at war's end. Her story is told in AUTOBIOGRAPHY OF PRINCESS LOUISE, by Lieut Col R S MacLeod ED (printed in Pakistan, for the Regt, 1987). Another secondary source for the Regt is THIS HUSSAR REMEMBERS, by Maj H R S 'Tim' Ellis DSO (privately, Saint John, NB, 1990).

THE 8th CANADIAN HUSSARS (PRINCESS LOUISE'S), 1962-1987
Maj G H MacDonald * Published by the Regt, no details shown, 1987. Blue, gold, Regtl crest, 11.5 x 8.5, -/162. 4 fps, 364 mono phots (incl many captioned groups and portraits), no maps, no appendixes, no Index.
* A good narrative and pictorial history of the 25 years following the Regt's NATO deployment in Germany. Detachments went to Egypt and Cyprus, then back to NATO duties in Germany. A great many individuals are named in the text, and lists of officers and NCOs appear at frequent intervals. A good source also for those interested in AFVs (Centurion, Leopard, Ferret, Cougar, Lynx). R/1 V/4. PC. JRD.

Fort Garry Horse

THE GATE
A History of the Fort Garry Horse
Capt G T Service and Capt J K Marteinson CD * Commercial Printers, Calgary, for a Regtl Committee, 1971. Blue, gold, Regtl crest, 10.0 x 6.75, -/228. 120 mono phots, 4 cld ills, 9 maps, no Index. Apps: H&A (WWI and WWII), list of former COs.
* This Regt had its roots in an early western Militia unit, the Boulton Mounted Corps, which took part in the suppression of the North West Rebellion of 1885. It was reconstituted as the Fort Garry Horse in 1912, and the title of the book derives from the entrance gate of the fort depicted in its cap badge. The bulk of the narrative is devoted to an interesting and informative account of the Regt's services in the two world wars. It was mobilised in 1914 but not despatched overseas. Many of its personnel then joined 6th Cdn Inf Bn CEF. In 1916 the Regt was sent to the Western Front where it served under its own title as part of the Cdn Cav Bde (together with the Royal Canadian Dragoons and Lord Strathcona's Horse). Mobilised again on 3 September 1939, the Fort Garrys moved to England in late 1941 and were equipped with Sherman tanks. On D-Day they went ashore at Bernieres-sur-Mer with 3rd Cdn Inf Div. Thereafter their operations were typical of many other Canadian Army units - the Normandy battles, the Falaise Gap, the reduction of the Channel ports, the Scheldt estuary battles, the Hochwald Forest, the Rhine crossings, and the final advance into Germany. All of this is described in entertaining detail. After the war, the Fort Garry Horse served with NATO in Germany and with UN forces in Cyprus before being disbanded on 15 June 1970. The book is a handy summary of the Regt's entire history. R/2 V/4. PC. JEB.

VANGUARD - THE FORT GARRY HORSE
The Fort Garry Horse in the Second World War
Anon * Republished by the Fort Garry Horse Association, Altona, Winnipeg, 1980. Stiff card, red, gold, 'Knight in armour' motif, 9.25 x 6.0, x/198. Fp, 40 mono phots, 13 line drawings, 2 cartoons, 8 maps (5 printed in the text, 3 bound in), no Index. Apps: Roll of Honour (KIA, WIA and MIA, with dates), H&A, extracts from 'C' and 'B' Squadrons' War Diaries, notes on reinforcements, idem specific actions.
* Despite its sub-title, the book includes a brief but useful summary of pre-1939 services. The Regt was reformed in 1912 from 'A' Sqn of the 18th Mounted Rifles and fought with distinction on the Western Front (where, in 1917, Lieut Harcus Strachan won the VC when leading a mounted charge through a line of German machine guns armed only with his sword). The bulk of the narrative, naturally, deals with events following 6 June 1944 and the long hard march to the Rhine and beyond. The material is authoritative, based firmly on War Diaries and the views of the personnel who were there. R/4 V/4. MODL. JRD.
Note: this book was first produced in Holland in 1945. The original version had soft card covers (blue, gold), with two additional maps but fewer illustrations. The printer was Uitgevers-Maatschappij, C Misset NV, of Doetinchem. The print run is not known. The 1980 edition, as recorded here, was limited to 250 copies.

Governor General's Horse Guards

HISTORICAL RECORD OF THE GOVERNOR GENERAL'S BODYGUARD AND ITS STANDING ORDERS
Capt Frederick C Denison * Hunter, Rose & Co, Toronto, 1876. Red, gold, ornate Victorian embellishment, 6.0 x 4.75, iii/87. No ills, no maps, no formal appendixes, no Index.
* The historical content is a straightforward account of the war of 1812, the Upper Canada Rebellion of 1837-1838, and the Fenian Raid of 1866.
R/5 V/3. UWOL. DKD.

THE GOVERNOR GENERAL'S BODY GUARD OF CANADA
A History of the Origin, Development and Services of the Senior Cavalry Regiment in the Militia Service of the Dominion of Canada
Capt Ernest J Chambers * E L Ruddy, Toronto, 1902. Blue, gold, 'Charging cavalryman and Regtl crest' motif, 12.5 x 10.0, viii/128. 32 mono phots, no maps, no Index. Apps: list of former officers, muster roll, nominal roll of GGBG personnel who served in the North West Canada campaign of 1885, idem those who served in South Africa (Anglo-Boer War), list of Staff Sergeants and Sergeants (as serving with the Regt in 1902).
* This is a much expanded and updated work compared with Denison's book of 1876 (vide preceding entry). It covers the complete history of the GGBG from 1793 through to the end of the Anglo-Boer War. The additional coverage includes the Fenian campaign of 1870 and services in South Africa. Like all of Chamber's histories, the narrative is well written, full of detail, and having many references to individual members of all ranks. The printer, E L Ruddy, worked to his usual high standards with the binding and the quality of reproduction of the pictures.
R/5 V/4. AMOT/UWOL/MODL. DKD/RP.

SOLDIERING IN CANADA
Recollections and Experiences
Lieut Col George T Denison * George N Morang & Co Ltd, Toronto, 1901. Seen rebound in red cloth (the original covers were soft card, 'Mounted horseman' motif, red, black), 8.0 x 5.5, x/357. Fp, 7 mono phots (mainly portraits), one map, no appendixes, Index.
* Twenty-five years after compiling the first official history of the Regt, Denison produced this his personal memoir. He had retired in 1898 having formerly risen to command the Regt and having been much involved in the growth of the Militia movement in general. His father and grandfather had likewise served many years with various Militia units. His narrative covers every aspect of soldiering in Canada from the War of 1812 through to the North West Rebellion of 1885, the raising of the Active Force, the Fenian Raids, and the despatch to the Sudan of the Nile Voyageurs. He also provides much detail concerning the rebellion of 1837-1838. His book is the only contemporary general account of Canadian cavalry pre-1895.
R/5 V/4. PC. RP.
Note: the Governor General's Bodyguard kept its title until 1936. It was then amalgamated with the Mississuaga Horse and redesignated the Governor General's Horse Guards.

THE 4th CANADIAN MOUNTED RIFLES, 1914-1919
S G Bennett * Murray Printing Co, Toronto, 1926. Blue, gold, Regtl crest, 9.75 x 6.5, xv/336. Fp (a fine map of Flanders, pasted in), 18 mono phots, 6 line sketches, 5 other maps (all finely executed, bound in), Glossary, Index. Apps: unit nominal roll (pages 160-327, all who served, with name of original unit before joining 4 CMR, and with notes on casualties, awards, and promotions).
* A superb history, well presented, and a pleasure to handle. Under the Hughes edict, 4 CMR was raised in Ontario in 1914 from volunteers coming forward from the Governor General's Bodyguard, the 2nd Dragoons, the 9th Mississuaga Horse, and the 25th Brant Dragoons. Initially it trained in Canada, partly at its own expense, as a mounted unit. It was then told that it would fight dismounted and so sailed for England in July 1915 without its recently purchased horses. It landed in France in October 1915 and was in the line a month later at Bailleul. It stayed on the Western Front throughout the war - Sanctuary Wood, the Somme, Vimy Ridge, Passchendaele (where Pte Thomas Holmes won the VC), and the campaign of 'the last 100 days'. The narrative is based directly upon the facts stated in the War Diary and is clear and reliable. The basic facts, however, are leavened with a good running commentary upon the main events, with many officers and men being named in the text (awards, postings, casualties, etc). The huge appendix is, of course, a prime source for genealogists. The unit is perpetuated by the Governor General's Horse Guards. R/4 V/5. NYPL/MODL. AMM/RP.

THE GOVERNOR GENERAL'S HORSE GUARDS

Anon * Printed by L'Eclaireur Ltd, Beauceville, QP, for The Canadian Military Journal, 1954. Soft card, blue/red/silver, Regtl crest, 9.25 x 6.0, -/243. 2 fps, 25 mono phots (plus one page of photo portraits of WWII COs), 4 maps (all printed on the end-papers), Glossary, no Index. Apps: Roll of Honour (WWII only), list of former officers (1810-1952), roll of all ranks who served in WWII (names and initials only), notes on The Women's Auxiliary, idem the Regtl Association.
* Like most Canadian regiments, the GGHG has an extremely complex lineage. It traces its roots to Button's Troop of Cavalry (1810) and Denison's Troop of Cavalry (1822). The author of this book makes brief mention of the subsequent mergers and the services of these predecessor units in the War of 1812, the rebellions of 1837, 1866 and 1885, and the Canadian Contingents in South Africa. In 1914, the Regt provided drafts for 3rd Cdn Infantry Bns CEF and for 4th Cdn Mounted Rifles CEF, but did not serve overseas as an integral unit. The bulk of the book is devoted to WWII when 1st GGHG served in England (October 1941 to November 1943), in Italy (December 1943 to February 1945), and in NW Europe (through to the end of the war). It saw much hard fighting under its wartime designation of 3rd Armoured Reconnaissance Regt, mounted on tanks. The descriptions of campaign services are good, but few individuals are mentioned by name and they are not identified in the picture captions. R/3 V/3. NYPL/MODL. JRD.

4th Princess Louise Dragoon Guards

THE PRINCESS LOUISE DRAGOON GUARDS - A HISTORY

Lieut Col H M Jackson * Printed by Richardson, Bond & Wright, Owen Sound, Ont, 1952. Blue, silver, Regtl shoulder flashes, 9.5 x 6.25, xiv/292. Fp, 43 mono phots, 3 maps, Glossary, no Index. Apps: Roll of Honour (KIA, WIA and POW, with dates), H&A (WWII), list of officers (1914-1918), idem COs (WWII), summary of monthly casualty statistics (1941-1945).
* A very readable narrative covering a long period of time. There is reference to events in 1812, and a short chapter describing the Regt's services in WWI (as 8th Cdn Mounted Rifles), but the bulk of the book is then devoted to WWII. Arriving in England in 1939, it served as an armoured car unit with 1st Cdn Inf Div under the title 4th Reconnaissance Regt. It fought in Italy and NW Europe, and these operations are described in interesting detail (with many individuals and minor actions mentioned). R/3 V/4. NYPL/MODL. JEB/JRD.

The Halifax Rifles

A CENTURY OF RIFLES, 1860-1960
The Halifax Rifles (RCAC) (M)

John Gordon Quigley * William Macnab & Son Ltd, Halifax, NS, n.d. (c.1960). Stiff card, green, silver, 9.0 x 6.0, xviii/230. Fp, 26 mono phots (incl 3 large fold-outs of the entire Regt), no maps, no Index. Apps: H&A (incomplete), list of former COs, nominal rolls, notes on local 'regimental families'.
* This is a chronology illustrated with pictures and many stories regarding local families whose sons and fathers served with this Militia unit. It never went overseas as an integral unit, but many of its members served with CEF Bns during WWI and with other Regts in WWII. Some of the awards which they gained are listed in the appendix. The book is of interest mainly as a reflection of the social history of Halifax and the evolution of the Militia in general. R/1 V/3. MODL. MCJ.

Grey and Simcoe Foresters

FIGHTING MEN

Leslie M Frost * Clark, Irwin & Co Ltd, Toronto, 1967. Drab olive, gold, 8.5 x 5.5, xxv/262. 27 mono phots, no maps, Bibliography, Chapter Notes, Index. Apps: unit nominal roll for 'C' Coy, 157th Cdn Inf Bn CEF (with serials, ranks, records of service, casualties, awards, home addresses, etc), idem 'B' Coy, 177th Cdn Inf Bn.

* This is not a unit history but an account of the WWI services of 393 Militia men who volunteered from the Orillia area of Southern Ontario. Previously they had served with 35th Regt of Simcoe Foresters. More than 60.0% were to become casualties when they went to France. Most went overseas with 157th and 177th Cdn Inf Bns CEF, but these were then broken up to provide drafts for several other Bns. The title is recorded here because the 157th Bn is today perpetuated by The Grey and Simcoe Foresters. The book provides a helpful summary of the very complex origins of the Regt, but its main value is to genealogists interested in the Orillia area. R/3 V/5. PC. JRD.

GREY AND SIMCOE FORESTERS
An Unofficial History of the Grey and Simcoe Foresters Regiment, 1866-1973
Brig Tom Rutherford, Maj Campbell Raikes, Lieut Col N E MacDonald, W J Carmichael and Capt George Wakefield * Published by the Regt, Owen Sound, Ontario, n.d. (c.1974). Stapled soft card, green, silver, Regtl crest, 11.25 x 8.5, xx/88. Fp, 236 mono phots (almost entirely of groups of personnel and individual officers, at various dates from pre-WWI to post-WWII, all fully captioned), no maps, no Index. Apps: Roll of Honour (WWII, with much detail), list of former officers (1866-1936), unit nominal rolls [incl a roll of personnel of the 26th Army Tank Bn (Grey and Simcoe Foresters) who embarked for the UK in June 1943], notes on Battle Honours, idem Regtl music, idem the Regtl Association.
* The narrative is a very condensed account of a Regt formed in 1936 by the amalgamation of two of Canada's oldest units - The Grey Regt and The Simcoe Foresters. Earlier known as the 31st and 35th Regts of Militia, they had served against the Fenians and in South Africa, and had raised drafts for CEF units in WWI. They trained and drafted so many men that they were granted seven Battle Honours for that war. The G&SF converted to the armoured role in WWII, sailing for the UK with their tanks in June 1943 but, sadly, being disbanded only two months later. This little book contains little information concerning active services, but it is packed with names and captioned pictures of personnel. For genealogists in general, and for those interested in Southern Ontario in particular, it is a fine source of reference. R/4 V/4. PC. JRD.

FORESTERS - THE CANADIAN QUEST FOR PEACE
Brian A Brown * The Boston Mills Press, Erin, Ont, 1991. Grey, gold, Regtl crest, 10.5 x 7.75, -/176. Fp, 76 mono phots (incl captioned portraits and groups), 8 line drawings, 3 maps, no appendixes, Index.
* Published to commemorate the formation, 125 years earlier, of the Regt's predecessor units, this book updates the record described in the previous entry. Naturally it covers the same ground, but it is not rated so highly as a source of reference. However, it does include information for the period 1973-1990, and this is useful in tracking the evolution and deployment of Canadian armour in recent years. Lists of officers and NCOs appear at frequent intervals in the text, and the captioned pictures will be helpful to family historians. R/1 V/3. PC. JRD.

SCARLET TO GREEN
The Colours, Uniforms and Insignia of The Grey and Simcoe Foresters
Maj Murray M Telford CD * Printed by Ampersand, Guelph, Ont, for The Boston Mills Press, Erin, Ont, 1987. Illustrated soft card, white, grey/black, 'Standing rifleman' motif, dimensions not recorded, -/64. Numerous illustrations of every kind, Glossary, Bibliography, no Index.
* The period covered is 1866 to the 1960s. The narrative element consists of short accounts of the various root Regts - The Greys, the 31st Grey Bn of Infantry, The Simcoes, and the 'perpetuated' 147th and 248th Cdn Inf Bns CEF. The illustrations are the main feature. They illustrate all aspects of Dress, insignia, helmet plates, cap badges, and so forth. A useful adjunct to the formal histories of the Regt. R/2 V/3. PC. RP.

Elgin Regiment

THE ELGINS
The Story of the Elgin Regiment (RCAC)
Capt Leonard A Curchin and Lieut Brian D Sim * Printed at the Sutherland Press, St Thomas, Ont, for the authors, 1977. Blue, gold, Regtl crest, 11.25 x 8.5, vii/150. Fp, many mono phots, 3 cld plates, 6 maps, Glossary, Index. Apps: Rolls of Honour (for the Mackenzie Rebellion, South Africa, WWI), various nominal rolls (those who served with the 91st Cdn Inf Bn CEF, etc).
* A superficial but interesting account of the Regt from 1866 to 1986. The story covers services in Canada, South Africa, the Western Front (WWI), and Italy and NW Europe (WWII). The two main strengths of this book are the nominal rolls and the several dozens of photographs of members of the Regt (peacetime and wartime) which are fully captioned with the names of those depicted. In NW Europe (WWII), the Regt served as 25th Cdn Armd Delivery Regt. R/2 V/4. AlmMM/MODL. RP.

Ontario Regiment

THE 116th IN FRANCE
Anon ('a former Adjutant', probably E P S Allen) * The Hunter-Rose Company Ltd, Toronto, Ont, 1921. Grey, gold, 8.25 x 6.25, -/111. Fp, 49 mono phots (mainly named groups and individuals), one map, one sketch, no Index. Apps: Roll of Honour (with home addresses).
* Recruited mainly from Militia men in the County of Ontario, the 116th Cdn Inf Bn CEF was authorised in October 1915 and arrived in France in February 1917. It fought in several great battles, including Vimy Ridge, Hill 70, Passchendaele, Poperinghe, and Cambrai. Some officers are mentioned in the text, but this is a bare statement of facts and events with little attempt at comment or analysis. The Bn later became 1st Bn, The Ontario Regt. R/4 V/3. TPL/RMCL. JRD.

HISTORY OF THE ONTARIO REGIMENT, 1866-1951
Capt Lex Schragg * General Printers, Oshawa, 1952. Dark blue, gold, Regtl crest, 9.25 x 6.25, -/286. 2 fps, 149 mono phots (incl groups of personnel and portraits of COs from 1866 to 1951), 3 maps (one printed in the text, 2 on the end-papers), no Index. Apps: Roll of Honour (WWII only), list of former officers.
* Despite the dates quoted in its title, this book is essentially the story of an outstandingly efficient tank Regt in WWII. Under the designation 11th Cdn Armoured Regt, it fought throughout the campaigns in Sicily and Italy until February 1945 when it moved to Holland for the final advance into Germany. It developed various battlefield techniques of its own. The Regtl Provost worked as para-medics and stretcher-bearers whenever the unit was in action, all tank crews were trained in mine clearance, and every Troop learned the specialised skills of street clearance by night. As a result, the Regt won the respect of the many Infantry and other units with which it worked in the field. The narrative contains few names of individual members, but gives a clear picture of the various actions in which the Regt was engaged (particularly on mainland Italy). The book has no 'Honours & Awards' appendix, but award winners are named at appropriate points in the text. An Index would have been helpful. R/3 V/3. NYPL. JRD.
Note: a brief WWII history, having 44 pages, was printed for the Regt in Harlingen, Holland in 1945. The compilers were Maj J E Slinger and Capt D McNichol.

Queen's York Rangers

HISTORY OF THE 12th REGIMENT, YORK RANGERS
With Some Account of the Different Raisings of Militia in the County of York, Ontario
Capt A T Hunter * Murray Printing Co Ltd, Toronto, n.d. (c.1912). Dark maroon, white, Regtl crest, 10.75 x 8.0, -/90. 35 mono phots, 2 maps, no Index. Apps: list of former officers, unit muster roll, shooting competition results (1885-1910).

* This is mainly a story of routine peacetime training and Regtl ceremonial. The 12th Regt was formed in 1885 from several old Militia units in York County (and including the 3rd Regt of York Militia, raised in 1812). By 1912, when this book was published, the Regt was centred on the city of Toronto. The author, a Company Commander, provides a lightweight but informative account of the Regt's forebears and achievements. Apart from the appendixes listed on the previous page, he also provides officers' service records (1862-1912), a roll of staff serving with the York-Simcoe Bn and The York Ranger Companies (1885), and quotes a memorandum on the York Volunteers at the Battle of Queenston Heights.
R/4 V/3. MODL/UMiamiL. AMM/HIS.

THE TWENTIETH

The History of the Twentieth Battalion (Central Ontario Regiment), Canadian Expeditionary Force, in the Great War, 1914-1918

Maj D J Corrigall DSO MC * Stone & Cox Ltd, Toronto, for the Trustees of the Twentieth Canadian Battalion, 1935. Green boards, blue spine, gold, 9.5 x 6.5, xvii/586 in total (the narrative pages and appendixes are numbered up to 323, the nominal roll is numbered, separately, up to 263). 2 fps (one being a fold-out landscape photograph of the entire Bn, taken in Toronto, 1914), 7 other mono phots, one cld plate (the Colours), 31 maps, no Index. Apps: nominal roll (see below), notes on Battle Honours, idem the affiliation with the Queen's Royal Regt (West Surreys).
* This is a massive compilation of names, facts, statistics and historical narrative. The scholarship is deeply impressive. Of the 586 pages, nearly a half are devoted to a nominal roll which lists every officer and man who served with the Bn. For each, there is a note of his date of joining and leaving, his previous and later services with other units, his Regtl number, highest rank held, and any awards gained. As appropriate, there is a note of whether he was killed, wounded, died of disease, presumed dead, or taken prisoner. The other (first) half of the book is a very good account of the Bn's services on the Western Front where two of its members won the VC - Sgt Frederick Hobson and Lieut W L Algie. Finally, there is a chapter which deals with the redesignation as The West Toronto Regt and, in 1925, the amalgamation with the 2nd Bn York Rangers to form The Queen's York Rangers (an Active Militia unit). R/4 V/5. UWOL/NYPL. SS/CSM.

THE QUEEN'S YORK RANGERS

The Queen's York Rangers - An Historic Regiment

Stewart H Bull * The Boston Mills Press, Erin, Ont, 1984. Green, silver, 10.25 x 7.75, -/248. Fp, 66 mono phots (incl 12 portraits of COs, post-WWII), 13 line drawings, 21 maps, Index. Apps: list of former COs (1919-1984), idem SNCOs (1944-1983), idem honorary appointments in the Regt (1906-1974), notes on discipline, the Colours, etc.
* The Regt originated as an American Loyalist scouting unit which fought the French at Quebec in 1775 (the Seven Years War), fought the Revolutionaries in the War of Independence (1776-1782, winning the Battle of Brandywine in 1777), and then accepted defeat by withdrawing to Canada. The distinction '1st Americans' was bestowed after Brandywine by King George III, and the Regt retains it to this day. The Rangers fought at Detroit and Queenston Heights in the War of 1812, and all of these events are given fair coverage in this book, as are the various home-grown rebellions. When war broke out in 1914, the Regt mobilised but never served overseas. Instead, it provided drafts for various CEF units, notably the 20th Cdn Inf Bn CEF (vide preceding entry). Also, in 1916, it provided men for 2nd Cdn Railway Troops (vide Index of Canadian Units). The Regt was unlucky in WWII because it was never mobilised for active service. Most of the officers and men melted away between 1939 and 1942, going off to join other units which had better prospects of going overseas. The Regt was stood down in October 1943, its title at that time being The Queen's York Rangers (1st American Regiment). In 1947, it was reconstituted as 25th Armoured Regt, Canadian Army Reserve. Coverage of the

1947-1948 period is good, with interesting comments on the changing structure of the Army. R/1 V/4. MODL. JRD.
Note: reference should be made to the 'Colonial North America' section of this bibliography for further information regarding The Queen's Rangers during the Revolutionary period and its immediate aftermath.

Sherbrooke Regiment

THE SHERBROOKE REGIMENT
The Sherbrooke Regiment (12th Armoured Regiment)
Lieut Col H M Jackson MBE ED * Christian Brothers Press, Montreal, for the Regt, 1958. Red, black, 9.25 x 6.25, -/229. Fp, 22 mono phots (plus five pages of small studio portraits of individual COs, other officers, and RSMs, 1882-1957), 2 line drawings, one map, no Index. Apps: Rolls of Honour (very detailed, for WWI and for WWII, with causes, dates, locations, and including non-fatal casualties and POW), H&A (including 17 individual citations), list of officers (at 6 June 1944), notes on The Bishop's School Cadet Corps, idem rifle competitions, etc.
* This comprehensive history traces the evolution of the Regt from 1866 (when it was mobilised for duty at the time of the Fenian incursions). It was mobilised again in December 1915 for service overseas under the wartime designation 117th Cdn Inf Bn CEF. It arrived in England in August 1916, but was disbanded shortly afterwards and its personnel sent as reinforcements to other units. The Roll of Honour and H&A appendixes therefore relate to officers and men killed, wounded, and/or decorated while serving with those other Bns. The Regt was redesignated The Sherbrooke Regt (MG) in 1936 and mobilised for war in May 1940. After coastal defence duties in Newfoundland, its role was changed yet again, this time to armour. It moved to England in 1942 for further training and was equipped with Sherman tanks. As part of 2nd Cdn Armd Bde, it landed at Bernieres-sur-Mer on D-Day and fought throughout the NW Europe campaign. In one of its earliest battles in Normandy (at Buron), it lost twenty-one tanks. Apart from having a lively narrative, this book is laced liberally with explanatory footnotes, additional lists of personnel, and fully captioned illustrations. An excellent source for medal collectors and for genealogists. R/3 V/4. NYPL/MODL. JRD.

Le Régiment de Trois-Rivières

HISTOIRE DU REGIMENT DE TROIS-RIVIERES
Les Soldats-Citoyens, Histoire ... 1871-1978
Jean-Yves Gravel and Michel Grondin * Les Presses de L'Imprimerie du Bien Publique, Trois Rivierès, QP, 1981. Illustrated soft card, full colour, 'Tank in Italian village' motif, 8.75 x 6.0, -/153. Fp, 30 mono phots, 8 maps, Chapter Notes, Bibliography, Index. Apps: Rolls of Honour (with full and helpful details for WWII, Indo-China 1973, and Cyprus 1977), H&A, list of COs (1871-1981), idem 2 i/c (1968-1980), idem RSMs (1930-1965), notes on Battle Honours, Dress, traditions, and unit affiliations.
* A comprehensive history, written in French but with some notes in English. The Regt originated in 1871 as a Volunteer infantry unit - the Bataillon Provisoire de Trois-Rivières. It underwent several changes of title, provided men for the CEF in WWI (it perpetuates the 178th Cdn Inf Bn), became a mechanised unit in 1936, and fought in WWII in Sherman tanks. Coverage of the eighteen months in Italy is particularly good - Termoli, Ortona, the Liri Valley, etc. R/2 V/5. PC. JRD.

1st Hussars

A HISTORY OF THE FIRST HUSSARS

Anon (Lieut Foster Clark) * Hunter Printing (London) Ltd, London, Ontario, 1951. Stiff card, pale blue, dark blue, Regtl crest, 9.0 x 6.0, -/172. Fp, no other ills, one map (bound in), no Index. Apps: Roll of Honour (KIA, DOW and MIA, with dates and locations, WWII only), list of COs (1872-1950), list of Regtl and attached officers who served during WWII (with their awards, as appropriate), notes on D-Day training.

* The Regt had its beginnings in 1856 as the First London Volunteer Troop of Cavalry. Amalgamated with several other Militia mounted units in Western Ontario, it became the 1st Hussars Regt in 1872. Its members provided the bulk of the 7th Cdn Mounted Rifles CEF for service on the Western Front (where it several times had its role and designation changed). All of this is covered in brisk style, also the inter-war years, but most of the narrative is then given to services in WWII. After three years' training in England, and designated 6th Cdn Armoured Regt, the 1st Hussars went ashore on D-Day on the beaches between Courseulles and Bernieres-sur-Mer. They succeeded in reaching their first day objective (the Caen-Bayeux railway) but, five days later, they ran into a strong Panzer force. The brunt of the action fell on 'B' Squadron. It lost nineteen of its twenty-one tanks in the battle, and not a single officer was unscathed at the end of the day. The author provides skilful coverage of the Normandy 'break out' battles, the closing of the Falaise Gap, the capture of the Calais cross-Channel guns, and the later battles in Holland and Germany. During this period, the Regt gained seventy-two decorations - more than any other comparable unit in the Canadian 1st Army. Apart from the details given in the appendix, lists of casualties are inserted in the text for various key dates. R/4 V/4. UWOL. JRD.

A HISTORY OF THE FIRST HUSSARS REGIMENT, 1856-1980

Anon ('A Regimental Committee') * Publication details not shown, n.d. (c.1981). Blue, gold and silver, 9.25 x 6.25, viii/195. 7 mono phots, 2 maps, Glossary, no Index. Apps: Roll of Honour (WWII), list of former COs, idem former officers (WWII only), notes on training, idem the Regtl Association.

* The first chapter is a summary of the early years and WWI. The bulk of the book is then given to WWII and to post-1946 administrative matters (the change from armour to civil defence, then back to armour, etc). R/3 V/3. PC. MCJ.

Royal Canadian Hussars

THE LONG RIDE

A Short History of the 17th Duke of York's Royal Canadian Hussars

Maj Harwood Steele MC * Gazette Printing Co Ltd, Montreal, 1934. Soft card, sand, black, 'Officer and badge' motif, 8.5 x 6.0, -/48. Fp, 15 mono phots, various vignettes, no maps, Bibliography, no Index. Apps: list of COs (1812-1934), list of officers serving at the time of publication.

* This is a graphic account, written in racy style, of one of the units which, in 1958, came together to form the modern Royal Canadian Hussars (Montreal). The 17th claimed its origins as No 1 Troop, Royal Montreal Cavalry, raised in 1812. It was engaged in suppressing the Rebellion of 1837 and the Fenian Raids of 1866 and 1870. The distinction 'Duke of York's' was granted in 1897 and, shortly afterwards, a contingent served in the South African war. Mobilised in 1914, the Regt soon lost most of its strength when many officers and men volunteered to join the new CEF units. The remainder joined 5th Cdn Mounted Rifles CEF when it was formed in 1915 for service in France and Flanders. A pleasant little book, well illustrated, and informative. R/4 V/3. MODL. AMM.

7th CANADIAN RECONNAISSANCE REGIMENT IN WORLD WAR II
An Historical Account of the 7th Canadian Reconnaissance Regiment (17th Duke of York's Royal Canadian Hussars) in the World War, 1939-1945
Capt Walter G Pavey * Harpell's Press Cooperative, Gardenvale, QP, for the Regt, 1948. Grey, blue/green, Regtl crest, 10.75 x 7.75, -/139. Fp, 92 mono phots, 7 maps (5 printed in the text, 2 bound in), no Index. Apps: Roll of Honour (with dates), H&A.
* Mobilised in May 1940, initially as a motor-cycle unit, the Regt's first claim to fame in WWII was its assault on a fair ground at Truro, Nova Scotia, in July 1941. A booth attendant shot a soldier in the leg. On the following evening, 500 of his RCH comrades reduced the site to rubble. Shortly afterwards they were moved to England. Equipped with Humber armoured cars (and later with Daimlers), they fought with the same fierce spirit, as Recce Regt for 3rd Cdn Inf Div, from D+5 through to Appledoorn at war's end. The narrative contains good coverage of its widely spread actions in Normandy and on the German border.
R/4 V/4. MODL/NYPL. JRD.

British Columbia Regiment

A SHORT HISTORY OF THE 7th BATTALION, CEF
Maj T V Scudamore VD * Anderson & Odlum Ltd, Vancouver, BC, n.d. (1930). Red, black, 8.0 x 5.5, -/55. No ills, no maps, no Index. Apps: Roll of Honour (KIA, DOW and MIA, all ranks, with dates), list of officers (serving in 1914).
* Prior to 1939, the Regt had traditionally been an Infantry unit but with strong roots in the late 19th Century Militia Artillery units of Victoria and Vancouver. In WWI, its personnel volunteered for overseas service with three Cdn Inf Bns of the CEF - 7th, 62nd, and 178th. The 7th were in action by February 1915 and faced their first gas attack at St Julien, in the Ypres sector. The Bn stood fast and most of them, including the CO, died. The Bn went on to win two VCs later in the war - Pte M J O'Rourke and Pte W L Rayfield. Of the men disbanded in 1919, only thirty-two had not suffered at least one wound in action. All of this is dealt with in a very condensed fashion, half of the book being taken up with the Roll of Honour. R/4 V/3. NYPL. MP.

THE STORY OF THE BRITISH COLUMBIA REGIMENT, 1939-1945
Maj Douglas E Harker * Publication details not shown, n.d. (c.1951). Soft card, grey, brown, Regtl crest, 10.5 x 8.0, -/120 (not numbered). Fp, 19 mono phots, one line drawing, no maps, no Index. Apps: Roll of Honour, H&A (some with citations), list of COs (1939-1945).
* A lucid account, readable and informative, but published to 'economy' standards. Mobilised in August 1939, the Regt served guard duties at home before converting to the armoured role. It moved to England in 1942 with the designation 28th Cdn Armd Regt (BCR), and landed in Normandy in July 1944. A few days later, in a confused action during Operation Totalise (the closing of the Falaise Gap), it was caught in an exposed position by 12th SS Panzer Div and all of its forty-four tanks were destroyed. After regrouping, 'the Dukes' went on to serve with great credit in Belgium, Holland and Germany. Casualties throughout the war were 114 killed and 225 wounded, and they are listed in the appendix. The book contains much useful information for those with the patience to find it.
R/4 V/3. MODL. AMM.

THE DUKES
The Story of the Men who Served in Peace and War with the British Columbia Regiment (Duke of Connaught's Own), 1883-1973
Maj Douglas E Harker * Published by the Regt, 1974. Green, gold, 9.75 x 6.5, vi/438. Fp, 31 mono phots, 3 line drawings, no maps, Bibliography, Index. Apps: Roll of Honour (KIA and WIA, for WWI, KIA, WIA and POW for WWII), H&A (WWI and WWII), notes on Regtl reorganisations, Battle Honours (South Africa, WWI, WWII), a 'Chronology of the Regt (1866-1973)'.

* This is not only an updated history by the same author (vide preceding entry), it is a vastly improved quality of book in every respect. Utilising the information contained in his first book and in the 7th Bn history by Scudamore (vide the preceding page), plus other sources, he brings together the complete evolution and services of the BCR and its various predecessor units. All of the major events are covered, the numerous changes of title and role, services in WWI and WWII, and post-war events through to 1973. There is an interesting account of the Regt's rescue work during the disastrous Fraser Valley floods of 1948, also an assessment of the difficult years when it was deployed as part of the Civil Defence organisation. The BCR resumed its full military role in 1965 as a Reconnaissance Regt (Militia). Plenty of individual members are mentioned, and the narrative is interesting even to the non-specialist reader. R/2 V/5. PC. JRD.

Algonquin Regiment

WARPATH
The Story of the Algonquin Regiment, 1939-1945
From Tilly-la-Compagne to the Kusten Canal
Maj G L Cassidy DSO * Paperjacks Ltd, Markham, Ontario, 1980. Illustrated soft card, red/white/black, 'Tank and soldiers' motif, 8.5 x 5.25, -/381. 30 mono phots, 19 line drawings, 2 cartoons, 18 maps, no appendixes, no Index.
* The Regt originated as a Volunteer Militia unit in Sault St Marie, Southern Ontario, in 1863. It was reformed in 1900 as the 92nd Algonquin Rifles. It did not see active service in WWI, but many of its members joined various units of the CEF. There is brief coverage of those early years, but the bulk of the book is devoted to WWII. Mobilised in July 1940, the Regt served in Newfoundland and Nova Scotia on local defence duties before arriving in England in June 1943. It landed in France (at Courseulles) on 24 July 1944, its first battle being at Tilly-la-Compagne. An element of 4th Cdn Armd Div, it took part in the Falaise battle, the forcing of the Leopold Canal, and the winter campaign in Holland, and then fought its last action on the Kusten Canal. Coverage of the fighting in NW Europe is excellent, with many individuals and minor actions being given a mention. Although this edition of the book lacks any appendixes, lists of awards and casualties appear frequently throughout the narrative. R/1 V/4. PC. JRD.
Note: the version recorded above is the 1980 reprint of the original edition produced by Ryerson Press, Toronto, in 1948. Copies of that edition are seen only rarely. It is a casebound book (olive green cloth, 9.25 x 6.25, xvii/372). Unlike the 1980 edition, it is well provided with appendixes - Roll of Honour (KIA and DOW), H&A, unit nominal roll (all ranks who served, July 1940 to January 1946). It is not known why the publishers of the second edition chose to omit these very important appendixes. Also, given that the narrative contains many names of places and people, an Index would have been helpful.

12th Manitoba Dragoons

XII MANITOBA DRAGOONS, 1885-1991
A Tribute
Bruce Tascona * Friesen Printers, Altona, Manitoba, for the Regtl Association, 1991. Maroon, silver, Regtl crest, 11.25 x 8.5, vii/185. 280 mono phots (incl 85 named groups and portraits), 23 sketches and cartoons, 22 maps (19 printed in the text, 3 on the end-papers), Bibliography, no Index. Apps: Rolls of Honour (KIA for South Africa, WWI, and WWII, plus DOW for 1919-1921), H&A (South Africa, WWI, and WWII), list of COs (95th Manitoba Light Infantry and Manitoba Dragoons, 1885-1946), casualty statistics, notes regarding vehicles used in WWI, notes on the Veterans' Association.
* Starting as 91st Winnipeg Battalion of Infantry in 1885, the Regt was soon given the title 95th Manitoba Light Infantry. Disbanded in 1892, some elements were retained to form The Corps of Manitoba Dragoons based in Virden and Portage-la-

Prairie. Volunteer drafts served with other Canadian units in the Anglo-Boer War. The book then traces the constant changes of organisation preceding WWI and the chaotic formation of the Canadian Expeditionary Force. The Regt did not serve intact, but some personnel fought on the Western Front with the 5th Cdn Infantry (Western Cavalry) Bn CEF. This unit's services are well recorded here (Second Ypres, Festubert, Mont Sorrel, etc, through to the pursuit to Mons). In 1921, the XII Manitoba Dragoons were reactivated as Militia Cavalry with a strength of three Squadrons. They mobilised in May 1941 as 2nd Armoured Car Regt (later changed to 18th Armoured Car Regt). Arriving in England in 1942, they were equipped with Staghounds which they took to Normandy on 8 July 1944. Repeated changes of role and title after the war culminated with disbandment in 1965. This is a very complete history, packed with names and reference details. The lack of an Index is lamentable. R/1 V/4. PC. JRD.

REGIMENTAL HISTORY OF THE 18th ARMOURED CAR REGIMENT (XII MANITOBA DRAGOONS)
France, Belgium, Holland, Germany, 8 July 1944 – 4 May 1945
Capt C E Henry * Nederlansche Diepdruk Inrichting NV, Deventer, Holland, 1945. Soft card, wire coil spine, grey, red, Regtl crest, 8.5 x 5.5, i/151. Fp, 23 mono phots (of poor quality), one map (folding, bound in, at rear), no Index. Apps: Roll of Honour, H&A, details of the Regt's operations and movements, notes on weaponry and vehicles, full nominal roll (all ranks, with serial numbers, home addresses, incl attached Corps, liaison, and interpreter personnel).
* The author plunges directly into the North West Europe campaign. The Regt was heavily engaged in wide-ranging scouting work during the operations to close the Falaise Gap. It lost thirteen of its Staghound armoured cars around Trun and Granville. On one occasion, they met a German horse-drawn column, killing seventy horses and two hundred men. On another, they captured a German field hospital. The Regt advanced into Belgium (the capture of Ostend) and fought in Holland and on the German border (Kusten Canal, Oldendorf and Oldenburg) as an element of 2nd Canadian Corps. The narrative mentions many members by name and the various appendixes are helpful. R/4 V/4. NYPL. JRD.
Note: it is understood that this book was subsequently reprinted, but no other details are available.

South Alberta Light Horse

HISTORY OF THE 31st CANADIAN INFANTRY BATTALION, CEF
From its Organisation in November 1914 to its Demobilisation in June 1919, Compiled from its Diaries and Other Papers
Maj H S Singer and Mr A A Peebles * Printed by Knight Bindery, Calgary, for the 31st Cdn Bn Assn, 1939. Light blue, black, 9.0 x 6.0, xiv/515. Fp, 14 mono phots, 8 maps, no Index. Apps: a complete nominal roll (mentioning KIA, DOW, WIA, MIA, POW, and individual awards).
* When war was declared, the South Alberta Light Horse's two predecessor units of that period – 15th Light Horse and 23rd Alberta Rangers – supplied trained men to form new CEF units – the 12th and 13th Cdn Mounted Rifles respectively. These units were soon broken up to provide infantry reinforcements on the Western Front. Both Regts also supplied men for the 31st, 113th, 175th, and 187th Cdn Inf Bns CEF, all of which served overseas. This book is the only known record of any of them. A large-scale work containing much detailed information, it covers all the great battles of the Western Front in which the CEF took part. It has two defects – the lack of an Index, and the absence of any dates in the otherwise admirable nominal roll appendix. R/4 V/4. UWOL. DJB/JEB.

A SHORT HISTORY OF THE 29th CANADIAN ARMOURED RECONNAISSANCE REGIMENT (SOUTH ALBERTA HORSE)

Maj G L MacDougall * Spin's Publishing Co, Amsterdam, Holland, n.d. (1945). Seen only as a rebound facsimile, 7.25 x 5.0, -/87. No ills, no maps, no Index. Apps: Roll of Honour (KIA, DOW, and WIA), H&A, list of officers, idem SNCOs (at 8.4.45).
* The South Alberta Light Horse was not ordered to mobilise until May 1940 and, by that time, many of its members had voluntarily gone off to join the Princess Patricia's Canadian Light Infantry and the Edmonton Regt. When the call came, the Regt made up its numbers by absorbing several local Militia units and was designated, after arrival in England, 29th Cdn Armoured Regt. Equipped initially with (Canadian) Ram tanks, it trained in England for the next two years and was re-equipped with (American) Sherman tanks. As part of 4th Cdn Armd Div, it went ashore in Normandy on 24 July 1944 and was heavily involved in the Falaise Gap battle. At St Lambert-sur-Dives, Maj David Currie won the VC when he commanded a small force of tanks, SP guns, and infantry which, for 36 hours, held off desperate German columns attempting to escape eastwards (and inflicting severe losses upon them). Currie's VC was the only such award to a member of the Royal Canadian Armoured Corps since it was formed in 1940. Although quite condensed, the narrative of this little book is readable and contains a lot of useful detail.
R/5 V/3. MODL. AMM.

KEEN-EYED PRAIRIE MEN

A Summary History of the South Alberta Light Horse and of Medicine Hat and District Military Units

Capt J A MacDonald * Published by the Regt, no other details shown, 1976. Disbound facsimile TS, Regtl crest, -/23 (pages not numbered). No mono phots, 3 line drawings (poorly executed), one map (Alberta, also very poor), no Index. Apps: lineage chart of major military units raised in Medicine Hat and district.
* As noted elsewhere, Canadian unit histories vary widely in their quality of content and presentation. This item is one of many cyclostyled or photo-copied pamphlets which are all that are available for several long-established Regiments. This one is listed here only because it makes superficial reference to otherwise unrecorded units - the Rocky Mountain Rangers (formed in South East Alberta in 1885 during the North West Rebellion and disbanded shortly afterwards), and a few others. The South Alberta Regt, which absorbed so many of the early Militia units in that Province, was re-titled South Alberta Light Horse in 1958.
R/4 V/2. PC. RP.

Saskatchewan Dragoons

THE SUICIDE BATTALION

46th Battalion, Canadian Infantry, CEF

James L McWilliams and R James Steel * Hurtig Publishers, Edmonton, Alberta, 1978. Dark blue, gold, 9.25 x 8.25, -/226. No ills, one map (printed on each end-paper), Bibliography, Index. Apps: H&A (incomplete), nominal roll (incomplete), biographical notes on some of the people mentioned in the narrative.
* The authors admit that many other military units could claim to have been a 'suicide battalion', but their story is otherwise an impartial and reliable account of the 46th Cdn Inf Bn CEF. It was one of several such units raised during WWI in the districts of Moose Jaw and Valcartier with officers and men who had served previously with the 95th Saskatchewan Rifles (the Militia unit which, in 1958, would evolve as The Saskatchewan Dragoons). The 46th Bn arrived in England at full strength in October 1915 and was immediately stripped of 800 officers and men who were sent as reinforcements to other CEF units already serving on the Western Front. Absorbing fresh drafts from home, the Bn moved to France in August 1916. The book gives a vivid account of trench warfare and is based upon a variety of sources - letters, diaries, official documents, and interviews with elderly survivors. On 1 November 1918, Sgt Hugh Cairns DCM won a posthumous VC at Audenarde, Belgium, the last VC of WWI to a Canadian. R/3 V/3. MODL. AMM/RP.

The King's Own Calgary Regiment

THE CALGARY REGIMENT
Lieut R G Maltby * Printing Works De Jong & Co, Hilversum, Holland, n.d. (1945). Stiff card, yellow, black, Regtl crest and tactical sign on front cover, 9.25 x 6.0, -/17. No ills, 2 maps (bound in), no Index. Apps: Order of Battle for 1st Cdn Armd Bde, 'Highlights' of the Bde, comments by senior officers.
* In 1936, the Calgary Regt opted to become an Infantry Tank Bn (Canada's first). Mobilised in February 1941, it became 14th Army Tank Bn (Calgary Regt) and arrived in England in July. Equipped initially with Bren carriers and Matilda tanks, it re-equipped with Churchills and took them to Dieppe in 1942. After that disaster, the survivors were reinforced, regrouped, and moved to Sicily. It saw some action on that island, and was then fully committed to the campaign on mainland Italy. In February 1945, the Regt moved to Holland and finished its war in the fighting around Arnhem and in the Reichswald Forest. This laconic diary of events mentions few individuals and is too condensed to be really useful. R/5 V/2. MODL. AMM/RP.

THE CALGARY REGIMENT
Dick Maltby (presumably the same author as noted above) * Copy-time, Vancouver, BC, for 50/14 Veterans' Association, 1990. Illustrated soft card, plastic ring spine, 11.0 x 8.5, -/247 (plus blank pages). Fp, 199 mono phots, 21 cartoons, 11 line drawings, 25 maps, Glossary, Bibliography, no Index. Apps: unit nominal roll (WWII), verbatim messages to the Regt from Montgomery, MacKenzie King, etc.
* An 'economy' production, facsimile typescript, poorly reproduced illustrations, and many blank pages. In sum, an unattractive item. And this is a pity because the text provides a mass of detail and incorporates many worthwhile anecdotes and reminiscences gathered from individual former soldiers who fought at Dieppe and in the operations in Italy and NW Europe (under the designation 14th Armoured Regt). The author includes some references to the Regt's origins, and gives a very helpful account of the WWI services of 50th Cdn Inf Bn CEF. R/2 V/4. PC. JRD.

British Columbia Dragoons

A SHORT HISTORY OF THE 31st BRITISH COLUMBIA HORSE
Lieut Col C L Flick CMG CBE * The Reliable Press, Vancouver, BC, 1922. Soft card, grey with two gold stripes, dark blue, Regtl crest in gold, 8.75 x 6.25, -/40. Fp, 12 mono phots, no maps, no Index. Apps: H&A (WWI), list of officers, unit nominal roll (at 27 August 1914).
* Raised in British Columbia in 1908 as a Cavalry unit, the Regt mobilised in August 1914 and then saw its membership depart to join various CEF units destined to proceed overseas (notably the 2nd Cdn Mounted Rifles). The narrative contains little information concerning the subsequent war services of these men. The book was published shortly after reconstitution, in November 1920, as the 5th British Columbia Light Horse. A pretty little book, desirable more for its rarity than its value as a source of information. R/5 V/2. TPL/MODL. AMM.

SINEWS OF STEEL
The History of the British Columbia Dragoons
R H Roy * Charters Publishing Co Ltd, Brampton, Ont, for The Whizzbang Association, 1965. Maroon, gold, Regtl crest, 9.25 x 6.25, xiii/469. 2 fps, 24 mono phots (incl portraits), 7 maps, many footnotes, no Index. Apps: Roll of Honour (KIA and WIA, with dates), H&A, list of officers (1908-1963), annual strengths (all ranks, 1921-1963), list of Honorary Colonels, notes on badges and the Colours, etc.
* The Regt has its origins in the Okanagan Valley of British Columbia. After a false start, the men of the valley formed themselves into the British Columbia Horse in 1908. The author of this comprehensive and satisfying history takes his reader through the complexities of those early Militia years, the chaotic despatch of the first contingents of the CEF to France, the formation of 2nd Cdn Mounted Rifles, and its dreadful experiences on the Western Front (particularly on Vimy

Ridge). The difficult inter-war years and WWII services (as 9th Cdn Armd Regt) are clearly described, with liberal mention of individual members. The Regt arrived in England in November 1941, fought in Italy (mounted on Sherman tanks) until early 1945, then moved to Holland. During the final weeks of the war it served as an Armoured Car Regt (mounted on Humber scout cars and GMC semi-armoured vehicles). In such a large-scale work, with so many personnel, places and units mentioned in the narrative, the author's decision to omit an Index is hard to understand. R/4 V/4. MODL. JRD.

THE 2nd CANADIAN MOUNTED RIFLES (BRITISH COLUMBIA HORSE) IN FRANCE AND FLANDERS

Lieut Col G Chalmers Johnston DSO MC (edited by M V McGuire, H R Denison and G W Pearson) * The Vernon News Printing & Publishing Co, Vernon, BC, n.d. (c.1932). Blue, black, Regtl colours stripe across front cover, 9.0 x 6.25, -/174 (last four pages blank). Fp, 23 mono phots (mainly battlefield views), no maps, Glossary, no Index. Apps: Roll of Honour (KIA, DOW and WIA), H&A, list of officers who served, idem SNCOs, unit nominal roll (the names of those on the strength at 22.9.1914, with later reinforcements added).

* This is a careful and detailed history of 2 CMR from the time of its formation until its return home for disbandment in 1919. It arrived in England in September 1915 and then moved to the Western Front where it fought in all the great Canadian battles in the infantry role. The book has good accounts of Mont Sorrel, Maple Copse, Loos, Passchendaele, Arras, Canal du Nord, etc. The narrative is based upon the diary kept throughout that period by Chalmers Johnston, with later checking of facts and figures by the three editors named above. There are not many references to individual officers and men, but the book gives a detailed picture of movements and actions. R/4 V/4. MODL. AMM.

Note:

It will be seen that the preceding pages do not carry entries for the following regiments:

7th/11th Hussars
Prince Edward Island Regiment (RCAC)
19th Alberta Dragoons
14th Canadian Hussars
Le Régiment de Hull (RCAC)
Windsor Regiment (RCAC)

Enquires were raised c.1989-1990 with each of the regimental authorities and, from the information received, it appears that none of them had at that time produced a formal history of the style and quality which qualifies for inclusion in this bibliography.

ARTILLERY

Until 1883, the abbreviation RCA signified Regiment of Canadian Artillery but, in that year, Queen Victoria granted the distinction 'Royal' to several Regiments and Corps of the Permanent Force. The title changed to Royal Canadian Artillery and so the abbreviation remained unchanged. In 1905, it was decided to restyle the Field Regiments as Royal Canadian Horse Artillery (RCHA) while all the other Regular and Militia units continued as Royal Canadian Artillery (RCA).

In 1914, under the Hughes edict, temporary designations were given to all units being formed for service overseas with the Canadian Expeditionary Force. The Artillery Regiments were designated Brigades, the RCHA-based units were styled Canadian Field Artillery (CFA), and the heavier units Canadian Artillery (CA). The titles of the books listed on the following pages reflect these changes.

R.C.H.A. - RIGHT OF THE LINE
An Anecdotal History of the Royal Canadian Horse Artillery from 1871
Maj G D Mitchell MC CD * Published by the RCHA History Committee, Ottawa, 1986. Red, gold, 8.75 x 10.75 (landscape), x/303. Fp, 175 mono phots, 5 line drawings, 24 maps, Glossary, Bibliography, Index. Apps: eight in total, incl Roll of Honour, H&A, list of former COs, idem RSMs, notes on the RCHA Band, idem weaponry, a diary of key dates and events, etc.
* A very readable account which commences with the raising of the first two Regular Batteries of Artillery in 1871, then moves on to the creation of the RCHA in 1905, and the Regt's main campaigns - North West Canada (1885), South Africa (1899-1902), WWI (1914-1919), WWII (1939-1945), Korea (1950-1954), and duties with the UN in Cyprus (1965-1975). In May 1940, 1 RCHA landed at Brest and was within 100 miles of Paris when it was ordered to turn around and re-embark for England. It was the only Artillery unit under British command to bring its guns away from France. There are dozens of reminiscences by named individuals quoted throughout the narrative (hence the book's sub-title). An unusual format for a Regtl history, but one which works well and which captures the spirit of the RCHA over eight decades. R/2 V/5. RAI. AMM.

THIRD REGIMENT, ROYAL CANADIAN HORSE ARTILLERY, 1953-1983
Anon * Leech Print, Brandon, Manitoba, 1983. Soft card, stapled, Regtl crest, 8.75 x 6.0, -/32. Fp, 67 mono phots (incl COs and RSMs for the period), one line drawing, no maps, no appendixes, no Index.
* The Regt was formed in 1951 as 79th Field Regt RCHA for NATO service in Germany. Initial equipment was the 105 mm gun-howitzer, replaced in 1952 by the 25-pounder. In 1954, the Regt moved to Korea for six months, then returned to Germany via Canada. In the 1970s and early 1980s, it formed part of 1 Cdn Bde Group (Air Mobile), with detachments serving in Cyprus and Norway and its home base being Camp Shilo, Manitoba. The booklet commemorates the 30th Anniversary of formation and is mainly pictorial in content. R/4 V/1. RCAM. JRD.

THE GUNNERS OF CANADA
The History of the Royal Regiment of Canadian Artillery, 1534-1967
Col G W L Nicholson CD * McClelland & Stewart Ltd, for the RCA Association, Toronto. Two matching volumes, dark blue, gold, Regtl crest, 10.0 x 6.25.
Volume I : 1534-1919. Published in 1967, xiv/478. Fp, 48 mono phots, 8 sketches, 18 maps, Index. Apps: eight in total, incl H&A, list of COs, etc.
Volume II : 1919-1967. Published in 1972, xvi/760. Fp, 57 mono phots, 5 sketches, 21 maps, Bibliography, Index. Apps: H&A, list of COs, etc.
* A Regtl history on the grand scale. Both volumes are eminently readable, with many references to individuals of all ranks, to specific actions, and to various units and sub-units. The author covers a lot of ground - the earliest days of

gunnery in Canada, the War of 1812, the Fenian Raids, the South African war, and the two world wars (for which the coverage is excellent). The maps are helpful, and the illustrations are well captioned. R/3 V/5. PCAL/RAI. AMM.

THE ROYAL REGIMENT OF ARTILLERY, OTTAWA, 1855–1952

Lieut Col H M Jackson MBE ED * Printed by the Industrial School for the Deaf, Montreal, 1952. Blue, red, RCA crest, 9.5 x 6.5, -/418. 2 mono phots, 7 maps (5 printed in the text, 2 on the end-papers), Bibliography, no Index. Apps: Roll of Honour (1st Field Bde CFA, 1914-1921), H&A (idem, incl some citations), list of former officers.

* The title may be confusing to non-Canadian readers. The subject matter of the book is in fact the history of artillery units originating in and around Ottawa during the stated period. The author traces their evolution and services as Militia units, their services in South Africa, and, as 1st Field Bde CFA, with the CEF in France and Flanders. Their successor in WWII was 51st Bty, 1st Anti-tank Regt, which fought in Italy and NW Europe. An interesting and well presented history. R/3 V/4. NYPL/MODL. JEB/AMM.

THE ORIGIN AND SERVICES OF THE 3rd (MONTREAL) FIELD BATTERY OF ARTILLERY
With Some Notes on the Artillery of By-gone Days, and a Brief History of the Development of Field Artillery

Capt Ernest J Chambers * E L Ruddy, Montreal, 1898. Black, gold, Bty badge, 10.5 x 8.25, -/84/xxxvi. Fp, 25 mono phots, 8 line drawings, no maps, no Index. Apps: list of former and serving officers, list of subscribers (whom the author charmingly describes as 'The Roll of Honour').

* The opening chapters are a eulogy of the Bty's past record and of its senior officers, with some very generalised comments regarding the evolution of field gunnery. There is then some mention of the Fenian Raids (in which the Bty played a very minor role) and its various 'aid to the civil power' commitments between 1855 and 1885 (which are much more interesting). Nominal rolls are scattered throughout the text, and some of the captioned group photographs are useful to genealogists and students of Dress and insignia. As usual with Chambers' books, the last 36 pages carry commercial advertisements. This is an attractive Militia history which, as much as anything, is a window on Montreal society at the turn of the century. R/4 V/4. MODL/UWOL. AMM.

VANCOUVER DEFENDED
A History of the Men and Guns of the Lower Mainland Defences, 1859–1949

Peter N Moogk and Maj R V Stevenson * Antonson Publishing Ltd, Surrey, BC, 1978. Brown, gold, 9.25 x 7.0, -/128. Fp, 80 mono phots, 11 line drawings, 3 maps, Bibliography, Chapter Notes, Index. Apps: list of all Militia Artillery units between 1866 and 1949, and their fate.

* The defence of Vancouver was initially a Royal Engineers responsibility. Following the withdrawal of Imperial garrisons, local defence was taken over by a newly raised Militia unit - The Westminster Volunteer Rifles. From 1866, the Rifles were augmented by local Artillery units under a succession of titles which are recorded here in great detail. During WWI, they provided drafts for the 31st, 68th and 85th Btys CFA, and in WWII they manned coastal batteries throughout the coastal areas of British Columbia. The need to man the searchlights operating in conjunction with these batteries was met by disbanding the British Columbia Hussars and transferring the personnel to the new 1st Searchlight Regt RCA. The long tradition of locally-manned Artillery units came to an end with the disbandment of 102nd Coast Regt (Reserve) in 1954. An interesting account, with many officers mentioned in the text. R/4 V/5. PC. JRD.

HISTORICAL RECORDS OF THE NEW BRUNSWICK REGIMENT, CANADIAN ARTILLERY

Capt John B M Baxter * The Sun Printing Co Ltd, St John, NB, 'for the Officers of the Regt', 1896. Blue, gold, Artillery helmet plate motif, 8.25 x 6.0, viii/259. Fp, 22 mono phots, no maps, Index. Apps: list of former officers (by Bty, 1793-1896), Bty muster roll (at 1893).

* This handsome book is an account of the oldest Canadian Militia Artillery unit. The narrative covers the period 1793 to 1896. The Regt, of ten Coys (later designated Btys), never saw active service, but the book is an important example of socio-military history. It is, in effect, a commentary upon the role and place of the Militia in the life of the Province during that period. There are some useful notes on officers and ORs, organisation and designations, fortifications, the band, and so forth. R/5 V/4. RAI/ASKBC. AMM/CB.

FROM THE ST LAWRENCE TO THE NORTH SASKATCHEWAN
Being Some Incidents with the Detachment of 'A' Battery, Regiment of Canadian Artillery, who Composed part of the North West Field Force in the Rebellion of 1885
Alexander Laidlaw * Publication details not known, seen only as a bound photocopied volume, 8.25 x 5.5, -/43. No ills, no maps, no appendixes, no Index.
* A prolix but readable account by one member of the Bty. He describes the march northwards from Quebec and the Battle of Fish Creek. The text includes numerous references to individual personnel which might be useful to a genealogist. R/5 V/2. MODL. AMM.

50 ANS D'ACTIVITES AVEC LE 6e REGIMENT D'ARTILLERIE, QUEBEC ET LEVIS, 1899-1949
Anon * L'imprimerie La Flamme Lte, Quebec, 1949. Paper, blue, red, Regtl crest, 9.75 x 6.5, -/18 (not numbered). Fp, 11 mono phots, no maps, no appendixes, no Index.
* Written in French and based upon notes compiled by various officers for a proposed full history. There is useful reference to individual officers, and a WWII chronology for each of the four Btys, but the research value is very limited. R/5 V/1. NYPL/NDHQL. RBM/MAR.

WORLD WAR I

SOS - STAND TO!
1st Field Brigade, 1st Canadian Division
Sgt Reginald Grant * D Appleton & Co, New York City, 1918. Green, gold, 7.5 x 5.25, x/297. Fp, 6 mono phots, no maps, no appendixes, no Index.
* An autobiographical account by a gunner who served on the Western Front from 1914 to 1917 (when he was wounded, and returned to Canada). An interesting individual view of Ypres, Sanctuary Wood, the Somme, and Vimy Ridge, but in most ways of limited research value. R/4 V/1. USL. JRD.

GUN-FIRE
An Historical Narrative of the 4th Brigade CFA in the Great War (1914-1918)
Lieut J A MacDonald CFA * The Greenway Press, Toronto, 1929. Black, red, 'Gun' motif glued onto front cover, 9.5 x 6.0, vi/264. Fp, 10 mono phots, 22 chapter head line drawings, 11 maps, no Index. Apps: Roll of Honour (KIA and DOW), H&A, list of COs and OCs for each Bty, Bde nominal roll (with dates of death and wounds), skeleton histories for each of the eight Btys associated with the Bde.
* The volume is divided into two 'Books'. The first is a detailed account of the Bde's formation, move to England, landing in France, and subsequent services on the Western Front. This is readable and interesting, with many officers mentioned in the text. The second part deals quite fully with 15 and 16 Btys which served with the Bde until 1916 but were then transferred to 6 Bde. A useful source for the genealogist and for students of WWI field gunnery. R/4 V/4. MODL. AMM.

THE 2nd CANADIAN HEAVY BATTERY IN THE WORLD WAR, 1914 TO 1919
Record of the Battery from Mobilisation in 1914 to Demobilisation in 1919, Including Battle Engagements and Battery Positions
J A Argo * Woodward Press, Montreal, for the 2nd CHB Old Boys' Association, Montreal, 1932. Soft imitation leather covers, maroon, black, 6.25 x 4.0, i/117. No ills, 6 maps (bound in), no Index. Apps: Roll of Honour (KIA, DOW and WIA), unit nominal roll (with H&A details included).
* This curious book is a combination of technical information concerning the Bty's deployments and much irrelevant comment regarding the progress of the war in general. Few members of the Bty are named in the text, but the nominal roll appendix is certainly of interest to family researchers and medal collectors. The Bty was formed in November 1914 and recruited mainly in Eastern Canada.
R/4 V/3. MODL. JEB/AMM.
Note: a copy has been seen with stiff card covers (red/black) and a rear pocket for the maps. This may have been the original binding format.

THE SEVENTH
The Seventh Canadian Siege Battery
T W L MacDermont * Published by The Seventh Canadian Siege Battery Association, 1930. Black, gold, Bty badge, 8.5 x 5.75, -/144. Fp, 6 mono phots, 8 maps, Bibliography, no Index. Apps: Bty nominal roll (with details of deaths, wounds, awards, ranks and service numbers).
* The Bty served at Vimy Ridge, Lens, Hill 70, Passchendaele, Arras, Canal du Nord, Valenciennes, and Mons. This is a sound workmanlike history which contains all of the required information. R/3 V/4. MODL. JEB.

FROM OTTERPOOL TO THE RHINE
With the 23rd Battery, Canadian Field Artillery
Capt J D McKeown MC and Lieut R S Gillespie MC * W Charles & Son, London, UK, n.d. (c.1919). Dark blue, gold, Artillery crest on rear cover, 7.5 x 5.0, -/48. Fp, one mono phot (a Bty crossing the Rhine, 13.12.1918), no maps, no Index. Apps: full unit nominal roll (with some details of casualties and awards).
* The Bty was raised at Shorncliffe (UK) in 1915 and equipped with howitzers. Its first taste of war, and its first casualties, occurred at Otterpool Camp on 13 October during a Zeppelin bombing raid. The Bty landed in France in January 1916 and served subsequently on the Western Front through to the end of the war (and crossed into Germany at Bonn). Amongst its misadventures was a serious gas attack at Pozieres and a direct hit on its wagon lines at Guillaucourt. This is a very brief record, but the basic facts are presented clearly and many individuals are named in the narrative. R/5 V/3. NYPL (on microfilm only). JRD.

BATTERY ACTION
The Story of 43rd Battery, CFA
H R Kay, G McGee and F A McLennan * Warwick Brothers & Rutter, Toronto, n.d. (c.1920). Red, gold, 7.75 x 5.0, -/305. Fp, 7 line drawings (by James Frise), one map (bound in), no Index. Apps: Roll of Honour, nominal roll of all ranks who served overseas.
* The Bty was raised in Ontario and served on the Western Front. The narrative is clear and informative, with plenty of individuals and incidents mentioned. The lack of an Index is lamentable in a book of this length, and it would have benefitted from more appendixes. R/4 V/3. PALO. JEB.

THE HISTORY OF THE FIFTY-FIFTH BATTERY, CFA
D C McArthur * H S Longhurst, at the Robert Duncan Press, Hamilton, Ontario, 1919. Leather, blue, gold, Div flash, 7.5 x 5.25, -/94. Fp, 18 mono phots, 3 maps (bound in), no Index. Apps: Roll of Honour, list of former officers, unit nominal roll (with details of awarded included).
* A straightforward Bty history, dealing mainly with movements and engagements. The nominal roll does not include details of ranks or service numbers and is

therefore of limited reference value. A useful little book as far as it goes, but it does not go quite far enough. R/4 V/3. NYPL/RAI. AMM.

THE 60th BATTERY BOOK
Anon * Canada Newspaper Co Ltd, London, for the Battery Association, 1919. Purple, gold, CFA crest, 7.25 x 4.75, -/190. 31 mono phots, 7 maps, no Index. Apps: Roll of Honour, H&A, list of former COs, idem former officers, unit nominal roll (with much detail), notes on 'Regimental personalities', idem the Bty flag.
* A substantial record, produced at speed soon after the Armistice. The narrative contains plenty of good factual information regarding the Bty and its work on the Western Front, with abundant references to individual officers and men who served with it. Most of the photographs are unique to this book, and are reasonably well printed. R/4 V/4. RAI. AMM.

THE STORY OF THE SIXTY-SIXTH BATTERY, CFA
Anon * Turnbull & Spears, Edinburgh, 1919. Red, gold, 7.75 x 5.25, xii/148. Fp, 13 mono phots, 3 maps, no Index. Apps: H&A, unit nominal roll (with service details and home addresses).
* Like the book noted in the preceding entry (60th Bty), this publication was produced in the United Kingdom while the Bty was waiting for shipping to become available to take them home for demobilisation. Although slightly slimmer, it has the same sort of format and content, and presumably was based upon the War Diary. R/4 V/4. NYPL/MODL. AMM.

WAR DIARY, SECOND C.D.A.C
Extracts from the War Diary and Official Records of the Second Canadian Divisional Ammunition Column
Lieut H D Clark and Staff Sgt Roy F Logan * J & A McMillan, St John, NB, 1921. Brown, black, 'Soldier with mules and Div patch' motif, 8.5 x 5.75, -/166. Fp, 7 mono phots, no maps, no Index. Apps: Roll of Honour (all causes, with dates), H&A (with Gazette dates), unit nominal roll (upon landing at Le Havre, 17.9.1915), officers' postings, plus 8 others (quotations and statistics).
* With 825 all ranks and 902 horses, the unit trained in Canada and England with 13 pdr and 18 pdr field guns. Once arrived in France, in September 1915, each of the four Sections commenced its primary task of hauling ammunition up to various British and Canadian Artillery positions in the forward areas. Much of this work was done at night and under fire. The authors admit that their book is not a complete day-by-day record, but it does give a useful picture of a little-known aspect of gunner work on the Western Front. Incidents resulting in casualties or awards are described in clear detail. R/5 V/4. UWOL/TPL. JRD.

WORLD WAR II

BATTERY FLASHES OF W.W. II
A Thumb-nail Sketch of Canadian Artillery Batteries during the 1939-1945 Conflict
D W Falconer * Published privately in Canada, no details shown, 1985. Illustrated stiff card covers, red, white, 9.0 x 6.0, xii/514. 4 mono phots, 4 cld plates, Bibliography, Glossary, no formal appendixes, Index.
* The title of this large-scale work is very misleading. It does indeed have a section (well illustrated) which deals with the cloth insignia worn on battle dress, but the main purpose of the book is to record the dates of formation, mobilisation, reorganisation, designation, amalgamation, moves, locations, and (where applicable) disbandment of every single Bty of the RCHA and RCA mobilised for service in WWII. There is an almost incredible amount of information for each Bty, few being given less than half a page of text and many having much more. Every type of Bty is covered, including Air OP, training units, holding units, etc. A true labour of love by the author. R/2 V/5. RAI/MODL. AMM.

THE STORY OF THE FIRST MEDIUM REGIMENT, RCA, 1940-1945
Lieut R Y Walmsley and Lieut B J P Whalley * Spin's Publishing Co, Amsterdam, Holland, n.d. (c.1945). Stiff card, yellow, white/red/black, 'Maple leaf with 5.5 gun' motif in gold, 7.5 x 5.25, -/121. No ills, no maps, no Index. Apps: Roll of Honour (KIA, DOW and WIA), H&A, list of officers (incl non-RCA attached).
* The Regt was raised from Btys resident in Quebec, Ontario and Prince Edward Island in August 1939. This is a retrospective of its hardships, its own brand of humour, and individual acts of courage. No attempt is made to include operational data, and few personnel are mentioned in the text. The Regt trained in England from 1940 to 1943 and then moved to mainland Italy via Sicily. It was transferred to Holland in March 1945 for the final advance into Germany, but most of the pages are devoted to the Italian campaign. R/4 V/2. NYPL/MODL. JRD/AMM.

2nd CANADIAN MEDIUM REGIMENT, RCA
Regimental History, 18th January 1942 - 30th June 1945
Maj John G Osler * Nederlandsche Diepdruk Inrichting NV, Deventer, Holland, n.d. (c.1945). Soft card, yellow, black, RCA crest in red, 7.25 x 5.25, -/119. 28 mono phots, no maps, no Index. Apps: Roll of Honour (KIA, DOW and WIA), H&A, list of officers (incl non-RCA attached), diary of moves and locations.
* The Regt was raised in January 1942 from Btys resident in Quebec and Ontario. It trained in England in 1942-1943 and then, like so many other RCA units of that period, fought in Italy until being transferred to Holland in March 1945. The book has a good readable narrative, with some officers mentioned in the text.
R/4 V/3. MODL. AMM.

PAR LES BOUCHES DE NOS CANONS
Histoire de 4e Regiment d'Artillerie Moyenne, 4th Canadian Medium Regiment, Royal Canadian Artillery, 1941-1945
Jacques Gouin * Gasparo Ltee, Quebec, 1970. Stiff card, dark blue, white, 'Cannon balls' motif, 10.0 x 8.0, -/268. 63 mono phots, 3 line drawings, 18 maps (bound in), Bibliography, no Index. Apps: Roll of Honour, H&A, list of COs, idem officers, unit nominal roll (all ranks).
* Written in French, this is a plain factual narrative account of a Quebec-raised Artillery Regt in the Normandy and NW Europe campaigns. It covers the first three years of training in Canada and the UK (1941-1944), and then the landing in France and the advance to Germany (July 1944 - May 1945). The Roll of Honour is very detailed, giving each man's name, number, Bty, and the date and cause of death. Of particular interest to serious gunner researchers is the Bibliography (which runs to five pages) and the 'References' section (which covers twenty-one pages). R/3 V/4. RAI/MODL. AMM.

THE HISTORY OF THE 5th MEDIUM REGIMENT, RCA
Lieut Robert J Giles * Publisher's details not shown, printed in Holland, 1945. Soft card, white, black, 'Wings, anchor and globe' motif in gold, 11.5 x 9.25, -/48. No ills, no maps, no Index. Apps: Roll of Honour, H&A.
* This short history covers the Regt's time in Italy from January 1944 to March 1945 (when it moved to Holland). The narrative is based upon the recollections of the author and some of those who served with him. R/4 V/1. PC. JRD.

HISTORY OF THE 7th MEDIUM REGIMENT, RCA
From 1st September 1939 to 8th June 1945, World War II
Capt A M Lockwood and Maj W H Gillespie * H J Jones & Son, London, 1946. Blue, gold, RCA crest, 9.5 x 6.25, -/129. Fp, 11 mono phots, 8 cartoons, 5 maps (bound in), Glossary, no Index. Apps: Roll of Honour (KIA and WIA, with much detail), H&A (with dates), list of officers (at various key dates), idem BQMSs, BSMs and Staff Sgts (with promotion dates), Bty locations (by month and year), etc.
* Formed at the outbreak of war, the Regt was reorganised in February 1941 with three Btys - 12th, 45th and 97th, each of two Troops of four guns. After nearly

three years of training in England, the Regt took its 25-pounders to Normandy on on 9 July 1944 and moved straight into the battle for Carpiquet airfield. The narrative, arranged in a very clear diary format, then covers the Regt's travels through France, Belgium, Holland and Germany as part of 2nd Army Group RCA (1st Cdn Army Troops). An exceptionally fine history, with first class appendixes. R/4 V/4. NYPL/MODL. JRD.

THE HISTORY OF THE SECOND FIELD REGIMENT, RCA, SEPTEMBER 1939 - JUNE 1945
Anon * Publication details not shown, n.d. (c.1945). Soft card, dark orange, black, 9.5 x 6.5, xxiv/79. No ills, no maps, no Index. Apps: Roll of Honour (KIA, DOW, WIA, MIA and POW), H&A, lists of officers (with dates), unit nominal roll (at embarkation, 8.12.1939).
* The Regt consisted of 7th Field Bty (Montreal, QP), 8th Field Bty (Moncton, NB), and 10th Field Bty (St Catherine's, Ont). Under the title 2nd Field Bde RCA, the Regt was raised at the outbreak of war and trained in its home towns. It was retitled 2nd Field Regt in November and a month later embarked for the UK aboard the SS Empress of Britain. The book has good coverage of training in England with 25-pounders and then the move to the Mediterranean. The Regt fought in Sicily (the battle at Regalbuto) and mainland Italy (Moro River, Ortona, Cassino, the Gothic Line, Rimini, etc) before moving to Holland in March 1945 (the actions at Deventer and Zutphen). The book has plenty of detail, with individual casualties mentioned throughout. The appendixes are extensive. R/5 V/4. PC. JRD.

HISTORY OF 5th CANADIAN FIELD REGIMENT, RCA
September 1st 1939 to July 31st, 1945, World War II
Anon * Publication details not shown (probably in Holland), n.d. (c.1945). Soft card (stapled), black/beige, black, Bty crests, 9.75 x 8.25, -/25. No ills, no maps, no Index. Apps: Roll of Honour (KIA, WIA and POW, with dates and Btys), H&A, list of officers who served.
* This very condensed account covers the Regt's services in the UK and in NW Europe. It is based upon the War Diary, and is therefore an accurate record of dates and movements. The most useful parts of the narrative refer to the battles at Authie, Carpiquet airfield, Caen and Falaise. The Regt formed part of 2nd Cdn Inf Div and the component Btys were - 5th (Westmount, QP), 28th (Newcastle, NB), 73rd (Magog, QP), and 89th (Woodstock, NB). Probably useful in the main to family historians and medal collectors. R/4 V/1. PC. JRD.

THE SIX YEARS OF 6 CANADIAN FIELD REGIMENT, ROYAL CANADIAN ARTILLERY
September 1939 - September 1945
Maj Arthur K Kembar, Lieut W T Grundy, and R B Dale Harris * Town Printing Office, Amsterdam, Holland, September 1945. Soft card, beige/blue, RCA crest, 7.5 x 5.25, -/128. No ills, 4 maps (one printed in the text, 3 bound in), no Index. Apps: Roll of Honour (KIA and DOW, with dates), list of officers.
* The Regt was stationed in the UK from 1940 to 1944. It finally saw action in Normandy (after landing on 9 July) at Carpiquet airfield, Orbec and St Germain-la-Champagne. As a unit of 2nd Cdn Inf Div, it advanced into Holland and Germany and was engaged in the actions at Eindhoven, Flushing, Groesbeek, Groningen, and Oldenburg. For most of this time, the Regt gave fire support to 6th Inf Bde which comprised the South Saskatchewan Regt, Queen's Own Cameron Highlanders of Canada, and Les Fusiliers Mont-Royal. Individuals are named throughout the narrative, mainly in those sections which refer to actions with the enemy. The Regt consisted of 13th Field Bty (Winnipeg), 21st Field Bty (Saskatoon), 91st Field Bty (Calgary), and 111th Field Bty (Nelson). R/3 V/3. RMCL/NYPL/MODL. JRD.

HISTORY OF THE 11th CANADIAN FIELD REGIMENT, RCA
From 1 September 1939 to 5 May 1945
Capt A G Campbell * Kemink em Zoon NV, Holland, for 29th Bty RCA Veterans Association, n.d. (c.1945). 'Perfect' bound, soft card, mottled grey, black, 9.5 x 6.0, -/205. No ills, no maps, no Index. Apps: Roll of Honour (KIA, WIA and POW),

H&A.
* A factual account of the Regt's locations, movements and engagements during WWII. With 205 pages it is a substantial production, and contains much useful information, but the narrative is curiously lifeless. Few members of the Regt are mentioned by name and some readers may find the whole work rather hard going. The lack of illustrations is a barrier to understanding the spirit of the Regt, and the lack of an Index inhibits the worth of the book as a source of reference.
R/4 V/2. AldMM. RP.
Note: this history was republished by the Regimental Association in Toronto on the occasion of the 1966 Reunion. The general quality of production is superior to the Dutch 'economy' first edition. It has stiff card covers, beige and black, quarto, with 59 mono phots (mainly individual and group pictures, with the names of those depicted). The appendixes are much improved and include a list of officers (at 9.2.1940) and a complete Regtl muster roll (with notes on casualties). It is reported that the narrative is the same as that used in the first edition, but the overall length of the book has increased to v/289 to accommodate the expanded appendixes and the new illustrations pages. The modified title reflects the latter feature - HISTORY AND PHOTOGRAPHS OF THE 11th CANADIAN FIELD REGIMENT, RCA.

INTO ACTION WITH THE 12th FIELD REGIMENT, 1939-1945
Capt T J Bell MC * Publication details not shown, n.d. (probably Holland, c.1945). Stiff card covers with leather spine, 'Landing craft' motif, white/black/green, green, 9.5 x 6.25, -/160. 44 mono phots, 54 line drawings (by Sgt J Daimer), one map (pasted onto rear cover), no Index. Apps: Rolls of Honour (separate lists for KIA, DOW and WIA, with dates), H&A, list of officers (6.6.1944), idem officers who took part in later operations (with dates), diary of locations between September 1940 and May 1945.
* The Regt comprised 16th and 43rd Field Btys from Guelph, Ontario, and 11th Field Bty from Hamilton, Ontario. It arrived in England in July 1941 and did not see action until D-Day. It took part in the actions at Panville, Norrey-en-Bessin, Le-Mesnil-Patri, Buron, the Falaise Road, etc, all in the Normandy bridgehead. The Regt was caught in the fiasco on 14 August when the RAF bombed the Allied lines at Quesney Wood. The losses included 13 killed, 53 wounded, and most of the guns and vehicles of 16th Bty destroyed. There is good coverage of the advance into Belgium and the winter campaign with 3rd Cdn Inf Div. R/4 V/3. RMCL/NYPL. JRD.

THE HISTORY OF 13 CANADIAN FIELD REGIMENT, ROYAL CANADIAN ARTILLERY 1940-1945
Lieut W W Barrett * Publication details not shown, possibly Holland 1945, but more probably Canada at a later date. Black, gold, 10.5 x 7.0, -/188.
84 mono phots (incl 4 pages of small portrait photographs of officers and SNCOs), 22 sketches, 9 maps (bound in), no Index. Apps: Roll of Honour (KIA and WIA, with dates), H&A (with edited citations for all 'immediate' awards of the MC and MM), list of officers, idem SNCOs, Regtl nominal rolls (at November 1941, June 1944, May 1945, and 'miscellaneous').
* The Regt arrived in England in November 1941 and formed part of 3rd Cdn Inf Div. It comprised 44th Bty from Prince Albert, Saskatchewan, 62nd Bty from Duncan, BC, 78th Bty from Red Deer, Alberta, and 22nd Bty from Gleishen, Alberta. It took part in the D-Day landings and in many of the Normandy actions - at Amblie, Sequeville-en-Bessin, Bretteville, Carpiquet airfield, etc. Later it was involved in the reduction of the German garrisons at Calais and Boulogne, and fought in the winter campaign in Holland. Each chapter concludes with a list of officers and ORs, stating what they did during the period under review. This is an interesting history, with many footnotes throughout. The standard of compilation and presentation is so good that it suggests a work started in Holland but then completed after the author had returned to Canada. R/4 V/4. NYPL/MODL. JRD/AMM.

THE HISTORY OF THE 14 FIELD REGIMENT, ROYAL CANADIAN ARTILLERY, 1940-1945
Lieut G E M Ruffee and Lance Bombardier J B Dickie * Wereldbiblioteek NV, Amsterdam, September 1945. Illustrated soft card, 'Field gun in action' motif, full colour, 8.0 x 5.25, -/61. No ills, no maps, no Index. Apps: Roll of Honour (with separate lists for KIA and WIA), H&A, list of officers, notes on the Regtl song, list of poems by D W Bangs.
* The Regt comprised 34th Bty from Belleville, Ontario, 66th Bty from Montreal, and 81st Bty from Shawinigan Falls, QP. While still under training at Petawawa, all of the guns and vehicles of 66th Bty were lost in a fire of unknown origin. After this inauspicious start to its war, the Regt moved in July 1941 to England. As part of 3rd Cdn Div, it landed in Normandy on D-Day and served in several of the bridgehead battles before the breakout. Subsequent actions were the clearance of the Channel coast (Boulogne, Calais, Cap Gris Nez) and the advances into NW Europe (The Scheldt, Calcar, the Hochwald, Cleve, etc). The battle descriptions are excellent and individual members are mentioned throughout (hence an Index of Places and Persons would have been a good idea).R/3 V/3. NYPL/RMCL/MODL. JRD.

A BRIEF HISTORY OF MILITIA UNITS ESTABLISHED AT VARIOUS PERIODS AT YARMOUTH, NOVA SCOTIA
Lieut Col W D King OBE ED RCA * The Lawson Publishing Co, Yarmouth, NS, 1947. Soft card, cream, dark blue, red/blue diagonal stripe, 7.75 x 5.0, -/32. 4 mono phots, one line drawing, no maps, no appendixes, no Index.
* A brief muddled account, full of useful detail for the period 1812 to 1946. Most of the local Militia units were Artillery. This item is listed here because the 14th Field Regt formed at Petawawa included men drawn from Nova Scotia.
R/5 V/2. MODL. AMM.

FIFTEENTH CANADIAN FIELD REGIMENT, ROYAL CANADIAN ARTILLERY, 1941-1945
Capt R Spencer * Printed by Meizer's Boek-en Handelsdrukkeriz, for Elsvier, Wormerveer, Holland, 1945. Green, gold, RCA crest, 10.5 x 7.5, -/303. Fp, 72 mono phots, 10 cartoons and drawings, 15 maps (13 printed in the text, 2 bound in), no Index. Apps: Rolls of Honour (KIA and WIA, with dates, locations and causes, by Bty), H&A (by Bty), list of Regtl COs and Bty OCs (with dates), list of RSMs.
* The Regt was raised by Lieut Col P L Park in January 1941. The constituent Btys were 17th (Winnipeg), 95th (Calgary), and 110th (Broadview, Sask). The first RCA Regt to equip with 25-pounders, it arrived in England in August 1942. Landing in Normandy on 20 July 1944, the Regt saw almost non-stop action through to Wiefelstede (Germany) at war's end. One terrible task was that of removing 186 bodies from the Town Hall at Heusden, these being Dutch civilians murdered by the Germans. The comprehensive narrative is supported by extensive margin notes which explain the activities of each Bty on a day-by-day basis. Each incident resulting in the award of a medal is explained in detail. Although printed on mediocre paper, the book is a desirable collector's and researcher's item. R/5 V/4. UWOL/MODL. JRD.

HISTORY OF 17 CANADIAN FIELD REGIMENT, RCA
5th Canadian Armoured Division
Anon * J Niemeijer's Publishing Co, Groningen, Holland, 1946. Black, gold/red/blue, RCA crest, 8.5 x 5.5, -/108. 2 fps, 27 mono phots, 5 drawings, no maps, no Index. Apps: Roll of Honour (KIA, DOW and WIA), list of officers who served, idem WOs and BQMSs, idem OCTU candidates, notes on Battle Honours.
* Formed in February 1941, the Regt trained in Canada with 18 pdrs and 4.5 inch howitzers before re-equipping with 25 pdrs upon arrival in the UK in November. The following two years of training are well described. The Regt then moved to Italy and provided support for various Bdes of 4th Indian Div. The final move was to Holland, in March 1945, but meanwhile the Regt had seen much action at Orsogna and Campobasso, and on the Gustav, Hitler, and Gothic Lines. The last battles were 's-Hertogenbosch, Arnhem, Otterloo and Leeuwarden. This is a good quality production, printed on excellent paper (for that period). Several awards are mentioned in the narrative. R/4 V/4. NYPL/MODL. JRD.

19th CANADIAN ARMY FIELD REGIMENT, ROYAL CANADIAN ARTILLERY
Regimental History, September 1941 - July 1945

Anon (thought to have been Capt F K Brown) * Word Weavers, Vancouver, for the author, 1989. Blue, gold, 11.25 x 8.75, v/140. Fp, 17 mono phots, no maps, no Index. Apps: Roll of Honour (KIA, DOW, WIA and POW), H&A, list of COs, idem all officers serving 6.6.1944, idem all officers who served with RHQ and each Bty, summary of principal events, etc.

* The Regt was formed in September 1941 and it comprised 55th Field Bty (London, Ont), 63rd Field Bty (Guelph, Ont), and 99th Field Bty (Wingham, Ont). In 1942 it had the curious task of manning and operating an armoured train (equipped with 75 mm guns and a 36 inch searchlight) covering 275 miles of the British Columbia coastline against possible Japanese attack. A year later the Regt was trained to operate in the self-propelled artillery role. Arriving in England, it was equipped in October 1943 with the Priest - a 105 mm gun mounted on a tank chassis. With this formidable kit, the Regt landed on D-Day at St Aubin-sur-Mer in support of The North Shore (New Brunswick) Regiment. Subsequently it fought in the various Normandy battles and then right through to Germany as an element of 2nd Army Group RCA. The narrative is packed with names (all ranks), and the battle scenes are described in clear detail. This is a fitting tribute to a Regt which gained a reputation for using its SP guns in a highly mobile and aggressive style.
R/3 V/4. PC. JRD.

Note: the book described above is an updated version of a first edition printed for the Regt by Niederlansche Diepdruk Inrichting NV, Deventer, Holland, in late 1945. That original version had an illustrated front cover ('105 mm SP gun with flags and RCA crest' motif, multi-coloured, octavo, -/131) and had a print run of 1200 copies. The 1989 edition was produced for the Regtl Reunion with a limited print run of 40 copies. A copy of the 1945 edition is to be seen at the MOD Library, London.

THE HISTORY OF THE 23rd FIELD REGIMENT (SP), RCA
April 1942 to May 1945

Lieut Lawrence N Smith RCA * St Catherine's Standard, St Catherine's, Ontario, 1945. Soft card, sky blue, black/red, 'SP gun' motif, 10.75 x 8.0, -/81. 39 mono phots, no maps, no Index. Apps: Roll of Honour (KIA, WIA and POW), H&A, list of COs (1942-1945), locations (1944-1945), list of officers posted out to named units and soldiers sent to OCTU.

* The Regt (31st, 36th and 83rd Btys) was raised in May-July 1942. It landed in England in July 1943, then in France a year later. This is a workmanlike account, by the Regtl IO, of services performed throughout the NW Europe war and which ended at Oldenburg (at the time of the German capitulation). The Regt fought with field guns mounted on Ram tank chassis. Many individuals of all ranks are named in the narrative. R/4 V/3. MODL. AMM.

THE 23rd CANADIAN FIELD REGIMENT (S.P.), ROYAL CANADIAN ARTILLERY

Gnr Alex Morrison and Gnr A L Bronetto * Printed by J Scheen, Lochem, Holland, 1945. Stiff card covers with cloth spine, beige-blue boards and red spine, blue, 'S.P.' lettering on front cover, 12.75 x 9.75, -/72. 121 mono phots, 26 line drawings, one map (folding, bound in), no Index. Apps: Roll of Honour (25 names, with biographical notes for each, plus names of all WIA with dates and locations), H&A (with individual portrait photographs),list of Battle Honours.

* While Lieut Smith was producing his account in Canada (vide preceding entry), two Gunners of the Regt were busily assembling this essentially pictorial history in Holland. The two complement each other extremely well. Morrison and Bronetto give little detail of the Regt's fighting services but instead concentrate upon its personnel. Their book is an ideal source for family historians and medal collectors.
R/4 V/3. NYPL. JRD.

CINQUANTE-QUATRE
Being a Short History of the 54th Canadian Infantry Battalion
John Beswick Bailey * Publication details not shown, 1919. Stiff card, black, brown, 9.0 x 5.75, iii/108. 3 fps, 15 mono phots, no maps, no Index. Apps: H&A (with dates), unit nominal roll (with details of casualties, transfers, home addresses, etc), unit strength statistics, notes on captured trophies.
* Raised at Nelson, BC, in May 1915, the Bn moved to England six months later. Its first action was a raid in the area of Ypres. Thereafter it was constantly in and out of the front line and took part in dozens of now forgotten attacks, raids and skirmishes. The author describes them in interesting detail, but too often neglects to specify the locations or to specify the individuals involved. The book is useful mainly for its appendixes. They occupy half the page space. The French nick-name (as in the book's title) is not explained. The first recruits came mainly from the interior of British Columbia, where many of the loggers were French-speaking, and this may be the reason for it. After WWI, the Bn was perpetuated by The Kootney Regt, at that time a Militia Infantry unit. In 1936 it was redesignated as 24 (Kootney) Field Bty RCA, and it is for this reason that the book is listed here. The contents do not, of course, cover anything other than WWI services.
R/4 V/4. NYPL. JRD.

GUNNERS, WORLD WAR II
166th (Newfoundland) Field Regiment, Royal Artillery
Edward W Chafe * Creative Publishers, St John's, Newfoundland, 1987. Blue, gold, 9.0 x 11.0 (landscape), vii/162. Approx 350 mono phots (mainly individuals and groups identified in the captions), 2 maps (printed in the text), Index. Apps: Roll of Honour (with some details of dates and locations of graves), H&A, general unit muster roll (with service details), notes regarding the Regt's formation.
* The Regt gained the designation shown in the title of this book in July 1942. It was a British, not Canadian, Army unit, but it is listed here for the sake of clarification. The 166th was a wartime unit formed from British-born army (gunner) personnel and volunteers from Newfoundland. It fought in the Tunis campaign and then landed at Taranto in October 1943. Equipped with 25-pounders, it gave support to a wide variety of Canadian, British and Indian formations throughout the Italian campaign - notably at Paglieta Ridge, Cassino, Casalbordino, and Monte Catarelto. The final deployment, on the Gothic Line, was in February 1945. The Regt was then withdrawn from battle and officially disbanded a few months later at St John's. This is essentially a pictorial history, the great number of clearly captioned photographs and the appendixes representing a rich source of information for genealogists. R/1 V/4. PC. JRD.

HISTORY OF THE 3rd ANTI-TANK REGIMENT, RCA
October 1 1940 - May 8 1945
Anon * Jan de Lange, Deventer, Holland, 1945. The only copy seen is mutilated, hence details of original covers not known, -/47. No ills, one map (centre spread), no Index. Apps: Rolls of Honour (separate lists for officers and ORs - KIA, WIA), H&A, list of officers who served.
* 3rd A/T Regt was one of the earliest such units in the Canadian Army, being formed on 1 October 1940 from various Militia Btys in Eastern Canada. A year later it sailed for England where it remained until June 1944. Landing in Normandy on D-Day, 94th Bty lost most of its 'H' Troop when, on 7 June, it was overrun by a German counter-attack. Only 12 men survived unhurt. The Regt suffered further losses when, on 14 August, 105th Bty was bombed by the RAF. As part of 3rd Cdn Inf Div, the Regt subsequently took part in the clearance of the Channel ports, the advance into Belgium and Holland, the battle for the Reichswald Forest, and the river crossings into Germany. During most of the campaign, the Regt was equipped with towed 6-pounders and M10s. R/4 V/3. PC. JRD.
Note: reprinted in facsimile in 1955 by Kellaway Printing, Calgary.

THE HISTORY OF THE 5th CANADIAN ANTI-TANK REGIMENT
10 September 1941 - 10 June 1945
Maj J M Savage, Capt J P Claxton and RSM W Cunningham * Printed by J H Scheen, Lochem, Holland, n.d. (1945). Seen rebound, 8.0 x 5.25, xxxi/83. Fp, 42 mono phots (some of named officers), 6 line drawings, no maps, no Index. Apps: Roll of Honour (KIA, DOW and WIA, with dates), H&A, list of officers who served.
* The Regt first assembled at Camp Sussex, New Brunswick, in February 1942. The constituent elements were 3rd, 65th (see following entry) and 96th A/T Btys. They arrived in England four months later and remained there until 23 July 1944 when they went ashore at Gray-sur-Mer. Thereafter, the Regt was almost continuously in action around Caen, in the Falaise battle, the race for Holland, and the bitter winter stalemate on the Maas River. At war's end it was concentrated at Rostrup. The authors provide interesting coverage of its time in England and on the Continent, some officers receiving a mention in the text. R/5 V/4. DND. JRD.

THE HISTORY OF THE 65th CANADIAN ANTI-TANK BATTERY, RCA
9 September 1941 - 20 September 1945
Anon * J H Scheen, Lochem, Holland, n.d. (1945). Seen as rebound photo-copy with 'Vehicles and guns in convoy' motif on front cover, 8.5 x 5.5, xxviii/36. Fp, 28 mono phots, 5 line drawings, no maps, no Index. Apps: Roll of Honour (KIA and WIA), H&A, list of COs, Bty muster roll (May 1942 to May 1945).
* Recruited originally as 65th Field Bty at Grenfell, Saskatchewan, it mobilised in September 1941. It was then redesignated as an anti-tank unit and joined 5th Cdn A/T Regt at Camp Sussex (vide preceding entry). During the Regt's two years of training in Canada, it received the new 17-pounder gun, probably the best such weapon to be developed by the Allies during the war. The Bty's adventures in NW Europe are much the same of those of most other Canadian gunner units, although it did for a while operate as an infantry unit. The story was seemingly written by several officers of the Bty. The result is readable and informative. The illustrations are mainly contemporary snapshots and are evocative of the period.
R/5 V/4. MODL. AMM.

HISTORY OF THE SIXTH ANTI-TANK REGIMENT
G T Heintzman, W A Hand and E H Heeney * W A Swope, West Vancouver, BC, 1989. Blue, gold, 9.5 x 6.0, -/39. Fp, 57 mono phots, 3 maps (one printed in the text, 2 on the end-papers), Glossary, no Index. Apps: Roll of Honour, H&A.
* This brief history is mainly a basic record of fact - dates, locations and movements. There are few references to individual members of the Regt, although a large number are identified in the picture captions. The narrative covers the period from the unit's arrival in the UK on 31 August 1943 through to its landing in France on 9 July 1944 and then its subsequent services as part of 2nd Cdn Corps. Although very condensed, the battle descriptions are good. The Regt comprised 33rd, 56th, 74th and 103rd A/T Btys. R/2 V/3. MODL. JRD.
Note: the edition reported above is a facsimile reprint of the original (and much rarer) edition published in Toronto in 1946.

A HISTORY OF THE 7th ANTI-TANK REGIMENT, RCA
Anon * Publication details not shown, n.d. (possibly Holland, 1945). Soft card, red, black, 8.5 x 6.75, -/22. No ills, no maps, no appendixes, no Index.
* A very incomplete booklet, produced as a memento for the officers who served (ORs are not mentioned). The Regt was formed in England on 25 July 1941, based upon 104th Bty from Fredericton, NB. It was joined by 111th and 113th Btys, each of which were made up from men drawn from various Field Btys. The Regt served in Italy from December 1943 until the exodus of Spring 1945 when it joined the 1st Cdn Corps in Holland. As far as it goes, the narrative is interesting.
R/3 V/1. PC. JRD.

A HISTORY OF 2 CANADIAN HEAVY ANTI-AIRCRAFT REGIMENT, 1939-1945
Maj J E Wilson, Maj D N Byers, Cape F E E Darling, and BQMS J S Phelps * Produced in Soesterberg, Holland (printer not named), August 1945. Illustrated soft card, 'HAA gun and crew' motif, beige, 9.5 x 6.25, i/59. No mono phots, 48 line drawings, no maps, no appendixes, no Index.
* This brief record covers the Regt's arrival in the UK on 19 August 1941, its landing in France on 19 June 1944, and its subsequent services in NW Europe as a mobile unit of 2nd Army Group RCA. The component Btys were 1st, 8th and 11th HAA Btys. Action incidents are well described, and many individuals are named in the text. R/4 V/2. NYPL. JRD.

HISTORY OF 1st CDN LAA REGIMENT RCA (LANARK & RENFREW SCOTTISH REGT) From 10 March 1941 to 29 June 1945
Anon * Produced by the Regt, no other details shown, n.d. (c.1945). Facsimile quarto TS, stapled, -/28. No ills, no maps, no Index. Apps: Roll of Honour (with dates and locations), list of officers, etc.
* The Regt landed in England in late 1939 and early 1940 and was issued with 25-pounder field guns. The advent of the Blitz revealed an urgent need for more anti -aircraft units. The Regt's 25-pounders were replaced by Bofors guns and it was redesignated 1st Cdn LAA Rgt. In 1942 its guns brought down two German raiders over England's south coast. It then moved to Sicily, giving A/A cover at Messina. After further service on the mainland at Frosinone, it was withdrawn and retrained in the infantry role with a new title - 89/109th Cdn Inf Regt (The Lanark & Renfrew Scottish). Six weeks later it moved to the front, on the Conca River. After further battles at Foglia, Misano, Godo and San Pancrazio, it moved to Belgium and was re-converted to the LAA role. At war's end the Regt was at Ede, in Holland, where it was disbanded. A very inadequate record of a fine fighting unit.
R/5 V/1. PC. JRD.

THE HISTORY OF THE THIRD CANADIAN LIGHT ANTI-AIRCRAFT REGIMENT From 17 August 1940 to 7 May 1945, World War II
Anon (Lieut Col G G K Peake DSO RCA) * Kellaway Printing Ltd, Calgary, n.d. (1946). Yellow with maroon spine, red, Regtl crest, 8.5 x 5.5, ii/57. No ills, one map, no Index. Apps: Roll of Honour (KIA and WIA), H&A, list of COs (1941-1945), list of personnel selected for OCTU.
* A straightforward factual account written by one of the COs (1944-1945). Raised in Western Canada in August 1940, the Regt arrived in England in early 1941 and comprised 15(38)th, 16th, 17th and 53rd LAA Btys. A large detachment of the Regt, less its guns, had a supporting role in the Dieppe Raid. In 1943, 53rd Bty was transferred out. The original constituent Btys, equipped with 40 mm Bofors, landed in Normandy on 6 July 1944 and then served though to the Reichswald and to Wardenburg, in Germany. R/4 V/4. MODL. AMM.

HISTORY OF THE 4th CANADIAN LIGHT ANTI-AIRCRAFT REGIMENT From 18 February 1941 to 8 May 1945
Anon * Publication details not shown, n.d. Facsimile quarto TS, stapled, -/97. 3 mono phots, no maps, no Index. Apps: Roll of Honour (all causes, with locations and dates), H&A, lists of COs and other officers, details of enemy aircraft destroyed, diary of movements.
* Despite the 'economy' standards of production and the numerous spelling errors, this is a valuable record. It covers the usual background details (raised December 1940, moved to England August 1941, pre-invasion training in the UK, etc), but then launches into an absorbing account of the Regt's services following its D-Day landings. The Regt was equipped with towed 40 mm Bofors and was heavily involved in defending the Normandy bridgehead. In the first two months in France, it was credited with sixty-one 'kills', a record for any such Allied anti-aircraft unit in the European theatre of operations. Later, as the Luftwaffe became less active, the Regt's guns were often used - with spectacular results - in the ground attack

role. Few members are mentioned in the narrative, but the appendixes are excellent and certainly helpful to genealogists and medal collectors. For the military historian, this item provides a perspective on the Normandy campaign which may not be evident in more generalised accounts. R/5 V/4. PC. JRD.

5 CANADIAN LIGHT ANTI-AIRCRAFT REGIMENT
Regimental History, 1 May 1941 - 8 May 1945
Capt A Noblston * De Waal, Groningen, Holland, October 1945. Illustrated soft card, 'Soldier and aeroplane' motif, beige/red/blue, black, 9.25 x 6.25, -/64. No ills, no maps, no Index. Apps: Roll of Honour (KIA, DOW, DOD and WIA), H&A, lists of sports team members.
* The Regt was formed in March 1941 at Camp Petawawa, Ontario. Its Btys were the 41st (Simcoe and Dundas, Ont), the 47th (Cobourg, Ont), and the 88th (Dartmouth, NS). It sailed in November and was deployed in the anti-aircraft defence of South East England. It then served in Italy from 1943 to early 1945 when it moved to the Dutch-German border. Luftwaffe activity had by then sunk to such a low level that the Regt lost its guns and converted to the infantry role. It was deployed as such in the fighting around Nijmegen and on the Waal. Although brief, the narrative gives a good account of all these operations, with many individuals mentioned by name. R/4 V/3. UWOL. JRD.

REGIMENTAL HISTORY OF THE 6th CANADIAN L.A.A. REGIMENT
Anon * D W Falconer, Victoria, BC, 1978. Soft card, spiral bound, blue, black, RCA crest, 11.0 x 8.5, -/35. No ills, no maps, no Index. Apps: list of officers who first embarked with the Regt, and of those serving at disbandment.
* For such a slim publication, it contains a surprising amount of information. The component Btys were the 1st, 30th and 112th. They arrived in England in 1942 after some training and local defence duties in Canada and Alaska. It landed in Normandy in July 1944, was badly bombed by both the Luftwaffe and the RAF, and shot down many enemy aircraft (including, during the closing stages of the war, five of the new jet-propelled Me262s). The author's claim that his Regt destroyed more aircraft than any other conflicts directly with the same claim made by the 4th Cdn LAA Regt, but that is a matter for historians, not bibliographers. The operational content of the booklet is limited, but it contains some good biographical notes in respect of various officers. R/1 V/3. PC. JRD.
Note: the version recorded above is a facsimile reprint of a first edition, printed probably in Holland in 1945. The latter is, of course, a rarity.

THE HISTORY OF THE 8th CANADIAN LIGHT ANTI-AIRCRAFT REGIMENT, RCA
Capt W S Russell * NV Drukkerij Onnes, Amersfoort, Holland, 1945. Red, gold, RCA crest, 9.25 x 6.0, -/124. Fp, 15 mono phots, 27 line drawings, 2 maps (one printed in the text, one folding, bound in at the rear), no Index. Apps: Rolls of Honour (KIA, DOW, WIA and POW, with dates), H&A, lists of officers (at various dates, with details of their appointments).
* Mobilised in 1940 from Militia Artillery units in Quebec Province and Nova Scotia, the Regt was several times re-structured before moving to England in 1942. It was equipped with the 40 mm Bofors gun and trained in both the anti-aircraft and anti -tank roles. On 7 July 1944, shortly before embarking for Normandy, it became the only Canadian unit to shoot down a V1 weapon. In Normandy it was twice bombed by 'friendly' aircraft of the USAAF and the RAF, suffering casualties on both occasions. As part of 4th Cdn Armd Div, the Regt served in Holland and was on several occasions deployed in support of infantry units for anti-tank and assault tasks. The descriptions of its time in England and on the Continent are excellent, although few personnel are named. The book is exceptional for the quality of its paper and binding, and the professional arrangement of the contents. Other unit histories produced in Holland at that time were usually of a lower standard (a fact which simply reflects the lack of printing materials at the end of the war). R/4 V/4. NYPL. JRD.

THE STORY OF THE 69th LIGHT ANTI-AIRCRAFT BATTERY, RCA

BSM T G Rimmer and Gnr H C Boyle * T H Best Printing Co Ltd, Toronto, n.d. (c.1947). Black, gold, RCA crest, 9.25 x 6.25, xi/179. Fp, 8 mono phots, 12 line drawings, 2 maps (printed on the end-papers), no Index. Apps: Roll of Honour (KIA and WIA), H&A, unit nominal roll (with home addresses), Bty chronicle of movements (10.1.1941 to 25.8.1945).

* The Bty, raised in 1941 at Brantford, near Toronto, was an element of the 4th Cdn LAA Regt (noted elsewhere, vide Index). It sailed from Halifax, NS, in August 1941 and spent the next three years in England. Its first success was the destruction of a Ju88 in 1942. Landing in France on D+7, it went on to serve in NW Europe to war's end. A highlight was the day when it shot down five German aircraft in quick succession around Carpiquet airfield, near Caen. All of this is told in clear and interesting detail. Few individuals are named in the text, but the unit nominal roll is quite detailed. R/4 V/3. NYPL. JRD.

1st CANADIAN SURVEY REGIMENT AND 2nd CANADIAN SURVEY REGIMENT, ROYAL CANADIAN ARTILLERY

Italy, North West Europe, 1940–1945

Bill Manning and Walt Boddy * Privately, by W J Manning, Kelowna, BC, 1987. Illustrated soft card, taped spine and plastic casing, 11.0 x 8.5, -/208 (plus 4 blank). Fp, 26 mono phots, one cartoon, no maps, no appendixes, no Index.

* A compendium of memoirs written by fifty-seven different former members and recording their reminiscences of service in Canada and Europe. The material has plenty of references to individual former members of the two Regts, but there is little in the way of operational data and the lack of appendixes or an Index are a weakness in what might have been a useful source. R/3 V/2. NLC. JRD.

Note: reference may be made to THE STORY OF 1st CANADIAN SURVEY REGIMENT, RCA, 1939-1945, by Capt T M Gavin (printed in Holland, 1945). No copy of this item has been traced, but presumably it deals more with the day-to-day work of a Survey Regt than the book described above.

ENGINEERS

In 1904, the 'Royal' prefix was granted by King Edward VII to all Engineer units in Canada. In 1914, under the Hughes edict, the new wartime units were not permitted to incorporate this distinction in their designations. Those which went overseas with the CEF were designated Canadian Engineers (CE). Units which remained at home, and which did not form part of the CEF, continued to enjoy the 'Royal' distinction throughout the war. The titles of the books listed on the following pages reflect these changes in style.

THE HISTORY OF THE CORPS OF ROYAL CANADIAN ENGINEERS
Col A J Kerry OBE and Maj W A McDill * Printed by Thorn Press, Toronto, for the Military Engineers Association of Canada, Ottawa. Two matching volumes, blue, gold, Corps crest.
Volume I : 1749–1939. Published in 1962, xx/389. Fp, 41 mono, 8 maps.
Volume II : 1936–1946. Published in 1966, xix/713. Fp, 102 mono phots, 12 maps.
The maps are in part printed on the end-papers, in part bound in. Each Volume has its own Glossary, Index and Appendixes for H&A (statistical summaries only), lists of some former officers, Orders of Battle, and lists of major actions.
* The authors succeeded in condensing a mass of detailed information, supported by extensive chapter notes, into a readily digestible narrative. There is much here to interest both the general reader and the specialist researcher (for whom the Indexes are a vital aid). The maps, drawn by Cpl H Heinrichs, are exceptionally clear and attractive. R/3 V/5. PCAL/MODL. JEB/RH.

WORLD WAR I

4th CANADIAN DIVISION SIGNAL COMPANY, CANADIAN ENGINEERS
With the 4th Canadian Divisional Signal Co, CE
Anon * No publication details shown, n.d. Stiff card, felt, brown, gold, CE crest, 9.0 x 6.5, -/111. Fp, 17 mono phots, one map (bound in), no Index. Apps: Roll of Honour (names only), unit nominal roll (incl details of KIA, WIA, awards, all arranged by Section).
* Men of the Coy were attached to various Artillery and Infantry Bdes in France and Flanders. This account of their work is fairly well presented, but the unit nominal roll is particularly useful to genealogists and medal collectors.
R/5 V/3. PC. JRD.

FROM THE RIDEAU TO THE RHINE
The 6th Field Company and Battalion, Canadian Engineers, in the Great War
Maj K Weatherbe MC * The Hunter-Rose Co Ltd, Toronto, 1928. Blue, gold, CE crest, 7.25 x 6.5, xiv/519. Fp, 135 mono phots, 10 sketches, 27 maps (bound in), no Index. Apps: Roll of Honour, H&A, nominal roll.
* A very complete history of the unit, written by one of its officers. It is based partly upon his own experiences and partly upon the War Diary. Many of the photographs are individual members of the unit, and the nominal roll is a prime source for genealogists. Many of the maps are reproductions of official trench maps. R/3 V/4. NYPL/UWOL/MODL. MCJ.

WITH THE TENTH FIELD COMPANY, CANADIAN ENGINEERS, CEF
Harold S Turner * A set of three booklets produced in Goderich, Ontario, noted in a catalogue as 'quarto, with illustrations'.
Vimy Pilgrimage, published in 1936
Nominal Roll, published in 1937
25th Anniversary, published in 1941
Not seen, but reported to be concerned mainly with survivors, cemeteries and monuments. No other details known, but certainly rare. NYPL. RP.

THE STORY OF THE 11th BATTALION, CANADIAN ENGINEERS
From March 26th 1918 to November 11th 1918
Anon * Gale & Polden Ltd, Aldershot, n.d. (c.1919). Stiff card, grey, dark blue, CE crest, 7.0 x 4.75, -/28. No ills, no maps, no appendixes, no Index.
* A brief anecdotal account which quotes the names of some officers and men but which is otherwise too generalised to be useful. The unit was raised in March 1918 and served on the Western Front during the last five months of the war.
R/4 V/1. MODL. AMM.

WORLD WAR II

GREEN ROUTE UP
Royal Canadian Engineers - 4 Canadian Armoured Division - Second World War
Lieut M O Rollefson * Mouton et Cy, The Hague, Holland, 1945. Pea green, black, RCE crest in gold, 11.5 x 8.75, -/119. Fp, 61 mono phots, 7 cld ills, 46 line drawings, 7 maps (bound in), no Index. Apps: Roll of Honour (KIA and WIA), H&A.
* This is the story of 4th Cdn Armd Div Engineers - 6th Field Park Sqn and 8th and 9th Field Sqns. They were mobilised in Toronto and Western Canada in May and June 1941, reached England in June 1942, and landed in France in July 1944. They built bridges, floated rafts, and lifted mines across France, Belgium, Holland and Germany until they reached Wilhelmshaven in May 1945. Only sappers could achieve a book with illustrations of this quality. The maps are excellent, the paintings of bridges superb, the photographs well selected, and the forty-six sketches of named 'characters' outstanding. R/4 V/4. MODL. AMM.

THE STORY OF 2nd BATTALION, RCE, 1940-1945
The Story of 2nd Bn, Royal Canadian Engineers
Anon (thought to have been Maj S Slater and Capt A W Lees) * Publication details not shown, Zwolle, Holland, 1945. Black, red/gold, RCE crest, 11.25 x 8.0, -/89 (not numbered, 9 blank). Fp, 137 mono phots, no maps, no Index. Apps: H&A, chronicle of movements (5.9.1940 to 19.6.1945, shown for Bn HQ and for each Coy), four pages of music.
* Written as a memento for those who served. The authors commence with a brief account of military engineering in Canada from the earliest days. They then cover the formation of the Bn in 1940 at Camp Borden, Ontario, and the move to England a few months later. The next four years of living and training in the UK are interestingly described, though with little mention of individuals. The Bn landed in France in July 1944 and was employed on repairing the much-contested Carpiquet airfield, near Caen. It performed similar repair duties at other locations as the Allies moved north into Belgium, Holland and Germany. The book is useful as a record of sapper tasks behind the main battle lines. R/4 V/3. RMCL. JRD.

HISTORY OF THE SIXTH CANADIAN FIELD COMPANY, ROYAL CANADIAN ENGINEERS 1939-1945
CQMS S A Flatt ('And a Committee') * Wrigley Printing Co Ltd, Vancouver, BC, n.d. 20 pages of small snapshot photographs and portraits, 17 line drawings (chapter heads), 4 maps, no Index. Apps: Roll of Honour (KIA and WIA), H&A, list of COs.
* Originally formed in May 1912, the Coy was enlarged as a training and draft-finding unit in WWI. Between the wars it was a Militia unit. This readable account paints that background and then covers the Coy's mobilisation in September 1939, its early work-up training in Canada, the move to England, further specialist training, and the D-Day assault. The story moves on to the siege of Calais, the Scheldt clearances, Nijmegen, the Rhine crossings, and the race across Germany. Evidently based upon Part I and Part II Orders, the narrative includes many names and much good detail. R/4 V/4. RCSL/MODL. PJE/AMM.

THE TWENTY-THIRD STORY
The Story of the Twenty-Third Field Company, Royal Canadian Engineers 1939-1945
Anon (thought to have been Lieut Col M L Tucker) * London Print & Lithograph Company, London, Ontario, 1947. Royal blue, red, Unit crest, 9.5 x 6.5, iii/86. 26 mono phots, no maps, no Index. Apps: Roll of Honour (with locations of burials).
* Written in diary form, the story covers the period from July 1943 (departure from Canada) to September 1945 (disbandment in England). The Coy landed in Normandy on 10 July 1944 and subsequently served with the Canadian Corps through Holland to the Ems Canal at war's end. One unusual episode was the period of eight months when an Intelligence Section was attached to the Company. It controlled secret agents operating behind enemy lines. Another unusual episode was the evacuation of survivors from the Arnhem landings while operating in conjunction with 204th Field Coy of the Royal Engineers.
R/4 V/3. MODL. AMM/JRD/RH.

REGIMENTAL HISTORY
85 Bridge Coy (June 1941 - May 1945)
Anon * J J de Erven Tijl Ltd, Holland, 1945. Soft card, blue, black, Unit crest, 8.75 x 6.0, xi/82. One cld ill (Divsl flashes), no maps, no Index. Apps: Roll of Honour (KIA and WIA), notes on Battle Honours.
* This wartime unit - originally designated No 1 Cdn Bridge Coy - was raised in June 1941 in the Montreal district. Its personnel were all specialists, drawn from a number of RCASC and other RCE units. It landed in Normandy in July 1944 after training in England. It served throughout the NW Europe campaign under the command of various British, Canadian and Polish Divisions. The text consists of short narrative chapters for each Platoon, written by the men, not the officers. The result is a frank commentary on army life which puts some of the more formal histories into perspective and which gives the book a 'family' flavour.
R/4 V/3. NYPL/CWM. RBM/MAR/RH.

LINE CLEAR FOR UP TRAINS
A History of No 1 Canadian Railway Operating Group, RCE, 1943-1945
Allin John Mandar * Museum Restoration Service, Bloomfield, Ontario, 1991. Blue, gold, 8.75 x 5.5, -/112. Fp, 39 mono phots, 7 maps (3 printed in the text, 2 bound in, 2 printed on the end-papers), Glossary, no Index. Apps: notes on gift parcels.
* The Group was authorised in March 1943 as part of the plan for the invasion of North West Europe. It was evident that there would be a need for personnel able to reactivate and operate the rail system in France and Belgium in support of the combat formations. The Allies agreed that the Canadians were the best qualified for this task (thus following the precedent set in WWI). The book tells the story of No 1 Group which incorporated telegraph, repair, operating, and maintenance sub-units. A well written account of a vital behind-the-scenes element in the war, but with few individuals mentioned by name. R/1 V/3. PC. JRD.

RAILWAY CONSTRUCTION CORPS

THE WAR AND THE 7th C.R.T.
Anon * Publication details not shown, 1920. Stiff card, brown, black, unit crest, 9.0 x 6.0, -/67. Fp, 2 plates on mono phots (14 in total), no maps, no Index. Apps: unit nominal roll (with details of casualties, H&A, home addresses, for all ranks), H&A (statistical summary only).
* The need to increase transport capacity behind the Western Front led, in 1916, to the call for more railway construction units. The 257th Cdn Railway Construction Bn CEF commenced recruitment in Ontario, Quebec and New Brunswick in January 1917. It arrived in England in February, was retitled 7th Bn, Cdn Railway Troops, and landed in France in April. Based upon the War Diary, the narrative gives a compact but clear account of rail, bridge, and trench construction behind the main battle lines. A typical unit history, intended mainly for those who served, it contains many references to individual officers and to locations, awards, casualties, etc. Although there is no H&A appendix as such, Chapter IV is devoted entirely to promotions and decorations for the year 1917. The Bn returned to Canada for disbandment in 1919. R/5 V/3. BCPL. RBM.
Note: although it was published anonymously, it is evident from the contents that the compiler and editor was Capt the Rev J R O'Gorman. The book is 'dedicated to the officers and men ...' by the Bn Co, Lieut Col L T Martin, and he is wrongly recorded in some library catalogues as having been the author.

FRANCE AND FLANDERS
Four Years Experience, Told in Poem and Story
Sapper W Brindle * S K Smith, St John, New Brunswick, 1919. Green, black, Corps crest, 8.75 x 5.5, -/84. 2 fps, 6 mono phots (incl named groups), no maps, no appendixes, no Index.
* Despite its very vague title, this little book is an interesting account of the work of a unit of the Canadian Railway Construction Corps. Although not clearly specified, it seems to have been the 12th Bn, Cdn Railway Troops, CEF. The author describes the building of military railways leading into the Ypres Salient in 1916, the construction of bridges across the Yser, a line through Barincourt in 1917, and other tracks and marshalling yards to serve the forward positions. For much of the time, his unit was under aerial and artillery bombardment. His book reveals an aspect of the huge logistical effort needed to supply food, fuel, stores, and ammunition to the combat troops on a daily basis and in preparation for the various major offensives. R/5 V/3. PC. JRD.

THE 127th BATTALION, CEF, 2nd BATTALION RAILWAY TROOPS
Lieut Col H M Jackson MBE ED * Industrial Shops for the Deaf, Montreal, n.d. (probably 1950s). Green, black, 6.5 x 4.0, -/186. 4 fps (portraits of COs), no other ills, no maps, no Index. Apps: Roll of Honour (KIA, DOW, DOD, WIA and MIA, all by year), H&A (with six representative citations), list of officers who embarked (21.8.1916), officers' duties (by named individuals), list of attached units.
* In November 1915, the York Rangers were granted permission to raise a complete Bn for service with the CEF. Despite having already supplied twice their pre-war establishment as drafts for other CEF Bns, the Regt found 1100 all ranks from York County, Southern Ontario. As 127th Cdn Inf Bn, they reached England in August 1916. Many of the officers and ORs had worked in the engineering and railway industries so, when the Railway Construction Corps was formed, the Bn was assigned to it as 2nd Bn, Cdn Railway Troops. This book is an excellent account of its work, usually under shell-fire, constructing light railway tracks at Bapaume, Messines, Ypres, Arras, etc. In April 1918, it was thrown into the line to fight as infantry. Some officers are mentioned in the text, and the appendixes are most detailed, but the main interest of the book is the coverage of combat engineering. R/4 V/4. MODL. JRD/AMM.
Note: the Bn is perpetuated by the Queen's York Rangers. For details of Canadian railway operating units in WWII, note A J Mandar's book on page 133.

SIGNALS

HISTORY OF THE ROYAL CANADIAN CORPS OF SIGNALS, 1903–1961
John S Moir * Published by the Committee of the Corps, Ottawa, 1962. Blue, gold, Corps crest, 10.0 x 6.5, -/366. Fp, 21 mono phots, 15 maps (10 printed in the text, 2 cld, folding, bound in, 2 printed in the end-papers), Glossary, Index. Apps: Roll of Honour (all ranks, WWII and Korea), H&A (WWII and Korea), list of former senior officers.
* A superb Corps history which covers the early days, WWI service on the Western Front, developments during the inter-war years, and the work of the Corps during WWII. The latter involves some excellent descriptions of operations during the Dieppe raid, in Sicily and on the Italian mainland, and the Normandy landings through to the end of the war. The book concludes with the work of the Corps during the war in Korea. The narrative is readable and interesting for the non-specialist and is supported by very good illustrations and maps.
R/3 V/5. PCAL/MODL. RP.

1 CANADIAN SPECIAL WIRELESS GROUP, ROYAL CANADIAN CORPS OF SIGNALS
Souvenir Booklet, 1944–1945
Mel Howey * Static Press, Darwin, Australia, 1945. Seen as a bound photo-copy, 10.75 x 7.25, ii/32. 89 mono phots, one line drawing, no maps, no Index. Apps: unit muster roll.
* Apart from the heroic defence of Hong Kong in December 1941, Canada's armed forces were not involved in Allied WWII operations in the Western Pacific. This little publication is unique because it reveals the existence of a Canadian unit which otherwise might have passed unnoticed. It records the short history of a Special Wireless Group which was formed in Victoria, British Columbia, in June 1944. After travelling via San Francisco and Brisbane, it arrived in Darwin in April 1945. Presumably its task was to monitor Japanese radio communications during the remaining months of the war, but this is not specified in the narrative (most of which is taken up with sport and entertainment). The pictures are mainly 'tourist' snapshots. The true function of the unit was probably still subject to the constraints of censorship at the time the booklet was written. Further research might reveal a most unusual story. R/5 V/2. MODL. AMM.

INFANTRY

MEN IN KHAKI
Four Regiments of Manitoba
Roy St George Stubbs * The Ryerson Press, Toronto, 1941. Khaki, ochre, 8.0 x 5.5, viii/72. No ills, no maps, no appendixes, no Index.
* The book deals with four Regts - the Royal Winnipeg Rifles, the Winnipeg Grenadiers (MG), the Queen's Own Cameron Highlanders of Canada, and the Winnipeg Light Infantry (MG). The simple narrative is divided equally into four parts, with eighteen pages being devoted to each Regt and covering its history up to 1940. It is possible that this slim volume was written to boost public morale, or for the information of new recruits in the Winnipeg area. As 'potted histories', the four sections are a useful starting point for further study, and they include a surprising number of references to key events and to individuals.
R/4 V/2. RCSL. PJE.

Brigades

NOVA SCOTIA OVERSEAS HIGHLAND BRIGADE, CEF
A Short History and Photographic Record of the Nova Scotia Overseas Highland Brigade
Lieut Col A H Borden * The Mortimer Printing Co Ltd, Halifax, NS, n.d. (c.1916). Brown, red, 4 Regtl crests, 12.5 x 9.5, -/47. Very many mono phots, no maps, no appendixes, no Index.
* This is a photographic record of the officers and men who were at the time (c.1916) serving with the Nova Scotia Bde - 85th, 185th, 193rd, and 219th Cdn Inf Bns, CEF. It is a massive piece of wartime research and compilation. The author succeeded in obtaining a 'head and shoulders' photograph of a very large number of individuals, and each is captioned with their names, ranks, service numbers, unit, and home town. Every page is taken up with such pictures, and there is no narrative content. An excellent source for Nova Scotia genealogists, and for medal collectors. R/4 V/2. PC. JEB.

A SHORT HISTORY - THE TENTH CANADIAN INFANTRY BRIGADE
Maj R A Paterson * DeJong & Co, Hilversum, Holland, 1945. Soft card, green/gold/black, 5 Regtl crests, 9.5 x 6.25, -/78. No ills, 8 maps, no Index. Apps: various lists of officers serving with the Bde HQ and each constituent Regt at various dates between July 1944 and May 1945.
* A bare calendar of events in the story of 10th Cdn Inf Bde. It was formed in April 1943 and fought throughout the NW Europe campaign. Its component infantry elements were the Argyll & Sutherland Highlanders of Canada (Princess Louise's), the Algonquin Regt, and the Lincoln & Welland Regt. The Bde Support Group consisted of the 10th Independent MG Coy (New Brunswick Rangers), the 29th Cdn Armoured Recce Regt (South Alberta Regt), the 15th Cdn Field Regt RCA, the 3rd Cdn Anti-tank Regt RCA, 70th Cdn Light Anti-aircraft Bty RCA, 9th Cdn Field Sqn RCE (or elements thereof), plus the usual logistical sub-units. The Bde fought at Tilly, Fleury-sur-Orne, and Quesnoy, during the Normandy campaign. At St Lambert-sur-Dives, on 18 August 1944, Maj D V Currie of the South Alberta Regt formed a mixed force of tanks and infantry which, for 36 hours, prevented German columns from breaking out of the Falaise Pocket. He was awarded the VC. This and other actions are described in brisk detail, the narrative being based mainly upon the War Diaries. Apart from the appendixes, the book contains few references to individual officers and men. R/3 V/3. RMCL/NYPL. JRD/MAR.

The Canadian Guards

THE ORIGINS AND SERVICES OF THE PRINCE OF WALES' REGIMENT Including a Brief History of ...

Capt Ernest J Chambers * E L Ruddy, Montreal, 1897. Leather, plum, gold, 'Fleur de Lys and crest' motif, 12.0 x 8.5, v/94/xxii (the latter being commercial advertisements). Fp, 34 mono phots (incl officers and groups, captioned), 13 sketches (chapter heads), no maps, no Index. Apps: list of financial contributors to the cost of the Militia, list of officers (1854-1896).

* A book with a very long sub-title which explains the scope and purpose of its publication. The first 45 pages describe the Militia movement of the early French Canadian and British Canadian periods, the role of the Militia in the campaigns of 1812 and 1837, and the growth of the Montreal Volunteers. Then follow six chapters regarding the raising of the Prince of Wales' Regiment in 1860, its services in The Trent Affair, the Fenian Raids, and the Northwest Rebellion. The narrative is interspersed with quotations from officers' letters and official documents. The book follows the usual Chambers style, is beautifully produced, and is useful as a general reflection of the social history of the Montreal area. R/4 V/4. UWOL/NYPL/RCSL. PJE.

Royal Canadian Regiment

A STORY OF THE OXFORD RIFLES, 1798-1954

Herbert Milnes * Woodstock Print & Litho Ltd, Woodstock, Ontario, 1974. Soft card, stapled, green, white, 8.5 x 5.25, ii/28. Numerous ills (badges, swords, former COs), no maps, no Index. Apps: list of COs (1798-1954).

* Recruited from the Burford, Blenheim, and Oxford areas, the Regt fought in the War of 1812 as the 1st and 2nd Oxford Companies. The title changed to Oxford Rifles in 1863 and the unit served in the Fenian affair of 1866. It was mobilised as 168th Cdn Inf Bn CEF in 1915, but saw no active servive. It provided drafts (2500 men) for other units. The Rifles were not mobilised for active service in WWII, so most of its members enlisted in the Elgin Regt. The Oxfords lost their identity in 1954 when they were absorbed into the Royal Canadian Regt. This is a very condensed history, of limited research value other than as a genealogical source for this part of Southern Ontario. R/4 V/1. PC. JRD.

THE STORY OF THE SEVENTH REGIMENT, FUSILIERS OF LONDON, CANADA, 1899-1914

Col Francis B Ware DSO VD * Hunter Printing Co, London, Ontario, for the Regt, 1945. Red, black, Regtl crest, 9.0 x 6.5, xiii/190. Fp, 5 mono phots, no maps, no appendixes, no Index.

* Despite the dates given in its title, this book covers the evolution and services of the Regt from 1866 (Fenian Raid, as 7th Bn, Prince Arthur's Own) through to 1943 [occupation of Kiska, as The Canadian Fusiliers (City of London Regt)]. The main value of the work is its coverage of the Militia movement in Southern Ontario during the fifteen years preceding WWI, particularly from the social point of view. The narrative is packed with names, especially those of families resident in the area of London, so the book is very useful to local family historians. However, the author also gives some helpful information regarding the Fenian and Riel affairs, and the despatch of drafts to South Africa (as part of the various Contingents), and to France (as elements of 1st Cdn Inf Bn CEF). All of these events, at home and overseas, are presented in an easily consulted year-by-year sequence. The Regt underwent many changes of title until, in 1954, it became 3rd Bn, Royal Canadian Regt (London & Oxford Rifles), a Militia unit. R/4 V/4. UWOL/MODL. JRD.

THE ROYAL CANADIAN REGIMENT
1883–1933
R C Fetherstonhaugh * Gazette Printing Co Ltd, Montreal, for the Regt, 1936. Dark blue, gold, Regtl crest, 9.5 x 6.5, xi/467. Fp, 46 mono phots, 3 cld plates (the Colours, uniforms), 7 maps (bound in), Index. Apps: Roll of Honour (KIA in the 1885 Northwest Rebellion, KIA, DOW and WIA in the Anglo-Boer War, KIA and DOW for WWI, with dates), H&A (awards for WWI, plus LS&GC awards, 1904-1932), list of Commandants (1883-1919), idem COs (1896-1935), idem all officers who served (1883-1919, with details of ranks held, active services, awards, etc, for all their campaigns, incl the Yukon Field Force of 1893), notes on Battle Honours.
* A thoughtfully written history which covers a great deal of ground. In effect, it is Volume I of a pair (vide following entry). It opens with detailed accounts of the 1885 Rebellion and the less widely known Yukon Field Force. There is then equally good coverage of the Anglo-Boer War when the Regt took part in several significant operations including Doorn Kop, Zand River, Driefontein, Paardeberg, and Modder River. WWI opened pleasantly for the Regt, with a year as garrison force in Bermuda, but the Regt was then plunged (late 1915) into the Ypres Salient, the Somme, Vimy Ridge, Passchendaele, Amiens, Arras and Cambrai, as part of 7th Bde, 3rd Cdn Div. The Western Front period is described in very clear detail, with many individuals mentioned by name. The illustrations are very good, and fully captioned with the names of those depicted. Militaria collectors will find interest in a page devoted to badges and buttons as used at different periods. A very professionally presented history. R/4 V/5. UWOL/NYPL. JRD.
Note: this volume was reprinted for the Regt in 1981 by Centennial Press & Litho Ltd, of Fredericton, New Brunswick (blue, gold, Regtl crest, 9.5 x 6.25, with identical contents).

THE ROYAL CANADIAN REGIMENT
Volume II : 1933–1966
Lieut Col G R Stevens OBE * The London Printing & Lithographing Co Ltd, London, Ontario, 1967. Blue, gold, Regtl crest, 10.25 x 7.25, xii/420. Fp, 53 mono phots, one cld plate, 12 maps (10 bound in, two printed on the end-papers), 4 Indexes (General, Allied Units, Enemy Units, Canadian Units). Apps: Rolls of Honour (WWII and Korea), H&A (idem), lists of Colonels, Honorary Colonels, Honorary Lieut Cols, and former COs, with biographical notes.
* Another well written history, this one covering the Regt's services in Sicily, in mainland Italy, NW Europe, Korea, post-war Germany (NATO), and Cyprus (UNO). The illustrations are interesting and fully captioned. In WWII, the Regt served in the 1st Inf Bde, 1st Cdn Inf Div. Later it served in Korea and completed several tours of duty as part of the NATO forces based in Germany. Although some of the latter material is somewhat dry, it serves to illustrate Canada's post-war military strategy and places the Regt's story in the context of international events.
R/3 V/5. PC. JRD/RH.

ONE HUNDRED YEARS
The Royal Canadian Regiment, 1883–1983
Ken Ball and C P Stacey * Collier Macmillan (Canada), Ontario, 1983. Black, gold, 10.25 x 10.25, -/184. 169 mono phots, 15 cld plates, no maps, no appendixes, no index.
* Essentially a pictorial record, published to mark the Regt's centennial. The pictures are of a superb quality, but the historical reference value is mainly visual. R/1 V/3. PC. DBP-P.

55 AXIS
With the Royal Canadian Regiment, 1939–1945
Maj Strome Galloway ED * Provincial Publishing Co Ltd, Montreal, for the Regt, 1946. Illustrated covers, red/blue/grey/white, 'Route map of NW Europe' motif, 8.0 x 5.5, -/232. Fp, 21 mono phots, 2 maps (printed on the end-papers), no Index. Apps: Roll of Honour (KIA, DOW and DOD), list of COs (with biographical notes), itinerary of moves and locations (15.11.1939 to 1.10.1945).

* The title derives from the Regt's tactical number, 55. It was the first Canadian Army unit to arrive in England. It then served in Sicily and mainland Italy, taking part in the heavy fighting at Ortona, in the Liri Valley, on the Gothic Line, and in the Po Valley approach battles. Early in 1945, it moved to Holland for the final push into Germany as part of 1st Canadian Army. A clear narrative, with many individuals named. Much of this material is incorporated in Stevens' later 'Vol II' history (vide preceding page), but Galloway's account was written immediately after the German surrender and is arguably fresher and more vivid. Ideally, the two should be consulted in conjunction. R/3 V/3. NYPL/RMCL/MODL. JEB/RH.

A REGIMENT AT WAR
The Story of the Royal Canadian Regiment, 1939-1945
Col Strome Galloway ED CD * No publication details shown, 1979. Illustrated stiff card, cream, red, 8.0 x 5.5, -/238. Fp, 17 mono phots, one line drawing, no maps, no Index. Apps: Roll of Honour (deaths, all causes), list of COs (1939-1945, with biographical notes), unit itinerary.
* This is basically a reprint of 55 AXIS (vide preceding entry), but with the addition of a new Chapter XIII - 'The Kiska Connection'. This describes the work of The Canadian Fusiliers (City of London Regiment) on the island of Kiska, in the North Pacific, between July and November, 1943. The Canadian Fusiliers became the 3rd Bn, Royal Canadian Regt, in 1954. R/3 V/3. MODL. AMM.

SOME DIED AT ORTONA
The Royal Canadian Regiment in Action in Italy, 1943
Strome Galloway * Published by the Regt, no other details shown, n.d. (c.1983). Illustrated stiff card, cream, red, 'War graves' motif, 8.0 x 5.5, -/223. 37 mono phots, 2 line drawings (badges), no maps, Glossary, no appendixes, no Index.
* The narrative is based upon the diary of a Company Commander during his active service between 11 July and 31 December, 1943. It covers, therefore, the battle for Sicily and the first half of the campaign in mainland Italy. Sadly, his diary for 1944 was lost. The book is readable and informative. To balance the lack of formal appendixes, it contains several rolls of officers inserted in the narrative at various points, and there is also some mention of their awards. All but two of the illustrations are photographs of named individuals (all ranks).
R/2 V/4. MODL. AMM.

Princess Patricia's Canadian Light Infantry

PRINCESS PATRICIA'S CANADIAN LIGHT INFANTRY
Jeffery Williams * Compton Press Ltd, Salisbury, UK, for Leo Cooper, 1972. Blue, gold, 8.75 x 5.75, xii/110. Fp, 31 mono phots, no maps, no Index. Apps: outline of the Regt's services (1914-1972).
* Like most books in Leo Cooper's pleasantly produced 'Famous Regiments' series, this one is aimed at the 'popular' market - hence no Index and none of the usual personnel appendixes, and only 110 pages to cover a long and illustrious story. The Regt had a curious inception. A Captain of Militia, Andrew Hamilton Gault, was sufficiently wealthy for him to offer to pay, in 1914, for the raising of a new Regt to fight in the European War. In return, the Minister of War, Hughes, agreed that it should proceed overseas under its own title instead of a numerical designation as allocated to (almost all) other CEF units. Gault was granted permission to use the name of the daughter of the Duke of Connaught, Queen Victoria's third and favourite son, who was at that time Governor General of Canada. Recruitment came mainly from former soldiers of the British Army who had emigrated to Canada after the South African war of 1899-1902. At one stage, every Regt of the British Army (with one exception) was represented in the PPCLI's ranks. Very few of these men were to survive the Western Front. The author of this book fought with the Regt in WWII and Korea, so he has first-hand knowledge of his material, but the result is basically an 'outline' history. R/1 V/3. MODL. RP.

PRINCESS PATRICIA'S CANADIAN LIGHT INFANTRY, 1914-1919
Ralph Hodder-Williams * Printed by R R Clark Ltd, Edinburgh, for Hodder and Stoughton, London, 1923. A matching pair of volumes, red/brown, gold, 9.0 x 6.25.
Volume I : Fp, 6 mono phots, 11 maps, no Index, xix/411.
Volume II : no ills, no maps, Index (for both volumes), i/391. Apps: Roll of Honour, H&A, list of COs, list of officers, unit nominal roll (all ranks who served).
* An excellent unit history, presented in an unusual style. The narrative, with all the illustrations and maps, are contained in Volume I. The extensive appendixes are contained in Volume II. It is important, therefore, that any prospective purchaser of this work should acquire both volumes rather than one or the other. The author opens with an account of the remarkably short period in which the Regt was raised for war in 1914. He then provides a solid workmanlike description of its fighting services from St Eloi through to the final actions on the Canal du Nord, with sufficient references to individual officers and men to give the story a human dimension. R/4 V/5. ASKBC/UWOL/MODL. JRD/CB.

PRINCESS PATRICIA'S CANADIAN LIGHT INFANTRY, 1919-1957
Volume III
G R Stevens OBE * Southam Printing Co Ltd, Montreal, for the Regtl Historical Committee, 1958. Red, gold, 9.0 x 5.75, xvi/411. Fp, 32 mono phots, 11 maps (bound in, of excellent quality), no Index. Apps: list of former COs, with portraits and biographical notes for each.
* The Regt was stationed in England for three years before taking part in the invasions of Sicily and mainland Italy. In early 1945, it moved to Holland for the final battles of the war. Two PPCLI Battalions served in Korea. This is a long and very detailed narrative account by a skilled historian, but it lacks flair. Few individuals are mentioned by name, and the lack of appendixes, or an Index, is surprising in a work of this magnitude. R/3 V/3. AldMM/NYPL/MODL. RP.

ONCE A PATRICIA
Memoirs of a Junior Infantry Officer in World War II
Col C Sydney Frost CD * Vanwell Publishing Ltd, St Catherine's, Ontario, 1988. Light blue, gold, 9.25 x 6.0, -/564. 66 mono phots, 8 maps, Chapter Notes, Glossary, 2 Indexes (General, and Units). Apps: notes on Maj Gen C Vokes, idem HRH Princess Patricia of Connaught, idem the Regtl song.
* This is the personal story of a young PPCLI officer's experiences in Canada, England, Sicily, Italy, France, Belgium, Holland, and Germany. The period covered is June 1942 through to October 1945. It is mainly a racy and readable account of front-line action, with many officers being named in the text. The introductory chapters, and accounts of four post-war pilgrimages to the battlefields, are interesting but perhaps less relevant. The photographs, although mostly 'snapshots', include many identified members of the Regt and are quite good.
R/1 V/4. MODL. AMM.

PRINCESS PATRICIA'S CANADIAN LIGHT INFANTRY
Maj R B Mainprize CD * Publication details not shown, n.d. Maroon, gold, 9.5 x 6.25, iii/170. Fp, no other mono phots, one cld plate, Glossary, no Index. Apps: Roll of Honour, H&A, unit nominal roll.
* A useful narrative account, but the main value of this book is to be found in the roll of all PPCLI personnel who served in WWII. The book is therefore a most useful adjunct to Stevens' 'Volume III' as described above. R/4 V/4. MODL. JRT.

PRINCESS PATRICIA'S CANADIAN LIGHT INFANTRY
Regimental Manual
Anon * Regtl Executive Committee, Calgary, 1969. Soft card, grey, black, Regtl crest, 9.0 x 6.0, -/36. Fp, 30 mono phots, 8 line drawings (badges), 2 maps, no Index. Apps: list of COs (1914-1969).
* This is essentially an aide-memoir, designed to be given to all ranks. It covers briefly the traditions and music of the PPCLI (Regular) and the Loyal Edmonton Regt (3rd Bn, PPCLI, Militia). R/3 V/3. MODL. AMM.

Royal 22e Régiment

HISTOIRE DU ROYAL 22e REGIMENT
Charles-Marie Boissonnault and Lieut Col L Lamontagne CD * Editions du Pélican, Québec, pour la Régiment, 1964. Red, gold, Regtl crest, 9.0 x 5.75, -/414. 63 mono phots, 6 cld plates, one line drawing (cap badge), 16 maps (2 printed in the text, 14 bound in), no Index (but a detailed 'Contents' page at the rear of the book). Apps: H&A (all ranks, WWII), list of former COs (with a studio portrait of each).
* Written in French, the first language of this famous old Regt recruited from the French-speaking population of Quebec Province and based in The Citadel, Quebec City. The Regt is best known as 'the van doos'. The opening pages of this book deal with the early years, but most of the narrative is then devoted to services in Sicily, Italy, and Germany (1943-1945). R/3 V/4. PCAL. RP.
Note: 3000 copies printed, of which 100 were 'de luxe edition' copies, numbered.

LES ARCHIVES REGIMENTAIRES DES FUSILIERS DU SAINT LAURENT
Leopold Lamontagne * L'Imprimerie Blais, Rimouski, Ottawa, 1943. Illustrated soft card, grey, black, 'Map of the Gaspe Peninula' motif, 9.25 x 6.25, -/247. 35 mono phots, no maps, no Index. Apps: list of all Militia officers of Lower St Laurent from 1775 to 1942, list of the Staff of various School Corps in the area (1943).
* Written in French. A comprehensive survey of part-time soldiering in the St Laurent area over a long period of time, and doubtless of particular interest to French-Canadian genealogists. The Regt was raised in 1869. Post-WWI, it perpetuated the 189th Cdn Inf Bn CEF. In 1954, it was amalgamated with the Régiment de Montmagny to form the 5th (Militia) Bn of the Royal 22e Régiment.
R/3 V/3. RMCL/NYPL/MODL. JRD/AMM.

LE REGIMENT DE MONTMAGNY, DE 1869 A 1931
Lieut Joseph-A Lavoie * Ancien du Regt de Montmagny, n.d. (c.1932). Deep blue, gold, 10.0 x 7.0, v/xiii/117. Fps (three), 16 mono phots, no maps, Index. Apps: H&A (1869-1931), list of COs and other officers (1869-1931), notes on shooting cups and medals (1928-1931), list of campaign and long service awards presented to officers, verbatim report presented by the author to the officers of the Regt in 1929 - 'Conférence sur les Canadiens-francais comme Militaire au Canada'.
* Written in French. Not so much a history as a compilation of lists, the two longest naming all officers who served between 1869 and 1931, the other giving biographies (with photographic portraits) of all former COs. A mere six and half pages tell the story of the Regt's activities. Two group photographs show all officers serving in 1925 and 1930 (fully captioned). The Regt was amalgamated in 1954 with the Fusiliers du St Laurent to form the 5th Bn (Militia) of the Royal 22e Régiment. R/5 V/3. RCMI/CWM. AM/MAR.

LES BATAILLONS ET LE DEPOT DU ROYALE 22e REGIMENT
Vingt Ans D'Histoire, 1945-1965
Jacques Castonguay * Produced by the Regt, La Citadelle, Quebec, 1974. Red, gold, Regtl crest, 9.0 x 6.0, -/288. 58 mono phots (incl named groups), one line drawing, 7 maps, Bibliography, no Index. Apps: Roll of Honour (for Korea), H&A (for each Bn), list of officers (at 1965, by Bn), list of COs (1945-1946).
* Written in French. A comprehensive history for the period specificed in the subtitle. All six Regular and Militia Bns are covered, with good descriptions of their activities in Korea, Cyprus, and at the famous depot, La Citadelle.
R/2 V/4. PC. JRD.

HISTOIRE DU 22e BATAILLON CANADIEN-FRANCAIS
Tome I : 1914-1919
Col Joseph Chaballe * Les Editions Chanticler Ltée, Montreal, 1952. Black, gold, 8.0 x 5.25, -/412. Fp, no other ills, no maps, no appendixes, Index.
* Written in French. A purely narrative account, with many individuals mentioned. There is extensive coverage of the fighting in the Ypres Salient, and at St Eloi,

Zillebeke, and Mont Sorrell. The Regt was permitted to serve overseas with its pre-war number, as 22nd Cdn Inf Bn CEF, hence the title of this book.
R/3 V/3. MODL. AMM.
Note: a soft card cover edition, also imprinted 1952, has been noted. The covers are grey, red/black, with a 'Regtl crest and Vimy Ridge memorial' motif. The contents are identical. Despite the book's 'Tome I' sub-title, no later volumes have been traced. Consequently, researchers looking for information on the Regt's services in WWII should consult Boissonnault and Lamontagne (first entry on the preceding page), and, for Korea and the post-war years, that same book plus Castonguay (fourth entry on the preceding page).

L'EPOPEE DU VINGT-DEUXIEME
Claudius Corneloup DCM MM * La Presse, Montreal, 1919. Marbled boards, leather spine, gold (on spine only), 7.25 x 5.5, -/150. Fp, 14 mono phots, one map (bound in), no appendixes, no Index.
* Written in French (the title translating as 'The Epic of the Twenty-second'), this is a personal memoir. The author, who had previously served with the French Foreign Legion, was the Regimental Sergeant Major during the 22nd's time on the Western Front. Written as a paean to the dead, the narrative gives prominence to various individual acts of bravery, to French-Canadian unity, and to the soldiers' disenchantment with British military leadership. Pages 18-20 carry a list of the 34 officers of the Regt at the time of its arrival in France in September 1915, with a note of what happened to each. The photographs are mainly of officers who died. A moving book, helpful for an understanding of French-Canadian attitudes to the war. R/4 V/3. CRLC/CWM. RBM/MAR.
Note: the casing described above may be a 'de luxe' presentation edition. Another version, having a commercial binding (light brown, black) has been reported.

Queen's Own Rifles of Canada

ILLUSTRATED HISTORICAL ALBUM OF THE 2nd BATTALION, THE QUEEN'S OWN RIFLES OF CANADA, 1856-1894
Capt E F Gunther and H Bruce Brough * The Toronto News Co, Toronto, for the Regt, 1894. Rifle green, gold, Regtl crest, 8.0 x 5.75, -/80. 114 mono phots, one line drawing, no maps, no Index. Apps: Roll of Honour, unit nominal roll (listed HQ and Coys, 1894).
* Formed in Toronto from six local Militia Rifle Companies, the Regt was mobilised for service against the Fenians in 1866. This slim volume contains 16 pages of historical narrative (written by Gunther) and 12 pages of nominal rolls (compiled by Brough). The numerous photographs are mainly studio portraits of individual officers and SNCOs, all of whom are identified. An evocative record of the period.
R/5 V/3. MODL. AMM.

THE QUEEN'S OWN RIFLES OF CANADA
A History of a Splendid Regiment's Origin, Development and Services, including a Story of Patriotic Duties well Performed in Three Campaigns
Capt Ernest J Chambers * R G McLean, for E L Ruddy, Toronto, for the Regt, 1901. Red and green, cloth boards with leather spine, gold, Regtl crest, 12.0 x 9.0, -/156. Numerous mono phots, no maps, no Index. Apps: list of officers, with biographical notes.
* The sub-title tells most of the story. The 'three campaigns' were the Fenian Raid of 1866, the Riel (Northwest) Rebellion of 1885, and the Anglo-Boer War of 1899-1902. As with all Chambers' narratives, the style is florid and adulatory, but very readable and full of references to officers and their individual services.
R/4 V/4. AMOT/UWOL/NYPL/MODL. MCJ.

THE QUEEN'S OWN RIFLES OF CANADA, 1860-1960
One Hundred Years of Canada
Lieut Col W T Barnard ED CD * Printed by T H Best Printing Co Ltd, for Ontario Publishing Ltd, 1960. Rifle green, silver, Regtl crest, 9.25 x 6.0, xiii/398. Fp, 34 mono phots, 18 maps (9 printed in the text, 7 bound in, 2 printed on the end-papers), Bibliography, Index. Apps: Rolls of Honour (see below), H&A (idem), list of former COs, notes on Battle Honours, etc.
* An admirable history which covers every event in the Regt's life from formation in 1860 through to the Korean war and the late 1950s. The campaigns in which it took part were - Fenian Raid (1866), Riel Rebellion (1885), South Africa (1899-1902), Europe (1943-1945), and Korea (1953-1954). During WWI it acted as a training and draft-finding unit for the CEF. The 'Roll of Honour' appendixes are unusual. They list the men who died in action (2.8.1866) during the Fenian Raid, in South Africa with the Canadian Contingents (1900), in WWI (former members who died while serving with named CEF units), in WWII, and in Korea. The 'Honours & Awards' appendix has only a numerical summary for WWI, but a full list of names for WWII. A first-class research source, with very good maps drawn by Capt R A With. R/3 V/5. PCAL. RP.
Note: known to exist, but not seen, is A SHORT HISTORY OF THE QUEEN'S OWN RIFLES OF CANADA, by the same author, W T Barnard, and produced by MacKinnon & Atkins, 1954.

Black Watch (Royal Highland Regiment) of Canada

THE 5th REGIMENT, ROYAL SCOTS OF CANADA HIGHLANDERS
A Regimental History
Capt Ernest J Chambers * The Guertin Printing Co, Montreal, for the author, on commission to the Regt, 1904. Red, gold, 12.0 x 9.0, -/90. Fp, numerous mono phots (uniformed officer portraits, captioned), no maps, no appendixes, no Index.
* Another of Chambers' attractive histories, full of names and a mirror of contemporary Canadian society. The photographs are particularly useful for students of uniform and personal accoutrement. The Regt was one of the Black Watch's forebears. R/4 V/4. AMOT/MODL. RP.

THE STORY OF THE THIRTEENTH BATTALION, 1914-1917
The Royal Highlanders of Canada
Stuart Martin * W Charles & Son, London, UK, n.d. (c.1918). Seen part-rebound, grey, black, Regtl crest, 7.0 x 4.5, -/19. Fp, one mono phot, no maps, no Index. Apps: list of COs (1914-1917).
* The 5th Royal Highlanders of Canada mobilised in Montreal in August 1914, and embarked for England a few weeks later as 13th Cdn Inf Bn CEF. It did not land in France until February 1915 but, thereafter, it served almost continuously on the Western Front. The story is told here very briefly and very inadequately, and ends in August 1917. R/4 V/1. MODL. AMM.
Note: this pamphlet is one of a series by the same publisher, two others being brief accounts of the 10th and 28th Cdn Inf Bns CEF.

THE 13th BATTALION, ROYAL HIGHLANDERS OF CANADA, 1914-1919
R C Fetherstonhaugh * Published by the Regt, Toronto, 1925. Black, gold, Regtl crest, 9.0 x 6.5. xv/344. Fp, 20 mono phots, 3 maps (folding, bound in), no Index. Apps: Roll of Honour, H&A, list of former COs (with studio portraits).
* A substantial and detailed account of the Bn's movements and battles between February 1915 and November 1918. Most officer casualties are noted in the text as they happened. The text also includes quotations from operational orders and, as expected from this author, the entire work is lucid and authoritative. The Bn is perpetuated by the 3rd Bn (Militia) of the Black Watch of Canada.
R/4 V/4. NYPL/UWOL/MODL. MCJ/JBC.

THE 42nd BATTALION, CEF, ROYAL HIGHLANDERS OF CANADA, IN THE GREAT WAR
Lieut Col C Beresford Topp DSO MC * Gazette Printing Co Ltd, Montreal, 1931. Red, gold, Regtl crest, 9.25 x 6.0, xii/412. Fp, 21 mono phots, one line drawing, 9 maps (folding, bound in), no Index. Apps: table of casualty statistics, unit nominal roll (36 pages), Battle Honours, Operation Order for Vimy Ridge (9.4.1917), list of the Bn's main engagements, itinerary of its movements, Bn songs.
* A comprehensive and intimate account of the Bn's services on the Western Front, with many members mentioned by name and eyewitness accounts woven in. The author covers periods of front-line combat and behind-the-lines rest and recovery equally well. At Parvillers, on 12 August 1918, Pte Thomas Dinesen won the VC in ten hours of continuous hand-to-hand fighting. The book is attractive to handle, the maps are very good, and the nominal roll exceptionally useful. The lack of an Index is a serious omission in a history of this quality. R/3 V/4. PCAL/UWOL. RP.

CANADA'S BLACK WATCH
The First Hundred Years, 1862-1962
Col Paul P Hutchison ED * T H Best Printing Co Ltd, Don Mills, Ontario, for the Royal Highlanders of Canada Armoury Association, 1962. Dark blue, gold, Regtl crest, 9.25 x 6.0, xxiii/340. 106 mono phots, 4 cld plates, 33 line drawings, 2 maps (printed on the end-papers), no Index. Apps: H&A (WWI and WWII), list of former Honorary Colonels, idem COs, idem RSMs, idem RPMs, notes on Battle Honours.
* The Regt was formed in 1862. It served in the Fenian disturbances of 1866 and 1870, in WWI (as 42nd Cdn Inf Bn CEF, on the Western Front), and in WWII (with a detachment in the Dieppe raid, and then an entire Bn landing in Normandy on 6 July 1944). As 2nd Royal Highlanders of Canada, they fought in Korea with the Commonwealth Div. Amongst the 106 photographs, there are about 40 of individual officers and men (studio portraits). R/3 V/4. PCAL/MODL. JBC/LM.
Note: known to exist, but not seen, is WARTIME ACTIVITIES OF THE BLACK WATCH (RHR) OF CANADA, DURING THE SECOND WORLD WAR, also by Col P P Hutchison. His major work, the CANADA'S BLACK WATCH book as recorded above, was reprinted for the Regt in 1987 by Museum Restoration Service, Bloomfield, Ontario.

Governor General's Foot Guards

HISTORY OF THE 2nd BATTALION
The History of the 2nd Battalion (Eastern Ontario Regiment), Canadian Expeditionary Force, in the Great War, 1914-1919
Col W W Murray, OBE MC * Printed by W Mortimer Ltd, Ottawa, for 2nd Bn CEF Historical Committee, 1947. Wine red, black/silver, 9.25 x 6.25, xix/408. 2 fps, 17 mono phots (indexed, all portraits of officers), 29 maps, no Index. Apps: Roll of Honour (KIA, DOW, and DOD), H&A, list of officers (22.9.1914 to 30.4.1919), notes on Battle Honours, idem the Colours, idem the Bn Association.
* The Bn was formed at Valcartier (QP) in August 1914, its personnel having volunteered from several pre-war Militia units. It sailed for England two months later and arrived in France in February 1915. The author of this authoritative book gives an excellent account of the following years of violent and bloody trench warfare, particularly that of the Ypres Salient and the Somme (where, in the space of six weeks, the Bn was effectively wiped out). In total, throughout the war, 5326 officers and men passed through the Bn. Of these, 52 officers and 1227 ORs lost their lives. The Bn returned to Kingston, Ontario, in April 1919 and is perpetuated by The Governor General's Foot Guards. The layout is rather old-fashioned for a book published in 1947, but the narrative is detailed and contains all the information most researchers are likely to require.
R/3 V/4. RCSL. JRD/RP.

AN HISTORICAL SKETCH OF THE SEVENTY-SEVENTH BATTALION, CANADIAN EXPEDITIONARY FORCE
Having Particular Reference to the Military Records of the Members of this Battalion
Anon * War Publications Ltd, Ottawa, 1926. Seen rebound in buff, gold, 10.25 x 6.75, iii/410. Hundreds of mono phots, no maps, Index. Apps: Roll of Honour, H&A (with separate list of MID), list of officers, idem SNCOs, unit nominal roll (with some biographical notes), notes on POW.
* The Bn saw no fighting, but this record is a prime source for family historians in the area around Ottawa. Raised locally in July 1915, the Bn disembarked at Liverpool a year later and was immediately broken up to provide drafts for other units. All these postings are noted, thus enabling the researcher to trace a man's later services. The book is divided into five parts. The first two contain the narrative and the nominal rolls. The other three parts contain several hundreds of captioned photographs of individual officers and men, plus some uncaptioned groups. The Bn was perpetuated by the Governal General's Foot Guards (5th Bn, The Canadian Guards). R/4 V/5. MODL/UWOL. AMM.

REGIMENTAL HISTORY OF THE GOVERNOR GENERAL'S FOOT GUARDS
Anon (but attributed to Lieut Col G T Baylay DSO, Maj A R Jessup, and Lieut Col W G Wurtele) * Printed by Mortimer Ltd, Ottawa, Ontario, for the Regt, 1948. Soft card, light blue, dark blue, Regtl crest, 9.75 x 6.5, ix/268. Fp, 40 mono phots, (incl 9 large fold-outs, captioned groups of personnel), 5 maps (cld, folding, bound in), Glossary, no Index. Apps: Roll of Honour, H&A (4 VCs for WWI, full listing for WWII), unit nominal roll (WWII), notes on the Regtl Rifle Association, names of the members of the Bisley Teams (1874-1939), notes on Regtl dress and customs, the Colours, Battle Honours, etc.
* There were two Regts of Militia Artillery in Ottawa in 1872, but no infantry units. On the authority of Queen Victoria, a Regt of Foot Guards was raised and given the title of the viceroy, i.e. Governor General's Foot Guards. In 1885, the Regt sent a Company to serve in the North West Rebellion campaign. It fought in the Battle of Cut Knife Hill (Creek), and there is a good account here of that affair. In August 1914, the Regt provided a Company for the newly-raised 2nd Cdn Inf Bn CEF (the 'Iron Second'), and later provided drafts for the 47th and 77th Bns. Four Victoria Cross winners were connected with the GGFG in various ways. They were Cpl L Clarke, Lieut M F Gregg, Cpl F Konowal, and Maj O M Learmouth. The Regt was mobilised again in 1939 and converted to the armoured role in August 1942. As 21st Cdn Armd Regt, it fought in the NW Europe campaign from June 1944 onwards as an element of the 4th Cdn Armd Div.
R/4 V/4. PC JRD/MAR.
Note: the 'soft card' version reported above is that most commonly seen. Two other versions were produced, one in conventional hardback, another having a 'de luxe' binding embossed with the Regtl crest.

Canadian Grenadier Guards

A BRIEF OUTLINE OF THE STORY OF THE CANADIAN GRENADIER GUARDS
And the First Five Months of the Royal Montreal Regiment in the Great War
Anon (Brig F S Meighen) * Gazette Printing Co Ltd, Montreal, 1926. Stiff card, maroon (blind), Regtl crest in gold/silver, 8.25 x 5.25, -/75. One line drawing (no other ills), one map, no appendixes, no Index.
* An unusual item, with brief diary-type entries detailing events in the lives of the two Regts, interspersed with pieces of poetry. The first third of the book deals with the Royal Montreal Regt, formed in August 1914 by combining men from three Militia units and later designated 14th Cdn Inf Bn CEF. It reached France in February 1915. These notes terminate in June 1915. The author then deals with the mobilisation of the CGG in July 1915 as 87th Cdn Inf Bn CEF. This Bn landed in France in August 1916, and it is recorded here in greater detail. The

entries cover this Bn's fighting record on the Western Front and then the return to Montreal for demobilisation in June 1919. This is not a formal history, very few individuals are named, but it somehow contrives to be a useful source of reference despite lacking most of the customary features. R/5 V/3. MODL. AMM.

HISTORY OF THE CANADIAN GRENADIER GUARDS, 1760-1964
Col A Fortescue Duguid DSO OBE ED * Gazette Printing Co Ltd, for the Regt, 1965. Dark blue, gold, 9.0 x 5.5, xxiii/520. Fp, 109 mono phots, 44 maps (all folding, bound in), no Index. Apps: Roll of Honour (WWI and WWII, all ranks, with dates), H&A (idem, incl MID), list of COs, idem other officers, notes on Battle Honours.
* A monumental work which covers a very wide variety of service - raids and rebellions during Canada's formative years, WWI infantry service in France and Flanders, and WWII service as an armoured (tank) unit in NW Europe. The narrative is packed with names throughout, and should have been indexed. There are also numerous lists of names at certain key points in the main body of book, plus the massive appendixes which run to 147 pages. R/3 V/4. PCAL. RP.

Victoria Rifles of Canada

THE 24th BATTALION, CEF, VICTORIA RIFLES OF CANADA, 1914-1919
R C Fetherstonhaugh * Gazette Printing Co, Montreal, for the Victoria Rifles of Canada, 1930. Green (pebbled), gold, 9.25 x 6.25, i/318. Fp, 13 mono phots, 4 sketches, 8 maps (bound in), no Index. Apps: Roll of Honour, H&A, list of officers who served.
* A very detailed - almost 'shot by shot, casualty by casualty' - account of the Bn's services on the Western Front. The appendixes are very comprehensive.
R/4 V/4. NYPL/UWOL. MCJ.

THE VICTORIAN - 1st BATTALION, 1940-1941
Anon * Publication details not shown, n.d. (c.1942). Stiff card boards, cloth spine, green/black/red/white, 11.25 x 8.75, -/37. Fp, 51 mono phots (incl 29 fully captioned groups), no maps, no Index. Apps: Roll of Honour (two men), list of former officers (1862-1940), notes on Battle Honours (South Africa, and WWI as 24th Cdn Inf Bn CEF).
* An extended sub-title states - 'With this Anniversary Issue, the 1st Battalion Victoria Rifles of Canada on 25th July 1941 marked its First Year of Active Service in the Second World War'. It is mainly a pictorial record of home defence duties in 1941 in Newfoundland. The narrative includes a very brief summary of the Regt's origins, but the only likely value of this publication is for family historians who may find a relative in the group photographs. R/4 V/2. PC. JRD.
Note: the Bn was later stationed at Sussex, New Brunswick. It then moved to the UK where, upon arrival in late 1944, it was broken up to provide battle casualty replacements for other units in Holland.

Royal Rifles of Canada

THE ROYAL RIFLES OF CANADA
Allied with The King's Royal Rifle Corps, 1862-1937
Anon ('Regimental Committee') * T J Moore & Co Ltd, Quebec, 1937. Soft card, rifle green, silver, Regtl crest, 9.25 x 6.0, -/21. 11 mono phots, 2 line drawings (badges), no maps, no Index. Apps: Roll of Honour (no dates), H&A (statistical summary only), list of COs (1862-1937), list of serving officers (at 1937).
* A souvenir item published to celebrate the Regt's 75th Anniversary. Raised from a variety of Militia Companies, it provided detachments during both Fenian Raids (1866 and 1870), the Riel Rebellion (1885), and the war in South Africa (1899-1900). In WWI, it provided drafts for the 12th and 171st Cdn Inf Bns CEF. All of this is covered here very superficially. R/4 V/1. MODL. AMM.

ROYAL RIFLES OF CANADA, 'ABLE AND WILLING', SINCE 1862
A Short History
Arthur G Penny * Publication details not shown, n.d. (1962). Soft card, green, red, Regtl crest, 9.0 x 6.0, -/62. 8 mono phots, no maps, no Index. Apps: H&A (Hong Kong only), list of officers (at March 1962).
* Originally one of six Independent Rifle Companies raised in Quebec City in 1862, this unit was absorbed into The Royal Rifles in 1900. Contingents were sent to South Africa, and drafts were provided for many CEF infantry units in WWI. The title was changed to Royal Rifles of Canada in 1920. The Regt was mobilised in May 1940 for defence duties in Newfoundland, but it then sailed for Hong Kong in November 1941. This little book does include a useful account of the Japanese invasion of that Colony, but a much fuller record will be found in THE ROYAL RIFLES OF CANADA IN HONG KONG, 1941-1945, by Capt G S Garneau and Capt E L Hurd, in the Hong Kong section of this bibliography (vide the Index of Authors). Penny's 'short history' is exactly what he claims for it - it is a summary of larger events. R/4 V/2. MODL. JRD.

Les Voltigeurs de Québec

This Regt traces its roots to 1862 and the formation of the 9th Bn, Volunteer Militia Rifles. It underwent the usual succession of title changes and roles until 1954 when it was amalgamated with Le Régiment de Québec and gained its present title in 1958. Only two histories have been recorded, and both are reported to be of a fairly superficial nature - LES VOLTIGEURS DE QUEBEC, 1862-1952, NOTES HISTORIQUES (produced in 1952), and LES VOLTIGEURS DE QUEBEC, 1862-1962, ALBUM DU CENTENAIRE (produced in 1962).

Royal Regiment of Canada

HISTORY OF THE 10th ROYALS AND THE ROYAL GRENADIERS
From the Formation of the Regiment until 1896
T E Champion * The Hunter Rose Co Ltd, Toronto, 1896. Red, gold, 'Grenadier' motif, 7.5 x 5.0, -/279. Fp, approx 50 mono phots, 2 line drawings, no maps, Index. Apps: Roll of Honour (KIA and WIA, 1885), list of former officers, nominal roll (all ranks who served in the 1885 campaign), notes on rifle matches.
* The 10th Bn Volunteer Rifles, formed from seven Militia Rifle Companies in March 1862, became the 10th Bn Royal Grenadiers in August 1881. This is a well written history, with many anecdotes woven into the narrative. The author supports his factual information with numerous quotations from General Orders. The photographs are mostly studio portraits of officers. R/4 V/4. MODL. AMM.

THE ROYAL GRENADIERS
A Regimental History of the 10th Infantry Regiment of the Active Service Militia of Canada
Capt Ernest J Chambers * Browne Searle Printing Co, Toronto, for E L Ruddy, Toronto, 1904. Cloth boards with leather spine, red/blue, gold, Regtl crest, 12.0 x 9.25, -/128/xiii. Several mono phots, no maps, no Index. Apps: list of officers (with biographical notes for each).
* Another of Chambers' finely produced Militia histories. As usual, the final run of pages (xiii) are commercial advertisements, and these in themselves are a commentary upon the times in which the book was written. The Regt later evolved as The Royal Regiment of Canada. R/4. V/3. AMOT/UWOL/NYPL. RP.

A BRIEF HISTORY OF THE ROYAL REGIMENT OF CANADA
Allied with The King's Regiment (Liverpool)
Anon * Publisher's details not shown, Toronto, 1948. Soft card, light blue with red quarter stripe, Regtl crest, 6.0 x 3.5, -/135. No phots, 2 line drawings (badges), no maps, no Index. Apps: list of COs (1862-1948).
* A book designed for presentation to all ranks. It draws together the histories

of the RRC's forebears - the Royal Grenadiers (1862-1936) and the Toronto Regt (1920-1936) which amalgamated in 1936 to become the Royal Regt of Toronto Grenadiers, this then being redesignated the Royal Regt of Canada in 1939. This is a compact, succinct, and useful aide-memoire, with few persons named but with a great deal of factual information. R/4 V/3. MODL. AMM.

A BRIEF HISTORY OF 3rd BATTALION, CEF (TORONTO REGIMENT), 1914-1919
A Brief History of the 3rd Bn CEF (Toronto Regiment), Now The Toronto Regiment (Allied with The King's Regiment, Liverpool)
Anon * Apparently produced by the Battalion Association for its own members and their families, no details shown, 1934. Stapled card, grey, gold/red, Bn crest, 6.0 x 3.5, -/49. No ills, no maps, no Index. Apps: H&A (statistics only), list of officers (1914-1934), nominal roll for all ranks who embarked in 1914 and returned in 1919.
* The Bn was formed at Valcartier (QP) in August 1914 with volunteers from the 2nd Queen's Own Rifles of Canada, the 10th Royal Grenadiers, and the Governor General's Bodyguard. After service in the Ypres Salient in 1915, it went into the Battle of the Somme in 1916 and there lost 27 officers and 682 Other Ranks. Total losses during the war were 181 officers and 4592 ORs. After occupation duties in Germany, the Bn returned to Toronto in April 1919 and was disbanded. Shortly afterwards, the Non-Permanent Active Militia was created. The Bn was then reconstituted as The Toronto Regt (which perpetuated the 3rd Cdn Inf Bn CEF, and also 124th, 170th, and 204th Bns). R/5 V/2. NYPL (microfilm only). JRD.

BATTLE ROYAL
A History of the Royal Regiment of Canada, 1862-1962
Maj D J Goodspeed CD * Printed by Charters Publishing Co Ltd, Toronto, for the Regt, 1962. Blue, silver, Regtl crest, 9.0 x 6.0, -/703. 2 fps, 77 mono phots, 2 cld plates, 24 maps (22 printed in the text, 2 on the end-papers), Bibliography, Index. Apps: Rolls of Honour (WWI, for the founder Regts, WWII for the RRC), H&A (WWI and WWII, incl foreign awards), list of Colonels-in-Chief, idem Honorary Colonels, idem Honorary Lieutenant Colonels, idem COs.
* As indicated by the dates in its sub-title, this imposing book covers the history of the RRC's origins, the services of the two main forebear Regts, their services in WWI, the amalgamation in 1936, and then the events of WWII (the Dieppe Raid, the Normandy battles, and the advance into Belgium, Holland, and Germany). An outstandingly good history. R/3 V/5. PCAL/MODL. RP/RH.
Note: the first (1962) edition was revised and republished in 1979 (Charters Publishing Co Ltd, Brampton, for the Regtl Association, soft card, red/brown, white, Regtl crest, 8.0 x 5.0, -/754). The author was again Goodspeed, by now Lieut Col. The narrative for the period 1862-1962 is the same as that found in the book noted above. However, the second edition was expanded by the addition of 51 pages of new text and 32 new illustrations (plus a separate Index to cover the added material), all relating to the period 1962-1979. The Regt saw no active service during this time, so the story is concerned mainly with social, ceremonial, and training activities. RH.

Royal Hamilton Light Infantry (Wentworth Regiment)

THE ORIGIN AND OFFICIAL HISTORY OF THE THIRTEENTH BATTALION OF INFANTRY AND A DESCRIPTION OF THE EARLY MILITIA AND THE NIAGARA PENINSULA IN THE WAR OF 1812 AND THE REBELLION OF 1837
The Thirteenth Battalion of Infantry - Hamilton - Canada
Lieut Col E A Cruikshank * E L Ruddy, Hamilton, Ontario, for the Regt, 1899. Blue/red, leather spine and quarters, gold, 10.0 x 8.0, -/88/Lx. Fp, 53 mono phots (mostly captioned groups and portraits), 7 line drawings (chapter heads), no maps, no Index. Apps: list of former officers (with career details), records of shooting competitions (with team members named, 1863-1899).
* The story begins in the summer of 1782 when some Loyalist ex-soldiers of

Butler's Corps of Rangers founded a settlement on the west bank of the Niagara River. They and their sons formed the first Canadian Militia Companies in that area, and fought the Americans in the War of 1812. They were mobilised again, under a variety of unit titles, for the 1837 Rebellion. In 1862 they were given a new organisation under the title of 13th Battalion and served as such against the Fenians in 1866. The book also contains useful information regarding the Regt's activities through to 1899. Having been produced by E L Ruddy, its format and style of presentation is very similar to those written by Capt Ernest Chambers (as noted elsewhere in this bibliography). The 13th was absorbed later into the Royal Hamilton Light Infantry. R/4 V/3. AMOT/UWOL/MODL. JRD.
Note: seen also in modern facsimile reprint with soft card covers.

RECORDS OF THE FOURTH CANADIAN INFANTRY BATTALION IN THE GREAT WAR, 1914-18
Capt W L Gibson * The Maclean Publishing Co Ltd, Toronto, 1924. Green, gold, 9.75 x 6.5, -/274. Fp, 16 mono phots, no maps, no Index. Apps: a nominal roll of every man who served, with his service number, rank, date of enlistment, details of death or wounds (as applicable), awards, and home address at demobilisation. A separate roll lists all awards, with full citations in most cases (where applicable).
* This is the story of 4th Cdn Inf Bn CEF, a unit which is perpetuated by the RHLI. The narrative content is very slender, the bulk of the book being devoted to the very impressively researched appendixes. A fine source for genealogists.
R/4 V/4. NYPL. MCJ.

SEMPER PARATUS
The History of the Royal Hamilton Light Infantry (Wentworth Regiment), 1862-1977
Brereton Greenhous and Kingsley Brown (Senior and Junior) * W L Griffith Ltd, for the RHLI Historical Association, Ontario, 1977. Illustrated stiff card, red/white, white, 9.0 x 6.0, xvii/446. Fp, 123 mono phots, 28 cld ills, 7 maps (6 printed in the text, one on the end-papers), Index. Apps: Roll of Honour (WWII only), list of COs (1862-1977), idem Honorary Colonels, idem RSMs (1862-1976), idem Bandmasters (1866-1968), idem Bugle Majors (1918-1967), numerous notes regarding the Colours, the evolution of the Regt, the Memorial Silver Bugles, the Regtl Museum, and affiliated Regts.
* A well written account covering a long period of service in variable detail. The story opens with a good description of the Battle of Ridgeway, Ontario, in May 1866 (the Fenian incursion), and then moves on to members' services in the South African war. The WWI section is fairly sparse because the Regt as such did not go overseas and its members served with a large number of CEF units. The bulk of the narrative is then devoted to WWII. The Regt's role in the Dieppe raid, where its Chaplain, Hon Capt John Foote, won the VC, is covered in detail. This is a sound unit history which also covers post-war developments.
R/1 V/4. MODL. JEB/JRD.
Note: published simultaneously in a card cover (as reported above) and in a hardback (cloth) version. Details of the latter are - green, gold, Regtl crest, 9.5 x 6.5, identical contents.

Princess of Wales' Own Regiment

HISTORICAL CALENDAR - 21st CANADIAN INFANTRY BATTALION (EASTERN ONTARIO) REGIMENT
Belgium - France - Germany, 1915-1919
Anon * Gale & Polden Ltd, Aldershot, UK, 1919. Stiff card, cord binding, grey, green, Bn badge, 6.5 x 4.25, -/72. Fp, 5 mono phots (4 of COs, with biographical details), one cld ill, no maps, no Index. Apps: Roll of Honour (with dates and causes, but no ranks), H&A (with officers arranged in order of precedence of award, but the ORs' awards arranged by Gazette date), list of officers who served (with details of KIA, WIA, etc), list of RSMs, idem RPMs, notes on Battle Honours.
* This is the record of a CEF Bn raised in October 1914 in Kingston, Ontario, and

compiled as a souvenir for those who served (and families of those who did not survive). The Bn sailed for England in May 1915, landed in France in September, and served thereafter as part of 4th Bde, 2nd Cdn Div. The narrative gives little detail regarding formation, training, or routine active service. Instead, it focuses on a chronology of movements in and out of the line, with just the main battles highlighted. The principal value of the book, for many researchers, is to be found in the excellent appendixes. The Bn is perpetuated by the Princess of Wales' Own Regiment. R/5 V/3. MODL/IWM. AMM.

THE PRINCESS OF WALES' OWN REGIMENT (MG)
J D MacKenzie-Naughton * Publisher's details not shown, Kingston, Ontario, 1946. Red, gold, Regtl crest, 7.75 x 5.25, -/74. Fp, 15 mono phots, no maps, no appendixes, Index.
* The Regt was raised originally in 1855 as the Kingston Rifles and saw active service during the Fenian Raid of 1866. The book gives a useful account of those early years, with lists of all officers serving in 1873, 1876, 1877, and 1881. Some men served in the Canadian Contingents during the Anglo-Boer War, and their names also are listed. The Regt was mobilised in 1914 and most of its members went to France as the 21st Cdn Inf Bn CEF. It fought at Loos, Courcelette, Vimy Ridge, Hill 70, etc. Coverage of these events is fairly superficial, and few individuals are named in the text. The title Princess of Wales' Own was adopted in 1920. The Regt converted to the machine-gun role in 1936. Lists of officers serving at those dates are included. The Regt was not mobilised in 1939, so a large number of its officers and men volunteered to serve with the Stormont, Dundas and Glengarry Highlanders. Authority to mobilise the 1st Bn POW's Regt was received in 1942, but it did not proceed overseas and was disbanded a year later. This booklet lacks any significant historical content, but it is useful as far as it goes, particularly in the absence of any other record for the Regt.
R/3 V/3. NYPL/UWOL/MODL. JRD.

Hastings and Prince Edward Regiment

THE REGIMENT
Hastings and Prince Edward Regiment
Farley Mowat * T H Best Printing Co, Toronto, for McClelland & Stewart Ltd, Ontario, 1955. Grey, gold, Regtl crest, 9.25 x 6.25, xix/312. No ills, 16 maps, Glossary, no appendixes, no Index.
* Although the book lacks many of the features which one would hope to find in a good unit history, the narrative is at least well written. The author served with the Regt throughout WWII. In 1940 it served briefly in France, returned to the UK for further training, landed in Sicily in July 1943, fought on the Italian mainland until early 1945, and then took part in the final battles for Germany. Few individuals are mentioned, the story being based mainly upon the Regt's movements and engagements. R/3 V/3. NYPL/UWOL/MODL. JRD/RH.
Note: the book was reprinted in paper-back in 1972, 1973, and 1977, the latter version having an Index. Examples of these editions are much easier to acquire than the original 1955 edition.

DUFFY'S REGIMENT
Kenneth B Smith * T H Best Printing Co Ltd, Don Mills, Ontario, 1983. Light blue, gold, Regtl crest, 9.25 x 6.0, xxiv (not numbered)/222. 54 mono phots, 2 maps, Bibliography, no appendixes, no Index.
* This is the story of the Hastings and Prince Edward Regt but woven around the career of Angus Duffy. Joining as a private soldier in 1930, he became the RSM in 1939, served throughout the Sicily and mainland Italy campaigns, and was granted a Commission in 1949. In 1958 he became the 1st Bn's CO and was appointed Honorary Colonel in 1976. The book, therefore, is the story of a man and his Regt. The narrative is informal and anecdotal, but it gives a useful view

of the Hastings and Prince Edwards during Duffy's fifty years of service.
R/2 V/3. MODL. AMM/JRD.
Note: another anecdotal record is AND NO BIRDS SANG, by Farley Mowat (McClelland & Stewart, Toronto, 1979). The author was Bn IO during the WWII period.

HONOURS AND AWARDS, 1939-1945, THE HASTINGS AND PRINCE EDWARD REGIMENT
Capt R D Bradford * H Brittle Publishing Ltd, Arnprior, Ontario, for the Regt, 1986. Illustrated board, full colour, 8.5 x 5.5, viii/115. 60 mono phots (mostly named groups and individuals), 21 cld ills (medals and ribbons), 4 maps (one printed in the text, 4 cld, bound in), Glossary, no Index. Apps: H&A (with theatre and Gazette dates, incl MID).
* The book contains a brief account of the Regt's fighting services in Sicily, on mainland Italy, and in the Rhine crossings, but its main purpose is to describe how the Regt came to win its various Battle Honours and how each member gained his decoration or award. There is also an account of the origins and history of each of the medals normally awarded to military personnel during that period. Useful mainly to medal collectors and family historians. R/3 V/4. PC. JRD.

Lincoln and Welland Regiment

HISTORY OF THE LINCOLN AND WELLAND REGIMENT
Maj R L Rogers * Printed by Industrial Shops for the Deaf, Montreal, for the Regt, 1954. Red, black, Regtl crest, 9.25 x 6.0, -/465. Fp, 12 mono phots, 11 maps, Glossary, no Index. Apps: list of former COs (incl those of the original forebear units), list of former officers (incl WWI, with biographical notes), nominal roll for the Regt (1939-1946).
* A useful narrative history, devoted mainly to WWII and heavily laced with lists (all alphabetically) of officers and men who were killed, wounded, taken prisoner, and so forth, with dates and locations, during the NW Europe campaign. The first 98 pages of the book deal with the evolution of the Regt and its forebears from 1794 to 1939. This is a pleasingly produced record which meets all the usual requirements. R/3 V/4. AMOT/UWOL/MODL. RP.

Lorne Scots (Peel, Dufferin and Halton Regiment)

A BRIEF HISTORICAL SKETCH OF THE LORNE SCOTS
Peel, Dufferin and Halton Regiment
Anon (Regtl HQ Committee) * Charters Publishing Co Ltd, Brampton, Ontario, 1943. Stiff card, 'Regtl crest and Campbell of Argyll tartan' motif, 6.0 x 3.5, -/24. One cld ill (Colours of the Peel and Dufferin Regt), 4 line drawings (badges), no maps, no Index. Apps: notes on Battle Honours.
* This pocket-sized booklet was designed as an introduction for new recruits. Succinctly written, it draws together the historical threads from which The Lorne Scots descended, from 1793 to the outbreak of WWII.
R/4 V/2. MODL/NYPL. AMM.

HISTORICAL RECORD - 76 OVERSEAS
Historical Record of the 76th Overseas Battalion of the Canadian Expeditionary Force
The Rev E R J Biggs BA BD * The Hunter-Rose Co Ltd, Toronto, Ontario, 1916. Wine red, gold, Bn crest, 9.5 x 6.25, -/73. Fp, 14 mono phots (groups of officers, the SNCOs, the Band, the MG Section, and each Platoon, all identified by name, at Camp Niagara, 1915), no maps, no Index. Apps: Roll of Honour (2 men died in Canada), unit nominal roll (with details of marriages, officers' and NCOs' previous military careers), names of athletic event winners, etc.
* King's Regulations required each unit to maintain a record of its services, and this is a remarkably detailed response to that instruction. Despite the Bn's title, it never went overseas (although a draft of 300 men did cross over to England in

November 1915 to reinforce other CEF units). The narrative describes the Bn's training and other activities in Canada in 1915 and 1916. It is packed with the names of officers and men, and the rolls of personnel are a goldmine for genealogists concerned with families at that time resident in Southern Ontario. The Bn was formed from men of The Peel Regt and The Halton Regt, and is perpetuated by The Lorne Scots (Peel, Dufferin and Halton Regiment). R/4 V/4. NYPL. JRD.

THE LORNE SCOTS (PEEL, DUFFERIN AND HALTON REGIMENT)
(Allied with XX The Lancashire Fusiliers)
Col R V Conover OBE VD (and Committee) * Charters Publishing Co Ltd, Brampton, Ontario, for the Regt, 1962. Stapled soft card, green, beige, with strips of Campbell of Argyll tartan attached, 6.5 x 3.75, -/52. Fp, 3 mono phots, 2 cld ills, no maps, no Index. Apps: list of former COs, idem Honorary Colonels, idem Lieutenant Colonels.
* This booklet is the only other known published record of the Regt. It describes the early Militia movement in a strongly Scottish part of Ontario where, by 1846, the volunteer units had been organised into six Militia Bns. Training and command problems were met by another major reorganisation in 1866 when the existing units were grouped as the 36th Peel Bn and the 20th Halton Bn. The Governor General of Canada, the Marquess of Lorne, later agreed to the inclusion of his own name in the combined Regtl title. There were many changes between 1866 and 1936 when the present title was consolidated, and they are recorded here in some detail. The appendixes list the senior officers for all of the ancestor units up to 1935, and then for The Lorne Scots from 1936 through to 1961. The Regt did not serve overseas in WWII, but it provided various complete Army and Divisional Defence Platoons for service in Italy and NW Europe. R/4 V/2. PC. JRD.

The Perth Regiment

THE FIGHTING PERTHS
The Story of the First Century in the Life of a Canadian County Regiment
Stafford Johnston * Printed by B-H Press, Stratford, Ontario, for the Perth Regt Veterans' Association, 1964. Soft card, blue/gold/black, black, 9.0 x 6.0, vi/136. 8 mono phots (mostly cap badges), 10 sketches and cartoons (by Jack M Dent), one map (bound in), no Index. Apps: Roll of Honour (WWII only), H&A (idem), list of COs (1866-1964), notes on Battle Honours.
* Originating as a Militia infantry unit at Stratford, in 1858, the Regt underwent various amalgamations and redesignations during the 100 years under review. During WWI it provided drafts for CEF units, particularly the 18th Cdn Inf Bn. Retitled The Perth Regt in 1920, it was equipped as a Machine-gun Bn in 1936, but was then converted to the lorried infantry role in 1939. The 1st Bn sailed for England as dismounted infantry in 1941, then moved to Italy in 1943. After hard service on the Adriatic coast and in the Appenines, it moved to Holland in 1945 and returned to Canada in 1946. The 2nd Bn remained in Canada throughout the war for recruiting and training duties. The coverage of 1st Bn's experiences in Europe is written clearly, and there are plenty of references to individuals and to lesser engagements. R/3 V/4. MODL/CWM. JRD.
Note: known to exist, but not seen, is IN MEMORIAM - THE PERTH REGIMENT - 4th SEPTEMBER 1939 TO 8th MAY 1945, printed in Sneek, Holland, in 1945.

Highland Light Infantry of Canada

1st BATTALION, THE HIGHLAND LIGHT INFANTRY OF CANADA, 1940-1945
Jack Fortune Bartlett * Published by the HLI of Canada Association, Galt, Ontario, 1951. Dark green, gold, Regtl crest, 8.5 x 5.75, -/126. 9 mono phots (all at the rear, on unnumbered pages), 4 maps (folding, bound in), no Index. Apps: Roll of Honour (KIA and DOW), H&A (names, ranks and serials).
* Despite its title, this book includes (Chapter 17) a summary of the Regt's entire history, from 1866 when its forebear was embodied as the 29th Waterloo Bn (Militia

Force) at Galt, Ontario. By 1915 it had become the 29th Regt, Highland Light Infantry of Canada. Its role in WWI was to act as recruiting and training depot for the 1st, 18th, 34th, 71st, 111th, and 122nd Cdn Inf Bns CEF. It was mobilised for active service in May 1940 and the 1st Bn arrived in Scotland a year later. After three years' training and defence deployments in the UK, the Bn landed at Bernieres-sur-Mer on 6 June 1944. Subsequently it was engaged in the Normandy battles as an element of 3rd Cdn Inf Div. After the clearance of the Channel ports and the harsh winter campaign in Holland, its final difficult battle was the Reichwald Forest. These operations are described in clear detail. Officers and men who gained awards are mentioned in the narrative, with interesting descriptions of the circumstances which led to those awards. A 2nd Bn was formed at Galt as draft-finding unit for 1st Bn, and a 3rd Bn was raised in 1945 for service with the Canadian Army of Occupation in Germany. With such a large story to tell, it is surprising that the author and his sponsors did not produce a much bigger book, with more illustrations, maps and appendixes. R/4 V/3. RMCL/NYPL/MODL. JRD/RH. Note: the name of the author is shown on the outer casing but not on the title page.

BLOODY BURON

Capt J Allan Snowie * Printed by The Boston Mills Press, Erin, Ontario, 1984. Black, gold, 8.75 x 11.0 (landscape), -/120. Fp, 70 mono phots (incl two large group pictures printed on the end-papers), 4 maps, Glossary, Bibliography, no Index. Apps: Roll of Honour (specifically, those killed at Buron), H&A (for Buron, with full citations), Bn nominal roll.

* Like most modern Canadian regiments, the HLI has an extraordinarily complicated lineage. It can in fact trace its roots back to the North Waterloo Mennonite Teamsters which were raised for service in the War of 1812. This particular book deals solely with one event in the HLI's history - the action at Buron, Normandy, when the Bn was ordered to assault the village in daylight across open ground. It was their baptism of fire. The author describes the events leading up to this intense and bloody action, and the minutiae of the battle itself. A most unusual form of unit history, and of great interest. R/1. V/4. AldMM. RP.

Stormont, Dundas and Glengarry Highlanders

STORMONT, DUNDAS AND GLENGARRY HIGHLANDERS
A Brief History, 1784-1945

Anon * Publisher's details not shown, Cornwall, Ontario, n.d. (c.1946). Seen only as a library-bound photo-copy, 8.5 x 5.5, -/39. 4 mono phots, one line drawing (cap badge), no maps, no Index. Apps: Roll of Honour (WWII only), H&A, list of officers (1916 and 1940, the latter illustrated).

* This little book was compiled as a memento for all ranks who returned from NW Europe in 1945. It gives a condensed summary of the 19th Century campaigns, the contribution to the CEF in WWI, and its services in WWII (the UK from 1941 to 1944, NW Europe from D-Day to war's end). The narrative lacks detail, but it is a handy summary of events. R/4 V/2. MODL. AMM.

THE STORMONT, DUNDAS AND GLENGARRY HIGHLANDERS, 1783-1951

Lieut Col W Boss * The Runge Press Ltd, Ottawa, 1952. Blue, silver, Regtl crest, 9.25 x 6.25, x/449. Fp, 15 mono phots (plus 5 pages of small photographs of former COs, 1885-1949, and a similar pictorial page of Honorary Colonels, 1921-1949), 2 maps (one printed in the text, one on the end-papers), no Index. Apps: Rolls of Honour (The War of 1812, the Rebellion of 1837-1839, WWI, and WWII, with ranks and dates), H&A (The War of 1812, WWI, and WWII), unit muster roll for the 154th Overseas Bn (Highlanders) CEF (with much personal detail), a similar roll for the SDGH in WWII, lists of officers who served with all the predecessor Regts between 1783 and 1951 (too numerous to nominate here).

* This is an outstanding regimental history, flawed only by the lack of an Index. The SDGH trace their roots back to 1st Bn, The King's Royal Regiment of New York, one of the Loyalist units whose members moved to Canada after the American War

of Independence. There is good coverage of the War of 1812 (when the Glengarry Fencibles were much involved), and the major changes which followed enactment of the Militia Act of 1855. A detachment of 28 men from the Dundas and Glengarry Highlanders served in South Africa with the 1st Canadian Contingent, and they are named here. In WWI, the Regt recruited and trained drafts in large numbers for the 2nd, 21st, 38th, 73rd, and 154th Bns of the CEF. The latter, the 154th, was particularly representative of the local population, but it was soon broken up to provide drafts for other units. One of these men, Sgt C J P Nunney DCM MM, won the VC in 1918 while serving with 38th Cdn Inf Bn near Drocourt, France. The Regt was mobilised in June 1940 and arrived in England in 1941. It landed at Bernieres-sur-Mer on D-Day as part of 9th Bde, 3rd Cdn Div, and fought throughout the NW Europe campaign before returning to Cornwall, Ontario, in December 1945. A 2nd Bn had remained in Canada for local defence duties and to train reinforcements for the 1st Bn. A 3rd Bn was formed in June 1945 for occupation duties in Germany. This is a massive compilation - it contains lucid descriptions of active services, helpful explanations of the various changes in organisation, and many lists of officers inserted in the text. The extensive appendixes are, of course, a goldmine for genealogists. R/3 V/4. UWOL/RMCL/MODL. JRD.

Le Régiment de la Chaudière

PRECIS HISTORIQUE DU 17ieme BATAILLON D'INFANTERIE DE LEVIS
Depuis sa Formation en 1862 jusqu'a 1872, Suivi des Ordres Permanents du Meme Corps
Capt L G Desjardins * Des Presses a Vapeur de L'Echo de Levis, Levis, QP, 1872. Seen only in microfiche form, details of original casing not known, i/89. No ills, no maps, no Index. Apps: list of officers.
* Written in French. This is a chronological account of the ten years following formation. In condensed style, it lists all important parades, annual camps, Coy strengths, etc, with two short chapters regarding the Regt's role during the Fenian Raids of 1866 and 1870. Tables within the narrative list all officers who served with each of the seven Coys (showing their dates of Commission, promotions, and appointments). The book concludes with quotations from Regtl Standing Orders regarding the duties of various persons (Canteen Sergeant to Adjutant).
R/5 V/3. NLC. MAR.

LE REGIMENT DE LEVIS
Histoire et Album
G E Marquis * Publisher's details not shown, Levis, QP, 1952. Soft card, pale green, black, Regtl crest, 8.0 x 5.5, -/292. 38 mono phots, vignettes, no maps, no Index. Apps: list of former officers.
Written in French. This is a comprehensive history, covering the period from 1862 through to 1954 when the Régiment de Levis was amalgamated with the Régiment de la Chaudière. R/4 V/4. MODL. AMM.

LE GESTE DU REGIMENT DE LA CHAUDIERE
Maj Armand Ross DSO and Maj Michel Gauvin DSO * Drukkerij van Veen & Scheffers, Rotterdam, Holland, n.d. (c.1945). Maroon, gold/silver, Regtl crest, 8.75 x 5.5, -/179. 45 mono phots, 32 line drawings, 2 maps, Glossary, no Index. Apps: Roll of Honour, H&A, unit nominal roll.
* Many Canadian units arranged for their WWII services to be recorded immediately after the German surrender and while they were still stationed in Holland. Given the pressures of time and the lack of good quality printing materials, these books were remarkable achievements. This example is unusual for its high standard of production and for the fact that it is printed in French (thereby posing a problem for the Dutch type-setters). R/4 V/4. MODL. AMM.

LE REGIMENT DE LA CHAUDIERE
Jacques Castonguay and Armand Ross * Imprimerie L'Eclaireur, Beauceville, QP, 1983. Maroon, gold, Regtl crest, 8.75 x 6.5, xi/644. 4 fps (cld), 155 mono phots, 4 line drawings, 19 maps (18 printed in the text, one bound in), footnotes, no Index. Apps: Roll of Honour (WWII only), H&A (idem), list of Honorary Colonels and Honorary Lieut Cols (1930-1983), idem COs (1869-1982), idem 2 i/c (1939-1945), idem RSMs (1939-1983), idem POW (1939-1945), nominal roll (all ranks, 1939-1945), notes on the Mobilisation Scheme, D-Day Orders.
* Written in French. A very detailed account of the Regt from the 1860s through to 1983. A wealth of portraits, maps, and charts traces the development of this, a typical French-speaking Militia regiment, from its diverse early decades through to the 1980s. The main focus of the book is the WWII period. Individual officers and men are freely mentioned throughout, and the personnel photographs are all fully captioned. Apart from the lack of an Index, this is an exemplary history. R/2 V/4. CWM. MAR.
Note: 2950 copies printed, of which 150 were a 'de luxe' edition.

Les Fusiliers Mont-Royal

CENT-VINGT JOURS DE SERVICE ACTIF
Récit Historique très Complet de la Campagne du 65eme au Nord-Ouest
Charles R Daoust * Eusebe-Sénécal et Fils, Montreal, 1886. Soft card, grey, black, Regtl crest, 8.0 x 5.5, -/242. Fp, no mono phots, 37 line drawings (portraits of officers, with some NCOs, of the two Bns), no maps, no Index. Apps: chronology.
* Written in French. The two Bns of the 65th Regt of Canadian Militia were mobilised in 1885 for service in North West Canada. The narrative covers the period 28 March to 20 July, hence the 'one hundred and twenty days' referred to in the book's title. The contents are presented in the form of an expanded diary, with lists of officers and SNCOs inserted in the text. R/5 V/4. MODL/CWM. AMM/MAR.

HISTOIRE DU 65ieme REGIMENT CARABINIERS MONT-ROYAL
Capt Ernest J Chambers * La Compagnie D'Imprimerie Guertin, Montreal, 1906. Dark maroon, gold, Regtl crest, 12.0 x 9.0, -/151. Fp, 75 mono phots, 4 line drawings, no maps, no appendixes, no Index.
* Another of Chambers' opulent socio-military compilations, but this one being written in French. The portraits and group photographs of personnel are, as usual, well reproduced and fully captioned. The Regt recruited from the French-speaking population of Montreal. R/4 V/3. MODL. AMM.

CENT ANS D'HISTOIRE D'UN REGIMENT CANADIEN FRANCAIS
Les Fusiliers Mont Royal, 1869-1969
Anon * Les E D Marquis Ltd, Montreal, 1971. Illustrated soft card, full colour, 'Steel helmet, rifle, and badges' motif, 8.5 x 5.5, -/434. 140 mono phots (incl many identified portrait and group pictures), 5 line drawings, 9 maps (7 printed in the text, 2 bound in), no Index. Apps: Roll of Honour (WWII only), H&A (idem), list of COs (1869-1969), idem RSMs (1902-1969), idem Honorary Colonels (1901-1965), idem serving officers (1969), notes on Battle Honours.
* Written in French. The Regt perpetuates the 69th and 150th Cdn Inf Bns CEF. This is the definitive history of the Regt, its forebears, and affiliated units. It includes good coverage of the Regt's role in the Dieppe Raid of 1942 and subsequent (1944-1945) services in the advance from Normandy to the Dutch/German border. R/3 V/4. MODL. JRD/AMM.
Note: 2750 copies printed, of which 250 were a 'de luxe' edition.

Princess Louise Fusiliers

HISTORY OF THE HALIFAX VOLUNTEER BATTALION AND VOLUNTEER COMPANIES, 1859-1887
Maj Thomas J Egan * A & W Mackinlay, Halifax, Nova Scotia, 1888. Red, gold, Regtl motto, 7.5 x 5.0, viii/172. Fp, 2 line drawings (uniforms), no maps, no Index. Apps: list of officers, roll of members who served in the 1885 campaign.
* A book divided into two parts. The first describes the formation of the Halifax Volunteer Bn in May 1860, and its subsequent training and ceremonial duties. The second part consists of several short histories of each of the Regt's forebears - The Scottish Rifles, the Chebulco Greys, the Mayflower Rifles, the Dartmouth Rifles, the Dartmouth Engineers, etc. Nominal rolls appear at several points in this section. The book is a fascinating glimpse into the social structure and military ethos of Nova Scotia during that period. R/4 V/3. MODL. AMM.

1885 EXPERIENCES OF THE HALIFAX BATTALION IN THE NORTH-EAST
Robert A Sherlock * Museum Restoration Service, Bloomfield, Ontario, 1985. Stapled illustrated paper, 'Soldiers with a table' motif, brown, 11.0 x 8.25, -/28. 14 mono phots (mostly uncaptioned groups), one map, no appendixes, Chapter Notes, Index.
* A pamphlet which describes the sudden mobilisation, on the morning of 11 April 1885, of two Coys of the Halifax Garrison Artillery, three Coys of the 63rd Halifax Rifles, and of three Coys of the 66th Princess Louise Fusiliers, in response to the Riel Rebellion. By evening, the composite 'Halifax Battalion' was entrained and on its way to Moose Jaw, Sasketchewan (2000 miles from Halifax). In the event, it saw little action. However, the episode demonstrated the flexibility of the Militia system and the importance of the Canadian railway system.
R/2 V/2. PC. JRD.

THE STORY OF THE 64th BATTALION, CEF, 1915-1916
Lieut Col G C MacHum * Industrial Shops for the Deaf, Montreal, 1956. Red, black, 9.0 x 6.0, -/94. 8 mono phots, no maps, no Index. Apps: unit nominal roll.
* This fairly slim volume is arranged in two parts. The first is a superficial narrative account of a local CEF unit which embarked for Europe on 31 March 1916. The second, very much longer, section is a roll of every man who sailed. The Bn was perpetuated by the Princess Louise Fusiliers.
R/3 V/3. UWOL/NYPL. JEB/RP.

Royal New Brunswick Regiment

HISTORICAL RECORDS OF THE 62nd ST JOHN FUSILIERS (CANADIAN MILITIA)
Maj E T Sturdee * J & A McMillan, St John, New Brunswick, 1888. Red, gold, Regtl crest, 7.75 x 5.75, ii/139. No ills, no maps, no Index. Apps: list of officers (with brief notes of their services), Rules of the Volunteer Corps, Dress Regulations, Rules for Enrolment, Promotion, etc.
* Originally raised in 1860 as a Company of the 1st Bn of St John County Militia, the unit soon absorbed other New Brunswick Companies and became The St John Volunteer Battalion. Mobilised briefly for the 1866 and 1885 campaigns, it saw little or no action in either. This is essentially a routine account of part-time soldiering in 19th Century Canada. R/5 V/3. MODL. AMM.
Note: the Regt amalgamated in August 1946 with The New Brunswick Rangers to form The South New Brunswick Regt. Four months later it was retitled The New Brunswick Scottish. This unit amalgamated in 1954 with The Carleton and York Regt to form 1st Bn, The New Brunswick Regt (Carleton and York).

THE STORY OF THE FIGHTING 26th
The Glorious Story of the Fighting 26th, New Brunswick's Own Infantry Unit in the Greatest War of all Ages
R W Gould and S K Smith * Montreal Standard, Montreal, for the authors, n.d. (c.1920). Soft card, stapled, grey, Bn badge, 15.25 x 10.5, -/48. 4 fps, 66 mono phots (mostly named portraits), no maps, no Index. Apps: nominal roll of all ranks at embarkation.
* Not so much a book as a collection of contemporary newspaper articles. Half of the pages are taken up, either in whole or in part, with advertisements. As the triumphalist sub-title might imply, this was basically a commercial publishing venture, not a serious attempt to record history. There is some coverage of the Bn's battles in France and Flanders, but its accuracy should not be taken at face value. R/4 V/2. NYPL. JRD.
Note: the Bn is perpetuated by 1st Bn, RNB Regt (Carleton and York).

THE 104th NEW BRUNSWICK BATTALION IN THE FIRST WORLD WAR, 1914-1918
Harold G Kimball * Unipress, Fredericton, NB, 1962. Soft card, stapled, red, black. Regtl crest, 8.5 x 5.25, -/20. 10 mono phots (groups of personnel, not identified), no maps, no Index. Apps: list of CEF units recruited in the Province of New Brunswick.
* This very limited account serves only to emphasise the chaos which surrounded the formation of the CEF in 1914-1915, and the arbitrary way in which Canada's volunteer soldiers were despatched to the Western Front with comrades with whom they had not properly trained, and commanded by officers whom they barely knew. After much indecision and several changes of designation, the first New Brunswick volunteers sailed for England in 1916 as 104th Cdn Inf Bn CEF. The unit was progressively milked to reinforce other Bns and finally, in early 1918, was disbanded. R/3 V/1. PC. JRD.

1st BATTALION, THE NEW BRUNSWICK RANGERS
A Brief Account of the Unit's Exploits in World War II
P R Robinson * Publication details not shown, n.d. Soft card, stapled, mottled green, blind, Regtl crest, 6.0 x 9.5, -/47. 6 mono phots (groups of personnel), 16 line drawings, no maps, no Index. Apps: Roll of Honour (KIA, DOW, and DOD, all listed separately, with ranks and serials), H&A (with ranks and serials), nominal roll (all ranks, at March 1945), notes on the principal actions in which the Bn was engaged.
* The Rangers were mobilised at St John, New Brunswick, on 28 August 1939. Until 1943, they were employed in coastal defence duties in north east Canada, but then moved to England where they became 10th Canadian Independent Machine Gun Company (New Brunswick Rangers). It was the only such unit in the 4th Cdn Armd Div. It landed in France in July 1944 and fought throughout the NW Europe campaign. The narrative is interesting as far as it goes, but the appendixes are probably the best feature of this modest little book. R/4 V/2. PC. JRD.

NORTH SHORE (NEW BRUNSWICK) REGIMENT
Will R Bird * Unipress, Fredericton, NB, for the Brunswick Press, 1963. Dark blue, gold, Regtl crest, 9.5 x 6.5, -/629. Fp, 98 mono phots (incl 3 pages of small individual portraits of former COs, 1864-1960), 12 maps (11 bound in, one printed on each of the end-papers), Glossary, Index. Apps: Roll of Honour (KIA and WIA, for WWII only), list of former officers, notes on Battle Honours (for WWI and WWII).
* A fine big book which opens with a good account of the original County Militias (Northumberland, Gloucester, and Restigouche) between 1811 and 1867, with rolls of their officers. In 1870, these Militias evolved into the 73rd Northumberland (New Brunswick) Battalion of Infantry, later the 73rd Infantry Regt. This was mobilised in 1914 but for home duties only. The majority of the officers and men volunteered for service overseas and went to the Western Front with the 26th Cdn Inf Bn CEF and fought at Arras, Hill 70, Ypres, Amiens, etc. The author does,

however, make plentiful mention of officers and NCOs who served with other CEF units. The Regt was redesignated North Shore (New Brunswick) in 1922, and carried this title in WWII. Mobilised in 1940, it arrived in England in 1941, and went ashore in Normandy, at St Aubin, on 6 June 1944. After the Normandy battles, where it lost all its vehicles and 37 dead when bombed by the US Army Air Force, it took part in all the main operations fought by 3rd Cdn Div (the Scheldt, the Breskens Pocket, the Waal, the Hochwald, etc). One claim to fame is that the Regt lost only four men taken POW by the Germans throughout the NW Europe campaign. The narrative is packed with names (making the Index particularly useful), and most of the officers appear in the well captioned photographs. The Regt is now titled 2nd Bn, Royal New Brunswick Regt (North Shore). R/3 V/5. MODL. JEB/JRD/RH.
Note: reference may be made also to THE SCARLET DAWN, by Hon Maj R M Hickey (Tribune Publishing Co Ltd, Campbellton). Hickey was Chaplain to the Regt in NW Europe.

INVICTA
The Carleton and York Regiment in the Second World War
Robert Tooley * New Ireland Press, Frederiction, NB, 1989. Light blue, gold, Regtl crest, 9.25 x 6.25, xv/471. Fp, 25 mono phots, 30 maps (bound in), Glossary, Bibliography, Index. Apps: Roll of Honour (KIA, DOW, DOD, WIA, MIA, all with dates), H&A.
* This Regt had a very short life-span. It was formed in 1936 by the amalgamation of the Carleton Light Infantry with the York Regt (both of which had long and convoluted histories). Mobilised in September 1939, it moved to England three months later and formed part of the anti-invasion force. In 1943, a detachment was sent to North Africa to gain battle experience, these troops being amongst the very few Canadians to serve in that theatre of war. The complete Regt landed in Sicily on 10 July 1943 and saw some hard action on the island. Crossing to the mainland at Reggio Calabria on 3 September, it subsequently fought all the way up the peninsula to Rimini before being withdrawn for transfer to Holland in March 1945. Its final actions were fought at Apeldoorn, Ham, and on the Grebbe. The narrative is well written and full of vivid descriptions of minor episodes within the larger framework. Rolls of officers are inserted in the text at key dates. In 1954, the Carleton and York Regt amalgamated with the New Brunswick Scottish to form 1st Bn, Royal New Brunswick Regt (Carleton and York).
R/1 V/5. CWM. JRD.

West Nova Scotia Regiment

WEST NOVAS
A History of the West Nova Scotia Regiment
Thomas H Raddall * Publisher's details not shown, Toronto, 1947. Brown, gold, Regtl crest, 9.5 x 6.25, -/326. 2 fps, 95 mono phots, 10 maps, no Index. Apps: Roll of Honour (KIA, all ranks).
* Chapter I is a summary of the Militia tradition in Nova Scotia from 1697 (when the French established the first local unit) through to the formation of the West Novas and their services in WWII. Most of the chapters are in fact devoted to the period 1939-1945. The Regt served in Sicily, mainland Italy, and NW Europe with 1st Cdn Div. Page 318 carries a list of the twenty-one major actions in which it took part. This is a good readable narrative history which could have been improved by the addition of more reference appendixes and an Index.
R/4 V/4. UWOL/NYPL/MODL. JEB/RH.
Note: the book was first produced with a limited print run of 1000 (numbered) copies. It was reprinted in 1986 without amendment. The second edition has a similar brown casing with gold lettering. No publication details are shown in either this or the original (1947) edition.

Nova Scotia Highlanders

OVER THE TOP WITH THE 25th
Chronicle of Events at Vimy Ridge and Courcelette
Lieut Ralph Lewis * H H Marshall, Halifax, Nova Scotia, 1918. White, black, 9.5 x 6.5, -/59. One mono phot, 2 maps, no appendixes, no Index.
* A brief summary of events. Some officers and men are mentioned in the text. Limited, but interesting as far as it goes. The Bn is perpetuated by the Nova Scotia Highlanders. R/5 V/1. TPL. JEB.

THE TWENTY-FIFTH BATTALION, CANADIAN EXPEDITIONARY FORCE
Nova Scotia's Famous Regiment in World War One
F B MacDonald CD and John J Gardiner * J A Chadwick, Sydney, NS, 1983. Soft card, 8.5 x 5.5, -/211. Fp, 9 mono phots (incl one of badges), no cld ills, no maps, Glossary, no Index. Apps: H&A (statistical summary only), list of former COs, Bn nominal roll, notes on Battle Honours.
* A retrospective account of the 25th Cdn Inf Bn CEF, and an improvement on the Lewis booklet noted in the preceding entry. The authors followed the unusual but academically sound route of tracing and interviewing numerous elderly veterans who had served with the Bn on the Western Front, and then relating their recollections to the facts as stated in the contemporary Bn War Diary. The former source gives colour (but not necessarily accuracy), while the latter gives total accuracy (but little emotion). The combination produces a result both interesting and authoritative. R/1 V/4. PC. MCJ.

THE EIGHTY-FIFTH IN FRANCE AND FLANDERS
Lieut Col Joseph Hayes DSO * Royal Print & Litho Ltd, Halifax, NS, 1920. Green, gold, Regtl crest, 9.5 x 6.5, -/362. Fp, 22 mono phots, one map (loose in rear pocket), no Index. Apps: unit nominal roll, list of officers (with service details).
* Sometimes known as 'the Highlanders without kilts', they distinguished themselves at Vimy Ridge and held Hill 145. Like the 25th Bn, this unit also is perpetuated by the Nova Scotia Highlanders. R/4 V/4. RMCL/NYPL. JEB.

106th OVERSEAS BATTALION, CEF, NOVA SCOTIA RIFLES
A Short History and Photographic Record
Anon * The Mortimer Printing Co Ltd, Halifax, NS, 1916. Stiff card, light brown, black/silver, Bn badge, 12.0 x 9.5, ii/47. 896 mono phots, no maps, no formal appendixes, no Index.
* An unusual wartime publishing venture, aimed presumably at the families of the men serving with the Bn. Just one page of narrative is devoted to the story of the Bn's formation and training in 1915-1916. The remainder of the book consists of 896 head-and-shoulder portraits of the Bn's members, arranged by Platoon and giving, in most cases, their home towns. Of little interest to the military historian, but probably useful for genealogists and medal collectors. R/5 V/1. CWM. MAR.
Note: the sole narrative page contains a number of fervent patriotic references to 'the Fiery Cross' and Roderick Dhu MacNeill. He was a prominent fighting Hebridean chieftain of the late 17th Century. Readers wishing to know more about these baffling allusions should consult any works which deal with that period in Scotland's history.

NO RETREATING FOOTSTEPS
The Story of the Nova Scotia Highlanders
Will R Bird * Printed by The Kentville Publishing Co Ltd, Kentville, NS, for the Regt, n.d. (c.1951). Blue, gold, Regtl crest, 9.5 x 6.0, -/398. Fp, 18 mono phots, 6 maps, no appendixes, no Index.
* The Nova Scotia Highlanders were established in 1936 at Amherst. They landed in Normandy as an element of 3rd Cdn Div. Some of the Regt's men were captured and, in a notorious incident, were murdered on the orders of Gen Kurt Meyer. This book is a substantial and complete unit history, flawed by the lack of appendixes

and an Index. The illustrations and maps are very well presented.
R/4 V/4. NYPL/UWOL/CWM. JEB.
Note: the first (c.1951) edition was restricted to a print run of 1000 copies. There have been two subsequent facsimile reprints (not seen).

NORTH NOVA SCOTIA HIGHLANDERS
Lieut Col D F Forbes * Printed in Varel, Germany, 1945. Stiff card, blue, gold, 5.5 x 4.0, -/32. No ills, no maps, no appendixes, no Index.
* Formed in June 1940 from four Militia units, the Regt landed in England in July 1941, and then in Normandy on 6 June 1944. By war's end it was in Leer, North Germany. Although very brief, the narrative is lucid and readable, and includes many references to officer casualties and awards. R/4 V/3. MODL. AMM.

THE CAPE BRETON HIGHLANDERS, 1939-1945
Anon * Publication details not shown, n.d. Soft card, facsimile Regtl tartan, Regtl crest, gold/silver, 7.75 x 5.5, -/18 (not numbered). No ills, no maps, no appendixes, no Index.
* A booklet, professionally printed, which is simply a Roll of Honour of all those members of the Regt who lost their lives in Italy and NW Europe between 15 January 1944 and 1 May 1945. The names are listed chronologically - according to the dates of death - and show each man's Service number, the Coy with which he was serving, the cause of death (KIA, DOW, etc), and the name of his home town. R/4 V/1. PC. RP.

Le Régiment de Maisonneuve

LE REGIMENT DE MAISONNEUVE VERS LA VICTOIRE, 1944-1945
Gerard Marchand * Les Presses Libre, Montreal, 1980. Illustrated stiff card, cream, brown/black, 'Infantryman' motif, 9.0 x 6.0, -/266. More than 100 mono phots, 10 maps, no Index. Apps: Roll of Honour.
* Written in French. A good workmanlike history, well illustrated, with helpful supporting maps. R/3 V/4. MODL. AMM.

BON COEUR ET BON BRAS
Histoire du Régiment de Maisonneuve, 1880-1980
Jacques Gouin * Mediabec Inc, Montreal, 1980. Soft card, full colour, Regtl crest, 9.0 x 6.0, -/303. 5 fps, 72 mono phots (incl many named portraits), 9 maps, Bibliography, Index. Apps: Rolls of Honour (WWI and WWII, very detailed), list of COs (1880-1980, with biographical notes).
* Written in French. It covers the period 1612 to 1980 in good uniform detail, but with the main focus on services in WWI and WWII. The Regt perpetuates the 41st and 206th Bns CEF. R/2 V/5. PC. JRD.

Cameron Highlanders of Ottawa

THE DUKE OF CORNWALL'S OWN RIFLES
A Regimental History of the Forty-third Regiment, Active Militia of Canada
Capt Ernest J Chambers * E L Ruddy, Ottawa, 1903. Cloth boards with leather spine, red/blue, gold, Regtl crest, 11.5 x 9.0, -/70/xii (the latter being commercial advertisements). Many mono phots (mostly high quality studio portraits of officers), no maps, no appendixes, no Index.
* As noted elsewhere in the Canadian section of this bibliography, Capt Chambers was a professional author who, for several years at the turn of the 20th Century, earned his living (at least in part) by compiling regimental histories. He almost always worked in conjunction with a printer by the name of E L Ruddy, a man who clearly must have had a skilled workforce and very good printing and print-finishing machinery. Chambers, Ruddy, and the client Regiment, presumably made contractual arrangements regarding the work to be done and the profits to be made. The financial terms must have been very sensible because, unfailingly,

Ruddy used only the best materials and assembled an end-product of high quality. Chambers, for his part, always wrote in a laudatory florid style, made flattering references to all senior officers and local dignatories, included numerous studio portraits, and generally ensured that his work would be pleasing to the wealthiest sectors of local society. He further increased the profit potential by having a number of pages at the rear of each book which carried commercial announcements. The advertisers were firms anxious to associate their products and services with the prestige of the County's, or city's, own Militia regiment and its influential members. All of this should have militated against the writing of good history. Instead, Chambers produced excellent historical accounts which have stood the test of time. Apart from being accurate records of events, they capture the social and military ethos of the period in which they were written. Further, because his client regiments had often been involved in events in which the British Army had taken no part, he described various battles and scuffles which otherwise might not have been recorded elsewhere. Certain 'aid to the civil power' deployments, and the Fenian and Riel campaigns, are cases in point. This book is typical of his work. The Duke of Cornwall's Own Rifles were forebears of the Cameron Highlanders of Ottawa. R/4 V/4. AMOT/UWOL/MODL. RP.
Note: the Cameron Highlanders of Ottawa recruited mainly in and around the city of that name. The Regt must not be confused with the totally separate Queen's Own Cameron Highlanders of Canada, a Regt which was based in Winnipeg and which recruited mainly in Western Canada (primarily the Province of Manitoba). Refer to the Index of Units for details of this Regt.

THE HISTORY OF THE 1st BATTALION, THE CAMERON HIGHLANDERS OF OTTAWA (MG)
Lieut Col Richard M Ross OBE ED * Runge Press Ltd, Ottawa, n.d. (c.1946). Case-bound, with printed reproduction of the Regtl tartan and Regtl crest superimposed, 9.5 x 6.0, -/96. Fp, 7 mono phots, 6 maps, no Index. Apps: Roll of Honour.
* A well written straightforward account which covers the period from September 1939 to December 1945. Based upon the individual Company War Diaries, it is clearly authentic and reliable in every way. Like all MG Bns, it was split up while on active service and its sub-units allocated to various different formations. They went ashore on the Normandy beaches on 6 June 1944 and fought throughout the NW Europe campaign. A nicely presented record, with many individuals of all ranks mentioned in the text. R/4 V/4. AMOT/UWOL/NYPL. RP.

Royal Winnipeg Rifles

THE 90th REGIMENT
A Regimental History of the 90th Regiment, Winnipeg Rifles
Capt Ernest J Chambers * Publication details not shown, but most probably printed by E L Ruddy, for Chambers and the Regt, n.d. (c.1906). Blue, gold, 12.0 x 9.0, x/99/xv (the latter being commerical advertisements). Fp, 55 mono phots, no maps, no Index. Apps: list of former officers (with details of their services).
* Another of Chambers' opulent histories. He describes the raising of the first Militia units in Manitoba and their role in the Fenian Raid campaign of 1870-1871. He then passes to the specific story of the Winnipeg Rifles, their part in the suppression of the 1885 Riel Rebellion, and the various changes in the Regt's status and organisation. The final chapter deals with its contribution to the war in South Africa when a number of Winnipeg Rifles officers and men joined the two Canadian Contingents. R/4 V/3. MODL/UWOL. JMAT.

SIX THOUSAND MEN OF CANADA
Being the History of the 44th Battalion, Canadian Infantry, 1914-1919
E S Russenholt * De Montfort Press, Winnipeg, for the Bn Association, 1932. Green, gold, Div patch, 9.75 x 6.5, xii/364. 4 fps, 50 mono phots, 5 sketches, 10 maps (bound in), no Index. Apps: H&A, unit nominal roll (with notes on casualties, thereby substituting for the lack of a 'Roll of Honour' appendix).
* The title of the book refers to the number of men who passed through the Bn

during its time on the Western Front. Like so many other CEF units, the 44th had little chance to adequately prepare itself for war. Raised in December 1914 with Militia volunteers from the 90th Winnipeg Rifles, the 100th Winnipeg Grenadiers, and the 106th Winnipeg Light Infantry, the Bn started to train as an integral unit but was repeatedly milked to provide drafts for other CEF units. Having survived the threat of disbandment, it finally embarked as part of 4th Cdn Div. Arriving in France in 1916, it soon lost 200 men at Regina Trench. Reinforced with drafts from New Brunswick, it moved to Vimy. The battles of that period are described here in great detail. This is a good history, with many individuals and incidents mentioned in the text. The 44th Bn is perpetuated by the Royal Winnipeg Rifles. R/4 V/4. TPL/MODL. JRD/AMM.

THE WINNIPEG RIFLES
Fiftieth Anniversary, 1883-1933
Anon ('the Anniversary Committee') * Publisher's details not shown, Winnipeg, n.d. (1933). Soft card, tan, green/black, 10.0 x 8.0, -/59. 52 mono phots, no maps, no Index. Apps: H&A (VCs only), list of former officers, notes on the Regtl music.
* A brief summary of the Regt's history, intended simply to mark the half-century anniversary celebrations. R/4 V/2. NYPL. JRT/RP.

SEVENTY-FIFTH ANNIVERSARY - ROYAL WINNIPEG RIFLES, 1883-1958
Anon * Publication details not shown, (1958). Soft card, rifle green and cream, black, 'Shako and cap' motif, 10.0 x 8.0, -/64. Fp, more than 100 mono phots, approx 40 line drawings, one map, no Index. Apps: list of COs (1883-1958), notes on Battle Honours.
* A souvenir, celebrating the 90th Winnipeg Rifles (1883-1920), the Winnipeg Rifles (1920-1935), and the Royal Winnipeg Rifles (1935 onwards). The narrative gives an outline of services on the Nile (1884, when some members joined the Nile Voyageurs), the Northwest Rebellion (1885), South Africa (1899-1900), and the two world wars. Many individuals are named in the text, and the photographs include many captioned portraits of past and serving members. R/4 V/2. MODL. AMM.

LITTLE BLACK DEVILS
History of the Royal Winnipeg Rifles
Bruce Tascona and Eric Wells * Frye Publishing, Winnipeg, Manitoba, 1983.
Green, silver, Regtl crest, 9.5 x 6.5, x/241. Fp, 137 mono phots, 17 cld ills, 16 maps (8 printed in the text, 8 bound in), no Index. Apps: Rolls of Honour (DOD in the 1884 Nile campaign, KIA in the 1885 North West Rebellion and the South African War, then KIA and DOW, with dates, for WWI and WWII), H&A (Nile, South Africa, WWI and WWII, with citations, plus pictures of VC winners), list of former officers (1883-1983), history of the 'shooting rifles', notes on Battle Honours.
* The Regt was founded in 1883 (vide preceding entries) and the first active service by any of its members was the Nile Expedition of 1884. The detachment suffered no battle casualties, but the CO and eleven others died as the result of disease or drowning accidents. A year later, the Regt was mobilised in response to the Riel Rebellion. There is good coverage of the battles of Batoche and Fish Creek (where the Sioux distinguished their rifle green jackets from the red coats of the North West Mounted Police by referring to them as 'little black devils', a soubriquet adopted for the Regtl motto - 'Hosti Acie Nominati'. The authors make brief reference to the 39 men who went to South Africa for the Anglo-Boer War before giving very comprehensive coverage to the Regt's WWI services (when most of its personnel managed to stay together as the 8th Cdn Inf Bn CEF and retained their own cap badge). It fought in all the main Canadian battles between 1915 and 1918 (Second Ypres, Gravenstafel, Festubert, Mont Sorrel, the Somme, Amiens, Canal du Nord, etc). Four Bns were mobilised or newly raised in WWII, and the 1st Bn went ashore in Normandy on D-Day. At Putot-en-Bessin, on 8 June, and only two days after landing, 18 men of the Regt were taken prisoner by the 26th Panzer Grenadier Regt and murdered. The Regt served in NW Europe through to war's end, returning to Winnipeg on Christmas Eve, 1945. The narrative mentions

very few individuals, but is an excellent account of the Regt's services as a whole. R/1 V/4. MODL. JRD.

Essex and Kent Scottish

HISTORY OF THE 21st REGIMENT OF ESSEX FUSILIERS
Of Windsor, Ontario, Canada
Lieut William H Aston * The Record Printing Co Ltd, for the Regt, February, 1902. Red, white, pages with rounded corners and gold blocked all around (AEG), 9.25 x 6.25, -/128. 2 fps, 44 mono phots (incl 30 studio portraits and 9 groups, all personnel identified in the captions), no maps, no Index. Apps: Roll of Honour (20 men who died while serving in South Africa with the 1st Cdn Contingent), list of officers, idem SNCOs, notes on the Regtl music.
* This excessively rare book was published to mark the opening of the Regt's new Armouries, and is comprehensive in every way. The author covers the story of the Regt and its forebears from 1812 onwards, with references to the earlier associated unit titles - 23rd Bn Volunteer Light Infantry, The Essex Volunteer Light Infantry, the 24th Kent Bn, etc. As the 21st Regt of Essex Fusiliers, the unit was formed in June 1885 as a specific response to the Riel Rebellion, but it took no part in that campaign. The author's account of an earlier rebellion - the 1837 affair in Upper Canada - is more detailed than in any other unit history seen by this reporter. The author also describes the Regt's 'aid to the civil power' duties during the Street Railway Strike of July 1899. Soon afterwards, a large proportion of the Regt volunteered for service in South Africa, but the book contains little detail of their experiences (other than the fate of those who did not return home). A well written narrative, especially with regard to events in the Toronto and Windsor district of Southern Ontario, and with many officers mentioned throughout. R/5 V/4. UWOL. JRD.

1st BATTALION, THE ESSEX SCOTTISH REGIMENT
1st Battalion The Essex Scottish Regiment (Allied with the Essex Regiment), 1939-1945 - A Brief Narrative
Capt R W Meanwell * Gale & Polden Ltd, Aldershot, 1946. Soft card, beige/cream, green, Macaulay tartan embellishment, Regtl crest, 10.0 x 6.25, vii/93. Fp, 92 mono phots, one map, no Index. Apps: Roll of Honour, H&A, list of officers.
* The Regt arrived in England in July 1940. It fought at Dieppe, and then later in the Caen (Normandy) battles, at Cleve (the Rhine crossings), and in the Hochwald Forest (where Maj F A Tilston gained the VC). Despite its superb fighting record, the Regt is not well recorded in this book. According to the author, 'reference to individuals by name was not deemed advisable'. There are very few references to other units or to larger events. The book meets no more than the author's declared aim - 'to produce a brief dispassionate chronological narrative'. The Regt was later retitled The Essex and Kent Scottish. R/4 V/2. NYPL/MODL. JRD.

48th Highlanders of Canada

HISTORY OF THE 48th HIGHLANDERS
The 48th Highlanders of Toronto, Canadian Militia
Alexander Fraser * E L Ruddy, Toronto, Ontario, 1900. Red/green, Regtl crest, 11.5 x 9.0, -/96/xxxi (the latter being commercial advertisements). Fp, 60 mono phots (incl 49 captioned portraits of officers and musicians), numerous line drawings, no maps, no Index. Apps: list of officers (with promotion dates), list of subscribers, notes on Regtl music.
* The raising of the Regt was Gazetted on 16 October 1891 and it paraded for the first time just six months later with a strength of six Rifle Coys and a Bugle Band. This book was published in 1900, so it contains no references to active services. Its greatest interest is to be found in the late Victorian social structure of the Toronto district and the local inheritance of Scottish music and traditions. All of this is well reflected in the narrative and in the charming photographs. To provide

his narrative with additional bulk, the author included some interesting summaries of the Canadian and North American war services of the British Army's Highland Regts which garrisoned those territories between the mid-18th and mid-19th Centuries - the old 42nd, 71st, 74th, 78th, 79th, 84th, and 93rd Regts. A first class source for students of military pipe music, of Scotland's military heritage, and of Scottish-Canadian genealogy in that area. R/4 V/4. UWOL/NYPL/MODL. JRD.

THE RED WATCH
With the First Canadian Division in France
Col J A Currie * McClelland, Goodchild & Stewart Ltd, Toronto, 1916. Red, black, Regtl crest (48th Highlanders), 8.25 x 5.5, -/308. Fp, 16 mono phots, 2 maps, Index. Apps: unit nominal roll.
* A book written by its first CO (1914-1915) in a personal but informative style, it is the story of the formation and early services of the 15th Bn CEF (48th Highlanders of Canada). One of the first units to proceed overseas, it formed part of the 3rd Cdn Inf Bde and was known as 'the Red Watch'. The author was invalided back to Canada in 1915, but his account provides a useful record of the Bn's formation in Toronto in August 1914, its move to England in October, and then to France in February 1915. Many officers are named in the narrative and in the one group photograph. R/4 V/3. MODL. AMM.

48th HIGHLANDERS OF CANADA, 1891-1928
Kim Beattie * The Southam Press, Toronto, for the Regt, 1932. Dark blue, gold, Regtl crest, 9.5 x 6.25, -/434. Fp, 15 composite mono plates, 7 maps (drawn by E W Haldenby), no appendixes, no Index.
* As far as it goes, this is an attractive and well prepared unit history. The lack of appendixes and an Index severely reduces its worth as a source of reference. Many individuals and their awards are mentioned in the text but, in a book having 434 pages, tracing them is a laborious task. Despite the dates shown in its title, the book is devoted mainly to WWI services on the Western Front.
R/4 V/3. PCAL/NYPL/CWM. LM/RP.

DILEAS
A History of the 48th Highlanders of Canada, 1929-1956
Kim Beattie * T H Best Printing Co Ltd, Toronto, Ontario, for the Regtl Association, 1957. Red, gold, Regtl crest, 9.25 x 6.25, xvii/847. Fp, 46 mono phots, 11 maps (9 printed in the text, 2 on the end-papers), no formal appendixes, Index.
* Twenty-five years after writing the Regt's first major history (vide preceding entry), Kim Beattie was asked to write this second and updated record. Very few authors have such a long association with the same Regt. His 1957 work is written on a monumental scale. It is packed with names, dates, incidents, key events, and all the other information any reader is likely to require. Crucially, this book is furnished with an Index. There are still no appendixes, but people and places can be found in the Index. The illustrations are superb and fully captioned. The focus of the narrative is on WWII - mobilisation, the move to England, the battles in Sicily and mainland Italy, the move to Holland, the advance into Germany in 1945 as part of 1st Cdn Div, and the return to Canada. The Regt's seventeen major battles are well documented, with an entire chapter being devoted to each.
R/3 V/4. NYPL/MODL/CWM. JRD.
Note: although not imprinted as such, this book is effectively Volume II of the Regiment's history. 'Dileas' translates from the Gaelic as 'Faithful', or 'Loyal'.

Argyll and Sutherland Highlanders of Canada (Princess Louise's)

HISTORICAL RECORDS OF THE ARGYLL & SUTHERLAND HIGHLANDERS OF CANADA (PRINCESS LOUISE'S)
Formerly 91st Regiment, Canadian Highlanders, Canadian Militia, 1903-1928
Lieut Col Walter H Bruce, Lieut Col William R Turnbull, and Lieut Col James Chisholm * Robert Duncan & Co, Hamilton, Ontario, for the Regt, 1928. Full leather,

gold, 9.5 x 6.5, iv/99. Two fps, 25 mono phots (mostly portraits of officers), no maps, no Index. Apps: Roll of Honour (officers only, with dates, Bns, and locations), lists of officers who served (1903-1926), idem Adjutants, idem Quartermasters, idem RSMs, idem RPMs, etc, etc, all with dates and medal entitlements.
* The Regt was raised in 1903 following representations by Scots and Canadians of Scottish descent who had settled in the area of Hamilton, Ontario, and who had lobbied for a local 'Highland Militia' unit. Its initial title was 91st Regt, Canadian Highlanders, this number being the same as that of the British Army's Princess Louise's Argyll & Sutherland Highlanders. The Canadian unit's present title, as shown in the title of this book, was granted in June 1927. The Regt volunteered for overseas service in 1914 but, due to the notorious ruling by Sir Sam Hughes, was confined to recruitment and training tasks on behalf of various Bns of the Canadian Expeditionary Force. The Regt's pipers went to the 19th and 173rd Cdn Inf Bns CEF. This book's narrative makes almost no reference to WWI but concentrates instead upon pre- and post-war events. The range of appendixes is exemplary, and a model for all compilers of regimental history books. The 'Roll of Honour' lists those former Argyll officers who lost their lives while serving overseas with various CEF units. R/4 V/4. NYPL/MODL. JRD.

THE ARGYLL AND SUTHERLAND HIGHLANDERS OF CANADA (PRINCESS LOUISE'S) 1928-1953
Lieut Col H M Jackson MBE ED * Printed by the Industrial Schools for the Deaf, Montreal, for the Regt, 1953. Green, red, Regtl crest, 9.25 x 6.0, -/407. Fp, 38 mono phots (mostly named officers), 11 maps, no Index. Apps: Roll of Honour (KIA, WIA, DOW, and POW), H&A, list of former COs, idem former officers, nominal roll (all ranks, 1940-1946).
* While the narrative does indeed deal with pre- and post-war events, this is essentially a WWII history (devoted mainly to the Regt's services in NW Europe). The book is a straightforward, complete, and well rounded narrative record, based upon the War Diary. Both the binding and the paper are somewhat inferior in quality, and the surviving copies seen have not worn well over the years since the book was published. Another disappointment is the lack of an Index - a serious handicap in a book of this length. R/3 V/4. PCAL/NYPL/MODL. RP.
Note: the book was published with a Corrigenda slip listing thirty corrections (tipped in after the title page).

Lake Superior Scottish Regiment

FROM THUNDER BAY THROUGH YPRES WITH THE FIGHTING 52nd
M C Millar * Printed in Fort William, Ontario, 1918. Paper covers, brown, black, 7.5 x 5.5, Regtl crest, -/101. Two mono phots, no maps, no appendixes, no Index.
* Private Millar served with the Scout Section of the 52nd Cdn Inf Bn CEF and was invalided in 1917. Basically an autobiographical account, the book is limited to one man's experiences and memory. However, he does seem to have had a dependable recollection of the names of places and people, and this is as good an account of the Bn's services during the middle years of the war as one is likely to obtain in such circumstances. The 52nd Bn is perpetuated by the Lake Superior Scottish Regiment. R/5 V/3. TPL. MCJ.

IN FACE OF DANGER
The History of the Lake Superior Scottish Regiment
Lieut Col George F G Stanley * Published by the Regt, Port Arthur, Ontario, n.d. (1960). Blue, silver, 9.25 x 6.25, -/357. Fp, 43 mono phots, one line drawing, 23 maps (21 printed in the text, 2 on the end-papers, all drawn by Maj C C J Bond), no Index. Apps: Roll of Honour (KIA and DOW for WWI, with dates, for 52nd Bn CEF, then KIA, DOW and WIA for the LSR in WWII), H&A (WWI and WWII), list of COs (1886-1958, with dates, for the 96th Algoma Rifles, the 96th Lake Superior Regt, the 52nd Bn CEF, and then the modern Regt, post-1921).
* The roots of the Regt are in Port Arthur, Ontario, where a Company of Rifles was raised in 1885 and named the 96th Bn (Algoma Rifles) a year later. Disbanded

in 1896, it was reactivated in 1905 and given the title Lake Superior Regt. In 1914 it provided drafts for various CEF units, but then increased its strength sufficiently to provide a complete Bn for duty overseas. Numbered 52, it went to France in 1916. It fought in most of the Canadian Corps' great battles such as Mont Sorrell, Vimy Ridge, and Passchendaele. Several of the 52nd's men were full-blooded Canadian Indians. Two were awarded the DCM and two the MM. The Regt was again mobilised in 1940 and converted to the motorised infantry role. It went ashore in Normandy on 20 July 1944 as part of 4th Bde, 4th Cdn Armd Div. The Regt's contribution to both world wars is described lucidly in this book, but there are few references to individual officers and men. The Regt was later retitled the Lake Superior Scottish Regt. R/3 V/4. MODL. JRD.

North Saskatchewan Regiment

A RESUME OF THE STORY OF 1st BATTALION, THE SASKATOON LIGHT INFANTRY (MG) Canadian Army Overseas

Lieut Col D E Walker DSO ED * General Printing & Bookbinding Ltd, Saskatoon, n.d. (c.1946). Stiff card, black, gold, Regtl crest, 10.0 x 7.0, -/139. Fp, 210 mono phots, one cld ill (the Colours), 5 maps, no Index. Apps: list of former officers, music of the Regtl march, four poems by Sgt W A MacKay.

* This account covers briefly the story of 5th Cdn Inf Bn CEF in WWI, and of 1st Bn Saskatoon LI in WWII. Having mobilised on 1 September 1939, 1st Bn moved to England only three months later. Deployed initially as part of the anti-invasion force, it trained in the UK for three years before moving to the Mediterranean theatre for the invasions of Sicily and mainland Italy. It was the Machine-gun Bn of the 1st Cdn Inf Div. The Division moved to Holland in early 1945 and took part in the final assault on the German homeland. The book seems to have been written mainly as a souvenir for those who served, but very few of them are named in the narrative or in the picture captions. The book is useful mainly as a record of the major actions in which units and sub-units of the Bn were engaged. It was later redesignated 2nd North Saskatchewan Regt (Saskatoon Light Infantry). R/4 V/3. MODL/RMCL. AMM/JRD.

Note: a useful additional source is 1st BATTALION, THE SASKATOON LIGHT INFANTRY (MG), HONOUR ROLL, 10th JULY 1943 TO 8th MAY 1945, SICILY, ITALY AND HOLLAND, anon (Gale & Polden Ltd, Aldershot, 1945). This is a booklet of only 15 pages, but it contains the Roll of Honour which might otherwise have appeared as an appendix to the book by Walker (as above).

Regina Rifle Regiment

THE STORY OF THE TWENTY-EIGHTH (NORTH WEST) BATTALION, 1914-1917

G E Hewitt * W Charles & Son, London, UK, for the War Records Office, 1918. Paper covers, stapled, grey, black, Bn badge, 7.25 x 4.75, -/24. Fp, no other ills, no maps, no Index. Apps: list of major engagements in which the Bn took part (St Eloi Craters, Hooge, Courcelette, Vimy Ridge, etc), list of COs.

* The Bn was formed in Saskatchewan in late 1914. This is a very brief record of service on the Western Front as an element of the 6th Inf Bde, 2nd Cdn Div. It is unclear why the narrative ends with Passchendaele, but the descriptions of earlier actions (particularly at the St Eloi Craters on 3 April 1916) provide a useful record. The Bn is perpetuated by the Regina Rifle Regt. R/4 V/1. PC. JRD.

THE HISTORY OF THE 28th (NORTHWEST) BATTALION, CEF October 1914 - June 1919

Maj D G Scott Calder ED * Published by the Regina Rifle Regiment, n.d. (c.1961). Facsimile TS, in soft card covers, black with red spine, white, Bn badge, 12.75 x 8.0, -/277 (folios printed one side only). No ills, 85 maps (free-hand drawn, on unnumbered folios, bound in), Index. Apps: list of COs, idem Adjutants, idem RSMs and SNCOs (all with details of service), notes on the Colours.

* Formally established on 1 November 1914, the Bn recruited its personnel from

five Militia units in and around Regina (notably the 95th Saskatchewan Rifles). The first 2 i/c was Maj Alexander Ross. He assumed command in September 1916 and continued as CO until October 1918 when he was promoted to command the 6th Cdn Inf Bde. As an additional sub-title explains, this record is based mainly upon his personal diary - 'The Memoirs of Brig Gen Alexander Ross CMG DSO VD'. Scott Calder edited the memoirs and added much useful information regarding the Bn's predecessors (1907-1914) and the post-war organisation of the Militia. This describes the Bn's 'perpetuation' as 1st Bn South Saskatchewan Regt in 1920, and the reorganisation of 1925 which led to the formation of the Regina Rifle Regt. The narrative covers the three years of fighting on the Western Front, Ross's original material being much expanded by Scott Calder with quotations from the War Diary and Regtl Orders, plus numerous lists of awards and casualties inserted in the text and which might otherwise have appeared as appendixes. A prime source for genealogists. R/4 V/5. UCSRL. RBM.

1st BATTALION, THE REGINA RIFLE REGIMENT, 1939-1946

Capt Eric Luxton * Commercial Printers Ltd, Regina, for the Regina Rifles Association, n.d. (c.1946). Soft card, spiral bound, black, silver/brown, Regtl crest, 12.0 x 9.0, -/70. 40 mono phots (of poor quality), one map (poorly drawn), no Index. Apps: Roll of Honour, H&A, list of COs (with portrait photographs and biographical notes).

* This slim book has an unusual style of presentation, and generally gives the impression of having been assembled under the pressures of time and cost. This is a pity, because the narrative, although condensed, is readable and informative. The Bn went ashore on D-Day as part of 7th Inf Bde, 3rd Cdn Inf Div, at Courseulles. It had a hard campaign in Normandy, and another in Holland during the winter of 1944-1945. The author, who presumably served with the Bn, gives a lucid account of its experiences. R/3 V/3. AldMM/RMCL. RP.

South Saskatchewan Regiment

THE MARCH OF THE PRAIRIE MEN
Being a Story of the South Saskatchewan Regiment

Lieut Col G B Buchanan MBE * Midwest Litho Ltd, Saskatoon, Saskatchewan, 1957. Stiff card, blue/green/gold/purple/white, with blind cream spine, Regtl crest, 11.0 x 8.5, vi/75. Fp, 27 mono phots, 17 line drawings (chapter heads), one map, Glossary, no Index. Apps: Roll of Honour (all ranks, KIA, DOW and DOD, incl those who lost their lives while serving with other units), H&A, notes on Battle Honours, lineage of the Regt, statistical summary of casualties (WWII).

* The story opens with a brief summary of the Regt's evolution - 20th Mounted Rifles (1908), 152nd Cdn Inf Bn CEF, The Weyburn Regt (1924), and Saskatchewan Border Regt (1924). Thereafter, the narrative is devoted mainly to WWII. The Regt took part in the disastrous Dieppe Raid on 19 August 1942 when the CO, Lieut Col C C I Merritt, won the VC. On 6 July 1944, the Regt landed again in France. It fought in the battles around Caen (Bourgebus Ridge, Falaise Gap, etc) as part of 6th Inf Bde, 2nd Cdn Div. After the breakout, it served in Holland and on the German border (The Scheldt, Hochwald Forest, and Oldenburg). Some officers are mentioned in the text, but the main strength of this attractive book is to be found in its excellent descriptions of the major battles. R/3 V/3. NYPL/MODL. JRD.

Rocky Mountain Rangers

ROCKY MOUNTAIN RANGERS
First Battalion, CAAF, 1885-1941

Anon * Publication details not shown, n.d. (c.1941). Seen only in micro-fiche form, details of original casing not known, -/60. 56 mono phots, no maps, no Index. Apps: lists of officers, idem SNCOs, unit nominal roll.

* Only six pages are to given to the Regt's history. The bulk of the booklet is devoted to photographs of officers serving in 1941, and group pictures of the

SNCOs, the Regtl Band, the Regtl Bugle Band, Bn HQ personnel, and each of the eighteen Platoons. The pictures are all captioned with the names of those depicted. R/5 V/3. NLC. MAR.
Note: known to exist, but not seen, is ROCKY MOUNTAIN RANGERS - FIRST BATTALION CA (AF), 1885-1941, anon (Provincial Publishing Co, Montreal, 1946). There may be also a second version of this very rare publication, covering events up to 1943.

Loyal Edmonton Regiment

HISTORY OF THE 101st REGIMENT, EDMONTON FUSILIERS, 1908-1913
Capt H N Kennedy * Pierce & Kennedy, Edmonton, Alberta, n.d. (c.1914). Soft card covers secured with red cord, brown, Regt crest, 8.5 x 11.75 (landscape), 44 pages of text and illustrations, with 36 unnumbered pages of commercial advertisements. Fp, 18 mono phots, no maps, no Index. Apps: nominal roll.
* This is a very localised account of Militia soldiering over a short span of time. Its main value is the nominal roll, some biographical notes regarding officers, and the fifteen photographs of groups of personnel and individuals, all fully captioned with their names. An unusual and attractive item, of interest to local genealogists. The Regt was a forebear of The Loyal Edmonton Regt (3rd Bn, Princess Patricia's Canadian Light Infantry). R/5 V/2. UAL/MODL. JRD.

A CITY GOES TO WAR
History of the Loyal Edmonton Regiment (3 PPCLI)
Lieut Col G R Stevens OBE * Printed by Charters Publishing Co Ltd, Brampton, Ontario, for The Edmonton Regiment Association, 1964. Orange-red, Regtl crest, 10.25 x 6.75, -/431. Fp, 38 mono phots, 11 maps (folding, bound in), Index. Apps: Rolls of Honour (WWI, as 49th Cdn Inf Bn CEF, and WWII, as The Edmonton Regt and The Loyal Edmonton Regt), H&A (idem), list of former COs (with artists' sketches and biographical notes for each).
* An excellently presented account of services in WWI (the Western Front) and WWII (Sicily, mainland Italy, NW Europe). The narrative is fluent and readable. It covers all the major actions and moves, but is well laced with references to individual members and to minor incidents. The book is well printed and bound, and the maps are particularly good. For no obvious reason, the sub-title is shown on the dust-jacket but not on the title page. Similarly, the author's military rank appears on the dust-jacket but not on the title page. R/2 V/5. AldMM/MODL. RP.

Queen's Own Cameron Highlanders of Canada

THE QUEEN'S OWN CAMERON HIGHLANDERS OF CANADA
Twenty-fifth Anniversary Souvenir
Lieut Col J D Sinclair VD * Publisher's details not shown, Winnipeg, Manitoba, 1935. Soft card, grey, black, Regtl crest, 9.0 x 6.0, -/99. Fp, 32 mono phots (mostly captioned individual portraits), no maps, Chapter Notes, no Index. Apps: Roll of Honour (statistics only, for 16th, 27th, 43rd, 79th, 174th, and 179th Cdn Inf Bns CEF), H&A (idem), lists of officers (at 1910, with later war services, and at 1935).
* The early title - 79th Cameron Highlanders of Canada - was adopted in February 1910. The Regt was based in Winnipeg. In August 1914, it asked to be sent to France. Instead, its personnel were dispersed amongst several CEF units (vide the Roll of Honour appendix above) which embarked for England on various dates during the following two years. In this book, the services of each of those Bns are recorded separately, with good mention of key dates and events. The present title - Queen's Own Cameron Highlanders of Canada - was granted in 1923.
R/5 V/3. MODL. AMM/JRD.

WHATEVER MEN DARE
History of the Queen's Own Cameron Highlanders of Canada, 1935-1960
R W Queen-Hughes * Printed by Bulman Brothers Ltd, Winnipeg, Manitoba, for the Regt, 1960. Blue, silver, Regtl crest, 9.0 x 6.0, xi/247. Fp, 61 mono phots (incl all COs, 1934-1947, groups of officers, WOs and SNCOs, all named in captions), 10 maps (9 printed in the text, one on the end-papers), Glossary, no Index. Apps: Roll of Honour, H&A, Battle Honours (WWI and WWII), list of members of the 50th Anniversary Committee.
* The Regt was raised in 1910 by new recruitment and by absorption of older local Militia units. The narrative traces its role in WWI (when its membership served with the CEF units listed in the preceding entry), and in WWII (when it served under its own designation). The Regt arrived in England in 1940 and was stationed in Aldershot. It formed part of the assault force at Dieppe on 19 August 1942 and suffered heavy casualties in that disaster. It returned to the French coast on 7 July 1944 and went on to serve in the Normandy battles, the clearance of the Scheldt, and the winter campaign on the Dutch-German border. This is a good detailed history, devoted mainly to the WWII period, with abundant references to individuals and to engagements major and minor. The Regt has a strong musical tradition, and Scottish pipers will find many interesting references to that instrument in this book. R/3 V/4. MODL. JRD.

THE LION RAMPANT
A Pictorial History of the Queen's Own Cameron Highlanders of Canada
G C A Tyler * The Public Press, Winnipeg, Ontario, 1985. Blue, gold, 8.75 x 11.25 (landscape), x/134. Fp, 212 mono phots, 3 cld plates, 3 maps, no Index. Apps: H&A, list of former COs, idem RSMs, notes on Battle Honours.
* This is basically a centenary celebration publication. It traces, in pictorial format, the entire history of the Regt and of its forebears. The illustrations are well selected and well presented, and successfully evoke the times which they depict. The narrative content is correspondingly limited, but the appendixes are useful as a reference source. R/1 V/2. MODL. JRT.

The Westminster Regiment

THE WESTMINSTER'S WAR DIARY
An Unofficial History of the Westminster Regiment (Motor) in World War II
Maj J E Oldfield MC * Printed by Mitchell Press Ltd, Vancouver, for the Regt, 1964. Maroon, gold, Regtl crest, 9.25 x 6.0, -/209. Fp, 10 mono phots, 5 line drawings (cartoon), 3 maps (folding, bound in), no appendixes, no Index.
* The Regt had two frustrating years of training and waiting in England before getting into action in Italy. After a year of hard fighting there, it was brought north for the final months of the war in Holland. The author states in his Introduction that the Regtl Committee needed sixteen years to assemble and approve the draft for this book. After such a prolonged effort, the reader might have hoped to find an Index and some reference appendixes, features which were not included. The narrative itself reads well, is full of exciting incidents, and is packed with names. R/3 V/3. PCAL/MODL. LM/RP.
Note: only one published record for WWI has been traced. It is entitled 131st WESTMINSTER OVERSEAS BATTALION, 1916, by Homer E Leash (Evans & Hastings, Vancouver, 1916) and consists mainly of portraits of personnel serving circa 1915-1916.

THE ROYAL WESTMINSTER REGIMENT, 1863-1988
125 Years of Loyal Service
Pro Rege et Patria - For King and Country
Anon * Published by the Regt, no other details shown, 1988. Paper, red, white, Regtl crest, offset litho, stapled, 11.0 x 8.5, -/70. More than 100 mono phots, no maps, no Index. Apps: list of Honorary Colonels, idem COs of the Volunteer Rifles, the Seymour Bty, and the Active Service and Militia Bns (1863-1985).

* A potted history presented in magazine format, with a large number of poorly printed monotones and a condensed narrative covering the entire period. In WWII, Maj John Mahoney won the VC as a Company Commander with the Regt (River Melfa, 24 May 1944), and this and other episodes receive some mention, but the booklet is basically a lightweight effort. R/2 V/2. PC. RP.

Calgary Highlanders

GALLANT CANADIANS
The Story of the Tenth Infantry Battalion, 1914-1919
Daniel G Dancocks * The Calgary Highlanders Regtl Funds Foundation, Calgary, Alberta, 1990. Blue, gold, 11.25 x 9.0, vii/251. 93 mono phots (incl technical illustrations of the Ross rifle), 17 maps, Glossary, Index. Apps: H&A, list of former officers, notes on Battle Honours, the Canadian Army Order of Battle (at 11 November 1918), statistical summary of casualties.
* Raised in September 1914 as 10th Bn CEF, the unit's founder members were mostly Militiamen from the 103rd Calgary Rifles and 106th Winnipeg Light Infantry. On the instruction of Sam Hughes, controversial Minister of Militia and Defence, the 10th Bn was sent into action on the Western Front armed with the Ross rifle. Popular with snipers and hunters as a single-shot weapon, it over-heated and jammed when fired 'rapid'. The Bn arrived in France in February 1915. Many of its men threw away their Ross weapons after the early engagements and re-equipped themselves with British Lee-Enfields salvaged from the battlefield. On 22 April, 1915, while occupying trenches at St Julien, near Ypres, they were drenched with German gas. Despite heavy losses, they launched a successful counter-attack which attracted much admiration. That date is still toasted on Regtl occasions. The Bn was later issued with gas masks and helmets, but still suffered a total of 4500 casualties in the ensuing battles (notably Festubert, Mont Sorrell, and Hill 70). The Bn fought on to the end of the war and crossed the Rhine to form part of the Allied occupation force before returning to Canada in April 1919. It was disbanded a year later, but was then reactivated as 1st Bn, Calgary Highlanders. This book is a comprehensive account of its WWI services, the narrative being packed with names and incidents. An excellent source for everyone interested in the social and military history of Alberta. R/1 V/5. PC. JRD.

THE STORY OF THE TENTH CANADIAN BATTALION, 1914-1917
J A Holland * W Charles & Son, London, UK, n.d. (1918). Soft card, grey, black, Regtl crest, 7.25 x 4.75, -/35. Fp, one other mono phot, no maps, no Index. Apps: list of COs (1914-1918).
* Raised in August 1914, the Bn sailed for England two months later and landed in France in February 1915. The descriptions of trench warfare are basic and straightforward, with few individuals named. The narrative ends with the events of November 1917. The Bn is perpetuated jointly by the Royal Winnipeg Rifles and the Calgary Highlanders. R/5 V/1. MODL. AMM.

HISTORY OF THE CALGARY HIGHLANDERS, 1921-1954
Maj Roy Farran DSO MC * The Bryant Press Ltd, Toronto, 1955. Green/gold, green/ gold, Regtl crest, 8.25 x 5.75, ix/223. Fp, 20 mono phots, 2 maps, no appendixes, no Index.
* Despite the dates in its title, this book has one complete chapter devoted to services in WWI when, as 10th Cdn Inf Bn CEF, the bulk of the Regt's membership fought on the Western Front. Their finest hour was the defence of Kitchener's Wood, on 22 April 1915. The rest of the book deals with WWII. The Regt arrived in England in September 1940, landed in Normandy on 6 July 1944, and fought at Fleury-sur-Orne, Tilley-la-Campagne, Bretteville, and on the Escaut Canal. There is good coverage also of the later battles - Walcheren Island, Groningen, and Neuenkoop - as part of 2nd Inf Bde, 1st Cdn Div. Few individuals are named other than some officers during the inter-war years. R/3 V/3. RMCL/UWOL/MODL. JRD.

Les Fusiliers de Sherbrooke

LES FUSILIERS DE SHERBROOKE, 1910-1980
Lieut Denise Rioux * Published by the Regt, Sherbrooke, QP, 1980. Soft card, black, white, 9.0 x 6.0, -/68. No ills, one map, Bibliography, no Index. Apps: list of COs (1910-1978), list of former officers (no dates), idem Honorary Colonels, notes on Battle Honours, chronicle of events (1910-1975).
* Written in French. In WWI, the Regt contributed officers and men to the 163rd Cdn Inf Bn CEF, which it perpetuates. WWII services are barely mentioned in this very slender history. R/1 V/2. PC. JRD.

Seaforth Highlanders of Canada

HISTORY OF THE 72nd CANADIAN INFANTRY BATTALION, SEAFORTH HIGHLANDERS OF CANADA
Bernard McEvoy and Capt A H Finlay * Cowan & Brookhouse, Vancouver, BC, 1920. Red, gold, Regtl crest and tartan, 9.0 x 6.0, xxiv/311. Fp, 60 mono phots (incl named portraits and groups), one line drawing, 3 maps (bound in), Glossary, footnotes, Index. Apps: H&A (with dates and locations), diary of events (1909-1919), list of officers (with service details), nominal roll for France and Flanders (with much individual detail).
* The Regt was raised from the large Scottish community in and around Vancouver in 1910. Called out for security duties in Nanaimo in 1913, it next mobilised in August 1914 for expected service in France. This was blocked by the Hughes edict, so many of the officers and fifty-two ORs volunteered for service with the 16th Cdn Inf Bn CEF. The Regt then appealed, in May 1915, for permission to serve as an integral unit under the CEF arrangements. This was granted, and it sailed for England a year later as the 72nd Cdn Inf Bn (Seaforth Highlanders of Canada) CEF. Service in the front line commenced in August 1916 at Kemmel. While living in the trenches, and according to the authors, Pte A E McGubbin invented the 'Tommy' cooker. It was quickly adopted throughout the army. The Bn fought at Vimy Ridge, Passchendaele, Amiens, Cambrai, on the Hindenburg Line, and at Valenciennes before leaving France in May 1919 (the last CEF unit to depart). The narrative is full of incident and individual names, and gives particularly good accounts of front-line service. R/4 V/5. NYPL/RMCL/MODL. JRD.
Note: the Regt raised another Bn for WWI service and it is recorded briefly in SOUVENIR, 231st OVERSEAS BATTALION, CEF, 3rd BATTALION SEAFORTH HIGHLANDERS OF CANADA, this being a pamphlet of 31 pages (plus ten of commercial advertisements). It was produced by Clarke & Stuart, Vancouver, 1917, author not stated.

THE SEAFORTH HIGHLANDERS OF CANADA, 1919-1965
Reginald H Roy CD * Printed by Evergreen Press, Vancouver, for the Regt, 1969. Beige, gold, Regtl crest, xxiv/559/64 (the latter being unnumbered folios which follow the Index and which carry a complete WWII nominal roll). 53 mono phots (incl many large captioned groups of personnel, plus named portraits), 2 cld plates, 8 maps (folding, bound in, very detailed), Index. Apps: Roll of Honour (KIA, WIA and POW for WWII), H&A (WWI and WWII), list of former COs, idem RSMs, idem RPMs, full nominal roll (WWII, with details of individual services, KIA, DOW, WIA), notes on Battle Honours for WWI and WWII.
* Despite the dates given in its title, this magnificent book concentrates almost entirely upon the Regt's services in WWII (Italy, Holland and Germany). Most of the regimental histories published in Canada are very good in one way or another, but this one meets the needs of every category of general reader and specialist researcher. R/3 V/5. PCAL. RP.
Note: reference may be made also to ACTION WITH THE SEAFORTHS, by Charles A Johnson (Vantage Press, New York, 1954).

Canadian Scottish Regiment (Princess Mary's)

THE HISTORY OF THE 16th BATTALION (THE CANADIAN SCOTTISH), CANADIAN EXPEDITIONARY FORCE, IN THE GREAT WAR, 1914–1919
Lieut Col H M Urquhart DSO MC ADC * The Macmillan Company of Canada Ltd, Toronto, for the Trustees of the Regtl Association, 1932. Maroon, gold, Regtl crest with 'The Sixteenth' motif, 9.5 x 6.5, xx/853. Fp, 22 mono phots, 11 maps (cld, folding, bound in), no Index. Apps: Roll of Honour, H&A, unit nominal roll (with details of each individual's military service), notes on the Canadian Militia forces (1812–1914), etc, 14 appendixes in total.
* A wonderfully researched and presented history, rich in detail, and a goldmine for genealogists and medal collectors. Half of this massive book's 853 pages are devoted to the nominal roll – every officer and OR who served with the Bn between 1914 and 1919, with details of his date of joining, wounds, death, awards, and so forth. The Bn won four VCs – a record for any comparable CEF unit in that war. The maps are exceptionally fine, and the illustrations are of good quality. The lack of a narrative Index is the only defect in a history which is otherwise exemplary. R/4 V/4. NYPL/RMCL/MODL. LM/SS.

THE CANADIAN SCOTTISH
History of the Regiment from Mobilisation to Present Day
Anon * Printed by W Anton Abels, Utrecht, Holland, c.1945. Soft card, grey, red, Regtl crest, 9.0 x 6.0, –/31. Five line drawings, no maps, no Index. Apps: H&A (statistical summary only).
* The Regt mobilised two Bns on 26 August 1939. This is a very brief summary of the subsequent activities of the 1st Bn. It arrived in England in September 1941, trained for nearly three years, then went ashore in Normandy as part of the D-Day assault force. At war's end, it was in northern Germany. This worthy but superficial record mentions a few officers by name, but it leaves many questions unanswered. R/4 V/1. MODL. AMM.

READY FOR THE FRAY – DEAS GU CATH
The History of the Canadian Scottish Regiment (Princess Mary's), 1920–1955
R H Roy * Printed by Evergreen Press Ltd, Vancouver (BC), for the Regt, 1958. Maroon, gold, Regtl crest, 9.75 x 6.5, xiii/509. 2 fps, 37 mono phots (plus one page of individual portraits of Honorary Colonels and Honorary Lieut Cols), 6 maps (bound in), no Index. Apps: Roll of Honour (KIA and WIA, with dates), roll of POW, H&A, notes on Battle Honours (WWII), notes on the Women's Auxiliary (1940–1955), idem the Cadet Corps, list of Colonels-in-Chief, idem Honorary Colonels (1929–1956), idem Honorary Lieut Cols (1922–1948), idem COs (for 1st and 2nd Bns, 1922–1954), idem Acting COs (1943–1954, with dates).
* The first two chapters cover the period 1920 to 1938. The bulk of the narrative then deals with the Regt's services in WWII. It was one of only three Canadian Regts with two Bns already in existence before the declaration of war. The 2nd remained in Canada and was disbanded in 1943. The 1st arrived in England in 1941, then landed in France on 6 June 1944 at Courseulles as part of 7th Bde, 3rd Cdn Inf Div. Having fought in the Normandy battles, it saw hard action in the operation to reduce the German garrison in Calais, the clearance of the Scheldt, the forcing of the Leopold Canal, and the bitter winter campaign on the Dutch-German border. The end of the war found the Bn at Oldendorf. At the outbreak of the Korean war (June, 1950), some men volunteered for service there with 25th Inf Bde. In 1951, elements of the Canadian Scottish went to Germany as 'D' Coy, 1st Canadian Highland Regt, to serve under NATO command. This is a detailed history, very well supported with extensive footnotes and a good range of appendixes. R/3 V/4. NYPL/MODL. JRD.
Note: reference may be made also to THE BRAZIER, this being the 50th Anniversary Souvenir edition of the Regtl magazine (card covers, 20 pages).

Irish Fusiliers of Canada (Vancouver Regiment)

A PICTORIAL RECORD AND ORIGINAL MUSTER ROLL, 29th BATTALION
29th (Vancouver) Battalion, CEF
John N McLeod * R P Latta & Co, Vancouver, for the Bn Association, 1919. Black, gold, Regtl crest, 10.25 x 14.0 (landscape), -/64. Fp, 47 mono phots (mostly of personnel), no maps, no Index. Apps: Bn nominal roll (incl a note of the pre-war Militia regiment from which each officer and man had volunteered to join the Bn).
* The 29th Cdn Inf Bn CEF was raised in November 1914 with volunteers who formerly had served with Militia units in the Vancouver area. The narrative deals mainly with the period of training in Canada and England (Shorncliffe). The Bn crossed over to France in September 1915. It saw much action on the Western Front, but coverage of this period is curiously slender. In September 1917, near Lens, CSM Robert Hanna, an Irish-Canadian from Kilkeel, County Down, led a rush against a German strong-point and was awarded the VC. This booklet's main value is the muster roll. R/5 V/2. PLV. JRD.

VANCOUVER'S 29th
A Chronicle of the 29th Canadian Infantry, in Flanders Fields
H R N Clyne MC * Tobin's Tigers Association, Vancouver, BC, 1964. Light brown, red, Bn crest, 8.75 x 5.5, viii/166. One mono phot, one map, Index. Apps: 7 in total, incl detailed H&A and notes on the capture of Hill 70.
* Published nearly half a century after the events which it describes, this book is a useful history of 29th (Vancouver) Bn CEF on the Western Front. It fought at St Eloi, on the Somme, at Vimy Ridge, Hill 70, Lens and Passchendaele, and then at the assault on the Hindenburg Line. Unlike many such publications, this one contains a lengthy account of the post-Armistice march into Germany and the occupation of the Rhineland. R/2 V/4. FFL. RP.

FROM B.C. TO BAISIEUX
Being a Narrative of the 102nd Canadian Infantry Battalion
L McLeod Gould MSM CdeG * Thomas R Cusack Presses, Victoria, BC, 1919. Dark green, gold, 9.0 x 6.0, -/134/98 (the latter being the nominal roll). Fp, 8 mono phots, one map, no Index. Apps: unit nominal roll (every officer and OR who passed through the Bn, with full details of joining and leaving dates, deaths, wounds, H&A, home addresses, etc).
* Sgt Gould worked on the Bn HQ staff and he was responsible for all personnel records and for maintaining the War Diary. With this material available to him, he was uniquely placed to compile this exceptionally detailed record. Every single significant event in the life of the Bn is recorded in the narrative. The 98 pages of the personnel appendix are, of course, a prime source for genealogists.
R/4 V/4. PCAL/NYPL/MODL. LM.
Note: it is understood that a modern facsimile reprint has been produced. The 102nd Bn, like the 29th Bn, is perpetuated by The Irish Fusiliers of Canada. As far as can be established, no modern history of the Fusiliers has yet been published.

Royal Montreal Regiment

THE ROYAL MONTREAL REGIMENT, 14th BATTALION, CEF, 1914-1925
R C Fetherstonhaugh * The Gazette Printing Co, Montreal, 1927. Red, gold, 9.5 x 6.25, xv/334. Fp, 21 mono phots, 6 maps, no Index. Apps: Roll of Honour, H&A, roll of men commissioned from the ranks, diary of movements and locations, statistics.
* Written by a professional military historian, this is a better-than-average record of a CEF infantry unit which saw much action on the Western Front. It contains an attractive blend of basic facts, anecdotes, and references to Regtl characters. The principal actions in which the Bn took part are described here very fully - Ypres (1915), Festubert, Givenchy, Messines, Ypres (1916), the Somme, Montreal Crater, Vimy Ridge, Hill 70, Ypres (1917), and the Hindenburg Line. Numerous minor raids also receive good coverage. R/3 V/4. ASKBC/UWOL/MODL. JBF/CB.

THE ROYAL MONTREAL REGIMENT, 1925-1945

R C Fetherstonhaugh * Gazette Printing Co Ltd, for the Regt, Westmount, QP, 1949. Blue, gold, 9.5 x 6.5, ix/298. Fp, 89 mono phots, 6 maps (bound in), Index. Apps: Roll of Honour, H&A, list of former officers (with portraits), idem SNCOs, notes on the evolution of the Regt, 1914-1945.

* The period from 1925 to 1939 is covered in the first twelve pages. Thereafter, the book concentrates upon the events of WWII. The Regt landed in Normandy on 26 July 1944 and served as defence unit for HQ 1st Canadian Army. Its movements and operations are described lucidly, with many individual members being named in the text. All photographs are likewise well captioned with names and ranks. This is a sound workmanlike history, containing all of the information which most researchers are likely to require. R/3 V/4. RMCL/NYPL/MODL. JRD.

Irish Regiment of Canada

THE STORY OF THE IRISH REGIMENT OF CANADA, 1939-1945
Dedicated to the Soldiers of The Irish Regiment of Canada

Maj Gordon Wood * Printed by Hepkema, Heerenveen, Holland, n.d. (1945). Soft card, aquamarine covers, beige spine, black/silver, Regtl crest, 8.25 x 5.25, -/87. Fp, 2 line drawings, 4 maps (bound in), no Index. Apps: Roll of Honour (KIA, DOW, DOD, and MIA, with locations and dates), H&A (with dates), notes on casualties, notes on battle procedures.

* In WWI, various Irish-Canadian community groups in Toronto sponsored the raising of the 110th Bn CEF. It went overseas, but was soon broken up to provide reinforcement groups for other CEF units. Similar Irish community-led efforts led to the formation of the 108th and 208th Bns, both of which reached the Western Front and there suffered heavy casualties. After the war, 208th Bn provided the basis for a newly established Militia unit, The Irish Regiment of Canada. In the 1930s it retrained as a Machine-gun unit. Following mobilisation and early home defence duties, the Regt's 1st Bn moved to England in 1942 and thence to Italy in 1943. The author gives a good account of this campaign, particularly the battle at Coriano. The Bn moved to Holland in February 1945 for the final battles of the war. A 2nd Bn was raised to provide drafts for the 1st Bn. This is a compressed history, produced under the difficult conditions prevailing in post-ceasefire Holland, but the narrative provides all of the basic facts and the appendixes are thought to be complete. R/4 V/3. RMCL/MODL. JRD.

Toronto Scottish Regiment

CARRY ON
The History of the Toronto Scottish Regiment (MG), 1939-1945

Maj D W Grant * Printer's name and location not shown, published 'by authority of the Commanding Officer', 1949. Blue/silver, blue/silver, Regtl crest, 9.75 x 7.25, xiii/177. Fp, 47 mono phots, 2 cld ills, 22 line drawings, 8 maps (2 printed in the text, 6 bound in), Glossary, no Index. Apps: Roll of Honour, H&A, list of officers, statistical summary of officers and ORs who suffered non-fatal wounds.

* The Regt arrived in England early in the war and had the distinction of providing the King's Guard at Buckingham Palace on 21 April 1940. It was the first Canadian Militia unit to be so honoured (the previous Guard being furnished by the 22nd Regt, the 'Van Doos', a Permanent Force unit). Following the German invasion of France in May 1940, the Regt moved to Brest but was withdrawn two days later (14 June) when it became obvious that France was lost. Its first action was the Dieppe raid in 1942, but this event is poorly covered here and only a few individuals are mentioned. It trained in England with 2nd Cdn Div and in 1944 crossed the Channel for the third time. It fought throughout the NW Europe campaign in the machine-gun role. This is a useful history as far as it goes, but only a handful of members are named in the text and picture captions, and the narrative is patchy. R/3 V/3. NYPL/MODL. JRD.

Royal Newfoundland Regiment

Because the Colony of Newfoundland did not become an integral part of the Dominion of Canada until 1949, the records of the Royal Newfoundland Regt are listed in this bibliography under a separate heading (vide the Index of Units).

Disbanded Regiments

Irish-Canadian Rangers

THE IRISH-CANADIAN RANGERS
Anon * Gazette Printing Co, Montreal, 1916. Green, gold, 199th Bn CEF cap badge, 9.0 x 6.0, -/57. Fp, 25 mono phots (mostly identified groups and individuals), one line drawing, no maps, no Index. Apps: list of former officers of the 55th Bn of Militia.
* This booklet tries to cover a lot of ground in a very few pages. In 1867 a new Militia unit was raised under the title 55th Megantic Bn of Infantry. It later gained the title Irish-Canadian Rangers. In the Spring of 1915, a Col Gascoigne raised the 60th Bn CEF with volunteers coming forward from several Militia units. One of his Companies consisted entirely of men from the Irish-Canadian Rangers. The 60th went to the Western Front and there is some account of its role in Second Ypres in this booklet. At the same time, moves were afoot to form another CEF unit in the Montreal district with personnel drawn in part from the Rangers. It was authorised in February 1916 with the designation 199th Cdn Inf Bn CEF. Having completed his account in that same year, the author describes only the raising of this Bn, not its subsequent experiences. The main value of this item is its description of the manner in which the 199th was formed and the names of officers and men who were associated with it. R/5 V/2. RMCL/UWOL. JRD.
Note: the Irish-Canadian Rangers were disbanded in 1936.

Note:

It will be seen that the preceding pages do not carry entries for the following regiments:

Brockville Rifles
Lanark and Renfrew Scottish Regiment (but note page 128)
Le Régiment de Joliette
Le Régiment du Saguenay
Winnipeg Grenadiers
Scots Fusiliers of Canada
Yukon Regiment

Enquiries were raised c.1989-1990 with each of the regimental authorities and, from the information received, it appears that none of them had at that time produced a formal history of the style and quality which qualifies for inclusion in this bibliography.

MACHINE-GUN UNITS

THE CANADIAN 'EMMA GEES'
A History of the Canadian Machine-gun Corps
Lieut Col C S Grafton VD * Printed by Hunter Printing, London, for the CMGC Association, 1938. Maroon, black, 'Corps crest with gunner in trench' motif, 9.75 x 7.0, -/218. Fp, 12 mono phots, one line drawing, 4 maps, no appendixes, no Index.
* Excellent coverage of the raising and subsequent services of the Corps and of its many units and sub-units. Although the book has no formal appendixes, there are numerous nominal rolls of officers scattered throughout the text, Company by Company, and as at 22 February 1918. The organisation of the Corps is explained in tabular form. A very helpful record which would have benefitted greatly from the provision of an Index. R/3 V/4. RMCL/UWOL. MCJ.

CANADIAN MOTOR MACHINE GUN BRIGADE
With the British Fifth Army, March-April, 1918
Lieut Col William K Walker DSO MC * Publication details not shown, Ottawa, 1957. Soft card, ochre, maroon, 6.25 x 4.5, -/18 (not numbered). Fp, 2 mono phots, no maps, no Index. Apps: Roll of Honour (officers only, KIA and WIA).
* A very brief account by the officer who commanded the Bde (consisting of four Companies). Little detail, but many officers named in the text. R/5 V/2. MODL. AMM.

REGIMENTAL HISTORY OF THE 11th MACHINE GUN BATTALION, CANADIAN MACHINE GUN CORPS
Organised 1st June 1919, Disbanded 14 December 1936
Lieut Col Francis Layton * Facsimile TS, no details shown, 1954. Soft card, stapled, light blue, black, CMGC crest, 13.5 x 7.75, ii/25. No ills, no maps, no Index. Apps: Roll of Honour (WWII, Korea and later).
* An apparently unpublished history for the period described in the sub-title. Most of the limited narrative is taken up with the results of shooting competitions and with scarcely any mention of other events or Bn personalities. Many of its one-time members subequently served with other Corps and Regts, hence the appendix noted above. R/5 V/1. ASKBC. CB.

SPECIAL FORCES

THE FIRST SPECIAL SERVICE FORCE
A War History of the North Americans, 1942-1944
Lieut Col Robert D Burhans * Infantry Journal Press, Washington, DC, 1947. Blue, red/white, SSF shoulder flash, 9.5 x 6.25, xiii/376. Fp, 118 mono phots (incl studio portraits), one cld ill, 13 maps (11 printed in the text, 2 printed on the end-papers), no Index. Apps: unit nominal roll (with each man's name, rank, home town and country of origin), plus Roll of Honour on pages 303-314.
* The story of a short-lived but truly remarkable unit. In 1942 it was decided by the Allies that a force should be raised for special operations in the least accessible parts of Europe. The specification was for a self-contained Battalion, 1200 strong, trained to arrive on target by parachute, to fight in mountain terrain in winter, to operate Allied and captured equipment equally well, and to have a high level of individual survival skills. The American and Canadian governments agreed to fund such a unit, each providing half of the volunteer recruits and half of their kit. Selection preference was given to men having a background in mining, fur trapping, backwoods prospecting, and logging. Initial training commenced at Helena, Montana, and plans were made to attack oil installations in Rumania and hydro-electric plants in Norway. Such suicidal schemes were soon abandoned and the unit's first operation was the unopposed occupation of Kiska. The scene then changed to Italy where the Allies were blocked in the mountains south of Rome. The SSF fought a spectacular action on Monte la Difensa, an episode later adapted as the scenario for a Hollywood film - 'The Devil's Brigade'. It next fought in the Anzio beach-head and took part in the 'Anvil' landings in the south of France. The need for small elite forces had, by that stage of the war, largely evaporated. The SSF was disbanded at Nice in December 1944 and its men dispersed. The Americans went mainly to 474th Infantry Regt, US Army, and the Canadians provided drafts for several units of their own army. The author has compiled here an exemplary account of this unique unit which operated under US command but which was truly bi-national. He covers the successes but also the problems. Canadian Sergeants, for example. drew less pay than the American enlisted men (private soldiers). There were difficulties also in connection with the two very different systems of granting awards for gallantry. A good story. R/3 V/4. NYPL. JEB/RH.
Note: reference may be made also to THE DEVIL'S BRIGADE, by Robert H Adleman (Chilton Books, Philadelphia, 1966).

OUT OF THE CLOUDS
The History of the 1st Canadian Parachute Regiment
John A Willes * Port Perry Printing Ltd, Kingston, Ontario, 1981. Red, gold, Regtl crest, 9.0 x 6.5, -/251. 82 mono phots, 4 maps, no Index. Apps: Roll of Honour (KIA, WIA, and POW for the period November 1943 to May 1945, with names, ranks, and dates), H&A (names and ranks), unit nominal roll (with details of where and when each individual qualified as a parachutist).
* This wartime unit was based in England, its personnel arriving from parachute training bases as far afield as Fort Benning (USA), Camp Shilo (Canada), and RAF Ringway (UK). It dropped in Normandy on D-Day with 6th British Airborne Div and fought on the east flank of the beach-head area. It returned to England to refit and to absorb replacements for its battle casualties, then took part in Operation Varsity (the Rhine crossings). It was during this operation that one of the Regt's NCOs, Cpl F G Topham, won his VC. The Regt was disbanded at the end of the war but, in the 1950s, three Canadian infantry Regts were trained in the parachute role - Royal Canadian Regt, Princess Patricia's Canadian Light Infantry, and the Royal 22e Regt. In 1970, the Canadian Airborne Regt was formed, with a permanent HQ at Camp Petewawa, Ontario. This is a satisfying history, with plenty of detail and good illustrations. R/1 V/4. MODL. JEB.
Note: reprinted without amendment in 1984.

MEDICAL SERVICES

SEVENTY YEARS OF SERVICE
A History of the Royal Canadian Army Medical Corps
Col G W L Nicholson CD * Borealis Press Ltd, Ottawa, 1977. Plum, gold, RCAMC crest, 8.75 x 5.5, xiv/388. Fp, 73 mono phots, 5 maps, Chapter Notes & Sources, Index. Apps: H&A (22 pages, all awards to all personnel for the entire period, incl VCs to Capt B S Hutcheson and Capt F A C Scrimger).
* The RCAMC was formed in 1904 and disbanded in 1974 (at the time of the unification of Canada's armed forces). A good solid account of military doctors and nurses and their work, from the Boer War through to the Korean conflict. R/2 V/4. MODL. RP.

CANADA'S NURSING SISTERS
Col G W L Nicholson * A M Hakkert Ltd, Toronto, 1975. Blue, gold, 9.25 x 6.0, x/272. Fp, 75 mono phots, 5 maps, Bibliography, Index. Apps: list of Matrons-in-Chief or equivalent (1904-1975), idem Matrons of units which served overseas (1914-1945), idem Matrons of Veterans' Hospitals and Homes (1915-1974).
* Full of names and anecdotes, this is the history of the Canadian Nursing Service. Some nurses had accompanied the Field Forces during the North West Rebellion of 1885, but it was the Anglo-Boer War of 1899-1902 which highlighted the need for a formal nursing establishment. The CNS was formed on 1 August 1901 and it subsequently rendered invaluable service in many theatres of war in WWI, WWII and Korea. Its personnel also served at various bases in Germany from 1945 onwards. R/3 V/5. MODL. AMM.

THE STORY OF THE ROYAL CANADIAN DENTAL CORPS
Lieut Col H M Jackson MBE ED * Industrial Shops for the Deaf, Montreal, for the RCDC, 1956. Green, yellow, 9.25 x 6.0, xvi/475. Fp, 11 mono phots, 3 maps, Index (for the nominal roll only). Apps: 15 in total, incl a nominal roll of officers who served in various posts between 1904 and 1956 (with their promotion dates), lists of Dental Companies serving in Canada and overseas, Staff appointments, etc.
* In broad terms, this is the story of the Canadian armed forces in the two world wars. Dental personnel accompanied the fighting troops to every theatre of war, even being attached to Special Forces. A good readable history, interesting even to the non-specialist. R/3 V/4. NYPL/MODL/RCSL. RP.

WORLD WAR I

HISTORY OF THE CANADIAN FORCES IN THE GREAT WAR
The Medical Services
Sir Andrew MacPhail OBE * F A Acland, for the Government of Canada, Ottawa, 1925. Maroon, gold, 10.0 x 7.0, viii/428. No ills, one map (bound in), Index. Apps: Roll of Honour, H&A.
* As might be expected, in view of its sponsorship, this is a comprehensive and totally authoritative history of the Canadian Army's medical branch in WWI. The book is one of the very few tangible results to emerge from the aborted OFFICIAL HISTORY project described earlier (vide the Canadian 'General Reference' section of this bibliography). R/4 V/5. PC. JRT.

WAR STORY OF THE CANADIAN ARMY MEDICAL CORPS, 1914-1915
Volume I : The First Contingent - To the Autumn of 1915
Col J G Adami * The Musson Book Co Ltd, Toronto, for the Canadian War Records Office, 1918. Red, black, 7.5 x 4.75, viii/286. Fp, one mono phot, 11 (bound in), no appendixes, no Index.
* A quite detailed book, and possibly of use to the medical historian. The writing is uninspired and its utility is limited by the lack of an Index. Lists of awards appear at several points in the narrative, with full citations and verbatim recommendations for MID. They refer mainly to Second Ypres, Festubert and 'Plug Street'.

This is one of those publications which contains a lot of good material, but which fails to satisfy because the contents are so clumsily presented. It is not surprising that plans to publish a Volume II (and presumably even more volumes thereafter) were abandoned by the publishers after they had launched this first volume.
R/3 V/3. RCSL/NYLP. RP.

THE C.A.M.C. WITH THE CANADIAN CORPS DURING THE LAST HUNDRED DAYS OF THE GREAT WAR
Col A E Snell CMG DSO * F A Acland, Ottawa, 1924. Brick red, gold, 10.0 x 6.5, ix/292. No ills, four organisational charts, 7 maps (loose in rear pocket), no Index. Apps: list of medical and dental officers, notes on establishments, Order of Battle of the Canadian Army Corps (August-November, 1918).
* Written in an impersonal and formal style, this is an important source for the specialist researcher. The book provides much detail concerning the organisation of the CAMC during the final months of the war and gives a good account of the medical work undertaken during that period. R/4 V/4. MODL. AMM.

No 1 CANADIAN GENERAL HOSPITAL
Col K Cameron CMG VD CAMC * The Tribune Press, Sackville, New Brunswick, 1938. Maroon, gold, 9.5 x 6.5, xvii/667. Fp, more than 100 mono phots, 12 maps (bound in), Glossary, 2 Indexes (General, and Personnel). Apps: H&A, list of officers, idem SNCOs, full unit nominal roll.
* This immensely detailed account begins with the mobilisation of 'V' Field Ambulance CAMC in Quebec at the outbreak of war. It expanded on 1 September 1914 to become No 1 General Hospital, landed in England a month later, and moved to France in May 1915. It was eventually demobilised in Montreal in April 1919. The narrative is packed with names, details of awards, and medical statistics. An exemplary history, and a prime source for several different categories of collector and researcher. R/4 V/5. MODL. AMM.

No 3 CANADIAN GENERAL HOSPITAL (McGILL), 1914-1919
R C Fetherstonhaugh * The Gazette Printing Co, Montreal, for the Faculty of McGill University, 1928. Red, gold, University seal, 9.5 x 6.25, x/274. Fp, 38 mono phots, one diagram (layout of the hospital at Boulogne), no maps, no Index. Apps: Roll of Honour (those who died while serving with the hospital, and those who died later while serving with other units), H&A (idem), general nominal roll (all who served, with ranks and dates), establishment statistics, list of ORs who were granted Commissions.
* Based upon the War Diary, letters, and personal records, this is a fluent and non-technical account of a 'lines of communication hospital' which handled many thousands of casualties from the battles at Loos in 1915, the Ypres Salient, the Somme in 1916, Vimy Ridge in 1917, and the great offensives of 1918. The volunteer staff was formed in March 1915 from doctors and students at McGill University, and nurses from the Royal Victoria and Montreal General Hospitals. The official establishment was 1014 beds. Many of the staff are named in the text.
R/4 V/4. PC. JRD.

No 4 CANADIAN HOSPITAL
The Letters of Professor J J Mackenzie from the Salonika Front
Kathleen Cuffe Mackenzie * The Macmillan Company of Canada Ltd, Toronto, 1933. Dark blue, gold, 8.75 x 5.75, -/247. 12 mono phots, no maps, no appendixes, no Index.
* Unfortunately, the contents are no more than the sub-title might imply. Prof Mackenzie was a biologist who was sent to Salonika to work as the patholigist attached to No 4 Canadian General Hospital. He makes few comments regarding the nature of that campaign or of the medical work in which he was engaged. Perhaps his wife thought that his letters would interest somebody, somewhere.
R/4 V/1. RCSL. RP.

STRETCHER-BEARERS AT THE DOUBLE
History of the Fifth Canadian Field Ambulance which Served Overseas During the Great War of 1914-1918
Frederick M Noyes * The Hunter-Rose Co Ltd, Toronto, n.d. (1937). Blue, gold, 9.25 x 6.25, vi/328/13 (the latter not numbered - the unit nominal roll). Fp, 172 mono phots, 14 sketches, 8 maps (bound in), no Index. Apps: Roll of Honour (KIA, DOW and MIA, plus post-war deaths up to 1935, with dates), unit nominal roll (incl awards and home addresses).
* Raised by Maj George Devey in November 1914, 5th CFA formed part of the Second Contingent of the CEF. The narrative provides a comprehensive account of services on the Western Front - St Eloi, Vimy Ridge, Passchendaele, Lens, Cambrai, Canal du Nord, etc. The illustrations are of superb quality, many being identified groups and individuals. A fine work of dedicated research, and a good source for genealogists. R/4 V/4. RMCL/MODL. JRD.

HISTORICAL RECORD OF NUMBER 8 CANADIAN FIELD AMBULANCE, 1915-1919
Lieut Col J N Gunn DSO and S/Sgt E E Dutton * The Ryerson Press, Toronto, 1920. Dark red, gold, 'Ypres Cloth Hall in ruins' motif, 9.25 x 6.5, xii/169. Fp, 5 mono phots, 2 line drawings, no maps, no Index. Apps: Roll of Honour (KIA, DOW and WIA), H&A.
* The unit commenced training, from scratch, in Alberta on 5 January 1916. It landed at Liverpool on 9 April and was in France a month later. This urgency was a reflection of the enormous and increasing Canadian flow of casualties. The unit was in the thick of the action on the Western Front through to the end of the war. It returned to Calgary on 1 April 1919. The narrative lacks sparkle, but the book is in general terms a worthy record. Four of the five photographs are fully captioned groups of officers and NCOs. R/4 V/4. MODL. AMM.

WORLD WAR II

OFFICIAL HISTORY OF THE CANADIAN MEDICAL SERVICES, 1939-1945
Lieut Col W R Feasby BA MD * Edmond Cloutier (Queen's Printer & Controller of Stationery), for the Ministry of National Defence, Ottawa. Matching pair, maroon, MND crest, 10.0 x 6.5.
Volume I : ORGANISATION AND CAMPAIGNS. Published 1956, xii/568. Fp, 25 mono phots, 4 cld ills, 19 maps (7 printed in the text, 10 folding, bound in, 2 printed on the end-papers), Glossary, Index. Apps: various charts and notes regarding organisation and Orders of Battle, list of all senior officers down to the rank of Colonel (with their appointments).
Volume II : CLINICAL SUBJECTS. Published in 1953, xv/537. Fp, 7 mono phots, 4 cld ills, no maps, Index. Apps: 33 tables of statistics.
* A very substantial record which covers the work of all the Canadian medical services in WWII, but with the emphasis on the Army. Volume I can be enjoyed by both the general and the specialist reader. It covers early training in England and then the campaigns in Italy and NW Europe. Volume II is aimed mainly at the reader who is medically qualified. It deals in detail with the incidence and treatment of infectious diseases, wounds, surgical techniques, pioneering work with penicillin, the diagnosis of battles neuroses, and other technical subjects. The maps - all concentrated in Volume I - were drawn by Capt C C J Bond and are of excellent quality. R/4 V/5. RMAS. JRD/RP/RH.

ELEVEN MEN AND A SCALPEL
John Burwell Hillsman MD * The Columbia Press Ltd, Winnipeg, for the author, 1948. No ills, no maps, no appendixes, no Index.
* The author served with No 8 Field Surgical Unit in England, France, Holland and Germany. Basically a memoir, the book does highlight the extraordinary hazards of field surgery (the role of a FSU being the treatment of casualties too severely wounded to be moved immediately to a rear area). Plenty of human interest, and clearly of value to the medical researcher. R/4 V/3. FFL. RP.

OTHER CORPS

WAIT FOR THE WAGGON
The Story of the Royal Canadian Army Service Corps
Arnold Warren * McClelland & Stewart Ltd, Canada (no other details given), 1961. Dark blue, silver, 9.25 x 6.25, xL/413. 63 mono phots plus 24 small studio portraits, 2 maps (printed on the end-papers), Glossary, Index. Apps: Roll of Honour (WWI and WWII, listed year by year), H&A (WWI, WWII, and Korea), list of former officers, notes on the Corps badge, Corps march, flag, and motto.
* An account which covers the story of the CASC (later RCASC) from its formation in 1904 through to 1961. The narrative deals well with organisational and technical matters, but this material is leavened with numerous anecdotes, references to individual officers and men, and specific combat incidents. The appendixes are particularly detailed for such a large-scale history. The Roll of Honour, as an example, includes the names of personnel who died while serving on detachment with the British Army. The H&A appendix includes MID and foreign awards. A worthy record. R/2 V/5. MODL/PCAL. RP.

TO THE THUNDERER HIS ARMS
The Royal Canadian Ordnance Corps
William F Rannie * Published privately, Lincoln, Ontario, 1984. Soft card, 'Perfect' binding, ivory, blue, Corps crest and colours, 8.75 x 5.75, -/360. 53 mono phots, one map, no Index. Apps: Roll of Honour (KIA, WWII only, all ranks), H&A (WWI and WWII), Corps Order of Battle (1939-1946), summary of 'milestone' dates in the history of the Corps.
* The narrative traces the evolution of the Corps from the second half of the 19th Century through to disbandment in 1974. It covers a wide field of service - WWI in France and Siberia, WWII in Sicily, Italy and NW Europe, then the later commitments in Korea and with various other UN Contingents (Kashmir, Congo, Cyprus, Lebanon, and elsewhere). This is a broad-brush description of a long and complicated series of events which appears to be complete and authoritative in every way. R/3 V/4. AldMM/MODL. RP.

CANADA'S CRAFTSMEN
The Story of the Corps of Royal Canadian Electrical & Mechanical Engineers, and of the Land Ordnance Engineering Branch
Col Murray Johnston * Published by the RCEME Association, n.d. (c.1984). Soft card, 'Perfect' binding, blue, gold, 3 Corps crests, v/291. 90 mono phots, no maps, Bibliography, Index. Apps: list of Colonels Commandant and Corps Commanders, Corps Order of Battle (WWII).
* The author traces the evolution of the Corps from 1903 - the year in which the Canadian Stores Department was formed - through to the 1980s. The Corps was formally established in its own right - as the RCEME - in 1944. Its immediate parent was the Royal Canadian Ordnance Corps, with many of its founder personnel being transferred in from that Corps. R/2 V/5. AldMM. RP.

SCARLET TO GREEN
A History of Intelligence in the Canadian Army, 1903-1963
Maj S R Elliott CD * Hunter-Rose Co Ltd, Toronto, 1981. Dark green, silver, Corps crest, 9.25 x 6.25, xix/769. Fp, 51 mono phots, one cld ill, 2 line drawings, 23 maps, Glossary, Bibliography, Index. Apps: Roll of Honour (WWII), H&A (WWII), list of officers, idem SNCOs, plus 24 'Personnel and Organisation' appendixes.
* This monumental work describes the formation of the first 'Guides' (or Reconnaissance unit) in February 1862, and their services during the Fenian Raids and Riel's Rebellion. The founder members were expanded into a Corps of Guides on 1 April 1903, and this later evolved into a full-scale Intelligence Corps. The book contains only sketchy references to WWI (33 pages), but WWII is given detailed treatment (435 pages). Intelligence gathering and processing, counter-Intelligence, and the processing of POW is all covered in good style. The narrative concludes

with Korea and Cyprus. The numerous group photographs are well captioned with the names of those depicted. A remarkable work of reference. R/3 V/5. MODL. AMM.

IN THIS SIGN
Maj Walter T Steven * The Ryerson Press, Toronto, 1948. Brick red, gold, badge of the CCS, 8.75 x 5.75, xiii/182. 18 mono phots, one line drawing, no maps, no Index. Apps: Roll of Honour (nine Chaplains died), H&A, list of officers, notes on senior posts and their successive incumbents.
* The story of the Canadian Chaplains Service (Protestant). Before WWII, Chaplains were nearly all appointed regimentally, one per 1000 men. There is some mention here of their work in WWI, but this history deals with WWII chaplaincy - in Italy and NW Europe - under the umbrella of the CCS. The narrative is highly readable, with plenty of anecdotes and references to individuals. R/3 V/4. MODL. AMM.

WORLD WAR I

THE SAGA OF THE CYCLISTS
W D Ellis * Published by the Canadian Corps Cyclist Battalion Association, Toronto, 1965. Soft card, red, black, Association badge, 8.75 x 5.75, v/93. No ills, 3 maps, no appendixes, no Index.
* This is an anecdotal account, compiled long after the event and, to quote from the Preface: '... in defence of the gas-pipe cavalry'. Five Divisional Cyclist Coys were formed between 1914 and 1916. Their purpose was reconnasissance, traffic control, despatch riding, POW escorts, etc. Three of the Coys were combined in May 1916 into a single Corps Cyclist Bn which saw considerable front-line action. Not surpisingly, given the exposed nature of their duties, the Cyclists suffered heavy casualties. Few of them are named in this account. R/3 V/2. MODL. AMM.

THE CANADIAN FORESTRY CORPS
Its Inception, Development and Achievement
C W Bird and Lieut J B Davies * HM Stationery Office, London, 1919. Grey-blue, rust, 10.5 x 6.75, -/51. Fp, 48 mono phots, 2 maps, no appendixes, no Index.
* A very bare account of an unusual aspect of the Allied war effort in WWI. In February 1916, a force of 1600 experienced loggers was formed as 224th Cdn Forestry Bn for the felling and processing of timber in Scotland, Southern England and France. The Corps was later expanded by the formation of 230th, 238th and 242nd Forestry Bns. Chapter 3 gives some detail of the senior personnel involved. R/4 V/2. NZMODL/NYPL (the latter, microfiche only). HEC.

THE BLACK BATTALION
Canada's Best Kept Military Secret
Calvin M Ruck * Nimbus Publishing Ltd, Halifax, NS, 1987. Soft card, grey, pink, unit crest in gold, 9.0 x 6.0, iii/125. Fp, 62 mono phots (many of personnel, fully captioned), no maps, Bibliography, Chapter Notes, Index. Apps: unit nominal rolls for No 2 Construction Bn CEF and 106th Cdn Inf Bn CEF, extracts from military documents, notes on the political debate, etc.
* The first black people to arrive in Canada were soldiers (and their families) who had served in the ranks of Loyalist Regiments during the American War of Indepe-ndence. The majority settled in Nova Scotia and New Brunswick. The first Canadian to win the Victoria Cross was in fact a Nova Scotian negro - Petty Officer William Hall RN (in India, 1857). Large numbers of black Canadians tried to volunteer for overseas service in 1914, but racial discrimination kept them out of the newly-formed CEF. In 1915, after much debate, a few of them were admitted into the ranks of the 106th Inf Bn (Nova Scotia Rifles). Upon arrival in England, the Bn was disbanded to provide reinforcement drafts for several other Infantry units. In 1916, after further acrimonious political wrangling at home, the all-black No 2

Construction Bn CEF was formed at Pictou, Nova Scotia. It went to France a year later and was deployed in the Jura (at Peronne and Alencon). It was attached to the Canadian Forestry Corps, producing lumber for military construction work. The author does not go into the detail of its services but concentrates instead upon the social and political factors which governed the recruitment of black soldiers in WWI and the recorded experiences of those who survived. The book is a well rsearched examination of military service by 'Canada's black patriots', with abundant social, political and biographical detail. R/1 V/5. MODL. JRD/RBM.
Note: reported to have been reprinted in 1991.

WORLD WAR II

DIARY OF 65 CANADIAN TANK TRANSPORTER COMPANY
Royal Canadian Army Service Corps
Norman Lafrance * Barb's Typing & Printing Service, Coldwater, Ontario, for the 65th Association, 1983. Soft card, plastic clip spine, blue, gold, RCASC crest, litho offset text, 11.0 x 8.5, -/199. More than 100 mono phots, 11 maps, no Index. Apps: H&A (page 34, incl GM awarded to Capt T F Chandler), unit nominal roll (the names arranged by Platoon, with home addresses, at June 1945).
* A chaotically arranged and totally absorbing record of a vital aspect of mechanised warfare. Compiled as a memento for former members and their families, the book is packed with maps, tables of statistics, personal anecdotes, extracts from orders and official reports, diaries of movements and deployments, rolls of personnel, and many photographs from private collections. Even for the non-specialist reader, this is a splendid publication, full of interest. R/4 V/4. PC. RP.

THE PAY SERVICES OF THE CANADIAN ARMY OVERSEAS IN THE WAR OF 1939-1945
Capt J D Londerville RCAPC * The Runge Press Ltd, Ottawa, for the RCAPC Association, 1950. Dark blue, yellow, Corps crest, 9.25 x 6.0, -/315. 21 mono phots, 2 maps (printed on the end-papers), Glossary, Bibliography, no Index. Apps: notes on organisation.
* The Royal Canadian Army Pay Corps was formed in 1907, allowed to wind down between 1930 and 1935, and then resuscitated (as part of the Militia) in April 1938. There is nothing in this thoroughly worthy account to stir the soul, but it does give a complete picture of a behind-the-scenes administration of great importance to the serving soldier and his family. Numerous officers are mentioned in the text. The photographs capture the feel of the period but, sadly, the people who appear in the pictures are not identified. R/3 V/4. MODL. AMM.

WOMEN'S SERVICES

ATHENE - GODDESS OF WAR
The History of the Canadian Women's Army Corps
W Hugh Conrod * Writing & Editorial Services, Dartmouth, NS, 1983. Brown, 9.0 x 6.0, -/315. Fp, 84 mono phots, 25 line drawings, no maps, no appendixes, no Index.
* The CWAC was formed in 1941 and disbanded in 1946. Like other similar Corps in other Commonwealth countries, it recruited young women who could take over military tasks and thereby release male soldiers for combat duties. The 'quacks' (the unflattering pronunciation of CWAC) filled thousands of such posts in Canada, in the UK and, after 1944, on the Continent. Many were killed before they could complete their service. This very readable book is based upon official records, private letters, and personal interviews. Many former CWAC members are named in the narrative. R/1 V/3. FFL. RP.

HERE COME THE KHAKI SKIRTS - THE WOMEN VOLUNTEERS
A Pictorial Review of the Canadian Women's Army Corps during the Second World War
Ada Arney CD * Highway Bookshop, Cobalt, Ontario, 1988. Maroon, gold, 11.5 x 9.0, xiv/169. Fp, more than 100 mono phots, no maps, no appendixes, Glossary, no Index.
* The limited narrative simply sets the scene for the pictures. These have been selected from a number of official and archive sources. Some are trite and ordinary, others are highly evocative of the war years. Many are captioned with the names of those depicted. A generalised tribute, certainly of interest to the social historian. R/3 V/1. MODL. AMM.
Note: another source is GREATCOATS AND GLAMOUR BOOTS - CANADIAN WOMEN AT WAR, 1939-1945, by Carolyn Gassage (Dundurn Press, Toronto, 1991). This is another generalised account but, in this case, the author deals with women who volunteered for all three services. It is based in part upon official documents and in part upon personal reminiscences.

POLICE

THE CANADIAN PROVOST CORPS
Silver Jubilee, 1940–1965

Lieut Col Q E Lawson MBE, Lieut Col R I Luker MC, Maj A F Ritchie, and Capt P A H Dupille * Mortimer Ltd, Ottawa, 1965. Blue, silver, Corps crest, 9.25 x 6.25, –/96. Fp, 66 mono phots (mainly identified groups and individuals), no maps, no Index. Apps: Roll of Honour (with dates), H&A.

* Military policemen had been appointed at District Depots before the war, but the Corps came into being as a complete entity on 1 November 1940. By the end of the war, it had grown to a strength of 8000 all ranks. Trained primarily in traffic control and POW processing duties, they fought as infantry at Dieppe in August 1942. Later services in Sicily, Italy and NW Europe receive only casual mention in this book. Post-war establishment was about 250 all ranks (except during the Korean War when it rose to 1500). Members of the Corps have served in many of Canada's numerous subsequent UN deployments, and these are well described. R/4 V/3. PC. JRD.

HISTORY OF THE ROYAL NORTH-WEST MOUNTED POLICE
A Corps History

Capt Ernest J Chambers * The Mortimer Press, Montreal, n.d. (c.1907). Red/beige, gold, 'Corps crest and mounted police officer' motif, 12.0 x 9.0, –/158/xxxvii. Numerous mono phots of early senior officers, no maps, no Index. Apps: list of former and serving officers.

* The ever-industrious Capt Chambers (vide Index of Authors) did not confine his attentions to Canadian Militia units. The fact that the last section of this book (pages xxxvii) consists entirely of paid advertisements would suggest that he was amongst the small minority of authors to have made money out of writing history. The basic format of the book is the same as his Militia histories. It is produced to a high standard and is illustrated with beautifully presented photographs. The narrative covers the period from 1873 through to 1906 and provides an excellent starting point for the publications listed hereafter. R/5 V/4. AMOT. RP.

RIDERS OF THE PLAINS
A Record of the Royal North-West Mounted Police, 1873–1910

A L Haydon * Andrew Melrose, London, 1910. Seen in library rebinding, details of original casing not known, 8.5 x 5.5, xvi/385. Fp, 28 mono phots, 4 maps (2 printed in the text, 2 bound in), Bibliography, Index. Apps: 10 in total, incl Roll of Honour (KIA and DOW during the North West Rebellion), list of former Commissioners, idem some former officers.

* Formed in 1873, the RNWMP was the only disciplined armed force in the wilder tracts of pioneering Canada, and it fulfilled both a police and a para-military role. The citizens for whom they were responsible were a mixed crowd – fur trappers, gold prospectors, Indians, lumberjacks, farmer settlers, and so forth. It was during this period that the Corps began to gain the romantic popular image – inherited by the RCMP – which has never been lost. This book is a detailed historical account of the first thirty-seven years, a period which witnessed the creation of modern Canada. R/5 V/5. PCAL. LM/RP.

THE ROYAL CANADIAN MOUNTED POLICE

R C Fetherstonhaugh * Carrick & Evan Inc, New York, 1938. Red, black, 10.25 x 6.25, impagination not recorded. 16 mono phots, 5 maps (2 printed in the text, 3 bound in), Index. Apps: Roll of Honour (61 names, KIA and DOW, 1873–1937), list of fathers/sons who served, list of RCMP who also held honorary Militia rank, Chronology.

* The narrative covers the evolution of the RNWMP from 1873, the change of title and organisation, the Rebellion of 1885, fights with US Indians, the story of the 245 men who volunteered for the South African war (1899–1902), the Winnipeg

General Strike of 1919, and some notable criminal cases of the 1920s and 1930s. A good general account by a professional writer (vide Index of Authors). R/4 V/4. SLV. RP.

THE ROYAL CANADIAN MOUNTED POLICE

L Charles Douthwaite * Blackie & Son Ltd, London & Glasgow, 1939. Red, gold, 8.5 x 5.5, vi/281. Fp, 15 mono phots, one map (bound in), no Index. Apps: list of former Commandants.

* A good readable history of the Force from 1873 to 1937. The book would have benefitted from an Index and some more appendixes but, as far as it goes, it is a satisfactory source. R/2 V/3. PC. RLP.

THE LIVING LEGEND
The Story of the Royal Canadian Mounted Police

Allan Phillips * Cassell & Co, London, 1957. Red, gold, 8.5 x 5.5, iv/230. No ills, no maps, no appendixes, Index.

* The sub-title is not strictly accurate. The book is not so much a history of the RCMP as a compendium of incidents and notorious criminal cases from the 1930s and 1940s. Its research value is no more than marginal. R/2 V/2. PC. RLP.

THE MOUNTIES
The History of the Royal Canadian Mounted Police

Jim Lotz * Printed in Hong Kong, for Bison Books, 1984. Black, gold, 12.25 x 9.25, -/160. 128 mono phots, 42 cld ills, 9 line drawings, no maps, no appendixes, Index.

* A typical Bison Books publication. The well written and liberally illustrated narrative covers the evolution of the Mounties from formation in 1873 (as the RNWMP) through to the 1980s. The author provides lucid accounts of the Indian pacification campaigns, the Yukon Gold Rush, counter-espionage work during WWII, and modern crime detection. R/1 V/4. SLV. PS.

Note: an earlier but similarly illustrated book is THE PICTORIAL HISTORY OF THE ROYAL CANADIAN MOUNTED POLICE, by S W Horrall (McGraw-Ryerson Ltd, Canada, 1973). With more than 200 pictures on 256 pages, it was published to mark the force's Centenary. It contains a Roll of Honour naming the 146 personnel who died on duty during that century (with cause of death stated). Another general source, with good illustrations of uniforms, is THE ROYAL CANADIAN MOUNTED POLICE, 1873-1987, by David Ross and Robin May (Osprey Publishing, 'Men at Arms' series, London, 1988). The specialist researcher is recommended to consult RECORDS OF THE RCMP, compiled by Joanne Poulin and published in 1975 as part of the Public Records General Inventory series by the Public Archives of Canada, Ottawa. This is a guide, written in French and in English, to all the RCMP records held in those Archives.

Provincial Police Forces

O.P.P.
The History of the Ontario Provincial Police Force

Dahn D Higley * The Queen's Printer, Toronto, 1984. Blue, gold, 9.25 x 6.0, -/668. 231 mono phots, 2 line drawings, no maps, Index. Apps: list of ranking officers (1909-1964), Force nominal roll (original members, 1910), list of holders of the Queen's Commission.

* A detailed and significant history which covers events from the force's first raising - as the Niagara River Frontier Police, in 1865 - through to its reorganisation as the Ontario Provincial Police in 1909, and then through to 1984. R/2 V/5. SLV. PS.

Note: a similar but less substantial record is A CENTURY OF SERVICE - A HISTORY OF THE WINNIPEG POLICE FORCE, 1874-1974, by Robert Hutchison (Inter-Collegiate Press of Canada, for the City of Winnipeg Police Force, 1974).

PART 5

Europe

NOTES

INTRODUCTION

Great Britain's world-wide commitments in the opening years of the 19th Century were such that her Regular Army was, once again, severely over-extended. The shortage of manpower was met, at least in part, by the creation of additional Regiments recruited from a wide variety of non-British populations.

References to a few of these temporary units appear on the following pages and in other sections of this bibliography, but the majority faded away without trace. It is understandable that this should have been so. Often their ranks consisted of officers and men who were fighting for the Crown as a means of returning to their native lands. Many of the emigré and refugee soldiers were deeply opposed to the Revolutionary and Napoleonic regimes on political or religious grounds, others wanted simply to liberate their own people from alien occupation. Others again were mercenaries who were following their professional vocation, seeking nothing more than adventure, loot, victuals and pay. Few of them - patriot or soldier of fortune - possessed either the means or the motivation to record their services once the fighting had come to an end.

For a closer examination of this subject, reference should be made to THE JOURNAL OF THE SOCIETY FOR ARMY HISTORICAL RESEARCH. A series of articles was published in the Journal during the period 1942-1944, and there may be others at different dates.

The following random sample of unit titles will serve to illustrate the multi-ethnic and multi-national composition of British military forces during those times. It also reflects the Government's efforts to unite disparate groups in a common cause, thus setting a precedent for the raising of the 'Free' forces in WWII.

The Albanian Regiment
The Anglo-Corsican Regiment
The British Legion of St Domingo
Brodrick's Albanians
Charmilly's Uhlans Britanniques de St Domingo
Les Chasseurs Britanniques
La Chatre's Loyal Emigrant Regiment
The Corsican Light Dragoons
The Dutch Brigade (of 1795)
The French Emigrant Artillery
The Helvetic Legion
The Minorca Light Dragoons
La Tour's Loyal Foreigners

The British Army was similarly under-manned when, in 1854, it was committed to the war in the Crimea. New Corps (Legions) were recruited in Germany, Switzerland and Italy. These short-lived units are described in THE EXTINCT REGIMENTS OF THE BRITISH ARMY, by A E Sewell, in THE JOURNAL OF THE ROYAL UNITED SERVICE INSTITUTION, Vol XXXI, No 38, 1887.

In those parts of Europe where Great Britain had a long-term commitment - Malta, Gibraltar and the British Home Islands - units were raised at various times with a permanent establishment (rather than a temporary 'hostilities only' role). It is not surprising that such units have subsequently attracted the interest of historians and publishers, and so been recorded in print. The local forces of Malta and the Home Islands have been particularly well served in this regard.

CHANNEL ISLANDS - GENERAL

MEMORANDUM ON THE CHANNEL ISLANDS MILITIA
Col E W C Wright and O H Morshead * 'Confidential Report for the War Office', 1869. Seen in facsimile, details of original binding not known, -/27. No ills, no maps, no Index. Apps: two tables of costs.
* A report based upon a careful examination of the organisation and roles of the Militias of Guernsey, Jersey, Alderney and Sark. Many of the authors' recommendations were later followed through. A valuable source. R/5 V/5. NAM. CEP.

THE CHANNEL ISLANDS MILITIA
Its Present Constitution Considered with Criticisms on the Government Plan of Reform and a Counter-proposal for the Re-organisation
Anon ('A Guernsey Militia Officer') * Thomas Bichard, Guernsey, 1874. Soft card, blue, 8.25 x 5.0,-/43. No ills, no maps, no Index. Apps: tables of organisation.
* A counter-blast to the suggestions of Wright and Morshead (see preceding entry). Useful because it sets out the arguments in great detail. The narrative includes some history and analysis of the Militia units of both Guernsey and Jersey.
R/5 V/3. PLG. CEP.

GUERNSEY

THE ROYAL GUERNSEY MILITIA, 800-1895
A Brief Sketch of its Services
Lieut Col J Percy Groves * Frederick Clarke, Guernsey, 1895. Red, gold, 9.25 x 7.25, -/97. No ills, no maps, no appendixes, no Index.
* The author commanded the Royal Guernsey Artillery and, as librarian of the Priaulx Library, had access to the old Militia archives. Drawing heavily upon those records, he traces the history of the Militia over a period of nearly nine hundred years. As he explains, the Militia played an important role in island life and was a key element in the island's constitutional status. R/4 V/1. PLG. CEP.

PROCEEDINGS IN THE ISLAND OF GUERNSEY ...
Relative to the Dismissal of Colonel Guille from the Command of the North or 1st Light Infantry Regiment of Militia by Major General Bayly, the Present Lieutenant Governor
Anon * Printed and published by H Brouard, St Peter Port, 1819. Soft card, blind, blue, 8.25 x 5.25, viii/42. No ills, no maps, no appendixes, no Index.
* A detailed record of a notable post-Napoleonic War scandal which centered upon the constitutional question of whether or not a Lieutenant Governor had the authority to sack officers of the Militia. The row went to the highest levels in the British Government before Col Guille was restored to his command. This valuable source is a verbatim reprint of official documents and letters, and is noted here because it deals with several important aspects of Militia administration.
R/5 V/4. PC. CEP.
Note: a second edition (viii/53 pages) was published a year later with an appendix containing details of the Lieutenant Governor's retraction.

ROYAL GUERNSEY
A History of the Royal Guernsey Militia
Victor Coysh * Guernsey Press, 1977. Soft card, blue, yellow, Militia crest, 7.75 x 6.0, -/64. 6 mono phots, no maps, Bibliography, no Index. Apps: text of a typical 18th Century Commission, personal memoirs (1920s-1930s).
* A useful but not always accurate account of the period 1327 to 1946. Until 1750, local defence was provided by the island's Parish Companies, but the wars with France caused these armed bands to be expanded and reorganised. Their importance increased sharply during the Revolutionary and Napoleonic Wars. Training was continued after Waterloo, but another hundred years were to pass

before the Militia was called to active service. In August 1914, the RGM included two Bns of infantry. Their training was intensified and, in March 1915, a party of 245 all ranks travelled to Fermoy, Ireland, where they became a Coy of the 6th (Service) Bn Royal Irish Regt. Shortly afterwards a similar party embarked to become a Coy of 7th (Service) Bn Royal Irish Fusiliers. The RGM also found men to become a Divsl Ammunition Column for 9th (Scottish) Div. These troops all saw service in France and Flanders. After some debate, the War Office gave authority in 1916 for the establishment of a new Regt so that the men of the island could attest for overseas service under their own Colours. Entitled the Royal Guernsey Light Infantry, it recruited former Militiamen and wartime volunteers and raised two Bns - 1st (Service) Bn RGLI and 2nd (Reserve) Bn RGLI. The 1st Bn landed in France in September 1917 with 29th Div, was heavily mauled at the Battle of Lys in April 1918, then transferred to GHQ Troops. The 2nd Bn remained on the island as the garrison force and draft-finding unit for the 1st Bn. After the war, the RGLI was disbanded but part-time soldiering continued under the aegis of the RGM. When the Germans invaded in 1940, the RGM went into suspended animation and has not since been revived. R/3 V/2. CFHT. PJE.

THE ROYAL GUERNSEY MILITIA
Interesting History from 1203 to 1916
Edith Carey * The Star, Guernsey, 1916. Soft card, buff, 3.5 x 4.75, -/16. No ills, no maps, no appendixes, no Index.
* Written by a noted local historian, this little pamphlet was produced as a morale booster at the time when the newly-formed RGLI was training and preparing for service overseas. R/4 V/1. PC. CEP.

DIEX AÏX: GOD HELP US
The Guernseymen Who Marched Away, 1914-1915
Maj Edwin Parks * Guernsey Museums and Galleries, Guernsey, 1992. Illustrated soft card, red/sepia, yellow, 7.75 x 8.25 (landscape), xvi/172. Fp, 18 mono phots, 8 maps, Bibliography, Chapter Notes, no Index. Apps: Roll of Honour (for all six Guernsey-raised units, KIA, DOW and WIA, with locations of burials), H&A, list of officers, idem SNCOs, unit nominal rolls.
* Guernsey provided the officers and men for six separate units in WWI - two Coys of infantry for 16th (Irish) Div, a Divsl Ammunition Column for 9th (Scottish) Div, a Quarry Coy RE, an Army Troops Coy RE, and the Royal Guernsey Light Infantry (a Service Bn and a Reserve Bn). A total of 4000 all ranks served with these units - a very large number for such a small island. The book is a compilation, drawn from many archival sources, of nominal rolls for each unit, with details of casualties, awards, etc. In the case of non-Guernseymen who were posted to the RGLI in France as battle casualty replacements, the same degree of detail is provided (most of these men were from Staffordshire). An exceptionally helpful source for genealogists and medal collectors. R/1 V/5. PLG. RP.
Note: this book is No4 in a series of monographs published by the Guernsey Museums and Galleries, each of which deals with a facet of island history and culture.

NORMAN TEN HUNDRED
A Stanley Blicq * Guernsey Press, St Peter Port, 1920. Illustrated soft card, buff, black, 7.25 x 4.75, -/104. No ills, 4 sketch maps (inaccurate, and two transposed), no appendixes, no Index.
* A personal memoir by a man who served with 1st Bn RGLI during its time on the Western Front, 1917-1918. A soldier's reminiscences of life in the ranks, it was written from memory and in a style favoured by popular journalists of the period. The book contains a number of factual errors. The paper and binding are of poor quality. A collector's curiosity. R/4 V/1. PLG. CEP.

THE ROYAL GUERNSEY MILITIA
A Short History and List of Officers
Maj Edwin Parks * La Société Guernesaise, Guernsey, 1992. Soft card, cap badge, scarlet, black, 10.5 x 7.25, -/101. 16 cld ills (uniforms), one map, Bibliography, no Index. Apps: list of all officers who served (1800-1940).
* Painstakingly compiled over a period of years from a number of official sources, nearly half of this book consists of lists of officers who served with the RGM from 1800 to 1940 (when the arrival of the Germans brought its activities to an end). The lists are complete from c.1800 onwards, but the author also lists a great many names of pre-1800 officers (leaving space for additional names which a researcher might later discover for himself). One list of wide interest is that of officers who, having at some stage been granted a Lieutenant Governor's Commission in the local Militia, subequently obtained a Commission in the Armies of the Honourable East India Company (Hodson of Hodson's Horse was one such), or a King's Commission in the British Army or Indian Army. These lists are prefaced by a short outline history, but the book is intended to complement rather than replace the works by Groves, Coysh, and Carey (vide preceding entries). It also complements the same author's listings of WWI personnel (vide preceding page). A unique feature are the sixteen coloured plates, these being photographic reproductions of a series of late 19th Century paintings by Lieut Col J Percy-Groves (a former officer of the Royal Guernsey Artillery). They illustrate the Militia uniforms of the period and had not been published previously. The book is a prime source for medal collectors, genealogists and military modellers. R/1 V/5. PLG. RP.

THE ROYAL GUERNSEY LIGHT INFANTRY
Standing Orders and Duties of Officers
Anon * Gale & Polden Ltd, Aldershot, 1921. Soft card, buff, black/red, Regtl crest, 6.0 x 4.0, -/29. No ills, no maps, no appendixes, no Index.
* Bearing the instruction 'Always to be carried on the Person', this booklet is of a standard format for such publications. However, the insular nature of the unit's origins are reflected in the scope of the Orders which cover everything from 'The Powers of the Lieutenant Governor commanding Troops' to 'Duties of the Sergeants' Mess Caterer'. It should be noted that these Standing Orders were authorised in 1921, and yet the RGLI referred to in the WWI accounts was disbanded in 1920. The explanation is that the designation Royal Guernsey Light Infantry (Militia) had existed over very many years before the war. The RGLI authorised by the War Office in 1916 was a wartime unit of the British Army. The war over, the War Office no longer needed it. Following its disbandment the RGLI title continued to be used by the infantry element of the Royal Guernsey Militia. It was to this unit - the RGLI(M) - that the Standing Orders refer. The RGLI(M) was itself disbanded in 1928. R/4 V/1. PC. CEP.

JERSEY

BALLEINE'S HISTORY OF JERSEY
Revision of the Original Book, Dedicated to his Memory
Marguerite Syvret and Joan Stevens * The Garden City Press Ltd, Letchworth, Northants, UK, for La Société Jersaise, St Helier, 1981. Illustrated case-binding, 'View of St Aubin's Bay' motif, blue, gold, 10.0 x 7.5, xiv/306. Fp, 22 mono phots, 12 cld ills (topographical), 13 line drawings, 2 maps (printed on the end-papers), Glossary, Bibliography, Chapter Notes, Index. Apps: Roll of Honour (2 names only, Lieut W A McRae VC and Capt A M C McReady-Diarmid VC).
* The definitive work on the history of Jersey. Events are set against the broader canvas of world and European history. The book appeals, therefore, to a wide readership and is likely to remain the standard reference work for many years to come. The narrative contains many references to the Royal Jersey Militia which traces its roots back to 1336 and the Hundred Years War. R/1 V/5. JL. JFE.
Note: the first edition of this book was published in 1950. As a matter of record,

the Royal Jersey Militia included three Bns of infantry at the outbreak of war in August 1914. Some of these men were unfit and most were only semi-trained. By March 1915, however, a first contingent of 230 all ranks was ready to join 7th (Service) Bn Royal Irish Rifles in Ireland. They subsequently landed in France in August 1917 as an element of 16th Div. Other drafts followed later. In 1916 the War Office authorised the raising of the Royal Jersey Garrison Bn, a wartime unit which remained on the island throughout the war. By the end, 862 Jerseymen had died in the conflict, most of them on the Western Front and none of them in a Jersey-badged unit. In 1940, some members of the Royal Jersey Militia managed to evade the occupation and were posted to the Hampshire Regt. The RJM still existed on paper during the occupation, but was finally disbanded in 1954. Then, following an appeal by the British Government in 1987, the States of Jersey agreed to make a contribution to UK defence by funding a local Royal Engineers unit, Territorial Army. Recruitment and training commenced early in 1988 with the HQ in the old Royal Engineers Yard at Mount Bingham, St Helier. The title of the new unit is The Jersey Field Squadron RE (The Royal Militia of the Island of Jersey). Bearing in mind that the Jersey Militia was first raised by Royal Command in 1336, the new unit can claim to have the longest history of any in the British Army. Also, it shares with the Royal Monmouthshires the distinction of bearing two 'Royal' titles.

THE BATTLE OF JERSEY

Richard Mayne * Phillimore & Co, Chichester, UK, 1981. Red, gold, 10.0 x 7.5, xii/116. Fp, 34 mono phots, 10 cld ills, 2 maps (printed on the end-papers), Bibliography, Index. Apps: list of participating officers (1781), plus 14 other short appendixes relating to barracks, songs, personalities, passwords, fortifications, etc.
* A clear account of the last occasion, in January 1781, when French troops fought on British soil. Most of the defending soldiers were local Militia. Full of information regarding the build-up and the battle itself. R/1 V/5. CFHT. PJE.

SOUVENIR DU CENTENAIRE

Bataille de Jersey et la Celebration du Centenaire, 1881, avec Gravures

Anon * Printed by Huelin & Le Feuvre, for La Nouvelle Chronique de Jersey, 1881. Royal blue, gold, 'Laurel wreath' motif, 6.75 x 4.5, x/121. Fp, 8 engraved plates, one map (bound in), no Index. Apps: verbatim documents regarding the granting of the 'Royal' prefix (in 1831).
* Written in French (the official language of the period), and published to mark the 100th Anniversary of the Battle of Jersey. The book is 'a tribute to the brave and loyal Major Pierson of the 95th Regt of Foot who rallied the military forces of the island to defeat the French invaders led by Baron de Rullecourt'. It covers the history of the Jersey Militia from the Norman Conquest through to 1781 and includes an account of the trial of the Lieutenant Governor, Mois Corbet. The narrative describes the celebration ceremonies in detail and stresses the loyalty to the Crown of all those involved. R/5 V/4. PC. JFE.

SARK

CANNON AND MUSKET

The Defences of Sark

Christopher Murphy * Extract from The Transactions of La Société Guernesaise, (Part IV, Vol XXII, 1989), Candie Museum, St Peter Port, Guernsey. Soft card, beige.
* This four-page pamphlet is the only account in print of the Sark Militia, first formed in 1572. Traditionally commanded by the Seigneur of Sark, in the rank of Lieutenant Colonel, it consisted of approximately 100 men who could be called out at any time of threat of their small island. The 'Royal' title was granted in 1831 and the unit was organised as Light Infantry. It converted to the artillery role in 1881 and was disbanded in 1900. R/1 V/3. PC. CEP.

THE ROYAL SARK MILITIA

Bertha J Hurden * Guernsey Press Co, for the author, 1992. Illustrated soft card, pale blue, dark blue, '1850s Shako plate' motif, 8.25 x 5.75, ii/43. Fp (portrait of the last CO), 8 mono phots, no maps, list of sources, no Index. Apps: notes on uniforms.

* Apart from the minor item noted on the preceding page, very little work has been done on the history of the Royal Sark Militia. In this booklet, Mrs Hurden has pulled together all the available sources concerning the Regt, from its earliest roots through to the final disbandment of 1900. In contrast to the account by Murphy (vide preceding page), Mrs Hurden traces the origins of the Regt, or at least its forebears, to the 14th Century. Her booklet is a valuable record of a Regt which otherwise was in danger of being entirely forgotten. If her account has a weakness, it is with regard to uniforms. She states that little is known, but some examples and artefacts have in fact survived the passing years. R/1 V/4. PLG. CEP.

THE ISLE OF MAN

A MILITARY HISTORY OF THE ISLE OF MAN
B E Sargeant * Buncle & Co Ltd, Scotland, 1947. Light blue, black, 8.5 x 5.5, -/94. No ills, one map, Index. Apps: list of all Manx units (at 1811, 1863, and 1943).
* Five chapters deal with different aspects of Manx military history (Fortress, Militia, Fencible, Cavalry and Volunteer units), and three more deal individually with events during the Victorian, WWI and WWII periods. It was during the two world wars that the island was used by the British as a dumping ground for POW and civilian political internees. Local units were much involved in guarding these camps. Written in a dry 'diary' format, but full of good factual reference material. R/4 V/3. CFHT. PJE.

THE ROYAL MANX FENCIBLES
B E Sargeant * Gale & Polden Ltd, Aldershot, 1947. Red, black, 8.5 x 5.5, -/101. Fp, 4 mono phots, one map, no Index. Apps: list of officers of the four Corps of Manx Fencibles.
* Another basic factual account from an author who seems to have compiled a number of very useful records of local Corps and units. This one covers the period 1779 to 1811. A chapter is devoted to each of the four Corps of Fencibles, with much attention given to matters of Dress, accoutrements, parades, Courts Martial, etc, all based upon original documents and published sources. R/4 V/4. CFHT. PJE.

ISLAND AT WAR
The Remarkable Role Played by the Small Manx Nation in the Great War, 1914-1918
Margery West * Western Books, IoM, 1986. Leather, black, gold, 8.5 x 6.0, vi/234. Fp, 65 mono phots, no maps, Bibliography, no Index. Apps: Roll of Honour (very detailed, for all men originating in the island and who lost their lives in WWII), H&A (also very detailed).
* Written by a journalist in memory of her father, this is an easily readable account of the events of WWI as they applied to the Isle of Man and to local men who served in various capacities around the world. Most of them, in fact, joined the British Army or the Royal Navy. There is also some mention of the POW camps. Quite generalised, but helpful background reading. For the genealogist, the appendixes are invaluable. R/1 V/3. CFHT. PJE.

ISLES OF SCILLY

Unlike the Channel Islands and the Isle of Man, the Isles of Scilly are constitutionally part of the United Kingdom. Their military history does not, therefore, come within the scope of this bibliography. Even so, the following information may be of interest.

The islands have a long and interesting military history, but the services of the few locally raised units are not well recorded. Some documents concerning the Scillonian Fencibles have survived, but they have not been developed in book form. A local school-master, John P Osbourne, compiled an extensive account of the role of the islands in WWI and WWII, the information being presented in facsimile TS:

SCILLONIAN WAR DIARY, 1914-1918, in three volumes
SCILLONIAN WAR DIARY, 1939-1945, in four volumes

These were produced privately in 'Perfect' bound soft card covers, the WWI series including some mention of the Isles of Scilly Volunteers. The contents are an amalgam of reminiscences, extracts from newspapers, maps, official documents, and poorly reproduced photographs. A limited number of copies were circulated, mainly in the islands, and a complete set can be viewed in The Museum, Hugh Town, St Mary's.

GERMANY

HISTORY OF THE KING'S GERMAN LEGION

N Ludlow Beamish * Thomas & William Boone, London, 1832. Two matching volumes, both in marbled boards with leather spines and quarters, gold on red, 9.0 x 5.5.
Vol I : xxxi/387. 9 mono plates (uniforms), 4 maps, no Index. Apps: list of officers KIA and WIA at Talavera, etc.
Vol II : xvii/672. One mono plate, 5 maps (4 printed in the text, one bound in), Bibliography, no Index. Apps: 200 pages of Returns, verbatim documents, Orders, casualty returns, unit strengths, Errata, etc.
* A typical and monumental early 19th Century work, packed with detail of every kind, military and political. Volume I opens with a description of the condition of the Hanoverian Army during Napoleon's advance into that country. The author continues with the recruitment of mercenary volunteers from Hanover, the transport of these men to England, their organisation and training, their return to the Continent, their fighting services (particularly at Austerlitz), and then their posting to Ireland. The Legion moved next to the Iberian Peninsula to fight under Wellington. The first volume, of twenty-two chapters, ends with the siege of Badajoz. Volume II has seventeen chapters. It opens with the capture of Badajoz and continues with all the great Peninsula battles in which the KGL was engaged - Cuidad Rodrigo, Salamanca, etc. The author covers also those elements of the Legion which were detached for service in Sicily and the Netherlands. After Toulouse, they were reunited as the Army of the Netherlands and as such took part in the Battle of Waterloo. He concludes with the disbandment of the KGL following Napoleon's exile to St Helena. R/5 V/5. NAM. PJE.

THE WHEATLEY DIARY
A Journal and Sketch-book kept during The Peninsular War and The Waterloo Campaign

Edmund Wheatley (edited by Christopher Hibbert) * Longmans, London, 1964. Beige, gold, 8.75 x 5.5, xvi/94. Fp, 18 line drawings (some cld), plus other minor line sketches, 4 maps, no appendixes, Index.
* Wheatley was one of only two British officers serving with 5th Line Bn, King's German Legion, when it fought its way from San Sebastian to Bayonne in 1813-1814. His original observations on that campaign are here expertly edited and annotated by Hibbert, and they represent one of the very few published records. Although initially a Hanoverian force, with eight Light Infantry Bns, two Regts of Dragoons, three of Light Dragoons, plus artillery and engineer units, the Legion's ranks were progressively diluted with recruits of poor quality from many other countries as the war went on. Even so, it played a valuable role in the defeat of French forces in Spain and, later, in Belgium. This is not a unit history per se, but is certainly a most useful reference source. R/2 V/3. DCLS. RP.

ON THE ROAD WITH WELLINGTON

August L F Schaumann (edited by Anthony M Ludovici) * William Heinemann Ltd, London, 1924. Blue, gold, 9.0 x 6.0, xxi/416. Fp, 19 cld plates (landscapes, battle scenes, officers), no maps, no appendixes, no Index.
* At age 30, the author of these diaries joined the KGL as a Commissary. Between 1808 and 1812, he served from Portugal to France with the Legion and, occasionally, with British units (32nd Foot, 18th Hussars, 9th Light Dragoons). He recorded the war in great detail and made many interesting observations on the campaign as seen at regimental level. The narrative contains a wealth of good reference material. R/4 V/3. NAM. PJE.

Note: the KGL must not be confused with similarly titled British German Legion which was raised for service in the Crimean War and which comprised two Regts of Light Dragoons, three Jager (Rifle) Corps, and six Regts of Infantry. Vide the Index of Authors - C C Bayley.

THE KING'S GERMAN LEGION

Otto von Pivka * Osprey Publishing Ltd, Reading, Berkshire, 1974. Illustrated soft card, 'KGL soldier with pistol' motif, full colour, 9.5 x 7.25, -/40. 17 mono phots, 22 cld ills, 2 maps, no appendixes, Bibliography, no Index.

* Of the three sources listed on the preceding page, only the 1832 work by Ludlow Beamish can be regarded as a full Regtl history. For obvious reasons, it is expensive to acquire and can be found in only a limited number of libraries. This being so, the researcher is advised to consult the slim but well researched booklet described above. Another of Osprey's 'Men at Arms' series, it provides in condensed format an account of the Legions's formation, Order of Battle, various titles (as Hanoverian Army and Prussian Army), its battles between 1808 and 1814, and much else besides. The 'year of victories', 1812, and the battles in Spain and France leading to the great battle at Waterloo, are particularly well summarised. As usual with the 'Men at Arms' books, this one is beautifully illustrated with pictures of uniforms, weapons, equipment and the Colours. The bibliography refers mainly to records and books of German origin, and this is useful to researchers unfamiliar with sources printed in that language. The author even managed to include the names of the Regtl Commanders and Adjutants, and this feature may be useful to genealogists. A most handy source of reference. R/1 V/4. ANL. MCND'A.

GIBRALTAR

THE GIBRALTAR REGIMENT

Stand Easy Commemorative Journal, 50th Anniversary

Maj G J Valerino ED (and other officers) * Cams International, location not stated, n.d. (1989). Illustrated soft card, stapled, full colour, 'Soldier with keys' motif, 11.75 x 8.25, -/61. 57 mono phots, 35 cld ills, no maps, no appendixes, no Index.

* In March 1939, the British Government authorised the raising - from Gibraltar's male population - of a part-time volunteer unit. The intention was to train these men primarily as anti-aircraft gunners. The first forty-eight members of the GDF (Gibraltar Defence Force) were mobilised on 3 September and placed under command of 19th A/A Bty RA (later incorporated into 82nd Heavy A/A Regt RA). The initial establishment was soon increased by the formation of Signals, Transport, and Medical Sections which worked with British Army units stationed in the Colony. On a war footing, the GDF manned some of the 9.2 inch coastal batteries and 3.7 inch A/A guns. Gibraltar was heavily raided on many occasions, mainly by aircraft of the Italian and Vichy French air forces, and the GDF shot down at least one of these bombers. Conscription of male Gibraltarians was introduced in 1944 (for a six months' term) and was continued through to 1971. Meantime, in 1958, the GDF was retitled The Gibraltar Regiment. In its modern form, the Regt is a part-Regular, part-Territorial Army infantry unit with strong artillery associations. Apart from routine training and ceremonial duties, it is Custodian of the Fortress Keys and was until recently responsible for the Rock Apes (the Barbary Macaque monkeys which inhabit the Upper Rock and which, by legend, are living symbols of the Colony's status as a Crown possession). This excellent magazine-style publication is full of historical reference material. Many former officers are named in the narrative, and there are useful details regarding local units raised in former years - the Genoese Guard of 1755, the Soldier Artificer Company of 1772, Los Carreteros del Rey (they saw active service with the British Army in Egypt in the 1880s), and the Gibraltar Defence Volunteer Force of 1915-1920. R/2 V/4. PC. JLC.

THE GIBRALTAR POLICE

The Second Oldest Police Force in Britain and the Commonwealth

Joe Garcia * Mediterranean Sun Publishing Co Ltd, Gibraltar, 1980. Illustrated soft card, facsimile TS, white/black, 9.5 x 6.5, -/62. 64 mono phots, no maps, Bibliography, no Index. Apps: Force nominal roll (all ranks, at 18.4.1980).

* A fairly sketchy little book, produced to mark the Force's 150th anniversary. The author wisely chose to highlight some of the more unusual events during that period, and this provides interest and entertainment. The illustrations are mainly of individual officers and groups of personnel. A useful source of reference as far as it goes, and certainly helpful to specialist reserchers. R/3 V/3. RCSL. PJE.

MALTA

HISTORICAL RECORDS OF THE MALTESE CORPS

Maj A G Chesney * William Clowes & Sons Ltd, London, 1897. Blue, gold, Maltese cross, 9.0 x 6.0, xii/210. Fp, 6 mono phots, 18 fine chromolithographs (14 of uniforms, 3 of the Colours), one map (Isle of Capri, 1808), Index. Apps: establishments and rates of pay for the Royal Malta Fencibles and Royal Malta Artillery (1815-1896), idem the Royal Malta Regiment of Militia (1888-1893), roll of Maltese who served (and were serving at the time of publication) in the British Army (with brief biographical details).

* Based primarily upon records available to the author in his capacity as Adjutant of the Royal Malta Regt of Militia, and from contemporary local records. The narrative covers the period 1798 to 1895 and describes actions in which Maltese units were engaged: removing the French from the island (1800), the expedition to Egypt (1801), the seizure of Elba (1801), the landings in Sicily, and the second seizure of Elba (1808). Volunteers from the Royal Malta Fencible Artillery took part in the Egypt campaign of 1882. Biographical notes regarding various officers and NCOs are scattered throughout the text, thus making the book a useful source for military historians and genealogists alike. The coloured plates are of superb quality. R/5 V/4. PC. HIS.

Note: reprinted by Midsea Books Ltd, Valletta, Malta, c.1987.

HISTORY OF THE ROYAL MALTA ARTILLERY
Volume I: 1800-1939

Brig A Samut-Tagliaferro CBE * Lux Press Ltd, for the author, Valletta, 1976. Dark red, gold, Corps crest with diagonal colours, 9.25 x 7.0, xii/496. 37 mono phots, 17 line drawings, 2 maps, Chapter Notes, Index. Apps: H&A, lists of former officers and SNCOs, idem Civil Commissioners and Governors of Malta, nominal rolls.

* An immensely detailed and very accurate study of the Corps by one of its former COs. It is the first formal account of the RMA's history and it incorporates brief accounts of all the Anglo-Maltese units from which the RMA evolved. The work is based upon a series of articles, by the same author, which had earlier appeared in THE MALTA LAND FORCE JOURNAL and THE ARMED FORCES OF MALTA JOURNAL between 1972 and 1976. R/4 V/5. PC. HIS/DAD.

Note: it is reported that the print run for this book was 300 copies. A Volume II has been drafted by Brig Samut-Tagliaferro, but he has not yet set a publication date.

A SHORT HISTORY OF THE ROYAL MALTA ARTILLERY
Abridged for Use in Regimental Schools

Anon ('A Committee of Officers of the RMA') * Criterion Press, Valletta, 1944. Soft card, Regtl crest, grey, black, 7.75 x 5.25, -/40. No ills, no maps, Bibliography, no Index. Apps: chronology of historical events.

* A booklet divided into two parts. The first covers the origins of the RMA, its formation in 1861, then in greater detail the WWI period and, finally, the Regt's expansion and vital services in defending the island in WWII. The second part consists of two essays by Sgt G B Harker AEC on Maltese and European history. A useful little reference book. R/5 V/2. MODL. AMM.

THE HISTORY OF THE KING'S OWN MALTA REGIMENT
And the Armed Forces of the Order of St John

Capt J M Wismayer * Said International Ltd, for Printwell Ltd, Valletta, 1989. Soft card, blue, white, 9.75 x 7.0, xvi/376. Fp (group of officers, Regimento di Malta, 1777-1798), very heavily illustrated with mono phots, plans of fortifications, maps and diagrams, Glossary, Bibliography, Index. Apps: Roll of Honour (1st, 2nd and 3rd KOMR, 3rd LAA Regt RMA, 11th HAA Regt RMA(T), and Static Group KOMR), H&A (for same units), list of Hon Colonels (KOMR, 1951-1972), list of COs (KOMR and 3rd Regt RMA(T), 1951-1956), full nominal roll (3/11th Regt RMA(T) at 31.3.1972), notes on RMA Dockyard Defence Bty, notes on the Order of St John, etc.

* This is the first full account, in English, of all the armies of St John up to 1798, and the modern Corps and units which evolved from them. The narrative covers in detail the history of the King's Own Malta Regt, the role of the Royal Malta Artillery during WWII, and then the amalgamation of the two Regts under the title Armed Forces of Malta in 1970. The text is liberally illustrated with maps and plans of Malta's fortications, plus tables of statistics regarding unit strengths, dispositions, and armaments. Very comprehensive. R/3 V/5. PC. DAD.
Note: published with a limited print run of 600 copies.

REGIMENTAL HISTORY - RMA AND KOMR
E G Montanaro and Sgt G B Harker MA AEC * Criterion Press, Malta, 1944.
Beige, black, 8.0 x 5.25, -/40. No ills, no maps, Bibliography, no Index. Apps: 'Date Chart' (a chronology of important events in Malta's history).
* Seemingly a private venture by its two authors, this booklet is a brief summary of Malta's military history from 1800 to 1944. Only the first twenty-four pages are of more than usual interest. They carry condensed histories of each of the local 19th Century units - Maltese Light Infantry (1800-1802), Maltese Pioneers (1800-1801), Maltese Militia (1801), Maltese Militia Coast Artillery (1801), Maltese Provincial Battalions (1802-1815), Maltese Veterans (1802-1815), Malta Coast Artillery (1802-1815), Royal Regiment of Malta (1805-1811), The Military Artificers, Sappers & Miners (1806-1817), Royal Malta Fencible Regt (1815-1861), Royal Malta Fencible Artillery (1861-1889), Maltese Militia (1852-1857), and Maltese Dockyard Battalion of Artillery (1853-1864). A most useful record of several otherwise forgotten units. R/4 V/3. PCAL. RP.

POLAND

AN ARMY IN EXILE
Lieut Gen W Anders CB * Macmillan & Co, London, 1949. Plum, gold, 8.75 x 5.5, xvi/319. Fp, 15 mono phots, 7 maps, no appendixes, Index.
* An autobiographical account, but the only comprehensive description of the Free Polish Army of WWII. Anders was a Div Commander when the Germans invaded his country in 1939. Escaping to Russia, he was permitted by the Soviets to gather together a force composed of other survivors. After much debate with the Allies, these men were removed from the Soviet Union via the Caucasus and Persia to the Middle East. After training and service in North Africa, and reinforced with more escapees, the 2nd Polish Corps moved to Italy under Anders' command and as an element of the 8th Army. The Poles took a prominent part in the Battle of Cassino and later fought all the way up the Adriatic coast to the valley of the Po, to Bologna and Milan. The Corps was then abruptly disbanded in circumstances which brought no credit to the Allies. With their homeland now occupied by the Soviets, perceived by the Communists as having been 'tainted' by Western ideas, the demobilised troops were obliged to disperse and to take up new lives elsewhere. Of necessity, the political factors dominate the story. A worthy record. R/3 V/4. NAM. PJE.
Note: Free Polish servicemen also fought for the Allied cause in the RAF and at sea in naval surface and submarine units.

3 DYWIZJA STRZELCOW KARPACKICH W ITALII
Album Fotograficsny
Anon * Archetipografia SA, Milano, Italy, for 3 DSK Historical Committee, 1945. Soft card, grey, white, red/white silk bootlace binding, 8.75 x 9.5 (landscape), -/128. Approximately 360 mono phots, no maps, no appendixes, Index (of photographers).
* Essentially a memento for all those who served in Italy with the 3rd Carpathian Division, and for the Italian friends whom they made along the way. It is a collection of photographs which show every aspect of the campaign, from action in the front line to the fun of off-duty activities in the rear areas. The pictures are not particularly good or well reproduced, but they capture perfectly the ethos of the 2nd Polish Corps (of which the 3rd Carpathian Div formed part) between June 1944 and July 1945. Each picture is accompanied by a caption in Polish, Italian and English. The Polish soldiers, each of whom had survived almost incredible adventures before reaching the Mediterranean theatre of war, fought with tremendous dedication in the Italian campaign. Their fervour caused them unnecessarily high casualties at their first battle, Cassino. Thereafter, they settled down to become dedicated professionals as they fought their way up the Adriatic coast to the valley of the Po. This book was published at a time when they still believed that they would return to a liberated Poland and that their sacrifices would be recognised by the Western governments which they had served so well. Neither of these beliefs was justified by subsequent events. In some ways, the fortunate ones were those who did not live to read this book but whose headstones are to be seen in the Polish war cemetery on the summit of Monte Cassino or hidden in the dingy suburbs of Bologna. To quote from their own Cassino memorial: 'For our freedom and yours, we soldiers of Poland gave our soul to God, our lives to the soil of Italy, and our hearts to Poland'. R/5 V/1. PC. RP.
Note: it is reported that other elements of the 2nd Polish Corps produced similar records in the summer of 1945 in Italy. If this is so, the above example may be regarded as representative of its genre.

PORTUGAL

OBSERVATIONS ON THE PRESENT STATE OF THE PORTUGUESE ARMY AS ORGANISED BY LT GEN SIR WILLIAM CARR BERESFORD, KB
With an Account of the Different Military Establishments and Laws of Portugal
Andrew Halliday MD * C Baldwin, London, 1811. Marbled leather all round, brown/ ochre, gold, 9.75 x 8.5, viii/149. No ills, 5 maps (printed on the end-papers), no Index. Apps: list of officers (at 16.7.1811, a total of 195 names).
* When General Junot entered Lisbon with the French Army in November 1807, the Portuguese Army was about 10,000 strong, demoralised and badly organised. It was disbanded on 5 March 1808. The French quitted Lisbon after the Treaty of Cintra, and Wellington then proposed a reformation of the Portuguese Army. In view of its past record, the task of raising and training the restructured force was given to officers of the British Army. A number of Portuguese were granted Commissions and they served alongside their British comrades. The chain of command bore some interesting similarities to that of the Armies of the Honourable East India Company. The title of the book is a good summary of its contents as far as administrative matters are concerned, but the narrative also includes a useful description of the campaign from March 1810 to July 1811. R/5 V/4. NAM. PJE.

ON THE PORTUGUESE LEGION
Anon * Printed by J Buttel Marshall, London, 1810.
* A bibliographic reference to this title has been seen. Nothing else is known about it. It may be a book or it may be little more than a broadsheet. Whatever it is, it is certainly very elusive.
Note: in the same category of rarity is A NARRATIVE OF THE LOYAL LUSITANIAN LEGION UNDER BRIGADIER GENERAL SIR ROBERT WILSON, by William Mayne (T Egerton, London, 1812). The name of Lusitania was given by the Romans to their Province in the western part of the Iberian Peninsula (and equating to latter-day Portugal), so this publication presumably refers to an Auxiliary Corps raised by the British in that region during the Peninsular campaign.

RUSSIA

CANADIANS IN RUSSIA, 1918-1919
Roy MacLaren * Macmillan of Canada, Toronto, 1976. Olive, black, 9.25 x 6.0, viii/301. 29 mono phots, 3 maps, Bibliography, Index. Apps: notes on Canadian airmen with the Volunteer Army, notes on Gregori Semenov.
* The story of the 6000 Canadian soldiers sent to North Russia and Siberia in 1918 to assist the White Army in its struggle with the Red Army. The narrative is a 'good read', but the lack of appendixes, the limited number of maps, and the absence of Chapter Notes prevent the book from becoming what would be otherwise a major source of reference. R/2 V/3. RCSL. RP.

ALLIED INTERVENTION IN RUSSIA, 1918-1919
And the Part Played by Canada
John Swettenham * George Allen & Unwin Ltd, London, 1967. Red, silver, 8.75 x 5.75, -/319. 22 mono phots, 8 maps, no appendixes, Chapter Notes, Bibliography (very extensive), Index.
* This work has its roots in material researched by the author for his contribution to CANADIAN EXPEDITIONARY FORCE, 1914-1919, by Col G W L Nicholson (vide the Index of Authors) which made only limited reference to the 1918-1919 operations in South Russia, North Russia and Siberia. The narrative is arranged in three parts and has two main strands - the issues and events of the Russian Civil War, and the intrigues and rivalries of the ten erstwhile Allies. The wide-ranging story opens with British operations in Kurdistan, Persia and South Russia (where the 1st Overseas Canadian Pioneer Detachment formed part of Dunsterforce). It then deals with operations based upon Murmansk (in which the Canadians had only a limited role) and Archangel (starting point for 16th Bde CFA in its advance to Tulgas and the Dvina River - vide following page). The third section of the book deals in depth with the inter-service wrangles which marred the operations in Siberia and neatly supplements the information given in J E Skuce's book (vide following entry). R/3 V/3. PC. JRD.

CANADIAN SOLDIERS IN SIBERIA
Canadian Siberia Expeditionary Force
J E Skuce * Access to History Publications, Ottawa, 1990. Beige/cerise, gold, CSEF patch on front cover, 11.25 x 8.25, v/149. 31 mono phots, 2 maps, footnotes, Bibliography, no Index. Apps: Roll of Honour (with dates, causes and locations), H&A, general CSEF nominal roll, plus eight others.
* A deeply researched account based upon previously unpublished archives. In early August 1918, a multi-national force began to assemble at Vladivostok to fight the Bolsheviks in Eastern Russia. Additionally to the soldiers of nine other countries there was the Canadian contingent, the CSEF. The Allied force advanced towards Omsk but then began to break up. It withdrew a year later. This book contains no details of the fighting in which the CSEF was engaged, but it does provide full details of the units and sub-units which took part in the ill-starred affair - 85th Bty CFA, 259th Bn CEF, 260th Bn CEF, and a Cavalry Squadron composed of men of the Royal North West Mounted Police. The military history content of this book is quite sparse, but the many rolls and other appendixes are a unique source for genealogists and medal collectors. R/2 V/4. CWM. JRD.
Note: published as a limited edition of 350 copies.

NREF - 16th BRIGADE CFA - 67th AND 68th BATTERIES

Anon (see below) * Publisher's details not shown on title pages, Toronto, Canada, n.d. (c.1920). Seen only as a photographic copy of a mutilated original, hence the details of the original binding are not known, 6.0 x 8.75 (landscape), -/55. Many ills (see below), probably no maps, no Index. Apps: Roll of Honour (KIA, DOW and DOD), H&A (2 pages), Bde nominal roll (3 pages, undated, all ranks).

* Prolonged enquiries have failed to unearth an original copy of this very rare book. The version described above is a one-off reproduction, held by the Library of Congress in Washington. It contains all of the original's 33 pages of text, but none of the 22 pages of illustrations. There is reference to the book being an 'album', so the missing pages presumably carried photographic half-tones. This guess is reinforced by the landscape format adopted by the printer/publisher. The Bde was formed specifically for service with the North Russia Expeditionary Force (the NREF of the book's title). It was commanded by Col C H L Sharman and his Introduction provides an over-view of the Allied activities in North Russia and the actions of his force. The bulk of the narrative consists of diaries of the 67th and 68th Btys by their respective COs - Maj F F Arnoldi and Maj Walter C Hyde. The diary of the 68th Bty includes an account of the Seletskoe Detachment, written by Lieut J Roberts. The book mentions many individual officers and men, but is little more than an outline history, produced as a souvenir of service for those who were there. R/5 V/3. LOC. RBM.

THE DIGGERS WHO SIGNED ON FOR MORE

Australia's Part in the Russian War of Intervention, 1918-1919

Bruce Muirden * Wakefield Press, Kent Town, South Australia, 1990. Illustrated paper-back, white/black, 7.75 x 5.75, -/115. 10 mono phots, 2 line drawings, 3 maps, Bibliography, no appendixes, Index.

* A fascinating account of the 200 Australian soldiers who, after the Armistice, volunteered to serve with the British Army against the Bolsheviks in North Russia. Two of these men, Cpl Arthur Sullivan and Sgt Samuel Pearse MM, each won the VC in August 1919 while attached to 45th Bn Royal Fusiliers. R/1 V/3. SLV. PS.

SICILY

ORDINI PERMANENTI PER IL REGIMENTO SICILIANO DI FANTERIA LEGGIERA NEL SERVIZIO DI SUA MAESTA BRITANNICA
Anon * Dalla Stamperia Regimentale (trans: The Regimental Press), Malta, 1813. Seen rebound in stiff card, red, blind, 8.0 x 6.0, -/59. No ills, no maps, no appendixes, no Index.
* Written (printed) in Italian, this is the second edition of the STANDING ORDERS FOR THE SICILIAN REGIMENT OF LIGHT INFANTRY IN THE SERVICE OF HIS BRITANNIC MAJESTY. Like most such publications, this one consists of regulations, rules governing distinctions of rank, codes of conduct, notes on guard duties, etc. Its interest is to be found mainly in the fact that it even exists. During the Napoleonic War, the ailing Kingdom of the Two Sicilies was Great Britain's ally. The French occupied its capital, Naples, and drove the Spanish Bourbon royal family to take refuge in Palermo, principal city of the island of Sicily. There was an obvious threat that the French would cross the Straits of Messina and capture this second half of the kingdom. The British were fully occupied with the campaign in Portugal and Spain, and had few troops to spare for the defence of the island. This task was entrusted to the Royal Navy. However, a number of military units were raised locally to man the coastal fortifications and port installations. This Regt was one such. The book appears to be the only published record of any of these short-lived Sicilian units. A collecting curiosity, and a memento of a largely forgotten episode. R/5 V/1. NLM. DAD.

SPAIN

A NARRATIVE OF THE BRITISH AUXILIARY LEGION
With Incidents, Anecdotes and Sketches of all the Parties Connected with the War in Spain, From a Journal of Personal Observations
Alexander Somerville * Muir, Gowans & Co, Glasgow, 1837. Three-quarters calf-skin, brown, gold, 8.25 x 5.0, -/288. No ills, no maps, no appendixes, no Index.
* The Civil War of 1835-1840 was one of a series of long-running disputes regarding rights of succession to the Spanish throne. King Ferdinand VII died in 1833, leaving his infant daughter Isabel as heir to the throne under a Regent, Dowager Queen Maria Christina. The child's uncle, Don Carlos, argued that the crown should pass only to male heirs (in this case, himself). Fighting, confined mainly to Northern Spain, broke out between 'the Christinas' and 'the Carlistas'. Bound by Treaty to support the Dowager Queen, Britain and France sent munitions, warships and thousands of men to her aid. A 'British Legion' was specially recruited in England for service in the war. It landed at San Sebastian in July 1835, but did not fight its first battle until the following year. The author of this account, a former officer of the Scots Greys, served with the Legion's 8th Regiment. He describes its operations in detail, with helpful references to many of the leading personalities. He also mentions the activities of the Royal Navy in securing the British lines of supply and landing sites. The narrative is readable and apparently authoritative. R/5 V/4. PC. TD.
Note: a Bn of Royal Marines served ashore, and its services are described in Vol II of BRITAIN'S SEA SOLDIERS, by Col Cyril Field RMLI, published in 1924.

THE MACKENZIE-PAPINEAU BATTALION
Canadian Participation in the Spanish Civil War
Victor Hoar * The Copp Clark Publishing Co, Toronto, 1969. Illustrated soft card, multi-coloured, 8.0 x 5.25, x/285. 25 mono phots (personnel, some captioned), 8 maps, Bibliography, Chapter Notes, Index. Apps: Roll of Honour (with home town, dates and locations), verbatim quotes from the Act regarding foreign enlistments.
* When Civil War broke out in July 1936, the Canadian and US Governments distanced themselves from the problems in Spain and did not subsequently sign the Agreement of Non-intervention. Many Canadians of left-wing or idealist views were, however, in sympathy with the Communist cause in that country. Despite the half-hearted official obstacles placed in their way, 262 Canadians (mainly from Ontario and Western Canada) succeeded in reaching Spain and fighting against the Republican forces as the MacKenzie-Papineau Bn. It was named after two Canadians who had led the rebellion of 1837. This detailed account describes the major actions at Jamara River, Brunete, Quinto, Belchite, Fuentes de Ebro, and during the retreats. A chapter is given to Dr Norman Bethune who created the Canadian Blood Tranfusion Service. Another chapter covers the story of Canadians taken POW, the last thirty of whom were repatriated in 1939. The author give good coverage of the fighting, naming many individuals in the narrative and describing their reception when they returned to Canada. R/3 V/5. PC. JRD.
Note: some of these men later fought in WWII with the armed forces of Canada.

AUSTRALIANS IN THE SPANISH CIVIL WAR
Amirah Inglis * Allen & Unwin Australia, North Sydney, 1987. Illustrated paper back, multi-coloured, 9.0 x 6.0, xvi/243. 36 mono phots, 5 line drawings, one map, Bibliography, Index. Apps: list of all Australians who served, with personal details.
* An unusual book which tells the story of the Australian men and women volunteers who travelled to Spain to fight for their personal convictions in the Civil War. Of the sixty-five persons involved, all but one fought on the Republican side. Fourteen were killed. R/1 V/2. PC. PS.

PART 6

The Middle East

NOTES

THE MIDDLE EAST
A Military Chronology

17th Century: the Honourable East India Company (HEIC) establishes its first trading bases in the Persian (Arabian) Gulf, at Bundar Abbas and Basra. The Portuguese are expelled from Muscat.
18th Century: much of the Middle East is still under the control, nominally at least, of the Turks, but the once mighty Ottoman Empire is in decline. Its subjects are held together by the Sunni Muslim faith. To the east, the Persian Empire also is in decline. It is the centre of the Shia Muslim faith.
1776: Hydar Ali of Mysore establishes diplomatic and trading links with Muscat.
1792: the Treaty of Jassy ends the fourth and last 18th Century war between Russia and the Turks. Catherine the Great annexes the Crimean khanates.
1793: the HEIC establishes a Residency in Kuwait. Its merchant ships are regular visitors to the Gulf from India. The Royal Navy provides protection from the pirate ships based at the southern end of the Gulf.
1797: Tipu Sultan, of Mysore, a friend of the French, renews the links with Muscat created in 1776 by Hydar Ali.
1798: the French invade Egypt. Three years later, they are ejected by the British and the Turks. The Royal Navy protects HEIC and other friendly shipping off Southern Arabia and in the Arabian Sea.
1799: in India, Tipu Sultan is killed in the Fourth Mysore War with the British. The indirect French link with Muscat is broken.
1799–1800: units of the HEIC's Bombay Presidency army briefly occupy Aden and Perim Island (at the southern approaches to the Red Sea). The Wahabis, a Sunni sect dominant in Eastern Arabia and including the ancestors of the present Saudi royal family, expand their influence to the Red Sea coast and to the Arabian Gulf. The HEIC moves into Muscat.
1807: as part of his plan to build an empire in the east, Napoleon Buonaparte enters into a treaty of friendship with Persia.
1808–1810: with the support of the Wahabis, the Quwasim pirates of Ras al Khaimah have gained in strength and daring. Their ships operate throughout the Gulf and across the Arabian Sea to the west coast of India. A major British expedition, consisting of Royal Navy and HEIC ships, with two thousand Indian and British Army troops, attacks Ras al Khaimah and other Gulf pirate ports. The HEIC now has four (Bombay Presidency) independent Residencies in the Gulf region - at Basra, Bushire, Muscat, and Baghdad.
1811: Quwasim piracy revives, with increasing ferocity over the next eight years. There is constant warfare between the Wahabis, who control Bahrain, Qatar, and Ras al Khaimah, to the west, and the Sultan of Oman to the east. Mohammed Ali, Pasha of Egypt, begins a large scale military operation to recover the Red Sea districts occupied by the Wahabis.
1812: the Treaty of Bucharest ends the latest war (1806–1812) between Russia and the Ottoman Empire. Bessarabia is separated from Moldavia and ceded to Russia.
1816–1818: Mohammed Ali despatches an army from Egypt to attack the Wahâbi capital of Dara'iyah (modern Riyadh). The city is besieged, then captured. The Wahabi leader, Emir Abdullah, is sent in chains to Constantinople and executed.
1819: the third major British expedition to the Gulf, against the Quwasim pirate base at Ras al Khaimah. It consists of ten HEIC Marine ships and two Royal Navy ships, with three thousand Indian and British Army troops (including the 47th and 65th of Foot). The force is supported by two ships and 600 men provided by the Sultan of Oman. The port is bombarded and occupied. The force then makes a show of strength along the entire Pirate Coast.
1820: suitably impressed, the Sheikhs of the Pirate Coast sign a General Treaty of Peace. This truce lays the foundation for the next one hundred and fifty-one years of British influence and protection in what will come to be known as The Trucial States (Abu Dhabi, Dubai, Sharjah, Ajman, Umm al Qaiwain, Ras al Khaimah, and Fujairah).

1821: subsequent to the defeat of a British force in Oman, operating in support of the Sultan, a further expedition is mounted from Bombay against the dissident tribe of the Beni Bu Ali. This time the British and Indian force is successful.
1821–1822: Greece has been part of the Ottoman Empire since 1460. The people now conduct a long and destructive war of independence. Great Britain, France, and Russia give support, their combined fleets destroying a Turkish and Egyptian fleet at Navarino in 1827. The Turks withdraw in 1830, formal independence is recognised in 1832. The Egyptians withdraw from Arabian Wahabi territory.
1835: the first Maritime Truce in the Gulf. The British impose an extension to the 1820 Treaty to forbid fighting between the Sheikhs of the Pirate Coast during the pearling season.
1837: a monthly mail packet service is started between Bombay and Suez. An Indian ship runs aground off Aden and is plundered by local Arabs. Aden's strategic importance starts to become apparent.
1839: Bombay Presidency forces take Aden by force. It becomes a key link in the chain of coaling stations which the introduction of steam power will necessitate on the maritime route to India.
1839–1840: another crisis for the ailing Ottoman Empire. The Pasha of Egypt, Mohammed Ali, has rebelled against his titular sovereign, Sultan Mahmud II, head of the Empire in Constantinople. Mahmud sends an army into Egyptian-controlled Syria where it is defeated by Mohammed Ali's forces. The Egyptians prepare to march into Anatolia and to give the Turks the coup de grace. The European powers threaten war against Egypt, and the status quo is maintained.
1853: Russia has already forced the Persians to cede their territories in the Caucasus. Now they threaten Turkish authority in Palestine and the Balkans. The Turks respond by declaring war on Russia.
1854: France and Great Britain go to Turkeys's aid by invading the Crimea.
1855: the Kingdom of Sardinia also declares war on Russia.
1856: the war ends with the Treaty of Paris. Meanwhile, Persia has annexed the disputed Afghan city of Herat. At year's end, a major expedition is mounted by the Government of Bombay to attack Persia. Under Outram and Havelock, the expedition is transported to the Gulf by Indian Marine ships. After heavy naval bombardments, the army goes ashore at Bushire and in the Euphrates delta. The Persians are defeated in a series of actions during the early weeks of 1857. The Bombay force withdraws when the Persians agree to relinquish Herat.
1858: the Mutiny in India leads to the transfer of power from the HEIC to the Crown. Former HEIC responsibilities in the Gulf remain with the Government of Bombay. In Aden, where a local Levy had been raised in the previous year, local defence will be in the hands of the Aden Troop - a unit consisting of officers and men from various regiments of the Indian Army. The Aden Troop will become an independent command, answerable to Bombay.
1860: the Lebanon contains one of the few Christian enclaves within the Ottoman Empire. An eruption of sectarian massacres leads to European intervention. The country is given special protected status under French influence.
1868: construction of the Suez Canal, financed by France and Egypt, is completed.
1869: the Sultan of Oman, who continues to receive active British support, expels the Wahabis from Buraimi. The HEIC Marine having been dismantled in 1863, the Royal Navy now assigns ships of its East India Squadron to the policing of the Arabian Sea and the Gulf. The Suez Canal is formally opened to the passage of shipping.
1875: Disraeli purchases, for Great Britain, a controlling interest in the Suez Canal operating company. There is an insurrection against the Turks in Bosnia and Herzegovina.
1877–1878: another war between Russia and the Ottoman Empire concludes with the Treaty of San Stefano. Turkey cedes the administration of Cyprus to Great Britain. The first local British-officered police units are formed.
1881: Colonel Arabi stages a coup in Egypt.
1882: the Mahdi, who has raised a rebellion in the Sudan, annihilates Hicks Pasha's Egyptian Army at El Obeid. The British bombard Alexandria and invade Eqypt.

1882–1896: the Gulf trade in firearms (gun running) grows to major proportions, with many of the weapons finding their way to the tribes of India's North West Frontier.
1891: the Sultan of Oman binds himself and his successors never to cede any part of his territory to any power other than Great Britain.
1892: the Trucial States agree that the British exclusively will handle their foreign affairs. The Sheikh of Kuwait will sign a similar agreement in 1898.
1895: Muscat, capital of the Sultan of Oman, is temporarily occupied by rebels. Two years later, with British assistance, order is restored.
1896: the Turks attempt to re-establish their authority in Kuwait.
1898: the first Zionist Congress is held in Basle. Zionist sentiments lead – initially on a small scale – to an increasing colonisation of Palestine by Jewish immigrants. This modest influx is tolerated by the Turks. In Crete, where the populace had rebelled against Turkish domination in 1878, European intervention results in the removal of the last Turkish troops and the granting of autonomy. Turkey has restored its domination – after numerous massacres – in Armenia.
1902: Abdulaziz al Saud (the future King Ibn Saud of Saudi Arabia) seizes control of Riyadh and declares himself Emir of Najd. The Turks, thwarted in their attempt to seize Kuwait, establish military posts at Umm Qasr and Bubiyan Island.
1904: Persia attempts to annex the islands of Abu Musa and Tunb from the Trucial Sheikhs. British diplomacy obliges them to withdraw without bloodshed.
1907: Russia and Great Britain agree to divide northern and southern Persia into respective spheres of influence.
1908: the British obtain the concession to explore and exploit the oilfields in South West Persia, north of the Shatt al Arab.
1909: ships of the Royal Navy and the Royal Indian Marine conduct, until 1914, a blockade of the Gulf in order to reduce the traffic in arms. Another wave of unrest in Armenia leads to further massacres of the civilian population.
1910–1913: the Albanians revolt against Turkish domination and win their autonomy in 1913. This unrest spreads into neighbouring countries and leads to two successive Balkan Wars – Bulgaria, Serbia, Greece and Montenegro, 1912, against Turkey, and Greece, Serbia, Montenegro and Turkey, 1913, against Bulgaria. When the map is redrawn in 1913, Turkey has lost almost all her continental European possessions.
1912–1915: an Arms Warehouse is established at Muscat to help control the firearms trade. The Omani tribes rise against their Sultan. Indian troops are sent to aid the Sultan. The Royal Navy bombards some rebel coastal towns. On land, the rebels attack Indian Army units but are crushed. A new Sultan remains firmly pro-British. Great Britain agrees that, administratively, Kuwait shall remain an autonomous unit of the Ottoman Empire. In Arabia, Abdulaziz al Saud receives British aid in driving the Turks from Eastern Arabia. They formally recognise him as ruler in 1915. In return, he undertakes not to interfere in the British-protected Gulf Sheikhdoms (where the Wahabis have been influential since 1800).
1914: war breaks out between the Central Powers (Germany and Austria-Hungary) and the Allied Powers (France, Belgium, Portugal and Great Britain, and their respective Empires). Despite her previously amicable relationship with the French and the British, Turkey opts to join the Central Powers. Her military forces in Palestine and Arabia are a threat to the Suez Canal and the sea route to India and Australasia. She has further forces in Mesopotamia which can strike at the oilfields in Persia. The British respond by despatching an expeditionary force from India to the Shatt al Arab, by disembarking in Egypt the first contingent of ANZAC troops who had been destined for England and then France, by reinforcing the small garrison in Aden, and by annexing the island of Cyprus and landing more troops there.
1915: the Turks occupy the Sinai peninsula and advance to the Suez Canal. They are stopped by British and ANZAC units which drive them slowly back towards Gaza. As a first step in supporting a planned Russian invasion of Turkey, Winston Churchill proposes a coup de main occupation of the entrance to the Black Sea. After a failed attempt by the Royal Navy to enter the Sea of Marmora, a military assault is launched in April. A multi-national force tries to occupy the Gallipoli

peninsula with landings at Cape Helles and Anzac Cove. Despite great gallantry by the Allied soldiers, poor planning and inadequate generalship lead to another failure. A second landing, at Suvla Bay in August, is even more seriously bungled. Meanwhile, in Mesopotamia, British and Indian forces have advanced headlong up the line of the Tigris with the aim of capturing Baghdad. They reach Ctesiphon, but are then driven back to Kut al Amara. Here they are trapped and besieged. Great Britain's problems are compounded when, in November, and with German and Turkish support, the Senussi tribes in Cyrenaica declare 'jihad' (holy war) and advance 120 miles into Western Egypt. After months of campaigning, the Senussi are driven back by a mixed force of British Army, South African, ANZAC, and Indian Army units. In Afghanistan, a German-Turkish mission tries to persuade the Amir to abandon his neutrality and to invade India. The Central Powers are establishing a significant military presence in Central Persia. Turkish forces in Yemen try to seize Perim Island, and come close to capturing Aden. In general terms, and despite their lack of industrial and maritime resources, the Turks are giving an excellent account of themselves. In December, all ANZAC troops are evacuated from Gallipoli.

1916: in January, the last remaining Allied troops in Gallipoli are withdrawn. They leave behind 46,000 dead. The intended occupation of Turkey never develops beyond an initial incursion. In Mesopotamia, all efforts to rescue the British and Indian units at Kut al Amara come to nothing. The British offer the Turks a bribe of two million pounds to secure their release. The offer is declined. After a siege lasting five months, they are starved into surrender. Of the 10,000 taken prisoner, 6000 will die in Turkish captivity. In June, an Arab uprising begins in the Hejaz (the western region of Arabia) against the occupying Turks. It is inspired by the Hashemite leader, Hussein, Sharif of Mecca, and two of his sons, Faisal and Abdullah, both of whom have been educated in Turkey. Faisal dreams of a free Hashemite kingdom, stretching from Hejaz north through the Jordan Valley to Syria. Excluded from Faisal's plan is any possible collaboration with Abdulaziz al Saud. The two families are blood enemies, and the tribesmen of the Wahabi sect take no part in the impending campaign. Abdullah's men - to the British, 'the Arab Army' - begin by attacking the railway line between Ma'an and Medina, causing the Turks to make a slow withdrawal from Arabia. Elsewhere, the British take control of the Straits of Hormuz by landing at Bundar Abbas. They move against the German and Turkish forces in Central Persia, and occupy Shiraz.

1917: Lawrence and 'the Arab Army' capture the key port of Aquaba. British, Indian, and ANZAC forces have ejected the Turks from Sinai and Gaza. Under Allenby, these combined armies drive north into Palestine and the valley of the Jordan. In Mesopotamia, British and Indian forces regain the ground lost at the time of the Ctesiphon/Kut al Amara disaster and finally occupy Baghdad.

1918: everywhere, Turkish resistance is crumbling. Allenby's forces advance into the Lebanon and Syria. The race for Damascus is won by Lawrence and 'the Arab Army', but its leaders lose cohesion and it crumbles away. Allenby pushes on to Homs and Aleppo and reaches the frontier of the Turkish homeland. The French, anxious to renew their connection with the Lebanon and to lay claim to a post-war share of the territorial spoils, land troops at Beirut and Alexandretta. They and the British are jockeying for future dominance in the region. The Turks surrender on 30 October. Within days, to forestall the French, a British force is sent hurrying north from Baghdad to occupy the Mosul oilfields.

1919: the Aden Troop is disbanded. Australian forces put down a revolt in Egypt.

1919–1921: with the destruction of the old Ottoman Empire, there is unrest and confusion throughout much of the Middle East. The Americans are invited to take control in Armenia (the Christian eastern region of Turkey). They decline. The British send garrison forces to Constantinople (Istanbul) and the Sea of Marmora coastal areas. They allow Greek troops and civilians to move into Western Turkey. The Turks drive them out and sack the port of Smyrna (Izmir) where 30,000 Greeks are massacred. The Turks launch genocide against the Armenians. Turkey's wartime hero, Kemal Ataturk, forms a strong national government. It challenges the British who soon withdraw their forces. Modern Turkey is born. In the Levant,

Northern Syria and the Lebanon are handed to France under a League of Nations mandate. Earlier promises to Hussein and his sons - of Hashemite independence - are overtaken by a European desire to impose stability in the region. Faisal becomes, briefly, King of Syria, but is then removed by the French. Great Britain's share of the spoils is a League of Nations mandate to administer Palestine and Southern Syria (now renamed Transjordan). On the order of the British Colonial Secretary, Winston Churchill, Hussein's second son, Abdullah, is installed as Emir in the capital, Amman. He arrives there with a small bodyguard of Arab soldiers who formerly had deserted from the Turkish Army to serve in 'the Arab Army'. The hero of the desert war, Lawrence, has been sent back to England. Abdullah's new military adviser is Peake. The two agree to expand the bodyguard to the size of a full Division, but are blocked by British objections. It is titled Arab Legion. A third British mandate applies to the former Ottoman provinces of Mosul, Baghdad, and Basra. Now known as Iraq, the area includes part of the homeland of the Kurds. They attempt to win autonomy, but are suppressed by British and Indian forces after two years of fighting. As a permanent policing force, the Iraq Levies are formed, and a British Military Mission begins to raise and train an Iraq Army. In Persia, an army officer named Reza Khan seizes power.

1920s onwards: in 1917, partly as a matter of wartime expediency, the Balfour Declaration had committed the British Government to assisting the Zionists in the creation of a Jewish national homeland in Palestine. The Palestinians had opposed the Declaration from the outset, and their resentment will increase as growing numbers of Jewish immigrants start to arrive in the country (particularly when Hitler's anti-semitic policies cause an exodus from Germany in the 1930s). For local security, the British Palestine Police are formed in 1920.

1925: Cyprus becomes a Crown Colony. Rebellion erupts in Syria. It is dealt with severely by the French. Abdulaziz al Saud, who has stayed quietly out of the war and the post-war arguments over territory, strikes at the Hashemites and occupies Mecca. The first oil concession is granted by the Sultan of Oman.

1926: Abdulaziz al Saud captures Medina and Jedda from the Hashemites, and declares himself King of the Hejaz (as well as Emir of Najd). Lord Plumer, High Commissioner in Palestine, raises the Transjordan Frontier Force (TJFF) to defend Transjordan, at the same time relegating the Arab Legion to the status of an armed gendarmerie. The TJFF consists of non-Bedouin Arabs, Jews, Yugoslavs, and others, all under the command of Arabs and British officers on secondment.

1928: Trenchard's scheme for using the Royal Air Force to police inacessible desert areas in Jordan and Iraq from the air is extended to Aden and the coastal areas north to Oman. The Aden Protectorate Levies are raised to guard the landing grounds.

1930: independence for Iraq is agreed, with the RAF retaining its bases at Shaiba and Habbaniyah. The Iraq Levies will be disbanded. Some personnel transfer to the new RAF Levies (Iraq) for the protection of those bases (from 1932 onwards). In Jordan, the TJFF has failed to subdue the Bedouin tribes. Glubb arrives from Iraq to put matters right. On his advice, the TJFF is withdrawn from the desert and instead given the task of dealing with gun-running and Arab/Jewish settler conflicts in the Jordan Valley. Glubb raises a new force, The Desert Patrol, with Bedouin tribesmen under British command. A camel-mounted gendarmerie, it is part of the Arab Legion but operates independently in policing its own people.

1932: Abdulaziz al Saud declares himself King ibn Saud of Saudi Arabia. Great Britain recognises his sovereignty. He has formerly agreed to have no territorial ambitions in the British-protected Gulf states or in the Aden Protectorate. Oil has been discovered in Bahrain, but most of the isolated and desperately poor Sheikhdoms will not for many years share in the oil wealth which soon will transform the futures of some of their neighbours.

1933: King ibn Saud pays an American deep drilling company to search for water. Instead, they discover oil. Standard Oil of California obtains the initial oil exploration concession. Other oil companies will join the search in future years as the vast scale of the Saudi Arabian reserves becomes apparent. The interest of the United States in Middle East affairs dates directly from that first 1933 concession.

1935: Persia is enjoying the financial benefits of the British-owned oil industry based upon Abadan. Reza Shah Pahlavi has forged his country into a strong nation. It is renamed Iran. The oil pipelines from Kirkuk to the Mediterranean coast are completed. Mussolini orders an intensive settler colonisation of Libya.

1936: there is an Arab Revolt in Palestine which severely tests the Palestine Police and British Army garrison. Wingate forms his counter-terrorist Night Squads.

1937: Aden is declared a Crown Colony. Egypt becomes independent under King Farouk. Great Britain retains military base facilities in the Canal Zone.

1939: despite the blandishments of London and Berlin, Turkey decides to stay neutral in this war. The immediate threat to British interests in the Middle East is her former ally. Italy has a powerful modern fleet, and an army in Tripolitania and Cyrenaica (territories which in 1912 she occupied by force and merged as Libya). She also has large military forces in Italian Somaliland, in Eritrea, and in Abyssinia (which she occupied by conquest in 1936).

1940: Italy declares war on the Allies. She tries to invade the Sudan, occupies British Somaliland, starts to bomb Aden, and drives sixty miles into Western Egypt before encamping. The latter force is then smashed by O'Connor who drives the Italians far back into their own territory. Large contingents of ANZAC troops disembark in Egypt. Preparations are made to destroy the Italian Army in East Africa. In the Eastern Aden Protectorate, still trying to keep the peace amongst fractious local tribes, the British form the Hadrami Bedouin Legion.

1941: after a failed first attempt by the Italians, Greece is attacked by Germany. British, Australian and New Zealand units are stripped from O'Connor's desert force and, with the Cyprus Regiment, they make a vain attempt to save Greece. Some of the survivors are evacuated to Egypt, others to Crete (which also is lost, after a valiant defence). Meantime, Indian forces have moved from the Western Desert to East Africa where, with British, South African, West African, East African, Free French and Free Belgian units, they assault the Italians in British Somaliland, Italian Somaliland, Abyssinia, and Eritrea. The Italians resist fiercely at Keren and Amba Alagi but, by November, the last of them have been rounded up. The Indians return to the desert where they are joined by the South Africans. Rommel has arrived with his Afrika Korps. He launches his first assault from El Agheila. It carries him forward 450 miles to Halfaya. The 9th Australian Division withdraws into Tobruk where it is besieged. The British attempt, without success, to raise the siege with Operation Battleaxe. They try again with Operation Crusader (1st New Zealand Division taking a key but costly role). Rommel is driven back to El Agheila. In this same year, there is much concern over developments further east, in Syria. Its Vichy French administration could conceivably allow the Germans to operate from its air bases. A coup in Iraq has produced a pro-German government headed by Rashid Ali. There are known Nazi sympathisers and agents in Iran. When German air force units arrive in Iraq, the British take action. Indian and British Army units move into the country and take control. A relief column, which includes Glubb's newly mechanised Desert Patrol from Jordan, raises the Iraqi's siege of RAF Habbaniyah. The British next invade Syria. The Vichy French resist strongly, and several Australian units suffer heavy casualties before the French capitulate. Next, Iran is occupied. The 'Persia and Iran Force' (Paiforce) is formed - mainly with Indian Army units - to meet three primary needs. First, to maintain Allied control - secondly, to contest an expected German penetration of the Caucasus, aimed at the Iranian and Iraqi oilfields - thirdly, to organise and protect an overland American supply route from the Gulf up to the Soviet Union (following the German invasion of the USSR). Meantime, the people and garrison of Malta are enduring continuous air raids by Italian and German bombers based in Sicily. The island is a vital base for British aircraft and submarines operating againt Rommel's maritime supply routes.

1942: despite losing so much of his fuel and other supplies to the Malta-based forces, Rommel attacks again in May, wins a major battle at Gazala, and captures Tobruk. In July, he makes another advance but is stopped by Auckinleck at El Alamein, only sixty miles from Alexandria. In August, Montgomery assumes command in the desert and, in October, launches the second El Alamein battle. Overwhelmed, abandoning many of his Italian infantry units, Rommel begins a long retreat which he has no realistic hope of reversing. American and British forces land in Algeria (Operation Torch) and start to drive east towards Tunisia. Hitler will try, too late, to pour in reinforcements. Having earlier transferred many of his bomber squadrons from Sicily to the eastern front (for Operation Barbarossa), he has long given up his plan to subdue and invade Malta. The island has survived its long travail and now strikes back even more strongly at the Axis supply routes. The fate of Axis forces in North Africa is sealed.

1943: the last German and Italian troops in Tunisia surrender at Cape Bon. The Soviets have won the Battle of Stalingrad. The Germans have failed to penetrate the Caucasus and thereby reach the oilfields of Iraq and Iran. Stalingrad and the second El Alamein battle are turning points in the war. Apart from the Australian campaign in New Guinea and the huge American campaign in the Pacific, all its future major land campaigns will be fought in Europe - on the eastern, southern, and north western fronts. Following a failed British attempt to seize Rhodes, Cos, and Leros, and following the Allied invasion of Sicily (Operation Husky), the Middle East becomes militarily less important. Many Indian units will be transferred from Paiforce to mainland Italy. In Jordan, the Desert Mechanised Force has expanded to Brigade strength. Trained for service in North Africa, it is never so required.

1944: the Germans are in retreat on the eastern front and, despite six major offensives since 1942, they have failed to defeat Tito's partisans in Yugoslavia. They begin to withdraw from Greece. Civil war breaks out between British-backed monarchists and Soviet-backed Communist factions. British and Indian Army units are landed in Greece to fight the Communist insurgents. Their campaign will continue into late 1945. The Communists are defeated and Greece is saved from becoming yet another Soviet satellite.

1945: the French try to re-establish themselves in Syria. They bomb Damascus.

1946: Emir Abdullah negotiates a treaty with Great Britain which ends the League of Nations mandate. Transjordan becomes The Hashemite Kingdom of Jordan, with Abdullah as its monarch. The Arab Legion is retained, with Glubb still in command. The last British, Indian, and Soviet forces are withdrawn from Iraq and Iran. All foreign troops leave Syria and the Lebanon. In Kuwait, where exploration has been suspended during the war, production and export of oil recommences.

1947: the British try to maintain the terms of the 1920 mandate in Palestine, but a combination of Jewish terrorism, American pressure, and post-war exhaustion at home are making the task impossible. The flood of Holocaust survivors attempting to enter the country - in conflict with the terms of the mandate and despite the fears of the Arab League - places the British in a position which they will have few regrets in abandoning. In this year, India is granted independence and is partitioned. Responsibility for affairs in the Arabian Gulf passes from the India Office to the Foreign Office.

1948: with the agreement of the United Nations, Great Britain's mandate in Palestine is ended. The last British troops depart and the new State of Israel is promptly attacked by Egypt, Syria, Iraq, and the Arab Legion (Jordan). The Transjordan Frontier Force has been disbanded (February), and likewise the British Palestine Police no longer exists (500 of its officers transfer to Malaya to serve in the new emergency there). Building on the wartime Palmach organisation, the Israelis quickly arm themselves, form a citizen army, and defeat the Arab assault.

1949: the First Arab-Israeli War is officially ended by a UN-brokered cease-fire, but spasmodic conflicts will continue through to the present day. In Syria, there are three military coups in rapid succession. Oil exports commence from Qatar. More oil is discovered in Eastern Arabia.

1951: the British Army still has bases in Egypt, Cyprus, and Aden, but there is a steady reduction in Great Britain's military commitment to the region (due in part to economic difficulties at home). There is no armed response when, in this year, the Iranians nationalise their mainly British-owned oilfields. An irregular Levy - soon to be titled Trucial Oman Scouts - is raised under Foreign Office control for service in the Trucial States (the six independent Sheikhdoms of Abu Dhabi, Ajman, Dubai, Ras al Khaimah, Sharjah, and Umm al Quwain). With British support,

Libya becomes independent, with King Idris as monarch. Great Britain retains garrison and military training facility concessions. In Jordan, King Abdullah is assassinated. He is succeeded briefly by Talal, and then by Hussein.
1952: the Sheikhdom of Fujairah becomes the seventh of the Trucial States. A rumbling dispute over the Buraimi Oasis - contested between Saudi Arabia and the Sultanate of Oman - escalates when the Saudis occupy a village claimed by Oman. There is an armed confrontation between American-backed Saudis and the British-backed Omanis. In Egypt, King Farouk is deposed by a military junta headed by Nasser. The new head of state is Naguib.
1954-1955: in Cyprus, Archbishop Makarios raises a campaign for Enosis (union with Greece). In 1955, Colonel Grivas launches the Eoka terrorist campaign against the British and against the minority Turkish-Cypriot population. In Egypt, Naguib is removed from office and replaced by Nasser. Israel mounts a massive raid against Egyptian forces in the area of Gaza.
1955: Nasser signs an arms deal with the Soviet Union. The British and Americans begin to reconsider their offer of aid to build the Aswan High Dam (on the Nile).
1956: in March, King Hussein dismisses Glubb and other British officers from the Arab Legion. In May, Nasser recognises Communist China. The Americans take this as an unfriendly act and, in July, withdraw their High Dam offer. Within days, Nasser nationalises the Suez Canal Company. In October and November, Anglo-French-Israeli forces invade Egypt and the Sinai. The Canal Zone is almost reoccupied when America intervenes with economic sanctions against the allies. The French and British are forced to withdraw. The Israelis retain, for the time being, the whole of the Sinai Peninsula.
1957: the British have lost face throughout the Middle East and have angered some of their Commonwealth partners. In January, Eden resigns as British Prime Minister and is replaced by Macmillan. In March, American pressure forces the Israelis to withdraw from the Sinai Peninsula.
1958: Nasser's 'Voice of the Arabs' radio broadcasts, and the flow of Soviet and American weapons, are subverting the old order in the British-protected Trucial States and in Oman. In the latter, with Saudi support, the Sultan's small army is attacked by dissident tribes under the inspiration of the Imam (the country's religious leader). An assault is launched against the Jebel Akdhar, the rebels' mountain stronghold, by British Army, RAF, and Trucial Oman Scouts units. A first attempt is called off through lack of resources, but a second attempt (in January 1959) will be successful. Alarm caused by the near loss of Britain's ally, the Sultan, leads to a sharp increase in British support. The Sultan's Armed Forces, with many more British Army officers joining its operational and training command structure, are expanded and upgraded. In Iraq, there is a coup d'état. King Faisal II is assassinated and a republic is declared. Egypt and Yemen federate as the United Arab Republic. They are joined by Yemen, forming the United Arab States. Hussein resists attempts to coerce him into making Jordan a fourth member. His throne threatened, he accepts British and American military support. British troops fly to Amman. The crisis passes. The United Arab States dissolve in 1961.
1960: Cyprus becomes a republic within the Commonwealth. The British retain sovereign base areas and training facilities, but the main British strategic reserve for the Middle East is now located in Kenya. More oil has been found in the Trucial States, and the oil exports of Kuwait and Oman have become powerful economic and political factors in the region.
1961: Kuwait becomes independent. Iraq immediately claims Kuwait for itself and prepares to invade. British forces are flown in from Kenya and deploy along the border. This, combined with the condemnation of the Arab League, persuades the Iraqis to back down. Two years later, they drop (for the time being) their claim. The British prepare to hand over power in Southern Arabia. Between 1958 and 1965, several of the Sheikhdoms are brought together - with Aden - as the Federation of South Arabia. The British declare their intention to leave Aden in 1968. The Aden Protectorate Levies are renamed The Federal Regular Army.
1962-1963: violence breaks out between Greek-Cypriots and Turkish-Cypriots in and around Nicosia. Some Greek politicians are still pressing for unification of the

island with their own country. A UN monitoring force is deployed, and a 'green line' drawn on the map to separate the two sides.
1963: governments of both Syria and Iraq are violently overthrown by the Ba'ath Party. It advocates a form of National Socialism, but is in effect a military junta. Nasser continues, as before, to negotiate various forms of alliance with Iraq, Syria, and Yemen, all of which are abortive or short-lived. Their main purpose is to arrange for the destruction of Israel.
1964: following revolution two years earlier, and with Egyptian encouragement and Soviet arms, Yemen is constantly trying to raise rebellion in Aden and amongst some of the tribesmen of the Western Aden Protectorate states. This leads to a short but intensive campaign in the Radfan mountains. The Yemenis have approximately 7500 men, the British raise a force consisting of various British Army, Federal Regular Army, and Royal Marines (45 Commando) units, with Royal Air Force support. The Yemenis are defeated.
1966: Egypt and Syria enter into (another) mutual defence pact. This also is aimed at Israel.
1967: the Third Arab-Israeli War (the Six Days War). By brilliant logistics and generalship, the Israelis reoccupy the Sinai, seize the West Bank of the Jordan, and take the Golan Heights from the Syrians. In November, the last British soldier departs Aden with no regrets. The Soviet Union and the Americans become the dominant foreign influences in the area, their conflicting interests muddied by Nasserite pan-Arabism and traditional inter-tribal quarrels. China continues to fuel tribal unrest in the Sultanate of Oman.
1968: the Battle of Karameh (Jordan). Units of the Palestine Liberation Organisation make a successful stand against an Israeli Army raid. The PLO's credibility and influence receives a boost.
1969: King Idris of Libya is overthrown and forced into exile by a military coup. Colonel Gadaffi comes to power. The British Army, which at the cost of its own blood and that of several Commonwealth armies had given Libya its freedom in WWII, is obliged to withdraw its garrison and training units six months later.
1970: a civil war in Yemen is ended with Saudi intervention. A continuing war of attrition between Israel and Egypt, with Israel making deep penetration raids into Egyptian territory, causes Nasser to ask for Soviet assistance. Moscow supplies combat troops and pilots to reinforce the training cadres already in the country. Nasser dies soon afterwards. He is replaced by Sadat, a former Chief of Staff of the Egyptian Army whom the British had imprisoned in 1941 for his pro-Nazi sympathies and active subversion.
1971: the seven Trucial States have federated to form the United Arab Emirates. The Trucial Oman Scouts are renamed The Union Defence Force. Great Britain completes her gradual withdrawal from the Gulf. Having first gone there in the 17th Century for trade, her role has evolved through several diverse phases - the destruction of piracy, the suppression of slavery and slave-running, the arms blockade, the reconciliation of traditional tribal enemies, and guidance to their leaders in making best use of their new oil wealth. Diplomacy and minimal military interference have transformed the politics of the region. Only one problem remains unresolved - the Dhofar province of Oman. Its mountain tribesmen have not shared in the Sultan's oil revenue and have been left largely to their own devices. In 1965, a rebellion started to gather pace and erupted when the British departed Aden in 1967. The (Marxist) People's Democratic Republic of Yemen - which had evolved from the ill-fated South Arabian Federation created by the British before their withdrawal - provides weapons, training, and idealogical support. The former Sultan of Oman has been replaced (1970) by his son. The British agree to meet his request for military assistance. The Sultan's Armed Forces - still consisting mainly of Baluchi rank and file - are expanded and modernised by British officers serving on contract. A major campaign, lasting five years and involving the Royal Air Force, the SAS and other British Army personnel, plus units on loan from the armies of Jordan and Iran, finally defeats the rebellion.
1973: the Fourth Arab-Israeli (Yom Kippur) War. Egypt launches a surprise attack across the Suez Canal and drives Israeli forces back into central Sinai. After

several days of severe tank warfare, the Egyptians are driven back. Israeli units cross the Canal into Egypt and advance towards Cairo. Even though Soviet troops had been expelled from Egypt a year earlier, the conflict takes on a 'third world war' dimension when Soviet and American surveillance aircraft start to overfly the battlefield. The Americans, through Kissinger, mediate a disengagement and persuade the Israelis to pull back into Sinai. The danger of a larger conflagration is averted.

1974: in Cyprus, in July, a coup is engineered by the Greek junta against Makarios. It is briefly successful. Five days later, Turkey launches a major amphibious and airborne invasion at Kyrenia and Nicosia, and occupies a fifth of the island. After heavy fighting, the UN negotiates a ceasefire. The 'green line', manned by troops from several Commonwealth and other countries, becomes a permanent feature across the entire island. In 1983, Turkey will declare a 'Muslim Republic of Northern Cyprus'.

1975: Iran agrees to stop aiding the Iraqi Kurds in their war against the regime in Baghdad. Civil war, based mainly upon age-old animosities between Christian and Muslim, erupts in the Lebanon. Over the next decade, the most attractive and cosmopolitan city in the Middle East will be reduced to rubble. The Suez Canal, blocked after the Yom Kippur War, is reopened to international shipping.

1976: Sadat abrogates the 1971 treaty with the Soviet Union.

1977: Sadat visits Jerusalem (the first time an Arab leader has set foot in Israel).

1979: revolution in Iran results in the overthrow and exile of the Pahlavi dynasty. The country becomes a cleritocracy, with the Ayatollah Khomeini as its head. The Soviet Union invades Afghanistan. The US Army's Delta Force makes an abortive attempt to rescue American citizens taken hostage in Teheran.

1980: Iran has been attempting to subvert the Shia majority in Southern Iraq. The Iraqi leader, Saddam Hussein, accuses Iran of breaching the 1975 accord, and of violating Shatt al Arab navigational agreements. He declares war on Iran and invades. Despite much secret Western aid for Iraq, neither side achieves anything other than major damage to its own economy and people.

1981: President Sadat of Egypt is assassinated by his own military.

1982: Israel hands control of the Sinai back to Egypt as part of a peace process. At the same time, in an ill-judged response to continuing PLO cross-border raids, Israel invades Southern Lebanon and occupies Beirut. Christian 'militiamen' seize the opportunity to massacre Palestinian civilian refugees.

1985: Israeli forces withdraw from most of Lebanon but retain a self-proclaimed 'security zone' in the southern part of that country.

1990: having failed to gain his objectives against the Iranians, and having failed to subdue the Kurds, Saddam Hussein renews Iraq's former claim to Kuwait and launches an invasion. The country is quickly overrun. The Western nations are alarmed by the loss of Kuwait oil and the threat to Saudi Arabian oil. America takes the lead in forming a Coalition - a multi-national force which includes Saudi, Egyptian, and Syrian units, a British Army armoured division and Royal Navy force, French Foreign Legion units, and contingents of various kinds (mainly medical) from several Commonwealth and other countries. The purpose of the Coalition, which has the backing of the UN, is to remove all Iraqi forces from Kuwaiti territory. Assembling the multi-national force, and conducting the largest air operation in history, occupies the final months of the year.

1991: on 24 February, Operation Desert Shield becomes Operation Desert Storm when Coalition forces commence their advance. For reasons which are at the time politically valid, but which will prove historically troublesome, the pursuit of the surviving Iraqi forces is halted at the border. Saddam Hussein remains in power.

1992: having failed in Kuwait, Sadam Hussein turns again upon the Kurds. The UN imposes 'no-fly zones' in an attempt to protect them. The Iraqi leader then begins operations to destroy a minority of his own people, the Marsh Arabs.

1994: after protracted negotiations arranged by Norway, the Israelis agree with the PLO to grant self-government to Gaza and the area around Jericho. Iraq is still subject to UN-approved economic sanctions but continues to be held firmly in the grip of the Sadam Hussein regime.

CYPRUS

CYPRUS 1878
The Journal of Sir Garnet Wolseley
Anne Cavendish (as editor) * Zavallis Litho, for the Cyprus Popular Bank Cultural Centre, Nicosia, 1991 (reprinted 1992). Illustrated soft card, dark green, gold, 'Wolseley's arrival' motifs, 10.75 x 8.5, xviii/204/xiv (the latter being the Index). 25 mono phots plus 54 contemporary prints and line drawings (all indexed), one map, Bibliography, Index. Apps: biographical notes.
* Following the Russo-Turkish war of 1877-1878, the British Government declared its opposition to the terms of the peace treaty imposed by Russia. It resolved to move a large deterrent force into the region. Amongst the troops assembled was a contingent (8470 all ranks) from India. Designated the Malta Expeditionary Force, it landed in Malta in May 1978, then moved to Cyprus one month later when the Turks ceded the island to the British in return for their continuing support. Sir Garnet Wolseley was appointed Governor and Commander-in-Chief, and this book is an edited version of the diary which he kept during his ten months in office (before he departed for South Africa and the Zulu campaign). The occupying force landed in Cyprus in June and July but, with Russia and Great Britain having quickly resolved their differences, it re-embarked within a few weeks and returned to India. The Journal is useful as a contemporary record, but Wolseley's references to the Indian units under his command are inaccurate and should be ignored (vide footnote). The local Turkish police - the Zaptieh - are mentioned in some detail, and the remarkable achievement of Lieut H H Kitchener RE in mapping the entire island is fully acknowledged. R/3 V/3. PC. MCND'A.
Note: according to Alan Harfield's THE INDIAN ARMY OF THE EMPRESS, 1861-1903, the Indian units included in the Malta Expeditionary Force, and which served briefly in Cyprus, were - 9th Bengal Cavalry, 1st Bombay Cavalry, two companies of the (Queen's Own) Madras Sappers & Miners, two companies of Bombay Sappers & Miners, 2nd (PWO) Goorkha Regt (The Sirmoor Rifles), 13th (The Shekhawattee) Bengal Native Infantry, 31st Bengal Native Infantry, 25th Madras Native Infantry, 9th Bombay Native Infantry, and 26th Bombay Native Infantry. This was the first time that Indian troops were deployed west of Suez.

THE LIFE AND TIMES OF A VICTORIAN OFFICER
Journals and Letters of Colonel Benjamin Donisthorpe Alsop Donne CB
Alan Harfield * The Wincanton Press, Wincanton, UK, 1986. Blue, gold, the Donne family crest, 10.0 x 7.0, -/231. Fp, 160 mono phots, 16 cld ills, 2 line drawings, 5 maps, Bibliography, Chapter Notes, Index. Apps: service record of Col Donne.
* Although devoted mainly to the military services of Col B D A Donne (1856-1907), this book contains valuable references to the formation and roles of the Cyprus Military Police and the Cyprus Police & Pioneer Corps. The former, raised from the old Turkish Zaptieh, was commanded by a British officer from August 1878 onwards. The latter was raised by Ordnance in November 1879 and had one third Turkish and two-thirds Greek-Cypriot recruits under a British commander. In March 1881, the Pioneer element of this unit was disbanded and the Police element absorbed into the Cyprus Military Police. As expected in a book by this author, the text includes a mass of information regarding uniforms, insignia and accoutrements, plus details of the services of many British officers (with Cyprus Gazette dates). The coloured illustrations, based mainly upon oil paintings in private collections, show the dress details of the Pioneers and of the Zaptieh of Military Police. R/2 V/4. AMOT. MCND'A.

CYPRUS PARTICIPATION IN THE WORLD WAR II
Nicos Panyiotou ('Prepared with the help of the Cyprus Veterans Association to mark the 40th Anniversary of the ending of World War II', parallel text in Greek and English, the latter compiled by Priamos Loizides) * Theopres Press Ltd, for the Cyprus Popular Bank Group, Nicosia, 1985. Soft card, 'Regtl crest and colours' motif, grey, black, 6.75 x 9.5, -/79. 68 mono phots, no maps, no Index. Apps: H&A (incl three verbatim citations).

* Despite its generic title, this little book is essentially the story of the Cyprus Regt. Raised in September 1939, largely at the instigation of Sir William Battershill KCMG, Governor and C-in-C, it had recruited 30,000 men by the end of the war (25,000 from the island population, 5000 in Egypt). Only four months after being formed, it had two Mule Companies serving in France (the first Colonial troops to join the BEF). They were evacuated via Dunkirk in May/June 1940 and, after six weeks in England, moved to East Africa where they rendered valuable service under fire at the Battle of Keren. In the meantime, other Detachments, totalling 10,000 men, had been sent to Egypt. The Regt's infantry, pioneer and transport units served in the Western Desert and Greece. At the fall of Greece, 2500 men were cut off in the Peleponnese and forced to surrender. Some survivors from the Greece campaign managed to reach Crete and fought in the defence of that island. One of these men, Pte Jack Theodoulou, again evaded capture. Single-handed, he hi-jacked a German auxiliary schooner, threw the crew overboard, and sailed to Palestine. For this exploit, and for the intelligence information he had gathered, he was awarded the DCM. In the Italian campaign, various Cyprus Regt units did important work, particularly the Mule Companies at Cassino between February and May, 1944. The Regt was disbanded at the end of 1946. R/3 V/4. PC. MCND'A.

50th ANNIVERSARY OF THE CYPRUS REGIMENT, 1939-1945
Anon * Press & Information Office, Republic of Cyprus, Nicosia, 1990. Soft card, Regtl crest, cream, black, 9.5 x 6.75, -/23. 8 mono phots, no maps, no appendixes, no Index.
* The brief narrative covers the same ground as noted in the preceding entry, with the added information that the Regt gained twenty-three awards for gallantry (12 to officers, 11 to ORs). The Regt should not be confused with the Cyprus Volunteer Force which was raised, with a strength of 5000 all ranks, to aid the British Army in local defence duties on the island. The CVF was disbanded in 1943 when the earlier threat of a German invasion had receded. R/3 V/3. PC. MCND'A.

POLICE AS PEACE-KEEPERS
The History of the Australian and New Zealand Police serving with the United Nations Force in Cyprus, 1964-1984
Gavin Brown, Barry Barker and Terry Burke * UNCIVPOL (Victoria) Club, Melbourne, 1984. Blue, silver, 9.75 x 6.75, xv/240. 30 mono phots, 75 cld ills, phots on end-papers, 9 maps (indexed), Bibliography & Sources, Index. Apps: 11 in total, incl Roll of Honour (died on duty), list of Contingent Commanders, nominal rolls, copies of Statements and Directives.
* As part of the UN peace-keeping effort following the Turkish invasion of 1964, Australia and New Zealand agreed to send Contingents of civil (unarmed) police officers to the island. By 1984, twenty Australian Contingents had been provided (616 officers in total), with six New Zealand Contingents (60 officers). This book is a well-illustrated record of the first twenty years of a continuing commitment. The authoritative narrative recounts a little-known aspect of the island's recent troubled history. R/2 V/5. ANL. MCND'A.

IRAQ

THE IRAQ LEVIES, 1915-1932
Brig J Gilbert Browne * Royal United Services Institution, London, 1932. Sand brown, unit crest with two diagonal blue stripes, 10.0 x 7.25, vii/88. Fp, one mono phot, 3 maps (good quality, folding, bound in), Index. Apps: H&A (British, Indian, and Iraqi personnel, all ranks).
* The Iraq Levies were formed in 1919-1920 from various wartime irregular units (such as the Arab Scouts) which the British had deployed to gather intelligence along and behind Turkish lines in Mesopotamia. By 1922 it was a regular disciplined all-volunteer force with a strength of 6199 all ranks (with cavalry, artillery, and infantry sub-units). The rank and file were mainly Marsh Arabs, Turkomans, Kurds, and Assyrian Christians. Most of the Arabs were transferred, during the 1920s, to the Iraq Army (which was being developed and trained by a British Military Mission and which gradually took over many of the Levies' responsibilities). In 1928, the Levies passed from Colonial Office to Air Ministry control. When Iraq became independent in 1932, the Iraq Levies were disbanded, but many of its personnel (mainly the Assyrian Christians) joined the new RAF Levies, Iraq. This unit had the primary task of providing security for the bases and landing grounds which the RAF retained under the terms of the 1930 Anglo-Iraqi Treaty. In 1948, the RAF Levies became part of the RAF Regiment. They were disbanded in 1955 when, by mutual consent between the two governments, the Anglo-Iraqi Treaty was terminated. This well written book covers events up to 1932, with good coverage of the campaigns against the Kurds and with many individuals mentioned by name. R/4 V/5. PCAL. RP.
Note: for an account of the RAF Levies and their WWII services, reference should be make to IMPERIAL SUNSET, by James Lunt (Macdonald, London, 1981). Additional sources are IRAQ, 1900 TO 1950, by Stephen H Longrigg (Oxford University Press, 1953), THE CAVALRY REGIMENTS OF THE IRAQ LEVIES, by J G Browne (article, Cavalry Journal, 1928), and KURDS, TURKS, AND ARABS, by C J Edmonds (Oxford University Press, 1957).

ADEN

ADEN TROOP
A Summary of the War Diary of the Aden Troop, 1914-1918
Anon * The Pioneer Press, Allahabad, India, 1921. Maroon, 10.75 x 8.5, -/81. No ills, one map (loose, in rear pocket), no appendixes, no Index.
* A very detailed record, in diary form, of the Troop's operations against the Turks on the Yemen frontier, and during the period in 1915 when the Turks made a determined effort to occupy Aden and Perim Island. The Troop was a small composite force consisting of a Camel Company and in Infantry Company, each of which in peacetime had as few as two British officers and fifty or sixty sowars and sepoys on their strengths. All ranks were volunteers from a variety of Indian Army regiments who chose to serve a term of duty in Aden for variety and the prospect of action. The period covered in this publication saw plenty of the latter during the early stages of the war, and the unit was much reinforced during this time, but Aden became a backwater when, in 1917, Lawrence and 'the Arab Army' obliged the Turks to withdraw from most of Arabia. Few individuals are named in this account, but it is a sound factual source for dates and events.
R/4 V/3. IOL. RGB/RP.
Note: reference may be made also to ADEN UNDER BRITISH RULE, 1839-1967, by R J Gavin (C Hurst & Co, London, 1975).

PALESTINE

ECHO OF THE BUGLE
Extinct Military and Constabulary Forces in Palestine and Transjordan, 1915-1967
Marcel Roubicek * Franciscan Printing Press, Jerusalem, 1975. Stiff glazed card, illustrated (front and rear covers) with facsimile reproductions of a British proclamation of 1918, main title in red, 9.5 x 6.75, vi/130 (numbered 7 to 134).
42 mono phots, 24 line drawings, one map (the administrative divisions of Palestine, 1939), no appendixes, no Index.
* A very curious book. The author was a 'Free Czech' officer who wrote in a colourful and intemperate style, equally anti-British, anti-Arab and anti-Jew. That said, the book displays evidence of prolonged and careful research. The narrative covers an extraordinary range of units, ranging from German and Turkish (WWI and the 1920s), to 'nationalist' groups (1930s), to the Palestine Police, to 'Free Czech' and 'Free Polish' formations (WWII). It notes every armed unit raised in Palestine/ Israel between 1915 and 1967, regardless of origin, purpose or political affiliation. The illustrations include photographs of people, graves, significant places, uniforms, badges and insignia. The author provides a plethora of information which it would be extremely difficult to find in any other source. R/4 V/4. PC. ACT.

WITH THE ZIONISTS IN GALLIPOLI
Lieut Col J H Patterson DSO * Hutchinson & Co Ltd, London, 1916. Blue, gold, 'Star of David' motif, 7.75 x 5.0, viii/306. No ills, 2 maps (one printed in the text, one folding, bound in), no Index. Apps: H&A (mainly recommendations for Imperial Russian awards).
* An autobiographical account, by the officer who commanded it, of the Zion Mule Corps. The men were mainly emigré and refugee Russian Zionist Jews who, having escaped from Turkish-occupied Palestine, arrived in Egypt and volunteered for the British Army. Trained as mule handlers, they gave fine service on Gallipoli (hauling supplies up from the beaches to the front-line). Their principal customers were the ANZAC troops and this is an interesting view of the support services needed to keep those troops in action. The story concludes with the evacuation to Alexandria (where GHQ Cairo authorised the payment of a bonus of £1.00 Sterling to each man 'as recognition of their good service on Gallipoli').R/4 V/4. RCSL. RP.

WITH THE JUDEANS IN THE PALESTINE CAMPAIGN
Lieut Col J H Patterson DSO * Hutchinson & Co, London, n.d. (c.1922). Light blue, black, 8.75 x 5.5, xi/13-279. Fp, 21 mono phots, one map (folding, bound in), no Index. Apps: Roll of Honour (KIA, DOW and WIA), H&A (incl MID), notes on the 'Care and Comfort Committee').
* In November 1917, the British Government authorised the historic Balfour Declaration which 'viewed with favour the establishment in Palestine of a National Home for the Jewish people' and undertook to 'use their best endeavours to facilitate the achievement of this objective'. Hand-in-hand with this announcement came the decision to raise a Jewish Infantry Brigade for service against the Turks. The author, who had already commanded Jewish troops on Gallipoli (vide the preceding entry) was given the task of forming the new unit. His account of the subsequent travels and fighting services of his men is an essential source for any study of the British presence in Palestine and the emergence of modern Israel. Plagued by inter-Jewish rivalries in England, and later by the anti-semitism of some British staff officers in the Egyptian Expeditionary Force, he and others succeeded in training (at Crownhill Barracks, Plymouth) the three new Bns. The rank and file were mainly Russian, British and American Jews. The War Office assigned them to the Royal Fusiliers (38th, 39th and 40th Bns). A total of 5000 all ranks were involved, two of the most notable being Jacob Epstein and Vladimir Jacotinksy. The Bde saw active service in Samaria and the Jordan Valley. Its performance

in the field was praised by Allenby, but the very existence of the Bde aroused the anger of the anti-Zionists. Readable and candid. R/4 V/4. UCL/ODUL. RP/JRStA. Note: a version having brown covers and gold embellishments has been seen.

SHIELD OF DAVID
The Story of Israel's Armed Forces
Yigal Allon * Wiedenfeld & Nicholson, London and Jerusalem, 1970. Pale olive, gold, 10.0 x 7.5, -/271. More than 100 mono and cld ills, 7 maps, no appendixes, Glossary, Index.
* Fully half of this finely produced book is concerned with operations in support of British objectives. The author, whose career permits him to write on this subject with unarguable authority, covers amongst other topics the history of the following units: the Zionist Mule Corps in the Gallipoli campaign, the 38th, 39th and 40th Bns Royal Fusiliers with Chaytor Force in Egypt and Palestine, the Jewish Settlement Police during the Arab Revolt in the 1930s, Wingate's Special Night Squads during the same period, and the Palmach force raised from personnel of Haganah. The Palmach was authorised, with some trepidation on the part of British commanders, in 1941. Axis forces were advancing through the Western Desert towards the Nile. There was a firm possibility that they would break through into Sinai and invade Palestine. The Palmach's task was to assist the British Army in defending that country and, if they failed, to conduct a 'stay behind' guerilla war against the occupying German and Italian armies. The Palmach was the organistion from which, seven years later, the Israeli Defence Force evolved. The narrative includes good coverage of the Jewish Bde in Northern Italy, the recruitment of Jews as espionage agents, and much else of interest. R/1 V/5. RMAS. RP.

SOLDIERS FROM JUDEA
Palestine Jewish Units in the Middle East, 1941-1943
Rabbi L Rabinowitz * Victor Gollancz, London, 1944. Blue, gold, 7.5 x 5.0, -/79. 8 mono phots, no maps, no appendixes, Glossary of Hebrew terms, no Index.
* To quote the author, 'this does not purport to be a complete history of the Palestine Jewish units during the first four years of WWII'. However, he does devote complete Chapters to the following: 51 (Middle East) Commando, 1039 Port Operating Coy RE, the Palestine Regt, RASC sub-units, and Jewish volunteers in the RAF and Royal Navy. He was Senior Jewish Chaplain MEF, 1941-1943, and his account contains many useful reminiscences. It deals not only with military achievements but also the cultural life of Palestinian Jewish units and their relations with Jewish communities with which they come into contact in the course of their travels. The removal of peacetime constraints led to greater freedoms and independence for women in uniform, a development which caused much debate in Orthodox and conservative circles. Large numbers of Jewish women volunteered for service with the ATS and worked in various theatres of war as drivers, linguists, cypher clerks, special agents and general clerical staff. The inclusion in the post-Independence Israeli Army of women soldiers was a natural progression of their WWII services to the Crown. R/4 V/3. RCSL. RP.
Note: published also in paperback.

WITH THE JEWISH BRIGADE
Bernard M Casper * Edward Goldstein, London, 1947. Black, gold, 7.5 x 4.75, -/128. Fp, no other ills, no maps, Glossary, no Index. Apps: Roll of Honour (names only, no ranks), quotations from various official statements and Press reports.
* Written by the former Senior Chaplain of the Bde, this is more an expression of Judaism than a military history. However, it does provide a useful record of the formation of the Bde at Burg al Arab (between Alexandria and El Alamein) on 20 September 1944, and its services in Italy between November 1944 and the end of the war. The Bde consisted of three Inf Bns, an Artillery Bty, and a Bde HQ. R/4 V/3. MODL. AMM.

WE WILL REMEMBER THEM

A Record of the Jews who Died in the Armed Forces of the Crown, 1939-1945

Henry Morris * Brassey's (UK) Ltd, London, 1989. Blue, gold, 'Star of David' motif on the spine, 11.25 x 8.25, xiv/289. Very many mono phots (portraits), no maps, no Index (but a detailed Contents page). Apps: Roll of Honour, H&A.

* Published as a memorial to Jewish men and women who lost their lives after joining British armed forces, either in Palestine or in the UK. The bulk of the book is taken up with the roll of the fallen. This shows each individual's rank, unit, date and location of death (where known). They served in every possible role as soldiers, sailors and airmen, and in the extremely dangerous (especially for a Jew) intelligence and espionage organisations. The last fifteen pages of the book are a useful account of the origins of several Jewish units rarely noted elsewhere: The Auxiliary Military Pioneer Corps, The Palestine Regt, and the Jewish RE and RASC Companies. R/1 V/4. NAM. RP.

Note: reference may be made also to AUSTRALIAN JEWRY'S BOOK OF HONOUR, WORLD WAR II, edited by G Pynt (Federation of Jewish Ex-Servicemen & Women, c.1973).

THE MIDDLE EAST COMMANDOS

Charles Messenger, Col George Young DSO, and Lieut Col Stephen Rose OBE * William Kimber, Wellingborough, Northants, 1988. Buff, gold, 9.5 x 6.25, -/176. 24 mono phots, 6 maps, Index. Apps: notes on Commando training, report on the Castelorizzo raid by 50 Cdo, report on the Layforce raid on Crete, notes on Irregular Warfare.

* This is mainly a book about British Army 'special' military activities in the Middle East, East Africa and Burma during WWII. It is recorded here because one of the units involved was 51 Cdo and this was composed mainly of Palestinians (Arab and Jewish volunteers). It should be noted also that 50 Cdo comprised a Troop of Spaniards. The story is of interest in tracing the evolution of modern 'special forces' and the employment of polyglot soldiers in a common cause. R/1 V/3. RCSL. RP.

SOUTH AFRICAN JEWS IN WORLD WAR II

Anon * Eagle Press, Johannesburg, for the South African Board of Jewish Deputies, 1950. Blue, gold, 8.5 x 5.75, xix/189. 39 mono phots, no maps, Glossary, Index. Apps: Rolls of Honour (KIA and WIA), H&A.

* The percentage of Jews in the SA armed forces was higher than the percentage of Jews in the SA population at large. This book describes the role they played in the Union Defence Force throughout the war. There are useful references to the East African and Western Desert campaigns, 6th SA Armoured Div in Italy, Jewish soldiers taken POW who later escaped and fought with the Partisans, and the services of Jewish men and women on the home front and in the medical and scientific research fields. There is reference also to South African Jews with the Jewish Bde in Italy and with other Commonwealth units. R/2 V/4. SANMMH. GTB.

A JOB WELL DONE

A History of the Palestine Police, 1920-1948

Edward Horne BEM * Anchor Press Ltd, Tiptree, Essex (UK), for the Palestine Police Old Comrades Benevolent Assn, 1982. Blue, silver, 8.5 x 5.75, -/616. 39 mono phots, ills of badges and insignia, one map, Index. Apps: list of former COs, details of rank structures, details of cups, shields and other trophies awarded annually for sport, drill, musketry and turn-out, chart illustrating the great diversity of Jewish political parties in Palestine (1945-1948).

* A well written comprehensive account covering the entire period. Many individual officers are named in the narrative, for which the Index is invaluable in such a large book. An attractive book, with many small incidents and actions interestingly described. R/3 V/4. MODL. RP/RLP.

TRANSJORDAN

THE STORY OF THE ARAB LEGION
Brig John Bagot Glubb CMG DSO OBE MC * Hodder & Stoughton, London, 1948. Red, gold, 8.75 x 5.5, -/371. Fp, 53 mono phots, 7 maps (5 printed in the text, 2 on the end-papers), no appendixes, Index.
* Trans-Jordan was one of several new countries to emerge after WWI from the wreckage of the former Ottoman Empire. In 1922, the League of Nations granted a mandate to Great Britain to administer it and to preserve the integrity of its borders. In the circumstances then prevailing in the region, it was vital to have a force capable of operating in desert areas inhabited by quarrelling Bedouin tribes. A start had been made when, in late 1920, Capt F G Peake recruited a hundred tribesmen. Within a year he had a thousand all ranks under command. This was the Arab Legion, a force which in later years gained a fine reputation for dash, smartness and fierce loyalty to the Hashemite ruling family. John Glubb, a Royal Engineer who had been severely wounded in WWI, joined the Legion in 1930 and subsequently commanded it during its most influential years. This book is his personal account, covering the years up to 1946. R/1 V/4. DCLS. RP.
Note: reprinted by the same publisher in 1952.

BEDOUIN COMMAND
With the Arab Legion, 1953-1956
Lieut Col Peter Young * William Kimber, London, 1956. Black, gold, 8.5 x 5.5, xiv/187. Fp, 22 mono phots, 2 maps (printed on the end-papers), Bibliography, no appendixes, no Index.
* The author, later Brigadier and eminent historian, served with the Arab Legion and this is his account of three years in command of one of the Legion's infantry battalions. It gives a good impression of what it was like to serve with Bedouin Arab soldiers and thus provides useful background reading. R/1 V/2. NAM. JL.

THE ARAB LEGION
Brig Peter Young DSO MC * Osprey Publishing Ltd, Reading, Berkshire, 1972. 'Perfect' binding, illustrated card covers, 'Arab soldier on camel' motif, red, black, white, 9.75 x 7.25, -/40. 31 mono phots (of excellent quality), 18 cld ills (by Michael Roffe), no maps, no appendixes, no Index.
* This is one of Osprey's well-known quick reference 'Men-at-Arms' series. Nicely presented, very condensed, readable. All aspects of the Legion's history are covered, albeit superficially. The story ends in 1956 when the Legion lost all its British officers and became The Jordan Arab Army. R/1 V/2. PCAL. RP.

GLUBB'S LEGION
Godfrey Lias * Evans Brothers Ltd, London, 1956. Blue, gold, 8.5 x 5.5, -/230. Fp, 16 mono phots, one map (printed on the end-papers), no appendixes, Index.
* Not a unit history, but a good general account. The narrative describes the growth and activities of the Legion through to 1956. R/1 V/3. DCLS. RP.

THE HASHEMITE ARAB ARMY
An Appreciation and Analysis of Military Operations
Brig S A El-Edroos * Fakenham Press Ltd, Norfolk, for The Publishing Committee, Amman, Jordan, 1980. Brown, gold, 10.25 x 7.25, xxxii/788. 67 mono phots (indexed), 38 maps (some in colour, of excellent quality, indexed), Bibliography, 4 Indexes (Places, Persons, Units, General). Apps: 14 in total, incl genealogical tree of the Hashemites, Orders of Battle for the Hashemite Arab Army (September 1916 and September 1918), Egyptian Expeditionary Force and Arab Northern Army (Megiddu, September 1918), The Arab Liberation Army and The Arab Legion (First Arab-Israeli War, 1948), the Jordan Arab Army (Third Arab-Israeli War, 1967), and the 3rd (Jordanian) Armoured Div (Golan Front, Fourth Arab-Israeli War, 1973).

* A monumental and very finely produced book, written by a former officer of the Pakistan Army. He traces the history of the Hashemites and the Hashemite Arab Army from the time of Sherif Hussein bin Ali, 'Father of the Arab Renaissance', through to the reign of his grandson, King Hussein bin Talal. The creation and survival of modern Jordan, and the contemporaneous evolution and services of the country's armed forces, are described in great detail. There are numerous generous references to Peake and to Glubb and to the part played by the British in preserving the country's integrity during difficult times. The maps are outstandingly helpful to an understanding of military operations in the Middle East in WWI, WWII, and the post-war Arab-Israeli conflicts. Apart from its obvious value to the purist military historian, the book is also a prime source for any student of Middle Eastern affairs in the 20th Century. R/3 V/5. RMAS. RP.

REGIMENTAL STANDING ORDERS OF THE TRANS-JORDAN FRONTIER FORCE, 1933

Anon * The Garden City Press, Letchworth, Hertfordshire, 1933. Dark blue, red stripes above and below the title, 'imperial British Crown and TJFF crest' motif in silver, 9.5 x 6.0, iii/111. Fp, one cld ill (grouped motor lorry, mounted cavalryman, and mounted camelier motif),no maps, Index. Apps: Roll of Honour, H&A, list of British officers (mainly originating from line Regts of the British Army, from the British Army's Reserve of Officers, and one - Lieut Col C A Shute - from the Indian Army), list of non-British officers (mainly native to the area, but some originating in Turkey, Yemen, Poland, Austria, Czechoslovakia and the Sudan), a similar list for WOs and S/Sgts (all for 1926-1933).

* The TJFF was formed in 1926 and disbanded in February 1948. Unlike the Arab Legion, it was a British Crown force, it was funded from British sources, and its role was to deal with banditry, insurgence, arms smuggling, and illegal infiltration in both Jordan and Palestine. In practical terms, much of its effort was directed at trying to keep the peace between the Arabs and the Jews along the length of the Jordan Valley. This book contains all the usual Standing Orders to be expected in any publication of the genre, but some (recruiting, weaponry, saddlery, signals and wireless) are specific to the TJFF and will interest the specialist researcher. Further, pages 4 and 5 carry a brief account of operations carried out between 1926 and 1932. A rare and absorbing insight into Great Britain's efforts to keep the peace in a region which has since witnessed a continuing turmoil.
R/5 V/3. PC. GC.

PART 7

British Colonial Africa, with West Africa

NOTES

BRITISH COLONIAL AFRICA

As noted elsewhere in this bibliography, a wide range of source material regarding the British presence in Africa is held at the Public Record Office, Kew, London. It is not the only such source. What is probably the second largest archive is held in the library of Rhodes House, Oxford. It was brought together by the Oxford Development Records Project (ODRP), a continuation of the Oxford Colonial Records Project.

Beginning in 1978, the ODRP distributed a questionnaire to a large number of people who had worked, in various capacities, in the former British Colonies in Africa. The emphasis was on the socio-economic aspects of their experiences in those countries - terms of service, living and working conditions, relationships with indigenous ethnic groups, and so forth. Amongst those approached were many who had served, between the 1920s and the 1960s, with one or more of the local police forces or with military forces such as the King's African Rifles, the Sudan Defence Force, and the Royal West African Frontier Force.

From the completed questionnaires, a number of academic researchers compiled a series of memoranda which were published in 1985 by the Rhodes House Library. Those of direct interest to military historians are:

THE THIN BLUE LINE, Studies in Law Enforcement in Late Colonial Africa, by Anthony Clayton (ODRP Report No 1)
THE BRITISH MILITARY PRESENCE IN EAST AND CENTRAL AFRICA, also by Anthony Clayton (ODRP Report No 2)
THE BRITISH MILITARY PRESENCE IN WEST AFRICA, by David Killingray (ODRP Report No 3)

Each Report includes a study of the relevant material, a bibliography, and an alphabetical listing of contributors (with details of their former services and their specific contributions to the project).

Lightly edited by the same two authors, and with a Glossary and updated bibliographies, these three reports were republished in 1989 under the title:

KHAKI AND BLUE, Military and Police in British Colonial Africa, by Clayton and Killingray, Ohio University Press, Athens, Ohio.

Working in conjunction with the ODRP, the Department of Sound Records of the Imperial War Museum selected sixty-eight of the contributors and made recorded interviews with each. They were all former military personnel (not police) and were chosen to represent a wide range of ranks, units, geographic areas, and periods of service. The recordings provide the basis for THE BRITISH ARMY IN AFRICA, 1919-1939, ORAL HISTORY RECORDINGS, published by the Imperial War Museum in 1986. Following the same format as the ODRP Reports, this is a simple facsimile quarto TS production, in soft card covers. It contains a detailed precis of each interview. It also contains very comprehensive Indexes, and indicates which of the interviews are available as a full transcript (two thirds of the total). The material is useful, but the title should be ignored. The British Army, as such, does not figure in the contents.

Many of those who responded to the ODRP questionnaire also donated their personal collections of photographs, personal papers, maps and memorabilia. Amongst this material is to be found a number of published and unpublished unit histories and reports which record the services of units for which no other comparable documentation is available. Neither East Africa nor West Africa ever generated more than a handful of formally published unit histories so, for the purposes of this bibliography, these regions have been treated as a special case. A number of ODRP items, all unpublished but some evidently intended for publication when first written, have been included in the following pages to ensure that the Corps and Regiments in question shall not become the ghosts of British African Colonial history. Items which appear in the Rhodes House Library cataloguing system are noted simply as 'RHL' holdings. Those items in the ODRP collections to which the Librarians have allocated a reference number, but which they have not yet (1993) included in the catalogue, are supported with a footnote which will enable the researcher to call for them.

An additional source which will certainly assist the researcher, and particularly in respect of the period which antedates that covered in the ODRP collections, is AFRICAN GENERAL SERVICE MEDALS, by R B Magor. Originally published circa 1970, it was compiled mainly with the needs of medal collectors in mind. However, it includes a great deal of information which the author gleaned from little-known primary sources. Further, his maps show several locations which were important at the time when certain battles or campaigns were being fought but which do not appear in modern atlases. The great strength of the book is its close scrutiny of the many small-scale localised punitive expeditions in West Africa and East Africa which resulted in the issue of a medal. These are familiar to collectors, but less so to historians in general. At the present time, an updated and expanded edition of this useful book is in course of preparation.

Another helpful source is UNKNOWN ARMIES - ORGANISATION, UNIFORMS, INSIGNIA - BRITISH EAST AFRICA - KENYA, TANGANYIKA, SOMALILAND, UGANDA AND ZANZIBAR, TO 1964, by Peter Abbot (Raider Books, Leeds, 1988). A booklet of 37 pages, it provides a short history of every unit formed during the period of British administration in the five territories. Half of the text describes uniforms and insignia.

The user of this bibliography will have noted that the Cabinet Office's official histories of the two world wars are not normally recorded. They are well known, and are not concerned with the activities of specific Regiments. Although they cover almost all aspects of WWI and WWII, there are some gaps. One of these is the history of military operations in and around German East Africa from 1916 (September) to 1918 (November). This was the period when the campaign was being fought almost entirely by African Colonial units for which published accounts are scarce. Those interested are advised to consult an unfinished draft account (which takes the story up to late 1917) held at the Public Record Office, Kew, London, under the reference CAB44/4-10. The first half of the campaign is, of course, covered in MILITARY OPERATIONS: EAST AFRICA, AUGUST 1914 - AUGUST 1916, by Charles Hordern (Oxford University Press, 1941).

Note:

The following pages have been arranged under three regional headings - West Africa, East Africa (with Egypt and the Anglo-Egyptian Sudan), and Central Southern Africa. The only country which presents a problem for the bibliographer is Northern Rhodesia. Geographically, it sits four square in Central Southern Africa and that is where it is located in this book. Indeed, its early history is tied closely to that of Southern Rhodesia. On the other hand, the north eastern area of Northern Rhodesia was at first administered by the Nyasaland authorities (whose police and armed forces were often sent there), and the military forces raised in Northern Rhodesia in WWI and WWII were deployed as though they were East African forces. The reader will wish to keep these anomalies in mind when studying the Chronologies and the bibliographic entries.

WEST AFRICA
A Military Chronology

15th Century: Portuguese navigators begin to explore the great curve of the West African coastline from Cape Verde around the Gulf of Guinea to the Cameroons. They are followed, during the next three centuries, by merchant traders from Holland, Spain, France, Scandinavia and England. They seek gold, ivory, slaves ('black ivory'), hides, beeswax, palm oil and hardwoods.
16th Century: the shipment of slaves to the West Indies begins. Sir John Hawkins is the first Englishman to engage in this trade.
17th Century: developments in the Americas increase the demand for cheap labour. The Europeans exploit to their own advantage the ancient West African custom of slave-catching. They collaborate with dominant coastal tribes in building a human export industry, based upon fortified coastal settlements and offshore island trading posts. These frequently change hands, often as a result of wars waged elsewhere.
18th Century: some of the British settlements are at times recognised as Crown Colonies. Others are maintained by commercial trading companies, operating with or without a Royal Charter. Their garrisons are mainly European mercenaries who are frequently struck by outbreaks of tropical diseases which give the Coast its reputation as 'the white man's grave'. The hinterland remains unexplored and unknown. The slave trade is at its height, but the Abolition Movement, led by Wilberforce, Buxton, Ramsay and others, causes a major swing in British popular sentiment. In 1772, the holding of slaves in the British Isles becomes illegal. Fifteen years later, in 1787, Freetown is established as a settlement for former slaves who have been set free.
19th Century: Parliament passes the Abolition Act. The Royal Navy commences an anti-slavery blockade of the West African coast. It will last half a century. There are no medals and little glory for the ships' companies, but they receive up to £60.00 in 'head money' for every slave they rescue. Naval bases to support the blockading ships are established at Freetown, Lagos and elsewhere. In 1811, slaving is declared a felony for British citizens. These changes cause friction with native rulers to whom the slave trade is a source of power and income. With some, the British make Treaties involving the payment of tribute and subsidies. There is armed conflict with those who are less amenable.
1816: Bathurst (Banjul) is founded as a naval base and settlement area for freed slaves. It is garrisoned by the Royal African Corps.
1821: The Gambia is placed under the control of the Governor of Sierra Leone.
1822: the Crown takes control of the Gold Coast settlements.
1823: the Gold Coast also passes into the control of the Governor of Sierra Leone. The new coastal settlements are defended by the newly-formed Royal African Corps of Light Infantry. The Corps has a short life-span, being annihilated at the battle of Isamankow (1824).
1829: the Sierra Leone Police Corps is raised.
1843: Crown control of The Gambia is separated from that of Sierra Leone. A Corps of Artillery is formed in the Gold Coast. A British Consulate, the first in the region, is established at Fernando Po. Commercial and military activity is still restricted to the coastal areas, but knowledge of the hinterland is growing steadily. Individual explorers such as Clapperton, Denham, Oldfield, Bowdich, Lander and Park have spent years wandering hundreds of miles northwards and making the first maps of the Southern Sahara, Lake Tchad and West Africa's complex river systems. Quinine is making the region a safer place for Europeans. Apart from the French, only the British trading companies are still expanding their interests.
1861: Lagos is declared a Crown Colony.
1863: the Gold Coast Artillery is disbanded. In Lagos, freed slaves under British officers form a new frontier force, Glover's Hausas. Two years later they are renamed the Hausa Constabulary (and later, the Lagos Constabulary).
1866: all British West African settlements are placed under the control of a single Governor, resident in Sierra Leone.
1868: a British Government committee decides that West Africa is of no benefit

to the Empire, and that no additional responsibilities should be accepted or Treaties made in that region.
1870–1871: the aftermath of the Franco-Prussian War causes France and Germany, for diverse reasons, to pursue expansionist policies in Africa. Imperialist ideas gain favour in England. The 'scramble for Africa' begins. The British Government changes its mind and is now prepared to extend its previously limited commitments. The new expansionist policy is in part justified by the need to stamp out the overland slave trade along the ancient 'Arab' camel routes from West Africa to the Sudan and beyond. Armed forces move into the hinterland and commence a long-running series of minor campaigns (particularly against the Ashanti, Yonnie and Fulani nations). The Maxim gun, and the quick-firing gun and high explosive shell, usually ensure a quick victory. The boundaries of the Colonies and Protectorates begin to take shape.
1872: the Dutch hand over their Gold Coast settlements to the British.
1873–1874: the Ashanti War (the sixth and largest so far). For the first time, the British move West African troops from their native territories to fight in another. With them are elements of the British Army.
1874: the Gold Coast settlements, with Lagos, become a separate Crown Colony.
1879: the Gold Coast Constabulary is raised from a nucleus of Hausa Constabulary.
1885: The Oil Rivers Protectorate is declared (the oil being palm oil). It is policed by The Oil Rivers Irregulars (the 'Forty Thieves').
1886: the Royal Niger Company forms the Royal Niger Constabulary.
1889: the British and the French make an agreement in principle regarding the boundaries of The Gambia. It is garrisoned by the West India Regiment.
1890: the Sierra Leone Frontier Police are formed.
1895: the British declare a Protectorate over the Lagos hinterland.
1896: Sierra Leone also is declared a Protectorate. The British make an unopposed entry into Kumassi, capital of the Ashanti. The king and his ministers are exiled.
1897–1898: the West African Frontier Force (WAFF, pronounced 'Woff'), is formed in Northern Nigeria. It consists initially of two locally-recruited Special Service Corps Battalions, the 1st and 2nd, based upon a nucleus of men from the Royal Niger Constabulary. They are followed by a Mounted Infantry unit, and a 3rd Battalion based upon a nucleus of Niger Coast Constabulary.
1898: the boundaries between the Gold Coast and the Nigerian Protectorates are agreed with the authorities in the neighbouring French territories.
1899: a similar agreement is made with regard to the adjacent German territories.
1900: despite having ejected their king and occupied their capital, the British have still not pacified the Ashanti. When a small expedition is mounted to find and seize 'the golden stool', symbol of kingship and spiritual power, the Ashanti react by laying siege to the British base at Kumassi. Six months of bush warfare follow. The British Army is fully occupied with the war in South Africa, so the campaign is conducted almost exclusively by black African units. The Special Service Corps Battalions are redesignated 1st and 2nd (Northern Nigeria Regiment) and 3rd (Southern Nigeria Regiment). Their strength is increased by a transfer of the remaining personnel of the Royal Niger Constabulary.
1901: Protectorates are declared over Ashanti and the Northern Territories of the Gold Coast. The remaining Colony and Protectorate forces (with the exception of the West African Regiment) are incorporated into the WAFF. The Lagos Constabulary becomes the Lagos Battalion, the Gold Coast Constabulary becomes the Gold Coast Regiment, the Sierra Leone Frontier Police become the Sierra Leone Battalion. The Gambia Company is formed with a nucleus of men from the Sierra Leone Battalion. Nigeria and the Gold Coast have Batteries of light man-portable howitzers.
1906: the Lagos Battalion is restyled 2nd Bn Southern Nigeria Regiment.
1914: with the unification of the Nigerian Protectorates, the Northern and Southern Nigeria Regiments are amalgamated as The Nigeria Regiment. The Mounted Infantry element is renamed 5th (MI) Battalion.
1914–1918: the initial WAFF task is to destroy the German forces in Togoland. The Gold Coast Regiment, with French support, achieves this aim within the first month of the war. The campaign in the Cameroons, in which units from all four Colonies

are employed, lasts until February 1916. In East Africa, the brilliant tactics of General von Lettow Vorbeck make it plain that the war there will be a long one. Experience has shown that African troops are better adapted than Europeans for fighting in bush and jungle conditions where the incidence of disease is high. By late 1916, the South African and East African troops have been joined by units of the WAFF - a Nigerian Brigade of four Battalions and a Light Battery, the Gold Coast Regiment with a Light Battery, and The Gambia Company. By the end of 1917 von Lettow Vorbeck has been driven out of German East Africa, but he remains at large until the Armistice. The Nigerians and the Gambians are repatriated in March 1918, but the Gold Coast Regiment (with its newly-formed Mounted Infantry element) remains until the end.

1922: the 5th (Mounted Infantry) Battalion of the Nigerian Regiment is disbanded.

1928: the WAFF is granted the 'Royal' prefix.

1936: with the growing threat of war with Italy, plans are made to create two RWAFF Brigades (one Nigerian and one Gold Coast) for possible service in East Africa (where the large Italian forces in Abyssinia, Italian Somaliland and Eritrea pose a threat to British interests in Kenya, British Somaliland, Aden, the Sudan, and the vital maritime route through the Red Sea and Suez Canal).

1940–1941: the two West African Brigade Groups, their officer and SNCO strengths augmented by hastily trained expatriate British residents and Rhodesian volunteers, sail for East Africa in June 1940 (just as France is collapsing and shortly before Italy enters the war as an ally of Germany). Italian forces overrun British Somaliland and invade the Sudan. They capture Kassala and Gallabat before being halted by the small lightly-armed Sudan Defence Force. Assigned to mixed Divisions alongside East African and South African Brigades, the two RWAFF Brigade Groups sweep through Italian Somaliland to Addis Ababa and beyond, playing a full part in the defeat of the much larger Italian forces. By the end of 1941 they have been shipped back to West Africa. In the meantime, the situation in that region has been changed radically by the decision of the French West African Colonies to adhere to the Vichy policy of collaboration with Germany. Britain's erstwhile allies are now potential enemies, standing on the frontiers of all four British Colonies, with large forces which include armour, aircraft and naval units based at Dakar. With its two RWAFF Brigade Groups away fighting in East Africa, the British Colonies are virtually helpless to defend themselves. The emergency decision is taken to expand the RWAFF establishment. Tens of thousands of rural tribesmen and many educated urban Africans respond to the appeal for volunteers. The officer and SNCO vacancies are filled with drafts from Britain. Their numbers are boosted, in 1941, by the arrival of 250 officers of the Free Polish Army. Few of these newcomers have any knowledge of Africa or of soldiering with black African troops, and they are hindered by a severe shortage of every type of weaponry and equipment, but they sustain a huge programme of initial and advanced training. The RWAFF reaches an eventual strength of twenty-eight Battalions. At the same time, and starting with almost nothing, the Colonies create the supporting arms needed for modern warfare - WA Engineer Corps, WA Army Service Corps, WA Signals, and WA Artillery (which absorbs the pre-war Nigerian and Gold Coast Light Batteries and forms new heavy and light anti-aircraft units). Other arms and Corps follow.

1942: by the end of the year, the Vichy French have ceased to be regarded as a threat. The now large and well trained British West African forces are no longer essential for home defence.

1943: in January, the War Office (which had in 1941 at last assumed responsibility from the Colonial Office) decides to despatch West African troops to Burma. They are formed into two complete Divisions - 81st (WA) in March and 82nd (WA) in August. They are equipped for mobile offensive operations in jungle. They have no armour, one Light Anti-tank/Anti-aircraft Regiment, and just twelve light howitzers. For first-line transport they have the Auxiliary Groups of the WA Army Service Corps. The men are able to carry 40 pound head-loads over the worst terrain in all weathers. Initially unarmed but otherwise trained soldiers, they boost the establishments of the Divisions to 25,000 all ranks. Additionally, the Colonies provide a complete Brigade of Heavy Anti-aircraft Artillery which will see service mainly in Assam. The embarkation of all these troops is a milestone because it is the first occasion when British African Colonial units have been sent to fight for the Crown outside their own continent.

1943–1945: 81st (WA) Div fights as an element of XV Indian Corps in the Second and Third Arakan campaigns from December 1943 to January 1945, operating mainly in the Kaladan Valley, isolated from other formations. Its 3rd (Nigerian) Bde is detached for service in the Second Chindit campaign. 82nd (WA) Div also joins XV Corps and fights through the Third Arakan campaign from December 1944 to May 1945. In January it relieves the 81st at Myohaung (capital of Arakan), an event which witnesses the largest ever concentration of units from all four West African Colonies. Both Divisions rely heavily upon air supply. The 81st (WA) Div is the first normal formation to be supplied entirely by air. With this and their ability to traverse the most difficult terrain without wheeled transport or pack animals, they win the respect of the Japanese as jungle fighters. Most of the actions are fought at Platoon or Company level, with little or no artillery support. Of the 530,000 Empire troops who serve in Burma, 340,000 are Indian Army, 100,000 are British Army, and 90,000 are West and East Africans.

1946: as the West African Expeditionary Force returns home, most of the wartime units and Corps are disbanded. The RWAFF reverts to its peacetime establishment and role as the Colonies begin to move towards Independence. Its units become the military forces of the newly independent States, starting with Ghana (Gold Coast) in 1957, or, as in the case of The Gambia in 1965, an armed constabulary. The RWAFF formally ceases to exist on 1 August 1960.

General reference:

The majority of West African unit histories are recorded on the following pages. For additional information regarding West Africa's role in certain specific wars and campaigns, reference should be made to other sections of this bibliography – Burma (pages 546–549), and East Africa (pages 253–266).

Note:

It will be seen that several of the histories recorded in the following pages, and also in the East Africa section, incorporate an 'Honours & Awards' appendix or annexure. Researchers specialising in such matters should keep in mind the possibility that some of these listings are incomplete. Awards to European officers were often recorded in the London Gazette with a reference only to their parent (British Army) regiments, not to the Colonial units with which they were serving at the time of their acts of gallantry. Consequently, they may have been overlooked when the authors of the Colonial units' histories were compiling their lists.

GENERAL AND EARLY HISTORIES

HISTORICAL RECORDS OF THE ROYAL AFRICAN CORPS
Maj J J Crooks * Brown & Nolan, Dublin, Belfast, Cork and Waterford, 1925. Maroon, black, 'Belt plate' motif, 7.25 x 5.0, viii/136 (plus 2 pages of advertisements). No ills, no maps, Bibliography, no Index. Apps: succession list of Colonels (with biographical notes, 1800-1819), list of officers (1800-1821), diary of events in Sierra Leone (1787-1800).
* The Corps was formed in 1800, as Fraser's Corps of Infantry, for the defence of the newly captured island of Gorée, off Cape Verde, West Africa. Recruitment had commenced in 1799 at Hillsea, Portsmouth, many of the men being convicts pardoned and released from the Royal Navy's nearby prison hulks. The title was changed to Royal African Corps in 1804, but this did not last long. The British Army was everywhere short of men, so the Corps had been given additional tasks in the West Indies. In 1806, the elements serving in the Caribbean were redesignated as the Royal West India Rangers and, two years later, those still serving in West Africa became the Royal West African Rangers. This transformation, its causes and effects, are interestingly described in this book, as are the hard campaign services of the Corps in Sierra Leone, Senegal and the Cape of Good Hope. The narrative is based upon material drawn from the London Gazette, contemporary Army Lists and State papers at the PRO. It also contains excerpts from the author's other major work, THE HISTORY OF THE COLONY OF SIERRA LEONE. R/5 V/4. MODL/NAM. AMM/HIS.
Note: for more details of 19th Century West African defence, refer also to THE ORIGINS OF THE NIGERIAN ARMY - A HISTORY OF THE WEST AFRICAN FRONTIER FORCE, 1897-1914, by Sam C Ukpabi (Gaskiya Corp Ltd, Zaria, Nigeria, 1987).

THE HISTORY OF THE ROYAL WEST AFRICAN FRONTIER FORCE
Col A Haywood CMG CBE DSO and Brig F A S Clarke DSO * Gale & Polden Ltd, Aldershot, 1964. Blue, gold, Force crest, 9.5 x 6.0, xv/540. Fp, 42 mono phots, 50 maps, Glossary, Index. Apps: Roll of Honour (European personnel only), H&A (all periods, with citations for VCs), note on campaign medals, Orders of Battle (for various years), list of Inspectors-General, Dress Regulations (1903), etc.
* A magnificent book, written with great attention to detail and a model of what a good Regtl history should be. The narrative is divided into two parts. The first was written by Haywood and covers the evolution of the WAFF up to 1919 (with very full coverage of WWI operations in East Africa). The second was written by Clarke and covers the period 1920 to 1961 (with an account of the Southern Cameroons commitment of 1959-1960). Clarke's coverage of the Burma campaign is not entirely free of errors, and the maps are not completely reliable, but these points can be identified from other sources. This was one of the last of Gale & Polden's major high quality productions. R/4 V/5. NAM. BCC/JALH.
Note: autobiographical accounts of the early years are:
WITH THE WEST AFRICAN FRONTIER FORCE IN SOUTHERN NIGERIA, by Lord Esme Charles Gordon-Lennox (H J Ryman, London, 1905)
BARRACK AND BUSH, by H C Hall (George Allen & Unwin, London, 1923)
FIVE YEARS HARD, by F P Crozier (Jonathan Cape, London, 1932)

REPORT ON THE NIGER SUDAN CAMPAIGN (1897)
With Miscellaneous Documents, including the Military Report by Maj Arnold (3rd King's Own Hussars), Commandant, Royal Niger Constabulary
Sir George Taubman Goldie and Maj A J Arnold * Witherby & Co, London, n.d. (c.1897). Seen only in library binding, 13.0 x 8.0, -/23. No ills, 3 maps (folding, pasted in at the rear), no appendixes, no Index.
* Although the British had brought an end to slave-trading in the coastal areas, the traders continued to thrive in the sub-Saharan region. In 1897, pursuing the anti-slavery crusade launched nearly a century earlier, they decided to stop the Muslim rulers of the Sokoto-Gandu Empire from raiding their weaker neighbours. An expedition of 513 men of the Royal Niger Constabulary, 1000 Hausa Irregulars, and

30 Europeans, was formed under Maj A J Arnold. They were equipped with rockets, field guns and Maxim guns. A series of engagements was fought at Bida and Ilorin, the Royal Niger Company troops forming square and beating off repeated charges by up to 30,000 mounted Fulanis. Overwhelming fire-power inflicted huge losses on the tribesmen, the Emir Sulimain signed a peace treaty, and the region was taken over by the Company. This record is simply Maj Arnold's final report combined with related Company papers. R/5 V/4. NAM. JALH.
Note: there is another account of this campaign. Written by Lieut Seymour Vandeleur, it is entitled CAMPAIGNING ON THE UPPER NILE AND NIGER.

THE GOLDEN STOOL
An Account of the Ashanti War of 1900
Maj Frederick Myatt MC * William Kimber, London, 1966. Green, gold, 9.5 x 6.0, -/192. No ills, 3 maps, Bibliography, no appendixes, Index.
* One of several books describing military operations against the Ashanti, this was written by a former officer of the Gold Coast Regt and it makes useful references to the African troops and police who took part - Central African Rifles, the Gold Coast Constabulary, the Sierra Leone Frontier Police, etc. R/2 V/4. NAM. JALH.
Note: additional details of this and other early campaigns in West Africa can be found in AFRICAN GENERAL SERVICE MEDALS, by R B Magor (printed by The Ganges Printing Co, Calcutta, for the author, n.d.).

TRIBES OF THE NIGERIAN MILITARY FORCES
Their Customs and Markings
Anon * Government Printer, Lagos, 1943. Paper covers, dark green, black, 7.25 x 5.0, -/27/iv. 28 line drawings (on the last four pages), one map (double page, showing the principal tribal areas), no appendixes, no Index.
* A pamphlet for the instruction of newly joined European personnel, it gives a brief history of Nigeria (geography, administration, religions, tribal customs, etc). Its main interest is found in the 'notes on the tribes most commonly represented in the Army', and in the line drawings (by P G Harris) which illustrate each tribe's traditional facial markings (scars). R/5 V/3. IWM/NAM. JALH.

THE GREAT WAR IN WEST AFRICA
Brig Gen E Howard Gorges CB CBE DSO * Hutchinson & Co Ltd, London, n.d. (c.1920). Red, black, 9.25 x 6.0, -/284. Fp, 191 mono phots, 15 maps (12 printed in the text, 3 folding, bound in), Index. Apps: list of officers of the West African Regt at July 1914, idem those serving with the West African Frontier Force in 1915, notes on British and French naval forces (Cameroons, 1914-1916), Order of Battle of the Anglo-French Expeditionary Force (Cameroons, 23 September 1914).
* A pleasingly readable description of the circumstances leading up to the actions, in 1914, against the German garrisons in Togoland and the Cameroons, together with a good account of the fighting and the subsequent occupation of those territories. There are few published histories of the campaign - this book is said to be the best. The Order of Battle appendixes are particularly helpful.
R/4 V/5. RMAS. RP.
Note: reference should be made also to WEST AFRICAN EXPEDITIONARY FORCE, CAMEROONS, NOMINAL ROLL OF EUROPEANS OF THE BRITISH FORCE, OCTOBER 1915, anon, produced at the Government Printing Office, Duala, 1915. The 51 pages include a roll of casualties. Another helpful background source is THE GREAT WAR IN AFRICA, 1914-1918, by Byron Farwell (Viking, UK, 1987).

THE FORGOTTEN WAR
The British Army in the Far East, 1941-1945
David Smurthwaite (as Editor) * National Army Museum, London, 1992. Illustrated soft card, 'Indian and African troops in jungle' motif, 11.5 x 8.0, iii/204. Many mono phots, 21 cld ills (medals, unit signs, etc), 5 line drawings, 6 maps, Bibliography, Index. Apps: list of contributing authors, chronology of events.

* A general view of the entire British (Empire) military effort in the Far East during WWII, but with the emphasis on Burma. The book is in fact noted under the 'Burma' section of this bibliography, but it is duplicated here because it includes a section written by a former RWAFF officer, John Hamilton, and headed 'African Colonial Forces'. It is a condensed but comprehensive account of the operations in the jungle of the two West African Divisions (81st and 82nd), the Nigerian Chindits (3rd WA Brigade), the East African Division (11th), and the two East African Independent Brigades (22nd and 28th). The raising and unusual organisation of the West African formations - with their Auxiliary Groups of carriers (porters) - is outlined in interesting detail. R/1 V/3. NAM. RP.

The West African Regiment

THE LEOPARD
The Regimental Journal of the West African Regiment
Anon * Gale & Polden Ltd, Aldershot, 1926-1928. Seen casebound, cloth, green, 16.0 x 7.0, the pages numbered -/88 and -/180 successively. Some mono phots, line drawings and maps, no appendixes, no Index.
* This is the only published record of the West African Regt, a unit which had an identity quite separate from that of the WAFF/RWAFF. It had its origins in a decision, made in 1896, to declare a Protectorate over some of the territory adjoining the Crown Colony of Sierra Leone. The new British administration tried to impose a 'hut tax'. It was resisted, and 1000 British subjects (European and Creole) were massacred. The rebellion was suppressed in part by the West India Regt and the Sierra Leone (Native) Company, Royal Artillery, but the brunt of the work was done by the Sierra Leone Frontier Police (later reformed as the Sierra Leone Bn of the WAFF). There was a clear need for a force which could take over the internal security role in this Province on a permanent basis. Two years later, in 1898, the West African Regt came into being. The rank and file were locally-recruited tribesmen, the senior ranks and officers were recruited in Great Britain. It was administered not by the Colonial Office but by the War Office. Apart from local policing duties, the Regt took part in the Ashanti campaign (1900) and the Cameroons expedition (1914-1916). It was disbanded in 1928. No formal history book was ever published, but the Regt produced its own regular Journal between 1926 and 1928. It ran to just eight issues before being discontinued at disbandment. This item, therefore, is a complete run of issues, arranged in two parts (each of four issues), the whole bound in a single casing. It seems likely that Gale & Polden produced a limited number, in this format, circa 1929, for former officers and their friends. Apart from the usual spread of Regtl news and gossip to be expected in this type of publication, there are four good articles on the Cameroons campaign. R/5 V/4. NAM. JRStA.

DIVISIONS

JUNGLE COMMANDO
The Story of the West African Expeditionary Force's First Campaign in Burma
Anon (George Kinnear) * Produced for the Ministry of Information by PR Branch, GHQ West Africa, n.d. (May, 1945). Illustrated paper covers, 8.5 x 6.0, vi/34. Fp, 25 mono phots, Divsl sign (inside rear cover), one map (inside front cover), no appendixes, no Index.
* A condensed account of the 81st (WA) Div in Burma up to July 1944. A 'utility' production, designed for popular consumption and not always entirely accurate. The subjects covered are - First Kaladan campaign, the Battle of Pagoda Hill, and the actions at the Kyingri Box. The 1st Sierra Leone and the 1st Gambia Bns are given good coverage in the narrative, but there is a useful account also of 'Wingate's Woffs' - 3rd (West African) Brigade. R/3 V/2. NAM/IWM. JRStA/JALH.
Note: 30,000 copies were printed. It is possible that a co-author was Maj Sydney Butterworth who, like Kinnear, was a War Correspondent. He later wrote THREE RIVERS TO GLORY, a fictionalised account of the WA Artillery (in Sierra Leone and with 81 Div in the First Kaladan campaign). For more precise details, reference should be made to 81 (WEST AFRICAN) DIVISION, REPORT ON THE CAMPAIGN IN BURMA, WINTER 1943 - SPRING 1944, by Maj Gen C G Woolner CB MC, the Divsl Commander. A copy is held at the National Army Museum, London. It has v/59 pages, duplicated TS, and is a complete analysis. Written in the first person, it clearly reflects much of Woolner's own thinking and conclusions.

BURMA, 1943-1944
Memories of the First Kaladan Campaign, 81st (West African) Division
Brig P J Jeffreys DSO OBE * Published by the 81 (WA) Division Club, originally compiled in 1945, 'reviewed' in 1992. Paper covers, facsimile octavo TS, -/56. No ills, 2 sketch-maps, no appendixes, no Index.
* The author was GSO(1) of the Div. He joined it one day before it sailed from West Africa and had no West African experience. This account, made from contemporary notes and expanded with some reminiscences in 1992, gives a vivid picture of the problems encountered when the Division broke through hilly jungle country to first penetrate the Kaladan Valley. The fierce Japanese resistance, and the heavy fighting in the flat open paddy fields of the lower Kaladan, are well described. There are useful assessments of the Divisional Commander, Woolner, and of the personalities of other senior officers. R/4 V/3. NAM/IWM. JALH.
Note: 400 copies were made and distributed, mainly to members of the Club.

81 (WA) DIV SIGS: SIGNAL REPORTS ON KALADAN AND KALAPANZIN OPERATIONS (1943-1944)
Lieut Col T E Dobson * Unpublished MS, 1944. Disbound foolscap, -/12. No ills, no maps, no appendixes, no Index.
* A contemporary report which describes the problems of providing wireless (radio) communications for the Division while operating in jungle with either minimal transport or, after April 1944, with man-packing only. The Division was totally reliant upon supplies delivered from the air. All supply demands were channelled to the Divsl Rear HQ at Comilla. This was 200 miles away (and more, as the Division advanced southwards). Efficient signals were of crucial importance if the required loads were to arrive at the right place and at the right time. A unique source, of interest to communications and air supply specialists. R/5 V/3. NAM. JALH.
Note: also held at the NAM are two other similar reports: 81 (WA) DIV SIGNALS - KALADAN OPERATIONS, OCTOBER 1944 TO FEBRUARY 1945, and 3 (WEST AFRICAN) BRIGADE SIGNALS SECTION, REPORT ON OPERATIONS, PERIOD 1943-1944. The latter is especially important because it deals with 'Special Force (Chindit) Signals', and provides vivid detail of conditions in White City during the violent Japanese assaults in April 1944, and at the Aberdeen stronghold (manned almost entirely by West African troops).

81 (WEST AFRICAN) DIVISION - REPORT ON EXPERIENCE OF AIR SUPPLY
January 1944 to June 1944
Maj K C Christofas * Unpublished TS, 1944. Disbound foolscap, -/66. No ills, one map, no Index. Apps: 19 in total, technical and statistical.
* 81 (WA) Div was, to quote Slim, 'the first normal formation to rely completely on air supply'. This report was written by the officer who, at short notice and then by trial and error, created and managed the organisation which, for five months, kept 20,000 troops fed, clothed and armed entirely from the air. Some limited experience of air supply had been gained during Operation Longcloth in the previous year, but 1944 saw the technique developed to the full. It is unlikely that a more detailed account of the day-to-day working of air supply has ever been written. R/5 V/5. NAM. JALH.

KALADAN RETURN
The Second Campaign of the 81st West African Division
Anon * Printed by M L Sabharwal, Roxy Press, Delhi, for PR Services (West Africa), n.d. (c.1946). Soft card, Divsl sign, 7.25 x 5.5, i/45. Fp, 31 mono phots, 7 line drawings, one map (folding, pasted in at the rear), no Index. Apps: H&A, with statistical summary of awards up to 31.1.1946, all ranks, incl 3rd (West African) Bde, Order of Battle.
* This is a more accurate and less journalistic account than JUNGLE COMMANDO (vide preceding page). It covers the Second Kaladan campaign, from July 1944 to January 1945. The illustrations include photographic portraits of the new GOC, Maj Gen F J Loftus-Tottenham, of two Bde Commanders, of the CRA, and of four Africans awarded the DCM. R/4 V/3. IWM. JALH.
Note: for greater detail, reference should be made to 81 (WEST AFRICAN) DIVISION, THE SECOND KALADAN CAMPAIGN, AUGUST 1944 - JANUARY 1945, this being an unpublished official report (a copy of which is held at the NAM). It consists of iii/58 pages, plus 15 pages of appendixes. The compiler is thought to have been Lieut Col E A T Boggis, the GSO(1), and is primarily a plain statement of facts. Appendix 'C', however, is written in a more personal style and may be the work of Loftus-Tottenham, the Divsl Commander who replaced Woolner.

ARAKAN ASSIGNMENT
The Story of the 82nd West African Division
Anon * Printed by Roxy Press, New Delhi, for PR Services (West Africa), n.d. (c.1946). Illustrated paper covers, 8.0 x 5.5, -/44. Fp, 24 mono phots, one cld ill, one line drawing, one map (folding), no Index. Apps: Divsl Order of Battle, summary of H&A up to 28.2.1946 (no names).
* A brief history, useful only as a general background. It covers the Div's operations in the Arakan in 1944-1945 and, while similar to the equivalent items published by the PR Services for 81st (WA) Div, this one is more informative. The illustrations include photographic portraits of the two successive GOC - Maj Gen McI Bruce and Maj Gen H C Stockwell - of the three Bde Commanders, and of two African soldiers awarded the DCM. R/3 V/3. IWM. JRStA.

82nd WEST AFRICAN DIVISIONAL ARTILLERY
Maj H B Heath and Brig R H M Hill * Published by HQ RA, 82 (WA) Div, SEAC, June 1945. Seen in library binding, 12.75 x 8.0, -/44 (plus 10 not numbered). No ills, no maps, no Index. Apps: casualty statistics, list of Regts under command or in support, verbatim XV Corps Special Order of the Day to 82 (WA) Div, notes on 22 (EA) Bde.
* Written soon after the conclusion of the fighting in the Arakan, and intended to underscore the lessons learned, this is a strictly factual account. Perhaps its main value to many researchers is that it shows the movements and roles of the individual Batteries. Detailed and authoritative. R/5 V/4. IWM. JALH.

ARTILLERY

THE GOLD COAST ARTILLERY, 1851-1863
Maj J J Crooks * Reprinted from the Journal of the Royal Artillery, Vol XXXVIII, No 12, March 1912, Royal Artillery Institute, Woolwich (London). Paper covers, brown, 8.5 x 5.5, -/7. No ills, no maps, no appendixes, no Index.
* This little pamphlet describes the organisation, establishment, and pay scales of a short-lived unit formed in 1851 from 'slaves and pawns amongst the Fantee tribe' to augment local garrisons of the West India Regt. The Corps took part in four minor expeditions against the Ashantee between 1852 and 1863, but was then disbanded following a mutiny. The latter was probably the consequence of poor leadership. Many of the British officers succumbed to local diseases or were invalided back to England. Of those who survived, many neglected their duties by 'moonlighting' on other and more gainful employments. A limited but interesting glimpse into the early British presence in West Africa. R/5 V/2. PC. JRStA.

KALADAN MORTARS, OR A WALK ON A KNIFE EDGE
Maj M S Clarke MBE * Facsimile TS in binder, 11.0 x 8.5, vii/33/12 (the latter being the appendixes). 11 mono phots, 2 line drawings (101st Mortar Bty flag and 81st WA Div flash), 7 maps (6 reproduced in the text to show the route followed, one inside the rear cover), no Index. Apps: 7 in total, verbatim Operation Orders and Reports.
* A most interesting and detailed account by its eventual CO of the formation of 101 Mortar Bty, 41 Mortar Regt, West African Artillery, and its services in Burma. The personnel were drawn from the 'carriers' of the Light Regt of 81 (WA) Div and the Nigerian Bty of its LAA/Anti-tank Regt. The author gives full information regarding the difficulties encountered during the Second Kaladan campaign from September 1944 to January 1945. The 3 inch mortar was the West Africans' most effective (and often only) support weapon. This candid first-hand account is well written and provides a clear picture of the ways in which the weapon was employed. R/4 V/4. IWM/NAM. JALH.

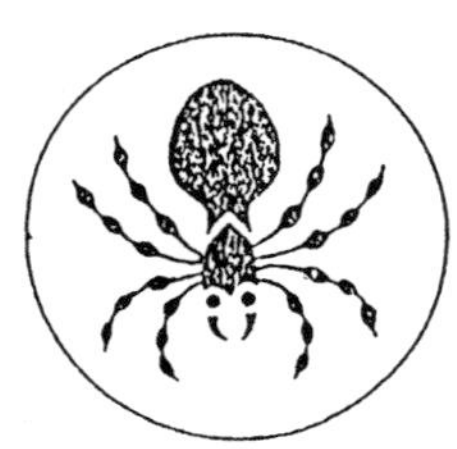

ENGINEERS

THE DEVELOPMENT, TRAINING AND OPERATIONS OF THE WEST AFRICAN ENGINEERS AND THE OPERATION OF WORKS SERVICES IN WEST AFRICA TO 1949

Brig H W Baldwin OBE * No publication details shown, March 1981. Seen in library bindings, brown, gold, 12.0 x 8.0, -/26. No ills, no maps, no Index. Apps: list of Engineer units raised in West Africa, notes on expenditure, list of Chief Engineers and of CRE (Areas and Districts), list of RE officers commanding post-war West African Field Squadrons.

* A brief outline of the services of all WA Engineer units during WWII, plus civilian works undertaken by such units in the immediate post-war period. Written, according to the author, to correct the lack of coverage in other and more generalised Engineer histories, and based in part upon information obtained from officers who served. R/5 V/3. IWM. JALH.

THE 2nd AND 3rd (GOLD COAST) FIELD COMPANIES

Brig H W Baldwin OBE * No publication details shown, dated May 1981. Seen in a single library binding, buff, gold, 12.0 x 8.0. Two facsimile TS volumes bound as one, folios numbered successively but irregularly, approx -/180.

Volume I : Formation and the Campaign in East Africa. 28 mono phots, 12 maps (9 printed in the text, one bound in, two loose in rear pocket), no Index. Apps: notes on the work done by both Field Coys from Wajir to El Wak (Kenya), and in the major actions at Buro Erillo, the Juba River crossing, and the Battle of Uaddara (Waddara) through to the capture of Gondar (Abyssinia), notes on the East African Road Construction Corps.

Volume II : In West Africa between the Campaigns, and the Campaign in Burma. 8 mono phots, 13 maps (12 printed in the text, one bound in), no Index. Apps: notes on 4th (WA) Field Coy at Ru-Ywa, notes on the Guerilla Party (Arakan, October 1944), history of 82nd (WA) Div Engineers.

* The narrative is a much expanded version of an article written for the Royal Engineers Journal. With the pre-war RWAFF having no integral sapper element, it was decided in 1939 to raise three Field Coys as the nucleus of a new West African Engineers Corps. The 1st Field Coy was formed in Nigeria, the 2nd and 3rd in the Gold Coast. The other ranks were newly recruited tribesmen. The officers and SNCOs were mainly volunteers from the British population resident in those Colonies. The majority of the personnel, both African and European, had formerly been employed in the mining and civil engineering industries. Volume I provides an interesting record of their adventures while under training, the move to Kenya, and then their role in the East African campaign. It concludes with the return to West Africa in 1943. Volume II deals with the re-fit period, the move to Burma, and the work done there. These two volumes were apparently a private venture by an author wishing to ensure that the services of the short-lived WA Engineers should not be forgotten by history. The result is a well written and certainly helpful source of reference. R/5 V/4. IWM/MODL. JALH/ECL.

THE GAMBIA REGIMENT

WITH AFRICANS IN ARAKAN

David M Cookson * Facsimile TS, unpublished, Foreword dated April 1969.

* This is a personal memoir by a former officer who served with 1st Bn The Gambia Regt in Burma, 1943-1944. The document consists of 95 facsimile foolscap pages, printed one side only, comprising 70,000 words arranged in 12 chapters. It has no Index and no appendixes (other than a list of subscribers and a Foreword written by Lieut Gen Sir Anthony Read KCB CBE DSO MC who had assumed command of the Bn after the Battle of Pagoda Hill). It is the basic story of the Bn's 'D' Company. Well written and convincing, the narrative covers all the main events, including the fight at Frontier Hill (Kaladan Valley) as part of Hubforce. It is unfortunate that the author referred to his brother officers by the forenames only, and this limits the research value of his work. However, nothing else has been written about the Bn and, as far as it goes, it is a very useful record. Several dozen copies were produced for members of the Regt and of the 81st (West African) Division Club. R/5 V/3. IWM/NAM. JRStA.

THE NIGERIA REGIMENT

A SHORT HISTORY OF THE NIGERIA REGIMENT, RWAFF
Lieut Col A S Taylor * West African Printing & Stationery Services, Nigeria, n.d. (c.1930). Soft card, buff, black, 8.25 x 6.5, -/19. No ills, 2 maps (bound in), no Index. Apps: H&A (for WWI, 3 DCMs, one MM, with citations).
* A condensed history compiled as a Regtl teaching aid. It tries to cover, very sketchily, the origins of the Regt, its West African campaigns between 1873 and 1910, and its services in West and East Africa in WWI. In only nineteen pages, this is just not possible. The two maps (Nigeria and the Gold Coast) are helpful, but this booklet is otherwise remarkable only for its rarity.
R/5 V/2. MODL/NAM. AMM.

WITH THE NIGERIANS IN GERMAN EAST AFRICA
Capt W D Downes MC * Methuen & Co Ltd, London, 1919. Red, black, 9.0 x 5.5, xiii/352. Fp, 30 mono phots, 5 maps (4 sketch maps, plus one large folding, bound in at the rear), Index. Apps: Roll of Honour (British officers and NCOs, KIA, WIA and DOD), H&A (for the Nigerian Bde for the entire campaign, all ranks, with precis of citations and dates of award), summary of British and Indian units in the field at the end of 1916, notes on effective strengths in 1917.
* This is the story of the Nigerian Brigade as constituted in WWI - 1st, 2nd, 3rd, and 4th Bns of the Nigeria Regt, plus a Nigerian Battery of light artillery. Its men had already served 18 months in the Cameroons, and had returned home, but were then reorganised for service in East Africa. They departed Lagos in November 1916. Operations and battles are described in fluent detail, with numerous eyewitness accounts by officers who took part. The book also contains a brief summary of the origins of the Nigeria Regt (from 1863 when the Hausa Armed Police were formed). R/4 V/5. NAM/IWM. JRStA.
Note: a pamphlet of 17 pages, entitled NIGERIAN SOLDIERS IN EAST AFRICA (anon, Lagos Government Printer, 1917) has been seen.

A SHORT HISTORY OF THE 1st (WEST AFRICAN) INFANTRY BRIGADE IN THE ARAKAN, 1944-1945
C R A Swynnerton * Ife-Olu Printing Works, Lagos, 1949. Brown boards, purple spine, black, 8.5 x 5.25, xii/88. No ills, 4 maps (on unnumbered pages at the rear), no Index. Apps: casualty statistics, chronology of Bde HQ moves and locations (12.12.1944 to 14.4.1945).
* This account was first published in 1945 (printed by Thacker's Press & Directories Ltd, Calcutta). The second edition, as recorded here, was produced four years later in expanded form. The story is that of 1st, 2nd and 3rd Bns, The Nigeria Regt, between December 1944 and May 1945. The author was the Bde commander. As the Preface to the second edition states: 'Since the first edition of this history was published, more information has come to hand regarding the strength and movements of the enemy. This information was obtained at a conference held in Rangoon in April 1946 and attended by senior officers of 82nd (WA) Division on one side and senior officers of the Japanese 54th Division, our opponents, on the other. The Japanese officers included Lieut Gen Miyazaki, Divisional commander, and Maj Gen Koba, Commander of the Infantry Group of the 54th Division'. An unusual and clearly important record. R/4 V/4. IWM/MODL. AMM/JALH.

THE NIGERIA REGIMENT
Spearhead of Victory - Yan Jagaban Nasea
Anon (possibly Col A Haywood) * No publication details shown, possibly at Lagos, 1944. Illustrated paper, blue, white, 8.0 x 5.0, -/28. No photographic ills, 23 line drawings, one map (tribal areas of Nigeria), no Index. Apps: Battle Honours.
* A wartime propaganda item, with three introductory pages referring to 81st (WA) Div and its Chindit Bde. The main attraction of this item are the excellent line drawings (portraits) of individual Nigerian soldiers, each with personal details of origin and army service. R/5 V/1. IWM/NAM. JALH.

THE CAMPAIGN IN BURMA, DECEMBER 1943 - FEBRUARY 1945
Anon * No location or date shown, facsimile TS, 11.75 x 8.25, -/20 (unnumbered). No ills, no maps, no appendixes, no Index.
* An informal account of 4th Bn The Nigeria Regt's role in 81st (WA) Div's two Kaladan campaigns, and possibly the work of two different officers. The story is told in very condensed form but with candid appraisals of setbacks and mistakes. Some details of casualties and awards are listed within the narrative.
R/5 V/3. IWM. JALH.
Note: THE CAMPAIGN IN BURMA is the title of another similar account, compiled by Lieut Col Frank Owen OBE and published by HMSO, 1946. It deals with the entire campaign, not just the services of 4 NR.

THE JEEP TRACK
The story of the 81st West African Division fighting on the Arakan Front in Burma
Capt John Cattanach * Regency Press, London & New York, 1990. Illustrated stiff card, 7.75 x 5.5, -/79. One mono phot, no maps, no appendixes, no Index.
* A booklet which deals with the actions of 4th Bn The Nigeria Regt in the First Kaladan campaign (December 1943 to March 1944), but badly written and frequently inaccurate. The main protagonist, Smythe, appears to be a figure of fiction, although other personnel named in the narrative are known to have served.
R/1 V/1. IWM. JALH.

RECORD OF OPERATIONS OF 7th BATTALION, THE NIGERIA REGIMENT
Burma, April-July, 1944
Lieut Col C P Vaughan DSO * Publication details not shown, n.d. (c.1954). Stiff card, tape spine, buff/green purple, 'Palm tree' motif, 13.0 x 8.0, -/62. No ills, one map (sketch, in the text), no Index. Apps: copy of Operational Movement Order (to Mawlu, 11.4.1944), summary of casualties (7 NR and Japanese).
* The frank personal diary of Lieut Col Vaughan regarding 35 Column as a part of the Second Chindit force. He was evacuated, wounded, on 16 July. His diary continues through to 22 July and is a detailed record - not only of daily events and mileages covered but also his own assessments and reactions to events. The original diary was presented to the IWM Department of Documents (together with other papers relating to the Second Chindit campaign). The version recorded here, expanded and with an Introduction and explanatory notes, was produced by the author ten years later. The Introduction incorporates a list of officers and WOs who served with 29 and 35 Columns. R/5 V/4. IWM. JALH.

CHINDIT COLUMN
Charles Carfrae * William Kimber & Co Ltd, London, 1985. Green, gold, 9.5 x 6.0, -/194. 13 mono phots, 4 maps, no appendixes, Index.
* An autobiography by an officer who served with 10th Bn The Nigeria Regt in West Africa between 1940 and 1943, and then with 7th Bn in Burma until August 1944. The 7th was assigned to Wingate's Special Force and operated in the deep penetration role as 29 and 35 Columns in the Second Chindit campaign. This is a good individual account of Africans as Chindits. R/1 V/4. IWM/NAM. JRStA.

THE MARCH OUT
The End of the Chindit Adventure
James Shaw (otherwise Jesse Shaw) * Rupert Hart-Davis, London, 1953. Maroon, silver, 8.0.x 6.0, -/206. Fp, 3 mono phots, one map, no appendixes, no Index.
* The author was a Vickers machine-gunner Sergeant who was air-lifted into the 'Aberdeen' block in April 1944 as a reinforcement to 12th Bn The Nigeria Regt. He joined the unit after marching to 'White City' at Henu. In late May, he and the rest of the 12th Bn made 'the march out' to Hill 60 and Mogaung. His book is one of the very few accounts by an NCO. R/3 V/4. IWM/NAM. JALH.
Note: as Jesse Shaw, the same author wrote SPECIAL FORCE - A CHINDIT'S STORY (Alan Sutton, 1986).

THE SIERRA LEONE REGIMENT

HISTORY OF THE SIERRA LEONE BATTALION OF THE ROYAL WEST AFRICAN FRONTIER FORCE

Lieut R P M Davis * Government Printer, Freetown, 1932. Brown, black, 8.25 x 5.5, x/147/xv. No ills, one map (folding, pasted in at the rear, Cameroons, 1914), Bibliography, Index. Apps: Roll of Honour (all ranks, with causes, the Cameroons campaign, 1914-1916), list of all officers who served (1914-1918), notes on the presentation of Colours in 1922 (with the names of all officers, BNCOs and ANCOs who were present on that occasion).

* A good detailed history for the period from August 1829 (raising of the Sierra Leone Police) through to 30 June 1928 (when the Bn took over the garrison barracks at Freetown from the about-to-be-disbanded West African Regt). It has clearly written coverage of all the main punitive expeditions (Ashanti 1900, Kissi 1905, etc) and the Bn's services in the Cameroons campaign. Probably the best Bn history of any Colony in West Africa. R/5 V/4. NAM. JA/JALH.

Note: it is believed that this book was first published in 1929 with a print run of 250 copies. The version recorded above and dated 1932 is said to be identical in all respects.

HISTORY OF THE 1st Bn, THE SIERRA LEONE REGIMENT, ROYAL WEST AFRICAN FRONTIER FORCE, 1939-1945

Anon (Capt Peter Clements, Maj John Bull, and other members of the Bn) * 'India, Madras Province, November, 1945'. Soft card, pale yellow, black, 8.0 x 5.25, -/60. No ills, 2 poorly executed maps (bound in), no Index. Apps: Roll of Honour (KIA and WIA, all ranks), lists of officers, WOs, BNCOs and ANCOs (as serving in July 1943 and July 1945), verbatim Orders of the Day issued by 81 Div, by XV Corps, and by Supreme Commander SEAC.

* A clear basic account, containing much useful detail of the Bn's services in Burma but with certain key dates not mentioned. It is possible that all units of the Div were ordered to produce narrative accounts of their recent services in the Arakan. Any plan to combine these reports and use them for the production of a full Divsl history was never carried through, but various original texts have survived. Some are one-off drafts, others are facsimile typescripts which were reproduced in varying quantities, cyclostyled on paper of poor quality. This item is an exception because it was professionally type-set and published in a bound octavo format as described above. It was produced at Karvetnagar, in the Province of Madras, while the Bn was waiting to return home. Demand soon overtook supply and the text of the book was reproduced in cyclostyled TS (quarto format) after the Bn had arrived back in Freetown. This version has 42 pages, unbound, and it contains some errors. R/5 V/4. RMAS/IWM. RP/JALH.

DESERT, JUNGLE AND SAND
A Memoir

Philip van Straubenzee * Pentland Press, Durham, 1991. Green, gold, 8.25 x 6.0, xv/124. Fp, 24 mono phots, 5 maps, Glossary, no Index. Apps: Special Orders of the Day, etc.

* The author was Adjutant of 3rd Bn The Gold Coast Regt from formation in 1940 through to the end of the Abyssinia campaign. He then commanded 1st Bn Sierra Leone Regt in Burma from October 1944 to March 1945 (the period of the Second Kaladan campaign). Capt Peter Clements (vide preceding entry) was his Int Officer during that time. This account provides a helpful contribution to the histories of both Bns. It incorporates a substantial verbatim extract from the work compiled by Clements, Bull et al. The narrative makes frequent mention of individuals and of actions to which van Straubenzee was an eyewitness. R/3 V/3. PC. JRStA.

THE SIERRA LEONE ARMY
A Century of History
E D A Turey and A Abrahams * Macmillan Publishers Ltd, London, 1987. Illustrated laminated boards, 'Troops being inspected' motif, dark green, red/gold, 8.5 x 5.5, iv/180. 16 mono phots, 3 maps, Bibliography, Index. Apps: H&A (WWII only), list of COs (1902-1987), notes on WAFF operational tactics (c.1902).
* Until about 1819, the defence of Sierra Leone was in the hands of the Royal African Corps - an all-European force (vide Maj J J Crooks in the Index of Authors). This was replaced by the 2nd Bn West India Regt. An early local police force was revitalised in May 1890 and retitled the Sierra Leone Frontier Police. Following the Hut Tax War (1898-1899), the Frontier Police were again reformed, in 1901, as the Sierra Leone Bn of the West African Frontier Force. It took part in the Kissi War (1905) and the Cameroons campaign (1914-1916). In WWII, as 1st Bn The Sierra Leone Regt, it served in Burma with 81st (WA) Div. The RWAFF was disbanded in August 1960, but the Sierra Leone Regt retained its Empire title as an element within the Royal Sierra Leone Military Forces when the country became independent in 1961. The Army seized power by a coup d'état in 1967 and the country became a republic in 1971. The 'Royal' prefix was discarded at that time. This is a comprehensive record which covers nearly two centuries of Sierra Leone's military history. R/3 V/5. MODL. AMM.

THE GOLD COAST REGIMENT

THE GOLD COAST REGIMENT IN THE EAST AFRICAN CAMPAIGN
Sir Hugh Clifford KCMG * John Murray, London, 1920. Brown-grey boards, black leather spine, gold, 8.75 x 5.75, ix/306. Fp, 7 mono phots, 5 maps (3 printed in the text, 2 bound in), Index. Apps: H&A, Regtl strength (tabular format), notes on the history of the Mounted Infantry of the Gold Coast Regt.
* A book which covers the services of the Regt in East Africa between mid-1916 and mid-1918. Very readable, and a good 'human interest' view of the operations against von Lettow Vorbeck's Schutztruppe. Many names, European and African, are mentioned in the narrative and are well indexed. Some of the photographic illustrations are of particular interest because they are not widely published elsewhere. R/3 V/4. NAM/IWM. BCC/JRStA.
Note: the version recorded above may be a 'de luxe' edition. The same book is often seen in red cloth boards with black titles. Reference should be made also to BATTLE FOR THE BUNDU, by Charles Miller (Purnell's Book Services, London, 1974).

HISTORY OF 3rd BATTALION, THE GOLD COAST REGIMENT, RWAFF, IN THE ARAKAN CAMPAIGN, OCTOBER 1944 - MAY 1945
Anon (known to have been Lieut Col F J Goulson DSO, Brig E W D Western DSO, and Capt M D I Gass) * John Cordle Ltd, Premier Press, Felixstowe, UK, n.d. Soft card, stapled, light blue, dark blue, 'RWAFF palm' motif, -/30. No ills, six maps (drawn by Lieut A Morris), no Index. Apps: list of officers and BNCOs (at 24.10.1944).
* A good record, condensed but detailed, of the services of 3rd Bn The Gold Coast Regt in the Arakan during the period stated in the title of the book. They included Goppe (4 November to 5 December 1944), the action at Gyethinka Chaung, the Road Block (6 March to 9 March 1945), the heavy fighting and (subsequent) advance from the Ru-Ywa Bridgehead (21 February to 2 March 1945), and the actions at Shawlin Taung (14 March to 26 March 1945) and Tamandu-Taungup (1 April to 11 May 1945). R/5 V/3. NAM. ECL.
Note: one of the authors, 'Tank' Western, had a special interest in this little book because he had raised the Bn at Winneba, Gold Coast, in 1939 and commanded it in the Abyssinian campaign. His award of the DSO reflected his Bn's service in that campaign.

ABYSSINIA ADVENTURE
J F MacDonald * Cassell, London, 1957. Green, gold, 8.0 x 6.0, x/213. No ills, one map, no appendixes, no Index.
* A work of 'faction'. It purports to be the story of the so-called '5th West African Askaris' in the East African campaign of 1940-1941. The events described were in fact those experienced by 3rd Bn The Gold Coast Regt and as viewed by the author (a Rhodesian Major serving with the Bn). The names of other people named in the text are entirely fictional. The book is well written and is certainly helpful as a reflection of what happened, but it is otherwise an eccentric effort which did not endear the author to his former brother officers.
R/3 V/2. IWM. JALH/ECL.
Note: this book should not be confused with another having a similar title and dealing with the same campaign - ABYSSINIA PATCHWORK. This was a general (factual) account written by the war correspondent, Kenneth Gandar Dower, and published by Frederick Muller, London, in 1949.

THE HISTORY OF THE 5th Bn, THE GOLD COAST REGT, 1939-1946

Lieut Col A F Giles ('and others') * Duplicated TS, no publication details, n.d. (c.1946). Seen disbound, 11.75 x 8.25, -/54. No ills, 3 maps, no Index. Apps: H&A (all ranks).

* A badly typed and poorly presented record which is full of interesting detail. It covers the period from 15 December 1943 to 24 January 1945 when 5th Bn The Gold Coast Regt was fighting in the Kaladan Valley as part of 81st (WA) Div. Most of the pages deal with the campaign in general terms, but the last twelve pages describe specific engagements and patrols in which Bn sub-units took part. Several officers had a hand in compiling this account, but Maj C G Bowen (vide following entry) was not one of them. Presumably he decided, some months later, to produce his own record in his own way. The Giles (et al) account is strictly factual and avoids subjective comment. Bowen expresses his own personal views. The researcher is advised to consult both of these sources. R/5 V/4. NAM. JALH.

WEST AFRICAN WAY
The Story of the Burma Campaigns, 1943-1945
5th Bn Gold Coast Regiment, 81 West African Division

Anon (Lieut Col C G Bowen) * Ashanti Times Press, Obuasi, Ashanti, The Gold Coast, n.d. (c.1946). Soft card, brown, black, 10.0 x 8.0, -/84/xii. No ills, 8 maps (seven bound in, to illustrate individual engagements, one large folding, bound in at the rear, showing the Kaladan area), no Index. Apps: Roll of Honour, H&A (including extracts from citations for awards to Africans), reports on patrols carried out by Maj H Olszewski, Capt A W Gauld and Lieut Rother, notes on mileages covered.

* A well written, detailed and accurate account of 5th Bn The Gold Coast Regt in both Kaladan campaigns, with many illuminating comments on the problems and tactics of jungle fighting. The author, in his Foreword, states: 'This book ... has not been compiled from official records ... I simply wanted to write a story of what I saw, heard and felt ... I wanted people to know what the African did rather more than they would in sifting the mass of facts and figures in an official history'. R/4 V/4. NAM/IWM. JALH.

THE HISTORY OF THE 7th BATTALION, THE GOLD COAST REGIMENT

Maj K M Scott * Duplicated TS, no publication details shown, n.d. (c.1945). Seen disbound, 11.75 x 8.25, -/36 (plus 8 unnumbered pages). No ills, one map, no Index. Apps: notes on the organisation of the RWAFF Bn (1943), plus four poems.

* As mentioned elsewhere, several unit histories were drafted while 81st (WA) Div was waiting (for eight months) for shipping to become available so that it could return home. This is another such, never formally published. It describes the services of the wartime 7th Bn from formation in August 1940 through to disbandment in April 1946. A plainly written story which does not gloss over the errors and setbacks. R/5 V/3. NAM. JALH.

THE FIRST KALADAN CAMPAIGN
THE SECOND KALADAN CAMPAIGN

Maj P B Poore MC * Transposed from original TS, n.d. (c.1991). Seen in library binding, 11.75 x 8.25, -/118 (with two title pages as shown above). Fp, 28 mono phots, 12 line drawings, no maps, no Index. Apps: notes on the organisation of a RWAFF Battalion.

* No details of location or date are available, but this would appear to be a recently (1991) edited and tidied-up version of a draft prepared by the author many years earlier (this can be seen at the IWM). The story is based partly upon Scott's account (vide preceding entry) and partly upon Poore's memory and letters which he wrote home from Burma. He was an OC Coy with 7th Bn throughout the period 1943 to 1945 (First and Second Kaladan campaigns). The narrative is candid and detailed, with full explanations of the various problems encountered. His references to the general situation and to other units are not, however, as reliable as his comments on his own Bn. R/5 V/4. IWM/NAM. JALH.

AUXILIARY GROUPS

HISTORY OF THE 4th WEST AFRICAN AUXILIARY CORPS, SIERRA LEONE REGIMENT, ROYAL WEST AFRICAN FRONTIER FORCE, 1941-1945

Capt R R Ryder MBE * No publication details shown, but probably produced at Karvetnagar, Madras Province, 1945. Facsimile TS, seen disbound, 13.25 x 8.5, -/40. No ills, no maps, no Index. Apps: Roll of Honour, H&A, list of officers, WOs, BNCOs, and ANCOs who disembarked at Bombay (17.8.1943), idem for those serving in December 1945, notes on Hubforce (compiled by Lieut H R Hikins), notes on 'head load scales' (portage loadings per unit).

* Alone among Empire formations, and in conformity with the conditions and customs of the region, the WAFF/RWAFF employed 'carriers' (porters) to head-load heavy weapons (including light artillery), equipment and supplies. Experience gained in the Ashanti campaign of 1900 led to carriers being enlisted, uniformed and given military training. WAFF Battalions and light batteries had an establishment of such men, sufficiently trained to enable them to replace a rifleman or gunner if needed. In the East African campaign of 1916-1918, a Carrier Corps raised in Sierra Leone gave additional support to the WAFF combat units. When, in 1940, it was decided to start expanding the West African Forces (including a full range of supporting arms and services), it was decided also that the new WA Army Service Corps would incorporate a number of Auxiliary Groups of carriers. The first Groups were formed in 1941, each intended to 'lift' a complete Brigade Group. When the two WA Divisions were formed in 1943, each required an additional Group to 'lift' the Divsl HQs and Divsl Troops. These Groups, each of 2000 men (1650 carriers and 350 armed NCOs and ORs), when combined with the combat units' own carrier elements, increased the strength of a WA Division to 25,000 men (at least 50% more than a normal Division having normal transport). Their primary role was to carry, but they also cleared and levelled airstrips and dropping zones, collected and distributed air-delivered supplies, and at times manned the defensive perimeters. These tasks freed the combat units to concentrate on patrolling and fighting. Those without arms soon began to acquire them. Later it became official policy to arm all ranks, but they still carried the same loads of 40 lbs or more. Initially regarded as second-rate soldiers, their stamina and amazing ability to manage even the lost awkward loads in jungle, where even an unloaded man found it difficult to move, earned them the praise and admiration of their comrades. The Appendix by Lieut Hikins well illustrates the untiring work and contribution of Auxiliary Group men during the two weeks' long defence of Frontier Hill by Hubforce (by 1st Bn The Gambia Regt, 7/16th Punjab Regt, with the Tripura Rifles under command). The formation badge of 82nd (WA) Div aptly illustrated their work. It consisted of a carrier's head-load, pierced by crossed spears, signifying 'Through our carriers we fight'.
R/5 V/4. IWM/NAM. JALH.

POLICE

THE GOLD COAST POLICE, 1844-1938
W H Gillespie * Government Printer, Accra, The Gold Coast, 1955. Stiff card, light blue boards with dark blue spine, black, GCP crest, 8.5 x 5.75, -/89. 6 mono phots, some line drawings of uniforms, no maps, Index. Apps: Roll of Honour (1930-1953), H&A (with names and years of award for the George Medal, King's Police Gallantry Medal, Colonial Police Medal for Gallantry, Colonial Police Medal for Meritorious Service, etc), list of former officers (with biographical details, 1894-1953), notes on criminal statistics.
* A clear straightforward account of the Force's evolution and operational role during the stated period. As can be seen from the list of appendixes, this is an excellent source of reference also for genealogists and medal collectors.
R/4 V/5. MODL. RP.

THE POLICE IN MODERN NIGERIA
Origins, Development and Role
Tekena M Tamuno * Ibadan University Press, Ibadan, Nigeria, 1970. Royal blue, gold, 8.75 x 5.5, xvi/332. Fp, 12 mono phots, one map (bound in), Glossary, Bibliography, Index.
* A detailed and competent analysis which first sets out the historical background and then describes in condensed form the many events in which the Force was involved up to 1970 (dealing with riots and strikes, maintaining internal security, etc). Readable and interesting. R/3 V/5. MODL. AMM.

Notes:

1. Reference should be made also to THE COLONIAL POLICE, by Sir Charles Jeffries, KCMG OBE (vide the 'Index of Authors').

PART 8

East Africa
with Egypt, and the Anglo-Egyptian Sudan

NOTES

EAST AFRICA
with EGYPT and THE ANGLO-EGYPTIAN SUDAN
A Military Chronology

15th Century: Portuguese navigators, seeking a sea route to the Indies and the legendary kingdom of Prester John, explore the west coast of Africa. By the end of the century they have rounded the Cape of Storms (soon renamed the Cape of Good Hope). They reach Malindi, on the coast of modern Kenya, and sail on to the Malabar coast of India.
16th Century: the Portuguese discover the island of Madagascar. They establish fortified trading posts up the east coast of Africa, the most important being on the island of Mozambique. From India, they explore eastwards to the Moluccas (the Spice Islands) and reach China and Japan. Dutch, French and English maritime traders follow in their wake.
17th and 18th Centuries: Portuguese power wanes. Islam is spread along the coast of East Africa by Arab trading dhows coming south from Arabia. The Sultans of Oman take over the island of Zanzibar and develop it as a major slave market. The French establish themselves in Madagascar and occupy the smaller islands of the western Indian Ocean - Mauritius, Reunion, and the Seychelles.
19th Century: the sparse Arab and European coastal footholds slowly grow in size. Arab slavers push deep into the hinterland, creating a network of contacts with dominant local tribes. They catch or purchase 'black ivory' - people of the weaker tribes - and use them to carry 'white ivory' - elephant tusks - on the long trek to the coast. The tusks are shipped to Europe and China. Some of the slaves are sold to American traders (who find the Royal Navy's patrols less effective here than around West Africa), but most are exported to the world of Islam. In Europe, there is growing curiosity regarding the source of the Nile. The tales of Darkest Africa brought home by the early travellers cause the missionary and humanitarian movements to campaign for European intervention. David Livingstone embodies the belief that 'the three Cs - Christianity, Commerce and Civilisation' - are needed in tropical Africa. With the 1880s, the 'scramble for Africa' begins. A fourth 'C' is added to the list - Conquest. France and Germany and Leopold, King of the Belgians, join the race. The Khedives of Egypt expand their rule southwards up the Nile. The Suez Canal is completed. The Red Sea, and its coastal areas, becomes vital to British strategic interests in India and the Far East. By the end of the century, only the Coptic Christian kingdom of Abyssinia retains its independence.
1801: the British expel the French from Egypt and return it to Turkish suzerainty.
1805: Muhammed Ali seizes power in Egypt and, from 1808, rules as Khedive (or Viceroy) to the Sultan of Ottoman Turkey. He initiates a policy of modernising his country and expanding into Abyssinia, Arabia and the Sudan.
1814: France cedes Mauritius and the Seychelles to the British.
1820-1822: the Khedive conquers northern Sudan. In 1823 he founds Khartoum.
1840: the Sultans of Oman take power in Zanzibar. A British Consul is appointed.
1852: many British politicians object to spending money on overseas commitments. Disreali declares the view that 'Colonies are a millstone around our necks'.
1853-1856: on his second expedition, Livingstone discovers the Victoria Falls and the Central Zambezi Valley.
1854: the Khedive grants the Suez Canal concession to de Lesseps.
1856: Zanzibar is separated from Oman. It is estimated that Arab traders are killing or enslaving nearly 100,000 Africans each year. The Royal Navy's patrols are having little effect in stopping the trade (due to lack of local shore bases).
1857: Burton and Speke reach Lake Tanganyika, and Speke, alone, Lake Victoria.
1858-1864: Livingstone is British Consul on the coast. He travels inland and finds Lake Nyasa (previously discovered by the Portuguese).
1859: de Lesseps commences construction of the Suez Canal.
1860-1863: Grant and Speke discover that Lake Victoria is the main source of the White Nile. They follow the river northwards and meet Baker who, in 1864, finds another White Nile source, Lake Albert.

1862: the French establish a base at Obock, in Somalia.
1866: Turkey grants the Red Sea ports of Suakin and Massawa to the Khedive of Egypt. Livingstone begins his last expedition.
1867: the 'mad Emperor' Theodore of Abyssinia, his overtures of friendship to Queen Victoria ignored, has imprisoned British missionaries and envoys. General Napier, leading a major force of British Army, Indian Army, and Royal Navy units, marches to Theodore's capital, Magdala, and captures it. Theodore kills himself and the British withdraw in 1868.
1869: the Suez Canal is opened. Baker is commissioned by the Khedive to establish a Province of Equatoria (southern Sudan and the northern part of modern Uganda). He begins the fight against the Arab slavers in the area.
1870: an Italian trading company takes over Assab, on the Red Sea. The Khedive occupies Berbera, on the Gulf of Aden.
1871: Livingstone, feared lost, is found near Lake Tanganyika, by Stanley.
1873: having devoted his life to the exploration of Africa and the destruction of the slave trade, Livingstone dies on 1 May.
1874: the Egyptian conquest of eastern Sudan is completed.
1875: Stanley makes the first circumnavigations of Lakes Tanganyika and Victoria. Disraeli purchases the Khedive's shares in the Suez Canal Company.
1876: the Khedive's government is bankrupt. An international debt commission is formed to protect European (mainly French and British) interests in Egypt.
1877: the Sultan of Zanzibar agrees to allow the Royal Navy to recruit local men for military service. Lieut Lloyd Mathews RN, of HMS London, raises 300 Zanzibari Arabs. They are the first East African troops to be trained on European lines. Later their numbers rise to 1300 all ranks, with Mathews permitted by the Admiralty to carry the title of Brigadier General in the Sultan's Army.
1878: the Livingstonia Central Africa Company (generally known as the African Lakes Company) is formed by Scottish missionary, humanitarian and commercial interests with the intention of putting his ideas into practice around Lake Nyasa.
1879: Egypt becomes a constitutional monarchy under Turkish suzerainty and the 'dual control' of France and Great Britain with a new Khedive, Tewfik. Gordon, who had taken over from Baker, resigns his governorship of Equatoria.
1881: the Mahdi, a messianic Islamic leader named Muhammed Ahmed, launches a rebellion in the Sudan. Colonel Arabi stages a coup in Egypt.
1882: the Mahdi's forces annihilate Hicks Pasha's Egyptian Army at El Obeid. Turkey declines to take any action in Egypt. A British fleet, the French fleet having withdrawn, bombards Alexandria and puts ashore an invasion force under the command of Wolseley. At Tel-el-Kebir, his British, Indian and Maltese troops defeat Arabi's army. The country is now effectively controlled by the British.
1884: Gordon, sent back to the Sudan with the task of evacuating the Egyptian garrisons, is besieged by the Mahdists in Khartoum. A major expedition, led by Wolseley, moves slowly southwards with the aim of rescuing him. The British and Egyptian Armies rely on the waters of the Nile as a means of transport. They are assisted by the Nile Voyageurs - expert boat handlers from Canada. They are the first men of the self-governing Colonies to come to the aid of 'the mother country' in a foreign war. Far to the south, Carl Peters of the German East Africa Company, is signing treaties with local chiefs on the mainland opposite Zanzibar.
1885: Wolseley arrives too late to save Gordon. Khartoum falls to the Mahdists and he is killed. An Australian volunteer contingent, raised in New South Wales, lands in March at Suakin. They are the first troops from any Australian Colony to fight for the Crown outside Australasia. Some Egyptian Army garrisons in southern Sudan continue to hold out against the Mahdists, but the Egyptian forces in the rest of the Sudan and in the Horn of Africa are withdrawn. The Mahdi dies in June. British forces also are withdrawn from the Sudan and the country is left to its own devices for the next decade. Elsewhere, the British occupy Berbera and declare a Protectorate of Northern Somalia. The Italians, at the invitation of the British, assume control of Massawa. Germany declares a Protectorate in East Africa. A boundary commission is formed to delimit the German and British spheres of control

as far west as Lake Victoria.
1887: the British occupy Kismayu, Jubaland. Around Lake Nyasa, the strain of conducting 'the Slavers War' is placing the African Lakes Company in difficulty.
1888: Rhodes conceives the 'Cape to Cairo plan'. He wants to create a series of British Colonies and Protectorates, connected by railway, to link South Africa with Egypt. The British Imperial East Africa Company is chartered. It intends to exploit the region of the great lakes and to take over British interests previously vested in the Sultan of Zanzibar. The French transfer their Somalia base to Djibouti.
1889: Menelik becomes Emperor of Abyssinia. He recognises the British Somaliland Protectorate. He signs a treaty with the Italians which gives them two Protectorates in the north-east corner of Somalia but which they also interpret as giving them control of Abyssinia itself. The French are planning their own sphere of influence - east to west - from the Atlantic Ocean to the Indian Ocean. They supply arms to Menelik. Emin Pasha, who continued to maintain a small Egyptian Army force in the southern Sudan following the death of Gordon, leaves Equatoria for the coast with Stanley. Most of his troops stay behind, under Selim Bey. The Sultan of Zanzibar yields to Italy his claims east of the Juba River. Johnston, the British Consul in Mozambique, is instructed to make treaties with the chiefs north of the Zambesi. Rhodes pays the cost of his expedition and subsidises the struggling African Lakes Company.
1890: Carl Peters of the German East Africa Company signs a treaty with the King of Buganda. Within months, Germany renounces the treaty in favour of Great Britain and likewise abandons all former claims in Equatoria, Nyasaland, and Witu. In return, the British concede ownership of the North Sea island of Heligoland (which in 1814 had been ceded to Great Britain by Denmark). Germany also agrees that Zanzibar, long an informal British Protectorate, should formally become one. The French agree to all of this in exchange for British recognition of their position in Madagascar. In December, Lugard, with a small force of Sudanese and Swahili troops and a Maxim gun, signs a treaty on behalf of the Imperial British East Africa Company with the King of Buganda. One clause provides for 'a standing army which the officers of the Company ... will ... organise like a native regiment in India'.
1891: Johston, as Commissioner, declares a British Protectorate over 'the territories under British influence north of the Zambesi' (the Nyasaland Districts and North East Rhodesia). The main aim is to preclude the Portuguese from the former and the Germans from the latter. He enrols a small armed force with Sikh volunteers from the Indian Army. The British Government authorises the British South Africa Company to operate north of the Zambesi and it makes treaties with the chiefs in Barotseland (North West Rhodesia). Far to the north, Lugard receives a small reinforcement of Sudanese and Swahili soldiers. While campaigning against the Bunyoro on behalf of the King of Buganda, he encounters Selim Bey's Sudanese troops, west of Lake Albert. Cut off from their Egyptian paymasters, they are living off the land with no clear role. They are taken in hand by Lugard who places 500 of them, under the Egyptian flag, in small forts along the Buganda/ Bunyoro border. He takes 100 more back to Kampala.
1892: Lugard wins the Battle of Mwengo, near Kampala. He is sustained by funds from the Church Missionary Society.
1893: once again out of money, the Imperial British East Africa Company can barely maintain its responsibilities in Uganda. It considers abandoning the entire territory, but Owen proceeds to enlist - under the Union flag - 450 of Lugard's fort garrison Sudanese. To the south, the Nyasaland Districts are renamed the British Central Africa Protectorate. Its armed forces consist of 200 Sikhs and 150 African soldiers.
1894: under pressure from missionary and humanitarian interests, the British Government declares a Protectorate over Uganda. Another 400 Sudanese, formerly in Egyptian pay, are enlisted for Crown service. They are told that they will be given new uniforms (which do not arrive) and will be paid in trade goods (which are not available).
1895: in July, the Imperial British East Africa Company finally collapses. The

Protectorate of British East Africa is declared (broadly, modern Kenya with Jubaland west of the Juba River). The East African Rifles are formed. The ranks comprise Sudanese, Swahili, Punjabis and locally recruited tribesmen in equal numbers. On 1 September, the Sudanese soldiers recruited earlier by Lugard and Owen are given the title Uganda Rifles. Led by a variety of British officers, they are still unpaid.

1896: Emperor Menelik having renounced his treaty with them, the Italians invade Abyssinia from Eritrea. They are heavily defeated at the Battle of Adowa. As a result, Italy, France and Great Britain are each obliged to sign new treaties with Menelik which reduce the extent of their holdings in Somalia (but Italy retains Eritrea). In Egypt, eleven years after the death of Gordon, the British mount an expedition for the reconquest of the Sudan. An Anglo-Egyptian force, commanded by Kitchener, marches south up the Nile. In Nyasaland, the Central African Rifles are formed with newly-recruited Africans and a cadre of Indian Army volunteers.

1897: the French Colonel Marchand is known to be heading towards Equatoria from the west. France has thoughts of claiming the territory before Kitchener can reach it. Three Companies of Uganda Rifles are ordered north to intercept him. War weary, unpaid, their uniforms in tatters, they desert en masse and go to Fort Lubwa's, on the shore of Lake Victoria. They murder Capt Thruston and two other officers. Loyal Sudanese of the Uganda Rifles, with the East African Rifles, bring the mutineers to battle. Those not killed in action are hanged.

1898: with the benefit of modern firepower, Kitchener destroys the Mahdists at the Battle of Omdurman. Further south, Marchand has reached Fashoda, on the Upper White Nile. A French expeditionary force from Abyssinia fails to join him. When confronted by Kitchener, who is authorised to eject him by force if necessary, he withdraws. His government lacks sufficient sea power to risk conflict with Great Britain, but 'the Fashoda incident' almost triggers a European war. Elsewhere, the Central African Rifles are retitled the Central African Regiment (CAR). British Somaliland, which so far has been garrisoned by the Indian Army and administered by the India Office, is passed to the Foreign Office.

1899: the Sudan is declared an Anglo-Egyptian Condominium. The 'mad mullah', Hajji Muhammad Ahmed bin Abdulla Hassan, begins raiding in Somalia (as he will, intermittently, for the next twenty years). In Nyasaland, 2 CAR is raised, under War Office control, for service overseas. Without proper uniforms and lacking any weapons, it is sent to Mauritius as a garrison force. The Mauritians protest strongly at being garrisoned by black troops in general, and by 2 CAR in particular.

1900: 2 CAR is withdrawn from Mauritius and sent to Berbera, Somaliland, where it receives its uniforms and rifles. With most of the British Army's regiments engaged in the war against the Boers in South Africa, the British are hard pressed when trouble erupts in West Africa. Half of 2 CAR is shipped around from Somaliland to join 1 CAR in the fight against the Ashanti (the 'War of the Golden Stool').

1901: the second half of 2 CAR arrives from Somaliland to deal with insurgents in The Gambia and with West African Regiment mutineers in the Gold Coast.

1902: from 1 January, the armed forces of the British Protectorates in East Africa are reorganised and incorporated into a new Regiment - the King's African Rifles. Initially it has five Battalions - the 1st and 2nd (formerly 1 CAR and 2 CAR) in Nyasaland, the 3rd (formerly the East African Rifles) in Kenya, and the 4th and 5th (formerly the Uganda Rifles) in Uganda. The latter (the 5th) is an Indian unit, while the others - 1st, 2nd, 3rd and 4th - have black African other ranks and NCOs. The patient Sudanese who served Lugard and Owen so well have all (apart from those who mutinied) gone home. Later in the year, a 6th Bn is raised in Somaliland from the local levies.

1902-1904: all Battalions of the KAR are at one time or another engaged in the campaign against the 'mad mullah' in Somaliland.

1904: its Indians being time-expired, the 5th Bn is disbanded. The British Central Africa Protectorate is renamed Nyasaland.

1908-1910: inconclusive operations against the 'mad mullah' end with British forces abandoning the hinterland and withdrawing to the coast. 6 KAR is disbanded.

1911: as an economy measure, 2 KAR is disbanded. Many of its askari take service with the Germans across the border. The two areas north of the Zambezi and so far administered separately by the British South Africa Company are merged to form Northern Rhodesia. Local security is maintained by an armed constabulary – the Northern Rhodesia Police.
1912: a Camel Constabulary is formed in Somaliland. Two years later it will be replaced by the Somaliland Camel Corps.
1914–1916: when war comes, the task of the three remaining KAR Battalions, and of the Northern Rhodesia Police ('on active service'), is to guard the borders of their respective territories. In German East Africa, Lieut Col Paul von Lettow Vorbeck has a small force of Europeans and askari to defend a huge area. He repulses an early attempted invasion by Indian forces at Tanga. The British have forgotten lessons learned during the 'guerilla' phase of the recent Anglo-Boer War. More troops are assembled from India and South Africa, but they make little headway. Logistics and tropical disease are their main obstacles.
1916–1918: 2 KAR is reformed in Nyasaland in January 1916, and 5 KAR in June (the latter to garrison Jubaland and the Northern Frontier District of Kenya). In February 1916, the great Boer leader, Jan Smuts, receives more troops from South Africa and Great Britain and launches a major invasion of German East Africa. A quick and decisive result is expected. His main thrust is southwards from Kenya. A second force (which includes 1 KAR and the Northern Rhodesia Police) advances north from Nyasaland, and a third force (3 KAR and Belgian units) attacks the north-east sector. The Germans skilfully fall back to the south-east sector of their territory, evading encirclement and exhausting their pursuers. Smuts' Indian and European troops are suffering heavy losses from sickness and supply shortages. At last it is accepted that the best soldiers to fight in Africa are Africans. The KAR is rapidly expanded. By January 1917 it has twelve Battalions. By the end of the war it will have twenty-two. 6 KAR is reformed with ex-German askari in two Battalions, and 7 KAR is raised with Swahili and Zanzibaris. By late 1917, von Lettow Vorbeck is being harried from one place to another, the strength of his guerilla force steadily eroded. Finally, having held out to November 1918, he surrenders in Northern Rhodesia to the Northern Rhodesia Police and to 1/4 KAR. Since 1916, the campaign has been fought mainly by black African units – those raised locally and those from Nigeria, the Gold Coast, and The Gambia.
1919–1939: the KAR is reduced to six Battalions (numbered 1 to 6). Its role is seen as primarily IS (internal security). There is constant pressure to reduce its size, or even to convert it to an armed constabulary.
1919: German East Africa becomes Tanganyika Territory, administered by the British under a League of Nations trusteeship. 6 KAR is recruited in the Territory, but it can be used only for internal duties, not for 'foreign wars'.
1920: the British East Africa Protectorate becomes the Crown Colony of Kenya. In Somaliland, the 'mad mullah' fights his last campaign. The Royal Air Force plays a key role in suppressing the insurgency. The mullah's men are captured or dispersed into the desert. He himself evades capture but, in November, falls ill and dies.
1922: the Somaliland Camel Corps' two Companies are reinforced by a Company of askari from Nyasaland. 1 KAR and 2 KAR will provide a routine detachment every year through to 1940.
1924: the British South Africa Company's charter in Northern Rhodesia expires. The Territory becomes a formal British Protectorate.
1925: following mutinies in the previous year amongst the Sudanese units of the Egyptian Army, the British raise the Sudan Defence Force. Jubaland is ceded to Italian Somaliland and 5 KAR is disbanded at the end of the year.
1930: 5 KAR is reformed, but all KAR Battalions are reduced to half strength.
1933: the military wing of the Northern Rhodesia Police is formalised as the Northern Rhodesia Regiment.
1935–1936: ignoring the half-hearted League of Nations protests and sanctions, Mussolini's Italy invades and conquers Abyssinia. The Emperor Haile Selassie's unsophisticated army is overwhelmed by aerial bombing, mustard gas, tanks and

artillery. The arrival of powerful Italian forces on the borders of Kenya and British Somaliland, combined with the growing political ties between Mussolini and Hitler, sets the alarm bells ringing in Nairobi and London. If war comes, Italy can occupy the entire Horn of Africa, invade weakly defended Kenya, establish a naval base at Mombasa, and dominate the Indian Ocean maritime routes to the Cape and to India and the Far East. Plans are made to form two Brigade Groups from KAR units, if required, and half of the KAR Battalions are brought up to full strength. The Coast Defence Unit, KAR, is formed at Mombasa. East African soldiers are, for the first time, trained to operate coastal artillery, searchlights, and radio networks.

1937: the Kenya Regiment is raised from volunteer white settlers. A Territorial Force unit, it is intended to perform internal security duties in an emergency and to provide officers and NCOs for any future expansion of the KAR. The Northern Rhodesia Regiment (NRR) is reorganised on the KAR model so that it can be integrated into a KAR Brigade, if necessary.

1939: 7th (Uganda Territorial) Bn is raised for internal security duties in the event that 4 KAR is sent outside the Protectorate. It is embodied in September, and all KAR Battalions are brought up to full strength by local recruitment and with additional officers and NCOs from the Kenya Regiment and from Southern Rhodesia. Action is taken to raise more KAR Battalions and, for the first time, to create the services and supporting arms needed for modern warfare (artillery, engineers, etc).

1940: the Italians at last declare war. They invade Egypt from Cyrenaica, but are driven out with heavy loss by O'Connor's British and Indian Divisions. They also mount an incursion into the Sudan, but are then deterred by the lightly equipped Sudan Defence Force. They overrun British Somaliland in August. The garrison, which includes 1 NRR, 2 KAR, and 1 (EA) Light Battery, is evacuated by the Royal Navy. Also rescued is Nyasaland Company (2 KAR) of the Somaliland Camel Corps. The Somali Companies are disbanded and the men return to their homes. Two KAR Brigades deploy to defend the northern frontier of Kenya and are reinforced by two Brigades of the Royal West African Frontier Force and a Brigade from the Union of South Africa.

1941: all Italian forces in East Africa are destroyed after being attacked from north and south. The northern thrust consists of 4th and 5th Indian Divisions (fresh from the Western Desert) and the Sudan Defence Force. The southern thrust is made by 11th (African) and 12th (African) Divisions supported by 1st (South African) Division. The two forces meet at Amba Alagi. The Indians and the South Africans move to Egypt, the West Africans return home to refit. Units from the Free French and Belgian colonies join 25th and 26th (EA) Brigades for the final stage of the campaign - after the rains - culminating in the capture of Gondar.

1941-1942: the Somaliland Camel Corps is reformed as an armoured car unit. Irregular Somali Companies are raised as POW camp guards and are later used to patrol the border with Vichy-controlled Djibouti. Two Somali KAR Battalions (71 and 72) are raised. In Italian Somaliland, now British administered, the Somalia Gendarmerie are formed (with a military wing).

1942: Japan has entered the war and East Africa begins to look to the east. Soon Africans will be fighting for India just as in the past Indians fought for the Crown in Africa. A proposal to immediately send East African troops to Burma proves impracticable, but 21 (EA) Brigade moves to Ceylon. With more officers and NCOs from the United Kingdom and Southern Rhodesia, the KAR and the NRR are further expanded (to forty-four and eight Battalions respectively). All the main supporting services and arms have been further increased. The Coast Irregulars are raised for 'hit and run' and scouting operations. They will be renamed the East African Scouts. Concern over future Japanese intentions focuses upon the island of Madagascar. If the Vichy French administation grants free access, as they did in Indo-China, the Japanese can use it as a forward operating base to attack Allied shipping in the Mozambique Channel or even as a springboard to invade mainland Africa. The Royal Navy attacks Diego Suarez and puts ashore a British and then East African force. A second landing is made at Majunga.

The French resist fiercely but, with the arrival of a South African Brigade, they are driven nearly 1000 miles down the length of the island to Ambavalao (where they surrender). The KAR is given the task of providing a garrison force for Madagascar and for the islands of the western Indian Ocean.
1943: the irregular Somaliland Companies are formally established as the Somaliland Scouts. In May, authority is given for the creation of 11th (East African) Division. It moves to Ceylon. After eleven months of jungle training, it joins XIVth Army in Burma. Its component elements come from Uganda (three rifle Bns), Kenya (two Bns), Tanganyika (two Bns), Nyasaland (three Bns), and Northern Rhodesia (one Bn), with their own supporting artillery, engineer, signals, and transport units.
1944: the East African Scouts are attached to 81st (West African) Division in the Kaladan Valley and are the first East African troops to see action in Burma. They serve from January to June and are then disbanded. In July, 11 (EA) Division is given the task of opening the way into Central Burma. Its objective is Kalewa, on the Chindwin River. To get there it must force a passage through the disease-ridden Kabaw Valley. From August to November, the Division fights two enemies - the Japanese and the monsoon. At times reliant solely upon air supply, it crosses the Chindwin in early December and creates a bridgehead (to be exploited by XXXIII Corps). Its job done, the Division is flown out to Assam for rest and refit. It will see no further action.
1945: 22 and 28 (EA) Brigades have arrived in Burma from Ceylon. 28 Brigade is quickly committed to battle. Its men come from Somaliland (71 KAR), from Uganda (7 KAR), and from Tanganyika (46 KAR). Aiming for Meiktila, the Brigade leads the drive by IV Corps down the Gangaw Valley. The Japanese react violently, and there is heavy fighting until April. The Brigade is then withdrawn to India, having had more casualties than any other East African Brigade, but having inflicted severe losses on its opponents. Meanwhile, between December 1944 and April 1945, 22 (EA) Brigade (comprising 1 KAR, 1 RAR, and 3 NRR), has been attached to XV Corps in the Arakan. It mops up the Japanese garrison on Ramree Island before joining 82 (WA) Division for operations around Taungup and Prome. In June, it crosses the Arakan Yomas to join XII Army. It assists in clearing the desperate starving Japanese in the Pegu Yomas, and rounding up the stragglers after the surrender in August. It is then repatriated directly from Rangoon. As the year ends, 11 (EA) Division and 28 (EA) Brigade begin to return home from India. The Kenya Regiment, its wartime training task completed, is disbanded.
1946: the KAR is quickly scaled down to seven battalions (numbered 1 to 6, plus 2/3rd Bn). The NRR is reduced to one battalion. 11 (EA) Division is disbanded.
1950: the Kenya Regiment is reformed. Italian Somaliland is returned to Italian control under a United Nations trusteeship.
1951-1952: 1 KAR and 2 KAR each serve tours of duty in Malaya, working with British Army and other Commonwealth units in the long campaign against the Communist-led insurgency. Two additional units are raised to replace them - 23 KAR and 26 KAR.
1952: sabotage and killings by Mau Mau (Kikuyu) gangs cause a State of Emergency to be declared in Kenya. British Army units are brought in to support the KAR and the Kenya Police. Southern Rhodesia sends air support. A savage campaign develops in the forests of the Aberdare Mountains and in parts of the Rift Valley. A unique feature of British tactics is the deployment of 'psuedo gangs' - former Mau Mau members who have changed sides, operating under British officers who disguise themselves as 'forest fighters'.
1953: Southern Rhodesia, Northern Rhodesia, and Nyasaland form a Central African Federation. 1 KAR, 2 KAR, and 1 NRR will constitute the Federation's armed forces.
1956: the Anglo-Egyptian Sudan becomes independent. The Sudan Defence Force is disbanded.
1957: progressive 'Africanisation' of the KAR's command ranks is commenced with the introduction of the rank of Effendi.
1960: the Mau Mau emergency is officially ended in January. The Kenya Regt becomes multi-racial. The political 'winds of change' are blowing hard throughout East Africa. The first major change, in this year, is the unification of British

Somaliland and Italian Somaliland to create the Republic of Somalia. Unlike its southern neighbours - when their turns come - it does not join the Commonwealth. In due course, the Soviets will exploit Somalia as a convenient base from which they will spread their political and military influence in other parts of Africa.
1961: Zanzibar prepares for independence. Promises of 'freedom' encourage local Africans to attack the Arabs. Order is restored by 5 KAR flown in from Kenya and 6 KAR from Tanganyika. It is arranged that the British Army's strategic force based in Kenya will remain there until such time as the region's transition to independence has been completed. Tanganyika becomes independent in December. 6 KAR and 26 KAR are retitled 1st and 2nd Tanganyika Rifles.
1962: Uganda becomes independent in October. 4 KAR reverts to its old title of Uganda Rifles.
1963: between February and June, outbreaks of lawlessness and general strikes in Swaziland cause the despatch from Nairobi to Mbabane of a Battalion Group based upon 1st Bn The Gordon Highlanders. They help local police to arrest the key trouble-makers before handing over to 1st Bn The Loyal Regiment. Peace is restored and Swaziland will become independent in 1968. Meanwhile, Zanzibar and Kenya approach their own independence celebrations. The formal handovers take place in December. The Kenya Battalions - 3 KAR, 5 KAR, and 11 KAR (formerly numbered 7, formerly 2/3) - temporarily retain those designations. Later they will become 1st, 2nd, and 3rd Kenya Rifles. The Kenya Regt is disbanded.
1964: as the year opens, British plans for a smooth transition of military power come under strain. The Central African Federation has been dismantled and 2 KAR (in Nyasaland) disbanded. In January, the Sultan of Zanzibar is overthrown by a coup d'état. He escapes to London via Tanganyika. Elsewhere, bemused by the rapid pace of events and by the actions of some local politicians, the Askari of several units are in an unsettled state. On 20 January, at Dar es Salaam, there is a mutiny by 1st Tanganyika Rifles. Order is restored by 45 Commando, Royal Marines, helicoptered ashore from HMS Centaur at the request of President Nyere. At the same time, 2nd Tanganyika Rifles at Tabora arrest all their officers. Within hours, there is a mutiny by the Uganda Rifles at Jinja. It is suppressed, at the request of the Ugandan Government, by British Army units (1st Bn Staffordshire Regiment and two companies of the Coldstream Guards) flown in from Kenya. There is a third mutiny, this time at Lanet, in Kenya, when 11 KAR takes over its barracks and breaks into the armoury. Elements of 3rd Regiment, Royal Horse Artillery, quickly arrive from Gilgil and disarm the mutineers. By mid February, the risk of further disorders has greatly diminished. In April, Zanzibar is federated with Tanganyika to form Tanzania, with China exerting much influence on the country's affairs. The Tanganyika Rifles are again renamed, this time as The People's Defence Force. In July, Nyasaland gains its independence as Malawi. 1 KAR is retitled 1st Malawi Rifles. In October, Northern Rhodesia becomes independent as Zambia. The Northern Rhodesia Rifles are retitled 1st Zambia Rifles.
1968: Mauritius becomes independent. Its military arm is the Special Mobile Force.
1971: the Seychelles become independent. Apart from the unresolved problem of breakaway Southern Rhodesia, Great Britain has shed herself of all responsibility for the peoples of continental Africa and the Indian Ocean islands in the space of just fifteen years. The KAR, a regiment which uniquely had bonded all the diverse racial and tribal groups between the Horn and Lake Nyasa, has become a series of national armies.

GENERAL REFERENCE

PERMANENT WAY
M F Hill * The English Press Ltd, Nairobi, in association with Hazell, Klatson & Viney Ltd, Aylesbury and London. Two matching volumes, green, gold, 10.0 x 7.5.
Volume I : The Story of the Kenya and Uganda Railway, East African Railways & Harbours. KUR&H crest on front cover, xii/582. 20 mono phots (sepia), 2 maps (bound in), footnotes, no appendixes, Index.
Volume II : The Story of the Tanganyika Railways. EAR&H crest on front cover, xii/295. 43 mono phots (sepia), 2 cartoons, one map (bound in), footnotes, Index. Apps: financial reports (1920-1948), table of principal commodities carried (1924-1948).
* The key to the European conquest of any new territory was transport. Explorers could move on foot, but trading companies and military commanders needed to move men and materiel in numbers and in quantity. East Africa has no system of navigable rivers connecting it with the Indian Ocean. Unlike Egypt or India, for example, the new arrivals could not utilise water transport to reach the hinterland. The motor vehicle was in its infancy, so a railway system was vital if the great African plateau - four thousand and more feet above sea level - was to be pacified and developed. The sub-titles to these two books are slightly misleading. The narratives do not deal exclusively with questions of track, locomotives and rolling stock. Instead, they cover the entire story - political, financial, technical and military - of the British advance into Kenya and Uganda, and the subsequent occupation of Tanganyika. The period covered extends from the 1880s through to circa 1943 (although some of the pictures were taken in 1944-1946, and the appendixes include material for 1948). The author highlights the role of local military forces in the construction of the railways (work in which officers of the Royal Engineers took a major part). He also explains how and why the railways were so important during WWI and WWII. Volume I, for example, has two chapters, devoted to WWI, which make numerous references to South African and Indian forces and to the NRR, the WAFF, and the KAR. A first-class background source. R/4 V/5. KHCL. JHFPJ.

THE KING'S AFRICAN RIFLES
A Study in the Military History of East and Central Africa, 1890-1945
Lieut Col H Moyse-Bartlett MBE * Gale & Polden Ltd, Aldershot, 1956. Black, gold, Regtl crest, 9.75 x 6.0, xix/727. Fp, 40 mono phots, 58 maps (47 printed in the text, 11 bound in), Glossary, Bibliography, Index. Apps: Bn locations (1939-1945), notes on uniforms, idem Bn bands, idem campaign medallic awards.
* Just as Haywood and Clarke's history of the RWAFF is a tour de force in its field, so does this huge work by Moyse-Bartlett stand head and shoulders above anything else ever written about East African soldiers. Very deeply researched, cogently arranged, the narrative contains a mass of information which reflects the book's sub-title. The author does not simply recount the services of the KAR. He sets them in the larger context of Europe's exploration of, and exploitation of, the eastern half of the African continent. From page 475 onwards, he covers the events of WWII - the campaigns in Somaliland, Abyssinia and Eritrea in 1941, in Madagascar in 1942, and in Burma in 1944-1945. Many British officers, and some African ORs, are named in the text. A superb book. R/4 V/5. IWM/NAM. BCC/RP.

THE KING'S AFRICAN RIFLES
Lieut Col H Moyse-Bartlett MBE * Printed by Regal Press Ltd, Nairobi, for the Regtl Committee, n.d. (c.1952). Stiff card, stapled, green, black, 7.25 x 5.0, -/16. No ills, no maps, no appendixes, no Index.
* As the Foreword by Maj Gen W A Dimoline explains, the KAR had no permanent establishment of European personnel. Officers, WOs, and some specialist NCOs, served with KAR Bns on secondment from their parent British Army units, usually for two or three years, sometimes longer. During the 1950s, almost all of the Subalterns were National Service officers, serving in East Africa for only

eighteen months. This booklet was intended to give new arrivals some idea of the KAR's history and its Regtl spirit. R/4 V/1. PC. RP.

THE KING'S AFRICAN RIFLES

Lieut Col H Moyse Bartlett MBE * Unpublished quarto TS with many MS annotations, n.d. (c.1971-1972). Disbound in single folder, -/171. No ills, no maps, no Index. Apps: list of Regtl days of the post-war Bns.

* Moyse-Bartlett's major history (vide preceding page) concluded with the events of 1945. At a later date, he was asked to compile a more condensed version, with the story continued through to the transformation of the constituent Bns into the armies of the newly independent parent countries. The book was to have been published by Leo Cooper in the FAMOUS REGIMENTS series, but the project was shelved. This is the author's original typed working draft, with many alterations and deletions in his own hand which would have reduced the length of the text if it had been published. It covers the evolution of the Regt from its earliest days and its services in WWI and WWII. It then breaks fresh ground by describing the post-war commitment to the campaign in Malaya and the much larger commitment to the Mau Mau campaign. The story concludes with the demise of the old KAR in the 1960s. This is the only connected history of the Regt from beginning to end. R/5 V/4. RHL. JALH.

Note: Rhodes House Library reference MSS.Afr.s.1715-197 (Box 12-C).

K.A.R.

Being an Unofficial History of the Origins and Activities of the King's African Rifles

W Lloyd-Jones * Arrowsmith, London, 1926. Maroon, gold, 'Askari' motif, 9.5 x 5.5, -/296. Fp, 37 mono phots, one line drawing, one map, Bibliography, no appendixes, Index.

* The sub-title - 'unofficial account' - is somewhat misleading. This is a sound authoritative description of the Regt's roots and services between 1890 and 1925. It covers the anti-slavery and punitive operations of the period, the campaign against von Lettow Vorbeck, and the 1920 campaign against the 'Mad Mullah'. Written in a pleasingly readable style, the narrative includes many helpful commentaries on Regtl attitudes, with quotations from the citations for a number of individual gallantry awards. R/3 V/4. MODL/RHL/IWM. DJB/RP.

Note: the same author wrote HAVASH, this being a memoir of his travels and his services in Kenya, Abyssinia, and Somaliland as a KAR officer from 1910 onwards (Arrowsmith, London, 1925). For information regarding an even earlier period, reference should be made to THE RISE OF OUR EAST AFRICAN EMPIRE - EARLY EFFORTS IN NYASALAND AND UGANDA, by Capt F D Lugard DSO (William Blackwood & Sons, Edinburgh and London, 1893, in two volumes).

THE INFANTRY OF EAST AFRICA COMMAND, 1890-1944

Anon * East Africa Command, in collaboration with the Ministry of Information, East Africa, Nairobi, n.d. (c.1944). Soft card, dark brown, white, 9.75 x 7.25, -/40. Fp (pencil sketch, '1890 Askari greeting 1944 Askari'), 42 mono phots, 14 cld ills (unit flashes), 9 line drawings, one map (bound in, showing the territories in which Askari were recruited), no appendixes, no Index.

* A compilation of brief histories for each of the infantry units which came under East Africa Command during WWII - the principal KAR Bns, The Northern Rhodesia Regt, The Rhodesian African Rifles, The Mauritius Regt, The Kenya Regt, The East African Scouts, The Somaliland Scouts, and the 71st and 72nd Somali Bns KAR. Each account occupies roughly one page and is accompanied by a colour print of that unit's flash. A centre double page has a family tree showing the evolution of all of these units and their relationship with each other. The chart is incomplete because some smaller units are not mentioned. It also has some inaccuracies regarding 5 KAR and some Somaliland units. However, this attractive little book does provide a useful bird's-eye view. R/5 V/4. PC. GTB.

Note: given the huge expansion of East Africa's armed forces during WWII, the listings of units in this booklet - which in any event deals only with infantry - are far from complete. Additional information can be found in the papers of Maj M W Beedle, deposited by him in the National Army Museum Archives (reference 8403-26-11). Amongst other interesting items is a folder containing thirty-eight loose folios, drawn in crayon circa 1960, which illustrate almost all of the hat flashes and badges of the KAR Bns and East African supporting arms raised during WWII. Each sketch is accompanied by a hand-written note which describes the badge in detail and quotes the authority for its design and issue. These notes include important comments on possible errors in Moyse-Bartlett's listings of wartime KAR Bns . JALH.

World War I

INDIAN ARMY IN EAST AFRICA 1914-1918

S D Prahan * Kay Printers, New Delhi, 'First Published in India in 1991 by Mrs A H Marwah on behalf of the National Book Organisation', 1991. Green, white, 8.5 x 5.5, xi/172. No ills, 14 maps, Bibliography, chapter notes, Index. Apps: notes on the Settlement of Versailles, Order of Battle (5.3.1916), list of veterans interviewed by the author.

* Prahan, Reader in History, Punjabi University, Patiala, has the twin gifts of clarity and compression. The first chapter - 'The Indian Army before the First World War' - covers the period from 1678 to 1914 in five remarkably lucid pages. The Indian Army's status in 1914, and the attendant political framework, is covered in fourteen pages. The bulk of the narrative then concentrates upon the role and activities of Indian Expeditionary Force 'B' in the East African campaign between September 1914 and September 1917. It is crammed with information on who did what, where, and when, and is based largely upon the unpublished IEF War Diary. The text is heavily supported with chapter notes throughout. The theme is essentially a statement of movements and engagements, offering little in the way of analysis. Despite some type-setting errors, the book is easy to read and is well indexed. R/1 V/4. CFHT. SODW.

Note: reference may be made also to the JOURNAL OF THE UNITED SERVICE INSTITUTION OF INDIA, April 1919, Vol XLVIII, pages 244-261. This has a useful article by Brev Col G M Orr DSO, 11th Lancers, and having the same title as that chosen by Prahan - THE INDIAN ARMY IN EAST AFRICA.

THREE YEARS OF WAR IN EAST AFRICA

Capt Angus Buchanan MC * John Murray, London, 1919. Pale green, dark green and black, 'Soldier with palm tree' motif, 8.75 x 5.5, xvii/247. Fp, 7 mono phots, 3 maps (bound in), no appendixes, Index.

* Buchanan was a Canadian officer with the 25th (Service) Bn (Frontiersmen), Royal Fusiliers. This (British Army) unit was in East Africa from May 1915 until late 1917 (when it was re-embarked for England). During that time it saw much action, being almost wiped out at the Battle of Mahiwa. This is an unsophisticated but enjoyable memoir which includes the author's observations on the country and its wildlife. The 'historical' content is limited, but the author was one of the very few British officers to commit his experiences to paper while they were still fresh in mind. Useful background reading. R/4 V/2. RCSL/RHL. TAB.

Note: for further information concerning The Legion of Frontiersmen, refer to the Index of Authors (Geoffrey A Pocock). For comprehensive accounts of the entire campaign, reference may be made to BATTLE FOR THE BUNDU - THE FIRST WORLD WAR IN EAST AFRICA, by Charles Miller (Purnell Book Services Ltd, London, 1974) (first published by Macdonald and Janes), and to TANGANYIKA GUERILLA, by Maj J R Sibley (Ballantine, USA, 1971, and Pan Books Ltd, London, 1973).

World War II

ASKARIS AT WAR IN ABYSSINIA
Kenneth Gandar Dower * East African Standard Ltd, Nairobi, for the East Africa Command, by the Ministry of Information, East Africa, n.d. (c.1943). Illustrated soft card, pale buff/sepia, dark blue, 'Charging Askari' motif, 9.5 x 7.25, iv/55 (plus four plates of illustrations, not numbered). 123 mono phots (incl 64 portraits of African award winners), 5 sketches, one map (pasted inside the rear cover), no appendixes, no Index.
* Presumably intended to boost public morale, the narrative is written in simple English and seems to have been aimed at an African (rather than European) readership. The value of the book, apart from its good range of photographs, is to be found in the fact that the author made a clear attempt to interpret the war from the viewpoint of the Askari and his family. Many individual African soldiers are mentioned in the text. Unusual and interesting. R/5 V/3. NAM. JALH/GR.
Note: another official source - of greater substance - is THE ABYSSINIAN CAMPAIGNS, THE OFFICIAL STORY OF THE CONQUEST OF ITALIAN EAST AFRICA, anon, (HMSO, London, n.d.). Thought to have been published in 1942, this too was aimed at a wide readership but, in this case, European rather than African.

THE FIRST TO BE FREED
The Record of British Military Administration in Eritrea and Somaliland, 1941-1943
K C Gandar Dower * Published by the East Africa Command in conjunction with the Ministry of Information, East Africa, Nairobi, n.d. (c.1943). Illustrated soft card, 'Army personnel/Somali girl' motif (on front and rear covers respectively), red, white, 9.0 x 5.75, -/72. Fp, 34 mono phots, one line drawing, 2 maps, no appendixes, no Index.
* Another wartime publication, well written, and clearly intended for propaganda purposes. It deals with the work of the military administration in the wake of the ejection of Italian forces. A unique feature are the passages which describe the raising and intended role of the Eritrea Police and the Somalia Gendarmerie.
R/4 V/3. RHL. JALH.

THE KING'S AFRICAN RIFLES IN MADAGASCAR
Kenneth Gandar Dower * Published by the East Africa Command in conjunction with the Ministry of Information, Nairobi, n.d. (c.1943). Illustrated soft card, sepia/red, 9.0 x 6.75. 87 mono phots (interesting but poorly reproduced, in sepia), 2 maps (cld, of excellent quality), no appendixes, no Index.
* A popular account, by the War Correspondent who accompanied it, of the work done by 22 (EA) Bde between 4 May and 6 November, 1942. He explains briefly the main landings at Diego Suarez, but then concentrates upon the landings at Majunga [spear-headed by 29 (British) Bde and exploited by 22 (East African) Bde]. The 600 miles march down the length of the island to Ambavalao is described in concise detail. The clearly drawn maps are helpful. R/4 V/3. PACL/MODL. LM/AMM.
Note: the author later wrote a personal account, with the title INTO MADAGASCAR.

RHINO REVIEW
The History of the East African Forces in the Burma Campaign, 1943, 44, 45
Maj T D Bridge, George Kinnear and Gerald Hanley * The Statesman Press, Calcutta, January 1946. Illustrated paper covers, 'KAR bugler and East African unit badges' motif, 14.25 x 9.75, -/43. Fp, 93 mono phots, 19 line drawings, 2 maps (one tipped in at the rear, one printed on outside rear cover), Index. Apps: H&A (page 35, incomplete), Order of Battle (with names of officers commanding the Div elements).
* This unusually proportioned booklet, liberally illustrated, was produced on the initiative of Maj Bridge in the space of a few weeks in October 1945 while waiting to depart India. His co-authors were both War Correspondents. Their aim was to ensure that the services of East African forces in Burma should be recorded before they were dispersed and disbanded. Of the 530,000 Empire and

Commonwealth troops who served in that theatre of war, 340,000 were Indian, 100,000 were British, and 90,000 were Colonial troops from West and East Africa. The vast majority of the Africans were not professional soldiers but hastily trained volunteer tribesmen. The sub-title of this useful booklet is not entirely accurate. The narrative makes no mention of 22 and 28 (EA) Independent Bdes or of the East African Scouts. It deals solely with the work done by 11 (EA) Div, and the main title derives from the 'Black Rhino' flash worn by that Division.
R/4 V/4. NAM/IWM/RHL. RP/JALH.

MONSOON VICTORY

Gerald Hanley (Honorary Capt) * Collins, London, 1946. Yellow, gold, 8.0 x 5.75, -/256. Fp, 12 mono phots (all official PR pictures), no maps, no appendixes, no Index.
* Collins was a War Correspondent attached to 11 (EA) Div. He had already co-authored RHINO REVIEW (vide preceding entry), so this book - MONSOON VICTORY - was his later personal account of his time with the Division in the Kabaw Valley in 1944. As such, it has several weaknesses. The overall tone is condescending towards East African soldiers in general, and he neglects to mention any units other than those of the KAR. His account contains few observations on the tactics and strategy of either the Allies or the Japanese. However, and allowing for these limitations, he paints a general picture of what it was like for East African troops to find themselves fighting Asiatics in a country far from their own.
R/4 V/2. PC. RH.

BEYOND THE CALL OF DUTY
African Deeds of Bravery in Wartime

Salmon E Marling * Macmillan & Co, London, 1952. Illustrated stiff card, 'Medical Orderly with wounded Askari', motif, 7.25 x 5.0, xiv/49. 6 line drawings, no maps, Glossary, no Index. Apps: citations for the awards described in the main narrative (four pages).
* 'The MS for this book was received from the East African Literature Bureau at whose request it was written'. Presumably intended as a 'reader' for use in East African schools, written in simple English, it covers eight officially recognised acts of bravery by East African soldiers during WWII - four in Abyssinia, one in Madagascar, and three in Burma. Little has ever been written about individual Askari, hence this slim volume is a rarity. R/4 V/2. NAM. JALH.

The Mau Mau Campaign

COUNTER INSURGENCY IN KENYA
A Study of Military Operations in Kenya

Anthony Clayton * Kenya Litho, for Transafrica Publishers, Nairobi, 1976. Illustrated soft card, red, white, 8.5 x 6.5, viii/63. 12 mono phots (centre section, folios not numbered), one map, footnotes, no appendixes, no Index.
* The Mau Mau emergency began in 1952, was officially declared to be at an end in 1957, but continued to cause problems until 1960. This brief account, written by a lecturer in history at the RMA Sandhurst, covers the entire period. It is a sound and balanced account of a controversial episode but, like several other books on the same subject, it is diminished by the lack of those features which would assist a researcher - there is no Index and no appendixes which might have detailed the Crown units engaged, their casualties, the financial costs, etc.
R/3 V/3. NAM. JALH.
Note: to obtain a contrasting interpretation of the campaign, reference should be made to MAU MAU GENERAL, by Waruhiu Itote, otherwise known as General China (East African Publishing House, Nairobi, 1967). Educated by the Church of Scotland Mission, he served as a Corporal with 36 KAR in Burma. That experience caused him to question the status quo in this own country. Joining the Mau Mau movement, he became a leading 'forest fighter'. His thoughtful autobiography is well written, concise, and a valuable insider's record of strategy and tactics.

DIVISIONS

REPORT ON THE OPERATIONS OF 11th (AFRICAN) DIVISION BETWEEN FEBRUARY 14th AND APRIL 6th, 1941
During which the Division advanced from the River Tana to Addis Abeba (sic)
Anon * Facsimile foolscap TS in soft card covers, buff, black, small Italian map ('Africa Orientale') pasted on the front cover, n.d. (c.1941), iii/28/xi (the latter being the appendixes). 25 mono phots (Italian postcards pasted in), 7 maps (one reproduced in the text, 6 folding, bound in at the rear), no Index. Apps: notes on moves and locations, casualty statistics, details of Italian prisoners taken and equipment captured.
* The ODRP Report credits the authorship to Capt James Walker, Adjutant of 6 KAR, but this is most improbable. It is more likely to have been compiled by one or more officers of the Divsl Staff, acting upon an instruction from GHQ Nairobi. The document states the basic facts of the Div's movements and actions. It is believed that no more than a dozen or so copies were made and distributed.
R/5 V/3. RHL/NAM. JALH.
Note: Rhodes House reference MSS.Afr.s.1715-284 (Box 17).

AN ACCOUNT OF THE OPERATIONS OF 11 (A) DIVISION IN ABYSSINIA FROM THE FALL OF ADDIS ABABA ON APRIL 6 TO THE SURRENDER OF GENERAL GAZZERA ON JULY 3, 1941
Anon * Facsimile foolscap TS in soft card covers, strawberry, black, dated 1941, vi/61. Fp, 5 mono phots, two sketches (panoramas), 11 maps (bound in), no Index. Apps: locations of all units on 6.4.1941, Orders of Battle (four, at various dates).
* Written in the immediate aftermath of the campaign, this account is evidently based upon operational documents and unit War Diaries and is therefore entirely reliable. It covers in precise detail the events of mid-1941 as experienced by 1st Nigerian Bde and 22nd (EA) Bde (Fowcol) in the south and west, and by 1st (SA) Inf Bde (Pincol) in the north (around Amba Alagi). It gives a clear picture of Wingate's destruction of Col Mareventano's force and includes an interesting analysis of how various administrative problems were overcome. This is a primary source for the post-Addis Ababa phase of the campaign. R/5 V/4. NAM. MWB.

12th AFRICAN DIVISION - HISTORY OF GONDAR OPERATIONS
Anon * Facsimile foolscap TS, seen disbound, dated 1942 but no other details shown, -/29 (15 of text, 12 of appendixes, 2 not numbered). No ills, no maps, no Index. Apps: tables of battle casualty statistics, Orders of Battle (for 7.11.1941 and for the main attack).
* A detailed record of the operations leading to the surrender of the Italian forces at Gondar, November 1941. The text seems to have been based very largely upon unit War Diaries and is therefore reliable. R/5 V/3. IWM. JALH.

Note:

To place these unpublished records in the context of a commercially published account, reference should be made to AN IMPROVISED WAR - THE ABYSSINIAN CAMPAIGN OF 1940-1941, by Michael Glover (Leo Cooper, London, 1987). Further important references to the Abyssinia campaign will be found in the South Africa section of this bibliography.

22 BRIGADE

East Africa, 1941

REPORT ON THE OPERATIONS OF 22nd EAST AFRICAN INFANTRY BRIGADE BETWEEN JAN 23rd AND JUN 21st, 1941
Anon * Publication details not shown, probably reproduced at GHQ Nairobi, 1941. Facsimile foolscap TS on soft card covers, fawn, -/30. See footnote for ills and maps, no Index. Apps: Order of Battle of Bole Column.
* This is a terse but complete description of the Bde's remarkable advance from the Tana River through Jubaland, Italian Somaliland and Abyssinia, leading to the occupation of Addis Ababa, and thence past the lakes to the capture of Gimma. Crossing huge distances over harsh terrain, the Bde fought and advanced for five months without pause. Its component elements were 1 KAR, 5 KAR and 6 KAR (from Nyasaland, Kenya and Tanganyika respectively). It was supported by 22 Mountain Bty RA and 54 Field Coy, EA Engineers, and had several Nigerian and South African units under command at various times. The Report is based upon the Bde War Diary, situation reports, and operation orders, and was compiled immediately after the conclusion of that phase of the campaign. R/5 V/4. NAM/RHL. MWB/JALH.
Note: two copies have been sighted. The NAM copy has 10 maps (bound in) but no illustrations. The RHL copy has no maps, but it has 15 Italian postcards pasted in. An additional source is THE TWO THOUSAND MILE WAR, by W E Crosskill (Robert Hale, London, 1980). Crosskill was the Brigade Intelligence Officer during the period described above. The second half of his book is devoted to the operations around Gondar.

Madagascar, 1942

ACCOUNT OF THE OPERATIONS OF 22 (EA) INFANTRY BRIGADE IN MADAGASCAR 10 September - 6 November, 1942
Capt Robin R Thorne * Produced by 'Bde HQ, Madagascar, 1943'. Facsimile foolscap TS in soft card covers, buff, pinned, iii/63. No ills, 13 maps, 2 sketch plans, no Index. Apps: Bde Order of Battle, French Order of Battle, notes on air support, notes on the Bde Group, summary of events.
* A detailed but very readable account of the role of the Bde in ensuring that the Japanese would not be permitted by the Vichy French to use the island as a forward operating base. The Bde landed on the north east coast at Majunga after 29th Independent Bde (British Army) had created a beach-head. It advanced 660 miles in only eight weeks. Along the way, it defeated a Vichy force of 6000 men, took 3000 prisoners, and captured 16 field guns, 52 heavy machine-guns, and 23 mortars. In the process, the Bde lost 4 British officers and 23 African ORs killed, and 7 British officers and 75 African ORs wounded. The narrative includes, inter alia, a detailed account of the initial actions at Majunga by 29 Bde.
The value of the operation, and the need to occupy the island, was demonstrated when a Japanese submarine attacked and seriously damaged the elderly battleship HMS Ramillies at Diego Suarez, shortly after the initial British landings there.
R/5 V/4. NAM. JP.
Note: it is known that just ten copies of this Report were printed and distributed. Capt Thorne was the Brigade Intelligence Officer.

Burma, 1945

OPERATIONS OF 22 EAST AFRICAN BRIGADE
From 15 March to 16 May, 1945
Brig R F Johnstone * Facsimile foolscap TS, dated 1 June 1945. Seen disbound, in a folder, -/12. 7 mono phots (aerial recce, loose), 4 maps (original issues, with the Bde's route and locations traced in), no Index. Apps: casualty statistics.
* A straightforward narrative of the most active period of the Bde's services in Burma, written within a month of the end of the operations by its Brigadier and intended to bring out the lessons learned from them. The Bde as it served in Burma was much changed from that which had served in the East Africa campaign. Only 1/1 KAR remained. The other two Bns were from the Rhodesias - 3 NRR and 1 RAR. The Bde had difficulties with its air supply because, unlike formations from West Africa, it did not have its own trained Auxiliary porters.
R/5 V/4. IWM (Documents). JALH.

OTHER CORPS

World War I

THE CARRIER CORPS
Military Labor in the East African Campaign, 1914-1918
Geoffrey Hodges * Greenwood Press, New York and London, 1986. Buff, black, 9.5 x 6.0, -/244. Fp, 9 mono phots, 2 maps, Glossary, Bibliography, Index. Apps: labour recruitment statistics (Kenya and Uganda), notes on pay, notes on medical considerations, death rates, equipment.
* Meticulously researched, poorly printed but nicely bound, this book is a microscopic examination by an American academic of all aspects of Great Britain's need for muscle-power in trying to defeat von Lettow Vorbeck. Given the lack of roads and railways in East Africa at that time, the fighting men could be sustained in action only if they had an immense retinue of porters to carry the food and ammunition which they needed. As the author makes clear, this was a campaign uniquely influenced by logistics. The British recruited, at one time or another during the war, a total of 500,000 men as 'native carriers'. Of these, 180,000 came from the tribes of Kenya. Others came from Uganda and the neighbouring territories. They handled 50-pound loads through semi-desert, bush and swamp, and suffered severe hardship in the process. Although non-combatants, the men of the Carrier Corps had more casualties than all of the fighting formations combined. The African Native Medical Corps was available to care for them, but the book demonstrates that the human cost of the East Africa campaign, which dragged on for four years, was much higher than the official 'military' casualty lists might imply. This is a fascinating insight into bush warfare. R/1 V/5. RMAS/RCSL. RP.

THE AFRICAN NATIVE MEDICAL CORPS IN THE EAST AFRICAN CAMPAIGN
Maj G J Keane DSO and Capt D G Tomblings ANMC * The Cornwell Press Ltd, London, n.d. (c.1920). Dark blue, gold, 9.0 x 6.0, -/63. Fp, 7 mono phots, no maps, no Index. Apps: Roll of Honour, list of officers and BNCOs, idem African SNCOs, nominal roll of ORs recruited from various Missions, notes on scales of pay and equipment, etc.
* In August 1914, the Uganda Stretcher Bearer Corps (later retitled Uganda Native Medical Corps) was raised in haste in Kampala. It was soon found that the men's educational standards were too low for the duties required of them, so later intakes were recruited mainly from various Mission schools throughout Uganda. The UNMC was disbanded following the capture of Tabora, but it was soon reactivated and then expanded as the African Native Medical Corps. From 1917 onwards, new recruits were trained at Dar-es-Salaam and then posted to forty different Field Ambulances and military hospitals located everywhere between Abyssinia and Nyasaland. The text of this excellent history incorporates several lists of awards, and a roll of former UNMC personnel who transferred to the ANMC in April 1917. The story concludes with disbandment in 1919. R/5 V/5. AL/MODL. GTB.

World War II

THE EAST AFRICAN ELECTRICAL AND MECHANICAL ENGINEERS
Anon * East African Standard Ltd, Nairobi, 1943. Glossy paper, 'African fitter' motif, black, white, superimposed Corps colour stripes (blue, yellow, red), 9.0 x 6.0, -/24. Fp, 32 mono phots, no maps, no appendixes, no Index.
* Written entirely in Ki-Swahili and presumably intended as a morale-booster for the men of the Corps and their families, this is a broad-brush description of the Corps and its work at that stage of the war (1943). The historical value is almost nil, but the fact that the book even exists is a reminder of East Africa's contribution to the Allied war effort. R/5 V/1. MODL. AMM.

THE STORY OF THE EAST AFRICAN ARMY EDUCATION CORPS

Maj F G Sellwood OBE MC * East African Standard Ltd, Nairobi, 1943. Illustrated soft card, 'EAAEC personnel' motif, black/white, 8.5 x 5.5, -/10/ii. Fp, 11 mono phots, no maps, no appendixes, no Index.

* The Corps was formed in Nairobi on 7 February 1942. Its initial task was to create a programme for the teaching of Ki-Swahili - East Africa's lingua franca - to newly arrived European officers and BNCOs who had no previous experience of the region and its people. Even locally enlisted Europeans, who had grown up with the language, needed some instruction so that they could add military terminology to their usual vocabulary. The programme was then extended by the creation of a central school at which African language instructors were trained to teach the language, at unit and sub-unit level, to the men of the new KAR Bns and the newly formed Corps. Most Africans spoke (still speak) more than one language over and above that of their own tribe. Ki-Swahili is spoken freely from Southern Somaliland and Southern Sudan down to Southern Tanganyika (Tanzania), but it is not of uniform quality. The sophisticated Ki-Swahili of Eastern Kenya (the word means 'the language of the people of the coast') is very different to the 'bush' or 'upcountry' Swahili commonly heard in, for example, the northern Districts of Uganda. Indeed, many inland Africans find pure Ki-Swahili almost incomprehensible. With all of this in mind, there was a clear and immediate need for the EA Army Education Corps and its special skills. The Corps also assumed responsibility for ASKARI, the EA Command soldiers' newspaper (printed in Swahili) and for some of the broadcasts put out by local radio stations. This is a very condensed summary of work which, at the time, was vital in providing cohesion to a fighting force drawn from a wide variety of geographical locations and tribal groupings. R/5 V/2. MODL/IWM. AMM.

A SPEAR FOR FREEDOM

Anon * Printed in Nottingham, by HMSO, for the Ministry of Information, n.d. (c.1944). Illustrated soft card, 'African soldier' motif, black/white, 4.00 x 7.00 (landscape), 43 mono phots (one per page), no maps, no appendixes, no Index.

* A photographic essay, presented in 'comic book' format. It tells the story of Kasarishu, a representative enlistee into the East African Military Labour Service. It seems to have been sponsored by the EA Intelligence Corps (the pictures are credited to Capt A A Dickson of that Corps). It was clearly intended for publicity purposes, to encourage recruitment and to reassure the families of young men who had volunteered to leave their villages for wartime service. A curiosity, of minimal research value. R/5 V/1. USCL. TP.

AFRICANS IN KHAKI

D H Barber * Edinburgh House Press, London, 1948. Illustrated soft card, khaki/white/black, 7.25 x 4.75, viii/120. 22 line drawings (by Mary Gernat), one map, no appendixes, no Index.

* A personal memoir by a young British officer, of strong Christian convictions, who served in WWII with the African Pioneer Corps. The narrative tends to wander from passages of personal philosophy to accounts of daily happenings, but it is interesting as a mirror of the culture shock experienced by a nice young man plunged into a totally new world. Some of his brother officers were British, others were Mauritians and Palestinians (Arab and Jew). He served with 8999 Company which had in its ranks tribesmen from various parts of Uganda (Pagan, Anglican, Roman Catholic and Muslim). The Coy was employed on logistic duties in Egypt from 1942 to 1945. The author makes some interesting observations on the men under his command during that time and his account is the only known published record of the Corps. R/4 V/1. RMAS. RP.

EGYPT AND THE SUDAN

THE FIGHTING SUDANESE
H C Jackson * MacMillan & Co Ltd, New York and London, 1954. Red, gold, 7.5 x 5.0, xvi/85. No ills, 2 maps (one printed in the text, one bound in at the rear, folding), no appendixes, no Index.
* A generalised account of the Sudanese warrior from post-Omdurman to post-WWII. The author discusses the fighting traditions and qualities of the various tribes of the Sudan, but the bulk of his narrative is devoted to the services of the Sudan Defence Force during the Darfur insurgency of 1921 and the attempted Italian invasion of 4 July 1940. It was on this date that a major assault by 10,000 Italian troops, backed by artillery, armour and bomber aircraft, was blocked by 600 lightly armed soldiers of the SDF. The Italians were held and finally driven back into Eritrea when more Allied forces moved up from Kenya, Uganda and South Africa. Sadly, this brilliant episode, and the role of the SDF, is covered here very inadequately. The book is useful as far as it goes, but is a lost opportunity in terms of recording the history of a remarkable Regt. R/4 V/2. PCAL. RP.
Note: further background reading is provided by FIRE AND SWORD IN THE SUDAN - FIGHTING AND SERVING THE DERVISHES, 1879-1895, by Col R Slatin Pasha CB CMG (first published in 1896, revised 1897, republished in facsimile by Lionel Leventhal, London, 1990).

NOTE ON THE HISTORY OF THE CAMEL CORPS
El Miralai G A V Keays Bey * Published in the SUDAN NOTE & RECORD, Vol XXII, 1939, Part I, pages 103-123. No ills, no maps, no Index. Apps: 'Actions and Patrols in which the Camel Corps has taken part' (1884-1930), 'Officers who have Commanded the Camel Corps' (1898-1939).
* The Eyptian Camel Corps was raised in 1883 for service in Lower Egypt. Initial strength was 20 native troopers of the Egyptian Army, commanded by Lieut R A Marriott, Royal Marines Artillery. The establishment soon increased to 6 British officers and 200 Egyptian rank and file. The Corps served with the Field Column during the Gordon Relief Expedition (1884-1885) and gained a fine reputation as a reconnaissance unit. During the 1896 campaign for the reconquest of the Sudan, it fought at Firket, Hafir and Atbara. By 1901 it had moved its HQ to Kordofan and began recruiting Sudanese in place of Egyptians as officers and as troopers. Its role for the next 40 years was essentially IS and 'maintaining the presence', with a remarkable ability to swiftly cover hundreds of miles of broken country when responding to an emergency. Mechanisation was commenced in the mid-1930s and was complete by 1937. R/4 V/2. RSCL. GC/RP.

TALES OF THE SUDAN DEFENCE FORCE
To the Former Bimbs and Beys of the Sudan Defence Force
John Orlebar * Published privately, facsimile typescript, no details shown, 1981. Soft card, stapled, cream, black, SDF badge, 9.75 x 7.25, -/86. Fp, one other mono phot, 3 maps, one diagram, Glossary, no appendixes, no Index.
* As the title suggests, and as the author confirms in his Foreword, 'this is not a history of the SDF'. It is an anthology of reminiscences and anecdotes by former officers. Amusing and informative, their tales illuminate the special relationship which existed between the British and the diverse unsophisticated tribesmen with whom they shared their lives as soldiers of the Crown. The period covered is 1919 to 1950, so the material is not restricted solely to peacetime patrols and skirmishes. It includes several useful accounts of WWII services which receive scant attention in the official histories, e.g. actions against the Italians at Kassala, the battle for Keren, and joint operations with the LRDG around Kufra. Many officers are named and quoted in the text, and there are references to now forgotten formations such as the Motor Machine Gun Companies, The Sudan Horse, and The Sudan Artillery. In 1956 the Sudan became an independent State. The SDF was disbanded, its traditions and its men providing the basis for the new Sudan Army. R/4 V/2. RCSL. RP.
Note: the author later produced a Volume II, this again being a collection of anecdotes but relating mainly to WWII (Crossprint, Newport, Isle of Wight, 1986).

AUSTRALIANS AND EGYPT, 1914-1919

Suzanne Brugger * Melbourne University Press, Melbourne, 1980. Brown, gold, 8.5 x 5.5, v/178. 8 mono phots, 2 maps, no appendixes, Glossary, Bibliography, Index.
* A book which describes the impact of Australian troops upon the civil population of Egypt after their arrival in late 1914, during their deployments on the Canal and in Sinai during the war, and, most significantly, after the cessation of hostilities in 1919. The author discusses the actions of the Australian Mounted Div and the ANZAC Mounted Div in suppressing the post-war uprising during which a number of regrettable incidents occurred. She maintains a sound dispassionate approach to a disagreeable subject, with interesting descriptions of the Rural Pacification Schemes in the Nile Delta. The text is supported by a formidable number of Chapter Notes. R/1 V/4. ANL. MCND'A.

THE CAMPAIGN OF 1884-1885

RECORDS OF THE NILE VOYAGEURS, 1884-1885
The Canadian Voyageur Contingent in the Gordon Relief Expedition

C P Stacey * The Champlain Society, Toronto, 1959. Red, gold, 9.75 x 6.5, x/285. Fp, 8 mono phots, 2 maps, Index. Apps: nominal roll ('The Canadian Voyageur Contingent and Wheelsmen'), biographical notes on 'chief persons' mentioned in the quoted documents.
* To quote from the 51 pages of the Introduction: 'In the year 1884, a force of nearly 400 boatmen, commanded by a Toronto Alderman, went to Egypt to take part in the Expedition to relieve General Gordon. This was the first occasion when Contingents from what were called "self-governing Colonies" assisted the Mother Country in an overseas war'. The documents published in the book are arranged in five parts - records relating to the raising of the Voyageurs in August and September of 1884, the diary of Lieut Col F C Denison, papers relating to the activities of the Voyageurs in Egypt-Sudan, extracts from the diary of Maj Mordaunt Boyle, and documents relating to the Wheelsmen. This unique volunteer force was raised from an extraordinary cross-section of Canadian social classes - Salteaux Indians from Manitoba, Iroquois Indians from Quebec, officers of the Militia, backwoodsmen, professional river pilots and young men in search of adventure. Their task was not to fight but to assist the British Army in its efforts to transport supplies up the Nile and over various stretches of cataract which were impeding the advance south to Khartoum. R/4 V/5. RCSL. TAB.
Note: printed only as a limited edition of 600 copies.

THE AUSTRALIAN CONTINGENT
A History of the Patriotic Movement of New South Wales and An Account of the Despatch of Troops to the Assistance of the Imperial Forces in the Soudan

Frank Hutchinson and Francis Myers * Thomas Richard, Government Printer, Sydney, 1885. Leather, red/gold, 8.5 x 5.5, iii/285. No ills, no maps, no Index. Apps: 'List of the Contingent sailing to the Soudan', 'The Patriotic Fund', 'Resolution of the Imperial Parliament concerning Colonial Troops in the Soudan', 'Record of the Campaign'.
* The first 172 pages are devoted to the speeches of the Colonists when confronted by the news of Gordon's death. A great surge of patriotic fervour resulted in the despatch of a force of volunteers to Egypt. It arrived at Suakin in March 1885, fought one skirmish in which three men were killed, and then re-embarked for Australia six weeks later. Operations in the field are covered in one appendix of three pages. The book is therefore little more than a mirror of public attitudes towards Queen and Empire. The style of writing is typically florid and jingoistic. A classic work of the period. R/3 V/3. ANL. MCND'A.

SOLDIERS OF THE QUEEN
War in the Soudan
Ralph Sutton * M S Simpson & Sons Pty Ltd, Sydney, for the NSW Military History Society and the Royal New South Wales Regt, 1985. Red, gold, 8.5 x 6.5, xxvii/321. Fp, 51 mono phots, 19 cld ills, 4 line drawings, 5 maps (3 printed in the text, two bound in, folding), Bibliography, Index. Apps: unit nominal roll (NSW Contingent by Arms, with postings), 'Major Kitchener's Report on the Fall of Khartoum', 'Lieut Col Grove's Report on the Canadian Voyageurs' (with numerous officers and ORs named therein).
* A high quality production which marked the Centenary of the despatch of the NSW Contingent to the Sudan. The narrative provides a clear account of the political scene in early 1885 which led to the raising and despatch of 750 men, with 200 horses, to form the Suakin Field Force. In the event, the Contingent's deployment was very brief (see preceding entry), but the episode was significant as the first instance of an Australian Colony coming to the aid of The Mother Country. This book captures perfectly the popular sentiments of the period.
R/1 V/5. ANL. MCND'A.
Note: 1000 copies printed.

THE REHEARSAL
Australians in the Sudan War, 1885
K S Inglis * Rigby Publishers, 1985. Red, yellow, 11.0 x 8.0, -/176. 25 mono phots, 67 line drawings, 6 cld ills, one map, no appendixes, Bibliography, Index.
* A book covering the same ground as the two preceding entries, but with greater reliance upon illustrations. R/1 V/3. PC. PS.

BUT LITTLE GLORY
The New South Wales Contingent in the Sudan, 1885
Peter Stanley * Military Historical Society of Australia, Canberra, 1985. Illustrated soft card, brown, 9.75 x 6.75, vii/79. 14 mono phots, 14 sketches, 4 maps, Bibliography, no Index. Apps: Roll of Honour, nominal roll (with awards), notes on uniforms and equipment.
* This is yet another account of the Australian involvement in the Suakin episode, but with the needs of the medal collector taking pride of place. The information on the naming of the campaign medals, their presentation and subsequent survival rates, is particularly detailed. R/1 V/5. PC. PS.

BRITAIN, THE AUSTRALIAN COLONIES AND THE SUDAN CAMPAIGN OF 1884-85
Malcolm Saunders * University of New England, Armidale, NSW, 1985. Blue, gold, 9.75 x 6.5, xii/226. 12 mono phots, 7 line drawings, 2 maps, Chapter Notes, no appendixes, Bibliography, Index.
* Again, like the Sutton and Inglis accounts noted above, this is a detailed analysis of the role of the NSW Contingent, the factors which led to its embarkation, what happened when it reached the Sudan, and what happened when it returned home. The author discusses the impact of the event - of minor importance in contemporary military terms - upon the broader development of Australia's foreign policy and her later commitments in other wars. R/1 V/3. SLV. PS.

Note: one of the ad hoc units formed for this campaign was later recorded by Count Gleichen, a Lieutenant of the Grenadier Guards. His book, WITH THE CAMEL CORPS UP THE NILE, was published by Chapman & Hall, London, 1888 (reprinted by Scolar Press Ltd, Ilkley, Yorkshire, for E P Publishing Ltd, Wakefield, Yorkshire, 1975). The Camel Corps in this case was the Guard's Camel Regt, elements of which took part in the battles at Abu Klea and Abu Kru. Although a British Army unit account, the book is noted here to distinguish it from other books having a similar title and because it contains detailed information regarding camels and their use in war.

SOMALILAND

HISTORY OF THE SOMALILAND CAMEL CORPS

J G S Drysdale * Unpublished foolscap TS with some MS appendixes, no details of origin shown, 1935. Seen in library binding, buff, gold, -/191/xxvi (the latter being the appendixes), no Index. Apps: H&A, list of forts, notes on badges, idem arms and equipment, idem locations, idem the 'Mad Mullah'.
* A very detailed history of the Corps from formation in 1914 - when it replaced the Camel Constabulary - through to 1935, supported by a description of the British involvement in the Horn of Africa from 1870 onwards. Clearly intended for eventual publication, this draft sadly never found a publisher. In 1944, according to one authority, the men 'disbanded themselves by locking their officers in the Mess and disappearing into the bush with their weapons'. They seem to have decided that they would soldier no more. Nobody was injured in this affair. Included in the narrative is an 'appreciation' of the 'Mad Mullah' by 'Pug' Ismay, later General, later Peer. R/5 V/4. RHL. JALH.
Note: Rhodes House Library reference MSS.Afr.s.552.

HISTORICAL RECORD, SOMALILAND SCOUTS
K.Rs, 1940 para 1728

Maj V A C Ross and Lieut Col E Barry * Seen in a library binding together with various other papers under the title 'Abyssinia/Somaliland, 1915-1962', unpublished foolscap TS, -/14. No ills, no maps, no Index. Apps: list of officers, list of Coy Stations (January 1949 to January 1952), short statement by Brig A R Chater on 'the early days' (dated 23.12.1941), Special Order of the Day (by Chater).
* The authors presumably wrote their reports in accordance with the King's Regulation quoted in the sub-title. This 'Record' in fact consists of two successive reports - the first by Ross (who commanded to May 1945), the second by Barry (who commanded from May to July, 1945). Ross's report has ten pages, Barry's has just four. The unit had a strange evolution. It was first raised in July, 1941, by Chater, as a POW guard unit with the title Illalo Guard Bn. It was then deployed along the frontier with Vichy-controlled Djibouti and given a new title - Somali Frontier Guards. In May 1942 (before the Vichy French surrender of Djibouti), the unit was increased to six Coys and renamed The Somaliland Companies. At this time they seem to have been regarded as Irregular troops. Yet another change of title was authorised on 1 July 1943 when they became The Somaliland Scouts. They became a Lieutenant Colonel's command in May 1945 when two more Coys were added to the establishment. The additional men came from the recently disbanded 72nd (Somaliland) Bn KAR. This is an extremely brief but unique account of a period, and of long-ago units, which have all but disappeared down the plug-hole of history. R/5 V/3. RHL. JALH.
Note: two KAR Bns were formed in British Somaliland during WWII. The 72nd was a garrison and draft-finding unit, the 71st fought in Burma with 28 (EA) Independent Bde and served subsequently in South East Asia.

Note:

No formal histories of either The Somaliland Camel Corps or The Somaliland Scouts have yet been published. Apart from the WWII accounts noted on the preceding pages, information regarding military activities in the Horn of Africa is not easy to obtain. However, a considerable number of senior British officers have written personal memoirs - making reference to the periods in their lives when, as young men, they 'cut their teeth' in the 'Mad Mullah' campaigns conducted from time to time between 1901 and 1920.

UGANDA

A HISTORY OF THE 4th Bn, THE KING'S AFRICAN RIFLES
Formerly Known as The Uganda Rifles
Lieut Col E V Jenkins DSO * Government Press, Kampala, 1911. Green, black, 9.25 x 7.0, -/27. No ills, no maps, no Index. Apps: list of officers (6 pages, covering the period 1891 to 1911, with notes regarding deaths and injuries).
* An almost laconic account, by a former CO, of the origins of the Uganda Rifles. The author describes briefly the Regt's duties in connection with Boundary Commission escorts, and the constant conflicts with slavers, cattle raiders, and insurgents. He makes reference to many individual British military and civilian personnel. There is brief reference to the Imperial British East Africa Company (1888-1895) and to the Nandi campaigns of 1900 and 1905. The total span covered by this slim volume is 1885 to 1911. Its main value to many researchers is the appendix (list of officers). R/5 V/3. MODL/NAM. AMM/JALH.

UGANDA VOLUNTEERS AND THE WAR
By One of Them
Anon (Lieut C J Phillips) * Printed by Calcutta General Printing Co, Calcutta, published by A D Cameron, Kampala, Uganda, 1918. Medium brown, gold, 8.75 x 5.5, -/110. No ills, one map (mentioned in the text but not seen in the copy examined), no Index. Apps: list of UVR officers subsequently promoted or posted to other units, idem SNCOs, unit nominal roll (all ranks, European and Asian), Regtl Orders, notes on newly acquired territory, notes on the Buganda Loyalty War Fund, extracts from the Uganda Gazette.
* The UVR (Uganda Volunteer Reserve) was raised and trained for IS duties and for the defence of the country in the event of a German invasion. It did not take part in the East Africa campaign as an integral unit, although some MG and rifle sections were deployed on the south western border during the early stages of the war. The UVR's main function was as a source of experienced officers and NCOs who were attached to a bewildering range of other units - Buganda Rifles, Uganda Police Service Bn, Uganda Transport Corps, Uganda Rifle Corps, Uganda Native Medical Corps, East African Mounted Rifles, Bukakata-Lutobo Ox Transport Corps, Belgian Ox Transport Corps, East African Supply Corps, Uganda Protectorate Armed Vessels, and so forth. The narrative makes reference to many named individuals and to their war service. This aspect of the book, combined with the excellent appendixes, makes it a prime source for genealogist and medal collectors. The appendixes also incorporate verbatim official reports affecting Uganda which are not readily accessible elsewhere. The narrative is divided into numerous short chapters with some duplication of information (for which the author apologises). A unique source of reference. R/5 V/4. NUL/RCSL. GR.

BRIEF HISTORY OF THE 4th (UGANDA) BATTALION, THE KAR
Anon * East African Standard Ltd, Nairobi, 1951. Soft card, pale green, dark green, Bn crest, 8.5 x 5.5, -/17. 16 mono phots, no maps, no appendixes, no Index.
* An extremely brief history, printed in English and in Ki-Swahili. Its research value is restricted to its mention of all the Bns raised in Uganda from 1900 to 1951. R/5 V/1. NAM/RHL. JALH.
Note: Rhodes House Library reference MSS.Afr.s.1715/304 (Box 19). Vide also THE UGANDA JOURNAL, Vol 14, March 1950, pages 52-56 - 'With the 4th (Uganda) Bn KAR in Abyssinia and Burma'.

A BRITISH BORDERLAND
Service and Sport in Equatoria
Capt H A Wilson * John Murray, London, 1913. Dark green, black/white, 'Laurel' motif, 9.0 x 6.0, xxi/347. 18 mono phots, one map (bound in), no appendixes, Index.
* A personal account of the author's services with the 3rd and 4th Bns KAR in

Northern Uganda between 1902 and 1906. The narrative describes his work with the Anglo-German Boundary Commission and his participation in the 1906 campaign against the Nandi. He covers other matters of historical interest which are not widely known - the organisation of the KAR in its formative years, the method of constructing defence-works around 'up country' Government administrative buildings, and so forth. A useful source for an understanding of the role of the KAR during that period. R/5 V/3. ELJHU. TP.

SOLDIERING AND SPORT IN UGANDA
Capt E G Dion Lardner * Walter Scott Publishing Co, London, 1912. Dark blue, embossed blue, 9.0 x 5.5, xxi/289. Fp, 69 mono phots, one map (bound in), Glossary, no Index. Apps: notes on Uganda's trade prospects.
* The author served with 4 KAR in 1909-1910. His memoir is the expected mixture of comments regarding the country, its people, and its wildlife. The two aspects of this account which make it interesting are the passages which describe the friction between 4 KAR and the Belgian Colonial units along the Congo border, and the author's comments regarding the type of African which the Bn was recruiting in those pre-WWI days. A useful secondary source. R/3 V/2. EPL/OUL. TP.

SPORT AND ADVENTURE IN AFRICA
A Record of Twelve Years of Big Game Hunting, Campaigning and Travel in the Wilds of Tropical Africa
Capt W T Shorthouse DSO * Seeley Service & Co Ltd, London, 1923. Orange, black, 'Warusha warrior' motif, 8.75 x 5.75, -/316. Fp, 24 mono phots (of which six have a military content), one map (folding, bound in at the rear, showing the author's travels), no appendixes, Index (extensive, 6 pages).
* A narrative reminiscence. Pages 86 to 152 cover the author's service with 4 KAR during the WWI period in south western Uganda, and then on southwards to Portuguese East Africa (via Kisii, Kagara, Ukerewe, Mwanza, Tabora, Tunduru, Lioma, etc). Pages 192 to 235 cover service with 6 KAR in the final 'Mad Mullah' campaign in 1920 in Somaliland. This is a substantial and well indexed work, of better-than-average research value. R/3 V/3. PC. GR.
Note: the book recorded above is one of several written by officers who served in Uganda and neighbouring territories during the early days. Amongst these other sources are:

SOLDIERING AND SURVEYING IN BRITISH EAST AFRICA, 1891-1894, by J R L MacDonald (Edward Arnold, London, 1897)
SERVICE AND SPORT ON THE TROPICAL NILE, by Clement A Sykes (John Murray, London, 1903)
AFRICAN INCIDENTS, by A B Thruston (John Murray, London, 1900)
IVORY RAIDERS, by Harry A Rayne (William Heinemann, London, 1923)
CAMPAIGNING ON THE UPPER NILE AND NIGER, by Seymour Vandeleur (Methuen & Co, London, 1898).

JAMBO EFFENDI
Iain Grahame * J A Allen & Co, London, 1966. Grey, gold, 8.5 x 5.5, -/224. Fp, 20 line drawings (by Sheila Rogers), 2 maps (cld, one bound in, one printed on the end-papers), no appendixes, no Index.
* Unlike the titles listed above, this book relates to much later events. The author served with 4 KAR for seven years in the early 1950s and in the early 1960s. His memoir is a gentle and good-humoured description of the life of a Regimental officer during the time when the sun was setting on one of the Empire's furthest frontiers. He wrote not only about his Askari but also of their tribal homelands and their culture. Like many others who had served in Uganda in earlier years, he developed an affinity for the northern tribes which, at that time, were still living in a style untainted by Western values - above all, the Karamajong. The book is a nostalgic look back at African peacetime soldiering, combined with a brief account of the Mau Mau campaign. R/2 V/3. PC. RP.

KENYA

Battalions of the King's African Rifles

FIRST THIRD
History of the First Third Battalion, King's African Rifles, in Abyssinia, Somaliland and Eritrea
Maj J S Ross MBE * Publication details not shown, but the style of printing and presentation suggest an official source, n.d. Blue, black, 9.75 x 6.0, -/81. 12 mono phots, one map (bound in), no appendixes, no Index.
* It covers the organisation and operations of 1/3 KAR from September 1939 through to March 1942. As a Kenya-based Infantry Bn, 3 KAR had existed for many years but, in December 1939, it underwent a radical change of role. It was converted into a Machine-gun Bn. This was achieved by posting in the MG Platoons of other KAR Bns and posting out a corresponding number of riflemen. When it went north for the invasion of Italian-held territory it was assigned as Force Troops and its sub-units allocated to formations as needed. Subsequently it ceased to be an element of the KAR and became instead the 3rd (EA) Reconnaissance Regt - the title later changing to 3rd (EA) Armoured Car Regt. The narrative of this book is evidently based upon original sources (the War Diary, orders, reports, etc) and appears to be totally accurate. It even includes an account of how one of the Bn's Platoons was for a while pressed into service as 'Marines' with the East African coastal patrols. R/5 V/4. UCSRL. TP/JALH.
Note: this item is extremely rare. Protracted enquiries failed to locate a copy in any of the major United Kingdom military libraries or private collections.

THE DESERT AND THE GREEN
The Earl of Lytton (Noel Anthony Scawen Lytton) * MacDonald & Co, London, 1957. Green, yellow, 9.0 x 5.5, xiv/350. Fp, 18 mono phots, 2 line drawings, no maps, Index. Apps: the author's family tree.
* An autobiographical account of the author's military career (1920 to 1945). The book is listed here because it includes his account of service with 5 KAR between 1922 and 1926. Originally Commissioned into the Rifle Brigade, he was at one time an Instructor at the Royal Military College and a Staff Major at the War Office during WWII. Much of the narrative is given to personal matters, but some researchers will find interest in the KAR references and the many asides regarding Lytton's brother officers. R/2 V/2. ELJHU. TP.

5 KAR
1939-1945
Maj W D Draffan and Capt J W Howard * East African Standard Ltd, Nairobi, n.d. (c.1943). Soft card, blue, black, 'Arabic 5' motif, 7.75 x 5.25, -/23. No ills, 2 maps, no Index. Apps: list of COs (1917-1942), list of officers (those serving at 26.9.1939), notes on Battle Honours.
* A brief but useful account of 5 KAR's role in clearing the Italians out of Somaliland, and then its part in the Madagascar campaign. Presumably this account by Draffan and Howard was the precursor for the Draffan and Lewin account described below. The text incorporates plenty of detail regarding locations and movements, and makes numerous references to individual officers. It should be noted that the 5 KAR in question was that which had been disbanded in 1925 and then reformed in 1930. R/5 V/3. RMAS. RP.

A WAR JOURNAL OF THE FIFTH (KENYA) BATTALION, THE KING'S AFRICAN RIFLES
Col William Draffan MBE and T C C Lewin * Publication details not shown, n.d. (c.1946). Blue, gold, 8.75 x 5.5, -/151. No ills, 3 maps (folding, bound in at the rear), no Index. Apps: list of COs (1902-1945).
* A book which deals mainly with operations in Somaliland, Abyssinia, Madagascar

and Burma (especially the Kabaw Valley campaign). The book, which has far more substance and covers a longer period of time than the preceding entry, contains all of the information which most researchers are likely to require. The narrative is presented in a somewhat amateur format, but is very readable and easy to follow. R/4 V/4. RMAS/RHL. RP.

THE ELEVENTH (KENYA) BATTALION, KING'S AFRICAN RIFLES, 1941-1945
Anon (Maj P F Vowles) * Catholic Press, Bihar, India, n.d. (c.1946). Stiff card, blue, 7.0 x 4.5, -/32. No ills, no maps, no Index. Apps: H&A, list of officers and BNCOs who served with the Bn, notes on casualties (KIA, 2 officers and 16 ORs, WIA, 4 officers and 68 ORs).
* A slim but informative record of a wartime Bn formed at Jinja, Uganda, in February 1941, with men from a wide range of East African tribes. Employed initially as a POW guard unit at Naivasha, Kenya, the Bn embarked for Berbera, Somaliland, in April 1941. At the conclusion of the Abyssinia campaign, it returned to Kenya for further training. Men from Uganda and Tanganyika were posted away and it became an all-Kenyan unit. In June 1943 it sailed again, this time for Colombo, Ceylon. After eleven months of jungle warfare training on that island, it moved to Burma where it fought as part of 11 (EA) Div until late 1944. It was then withdrawn to Ranchi, in the Bihar Province of India. It remained at Ranchi for a year (the period when this little book was compiled and printed). Returning to Kenya, the Bn was wound down and many of its personnel were absorbed into 3 KAR. The text is based directly upon the War Diary and is therefore totally authoritative. R/5 V/3. NAM/AL. JALH/GTB.

The Kenya Regiment

THE STORY OF THE KENYA REGIMENT, TF, 1937-1959
Anon * The English Press, Nairobi, n.d. (c.1959). Stiff card, brown, diagonal stripe on front cover (Regtl colours, red/green/white), gold, Regtl crest, 5.0 x 3.75, -/24. Fp, no other ills, no maps, no Index. Apps: H&A (post-1952 only), list of original staff, list of Honorary Colonels, idem COs, idem RSMs.
* The Regt was disbanded in May 1963. This booklet covers the period from formation in June 1937 through to April 1959, and is a succinct and useful record. The Kenya Regt was a Territorial Force unit which initially was intended to provide 'aid to the civil power' in times of emergency. This approach soon changed as the prospect of war with Italy increased. From 1939 onwards, its main function was that of training young Europeans as officers and NCOs for service with other East African units (particularly the rapidly expanding KAR). The Regt was disbanded in 1945, reactivated in 1950, and then played a vital role during the Mau Mau campaign. R/5 V/4. NAM. JALH.

THE CHARGING BUFFALO
A History of the Kenya Regiment, 1937-1963
Guy Campbell (Colonel, Baronet) * Leo Cooper, in association with Secker & Warburg, London, 1986. Dull orange, gold, 9.5 x 6.25, ix/180. 30 mono phots, one map, Bibliography, Index. Apps: Rolls of Honour (for 1939-1945 and for 1952-1957), list of former officers, idem all other ranks (neither list complete).
* When it was raised in 1937, the Regt recruited almost entirely from the 'English' land-owning families when had begun to settle in Kenya from 1900 onwards. Just as the Auxiliary Force in India had an important social and sporting role for the ex-patriate community, so was the Kenya Regt at first viewed as a somewhat light-hearted part-time commitment. The outbreak of war with Italy changed all of that. The Regt played a key role by providing a flow of trained personnel to a variety of other East African units. The author summarises this background story, but then concentrates upon his Regt's participation in the suppression of the Mau Mau rebellion. He was hampered by a lack of source documents because so many

were lost when the Regt was disbanded in 1945, and the circumstances of its employment in the 1950s were not conducive to good paper-work. The narrative is therefore heavily anecdotal. The author succeeds, perhaps against the odds, in recounting a dark episode in Kenya's history with flair and humour.
R/1 V/4. PC. RP.

Other Kenya Regiments

THE STORY OF THE EAST AFRICAN MOUNTED RIFLES
Capt C J Wilson * East African Standard Ltd, Nairobi, n.d. (c.1938). Dark green, gold, 8.5 x 5.5, viii/130. 25 mono phots, 2 maps (printed on the end-papers), 3 topographical sketches, no Index. Apps: Roll of Honour, nominal roll (all ranks, with some biographical notes and details of awards), list of COs and other officers, diary of events (August 1914 to August 1916).
* A very readable account of this locally-raised WWI unit. The lack of an Index is a hindrance because the narrative is packed with references to individual members. The nominal roll is helpful to genealogists and medal collectors. The book is reported to be accurate and reliable as a source of reference.
R/3 V/4. PC. BCC.

THE HISTORY OF THE KENYA ARMOURED CAR REGIMENT, 1939-1941
Anon * Unpublished foolscap TS, no details shown, n.d. Seen in library bindings, -/55 (not numbered). No ills, 5 maps (loose in rear pocket), no Index. Apps: Roll of Honour, H&A, list of COs (during the East Africa campaign).
* A narrative account which covers the Regt's actions at El Wak (16.12.1940) through to the Italian surrender at Gondar (27.11.1941). It is written in a plain unadorned style, with no attempt at analysis. It reads, in fact, as though it was copied directly from the War Diary, and this may well have been the case. Like many other Armoured Car Regts, the KACR frequently operated over a wide area, with the Squadrons and Troops working separately and under the command of various formations. This history, therefore, throws light on the activities of units other than itself. R/5 V/4. IWM. JALH.
Note: a slip inserted before the title page of the copy seen states: 'Copied from an original by the Imperial War Museum, Local Service, Nairobi, Kenya, September 1945'. This suggests that one or more copies have survived in Kenya and elsewhere.

Kenya Police

THE KENYA POLICE, 1887-1960
M Robert Foran * Robert Hale Ltd, for the Government of the Colony and Protectorate of Kenya, 1962. Blue, silver, 8.75 x 5.5, xvi/237. 68 mono phots (of good quality), 2 maps, Index. Apps: list of senior officers.
* An excellent history, giving uniform coverage for the entire period. Foran was a police officer in Kenya for many years, and he is thought to have had access to official archives and files while compiling this account. R/3 V/4. MODL. JA.
Note: the same author also wrote a more anecdotal account entitled A CUCKOO IN KENYA - THE REMINISCENCES OF A PIONEER POLICE OFFICER IN BRITISH EAST AFRICA (Hutchinson & Co, London, 1936). It is a good secondary source for the early years.

Note:

Another author who wrote extensively about his years in pioneering Kenya was Richard Meinertzhagen. Military researchers will find useful material in ARMY DIARY, 1899-1926 (Oliver & Boyd, Edinburgh, 1960), and KENYA DIARY, 1902-1906 (from the same publisher, 1957).

TANGANYIKA

STANDING ORDERS OF THE 6th BATTALION, THE KING'S AFRICAN RIFLES, 1930
Anon * Government Printer, Dar es Salaam, n.d. (1930). Soft card, buff, black, 9.5 x 5.75, iii/70. No ills, no maps, Index. Apps: 12 in total, incl all the usual Instructions, plus some unique to African units, e.g. 'Scale of Baggage - British ranks', 'Scale of Baggage - African ranks'.
* An excellent source of factual material on the rules governing the conduct of a KAR Bn during the inter-war years. They cover the mundane routine of military life, plus some oddities which reflect the special ethos of the KAR during that period. One such admonition states: 'NCOs and men are forbidden to beat their wives without first obtaining permission from their Company Commander'. There is much detailed information regarding the wearing of the uniform, procedures for training, pay scales, musketry qualifications and prizes, and so forth. This is the only Standing Orders publication for a KAR Bn which has been traced.
R/5 V/3. RMAS. TP/AAO.
Note: an account of soldiering with 6 KAR during that period - the 1930s - was published in THE GUNNER, Nos 65 and 66, April and May, 1976. The two articles are headed KAR SUBALTERN and the author was D N W Irven. An additional source is HANDBOOK OF TANGANYIKA (2nd Edition, Government Printer, Dar es Salaam, 1958). Edited by J P Moffett, it contains much useful information on the history of 6 KAR.

SHORT HISTORY OF THE 6th (T.T.) BATTALION, THE KING'S AFRICAN RIFLES
Lieut Col C J M Watts * The General Printing & Stationery Co Ltd, Port Louis, Mauritius, 1950. Bound in full Morocco, brown, gilt, 7.0 x 5.0, -/23. No ills, no maps, no Index. Apps: H&A (statistical summary only, but with full citation for Sgt Nigel Leakey's VC award).
* 6th Tanganyika Territory Bn KAR evolved in 1918-1919 with the removal of that region from German administration. The author gives a sketchy account of the early days and the inter-war years, and then an even sketchier account of the WWII services of 1/6th, 2/6th and 3/6th Bns. The Kabaw Valley operation, in which 2/6th and 3/6th played a leading part, is covered here in just six lines. As an historical record, this booklet is totally useless. Its only appeal would be to collectors of rare ephemera. R/5 V/1. PC. RP.

ADUI MBELE (ENEMY IN FRONT)
Some Recollections of a Platoon Commander in the East African Campaign (1940-1941) and on the Brigade Staff in Madagascar (1942-1943)
John Pitt * Privately, by the author, at Woodstock House, Oxford, 1985. Soft card, yellow, black, facsimile TS folios, 11.75 x 8.5, iv/95. No ills, 2 maps (bound in), Bibliography, no appendixes, Index.
* The author was a pre-war forestry officer employed in Tanganyika. In 1939 he volunteered for military service and was Commissioned into the KAR. He served with 1/6 KAR in Abyssinia as a Platoon Commander and was then appointed Brigade Intelligence Officer with 22 (EA) Bde for the Madagascar campaign. He tells the story of how he and his brother 'bwanas' shared with their Askari the daily discomforts of life in the bush, and the dangers of leading them into battle. This is a good 'sharp end' view. R/5 V/2. IWM/NAM. MWB.
Note: the author made ten facsimile copies of his memoir and presented some of them to selected libraries.

Sgt N G Leakey, a Kenyan-born European who had volunteered for wartime service, was awarded a posthumous VC for his actions near Colito, Abyssinia, on 19 May 1941, while attached to 1/6th KAR. His body was never found. His was the only such award to a member of any KAR unit, in any war or campaign.

SHORT ACCOUNT OF THE ACTIVITIES OF THE 26th BATTALION, THE KING'S AFRICAN RIFLES

In Order to Place on Record the Achievements of this Newly Raised Unit in Their First Campaign

Lieut Col Sir Peile Thompson OBE * Unpublished foolscap TS, n.d. (c.1956). Single folder, i/48/iv (the latter being the appendixes). No ills, one map, no Index. Apps: list of all officers, BWOs and BNCOs who served during the Kenya Emergency, list of all attached personnel (officers and Sergeants of the Kenya Regt, Royal Corps of Signals, dog handlers).

* The operational period covered is 23.11.1954 to 1.4.1956. When the War Office decided in 1951 to deploy two Bns of the KAR in Malaya, it became necessary to raise two new Bns for home duties. They were given the numbers 23 and 26. The latter was formed in Tanganyika and built around a cadre of 6 KAR personnel. Because the Tanganyika Territory was administered by Great Britain under a United Nations mandate, its armed forces could not be used for 'overseas' wars, but they could be deployed in neighbouring Kenya. This is the story of 26 KAR's campaign services against the Mau Mau gangs in the Aberdares. At the end of that Emergency, it went to Mauritius to relieve 6 KAR as the resident garrison force.

R/5 V/4. RHL. JALH.

Note: Rhodes House Library reference MSS.Afr.s.1715-273 (Box 17).

NYASALAND

THE OFFICIAL SCRAP BOOKS OF 1st AND 2nd KING'S AFRICAN RIFLES

Anon (various contributors) * A series of foolscap-size volumes and photograph albums, numbered 1 to 7, into which numerous TS, MS, pictures, letters, reports, and newspaper cuttings have from time to time been pasted. The series forms part of the Dept of National Archives of Malawi, PO Box 62, Zomba.

* While explorers such as Burton and Speke were discovering 'the Darkest Africa' of the Upper Nile and Lake Victoria, far to the south in the area around Lake Nyasa an astonishing series of journeys was being made by David Livingstone. It was largely as a result of his discoveries that the British public became aware of the horrors of the slave trade. Uniquely, Great Britain's subsequent expansion in that part of Africa stemmed from the pressures exerted by the missionary and humanitarian movements. Around Lake Nyasa, the dominant Yao and Angoni tribes were waxing rich on the profits made from their alliance with the Arab slavers. The Livingstonia Central Africa Company tried to pursue his aims but, when it failed, the British Government took over and declared a Protectorate of British Central Africa in 1893. To police it, and to pursue the fight against the slavers, the Central African Rifles (later Regiment) was formed as a Crown unit. In 1902, the Regiment became part of the newly formed King's African Rifles. These volumes trace the entire story of those early years and the services of the Nyasaland Bns of the KAR in both world wars. Volume 7 deals specifically with the role of 2 KAR during the Malayan Emergency and concludes with the granting of Independence in 1964. The volumes are a primary source for any researcher able to gain access to the Archives in Zomba. R/5 V/4. DNAM. PRC.

HISTORY OF 1 (NYASALAND) KING'S AFRICAN RIFLES TO SEPTEMBER 1918

Col Humphrey P Williams OBE * Unpublished facsimile foolscap TS, disbound, n.d. (possibly 1950s), -/138. No ills, no maps, no appendixes, no Index.

* A unique and detailed history of the Bn from its origins as the Central African Rifles in 1895 through to the end of its services in the East African campaign in 1918. These chapters are complete and were seemingly intended for publication. Additional notes suggest that Col Williams intended to continue his account beyond that date, but he was possibly discouraged from doing so by the publication in 1956 of Moyse-Bartlett's major history of the KAR as a whole. However, the Williams account should be consulted because it includes details of several minor operations in which the Bn was engaged and which are not recorded elsewhere. R/5 V/4. RHL. JALH.

Note: Rhodes House Library reference MSS.Afr.s.1715-300 (Box 19).

AFRICAN ASSIGNMENT

Maj Gen Sir Francis de Guingand KBE CB DSO * Hodder & Stoughton, London, 1953. Cambridge blue, gold, 8.75 x 5.5, -/291. Fp, 26 mono phots, 8 line drawings, 7 maps (5 printed in the text, 2 on the end-papers), no appendixes, no Index.

* The author is best remembered as Chief-of-Staff, 8th Army (1942-1944) and Chief-of-Staff, 21st Army Group (1944-1945). However, as a junior officer of the West Yorkshire Regt, he spent six years in East and Central Africa. Seconded to the KAR, he served with 1st Bn in Nyasaland in 1926-1927, and this memoir is a unique commentary upon peace-time soldiering in the Protectorate during that period. The 'military' content is no more than superficial, but some researchers might find the book a useful secondary source. R/3 V/1. MODL. AMM.

THE EAST AFRICAN CAMPAIGN OF 1940-1941
As Seen by an Officer of the 1st Battalion, The King's African Rifles

Col Desmond J Bannister MC MBE * Unpublished foolscap TS and MS, in five file covers, -/103. No ills, one map, no appendixes, no Index.

* The author states: 'This book is not intended for the military student .. it is written in the form of a novel to make easier reading'. In the event, it is a clear account of 1 KAR's services with 22 (EA) Bde in the East African campaign. It

tells the story from the outbreak of war and the internment of enemy aliens through to 1941. Chapter 3 is certainly factual. It deals with the Bn's tribal composition and the characteristics of each represented tribe. R/5 V/3. RHL. JALH. Note: Rhodes House Library reference MSS.Afr.s.1715-1 (Box 1).

ACCOUNT OF 22nd Bn KING'S AFRICAN RIFLES IN ACTION
Burma [Khabaw (sic) **Valley], 1944**
Lieut Donald Bowie * Unpublished quarto TS, 1945. Ring binder, -/83. 8 mono phots (pasted in), 12 maps (5 sketch maps, 7 original one inch scale of the Kabaw Valley and Kalewa), no appendixes, no Index.
* The 22nd (Nyasaland) Bn served as an element of 26 (EA) Bde, 11 (EA) Div, in the Kabaw Valley from July to December 1944. This is an interesting unadorned account, evidently based upon the Bn's War Diary. Bowie was the Bn IO and was himself responsible for compiling the War Diary, so his narrative must be treated as totally reliable. The last nine pages describe the Victory Parade in London in 1946. R/5 V/3. RHL. JALH.

HISTORY OF 22nd Bn, KING'S AFRICAN RIFLES
Tamu-Kalewa
Anon (Lieut Donald Bowie as compiler) * Unpublished foolscap, 1945. Seen disbound in a file, buff, black/green, iv/20/8 (the latter being the appendixes), 14 mono phots (original prints, pasted in), one map (folding), no Index. Apps: H&A (immediate awards only, one MC, two DCMs, two MMs, two Certificates of Gallantry), list of Europeans serving with the Bn, operational reports.
* A simple but adequately detailed account of the Bn's part in operations between Tamu and Shwegyin, in the Kabaw Valley, and incorporating reports by individual officers on actions in which they were themselves engaged. The assessments by the CO, Lieut Col K H Collen, detailing both the good and the bad aspects of his Bn's performance, are candid and especially interesting. The narrative was compiled with a view to formal publication at a later date. R/5 V/4. IWM (documents). JALH.

A STORY OF THE GALLANT 22nd BATTALION, KING'S AFRICAN RIFLES
Brig K H Collen * Unpublished octavo TS, 1944. Seen disbound in a folder, -/47. No ills, no maps, no Index. Apps: Roll of Honour (KIA, September to December, 1944), H&A (immediate awards only, five in total).
* A selection of letters written to his wife by Collen while he was commanding the Bn and dated between 16.7.1944 and 21.12.1944. Despite the theoretical restraints of censorship, the letters are remarkably frank and detailed. It seems likely that Mrs Collen typed this record and gave the letters their collective title. R/5 V/4. IWM (Documents). JALH.

MAURITIUS

LES VOLONTAIRES MAURICIENS AUX ARMEES (1914-1918)
Liste Contenant 520 Noms, Avec une Preface et Des Annexes
Robert-Edward Hart * The General Printing & Stationery Co Ltd, Port Louis, Mauritius, 1919. Paper covers, stab sewn, beige, black, 8.25 x 6.0, -/96/I-IX (the latter being the Index). No ills, no maps, Index. Apps: three verbatim extracts from official publications, extolling the dedication and sacrifice of the people of Mauritius in the Allied cause.
* First visited by Arabs and Malays when it was still uninhabited, Mauritius was settled by the Portugese, claimed in 1715 by the French, captured in 1810 by the British, and formally ceded to Great Britain in 1814. During the following century it absorbed a wave of immigrant workers from India and other countries around the Indian Ocean. The population became multi-ethnic, multi-theistic and multi-lingual, with French being retained by the British as the official language. Anyone consulting this book should have these former events in mind. They resolve the questions of why it is not printed in English, and why it is that the 520 listed names reflect a number of different cultural roots. Apart from the laudatory extracts quoted in the appendixes, the book is an alphabetical listing of men who left the island during WWI to serve with the Royal Flying Corps, the Royal Marines, the Royal Army Medical Corps, the Mauritius Labour Battalion, in wartime factories and arsenals, and in various French and American Corps. Many of the surnames are clearly British, and it is possible that some of these men (mainly officers) were not Mauritian born. The author does not state the parameters which guided him in compiling his list, but each entry is accompanied by brief biographical and war service details (including deaths and wounds) which would assist a genealogist or medal collector. R/5 V/3. RCSL. TAB.

THE CALL OF DISTANT DRUMS
Lieut Col Alexander John Ward * The Pentland Press Ltd, Edinburgh, Cambridge and Durham, 1992. Charcoal, gold, 8.5 x 6.0, xvi/214. Fp, 55 mono phots (indexed), 5 maps, no appendixes, no Index.
* Joining the Argyll & Sutherland Highlanders in 1943, Sandy Ward went on to complete forty years of service to two British monarchs and five separate political authorities. The last of these was the Government of Zimbabwe, a country where he fought against the nationalist movement and then served it as Adjutant General of its new Army. Between times, he had for seven years (1967-1974) been the Commander of The Mauritius Special Mobile Force. Forty pages of this memoir are devoted to his time on the island. He explains the origins of the Force, its structure and purpose, and provides enough anecdotes to illustrate its 'regimental spirit'. There had been at one time a Mauritius Volunteer Force, but defence of the island was historically a task for the Royal Navy, for occasional British Army regiments and, from the outbreak of WWII, units of the King's African Rifles. The latter were withdrawn as their parent countries approached independence, and this led, in 1960, to the formation of the SMF. It could not be a Regular Army in the normal sense because it would always be too small to offer long-term career and promotion prospects. All ranks of the SMF, therefore, were selected from the Mauritius Police on two-year detachments. Having completed their time as soldiers, they then returned to normal police duties. This excellent arrangement is still in practice, and the Force has gained a fine reputation for its 'aid to the civil power' work in times of civil unrest and for its mountain and coastline rescue work. The book is an informative and entertaining account of the SMF (and of several African units with which the author was involved at various stages in his career). R/1 V/3. PC. RP.

PART 9

Central Southern Africa

NOTES

CENTRAL SOUTHERN AFRICA
A Military Chronology

1868: after a series of conflicts with the Boers, the tribes of Basutoland accept a measure of British protection. Apart from exploratory incursions by Portuguese traders, much of Central Southern Africa is yet untouched by European influences.
1885: the British Government declares a Protectorate over the northern part of Bechuanaland. In 1895, the southern part will be incorporated into Cape Colony.
1888: the territory south of the Zambezi River (later Southern Zambezia, later Southern Rhodesia) is the tribal homeland of two great nations - the Mashona, to the east, and the Matabele, to the west. In February, the chief of the Matabele, Lobengula, enters into a 'Treaty of Peace and Amity' with the British Government. Cecil Rhodes, an intensely patriotic Englishman who has made a fortune from the Kimberley diamond mines and who dreams of a British 'Cape to Cairo' rail and telegraph link, recognises his opportunity. He sends his associate, Dunnell Rudd, to negotiate with Lobengula a mineral prospecting concession. Believing that no more than ten Europeans will come to work in his territory, he readily accepts the offer of £100 sterling per month, plus 1000 Martini Henry rifles and 100,000 rounds of ammunition. The weapons are duly delivered, but not a promised gunboat intended to operate on the Zambezi.
1889: having obtained the Rudd Concession, Rhodes applies for a Royal charter to operate a trading company in Southern Zambezia. It is granted in October. Similar in terms to the charters of the Hudson Bay Company and the Honourable East India Company, it authorises the new British South Africa Company to raise its own police force. As a first stage to his plans, Rhodes will colonise Mashonaland.
1890: Rhodes and his associates recruit a 'Pioneer Column'. It has two elements - the British South Africa Company's Police (BSACP, with 300 men), and the Pioneer Corps (with 180 civilians; doctors, miners, lawyers, builders, butchers, tailors, etc, the nucleus of a civil community). Also in the Column are thirty-nine other civilians representing a number of commercial interests, and a correspondent from The Times (of London). The Column commences its trek in July. Scouting ahead and clearing a route for the waggons is Frederick Selous and Sir Leander Jameson. In September, having covered 400 miles without opposition, and having established Fort Victoria and Fort Charter along the way, the Column reaches Harare Kopje (soon stockaded as Fort Salisbury). The Pioneer Corps is disbanded so that its members can get on with their civilian jobs but are attested for Reserve service. At year's end, the Portuguese enter the disputed area of Manicaland. A small force of BSACP and Pioneer Corps Reservists from Fort Salisbury arrest two of the Portuguese officials and force their men to flee. During this little expedition, The Times correspondent is eaten by lions.
1891: the Portuguese arrive at Umtali with 200 European and 800 African troops. A scratch force of fifty BSAP and Reservists (jointly styled 'The Manica Rifles') move from Fort Salisbury. They meet the Portuguese in battle at Messikessi. Twenty Portuguese are killed, the rest withdraw in disorder. In December, due to the cost of maintaining them, the BSACP are disbanded. By proclamation, all European males between 16 and 60 years of age are made liable for military service. Following Boer practice, the settlers form themselves into the Mashonaland Horse and elect their own officers. The Europeans are rapidly establishing themselves amongst the friendly Mashona but, apart from hunters and prospectors, few have ventured into Lobengula's Matabeleland.
1892: in January, a new force - The Civil Police - is formed at Fort Salisbury (with detachments at Umtali, Victoria, and Tuli). Its strength is fifteen Mashona recruits and forty Europeans (mainly men of the former BSACP). Small municipal police forces are established in the rapidly developing townships of Salisbury, Umtali, and Victoria, for urban security. A volunteer unit is formed at Victoria (the Victoria Rangers).
1893: in July, a Matabele impi - acting without the authority of Lobengula - enters Mashonaland to attack the indigenous Maswina tribe. Coincidentally, they

kill some servants of European settlers and steal their cattle. Jameson meets the induna in parley and persuades it to go home. One maverick sub-induna fails to comply. The Victoria Rangers and a Burgher force take to the field and defeat the sub-induna, but the incident triggers a resolve to colonise Matabeleland by force. In July, the Mashonaland Border Police are raised to keep watch while Jameson assembles the invasion force. Under a variety of titles - Salisbury Horse, Victoria Rangers, Raaf Rangers, Victoria Column, Northern Column, Tuli Column, etc - it begins to cross into Lobengula's territory in October. Many of the volunteers have been promised, by Jameson, mining rights and land titles as reward for their services. Under his command also is a Crown unit - the Bechuanaland Border Police. After three pitched battles (Shangani River, Bembesi, Singesi) the invaders reach Lobengula's kraal at Bulawayo. A detachment searching for Lobengula runs into his escort (4000 warriors, some having Martini-Henry rifles). Thirty-five Europeans die. Rhodes and Jameson arrive at Bulawayo and more troops are brought north from Cape Colony to consolidate the victory - detachments of the Cape Mounted Riflemen, and of the West Riding Regiment and The Black Watch - but the fighting has ended. The volunteer units are disbanded and the Company starts to build a new township at Gwelo. It will be supervised by the Gwelo Town Police and the countryside will be patrolled by the newly formed Matabeleland Mounted Police.
1894: Lobengula dies in January. For the rest of the year, the Company establishes its administrative control and helps newly arrived settlers to establish themselves.
1895: on 3 May, Zambezia (north and south of the Zambezi River) is named, by Proclamation, 'Rhodesia'. Mashonaland and Matebeland are combined as Southern Rhodesia. The Rhodesia Horse Volunteers are formed in Matabeleland, with detachments at Gwelo, Belingwe and Gwanda. Similar units are raised in Mashonaland at Salisbury, Umtali and Victoria. They are then reorganised as two self-contained units - The Matabeleland Regiment (RHV) and The Mashonaland Regiment (RHV). In the newly acquired territory, an attempt is made to recruit 330 of Lobengula's best warriors as Matabeleland Native Police but, within a year, nearly all have deserted or been discharged. With encouragement from American mining interests, Jameson starts to secretly plan a raid into the Boer republic of the Transvaal. It is hoped to provoke a rebellion by the English-speaking community in that Republic against its Boer government (and thereby gain control of its mineral resources). With more men recruited from Cape Colony and Natal, he forms two wings for his column - one at Pitsani, the other at Mafeking. The force consists of 550 all ranks (mounted infantry, Maxim sections and artillery) from the Rhodesia Mounted Police and the recently disbanded Bechuanaland Border Police. He also secretly alerts the part-time Matabeleland Regiment (RHV) that they may be mobilised. On 29/30 December, his two wings march into the Transvaal and link up. They are met by fierce Burgher and Commando resistance.
1896: the Jameson column is forced to surrender on 2 January at Doornkop. Its casualties are 17 dead and 55 wounded. Jameson is arrested, tried, and jailed in England. His surviving men are exiled. The scandal causes the British Government to intervene. All armed BSAC units - military and police - pass to Crown control. The BSAC's future role will be administrative only. In March, the Matabele start a rebellion. Alarmed by the influx of Europeans and their loss of independence, they begin to attack settlements in their own territory and cross into Mashonaland. Several Europeans are killed. A scratch force consisting mainly of Americans and Canadians - Grey's Scouts - is raised at Bulawayo, and there is a rapid large scale mobilisation of Europeans throughout Southern Rhodesia. Offers of help come from all over southern Africa (including the Boer Republics). Recruitment for a Matabeleland Relief Force commences in April at Kimberley under the command of Lieut Col Herbert Plumer (later Field Marshal). Meanwhile, at the scene of the action, a Bulawayo Field Force has been formed with a plethora of self-help units operating under a variety of titles. The BFF contains the revolt until early June when the Matabeleland Relief Force arrives and takes over at Bulawayo. During the early skirmishes, Tpr Herbert Henderson, Matabeleland Regiment (RHV) has won Rhodesia's first Victoria Cross. The Relief Force operates throughout Matabeleland, protecting European settlements and suppressing the outbreak but, within days of

its arrival, there is trouble in previously peaceful Mashonaland. With insurrection in both tribal territories, the British are hard pressed. Yet more ad hoc volunteer units are raised and formed into a Mashonaland Field Force. The British Government, alarmed by the possible outcome to the disturbances, authorises the despatch of British Army units and detachments from Cape Colony, from Natal, and from a troopship docked in Beira (Portuguese East Africa). The strongest of these is the 7th Hussars. After a series of scattered but severe battles, Rhodes rides into the Matoppo hills to negotiate a peace with the Matabele chiefs. His only companions are three other Europeans and two bearers. The fighting in Matabeleland ceases shortly afterwards, but it will continue sporadically in Mashonaland until October, 1897. Meantime, in late 1896, the British South Africa Police - a permanent para-military Crown force - is established as a replacement for the various short-lived police forces which had preceded it. Its men are experienced campaigners, most having served previously with the BSAC Police, the Mashonaland and Matabeleland Mounted Police, the Bechuanaland Border Police, and the Matabeleland and Mashonaland Regiments (RHV). Additional recruits are men who first came into Mashonaland with the Mashonaland Field Force.

1897: the Mashonaland rebellion is officially declared at an end on 27 October. European losses during the two insurrections have been 262 civilians murdered and 451 soldiers and police killed in action, or died of wounds, or disease, or from accidental causes. Rhodes is still concerned that Germany or Portugal will occupy all or part of Northern Zambezia (later Northern Rhodesia). The region has two distinctly separate territories - the north west (Barotseland), and the north east (effectively a province of British Central Africa - the Protectorate which will be renamed Nyasaland in 1907). The north west is administered by officers of the BSAP and patrolled by the Barotseland Native Police. The north east is guarded by a force of volunteers from various Indian Army regiments and officered by members of the Bengal Staff Corps. In September, the Mashonaland Native Police are formed with recruits from Zululand and Northern Zambezia.

1898: the British Government increases its control over BSA Company affairs by appointing a Resident Commissioner.

1899: war with the Boer Republics - the Transvaal and the Orange Free State - is declared on 11 October. During the preceding months, Col Baden Powell has raised two new units for service in the impending conflict - the Rhodesia Regiment and the Protectorate Regiment. Other local units are amalgamated as the Southern Rhodesia Volunteers (SRV). They include a Troop of military cyclists. Baden Powell has moved to Mafeking with the Protectorate Regiment and elements of BSAP. Now he is besieged by the Boers. The Bulawayo railway workshops build a number of armoured trains (to be manned by the BSAP and the SRV).

1900: the Rhodesia Regiment and the SRV take part in operations for the relief of Baden Powell's force at Mafeking. The SRV cyclists serve with success in the Transvaal and the innovation is copied by the British Army. The Rhodesia Regiment is disbanded in October, but the SRV and the BSAP will fight on until war's end.

1901: the urban police forces - previously titled Mashonaland Constabulary and Matabeleland Constabulary - are combined as the Southern Rhodesia Constabulary.

1902: Cecil Rhodes dies in March, at Muizenberg, Cape Colony. His body is taken north to Matabeleland and buried at 'View of the World' (Malindidzimu). On 31 May the Anglo-Boer war ends with the signing of the Vereeniging Treaty.

1903: the BSAP No 1 Division (Bechuanaland) becomes the Bechuanaland Protectorate Police. No 2 Division (Matabeleland) and No 3 Division (Mashonaland) are merged, but still titled BSAP. At year's end, the BSA Native Police are formed.

1909: deposits of copper ore are discovered around Kitwe and Ndola, 300 miles north of the Zambesi. The Southern Rhodesia Constabulary is absorbed into the BSAP. The British Government relinquishes control of the BSAP and passes it to the Southern Rhodesia administration.

1911: north of the Zambesi, the Barotseland Native Police and the North East Rhodesia Constabulary are merged as the Northern Rhodesia Police.

1913: south of the Zambesi, the uniformed forces consist of a permanent force (the BSAP) and a part-time force (the Southern Rhodesia Volunteers). North of the Zambezi, the Northern Rhodesia Police are reorganised with a 'civilian wing' and a 'military wing'. The local Europeans are organised into a part-time volunteer force, the Northern Rhodesia Rifles. During this year, the Southern Rhodesia administation asks for a ten years extension to the British South Africa Company's Charter (due to expire in 1914). London grants approval.

1914: a small column of BSAP crosses into German South West Africa (GSWA) and captures the frontier post at Schuckmannsburg. The title 'Rhodesia Regiment' is reactivated for a new wartime force which recruits white Southern Rhodesians for service beyond its home territory. The first 525 all ranks - 1st Rhodesia Regiment (1 RR) - depart Salisbury on 14 November for Bloemfontein. They assist in putting down the Boer rebellion, move to Cape Town, and there embark for Walvis Bay, GSWA, in December. More white volunteers are recruited in Salisbury and formed as 2nd Rhodesia Regiment (2 RR, a separate regiment).

1915: 1 RR lands in GSWA. A junior member is 75 Bugler Arthur Harris, later Air Chief Marshal, Royal Air Force. The regiment is disbanded at the conclusion of the campaign, most of its men then joining other Southern Rhodesian units. 2 RR departs Salisbury in March for service in German East Africa (GEA). For home defence duties, the Rhodesia Reserve Volunteers are formed in February (disbanded in 1919). In July, for service in GEA, the Rhodesia Motor Volunteers are formed. Their CO is Capt Charles Duly DSO, the officer who had raised the first cyclist Troop in 1899. In August, also for service in GEA, the Southern Rhodesia Column (otherwise 'Murray's Column') is formed. It comprises men from the SRV, returned members of the disbanded 1 RR, and some seconded from the BSAP. North of the Zambezi, meantime, the Northern Rhodesia Police's 'military wing' forms a Service Battalion which, together with the mobilised Northern Rhodesia Rifles, joins the advance into GEA from the south (Nyasaland).

1916: in May, for the first time in Rhodesia, a black military unit is raised. Volunteer Matabele and Mashona tribesmen are recruited into 1st Bn Rhodesia Native Regiment (1 RNR) for service in GEA. They are joined there by troops from Basutoland and Bechuanaland.

1917: in common with other European units serving in the campaign against von Lettow Vorbeck, 2 RR is experiencing a high rate of sickness. Of the 1200 white Rhodesians who served, each was admitted to hospital at least twice and reported sick at least ten times. The regiment returns to Salisbury in April for rest and recuperation. Five months later it is officially disbanded, but two Companies depart for France where they will serve as part of the South African Infantry Brigade. Other ex-2 RR men follow the same route, but as reinforcement drafts for the British Army's King's Royal Rifle Corps. A second black unit - 2nd Bn RNR - is formed and sent to GEA (where the continuing campaign is now being fought almost entirely by African soldiers).

1918: 1st Bn RNR and 2nd Bn RNR are combined as 'The Rhodesia Native Regiment'. The undefeated von Lettow Vorbeck and his much reduced force surrenders to District Commissioner Horace Croad on 13 November (the formalities completed at Abercorn on 25 November).

1919: the RNR is disbanded on 31 January, the Rhodesia Reserve Volunteers on 6 March. During the war, in GSWA, GEA, and Europe, Southern Rhodesians have won two VCs, 166 MCs, 47 DCMs, and a large number of other awards. Of those who served, 732 have died on active service (443 with the British Army, Royal Flying Corps, etc, and 289 with Rhodesia-raised units). Sixty-four percent of white Rhodesians of military age have served in uniform.

1920: the SRV are retained, but much reduced in numbers (mainly as local rifle Companies). The BSAP has returned to its normal peacetime organisation, but the Northern Rhodesia Police retain their 'military wing'.

1923: Southern Rhodesia becomes a self-governing Colony and Northern Rhodesia a Crown Protectorate. The BSAC has ceased to have any administrative responsibilities and is concentrating upon the development of the enormously rich Kitwe/Ndola copperbelt.

1926: lack of interest in part-time soldiering, a reaction to the trauma of the war, has undermined the Volunteer system. The Legislative Assembly approves a Bill which obliges all white males between 19 and 22 years of age to attend military training. The Southern Rhodesia Defence Force (SRDF) is established, with Permanent and Territorial elements, plus Reserves as necessary. The BSAP, as the regular armed force, is declared to be 'the first line of defence'. The Act also authorises the creation of a Police Reserve and a Special Constabulary.

1927: the Southern Rhodesia Volunteers are disbanded. Under the new Territorial Force arrangements, most of its personnel transfer to The Rhodesia Regiment (this title being adopted for the third time in Rhodesia's history). It has two Battalions, the 1st (1 RR) in Mashonaland and Manicaland, the 2nd (2 RR) in Matabeleland. Other ex-SRV men form Mechanical Transport Companies or join small engineer and signals units. A Permanent Staff is formed, with a small nucleus of transferred BSAP personnel.

1933: the Permanent Staff is redesignated the Permanent Staff Corps (PSC). Its ranks include many outstanding sportsmen who represent their country in cricket, Rugby football, at Bisley, etc, so earning the Corps the soubriquet 'Permanent Sports Club'. North of the Zambezi, the 'military wing' of the Northern Rhodesia Police is given a separate establishment as the Northern Rhodesia Regiment (NRR). A regular force, it has European officers and (black) African other ranks.

1935: members of 1 RR form an 'Air Unit'. It is the country's first move into military aviation and is the seed of the future Southern Rhodesia Air Force.

1937: the NRR is reorganised to conform with the equipment scales and training methods of the King's African Rifles (which has its Battalions based in Uganda, Kenya, Tanganyika and Nyasaland). The intention is that the NRR's single Battalion can be Brigaded with KAR Battalions, if so required. The NRR's long-serving locally resident European officers are progressively replaced by British Army officers on secondment (again, conforming with KAR practice).

1939: in May, with war clouds rapidly gathering, there is a major reappraisal of Southern Rhodesia's military forces. The total white population is 69,000 (men, women, and children). Of these, 17,500 are males of military age, but this figure includes men whose skills are vital to the economy. Further, the ranks of 1 RR and 2 RR include men of greater education and experience than normally required for routine infantry work. It is decided to disband both Battalions and to redistribute their personnel to newly-formed or expanding specialist units - officer and NCO training, armoured car, artillery, engineer, signals, transport, medical. It is planned to provide a pool of qualified personnel to reinforce British and other Empire forces, plus some integral Southern Rhodesia units for attachment to larger Empire formations in the field. Most of these changes are effected in the following four months. On 27 August, the SR Air Unit No 1 (Cadre) Squadron, with its Audax and Hart biplanes, moves to Kenya in response to an urgent request from the British Government. Seven days before the declaration of war, it is the first Empire unit to proceed on active service. In September, SRTF units help to round up German nationals in Nyasaland and establish an internment camp at Hartley. Other units guard the Victoria Falls bridge against a possible German strike from South West Africa. In November, the Coloured Mechanical Transport Unit is formed for service in East Africa. With European officers, its ranks comprise Asians and men of mixed-race resident in Southern Rhodesia.

1940: at Nairobi, Air Unit No 1 is transferred to the Royal Air Force as 237 (Rhodesia) Squadron. The Territorial Force has been attested for overseas service. Four hundred white Rhodesians volunteer to serve (as officers and SNCOs) with the rapidly expanding Royal West African Frontier Force (in West Africa). Two hundred more go to Kenya and Somaliland to boost the strength of the King's African Rifles and the Somaliland Camel Corps. 1 NRR has also been sent to British Somaliland to strengthen the garrison force there. The Battalion is safely evacuated when the Italians invade in August. In Southern Rhodesia, compulsory service is introduced for all white males between 18 and 24 years of age, but many have already gone, voluntarily, to England to enlist in the Royal Navy, the British Army, and the Royal Air Force. Others are serving with the newly-formed SR Reconnaissance Unit, the SR Light Battery, the SR Signals Company, and the SR Medical Corps. In June, and

following the precedent of 1916, black Africans are enrolled for military service. The Rhodesian African Rifles (RAR) are formed in June. As a sub-unit of the RAR, the Rhodesian African Labour Corps is formed in July. In neighbouring Basutoland and Bechuanaland, volunteer tribesmen are joining a newly-raised Anti-aircraft Artillery Regiment, a Field Squadron of Engineers, and Pioneer units. They will serve in Egypt, Italy, and Assam.
1941: the East Africa campaign. The SR Armoured Car Squadron takes part in the removal of Italian forces from British and Italian Somaliland, Abyssinia, and Eritrea. Also serving in this campaign, as an element of 21 (EA) Brigade, is 1 NRR. The overall strength of the NRR is increased to eight Battalions. The RAR has two Battalions - 1 RAR as a front-line combat unit, 2 RAR as a depot unit. The SR Light Battery is affiliated to the Royal Artillery.
1942: the Madagascar campaign. In August, 3 NRR lands at Diego Suarez with 27 (NR) Brigade. After the fighting, it will remain in the Indian Ocean islands, as part of the garrison force, until July 1943 when it moves to Ceylon. Also guarding the islands and Madagascar are 2 NRR and 4 NRR.
1943: the SR Electrical & Mechanical Engineers are formed. The SR Armoured Car Regiment is in Egypt, training with 6th (South African) Division for future operations in Italy. 1 RAR departs Southern Rhodesia for Kenya (and later, Ceylon).
1944: 3 NRR and 1 RAR are in Ceylon. With 1 KAR (from Nyasaland), they form a unique combination of Battalions from the three neighbouring home territories. As 22 (EA) Independent Brigade, they move to Burma in December. At the same time, 1 NRR is evacuated from Burma to Assam, having fought through the monsoon in the tough Kabaw Valley campaign as a unit of 21 Brigade, 11 (EA) Division.
1945: 22 (EA) Independent Brigade is attached to XV Corps in the Arakan. It serves with 82 (West African) Division around Taungup and Prome before crossing the Arakan Yomas to join XII Army. From June to August, it operates in the Pegu Yomas. By the end of the year, most of Northern and Southern Rhodesia's servicemen have returned home. Southern Rhodesia's human contribution to the war has been - 9187 white males, 1510 females, 271 Coloureds and Asians, 15,143 blacks. Of the whites, 724 lost their lives. In addition, 2409 Rhodesians served with the Royal Air Force (mainly as aircrew). Of these, 498 lost their lives.
1946: the NRR quickly discards its seven war-raised Battalions. There is a similar winding-down in Southern Rhodesia, but the war-raised supporting arms and services are retained.
1947: the (white) Rhodesia Regiment is granted the distinction 'Royal'.
1948: the armed forces are reorganised as a much strengthened and rationalised Territorial Active Force. It consists of the SR Artillery, SR Engineers, SR Corps of Signals, 1st and 2nd Bns Royal Rhodesia Regiment, and SR Medical Corps. The war-raised (black) Rhodesian African Rifles are retained as part of this establishment. The Staff Corps is also retained, but without 'Permanent' in its title.
1950: Southern Rhodesia offers to contribute troops to the UN force in Korea. It is asked by the British Government to instead send troops to Malaya to support the anti-Communist campaign in that country. The 'SR Far Eastern Volunteer Unit' is formed at the end of the year under the command of Lieut (later Lieut Gen) Peter Walls.
1951–1956: Walls' unit arrives in Malaya in March, joins The Malayan Scouts, and is retitled 'C' (Rhodesia) Squadron, of the British Army's Special Air Service Regiment. The Squadron is disbanded in 1953. Also fighting in the Malayan jungles during this period are 1 NRR and 1 RAR.
1953–1954: the two Rhodesias and Nyasaland form the Central African Federation in December 1953. Their armed forces are restructured under a Central Africa Command in July 1954.
1956: all SR Territorial Force units are either disbanded or placed in 'suspended animation'.
1961: three new (white) units are formed - 1st Bn Rhodesian Light Infantry, the Armoured Car Regiment (reactivating the war-time title), and 'C' Squadron, Rhodesian Special Air Service Regiment (demonstrating continuity of spirit with the unit which had served with the British Army in Malaya). All three are full-time

Regular service units.

1963: the Central African Federation is dismantled. The Rhodesia Armoured Car Regiment (Selous Scouts), the RLI, and the SAS, have all been operating under Central Africa Command. They now revert to the control of their own government.

1964: on 1 January, the Southern Rhodesia Army is formally established. It has a balanced composition of combat and support services. In July, Nyasaland becomes independent as Malawi. 2 KAR is disbanded and 1 KAR is retitled 1st Malawi Rifles. In October, Northern Rhodesia becomes independent as Zambia. 1 NRR is retitled 1st Zambia Rifles.

1965: units or Corps with 'Southern Rhodesia' in their designation are re-titled as 'Rhodesia' (the 'Southern' is deleted). By a later order, the 'Rhodesia' becomes 'Rhodesian'.

1966: Bechuanaland becomes independent as Botswana, Basutoland as Lesotho.

1965–1980: for some time, the Rhodesian Government has been negotiating with London for its own future independence. Failing to obtain satisfactory terms, the Prime Minister, Ian Smith, makes a 'unilateral declaration of independence' on 11 November 1965. In view of their total loyalty to the Crown, and their many sacrifices in all Great Britain's wars since 1899, white Rhodesians feel betrayed by Harold Wilson's socialist government. Almost surrounded by Marxist and strongly nationalist regimes, they have only South Africa as an ally. Arms and instructors from the USSR, China, and Cuba feed a rising tide of violence along the country's borders. It is plunged into a bush war which involves a major mobilisation of military and economic resources. Not only the white population enlists into the much expanded army. Thousands of Mashona and Matabele enlist to fight for the same cause. Uniquely in all African military history, bi-racial units such as the reconstituted Selous Scouts are formed, with rank and responsibility determined by the individual's military skill, not the colour of his skin. London applies economic sanctions and the Royal Navy blockades the Mozambique Channel. The Rhodesians succeed for several years in containing the incursions, and even mount successful 'special operations' in hostile neighbouring countries.

1966: the BSAP form the 'Police Anti Terrorist Unit' (PATU). It will grow to a strength of 296 European Regulars and 184 European Police Reservists. Its sub-units operate in highly trained 'sticks' of five men.

1970: on March 2, the Smith government declares Rhodesia to be a republic. On 13 March, the Wilson government announces the withdrawal of the 'Royal' prefix from all Rhodesian units having it in its title.

1972: the Armoured Car Regiment is reformed.

1973: the 'Army Tracking Unit' is formed in September. In 1974 it will be retitled the Selous Scouts (in recognition of the daring of the famous pioneer, Frederick Selous).

1974: the 'Mounted Infantry Unit' is formed. Later it will adopt the title 'Grey's Scouts' - one of the famous Matabeleland Rebellion forces of 1896.

1977: a 'Psychological Operations Unit' is formed (too late to effect the outcome of the war).

1980: white Rhodesians tire of fighting a war which offers no prospect of victory. They accept black majority rule. Robert Mugabwe is installed as the first leader of the new Zimbabwe. For a time, the Mashona and the Matabele come close to inter-tribal war. The Mashona achieve political dominance and peace is restored. In an astonishing act of reconciliation, the black soldiers of the former Rhodesian Army and the former 'freedom fighters' merge to form the Army of Zimbabwe. Within two years, and apart from their campaign ribbons, it is impossible to tell which man fought on which side during the conflict. The price has been high. The Rhodesian armed forces had mobilised 64,200 men and women. Of these, 1047 have died. In addition, 581 Europeans, Asians and Coloureds - men, women and infants - have been murdered. The black civilian population has lost 3256 people murdered by the 'freedom fighters' and 535 killed by land mines. The number of 'freedom fighter' and 'criminal element' deaths - verified within the borders of Rhodesia - was 24,437.

BASUTOLAND AND BECHUANALAND

BASUTO SOLDIERS IN HITLER'S WAR
Brian Gray * Morija Printing Works, Morija, for the Basutoland Government, Maseru, 1953. Red, black, 8.75 x 5.5, x/97. Fp, 41 mono phots, 6 general regional maps (folding, bound in), detailed Index. Apps: H&A (all ranks).
* Basuto volunteers were trained in a variety of specialist and semi-specialist units - Field Artillery, Heavy Anti-aircraft Artillery, Field Engineers, Pioneers and Infantry. Their early services were in Palestine and Lebanon, but their most important campaign was Italy. A well-written and interesting account, produced to a very good standard. R/4 V/4. PCAL/MODL. RP.

TEN THOUSAND MEN OF AFRICA
The Story of the Bechuanaland Pioneers and Gunners, 1941-1946
Maj R A R Bent RPC * HM Stationery Office, London, for the Government of Bechuanaland, 1952. Red, gold, 8.5 x 5.5, xii/128. Fp, 41 mono phots, 3 maps (2 printed on the end-papers, one bound in), Index. Apps: 13 in total, incl Roll of Honour (KIA, all ranks, with details), H&A (all ranks), list of COs, lists of officers, idem British and Basuto WOs and SNCOs.
* In proportion to its population, Bechuanaland made a major contribution to the British cause in both world wars. Troops were sent to France in WWI, but this book tells the story of the WWII generation which served in Syria, Palestine, Egypt, the Western Desert and Italy. Under British officers, they served as Field Engineers and as Heavy Anti-aircraft gunners. A well-written and informative account. R/4 V/4. PCAL/MODL. RP.

NORTHERN RHODESIA

THE STORY OF THE NORTHERN RHODESIA REGIMENT
W V Brelsford ('and others') * Government Printer, Lusaka, NR, 1945. Pale olive green, dark green, Regtl crest, 9.75 x 7.25, viii/134. 61 mono phots, 4 cld ills (the Colours and uniforms), 2 line drawings, 5 maps, Index. Apps: H&A (WWII only, incomplete), list of former COs (incl Barotse Native Police, NE Rhodesia Constabulary, and Northern Rhodesia Police).
* In 1891, the British South Africa Company was authorised to start operating north of the Zambesi, in Barotseland (North West Rhodesia). The local chiefs needed the Company's help in defending themselves against their neighbours, the Ndebele, and the Company wanted to prevent any incursions by other European powers. Treaties were signed, and initially the area was supervised by officers of the British South Africa Company Police. They were succeeded in 1899 by the Barotse Native Police. Meanwhile, the British Government had declard a Protectorate over the area known as North East Rhodesia and, in 1900, it authorised the formation of the North East Rhodesia Constabulary. In 1911, the latter was combined with the Barotse Native Police to form the Northern Rhodesia Police (NRP). In 1913, the NRP were split into two parts - one wing continuing as a civil force, the other as a military force. In 1914, the military wing formed a Service Bn which fought in the East Africa campaign. In 1933, the military wing was made completely separate and named The Northern Rhodesia Regiment (NRR). Four years later, with war clouds gathering, it was restructured along the same lines as The King's African Rifles. In WWII, it raised eight Bns (numbered 1 to 7, plus 2/2nd Bn). The book has good coverage of the 1st Bn's role in the Battle of the Turgan Gap (Somaliland, 1940), and 1st and 3rd Bns' later services in Burma. A nicely presented book, the narrative telling the story not only of the Regt but also of its homeland and origins. Two chapters are devoted to medals, uniforms, badges, equipment, and the Colours (all in useful detail).
R/4 V/4. IWM/NAM. BCC/JALH.
Note: reprinted in facsimile in 1990 by Galago Publishing, Bromley, Kent.

CEYLON TO THE CHINDWIN
1st Battalion, The Northern Rhodesia Regiment
Capt Malcolm J C Monteith * Government Printer, Lusaka, NR, 1946. Stiff card, cream, black, 9.0 x 7.0, -/44. No ills, no maps, no Index. Apps: Roll of Honour (all ranks), H&A (one MC, one MM), list of officers (at July 1944), list of British and African NCOs (at July 1944), notes regarding 'the Japanese soldier'.
* The Bn was stationed in Ceylon from 1942 to July 1944, then moved to Burma. The narrative is a fairly condensed account of its progress, as an element of 21 Bde, 11 (EA) Div, from Chittagong to the Chindwin via the Imphal Plain. Many individuals are mentioned by name, and the work is helpful as far as it goes, but it could have been improved by the provision of some maps and an Index. The narrative ends with the events of March 1945. R/4 V/3. MODL. AMM.

BURMA, 1945-1946
3rd Battalion, The Northern Rhodesia Regiment
Lieut Col J W E MacKenzie * Government Printer, Lusaka, NR, 1946. Stiff card, cream, black, Regtl crest, 9.0 x 7.0, -/32. Fp, 5 mono phots, 4 pages of cld ills (showing 14 formation flashes), one map, no Index. Apps: Roll of Honour (all ranks).
* The Bn was formed in Lusaka in February 1940, moved to Madagascar in 1942, returned home in February 1944, sailed then to Ceylon, and arrived in Burma in December of that year. It fought on to the end of the war as an element of 22 (EA) Independent Bde. This short account, written by the Bn's CO, provides a condensed but useful picture of the advance from Chittagong, through Akyab to Prome, Rangoon, and Taungoo. Many British and African members are mentioned in the text (with several gallantry award citations quoted in full). The Bn was disbanded in April 1946. R/4 V/3. MODL. AMM.

96 INDEPENDENT GARRISON COMPANY (NORTHERN RHODESIA REGT)
Col John H S Martin * Unpublished MS, quarto, disbound, -/24. No ills, no maps, no appendixes, no Index.
* The author raised and trained the Company, eventually bringing it to such a standard of smartness that it was selected to mount a Guard of Honour for the GOC-in-C, East Africa Command. There were several Independent Garrison Companies in that Command during WWII, and they seem to have been employed as POW camp guards. The KAR had at least six such Companies (numbered between 97 and 108), but no written record has been traced for any of them. The 96 Independent Garrison Company was the only unit of this type to be raised within the NRR.
R/5 V/3. RHL. JALH.
Note: Rhodes House Library reference MSS.Afr.s.1715-179 (Box 11).

DECORATIONS FOR AFRICAN TROOPS OF THE NORTHERN RHODESIA REGIMENT
For Service in Somaliland, 1940
G H Wilson * Unpublished facsimile TS, quarto, 1941. Seen in library folder, grey, -/12/ii (the latter being the appendixes). No ills (although the author clearly intended to include four pictures), one map (bound in), no Index. Apps: H&A (the names of all recipients, with details of their tribes, villages, chiefs, and Regtl sub-units).
* A succinct narrative, intended for publication, of the part played by 1 NRR in the Battle of the Turgan Gap during the Italian invasion of British Somaliland in August 1940. It concentrates upon the role of four Africans who were awarded the DCM in recognition of their exploits during the battle. There is interesting analysis of the characteristics of each of the men's tribes, and commentory upon the reaction of the 'Jocks' of the Black Watch to the black soldiers of the NRR when they found themselves serving together in the field (they acknowledged them 'as comrades of the line'). The work of the EA Light Bty at the Turgan Gap is mentioned, and there is a good account of the NRR Corporal (one of the DCM winners) who, when his section was cut off, led it on a sixty miles detour and brought his men safely in with all their weapons and equipment. The H&A appendix lists the awards of three DCMs, one DCM with East Africa Force Badge, one MID with East Africa Force Badge, and thirty-six unaccompanied East Africa Force Badges. R/5 V/4. RHL. JALH.
Note: Rhodes House Library reference MSS.Afr.s.1171.
The East Africa Force Badge was introduced on his own initiative by the General Officer Commanding, East Africa Force, Lieut Gen D P Dickinson DSO OBE MC.
A former Inspector General of the KAR and of the RWAFF, he felt strongly that the troops who had been engaged in the defence of British Somaliland, and deployed along the Kenya and Italian Somaliland borders, should be eligible for a distinctive award which would fill a gap in the normal range of gallantry medals and written Commendations. A Nairobi jeweller produced one hundred Badges to Dickinson's design and, of those actually awarded, the majority went to men who otherwise would have received a GOC's Commendation. Dickinson resigned on health grounds in October 1940 and the award of the Badge was thereafter discontinued.
For other details, vide the Journal of the Orders & Medals Research Society, Vol 32, No 1, Spring 1993, page 31, an article by G A Mackinlay.

SOUTHERN RHODESIA
General Reference

RAGTIME SOLDIERS
The Rhodesian Experience in the First World War
Peter McLaughlin * Mardon Printers, Bulawayo, for Books of Zimbabwe Publishing Co, 1980. Illustrated soft card, red, white/black, 'Troops crossing river' motif, 8.5 x 5.5, xvi/159. 37 mono phots, 3 maps, Index. Apps: H&A ('Honours won by Rhodesian residents for war services'), diary of main events during WWI, units in which Rhodesians served.
* The author states - 'This is a popular history aimed at the general reader'. In the event, he compiled a surprisingly detailed narrative which is full of useful facts and figures. Based upon original material now held in the National Archives of Zimbabwe, Harare, it is well presented and very readable. The book covers the history of Southern Rhodesia's uniformed services between 1914 and 1919 - the British South Africa Police, the BSAP Mechanical Transport Company, the 1st and 2nd Rhodesia Regiments, the 1st and 2nd Rhodesia Native Regiments, and the Rhodesia Company of the King's Royal Rifle Corps (which fought on the Western Front and in Salonika). There are interesting references also to Rhodesians who flew with the Royal Flying Corps and to Rhodesians who served at home.
R/2 V/4. PC. GTB.
Note: the book was published simultaneously in a hardback (casebound) edition, with identical contents.

WAR HISTORY OF SOUTHERN RHODESIA, 1939-1945
J F MacDonald * The Rhodesia Printing & Publishing Co Ltd, for the Government of Southern Rhodesia, various dates (see below). Two matching volumes, dark blue, silver, 9.25 x 6.25.
Volume I : 1939-1942. Published in 1947, xiv/353. Fp, 78 mono phots, 7 cld ills, 11 maps (3 cld, folding, bound in, 8 printed in the text).
Volume II : 1943-1945. Published in 1950, pages numbered 354 to 673, plus 14 not numbered. Fp, 83 mono phots, 11 cld ills, 11 maps, Index (for both volumes). Apps: Roll of Honour (Europeans and Africans, arranged alphabetically, but showing only their surnames and initials - no reference to their ranks, units or awards), various statistics for numbers of men who served, casualties, and awards.
* A general description of the Colony's contribution to the Allied cause in WWII. A great many white Southern Rhodesians served overseas with non-Rhodesian units - the Royal Air Force, King's African Rifles, Royal West African Frontier Force, Royal Artillery, 6th South African Armoured Division, etc - so the author is obliged to bounce around the world while trying to cover their diverse services in the various theatres of war. Despite the scale of his work, he succeeds in keeping track of them and, at the same time, mentioning many by name (thus making the Index a valuable aid to the researcher). He also covers in good detail the work done by the Colony's own integral units - 4th (Rhodesian) Anti-tank Bty RA, 17th (Rhodesia) Field Bty RA, Rhodesian African Rifles, etc. While exemplary in every other way, this nicely presented two-volume history would have been greatly improved by the provision of more reference appendixes. Further, the 'Roll of Honour' would have been more useful and reliable if the author had shown each man's rank and unit (or service). R/3 V/3. RMAS. RP/RH.
Note: subsequently reprinted in facsimile and with new Introductions by the very good Rhodesiana Reprint Library (as part of its 'Silver' series, at Bulawayo, in the 1970s).

LION WITH TUSK GUARDANT
J F MacDonald * The Rhodes Printing & Publishing Co Ltd, Salisbury, SR, 1945. Dark brown, light brown, 'Lion with tusk, and Rhodesia' motif, 9.75 x 7.5, xiv/136. Fp, no mono phots, 4 line drawings, 6 maps, no appendixes, no Index.
* This book seems to have been a precursor to the major history, by the same author, described in the preceding entry. It deals mainly with the services of white Rhodesians in WWII. It opens with a summary of the first three years of the war. The background to the story, interestingly explained here, was the Nairobi Conference of 1938 which examined, amongst other defence problems in East Africa, the difficulties of raising a balanced military force in Southern Rhodesia at that time. The total white population was only 69,000, and just 17,500 were males of military age. With this limitation, it was concluded that, in the event of war, the Colony would be able to do little more than provide drafts for other Empire and Commonwealth units. When the call came, in September 1939, the Colony responded by despatching, within weeks, 600 volunteer officers and men to West and East Africa. Of these, 400 sailed in the SS Strathaird to join the Royal West African Frontier Force. They were distributed amongst The Gambia, Nigeria, Gold Coast, and Sierra Leone Regts. At the same time, 200 went to Somaliland to reinforce the Somaliland Camel Corps and to Kenya to join The King's African Rifles. Other white Rhodesians joined the Royal Navy, and No 1 Sqn, Southern Rhodesian Air Force, was integrated into the Royal Air Force as 237 Sqn. From 1940 and 1941 onwards, when the Colony began to recruit black Africans for its newly authorised local military units, the command ranks were filled by hundreds more white Rhodesian volunteers. Also in 1940, a contingent of 700 white Rhodesian volunteers landed at Port Tewfik and were distributed amongst British Army units then refitting in Egypt. Of these, 79 went to the Royal Horse Artillery, 56 to the 11th Hussars, 127 to the King's Royal Rifle Corps (following the precedent set in WWI), and others went to Line Regiments, the Royal Engineers, and the Royal Corps of Signals. R/4 V/3. AL. GTB.
Note: the 'lion with tusk' motif appeared on many of the Colony's unit badges.

Unit Histories

GUNNERS
A Narrative of the Gunners of Southern Rhodesia during the Second World War
Anon ('Tort') * Rustica Press Ltd, Wynberg and Cape Town, RSA, for The Southern Rhodesia Artillery Association, Salisbury, SR, 1947. Red, blue, Regtl crest, 8.75 x 5.5, -/383. Fp, approx 100 mono phots, 4 maps (printed on the end-papers), Glossary, no Index. Apps: Roll of Honour (KIA and WIA), H&A, nominal roll (all ranks who served), roll of members taken POW.
* Mainly an account of 4th (Rhodesian) Anti-tank Bty RA and 17th (Rhodesia) Field Bty RA in the East African, Western Desert, and Italian campaigns. The book is a well written blend of descriptive narrative and quotations from the reminiscences of some of the Association's members. The binding is adequate, but the text paper is of poor quality (copies of this book in good condition are hard to find). The illustrations are excellent, rarely seen elsewhere. R/2 V/4. PC. RP.
Note: a number of white Rhodesians served initially in North Africa with 4th Regt, Royal Horse Artillery, an element of 7th Armoured Div (British Army). Many later transferred to 17th (Rhodesia) Field Bty RA, an element of 6th (South African) Armoured Div, and fought with it in the Italian campaign.

THE 2nd RHODESIA REGIMENT IN EAST AFRICA
Lieut Col Algernon Essex Capell DSO * Simson & Co Ltd, London, 1923. Dark blue, gold, 9.25 x 6.0, iv/132. No ills, 7 maps (6 printed in the text, one bound in), no Index. Apps: Roll of Honour, H&A, list of COs, summary of casualties, nominal roll.
* A good detailed account of 2 RR's work in East Africa in WWI. A white unit, raised specifically for service in that campaign and drawing its recruits from the pre-war Southern Rhodesia Volunteers and the settler community at large, it saw a

considerable amount of action during its short existence. It also, in common with other white units, suffered heavy losses from disease and the general wear and tear of bush warfare. It was disbanded in 1917. There was no longer an adequate flow of replacement drafts, and the decision had in any event been made to pursue the campaign with mainly black African troops. The nominal roll in this book is particularly helpful to medal collectors and genealogists. It shows details of attestation dates, highest ranks held, whether killed or wounded, and any awards made. R/4 V/4. RMAS. BCC/RP.

THE RHODESIAN AFRICAN RIFLES
Christopher Owen * The Pitman Press Ltd, Bath, for Leo Cooper, London, 1970.
Grey, black/gold, 8.5 x 5.5, -/75. 8 mono phots, 3 maps, Bibliography, no Index.
Apps: Roll of Honour (incomplete).
* A superficial and disappointing example of the Leo Cooper 'Famous Regiments' series of popular unit histories. The Regt was raised from Mashona and Matabele tribesmen in June 1940. It fought so well in the Burma campaign that, post-war, it was retained in the Order of Battle of the permanent Rhodesian Army. Subsequently it served under British Army command in the Malayan Emergency and, from 1965 to 1980, fought loyally against the 'liberation' forces in support of the Ian Smith regime. The author deals here only with the Burma period (1944-1945). He states that he was obliged to work without access to official records. Sadly, this obstacle shows in his work. Even sadder, this will probably be the only book ever to be published about this fine Regiment. R/1 V/2. AJW/RP.
Note: an American edition was produced by Hilary House Publishers, New York, also in 1970. The contents are identical, but the casing is brown with gold.

THE WAR OF 1965-1980

CONTACT
A Tribute to Those who Serve Rhodesia
John Lovett * Galaxy Press, Salisbury, Rhodesia, 1977. Grey, black, 11.75 x 9.75, x/228. Abundantly illustrated throughout (interesting high quality photographs on almost every page), one map, no Index. Apps: Roll of Honour, H&A.
* As the sub-title suggests, this is not a Regtl history. However, it contains such a huge mass of information on individuals, acts of gallantry, citations for awards, casualties and anecdotes that it is a prime source for research on the warfare of the UDI period. The book was printed in large numbers, but second-hand copies are difficult to obtain, even in Zimbabwe. R/4 V/4. PC. AJW.
Note: a follow-up book, CONTACT II, which covers the period 1978-1980, is also a reference source of great worth and is equally difficult to acquire.

THE INCREDIBLES
The Story of the 1st Battalion, The Rhodesian Light Infantry
Geoffrey Bond * Sarum Imprint, Salisbury, 1977. Illustrated soft card, khaki, black, 8.25 x 5.75, -/159. Fp, 22 mono phots, no maps, no Index. Apps: Roll of Honour (KIA and WIA, 21.9.1960 through to 29.9.1972), list of COs.
* Prior to 1960, Southern Rhodesia did not have a Regular force of white troops. In that year, a recruiting drive was launched in the UK and Southern Africa and this resulted in the formation of 1st Bn RLI. This breezily-written account of the Bn's first twelve years is based mainly upon interviews with former and serving personnel. There is frank coverage of the early disciplinary problems, the training programme, off-duty activities, and operations in the field. Events post-1972 are not discussed (as a result of security restrictions, no doubt). The story relies heavily upon anecdotal material and contains many references to individual officers and men. To balance the lack of appendixes, the last two short chapters deal with unit slang, customs, Dress, the Colours, etc. R/2 V/4. PC. RBM.
Note: an additional source is the autobiographical A MARTYR SPEAKS - JOURNAL OF THE LATE JOHN ALAN COEY, published by New Puritan Library, Fletcher, North Carolina, 1988. Coey was an American undergraduate, a Christian fundamentalist and right-wing activist who joined the Rhodesian Army in 1972. He served with the SAS Regt but was killed in action in 1975 while serving with the RLI. His Journal, while incorporating heavy doses of his own personal philosophies, makes useful reference to many minor actions and obscure sub-units not often mentioned elsewhere.

SELOUS SCOUTS - TOP SECRET WAR
Lieut Col Ron Reid-Daly and Peter Stiff * Printpak, Cape Town, for Galago Publishing, Alberton, RSA, 1982. Brown, white, 9.75 x 7.0, -/432. Fp, 89 mono phots (indexed), 16 cld ills (indexed), 15 maps (indexed), Bibliography, Index. Apps: H&A (statistical summary only).
* Reid-Daly commanded the elite Selous Scouts during the Rhodesian Bush War and the book is largely a record of his personal reminiscences. Named after one of the country's pioneer settlers, the Scouts had one simple objective - 'the clandestine elimination of terrorists and terrorism both within and outside Rhodesia'. The emphasis was on 'clandestine'. Border and cross-border operations were conducted in the greatest secrecy and, even after the war ended with Independence for Zimbabwe in 1980, it was not possible to include 'Roll of Honour' or 'Honours & Awards' appendixes in this book. A bi-racial force, the Scouts were raised in 1973 and abruptly disbanded (not surprisingly) in 1980. This is an excellent source of information on soldiering under conditions of unorthodox warfare. R/1 V/4. PC. GTB.
Note: two versions were published. A limited edition of 1000 copies was produced in a leather binding. An unlimited edition had a standard casing as described above.

SELOUS SCOUTS
Rhodesian War - A Pictorial History
Peter Stiff * Galago Publishing (Pty) Ltd, Cape Town, RSA 1984. Brown, white, 13.0 x 9.75, -/176. 461 mono phots, 18 cld ills, sketches, cartoons and charts, Bibliography, photographic credits, no appendixes, Index.
* Published two years after the preceding entry, this book has a substantial narrative (70,000 words), but it is essentially a photographic supplement to its predecessor. Again, for reasons of security, few members are mentioned by name. The quality of the pictures is excellent and they are highly evocative of the period. R/2 V/4. PC. DJB.

THE ELITE
The Story of the Rhodesian Special Air Service
Barbara Cole * Three Knights Publishing, Pietermaritzburg, RSA, 1984. Blue, gold, 9.75 x 6.75, x/449. 49 mono phots, 46 cld ills, 25 maps, Bibliography, Glossary, Index. Apps: Roll of Honour, chronology of military events (1888-1980).
* The first 23 pages deal with the roots and origins of the RSAS in North Africa (during WWII) and in Malaya (the post-war Emergency period). The bulk of the book then describes 'anti-terrorist' operations during the long years of the Ian Smith administration. Much detail on specific cross-border missions - and a suprising number of individual personnel - are noted in the narrative. A prime source for all students of 'special operations'. R/2 V/5. PC. DJB.
Note: reference should be made also to LONG RANGE DESERT GROUP - THE STORY OF ITS WORK IN LIBYA, 1940-1943, by W B Kennedy Shaw (Collins, London, 1945). This includes useful references to pioneering Rhodesian involvements in clandestine deep-penetration warfare.

THE ELITE
Rhodesian Special Air Service
Barbara Cole * Three Knights Publishing, Amanzimtoti, RSA, 1986. Illustrated boards, 'Bush warfare' motif, 12.0 x 8.0, -/168. Approx 400 mono phots and cld ills, Glossary, chronology of events (1890-1980). Apps: Roll of Honour.
* This book covers largely the same ground as the book of the same title noted in the preceding entry, but it is in essence a pictorial supplement. The narrative tells the story of the resurrection of the British Army's 'C' (Rhodesian) Squadron of the SAS Regt in 1961. It was ear-marked as a special unit to be placed at the disposal of the newly formed Central African Federation. Following the disintegr-ation of the Federation, only two years later, and the dismemberment of the Squadron, a remnant nucleus of 31 officers and men started to rebuild what was to become a superb bush warfare unit, the Rhodesian SAS. The illustrations provide a fresh perspective to the more factual information found in the earlier work by the same writer. R/2 V/3. RMAS. RP.
Note: 500 copies were printed in a 'de luxe' leather binding, with an unlimited version in a standard commercial binding as noted above.

Police

THE HISTORY OF THE BRITISH SOUTH AFRICA POLICE
Peter Gibbs * Kingstons Ltd, Salisbury, SR, for the Commissioner of the BSAP, 1974. Two matching volumes, dark blue, white, BSAP crest in orange (on front covers and spines), 9.0 x 6.5.
Volume I : The First Line of Defence, 1889-1903. Fp, 8 mono phots, one map, Glossary, Bibliography, no appendixes, Index, ix/266.
Volume II : The Right of the Line, 1903-1939. Fp, 12 mono phots, 2 maps, no appendixes, Index, xv/244.
* The definitive history of the BSAP (which had its roots in the short-lived BSA Company Police which were formed to escort and protect the first European settlers in Mashonaland). The BSACP were organised on the lines of a British regiment of cavalry and operated in a quasi-military role. Volume I covers the raising of the

BASCP, the occupations of Mashonaland and Matabeleland, the Jameson Raid incident, the suppression of the Mashona and Matabele rebellions, the Relief of Mafeking in 1900, and the story of the various police forces which came and went in Central Southern Africa between 1891 and 1897 (when the British South Africa Police - with no reference to the Company - was authorised and recruited). Volume II covers the BSAP's evolving role as a peacetime civil police force and as a wartime fighting unit (the capture of Schuckmansburg, GSWA, and Murray's . Column, GEA and Nyasaland, during WWI). The story concludes with BSAP activities immediately prior to the outbreak of WWII. To balance the lack of appendixes, both Volumes mention many individuals by name and these are well indexed.
R/4 V/5. RCSL/MODL. GTB.

MEN WHO MADE RHODESIA
A Register of Those who Served in the British South Africa Company's Police
Col A S Hickman * The British South Africa Company, 1960. Dark blue and old gold (the Force Colours), BSAC crest, 10.0 x 6.0, -/462. Fp, 22 mono phots, 2 maps (bound in), no appendixes, Index.
* The classical record of the BSACP - authorised in 1899 and disbanded in 1891. The first 85 pages tell the story of the unit's origins and pioneering services in protecting the settlers and merchants who were flooding into Mashonaland and Matabeleland. Never exceeding Battalion strength, and with only limited British Army support, it ensured an (initially) peaceful British conquest of the area which would later be known as Southern Rhodesia. The occupation was so peaceful, in fact, that the Force was soon disbanded (with just forty men being retained in service as a civil force, the Mashonaland Police). The bulk of the text is then devoted to a compilation of detailed biographical notes on each of the 897 men who served with the BSACP. They were recruited from a very broad range of European adventurers and soldiers of fortune. The book is a primary source for genealogists and medal collectors. R/2 V/5. PC. RP.
Note: available in reprint.

FRONTIER PATROLS
A History of the British South Africa Police and Other Rhodesian Forces
Col Colin Harding CMG DSO * G Bell & Son Ltd, London, 1938. Blue, gold, 9.0 x 6.0, xii/372. Fp, 21 mono phots, 2 maps (bound in), Index. Apps: 16 in total, incl Rolls of Honour (1893, 1896, 1897, and 1914-1915), H&A (WWI only, all ranks, incl 14 DSO recipients, 20 DCMs, 14 MSMs, 163 MID, foreign awards, etc).
* A sound history of the early days, with good coverage of the Jameson Raid, the Mashona and Matabele rebellions, the Anglo-Boer War of 1899-1902, and the WWI campaigns in German South West Africa and in East Africa. It includes useful references to the Rhodesia Field Force, Northern Rhodesia Regt, 2nd Rhodesia Regt, and the Rhodesia Native Regt. R/3 V/4. VS/PS.
Note: first published in November 1937, reprinted in March 1938.

THE REGIMENT
An Outline History of the British South Africa Police
Richard Hamley * Mardon Printers of Rhodesia, for T V Bulpin and Books of South Africa (Pty) Ltd, Cape Town, 1971. Illustrated boards, 12.0 x 10.0, vi/119. No mono phots, 71 line drawings, no maps, Index. Apps: notes on badges.
* The author provides a condensed history of the Force, but his work is useful mainly for information on its uniforms, badges, insignia, and so forth.
R/2 V/3. PC. DBP-P.
Note: a useful additional source is BLUE AND OLD GOLD - A SELECTION OF STORIES FROM 'THE OUTPOST', THE REGIMENTAL MAGAZINE OF THE BRITISH SOUTH AFRICA POLICE, anon (Howard B Timmins, Citadel Press, Cape Town, n.d., c.1953). As the sub-title makes clear, this is not a formal history but an interesting anthology of articles brought together in a single attractive binding. The period covered is 1890 to 1950.

PART 10

South Africa (Union and Republic)

NOTES

ORDER OF PRECEDENCE
of the Regiments and Corps
as authorised, 1980

The following information has been extracted from the South African Defence Force Order, dated 1 March 1980, which listed all of the Force's elements, with their designations and order of precedence at that time.

Unlike Great Britain, South Africa gives precedence to its Army. The combat services are listed thus - SA Army, SA Air Force, SA Navy, SA Medical Services. This sequence reflects the South African custom of designating its military units (the Regiments and Corps, and the sub-units within them) in accordance with their original dates of establishment.

The SA Army's constituent Corps carry titles similar to those found in, for example, the British Army, but some are unique. The most noticeable feature is the location of the Corps of Infantry. Contrary to the custom in other former Empire countries, the Infantry take precedence over the Armoured, Engineer, and Signals elements:

SA Staff Corps
SA Artillery
SA Infantry Corps
SA Armoured Corps
SA Engineer Corps
SA Corps of Signals
SA Personnel Corps
SA Ordnance Corps
SA Technical Corps
SA Corps of Military Police
SA Special Service Corps
SA Corps of Bandsmen
SA Caterers Corps
SA Civil Defence Corps
SA Ammunition Corps
SA Corps of Professional Officers
SA Army Intelligence Corps
SA Army Women's Corps
SA Cape Corps
SA Indian Corps
SA Supporting Services Corps
SA Finance Services Corps

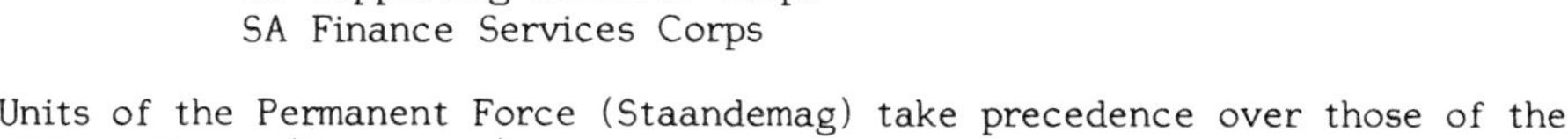
Units of the Permanent Force (Staandemag) take precedence over those of the Citizen Force (Burgermag).

Researchers working on South Africa's pre-1961 military history will find most of the unit titles with which they are already familiar listed under the Citizen Force groupings. Details of their published histories appear later in this bibliography under the appropriate headings. However, it should be noted that the majority of the units listed on this and the two following pages have not yet produced such a record.

SA Artillery

Cape Field Artillery
Natal Field Artillery
Transvaal Horse Artillery
Cape Garrison Artillery
plus sixteen post-1961 Citizen Force regiments of artillery

SA Infantry Corps - Permanent Force

1 Infantry Bn
1 Parachute Bn
2, 3, 4, 5 and 6 Infantry Bns
State President's Guard
1 Reconnaissance Commando
7 and 8 Infantry Bns
11 Commando
3, 4 and 5 Reconnaissance Commandos
Reconnaissance Commando Base Unit
51, 52, 53 and 54 Infantry Bns
44 Parachute Bn
61 Mechanised Bn Group

SA Infantry Corps - Citizen Force

The Natal Carbineers
Durban Light Infantry
Cape Town Rifles (Dukes)
First City Regiment
Kaffrarian Rifles
Cape Town Highlanders
Kimberley Regiment
Transvaal Scottish Regiment
Witwatersrand Rifles
Rand Light Infantry
Regiment Botha
1 Regiment De La Rey
Regiment De Wet
Regiment Louw Wepener
Regiment Langenhoven
South African Irish Regiment
Regiment Christian Beyers
Regiment Grootkaroo
Regiment Westelike Provinsie
Regiment Uitenhage
Johannesburg Regiment
Regiment Noord-Natal
Regiment Universiteit Stellenbosch
Regiment President Kruger
Regiment Piet Retief
Regiment Oosrand
Regiment Hogeveld
Durban Regiment
Regiment Bloemspruit
Regiment Skoonspruit
1 Regiment Noord-Transvaal
Regiment Springs
Regiment Erongo
Regiment Namutoni
Regiment Noord Natal
2 Regiment Noord-Transvaal
2 Regiment De La Rey

Regiment Boland
Regiment Algoabaai
Regiment Dan Pienaar
2 Parachute Battalion
3 Reconnaissance Commando
3 Parachute Battalion
University of Pretoria Military Unit
University of Orange Free State Military Unit
University of Port Elizabeth Military Unit
Potchestroom University for Christian Higher Education Military Unit

SA Armoured Corps – Permanent Force

1 Special Service Battalion
2 Special Service Battalion

SA Armoured Corps – Citizen Force

1 Natal Mounted Rifles
Umvoti Mounted Rifles
1 Light Horse Regiment
Prince Alfred's Guard
Pretoria Regiment
Regiment President Steyn
Pretoria Highlanders
Regiment Windhoek
Regiment Oranjerivier
Regiment Mooirivier
Regiment Molopo
3 Armoured Personnel Carrier Squadron
5 Forward Delivery Squadron
2 Natal Mounted Rifles
2 Light Horse Regiment
Regiment Vrystaat
Regiment Tafelberg

Notes:

1. The Cape Corps, still maintaining one of the oldest unit titles in South African military history, was organised in the 1980s as a Citizen Force training cadre, based in Cape Town.

2. Supporting Service Corps was the designation given to six bi-racial battalions deployed on security duties around the black townships.

NUMBERED UNITS AND FORMATIONS

The preceding three pages list the Corps and Regiments as they stood in 1980. In earlier years, the soldiers of South Africa had at times served in units which were designated according to one or more numerical systems. This is a large and complex subject covered more fully by Maj G Tylden and by E H J Shaw (vide the Index of Authors), but the details shown below will provide a framework against which the book titles recorded on the following pages can be better understood.

1912–1913

With the declaration of the Union of South Africa in 1910, it became clear that a measure of rationalisation was needed with regard to the disparate military and police units at that time in existence. Beginning in 1912, they were brought under the aegis of the Union Defence Force (UDF) and were given numbers, thus:

South African Mounted Rifles – Permanent Force

1st SA Mounted Rifles (Cape Mounted Police)
2nd SA Mounted Rifles (Natal Police and Orange Free State Police)
3rd SA Mounted Rifles (Natal Police)
4th SA Mounted Rifles (Transvaal Police)
5th SA Mounted Rifles (Cape Mounted Police)

Mounted Rifles – Active Citizen Force

1st Mounted Rifles (1st Natal Carbineers)
2nd Mounted Rifles (2nd Natal Carbineers)
3rd Mounted Rifles (Natal Mounted Rifles)
4th Mounted Rifles (Umvoti Mounted Rifles)
5th Mounted Rifles (Imperial Light Horse)
6th Mounted Rifles (Cape Light Horse)
7th Mounted Rifles (Southern Mounted Rifles)
8th Mounted Rifles (Middellandse Ruiters)
9th Mounted Rifles (Hogeveld Ruiters)
10th Mounted Rifles (Botha's Ruiters)
11th Mounted Rifles (Potchefstroom Ruiters)
12th Mounted Rifles (Krugersdorp Ruiters)
13th Mounted Rifles (North Transvaal Berede Skutters)
14th Mounted Rifles (Steyn's Berede Skutters)
15th Mounted Rifles – never formed
16th Mounted Rifles (Eerste Vrystaatse Regiment)
17th Mounted Rifles (Western Province Mounted Rifles)
18th Mounted Rifles (Griqualand West Mounted Rifles)
19th Mounted Rifles (Transkei Mounted Rifles)
20th Mounted Rifles (Graaff-Reinet Ruiters)

Dismounted Rifles – Active Citizen Force

1st, 2nd and 3rd Regiments (Western Province Rifles)
4th and 5th Regiments (Southern Rifles)
6th Regiment (Middellandse Skutters)
7th Regiment (Hogeveld Skutters)
8th Regiment (De La Rey's Ruiters)
9th Regiment (Bechuanaland Rifles)
10th Regiment (Noordelike Transvaal Grenswacht)
11th Regiment (Oranje Skerpskutters)

12th Regiment (President Brand Regiment)
13th Regiment (Lichtenburg Ruiters)
14th Regiment (Karroo Skutters)

Infantry - Active Citizen Force

1st Infantry (Durban Light Infantry)
2nd Infantry (Duke of Edinburgh's Own Rifles)
3rd Infantry (Prince Alfred's Guard)
4th Infantry (First City/First Eastern Rifles)
5th Infantry (Kaffrarian Rifles)
6th Infantry (Cape Town Highlanders)
7th Infantry (Kimberley Regiment)
8th Infantry (Transvaal Scottish)
9th Infantry (Cape Peninsula Rifles)
10th Infantry (Witwatersrand Rifles)
11th Infantry (Rand Light Infantry)
12th Infantry (Pretoria Regiment)

1914-1915

The outbreak of war caught the infant UDF with too many commitments and too few resources. The Afrikaans-speaking population split into three parts - those who volunteered to fight for the British, those who took up arms against their own government, and those would not fight for anyone. Of the 90,000 men ready for service, 30,000 were allocated to put down the Boer rebellion at home while 60,000 were sent to invade German South West Africa. The attacking force consisted of Permanent Force units (SA Mounted Rifles), of Active Citizen Force units, and of a large number of Boer Commandos still organised as they had been in the war of 1899-1902.

At the conclusion of that remarkable campaign, the ACF units (Mounted Rifles, Dismounted Rifles and Infantry) returned home and, together with the Boer Commandos, were stood down. The Permanent Force units (SA Mounted Rifles) remained in South West Africa as a garrison force and to deal with a revolt by the Ovambo tribe.

1915-1918

South Africa did not have an army attested for overseas service. It was therefore decided to assist the Crown by raising an Expeditionary Force composed of entirely new (numbered) units. Many of the ACF men who had so recently returned from South West Africa volunteered to join these units (listed below) which selected them mainly upon the basis of where they lived rather than their previous regimental associations, thus:

1st SA Infantry Brigade, comprising

1st SA Infantry Regiment (Cape)
2nd SA Infantry Regiment (Natal and Orange Free State)
3rd SA Infantry Regiment (Transvaal and Rhodesia)
4th SA Infantry Regiment (men from the Cape Town Highlanders, the Transvaal Scottish, and the South African Caledonian Societies).

2nd SA Infantry Brigade, comprising

5th SA Infantry Regiment (Kimberley and Eastern Province)
6th SA Infantry Regiment (Durban, Eastern Province, Orange Free State)
7th SA Infantry Regiment (Transvaal)
8th SA Infantry Regiment (Transvaal)

3rd SA Infantry Brigade

9th SA Infantry Regiment ('The Sportsmen's Regiment')
10th SA Infantry Regiment (mainly Natal)
11th SA Infantry Regiment (Natal)
12th SA Infantry Regiment (various parts of the Union)

The 1st SA Infantry Brigade served in Egypt in 1915 and 1916, and then on the Western Front from 1916 to 1918. It suffered heavy battle casualties, particularly at the Battle of Delville Wood (July 1916). The 2nd and 3rd SA Infantry Brigades served in East Africa from 1915 to 1917. After experiencing heavy wastage from tropical diseases, they were replaced by African (Colonial) troops.

1919–1939

Military activity in South Africa ceased almost entirely after WWI. The numbering system was progressively abandoned and many units were either disbanded or were run down to the point at which they existed only on paper. Apart from the skeleton Permanent Force, only those ACF units which had their roots in the pre-Union period managed to keep their Regimental titles alive. The situation slowly began to recover in the mid-1930s when part-time training was resumed and new Afrikaans-speaking units were formed.

1939–1945

By the time war broke out, a system of Regimental naming (rather than numbering) was firmly re-established. Despite the divided loyalties in some sections of the Afrikaans-speaking population, the armed forces were able to expand rapidly when one in every three white South Africans of military age responded to the appeal for volunteers. The mounted units swiftly converted from horses to armoured cars, and the ancillary Corps were developed to meet the needs of modern warfare. Three Divisions were formed, equipped mainly for the infantry role:

1st SA Division (East Africa 1940-1941, Western Desert 1941-1942)
2nd SA Division (Western Desert 1941-1942)
3rd SA Division (elements in the Madagascar campaign, 1942)

By the time the second El Alamein battle had been won (October/November, 1942), South African forces in Egypt and Libya had become seriously depleted by battle casualties, by the surrender of the Tobruk garrison, and by the lack of reinforcement drafts from the Union. The survivors were withdrawn from North Africa and returned home for leave and reorganisation. The men, who initially had all volunteered for service outside the Union but not outside Africa, were now asked to re-attest for service overseas. Those who did so were regrouped into Combined Regiments or reinforced Regiments which went to Egypt for further training. Brought together as 6th SA Armoured Division, they arrived on the Italian mainland in 1943 and served in that campaign through to the end of the war.

Note: the information given on pages 308-310 is based upon original primary research by E H J Shaw, of Port Elizabeth, RSA.

SOUTH AFRICA - A MILITARY CHRONOLOGY

1488: the Portuguese navigator Bartolomeo Diaz makes landfall at Mossel Bay as he rounds the Cape.
1497: pursuing the European need for spices, the Portuguese mariner Vasco da Gama opens the sea route to India. Maritime traders from Portugal, and later Holland, will follow in his wake. The strategic importance of the Cape is not yet apparent.
1652: the Dutch East Indies Company (DEIC) establishes a permanent trading post for their merchantmen at Cape Town. The area is inhabited by Bushmen and Hottentots.
1659: the First Khoi-Khoi War. The Khoi-Khoi Hottentot clans resist Dutch settlement and are defeated by Regular troops of the DEIC. Local settlers form the Burgher Corps Infantry on a voluntary basis. The total white population of the Cape is still less than one thousand.
1672: compulsory military training for all white males between 16 and 60 years of age is introduced.
1673-1677: the Second Khoi-Khoi War. There is fighting around the area of Saldanha Bay. The Commando system, a form of militia with officers selected by election, starts to evolve.
1675: the San Hostilities commence. A campaign of raid and counter-raid between the Dutch and the indigenous Bushmen, this conflict will spread and will continue intermittently over the next two hundred years. The last clash will take place in 1861 on the border of Natal and Basutoland.
1688: Huguenot refugees arrive from France and settle in the Cape area. In time, their community will be absorbed by the Dutch.
1715: the DEIC formally approves the Commando system.
1779-1781: the First Frontier (Kaffir) War. Settler expansion brings clashes with the Xhosa tribes in the Fish River area.
1795: the Graaff Reinet and Swellendam Rebellions. Regular troops of the DEIC put down rebellions by local Burghers. Colonisation continues at a steady pace, aided by slave labour imported from the Dutch East Indies. The war in Europe then causes the British to occupy Cape Town. Invading British Army troops defeat a combined force of DEIC Regulars, Burgher Militia (Commandos) and Cape Coloured soldiers (the Pandour Corps) at Muizenberg.
1796: the British form the Cape Corps, a unit comprising the former Pandour Corps and newly recruited Eurafricans and Hottentots.
1799: a second rebellion at Graaff Reinet. British Regulars and Burghers loyal to the Crown defeat Burghers objecting to British rule.
1799-1803: the Third Frontier War. British troops and Burgher Commandos campaign against the Xhosa and Hottentot tribes on the Eastern Frontier.
1803: with the end of the Revolutionary War in Europe, the Cape is returned to Dutch rule. The British Army garrison departs.
1806: following the outbreak of the Napoleonic War, the British decide to reoccupy the Cape. Dutch Regulars, Burghers and Native Levies are defeated at the Battle of Blaauberg, north of Cape Town. The victors reactivate the former Cape Corps under a new title, the Cape Regiment.
1811-1812: the Fourth Frontier War. British Regulars and local Dutch Commandos keep up the pressure on the Xhosas on the Eastern Frontier.
1817: the Cape Regiment is disbanded.
1818-1819: the Fifth Frontier War. Again, Anglo-Dutch forces fight the Xhosa.
1820: the British try to form a human buffer between Cape Colony and the lands of the Xhosa tribes. Following a publicity campaign in Great Britain, 4000 new settlers are brought to South Africa and are given land on the Eastern Frontier beyond Algoa Bay (the Fish River). Many soon move on elsewhere, the farms being too small.
1827: the Cape Mounted Riflemen are established. A Regular force, later to win much fame, its men are newly-recruited Europeans and former members of the Cape Regiment.

1828: the Fetcani Expedition. Anglo-Dutch forces and Native Levies defeat the Amangwane (a Xhosa tribe) who had invaded Cape Colony in the Umtata River area.
1834–1835: the Sixth Frontier War. The Xhosa again invade Cape Colony and are engaged by British Regulars, Burgher Commandos and Native Levies. The results are indecisive.
1836–1840: the period of the Great Trek. There is an exodus from the frontier areas of the Cape by those families, originally Dutch and French, who now seek a new life away from British influence and control. Collectively they are known as Boers (literal translation, farmers). They travel by ox-drawn waggon towards the north and east where they establish the Independent Republics of Natal, the Orange Free State, and the Transvaal. Many of these Voortrekker convoys are massacred en route, but a combination of modern weapons and desperate courage defeats the Matabele in the Transvaal and the Zulu at Blood River in Natal.
1842: the British pursue their appetite for territory by invading Natal. Their troops are defeated by the Boers at Congella. British reinforcements turn the tide and reoccupy Durban.
1845: the British invade the Orange Free State and beat the Boers at Zwartkopjes.
1846–1847: the Seventh Frontier War, the War of the Axe. There is more campaigning against the Xhosa on the Cape's eastern boundaries.
1847: the British declare Crown sovereignty over the whole of the Orange Free State. The Boers rise in rebellion against the occupation, but they are defeated at the Battle of Boomplaats in 1848.
1850–1853: the Eighth Frontier War. A force composed of British, Burgher, Fingo and Hottentot troops again face the Xhosa, this time at Boomah Pass.
1851: the British enter Basutoland and defeat its ruler, Chief Moshesh, at Viervoet.
1852: at the Battle of Berea, British Regulars again face the Basuto and this time are defeated. On 26 February, near Cape Town, the troopship Birkenhead sinks with heavy loss of life. Struggling with too many commitments and too few resources, the British formally recognise the independence of the Transvaal.
1852–1854: there is a series of engagements in Eastern and Northern Transvaal between Boer Commandos and local Bantu tribes.
1854: having failed to break the spirit of the Boers in the Orange Free State, the British declare their recognition of that Republic's independence. At the same time, and having established themselves firmly in the former Republic of Natal, they start to raise Volunteer units from the local English-speaking communities. This leads to the establishment of such later famous units as the Natal Carbineers and the Durban Light Infantry.
1855: the Frontier Armed and Mounted Police (FAMP) are raised to maintain law and order in the border tribal areas.
1857: the Boers in the Orange Free State raise a Regular (Permanent Force) unit, the Oranje Vrij Staats Artillerie.
1858–1868: Chief Moshesh is still leading the Basuto. Three separate campaigns are conducted against him during this period, each by Boer Commandos of the Orange Free State.
1868: the British annexe Basutoland and absorb it into the Empire.
1869: the Koranna Rebellion. Insurgent tribesmen are defeated by the FAMP.
1871: diamonds are discovered in Griqualand West, on the western border of the Orange Free State. The British promptly seize the area for themselves. Relations between the two-English speaking Provinces - Natal and the Cape Colony - and the two Afrikaans-speaking Republics - the Orange Free State and the Transvaal - become increasingly tense.
1873: gold is discovered in the Transvaal, at Pilgrim's Rest. The British do not immediately react, being preoccupied with the suppression of a major native rebellion in Natal. The Amahlubi, a Zulu tribe led by Chief Langalibalele, are coming under pressure from the British. Langalibalele mounts a rebellion. A

mixed force of British Regulars, Natal Volunteers, and Native Levies fight the Amahlubi near Eastcourt and the revolt is put down.

1874: a lesson of the Langalibalele Rebellion is the need for a police force in the Province. It is met by the establishment of the Natal Mounted Police. In this same year, the Boers in the Transvaal establish the Staats Artillerie, the Republic's first permanent full-time military unit.

1876-1877: the Sekukuni War. Transvaal Commandos, with the support of the Swazi impis, fight the Bapedi tribe of Chief Sekukuni near Lydenburg.

1877: the British march into the Transvaal and attempt to merge it into the Empire.

1877-1878: the Ninth Frontier War. The Xhosa are suppressed following six major battles.

1878-1879: the Griqualand Rebellion and the Sekukuni War. The British, with local supporting units, continue their attempts to suppress the tribes in Griqualand West and elsewhere.

1879: the Zulu War. After a long period of peaceful contact, the British fabricate an excuse to invade the heartland of the Zulu nation. One of their columns is annihilated at Isandlwana. British humiliation is partially redeemed by Welsh heroism at Rorke's Drift. At the same time, the Basuto rise against British control. Cape Colonial forces fight Chief Morosi and his warriors at the Battle of Morosi's Mountain.

1880-1881: the First (sic) Anglo-Boer War. Three years after having been invaded and occupied, the Boers of the Transvaal rise in protest. Their Commandos, mainly farmers and tradesmen, besiege the six main British Army garrisons and inflict severe defeats upon British Regulars at Bronkhorstspruit, Laing's Nek, Ingogo, and Majuba. Having been ejected from it, the British agree (again) to recognise the Republic's independence. During this same time, there are rebellions in the Transkei and Basutoland. The tribesmen give a rough handling to the Cape Colonial and loyal Burgher forces sent against them. British set-backs would have been even worse if the Cape of Good Hope Act, introduced two years earlier, had not permitted the raising of more of these part-time Volunteer units.

1882-1889: having rid themselves of the British, the Transvaal Boers are obliged to fight a series of battles with rebellious tribes in the northern and western areas of their Republic.

1884: huge deposits of gold, much larger than anything found previously, are discovered at Witwatersrand, in the Transvaal. British and other European businessmen are permitted by the Boers to move in and to exploit this new wealth.

1888: British Regulars and Zulu Levies defeat a Zulu insurgent movement. Its leader, Chief Dinizulu, is captured and exiled.

1889-1892: the emergence of Cecil Rhodes as an Empire builder. A British entrepreneur, he has made a fortune from the Kimberley (Griqualand West) diamond mines and from the Witwatersrand goldfield. Now he has gained from the Matabele a monopoly on the mineral rights in their tribal lands, north of the Transvaal. With his associates, he has formed the British South Africa Company, a financially and politically potent power in the region. The BSA Company Police escort the first column of settlers into Mashonaland. Rhodes claims the territory for the Crown.

1893: a Matabele induna invades Mashonaland. The incursion is soon crushed, but the incident causes Rhodes to authorise the colonisation of Matabeleland.

1895-1896: there is a similar problem in the Transvaal. The lure of gold is drawing in large numbers of speculators and adventurers from far and wide. The Republic's President, 'Paul' Kruger , is alarmed by the threat to the Boer way of life posed by these 'Uitlanders'. When pressed, he refuses to grant them the right to vote in local affairs. A column of Mashonaland Mounted Police (effectively BSA Company men) makes a provocative and illegal raid into the Transvaal from Bechuanaland. It is led by Sir Leander Jameson, a close colleague of Rhodes. Its objective is to inspire the 'Uitlanders' to overthrow Kruger and his administration. The raid fails when Jameson and his men are captured by local Commandos.

1895: Zambesia (Matabeleland and Mashonaland) are merged and renamed Rhodesia.

1896-1897: the Langeberg Rebellion. The Bechuana tribes protest at the enforced destruction of their diseased cattle. Cape Colonial forces, with Volunteers and Native Levies, put down the revolt after six major actions.
1899: continuing British pressure on his government, combined with the aftermath of the Jameson Raid, causes President Kruger, in desperation, to declare war on the British. The Orange Free State and the Transvaal join forces. Apart from some trained artillerymen, these consist almost entirely of farmers and their sons. They have little military training or organisation, but their way of life has made them expert horsemen, marksmen and foragers. They besiege the British bases at Mafeking, Kimberley and Ladysmith.
1900: the sieges are raised by the troops of Field Marshals Lord Kitchener and Lord Roberts. The British Government mounts a massive propaganda campaign throughout the world, depicting the Boers as a threat to the safety of the Empire. Contingents of Volunteers are raised in Australia, Canada, New Zealand, India and Ceylon. The British Army Regulars receive further support with the arrival of the Yeomanry, a Volunteer force recruited in Great Britain specifically for this purpose. The Boers are defeated after a series of set-piece battles in which they inflict heavy losses upon the Empire forces.
1900-1902: having been overwhelmed by weight of numbers, the Boers embark upon a hit-and-run guerilla war. Unable to suppress the roving Commandos, the British wage war upon their families. Farms are burned, food and livestock stolen, and non-combatants placed in concentration camps. Nearly 28,000 women and children die of disease and starvation in these camps.
1902: broken by the British strategy, the Boer leaders, Smuts, Botha and De Wet, capitulate. An Armistice is signed at Vereeniging on 2 May. At their peak, the Empire's forces in the field exceeded 500,000 men. The maximum strength of the Boer forces was about 65,000. At the time of the Armistice, they still have 22,000 men under arms. Having been defeated, the two Boer Republics are forced to become Colonies of the Empire. The British have achieved what they have wanted for the past thirty years - control of the world's richest sources of diamonds and gold.
1903: the Natal Militia Act converts the Volunteers into a Militia system.
1906: led by Chief Bambata, the Zulus rebel against a new hut tax. A police patrol is masssacred. The revolt is put down by units from Natal and the Transvaal.
1907: the Morenga Expedition. Police from the Cape assist the Germans in South West Africa where Chief Morenga has rebelled against European occupation.
1910: the Act of Union. The two former British Colonies - the Cape and Natal - are joined to the two former Boer Republics - the Orange Free State and the Transvaal - to form a new Union of South Africa.
1913: the police put down a violent strike by miners in the Witwatersrand gold fields.
1914: the Union declares war against Germany. Anti-British Boers revolt against the declaration. Their rebellion is put down by local Commandos led by two of the Crown's principal former opponents, Botha and Smuts. Neighbouring South West Africa, a well-established German colony, is invaded by Union Permanent and Active Citizen Force (ACF) troops. After six months of remarkable campaigning, the Germans are driven to surrender. The 67,000 South African troops engaged are then disbanded because their terms of attestation do not permit their deployment outside Southern Africa. A scheme is introduced for the recruitment of 'Imperial Service' units, attested for service in other regions of Africa and overseas.
1915: 44,000 white volunteers, with newly raised Cape Coloured infantry and Indian Stretcher Bearer Corps units in support, move to East Africa to join in the campaign against von Lettow Vorbeck. They achieve military success, but suffer heavy losses from tropical diseases. Most will be withdrawn during 1917.
1916: Union forces help to protect the Suez Canal by joining in the campaign against the Senussi. They then move to France and Flanders. They distinguish themselves at Delville Wood, Butte de Warlencourt, Arras, on the Somme, and at Lys and Messines. Nearly 58,000 South Africans will fight on the Western Front and a quarter will become casualties.

1917: South African artillery units and Cape Coloured infantry serve under Allenby in the Palestine campaign.
1919: the troops come home. In total, 231,600 South Africans have served in the war. Of these, 18,600 have died or been injured.
1920: the South African Air Force is formed.
1922: the South African Naval Service is formed. The Army is placed on a regular peacetime establishment, with new Staff, Engineer, Medical, Ordnance and Artillery Corps as elements of the Permanent Force. The old pre-Union part-time volunteer ACF regiments are preserved. They are called out for 'aid to the civil power' duties when miners in the Witwatersrand gold fields launch a very violent strike. There is trouble in South West Africa, caused by rebellious Hottentots.
1926: the South African Mounted Rifles are disbanded. National economies lead to severe cuts in the Permanent Force. Its strength is reduced to 151 officers and 1259 Other Ranks.
1929: more cuts result in the disbandment of forty-nine ACF units (nearly all of those which had been raised during the major reorganisations of 1913). The pre-1913 units survive, but in name only. All ACF training is suspended.
1933: the highly successful Special Service Battalion is formed to train, and provide work for, young unemployed whites.
1934: the Naval Service is abolished, but fifteen ACF units are reactivated and nine new ones created.
1937: a scheme is launched to produce a large reserve of pilots for the South African Air Force.
1939: some South Africans, particularly in the Afrikaner (formerly known as Boer) community, are opposed to siding with the British against Germany. With Great Britain's treatment of their forebears, and the heavy losses of the Great War, still fresh in mind, they would prefer neutrality. The South African authorities decide, therefore, that all military service shall be on a voluntary basis only. From a small and ill-prepared base, the nation quickly brings three Divisions up to full strength. The Air Force expands dramatically, as do various home defence and ancillary arms.
1940: 1st SA Division takes a leading role in removing the Italians from Abyssinia and Eritrea.
1941: 1st and 2nd SA Divisions move to the Western Desert. They suffer heavy losses in the battles around Sidi Rezegh.
1942: Tobruk is again under siege, but the in-depth defences created earlier by the British and the Australians have been allowed to fall into disrepair. The new defending force, which includes a large South African element, is forced to surrender. In October, South African artillery, armoured cars and infantry help to win the great victory at El Alamein. Far to the south, 7th SA Brigade assists in clearing the Vichy French out of Madagascar and possibly forestalling a Japanese occupation of that island.
1943: heavy casualties in the Western Desert have depleted the ranks of 1st and 2nd SA Divisions. They are brought home and regrouped as 6th SA Armoured Division. More volunteers are recruited and the Division is brought up to full strength. After a year of training at home and in the Middle East, it moves to mainland Italy and serves throughout that campaign.
1945: a total of 342,700 men and women, of all ethnic groups, have served full-time in the war, and 210,000 part-time. Of these, 38,200 have become casualties.
1950-1952: South Africa joins the United Nations effort in Korea by despatching No 2 Squadron SAAF. It flies 12,400 sorties, losing seventy-nine aircraft.
1957: a new Defence Act replaces the legislation of 1912, 1922 and 1932. The Union Defence Force is retitled the South African Defence Force. New styles of uniform and insignia are introduced, and a new system of honours and awards replaces the British decorations previously awarded.
1961: South Africa leaves the Commonwealth and becomes a republic. Anarchy in the Congo basin, following the Belgian withdrawal in the previous year, causes much concern in South Africa.

1965: Southern Rhodesia, under Prime Minister Ian Smith, makes a unilateral declaration of independence. The British Government pronounces the declaration to be illegal. It imposes economic sanctions and a maritime blockade. Bush warfare breaks out. In South Africa's two other neighbouring countries, Angola and Mozambique, similar campaigns are being conducted by various 'freedom' groups. These countries have been colonised by Portugal since the 16th Century, but Portuguese authority has been undermined by several United Nations resolutions and a weak economy at home. With the Belgians, French and British having already made hasty withdrawals from other parts of the continent, many white South Africans regard themselves as being the last remaining custodians of law and order.
1966: South West Africa had been annexed by Germany in 1884. A mandate to administer the territory was granted to South Africa in 1920 by the League of Nations, but this mandate is now unilaterally cancelled by the United Nations. South Africa disputes the decision and takes its case to the World Court in The Hague. The Court rules against the United Nations and South Africa continues to govern. The Soviet bloc, through its Angolan contacts, starts to sponsor a nationalist 'freedom' movement.
1975: a left-wing coup in Lisbon results in Portugal abandoning the long-running struggle to retain control of Guinea Bissau, Mozambique and Angola. Power is handed over to the left-wing leaders of Guinea-Bissau and Mozambique, and to the Soviet/Cuban-backed MPLA in Angola. There are two other powerful factions in Angola - the Chinese-backed FNLA and the socialist UNITA. Denied a role in their country's future by Lisbon's accord with the Communist MPLA, they appeal to the South Africans for military assistance. Pretoria responds with Operation Savannah - a deep penetration by the SA Defence Force which overruns large areas of Angola. The operation is actively supported by the US Central Intelligence Agency but condemned by the US Congress. After several clashes with Cuban-manned Soviet tanks, the South African force withdraws under pressure from 'world opinion'.
1980: despite the support of his powerful neighbour, Rhodesia's leader, Ian Smith, is obliged to hand over his country to the guerilla leaders. It is renamed Zimbabwe. The two main tribal groups, the Mashona and the Matabele, turn on each other.
1989: having for several years contained the SWAPO insurgents in South West Africa, Pretoria agrees under continuing United Nations pressure to hold a referendum in that country. The result is a foregone conclusion. SWAPO has close links with the MPLA in Angola, and has been receiving abundant resources from the Soviets. The nationalists obtain a majority at the polls and the South African forces withdraw under United Nations supervision. The territory becomes an independent country under the title Namibia.
1992: with the French, Belgian, British and Portuguese governments having abandoned their former responsibilities in most of the African continent, political and economic chaos have become widespread. Ancient tribal animosities, combined with a scramble for power, sustain a series of civil wars. Within the Republic of South Africa, there is a growing movement towards some form of multi-racial government. The concept of apartheid has been at last discarded. In response to a number of perceived internal and external threats, the nation has created one of the world's most efficient and best-equipped defence forces.
1994: free elections result in a black majority government, with Nelson Mandela as the nation's President.

GENERAL REFERENCE

THE ARMED FORCES OF SOUTH AFRICA

Maj G Tylden * Cape Town Times Ltd, for the Africana Museum, Johannesburg, 1954. Bright red, gold, 8.75 x 5.5, xvi/239. Fp, 3 mono phots, 68 line drawings (unit badges), no maps, Bibliography, Index of personal names of military interest, Index of Regtl mottoes and accronyms found on cap badges. Apps: short history of the Boer Commandos, idem The German Legion (1857), notes on sources consulted.
* The text opens with a short account (31 pages) of the evolution of the armed forces of South Africa, 1659 to 1946. The bulk of the book is then devoted to 628 entries dealing with the various military and police units raised in that region at one time or another. Arranged alphabetically, the entries provide condensed but vital information concerning dates of formation and disbandment, badges, uniforms, campaign services, and the like. Footnotes are provided throughout. An essential source for all research on South Africa's military history. R/5 V/4. PC. HIS.
Note: short-comings in this book were identified in AFRICANA NOTES AND NEWS (Africana Museum, Johannesburg) in March 1955, December 1958 and September 1960. The original work was republished in facsimile in 1982 (Trophy Press, Johannesburg), with the Addenda and Corrigenda from the AFRICANA NEWS AND NOTES incorporated at the rear. The Addenda provide details of 106 Town Guards and 68 District Mounted Troops. The 1954 edition is collectable for its rarity, but the 1982 version is the more complete source of reference. An additional source is OUR AFRICAN REGIMENTS, PAST AND PRESENT, by H G Murray (D Francis & Co, Bloemfontein, 1934).A booklet of 35 pages, it gives slightly more detail than Tylden of the units which came into being at the formation of the Union Defence Force in 1913. GTB.

INFANTRY IN SOUTH AFRICA, 1652–1976

Capt R J Bouch * Documentation Service, SA Defence Force, Pretoria, 1977. Black, silver, Springbok motif, 12.0 x 8.0, vi/276. 73 mono phots, 58 cld ills, 2 line drawings, 29 maps, Bibliography, no appendixes, no Index.
* The book traces the evolution of infantry warfare in South Africa from the time of the Dutch East Indies Company through to the Angola operations of the 1970s. Written in both English and Afrikaans, the narrative opens with an account of the early Hottentot and Cape Corps, the Cape Mounted Riflemen, Cape and Natal Police, the Impis of the Zulu Nation, and the Commandos and Artillery of the Boer Republics. The Union Defence Force was established in 1913, being based upon five Regts of SA Mounted Rifles and the infantry Regts of the Active Citizen Force. The author provides superficial but useful coverage of their expansion and active services in WWI and WWII. The second part of the book gives details of the infantry Regts of the modern SA Defence Force, National Service Training Units and the Active Citizen Force, placing them in an Order of Precedence (as in 1976). Most useful as a framework for further study. R/3 V/3. AL. GTB.

SHAMROCK AND SPRINGBOK

The Irish Impact on South African Military History, 1689–1914

Stanley Monick * Printed by The Freedom Press, Kempton Park, Johannesburg, for the South African Irish Regtl Assn, 1989. Green, black, combined 'Shamrock and Springbok' motif in white/black, 7.75 x 6.5, x/436. 38 mono phots, 5 line drawings (Regtl badges), 7 maps, Bibliography, Index. Apps: Roll of Honour (6th Inniskilling Dragoons, 1899–1902), unit nominal rolls (Upington's Foot, 'C' Coy Prince Alfred's Guard, etc), notes on the Regts of the Irish Bde (1775), idem 100th Regt of Foot.
* In effect, this is the scene-setter for the story of the South African Irish Regt, formed in 1914. The author has drawn together many and diverse strands to weave his tale. He shows how the birth of the Regt was a culmination of historical events far beyond the shores of Africa. After describing the raison d'etre of the Irish Bde in France and Austria-Hungary, he recounts the development of Irish nationalism, its impact in America and South Africa, the services of British Army Regts whose ranks were composed of Irishmen and sent to South Africa between 1795

and 1902, and the schisms provoked by the quarrels between the British and the Boers in the late 19th Century. He makes the point that the nationalist Irish Brigade fought during the war of 1899-1902 on the side of the Boers, while Irish Loyalists and Irish Regulars of the British Army fought against them. It was only after that war, and the subsequent emergence of a 'South African identity', that units of an Irish provenance were formed - the Cape Town Irish Rifles, 'C' Coy of Prince Alfred's Volunteer Guard, and the South African Irish Regt. This is a deeply researched authoritative work with a remarkably detailed Index (the author, Dr Monick, being an expert on indexing systems). Although the book does not have an 'Honours & Awards' appendix, lists of such awards appear throughout the text. R/1 V/5. PC. GTB.
Note: the same author subsequently (1992) produced a two-volume continuation work, dealing with the South African Irish post-1914 (vide page 344).

COLOURS AND HONOURS IN SOUTH AFRICA, 1783-1948
Dr H H Curson * Wallach's P & P Co Ltd, Pretoria, 1948. Buff, black, 9.5 x 7.0, xv/123. Fp, 56 mono phots (indexed, almost all of Regtl Colours), no maps, list of accronyms of all South African units. Apps: Regulations for the design of UDF Colours (at 1931).
* A primary source for students of Regtl Colours. Ironically, the Colours illustrations are printed in black and white, but the accompanying narrative and chronological tables are the definitive work on this specialist subject. Of interest to a wider readership are the references to Battle Honours and Regtl lineages. R/3 V/5. RCSL. RP.

SHORT HISTORY OF THE VOLUNTEER REGIMENTS OF NATAL AND EAST GRIQUALAND, PAST AND PRESENT
Col Godfrey T Hurst DSO OBE VD * Knox Publishing Co, Durban, 1945. Green, black, 8.5 x 5.5, vi/170. Fp, no other ills, no maps, Bibliography, no appendixes, no Index.
* An anthology of condensed unit histories, amongst which: Natal Mounted Rifles, Royal Durban Light Infantry, Royal Natal Carbineers, Umvoti Mounted Rifles, Natal Naval Corps, and 'other Corps no longer extant'. A useful source of reference and particularly helpful in respect of the smaller units which had a short life-span. Sixty-three different units are mentioned in this book. R/4 V/4. RCSL/JPL. VS/GTB.
Note: in the context of small defunct volunteer units, the following publications have been noted but not seen - NATAL COLONIAL SCOUTS, 1899-1900, anon (published in Durban by the NATAL MERCURY), HISTORY OF THE NATAL CARBINEERS (no other details traced), and HISTORICAL RECORD OF THE ZULULAND MOUNTED RIFLES (published in the ZULULAND TIMES ANNUAL,1924).

WORLD WAR I

UNION OF SOUTH AFRICA AND THE GREAT WAR, 1914-1918
Official History
Anon * Government Printer, Pretoria, for the General Staff, Defence HQ, 1924. Brick red, gold, Union coat of arms, 11.0 x 8.5, -/230. Fp, 23 mono phots, 28 maps, Index. Apps: list of every SA unit engaged (with summary of casualties for each), roll of the thirteen VC winners(with full citations).
* The book covers the whole of South Africa's contribution to WWI in concise but adequate detail. Although the Preface states that it does not attempt to assess or record the achievements of any individual units, the narrative does in fact contain good mini-histories of many which served on the Western Front - 71st, 72nd, 74th, 75th, 125th Siege Btys SAHA, 44th Bty RGA, Signal Coy, Medical Corps, Railway Coys, Cape Auxiliary Horse Transport Corps, and the SAASC Coys. Other chapters describe the formations deployed in various theatres of war, and the multifarious organisations created to support the front line troops. The maps and illustrations are adequate. R/4 V/4. SANMMH/RSAEL. GTB/PJE.
Note: published with a print run of 1000 copies.

THE CAMPAIGN IN GERMAN SOUTH WEST AFRICA, 1914-1915

Brig Gen J J Collyer CMG DSO * Government Printer, Pretoria, 1937. Brick red, gold, Union coat of arms, 8.5 x 6.5, vi/180. Fp (map of SW Africa), no ills, 16 other maps (all bound in), no appendixes, Index.

* The official account of the campaign to remove the Germans from what is now Namibia. The author opens with an explanation of the European colonisation of that corner of Africa and the evolution of the Union Defence Force. He then sets out very clearly the course of the campaign and the roles of the Southern Army, the Central Force (operating from Luderitzbucht), and the Northern Force (from Swakopmund). The campaign, fought entirely by SA Permanent Force, Active Citizen Force and Boer Commando units operating under their own high command and staff, was completed in 133 days. All of the major movements and actions are covered in detail, with helpful supporting maps. The book would have benefitted from the addition of some appendixes (lists of participating units, for example).

R/3 V/4. SANMMH/RSAEL. GTB/PJE.

Note: highly recommended as additional reading is URGENT IMPERIAL SERVICE - SOUTH AFRICAN FORCES IN GERMAN SOUTH WEST AFRICA, by Gerald L'Ange (Ashanti Publishing, Rivonia, Johannesburg, 1991). This is a serious retrospective examination of that campaign, with a superb range of photographic illustrations.

WITH BOTHA IN THE FIELD

Moore Ritchie * Longmans, Green & Co, London, 1915. Khaki boards with dark brown spine, black, gold, 7.5 x 5.0, xii/68. 2 fps, 82 mono phots (indexed), 5 maps (2 printed in the text, 3 bound in), no Index. Apps: casualty statistics.

* The author was a policeman who volunteered to join Botha's Bodyguard, a unit composed of 50 Afrikaans-speaking and 50 English-speaking police officers. His account covers two separate campaigns. The first was the suppression of the rebellion in 1914 when elements of the Union Defence Force and of some Boer Commandos rejected the decision of the Botha government to join Great Britain in the war against the Central Powers. Little has been written elsewhere about this episode. The second campaign was that conducted in GSWA (German South West Africa). The illustrations relate equally to both campaigns. A valuable addition to the record of South Africa's role during the early months of the war.

R/4 V/4. SADFA. GTB.

THE SOUTH AFRICANS WITH GENERAL SMUTS IN GERMAN EAST AFRICA, 1916

Brig Gen J J Collyer CB CMG DSO * Government Printer, Pretoria, 1939. Brick red, black, Union coat of arms, 8.5 x 5.5, xxi/299. Fp (map of East Africa), no ills, 22 other maps (bound in), no appendixes, Index.

* A detailed and readable record of the 48,500 men of the UDF who served under Smuts in GEA during 1916 and 1917. They were then withdrawn due to the high wastage caused by malaria and other tropical diseases (they were replaced in the field by black African units such as those of the much expanded King's African Rifles). The author sets the South African participation in the context of the opening phases of the campaign (1914-1915) and pays generous tribute to the British, African and Indian units involved. Lists of officers appear at various points in the narrative, but Collyer was Chief of Staff to Smuts and his style of presentation inevitably reflects the senior staff officers' overview of events.

R/3 V/4. AL/RSAEL. GTB/PJE.

Note: a variant having a green cloth casing has been noted (identical contents). For a possibly more balanced perspective of the campaign, reference should be made to THEY FOUGHT FOR KING AND KAISER - SOUTH AFRICANS IN GERMAN EAST AFRICA, by James Ambrose Brown (Ashanti Publications, Rivonia, Johannesburg, 1991). Unlike Collyer's work, this book is generously illustrated.

THE EAST AFRICAN FORCE, 1915-1919
An Unofficial Record of the Creation and Fighting Career ...
Brig Gen C P Fendall CB CMG DSO * H F & G Witherby, London, 1921. Brick red, gold, 'Askari' motif, 9.0 x 5.75, -/238. Fp, 20 mono phots (indexed), one map (bound in), no appendixes, Index.
* The author was a senior staff officer and this is his analytical account, based upon his diary and memory, of the formation and deployment of the Union's EAF. He did not take part in the fighting and does not attempt to describe it. Instead, he focuses upon the higher planning aspects of the campaign. After paying credit to the local and Indian forces which bore the brunt of the war during the early stages, he describes the formation of the EAF, its arrival in East Africa, the appointment of Smuts to command (and comments upon his suitability), the appointment of Van Deventer, the progression of the campaign into Portugese East Africa, and the negotiations for the armistice. The book contains substantial chapters on general problems of administration, veterinary and logistical problems, and medical problems (especially the high incidence of fever amongst European troops). The narrative ranges over other matters of interest - difficulties in obtaining fresh food, the difficulty of movement across areas of black cotton soil during the rains, and the work of the King's African Rifles and The Carrier Corps (vide Index, East Africa). A final section describes some of the outstanding personalities of the campaign and discusses why it was that von Lettow Vorbeck managed to keep going for so long. A thoughtful book, by a privileged observer. R/4 V/4. SANMMH. GTB.

THE HISTORY OF THE SOUTH AFRICAN FORCES IN FRANCE
John Buchan * Thomas Nelson & Sons Ltd, London, 1920. Dark blue, gold, Union coat of arms, 9.0 x 5.75, -/404. Fp, 17 mono phots, 22 maps (bound in), Index. Apps: H&A (for all SA personnel who served on the Western Front, with full citations for all VC awards to South Africans during WWI), notes on SA Heavy Artillery, Signal Coy (RE), Cape Auxiliary Horse Transport Coys, and medical services.
* The narrative gives some account of 1st SA Infantry Bde in the Libya campaign against the Turks and Senussi but, as the title implies, this is mainly a record of its services in France and Flanders. The period covered is 1916 (the Somme) through to 1918. Detailed and readable. R/2 V/4. AL. DJB/RP.

DELVILLE WOOD
Ian Uys * Uys Publishers, Rensburg, 1983. Khaki, white, 9.5 x 6.75, xi/298. 205 mono phots, 13 line drawings, one sketch, 13 maps, Glossary, Bibliography, Index. Apps: Roll of Honour, H&A, list of officers.
* The tragic story of 1st SA Infantry Bde and its heroic fight to capture and hold Delville Wood (14-19 July 1916). Deeply researched, analysed at Company and Battalion level, based upon personal recollections interspersed with official records, the book explains what was planned and what actually happened. In the space of five days, the 1st, 2nd, 3rd and 4th SA Infantry Bns gained one VC, 5 DSOs, 14 MCs, 12 DCMs, and 31 MMs, plus a few yards of shattered ground. In return, they lost 766 officers and men dead, and an unknown number wounded. R/1 V/4. AL. BCC.
Note: other books on this subject are MEMORIES OF DELVILLE WOOD, by J A Lawson (Maskew Miller, 1918), DELVILLE WOOD, by D Fourie, and THE SOUTH AFRICANS AT DELVILLE, by Richard Cornwall (Militaria Publications, 1977).

BASIC GUIDE FOR COLLECTORS OF SOUTH AFRICAN 1914-1918 MEDALS
E H J Shaw * Military Medal Society of South Africa, Johnnesburg, 1981. Stiff plastic, yellow, black, 11.75 x 8.25, -/35. No ills, no maps, Bibliography, Index. Apps: Addenda and Corrigenda.
* Despite its title, this little publication is useful to a wider range of researchers. It lists all UDF units extant during WWI. In addition to the Infantry, Mounted Rifles and Dismounted Rifles of the Permanent Force and Active Citizen Force, it covers all the Commando units, Defence Rifles Associations, Artillery and other specialist Corps (including the Air Force). Especially useful, as quick reference, are the listings of all the units which served in GSWA, GEAF and France/Flanders.

The work is one of several which describe the medallic awards to South Africans in various wars and campaigns. Most of them consist of little more than nominal rolls of recipients, and are therefore usually stocked by medal dealers rather than book dealers. R/4 V/3. PC. GTB.
Note: only 100 copies printed.

WORLD WAR II

EAST AFRICAN AND ABYSSINIAN CAMPAIGNS
South African Forces, World War II, Volume I
Neil Orpen * Purnell, Cape Town, 1968. Blue, gold, 10.0 x 6.0, xiv/390. 67 mono phots, 14 maps (11 printed in the text, 3 bound in), Bibliography, Index. Apps: notes on the UDF before 1933, the reorganisations of 1939, Italian Order of Battle (East Africa, June 1940), notes on the 1st SA Div, idem 11th (EA) Div, etc.
* This comprehensive record was the first of a series of semi-official histories compiled by the SA War Histories Committee in Johannesburg, and is 'completely authoritative'. The author was one of the most determined researchers of his country's military history. The great strength of this and other works which he compiled in the series is that they are based not only upon South African records but also Italian archives and eyewitness accounts. R/2 V/4. SANMMH. RP.

MUD, BLOOD AND LAUGHTER
Maurice Broll * War Fund Books, Cape Town, 1943. Buff, black, 7.5 x 5.0, -/132. 3 fps, 5 mono phots, 5 cld ills, one map, no appendixes, no Index.
* A readable account of 1st SA Div in the East African campaign of 1940-1941, presented in two parts. The first covers the move to Kenya and the period of training and preparation. The second describes the move north to Hargeisa in British Somaliland, and then the fighting advance through Abyssinia and the move to the Western Desert. The author served with the Division and his viewpoint provides a useful individual perspective. R/4 V/2. SANMMH. GTB.

WAR IN THE DESERT
South African Forces, World War II, Volume III
Neil Orpen * Purnell, Cape Town, 1971. Blue, gold, 10.0 x 6.0, xii/538. 67 mono phots, 20 maps (19 printed in the text, one bound in), Bibliography, Index.
Apps: notes on 'Braforce', 1st SA Div, 2nd SA Div, Order of Battle (17.10.1942).
* This is the complete story of the South African participation in the North African campaign from December 1940 through to El Alamein and late 1942. It is a definitive work, based upon South African, British, German and Italian records and reminiscences. R/2 V/4. SANMMH. RP.
Note: reference may be made also to RETREAT TO VICTORY - A SPRINGBOK'S DIARY IN NORTH AFRICA - GAZALA TO EL ALAMEIN, 1942, by James Ambrose Brown (Ashanti Publications Pty Ltd, Rivonia, Johannesburg, 1991.

THE FIGHTING THIRD
The Full Story of the Vital Battles in the North African Campaign fought by the Third South African Infantry Brigade, Consisting of the Imperial Light Horse, the Royal Durban Light Infantry, the Rand Light Infantry, and Ancillary Arms
Capt Ronald W Tungay * Printed by Unie-Volkspers Beperk, Cape Town, 1947. Dusky red, black, 8.25 x 6.0, x/410. 3 mono phots, no maps, no Index. Apps: Rolls of Honour (6 pages for KIA, with separate rolls for WIA and POW), H&A (3 pages), list of COs for each unit (1940-1943).
* A well written narrative account of services in Abyssinia and the Western Desert. It contains a wealth of detail covering events and actions between 1940 and 1943, with many individuals of all ranks mentioned in the text. Apart from those Regts named in the long sub-title, the book also makes reference to the Middellandse Regt and the Bde's attached Engineer, Signals and logistics units. R/3 V/4. SANMMH. GTB.

CRISIS IN THE DESERT

J A I Agar-Hamilton and L C F Turner * Rustica Press, for Oxford University Press, Cape Town, 1952. Black, gold, 9.75 x 6.5, x/368. Fp, no other mono phots, 37 maps (22 printed in the text, 15 bound in), Bibliography, Index. Apps: Order of Battle of all SA units in the Middle East (incl the smallest, in great detail).
* The turning point in the Desert War came between 26 May and 9 July 1942. This deeply researched account of the role played by SA forces during those critical six weeks is one of three such volumes produced by the Union War Histories Dept of the Office of the Prime Minister (the others were WAR IN THE SOUTHERN OCEANS and THE SIDI REZEG BATTLES, 1941). Its particular value is the light which it throws upon the actions of 1st SA Div in the retreat from Gazala, the fall of Tobruk, and then the last-ditch stand at El Alamein. The appendix appears to be unique to this book. R/2 V/5. SANMMH. GTB.

THE POLICE BRIGADE
6th SA Infantry Brigade, 1939–1945

Brig F W Cooper DSO * Printed by Cape & Transvaal Printers Ltd, Cape Town, for Constantia Publishers, Cape Town, RSA, 1972. Soft linen covers, white, black, Divsl sign, 8.5 x 5.5, -/142. 28 mono phots, 3 maps, no Index. Apps: H&A, list of all officers and RSMs who served (with 14 pages of sketches of those so named).
* A short but complete account of the services of 6th SA Infantry Bde. It comprised 1st and 2nd SA Police Bns (hence its name) and 2nd Transvaal Scottish. The period covered is June 1940 (when it was formed) through to June 1942 (when it went into captivity at the fall of Tobruk). R/2 V/2. SANMMH. GTB.

VICTORY IN ITALY
South African Forces, World War II, Volume V

Neil Orpen * Purnell, Cape Town, RSA, 1975. Blue, gold, 10.0 x 6.0, xiv/340. Fp, 64 mono phots, 14 maps (bound in), no appendixes (but some helpful annotations), Bibliography, Index.
* Mainly the story of 6th SA Armoured Div (including the British 24th Guards Armoured Bde) in Italy from the Battle of Cassino through to the end of the war. The narrative includes much interesting information regarding the efforts of the SA Engineer Corps in repairing the wrecked road and rail system as the Allies advanced slowly northwards. The SA Railway Construction Group alone had 10,000 men deployed in Italy. Compiled from South African, British, American, and German records. R/2 V/4. SANMMH. GTB.
Note: reference should be made also to WAR IN ITALY - WITH THE SOUTH AFRICANS FROM TARANTO TO THE ALPS, by Jack Kros (Ashanti Publications, Rivonia, Johannesburg, c.1990).

WITH THE 6th DIV
An Account of the Activities of the 6th South African Armoured Division in WWII

W L Fielding * Shuter & Shooter, Natal Witness, Pietermaritzburg, 1946. Blue-green, black, 7.5 x 5.25, xv/191. Fp (map of Italy), 22 mono phots, 4 other maps, no appendixes, no Index.
* The author was Tactical Intelligence Officer with 6 Div and he wrote this account while events were still fresh in his mind. The narrative covers the period from early 1943 (when the Div was formed) through to late 1945 (when it was broken up). It is a readable one-man's view of his country's main contribution to the Italian campaign, with useful coverage of all the units which served under 6 Div's command - Witwatersrand/De La Rey Regt, Royal Natal Carbineers, Natal Mounted Rifles, Combined Regt DSR, Prince Alfred's Guard, Pretoria Regt, Special Service Bn, and supporting Corps formations. R/3 V/3. AL/RSAEL. GTB/PJE.

NON-EUROPEAN UNITS

FIGHTING THEIR OWN WAR
South African Blacks in the First World War
A Grundlingh * Ravan Press, Johannesburg, 1987. Illustrated soft card, dark green, red, 8.5 x 5.5, x/200. No ills, no maps, Glossary, Bibliography (very extensive), no appendixes, Index.
* A deeply researched academic examination of the role of black South Africans in WWI. The narrative discusses white and black reactions to the call for more man-power and describes their impact upon contemporary and later social changes. There was much debate concerning the rights and wrongs of permitting men from the High Commission Territories of Swaziland, Bechuanaland and Basutoland to join the South African forces in East Africa and France, and whether or not they should be trained as combatants. Much of the story relates to the SA Native Labour Contingent, so this book is a useful adjunct to Clothier's account (vide following entry). The Bibliography alone makes this a valuable source of reference.
R/1 V/4. SANMMH. GTB.

BLACK VALOUR
The South African Native Labour Contingent, 1916-1918
Norman Clothier * University of Natal Press, Pietermaritzburg, 1987. Plasticated soft card, 'Sinking of the Mendi' motif, grey, red, 8.0 x 5.5, xvi/204. Fp, 21 mono phots, one map, Bibliography (16 pages), Index. Apps: Roll of Honour (of personnel lost in the SS Mendi, 7 pages).
* The SA Native Labour Contingent was raised (1916) for logistical work behind the lines on the Western Front. The personnel consisted of African troops under the command of white officers and SNCOs (21,000 all ranks). They served actively during the last two years of the war and rendered important service in sustaining the fighting troops. Disbanded in 1919, the unit is particularly remembered for the catastrophe which befell its 5th Bn in the early hours of 21 February 1917. It was being transported from Plymouth to Le Havre aboard the SS Mendi when, in the early hours of the morning, south of the Isle of Wight, the convoy encountered the SS Darro. The troopship was rammed and sank within 20 minutes. Amongst those lost were 616 officers and men of the SANLC. This is a well researched and clear account of the formation of the Corps, its services in France, and of the Mendi incident, with many personal recollections woven into the narrative.
R/1 V/5. AL. GTB.

SOLDIERS WITHOUT POLITICS
Blacks in the South African Armed Forces
Kenneth W Grundy * University of California Press, Berkeley (Calif) USA, 1983. Red, gold, 8.5 x 6.0, xiv/297. No ills, no maps, no appendixes, no Index.
* The book covers three main topics - the historical role of black South Africans in military service, their contribution to WWII, and their specific role (as police and para-militaries) in the post-war period of apartheid. The latter part covers the formation of the Black Combat Regts and the resuscitation, for the first time since WWI, of The Cape Corps. Useful statistics appear at various points in the text. R/1 V/4. SANMMH. GTB.
Note: The Cape Corps was disbanded in 1992.

THE STORY OF THE 1st CAPE CORPS (1915-1919)
Capt Ivor D Difford * Hortors Ltd, Cape Town, n.d. (c.1921). Glossy card boards, cloth spine, ivory/brown, gold, Corps crest, 10.0 x 7.0, -/448. 5 fps, 44 mono phots, 12 maps, Glossary, no Index. Apps: Roll of Honour (KIA, DOW and WIA), H&A (all ranks), list of former officers (with details of service), nominal roll (all ranks) with a record of service of officers while on detached service.
* The Cape Corps consisted of Cape Coloured personnel who volunteered for wartime service. Virtually unknown outside South Africa, the Corps is probably now largely forgotten inside its own country. The book is concerned mainly with

the men who served rather than with what they did. It contains a great deal of biographical information, and many of the individuals appear in captioned photographs. A first-class genealogical source, with an attractive presentation.
R/4 V/4. PCAL. RP.

WITH THE 2nd CAPE CORPS THRO' CENTRAL AFRICA
A History of the Battalion from its Formation in 1915 until its Return from East Africa
A J B Desmore * F W Ingram, at The Citadel Press, Cape Town, 1920. Greyish blue, black, 8.5 x 5.75, -/100. Fp, 11 mono phots (on 8 plates), no maps, no appendixes, no Index.
* A somewhat amateurish narrative which refers mainly to dates, locations and incidents. In direct contrast to the preceding entry (Gifford's account of the 1st Bn of the Corps), this book contains almost no reference to named individuals. Like the 1st Bn, the 2nd consisted of Cape Coloured men, recruited primarily in Cape Colony and commanded by European officers and SNCOs. It was trained in the infantry role and deployed as a defence force on the western border of Portugese East Africa. It did see some action, clashing with units of von Lettow Vorbeck's force when it made its return move to the north. The Bn seems to have been disbanded in late 1918 or early 1919. A moderately useful reference source, best read in conjunction with other accounts of that campaign. R/5 V/2. AL. GTB.

THEY LIVE BY THE SWORD
32 'Buffalo' Battalion
Col Jan Breytenbach * Lemur Books, Alberton (Transvaal), 1990. Dark green, white, 10.0 x 6.75, -/272. 42 mono phots, 2 maps (one printed in the text, one on the end-papers), Index. Apps: Roll of Honour (1975-1989, less Operation Savannah), H&A.
* The background to this book is the international pressure and internal unrest which, combined with the left-wing coup in Lisbon, caused Portugal to pull out of Angola in 1975 (vide the Chronology for South Africa). With the MPLA having won control of that country, the rival FAPLA and UNITA leaders appealed to Pretoria for support. One response was the appointment of Col Breytenach to create a multi-tribal Bn with men selected from both guerilla factions. The intention was to turn their past experience to advantage in fighting the MPLA and the Cubans. The book is his own account of how he selected his under-trained and ill-fed recruits, re-equipped them, brought them to fighting fitness and led them repeatedly into battle. When the cease-fire was declared in 1989, the men of the Bn could not return to their homes, nor could it move to Namibia (controlled by the MPLA-backed SWAPO). It was therefore sent, together with the mens' families and followers, to Pomfret, in Northern Cape Colony. This unique force, consisting of Portugese-speaking soldiers and English- and Afrikaans-speaking officers, black, white and coloured, was re-assigned to riot control duties in the tribally divided black townships within the Republic. The Bn prided itself on having no racial barriers within its own ranks and no tribal bias when operating in the townships, but it was disbanded in 1992 following accusations of using excessive violence. The book is a thought-provoking record of a remarkable unit. R/1 V/5. AL. GTB.

KOEVOET!
Jim Hooper * Southern Book Publishers, Bergvlei, Johannsesburg, 1988. Grey, white, 10.0 x 7.25, vii/236. 53 mono phots, 40 cld ills, no maps, no appendixes, Glossary, no Index.
* The Koevoet Special Police Unit was raised by the SWA authorities from Ovambo tribesmen to combat hostile incursions by SWAPO. It served on the Angola-Ovambaland border and gained a tough reputation before being disbanded in April 1989. The author, an American journalist, was attached to it from 1985 to 1987. He describes the daily life of the unit and its various engagements (in one of which he was wounded). Not a formal unit history, but the only published source of reference. R/1 V/3. AL. GTB.

ANGLO-BOER WAR, 1899-1902

THE COLONIALS IN SOUTH AFRICA, 1899-1902
Their Record, Based on the Despatches
John Stirling * William Blackwood & Sons, London & Edinburgh, 1907. Blue, gold, 9.0 x 5.75, xii/497. No ills, no maps, no appendixes, Index.
* An invaluable book which describes in detail all the Colonial Contingents which served. All of the Australian units are listed and described, as are those which went to South Africa from Canada, New Zealand and Ceylon. Further, and this is not made clear in the title, more than half of the book is devoted to units raised locally in Southern Africa. Apart from the better known units originating in Natal, Bechuanaland and Rhodesia, other more obscure formations covered here were Rimington's Guides, Brabant's Horse, Damant's Horse, Thorneycroft's Mounted Rifles, and so forth. The diversity of unit titles demonstrates the immense scale of Great Britain's military effort against the Boers. R/3 V/5. ANL. MCND'A.
Note: available in modern reprint by John Hayward.
The researcher interested in other little known units should note that a considerable number of non-white South Africans were recruited for Crown service between 1899 and 1902, particularly in Cape Colony. There were strong local political objections to any military training, or even basic weaponry skills, being given to non-whites, but these were overcome by the need for additional manpower. In the event, 198 non-white units are known to have borne arms on behalf of the British during the course of the war. Additionally, Bantus, Cape Coloureds and Bushmen were recruited as trackers, hospital orderlies, waggoners and storemen. No formal histories have been traced for any of these units, but an academic summary of the black experience in the Boer War can be found in ABRAHAM ESAU'S WAR - A BLACK SOUTH AFRICAN WAR IN THE CAPE, 1899-1902, by Dr Bill Nasson (Cambridge University Press, 1991). The narrative is certainly helpful, but the very extensive Bibliography and chapter notes (31 pages) are marred by numerous errors and should be ignored.

THE STORY OF THE IMPERIAL LIGHT HORSE IN THE SOUTH AFRICAN WAR, 1899-1902
George Fleming Gibson * G D & Co, no other details shown, 1937. Navy blue, gold, Regtl crest, 9.5 x 6.75, -/351/x. Fp, 33 mono phots (indexed), 6 maps (2 printed in the text, 4 bound in), no Index. Apps: H&A (incl MID), detailed list of tombstones and obelisks commemorating ILH personnel at 33 locations.
* A detailed and well researched history of the Regt from its raising in 1899 to its conversion to a Volunteer Corps in June 1902. The author writes with equal regard for the ILH and for its Boer opponents. The narrative is based upon War Diaries, personal anecdotes and Regtl Orders. It contains good detail of each engagement, with helpful supporting maps. Apart from the famous actions at Elandslaagte, Ladysmith and Mafeking, the author covers the less publicised Guerilla War engagements at Witklip, Cypherfontein and Hartebeestfontein, and the 'drives' in the Western Transvaal and the Orange Free State. The illustrations are mainly captioned photographs of Regtl personalities. R/4 V/4. SANMMHL/AL. GTB/PJE.
Note: copies with green covers and vi/351 pages have been noted. The contents appear to be identical.

NATAL VOLUNTEER RECORD
Annals and Rolls of Service in the Anglo-Boer War, 1899-1900
Anon (thought to have been H V Prisk) * Robinson & Co, Natal Mercury, Durban, 1900. Soft card, brick red, gold, 7.25 x 4.75, xii/204. No ills, no maps, Glossary, Index. Apps: Roll of Honour, lists of officers and SNCOs, muster rolls for all units.
* A short but useful record of the part played by the various Volunteer units of Natal, and the Natal Police, during the first year of the war. The following units are covered: Imperial and Volunteer Staffs, Natal Naval Volunteers, Natal Field Artillery, Hotchkiss Gun Detachment, Natal Royal Rifles, Natal Carbineers, Umvoti Mounted Rifles, Border Mounted Rifles, Natal Volunteer Veterinary Corps, Natal Volunteer Medical Corps and Murray's Horse. R/4 V/4. AL. GTB.

DIE HENDSOPPERS EN JOINERS
Die Rationaal en Verskynsel van Verraad
A M Grundlingh * Hollandsch Afrikaanche Uitgewers Maatschappije, Parow, 1977. Royal blue, white/blue, 9.0 x 6.5, viii/379. 6 mono phots, no maps, Glossary, Bibliography, no appendixes, Index.
* In English, the title is THE HANDSUPPERS AND JOINERS - THE RATIONALE AND MANIFESTATION OF TREASON. Not a unit history, the book nevertheless does explain the origins of The National Scouts and The Orange River Colony Volunteers. Both consisted of Boers, formally of the Orange Free State and the Transvaal Republic Armed Forces, who changed sides and attested for Crown service. One, surprisingly, was the brother of General de Wet. The author describes the circumstances leading to the formation of the two units, their deployments, conditions of service, and the post-war problems of re-integration. Many officers are mentioned in the text and the Bibliography is extensive. R/1 V/4. SANMMH. GTB.

CANADIAN CONTINGENTS

CANADA'S SONS ON KOPJE AND VELDT
A Historical Account of the Canadian Contingents
T G Marquis * Canada's Sons Publishing Co, Toronto, 1900. Royal blue, gold, 'figure of Victory with shield' motif, 8.5 x 5.25, xx/490. Fp, 90 mono phots (mainly individual officers), no maps, no Index. Apps: Roll of Honour (all Canadians KIA, DOW and DOD), muster rolls for 1st and 2nd Contingents and for Lord Strathcona's Horse, details of sailings of the transports.
* The definitive reference source for the three Contingents from Canada which took part in the Boer War up to the fall of Pretoria. The book is divided into two parts. The first deals with the 1st Contingent which consisted of eight Coys of infantry (125 men in each) recruited from all parts of Canada. They arrived at Belmont shortly after the battle and remained there, training and patrolling, before moving on to the major action at Paardeberg in February 1900. Subsequently they served at Poplar Grove, Abraham's Kraal, and the capture of Bloemfontein. The second part of the book describes the recruitment of the 2nd Contingent which consisted of four Squadrons of Mounted Rifles, three Btys of Artillery, and Lord Strathcona's Horse (see Index for other references to this unit). These arrived in South Africa in early 1900 and served initially in the Kenhardt district. The 1st and 2nd Contingents met at Bloemfontein and later fought on the Vet and Sand Rivers and at the taking of Kroonstad. Lord Strathcona's Horse subsequently joined Buller's army as scouts, while the Artillery element served at Mafeking. In September 1900, at Wolwe Spruit, the VC was won by Sgt Arthur Richardson, of Lord Strathcona's Horse. He was the first man to earn this award while serving with a Canadian unit under British command. R/4 V/4. RCMI. AM/GTB.

CANADIANS IN KHAKI
South Africa, 1899-1900
Anon * The Herald Publishing Co, Montreal, 1900. Illustrated stiff card, buff, red/black, 8.75 x 5.75, -/127. Fp, one mono phot, no maps, Glossary, Index.
* After a brief introduction to the war in South Africa, the book is taken up entirely with annotated nominal rolls for all the units and sub-units of the 1st and 2nd Contingents. The rolls are very detailed, showing the parent unit of every man who volunteered for South Afican service, with notes regarding previous active service, casualties, etc. Clearly, an excellent source for medal collectors and genealogists. R/4 V/5. MODL. AMM.
Note: an updated edition, with additional and corrected details,was published in 1917.

NEW BRUNSWICK MEN AT WAR
The South African War, 1899-1902
Daniel F Johnson and Byron E O'Leary * Copy Write Centre, St John, NB, for the authors, 1989. Stiff card and spiral spine, 8.5 x 7.0, ix/236. 16 mono phots (incl named portraits), no maps, Glossary, Index. Apps: Roll of Honour (extensive information regarding each casualty, for each NB unit), nominal roll (every man who enlisted in NB).
* The story of the volunteers born in New Brunswick, or residing therein, who volunteered for service in South Africa. Amongst the units named are the Royal Canadian Regt, Royal Canadian Dragoons, Lord Strathcona's Horse, South African Constabulary, 4th Cdn Mounted Rifles, and 10th Cdn Field Hospital. Apart from a brief history of each unit, the book is devoted entirely to a listing of biographical notes for each man. These are extremely detailed, and represent a rich source for genealogists. The notes also mention, where relevant, the later WWI services of each of these men. R/2 V/5. PC. JRD.

FROM QUEBEC TO PRETORIA
With the Royal Canadian Regiment
W Hart-McHarg * William Briggs, Toronto, 1902. Dark red, silver, Regtl crest, 7.75 x 5.5, -/276. Fp, 2 mono phots (both of the author!), 9 maps (8 printed in the text, one bound in), no Index. Apps: Rolls of Honour (KIA and WIA at Paardeberg, 18.2.1900 and 27.2.1900, plus DOD for the whole campaign).
* The author (later Lieutenant, Rocky Mountain Rangers) served with the RCR in South Africa as a Sergeant. Despite having himself been in the field with the Regt throughout the twelve months' deployment, his account is curiously impersonal and leaden. Few of his comrades are named in the narrative, although he does list the casualties incurred after each skirmish. Three chapters are devoted to the Battle of Paardeberg, thus providing a useful soldier's-eye view of the event. R/4 V/4. MODL. AMM.

AUSTRALIAN CONTINGENTS

OFFICIAL RECORDS OF THE AUSTRALIAN MILITARY CONTINGENTS TO THE WAR IN SOUTH AFRICA, 1899-1902
Lieut Col P L Murray * Printed by A J Mullett, Govt Printer, Melbourne, for the Dept of Defence, 1982. Dark green, gold, Royal coat of arms, 9.75 x 7.25, -/607. No ills, no maps, Index. Apps: Roll of Honour (KIA, DOW and DOD, listed by Contingent), H&A, unit nominal rolls (each Contingent).
* This is an official account of the Contingents sent by each of the six Australian Colonies. A section of the text is devoted to each Colony - New South Wales, Victoria, Queensland, South Australia, Western Australia and Tasmania - with a vast amount of information regarding dates, locations, engagements, casualties, and awards, for each unit and sub-unit. The lack of a Contents page is a weakness, but this is compensated by the provision of a very good Index. A definitive source. R/1 V/5. ANL. MCND'A.
Note: the version recorded above is the 1982 reprint of the original 1911 edition.

THE AUSTRALIANS AT THE BOER WAR
R L Wallace * AGPS, Canberra, for the Australian War Memorial, 1976. Tan, gold, 9.5 x 5.75, xv/420. 57 mono phots, 4 maps, Glossary, Bibliography, no appendixes, Index.
* A most comprehensive account of Australia's involvement in the war, with clear explanations of the factors leading to the decision by the six Colonies to send their volunteers to South Africa. The author gives interesting accounts of each action in which Australian and New Zealand troops were engaged. Australians won several Victoria Crosses in this war (Lieut F W Bell, Tpr J H Bisdee, et al), and the actions leading to their awards are described in detail. The illustrations and maps are outstanding, the Index first class. An entire chapter is devoted to the Court Martial and execution of Lieut Henry 'Breaker' Morant and Lieut Peter Handcock. R/1 V/5. ANL. MCND'A.

THE FORGOTTEN WAR

Australian Involvement in the South African Conflict of 1899–1902

L M Field * Melbourne University Press, Melbourne, 1979. Brown, gold, 8.75 x 5.5, xii/236. 8 mono phots, one map, Bibliography, Glossary, Index. Apps: Roll of Honour (statistics only), H&A (idem), notes on all the Colonial Contingents (incl Canada, New Zealand, India and Ceylon).

* A lucid account of all aspects (military, political and social) of Australia's involvement. The narrative is supported by voluminous notes, with explanations of how the different Contingents gained their unusual names. The author emphasises the particular value of these troops, their expert horsemanship, self-sufficiency, and mobility. There were no Australian journalists in the field during the last 18 months of the war so it was inadequately reported in contemporary Australian newspapers (hence the title of this book). R/1 V/5. ANL. MCND'A.

Note: an additional source is TO SHOOT AND RIDE – THE AUSTRALIANS IN THE SOUTH AFRICAN WAR, 1899-1902, by W M Chamberlain (Military History Society of Australia, 1967).

FOR QUEEN AND EMPIRE

A Boer War Chronicle

Ralph Sutton * Adept Printing Co, for the NSW Military History Society, 1974. Soft card, buff, brown, 'Queen Victoria' motif, Glossary, no Index. Apps: Roll of Honour, H&A, notes on 'Governments in NSW during the Boer War', 'Victoria Cross witness', 'Contingents despatched from NSW to South Africa, 1899–1902'.

* A book published to mark the 75th Anniversary of the outbreak of the war, and incorporating a wide range of useful material – actions in which NSW units were engaged (Spion Kop, Driefontein, Boschfontein), reprints of papers presented by veterans to the United Service Institution of NSW (1902–1905), chapters devoted to weaponry, topography, politics and descriptions of the units which served. The latter comprised the NSW Lancers, 'A' Sqn NSW Mounted Rifles, 1st Australian Horse, and 'A' Field Bty Australian Artillery. Capt Neville Howse, NSW Medical Staff Corps, won the VC at Vredefort while serving with the Contingents. An interesting narrative, good illustrations, good appendixes. R/1 V/4. ANL. MCND'A.

AUSTRALIANS IN WAR

With the Australian Regiment from Melbourne to Bloemfontein

Maj W T Reay * A H Massina & Co, Melbourne, 1900. Light brown, black, 7.5 x 5.0, –/382. No ills, no maps, no Index. Apps: Roll of Honour (Victorian casualties only, up to 1.9.1900, with names and locations for KIA, DOW, WIA, POW and invalided), list of officers of the First Australian Federal Regt.

* In October 1899, Tasmania, Victoria, South Australia and Western Australian all sent separate Contingents to South Africa. Upon arrival in Cape Town, they joined up with a New South Wales Contingent which had arrived earlier. A unique event then occurred. They were amalgamated under the title 'First Australian Commonwealth Regt'. This was a full year before the Federation of their parent states and the creation of the new Commonwealth of Australia. The book's 65 chapters cover all of this, operations in the field, and other related matters. The lack of any maps make the story difficult to follow, and the lack of an Index is an irritating omission. R/4 V/4. ANL. MCND'A.

THE AUSTRALIAN COMMONWEALTH HORSE

George Newbury * Privately by the author, Adelaide, 1990. Soft card, white, green/gold, unit crest, 11.75 x 8.25, iv/107. Fp, 30 mono phots, no maps, Glossary, no Index. Apps: Roll of Honour.

* A thoughtfully produced account of the eight Contingents, one from each Colony, which formed the ACH in South Africa between 1899 and 1902. The bulk of the text is devoted to a complete nominal roll for the Regt, with abundant related facts. Mainly for medal collectors and genealogists. R/1 V/4. AWM. PS.

FIRST QUEENSLAND MOUNTED INFANTRY CONTINGENT IN THE SOUTH AFRICA WAR 1899-1900

Maj Rex Clark * Military Historical Society of Australia, ACT Branch, 1971. Illustrated card, red, 'Trooper and badge' motif, 8.0 x 6.5, iii/26. 10 mono phots, no maps, no Index. Apps: roll of all members who served (with details of their campaign medals and clasps), H&A (incl 2 CBs, 1 CMG, 2 DSOs, 2 DCMs, 15 MID).
* The author compiled a series of these useful booklets, all similar in format and all geared to the needs of medal collectors and family historians. Amongst his other titles were - AUSTRALIAN CONTINGENTS TO THE BOXER REBELLION, 1900, THE FIRST VICTORIAN CONTINGENT TO THE SOUTH AFRICAN WAR, THE FIRST NEW SOUTH WALES CONTINGENT TO THE SOUTH AFRICAN WAR, and THE NEW SOUTH WALES CONTINGENT TO SUAKIN, 1885. R/2 V/3. PC. PS.

TASMANIANS IN THE TRANSVAAL WAR

Dr John Bufton * The Examiner & Weekly Courier, Launceston, for S G Loone, Hobart, Tasmania, 1905. Tan, gold, 9.25 x 7.5, xiii/534. 824 mono phots (mainly of individuals, arranged 24 to each page), no maps, no Index. Apps: Roll of Honour (shown as 'The Last Roll Call'), H&A (incl MID), 'Diary of the War'.
* This mammoth work covers every detail of the units raised in Tasmania for service in South Africa - First Tasmanian Contingent, First and Second Tasmanian Imperial Bushmen, three Contingents for the First Australian Commonwealth Horse. The narrative is arranged in twenty chapters and is based upon a wide range of sources - extracts from soldiers' letters and diaries, verbatim quotations from newspapers, official reports, speeches made by local dignatories, etc, all sensibly linked together and incorporating numerous nominal rolls and synopses of events. Information is given regarding Contingents despatched by other Australian Colonies, with their dates of departure and return. Eighty pages of photographic plates (fully captioned and indexed) carry the portraits of all Tasmanians who served, and the text includes details of their awards - two VCs (Lieut G G E Wylly and Tpr John H Bisdee), three CBs, three DSOs, three DCMs, and nine MID. A truly remarkable record of Tasmania's contribution to the war, and a formidable source of reference for genealogists and medal collectors. R/4 V/4. ADFA. MCND'A/PS.

ON THE VELDT
A Plain Narrative of Service Afield in South Africa

Maj R C Lewis * J Walch & Sons, Hobart, Tasmania, 1902. Brown, red, 7.5 x 5.25, xv/159. No ills, no maps (bound in), no Index. Apps: unit muster roll for the 1st Tasmanian Imperial Bushmen (incl notes on casualties, H&A, notes on ranks, etc).
* A nice old-fashioned format, with a helpful Contents page and summaries of events at the heading of each chapter. Written by the CO of the 1st Tasmanian Imperial Bushmen, the story is partly autobiographical, but it does provide good coverage of the unit's time in South Africa (where it saw much active service). R/4 V/4. ANL. MCND'A.

THE STORY OF THE SOUTH AUSTRALIA BUSHMEN'S CORPS, 1900

Edwin George Blackmore * Hussey & Gillingham, Printers, Adelaide, 1900. Seen in facsmile only, with soft card covers, orange, black, 7.0 x 5.0, -/32. No ills, no maps, no Index. Apps: lists of Executives and other Committee Members, unit nominal roll, notes on uniforms and equipment, idem pay scales and insurances, Balance Sheet (at 18.5.1900).
* The story of a unit raised entirely by private subscription and despatched to the South African war on 7 March 1900. With a strength of 100 men and 120 horses, it embarked for a year's service in company with similar Corps from Queensland, New South Wales, and Western Australia. The narrative gives no details of the unit's fighting services because it seems to have been written before the Corps had had time to get into action. Instead, it concentrates upon the evolution of the Bushmen Movement, the ways and means by which funds were raised, how the men were selected, how the officers were appointed, and how the scales of pay and equipment were decided. Of the £17,000 raised, only £9000 were needed

to mount the expedition. A remarkable little book, written by the Secretary of the unit's Executive Committe, and a rare insight into one of the ways in which the Anglo-Boer War was financed. R/5 V/3. AWM. MCND'A.

WESTERN AUSTRALIAN CONTINGENTS IN THE SOUTH AFRICAN WAR
John Burridge * Publication details not shown, Perth, WA, 1972. Illustrated stiff card, orange, black, 'Mounted trooper' motif, 8.25 x 6.0, v/49. 5 mono phots, no maps, no Index. Apps: detailed medal rolls for each Contingent, roll of nurses, H&A.
* A private research project by the well known publisher of facsimile editions of scarce Australian unit histories. The booklet provides useful basic information concerning each of the Contingents, and represents a handy source of reference for medal collectors and genealogists. R/2 V/3. PC. PS.

Note: numerous commemorative and celebratory items were published in Australia during the years following the return home of the various Contingents. Most are very brief, having no more than ten or twenty pages. They have not been recorded in this bibliography on the grounds that they do not contain sufficient detail to aid the researcher. The same applies to New Zealand (vide following page).

INDIAN CONTINGENT

THE HISTORY OF LUMSDEN'S HORSE
A Complete Record of the Corps from its Formation to its Disbandment
Henry H S Pearse * Longmans Green & Co, London, New York and Bombay, 1903. Red, gold, Regtl crest, cld banding on spine, 10.0 x 7.5, xii/506. Fp, 78 mono phots, 2 maps (one printed in the text, one bound in), Index. Apps: 9 in total, incl notes on formation, Adjutant's notebook, accounts and funds.
* Lieut Col D M Lumsden was on leave in Australia when, in December 1899, he heard of the outbreak of fighting in South Africa. He sent a message to the Government of India, offering 50,000 Rupees of his own money and 'his personal services' to raise a Regt of Cavalry for service against the Boers. The offer was accepted. He returned to Calcutta and recruited two Squadrons from the local British community. Enrollment was based upon each applicant's previous record with one of the Mounted Volunteer units and his perceived social standing (there were many complaints of snobbery). The Regt departed Calcutta in February 1900 (an extraordinary achievement in the circumstances) and returned in February 1901. It was then disbanded. This is an extremely detailed record, easy to read and consult, and a fine source of information regarding one of the Empire's least conventional units. R/4 V/5. IOL. VS/RGB.

LUMSDEN'S HORSE, SOUTH AFRICA 1900 AND JUBILEE REGISTER, 1900–1950
Maj H O Pugh * The Welsh Gazette, Cardiganshire, 1952. Paper covers, grey, blue, 8.5 x 5.5, -/39. Fp, 2 mono phots, no maps, no formal appendixes, no Index.
* A short but readable account of the Regt's brief existence, and including two lists of former members - those still living (in 1950), and those who had died in the interim. Apart from being a good source for genealogists, this little book provides an interesting and poignant tailpiece to the major history by Pearse (vide preceding entry). R/5 V/2. NAM. PJE.

Note: Volunteer Contingents travelled from Ceylon to South Africa to take part in the war of 1899–1902, but no free-standing publicatons, recording their services, have been traced. Officers and men of the Ceylon Mounted Rifles and the Ceylon Planters' Rifle Corps took part in the expedition. Such men formed a complete Company of the British Army's Gloucestershire Regt, and it is thought that other Ceylon volunteers were similarly used to bring a variety of units up to strength.

NEW ZEALAND CONTINGENTS

NEW ZEALANDERS AND THE BOER WAR
Soldiers from the Land of the Moa
Anon (attributed to Mrs Sarah E Hawdon) * Printed by William Brendon & Son Ltd, Plymouth (UK), for Gordon & Gotch, Christchurch (NZ), n.d. Soft card, black, 'Horseman' motif, 7.5 x 5.0, xiv/287. Fp, one mono phot, no maps, Index. Apps: notes on Sanna's Post, notes on Colonial contributions to the war (manpower and money)
* A useful description of the role played by all ten NZ Contingents. Many individuals are mentioned in the text, hence the Index is particularly helpful.
R/4 V/3. NZMODL. FC.
Note: referring to the book's sub-title, 'Moa' is the name given to any of New Zealand's extinct flightless birds. Another generalised account, and a good one, is THE NEW ZEALANDERS IN SOUTH AFRICA, 1899-1902, by D O W Hall (War History Branch, Dept of Internal Affairs, Wellington, 1949). It contains less narrative material than the (Hawdon) account, but it does have a 'Roll of Honour'. Halls' book, also, covers all ten NZ Contingents, most of which are recorded in separate publications under their own titles (vide the following entries). No such publication has been traced in respect of the 9th Contingent, but some information can be obtained from STILL JOGGING ALONG, by Pte J N Clarke (Otago Military Museum Publications, n.d.) which describes his experiences in 1902.

WITH THE NEW ZEALANDERS AT THE FRONT
A Story of Twelve Months Campaigning in South Africa
Cpl Frank Twisleton * Whitcombe & Tombs Ltd, Wellington, n.d. (c.1902). Marbled boards, red/black/blue, gold, 7.25 x 5.0, v/187. Fp, no other ills, no maps, no appendixes, no Index.
* First published as a weekly series of newspaper articles, the bulk of the story is a 'diary of events' as recorded by an NCO who reveals himself as having been a very correct and loyal soldier. In readable style, he made a detailed note of what he and his comrades did each day - facts, names, times, distances, rations, bivouacs, engagements, etc. The period covered is 1900-1901, and it is believed that he was serving with the 2nd NZ Contingent. The perspective is simply that of a fighting man concerned with the day-to-day business of working with his Section and following his orders. The result is a unique view of events around Kroonstad and Johannesburg, the pursuit of De Wet, the actions around Rhenoster Kop, and the advance to Pretoria. A final chapter offers some thoughtful suggestions on military administration and discipline. R/5 V/3. ATL. FC.

KIWI VERSUS BOER
The First New Zealand Mounted Rifles in the Anglo-Boer War, 1899-1902
Richard Stowers * Print House, Cambridge, NZ, 1992. Illustrated soft laminated card, 'Mounted rifleman' motif, full colour, 8.75 x 5.75, iv/276. Fp, 59 mono phots, one map (double spread, Transvaal and Orange Free State), Glossary, Bibliography, no Index. Apps: 23 in total, covering a wide range of topics - casualties, awards, POW, uniforms, medals, finances, etc.
* This is arguably the best account ever produced regarding the New Zealand involvement in South Africa. It focuses entirely upon 1 NZMR and its personnel. Indeed, nearly a third of the text consists of highly detailed biographical notes on each and every man who served (thus making the book a prime source for genealogists). Evidently a labour of love by the author, published by him privately, it represents a huge amount of painstaking research and is drawn from a variety of sources. The photographs are evocative of the period and include some of Boer personnel. R/1 V/4. NZMODL. HEC.
Note: this book is a much expanded version of FIRST NEW ZEALANDERS TO THE BOER WAR, 1899, compiled by the same author and published in 1983.

DIARY OF THE SECOND NEW ZEALAND MOUNTED RIFLES
On Active Service in South Africa from 24 February 1901 to 21 March 1901, also from 1 April 1901 to 8 May 1901
Montagu Craddock * Evening Star Co Ltd, Dunedin, n.d. (c.1905). Seen only as a photo-copy of an original, 8.0 x 5.5, -/50. Apparently no ills, no maps, no appendixes, no Index.
* As the title might imply, this is little more than a diary of movements and events. It has considerable research value, but this is limited by the lack of an Index or any appendixes. Locations are liberally mentioned, but not individuals. R/4 V/2. NZMODL. HEC.

OUR BOYS
A Souvenir of the Otago and Southland Contingent, March 24th 1900
Anon * Printed by Wilkie & Co, Dunedin, for the Otago and Southland Patriotic Committee, 24 March 1900. Illustrated paper covers, 'Mounted Trooper and Otago crest' motif, buff, white/red/gold, -/16 (not numbered). 164 mono phots, no maps, no appendixes, no Index.
* A pictorial record of the 13 officers, 143 ORs, and 8 nurses, who volunteered in the Otago and Southland district for service with the 4th NZ Contingent of Rough Riders. A prime source for researchers seeking a photographic portrait of any of those individuals. R/4 V/2. NZMODL. HEC.

FOURTH CONTINGENT, NEW ZEALAND ROUGH RIDERS
From Otago and Southland
Anon * Joseph Braitwaite, Dunedin, 1900. Illustrated paper covers, 'Patriotic flags and bunting' motif, brown, black, 10.5 x 7.5, -/27 (not numbered). Fp, 66 mono phots, no maps, no Index. Apps: nominal roll of those who served.
* Like the pamphlet described above, this also is a purely photographic record - mainly of personnel. The pictures are useful as a source of reference regarding details of uniform, insignia and accoutrements. R/5 V/2. ATL. JS.

WITH THE FOURTH NEW ZEALAND ROUGH RIDERS
James G Harle Moore * The Otago Daily Times Newspapers Ltd, Dunedin, 1906. Maroon, gold, 8.5 x 5.75, -/200. 18 mono phots, 2 sketches, no maps, no Index. Apps: Roll of Honour, H&A, unit nominal roll.
* A good workmanlike narrative account, with plenty of detail. The story has added interest when read in conjunction with one or both of the pictorial items noted above. R/4 V/4. PC. HEC.

THE KIMBERLEY FLYING COLUMN
Boer War Reminiscences, 'C' Squadron, New Zealand 5th Contingent
Trooper Frank Perham * Publisher's details not shown, Timaru, 1958. Stiff card, buff, black, 8.75 x 5.5, -/92. Fp, 6 mono phots, no maps, no appendixes, no Index.
* Based upon the author's diary and compiled fifty-six years after the events which he describes, the story is mainly autobiographical. Mr Perham recounts his pre-war experiences with the Volunteers, then the raising of his Squadron, the voyage to South Africa, the move north to Bulawayo and through Matabeleland to Kimberley, then the pursuit of De Wet. An interesting and unusual eyewitness account. Like the 4th Contingent, the 5th was raised from several different Volunteer units in both North Island and South Island. R/3 V/3. PC. HEC.

ON ACTIVE SERVICE WITH THE SILENT SIXTH
Being a Record Compiled by the Writer ...
Joseph Linklater * McKee & Co, Wellington, 1904. Blue, gold, 7.5 x 5.0, -/102. Fp, 2 mono phots, no maps, no Index. Apps: Roll of Honour.
* An account of the 6th NZ Mounted Rifles, presented in diary form. It contains all the facts - locations, actions, casualties - which most researchers are likely to require. R/4 V/3. ATL. JS.

THE SEVENTH NEW ZEALAND CONTINGENT
Its Record in the Field, Second South African Boer War, 1901-1902
Sgt K G Malcolm * Deslandes & Lewis, Wellington, 1903. Seen rebound only, 7.0 x 4.25, vi/44. Fp, 2 mono phots, no maps, no Index. Apps: Roll of Honour (KIA, DOW, DOD, and WIA).
* A brief record, covering the Contingent's services in the Orange Free State and the Transvaal between April 1901 and February 1902. Lacking in detail, with few individuals mentioned by name or date specified, the narrative lacks any great interest. Only the appendix possesses any research value. R/4 V/2. NZMODL. HEC.

THE COLLEGE RIFLES, WELLINGTON
Final Report and Summary of Thirteen Years' Volunteer Service
Anon * City Printing Co, Wellington, 1911. Paper covers, brown, black, dimensions not recorded, iv/25. No ills, no maps, no Index. Apps: H&A, list of officers, plus various other nominal rolls.
* A slim but useful pamphlet regarding an obscure unit. It is interesting as a reflection of the socio-military history of the Wellington area, and it is listed here because it includes a roll of members who volunteered for service in South Africa. R/4 V/1. NLNZ. HEC.

ARTILLERY

ULTIMA RATIO REGUM - THE LAST ARGUMENT OF KINGS
The Artillery History of South Africa
Commdt C J Nöthling * Government Printer, Pretoria, for the Military Information Bureau SADF, 1987. Black, gold, SADF cap and collar badges, 12.0 x 8.75, xii/432. 2 fps, very many phots, many maps and sketches, Bibliography, no Index. Apps: 'Short History of the Gunners Association'.
* This is another of the series noted elsewhere and is likewise printed partly in Afrikaans and partly in English. Published to coincide with the 75th anniversary of the creation of the old Union Defence Force (later SADF), it is well researched and covers the history of artillery in South Africa from the earliest days. It gives uniformly good coverage of the Anglo-Boer Wars, the two world wars (Africa East and North, the Middle East, France, Italy, etc), and the Angolan campaign. All aspects are dealt with in detail - gun and ammunition manufacture, orders of battle, traditions, fire control systems, and so forth. The names of individual officers appear at intervals throughout the narrative. A well balanced account. R/1 V/4. SANMMH. GTB.

YOUNG'S FIELD
A History of the Anti-aircraft School
Lionel Crook * Produced by the A/A Regt, A/A School, Kimberley, 1991. Black, gold, 'Gunners' motif, 12.0 x 8.5, ix/101. 27 mono phots, 8 cld ills, 2 maps, Glossary, Bibliography, Index. Apps: Roll of Honour, list of former officers, idem RSMs, notes on various guns used by the A/A at various periods.
* Young's Field has been a military base since 1938. The book gives a general account of its changing roles (military aviation in 1911, gunnery school in WWI, SA Marine Corps base, etc), but the main theme is the evolution of anti-aircraft artillery in South Africa over the past half century. An improvised weapon had been used against German aeroplanes in GSWA in 1915, but the first formal A/A Bty was formed at Young's Field in 1939. Other A/A units sprang from these roots and a good organisation chart explains their histories through to 1990. R/1 V/5. PC. GTB.

PRINCE ALFRED'S OWN CAPE VOLUNTEER ARTILLERY
Handbook of Drills, &c
Anon * Printed by Murray & St Leger, Cape Town, for the Corps, 1893. Leather, maroon, gold, 7.25 x 5.25, -/109. No ills, no maps, no appendixes, no Index.
* Although lacking any 'historical narrative' content, this publication is noted here as being the only known printed reference source for the Corps. The 'drills' referred to in the sub-title fall into three categories - cavalry skills, training with the Martini-Henry carbine, and gunnery drills. The latter are particularly detailed and will certainly interest researchers into coastal defence artillery. The Corps was equipped with a range of pieces which exemplified the late 19th Century transition from muzzle-loading guns to breech-loaders (7 inch 6.5 tons, 64 pounder 64 cwt, and 12 and 7 pounders BL). The text provides not only complete instructions for the manning of these weapons but also a technical description of their construction, ordnance and ballistic characteristics. R/5 V/5. SAPLCT. FRB.

WORLD WAR I

A HISTORY OF THE 71st SIEGE BATTERY, SOUTH AFRICAN HEAVY ARTILLERY
From July 1915, the Date of its Formation at Cape Town, to 11 November 1918
Anon * J Miles & Co, London, presumably for the author, n.d. (c.1920). Black, gold, Bty crest, 9.75 x 7.75, -/55. Fp (4 portraits of COs), 9 mono phots, no maps, no Index. Apps: Roll of Honour (incomplete), H&A, list of officers and SNCOs, unit nominal roll, diary of movements and locations.

* The 71st (Transvaal) Siege Bty had served in the GSWA campaign as No3 Bty of the SA Heavy Artillery (one of five Btys of that Regt). In 1915 the title was changed to 71st (South African) Siege Bty, Royal Garrison Artillery, and the unit moved to England and then to the Western Front. Although it was during that period an element of the British Army, the Bty kept its South African identity and the men continued to wear South African gunner cap badges. This booklet chronicles in commendable detail its activities from April 1916 onwards in the major actions of the following two years - Ypres, Somme, Ancre, Bullencourt, Menin Road, Lens, Cambrai, La Bassee, Lys, and the final advance. R/5 V/4. AL. GTB.
Note: genealogists may find some value in NOMINAL ROLL OF THE SOUTH AFRICAN HEAVY ARTILLERY, OVERSEAS EXPEDITIONARY FORCE, a pamphlet of 8 pages published (without imprint) in 1915.

A SHORT HISTORY OF THE 72nd (SOUTH AFRICAN) SIEGE BATTERY
Lieut H Bailey * F J Parsons Ltd, Hastings, UK, 1924. Black, gold, SAHA badge, 8.5 x 5.5, ii/8. No ills, no maps, no Index. Apps: Roll of Honour (KIA, DOW and WIA, with locations and dates).
* Although very brief, this a useful record of services in GSWA (as 'O' Bty, SAHA) and on the Western Front (from 1915 onwards, as 72nd Siege Bty, RGA).
The narrative is based upon the Bty War Diary and contains many references to dates, individuals and awards. R/5 V/3. AL. GTB.
Note: the Africana Library, Johannesburg, also holds Bailey's original typescript, bound in with numerous maps, aerial photographs and supporting documents. This collection contains more information than is to be found in the formally published account.

THE SOUTH AFRICAN FIELD ARTILLERY IN GERMAN EAST AFRICA AND PALESTINE, 1915-1919
Brig the Hon F B Adler MC VD ED, Maj A E Lorch DSO MC, and Dr H H Curson * J L van Schaik Ltd, Pretoria, 1958. Pale grey, dark blue, red/blue flash, 8.5 x 5.5, xvi/146. Fp, 14 mono phots (incl captioned groups), 2 line drawings (badges), 4 maps (one bound in, 3 loose in rear pocket), Bibliography, Glossary, Index. Apps: Roll of Honour (all ranks, with dates and locations), H&A (all ranks, names but no details), list of officers, idem WOs, NCOs and artificers.
* A clearly-written account which traces the movements and operations of 1st, 2nd, 3rd, 4th, 5th and 6th Btys SAFA in East Africa, Egypt and Palestine during WWI. A very professional compilation, presented in a publication of excellent quality. R/2 V/5. PCAL. RP.

KHAKI CRUSADERS
With the South African Artillery in Egypt and Palestine
F H Cooper * Central News Agency and Rustica Press, Wynberg, Cape Town and Johannesburg, 1919. Illustrated stiff card, 'Mounted Crusader and artillery at Jerusalem' motif, 8.5 x 5.5, -/92. Fp (folding aerial phot of Wadi Deir Ballut), 7 other mono phots (indexed), no appendixes, no Index.
* The book consists of nine essays written by the author during his service with the SAA in the Middle East and 'sent back to interest rather than instruct the people at home'. They were published in various newspapers during the war and then later gathered together for this book. The articles are well written, giving a good impression of life in that campaign as viewed by SA artillerymen, but they cannot be regarded as 'unit histories'. R/4 V/1. SANMMH/AL. GTB.

WORLD WAR II

THE NINE - O's - 1940-1945
A Brief History of the 500 Gunners who Joined ...
A A Lloyd * Shepco Printing, Durban, for the 50th Anniversary Reunion Committee, 1990. Stiff card, light brown, black, Regtl badge and Divsl flash, 11.75 x 8.25, -/33. Fp, 7 mono phots, 2 maps, no Index. Apps: Roll of Honour, H&A, list of former officers, unit muster roll, list of those taken POW.
* The full sub-title reads - 'A brief history of the 500 gunners who joined the 4th Light Brigade, South African Artillery, and whose Army enlistment number commenced with 90 and went on active service as 2nd Anti-tank Regiment, 2nd South African Division, in the North African campaign'. Apart from having one of the longest sub-titles on record, this little book's main interest is to be found in its observations regarding the comparative performance of artillery pieces used by British (South African) forces and their German opponents in the Western Desert and Italy. R/2 V/2. SANMMH. GTB.
Note: at the outbreak of war, gunner units in South Africa were still titled 'Brigades' and 'Batteries'. In January 1941, in line with the British Army's Royal Artillery organisation, 'Brigades' were redesignated 'Regiments'.

LOOK-IN AFTER FORTY YEARS
The Story of the Artillery Specialists, WAAS, 1941-1945
M H Hill * Marins Printing, Johannesburg, for the WAAS Reunion Committee, Cape Town, 1985. Illustrated card, 'WAAS magazine' motif, 9.0 x 7.0, Fp, 32 mono phots, no maps, no appendixes, no Index.
* A short superficial account of a small and little-known WWII Corps. To release able-bodied men for other duties, 450 members of the Women's Army Auxiliary Service (WAAS) were trained for range-finding and plotting work with the Coastal Artillery Batteries sited around South Africa's coastlines. They were not disbanded until August 1945. Those selected for this work were particularly proud of the privilege of wearing the Artillery cap badge in place of the WAAS badge. Many officers and NCOs are named in the text. R/2 V/2. AL. GTB.

Cape Field Artillery

GUNNERS OF THE CAPE
The Story of the Cape Field Artillery
Neil Orpen * The Standard Press Ltd, Cape Town, for the CFA Regtl Committee, 1965. Prussian blue, gold, Regtl crest, 9.5 x 6.25, ix/310. 76 mono phots, 8 maps (4 printed in the text, 2 bound in, 2 printed on the end-papers), 7 line drawings (artillery pieces and Regtl crest), Bibliography, Index. Apps: Roll of Honour (for the Tambookie campaign 1880-1881, Langeberg campaign 1897, Anglo-Boer War 1899-1902, GSWA 1914-1915, and WWII), list of former Honorary Colonels, idem COs, Battle Honours, notes on unit designations, list of officers (at 31.12.1964).
* This was the first of Col Orpen's typically thorough South African unit histories. His account covers the period 1856 to 1964, but is particularly good for the CFA's services in WWII (North Africa and Italy). R/2 V/5. SANMMH. BCC.

Natal Field Artillery

NATAL FIELD ARTILLERY
Centenary, 1862-1962
Anon * Natal Witness, Pietermaritzburg, 1962. Soft card, white, black, Regtl crest, 8.75 x 5.5, -/25. Fp, 23 mono phots (mainly former COs), no maps, no Index. Apps: Roll of Honour.
* Surprisingly, this is the only free-standing published record of one of South Africa's longest serving units. Founded as the Artillery Company of the Durban Rifle Guard in 1862, it was first mobilised for the Zulu War of 1879 (but saw no action). Expanded to Regtl status in 1892 as the Natal Field Artillery, it fought in

the Anglo-Boer War at Elandslaagte and in Northern Natal. In 1904 it absorbed the Durban Artillery element of the Natal Royal Regt and served in the 1906 rebellion. Mobilised again in 1914, it took part in the GSWA campaign. In WWII, the NFA saw much action, and suffered many casualties, in the Western Desert. Its period of service was July 1941 to July 1942 (when it went into captivity at the fall of Tobruk). The Regt was reconstituted after the war and, in 1962, became the Natal University Regt (NFA). All of this is covered in condensed but helpful detail. R/3 V/2. AL. GTB.

6th BATTERY

A Saga of Gunners in the Western Desert, 12 August 1941 – 13 June 1942

J A Newman and A G Vosloo * Mills Litho (Pty) Ltd, Cape Town, 1990. Red, black, gold, Regtl crest, 9.25 x 6.0, xi/75. Fp, 4 mono phots (incl one large fold-out of Bty personnel), 3 maps (bound in), Bibliography, Index. Apps: Roll of Honour, Bty nominal roll.

* 6th Bty was an element of the Natal Field Artillery, raised for war service in 1939. Serious training commenced in January 1941 at Potchefstroom where the Bty formed part of 2nd Field Regt (NFA) SAA. Arriving in Egypt via Port Tewfik, it was assigned to Operation Crusader (November 1941). Further action followed in the Gazala and Bardia battles, then in countering the Afrika Korps' assault on Tobruk in May and June of 1942. The Bty was over-run at Rigel Ridge and the survivors became POW for the next three years. A detailed and readable history. R/1 V/4. SANMMH. GTB.

Transvaal Horse Artillery

THE HISTORY OF THE TRANSVAAL HORSE ARTILLERY

Maj F B Adler MC VD * Alex White & Co (Pty) Ltd, Johannesburg, 1927. Dark blue, blue on white, Regtl crest, 7.5 x 5.0, ii/101. Fp, no other ills, no maps, no index. Apps: Roll of Honour, list of former COs, idem officers, idem 'Instructional and Subordinate Staff', idem 'Members Commissioned into Other Units', notes on annual camps and establishments, competitions and trophies, etc.

* A brief but authoritative history of the Regt from its formation on 17 March 1904 through to the end of 1926. The narrative gives good coverage for the WWI period and services during the Rand Revolt of 1922. The appendixes are particularly detailed. R/3 V/4. JPL. NO.

THE HISTORY OF THE TRANSVAAL HORSE ARTILLERY, 1904-1974

Neil Orpen * Alex White & Co (Pty) Ltd, Johannesburg, for the Transvaal Horse Artillery Regtl Council, 1975. Dark blue, gold, Regtl crest, 10.25 x 5.75, viii/275. Fp, 101 mono phots, 15 maps, Glossary, Bibliography, Index. Apps: Rolls of Honour (WWI, Rand Revolt, WWII), H&A (WWI and WWII, incl awards to former members who were posted away to other units during WWI), list of former COs, idem former officers, nominal roll of all members (1904-1926), notes on helmets, cap badges, etc (fourteen appendixes in total).

* One of the best of several excellent unit histories compiled by this author. As expected, the narrative is clear and concise, deeply researched, and the flow of events neatly presented. With Adler's book (vide preceding entry) having covered the early years so thoroughly, Orpen was free to concentrate upon the events of WWII. An attractive publication. R/2 V/5. SANMMH. BCC.

Note: a third history of the Regt, by Dr Stanley Monick, for the Regtl Council, was published in late 1993. Entitled WHEREVER DESTINY LEADS – THE TRANSVAAL HORSE ARTILLERY, 1975 TO 1992, it is a casebound Royal octavo volume having 699 pages, 200 mono phots, 3 cld ills, and four maps.

INFANTRY

PIET KOLONEL AND HIS MEN
A Personal Record of the 1st South West Africa Infantry Battalion (March 1940 – March 1943)
Anon ('GFR', 'Tweede in Bevel', Second in Command) * Publisher's details not shown, Durban, October 1944. Rust brown, black, 7.5 x 5.25, xiv/222. 8 mono phots, no maps, no appendixes, no Index.
* This is the only published record of the South West Africa Infantry Battalion. Prior to 1940 there had never been any military recruitment in the Mandated Territory. As part of the Union's war effort, this Bn was raised (mainly) from volunteer Afrikaners residing there. The unit became effective on 20 June of that year. Despite having no military experience, the men were soon trained to a good standard. Initially they were assigned to guard duties at POW camps in the Union. At the same time, they provided drafts for other units serving with the 1st SA Div in the Western Desert. When eventually the Bn arrived in Egypt (November 1942), it was too late. The second Alamein battle had been fought, and 1st SA Div was returning home to disband. To their dismay, the officers and men of the Bn were dispersed to various units of 6th SA Armd Div (then forming for future service in Italy). The Bn was run down and then disbanded. The final quarter of this well written and entertaining book describes the experiences of men who went on to fight with 6th Div in Italy. R/3 V/3. SANMMH. GTB.

SA INFANTRY CORPS - ACTIVE CITIZEN FORCE

CARBINEER
The History of the Royal Natal Carbineers
Prof Alan F Hattersley * Gale & Polden Ltd, Aldershot, 1950. Blue, silver, Regtl crest, 8.75 x 5.5, x/193. Fp, 12 mono phots, one cld ill, 3 maps, Index.
Apps: Roll of Honour (WWII only), H&A (WWII only).
* A book which reflects the history of European volunteer forces in Natal over nearly one hundred years. The Regt was formally embodied in 1855 and was then deployed from time to time against local tribes (notably the Zulu). Elements of the Regt were present at Isandhlwana (2 officers and 19 ORs being killed there). In the Anglo-Boer War, the Regt was part of the defence force at Ladysmith. Two Bns took part in the GSWA campaign (1914-1915) as 1st and 2nd Mounted Rifles. The 'Royal' prefix was granted in 1935 and retained until South Africa became a republic in 1962. In WWII, 1st RNC fought as infantry in the Abyssinia and Western Desert campaigns, and as armoured infantry in Italy (notably at Cassino and Monte Pezza). The 2nd RNC fought in the early stages of the Desert war as 6th SA Armoured Car Regt, but was disbanded after Second Alamein. It was in the Desert, at Alem Hamza, that Sgt Quentin Smythe won the VC. His was the only VC awarded to a South African soldier in WWII. The book is a workmanlike record, clear and concise. R/2 V/4. SANMMH. MP/HIS.
Note: published with a limited print run of 1000 copies.

LANGALIBALELE AND THE NATAL CARBINEERS
The Story of the Langalibalele Rebellion, 1873
R P Pears (et al) * Westcott Printing Co, Ladysmith, for the Ladysmith Historical Society, 1973. Grey, black, 'Memorial' motif, 9.0 x 5.75, -/91. Fp, 9 mono phots, one map (bound in), Bibliography, no Index. Apps: unit nominal roll (with details of casualties).
* The narrative falls into six elements - a brief account of the revolt by the Amahlubi tribe led by Chief Langalibalele, a description of the mountainous area in which the actions took place, the events of 3/5 November 1873 and the role of the Pietermaritzburg and Karkloof Troops, eyewitness accounts by members of the Amahlubi, the subsequent Military Enquiry, and individual accounts by ten officers and men of the Natal Carbineers. The latter part constitutes the bulk of the book. A useful supplement to the Regt's formal histories. R/1 V/3. AL. GTB.

THE NATAL CARBINEERS

The History of the Regiment from its Foundation, 15th January 1855, to 30th June 1911

Trumpet Major W H A Molyneux, Capt C N H Rodwell, and the Revd John Stalker * P Davis & Sons, Pietermaritzburg, 1912. Dark blue, gold, Regtl crest, 10.0 x 6.0, iv/384. Fp, 72 mono phots, no maps, no Index. Apps: unit nominal roll for the Anglo-Boer War (1899-1902, with notes of casualties), list of all officers who served (1855-1911), Chronology of the Regt (quoting relevant Proclamations, Bye Laws, Rules, etc).

* The narrative covers the establishment of Natal Colony and the formation of the Natal Carbineers under the Volunteer Ordnance of 1854. It moves on to the early operations against Bushmen incursions into the Colony from the Drakensburg Mountains, battles with the Zulu and Basuto, and so forth. The 1873 Langalibalele conflict is covered in some detail, as is the Regt's role in the 1878-1879 Zulu War. All members who served in these campaigns are listed, with details of those killed or wounded. The Second Anglo-Boer War is well covered, with much detail of operations at Ladysmith. The Regt returned home and was stood down in September 1900. It was mobilised again in 1906 for the 'hut tax rebellion' in Zululand, and there is liberal reference in this section to individual officers. The book does not have an 'Honours & Awards' appendix, but they are mentioned throughout the text. R/4 V/4. JPL. GTB.

THE DURBAN LIGHT INFANTRY

The History of the Durban Light Infantry, Incorporating that of the Sixth South African Light Infantry, 1915-1917

Lieut Col A C Martin MC VD * Hayne & Gibson Ltd, Durban, for the Regt, 1969. Two matching volumes, royal blue, silver, 9.75 x 7.25.

Volume I, 1854-1934: Fp, 39 mono phots, 2 cld ills, 6 maps, Bibliography, Index, xx/368. Apps: Roll of Honour (WWI, KIA and WIA), H&A (WWI), list of COs, idem RSMs and SNCOs

Volume II, 1935-1960: Fp, 57 mono phots, 2 cld ills, 14 maps, Bibliography, Index, xvii/487. Apps: Roll of Honour (WWII, KIA and WIA), H&A (WWII), list of COs, idem RSMs and SNCOs.

* This sumptuous pair of books is a tour de force by the author and a great credit to the publishers, Hayne & Gibson. Presumably they were instructed by the Regt that no expense should be spared, and they responded in full. All periods of the Regt's history are equally well covered, but some researchers will find the section which deals with the East African campaign (1915-1917) to be particularly helpful. A highly desirable possession for any library or collector. R/4 V/5. UWML. BCC/RP.

HISTORICAL RECORD OF THE DURBAN VOLUNTEER INFANTRY CORPS, 1854-1904

Anon (either A Milligan or A Dick) * Robinson & Co, Durban, 1905. Soft card, rust brown, black, 8.0 x 4.75, -/96. Fp, 14 mono phots, no maps, no Index. Apps: Roll of Honour (DLI only, 1899-1902), unit muster roll (DLI only, 1899-1902).

* The DLI originated in 1854 and was granted the 'Royal' title in 1935. This slim book has chapters devoted to each of the periods during which it was known by a different title - Durban Volunteer Guard (1854-1856), Durban Rifle Guard (1859-1869), Royal Durban Rifles (1873-1889), Natal Royal Rifles (1889-1895), and Durban Light Infantry (1895-1904). Each chapter gives details of dates of formation and (where relevant) dates of disbandment, with information on uniforms, shooting competitions, names of COs, etc. In the case of the post-1895 (DLI) period, there is even more detail. Many nominal rolls, particularly of officers, are interspersed throughout the narrative. A handy reference source. R/4 V/4. AL. GTB.

THE DUKES

A History of the Duke of Edinburgh's Own Rifles, 1855-1956

Angus G McKenzie * Galvin & Sales (Pty) Ltd, Cape Town, for the DEOR Regtl Council, 1957. Red, gold, Regtl crest, 9.0 x 5.5, -/234. Fp, 37 mono phots, 2 maps, no Index. Apps: Roll of Honour (WWII only), H&A (WWII only).

* The Regt was founded in Cape Town with the unofficial title The Cape Town Royal Rifles. In 1862, it was officially recognised as The Cape Town Rifles and, five years later, as The Duke of Edinburgh's Own Volunteer Rifles. The modern title, Duke of Edinburgh's Own Rifles (hence 'Dukes') was adopted in 1913 but, in WWI, it fought as 2nd South African Infantry (DEOR). This eminently readable book describes its role in the early campaigns - Transkei (1877-1879), Basutoland (1880-1881), Bechuanaland (1897), the South African War (1899-1902), and GSWA (1914-1915). Following the latter, the Regt was demobilised and its members were free to volunteer for the Imperial Service units being formed for service in East Africa and France. The bulk of the pages (170 of 231) are in fact taken up with the Regt's services in WWII - East Africa (El Wak, Addis Ababa, Gobuea and Amba Alagi), the Western Desert (Mersa Matruh, Gazala and El Alamein), and the Italian campaign (where it served as The Combined Regt DSR in the final weeks of the war). Coverage of the East Africa and Western Desert periods is especially detailed and interesting. R/3 V/4. AL. GTB.
Note: reference may be made also to DUKE'S VICTORY - CAMPAIGN IN EAST AFRICA, by Mary Hallett (Cape Times, 1941), this being a 16-page pamphlet describing the Regt's actions at El Wak, Camboleia and Amba Alagi.

THE DUKES
A History of the Cape Town Rifles 'Dukes'
Neil Orpen * Published by the Cape Town Rifles Dukes Assn, Cape Town, 1984. Blue, gold, 10.0 x 6.0, vi/325. Fp, 17 pages of small mono phots, 16 maps, Bibliography, Index. Apps: Rolls of Honour (for 'The Gun War', Basutoland, Langeberg, Bechuanaland, Anglo-Boer War, WWII, and the South West Operational Area, 1977-1983), list of former COs, idem Hon Colonels, idem Colonels-in-Chief, idem WOs, notes on unit designations, Battle Honours.
* A painstaking account which covers an unusually long period in South African military history (1854 to 1984). The contents encompass all the events mentioned in McKenzie's work (vide preceding entry), but Orpen supports that information with his useful additional appendixes. Further, he extends the story through to the conclusion of the Regt's involvements in the Angola and Namibia operations. R/1 V/5. SANMMH. GTB.

FIRST CITY, A SAGA OF SERVICE
Reginald Griffiths * Howard Timmins, Cape Town, 1970. Dark blue, silver, 9.25 x 6.75, xvi/292. 54 mono phots, 2 maps (bound in), Bibliography, Index. Apps: Roll of Honour (WWII), H&A (WWII).
* A complete history from 1875 to 1965. Raised originally as The First City Volunteers of Grahamstown, the Regt has always been known as First City. This book describes its various mobilisations for tribal and frontier operations of the late 19th Century, its contribution to the GSWA campaign, and its role in the WWII Italian campaign (when it was amalgamated temporarily with the Cape Town Highlanders from 1943 onwards). The narrative is not easy to read because it is much broken up with quotations from letters, nominal rolls, extracts from documents, and so forth. Much of this information would have been better presented in the form of appendixes. R/3 V/3. UWML. BCC/NO.
Note: an additional source is FIRST CITY VOLUNTEERS, THE CORPS HISTORY, 1875-1905, by T Hutchinson (a pamphlet of 29 pages, publication details not shown, n.d., but thought to be c.1906).

THE KAFFRARIAN RIFLES, 1876-1986
Nunc Animis
Francis L Coleman * Rustica Press, Wynberg, Cape, for The Kaffrarian Rifles Assn, 1988. Green, gold, Regtl crest, 10.0 x 6.5, xxii/327. 94 mono phots, 10 maps (9 bound in, one printed on each end-paper), Bibliography, Index. Apps: Roll of Honour (1876-1986), H&A (incl associated units), roll of men who enlisted in the Buffalo Mounted Rifles at the first meeting on 16 August 1876, roll of men who attended the Special Meeting on 29 November 1883, reference notes.

* The Regt originated in East London where, in 1876, eighty local Europeans came together to form a Volunteer defence unit. They were mobilised for the Basutoland and Transkei operations of 1880, but were then disbanded. Three years later, the same district produced the Kaffrarian Rifles and this Regt inherited the legacy of the former Buffalo Mounted Rifles. They took part in the Langeberg campaign of 1897 and then fought the Boers in the war of 1899-1902 (siege of Wepener). Under the new ACF system, the Regt was given the designation 5th Infantry and fought as such in GSWA in 1914-1915. In WWII, the Kaffrarian Rifles served in the Western Desert, but most them were captured at Tobruk. In later years, the Regt took part in operations in Angola. This is a well written history, nicely printed and bound, with many individuals named in the narrative. R/1 V/5. SANMMH. JRStA.
Note: reference may be made also to A BRIEF HISTORY OF THE KAFFRARIAN RIFLES, by Lawrence H Bailie (Daily Despatch, East London, 20 pages, 1964).

THE CAPE TOWN HIGHLANDERS, 1885-1970

Neil Orpen * Cape & Transvaal Printers Ltd, Cape Town, for the Cape Town Highlanders History Committee, 1970. Green, gold, 9.0 x 6.25, x/396. Fp, 117 mono phots, 14 maps, Glossary, Bibliography, Index. Apps: Rolls of Honour (Anglo-Boer War 1899-1902, WWI, and WWII), H&A (idem, plus 'periodic awards at the Union, 1910'), list of former COs, idem Hon Colonels, idem Colonels-in-Chief, idem RSMs, Battle Honours.
* A high class history of this famous kilted Regt. The narrative traces its founding in 1885 (when the Scottish section of The Dukes broke away to form their own Regt), through to its first campaign in 1897 (as part of the Bechuanaland Field Force). It then moves on to its role in the 1899-1902 war, a troubled episode which is described with restraint. The Regt served in the early WWI campaign to remove the Germans from SWA and was then disbanded. Many of the personnel promptly re-enlisted as Imperial Service troops and formed a nucleus for 'A' Coy, 4th SA Infantry (SA Scottish). These men took part in the suppression of the Senussi rebellion in Cyrenaica and then fought in France and Flanders. The bulk of the narrative is then devoted to service in WWII - the Desert battles of 1941, the two El Alamein battles of 1942, and the Italian campaign of 1943-1945. By 1943, the lack of trained man-power had caused a temporary amalgamation of this Regt with the First City Regt. The FC/CTH Combined Regt fought as such through to the end of the war (ultimately under American command). The WWII period is presented in masterful style, the narrative being well-laced with mention of named individuals and minor engagements. The maps are helpful and the pictures well captioned. The post-war coverage is concerned mainly with details of ceremonial, dress and unit badges. Following the success of this publication, the author was commissioned fifteen years later to write an extended account (vide following entry).
R/2 V/5. ANL/AL. MCND'A/GTB.

THE CAPE TOWN HIGHLANDERS, 1885-1985

Neil Orpen * San Printing Press, Simon's Town, for the Cape Town Highlanders Trust, 1988. Green, gold, 8.5 x 6.25, xii/164. Fp, 99 mono phots, 18 cld ills, 3 maps, Bibliography, Index. Apps: Rolls of Honour (Anglo-Boer War, WWI, WWII, Angolan Border), H&A (extensive, and incl LS&GC awards, Efficiency Medals, the John Chard Decoration, Jubilee and Coronation Medals, etc), list of RSMs, idem RPMs, notes on the Regtl Band and music, notes on command and control, 1985-1986.
* This was the last of Colonel Orpen's projects before his final illness. The opening pages summarise the Regt's earlier history, and the appendixes are a valuable adjunct to those found in the earlier book, but the main thrust of this history is the Regt's services in Southern Angola in the 1970s. The CTH was in fact the first ACF unit to cross the border. The illustrations are excellent and the maps helpful. The narrative is somewhat bland and lustreless, but all of the facts are clearly presented. R/1 V/5. SANMMH. RP.

A SHORT HISTORY OF THE CAPE TOWN HIGHLANDERS, SEPTEMBER 1939–FEBRUARY 1943
Regimental History of the Cape Town Highlanders
Maj W S Douglas MC * E & R Schindler, Cairo, Egypt, January 1944. Stiff card, buff, black, Regtl crest and 1st SA Div flash, 8.25 x 5.5, ix/51. Fp (map of Egypt), 32 mono phots, no other maps, no Index. Apps: Roll of Honour, H&A, notes on POW, idem captured enemy weapons.
* Although short, this is a useful record. It is based upon the War Diary and, having been compiled so soon after the events described, has an immediacy not always found in the accounts published later. It covers the Regt's experiences from mobilisation through to the amalgamation with the First City Regt for service in Italy. The main events were - acting as POW guards in South Africa, the move to North Africa, actions at Mersa Matruh, the subsequent battles of 1941–1942 (Gazala, First and Second Alamein), and then 1st SA Div's return to South Africa in 1943. R/5 V/3. SANMMH. GTB.

FIRST CITY/CAPE TOWN HIGHLANDERS IN THE ITALIAN CAMPAIGN
A Short History
L G Murray * Cape Times, for the author, Cape Town, 1946. Light brown, dark brown, 8.5 x 5.75, -/80. Fp, no other phots, 9 line drawings (chapter heads), one map (folding, bound in at the rear, showing FC/CTH Regt's route up the Italian mainland), no Index. Apps: Roll of Honour, Battle Honours (for both Regts), notes regarding their tartans.
* A short but accurate account of the services, between late 1942 and mid-1945, of the two (temporarily amalgamated) kilted Cape Regts on active service in Italy. R/4 V/3. JPL. NO.

THE HISTORY OF THE KIMBERLEY REGIMENT, 1876–1962
Dr H H Curson * Northern Cape Printers, Kimberley, presumably for the Regt, 1963. Black, gold, 9.25 x 6.0, xxiv/284. Fp, 113 mono phots, 6 maps, Bibliography, no Index. Apps: Roll of Honour (WWII), H&A (WWII), nominal roll (all ranks, WWII), notes on campaigns, local streets in Kimberley named after former officers of the Regt.
* Covers the period specified in the title, but concentrating mainly upon WWII. The Regt dates from 1899 when it emerged from an amagamation of the Diamond Fields Horse and the Kimberley Rifles. It sent two Bns for service in the GSWA campaign in 1914–1915, and was temporarily coupled with the Imperial Light Horse for service in Italy in 1943–1945. The narrative contains plenty of interesting detail for its time in Italy, and many individuals are named in the text. A good workmanlike history, spoiled only by the lack of an Index. R/3 V/4. SANMMH. BCC.

THE HISTORY OF THE TRANSVAAL SCOTTISH
Capt H C Juta * Hortors Ltd, Johannesburg, 1933. Green, with leather spine and quarters, gold, 10.0 x 7.5, xvii/152. Fp, 85 mono phots, various line drawings of insignia, 6 maps (2 printed in the text, 4 folding, bound in), Bibliography, Index. Apps: Roll of Honour, list of former COs, summary of the history of the 4th Bn, South African Infantry (1916–1919), idem The Scottish Horse (1902–1907).
* An excellent book which covers the original raising in 1902 through to 1932. The early years are described in particularly good detail. The account of the WWI period is more generalised, but the overall effect is informative. R/4 V/4. PC. BCC.
Note: a copy bound in brown cloth and bearing the imprint 1938 has been seen. The contents would appear to be identical.

WE BAND OF BROTHERS
Reminiscences from the 1st Infantry Brigade in the 1914–18 War
George W Warwick * Howard Timmins, Cape Town, 1962. Red, black, 'Bushveld tree' motif, 8.5 x 5.5, -/211. 14 mono phots, one map, Index. Apps: Roll of Honour (South Africans buried at Delville Wood), notes on casualties.
* A personal account by a soldier who served with 4th SAI (South African Scottish) in England, in Egypt (the Senussi campaign), and in France (Bernafay Wood, Trones

Wood, Delville Wood, Arras, and the Menin Road). Following a severe head wound, he was returned home and later became an Anglican minister. His account is an excellent 'soldier's view' of the war and the book is regarded as a classic in the South African bibliography of WWI. Numerous officers and ORs are mentioned in the narrative and their names are well indexed. R/3 V/3. SANMMH. GTB.

THE SAGA OF THE TRANSVAAL SCOTTISH REGIMENT, 1932–1950
Carel Birkby * Howard Timmins, Cape Town, for Hodder & Stoughton, 1950. Brown, gold, Regtl crest, 9.75 x 7.5, xxxii/749. 3 fps, 202 mono phots, 5 cld ills, line drawings of uniforms, 27 maps, Bibliography, no Index. Apps: Roll of Honour, H&A, list of former officers, idem WOs, idem POW, nominal roll of members, notes on Dress and uniforms.
* A massive work, almost more information that the reader can absorb. Most of the painstakingly researched narrative is devoted to the story of the Regt's three fighting Bns in the East African and Western Desert campaigns. Following the heavy losses in 1942 in Libya, the survivors joined the Combined Regt DSR which went to Italy in March 1945 (but saw no action there). The book is said to be unusually accurate and reliable. R/3 V/4. JPL. BCC.

THE BUGLE CALLS
The Story of the Witwatersrand Rifles and its Predecessors, 1899–1987
Stanley Monick * Printed by Gutenberg Book Printers, Pretoria, for the Witwatersrand Rifles Regtl Assn, 1989. Dark green, silver, Douglas Tartan embellishment with Regtl crest on front cover and spine, 9.75 x 6.75, xx/828. Fp, 102 mono phots, 11 line drawings, 57 maps (55 printed in the text, 2 folding, bound in), Bibliography, Index. Apps: Rolls of Honour (separately for 1899–1902, 1914–1918, 1939–1945, and 1946–1967), H&A (separately for 1899–1902 and 1946–1967, with awards for other periods listed in the narrative), unit nominal rolls (five in total, one for 1906, two for WWI, and two for WWII).
* A very comprehensive history of the Regt and its forebears (the Rand Rifles and the Railway Pioneer Regt). The narrative is clearly arranged in seven major chapters, and each period in the Regt's evolution, from original formation in 1903, is given equal coverage. Many individual members of the Regt are named in the text, this making the provision of a detailed Index a most welcome feature. The Bibliography section is extensive and is itself a useful source of reference. The photographic illustrations are not well printed, but the maps are well drawn and presented. An outstanding unit history. R/1 V/5. SANMMH. GTB.
Note: published with a print run of 2000 copies.

THE STORY OF MEN
A Brief History of Regiment De La Rey and The Witwatersrand Rifles and their Association
Capt S E van Broemsen * The Potchefstroom Herald, 1948. Dark green, black, 8.25 x 5.0, –/130. 3 mono phots, 5 line drawings, no maps, no Index. Apps: Roll of Honour (WWII), H&A (WWII).
* Regiment De La Rey was established in 1934. It was temporarily amalgamated in July 1943, in North Africa, with the survivors of the Witwatersrand Rifles. The marriage was a consequence of the shortage of trained men arriving from South Africa to replace battle casualties. The author covers their individual histories (from 1934 for the DLR and from 1903 for the WR) before concentrating upon the services of the combined regiment on mainland Italy. R/4 V/3. JPL. NO.

A SHORT HISTORY OF THE R.L.I.
Anon * H M Swann, Johannesburg, n.d. (1944). Card, light blue, black, Regtl crest on front cover, 8.0 x 6.0, –/10. No ills, no maps, no Index. Apps: H&A.
* A pamphlet which opens with a one-page history of the Regt, followed by a summary of services in WWII (mobilisation, the Western Desert, the return home, and preparations for Italy). R/4 V/1. AL. GTB.

RAND LIGHT INFANTRY, 1904-1964

Maj B G Simpkins JCD and Bar, MM * Rustica Press, Wynberg, for Howard Timmins, Cape Town, 1956. Dark blue, gold, Regtl crest, 10.0 x 6.5, xiii/371. Fp, 221 mono phots, 3 cld ills, 14 maps (12 bound in, 2 printed on the end-papers), Index. Apps: Rolls of Honour (WWI, Rand Revolt and WWII), H&A (WWI and WWII, with citations as available), lists of Colonels-in-Chief, Honorary Colonels and former COs, unit nominal rolls (for all ranks, 1915, 1922, 1941 and 1943, incl attached MT personnel and members of the Middellandse Regt), list of locations of graves of members of the Regt, notes on shooting competitions, notes on the history of the Regt's uniforms.

* A deeply researched history covering the period from October 1905 (when the Regt was first formed as the Transvaal Cyclist Corps) through to 1967 (year of publication). The book has thirty-seven chapters, three of which deal with the early years (Zulu Rebellion of 1906, first acquisition of 'armoured' cars in 1907, change of title to RLI in 1913). Six chapters then cover the fighting in GSWA in 1914-1915 as 11th Infantry ACF (RLI). Three more chapters deal with the Rand Revolt and the inter-war years. The bulk of the book (23 chapters) then describes in great detail the Regt's services in WWII - early training in South Africa, the move to the Western Desert in 1941 as part of 3rd SA Inf Bde and the battles of Bardia, Gazala and El Alamein. The RLI was frequently in the thick of the fight and suffered heavy losses. Returning home in late 1942, it was amalgamated with the Duke of Edinburgh's Own Rifles to form a Dukes/RLI combined unit. This was later amalgamated with the survivors of the Transvaal Scottish to form a Combined Regt DSR (an abbreviation for Dukes/Scottish/Rand). The DSR moved to Italy in March 1945 but saw no action there. A final chapter deals with post-war events. This is certainly one of the most complete histories of any South African unit. R/3 V/5. PCAL/JPL. GTB/JFHPJ.

Note: the author won his MM while serving as a CSM with the Regt at El Alamein.

COMMEMORATIVE BROCHURE

Issued by the Middellandse Regiment on the Occasion of its Fortieth Reunion

Anon * Printed by Framic (Pty) Ltd, for the Regtl Assn, 1989. Illustrated glossy soft card, white, green, 'Blazer badge' motif, 8.25 x 6.0, -/48. Fp, 24 mono phots, no maps, no Index. Apps: Roll of Honour (WWII), H&A (WWII), unit muster roll (for all personnel who embarked at Durban for North Africa on 10 June 1941), roll of officers and ORs who served with the RLI at El Alamein.

* The Regt was formed in 1935 to succeed 6th, 8th, 19th, and 20th Mounted Rifles which customarily recruited in the Graaff Reinet, Cradock, and Middelburg areas of the Karroo. The core of the booklet is a brief account of the Regt's mobilisation in July 1940, the move to Egypt one year later, its operations in the Western Desert, the withdrawal to the Tobruk perimeter, and the surrender on 21 June 1942. There is interesting coverage of the escape of Lieut Featherstone's Platoon. He and his men got away from Tobruk and, with the detached 'B' Coy, later fought at El Alamein as an element of the RLI. The bulk of the Bn was transported to Italy where many officers and ORs escaped from POW camps and joined the Partisan forces. A lot of information, presented in very condensed but readable form. R/1 V/3. JPL. GTB.

CLEAR THE WAY

The Military Heritage of the South African Irish

Dr Stanley Monick and Col O E F Baker * Printed by Perskor, Johannesburg, for the SA Irish Regtl Assn, 1992. Two matching volumes, glossy stiff card, green, silver, 10.0 x 7.0, each with Rolls, H&A, Bibliographies, Chapter Notes and Indexes.

Volume I : 1880-1945. x/680. Fp, 60 mono phots (indexed), 17 maps (bound in).

Volume II : 1946-1990. -/480. Fp, 55 mono phots (indexed), 2 maps (bound in).

* The main theme of this work is the contribution of the Irish community in South Africa to the country's military role, and with particular reference to the history of the South African Irish Regt. It is, therefore, a continuation of the broader historical perspective described in Dr Monick's SHAMROCK AND SPRINGBOK (vide the Index of Authors). Volume I, which carries the Imperial Crown on its front outer cover, deals with the services of the Regt in GSWA, its return home and demobilisation, and the services of its members following their re-enlistment in various Imperial Service units. The story then moves on to remobilisation for WWII, the abortive attempts to raise more than one Bn, the move to East Africa and that campaign, the move to the Western Desert, and then the chaotic ill-planned battle at Sidi Rezegh in November 1941. This is dealt with in detail and is important because it describes the Bn's actions in collaboration with 2nd Bn Botha Regt and 3rd Bn Transvaal Scottish (as 5th Bde, 1st SA Div). The Botha Regt is not well recorded elsewhere, so this section is a rare source of reference. The Bde was virtually wiped out in this battle and ceased to be part of the SA Order of Battle for the rest of the war. Volume II opens with the re-establishment of the Regt in 1946 as 22nd Field Regt, SA Artillery (SA Irish), and its experiences up to 1974. During this time, in 1960, the Regt reverted to the infantry role and South Africa left the Commonwealth. The cover of this Volume, therefore, does not have the Imperial Crown displayed in conjunction with the Regtl crest. Active service was resumed in 1975 when the Regt was committed to Operation Savannah. From then on, it was engaged almost continuously in the Border War (1976-1988). The final chapter deals with matters which might otherwise have appeared in the form of appendixes - Regtl traditions, the Regt's pipes, uniforms, insignia, etc, all well illustrated with photographs and sketches. This is an enormous work. It is based upon protracted research, is well indexed, and covers a long period of time in South African military history. R/3 V/5. SANMMH/JPL. GTB.
Note: although published in 1992, these two volumes will remain scarce because only 250 copies have been printed.

MOUNTED & MECHANISED

SPRINGBOKS IN ARMOUR
The Story of the South African Armoured Cars in WWII
Harry Klein * Purnell & Sons (SA) Pty Ltd, Cape Town, 1965. Black, silver, SA Tank Corps crest, 10.0 x 6.0, xvi/338. Fp, 35 mono phots (incl 2 pull-outs), 6 maps (4 printed in the text, 2 folding, bound in), Bibliography, Index. Apps: Roll of Honour, H&A.
* A readable and authoritative history of the SA Tank Corps from its formation in January 1940. The narrative covers its activities in the Abyssinia, Western Desert and Madagascar campaigns, through to April 1943. The Corps was then disbanded. Most of its constituent elements were absorbed into other SA and British units. R/3 V/5. SANMMH. NO.

PREPARE TO MOUNT
The Story of the 6th Mounted Regiment
Albert Plane * Howard Timmins, Cape Town, 1977. Lime green, white, Regtl crest, 8.75 x 5.5, -/70. 24 mono phots (indexed), one line drawing (badge), no Index. Apps: Roll of Honour.
* The author, who served with the Regt, claims that it was the last horse-mounted unit to be raised in any Empire country. Formed in June 1940, it lost its horses only eight months later. They were replaced by armoured cars, the unit changing its title to 3rd Mounted Commando Regt. Two months later it became the 10th Armoured Regt, SA Tank Corps. In December 1943 it was sent to North Africa but, upon arrival, was disbanded to provide drafts for other units and other services. This explains the wide variety of unit designations to be seen in the Roll of Honour. It includes the names of three men killed while serving with the Royal Navy. The narrative names many individuals. Several later became prominent in South African public life. One was the politician Sir De Villiers Graaf, another was the publisher of this book, Howard Timmins. The author denies that he intended to compile a formal history, but the book is in fact a very complete record of the Regt's three years' existence. R/3 V/4. SANMMH/AL. GTB.
Note: published with a limited print run of 300 copies.

EARLY MOUNTED UNITS

HISTORY OF THE CAPE MOUNTED RIFLEMEN
With a Brief Account of the Colony of the Cape of Good Hope
Anon * John W Packer, for Richard Cannon, London, 1842. Green, blind, 8.75 x 5.75, viii/32. Two cld ills (Standard and uniform), no other ills, no maps, appendixes, no Index.
* This is a curiosity, being the only Regtl history in the well-known Cannon series for a Colonial unit. Like most of Richard Cannon's books, it contains little of substance. Their main (and perhaps sole) redeeming feature are the pretty and well-executed colour plates. This CMR history has two good lithograph prints in the first (1842) edition as recorded here, but coarser wood engravings were used in a later edition. Full details of the latter are not available, but it is understood that the text remained unaltered. R/5 V/1. PC. VS.

REGULATIONS FOR THE INSTRUCTION AND MOVEMENTS OF THE CAPE MOUNTED RIFLES
Capt J W Goldsworthy * Printed by Saul Solomon & Co, Cape Town, 1878, for the Regt. Black roan, 9.0 x 6.0, viii/172. Several sketches (line drawings) connected with drill movements, no maps, no appendixes, no Index.
* A book devoted entirely to drill movements and bugle calls, with no 'historical reference' value. It is listed here for its great rarity. Goldsworthy was Adjutant of the Regt. R/5 V/1. PC. RP.

HISTORICAL RECORD OF THE CAPE MOUNTED RIFLEMEN
Anon * W A Richards & Son, Cape Town, 1893. Soft card, olive, black, 9.0 x 6.0, -/21. No ills, no maps, no appendixes, no Index.
* Little more than a pamphlet, this is a useful element within the overall record of the CMR (vide preceding and following entries). The story commences with the raising of the European Police Force in 1852 as an Armed Constabulary to fight marauders and Hottentot insurgents. A year later the title was changed to Frontier Armed and Mounted Police. Over the next two decades it was hard-worked, putting down tribal outbreaks and establishing the rule of European law. In 1878 it became part of the Corps of Cape Mounted Riflemen and lost it former identity. The story, which ends here in 1892, includes interesting detail of numerous frontier actions, the protection of settlers, and the recovery of stolen cattle. The names of casualties and the recipients of awards appear throughout. R/5 V/3. NAM. PJE.

RECORD OF THE CAPE MOUNTED RIFLEMEN
Basil Williams * Sir Joseph Causton & Sons Ltd, London, 1909. Full morocco, black, gold, Regtl crest, 8.5 x 5.25, iii/138. No mono phots, 10 cld ills (uniforms), one line drawing, one map (folding, bound in), Index. Apps: H&A, list of former COs, idem officers still serving.
* The first three chapters cover the origins of the Regt and describe some early frontier campaigns. The bulk of the narrative (page 58 onwards) deals with the Regt's role in the Anglo-Boer War (1899-1902). R/4 V/3. JPL. RP.

BOOT AND SADDLE
A Narrative Record of the Cape Regiment, the British Cape Mounted Riflemen, the Frontier Armed and Mounted Police, and the Colonial Cape Mounted Riflemen
P J Young * Maskew Miller Ltd, Cape Town, 1955. Blue, gold, Regtl crest, 8.5 x 5.5, xiv/193. 7 mono phots, one map, Bibliography, Index. Apps: 10 in total, incl list of former COs (with biographical notes), list of former officers, record of events (1797-1921), list of Commandants of the FAMP, records of service.
* A book which explains the various confusing unit designations found within the evolution of the Defence Forces of the Cape Colony, with clear accounts of those units' peacetime and campaign services, their organisation, and their armaments and dress. The following were all fundamentally an element of the same Corps - Cape Regt (1806-1826), Imperial Cape Mounted Riflemen (1827-1870), Frontier Armed and Mounted Police (1853-1878), Colonial Cape Mounted Riflemen (1873-1913), and the 1st South African Mounted Rifles (1913-1920). The 1st SAMR were unfortunately obliged to surrender to the Germans at Sandfontein in 1914. They were held POW, were then freed by Gen Myburgh, returned to service, and took part in the suppression of the Ovambo revolt of 1916. R/3 V/4. JPL. VS/JRStA.
Note: this book must not be confused with another having the same main title - BOOT AND SADDLE - BITS OF SOUTH AFRICAN LIFE IN BUSH AND BARRACKS, by H Marin-Humphreys (George Robertson, Melbourne, 1875). The latter is an autobiographical account (vii/150 pages) by an Australian who, as a Captain, served with the CMR between 1867 and 1870. It is a light-hearted yarn which deals principally with social and sporting activities.

A STORY OF THE CAPE MOUNTED RIFLEMEN, 1st AUGUST 1878 - 31st MARCH 1913, AND 1st REGIMENT SOUTH AFRICAN MOUNTED RIFLES, 1st APRIL 1913 - 1st APRIL 1926
Maj A E Lorch DSO MC * V&R Printers, Pretoria, 1958. Black, yellow, 8.5 x 5.5, -/119. 7 mono phots, 6 maps, no Index. Apps: 'Records of Men who Passed through the Ranks of the Regiment' (this being a list of private soldiers who later gained promotion and/or other distinctions), list of COs, idem Adjutants (CMR), notes on the Artillery Troop, idem Signalling Staff, idem Medical Staff (CMR).
* The author seems to have served with the CMR from 1890 to 1913 and, as a result, the narrative has a 'first-hand' air about it. The first two chapters deal with the formation of the Corps, the Morosi War (1879), the Matabeleland campaign

(1893), Pondoland (1894), Bechuanaland (1897), and the Le Fleur's Affair (1898). The bulk of the book is then devoted to operations during the war of 1899-1902 in great detail. The final chapter covers the Zulu Rebellion of 1906, the impact of the creation of the Union, and operations in GSWA (1914-1915). Lists of casualties and awards appear at regular intervals throughout the text, particularly in respect of the Anglo-Boer War. A goldmine for genealogists and admirers of this famous Regt. R/4 V/4. ASKBMC. CB.

WITH THE CAPE MOUNTED RIFLES
Four Years of Service in South Africa, by an ex-CMR
Alex K Granville * Richard Bentley & Son, London, 1881. Cloth, leather spine and quarters, light brown, gold, 8.75 x 6.0, xvi/262. No ills, no maps, no appendixes, no Index (but a good Contents page).
* An entertaining account of the author's experiences, from his recruitment into the Frontier Armed and Mounted Police (soon to become the CMR) through to his discharge in late 1880. He describes the 'steerage' passage from England, his initial training in South Africa, and then subsequent active service. He gives a 'soldier's view' of the battles of Ibeka, Kreli's Kraal, Lusisi, Umzintzani, Quintana, the annexation of St John's District, and finally the Basutoland campaign of 1879. Not a formal history, but an excellent supplementary source. R/4 V/3. AL. GTB.
Note: a similar book, and equally useful, is CAMP LIFE AND SPORT IN SOUTH AFRICA - EXPERIENCES OF KAFFIR WAR WITH THE CAPE MOUNTED RIFLES, by Thomas Lucas (Chapman & Hall, London, xiii/258, 1878).

THE ZULU REBELLION OF 1906
A Souvenir of the Transvaal Mounted Rifles, the first Regiment raised in the British Transvaal for Service beyond its Borders
W J Powell * Transvaal Leader, Johannesburg, 1906. Olive green, white/black, 'Troops in action' motif, 12.5 x 9.75, -/67. 99 mono phots, no maps, no Index. Apps: nominal rolls of 'A' Sqn Imperial Light Horse, 'B' Sqn SA Light Horse, 'C' Sqn Johannesburg Mounted Rifles, 'D' Sqn Northern Rifles, and the Transport.
* The book starts with a history (6 pages) of the 1906 Rebellion. This is followed by a detailed account of the part played by the Transvaal Mounted Rifles as viewed by a journalist who took part. The narrative is well written and is backed by excellent photographs. The author also provides brief but useful references to other Transvaal units of that period - Imperial Light Horse, Scottish Horse, CSAR Volunteers, Witwatersrand Rifles, and the Transvaal Cadets. R/4 V/4. AL. GTB.

SA ARMOURED CORPS - PERMANENT FORCE

THE SPECIAL SERVICE BATTALION (1933-1973)
Die Spesiale Diensbataljon
Cmdt W Otto, Brig J N Blatt, Col J Ploeger, and Maj F J Jacobs * Govt Printer, for the Documentation Service, SADF, 1973. Black, silver, SSB crest, 12.0 x 8.0, viii/147. Fp, 68 mono phots, no maps, Glossary, Bibliography, Index. Apps: Roll of Honour (KIA, DOW, DOD and POW), list of COs (with personal portraits), idem 2i/c, idem RSMs, list of officers serving at the conclusion of the Italian campaign, extract from the Govt Gazette authorising the establishment of the SSB, 28.4.1933.
* Written partly in English and partly in Afrikaans, this is the official record of a unit formed initially (1933) to provide employment and training for young men during the Depression years. Driven hard by RSM Whammond MC DCM MM, Sgt Maj A J Brand (Grenadier Guards), and Sgt P Flynn (Irish Guards), it achieved a high standard of military skill and served in the infantry role up until 1942. It then converted to armoured cars and fought with 6th SA Armd Div in Italy. Many individuals, with details of their awards, are mentioned in the text.
R/3 V/5. JPL. GTB.
Note: refer also to A SHORT HISTORY OF 1 SPECIAL SERVICE BATTALION, 1933-1983, by Lieut W A Dorning (Military Information Bureau, SADF, 1983), a 28-page booklet.

HISTORY OF THE NATAL MOUNTED RIFLES

Col G T Hurst * Knox Printing Co, Durban, 1935. Soft card, 'watered silk' paper covers, black, Regtl crest, 8.5 x 5.5, -/83. Fp, 29 mono phots, no maps, no Index. Apps: H&A, list of former officers (with casualty details), 'Rules & Regulations of the Royal Durban Rangers', notes on the Volunteer system in Natal.

* A history published to mark the Jubilee year of the founding of South Africa. It opens with a brief summary of the early Volunteer movement in Natal. A chapter is then given to the formation, organisation, arms, equipment and uniforms of the NMR. The rest of the narrative describes in succinct style the Regt's role in the Zulu War (1877-1879), the South African War (1899-1902), the Zulu Rebellion (1906), and WWI. R/4 V/4. NAM. PJE.

Note: the Regt produced a small casebound booklet of 16 pages under the title NATAL MOUNTED RIFLES - HISTORICAL NOTES, 1854-1942.

The date of publication seems to have been late 1942 or early 1943, i.e. shortly after the Regt's return home from the Western Desert. The narrative of this item covers briefly the early years, but then concentrates upon the Abyssinia and Desert campaigns. A fold-out map shows the unit's movements during that period. A useful adjunct to Hurst's 1935 history.

MY VERULAM TROOP

Being a Short Account of the Origin of the Verulam Troop of the Natal Mounted Rifles and of their Movements during the Period when they were Seconded to the Durban Light Infantry in the Zulu Rebellion of 1906

Capt A H Garnet-Blamey * Printed by the South Coast Herald Ltd, no other details shown, 1954. Light brown, silver, NMR crest, 9.0 x 7.75, -/30. Fp, 3 mono phots, one map (bound in), no Index. Apps: H&A (MIDs only, for the 1906 campaign), verbatim correspondence regarding the recommendation of a VC for the author (subsequently reduced to a MID).

* The author, who commanded the Troop during the campaign, states that the object of his book is to correct the accounts given in A HISTORY OF THE ZULU REBELLION, 1906, by J Stuart (Macmillan, 1913). His sub-title is a fair summary of the contents. R/4 V/3. SANMMH/AL. GTB.

NATAL MOUNTED RIFLES

Board of Management Centenary Appeal ...

Anon * EP & Commercial Printing, Durban, for the Regt, 1954. Stiff card, 'Tank and Rifleman' motif, white, black/green, 9.5 x 7.25, -/8. No ills, no maps, no appendixes, no Index.

* This fund-raising pamphlet appeared at a time when the Regt was building a new HQ in Walter Gilbert Road, Durban (as explained in the long sub-title). Its research value is to be found in the chronology of important events in the life of the Regt between 1854 and 1954. R/5 V/1. AL. GTB.

A COMPANY COMMANDER REMEMBERS

From El Yibo to El Alamein

A E Blamey * Publisher's details not shown, Pietermaritzburg, 1963. Green, gold, 8.5 x 5.5, vi/199. Fps, 12 mono phots, 2 maps (bound in), no Index. Apps: General Oliver Leese's instruction to 'every driver in XXX Corps' for the second Alamein battle.

* A readable and accurate account by an officer who served with 1st Natal Mounted Rifles. The period covered is 8.6.1940 (mobilisation) through to post-Alamein (the return to South Africa). During the intervening period, the Regt saw hard service in Abyssinia and the Western Desert. R/3 V/3. AL. NO.

ROUGH BUT READY

An Official History of the Natal Mounted Rifles and its Antecedent and Associated Units, 1854-1969

Eric Goetzsche * Interprint Pty Ltd, Durban, for the Regt, 1971. Dark green, silver, Regtl crest, 11.5 x 8.5, xxvii/408. Fp, 134 mono phots (indexed), 2 cld plates, 10 maps (bound in), Glossary, Bibliography, 2 Indexes (General, Military Units). Apps: Rolls of Honour (for each campaign, 1899-1945), H&A (for each campaign, with full citations for WWII),lists of former officers, nominal rolls (for each campaign), notes on cap badges, idem Battle Honours.
* This is a regimental history of exemplary quality - scholarly, deeply researched, well written. The author begins by tracing the Regt's roots in the Royal Durban Rangers, Victoria Mounted Rifles, Stanger MR, Alexandra MR, Border MR, Isipingo MR, East Griqualand MR, Durban MR, and Umzimkulu MR, through to 1894. He then describes the NMR'S role in the war of 1899-1902, the Zulu Rebellion of 1906, and in WWI. There is interesting coverage of the difficult inter-war years, conversion to dismounted status in 1934, and WWII services in East Africa, the Western Desert and Italy (where the NMR fought as an Armoured Reconnaissance Regt). The story concludes with the post-war period through to 1964. The appendixes are excellent. R/3 V/5. SANMMH. GTB/RH.

THE UMVOTI MOUNTED RIFLES, 1864-1975

Dr A J du Plessis * Printed by The Natal Witness, Pietermaritzburg, presumably for the Regt, 1975. Black, gold, Regtl crest in crimson, 11.5 x 8.25, ix/200. Fp, 124 mono phots, 9 maps, Bibliography, Index. Apps: Roll of Honour, H&A.
* A well researched history in which the author traces the origins and evolution of the Regt from its establishment in 1864 as the Greytown Mounted Rifles, its amalgamation in 1869 with the Natal Hussars, further amalgamation in 1887 with the Natal Carbineers, and then the secession of the Left Wing in 1893 to form the Umvoti Mounted Rifles. In 1913, the Regt absorbed, by amalgamation, the Zululand Mounted Rifles. Traditionally a horsed Regt, the UMR converted to the infantry role in 1937 and fought as such in WWII. In 1956 it became an armoured unit (which it still is at the time of writing, 1992). The narrative gives good coverage of the early campaigns - Zulu War (1879), Anglo-Boer War (1899-1902), and the Zulu Rebellion (1906). In WWI, the Regt fought in GSWA (including the Battle of Gibeon) under the title 4th SA Mounted Rifles. Mobilised again in 1939, the UMR fought in the Western Desert battles until ordered to surrender at Tobruk (only five men managed to escape). The UMR took no further part in WWII, although many of its personnel got away from POW camps in Italy and joined Partisan units in the mountains. There are numerous references to individual officers and men scattered throughout the text. R/3 V/5. SANMMH. GTB.

LIGHT HORSE CAVALCADE

The Imperial Light Horse, 1899-1961

Harry Klein * Howard Timmins, Cape Town, 1969. Red imitation leather, gold, Regtl crest (crossed flags with 'Imperium et Libertas' motif), illustrated end-papers, 11.0 x 8.75, -/200. 101 mono phots, 12 maps, Bibliography, footnotes, Index. Apps: Rolls of Honour (the roll for the war of 1899-1902 excludes 2 ILH, but includes men of the 5th Lancers and the Imperial Yeomanry killed while serving with the Regt. The roll for WWI is arranged by theatre - 1914 Boer Revolt, GSWA, and the 1922 Rand strikes. The WWII roll covers the ILH and the ILH/Kimberley Regt), H&A (1 ILH complete and incl 4 VCs, 2 ILH incomplete. The WWI listings are possibly incomplete. WWII awards are arranged under ILH for North Africa and under ILH/Kimberley Regt for Italy), lists of Colonels in Chief, Honorary Colonels, and COs (up to 1961, 1 ILH and 2 ILH), notes on Battle Honours, idem Dress.
* The narrative covers all the campaigns in which the Regt was engaged following inception in 1899 - Anglo-Boer War, the Boer insurgence of 1914, GSWA, the Rand Revolt, and WWII. Although the ILH did not serve under Smuts in East Africa,

many of its personnel went there with other units. The Regt converted to the infantry role in the 1930s. It fought as such in the Western Desert as an element of 3rd Bde, 2nd SA Div - roughly a quarter of its men becoming POW at the fall of Tobruk in June 1942. The Regt - specifically 1 ILH - then fought on as part of 1st SA Div until 1943 when the survivors joined the combined ILH/Kimberley Regt. Assigned to the new 6th SA Armoured Div, they served in Italy as motorised infantry from 1943 to 1945. Additionally, elements of 2 ILH served in the Desert. In 1961, when South Africa became a Republic, the Regt lost the 'Imperial' from its title. It then became The Light Horse Regt. This is a good readable history, with excellent illustrations. The author admits that a lack of source documents caused parts of his coverage of the early years to be somewhat sketchy, but the WWII coverage is complete and authoritative.
R/2 V/5. SANMMH. GTB/RH.

PRINCE ALFRED'S GUARD
With Notes Relating to the Volunteer Movement in Port Elizabeth
Quartermaster Sergeant Richard T Hall * Printed at The Port Elizabeth Advertiser Press, Cape Colony, 1906. Stiff card, red, black, Regtl crest, 5.75 x 4.5, -/421. Fp, approximately 40 mono phots (by R S Elmslie, mostly full page captioned groups and studio portraits of members), no maps, no appendixes, no Index.
* The Regt's pre-1906 evolution and campaign services are well covered in the histories produced by Perridge (1939) and by Orpen (1967), especially the latter (vide following entries). The main value of Hall's account is that he could devote 421 pages to a comparatively short period of years. As a result, this book has much more detail regarding minor events, named individuals, and the minutiae of Regtl life, than was possible for his successors. R/4 V/4. JPL. VS.

THE HISTORY OF PRINCE ALFRED'S GUARD
With Which is Affiliated the Royal Scots Fusiliers, 1856-1938
Maj Frank Perridge * E H Walton & Co Ltd, Port Elizabeth, 1939. Red, gold, 'Zulu war shield' motif (front cover and spine), 9.75 x 6.75, xv/208. Fp, 10 mono phots, 2 maps (printed on the end-papers), no Index. Apps: list of former officers.
* The narrative begins in 1856 with the raising of the Port Elizabeth Volunteer Rifle Corps and the provision of a guard for Prince Alfred in 1860. Active service in the field commenced in 1877 in the Transkei and, two years later, in Zululand. The author gives good detailed coverage of the campaign in Basutoland (1880) and Bechuanaland (1897), and then the Anglo-Boer War (1899-1902). The Regt was mobilised in 1914 and given garrison duties on the Cape Peninsula. A few months later, to the chagrin of its members, it was demobilised. Ninety percent of them promptly volunteered for service with other units. The book concludes with a basic factual account of the difficult inter-war years. This is a readable history which could have been much improved by the provision of an Index and more appendixes for reference purposes. R/3 V/3. UWML/ASKBC. BCC/CB.

PRINCE ALFRED'S GUARD, 1856-1956
Neil Orpen * Books of Africa (Pty) Ltd, Cape Town, 1967. Blue, gold, Regtl crest, 9.0 x 6.0, -/346. Fp, 80 mono phots, 5 cld ills, numerous line drawings, 11 maps, Bibliography, Index. Apps: Rolls of Honour (Transkei 1877, Basutoland 1880-1881, Bechuanaland 1897, Anglo-Boer War 1899-1902, and WWII), H&A (WWII only), list of former COs, idem Hon Colonels, idem all officers who ever served, notes on cap badges.
* An authoritative history, published to mark the Regt's centenary. The early campaigns are covered in some detail, but the author's main contribution in this regard is his addition of the Rolls of Honour and the bibliographic reference sources which do not appear in the books by Hall and Perridge (vide preceding entries). The other great strength of Orpen's account is his reporting of the Regt's WWII services. Initially, the PAG supplied drafts for 2nd SA Inf Bde in the Western Desert. Then, following the reorganisations of 1943, it came into its own as an armoured unit. Mounted on Sherman tanks, it moved to mainland Italy and

fought in that campaign through to the end of the war. Orpen gives detailed and readable coverage of the hard fighting on the Gothic Line during the winter of 1944-1945, with many officers and ORs mentioned in the text. R/3 V/5. UWML. BCC. Note: published as a limited edition of 1500 numbered copies.

THE PRETORIA REGIMENT
12th Infantry Battalion, Active Citizen Force of South Africa
Second to None
Anon * Govt Printing & Stationery Office, Pretoria, 1923. Soft card, dark grey, black, 9.5 x 6.0, -/16. 10 mono phots, no maps, no appendixes, no Index.
* This booklet is one of the very few published records of the Regt. It was intended to celebrate the Regt's tenth anniversary, in 1923. Services briefly described are - the 1914 Boer Rebellion, the 1914-1915 GSWA campaign, and the 1922 Rand strikes. The Regt's full title was Princess Alice's Own Pretoria Regt, but it was known as the 12th Infantry until 1928. In mid-1915, after returning home from GSWA, and in common with other ACF units, the Regt was demobilised because its members were not attested for service overseas. Most of the officers and men then joined the new Imperial Service units, some going to the Siege Btys SAHA and others to the twelve Bns of SA Infantry. A list of all personnel serving in 1923 is included in the text. R/5 V/2. AL. GTB.

REGIMENT BOTHA/REGIMENT PRESIDENT STEYN
Souvenir, June 1944
Anon * Govt Printer, Pretoria, 1944. Soft card, 'Tanks with flags' motif, white, black, 8.5 x 5.5, -/35. Fp, 6 mono phots, 19 excellent line drawings, no maps, no appendixes, no Index.
* This booklet, issued to commemorate the coupling of the two Regts for the Italian campaign as part of the 6th SA Armoured Div, is the only known history of either. Both Regts were formed in 1934, mobilised in 1940, and fought in the Western Desert before being brought back to South Africa after Second Alamein for amalgamation. A surprisingly detailed narrative for such a slim volume.
R/4 V/2. SANMMH. GTB.

ENGINEERS

A SHORT SKETCH OF THE HISTORY AND ORGANISATION OF THE CSAR ENGINEER CORPS
Prepared for the Colonel in Chief, the Rt Hon the Earl of Selbourne KG GCMG
Anon * Printed by the Transvaal Leader, Johannesburg, 1910. Half blue, half red, diagonal cloth overlay, gold, CSAREC crest, 9.0 x 11.5 (landscape), -/24. 27 mono phots, no maps, no Index. Apps: list of COs (1901-1910), idem Adjutants, list of Bisley prizes won by members of the Corps.
* The accronym in the title signifies Central South African Railway. The 'history' of the Corps, from foundation in 1901 through to 1910, is covered in just three pages. The other pages are taken up with unusual photographs of armoured trains, bridge building exercises, searchlights, and studio portraits of officers. The Corps was part of the Transvaal Volunteer Corps which ceased to exist in 1912 when the new Union Defence Force was being formed. R/3 V/2. SANMMH. GTB.
Note: reference may be made also to THE RAILWAY PIONEER CORPS, anon, a pamphlet of 17 pages published in Cape Town, c.1900.

NINE FLAMES
Ken Anderson * Purnell & Sons (SA) Pty Ltd, Cape Town, 1964. Dark blue, gold, red blocking on spine, 'Grenade' motif (hence the 'nine flames'), 9.75 x 6.0, xi/282. Fp, 16 mono phots, no maps, Index. Apps: Roll of Honour, H&A (statistical summary only).
* A good workmanlike history of the SA Engineers and their WWII services in East Africa, North Africa and Italy. A complete and well presented record, with many individuals and sub-units mentioned in the narrative. R/2 V/4. SANMMH. GTB.

SALUTE THE SAPPERS
Parts I and II
South African Forces, World War II, Volume VIII
Neil Orpen and H J Martin * Printed in Cape Town, published in Johannesburg by the Sappers Assn, Part I being issued as a single volume in 1981, Part II as a second volume in 1982, the pair then being described as Volume VIII of South Africa's semi-official war history. Matching bindings, blue, gold, SAEC crest on the spines, 10.0 x 6.0.
Part I : Fp, 69 mono phots, 15 maps, 4 line drawings, Bibliography, Index.
Part II : Fp, 84 mono phots, 20 maps, 5 line drawings, Bibliography, Index.
Apps: Roll of Honour (WWII only), H&A (WWI, WWII and subsequent operations up to 1982), list of former COs (all units, 1942-1945), notes on 8th Army Engineers, the Order of Battle (at 23.4.1945), notes on SAEC organisation (in 1982).
* As the above technical specification will suggest, this is an authoritative and complete account covering the period 1859 to 1982, but with the bulk of the narrative being given to operations during WWII. R/2 V/5. SANMMH. NO.

MINES ENGINEERING BRIGADE (SAEC)
A Short History of the Brigade (16 MEB Brigade), June 1940 - December 1946
Anon * Morefield & Field, Johannesburg, 1947. Card, white, black/red, 9.5 x 7.25, -/6. No ills, no maps, no Index. Apps: H&A, establishments, list of Trophies.
* A souvenir produced for the Bde's personnel at disbandment. Raised in 1939, the MEB recruited and gave basic and advanced military training to mining engineers who had volunteered for overseas service. It despatched Contingents of these experts to various SA Engineer units such as those involved in building the new Palestine-Lebanon-Syria railway. Later, after the fall of Tobruk and the serious losses in the Western Desert, the MEB recruited a further 1200 volunteers for full-time service (this despite the difficulties of obtaining the release of technical experts from South Africa's important mining industries). A very short but useful chronicle of South Africa's otherwise forgotten technical war effort.
R/5 V/2. SANMMH. GTB.

THE EIGHTH FIELD SQUADRON

A Brief History of the 8th Field Squadron (SAEC) which was a Field Squadron of the 6th South African Armoured Division, 1943–1945

D V Jeffrey ('and others') * Rostra Printers, Johannesburg, n.d. Plasticated soft card, dark blue, black, 10.5 x 7.5, viii/46. Fp (group of unit personnel), 39 other mono phots, 16 cartoons, one map, no Index. Apps: Roll of Honour, H&A.

* An informal history written 'to record our activities and to include mention of a few side-lights ... which will recall forgotten faces and incidents'. Although brief, the booklet covers a lot of ground - formation as an ACF unit in Cape Town in 1939, mobilisation in September 1940, training in South Africa until April 1943, embarkation for Egypt as part of 6th (SA) Div, then the move to Italy in April 1944. The Sqn took part in the mainland campaign through to the time of the German surrender, ending the war at Gorgonzola (Milan). R/4 V/4. AL. GTB.

THE STORY OF THE NINTH

A Record of the 9th Field Company, South African Engineer Corps, July 1939 – July 1943

* Maj J N Cowin * Gover, Dando & Co (Pty) Ltd, Johannesburg, 1948. Leather, red, gold, SAEC crest, 8.5 x 5.5, -/160. Fp, 27 mono phots, 24 line drawings, 4 maps (2 printed in the text, 2 on the end-papers), no Index. Apps: list of COs, idem RSMs, until nominal roll.

* A book divided into three parts - Formation and Growth, Active Service, and Swan Song (disbandment, July 1943). The Coy was formed as an ACF unit in July 1939, then mobilised for full-time duties in August 1940. Its war services began in Kenya and ended in Eritrea. The Coy then returned to Durban and was employed on local defence and IS duties before being disbanded. An excellent informative history, based upon a combination of Coy records and personal reminiscences. R/4 V/4. JPL/RCSL. PJE.

PRINTING IN THE FIELD BY THE SOUTH AFRICAN FORCES

Capt H G Cooper MBE * Associated Technical & Scientific Societies of South Africa, Johannesburg, 1946. Red, gold, 9.5 x 7.25, -/15. 5 mono phots, 2 line drawings, no maps, no appendixes, no Index.

* A brief but helpful account of the role of the Directorate of Printing & Stationery in the SA Forces in WWII. First delivered as a paper to a meeting of the Associated Scientific and Technical Societies of South Africa, it seems to have been then distributed in this format to other interested parties. The unit was formed in 1940 and the author served with it. He deals mainly with the technical aspects of map-making and map-printing while on active service in East Africa, the Western Desert, and Italy. Operating initially under the wing of 'Q' Services Corps, the No 1 Mobile Map Printing Coy was transferred to the SAEC in February 1942. It was disbanded in May 1946. A useful source for the specialist researcher. R/4 V/3. SANMMH. GTB.

SIGNALS

SUID AFRIKAANS SEINKORPS - SOUTH AFRICAN CORPS OF SIGNALS
Maj F J Jacobs, Lieut R J Bouch, Sophia de Preez and Richard Cornwell * Documentation Service, SA Defence Force, Pretoria, 1975. Black, silver, SACS crest and motto, 12.0 x 8.0, v/107. 67 mono phots, one map, no appendixes, no Index.
* This book covers the development of signalling and communications in South Africa from the earliest days of the Dutch East Indies Company through to 1974. It encompasses the British Colonial period, the Boer Republics, the Boer use of 'rapportryers' (despatch riders), and the British use of signal beacons and of heliograph and telegraph equipment in the war of 1899-1902. The Union Defence Force was established in 1912-1913, but the creation of a dedicated Signals Corps was still in transition when WWI commenced. Consequently, communications work was conducted in part by the SA Field Telegraph & Postal Corps and in part by the SA Corps of Signals Company (Royal Engineers). An autonomous SA Corps of Signals was formed in 1924 and was well established by 1939. It rendered valuable service in East Africa and during the Western Desert and Italian campaigns. Written partly in Afrikaans and partly in English, this book includes interesting references to the use of Telefunken and Marconi wireless equipment in 1915-1919 and the design of South African radar equipment first operated in December 1939. The narrative lacks detail, but it does provide a useful summary of a complex subject.
R/3 V/2. SANMMH. GTB.

SOUTH AFRICAN RADAR IN WORLD WAR II
Peter Brain, Sheilagh Lloyd, and F J Hewitt * Newset, Durban, for The SSS Radar Book Group, 1993. Paper covers, white, black, 'Mobile radar set' motif, 8.25 x 6.0, x/229. 60 mono phots, 8 line drawings, one map, Glossary, Index. Apps: notes on 'The Ghost', notes on the 'JB' set, list of personnel who attended courses.
* The book by Jacobs et al (vide preceding entry) does mention South African radar, but this later account by Brain et al covers the subject in far greater depth. Written in clear concise language, it is based mainly upon the recollections of ex-members of the Special Signal Services, SA Corps of Signals. Additional material, where appropriate, is drawn from the SADF archives. The book recounts how, in 1939, the Dominion governments were each invited to send to England their leading physicists for secret briefings by Sir Robert Watson-Watt and his team, the pioneers of 'RDF' (radar detection finding, later retitled 'radar'). South Africa failed to respond, but a New Zealand physicist, Dr Ernest Marsden, gave the South Africans all the latest information while travelling home via Cape Town. With these details, the South African scientists - most of whom later became the founder members of the SSS/SACS - were able to build their own experimental 'JB' set. It first operated in December 1939, and several such sets were later used operationally in East Africa, the Sinai Desert, and around the coasts of South Africa before being replaced by British-made sets. Members of the unit were initially all male, recruited from the universities, but the later composition was 50% men, 50% women. The unit could claim to have the highest proportion of post-graduate personnel of any unit in the Union Defence Force. The book, arranged in seven chapters, covers all aspects of the story - early research, the development of the 'JB' set, the construction of the coastal radar stations, the use of radar in aircraft, and so forth. It is a valuable addition to the published history of the evolution of modern radar. R/1 V/5. SANMMH. GTB.
Note: the initial print run was 600 copies.

OTHER CORPS

WE FOUGHT THE MILES
The History of the South African Railways at War, 1939-1945
Anon * Printed by Horters, Johannesburg, for the South African Railways, n.d. (c.1946). Grey, red, 'Soldier with rails' motif, 10.0 x 8.0, -/120. Fp, 136 mono phots, 4 cld ills, 4 maps, no Index. Apps: Roll of Honour (9 pages), H&A (6 pages).
* The only known record of the SA Railways & Harbours Bde in WWII. The first half of the book is devoted to its work on the home front. The second half describes its activities in East Africa, the Middle East, and Italy. There are many interesting sidelights to the logistical effort needed to sustain the front line forces, e.g. the construction at record speed of the railway from Haifa to Beirut, the repair and operation of Italian docks, and the work in Egypt and Italy of vehicle workshops (which repaired or assembled 100,000 trucks and 1096 armoured fighting vehicles). The narrative lacks detail, but does provide a useful overall record.
R/4 V/4. AL. GTB.

WAR RECORD OF THE UDFI, 1939-1946
War Record of the Union Defence Force Institutes (YMCA - Toc H)
Lieut Col T R Ponsford * Horters Ltd, Cape Town, n.d. (c.1948). Greenish grey, blue, 9.75 x 7.5, vii/235. Fp, 128 mono phots, no maps, no Index. Apps: unit nominal roll (with details of awards included).
* The UDFI was a military unit, raised in 1940 as part of the SADF 'Q' Services Corps, and commanded by the author of this book. It had an establishment of 488 all ranks (including 60 women). Sub-units served in every theatre of war in which South African troops were engaged. Its role was the provision of welfare services behind the lines and at isolated bases and construction sites. Apart from mobile canteens, film shows and libraries, it also cared for wounded troops in transit and for former POW during their repatriation. A well documented account of a small but important unit. R/2 V/4. JPL. GTB.
Note: a booklet of 46 pages with the unpromising title of No 19 RESERVE MT COMPANY - UDF ENTERTAINMENT UNIT, by G Marriot (Caxton Printing, Pretoria, n.d. c.1943) throws further light on the work of the 'Q' Services Corps.

MEN OF THE MIDLANDS
The Story of the Weenen-Klip National Reserve Volunteers
A Mervyn-Wood * Natal Witness, Pietermaritzburg, 1946. Stiff card, grey, black, 7.25 x 4.75, ix/63. 10 mono phots, no maps, no Index. Apps: muster rolls for A, B, and C Detachments.
* With most of its combat forces committed to the East Africa campaign, the Union commenced raising a local defence force in October 1940. Part-time, unpaid, and entirely voluntary, its recruits were men who were over-age, medically down-graded, time-expired from full-time service, or employed in 'key' civilian jobs. Standards of training and equipment increased sharply in 1942 when there was an anxiety that Japan might invade South Africa via Madagascar. In total, 27,000 men served in the NRV. This is the record of one such local unit, and it reveals an interesting aspect of South Africa's war effort and the temper of its white population during the most critical years. R/4 V/4. AL. GTB.

WAR EFFORT OF THE 19th BATTALION, SOUTH AFRICAN COASTAL DEFENCE CORPS
Lieut R B Archibald * Central Press, Durban, n.d. (c.1947). Soft card, white, dark blue, Corps crest, 8.0 x 5.0, -/19. No ills, no maps, no Index. Apps: list of former officers and NCOs.
* An extremely brief account of a little-known part-time volunteer unit which guarded the coastal area around Durban throughout the war. Entertaining and informative. R/4 V/2. SANMMH. GTB.

WOMANHOOD AT WAR
The Story of the SAWAS (South African Women's Auxiliary Service)
Gwen Hewitt * Frier & Munro, Johannesburg, 1947. Stiff card, grey, brown, 8.5 x 5.5, -/173. Fp, 75 mono phots, no maps, no appendixes, no Index.
* In WWII, 65,000 women volunteered for unpaid part-time service as welfare officers, cooks, clerks, drivers, etc, within South Africa's borders. They organised and ran canteens for the troops, recreational facilities, leave centres and many other 'troops comfort' services. A few volunteered for service in Egypt and Italy, work for which they received a salary. The service was disbanded in 1945.
R/3 V/4. SANMMH. GTB.
Note: recommended as an additional source is STRANGERS IN OUR MIDST, by Lucy Bean (Howard Timmins, Cape Town, 1970). The authoress was one of those who served in Italy, and she gives a good account of the work of the SAWAS in that country. She also covers Command 13, the SAWAS group based in and around Cape Town. The title of her book refers to the thousands of Allied servicemen whose ships called at Cape Town, Port Elizabeth and Durban while on passage between the Atlantic and Indian Oceans. Those men still recall with gratitude the almost overwhelming shore hospitality arranged for them by the SAWAS. This organisation must not be confused with the WAAS (Women's Auxiliary Army Service). This Service consisted of women who were full-time, paid, and employed specifically on military work connected directly to the war effort. As despatch riders, truck drivers, signallers, cypher clerks, ordnance technicians, etc, they were an integral element of the armed forces and were liable for service overseas (a first contingent moved to East Africa in September 1940 and others served in the Middle East). Curiously, the title of the WAAS was not prefixed by 'SA' (South African).

MILITERE GENEESKUNDE IN SUID-AFRIKA (1913-1983)
Maj A F van Jaarsvedt (and others) * Government Printer, Pretoria, for the Ministry of Information Bureau, 1983. Black, gold, 12.0 x 8.75, iii/119. 71 mono phots, 2 cld ills, 6 line drawings, no maps, Bibliography, no appendixes, Index.
* Printed entirely in Afrikaans. The title translates as MILITARY MEDICINE IN SOUTH AFRICA. It begins with a brief history of the fore-runners of the South African Medical Corps - the Cape Medical Staff, Natal Medical Corps, Transvaal Medical Staff Corps, and the medical services of the Boer Republics. There is then good coverage of WWI and WWII, and the book contains good illustrations of Colours and unit flashes. The extensive Bibliography is an aid to further research. This is the only published history of South African military medical services which has been traced. R/1 V/3. SANMMH. GTB.

POLICE

THE FIGHTING POLICE OF SOUTH AFRICA
J E M Thursby-Attwell * Natal Witness, Pietermaritzburg, n.d. (c.1926). Stiff card, buff, black, 8.75 x 5.5, -/207. 16 mono phots, no maps, no appendixes, no Index.
* The author states: 'This is not a historical record of the Police Forces of South Africa but a few interesting facts where honour, courage and self-sacrifice played a great part'. Despite the modesty of the claim, the book is in effect a most useful record of events in which various Corps of South African police played a noteworthy role - Isandhlwana and Rorke's Drift (1897), Wilson's Last Stand, or the Shangani Patrol (1893), the Ferreira Raid (1906), the Morengo Uprising (1907), the Bambata Rebellion (1905-1906), the Langeberg Campaign (1897), the Boer Rebellion (1914-1915), the Zandfontein Disaster (1914), the Transkeian Affair (1916), the Grahamstown Demonstrations (1917), the Bullhoek Affair (1916), the Bondelswarts Uprising (1916), the Tembu-Basu Troubles (1922), and the Witwatersrand Strike (1922). There is reference also to the services of the 5th (Police) Mountain Bty in Central Africa (1915). A final chapter deals with the black police of South Africa. R/5 V/3. SANMMH. GTB.

THE MOUNTED POLICE OF NATAL
H P Holt * John Murray, London, 1913. Red, gold, Corps crest, 8.75 x 6.0, xviii/366. 35 mono phots, no maps, Index. Apps: list of former and serving officers.
* The NMP was raised in 1874 by Maj (later Maj Gen Sir) T G Dartnell. This is a narrative account of its services in four major upheavals - the Zulu War (1877-1879), the two Anglo-Boer Wars (1880 and 1899-1902), the Zulu Revolt (1905-1906). The book also contains helpful references to the Reserve Territory Carbineers (later re-titled Zululand Police), the Natal Railway Police (amalgamated with the Natal Mounted Police in 1894), and the Natal Water Police (formed in that same year). The story includes numerous eyewitness accounts. A readable general history. R/5 V/4. PCAL/SLV. LM/PS.

NATAL PAST AND PRESENT
A History of the Natal Mounted Police, 1874-1894, and the Natal Police, 1894-1913
Maj Arthur A Wood * Bristol Typesetting Co, for Arthur H Stockwell Ltd, UK, 1962. Light green, white, 7.5 x 5.25, -/176. Fp, 11 mono phots, one line drawing, one map, Index. Apps: 5 in total, being verbatim copies of articles and editorials published by various Natal newspapers in 1961.
* The book is divided into three sections. Part I, to which half of the total narrative is devoted, is a history of the Natal Mounted Police (renamed Natal Police in 1894). It describes how the NMP was raised shortly after the Langalibalele Rebellion of 1873 (put down mainly by the Natal Carbineers) and then deals with events year by year through to 1913. Many individuals are named in the narrative, and the Anglo-Boer Wars and the Zulu Rebellions are quite fully covered (with casualties and awards listed in the text). There is useful reference also to the raising of the Water Police, the Railway Police, and the Indian and Native (Zulu) Police forces. In 1914 the Natal Police was reorganised into two Regts of the new Active Citizen Force - 2nd and 3rd SA Mounted Rifles. Part II is headed 'Epilogue (Personalities)'. This is mainly the author's reminiscences of his early service in the NP and his recollections of some of his fellow officers (one being South Africa's outstanding WWII leader, Maj Gen Dan Pienaar). Part III is the story of how the Colony of Natal became an unwilling member of the Union in 1910, and then subsequent events (up to 1961) in that region. The first two Parts are of particular interest to the police/military researcher and to the genealogist. R/3 V/4. SANMMH. GTB.

S.A. POLICE COMMEMORATIVE ALBUM
S.A. POLISIE GEDENKALBUM
The History of the South Africa Police, 1913-1988
Die Geskiendenis van die Suid-Afrikaanse Polisie, 1913-1988
Marius De Witt Dippenaar * Promedia Publications (Pty) Ltd, Silverton (Pretoria), 1988. Dark blue, gold, SAP '75th' motif, 11.75 x 9.0, xxviii/884. Fp, 332 mono phots (some sepia), 109 cld ills, no maps, Bibliography, chapter notes (extensive), no appendixes, no Index.
* Published to mark the SAP's 75th Anniversary, this book has parallel narratives and picture captions in both of South Africa's official languages. The layout is easy to follow and, even allowing for the duplication, still offers more than 400 pages of prime reference material in either language. The 'Album' in the title does not reflect the very high quality of the work. This is a deeply researched and academically presented history of South Africa as viewed from the police perspective. It does not have an Index, but the 'Contents' section covers ten pages and is both a synopsis of the book and, in effect, a chronology of post-1913 South Africa. A book compiled in this manner provides a wealth of information for researchers whose interests are not confined simply to police work. Apart from senior officers and award winners, few individuals are mentioned by name, so perhaps some appendixes (listing personnel who served) would have been beneficial, but the book is otherwise hard to fault. The Bibliography and chapter notes are very detailed, and the illustrations cover all aspects of the story.
R/1 V/4. AL. GTB.

NOTES

PART 11

India

NOTES

INTRODUCTION

Of the five former Dominions, and until recent times, India was the least well served in the matter of regimental histories. There are several reasons why this should have been so, but the most obvious is the fact that the rank and file were not familiar with the English language. With only the officers and their friends having an interest in the publication of a formal book, the economic factors and the motivations were different to those found in regiments of the British Army and in Canada, South Africa, Australia, and New Zealand.

Many of the histories which did make their way through the complicated process of conception, compilation, editing, printing and distribution are, to the eye of the modern reader, less than inspiring. The majority of those produced prior to the war of 1914-1918 are little more than bare diaries of dates and Stations, with active services noted in minimal detail. Such books are useful as far as they go, but the absence of commentary or analysis severely limits their interest. Some examples, those dated circa the 1890s and 1900s, are so skeletal that it is not easy to understand their intended purpose. With 450 publications listed in the following pages it is possible only to generalise on this subject. However, in broad terms, it is safe to say that, during the period up to 1947, when the British left the shores of India, the Infantry were not well recorded, the Cavalry were quite well recorded, and the Gurkha and Garhwali units were very well recorded. The balance has been redressed since India and Pakistan became independent nations. Several skilled historians have written balanced retrospective accounts which - although not always printed and bound to the highest standards - are exemplary in every other way. The overall result is that now - late in the 20th Century - few of the old Indian Army regiments are not recorded in one form or another.

In passing, it is worth noting that the history of a regiment as formally published is not always the same as that first drafted by the author. For a variety of reasons, usually associated with the publisher's production budget and technical limitations, an author's typescript may be edited or otherwise amended before it is committed to hard print. The final work may not therefore be as complete or detailed as originally conceived.

With this in mind, and for the purposes of in-depth research, it is often helpful to examine the author's original research notes and original drafts. In most cases, referring to the Commonwealth as a whole, these are no longer available. However, a substantial quantity of such material has survived in respect of various Indian Army histories. The National Army Museum, London, for example, has acquired some of this archive material and it can be viewed by holders of Reader's Tickets.

The Indian Army was astonishingly versatile. It was represented in almost every war or campaign, in almost every part of the world, in which Great Britain became embroiled between 1758 and 1947. At its peak, it was the largest professional all-volunteer standing army the world has ever known. Because it (and its fore-bears, the armies of the Honourable East India Company) existed over such a long period of time, the contribution of an individual regiment or unit - as recorded in its published history - is not always fully explained in the broader strategic or political contexts. The purpose of the following 'Chronology' and the 'General Reference' section is to provide the researcher with a useful number of sources which set the scene in that larger sense.

Other general background sources are the numerous Divisional histories published in respect of the second world war period. Inspired by the late Lieut Col Walter Hingston OBE, the 'Tiger' trilogy is particularly good. Those three volumes, and most of the other Divisional histories noted hereafter, strike a happy balance between, on the one hand, describing the strategic and tactical roles of the Armies and Corps of which those Divisions formed part, and on the other hand, making frequent references to individual officers and men serving with their component units and sub-units.

All Indian Army units were required to complete an annual DIGEST OF SERVICES, listing the main events of the year. During periods of active service, in wartime, these Digests were replaced by a War Diary. A few Digests were formally bound and distributed outside the narrow reporting channel to higher command, and they are noted in this bibliography. The majority were internal reports, never intended for a wide readership. Many have survived and are available for examination at the National Army Museum, London, or in the Oriental & India Office Collections, British Library. The Gurkha Museum, Winchester, has copies of most of the War Diaries of the Gurkha battalions which served during the period 1939-1946.

In addition to these official records, many units organised the production of periodic newsletters or bulletins. Compiled in the style of a 'house magazine', they were financed from Mess funds or by the regimental association. They appeared every six or twelve months and were circulated to all serving and retired officers and to friends of the regiment. The contents covered a wide range of topics - camps and parades, visits by senior commanders and dignatories, officers' marriages, regimental appointments, recent honours and awards, sporting activities, articles written by past and present officers regarding their wartime adventures and peacetime travels, and so forth. Of particular interest to genealogists and medal collectors are the obituaries, often detailed and usually found at the rear of such publications.

Two examples of this genre of 'unofficial history' have been noted in this bibliography - THE CENTRAL INDIA HORSE NEWSLETTERS, and THE SCINDE HORSEMAN. Attention is drawn also to a series entitled 14th PUNJAB REGIMENT YEAR BOOK, published annually from 1924 onwards by the Regimental Dinner Club, and printed (excepting the later editions) by Gale & Polden Ltd, of Aldershot. Researchers and collectors may encounter other comparable items, produced by other regiments, and will find them most useful (especially if they can examine a complete run of editions which give continuity to the comings and goings of personnel over a period of years).

Although the quality of authorship of individual Indian Army unit histories is unpredicatable - varying between the superb and the almost completely useless - the overall effect is comprehensive and pleasing. They are witness to the unique relationship between the British officer and the sowars and jawans with whom he shared the perils of war and the monotony of the cantonment. Over two centuries, it was impossible to separate the fate and fortunes of Great Britain from those of India. It was the Indian Army which bound the diverse religious and racial communities of the sub-continent to a common cause and helped to give them their sense of nationhood.

When the British eventually withdrew, in 1947, their departure was marred - especially in the Punjab - by a wave of blood-letting between the two major religious groups, the Muslims and the Hindus. The social historian might wish to note that, despite the appalling carnage caused by age-old prejudices within the civilian population, there was almost no trouble of any kind between serving soldiers. They remained loyal to their regiments and - even though they practiced conflicting religions - they held steady. No army has ever been put to a greater test.

INDIA
A Military Chronology

1498: the Portuguese navigator, Vasco da Gama, is the first European to reach India by sea. He is followed by maritime traders from Portugal, from Holland, and later, from France.
1599: the Dutch have well established coastal trading bases in India, Ceylon, and the East Indies, with powerful control over the important trade in preservative spices. The merchants of London resolve to break the Dutch monopoly in black peppercorns. By authority of Queen Elizabeth, they form the Honourable East India Company (the HEIC, known colloquially as 'John Company'). The new Company joins the expanding trade with the east.
1639: the first territorial acquisition. A local Rajah sells to the HEIC a plot of land on the Coromandel Coast. Fort St George is built at Madras.
1645: a small force of armed Europeans is formed to protect the Madras factories.
1661: King Charles II marries the Portuguese princess, Catherine of Braganza. Her dowry includes the Portuguese trading base at Bombay. A treaty between the two countries obliges the King to protect it. He leases the base, with its defence commitment, to the HEIC. The Company raises a small force of Portuguese and Deccanese mercenaries for this purpose. Apart from their enclave at Goa (which they will lose in 1961), the Portuguese withdraw entirely from India.
1668: having leased Bombay from the King since 1661, the HEIC now purchases the land outright.
1700: the third territorial acquisition. Three villages on the Hoogli River are purchased from the Moghuls. Fort William is founded at Calcutta.
1707: the decline of the Moghul Empire - after the death of Emperor Aurangzeb - leads to warfare between rival ethnic and religious factions. Large parts of the sub-continent slide into anarchy. The Company tries to protect its various trading concessions by forming alliances with friendly native rulers in the hinterland (those not already committed to the French). Involvement in affairs far distant from the coastal ports and factories follows an involuntary and haphazard course over many decades, but it will lead to the creation of three mighty administrative systems - the Presidencies of Madras, Bengal, and Bombay.
1744: war in Europe leads to seventeen years of conflict in India. France and her native ruler allies will come close to ejecting the HEIC entirely.
1748: the Company appoints Major John Stringer Lawrence as Commander-in-Chief, with the task of defending the three Presidencies, and upgrading their small irregular forces of watchmen and mercenary soldiers. Some of these are Indians, some are of mixed race, some are European adventurers, others are former slaves from East Africa. He commences the first recruitment of regular European units (artillery and infantry), and obtains the services of a British Army unit - Goodyer's Company, Royal Artillery. It arrives in time to fight, in August, at the Siege of Pondicherry. The British Army will maintain a continuous presence in India over the next 199 years.
1754: the first British Army infantry unit arrives - the 39th of Foot.
1757-1763: the Seven Years War (in Europe, Canada, and elsewhere) intensifies the conflict between the French and the HEIC. Robert Clive succeeds Stringer Lawrence as C-in-C. He raises more European units. More significantly, between 1757 and 1758, he raises the 1st Bengal Native Infantry and the 1st Madras Native Infantry, British-officered regiments in which the rank and file consist entirely of Indians armed, equipped, and trained to European standards, and attested for regular service. From this time forward, until 1858, the forces in India will consist of 'King's troops', 'Company European troops', and 'Company native troops'. At the Battle of Plassey (1757), Clive beats the Nawab of Bengal (an ally of the French), and the HEIC takes control of areas previously loyal to its competitor. By 1759, the last of the Dutch have left India. The Treaty of Paris, ending the Seven Years War, confirms the defeat of France's bid for supremacy in India (and in Canada, and elsewhere). In the event, France will continue to connive against the HEIC for several decades to come. Much of India

is still the domain of feuding warlords and two vigorous but restless warrior peoples - the Maharattas and the Sikhs.

1784: the India Act makes the HEIC answerable to the British Government for its policy and conduct. The Company is still concerned mainly with trade, but the continuing lawlessness in the interior causes it repeatedly to move into areas which offer no direct commercial advantage. More and more Presidential regiments are raised and trained to a superior standard.

1796: the British expel the Dutch from the island of Ceylon. They will declare it a Crown Colony in 1802.

1803: Wellesley (later Wellington) leads a force of British Army and Madras Presidency regiments against the Maharattas - who have French backing - and achieves a stunning victory at Assaye. Napoleon's dream of a French Empire stretching from the Atlantic Ocean to the Bay of Bengal is doomed. The British will now make peace with the Maharattas and with six hundred independent Principalities, many of which are the fractionalised remnants of the old Moghul Empire but some of which have always been independent. Only one region remains outside HEIC control - the north west.

1816: after several years of conflict, the British and the Gurkhas make peace. It is the beginning of an enduring friendship with the Kingdom of Nepal. The Treaty of Sagauli authorises the recruitment of Gurkhas into Crown service. Three such regiments are raised and become part of the Presidential Army of Bengal.

1818: following the protracted Kandyan Wars, the British finally subdue the native population of Ceylon and achieve total occupation.

1826: after two years of campaigning against the Kingdom of Ava, the HEIC gains a foothold in Burma. The King cedes Assam. It becomes part of India.

1839-1842: the First Afghan War. The British attempt to impose control in Afghanistan. They are driven out with heavy loss.

1842: the First China War. British merchants have a monopoly on the opium trade. Their warehouses are destroyed by the Chinese. The British respond with a Royal Navy fleet and a land force of British Army and Madras Army units.

1843: the British defeat the three Amirs of Scinde (in the lower Indus Valley) and take control of their territory.

1845-1849: the First and Second Sikh Wars result in control of the Punjab passing to the HEIC. Either by conquest or by treaty, the British have established their influence throughout the sub-continent. For the first time since the heyday of the Moghuls, all of India is at peace.

1852-1853: the Second Burma War. The British annexe the Province of Pegu (Lower Burma).

1857: the British have become over-confident. Disregard for established customs and religious taboos causes tension in the ranks of the Army of Bengal. In May, at Meerut, mutiny erupts and spreads rapidly throughout Northern and Central India. The total strength of the armed forces at this time is 24,000 King's troops (British Army), 19,000 HEIC European troops, and 226,000 HEIC native troops (including 7000 artillery gunners and drivers). Of the seventy-four regiments of Bengal Native Infantry, only fifteen remain completely loyal. There is similar disaffection in the cavalry and the artillery. Great Britain's position in India hangs in the balance. In September, a small ad hoc force of British, Indian, and Gurkha troops storms the walls of Delhi and drives out the mutineers. The tide is turned. Within two years, The Great Sepoy Mutiny will expire.

1858: the HEIC loses its mandate. Henceforth, the Crown will administer India.

1861: a long period of reorganisation commences. The three Presidencies will continue to administer their own military forces for internal security duties, but will make them available for overseas campaigns if required. Their allegiance is now to the Crown. With the exception of some Mountain and Bombay Native batteries, all other native-manned artillery units are disbanded. The former HEIC European regiments are transferred to the British Army.

1878: the Second Afghan War exposes defects in the new system. Proposals for the creation of a unified Indian Army are defeated, but the sharing of certain ordnance, administrative, and transport resources is agreed.

1885–1886: having imposed a treaty after the Second Burma War (1852-1853), the British now fight the Third Burma War, against King Thebaw. They annexe Upper Burma. They will mount a fourth and final campaign - this time against banditry - in 1887-1889. Burma is a Province of India from 1886 to 1937 when it will become a Crown Colony.
1886: the independent Punjab Frontier Force, formerly answerable only to the Punjab administration in Lahore, is transferred to the command of the C-in-C India, in Delhi. It is a major step towards unification of India's military forces.
1888: Napier reorganises the army so that its regiments are grouped in threes, with shared and standardised arrangements for training and reserves.
1895–1896: the abolition of the Presidential Armies is agreed. A new Army of India comprises four commands - Punjab (including the North West Frontier), Bengal, Madras (including Burma), and Bombay (including Scinde, Quetta, and Aden). The Regular forces are backed by Police Battalions (with military training), by the Volunteer Forces (30,000 part-time Europeans and Eurasians, with a primary responsibility for guarding India's 28,000 miles of railway track), and the Princely States Forces (110,000 all ranks, of whom 18,000 are trained for Imperial service, if needed).
1900: by the turn of the century, Indian troops have taken part in numerous campaigns on the frontier of their own country, and have served overseas in China, Burma, Persia, Abyssinia, Cyprus, Mauritius, the Sudan, the Arabian Gulf, and numerous other places where Great Britain's interests were at stake. Now they embark for their third visit to China. They join the international expedition to suppress the Boxer Rebellion.
1903: Kitchener (C-in-C India, 1902-1903) inaugurates a radical reform of the Army of India. Thirty-four military stations are closed, the remainder expanded and modernised. All references to the old Presidencies in unit titles are removed. The regiments are renumbered on a consecutive all-India basis. For example, the regiments of Bengal Cavalry retain their numbers up to 19, the Punjab Cavalry take the numbers 21 to 25, the Madras 25 to 28, and the Bombay 31 to 37. There are similar redesignations for the infantry, and in the same sequence - Bengal Army, Punjab Frontier Force, Madras Army, Hyderabad Contingent, and Bombay Army. The ten Gurkha regiments are not renumbered. It is ruled that future recruitment shall come mainly from the northern populations. The role of the army is redefined. It will train for the defence of the North West Frontier. The Indian Staff Corps (established since 1861) is disbanded and a new Staff College opens in Quetta. Combat regiments are grouped in three Corps, each of three Divisions with supporting services. Indian regiments are brigaded with resident British Army regiments in the ratio of two to one. Burma is made an independent command.
1904: disputes with the Dalai Lama result in a military expedition into Tibet. Its advance is contested. Led by Colonel G J Younghusband, a force of British and Indian Army troops reaches Lhasa after breaking through at Gyantse. The battle is fought, uniquely, at an altitude of 14,000 feet.
1914: as soon as war breaks out in Europe, Delhi is asked to contribute troops. An Indian Corps arrives at Marseilles in September. It consists of two Divisions of infantry (3rd Lahore and 7th Meerut), with a Brigade of cavalry (4th Secunderabad). Totally unprepared for European warfare, they are plunged straight into the first Battle of Ypres. Other Indian formations will deploy in East Africa, in Egypt, and in Mesopotamia. Reinforcements are sent to bolster the strength of the Aden Troop.
1915: the Indian Corps fights alongside the British Expeditionary Force at Neuve Chapelle and Loos until the end of the year. The infantry elements then transfer to Egypt and fight the Turks in the Sinai. The cavalry remains in France where it will fight on the Somme (1916) and at Cambrai (1917). Indian and Gurkha troops fight alongside British, ANZAC, Cypriot, and French soldiers in the Gallipoli campaign. In Mesopotamia, having pushed hard for Baghdad, Townshend is defeated at Ctesiphon and forced back down the Tigris to Kut-al-Amara. He is surrounded and besieged.
1916: in April, Townshend's force is starved into surrender. Elsewhere, Indian forces are fighting the Turks in Sinai and the Germans in East Africa.

1917: at the third attempt, and with the participation of units of the Indian States Forces, the Turks are finally ejected from Gaza. Allenby breaks through to Palestine and the Jordan Valley. He enters Jerusalem in triumph. In Mesopotamia, a new British-Indian army led by Maude captures Baghdad.
1918: the Turks collapse. Allenby races north into the Lebanon and Syria. Indians constitute the greater part of his army. Other Indian forces advance from Baghdad and occupy the oilfields at Mosul and Kirkuk. In East Africa, von Lettow Vorbeck is granted an honourable surrender.
1919: Great Britain joins the multi-national effort to suppress the Bolshevik revolution in Russia. Indian Army units are involved, and they fight in Trans-Caspia. Elsewhere, the defeat of Muslim Turkey by the infidel Christian provokes unrest throughout the Middle East and Asia Minor. Indian forces are engaged in putting down a national independence campaign by the Kurds. At home, Indian politicians are arguing for a greater role in the government of their own country. Gandhi's tactic of 'passive non-cooperation' with the civil authorities leads many Britons to fear the worst. Ignoring India's sacrifices and loyalty during the four years of world war, they conclude that they are faced with 'a second Mutiny'. In April, at Amritsar, Brigadier General Reginald Dyer orders the shooting - by Indian and Gurkha soldiers - of several hundred unarmed civilians. Despite the resultant anguish, the Indian Army stands fast.
1922: nearly one and a half million Indians volunteered for war service. Most have been demobilised. The army is now completely reorganised. The cavalry establishment is reduced to twenty-one regiments. The infantry is reduced to twenty regiments, each having four or five active battalions, a training battalion, and a Territorial battalion. The Corps of Pioneers is reconstituted with ten active battalions and three training battalions. The Gurkhas retain their pre-war establishment of ten two-battalion regiments.
1923: for some years, Commissions have been granted to eligible Indians by the Viceroy. In this year, it is decided to begin sending Indians to the Royal Military College, Sandhurst, where they will qualify for King's Commissions. 'Indianisation' of the command ranks will continue steadily during the coming years. Starting in 1923, increasing financial constraints will lead to more cuts in the establishment. Twenty-one active and two training battalions - comprising the Corps of Pioneers and the entire Madras Regiment - are disbanded. Seven other infantry battalions - from different regiments - are disbanded also. Some British Army units stationed in India make up their own depleted strengths by recruiting Indians into their ranks (as machine-gunners in the infantry, and as muleteers and drivers in the Royal Artillery).
1933: the Indian Military Academy is founded at Dehra Dun for the education and military training of Indian officer candidates. No longer will they be sent to Sandhurst.
1935: the Regiment of Indian Artillery (later re-titled the Royal Indian Artillery) is formed. The Indian Mountain Batteries will transfer from the Royal Artillery to the RIA in 1939.
1937: Burma, which has been a part of British India since 1886, becomes a Crown Colony, with its own administration and armed forces.
1939: even though the reforms of 1922 had been intended to prepare the Indian Army for duties other than internal security and defence of the North West Frontier, it again (as in 1914) finds itself unprepared for war against a first class enemy and involving modern weapons and equipment. A programme of expansion and technical improvement is set in train.
1940: still deficient in training and equipment, Indians are committed to battle against the Italians in the Western Desert, then in Abyssinia and Eritrea. Other units move to Burma to cover the border with Siam, and to Singapore to bolster the shaky defences of the Malay Peninsula.
1941: East Africa is cleared of Italian forces and the Indians return to the Western Desert. At year's end, in the east, the Japanese strike.
1942: together with British and Australian formations, the Indians are crushingly defeated in Malaya. They are driven out of Burma.

1943: 4th and 5th Indian Divisions have won a fine reputation in North Africa. The 4th is joined in Italy by the 8th and 10th. The 5th moves to Burma and joins the desperate fight to halt the Japanese tide. More Divisions are formed for the same purpose. They are joined in Burma by units of the Princely State Forces and of the Royal Nepalese Army. To counter the German threat to the Middle East oilfields, the 'Persia and Iraq Force' (Paiforce) is formed with mainly Indian Army units. Local pro-Nazi factions are suppressed, and the vital communications network (transporting American aid from the Arabian Gulf ports north to the hard pressed Soviet Union) is protected.
1944: after bitter fighting at Cassino, the battle line in Italy has moved north to the edge of the Po Valley. In total contrast to its capabilities in 1939, the Indian Army has become adept at mechanised warfare in a European setting. To the east, in Burma, the Japanese are being driven back by Indians and Gurkhas who are familiar with the techniques of aerial re-supply and ground-air cooperation. The cavalry have long since replaced their horses with Sherman tanks and Bren gun carriers. Indian forces are fighting the Communists in Greece.
1945: all fighting in Italy ceases in May. The starving Japanese are being driven from Burma into Siam where Indian forces will pursue them. Singapore is liberated with the ending of hostilities in that theatre in August.
1946: two and a half million Indian soldiers begin to return home. They find their country in turmoil. The war has weakened British resolve to continue governing a quarter of the world's population. It has also strengthened the nationalists' determination to govern themselves. All of this coincides with a radical change of government in the United Kingdom. Mountbatten is appointed Viceroy with the task of supervising a complete handover of power. Even while these events are unfolding, substantial elements of the Indian Army are still in action - fighting the nationalists in Sumatra and Java (Batavia) and trying to help the Dutch to re-establish their pre-war administration. Other Indian units are occupying Siam and Indo-China. The British Commonwealth Occupation Force in Japan (the BCOFJ) includes an Indian Army Brigade Group.
1947: chaos not seen since the collapse of the Moghuls sweeps across Northern India as old enmities and religious hatreds boil to the surface. The British depart in haste, having reluctantly agreed the Partition of a new (predominantly Hindu) India from (Muslim) West and East Pakistan. The former Indian Army is dismembered, some regiments (or their component parts) passing into service with the new Indian Army, others with the Pakistan Army. Several Gurkha regiments are transferred to the British Army and moved to England. The break-up marks the end of the largest all-volunteer military force the world has ever seen, unique in that it comprised men of three main racial streams (Aryan, Dravidian, and Mongolian), and four major religions (Hindu, Muslim, Buddhist, and Christian).
1948: Burma is declared an independent republic and leaves the Commonwealth.
1962: having conquered Tibet by force ten years earlier, the Chinese occupy the Aksai Chin area of Ladakh. To forestall any attempt to eject them, they cross the north east frontier and inflict a severe defeat on the Indian Army. They withdraw following an agreed ceasefire.
1965: continuing disputes, particularly over possession of Kashmir, lead to a major war between India and Pakistan.
1971: there is another full-scale conflict between the two countries. East Pakistan is overrun by Indian forces and subsequently emerges as independent Bangladesh. The hill tribes on the Indo-Burma border continue to rebel against Indian domination. The Army and the Assam Rifles (the armed constabulary) conduct a series of operations which conclude with the suppression of the insurgents in 1979.
1979: fulfilling the prophecies of three hundred years, the Russian Bear arrives in Afghanistan. Powerful Soviet forces enter Kabul and engage the hill tribes along the border with Pakistan. Massive American aid flows into Pakistan - partly to assist the Pakistan Army and partly to arm the Afghan tribesmen. The Soviets will withdraw following major changes in the ruling hierarchy in Moscow.
1983-1984: in the Eastern Punjab, there has been since 1947 a protracted and often violent campaign by fundamentalist Sikhs to break away from India and to

form their own independent country, Sikhistan (or Khalistan). A wave of murders leads to the introduction in some areas of President's Rule. In June 1984, the Indian Army launches a mechanised attack (Operation Blue Star) against the Sikh's holiest shrine - the Golden Temple, at Amritsar. The militants are defeated with the loss of 493 dead. The Indian Army's losses are 322 killed and wounded.
1989: Sri Lanka (Ceylon) has been independent since 1948, but has suffered from continuous and worsening religious and political factionalism. Parts of the island are now in a state of civil war. The Sri Lankan Government appeals to Delhi for a peace-keeping force to be established in the northern district (where there is a large population of Hindu Tamils). An Indian Army contingent arrives and begins to police the disturbed areas. It then launches an offensive against the 'Tamil Tigers'.
1993: despite continuing unrest in the Punjab and unresolved quarrels regarding the ownership of Kashmir, the armies of India and Pakistan are fulfilling important roles on the international stage by providing general officers and contingents of troops for several United Nations deployments.

GENERAL REFERENCE

A great many books have been written regarding the military history of the Indian sub-continent. Most are helpful in one way or another, a few are essential to a full understanding of the unit history books listed on the following pages. The representative publications listed below have been selected for their broad historical perspective.

A MATTER OF HONOUR
An Account of the Indian Army, its Officers and Men
Philip Mason * Purnell Book Services Ltd, London, by arrangement with Jonathan Cape, 1974. Blue, gold, 9.5 x 6.0, -/580. 27 mono phots, 10 maps, Bibliography, Index. Apps: a brief summary of the dates of the major reorganisations.
* A magnificent book which, as the sub-title suggests, concentrates upon the 'changing relations of officers and men, and to answer certain questions about their behaviour'. The author covers the entire period of British India and explains how it was that India's fighting forces gained such a fine reputation.
R/1 V/1. PC. RP.

BRITAIN'S ARMY IN INDIA
From its Origins to the Conquest of Bengal
James P Lawford * George Allen & Unwin, London, 1978. Red, gold, 9.0 x 5.5, -/342. No ills, 17 maps, Bibliography, Index. Apps: various Orders of Battle.
* Covers the period 1600-1764. A very readable and reliable account of the first 150 years of the British in India, particularly the military aspects and the use of Indian troops in tandem with British troops. The important early battles are exceptionally well described. R/1 V/4. NAM. PJE.

THE INDIAN ARMY AND THE KING'S ENEMIES
Maj Charles Chenevix-Trench * Thames & Hudson, London, 1988. Red, gold, 9.5 x 6.0, -/312. Fp, 70 mono phots, 20 maps, Bibliography, Index. Apps: chronology of events.
* A useful history of the Indian Army in the 20th Century. Based mainly upon personal accounts of individual services in WWI, on the NWF between the wars, and in WWII. R/1 V/3. NAM. PJE.

A ROLL OF HONOUR
The Story of the Indian Army, 1939-1945
Maj Gen J G Elliott * Cassell & Co Ltd, London, 1965. Beige, red, 8.5 x 5.5, -/392. 32 mono phots, 9 maps, Bibliography, Index. Apps: notes on military terms, Order of Battle, notes on air supply.
* A comprehensive account of the operations and campaigns in which Indian troops took part during WWII. A helpful framework for further research. R/1 V/4. PC. RP.
Note: published in the USA by A S Barnes & Co Inc, Cranbury, NJ, 1965, with a different main title - UNFADING HONOUR - and a light blue/silver casing.

ETHNOLOGICAL SOURCES

THE MARTIAL RACES OF INDIA
Lieut Gen Sir George MacMunn KCB KCSI DSO * Samson Low, Marston & Co Ltd, London, n.d. Black, gold, 9.0 x 5.5, xii/368. Fp, 15 mono phots, 7 cld ills (by Maj A C Lovat), 2 maps (folding, bound in), no appendixes, Index.
* MacMunn wrote more than two dozen books about India and he is acknowledged as having been unusually skilful in capturing on paper the special ethos of soldiering in that country. R/2 V/4. PCAL. RP.
Note: also recommended (by the same author) is THE ARMIES OF INDIA (Adam & Charles Black, London, 1911). It contains 72 attractive full plate coloured illustrations, also by Maj A C Lovat.

THE INDIAN ARMY
Its Contribution to the Development of a Nation
Prof Stephen P Cohen * Oxford University Press (India), New Delhi, 1990. Dark blue, gold, 8.75 x 5.5, xiii/254. No ills, no maps, Bibliography, Index. Apps: notes on the Indian States Forces.
* The author makes an analytical examination of the Indian Army from various aspects - recruitment and ideology, Indian popular attitudes towards the Army, the relationship with the Nationalist movement, British officers' attitudes, the conduct of wartime operations and, finally, the Army's legacy following Independence. An unusual approach to military history. R/2 V/4. PC. PJE.

REGIMENTAL ORIGINS AND LINEAGES

INDIA'S ARMY
Maj Donovan Jackson * Sampson Low, Marston & Co Ltd, London, n.d. (c.1940). Beige, pale blue, 5.5 x 4.5, xxi/584. Fp, 119 mono phots, 13 cld ills, numerous good line drawings of Regtl crests, no maps, no appendixes, no Index.
* This fat little book is an admirable 'ready reckoner' for facts, dates and Regtl lineages. It contains a 'potted history' of each Cavalry and Infantry Regt, and deals briefly with the Corps and the Princely State Forces. The Artillery are not mentioned. The tabular information - showing in outline each Regt's changes of title at various dates - is presented in readily understood form. Although dated 1940, the narrative applies only to events pre-1939. R/3 V/5. MODL. AMM.
Note: reprinted by D K Publishing, Delhi, 1986, but without the coloured plates.

SONS OF JOHN COMPANY
The Indian and Pakistan Armies, 1903-1991
John Gaylor * Spellmount Ltd, Tunbridge Wells, Kent, 1992. Red, gold, 9.5 x 6.0, ii/379. 31 mono phots, many line drawings (mainly Regtl badges and insignia), Glossary, Bibliography, seven Indexes (of Regts, for the periods 1903-1923, 1923-1947, 1947-1991, of Gurkha units, of Indian Volunteer, IDF and AF(I) units, of Frontier Corps, Scouts and para-military units, and of Indian State Forces). Apps: 5 in total (uniforms and badges, rank structures, Regtl changes of title and unit designations for 1903-1922 and 1922-1991, and notes on The Anglo-Indian Force of 1916-1920.
* A short introduction sets the scene by describing the early history of the Indian Army of the HEIC and Imperial periods. This is followed by several narrative chapters covering the evolution of India's military forces in the 20th Century. The bulk of the book then describes in concise detail the class composition, the badges, the wartime services and the Battle Honours of each Regt (both before and after Partition, India and Pakistan). Equal space is devoted to every pre-1947 unit, regardless of whether it was retained by the Indian Army, allocated to the Pakistan Army, or allocated to the British Brigade of Gurkhas. The book has some defects - the bibliographic footnotes contain minor errors, the Indexes might have been better arranged, the Artillery is barely mentioned, the publisher chose a disappointing quality of paper - but these quibbles should not detract from the overall worth of what is undoubtedly a tour de force. The book is a natural successor to the work by Donovan Jackson and is in many ways far more comprehensive (vide preceding entry). R/1 V/5. NAM. RP.

WARS AND CAMPAIGNS

FRONTIER AND OVERSEAS EXPEDITIONS FROM INDIA
Anon * Intelligence Branch, AHQ India, Delhi, n.d. (c.1913). A series of 7 volumes, each having approximately 500-800 pages, plus supplements to Volumes I and II.
* A splendid work of reference, highly readable, covering every border campaign and overseas expedition of the 19th and early 20th Century. The first five volumes deal with the NWF, Afghanistan and Burma. Volume VI recounts the 'foreign' expeditions to Africa, Ceylon, the islands of the Indian Ocean, Arabia,

Persia, the Malay Peninsula and China. Volume VII is devoted entirely to the Abor campaign of 1911-1912. Set in different type, and accompanying each combat account, is a list of all the units engaged (including 'friendlies' and carriers). An exceptional source of reference. R/5 V/5. CFHT. SODW.
Note: the complete set of volumes has been reprinted in facsimile by Mittal Publications, Delhi (no date shown). An additional and complementary source is BATTLE HONOURS OF THE BRITISH ARMY AND COMMONWEALTH, by Anthony Baker (Ian Allan, London, 1986). A survey of all such honours, with explanatory notes for each engagement or campaign, this large-scale work (-/398 pages) is full of easily accessible and useful information.

A POSTSCRIPT TO THE RECORDS OF THE INDIAN ARMY
An Attempt to Trace the Subsequent Careers and Fate of the Rebel Bengal Regiments, 1857-1858
Lieut Col H D Gimlette CIE * H H & G Witherby, London, 1927. Dark blue, gold, 8.75 x 5.5, -/222. No ills, no maps, Index. Apps: a list of units which did not mutiny.
* Whilst there is a smattering of inaccuracies in it, Gimlette's work provides a well-organised and thorough description of the disintregration of the Bengal Army during the Mutiny (and, despite the sub-title, he does cover events in early 1859). He arranges all relevant units under four categories - artillery and engineers, cavalry, infantry, irregulars and contingents. For each Regt he gives the date of formation, battles and campaigns in which it had formerly taken part, its location in 1857, and the names of British officers serving at that time (including those on attached duties). He then states whether the unit mutinied or was disbanded, and states when and where this happened. In the case of those which actively fought against the British, he relates the events leading to their eventual destruction. Where some remnants of mutinous units remained loyal, he describes their subsequent services. A most useful book which covers an important aspect of the Great Sepoy Mutiny not fully covered elsewhere. R/4 V/4. PC. CJP.

THE GREAT GAME
On Secret Service in High Asia
Peter Hopkirk * John Murray, London, 1990. Black, silver, 9.5 x 6.5, xiv/562. 39 mono phots, 5 maps (printed in the text), Bibliography, no appendixes, no Index.
* The Great Game was the Anglo-Russian rivalry for domination of Central Asia. The book begins with the plans of Tsar Paul to invade India in alliance with Napoleon and concludes with the Convention of 1907. In between lies a fascinating tale of warfare, guerilla campaigns, spying and exploration. The author describes Russia's wars of conquest against Persia, Turkey, and the khanates of Bokhara, Samarkand, et al. Many of Britain's wars were a direct result of this perceived threat to India - the First and Second Afghan Wars, the Persian War of 1856, and the Hunza, Chitral and Tibet expeditions. These events are covered here in clear detail, as are the epic journeys of explorers and spies such as Stoddart, Connolly, Hayward and Gromchevksy. The maps and illustrations are excellent. Any study of the British military presence in India must be viewed against the background described in this book. R/1 V/4. PC. CGB.

ROLE OF THE INDIAN ARMY IN THE FIRST WORLD WAR
Lieut Col Dr Shyam Narain Saxena * Bhavana Prakashan, Delhi, 1987. Green, white, 8.75 x 5.5, xiv/244. Fp, no other ills, 4 maps (of poor quality, bound in), Bibliography, Index. Apps: 81 pages in total, covering all manner of information on H&A, Orders of Battle, casualty statistics, the services of individual Regts, etc.
* A book based upon a doctoral thesis. The narrative content is not well presented and it is flawed by the author's use of the post-1922 titles when referring to each unit's WWI services. This requires the reader to be familiar with unit lineages in order to understand the meaning of the text. However, the facts are arranged in the form of a chronology of Indian Army and Imperial Service Troops' participation in the European, Middle Eastern and East African theatres of war, and this

makes the book an ideal source of quick reference. Furthermore, the extensive appendixes include brief summaries of each unit's services throughout the conflict (this information being drawn from their War Diaries and therefore reliable). The Bibliography and appendixes alone make this book a very handy source of detailed information. R/1 V/4. PC. RBM.

THE INDIAN CORPS IN FRANCE
Lieut Col J W B Mereweather CIE and Sir Frederick Smith * John Murray, London, 1919. Maroon, gold, 9.0 x 5.5, xviii/558. Fp, 19 mono phots, 8 maps (3 printed in the text, 5 bound in), no appendixes, Index.
* A much under-valued account of the Indian Army's role, between October 1914 and October 1915, in assisting the British and French Armies to halt the German drive towards Paris and the Channel ports. The fluently written narrative is packed with vivid accounts of trench fighting, with hundreds of officers and men being mentioned by name. It provides detailed coverage of First and Second Ypres, Neuve Chappelle, Festubert, Givenchy, and Loos. The lack of formal appendixes is balanced by numerous details of awards and casualties inserted in the text. Fortunately, the book has a good index. The authors complain bitterly in their Foreword that the War Office imposed illogical and unnecessary censorship on the first edition, a cri de coeur which strikes a familiar chord with later generations of military historian. This second (1919) edition is more complete and therefore more desirable. R/2 V/5. PC. RP.
Note: also recommended is WITH THE INDIANS IN FRANCE, by Sir James Willcocks GCMG KCB KCSI DSO (Constable & Co Ltd, London, 1920).

OFFICIAL HISTORY OF THE INDIAN ARMED FORCES IN THE SECOND WORLD WAR, 1939-1945
Dr Bisheshwar Prasad * Published by the Combined Inter-Services Historical Section (India and Pakistan), distributed by Orient Longmans, New Delhi, a series of 24 volumes published between 1954 and 1964, each volume having (on average) circa 460 pages.
* This monumental work covers all aspects of India's contribution to the Allied cause between 1939 and 1945. The narrative is packed with a huge amount of information regarding even the smallest fighting, logistical and medical units and sub-units, and yet it remains eminently readable throughout. It is a tribute to the skills of the editor, Dr Bisheshwar Prasad, that he was able to harness the energies of his Indian and Pakistan contributors even while their two countries were at war with each other. It should be noted that the dates given in the main title of the series are slightly misleading. In addition to covering events up to the Japanese surrender in August of 1945, he provides excellent accounts of the post-war occupation of Japan and Indo-China, and of the major effort in 1946 to secure the former Dutch East Indies. R/3 V/5. CFHT. SODW.

THE PRESIDENTIAL ARMIES

THE PRESIDENTIAL ARMIES OF INDIA

Lieut Col S Rivett-Carnac * W H Allen & Co, London, 1890. Red, gold, 'Imperial Crown and Vivat' motif, 9.0 x 5.5, xxiii/442. No ills, no maps, no Index. Apps: notes on Lord Napier of Magdala, idem operations in Upper Burma (1885-1886), idem the Native Armies of India.

* The early chapters cover Anglo-Indian history in general terms from the earliest days through to 1748, and then India's military history from 1748 to 1886. There are chapters on the HEIC's various Regiments of Artillery, Cavalry and Infantry, but the style is neither very readable nor very informative. R/3 V/1. MODL. AMM.

A ROUGH SKETCH OF THE RISE AND PROGRESS OF THE IRREGULAR HORSE OF THE BENGAL ARMY

With Hints for Improving the Regular and Irregular Cavalry of that Presidency, by an Old Cavalry Officer

Anon (Maj Gen Charles M Carmichael) * E Briere, Paris, n.d. (c.1854). Seen without covers, details of original binding not known, 8.25 x 5.5, viii/74. Fp, no other ills, no maps, no appendixes, no Index.

* A slim volume, useful mainly as a contemporary account of the formation and equipping of several Bengal Army Regiments of Irregular Horse (and including Skinner's). An extremely rare work. R/5 V/3. PC. BDM.

THE BENGAL NATIVE INFANTRY

An Historical Account ....

Capt John Williams * John Murray, London, 1817. Brown, gold, 8.75 x 5.25, -/387. Fp, plus 3 other cld ills (all full plates of uniforms), no maps, Corrigenda and Addenda, no Index. Apps: 15 in total, incl a list of serving officers (Bengal Army, 1760, sixty names in all), verbatim quotations from various General Orders.

* A useful secondary source for the early conquest of Northern India and the raising and organisation of the BNI. Although the book contains 387 pages, it does not contain as much information as this number might imply. The text is set in large characters with double line spacing, hence there are only 150 words (on average) on each page. The complete sub-title is - 'An historical account from its formation in 1757 to 1796 when the present Regulations took place, with supplementary notes to the year 1814, together with a Detail of the services on which several Battalions have been employed during that period'. The style is basic and factual, but the lack of an Index or any appendixes render the book unhandy as a source of reference. R/1 (as reported above) V/3. RCSL. RP.

Note: the version reported above is a modern facsimile reprint produced by Frederick Muller & Co, London, in 1970, with a limited print run of 550 copies. The original version, as produced in 1817, had a leather spine, marbled boards and gold blocking. Copies of that edition are very rarely seen.

HISTORY OF THE RISE AND PROGRESS OF THE BENGAL ARMY

Volume I

Capt Arthur Broome * W Thacker & Co Ltd, Calcutta, 1850. Red, gold, 'Flags, drum, gun and soldier' motif, 9.0 x 5.5, vi/629/lxxvi (the last being the appendixes). No ills, 6 plans and maps (in rear pocket), no Index (but good detailed chapter headings).

* This was seemingly the only volume published. It covers the period 1589-1767. The narrative is patchy, some sections being stimulating and very readable, other sections being tedious and over-written. A worthy attempt at a large and complex subject. R/3 V/3. PCAL. AMM.

A SKETCH OF THE SERVICES OF THE BENGAL NATIVE ARMY
To the Year 1895
Lieut F G Cardew * Superintendent of Government Printing, Calcutta, 1903. Dark green, gold, 8.5 x 5.5, v/576/ii. Two cld plates, no other ills, no maps, Bibliography, Index. Apps: list of Corps (arranged alphabetically), idem the Corps at 1895, list of services, idem battles, idem officers and their awards.
* Although it deals with the Bengal Native Army in its entirety, the book is particularly good as a source for the Bengal Artillery. Compiled originally by Cardew, it was edited and revised before publication by G W de Rhe-Philipe.
R/4 V/4. PCAL/RAI. AMM.
Note: available also in modern facsimile reprint.

THE BENGAL NATIVE INFANTRY, 1796-1852
Its Organisation and Discipline
Amiya Barat * F K L Mukhoppadhyay, Calcutta, 1962. Light red, black, 9.0 x 5.5, xii/341. 4 mono phots, 2 maps (printed on the end-papers), Bibliography, Index. Apps: list of former Commanders-in-Chief(Bengal), officer strengths of the BNI at various dates.
* A good secondary source. The early history of the BNI and the story of the mutinies are described from a fresh perspective. R/2 V/3. PCAL/NAM. PJE.

HISTORY OF THE MADRAS ARMY FROM 1746 TO 1826
With an Account of the European Artillery, Engineers and Infantry up to their Amalgamation with the Royal Army in 1861, and of the Native Cavalry and Infantry up to 1887
Lieut Col W J Wilson * Government Press, Madras, between 1882 and 1889. Five matching volumes, red, gold, 8.75 x 5.5, full Morocco.
Vol I : **1746-1780.** vi/396
Vol II : **1780-1799.** iv/383
Vol III : **1799-1816.** vii/408
Vol IV : **1817-1826.** ix/552, incl the Index for this and the earlier 4 volumes
Vol V : an album of 14 maps, all relating to Vols I - IV.
* An authoritative and (obviously) comprehensive account of the Madras Army for the period stated in the title. Volume IV is particularly readable and interesting in its coverage of the key period 1817-1826, and a final chapter summarises the events of the period 1827-1887. All four narrative volumes have appendixes - tables of unit strengths, casualties, and so forth. A highly desirable set of books. R/4 V/4. MODL. AMM.

HISTORY OF THE BOMBAY ARMY
Sir Patrick Cadell CSI CIE VD * Longmans, Green & Co, London, 1938. Red, gold, 8.75 x 5.5, xv/362. Fp, one other cld plate, 11 maps, Bibliography, Indexes. Apps: notes on the campaigns of the Bombay Army (with details of the units which took part), chronological list of Bombay Army unit designations (all arms), list of Bombay units raised during WWI, notes on amalgamations, idem the class composition of Bombay Regiments in 1895 and 1935.
* The narrative covers the period 1662-1937 in a generalised but always uniform and interesting style. Few individuals are named, but a great many Regiments receive a specific mention. An excellent over-view, with good appendixes, a helpful Bibliography, and a good Index. R/3 V/4. PACL/MODL. AMM.

THE ARMIES OF THE PRINCELY STATES

After the initial British conquests of the early and mid-19th Century, there were still six hundred independent Principalities in various parts of the sub-continent. Some were fractionalised remnants of the old Moghul Empire, others had long been free of any external control. Between them, they covered almost half of India's land mass and comprised a quarter of its teeming population. They varied widely in their geographical size and material wealth. The hereditary rulers of many of these States were permitted, by Treaty, to maintain their own private armies if they so wished.

Some of the Princes undertook to make available for Crown service a proportion of their armed forces whenever so requested. From modest beginnings in 1888, such forces were equipped and trained to Indian Army standards, and officers of the Indian Army were attached to them as advisors. Units trained in this way were known initially as Imperial Service Troops (IST), the title being changed in 1920 to Indian States Forces (ISF). Their first commitment was the Black Mountain Expedition of 1891 (in which the Jodhpur Sardar Rissala took part), their last were the 1945-1946 operations in Palestine (Jodhpur I.S. Lancers) and the contemporary operations in the Dutch East Indies (1st and 2nd Patiala I.S. Infantry). The ISF scheme was scrapped in 1947 when the Princes lost their sovereignty and their States were absorbed into the new nations of India and Pakistan. Over six decades, IST/ISF soldiers had fought alongside men of the British and Indian Armies in almost every theatre of war from Flanders in the west to China in the east. In addition, tens of thousands of their compatriots had been permitted by their Princes to enlist in the Indian Army (in WWII, there were 410,000 such volunteers).

The following pages show details of the books which have been published on this subject, but the researcher who requires more information should consult pages 50 to 58 of SONS OF JOHN COMPANY, by John Gaylor (vide Index of Authors). They explain the background in greater detail, with two important tables listing the ISF units which saw active service in WWII and those which were absorbed into the Indian Army following Partition. Primary sources of reference are:

IMPERIAL SERVICE TROOPS ARMY LIST (six-monthly Lists for the period July 1915 to July 1921), and **INDIAN STATES FORCES ARMY LIST** (six-monthly Lists for the period January 1922 to January 1946), all of which contain the war services of officers (British and Indian) with details of their awards.

ANNUAL REPORT ON INDIAN STATES FORCES
These are 'Strictly Confidential' annual reports compiled by the Military Adviser in Chief, with assessments of each of the State Forces, for the period 1922 to 1940.

ANNUAL REVIEW OF THE WORKING OF THE INDIAN STATES FORCES
These are 'Most Secret' annual reports, also issued by the Military Adviser in Chief, but containing even more sensitive assessments of the ability of each State Force unit to be employed on a war footing, for the period 1932 to 1946.

INDIAN STATES FORCES ANNUALS
Produced by the same source but having no security classification, the Annuals were aimed at a broad readership and were intended to be a chronicle of sporting activities, manoeuvres, parades, appointments, and so forth. They contain a good range of illustrations and provide details of honours and awards.

Complete runs of the ARMY LISTS, ANNUAL REPORTS and ANNUAL REVIEWS can be seen at the Imperial War Museum, London, and in the Oriental & India Office Collections, London. A complete run of the ANNUALS (the last mentioned, above) are held at the National Army Museum, London.

THE PRINCELY STATES
General Accounts

THE ARMIES OF THE NATIVE STATES
Anon * Printed by Whiting & Co Ltd, for Chapman & Hall Ltd, London, 1884. Blue, gold on black, 7.0 x 4.5, viii/172. No ills, one map (bound in), no appendixes, no Index.
* The material was first published as four long editorials in THE TIMES of London. Edited and reset for use in this book, the narrative is arranged under four main headings - 'The Mahratta States', 'The Mohamedan States', 'The Hindoo States', and 'The Frontier States'. The latter comprises both the North West States and the North East States. The armed forces of each of these States, as they stood in the 1880s, are described in brief but useful detail. Biographical notes are given for each Ruler, with comments upon his attitudes towards the British and towards the military. The final 'Conclusions' chapter argues that the Princely States were too powerful and that steps should be taken to reduce the size of their armies.
R/5 V/3. RCSL. PJE.

A HISTORY OF THE IMPERIAL SERVICE TROOPS OF THE NATIVE STATES
With a Short Sketch of Events in each State, which have led to their Employment in Subordinate Co-operation with the Supreme Government
Brig Gen Stuart Beatson CB * Office of the Superintendent of Government Printing, Calcutta, 1903. Blue, gold, 9.0 x 6.0, xvi/180. No ills, one map (loose in rear pocket), Bibliography, no Index. Apps: note on 'the Ruling Chiefs', statistics on numerical strengths of Imperial Service Troops (at 1903), designation of British officers, list of such officers, notes on awards.
* Despite its pompous sub-title, this books provides a good description of the structure and organisation of the IST system as it existed in 1903. The author compiled a short chapter in respect of each of the twenty-three State forces at that time participating in the scheme, and these historical summaries are most useful. R/5 V/4. IOL. BDM/AMcC.

THE NATIVE STATES OF INDIA
Sir William Lee-Warner KCSI * MacMillan & Co Ltd, London, 1910. Dark red, gold, 9.0 x 6.0, xxi/425. No ills, one map (bound in), no appendixes, no Index.
* Originally published in 1894 as THE PROTECTED PRINCES OF INDIA, this book addresses all aspects of those States which retained their independence after the British had completed their conquest of the sub-continent. The period covered is 1805 to c.1910. Chapter VIII, 'Obligations for the Common Defence', is a useful source for the military researcher. It describes the circumstances leading to the original formation of 'contingents' of 'native States troops' to assist the British in their campaigns from 1805 onwards. With the exception of the Nizam of Hyderabad's Contingent, they were gradually phased out. Later, in the 1880s, other States offered (or re-offered) to raise contingents under a new scheme to assist the Indian Army in time of peril. It was soon recognised that these disparate forces would need to be trained and equipped to a common standard if they were to fight alongside the forces of the Crown. It was against this background that the IST scheme was introduced. Only the Hyderabad Contingent retained its original title after the scheme's introduction. The author does not refer to individual State forces in detail, but his description of the political and military framework is clear and concise. R/4 V/2. MODL. RBM.
Note: reprinted by AMS Press, New York, 1971.

A SHORT HISTORY OF THE SERVICES RENDERED BY THE IMPERIAL SERVICE TROOPS DURING THE GREAT WAR, 1914-18

Maj Gen Sir Harry Watson KBE CB CMG CIE MVO * Government of India Central Publications Branch, Calcutta, 1930. Seen rebound, details of original binding not known, 8.5 x 5.5, vii/68. No ills, no maps, no Index. Apps: H&A (stated to contain some inaccuracies).

* A useful narrative account, with plenty of detail. Although the book should have been augmented with more appendixes, the author did manage to include a good range of reference material in the text - Stations, movements, active services, the names of British officers serving with the IST, casualty statistics, and so forth. R/5 V/3. IOL. AMcC.

THE INDIAN STATES FORCES
Their Lineage and Insignia

His Highness the Maharajah of Jaipur * Printed in India for Orient Longmans Ltd, distributed in the UK by Leo Cooper Ltd, 1967. Green, gold, 8.5 x 5.5, xxi/122. Fp, 4 mono phots, 172 line drawings of badges, no maps, no appendixes, Indexes (one for each State).

* To date, this is the only published record which attempts to describe the evolution and services of the Indian States Forces as a whole. The narrative is said to contain some inaccuracies, and the drawings are not entirely reliable, but this is a brave attempt at a large and complex subject. R/2 V/3. AMOT. AMcC.

61st CAVALRY
A Brief History of the Origins, Composition and Achievements of the Indian States Forces Cavalry Units from which it was Raised

Richard W Head * Produced by the author, facsimile TS, no publication details shown, 1978. Illustrated stiff card, plastic binding comb, grey, black, 'Regtl crest and two Mounted Sowars' motif, 11.5 x 8.5, ii/54. No ills, no maps, no appendixes, no Index.

* The 61st Cavalry, a Regular Regt of the Indian Army, was formed in 1951. This was shortly after all former Princely States units had been either disbanded or integrated into the Army. The Regt's formation was the result of a decision to preserve all the surviving horse-mounted units and to amalgamate them. It was further decided not to mechanise the Regt but to retain it as horsed cavalry for ceremonial duties. It is the sub-title of this work which gives the clue to its contents. Only one page is devoted to the post-Independence (61st Cavalry) period. This is followed by a brief summary of the IST/ISF schemes, with particular reference to ISF Cavalry units. The bulk of the pages is then given to a condensed history of each of those units. The author, the foremost expert in this field, provides a wealth of information not readily available elsewhere, with lists of Battle Honours, summaries of awards, names of officers, and so forth. R/5 V/4. IOL. AMcC.

Note: no more than a dozen copies were produced. Apart from the copy deposited with the India Office Library & Records, London, they were all presented to various authorities in India. The same author is currently compiling a book, to be entitled ARMIES OF THE INDIAN PRINCES, which will be a complete history of each of the forty-five State Armies and the (approximately) eight hundred Corps, Regts, units and sub-units which at one time or another served in them.

HISTORY OF THE 15th (IMPERIAL SERVICE) CAVALRY BRIGADE DURING THE GREAT WAR 1914-1918
Anon * Printed by Harrison & Son, for His Majesty's Stationery Office, London, 1919. Seen only as a photo-copy, details of original bindings and dimensions not known. No ills, 3 maps, -/35. Apps: Roll of Honour, H&A, list of former COs, idem former officers.
* An account, year by year, for the war period, with some years being more fully reported than others. The casualty list gives details by Regt, with dates and locations. A brief but useful source which covers the activities of the Kathiawar Signals Troop, Hyderabad Lancers, Mysore Lancers, Bhavnagar Lancers, Patiala Lancers, and the 124th Field Ambulance. R/4 V/4. IOL. AMcC.

RAJASTHAN STATES FORCES MEMORIAL - JAIPUR
Anon * By Authority ('Official'), Jaipur, n.d. (c.1956). Seen rebound, details of original binding not known, 8.0 x 6.0, ii/14. No ills, no maps, no Index. Apps: list of battles fought by each unit, list of contributors to the memorial.
* This little document was published to record the unveiling of a memorial to the fallen of the Rajasthan States Forces (incorporating Jaipur, Jodhpur, Udaipur, Bikaner and Alwar). However, the brief narrative does include some good historical information concerning the active services of these units. R/4 V/1. PC. AMcC.

Individual State Forces Accounts

A BRIEF STATEMENT OF BIKANER'S SERVICES IN THE GREAT WAR, 1914-1918
Anon * Government Press, Bikaner, n.d. Seen only as a photocopy, details of the original binding not known, State coat of arms on the title page, 8.5 x 5.5, i/35. No ills, no maps, no Index. Apps: Roll of Honour.
* As the title suggests, the narrative is very condensed. There is good coverage of the Ganga Risala (Camel Corps) which was despatched to Egypt in August 1914 (and where it remained until the end of the war). Awards to members of the Corps, including those to British Special Service Officers on attachment, are inserted in the text. Much of the remainder of the booklet covers financial matters and duties performed by the Maharajah, with verbatim extracts from telegrams and other papers which convey thanks for the good work done by the troops and by the State. A useful source for medal collectors in particular. R/5 V/3. BSI. AMcC.

BIKANER AND THE WAR
Being a Brief Narrative of the Various Contributions and Efforts of the Bikaner State towards the Successful Prosecution of the War
Anon * The Government Press, Bikaner, 31.12.1944. Paper covers, light brown, black, State coat of arms on the front cover, 8.5 x 6.0, iv/63. No ills, no maps, no appendixes, Index.
* A fairly typical State Government-inspired document which extols the personal virtues and efforts of the Maharajah. However, it also provides much useful detail on the valuable financial and practical support which he and his people had contributed to the Allied cause up to that point in the war (1939 to 1944). R/4 V/2. BSI. AMcC.
Note: this booklet was reprinted in 1947, again at the Government Press, Bikaner. The second edition differs from the first only to the extent that it has thirteen additional pages (updating the story from 1944 to 1947).

GWALIOR'S PART IN THE WAR
Mohammed Rafiullah * Printed by Hazell, Watson & Viney, London, 1920. Dark blue, gold, ornately embellished, 11.5 x 9.0, xiv/174. Fp, 56 mono phots, no maps, no appendixes, no Index.
* A slightly sycophantic account of the (very generous) activities of Gwalior's high society in raising funds and doing good works during WWI. The book, which is

finely produced, contains little information regarding the State's fighting forces and their active services. R/4 V/1. NAM. PJE.
Note: it is sometimes forgotten that the Princes not only provided men and materiel at their own expense during both world wars but also donated considerable sums of money from their own personal wealth and State treasuries.

OPERATION POLO
The Police Actions against Hyderabad, 1948
S N Prasad * Historical Section, Ministry of Defence, Delhi, 1972. Stiff card, green, black, 8.25 x 6.0, xii/199. 14 mono phots, 7 maps (bound in), Chapter Notes, Index. Apps: Order of Battle, Operational Instructions, list of COs who participated.
* This is one of a series of (originally) 'Secret' reports describing actions fought by the post-1947 Indian Army. Following the Partition of British India, the Muslim-ruled State of Hyderabad, a country the size of France, was not happy to find itself surrounded by the new Hindu-governed nation of India. The Nizam declared his intention to maintain his former independence. After several border incidents with neighbouring Indian Provinces, the Indian Government ordered the invasion of Hyderabad. Several hundred soldiers on each side lost their lives, but the campaign achieved a swift repression of Hyderabad resistance. This report concentrates upon the actions of the Indian Army units engaged, giving little space to the Hyderabad forces (other than showing their Order of Battle). However, as a source of reference, it is useful in showing how the Nizam's State Army units, and the State's former ISF units, attempted to maintain the status quo (as created by the original Treaty with the British). Operation Polo, the invasion of Hyderabad, was one of the first conflicts fought by the Indian Army under its own command and control. R/5 V/4. PC. RWH.

WAR EFFORT IN JAIPUR
Anon * The Information Bureau, Jaipur, July 1945. Illustrated paper covers, 'Photographic portrait of the Maharajah' motif, 8.0 x 6.0, iii/42. 18 mono phots, no maps, no appendixes, no Index.
* A useful account of Jaipur's contribution to the Allied cause in WWII. It is a fairly generalised story, but it includes some interesting details concerning the presentation of gallantry awards to non-ISF soldiers by His Highness the Maharajah when he acted on behalf of the King Emperor. R/4 V/2. PC. AMcC.

JAMMU AND KASHMIR ARMS
History of the Jammu and Kashmir Rifles
Maj Gen D K Palit VrC * Palit & Dutt, Dehra Dun, 1972. Bright blue, gold, 8.75 x 5.75, xv/305. Fp, 25 mono phots, 14 half-page lithographs of towns and scenes (at the beginning of each chapter), 6 maps (4 printed in the text, 2 on the end-papers), Index. Apps: extracts from the J&K Army List (1944), notes on the Regtl crest, Regtl marches, dates of raising of the fourteen Bns (8 during the period of the Raj, 6 post-1947), list of campaigns in which they served.
* As noted elsewhere, Gen Palit is a much-respected military historian, and this book is his professionally prepared narrative account of a famous Regt. It is an attractive, well illustrated and well written book. The story covers the entire period from medieval times through to post-Independence. It is, in effect, a complete history of Jammu and Kashmir. Part of the State's forces were dedicated to the IST/ISF arrangements. These elements served in WWI (German East Africa, and then the Third Afghan War), and in WWII (Iran, Syria, and Burma). The last part of the book deals with the conflicts with Pakistan. R/2 V/5. IOL. RGB.

HISTORY OF JAMMU AND KASHMIR RIFLES, 1820-1956
The State Force Background
Maj K Brahma Singh * Lancer International, New Delhi, 1990. Illustrated plastic-covered stiff card, 'Portrait of Gen Zorawar Singh' motif, 9.75 x 7.0, xiii/323. Fp, 23 mono phots, 11 cld ills, one line drawing, 21 maps, Bibliography, Index. Apps: H&A (from 1891 to 1956), list of former COs (from 1836 to 1957, incl Cavalry

and Artillery), lists of former officers, notes on the forts of the Jammu Rajahs, notes on war trophies, uniforms, diary of events (1815-1947), Battle and Theatre Honours up to 1948.
* The title is misleading. The book is not just the history of the Jammu and Kashmir Rifles. It describes also the origins of the State Army during the rule of Rajah Gulab Singh (a Dogra ruler and former General in the army of Ramjit Singh), and traces the services of the Artillery and Cavalry. The only previous record of the J&K Rifles was that given in the 1972 history by Palit (vide preceding entry). However, this later source, by Brahma Singh, is reported to be a step forward because it incorporates new unpublished material drawn from the Kashmir State Archives. R/1 V/5. NAM. AN.
Note: in October 1947, when Pakistan forces invaded Jammu and Kashmir, a spontaneous resistance movement evolved under various titles - Nubra Scouts, Punch Scouts, Border Defence Scouts, etc. Some months later they were organised as the Jammu and Kashmir Militia. In 1963, elements of the Militia became The Ladakh Scouts. They, in turn, in 1972, were established as part of the Indian Army with a new designation - The Jammu and Kashmir Light Infantry. All of this is described in HISTORY OF THE JAMMU AND KASHMIR MILITIA, by Maj Sita Ram Johri (Broca's Artistic Press, Srinagar, 1972).

WAR ON TWO FRONTS
Lieut Col Bhagwan Singh * Army Publishers, Delhi, 1967. Dark green, white, 8.75 x 5.75, iii/166. 3 mono phots, 2 maps, no Index. Apps: various verbatim commendatory messages.
* A personal account by the officer who commanded 1st Jammu and Kashmir Mountain Battery, ISF, during the first two years of WWII. An element of 5th Indian Div, the Bty served in the East African campaign. It saw action in Abyssinia, the Sudan, and Eritrea, distinguishing itself particularly in the Battles of Keren and Asmara. Soon afterwards it moved to Syria to fight the Vichy French for possession of Damascus. All of this is well covered, but the author gives much attention to the difficulties which he experienced with his British superiors. Even though his Bty was well trained and ready for war, several British Special Service Officers were appointed to it before it went into action. Of junior rank, they were placed over ISF officers of greater experience and seniority. They were removed after fierce protests had been lodged, but the affair caused such a bad atmosphere that Maj Bhagwan Singh was himself removed from his command in December 1941. His career suffered a temporary set-back, but later he rose to Lieutenant Colonel. The book is unusual in being a record of one of the very few ISF Artillery units. It is also demonstrates the difficulties which could arise if ISF units were handled in a clumsy way. R/2 V/4. PC. RWH.

THE INDIAN MILITARY REVIVAL
The Saga of the Fateh Shibji (4th Battalion, Jammu and Kashmir Rifles)
Maj G D Bakshi * Lancer International, New Delhi, 1987. Red, white, 8.75 x 5.75, xii/111. Fp (the Colours), 18 mono phots, no maps, Index. Apps: Roll of Honour, H&A (incl full citation for the Ashok Chakra awarded to Naik Sunder Singh, 1956), verbatim laudatory and congratulatory messages (1945 onwards).
* 'Fateh Shibji' translates as 'the ever-victorious Battalion', a claim substantiated by its distinguished history from formation in 1837 through to the present day. Originally the 4th Bn of the Army of the independent State of Jammu and Kashmir, it has retained its number in the modern Jammu and Kashmir Rifles (Indian Army). It served in various frontier campaigns in India, and then, as an ISF Bn, in Burma in WWII. During the Pakistani invasion of Kashmir, in 1947, it suffered heavy losses in the fighting around Poonch (Punch). This is a helpful account, containing all the information which most researchers are likely to require. R/2 V/4. PC. RWH.
Note: a variant of this book was published with identical contents but with an 'economy' illustrated hard cover showing a portrait of Gen Zorawar Singh.

8th BATTALION, THE JAMMU AND KASHMIR RIFLES
Golden Jubilee, 1940–1990

Anon * Bookmark, New Delhi, 1990. Stiff card, dark green, black, Regtl crest, 11.0 x 8.75, 34 pages (unnumbered). Fp, several portrait mono phots of Regtl officers and senior Indian Army officers, no maps, no Index. Apps: list of officers, idem Subedar Majors.

* A booklet produced by the Bn to mark the 50th Anniversary of its original raising as an ISF unit in 1940. Like many such units, it had been integrated into the Indian Army in 1947. It fought in the Kashmir War of 1947–1948, was disbanded in 1951, then re-raised in 1963. Although very slim, the booklet manages to include a brief Bn history, some reminiscences by former officers, two Rolls of Honour (for the Kashmir conflict of 1947–1948 and for the Indo-Pakistan War of 1965), and a list of recipients of various honours and awards. R/4 V/2. PC. RWH.

HISTORY OF THE JODHPUR STATE FORCES IN THE WAR, 1939–1946

Maj Gen R C Duncan CIE MVO OBE * Jodhpur Government Press, Jodhpur, 1946. Green, black, State coat of arms, 9.0 x 5.5, xiv/247. Fp, 81 mono phots, no maps, no appendixes, no Index.

* The quality of production of this book reflects the times in which it was published. The materials are poor, the text is badly printed, and the illustrations have not reproduced well. As a reference source, however, it is very good indeed. The author, who commanded the JSF during the war, organised the story into a series of chapters each of which describes in detail the services of a specific unit, i.e. Lancers, Infantry (by Bn), Transport Coy, Bodyguard, Training Centre, etc. Like many other Princely States, Jodhpur made a valuable contribution to the war effort. For example, the Lancers served in Iraq, Persia and Palestine. The 1st Infantry Bn was the first Indian unit to go ashore in Italy in 1943. The 54th (Jodhpur) Coy, RIASC, served in Baluchistan, Iraq, Palestine and Italy. All of this is lucidly explained, with many individual officers being named in the narrative. Honours and awards, with full citations and some studio portraits, are inserted at the appropriate juncture in each chapter. R/4 V/4. PC. CJP.

MILITARY KAPURTHALA, 1941

Anon * Printed by the Ripon Press (presumably for the State Government), 1941. Light blue, gold, 9.5 x 7.5, -/24. 15 mono phots, no maps, no appendixes, no Index.

* Much of the text is devoted to dutiful comments regarding the various former Maharajahs and their personal virtues. However, it makes some reference to the services of the State's armed forces during the Mutiny and in WWII. These passages are useful as a source for key dates and events. R/4 V/2. NAM. PJE.

THE HISTORY OF THE KOLHAPUR INFANTRY, 1845–1932

Capt L T Wilcock * The Times of India Press, Bombay, n.d. (c.1932). Green, blind, 7.5 x 5.0, -/71. One mono phot (portrait of the Maharajah of Kolhapur), 3 line drawings (incl the Regtl badge), no maps, no Index. Apps: list of former officers, medal roll for the Mutiny, roll of men who served in WWI.

* A fairly brief but interesting account of their services from 1857 (when they declined to join the mutinous HEIC Regt at that time stationed in Kolhapur), through to WWI (when many of the Sepoys volunteered for service with the Indian Army). The medal roll appendix has obvious value to medal collectors. R/4 V/4. PC. RJW.

REGIMENTAL HISTORY OF THE MALERKOTLA SAPPERS & MINERS

Maj B A Khan and Maj A H Khan * M Om Ria, Ludhiana, 1950. Seen only as a photocopy, unit crest on first end-paper, 9.0 x 6.5, xi/100. Fp (portrait of the Nawab of Malerkotla), 21 mono phots, no maps, no Index. Apps: list of COs (1894–1946), idem Seconds-in-Command, idem Coy Subedars.

* Malerkotla is in the Punjab, almost halfway between Delhi and Lahore. This strategically important location prompted an early Treaty between the HEIC and the ruling Nawabs. They provided troops to assist the British in various campaigns

over the next 150 years - Laswarree (1803), the First Afghan War, the Punjab campaign of 1845-1846, the suppression of the Mutiny, Second Afghan War, on the NWF in 1897-1898, the Boxer Rebellion (1900), WWI, Third Afghan War, and WWII. All of this is well covered here, particularly the unit's role in Burma in WWII. The prose is at times stilted and it contains a few grammatical errors, but these do not in any way detract from the clarity of the enjoyable narrative. Many individuals, of all ranks, are named throughout. This is one of the best of all IST/ISF unit histories. R/5 V/5. PC. AMcC.

PATIALA AND THE GREAT WAR
A Brief History of the Services of the Premier Punjab State
Anon ('Compiled from Secretariat and Other Records') * The Medici Society Ltd, London, 1923. Dark grey, gold, State coat of arms on front cover and spine, 9.0 x 6.0, iv/91. Fp, 49 mono phots (printed separately and then tipped in), no maps, no appendixes, no Index.
* Like some similar publications of the period, this one makes much of the personal role of the Maharajah in aiding the Allied war effort. This information will no doubt be useful to researchers interested in the general ethos of the Princely States and their relationship with the British. At the same time, there are enough references in the text to Patiala's IST units to make the book worthwhile as a source. R/5 V/2. AMOT. AMcC.

MILITARY HISTORY OF REWA STATE
Lieut Col Janardan Singh * Madha Printing Works, Alahabad, 1940. Green, black, 8.75 x 5.75, -/195. No ills, no maps, no Index. Apps: list of officers then serving (1940).
* Printed in Hindi. For those familiar with that language, the book provides an authoritative history of each unit which comprised the State Army. The author deals with all aspects - organisation, uniforms, weaponry, services, etc. During the reign of Maharajah Venkat Raman Singh (1895-1922) the Army was enlarged to a total strength of 5200 all ranks. Following his death, it was quickly reduced to 1700 all ranks and, later, to one Infantry Bn and a Transport Coy ISF. This is the only known history of a Princely State force printed in a language other than English. R/5 V/3. PC. RWH.

THE NAYAR BRIGADE OF TRAVANCORE
Selection from the Records of the Madras Government
Anon * Printed by the Superintendent, Government Press, Madras, 1898. Stiff card, white, black, 13.25 x 8.25, iv/137. No ills, no maps, no appendixes, no Index.
* The Brigade consisted of two Infantry Bns, British officered, which eventually joined the IST scheme of that period (late 1800s). Both still exist, as Bns of the Madras Regt, Indian Army. This is a detailed account which has Chapters covering the constitution of the Bde, its services, organisational changes, methods of officer selection, men's pay and allowances, the Commandant's duties and privileges, notes on supplies and stores, and much else of interest to the specialist.
R/5 V/4. PC. RWH.
Note: the copy seen is marked 'Confidential - To be kept in the Commandant's safe'. The evidence suggests that this is now a very rare collector's item.

BRITISH ARMY REGIMENTS ORIGINATING IN INDIA

Twelve regiments - three cavalry and eight infantry - at one time appeared in the Order of Battle of the British Army and yet had their roots planted firmly in the Armies of the Honourable East India Company. All of the infantry units, and one cavalry, are listed here in their original order of seniority.

Bengal Presidency

19th HUSSARS

THE NINETEENTH AND THEIR TIMES
Being an Account of the Four Cavalry Regiments in the British Army that have Borne the Number Ninteen, and of the Campaigns in which they Served
Col John Biddulph * Printed at the Edinburgh Press, for John Murray, London, 1899. Blue, gold, 9.0 x 6.0, xxi/330. Fp, 3 mono phots, 4 cld ills, 5 maps (bound in), Index. Apps: Roll of Honour (19th Hussars only - Egypt 1822, Suakin 1884, Sudan 1885), extracts from addresses given by various senior officers, report on Arab horses ridden by the 19th Hussars during the Nile campaign, 1885.
* Part IV, Chapter I, deals briefly with the formation, in 1858, of the 1st Bengal European Cavalry, and its transfer, in 1862, to the British Army (as the 19th Hussars). Ultimately, in April 1922, the Regt became 15th/19th The King's Royal Hussars. A well produced book, with excellent appendixes and Index. The bulk of the narrative refers to British Army services. R/3 V/4. PCAL. HIS.
Note: under current (1992) proposals, the 15th/19th The King's Royal Hussars will amalgamate with the 13th/18th Hussars.

ROYAL MUNSTER FUSILIERS

THE HISTORY OF THE BENGAL EUROPEAN INFANTRY
Now the Royal Munster Fusiliers, and How it Helped to win India
Lieut Col P R Innes * Printed by The Army & Navy Co-operative Society Ltd, for Simpkin, Marshall & Co, London, 1885. Royal blue, gold, 8.75 x 5.75, xii/572. Fp, no other ills, 4 maps (town plans, drawn in), Bibliography, Index. Apps: list of former officers, notes on Battle Honours (15), diary of events, war services.
* A narrative account covering the periods 1644-1756 (pre-formation) and 1756-1861 (Regtl history). It includes full details of all the actions and campaigns in which 1st and 2nd Bengal Europeans (under their various formal titles) took part. R/3 V/5. MODL. AMM/HIS.
Note: a second edition was published in the same year. The only change was the addition of two unnumbered pages of favourable reviews of the first edition.

THE ROLL OF OFFICERS OF THE 101st AND 104th FUSILIERS AND ROYAL MUNSTER FUSILIERS
Lieut Col S T Banning * Published privately in London, no other details shown, 1912. Seen in library binding, 8.5 x 5.5, ii/47. No ills, no maps, no appendixes, Index.
* The book comprises highly condensed data regarding the promotions and war services of officers who served with these three Regts. The listings commence in 1840 when the 101st was the 1st Bengal (European) Regt and when the 104th was the 2nd Bengal (European) Regt. R/4 V/3. MODL. AMM.

HISTORY OF THE ROYAL MUNSTER FUSILIERS
Capt S McCance * Gale & Polden Ltd, Aldershot, 1927. Royal blue, gold, Regtl crest, 10.0 x 7.5, vii/254. Fp, 32 mono phots, 4 cld ills, 20 maps, Index. Apps: H&A, list of former officers, nominal rolls, biographical notes regarding ten personalities connected with the Regt and regarding six VC winners.
* Volume I (of two) is arranged in two sections. Part I (1652-1860) deals with the Bengal (European) Regt, later the 1st (Bengal European) Fusiliers, and the

battles in which they and their forebears took part - Plassey (1757), Deig (1804), Bhurtpore (1826), Ghuznee (1839), the campaign in Burma (1852), and the suppression of the Mutiny (1857-1859). Many officers and casualties are mentioned in the narrative. Part II (1839-1860) deals with the 2nd Bengal (European) Regt, later 2nd (Bengal European) Fusiliers, in a similar way. The coverage is not as extensive because the period of time was shorter, but there are good accounts of the Second Punjab War (1848-1849), Burma (1852), and the Mutiny. Again, many officers are named in the narrative. R/4 V/5. MODL. AMM.

ROYAL SUSSEX REGIMENT

A SHORT HISTORY OF THE SECOND BATTALION, THE ROYAL SUSSEX REGIMENT
Lieut J H Dumbrell * C A Ribeiro, Singapore, n.d. (c.1925). Card, orange, black, 9.0 x 6.0, -/78. No ills, no maps, no appendixes, no Index.
* A condensed history from 1853 onwards. The Royal Sussex Regt was formed in 1881 by the amalgamation of the 35th (Royal Sussex) Regt of Foot with the 107th (Bengal Infantry) Regt. The 107th had started life, in 1854, as the 3rd (Bengal European Light Infantry) Regt. It was re-titled as the 107th when it became part of the British Army in 1861, but the author of this little book devotes only five pages to events before that date. R/4 V/1. NAM. PJE.

A HISTORY OF THE ROYAL SUSSEX REGIMENT
A History of the Old Belfast Regiment and the Regiment of Sussex, 1701-1953
G D Martineau * Moore & Tillyer Ltd, Chichester, n.d. (c.1954). Blue, gold, Regtl crest, 8.75 x 5.5, -/324. No ills, maps or appendixes relating to India, Bibliography, no Index.
* This author gives even less space to his Regt's old HEIC forebears (just one page, vide page 115). R/2 V/2. MODL. AMM.

Madras Presidency

ROYAL DUBLIN FUSILIERS
1st Battalion

A SKETCH OF THE SERVICES OF THE MADRAS EUROPEAN REGIMENT DURING THE BURMESE WAR
Anon ('By an Officer of the Corps') * Smith, Elder & Co, London, 1839. Red, gold, 9.0 x 5.5, vii/104. No ills, no maps, no appendixes, no Index.
* The author states that this book was written as a 'souvenir' for his brother officers. It is, in fact, an entertaining and informative record of the forgotten hard-fought actions of 1824-1826 (the First Burma War). R/5 V/3. RCSL. RP.

HISTORICAL RECORD OF THE HONOURABLE EAST INDIA COMPANY'S FIRST MADRAS EUROPEAN REGIMENT
Containing an Account of the Establishment of Independent Companies in 1645, The Formation of a Regiment in 1748, and its Subsequent Services to 1842
Anon ('By a Staff Officer', known to have been Brig Gen J G S Neill) * Smith, Elder & Co, London, 1843. Rust red, gold, Regtl crest superimposed upon a stand-of-arms on the front cover (in gold), and on the back cover (without gold), similar embellishments on the spine, 9.25 x 5.5, xxx/575. Fp, 8 lithograph ills, 3 lithograph plans, Index. Apps: 8 pages devoted to an abstract of Contents (arranged alphabetically).
* There are two variants of this work, both dated 1843. One is the 'anonymous' version, as described above, while the other credits Neill as being the author. The narrative and illustrations are identical in both cases. Before the 19th Century, the HEIC did not require its Regts to keep records. Neill himself joined the Regt in 1827. For the earlier periods, he was dependent upon the personal journals kept by its first Colonel, Stringer Lawrence, and upon general historical accounts of the period. His description of the First Burma War, based in part upon the

recollections of officers still serving at the time when he was compiling the book, are probably its most accurate and complete feature. In overall terms, the book is readable and full of interest - an outstandingly good Regtl history for its period. R/5 V/5. MODL. VS/CJP.

SERVICES OF THE 102nd REGIMENT OF FOOT (ROYAL MADRAS FUSILIERS) FROM 1842 TO THE PRESENT TIME

Col Thomas Raikes * Smith, Elder & Co, London, 1867. Red, gold, panels, 8.5 x 5.25, i/68. No ills, no maps, no appendixes, no Index.

* 'Being the sequel to The Services of the Madras European Regiment, by a Staff Officer', according to the author. This book, in other words, picks up the story from where Brig Gen Neill left it in 1842 (vide preceding entry). The period from 1842 to 1866 is covered in condensed narrative style, with good accounts of services in Burma and during the Mutiny. Casualties and awards are mentioned in the text (officers only). R/4 V/3. MODL. AMM.

REGIMENTAL RECORDS OF THE 1st ROYAL DUBLIN FUSILIERS, 1842-1904
Formerly the Madras European Regiment, 1st Madras Fusiliers, and 102nd Foot, By One who Served over 30 Years in it

Anon (known to have been Lieut Col S G Bird) * Printed by Biddle & Shipham, Guildford, Surrey, n.d. (1905). Dark blue, gold, Regtl crest, 8.5 x 5.5, viii/163/vi. Fp, 4 mono phots, 5 maps (bound in), no appendixes, Indexes.

* This work also picks up from where Neill left off. It covers the period 1842 to 1904 in chronological diary style, with details of moves and Stations, and with the names of many officers mentioned in the text. The campaigns covered are Burma (1852) and the Mutiny (this in very good detail, with much information on officer casualties). R/4 V/4. MODL. AMM.

Note: the Preface is dated 1904, but the text makes reference to events up to and including 1905.

THE REGIMENTAL RECORDS OF THE FIRST BATTALION, THE ROYAL DUBLIN FUSILIERS
Formerly The Madras Europeans, The Madras European Regiment, The First Madras Fusiliers, and The Royal Madras Fusiliers, 1644-1842, By One Whose Whole Service was Passed in the Corps and Who Had the Honour of Commanding it

Anon (reported to have been Col G J Harcourt) * Hugh Rees Ltd, London, 1910. Dark blue, gold, Regtl crest, 8.5 x 5.5, xiv/152. Fp, 11 mono phots, 2 maps (bound in), Glossary, Index. Apps: Regtl Orders, notes on organisation, memorials, list of former COs, idem former officers.

* This author went back to the beginning and covered the same ground as that covered by Neill (vide preceding page). He re-wrote that work 'to make it more clear and less prolix'. Written in a clear chronological format, it conforms nicely with the 1905 account by Bird (vide preceding entry). This author too gives interesting coverage of the major battles and mentions many officers by name. R/4 V/5. NAM/MODL. PJE/AMM.

NEILL'S BLUE CAPS
Being the Records of the Antecedents and early History of the Regiment variously known as the East India Company's European Regiment, the Madras European Regiment, the 1st Madras European Regiment, the 1st Madras European Fusiliers, the 1st Madras Fusiliers, the 102nd Royal Madras Fusiliers, and the 1st Battalion, Royal Dublin Fusiliers

Col H C Wylly CB * Gale & Polden Ltd, Aldershot, n.d. (c.1924). Blue, gold, Regtl crest, 9.75 x 7.25. Three matching volumes, published simultaneously.

Vol I : 1639-1826. -/330. Fp, 16 mono phots, 2 cld plates, 6 maps (5 printed in the text, one folding, bound in), Index. Apps: notes on uniforms.

Vol II : 1826-1914. -/229. Fp, 29 mono phots, 3 cld plates, 2 maps (bound in), Index. Apps: citations for four VC winners.

Vol III : 1914-1922. xii/248. Fp, 45 mono phots, 4 cld plates, 8 maps, Index. Apps: 22 in total, none relating to the HEIC period.

* Col Wylly was a professional historian and author. This massive compilation is one of his best works, the narrative being highly informative and fluently written. The first two volumes of the series cover the services of the Madras Fusiliers in their various guises from 1746 through to 1881 (when the 102nd Royal Madras Fusiliers were amalgamated with the 103rd Royal Bombay Fusiliers to form the Royal Dublin Fusiliers). The presentation and bindings of these three books is exemplary. R/4 V/5. PCAL. RP.
Note: refer to the 'Bombay Presidency' section for published records of the 2nd Bn Royal Dublin Fusiliers (vide facing page, 389).

ROYAL INNISKILLING FUSILIERS

THE ROYAL INNISKILLING FUSILIERS
Being the History of the Regiment from December 1688 to July 1914
Anon ('The Regimental Historical Records Committee') * Constable & Co Ltd, London, 1928. Violet, gold, 8.75 x 5.5, xxiii/673. Fp, 30 mono phots, 16 cld plates, 21 maps, Index. Apps: 8 in total, incl Roll of Honour (Waterloo and the war in South Africa, 1899-1902), H&A (1899-1902), list of former COs, idem former officers.
* Just one chapter, of 15 pages, deals with the 108th (Madras Infantry) Regt and its forebear, the 3rd (Madras Infantry) Regt. The latter was raised in 1853-1854, partly from Europeans already resident in India and partly by recruitment in Ireland. Its first campaign was the suppression of the Mutiny when it saw much action in Central India (1858). The 108th was redesignated the 2nd Bn Royal Inniskilling Fusiliers in 1881. R/3 V/4. PCAL. MP.
Note: another edition of this book, having green covering and pink lettering, and dated 1934, has been reported. The contents are seemingly the same of those of the first (1928) edition.

KING'S OWN YORKSHIRE LIGHT INFANTRY

HISTORICAL RECORDS OF THE ONE HUNDRED AND FIFTH REGIMENT OF LIGHT INFANTRY
Anon * Published by the Regiment, Meerut, no other details shown, 1871. Rifle green, black, 7.75 x 5.0, -/49. No ills, no maps, no appendixes, no Index.
* The narrative is arranged in two parts. The first deals with 2nd Madras (Light Infantry) Regt and is compiled from General Orders, Dress Regulations, extracts from Regtl records, etc, for the period 1839 to 1861. The second deals with the 105th (Madras Light Infantry) Regt, again drawing heavily upon official sources but with more detail and explanation. The period covered here is 1861 to 1871. The narrative is more worthy than stimulating. R/4 V/4. MODL/PCAL. AMM.

THE HISTORY OF THE KING'S OWN YORKSHIRE LIGHT INFANTRY
Volume II
Col H C Wylly * Percy, Lund, Humphries & Co Ltd, London, n.d. Royal blue, gold, Regtl crest, 9.0 x 6.0, vii/710. Fp, some ills but none relating to India, idem maps and appendixes, Index.
* This is essentially a KOYLI history. Despite its great length, the book has only 17 pages devoted to the 2nd Madras (European Light Infantry) Regt and its two successors (between 1839 and 1881). Like all other HEIC Regts listed on these pages, it passed into Queen's service in 1861 but still retained the Presidency association in its title until the reforms of 1881. R/3 V/4. NAM. PJE.

THE KING'S OWN YORKSHIRE LIGHT INFANTRY
Volume IV : Register of Officers, 1755-1945
Gen Sir Charles P Deedes * Lund, Humphries & Co Ltd, London, 1946. Royal blue, gold, Regtl crest, 9.0 x 6.0, -/247. Fp, no other ills, no maps, Bibliography, no Index. Apps: notes on the history of 'Purchase', the Regtl lineage (1755-1945), notes on allied Regts in Canada and Australia.

* A remarkable work of compilation. It consists of a complete listing of all those officers who held Regular Commissions and who served with the Regt during that entire period. The Register includes useful biographical information for many of those named, including those who served with the old 2nd Madras (European Light Infantry) Regt. R/3 V/3. NAM. PJE/HIS.

Bombay Presidency

ROYAL DUBLIN FUSILIERS
2nd Battalion

RECORDS OF HM's 1st REGIMENT OF BOMBAY EUROPEAN INFANTRY 'FUSILIERS'
Containing a Brief Account of its Formation in 1662 and Services to 1861
Anon (Lieut H Woodward) * Printed at The Observer Press, Poona, for the author, 1861. Originally in paper covers, seen rebound, 8.5 x 6.0, -/40. No ills, no maps, no Index. Apps: two verbatim speeches made to the Regt by Gen Sir Charles Napier.
* A booklet arranged in three sections. Part I (1662-1794) is a reprint of an article written by Woodward and first published in the EAST INDIAN UNITED SERVICES INSTITUTION JOURNAL in 1838. Part II (1662-1843) is an extract from an item first published in Bombay General Orders in 1843. Part III (1843-1861) is a brief history compiled from Regtl records. This third element consists of only four pages, but it does give a summary of actions in the Punjab and Mutiny campaigns, with several officers mentioned in the text. R/4 V/3. MODL. AMM.
Note: this booklet was published contemporaneously (1861) in England, at the press of T Kentfield, Newport, Isle of Wight. It differs from the Poona version in being of slightly smaller format (8.25 x 5.25) and having a slightly changed title.

HISTORICAL RECORD OF THE 103rd ROYAL BOMBAY FUSILIERS
Anon * Printed by A H Swiss, Devonport, for the author, n.d. (c.1876). Royal blue, gold, Royal coat of arms, 8.75 x 5.5, -/81/ix. No ills, no maps, no Index. Apps: list of former COs, idem officers (1824-1876), idem Adjutants (1798-1876), strength returns.
* The period covered is 1661-1876 and the condensed narrative is a detailed history of (successively) The Bombay Regt, the 1st Bombay (European) Regt, the 1st Bombay (European) Fusiliers, and the 103rd Bombay Fusiliers. It is written in diary style, with liberal mention of Stations, moves, and some officers' appointments. The main campaigns - Seringapatam (1799), Mahratta Wars (1817-1818), Aden (1839), Punjab (1848-1849) - are covered quite well, but the Mutiny only sketchily. R/4 V/3. MODL. AMM.

CROWN AND COMPANY
The Historical Records of the 2nd Batt, Royal Dublin Fusiliers, formerly 1st Bombay European Regiment, 1661-1911
Maj Arthur Mainwaring * Arthur L Humphreys, London, 1911. Green, gold, Regtl crest, 10.25 x 7.5, xxiii/437. Fp, 21 mono phots, 7 cld ills, one map (folding, bound in at the rear), no Index. Apps: 12 in total, incl list of former COs, idem officers.
* Well written and well produced. A large-scale work which provides good coverage of all its early campaigns before the Regt was transferred to the British Army in 1861. R/3 V/4. PCAL/RMAS. MP.

THE DURHAM LIGHT INFANTRY

THE DURHAM LIGHT INFANTRY
W L Vane * Gale & Polden Ltd, London, 1914. Dark green, gold, Regtl crest, 10.0 x 7.0, xii/334. Ills, Index. Apps: list of former COs, idem officers.
* A book which deals mainly with the DLI from 1881 to 1914. The information regarding 2nd Bombay (Light Infantry) Regt and 106th Bombay Light Infantry Regt is limited to just twelve pages. This is based upon extracts from Regtl records and

makes some mention of Kolhapur (1844), Persia (1856), and the Mutiny (1857-1859). The book is doubtless a helpful source for everyone interested in the DLI, but offers little for those concerned with the Regt's forebears and early roots. R/3 V/4. NAM. PJE.

FAITHFUL
The Story of the Durham Light Infantry
S G P Ward * Published by the Regtl HQ, DLI, London, 1962. Rifle green, silver, Regtl crest, 10.0 x 6.0, xx/574. Numerous ills, maps, appendixes, etc, but none relevant to the HEIC period.
* In contrast with Vane's earlier work (vide preceding entry), the narrative of this book includes a reasonably detailed account of the services of the 2nd Bombay European Light Infantry Regt between 1839 and 1862. It covers the same ground as that covered by Vane, but it makes mention of several officers and their services and describes the important Persia campaign in better detail.
R/1 V/3. NAM/MODL/PCAL. PJE/AMM.

THE PRINCE OF WALES'S LEINSTER REGIMENT (ROYAL CANADIANS)

THE HISTORY OF THE PRINCE OF WALES'S LEINSTER REGIMENT (ROYAL CANADIANS) Volume I
Lieut Col Frederick Ernest Whitton CMG * Gale & Polden Ltd, Aldershot, n.d. (c.1924). Blue with broad green band, gold, Regtl crest, 8.5 x 5.5, viii/483. Fp, 3 mono phots, 4 maps, no appendixes, Index.
* Chapters XIV and XX cover the period 1600-1864 and especially the Regt's services as 3rd (Bombay) Regt (1854-1861) and as 109th (Bombay Infantry) Regt (1861-1881). A good readable narrative, with helpful coverage of the Mutiny period (Central India, 1858). Volume II of this handsome pair of books covers the Leinster Regt in WWI and contains no references to the early years in India.
R/4 V/4. MODL/NAM. AMM/PJE.
Note: the 'Royal Canadians' element in the title was acquired in 1881 when the 109th amalgamated with the 100th (Prince of Wales's Royal Canadian) Regt.

THE DUKE OF WELLINGTON'S REGIMENT (WEST RIDING)

HISTORICAL RECORDS OF THE 76th 'HINDOSTAN REGIMENT'
From its Formation in 1787 to 30th June 1881
Lieut Col F A Hayden DSO * The Johnson's Head, Lichfield, 1909. Red, gold, 8.5 x 5.5, xiv/195. No ills, 7 maps (folding, bound in), no Index. Apps: list of officers (1788 to 1881), notes on uniforms, notes on the Colours.
* Unlike the Regts listed on the preceding pages, the 76th Regiment of Foot was never linked directly to the Armies of the HEIC. It was always a British Army unit. However, it spent so very many of its early years in India that it earned the soubriquet 'Hindoostan' and this fact alone justifies the inclusion of its history in this bibliography. The Regt's early Battle Honours speak for themselves - India (1780-1806), Seringapatam (1799), Mysore (1800), Allyghur (1803), Delhi (1803), and Leswaree (1803). This is a very detailed account, produced to a better-than-average standard for the period, but the various rolls of casualties (with details of dates and locations) are dispersed throughout the narrative instead of being concentrated at the rear of the book. There is no Index, so finding a named individual is not an easy task. The same applies to the 'Honours & Awards'. They include the Anglo-Boer War (1899-1902) awards but, again, they appear on random pages. These deficiences aside, the book is a good unit history. In 1881 the 76th linked with the 33rd to form The Duke of Wellington's Regiment (West Riding).
R/4 V/4. PCAL. RP.

Note: researchers wishing to know more about the lineages of Regiments of the British Army, including those which originated in India, are recommended to consult

A REGISTER OF THE REGIMENTS AND CORPS OF THE BRITISH ARMY
The Ancestry of the Regiments and Corps of the Regular Establishment of the Army

by Arthur Swinson (The Archive Press, London, 1972).

For immediate reference purposes, the following simplified version of some of those lineages may be of assistance (vide following page, Appendix I).

APPENDIX I

Simplified lineages of British Army Regiments of Infantry raised originally by the HEIC and which transferred to Crown service in 1861, and which lost their Presidency titles upon amalgamation in 1881

101st Regiment (Royal Bengal Fusiliers), formerly 1st Bengal Fusiliers
linked to the
104th Regiment (Bengal Fusiliers), formerly 2nd Bengal Fusiliers
to form the 1st and 2nd Bns respectively of
THE ROYAL MUNSTER FUSILIERS (disbanded in 1922)

107th Regiment (Bengal Infantry), formerly 3rd Bengal Light Infantry
linked to the
35th (Royal Sussex) Regiment of Foot
to form the 2nd Bn of
THE ROYAL SUSSEX REGIMENT (later 3rd Bn THE QUEEN'S REGIMENT)

102nd Regiment (Royal Madras Fusiliers), formerly 1st Madras Fusiliers
linked to the
103rd Regiment (Royal Bombay Fusiliers), formerly 1st Bombay Fusiliers
to form the 1st and 2nd Bns respectively of
THE ROYAL DUBLIN FUSILIERS (disbanded in 1922)

105th Regiment (Madras Light Infantry), formerly 2nd Madras Light Infantry
linked to the
51st (2nd Yorkshire, West Riding) Regiment of Foot
to form the 2nd Bn of
THE KING'S OWN YORKSHIRE LIGHT INFANTRY (later 2nd Bn THE LIGHT INFANTRY)

108th Regiment (Madras Infantry), formerly 3rd Madras Infantry
linked to the
27th (Inniskilling) Regiment of Foot
to form the 2nd Bn of
THE ROYAL INNISKILLING FUSILIERS (later THE ROYAL IRISH RANGERS)

106th Regiment (Bombay Light Infantry), formerly 2nd Bombay Light Infantry
linked to the
68th (Durham Light Infantry) Regiment of Foot
to form the 2nd Bn of
THE DURHAM LIGHT INFANTRY (later 4th Bn THE LIGHT INFANTRY)

109th Regiment (Bombay Infantry), formerly 3rd Bombay Regiment
linked to the
100th (Prince of Wales's Royal Canadian) Regiment of Foot
to form the 2nd Bn of
THE PRINCE OF WALES'S LEINSTER REGIMENT (ROYAL CANADIANS) (disbanded, 1922).

Note: the sole horsed Regiment recorded here (page 385) was the 1st Bengal European Light Cavalry. Raised in 1858, it transferred to Crown service in 1862 with the title 19th Hussars. By 1921 it had become 19th Royal Hussars (Queen Alexandra's Own). In April 1922, it amalgamated with 15th King's Hussars to form 15th/19th The King's Royal Hussars.

The two other HEIC horsed Regiments which transferred to the British Army were 2nd Bengal European Light Cavalry (as 20th Light Dragoons, 1861, later 20th Hussars), and 3rd Bengal European Light Cavalry (as 21st Light Dragoons, 1861, later 21st Hussars, then 21st Empress of India's Lancers, 1898).

DIVISIONS

AN ACCOUNT OF THE OPERATIONS OF THE 18th (INDIAN) DIVISION IN MESOPOTAMIA DECEMBER 1917 TO DECEMBER 1918
With the Names of all the Units which Served with the Division and a Nominal Roll of all the Officers
Anon (Lieut Col W E Wilson-Johnston DSO) * Printed by Finden Brown & Co Ltd, for St Martin's Press, London, n.d. (c.1920). Cloth-covered boards, leather spine, blue, gold, 'Elephant' motif, 10.25 x 7.5, iii/74. Fp, no other ills, 8 maps (cld, folding, bound in), no appendixes, no Index.
* The first half of this attractively produced booklet is a brief narrative account of the Division's services in Mesopotamia from the time it disembarked through to the end of the war. There are listings of all its constituent elements, and this information alone makes the publication a useful source of reference. The second half is a roll of all the British officers who served with every British and Indian Army unit which came under the Division's command during that period. The names are conveniently arranged under Div HQ, Bde HQs, Regts, and all ancillary units and sub/units. Self-evidently, a very helpful source for genealogists and medal collectors. R/4 V/4. RMAS. RP.
Note: two versions of this item have been seen. One (as recorded above) contains no illustrations other than the frontispiece. The other has an integral rear pocket in which are held (loose) twenty-one monochrome photographs.

THE TIGER STRIKES
Anon (Lieut Col W G Hingston) * The Government of India Press, Calcutta, 1942. Green, gold, with reversed lettering on white ground, 8.5 x 5.5, xviii/165. Fp, 65 mono phots, 7 maps (5 bound in, 2 printed on the end-papers), no Index. Apps: H&A (all ranks, by Regt).
* A detailed and very readable account of the 4th and 5th Indian Divs and the fighting in Somaliland, Eritrea, and the Western Desert. The period covered is September 1940 to June 1941. R/2 V/4. NAM. RP.
Note: a second edition was published in 1943 and there may have been others. The same text was published - in 1942 - in a Hindi edition and an Urdu edition.

THE TIGER KILLS
India's Fight in the Middle East and Egypt
Lieut Col W G Hingston OBE and Lieut Col G R Stevens * The Government of India Press, Bombay, 1944. Orange, black, 8.75 x 5.5, x/354. Fp, 66 mono phots, 12 maps, no Index. Apps: H&A (all ranks, by Regt).
* This book continues the story of the 4th and 5th Indian Divs, with emphasis on the 4th. Again, there is no Index. This is unfortunate because the broad-ranging narrative includes descriptions of many small-scale actions and the individual officers and men who were involved. Tracing them - in a book of 354 pages - is a particularly laborious task. R/2 V/4. NAM. RP.
Note: there was at least one reprint of this item. It does not contain the H&A appendix.

THE TIGER TRIUMPHS
The Story of Three Great Divisions in Italy
Anon (almost certainly Lieut Col G R Stevens OBE) * Printed by Whitefriars Press, London, for HMSO on behalf of the Inter-Services Public Relations Directorate, GHQ, New Delhi, 1946. Blue-grey, black on white labels, 8.25 x 5.25, -/212. Fp, 57 mono phots, 6 maps, no appendixes, no Index.
* The third of the officially-sponsored 'Tiger' trilogy, and again, researched and written to a high standard. This one deals with 4th, 8th, and 10th Indian Divs in the Italian campaign of 1943-1945. It describes all aspects of grand strategy, but it includes a great many references to minor engagements, to the movements of named units, and to acts of gallantry by named individual officers and men. R/2 V/4. RMAS. RP.
Note: a version having illustrated thin card covers has been seen. The front cover

has photographic portraits of three soldiers (British, Indian and Gurkha). The rear cover has the Divisional emblems, in colour.

FOURTH INDIAN DIVISION

Lieut Col G R Stevens OBE * McLaren & Son Ltd, Toronto, Ontario, Canada, n.d. (c.1948). Wine red, gold, 'Eagle' motif in black/red, 9.5 x 6.0, -/414 (plus 17 pages of appendixes, not numbered). 102 mono phots, 19 maps and diagrams, no Index. Apps: Roll of Honour (statistical summaries for each component unit), H&A (idem), lists of officers holding various Command and Staff appointments.

* The 4th was one of the most celebrated Divisions of WWII, combining some of the most illustrious Regts of the British and Indian Armies. It travelled 15,000 miles and suffered 25,000 casualties during its five years of service in Eritrea, Syria, the Western Desert, Tunisia, Italy, and Greece. It particularly distinguished itself at Cassino. This is a good readable account of those services, the narrative being well supported with helpful maps and a range of photographs not usually seen elsewhere. R/3 V/4. RCSL. RP.

Note: the traditions of 4th Div were retained after Partition. A substantial record (of 447 pages) was compiled by the professional historian K C Praval under the title THE RED EAGLES - A HISTORY OF THE FOURTH DIVISION OF INDIA. It was published in 1982 by Vision Books, of New Delhi. The period covered is 1940 to 1972, with the first twelve chapters being devoted to the Division's pre-Partition services.

BALL OF FIRE

The Fifth Indian Division in the Second World War

Anthony Brett James * Gale & Polden Ltd, Aldershot, 1951. Black, red, Divsl emblem, 8.75 x 5.25, xiv/481. Fp, 65 mono phots, 12 maps, no appendixes, no Index.

* Written in easy-going style, this informal history is a useful background account of Indian troops at war in Eritrea, in the Western Desert, in Burma, and then finally in the reoccupation of Singapore. The author provides plenty of action, with good details of the great battles at Kohima and Imphal. R/3 V/3. RMAS. RP.

GOLDEN ARROW

The Story of the 7th Indian Division in the Second World War, 1939-1945

Brig M R Roberts DSO * Gale & Polden Ltd, Aldershot, 1952. Black, gold, 'Arrow' Divsl emblem, 8.75 x 5.5, xxii/304. Fp, 41 mono phots, 7 maps (folding, bound in), Glossary, Index. Apps: Orders of Battle, Planning Directives for the Irrawaddy crossing.

* An interesting account which covers the entire story of the Div's formation in 1940, its initial training, active service in Burma, and the occupation of Siam. The introductory thumb-nail notes regarding each of the units which ever served under Divsl command during that time are particularly useful. They cover not only the Indian Army units but also those of the British Army, the Indian State Forces and East African forces. R/3 V/4. RMAS. RP.

THE FIGHTING COCK

Being the History of the 23rd Indian Division, 1942-1947

Lieut Col A J F Doulton * Gale & Polden Ltd, Aldershot, 1951. Yellow, red, Divsl emblem, 8.5 x 5.5, xvi/318. Fp, 13 mono phots, 20 maps (19 printed in the text, one folding, bound in), Index. Apps: H&A (statistical summary only), list of all Div and Bde commanders, Order of Battle at Imphal (June 1944).

* A good clear account of the Div's role in the Burma campaign and the final destruction of all Japanese forces in that theatre. It concludes with an interesting description of the reoccupation of Malaya (Operation Zipper). R/3 V/4. RMAS. RP.

Between 1945 and 1947 the Director of Public Relations, War Department, Government of India, published a series of booklets covering the individual histories of the WWII Divisions. They follow a consistent format, having between 44 and 48 pages within illustrated soft card covers. They have an average of 50 monochrome photographic illustrations, and each has a full colour centre-spread depicting a scene from the Division's wartime operations (drawn by official war artists). With the exception of ONE MORE RIVER and TEHERAN TO TRIESTE (which are slightly smaller), these booklets measure 7.0 x 4.75. They were printed at various presses in Bombay and New Delhi, and each contains at least one map. Their titles (as shown on their front covers) are listed below.

THE FIGHTING FIFTH
The History of the 5th Indian Division
As described in much greater detail in Anthony Brett James' book (vide preceding page), the 'Ball of Fire' Division saw active service in East Africa, North Africa, and Burma.

GOLDEN ARROW
The Story of the 7th Indian Division
The role of this Division also is duplicated by a much larger work - the book by Brig M R Roberts noted on the preceding page. However, the booklet gives a good account of Kohima and Imphal and the crossing of the Irrawaddy. In 1945, the Division was flown to Siam, so becoming the first Allied formation to re-enter South East Asia.

ONE MORE RIVER
The Story of the Eighth Indian Division
8th Indian Div started its overseas service in Iraq and then moved, in 1943, to Italy. Landing at Taranto, it pushed up the length of the peninsula in a series of major battles - breaking the Sangor Line, forcing the Rapido and turning the defences at Cassino, breaking the stubborn German resistance at Monte Grande, and, finally, forcing the Po River. It won four VCs along the way.

TEHERAN TO TRIESTE
The Story of the Tenth Indian Division
This booklet deals with 10th Indian Div's exploits in Iraq (under Maj Gen 'Bill' Slim), its role in the Libyan battles leading up to El Alamein, the following two years of garrison duties in Cyprus and Syria, and, finally, its fighting services in the Italian campaign (from Ortona onwards).

BLACK CAT DIVISION
17th Indian Division
This formation was committed to Burma from the early days when the British were in full flight from the invading Japanese. It remained in Burma right through to the end - when the starving remnants of the Japanese Army were making their own desperate retreat.

DAGGER DIVISION
Story of the 19th Indian Division
Raised in late 1941, the 19th was the first 'standard' Indian Division. Its troops were the first to breach the Japanese defence line in Burma and to raise the flag at Fort Dufferin. It crossed the Chindwin in November 1944, driving on to Mandalay and Rangoon during seven months of continuous fighting. The 19th's exploits are graphically described also in John Masters' personal memoir, THE ROAD PAST MANDALAY.

A HAPPY FAMILY
The Story of the 20th Indian Division
One of the few Indian Divisions in 14th Army trained specifically for the war in Burma. Raised in Bangalore in 1942, it commenced active operations in late 1943 and served from Imphal through to the end. It established 14th Army's first bridge-head across the Chindwin and its second such bridge-head across the Irrawaddy. Its final task was to round-up the Japanese in French Indo-China.

THE TWENTY-THIRD INDIAN DIVISION
Burma - Malaya - Java
The 'Fighting Cock' Division is well recorded in the book by Doulton (vide the earlier entry). This booklet gives coverage of the heavy fighting at the Kohima battle, the capture of Tamu, the reoccupation of Malaya in August 1945, and then its strange role on the island of Java - concurrently disarming the Japanese garrison, fighting the insurgent Indonesian nationalists, and caring for 65,000 former internees pending the arrival of a new Dutch administration.

THE STORY OF THE 25th INDIAN DIVISION
The Arakan Campaign
Formed in Southern India in August 1942 for the defence of that area in the event of a Japanese invasion, the 'Ace of Spades' Division had its baptism of fire in Arakan in February 1944. It served throughout the remainder of that campaign, the climax being the battle for Tamandu. Its victorious fight for the Kangaw road-block was considered by many to have been the fiercest battle of the entire Burma war, while its liberation of Akyab was the first convincing proof to the rest of the world that the tide had turned against the Japanese.

TIGER HEAD
The Story of the 26th Indian Division
This is a brief history of the Division said later by the Japanese to have been the opponent which they most feared. The 26th held the Allied monsoon line in the Arakan during two such seasons, repulsing every attack launched against it. Later it made a series of leap-frog landings down the coast to clinch the issue in the Arakan. It was the first Division to enter Rangoon, invading the city from the sea.

It is known that other booklets were published in this series (apart from the ten listed here). As condensed histories, they are all useful - particularly those which relate to Divisions for which no other record was ever produced. Only rarely are these title seen offered for sale. TK-C.

BRIGADES

THE JULLUNDUR BRIGADE IN FRANCE AND FLANDERS
Anon * Kraftwerk Print & Design Pvt Ltd, New Delhi, 1989. Illustrated card, 'Trench fighting and unit badges' motif, green, white, 9.0 x 7.0, vii/58. 36 mono phots, 3 maps, no appendixes, no Index.
* A short but fairly helpful history of the Bde's services on the Western Front from October 1914 to December 1915. It comprised 1st Bn Manchester Regt, 47th Sikhs, and 59th Scinde Rifles. It is not known who sponsored this booklet or why. The narrative describes events which had taken place sixty-five years earlier, so the unknown author should have had ample opportunity in which to compile some appendixes of casualties, awards, statistics, or other innovative material of historical interest. An oddity. R/3 V/2. PC. BDM.

CAVALRY

General Reference

THE INDIAN CAVALRY
History of the Indian Armoured Corps until 1940
Maj Gen Gurchan Singh Sandhu PVSM * Vision Books, New Delhi, 1981. Black, gold, 10.0 x 7.5, -/473. Fp, 8 mono phots, one cld plate, 15 maps, Bibliography, Index. Apps: a series of very helpful tables which detail the dates of raising, the changes of title, and the dates of disbandment or amalgamation of all the early Cavalry Regts, notes on early Volunteer Cavalry, Battle Honours, etc.
* An important book which covers a broad field, and the only substantial work which deals exclusively with India's mounted soldiers. The sub-title, with its reference to the Armoured Corps, is slightly misleading. The author starts with the early years and then traces the evolution of the Cavalry through to the time (1938) when the Indian Army began to mechanise. He includes much fine detail concerning the services of individual Regts during the preceding century and a half, explains the 'sillidar' system and its implications, and analyses the causes and effects of the various major reorganisations. He concludes with an account of the difficult conversion from the horse to the armoured car and the tank at the outbreak of WWII. Sadly, his publishers took little care with the type-setting, and the quality of paper and binding is not good. R/2 V/5. PC. CJP.

THE INDIAN ARMOUR
History of the Indian Armoured Corps, 1941-1971
Maj Gen Gurchan Singh Sandhu PVSM * Vision Books (incorporating Orient Paperbacks), New Delhi, 1987. Black, yellow, 9.5 x 7.0, -/570. 48 mono phots, 19 maps, Bibliography, Index. Apps: list of former Commanders, table of Regtl titles (1922-1971), notes on armoured fighting vehicles (armoured cars and tanks) used by the Corps, notes on unit class compositions, idem training establishments.
* Although not titled as such, this is effectively Volume II of the work described in the preceding entry. Written by the same author, it covers all aspects of the Armoured Corps in WWII (especially its work in Italy and Burma), the trauma of Partition, and the various Indo-Pakistan conflicts through to 1971. Like the first book, it is not particularly well produced, but it is deeply researched, well documented, readable, and packed with information. R/2 V/5. PC. CJP.

The Bodyguards

HISTORICAL RECORDS OF THE GOVERNOR-GENERAL'S BODYGUARD
Historical Records of the Viceroy's Body-guard
Lieut V C P Hodson * W Thacker & Co, London, 1910. Red, gold, 'Regtl crest and roll of Battle Honours' motif, 10.0 x 7.5, xiv/414. Fp, 7 cld plates, 12 mono phots (incl reproductions of lithographic portraits), no maps (but two of the cld plates are town plans), Bibliography, Glossary, Index. Apps: 16 various, incl war services of the Corps, alphabetical list of former officers, list of medical officers, idem veterinary surgeons, biographical notes on serving British officers, list of European Riding Masters and NCOs, idem Native Officers, etc.
* Described as an 'unofficial history' of the Bodyguard from its formation in 1773 to the end of 1908, this is a detailed work which certainly ranks as a formal history. Minutes from 'Secret Consultations' describe the raising and organisation of the Corps, and the early squabbles between Warren Hastings and General Clavering. The Bodyguard took part in many actions, and these are described in some detail (including little-known affairs such as the Battle of St George, on 23 April 1774). The Glossary and Bibliography are very good, with many items not often mentioned elsewhere. The Corps' principal campaigns were Mysore (1791-1792), Java (1811), the Mahratta Wars (1815-1818), the First Burmese

War (1824-1826), Gwalior (1843), the Sikh Wars (1845-1846 and 1848-1849), and the Burma War of 1885-1887. Occasionally there is confusion over the title of this excellent book. The outer casing refers to 'The Viceroy's Body-guard' (which highlights the other problem - Body-guard, Body Guard, Bodyguard). At the Durbar held in Allahabad on 1 November 1858, it was proclaimed that the Queen would assume henceforth the Government of India, and that her Governor-General would be restyled 'Viceroy and Governor-General'. The Corps, however, continued to be known as 'The Governor General's Bodyguard'. Following the reorganisations of 1862, the title 'Governor General's Bodyguard' came into general use, albeit without an official authorisation. The dedication at the front of the book is to the Earl of Minto - 'Viceroy and Governor-General of India' - so it seems that, as late as 1910, the author still felt it prudent to hedge his bets by using both titles.
R/4 V/5. NAM/IOL/RMAS. PJE/BR/CJP.
Note: the IOL holds a short article from THE CAVALRY JOURNAL, dated 1939, which may be useful for further research. It is entitled INDIA'S HOUSEHOLD CAVALRY - THE BODY-GUARDS.

SERVICES OF THE MADRAS BODY GUARD AND ITS OFFICERS
H Morgan * Published at Fort St George, 1866. Brown leather, gold, scrolled edgings, 9.5 x 6.0, -/23. No ills, no maps, no appendixes, no Index.
* This is mainly a compilation of extracts from General Orders between 1793 and 1859. The text gives a precise summary of the unit's services during that period but, with only twenty-three pages, the coverage is very superficial and of limited interest. R/5 V/2. BM. PJE.

SERVICES OF THE BODY GUARD OF HIS EXCELLENCY THE GOVERNOR OF MADRAS
Anon * Lawrence Asylum Press, Madras, 1886. Brown leather, gold, 8.25 x 5.25, -/34. No ills, no maps, no Index. Apps: list of former Commandants, idem Adjutants.
* A short history of the Corps, based upon General Orders, from its inception in February 1783 to 1886. It is therefore little more than an update on the item described in the preceding entry. The strength of the Corps at that time was 200 officers and men, half being Cavalry and half Infantry.
R/5 V/2. IOL. RGB.

RECORDS OF THE BODY GUARD OF HIS EXCELLENCY THE GOVERNOR OF MADRAS
Capt L W C Kerrich * Addison & Co, Madras, 1894. Maroon, gold, 9.0 x 5.5, -/47. No ills, no maps, no Index. Apps: list of former Commandants, idem Adjutants.
* Yet another amalgam of extracts from official documents, updated to 1894, but still lacking any worthwhile reference value or human interest. The period covered is again from formation in 1783 onwards. R/4 V/2. NAM. PJE.

RECORDS OF THE BODY GUARD OF H.E. THE GOVERNOR OF MADRAS
Capt R M Worgan * Hoe & Co, The Premier Press, Madras, 1910. Red, gold, Regtl crest, 8.5 x 5.0, -/75. No ills, no maps, no appendixes. Apps: list of Commandants (1783-1910), idem Adjutants (1826-1910).
* A better effort, with a more interesting selection of extracts from official documents, arranged chronologically and dealing with matters such as active services, pay, uniforms, etc. There is some reference to the Corps' role in the expedition against Tipu Sultan led by Lord Cornwallis in 1791-1792, and then in the 1801 expedition against the Poligars in Southern Madras. R/4 V/3. PC. JRS.

HISTORICAL RECORD OF THE BODY GUARD OF H.E. THE GOVERNOR OF MADRAS
Capt A E G Machonochie * Vest & Co, Madras, 1922. Red, gold, 8.5 x 5.5, -/95. No ills, no maps, no Index. Apps: list of former Commandants, idem Adjutants.
* Simply another update on the four items recorded above. This author follows slavishly the established format, thereby missing the chance to breath life and interest into the Corps' history. A curiously old-fashioned effort for a book published in 1922. R/4 V/3. NAM. PJE.

CAVALRY REGIMENTS

SKINNER'S HORSE (1st DUKE OF YORK'S OWN CAVALRY)

A SHORT HISTORY OF THE 1st DUKE OF YORK'S OWN LANCERS (SKINNER'S HORSE) 1803-1908

Maj H Roberts * Indian Daily Telegraph Press, Lucknow, 1908. Paper covers, green, black, 8.5 x 5.5, -/26. No maps, no ills, no appendixes, no Index.
* A general record, useful mainly as a quick reference source. Presumably it was produced for the instruction of young newly-joined officers. R/4 V/1. NAM. PJE.
Note: for an understanding of the origins of the Regt, reference should be made to SKINNER OF SKINNER'S HORSE, by Philip Mason CIE OBE (published by André Deutsch, 1979). The author had been asked by a leading American producer to write the 'book' for a film which he wanted to make about the famous soldier's life and times. The draft, based upon Mason's customary meticulous research, had been completed when plans for the film were abandoned. The story was published subsequently by André Deutsch as an historical novel - essentially factual but with fictional dialogue woven in. The book is accurate as a description of Skinner's private life and his military career.

SKINNER'S HORSE
The History of the 1st Duke of York's Own Lancers (Skinner's Horse) and The 3rd Skinner's Horse, now Amalgamated under the Designation, The 1st Duke of York's Own Skinner's Horse

Maj A M Daniels OBE * Hugh Rees Ltd, London, 1925. Blue, gold, 8.5 x 5.5, xvi/181. No ills, no maps, no Index. Apps: H&A (all ranks, with Gazette details), list of Commandants, idem officers serving in 1922, notes on the evolution of the Regt.
* A clear narrative, with plenty of detail of every kind. The early campaigns receive good coverage, followed by an interesting account of WWI services in France and on the NWF. The story concludes with the Third Afghan War. Extracts from the Bengal and Indian Army Lists for the years 1839, 1844, 1857, 1914 and 1923 are inserted in the main text. The 1st and 3rd Lancers were amalgamated in 1921 to form the 1st/3rd Cavalry. The title was changed again, in 1922, to the 1st Duke of York's Own Skinner's Horse. R/4 V/4. UWML/RMAS. BCC/RP.

THE LAST DAYS OF HORSED CAVALRY
An Account of Skinner's Horse between the Wars

Lieut Col E G Haynes * Facsimile TS, never formally published, seen in soft card bindings, 12.0 x 8.0, -/26. No ills, one map (showing Stations), no Index. Apps: list of officers (1930s).
* The author was Adjutant of the Regt from 1932 to 1936. This brief record describes the typical activities of a Cavalry Regt between 1920 and 1939.
R/5 V/2. IOL. CRDG.
Note: a further insight into Regtl life, during the period 1918-1942, can be found in HINDU HORSEMAN, by Lieut Col Denzil Holder (Picton Publishing, Chippenham, 1986). This is a good autobiography, concerned mainly with people, places and polo. The author was wounded in Eritrea and invalided from the Army in 1946.

SKINNER'S HORSE

Christopher Rothero * Printed by Staples Printers, Kettering, for Almark Publishing Co Ltd, New Malden, Surrey, 1979. Illustrated soft card, 'Group of officers and Sowars' motif, 7.25 x 8.25 (landscape), -/48. 17 pages of good black-and-white sketches, 6 pages of colour drawings of uniforms, Glossary, Bibliography, no Index.
* This is a different kind of unit history. Only three pages are devoted to narrative. The majority are given to excellently captioned illustrations of the Regt's uniforms, equipment and accoutrements (including its saddlery). An attractive record. R/2 V/3. PC. CRDG.

SWORN TO DIE

Lieut Col M A R Skinner * Lancer International, New Delhi, 1984. Patinated illustrated boards, 'Mounted Sowar' motif, full colour, 10.75 x 7.25, -/252. 20 mono phots, one cld plate, 34 line drawings and sketches, 3 maps (one printed in the text, two on the end-papers), Index. Apps: Roll of Honour (WWII and 1971), H&A (WWII and 1971), list of British and Indian officers serving at the time of amalgamation (May 1921), roll of recipients of the 1935 Jubilee Medal, idem the 1937 Coronation Medal, list of former COs, idem former officers (1921-1939).
* The first sixty-one pages cover the period 1921 through to 1939 and therefore repeat much which appears in the accounts by Haynes and Holder (vide preceding entries). The bulk of the book is then devoted to WWII. The Regt lost its horses and became mechanised in 1939. Equipped with light vehicles, it operated as a reconnaissance unit in the East Africa campaign and in the Western Desert with 4th Indian Div. After a spell on Cyprus and with Paiforce, it moved to Italy in June 1944 as an element of 10th Indian Div. The book concludes with an 11-page epilogue covering Partition and the Regt's participation in the 1948 Hyderabad Police Action and in the 1965 and 1971 wars with Pakistan. It includes details of casualties and awards for 1971. R/3 V/4. RMAS. RP.
Note: the author was a great-great-grandson of the Regt's founder. He compiled what is in effect Volume II of the Regt's history.

2nd ROYAL LANCERS (GARDNER'S HORSE)

DIGEST OF SERVICES OF IV CAVALRY

Anon * Punjab Frontier Press, Peshawar, 1920. Red, black, 7.0 x 5.5, -/138. No ills, no maps, no Index. Apps: list of former COs, idem officers, 'Who's Who' of IV Cavalry.
* A basic historical record, written in both English and Hindi. The Regt traced its origins back to 1838 and Cavalry of the Oudh Auxiliary Force. Absorbed into the Bengal Army in 1840 as the 6th Bengal Irregular Cavalry, it was subsequently designated 4th Regt of Bengal Cavalry (1861), later 4th Cavalry (1904), then 2nd Lancers (Gardner's Horse) at amalgamation with the 2nd Lancers in 1922.
R/5 V/3. USII. NKR/OSS.
Note: reference may be made to A SQUIRE OF HINDOOSTAN, by Narindar Saroop CBE (Nottingham Court Press, London, 1987), this being a biography of Col William Linneaus Gardner, founder of the 2nd Bengal Local Horse in 1803.

A BRIEF HISTORY OF THE 2nd LANCERS (GARDNER'S HORSE)
From 12th May 1809 to 12th May 1909

Anon * Pioneer Press, Allahabad, 1909. Royal blue, gold, 7.5 x 5.0, -/53. No ills, no maps, no Index. Apps: list of former officers, notes on the life of Col Gardner, nominal roll of British officers and VCOs serving in May 1909.
* The text is based mainly upon Regtl records and is essentially a summary of Stations and active service presented in diary form. Typically of its genre, it lacks colour and human interest. R/4 V/2. NAM. PJE.

A HISTORY OF THE 2nd LANCERS (GARDNER'S HORSE)
From 1809 to 1922

Capt D E Whitworth MC * Sifton Praed & Co Ltd, London, 1924. Khaki, blue, Regtl crest on front and rear covers, 8.5 x 5.5, xi/228. 3 sketches, 3 maps (bound in at the rear), no Index. Apps: H&A (WWI), notes on the war services of officers, notes regarding operations with the Mhow Cavalry Bde (November-December 1917), notes on horses, idem sillidar cavalry.
* The first forty-five pages are a synopsis for the period 1809-1914. The bulk of the narrative then deals with WWI services in good detail (the Western Front, Gaza, and the Palestine campaign). An attractive book, nicely printed and bound, and full of well presented information. R/4 V/4. NAM/RMAS. CSM/RGH.

A HISTORY OF THE 2nd ROYAL LANCERS (GARDNER'S HORSE)
Brig E W D Vaughan CB DSO MC * Printed by the Harrow Observer, Harrow, for Sifton Praed & Co Ltd, London, 1951. Blue, gold, Regtl crest, 8.5 x 5.5, xi/196. No ills, 4 maps (bound in at the rear), no Index. Apps: Roll of Honour (WWII), H&A (WWII), list of former COs, lists of former British officers and of VCOs, nominal roll of personnel taken POW with notes on those who escaped.
* The narrative deals mainly with WWII fighting in the Western Desert where the Regt was twice destroyed (at El Mechile and at Bir Hacheim). Later reformed, it saw service in Palestine, and in Iran and Iraq with Paiforce. A sound readable book. The Western Desert maps are particularly helpful, but the lack of an Index is lamentable. R/3 V/4. NAM/RMAS. RP.

3rd CAVALRY

ARMY LISTS - 5th CAVALRY
Anon * Dhoomi Dharam Das, Military Printers, New Delhi, presumably for the Regt, n.d. (c.1922). Seen in library binding, 9.75 x 5.5, -/63. No ills, no maps, no appendixes, no Index.
* This is nothing more than a reprint of Bengal and Indian Army Lists for the 5th Cavalry between 1841 and January 1922. British officers are listed, Indian officers are not, and this discrimination severely limits the worth of the book as a source of reference. The 5th Cavalry was merged in 1921 with the 8th Cavalry to form the 3rd Cavalry. R/4 V/1. PC. CJP.

REGIMENTAL STANDING ORDERS, 8th CAVALRY
Anon * R.A. Press, Jhansi, n.d. (c.1899). Red, gold, 8.0 x 5.0, ii/61/2 (the last two being the Index). Two lithograph diagrams of kit inspection layouts, no appendixes, no Index.
* Not a unit history, but the only known publication relating directly to the Regt. As might be expected in an item of this type, it contains nothing more than precise instructions regarding the duties to be performed by officers and men under various prescribed circumstances - inspection parades, issues of equipment, the posting of sentries, Regtl holidays, and so forth. R/5 V/1. PC. BDM.
Note: the 8th Cavalry was raised at Sultanpur (Oudh) in 1846 as the 17th Regt of Bengal Irregular Cavalry. A year later it was renumbered the 18th. It became the 8th Regt of Bengal Cavalry in 1861 and retained this number right through to the amalgamation, in 1921, with the similarly senior 5th Cavalry.

NOBODY'S OWN
The History of the 3rd Cavalry and its Predecessors, 1841-1945
Brig H W Picken * Published privately in Eastbourne, no details shown, 1962. Sky blue, gold, Regtl crest, 10.25 x 8.0, vi/209. 7 mono phots, one line drawing, one diagram showing the parade arrangements for the execution of mutineers, 8 maps, no appendixes, no Index.
* The title of the book reflects the facts that the 3rd was one of those few Regts which did not have a title which incorporated a reference to a member of the Royal family. This is a comprehensive and humorous account of the stated period, marred only by the lack of an Index. The Regt was the only Indian Cavalry unit to be captured at the surrender of Singapore. The 450 officers and men who survived were returned to India in 1945 and some continued in service when the Regt was then reconstituted. R/3 V/4. NAM. PJE.

HODSON'S HORSE (4th DUKE OF CAMBRIDGE'S OWN LANCERS)

10th DUKE OF CAMBRIDGE'S OWN LANCERS (HODSON'S HORSE)
Nominal Rolls, 1857–1912
Anon * Thacker Spink & Co, Calcutta, 1913. Royal blue with red quarters, gold, 10.0 x 6.5, -/94. No ills, no maps, no appendixes, no Index.
* This is a compendium of extracts from official Bengal and Indian Army Lists, showing the names of officers serving in each year and the Stations at which the Regt was at that time serving. A very bare and basic source. R/4 V/1. NAM. PJE.

HODSON'S HORSE [LATE 9th HODSON'S HORSE AND 10th D.C.O. LANCERS (HODSON'S HORSE)]
Nominal Roll of Officers who have Served with the Regiment, 1857–1928
Anon * Printed by The Civil & Military Gazette, Lahore, presumably for the Regt, 1929. Blue boards with red spine, gold, 10.0 x 6.75, -/330. No ills, no maps, no appendixes, Glossary, no Index.
* Like the preceding entry, this is nothing more than a series of extracts from Bengal Army and Indian Army Lists. However, it covers all the British officers who ever served with the original and amalgamated Regts during the stated period. Risaldar-Majors are listed from 1864 onwards and Indian officers from 1877 onwards. It is obviously more comprehensive than the 1913 publication, and would certainly be useful to genealogists or medal collectors wishing to trace any officer's services and promotions. R/5 V/2. PC. CJP.

WITH HODSON'S HORSE IN PALESTINE
Anon (shown as 'C.H.R.' - known to have been C H Rowcroft) * Thacker & Co Ltd, Bombay, n.d. (c.1919). Card covers, red cloth spine, black, 7.0 x 5.0, -/57. No ills, 5 maps (folding, bound in), no Index. Apps: H&A.
* The Regt served in Palestine from March 1918, and it is evident that the author was one of the officers who were there at the time. This booklet is useful, but to only a limited extent. R/5 V/3. NAM. PJE.

NARRATIVE OF WAR SERVICE, 9th HODSON'S HORSE, 1914–1921
Anon * Unpublished facsimile TS, n.d. (c.1922). Seen in library binding, black, gold, 13.0 x 9.0, -/54 (plus appendix pages, not numbered). No ills, 2 sketch maps, no Index. Apps: H&A, list of former officers, quotations from a selection of letters and Orders, an account of the Battle of Cambrai.
* A useful record of the 9th Hodson's Horse in France and Flanders from October 1914 to February 1918. The Regt then moved to Palestine and took part in the last great offensive against the Turks. The H&A appendix appears to be complete. R/4 V/3. NAM. PJE.

HODSON'S HORSE
Maj F G Cardew OBE * William Blackwood & Sons Ltd, Edinburgh and London, 1928. Blue, gold, 'Lancer' motif, 9.5 x 6.5, viii/402. Fp, 8 mono phots, 14 maps (6 printed in the text, 8 bound in), Glossary, Index. Apps: H&A (for all campaigns, for both founder Regts, from 1857 to WWI inclusive), list of former COs (with biographical notes), list of former officers (some with biographical notes), list of former Risaldar-Majors, notes on casualties, etc.
* A magnificent history - well written, authoritative, and finely produced. It contains good accounts of service during the Mutiny, the Second Afghan War, and WWI (the Western Front, Palestine, and Mesopotamia). This book is not only the primary source of reference for Hodson's Horse, it is also one of the best of all Indian Army histories. R/3 V/5. NAM/RMAS. RGH/RP.
Note: additional sources are THE LIFE OF HODSON OF HODSON'S HORSE, by Capt L J Trotter (Dutton's Everyman Library, Newcastle, 1927), and RIDER ON A GREY HORSE, by B J Clark (Cassell, London, 1958).

REGIMENTAL HISTORY - HODSON'S HORSE
Notes Covering the Period from the Conclusion of Volume I in 1921 to the End of 1939, the Arrival of the Regiment at Meerut
L E L Maxwell (Lieut Col) * Wellington Press, Meerut, 1939. Soft card, green, dark blue, 12.5 x 8.0, -/31. No ills, no maps, no appendixes, no Index.
* A brief summary of routine peacetime duties while the Regt was stationed first at Lahore (1921-1928) and later at Kohat (1928-1933), Sialkot (1933-1937), and Loralai (1937-1939). Presumably the author (who rose to command the Regt in 1944-1945), was referring to Cardew's major work (vide preceding entry) when he wrote 'Volume I' in his sub-title. Certainly his notes are a useful adjunct. In the event, a full-blown 'Volume II', covering the period through to 1947, was never produced. R/5 V/2. PC. BDM.
Note: sometime around 1930, Paramount Pictures of Hollywood decided to make a film version of LIVES OF A BENGAL LANCER, by Maj F Yeats-Brown. The Director insisted upon total authenticity. His location teams spent five years filming on the NWF and elsewhere in India, and Hodson's Horse was ordered to provide men and horses for many of the background sequences. The film, starring Gary Cooper and Franchot Tone, was launched in 1935. Many thousands of feet of film were never used in the final edited version. If these could now be found, they would be a unique record of the Regt (indeed, of all Indian Cavalry Regts) of that period.

A SHORT HISTORY OF HODSON'S HORSE
Lt Cdr the Hon Charles Willoughby RN (Retired) * Gale & Polden Ltd, Aldershot, n.d. (1946). Stiff card, blue, black, Regtl crest, 8.0 x 5.5, iii/57. Fp, no ills, no maps, no Index. Apps: list of Honorary Colonels, idem former COs.
* A very compressed but easily readable version of the Regt's history and lineage. Presumably intended for the instruction of newly-joined officers. R/3 V/2. NAM. PJE.
Note: the author, Willoughby, was the brother of Lord Middleton MC, an officer who served with the Regt from 1907 to 1923.

PROBYN'S HORSE (5th KING EDWARD VII's OWN LANCERS)

HISTORICAL RECORD OF THE SERVICES OF THE 11th BENGAL LANCERS (LATE 1st SIKH IRREGULAR CAVALRY), 1857-1872
With Supplement, Historical Record of the Services of the 11th Prince of Wales's Own Bengal Lancers, from March 1870 to March 1876
Anon * Government Press, Calcutta, n.d. (c.1876). Soft card, pink, black, 9.75 x 7.5, -/16/ii. No ills, no maps, no appendixes, no Index.
* The material is arranged in two sections. Part I covers briefly the services of 11th Bengal Lancers (1857-1870) in diary form, and including all its moves and Stations (with services during the Mutiny, Second China War, and the Umbeyla expedition). Part II deals mainly with changes of title and the appointment of the Prince of Wales as Honorary Colonel. The 11th Lancers and the 12th Cavalry were amalgamated in 1921 to form the 5th King Edward's Own Probyn's Horse.
R/5 V/2. MODL. AMM.

REGIMENTAL LISTS, XI KING EDWARD'S OWN LANCERS (PROBYN'S HORSE), 1857-1907
1st Regiment of Sikh Irregular Cavalry, XI Prince of Wales's Own Bengal Lancers
Gen Sir W R Birdwood GCMG KCB KCSI CIE DSO * Government of India Central Printing Office, Delhi, 1907. Red, gold, 9.5 x 6.5, -/234. No ills, no maps, no Index. Apps: war services of British officers, extracts from General Orders and Indian Army Orders (1857-1906).
* A compendium of extracts from Bengal Army and Indian Army Lists which made reference to the Regt and its forebears. British officers and Risaldars are listed from 1857 onwards, VCOs from 1876. The author commanded the Regt from 1875 to 1884. His hand-written note in a surviving 'presentation' copy states that he compiled this work 'on the occasion of the celebration of the Jubilee of my Regiment at Rawalpindi, in March 1907'. R/4 V/3. NAM. PJE/CJP.

A HISTORY OF THE XI KING EDWARD'S OWN LANCERS (PROBYN'S HORSE)
Capt E L Maxwell * A C Curtis Ltd, Guildford, 1914. Light maroon and dark red, gold, Regtl crest, 10.0 x 8.0, xi/163. Fp, 18 mono phots, 4 maps (bound in, two folding), no Index. Apps: list of former COs (1857-1909), verbatim letters from the Regt's original Letter Book.
* This is a book which began as a condensed history for use in the Regtl school and which later blossomed into a full-scale history. It suffers, according to the author, from 'the incomplete nature of the records', but it nevertheless paints a clear picture of the raising of the Regt in 1857, the death of Capt Wale, the appointment of Maj D M Probyn as Commandant, service in China under Hope Grant, the Umbeyla expedition, and so forth. A useful book, long on fine detail, short on historical perspective. R/4 V/4. NAM. BRW/RGH.
Note: an extremely rare additional source is SOUVENIR OF THE JUBILEE OF THE XI, KING EDWARD'S OWN LANCERS (PROBYN'S HORSE), RAWAL PINDI, 1907 (anon, printed for the Regt in 1907 by T & A Constable, Edinburgh). This is a presentation piece containing a compressed narrative history and 29 captioned mono phots. These serve to balance the lack of illustrations in other published records of the Regt. Some of them were in fact used by Maxwell in his 1914 history (vide preceding entry). It is thought that no more than 20 or 30 copies of this SOUVENIR were produced. Presumably they were intended for officers then serving, plus a few friends of the Regt.

NOTES ON THE SERVICES OF THE XII CAVALRY
Anon * The Civil & Military Gazette, Lahore, 1908. Black, gold, Regtl crest, 7.0 x 5.0, -/21. No ills, no maps, no appendixes, no Index.
* A very, very condensed description of the Regt's services during the Mutiny, Abyssinia, and Second Afghan campaigns. The 12th Cavalry amalgamated with the 11th Lancers in 1921. R/4 V/1. NAM. PJE.

THE HISTORY OF PROBYN'S HORSE (5th KING EDWARD'S OWN LANCERS)
Maj C A Boyle DSO * Gale & Polden Ltd, Aldershot, 1929. Maroon, with very fine Regtl crest on front cover in silver, gold, blue and scarlet, 10.0 x 7.5, xv/98. Fp, one other mono phot, 9 maps (cld, folding, bound in), no Index. Apps: Roll of Honour, H&A, list of former officers, notes on the career of Sir Dighton Probyn VC, idem Sir Hugh Gough VC.
* The narrative covers the entire period from the Mutiny through to the time of the amalgamation in just eighty-one pages of main narrative, hence there is little detail. The maps and appendixes are probably the most useful features.
R/4 V/3. IOL. RGH.

PROBYNABAD STUD FARM
The Property of Probyn's Horse (5th King Edward VII's Own Lancers)
Lieut Col E S MacL Prinsep * The Civil & Military Gazette Ltd, Lahore, April 1938. Full calfskin, brown, gold, with ribbon having the Regtl colours pasted diagonally across the front cover, 9.0 x 5.5, -/88. 2 mono phots, no maps, no appendixes, no Index.
* A publication which covers an aspect of horsed soldiering often overlooked by historians. It is the stud book for the Regt's own breeding programme for the entire period from 1864 to 1938. Probynabad was located near Bannu, on the NWF. The book gives details of sixty-six different brood mare lines maintained at the farm, and for all the stallions which stood there. An interesting volume for horsemen and specialist cavalry researchers. R/5 V/4. RMAS. RP.
Note: ironically, only two years after the book was published, the Regt lost its horse-mounted status and became mechanised.

AN ACCOUNT OF THE OPERATIONS IN BURMA CARRIED OUT BY PROBYN'S HORSE DURING FEBRUARY, MARCH AND APRIL, 1945
Maj B H Mylne MBE * Publication details not shown, printed in Rangoon, 1945. Seen in black boards with red spine, probably rebound, 10.0 x 6.0, -/76. 5 mono phots (of poor quality), H&A (all ranks), list of officers who served in the campaign.
* The Regt was equipped with Sherman tanks and the narrative describes their advance from Meiktila to Rangoon. A well written account, with good detail and with many references to individuals. The maps are crudely printed, but they show all the key features and are most helpful in supporting the narrative.
R/4 V/4. RMAS. RP.

6th DUKE OF CONNAUGHT'S OWN LANCERS (WATSON'S HORSE)

HISTORY OF THE 13th DUKE OF CONNAUGHT'S OWN LANCERS (WATSON'S HORSE) Formerly the 4th Sikh Cavalry, from the Date they were Raised in March 1858 to September 1908
Names of author(s), printers and publishers not known due to damage to the only copy seen. Apparently produced by the Regt for the instruction of young officers, c.1909. Format: 6.5 x 5.0, -/38. No ills, no maps, no Index. Apps: list of former COs, notes on the war services of the Regt.
* This is no more than a sketchy pamphlet, but it is the only published record of the 13th Lancers. The Regt has a complex and interesting history but, sadly, it never sponsored a full-blown history of itself. The Regt was raised in 1858 by Lieut H C Cattley as the 4th Sikh Irregular Horse. Lieut John Watson was associated with it for eleven years, giving it the soubriquet 'Watson's Horse', but this title was not formally authorised until 1904. By then, the Regt had ceased to be widely known by that name. The addition of 'Duke of Connaught's' to the title was the result of a dashing action by the Regt at Tel-el-Kebir (Egypt) in 1882. The battle was witnessed by the Duke who let it be known that he wished to be appointed the Regt's Colonel. This honour was confirmed two years later. In 1921, the 13th Lancers amalgamated with the 16th Cavalry to form the 13th/16th Cavalry. This was changed to 6th Lancers in the following year.
R/5 V/2. NAM. PJE/RS.

THE 6th DUKE OF CONNAUGHT'S OWN LANCERS IN ITALY September 1943 - May 1945
Maj F Brock * Printed by William Brown & Davis, Durban, South Africa, privately for the author, 1948. Soft card covers, fawn, black, 8.5 x 5.5, -/48. No ills, 5 maps (folding, bound in), no Index. Apps: H&A, summary of casualties.
* A readable account, with many junior officers and Indian ORs mentioned. It is based upon the Regtl War Diary and is therefore accurate and reliable.
R/4 V/4. PC. AGB.

THE LAST OF THE BENGAL LANCERS
Francis Ingall (Brigadier) * Leo Cooper, London, 1988. Blue, gold, 9.25 x 5.75, 19 mono phots, no maps, no appendixes, Index.
* The author commanded the Regt in Italy and this is his personal story. It makes no pretence at being a history of the 6th Lancers, but the descriptions of Frontier soldiering in the 1930s are historically and technically interesting. The coverage of the WWII period is patchy (or even entirely absent for the first half of the war), but Ingall was given the task of establishing, at Partition, the Pakistan Military Academy. This period is described in some detail, and is a unique account. The book is amusing and has value as a secondary source.
R/1 V/2. PC. RP.

7th LIGHT CAVALRY

HISTORY, VALOUR AND TRADITIONS OF THE 7th LIGHT CAVALRY, 1784-1984
Anon * Lancer International, New Delhi, 1984. Illustrated stiff card, full colour, 'Dismounted Sowar and Regtl crest' motif, 9.0 x 6.0, -/16. No ills, no maps, no Index. Apps: notes on awards, Battle Honours.
* An extremely condensed account of 3rd Madras Light Cavalry, later 28th Light Cavalry, later 7th Light Cavalry. R/3 V/1. PC. BDM.

THE 28th LIGHT CAVALRY IN PERSIA AND RUSSIAN TURKISTAN, 1915-1920
Maj J A C Kreyer and Maj G Uloth * Slatter & Rose Ltd, Oxford, for the Regt. 1926. Dark blue, gold, Regtl crest, 9.0 x 6.5, xx/203. Fp, 47 mono phots, 2 maps, no Index. Apps: Roll of Honour, H&A, list of British officers who served during that period, idem Indian officers.
* A good easily readable account of the period stated in the title. This is the only substantial record of the 28th Light Cavalry prior to its 1922 redesignation as the 7th Light Cavalry. Unlike most Indian Cavalry, it was not sent to France or to Egypt. Instead, in mid-1915, it was sent to East Persia. The task was to patrol the frontier and to prevent German infiltration. When the Russian Revolution broke out, the Regt moved north into Trans-Caspia and there it fought against the Bolsheviks. It later received the Battle Honour 'Merv' in recognition of the action fought at that location. The Regt could claim to be the only Indian Cavalry unit ever to have fought the Red Army. R/4 V/4. NAM. PJE.

WE LEAD
7th Light Cavalry, 1784-1990
Lieut Col C L Proudfoot * Lancer International, New Delhi, 1991. Illustrated boards, full colour, 'Mounted Sowar and Regtl crest' motif, 9.5 x 6.5, vi/258. Fp (badges), 38 mono phots, 16 cld ills, 10 maps (bound in), Index. Apps: H&A, list of officers, idem Risaldar Majors, notes on Battle Honours, the Guidon, biographical notes on Regtl sportsmen.
* This is the only comprehensive account of the Regt and its forebears ever written. The author went a long way towards rectifying the earlier neglect. His book has an enjoyable and well researched narrative which covers, in uniform depth, the raising of the Regt, its services as the Madras Lancers, the campaigns of the 19th Century (under various designations), the East Persia and Russia period, and its work in WWII. It fought in Burma, mounted first on Stuart light tanks, later on Shermans. The story then continues with the post-Independence years when the Regt, having retained its 1922 number, fought in each of the wars with Pakistan. In Kashmir it operated in the mountains at elevations up to 11,600 feet - a record by any standard. The illustrations and maps are helpful and well presented. R/2 V/5. PC. RWH.

8th KING GEORGE V's OWN LIGHT CAVALRY

DIARY OF THE SERVICES OF THE 1st MADRAS LANCERS, AND A TROOP EACH OF THE 3rd AND 4th MADRAS LIGHT CAVALRY ATTACHED, DURING OPERATIONS IN UPPER BURMA, 1886-87 AND 1887-88
Anon (stated to have been Lieut H L B Acton) * Lawrence Asylum Press, Madras, 1889. Black boards with brown spine and quarters, gold, Regtl crest, 9.5 x 6.5, -/234. No ills, no maps, no Index. Apps: list of men invalided back to India, idem men who died of disease in Burma, idem horses which died in Burma.
* A factual straightforward account of the Regt's part in the extensive campaign to deal with the chaos caused by King Thebaw, and to put down the banditry which was rife in the country at that time. The 1st Lancers became the 26th Light Cavalry in 1903, then amalgamated with the 30th Lancers in 1922 to form the 8th Light Cavalry. The narrative is based upon Regtl records and is thought to be entirely reliable. R/4 V/3. NAM. PJE.

HISTORY OF THE THIRTIETH LANCERS, GORDON'S HORSE
Former Titles: 4th Nizam's Cavalry; 4th Cavalry, Nizam's Contingent; 4th Lancers, Hyderabad Contingent
Maj E A Stotherd * Gale & Polden Ltd, Aldershot, 1911. Dark green, gold, Regtl crest, 7.5 x 5.0, vi/207. Fp, 14 mono phots, one map, Index. Apps: list of officers serving on 1.1.1911, plus a list of all former officers (both lists showing their individual service details).
* The 4th Nizam's Cavalry was raised in 1826 by Capt Sir John Gordon, an officer of the Coldstream Guards. Thereafter it took part in numerous 19th Century campaigns and was for many years almost continuously in action against minor warlords and minor criminal gangs in Central India. It became the 30th Lancers (Gordon's Horse) in 1903 when the link with Hyderabad was finally broken. A good solid Regtl history, full of detail. R/4 V/4. NAM/IOL/RMAS/RAI. RP/RGB/CJP.

A SUMMARY OF THE WAR DIARY OF THE 26th (K.G.O.) LIGHT CAVALRY, AUGUST 1915 TO OCTOBER 1918
Anon * The Pioneer Press, Allahabad, 1918. Royal blue boards, brown spine and quarters, gold, 8.5 x 5.5, -/92. No ills, one map (folding, bound in at the rear), no Index. Apps: H&A, list of officers attached to the Regt.
* An unadorned account, based directly upon the War Diary, of the Regt's services in WWI in Mesopotamia. R/4 V/3. NAM. PJE.

HISTORY OF 8th KING GEORGE'S OWN LIGHT CAVALRY
H G Rawlinson CIE * Gale & Polden Ltd, Aldershot, 1948. Light green, gold, Regtl crest and colours, 8.75 x 5.5, ix/142. Fp, 3 mono phots, 8 maps, Index. Apps: Roll of Honour (Burma, 1945), H&A (Burma, 1945), list of former COs, verbatim copy of the Order of the Day (2.4.1946).
* Rawlinson compiled a number of Indian Army unit histories (vide the Index of Authors) and this one is researched and compiled to his usual high standard. The narrative is particularly good with regard to the early years of the 26th Light Cavalry and for the services of the 30th Lancers during the Mutiny period. The coverage of WWII operations in Burma is curiously slender by comparison.
R/3 V/4. IOL. VS/CJP.

THE ROYAL DECCAN HORSE (9th HORSE)

HISTORY OF THE 1st LANCERS, HYDERABAD CONTINGENT, FROM 1816 TO 1903
Anon * The Times of India Press, Bombay, 1903. Limp covers, green, white, Regtl crest, 8.25 x 5.5, -/29. No ills, no maps, no Index. Apps: roll of officers serving in July 1903.
* As with so many of these little books produced by Indian Army units at the turn of the century, it is hard to understand their intended purpose. In this example, ninety years of very active service are crammed into less than thirty pages of text. The narrative's historical content, therefore, is no more than skeletal. Lacking most of the usual working appendixes (chronology, Battle Honours, etc), it was not even useful for the instruction of young officers. R/4 V/1. NAM. RP/VS.

A HISTORY OF THE HYDERABAD CONTINGENT
Maj Reginald George Burton * Office of the Superintendent of Government Printing, Calcutta, 1905. Green, gold, Regtl crest, 8.75 x 5.5, -/320/xc. Fp, one sketch (Mahratta camel gun in action), 9 maps and plans (bound in), Index. Apps: statements of unit strengths, notes on active services, list of British Residents (Hyderabad), list of former COs, notes on Treaties, etc.
* In sharp contrast to the preceding entry, this is a well organised and useful book. The Regt evolved from the period when the HEIC was entering into defence treaties with various independent Princely rulers. The Hyderabad Contingent was the only one which retained its original titles through to the major reorganisations of 1903. The author provides a clear explanation of the Regt's complex roots, its services to the HEIC and later the Crown, and in particular its role during the

the Mutiny (pages 143 to 245). There is liberal mention of awards and casualties throughout. Units of the Contingent served in Burma (1886-1887) and in Central Africa in support of British and Colonial African forces (1891-1892). The last three chapters are summaries of each of the Regts of the Contingent, with details of their uniforms and equipment. An admirable compilation. R/3 V/5. PC. CJP.

THE ROYAL DECCAN HORSE IN THE GREAT WAR
Lieut Col E Tennant * Gale & Polden Ltd, Aldershot, 1939. Green boards, Morocco spine and quarters, gold, Regtl crest, 10.75 x 7.5, xvii/181. Fp, no mono phots, 2 cld plates, 5 maps (folding, bound in at the rear), no Index. Apps: Roll of Honour, H&A (all ranks), list of former COs, list of officers (with posting dates).
* The narrative deals with the WWI services of the 20th Royal Deccan Horse and the 29th Lancers (Deccan Horse) in France and Palestine. A beautiful book to handle, it is printed and bound to a very high standard, but is sadly diminished by the lack of an Index. R/3 V/4. RCSL/RMAS. RP.
Note: the version reported here would seem to be a 'de luxe' edition. The same book, identical in all other respects, has been seen with conventional cloth binding (green, gold, Regtl crest).

ROYAL DECCAN HORSE
Account of Operations in Burma, January to May 1945
Anon * Thacker's Press & Directories Ltd, Calcutta, n.d. (c.1946). Soft card, green and yellow, black, Regtl crest, 8.5 x 5.5, ii/43. 5 mono phots, 2 maps (bound in, one folding), no appendixes, no Index.
* Although very brief, this is a superb 'read'. It is composed in the form of a highly detailed diary, and was obviously based upon an amalgam of personal reminiscences and the Regt's own War Diary. R/5 V/4. PC. RJW.

THE GUIDES CAVALRY (10th QUEEN VICTORIA'S OWN FRONTIER FORCE)

HISTORICAL RECORD OF THE SERVICES OF THE (QUEEN'S OWN) CORPS OF GUIDES 1846-1877
Anon * J Gray, Military Department Press, Lahore, February, 1877. Yellow, black, 12.5 x 8.0, -/42. No ills, no maps, no appendixes, no Index.
* This is the earliest known published record of the famous Corps first raised in 1846. Typically of its period, this publication is based upon formal Regtl records. Untypically, these are interesting, informative, and liberally sprinkled with references to individual officers and men, their awards, and their deaths and wounds. They also include some descriptions of fighting actions on the Frontier. R/4 V/4. NAM. PJE/DBP-P.

HISTORICAL RECORDS OF THE SERVICES OF THE (QUEEN'S OWN) CORPS OF GUIDES 1846-1885
Anon * Civil & Military Gazette Press, Lahore, 1885. Yellow, black, 12.5 x 8.0, -/62. 2 mono phots, no maps, no appendixes, no Index.
* Like the 1877 edition mentioned above, this account is based upon Regtl records and quotations from official despatches. Again, the narrative is well interspersed with details of casualties, medals, and officers' comings and goings. The story is updated to include the Corps' role in the Second Afghan War.
R/4 V/4. NAM. PJE/DBP-P.

RECORDS OF THE SERVICES OF THE QUEEN'S OWN CORPS OF GUIDES
Anon * Publication details not shown, 1888. Red, gold, 12.5 x 8.0, -/63. No ills, no maps, no appendixes, no Index.
* This book has substantially the same contents as the 1885 item described above. However, it is one page longer (updating the story 1887), and the binding is red, not yellow. That title, as can be seen, is slightly different.
R/4 V/4. NAM. PJE.

THE STORY OF THE GUIDES

Col G J Younghusband * Printed by R Clay & Sons Ltd, for Macmillan & Co Ltd, London, 1908. Maroon, gold, Regtl crest, 9.0 x 5.75, xvi/207. Fp, 15 mono phots, no maps, no appendixes, Index.

* This is arguably the most widely distributed Regtl history ever produced. At least five editions were published (vide footnote), and each was printed in large numbers. Its success owes more to the dash and brilliance of the actions which it describes than to the writing style of the author. The inspiration of Sir Henry Lawrence and formed in 1846, the Regt fought in almost every campaign on the Afghan frontier and heroically in the suppression of the Mutiny. It was formed as a composite Corps of Cavalry and Infantry with a centralised command, and it remained so until the 1921 reorganisations. During WWI, two further Infantry Bns were raised. In March 1921, the 1st and 2nd Guides Infantry became respectively the 5th and 10th Bns, 12th Frontier Force Regt. The 3rd Guides Infantry was disbanded. At that same time, the Guides Cavalry element became the 10th Queen Victoria's Own Corps of Guides Cavalry (Frontier Force).

R/1 V/4. NAM/RMAS/PCAL. WEL/RLP/CJP.

Note: a 1909 edition appears frequently in sales catalogues. It is slightly longer than the first edition, having xvi/217 pages, but the contents are identical. Two years later (1911) an expanded 'One Shilling' popular edition was published. This was followed (1918) by an even larger edition (xvi/245). Finally, a 'schools' edition was produced in 1921, the text having been abridged by J E Parkinson.

THE HISTORY OF THE GUIDES, 1846-1922

Anon (compiled by various officers) * Gale & Polden Ltd, Aldershot, 1938. Buff, gold, Regtl crest, 9.75 x 7.25, xv/347. Fp, 18 mono phots, 18 maps (11 bound in, 7 loose in rear pocket), no Index. Apps: 14 in total, incl list of former COs, idem officers (1858-1922), idem attached officers (1858-1914 and 1914-1922), idem Risaldar Majors and Subedar Majors, idem Medical Officers, H&A (1914-1921, with details for VC and IOM recipients), notes on Regtl organisation.

* A full and readable history of the Regt for the stated period, the clear narrative supported by maps and illustrations of fine quality. Originally a Corps of Pathans from the area of Mardan, the Guides were always 'at the sharp end' from their earliest days. An exemplary history (but no Index). R/3 V/4. IOL/RMAS. RGB/HLL.

THE HISTORY OF THE GUIDES
10th Cavalry (Q.V.O. Guides), 5/12 Frontier Force Regt (Q.V.O. Guides Infantry), With Pakistan Postscript, Part II : 1922-1947

Lieut Gen Sir George McMunn KCB KCSI DSO * Gale & Polden Ltd, Aldershot, 1950. Buff, gold, Regtl crest, 9.75 x 7.25, xv/208. Fp, 25 mono phots, 2 cld ills, 8 maps (bound in), Index. Apps: list of former Honorary Colonels, idem COs, idem Risaldar Majors (Cavalry) and Subedar Majors (Infantry), various lists of former officers (both Cavalry and Infantry), H&A (with details of the VC award to Capt Robert Shebbeare which was not mentioned in the 1938 history)(vide preceding entry).

* This work continues the story of the Guides from 1922 through to Partition. The author succeeded, very skilfully, in covering the widely divergent experiences of the Cavalry and Infantry elements following their segregation in 1921. The scope of the book is explained in its sub-title. During the period reviewed here, the Guides were much involved in their traditional work - policing the NWF (especially during the Waziristan operations of 1937). Light vehicles replaced the horses in 1940 and the Cavalry operated as a reconnaissance unit in the Western Desert and with Paiforce before converting to armoured cars and then tanks in India. The Guides Infantry units served during WWII in Persia, Iraq, and Kurdestan. Another exemplary history (this time with an Index). R/3 V/5. IOL/RMAS. WEL.

PRINCE ALBERT VICTOR'S OWN CAVALRY (11th FRONTIER FORCE)

HISTORY OF THE 1st PUNJAB CAVALRY
Anon * The Civil & Military Gazette Press, Lahore, 1887. Red, gold, 9.0 x 5.5, -/83/viii. No ills, no maps, no Index. Apps: Roll of Honour, H&A (Indian officers and ORs who received the OBI and the IOM), list of former officers.
* This is a short history for the period 1849 to 1883. It describes the class composition of the Regt, its services during the suppression of the Mutiny, various Frontier actions, and the Second Afghan War. The text is based mainly upon Regtl records and official reports, with numerous British and Indian officers receiving a mention. The Regt became the 21st Cavalry in 1903. R/5 V/3. IOL. BDM.

HISTORY OF THE THIRD REGIMENT, PUNJAB CAVALRY
Anon * Punjab Printing Co, for W Ball & Co, Lahore, 1887. Black, black on white label, 10.0 x 6.5, -/10. No ills, no maps, no appendixes, no Index.
* A short factual history covering the period 1849 to 1885. It is based upon Regtl Orders and official returns, but lacks any sort of useful detail. The 3rd became the 23rd in 1903, and was then amalgamated in 1921 with the 21st to form the 11th Prince Albert Victor's Own Cavalry (Frontier Force). R/5 V/1. NAM. PJE.

HISTORY OF THE 23rd CAVALRY (FRONTIER FORCE), LATE 3rd REGIMENT, PUNJAB CAVALRY
Anon ('compiled by officers of the Regiment') * Publisher's details not shown, n.d. (c.1910). Dark blue, black on white label, 9.5 x 6.5, -/17. No ills, no maps, no Index. Apps: list of personnel, list of Inspections (1849-1908), list of Stations.
* Another brief and very sketchy record, arranged year by year, from the date of raising (1849) through to 1909. An item which is certainly collectable for its rarity, but almost useless as a reference source. R/5 V/1. IOL/NAM. RGB/PJE.

SHORT HISTORY OF THE P.A.V.O. CAVALRY (11th FRONTIER FORCE)
Anon * Publisher's details not shown, n.d. (c.1936). Brown boards with black spine, gold, 7.5 x 5.5, -/21. No ills, no maps, no appendixes, no Index.
* This item is even more useless than that described in the preceding entry. It attempts to summarise the entire period from 1849 to 1935 in just twenty-one pages. It does not succeed. R/5 V/1. PC. RP.

SAM BROWNE'S CAVALRY (12th FRONTIER FORCE)

REGIMENTAL RECORDS, 5th REGIMENT, PUNJAB CAVALRY
Anon * W Ball & Co, Lahore, 1886. Black, blind, 9.5 x 6.5, -/69. No ills, no maps, no appendixes, no Index.
* A brief summary of services, based upon extracts from official records and lacking in detail. The Regt was retitled 25th Cavalry (Frontier Force) in 1903. R/5 V/1. NAM/IOL/USII. PJE/OSS.

HISTORY OF THE SECOND PANJÁB CAVALRY
From 1849 to 1886
Anon * Kegan, Paul, Trench & Co, London, 1888. Red boards, leather spine and quarters, gold, 12.25 x 9.75, -/71. 55 mono phots, no maps, no Index. Apps: list of former officers (with details of their services), list of British officers WIA, list of Stations.
* This is a good readable history, with many individuals of all ranks mentioned in the text. An outstanding feature of the book is the inclusion of fifty-five fully captioned group and single portrait photographs. Some show British officers, but the majority are of Indian officers and senior Indian NCOs. These are particularly impressive and evocative of the period. A pretty book. R/5 V/3. IOL/NAM. PJE.

REGIMENTAL RECORDS FROM 1886 TO 1912, 25th CAVALRY (FRONTIER FORCE)
Anon * Rai Sahib M Gulab Singh, Calcutta, 1912. Black, white, 9.75 x 6.25, -/47. No ills, no maps, no appendixes, no Index.
* A compendium of selected extracts from the Regtl records for the stated period. Useful only when consulted in conjunction with other sources. R/5 V/1. PC. VS.

2nd PUNJAB CAVALRY, REGIMENTAL HISTORY
Anon (compiled by various officers of the Regt) * Seen disbound, unpublished TS, compiled c.1920, 13.0 x 8.0, pages not numbered.
* The narrative is a 'digest of services' arranged in two sections. Part I covers 1849 to 1900 and is sparse but readable. Part II covers 1900 to 1919, and is an amalgam of extracts from various official records. A moderately useful source of reference for researchers having access to the National Army Museum in London. In 1903 the 2nd Punjab Cavalry became the 22nd Cavalry. During WWI it was designated 22nd Sam Browne's Cavalry (Frontier Force). It then combined with the 25th Cavalry to form, in 1922, Sam Browne's Cavalry (12th Frontier Force).
R/4 V/3. NAM. PJE.

SAM BROWNE'S CAVALRY (FRONTIER FORCE)
Anon * Seen disbound in two folders, unpublished TS, titled 'Part I' and 'Part II', and held at the NAM, London. The first folder covers 1849-1880, the second 1886-1933. The narrative is readable and informative. These papers are noted here because they are the only written record of the Regt (post-1920) other than the following list of officers who served in it. R/5 V/3. NAM. PJE.

22nd SAM BROWNE'S CAVALRY (FRONTIER FORCE)
Extracts from the Official Lists, giving Names of Officers who have Served in the Regiment from 1849 onwards (through to 1940)
Anon * Publisher's details not shown, n.d. Seen in brown leather binding, gold, Regtl crest, 13.0 x 8.5, -/142. No ills, no maps, no appendixes, no Index.
* Again, this is a 'one off' Sam Browne item which seems never to have been published formally. The volume consists of nothing more than copies of entries in various Indian Army Lists which have been pasted into a superior quality scrap-book. The lists of names might be useful to a genealogist but, in essence, the research value is nil. Even the title and sub-title are less than helpful. The '22nd' title had disappeared by 1922, so any officers listed 'through to 1940' could not have been serving members of that Regt. Presumably the officers so named (post-1922) were members of the new Sam Browne's Cavalry (12th Frontier Force). In 1937, under new training arrangements for the Indian Cavalry, it was removed from the Order of Battle and assigned as permanent training Regt for the 2nd Cavalry Group based at Ferozepore. In 1940 is was linked with 15th and 20th Lancers as the Indian Armoured Corps Training Centre. R/5 V/1. NAM. PJE.

JOURNAL OF THE LATE GENERAL SIR SAM BROWNE VC GCB KCSI, 1840-1898
Gen Sir Sam Browne (edited by, and published on the initiative of, his daughter) * William Blackwood & Sons Ltd, Edinburgh and London, 1937. Blue, gold, 9.0 x 6.0, -/80. Fp, no other ills, no maps, no appendixes, no Index.
* A terse but interesting account by Browne of his life and service in India. Packed with references to the great and famous of his period. He won his VC, and lost his left arm, during the Mutiny. The sword belt which he designed to overcome the absence of the limb is now in the collection of the National Army Museum. His narrative describes his experiences in the Second Sikh War, the Annexation of the Punjab, the Mutiny, and various Frontier skirmishes. His journal would have made an excellent starting-point for a full Regtl history, but his successors never followed that route. R/3 V/3. RMAS. WMTM/RP.

13th DUKE OF CONNAUGHT'S OWN LANCERS

A BRIEF HISTORICAL SKETCH OF HIS MAJESTY'S 31st DUKE OF CONNAUGHT'S OWN LANCERS, INDIAN ARMY

Col G F Newport-Tinley CB * Bombay Gazette Electrical Printing Works, Bombay, 1910. Grey boards with green quarters, gold, 9.75 x 6.75, iii/57. No ills, no maps, no Index. Apps: H&A (recipients of the OBI and IOM), list of former COs, list of former officers, list of campaigns, notes on uniforms, idem class compositions, list of Stations and movements.

* The words 'brief' and 'sketch' in the title of any unit history are too often an apology in advance for the inadequacy of the contents. This attractive little book is an exception to that general rule. Although very slim, it is full of useful facts, thoughtfully presented. The story covers the period from 1817, when the Regt was first formed as the 1st Regiment of Bombay Light Cavalry, through to 1910. The Regt rendered a wide range of services during that time - the First Afghan War, Second Sikh War, putting down the Mutiny in Central India, postings to Malta and Cyprus in 1878, the Sudan campaign of 1885. The appendixes are relevant and helpful. R/5 V/4. NAM. VS/RGH.

THE SCINDE HORSE (14th PRINCE OF WALES'S OWN CAVALRY)

RECORD BOOK OF THE SCINDE IRREGULAR HORSE
Volumes I and II

Gen John Jacob * Smith, Elder & Co, Cornhill, London, 1856. Matching pair, reversed calfskin, brown, pale blind lettering, 'Battle Honours with Laurel Wreath' motif, ornamental edging, 12.5 x 8.25.

Volume I : iv/340. Covers the period 8 August 1839 to 1 October 1851. Contains a hand-coloured double-page plan of 'The Battle of Meanee', and another of 'The Action at Goojerat', both originally published by James Wyld but thought to be integral to the book as published.

Volume II : vi/283. Covers the period 8 October 1851 to 13 June 1855. Contains a folding lithographed plan in two colours of 'The Town of Jacobabad', printed on glazed linen, and another similar of 'The Upper Sind', this drawn by Capt Macaulay from a map prepared by Maj John Jacob, both published by Smith, Elder & Co and almost certainly integral to the book, as published.

No other illustrations or maps in either volume, no appendixes, no Index.

* In the style of the period, the narrative is a detailed factual account of the Regt's formation, evolution, internal organisation, and campaign services. In addition to the pages recorded above, Volume I has two pages, inserted after page 70, which carry (verbatim) three letters written by Jacob to Napier. The Regt was embodied on 8 August 1839, many of the men being detached from The Poona Horse. Elements of the Regt were in action, against the 'Beloochi' tribes, only three months later. Much of the early service was against marauding robber bands and keeping the peace along the disturbed Scinde border (at the time of the disastrous British retreat from Afghanistan). During the Sikh Wars, the Regt fought with distinction at Meanee (27 February 1843), at the siege of Mooltan, and at Goojerat (21 February 1849). A very desirable pair of books. R/5 V/4. PC. BDM.

Note: both books were republished in 1902-1903. A set has been seen with matching dark brown cloth boards, light brown leather spine and quarters, and having iv/355 and -/283 pages. The printers were S M Soleiman & Sons, Sukkur (Vol I, 1902), and The Victoria Printing Press, Sukkur (Vol II, 1903). Although they have more pages than the 1856 edition, the text is identical. The appearance on the market of this new edition may have prompted a demand for copies with bindings tailored to meet individual tastes. Another pair, for example, has been seen with dark green boards, light green spines, red quarters and gold embellishments. The hand-coloured maps found in the 1856 edition are present in both of the reprints as reported here. Both of these (1902-1903) pairs also have the addition of an Index, but only in Vol I and only 'A to M'.

A SHORT HISTORY OF THE 35th SCINDE HORSE

Capt E D Giles * Thacker & Co, Bombay, 1909. Stiff card, olive green, dark green, Regtl crest, 8.25 x 5.5, -/21/ii. Fp, no other ills, no maps, no appendixes (apart from some brief notes on medals and trophies), no Index.

* This is a short history written by the Adjutant and intended for the instruction of newly-joined officers. Phrased in terse and bombastic language, it makes short and basically unhelpful references to each of the campaigns and battles in which the Regt took part. This booklet's reference value is minimal, but it has interest as a collectable rarity. R/5 V/1. IOL. RGB.

PRINCE OF WALES'S OWN, THE SCINDE HORSE
1839-1922

Col E B Maunsell * Butler & Tanner Ltd, London, for the Regtl Committee, 1926. Green, gold, Regtl crest, 10.0 x 7.5, xx/348. Fp, 45 mono phots, 22 maps, 5 line drawings, Index. Apps: Roll of Honour (British and Indian officers KIA, WIA and MIA), H&A, list of former COs, idem former officers, idem officers who served in WWI, notes on Battle Honours, idem the titles of the Regt, precis of the history of the Regt printed in Gurmukhi and Urdu (as hung in every Barrack Room), notes on the sillidar system.

* The book was published soon after the amalgamation, in 1921, of 35th Scinde Horse with 36th Jacob's Horse. Both component Regts had long and distinguished records. Their unification was totally logical because Jacob's Irregular Horse of 1839 vintage had been expanded by him into two Regts - the 1st and 2nd (later the 35th and 36th) in 1846. Maunsell deals briskly with their origins, early battles, and later 19th Century campaigns. He leaves it to the reader to consult Jacob's own book (vide preceding page) for the finer details. He does devote one complete chapter to the disaster at Maiwand when 3rd Scinde Horse was mishandled by the Cavalry Brigadier, but the bulk of his pages are devoted to the events of the early 20th Century. During WWI, 35th Scinde Horse remained in India, policing the NWF and finding drafts for service overseas. Then, in 1920, the Regt itself went overseas. It moved to Mesopotamia and won much acclaim for its rearguard action in 'the Manchester disaster'. The 36th Jacob's Horse, on the other hand, went to France in 1914 with the Indian Corps and fought dismounted at Festubert (January 1915), at Ypres, and on the Somme (1916). Its greatest battle was Cambrai (1917) when it repeatedly counter-attacked the advancing enemy. In 1918, the 36th moved to Palestine. It fought in Allenby's great final cavalry operations (the actions at Sharan, Megiddo, Abu Naj, and the advance to Damascus). The Turks defeated, the Regt was kept in Syria as a garrison force until 1921 and then returned to India for the amalgamation. Apart from the usual daily incidents, this book provides many interesting commentaries upon the practical incompetence of senior officers in France, the inadequacies of pre-war Cavalry training, relationships with the French Army and civilian population, and much else of value to the historian (both military and social). Most of the illustrations are uninspired, but the line drawings, and the photographic reproductions of six important paintings, reveal interesting aspects of 19th Century Regtl life. R/5 V/4. RMAS. BWR.

THE SCINDE HORSE
14th Prince of Wales's Own Cavalry, 1922-1947

Lieut Col K R Brooke * Deighton's Embassy Press, Haslemere, for the Scinde Horse Association, 1957. Green, gold, 9.75 x 7.5, xiv/90. 13 mono phots, no maps, no Index. Apps: list of former officers (WWI only), list of former COs, idem Risaldar Majors (1921-1947), notes on Battle Honours.

* The author states that this is a 'regimental biography' rather than a 'regimental history'. His meaning is obscure, but the book is, in any event, pleasantly readable and helpful. The period covered runs from amalgamation through to Partition. There is brief mention of the Regt's time at Quetta in the 1930s and the pre-war displays of horsemanship on the annual Meanee Day. The Regt became an armoured

unit in 1938 (being one of the first to mechanise), spent two years on the NWF, and then joined Paiforce in Syria. Sadly, it gained no Battle Honours in WWII because it saw no real action. R/3 V/4. NAM. PJE/TM.

THE SCINDE HORSEMAN
Special War Number, Autumn 1940 to January 1946
Maj F G Foster * Printed in Bombay, for the Regt, 1946. Paper covers, off-white, green, Regtl crest with diagonal stripes in red-green-red, 9.25 x 7.0, vii/110/v. 36 mono phots, one map (bound in), no appendixes, no Index.
* In common with many other Regts, it was the practice of the 14th Horse to produce an annual chronicle of its activities - sporting, social, training, etc. It was entitled THE SCINDE HORSEMAN. The item recorded here is a compendium of the issues produced during the war years. As a special 'one off' production, it was intended to celebrate the Regt's return to India in 1946 and as a memento for serving officers and friends of the Regt. The text includes rolls of officers serving at various dates, and some interesting photographs taken during the period (c.1940) when the Regt was engaged against lawless elements in Waziristan. A useful source for the genealogist and for the medal collector. Much of the text was later transposed almost verbatim by Brooke for inclusion in his book (vide preceding entry). R/4 V/4. PC. CJP.

15th LANCERS

REGIMENTAL STANDING ORDERS - 17th CAVALRY
Capt D D Wilson * Hugh Rees Ltd, London, 1909. Dark blue boards, cream spine, gold, Regtl crest, 8.25 x 5.25, -/98. No ills, no maps, no appendixes, no Index.
* This is exactly what its title states it to be. It is a compendium of instructions which cover the duties required of British and Indian officers, NCOs and Sowars, organisation and administration on the line of march, the care of the mules and horses, and so forth. The book has no historical content, but it is of interest as a reflection of the daily life of a Cavalry unit during that period. The 17th Cavalry amalgamated with the 37th Lancers (Baluch Horse) to form the 15th Lancers (February 1922). R/5 V/2. MODL. AMM.

THE STAR AND CRESCENT
Being the Story of the 17th Cavalry from 1858 to 1922
Maj F C C Yeats-Brown * Printed by The Pioneer Press, Allahabad, privately for the author, n.d. (c.1927). Dark blue boards with ivory pigskin spine, gold, Regtl crest, 9.75 x 6.5, xii/359. Fp, 57 mono phots, one map (folding, bound in), no Index. Apps: Roll of Honour, H&A, list of former officers.
* The author was 'the' Yeats-Brown, best known for his LIVES OF A BENGAL LANCER but also a skilled writer on a wide range of subjects and one-time Editor of THE SPECTATOR magazine. This history is arranged in a slightly chaotic format because many different sources for the various predecessor units have been quoted in parallel. Even so, it is a superb book. Almost half of the pages are devoted to the appendixes, the most interesting of which is that which lists all the British and Indian officers. Each entry gives details of the individual's military career and war services, and most are accompanied by a portrait photograph. The book was the author's own personal project, and the number of copies printed probably did not exceed one hundred (each impressed with a serial number). The four copies examined for the purposes of this bibliography have the serials 6, 42, 62 and 88. A very desirable book. R/5 V/5. NAM. RJW/RGH/CJP.

16th LIGHT CAVALRY

HISTORICAL RECORDS OF THE 2nd MADRAS LANCERS, NOW 27th LIGHT CAVALRY
Col J B Edwards * Christian Mission Press, Jubbulpore, 1907. Black, gold, 8.5 x 5.5, -/132. No ills, no maps, no Index. Apps: list of former officers, notes on the Regtl establishment (1819), notes on horses, Dress regulations (1820 and 1846).
* Based upon Regtl records and Standing Orders. Possibly of interest to the specialist Cavalry researcher, but basically dull and colourless. The 27th Light Cavalry was restyled the 16th Light Cavalry in 1922, without amalgamation.
R/5 V/2. USII/NAM. OSS/PJE.

HISTORY OF THE 16th LIGHT CAVALRY (ARMOURED CORPS)
Lieut Col C L Proudfoot * Publisher's details not shown, thought to have been produced in Calcutta, n.d. (c.1976). Blue, white, silver, Regtl crest, 8.5 x 6.0, viii/202. Fp, 16 mono phots, no maps, no Index. Apps: Roll of Honour (KIA and WIA, WWII only), list of officers serving in 1945, plus some of the more useful appendixes (transposed verbatim) from the earlier account by Col Edwards (vide preceding entry).
* The Regt did not lose its horses until 1941. Having become mechanised, it moved to the NWF where it remained for the next two years. It then transferred to Burma under the command of Lieut Col J N Chaudhuri (later General and Chief of Army Staff). The Regt saw active service in Burma, heading the drive to take Rangoon. A most useful and readable book. R/4 V/4. UWML/IOL. BCC.

THE POONA HORSE (17th QUEEN VICTORIA'S OWN CAVALRY)

HISTORICAL RECORDS OF THE SERVICES OF THE 3rd (THE QUEEN'S OWN) REGIMENT OF BOMBAY LIGHT CAVALRY
A booklet having this title - or with very similar wording - was published in 1877. The printer is reported as having been The Education Society's Press, Bombay, and the author was Maj A P Currie. Having only twenty-eight pages, its reference value is thought to be minimal. No surviving copies have been traced, and it is evidently a very rare item.

HISTORICAL RECORDS OF THE SERVICES OF THE 33rd (QUEEN'S OWN) LIGHT CAVALRY
Maj A P Currie and Capt M H Anderson * Publisher's details not shown, Poona, 1911. Green boards with black spine, gold, 9.5 x 6.5, -/208. No ills, no maps, no Index. Apps: list of Risaldar Majors, postings of British and Indian officers in and out of the Regt.
* Although Currie's name is shown as co-author, its inclusion would seem to have been mainly an act of courtesy and acknowledgement on the part of M H Anderson. This major history of the Regt is in every way more ambitious than Currie's first tentative record (compiled thirty-four years earlier). The text is based upon Regtl Orders and Regulations, but it does give useful accounts of the Regt's role in the First and Second Afghan Wars, the Scind battles, the Mutiny, and the expeditions to Persia and Abyssinia. R/5 V/4. USII/IOL. NKR/RGB/CJP.

HISTORICAL RECORDS OF THE SERVICES OF THE 33rd (QUEEN VICTORIA'S OWN) LIGHT CAVALRY
Anon ('compiled by officers of the Regiment' - known to have been M H Anderson, by then promoted Major, and his younger brother, Capt E S J Anderson) *
Printed by The Scottish Mission Industries Co, at the Orphanage Press, Poona, for the Regt, 1913. Blue boards, black leather spine and quarters, gold, 10.25 x 6.25, vii/274/ii (the last being the Index). 5 mono phots, 12 maps (bound in), Index. Apps: list of former COs, idem former officers, notes on campaign services.
* The book described in the preceding entry was published in 1911. In that same year, however, the 33rd was awarded (in June) the right to carry the Royal Cyphers on its badges. It was then granted (in December) the distinction of

having the Monarch's name included in its title. These changes appear to have been the trigger for republishing the Regt's history only two years later. The 1913 edition has only two pages of additional text. These carry the story through to November 1912. The first 208 pages are the same as the first 208 pages of the 1911 edition. Pages 214 to 225 are blank other than having folio numbers and the book title headings. As research sources, therefore, the two editions are of almost equal merit. R/4 V/4. IOL/NAM. CJP.
Note: it is possible that the bindings described for this (1913) book may be a 'de luxe' edition. A copy of the same book has been seen with olive green covers and gold lettering.

WITH THE 33rd Q.V.O. LIGHT CAVALRY IN MESOPOTAMIA
Capt E S J Anderson (as editor) * Printed by The Scottish Mission Industries Co, Poona, 1915. Cloth and leather, dark green, black, 9.75 x 6.25, -/49. Fp, one line drawing, no maps, no appendixes, no Index.
* In 1915, Maj M H Anderson, co-author of the history described in the preceding entry, was ambushed and killed by an Arab gang in Mesopotamia. This book consists of extracts from his diary and letters, edited and compiled by his younger brother, and is in essence a memorial. Presumably it was presented to his fellow officers and friends of the family, so the print run was probably very limited.
R/5 V/2. IOL. RGB/CJP.

HISTORICAL RECORDS OF THE POONA HORSE, 1882
Maj G C Hogg and Maj C M Erskine * Printed at The Education Society's Press, Bombay, for the Regt, n.d. (c.1882). Black, gold, 13.0 x 8.5, vii/36. 3 mono phots, no maps, no Index. Apps: list of former COs, idem former officers.
* Very brief indeed, and, like several other Indian unit histories published during that period, no more than a token effort. In 1903, The Poona Horse became the 34th (Prince Albert Victor's Own) Poona Horse. R/5 V/1. NAM. RP.

THE HISTORICAL RECORDS OF THE 34th (PRINCE ALBERT VICTOR'S OWN) POONA HORSE
Maj G M Molloy * Hugh Rees Ltd, London, 1913. Dark blue boards, light blue spine, gold, 9.0 x 6.0, ix/139. Fp, 5 mono phots, no Index. Apps: list of former COs, idem Honorary Colonels, idem Regtl officers.
* The 34th was the other Regt which, in 1922, was amalgamated to form the 17th Queen Victoria's Own Poona Horse which, in 1927, was redesignated as The Poona Horse (17th Queen Victoria's Own Cavalry). The 34th had, until 1903, been the 4th Prince Albert Victor's Own Bombay Cavalry (Poona Horse). Its 1922 amalgamation was with the 33rd Queen Victoria's Own Light Cavalry, formerly (pre-1903) the 3rd (Queen's Own) Bombay Light Cavalry. The author of this book traces the roots of the 34th Poona Horse from the early 19th Century in fairly general terms, but with sufficient detail to make it a useful source of reference.
R/4 V/3. IOL/NAM. PJE/CJP.

INDIAN CAVALRY OFFICER
Captain Roly Grimshaw
Col J Wakefield and Lieut Col J M Weippart (as editors) * Costello, Tunbridge Wells, 1986. Blue, gold, 9.0 x 6.0, -/224. 27 mono phots, one map, Chapter Notes, Index. Apps: notes on Indian ranks, Order of Battle (Indian Cavalry in France).
* Grimshaw served with the 34th PAVO Poona Horse in France and his account covers the period from 4 August 1914 to June 1915 (when he was wounded and repatriated). The book is an edited version of the diary which he kept during that short time. As published, the narrative falls into two parts - his own thoughts and experiences while on active service, and then the story of a typical Indian soldier (Ram Singh, Daffadar of Horse). The latter is based upon the reminiscences of various Indian officers and NCOs. Grimshaw's comments regarding the logistical difficulties of maintaining a Cavalry Regt so that it was battle-worthy, even when resting in a rear area, are revealing. R/1 V/4. PC. JG.

THE POONA HORSE (17th QUEEN VICTORIA'S OWN CAVALRY), 1817-1931
Various authors (see below) * Royal United Service Institution, London, 1933. Two matching volumes, olive green boards, red spines, 10.0 x 7.5.
Volume I : 1817-1913. Fp, 11 mono phots, 11 maps (10 printed in the text, one bound in), appendixes, Index, xxiv/276.
Volume II : 1914-1931. Fp, 12 mono phots, 15 maps, appendixes, Index, xviii/235.
* The authorship is given as Maj M H Anderson, Lieut Col E S J Anderson, and Col G M Molloy OBE (for Volume I), and Col H C Wylly (for Volume II). It should be noted that M H Anderson had been killed nearly twenty years before this history was published. It seems likely that the driving force was Wylly, with possibly some assistance from E S J Anderson and G M Molloy (who had written the QVO and PAVO histories before WWI). Alternatively, it may be that Wylly (an established historian) joined their names with his own as a gesture of acknowledgement of their earlier work. Whatever the explanation may be, this handsome pair of books is in a category totally different to the average run of Indian Army histories. The standards of research, writing, presentation, and binding, are of the highest. Volume I is a condensed and edited amalgam of the QVO history by the Anderson brothers (published in 1913) and the PAVO history by Molloy (also published in 1913). Volume II deals with the WWI services of the two Regts, their amalgamation in 1922, the redesignation of 1927, and other post-war events. This is entirely the work of Col Wylly, and it is written in his usual stylish manner. Both Volumes are provided with lengthy appendixes which, inter alia, list all former officers (giving details of their appointments and campaign services).
R/3 V/5. NAM/IOL/RMAS. RP/CJP.

18th KING EDWARD VII's OWN CAVALRY

HISTORY OF THE 6th KING EDWARD'S OWN CAVALRY
Anon * Publisher's details not known due to damage to the only copy seen, but thought to have been published c.1909. Seen rebound in black, gold, 9.25 x 6.25, -/47/Lxviii. No ills, no maps, no appendixes, no Index.
* The book is divided into two sections. The first forty-seven pages provide a clearly written chronology which contains much useful information. The unknown author presents this material under headings which name the Stations at which the Regt served between 1842 and 1909. Some of it is purely technical (unit strengths, class compositions, weaponry, equipment etc), but the passages describing actions in which the Regt was engaged, and how it survived the Mutiny, are fluent and easy to follow. He lists the Indian personnel who remained loyal and gives details of their services and awards. The second section is an extract for each year from the Bengal and Indian Army Lists (from 1.4.1842 to 1.1.1909) showing the names of all British officers who served. The senior Risaldars are listed from January 1858 onwards, and all Indian officers from January 1877 onwards. Despite the lack of Index and appendixes, a most helpful source of reference. R/5 V/4. PC. CJP.

REGIMENTAL HISTORY OF THE 18th KING EDWARD VII's OWN CAVALRY
Lieut Col L Lawrence-Smith * The Station Press, Meerut, 1938. White, silver, Regtl crest, 10.0 x 6.5, -/46. Fp, 2 mono phots, no maps, no Index. Apps: list of former COs, idem former officers.
* This is a short history from 1921 (the year of amalgamation of the 6th King Edward's Own Cavalry with the 7th Hariana Lancers) through to 1938 (shortly before mechanisation). R/4 V/2. NAM. PJE.

I SERVE
The Eighteenth Cavalry
Maj Gen Gurchan Singh Sandhu PVSM * Lancer International, New Delhi, 1991. Illustrated boards, 'Mounted Sowar and tanks' motif, full colour, 9.5 x 7.25, x/265. Fp, 53 mono phots, 8 cld ills, 4 line drawings, 32 maps, Glossary, Bibliography, no Index. Apps: H&A, list of former officers, idem Risaldar Majors, notes on uniforms.
* As can be seen from the two preceding entries, the 6th KE's Own Cavalry had made a modest effort (c.1909 and 1938) to publish accounts of their past services. The 7th Hariana Lancers, by contrast, never made the same effort to record their equally interesting and complex origins and adventures. This book makes good that previous neglect. The author covers the entire history of both founder Regts, under their changing titles, from 1842 through to 1990. He was commissioned into the Regt in 1944 and rose to command it in 1966. He writes with authority and in a pleasingly readable style, covering all the HEIC campaigns and the campaigns of the pre- and post-1947 Indian Army. He laces the story with items of Regtl gossip, personal anecdotes, descriptions of badges and buttons, and references to many individuals (such as the 'Regimental mascot', Admiral Sir Walter Cowan).
R/1 V/4. PC. JG.

19th KING GEORGE V's OWN LANCERS

A SHORT HISTORY OF THE 18th (P.W.O.) TIWANA LANCERS, 1858–1908
Anon * Superintendent of Government Printing, Calcutta, for the Regt, 1908. Red, white diagonal stripe, gold, Regtl crest, 9.5 x 6.5, vi/146. 2 mono phots (mounted and bound in), no maps, no appendixes, no Index.
* Only six pages are devoted to the Regt's history in conventional narrative terms. The other 140 pages are simply verbatim extracts from Bengal Army and Indian Army Lists of items relating to the Regt. The Tiwana Lancers changed their title in 1903, 1906 and 1910 before amalgamating with Fane's Horse in 1921 to form the 19th KGO Lancers. R/4 V/2. NAM. PJE.

ARMY LISTS – 19th LANCERS (FANE'S HORSE), 1860–1921
Anon * Publication details not shown, n.d. (c.1922). Blue, gold, 10.0 x 6.5, -/222. No ills, no maps, no appendixes, no Index.
* Simply a compendium of extracts from quarterly Bengal Army and Indian Lists for the period from January 1860 to January 1922 (less July and October 1920 which are ommitted). Indian officers are included from October 1876 onwards.
R/4 V/1. PC. CJP.

HISTORY OF THE 19th KING GEORGE'S OWN LANCERS, FROM 1858 TO 1921
Formerly 18th King George's Own Lancers and 19th Lancers (Fane's Horse), Amalgamated in 1921
Gen Sir Havelock Hudson GCB * Gale & Polden Ltd, Aldershot, 1937. Dark blue, red/grey stripe, Regtl crest, 10.0 x 7.0, xiv/370. Fp, 31 mono phots, 2 cld ills, 6 maps (folding, bound in), Bibliography, no Index. Apps: many, including Roll of Honour (KIA, WIA and MIA), H&A (with citations where applicable, for the entire period 1858–1921), list of Honorary Colonels, idem former COs, idem former officers.
* A superb publication, beautifully prepared and presented. Unfortunately, being such a useful source of reference, most copies seen in military libraries or being offered by dealers tend to be heavily 'thumbed' and 'shaken'. A copy in bright original condition is a joy to possess – if one can be found. It is extraordinary that, having expended so much trouble over the other details, the author and the publishers failed to recognise the need for an Index. The narrative covers the period from 1858 to 1921, with good descriptions of the Mutiny, Second Afghan War, the NWF (Tirah campaign), and WWI (the Western Front and Palestine).
R/3 V/4. IOL/RMAS/PCAL. RP.

THE SPIRIT OF A REGIMENT
Being a History of the 19th King George V's Own Lancers, 1921-1947
Brig J G Pocock * Gale & Polden Ltd, Aldershot, 1962. Blue, gold, Regtl crest, 9.75 x 7.25, xvi/114. Fp, 28 mono phots (indexed), 6 maps (indexed, 3 printed in the text, 3 folding, bound in), Bibliography, Index. Apps: Roll of Honour, H&A (1921-1947), list of former COs, idem Adjutants, idem Risaldar Majors, idem all Regtl officers, notes on Battle Honours.
* A workmanlike history for the stated period. In terms of overall quality, it is a worthy successor to Hudson's account (vide preceding entry) and has a similar style and format. Pocock went one better by taking the trouble to provide an Index. This is most helpful in view of the numerous name references in the main narrative. The Regt did not say 'goodbye' to its horses until 1941 and was then engaged only in training and coast-watching around Madras. Re-equipped with Sherman tanks, it finally went in action, in December 1944, in the Arakan.
R/4 V/5. NAM/RMAS. VS/RP.

19th KING GEORGE'S OWN LANCERS - WAR NEWS
September 1939 - December 1945
Anon * Publication details not shown, n.d. (c.1946). Black, yellow, Regtl crest, 10.0 x 7.25, ii/88. 78 mono phots, one map (bound in), no Index (but a good 'Contents' page). Apps: Roll of Honour (WWII), H&A (WWII), list of officers who served in WWII, notes on recruitment, notes on VCOs, officers' wartime marriages.
* A chronicle which covers all aspects of the Regt's experiences between 1940 and 1945 in considerable detail. The illustrations are interesting, but are very small and poorly printed. Less formal than Pocock's history (vide preceding entry), it represents a valuable additional source when the two are read in conjunction. At Partition, the Regt was assigned to the Pakistan Army as the 19th Lancers.
R/4 V/4. MODL. AMM.

20th LANCERS

15th LANCERS (CURETON'S MULTANIS), 1858-1908
Anon * Superintendent of Government Printing, Calcutta, 1910. Full Morocco, green, gold, 'Regtl crest and former Regtl titles' motif, 10.75 x 7.5, xxviii/172. No ills, no maps, Index. Apps: H&A, list of former COs, idem Risaldar Majors, idem former officers (with details of their war services), note on Regtl organisation.
* The book is essentially a compendium of extracts from official lists and reports. However, it does include an interesting account of the raising of the Regt, with good references to the Multani Pathans of the Derajat, and the Baluch tribes of the Sind Sagar Thal. The Regt became the 20th Lancers in 1921 when it amalgamated with 14th Murray's Jat Lancers. R/5 V/3. NAM. CJP.

THE CENTRAL INDIA HORSE (21st KING GEORGE V's OWN HORSE)

KING GEORGE'S OWN CENTRAL INDIA HORSE
The Story of a Local Corps
Maj Gen W A Watson CB CMG CIE * William Blackwood & Sons Ltd, Edinburgh, 1930. Fawn boards, red spine and quarters, gold, Regtl crest, 9.0 x 6.0, x/474. Fp, 4 mono phots, 4 maps (bound in), Index. Apps: H&A (all ranks, WWI only), list of former officers (WWI only).
* An excellent quality of production and a good readable narrative. Many individuals are mentioned in the text. The period covered is from 1858 through to the 1920s, the main events being the Mutiny, the Second Afghan War, the campaign in the Tirah, and WWI (Western Front and Palestine). The operations to suppress the Mutiny in Central India, and to round up the last of its leaders, were conducted in part by a number of ad hoc units which sprang up almost spontaneously and under the inspired leadership of young officers of junior rank. Amongst these units were Beatson's Horse, Meade's Horse, and Mayne's Horse. In time, these evolved

into the 38th and the 39th Central India Horse. In 1921, these two Regts merged their common roots and similar traditions to become the 21st King George's Own Central India Horse. This book is one of the best of all Indian Cavalry histories. R/4 V/4. RMAS/NAM/IOL. RP.

KING GEORGE V's OWN CENTRAL INDIA HORSE
The Story (Continued) of a Local Corps, being Volume II of the Regimental History
Brig A A Filose * William Blackwood & Sons Ltd, Edinburgh, 1950. Red, gold, 10.0 x 7.5, x/435. Fp, 4 mono phots, 2 cld ills, 13 maps (12 printed in the text, one bound in), Index. Apps: H&A (all ranks, WWII only).
* Although the format and dimensions of this book are not the same as those of Watson's account (vide the preceding entry), it is effectively the second part of a two-volume series (as indeed the sub-title claims). The opening chapters deal with the inter-war years. The second half of the book then deals with services in WWII (Eritrea, Western Desert, and Italy). The narrative is well written, full of good detail, and with many individuals of every rank mentioned. To quote a former officer of the Regiment: 'It is a model for the story of an Indian Cavalry regiment, having been written by a man whose prose was excellent, and who had the advantage of the publication being paid for by a benevolent Maharaja of Bahawalpur, an Honorary Colonel of the Central India Horse'. R/4 V/5. NAM. RP.

THE CENTRAL INDIA HORSE
Newsletters 1 to 24 - July 1940 to February 1946
Lieut Col R W Peters * Printed by C Murphy, at Thacker's Press, Bombay, for the Regt, n.d. (c.1946). Seen in blue cloth boards, gold, Regtl crest, and seen also in green full Morocco, 9.25 x 8.25, -/231. No ills, 7 maps (bound in), no Index. Apps: many, all to be found at the end of each Newsletter, the most useful being the H&A and the lists of officers.
* As the title suggests, this is a compendium of the Regt's customary quarterly Newsletters, reproduced and bound together in a single volume as a commemorative publication to mark the Regt's return to India. For obvious reasons, the material carries a great sense of immediacy. It reflects the day-to-day lives of all ranks, their adventures, their humour, their moves and postings, their awards, and their losses resulting from death or injury. The Regt travelled extensively in WWII, seeing action not only in East and North Africa and Italy, but also in Greece and with Paiforce. It is evident that Brig Filose drew heavily upon this source while compiling his formal history (vide preceding entry), but many of the details which lack of space in that book obliged him to ignore are to be found in these Newsletters. For example, most of the citations for gallantry awards (British and Indian) are quoted here in full. A most useful and interesting publication.
R/4 V/5. PC. CJP.

CAVALRY

Disbanded Regiments

HISTORICAL RECORD OF THE FOURTH 'PRINCE OF WALES'S OWN' REGIMENT, MADRAS LIGHT CAVALRY

Lieut Col W J Wilson * Printed by C Foster & Co, Madras, for the Regt, 1877. Soft card (with crudely stitched binding), blue, black, 9.5 x 6.0, -/96. No ills, no maps, no Index. Apps: an analysis of casualties (by type, ranks and Regt) for the Battles of Bangalore (6.3.1791), Assaye (23.9.1803), and Maheidpoor (21.12.1817), notes on the class composition of the 4th Regt of Cavalry at March 1811 and at October 1825, tables detailing entitlements to gratuities, pensions, batta, etc.

* A competent history compiled from records in the offices of the Madras Government and of the Adjutant General, supplemented by similar information taken from the records of the Regt itself. The narrative contains much detail concerning the internal organisation of the Regt. The author provides some sketchy coverage of its role in the Third and Fourth Mysore Wars, and the Second and Third Mahratta Wars, but then examines the period of the Mutiny in much greater depth. The 4th Regt of Madras Light Cavalry was disbanded in 1891, and this is the only known published record of its services. Apart from any other consideration, the book is interesting for its strange mixture of appendixes.

R/5 V/4. IOL/NAM. RGB/CJP.

A SHORT HISTORY OF THE 75th REGIMENT, INDIAN ARMY

Lieut Col H L Mostyn-Owen * HQ Luckdist Press, Lucknow, n.d. (c.1946). A booklet having viii/87 pages, one map, and some appendixes.

* These details were once noted in a dealer's catalogue, but prolonged enquiries have failed to unearth a copy so that it might be examined for the purposes of this bibliography. Little is known of the 75th Regt other than its having been one of several temporary armoured units raised in India during WWII and bearing numbers between 42nd and 76th. They seem to have had a great diversity of careers. Some lasted only a short time before being disbanded. Others took delivery of factory-new armoured cars and tanks and prepared them for battle use by fighting units in the field. Only one of these Regts - the 45th - was deployed in a combat zone (it fought in Burma, at Imphal and Kohima). The 75th, the subject of this publication, must have been doing a useful job because it was not disbanded until 1946. Mostyn-Owen commanded the Regt and his little book is self-evidently a great rarity. RP/CJP.

APPENDIX II

The numbering of Indian Army Cavalry Regiments
following the reorganisations of 1921–1922
with their final titles and dates of adoption
prior to Independence and Partition

Skinner's Horse (1st Duke of York's Own Cavalry), from 1927

2nd Royal Lancers (Gardner's Horse), from 1935

3rd Cavalry, from 1922

Hodson's Horse (4th Duke of Cambridge's Own Lancers), from 1928

Probyn's Horse (5th King Edward VII's Own Lancers), from 1936

6th Duke of Connaught's Own Lancers (Watson's Horse), from 1924

7th Light Cavalry, from 1922

8th King George V's Own Light Cavalry, from 1937

The Royal Deccan Horse (9th Horse), from 1927

The Guides Cavalry (10th Queen Victoria's Own Frontier Force), from 1927

Prince Albert Victor's Own Cavalry (11th Frontier Force), from 1927

Sam Browne's Cavalry (12th Frontier Force), from 1927

13th Duke of Connaught's Own Lancers, from 1927

The Scinde Horse (14th Prince of Wales's Own Cavalry), from 1927

15th Lancers, from 1922

16th Light Cavalry, from 1922

The Poona Horse (17th Queen Victoria's Own Cavalry), from 1927

18th King Edward VII's Own Cavalry, from 1936

19th King George V's Own Lancers, from 1937

20th Lancers, from 1922

The Central India Horse (21st King George V's Own Horse), from 1937

ARTILLERY

From its earliest days, the Honourable East India Company ensured that its three Presidential Armies - Bengal, Madras and Bombay - had the capability to take to the battlefield with a balanced force of Cavalry, Artillery, Engineers and Infantry. In 1748, the Presidencies each recruited their first units of Foot Artillery - so named because the gun detachments, while on the line of march, accompanied their pieces on foot. The guns were manned by Europeans (mainly Irishmen, selected for their physical strength) supported by native followers. Normally the guns were drawn by oxen, less frequently by horses or, on some occasions, by camels or elephants. The number of such units (Companies) grew steadily over the next hundred years.

In 1801, in Bengal, the first Troop of Horse Artillery was formed. Its designation derived from the fact that the pieces were always drawn by horses, with the gun detachments mounted on them. The personnel of these units were, as with the Foot Artillery, predominantly European. By 1825, there were twenty-four such units.

In 1827, in Bombay, it was decided to begin raising twelve Companies of Foot Artillery with European officers and Indian gunners.

In 1851, three Horse Light Field Batteries were formed, also with European officers and Indian gunners, to support the Punjab Irregular (later Frontier) Force.

Then came the Mutiny of 1857 and the consequent transfer of power to the Crown. The new administration was much concerned that, in the event of a second such uprising, it might not be able to suppress it. One way of reducing the risk was to ensure that the guns - 'the queen of the battlefield' - would in future be manned almost exclusively by European (British) personnel. In fact, only a small number of Indian gunners had been disloyal in 1857-1858.

Under the new policy, almost all of the former HEIC gunner units were transferred to the Royal Artillery (British Army). There were just two exceptions - four Companies of Bombay Native Artillery, and the six Batteries of the Punjab Frontier Force. The latter was, in any event, distinct and separate from the Indian Army. It was answerable not to the Commander-in-Chief, India, but to the Lieutenant Governor of the Punjab.

The years went by and the spectre of rebellion slowly faded. Their courage and fortitude during the Great War of 1914-1918 demonstrated beyond question the loyalty of the Indian Army's rank and file. It was decided, therefore, after a break of seventy-five years, to recommence the recruitment of Indian soldiers as artillerymen. At Bangalore, in 1935, 'A' Field Brigade, Indian Artillery, began to form. It was followed by a second - 'B' Field Brigade - in 1939-1940.

In 1939, the twenty-five Batteries of Indian Mountain Artillery, which had always been treated as a special case and which had not been transferred from the Indian Army to the British Army until 1925, reverted once more to the Indian Army and became an element of the Indian Artillery.

Although the old HEIC Artillery units lost their identities in 1862, they were perpetuated in the distinctive Honour Titles which still exist in the Royal Artillery. The origins of this heritage are apparent in the titles of some of the books recorded on the following pages. The entries are arranged under, first, those books which give a general account of Artillery in India, and then, secondly, the records of Batteries and their descendants which originated in each of the three Presidencies (in the sequence of their seniority).

ARTILLERY

General Reference

THE HISTORY OF THE ROYAL AND INDIAN ARTILLERY IN THE MUTINY OF 1857
Col Julian R J Jocelyn * Printed by Hazell, Watson & Viney Ltd for John Murray, London, 1915. Blue, gold, 'Indian Mutiny medal' motif, 9.25 x 6.0, xxvi/520. Fp, one mono phot, 14 engravings, 11 maps (folding, bound in), 28 sketch plans (printed in the text), Bibliography, Index. Apps: list of officers who served, summary of casualties, notes on organisation, idem battles, sieges, etc.
* An excellent book, full of detail, which deals almost exclusively with the period 1857-1858, but with a short chapter taking the story through to the amalgamation (in 1862) of most of the HEIC Artilleries with the Royal Artillery.
R/4 V/5. RAI. AMM.

BATTERY RECORDS OF THE ROYAL ARTILLERY, 1859–1877
Including HEIC (Foot) Artillery Companies, 1748–1862
Lieut Col M E S Laws OBE MC * Royal Artillery Institution, Woolwich, 1970. Dark blue, gold, RA crest, 8.75 x 11.0, vi/312. No ills, no maps, Index. Apps: notes on the Bengal Artillery, Madras Artillery, and Bombay Artillery.
* This book (Volume II of a long-term series) deals principally with Batteries of the Royal Artillery (British Army). In 1862, fifty-two Companies of Artillery which formerly had been in the service of the HEIC were transferred to the RA, and their former titles, Battle Honours, and other matters of interest, are recorded in this book. Consequently it is a complete and handy source of reference for early gunnery in India. R/2 V/5. RAI. AMM.

HONOUR TITLES OF THE ROYAL ARTILLERY
Maj Gen B P Hughes * Royal Artillery Institution, Woolwich, 1976. Blue, gold, 8.5 x 6.0, xii/222. 2 mono phots, 20 sketches, 21 maps, Bibliography, no appendixes, 2 indexes (Units, and Persons).
* An authoritative and very readable book which describes the circumstances which led to the award of an Honour title to certain Batteries of the RA. Twenty-five of them were (at the time of the event leading to the award) still in the service of the HEIC (pre-1862). The book has a section for each Bty, arranged chronologically, stating its evolution and services. Roughly one quarter of the material (including maps and illustrations) relate to the HEIC period. Information which might otherwise have appeared in the form of appendixes is instead shown in each section. R/2 V/5. MODL/RAI. AMM.

HISTORY OF THE REGIMENT OF ARTILLERY, INDIAN ARMY
Brig Gen Y B Gulati and Maj Gen D K Palit VrC * Palit & Dutt, Dehra Dun, 1971. Black, gold, 8.75 x 5.75, xiii/342. Fp, 12 mono phots, 3 cld plates, 11 maps, Index. Apps: H&A (WWII only, possibly incomplete), notes on nomenclature, list of units sent overseas in WWII, notes on anti-aircraft and coastal defences, idem the allocation of units at Partition, etc.
* For the reasons explained on the preceding page, the Indian Regiment of Artillery was not formed until 1935. There was a very rapid expansion from 1939-1940 onwards, and the Regt served overseas in many theatres of war and in many different roles. In August 1945, the King Emperor granted it the 'Royal' title (this distinction being discarded upon the proclamation of the Indian Republic in January 1950). A very comprehensive book, it has one chapter on the history of Indian gunnery prior to 1935, but the bulk of the narrative is devoted to a detailed account of the raising of new units and new branches in WWII, with an even more detailed description of the post-1947 campaigns. It concentrates upon the origins and war services of each unit, and is thereby an excellent source of reference.
R/1 V/5. NAM/IOL. MCJ/BCC/AMM.
Note: reprinted by Leo Cooper, London, 1972.

THE ANTI-AIRCRAFT BRANCH OF THE INDIAN ARTILLERY, 1940 TO 1947
Maj H Y Sawyer * Facsimile TS, no publication details shown, 1983. Seen in card covers, blue, blind, 11.5 x 8.5, -/42. No ills, no maps, Bibliography, no Index. Apps: list of Heavy A/A Regts, idem Light A/A Regts.
* A useful and quite detailed history of the various Regts and Btys which served in the anti-aircraft role. It is the only known source dealing specifically with this subject. R/5 V/3. NAM. PJE.

THE KAYE'S 2nd ANTI-TANK REGIMENT
Later 7 Fd 'The Gola of Gabot' - Some Facts and Experiences
M A Gani SJ * Publisher's details not shown, Islamabad, 1977. Plasticated soft card, dark red, gold, Regtl crest, 9.5 x 7.25, iii/88. Fp, 14 mono phots, one map, no appendixes, no Index.
* An expansive account written by an Indian officer who served with the Regt and eventually commanded it. The unofficial title 'The Kaye's' derived from the fact that, when raised in 1940, the first CO was Lieut Col J W Kaye RA. It consisted of 5, 6, 7 and 8 A/T Btys. On 15 August 1947, the Regt was transferred to the Pakistan Army. The narrative is readable and interesting, and gives good coverage of campaigning in Burma (1942-1944), Java (1945), and Kashmir (1947-1948). R/3 V/4. RAI. AMM.

IZZAT-O-IQBAL
The History of the Pakistan Artillery, 1947-1971
Maj Gen Shaukat Riza * School of Artillery, Nowshera, 1980. Dark blue, gold, 8.75 x 5.75, viii/458. Fp, 21 mono phots, 3 maps (bound in), no appendixes, Index.
* A good history of the Regiment of Artillery, Pakistan Army, covering formation, equipment, expansion, campaigns, etc. Training methods and aid received from American support programmes when the Regt was being raised are described in interesting detail. Various post-Partition active services are covered in detail, with specific references to the units engaged. R/3 V/4. PC. RWH.

BENGAL

MEMOIR OF THE SERVICES OF THE BENGAL ARTILLERY
From the Organisation of the Corps to the Present Time, with Some Account of its Internal Organisation
Capt E Buckle and J W Kaye * William H Allen & Co, London, 1852. Leather spine, red boards, gold, 9.0 x 5.5, xvi/592. 18 engravings (10 of medals, 8 of gun carriages), no maps, no Index. Apps: H&A, lists of former officers.
* A detailed and very useful account of the period 1748-1849. Some particulars of individual officer's services are stated to be inaccurate, but the book is basically a very reliable source of information. R/4 V/4. RAI/IOL. AMM.

HISTORY OF THE ORGANISATION, EQUIPMENT AND WAR SERVICES OF THE REGIMENT OF BENGAL ARTILLERY
Compiled from Published Works, Official Records, and Various Private Sources
Lieut Col Francis W Stubbs * Henry S King & Co, London. Three matching volumes, red, gold, 8.5 x 5.5. No ills, many maps and plans, Bibliography, no Index. Apps: numerous, miscellaneous, incl list of former officers, statistics of ammunition expended at various sieges, etc.
Volume I : 1748-1813. Published 1877, 35 maps and plans, xx/354.
Volume II : 1814-1837. Published 1877, 16 maps and plans, viii/274.
Volume III : 1838-1860. Published 1895, 37 maps and plans, xii/615.
* This rare and desirable set of volumes, not often found in combination, is an invaluable source of reference for the Bengal Artillery. The narrative also includes some information regarding the Madras and Bombay Artilleries.
R/5 V/5. RAI/IOL. AMM.

LIST OF OFFICERS WHO HAVE SERVED IN THE REGIMENT OF THE BENGAL ARTILLERY (1748-1860)
Maj Gen F W Stubbs * C Seers, Bath (UK), 1892. Rust red, gold, 11.25 x 8.75, iii/72. No ills, no maps, Bibliography, Index. Apps: notes on establishments, list of officers Commissioned from the ranks.
* Compiled by the author of the major history noted above, this work lists all officers who served with the Bengal Artillery during the period specified. Taken in combination with the previous three-volume narrative history, it provides an excellent additional source (particularly for medal collectors and genealogists). The listings do not provide details of war services, but they do specify awards granted, dates of promotion, and dates of death. R/4 V/4. RAI. AMM.

STATEMENT OF THE SERVICES OF 'C' BATTERY, 'C' BRIGADE R.H.A. (FORMERLY SHAH SOOJAH'S HORSE ARTILLERY)
Anon (thought to have been Capt W J Finch) * Publisher's details not shown, London, n.d. (c.1878). Paper covers, light blue, black, 8.5 x 5.5, -/8. No ills, no maps, no appendixes, no Index.
* A pamphlet which covers the period 1838-1877, but which deals primarily with events up to 1862. Originally the unit consisted of two Troops of Shah Soojah's Artillery. These were amalgamated in 1843 to form 5th Troop (Native), 1st Brigade, Bengal Horse Artillery. The text is a diary of stations, movements, and battles.
R/5 V/2. RAI. AMM.

RECORDS OF 3rd TROOP, 2nd BENGAL HORSE ARTILLERY (NOW No 1 DEPOT R.F.A.)
Anon (Maj Gen F W Stubbs) * Publisher's details not shown, Woolwich, 1904. Card covers, grey, black, 7.0 x 5.0, -/28. No ills, no maps, no Index. Apps: H&A (officers only), list of former officers, notes on stations, equipment, and unit designations.
* The period covered is 1825-1862. Although brief, this booklet is written in Stubbs' usual concise style, and is certainly useful. R/5 V/3. RAI. AMM.

A SKETCH OF THE HISTORY OF 'F' BATTERY, ROYAL HORSE ARTILLERY
Formerly 1st Troop, 1st Brigade, Bengal Horse Artillery
Maj A S Tyndale-Biscoe * Spottiswoode & Co Ltd, London, 1905. Red, black, 7.5 x 4.75, ii/64. Fp, 2 mono phots, 3 sketches, no maps, no Index. Apps: list of former COs, idem former officers.
* Half of the text is devoted to the period 1800-1862 when, as 1/1 BHA, the unit was in HEIC service. The narrative is based upon notes originally prepared by Maj Gen F W Stubbs, and includes details of stations, movements, changes in command, active services in the field, and so forth. R/4 V/4. RAI. AMM.
Note: the same information can be found in THE STORY OF 'F' TROOP, by Lieut Col C B Findlay (William May & Co Ltd, Aldershot, 1932, iv/84).

A SHORT HISTORY OF 'S' BATTERY, 1826-1926
Anon (shown as 'O.T.F.') * The Cabot Press, Bristol, 1926. Seen only in photo-copy form, 11.5 x 8.25, -/36. Apparently no ills, maps, appendixes, or Index.
* The Bty was first raised as 3rd Troop, 3rd Brigade, Bengal Horse Artillery, and this very brief history makes some reference to those early years.
R/4 V/1. NAM. PJE.

143rd (TOMBS'S TROOP), ROYAL ARTILLERY, A SHORT HISTORY
Formerly 2nd Troop, 1st Brigade, Bengal Horse Artillery
Maj A M Macfarlane * Instance Printers, Woolwich, 1968. Stiff card, Royal blue, gold, Bty crest (Tiger's head), 8.0 x 5.5, -/64. 4 mono phots, no maps, Bibliography, no Index. Apps: H&A, list of former COs, idem former officers, nominal roll for the siege of Delhi (1857).
* The first nine pages cover the period 1825-1862 when the Bty was in HEIC service. Although brief, the very readable narrative is packed with informative detail and interesting anecdotes. A model of its kind. R/2 V/4. RAI. RP.
Note: 500 copies printed. A second (revised) edition, and including one reproduction of a painting, was published in 1992 (-/73 pages).

THE BENGAL HORSE ARTILLERY, 1800-1861
The Red Men, A 19th Century Corps d'Elite
Maj Gen B P Hughes * Arms & Armour Press, London, 1971. Ochre, gold, 10.0 x 7.5, xiv/184. 20 mono phots, 4 cld plates, 14 maps, Bibliography, Index of Persons, Index of Units. Apps: extensive notes on uniforms, arms and armament, tactics, campaigns, medals, organisation and administration, etc.
* The Regt took part in all the major campaigns in India before being absorbed into the Royal Artillery in 1862. This is a very good narrative history, with most of the text being devoted to campaign services. It is regarded as the best overall history of the BHA. R/1 V/5. RAI/MODL. MJC/BCC/JRStA.

HISTORY OF THE 22nd (RESIDENCY) FIELD BATTERY, ROYAL ARTILLERY
Formerly 2nd Company, 3rd Battalion, Bengal (Foot) Artillery
Capt P A Brooke MC * The Pioneer Press, Allahabad, 1931. Royal blue, gold, 7.5 x 5.0, v/47. Fp, no other ills, 3 maps (bound in), no Index. Apps: list of former COs, idem battles and sieges, stations and movements.
* The book is arranged in two sections: pages 1-32 cover the period 1786-1862, while pages 34-42 apply to the period 1862-1930. The bulk of the first section deals with events during the Mutiny (and at Lucknow in particular). Brief, but clear and informative. R/4 V/4. RAI. AMM.

FROM RECRUIT TO STAFF SERGEANT
The Bengal Horse Artillery of Olden Time
N M Bancroft ('Late Sergeant, Bengal Horse Artillery') * Ian Henry Publications, London, 1979. Illustrated stiff card, red, black/white, 8.75 x 5.5, 24/ii/97/xiv. One mono phot, one map (printed in the end-papers), Bibliography, no Index. Apps: list of former COs, idem former officers, extracts from correspondence (1900) from HM the Queen's Secretary, record of service of the author.

* Three editions of this book are known to have been published (1885, 1900, and 1979). The third edition, as recorded here, is the best and the most complete. It includes an Introduction of 24 pages, written by Maj Gen B P Hughes, which describes the Bengal Artillery of the day, and an Epilogue, again by Hughes, which comments upon Bancroft himself. Basically a memoir of his services, the original narrative is a personal record (the only one ever written by an Other Rank of the Regt) which, in effect, is also a history of 2nd Troop, 1st Brigade, BHA, from 1841 to 1859. The commentaries by Hughes are most helpful in explaining to the modern reader the general background against which Bancroft led his life and the larger events of that period. R/1 V/5. RAI/MODL. AMM.

MADRAS

HISTORY OF THE SERVICES OF THE MADRAS ARTILLERY
With a Sketch of the Rise to Power of the East India Company
Maj F J Begbie * Franck & Co, at the Christian Knowledge Society's Press, Madras. Two matching volumes, seen rebound in green, blind (details of original binding not known), 8.75 x 5.25. No ills, no maps, Bibliographies (both volumes), no Indexes (but helpful chapter headings throughout).
Volume I : published in 1852, xviii/275. Covers the period 1600-1810.
Volume II : published in 1853, -/257/Lxvi (the latter being mainly the appendix). Covers the period 1811-1852.
* The 'sketch' mentioned in the sub-title consists of one chapter which is a summary of the founding and growth of the HEIC. For the rest, this substantial work deals exclusively with the evolution and campaigns of the Madras Artillery. Although in many respects a prime source of reference, the narrative does not always identify individual units by name or number, and this will frustrate some categories of researcher. Likewise, the lack of Indexes is an obstacle to ready reference. Only Volume II is provided with a (solitary) appendix. However, it is particularly useful to genealogists and medal collectors. Of 41 pages, it lists every officer who served with the Madras Artillery between 1748 and 1852. Thought to be complete and accurate, it gives their dates of service and details of their war services and awards. R/5 V/4. RAI. AMM.

LIST OF THE OFFICERS WHO HAVE SERVED IN THE MADRAS ARTILLERY FROM ITS FORMATION IN 1748 DOWN TO 1861
Maj John Henry Leslie * Publication details not shown, printed possibly in Derbyshire (UK), 1900. Card, buff, black, 11.5 x 8.75, iv/65. Fp, no other ills, no maps, Index. Apps: list of former COs.
* As stated in the title, this publication lists all the officers who served, and it is therefore an updated version of the appendix described in the preceding entry. It differs to the extent that it does not show their war services. However, useful details of promotion dates, awards, and dates of death (where appropriate) are given. R/5 V/3. RAI. AMM.

CAMEL HOWITZER BATTERY
Planned, Raised and Commanded by Captain J H Frith, Madras Artillery
Raised January 1819, Disbanded 15 May 1821
Capt J H Frith * 'Lithographed' at the Artillery Depot, Madras, 1837.
* Noted in a catalogue, but not seen. The only certain fact is that the book had six colour plate illustrations. One such picture (disbound) has been seen, and this bears the numeral '6'. If this is an accurate guide, it would suggest that the casing of the original book was unusually large - approximately 15.0 x 9.00. AMM.
Note: Frith also compiled a set of gunnery drills under the title REPOSITORY EXERCISE COMPILED FOR THE USE OF THE MADRAS ARTILLERY AT THE DEPOT OF INSTRUCTION, St THOMAS MOUNT. It was lithographed 'by authority' at Fort St George in 1830. Like his Camel Howitzer record, it has an outsize format. A copy of this very rare work is held at the Royal Artillery Institute.

THE HISTORY OF 'F' BATTERY, 'B' BRIGADE, ROYAL HORSE ARTILLERY
Formerly 'A' Troop, Madras Horse Artillery
Capt G E Wyndham Malet * F J Cattermole, Woolwich, 1878. Royal blue, gold, Regtl crest, 7.25 x 4.75, iv/41. Fp, no other ills, no maps, no Index. Apps: list of former COs, idem former officers, notes on changes in unit designations, notes on its campaign services (1808-1859).
* Half of the narrative deals with the period 1767-1861 when the Troop was in HEIC service. The text is an annual diary of stations, movements, changes in command, active service, etc. It relies heavily upon Begbie's major record (vide entry at the head of this page). R/5 V/4. RAI. AMM.
Note: first published in 1877. The second (1878) edition as recorded here is to be

preferred for research purposes (some errors having been detected in the first edition and subsequently corrected).

THE HISTORY OF 'J' BATTERY, ROYAL HORSE ARTILLERY
Formerly 'A' Troop, Madras Horse Artillery
Maj G E W Malet (updated by Maj P H Enthoven and Capt C A Sykes) * Charles Good & Co, London, 1903. Royal blue, gold, 8.75 x 5.5, x/133. Fp, no other ills, one map, no Index. Apps: list of former COs, idem former officers.
* A good reference work, based upon Regtl Orders but with a lot of detailed information of a wider nature. R/5 V/4. NAM/RAI. PJE/AMM.
Note: this is the third and updated version of two earlier editions (dated 1877 and 1898). It brings the story forward to the end of the Anglo-Boer War and includes (in the text) lists of casualties for that war. No copy of the first (1877) edition has been seen, but it is known that the second (1898) edition was printed in a slightly smaller format (7.25 x 4.75). Like the third edition, it has blue cloth covers with gold lettering. The pages are numbered viii/73.

SOME NOTES UPON THE ORIGIN AND SUBSEQUENT DEVELOPMENT (1805 TO 1861) OF THE MADRAS HORSE ARTILLERY
Maj John H Leslie * Printed by W H Lead, Leicester, for The Royal Horse Artillery Institution, London, 1907. Card, grey-green, black, 9.5 x 6.0, ii/8. Fp, 9 mono phots (all of uniforms), no maps, no appendixes, no Index.
* The title page refers to 'J', 'M', 'P', and 'R' Batteries, RHA, as represented in the year 1907. Of these, 'J', 'M', and 'P' still exist today (1993). This very slim booklet is nothing more than a reprint of an article (continuous text without section or chapter headings) first published in the Royal Artillery Journal. The material consists mainly of verbatim quotations from Governor General's Orders. It is of interest only for its information regarding uniforms. R/5 V/1. RAI. AMM.

Note: no published histories have been traced in respect of the Madras Foot Artillery.

BOMBAY

THE BOMBAY ARTILLERY
List of Officers (1748–1862)
Col F W M Spring * William Clowes & Sons Ltd, London, 1902. Cream-white leather spine, Royal blue boards, gold, BA crest, 8.5 x 5.5, xii/135. Fp, 5 sketches, no maps, Index. Apps: H&A, list of former COs, numerous lists and tables within the main body of the book.
* This was the last of three lists of officers of the HEIC Artilleries to be published (vide preceding pages, Maj Gen F W Stubbs, Bengal, and Maj John Henry Leslie, Madras). Of the three, this compilation by Col Spring is much the best. After opening with an outline chronology, he provides long lists of officers in their various appointments in each Company and Troop. Further, he gives details for each unit, showing its campaign services and changes of title. Separately, in a section of fifty pages, he states the records of service of every officer who served with the Bombay Artillery during the stated period (including notes on their campaign medals and their awards). R/4 V/5. RAI. AMM.

RECORDS OF 'E' BATTERY, 'C' BRIGADE, ROYAL HORSE ARTILLERY
4th Troop, Bombay Artillery, 1824–1876
Anon (reported to have been Maj T M Holberton) * Unpublished facsimile TS, copied from a MS first drafted in 1876, no other details shown, 11.5 x 8.5, -/63. No ills, no maps, no Index. Apps: notes on former officers, stations and movements, changes in unit designation.
* A good well-written memorial which covers the principal campaigns in which the 4th Troop was engaged - Mahratta Wars, First Afghan War, Persia, and the Mutiny. The text is based partly upon Regtl records and partly upon personal reminiscences. R/5 V/3. NAM. PJE.

HISTORY OF 'E' BATTERY, 'D' BRIGADE, ROYAL HORSE ARTILLERY, FROM 1820 TO 1876
Formerly 2 Troop, Bombay Horse Artillery
Maj Hubert Le Cocq * Curtis & Beamish, Coventry (UK), n.d. (c.1876). Paper covers, grey, black, 8.0 x 5.25, -/19. No ills, no maps, no Index. Apps: list of former COs, idem former officers.
* The brief narrative deals mainly with events prior to 1862. It gives the usual details of stations and movements, campaign services, and changes in title, and the four pages devoted to the Mutiny period are useful. R/5 V/3. MODL. AMM.

RECORDS OF 'D' BATTERY, 'C' BRIGADE, ROYAL HORSE ARTILLERY
Late 3rd Troop, Bombay Horse Artillery
Lieut Col T M Holberton * F J Cattermole, Woolwich, 1878. Seen in yellow, black, 9.5 x 6.0, -/64. No ills, no maps, no Index. Apps: list of former COs, idem former officers, personal reminiscences of certain engagements.
* A readable and quite full account of the period 1824-1872, with useful detail of the Troop's role in the First Afghan War and the Mutiny. R/5 V/4. NAM. PJE.

A SHORT HISTORY OF THE EAGLE TROOP, R.H.A.
Formerly 1st Troop, Bombay Horse Artillery
Anon * Publisher's details not shown, Hohne, Germany, 1955. Paper covers, buff, blue, 'Eagle' motif, 8.0 x 7.0, ii/40. No ills, no maps, no Index. Apps: list of former COs, stations and movements, notes on actions fought, changes in title.
* Two chapters (12 pages) cover the HEIC period (1811-1862) when the Troop served in the Deccan, First Afghan and Scinde Wars, and in the suppression of the Mutiny. This record, the only one known for this unit, was apparently compiled by one of its officers while he was serving in Germany and therefore having only limited access to source documents. There are some gaps in the coverage, but the booklet is certainly useful as far as it goes. R/3 V/3. RAI. AMM.

MOUNTAIN ARTILLERY

The following notes may assist any researcher having difficulty with the complex evolution of the Indian Army's Mountain Artillery.

The four Batteries of the Punjab Frontier Force were numbered 1, 2, 3, and 4 Mtn Bty on 15 December 1876. Subsequent additional Mtn Btys were numbered 5 to 10 as they were formed. Then, on 22 April 1901, and in order to distinguish them from the British Army's Mtn Btys, which also were numbered 1 to 10, the Indian units lost their numbers entirely. They were instead designated Kohat, Derajat, Peshawar, Hazara, Quetta Mtn Btys (and so forth). This nomenclature lasted little more than two years. On 2 October 1903, the Indian units were all assigned a number, this being their original number plus twenty. In this way they became 21 Kohat Mtn Bty, 22 Derajat Mtn Bty, etc.

Yet another change occurred on 29 November 1921 when it was decided to add eighty to their numbers and re-classify them as Pack Btys, thus 101 (Kohat), 102 (Derajat), 103 (Peshawar), etc.

On 31 July 1924, all these units were transferred from the Indian Army to the British Army, i.e. to the Royal Artillery. The transfers were rescinded on 1 August 1939 when the Indian-manned Mtn Btys were transferred to the Indian Regiment of Artillery which had been formed in 1935. In the meanwhile, however, tradition had triumphed when, on 1 May 1927, the 19th Century numbering system had been reinstated. The Mtn Btys then assumed the titles by which they are most easily recognised in the WWII campaign histories, thus: 1 Royal (Kohat) Mtn Bty, 2 (Derajat) Mtn Bty, etc. Their individual histories were, in the main, published in earlier years and this accounts for the unfamiliar Bty titles which appear in the titles of the books listed on the following pages.

GENERAL REFERENCE

THE HISTORY OF THE INDIAN MOUNTAIN ARTILLERY
Brig C A L Graham DSO OBE * Gale & Polden Ltd, Aldershot, 1957. Dark blue, gold, 9.0 x 5.75, xvi/470. Fp, 15 mono phots, 4 line drawings, 8 maps (bound in), Glossary, Index. Apps: extensive notes on Indian States Mountain Artillery, garrison Btys, survey units, etc.
* A first-class overall history. It covers the entire period from inception in 1840 through to post-WWII operations in Indo-China (1946). The author succeeded in striking a good balance between the evolution of the Corps, its campaigns, and various important technical factors. Many officers, and some ORs, are mentioned in the text. R/2 V/5. PC. BCC.

TALES OF THE MOUNTAIN GUNNERS
An Anthology, Compiled by Those who Served
C H T MacFetridge and J P Warren * William Blackwood, Edinburgh, 1973. Fawn, gold, 10.0 x 7.0, xix/327. Fp, 20 mono phots, 9 maps, no appendixes, no Index.
* A very good secondary source, especially when read in conjunction with Graham (vide preceding entry). R/1 V/3. PC. RP.

REGIMENTAL HISTORIES

ACTION IN BURMA, 1942–1945
Col J C Chaplin DSO OBE * Publisher's details not shown, London, 1984. Blue, gold, 8.5 x 6.0, xiii/212/xxii. Fp, 48 mono phots, 22 maps (bound in), no appendixes, Glossary, Index.
* This is the war history of 21 Mountain Regt RIA in Burma. It comprised 1, 6, and 37 Mtn Btys. Compiled by the officer who commanded the Regt from August 1944 to late 1945, it has a clear and graphic narrative, with many officers and ORs mentioned by name. Numerous citations for gallantry awards are quoted in the text (particularly for awards of the MC). A very helpful source. R/1 V/5. RAI. AMM.

REGIMENTAL HISTORY, 29th INDIAN MOUNTAIN REGIMENT, ROYAL INDIAN ARTILLERY
Anon (known to have been Lieut Col J M Hepper RA) * The Edwardes Press, Razmak, 1946. Card, blind, 8.0 x 6.0, -/39. No ills, no maps, no Index. Apps: Roll of Honour, H&A, list of COs, dairy of events (1942-1945).
* This was a pre-war Regt comprising 9 (Murree) Mtn Bty, 14 (Rajputana) Mtn Bty, and 38 Mtn Bty. The booklet has twenty-three pages of narrative followed by a diary of events and other appendixes. It was probably printed in very limited numbers as a memento for officers who served. R/5 V/4. RAI. AMM.

BATTERY HISTORIES

THE HISTORICAL RECORDS OF No 1 (KOHAT) MOUNTAIN BATTERY, PUNJAB FRONTIER FORCE
Formerly No2 Light Field Battery, PFF
Anon * The Punjab Government Press, Lahore, 1886. Royal blue, gold, 'Gun and crown' motif, 10.5 x 6.75, v/45. No ills, no maps, no appendixes, no Index.
* This is another volume in the useful HISTORICAL RECORDS OF THE REGIMENTS OF THE PUNJAB FRONTIER FORCE series (as noted elsewhere in this bibliography), all of which seem to have been published at roughly the same time. This one covers the period 1851-1886 in detailed diary form. It names all officers who served in the Bty during that time (with their dates of posting), and gives details of Stations, movements and campaign services. R/4 V/4. MODL. AMM.

HISTORICAL RECORD OF No 2 (DERAJAT) MOUNTAIN BATTERY, PUNJAB FRONTIER FORCE
Formerly No3 Light Field Battery, PFF
Anon * W Ball & Co (Successors to The Punjab Printing Co), Lahore, 1887. Dark brown, black on white label, 9.75 x 6.25, -/20. No ills, no maps, no appendixes, no Index.
* Although very similar in content to the 'standard' PFF series (as mentioned in the preceding entry), this book is quite different in outward appearance. This is explained by the fact that it was produced by a commercial printer instead of the usual official printer. It covers the period 1849-1886 in detailed diary form, and contains all the expected information regarding Stations, movements, officers' postings, campaign services, etc. A comprehensive and handy source of reference. R/4 V/4. RAI. AMM.
Note: this work was updated in 1905 and re-published in that year under a title which referred to '22nd Derajat Mountain Battery (Frontier Force) (Formerly No3 Light Field Battery), PFF'. This (second) edition was of similar format to the first, but was printed by The Albion Press, Lahore. The additional material increased the length of the book from -/20 pages to i/41 pages. It was then updated again and produced in 1921 by The Pioneer Press, Allahabad, with a brown casing and slightly larger format. The text covered the period 1849-1920, with additional material for 1905 onwards but without amendment to the earlier passages. As WWI services were included, the length doubled again (to ii/94 pages). Of the three editions, that dated 1921 is the best for research purposes. R/4 V/4. RAI/MODL. AMM.

No 3 (PESHAWAR) MOUNTAIN BATTERY, PUNJAB FRONTIER FORCE, BATTERY HISTORY
Formerly the Peshawar Mountain Train
Anon * The New Albion Press, Lahore, 1886. Red, gold, '7 pounder RML gun' motif, 8.25 x 5.75, i/78. No ills, no maps, no Index. Apps: list of former COs, idem British officers, idem Indian officers, H&A (one name only), notes on the origins of the unit, war services of the unit.
* The narrative covers the period 1853 to 1886. The total number of pages is 159, but half were left blank so that owners of the book could later add their own annotations. An excellent source. R/4 V/4. MODL. AMM.

THE HISTORICAL RECORD OF No 4 (HAZARA) MOUNTAIN BATTERY, PUNJAB FRONTIER FORCE
Formerly the Hazara Mountain Train
Anon * The Punjab Government Press, Lahore, 1888. Royal blue, gold, Bty crest, 10.0 x 6.0, x/97. No ills, no maps, no Index (but a detailed Contents page). Apps: Stations and movements, establishments and rates of pay.
* This is another example of the excellent PFF series of publications of that period. It covers the years 1849 to 1889 in detailed diary form, giving much information regarding officers' services and the Bty's role in the Second Afghan War and various Frontier operations. R/4 V/4. RAI. AMM.

THE HISTORICAL RECORD OF No 5 (OR GARRISON) BATTERY, PUNJAB FRONTIER FORCE
Formerly No 4 (or Garrison) Company, PFF
Anon * The Punjab Government Press, Lahore, 1886. Royal blue, gold, 'Gun and crown' motif, 10.5 x 6.75, i/8. No ills, no maps, no appendixes, no Index.
* No more than a simple pamphlet, this item covers the period 1851 to 1885. It contains details of Stations, movements, officers' postings in and out, etc, but there is nothing on active services for the simple reason that the Bty did not see any such service during that time. R/5 V/2. MODL. AMM.

BATTERY HISTORY, 106th JACOB'S PACK BATTERY
Formerly No 2 (Bombay) Mountain Battery
Anon * The Pioneer Press, Allahabad, 1923. Buff boards with black spine, black, 6.0 x 4.75, –/15. No ills, no maps, no appendixes, no Index.
* This is a narrative account of the Bty's services between 1843 and 1923. There is the usual condensed information regarding Stations and movements, but this is lacking in detail and is imprecise. The best aspects of the story are Maizar (1897) and the Great War (Gallipoli 1915 and Mesopotamia 1916–1919). A disappointing effort. R/5 V/1. RAI. AMM.

MOUNTAIN BATTERY, BURMA 1942
Pat Carmichael * Devin Books, Bournemouth, 1983. Buff, gold, 8.75 x 5.75, v/246. 13 mono phots, one map, no appendixes, Bibliography, no Index.
* A very graphic memoir by a wartime RA officer, on secondment, describing his time with 23 Mountain Bty, RIA, in Burma. The period covered is autumn 1941 through to late 1942 (when he was evacuated). R/1 V/2. RAI. AMM.

ENGINEERS

THE MILITARY ENGINEER IN INDIA

Lieut Col E W C Sandes * Mackays Ltd, Chatham, for the Institution of Royal Engineers, 1933 and 1935. Two matching volumes, red, gold, Corps crest, 9.5 x 6.5.
Volume I : xxiii/594. Fp, 17 mono phots, 18 maps (12 printed in the text, six loose in rear pocket), Index. Apps: notes on each of the component Corps (Bengal, Madras, Bombay), notes on the abolition of the Pioneers. Published in 1933.
Volume II : xxi/392. Fp, 40 mono phots, 9 maps (5 printed in the text, 4 loose in rear pocket), no appendixes, Index. Published in 1935.
* An excellent account of all aspects of the military, civil and marine engineering work done in India between 1640 and 1930 by the officers and men of the Corps of Engineers and of the Sappers & Miners. Having between them a total of nearly one thousand pages, the two volumes are self-evidently comprehensive and detailed. The engineers were involved in one way or another in every military operation fought on Indian soil from the earliest days. Of equal or even greater importance was their impact upon the country's development as a future nation. They were engaged in survey work, map making, road and bridge building, water purification and irrigation schemes, estuary and coastal navigation facilities, and much more besides. This is a completely authoritative record, interestingly written by an expert in his field. R/4 V/5. USII/NAM. PJE.

THE INDIAN SAPPERS & MINERS

Lieut Col E W C Sandes * W & J Mackay & Co Ltd, Chatham, for the Institution of Royal Engineers, 1948. Red, gold, Corps crest, 9.5 x 6.5, xxx/726. Fp, 30 mono phots, 55 maps (52 bound in, 3 loose in rear pocket), Index. Apps: condensed histories of King George V's Own Bengal S&M, Queen Victoria's Own Madras S&M, Royal Bombay S&M, Burma S&M, Indian State Forces S&M, Railway S&M, Indian Submarine Mining & Defence Light Units S&M, Indian Signals Unit S&M.
* The Honourable East India Company followed the example set by the British Army regarding the recruitment of personnel into the engineering services. Officers were members of a Corps of Engineers (Bengal, Madras or Bombay), all other ranks (including European NCOs) were members of a Corps of Sappers & Miners. The British abandoned this practice in 1855. All ranks were thereafter members of the Royal Engineers. The Indian Army, on the other hand, retained the distinction through to WWII. It is for this reason that the history of the Engineers (officers only) and of the Sappers & Miners (other ranks only) frequently overlaps or runs in parallel. On most operations, officers and men fought side-by-side and shared identical risks even though they were members of different Corps. The great strength of this history by Sandes is that it highlights the particular ethos of the Sappers & Miners and explains their own evolution and role. He covers the period 1759-1939 in uniform detail, making numerous references to individual men and their services. The maps are exceptionally helpful. R/3 V/5. NAM. RP.

THE INDIAN ENGINEERS, 1939-1947

Lieut Col E W C Sandes * The Institution of Military Engineers, Kirkee, 1956. Red, gold, 4 Corps crests, 9.5 x 6.5, xxx/534. Fp, 20 mono phots, 25 maps, Index. Apps: notes on the condition of the Bengal, Madras and Bombay Engineer Groups at the outbreak of war, 1939.
* A very thorough and readable history for the WWII period, the work of the Corps at home and overseas, and the impact of Partition. R/3 V/3. USII/NAM. BDM.

THE CORPS OF INDIAN ENGINEERS, 1939-47

Maj S Verna and Maj V K Anand * The Controller of Publications, for the Historical Section, Ministry of Defence, Delhi, 1974. Green, gold, 10.0 x 6.5, xii/486. 20 mono phots, 8 maps (bound in), Bibliography, Index. Apps: 38 in total and too abstruse to be described here (one is a 'list of officers who held senior engineering appointments during WWII', but the others are concerned with organisational and technical matters).

* This book covers the same ground as Sandes' account of the same period (vide preceding entry), but the authors concentrated far more upon the technical and essentially 'engineering' aspects than he did. They looked at the problems and the solutions which characterised the campaigns in East Africa, North Africa, Malaya, Burma, and South East Asia. Extremely detailed, and certainly a prime source for the specialist researcher. R/2 V/4. IOL. RGB/RH.
Note: the publication described above was the final volume of the 24-volume OFFICIAL HISTORY OF THE INDIAN ARMED FORCES IN WORLD WAR II.

HISTORY OF THE 10th INDIAN DIVISIONAL ENGINEERS
Lieut Col G F Hutchinson * Publication details not shown, 1946. Black, gold, 9.5 x 6.0, ii/63. No ills, 14 maps (RE survey maps, bound in), no Index. Apps: list of officers, notes on casualties.
* A good readable narrative account which covers the period from May 1944 to May 1945. Based upon the War Diary, and full of informative detail.
R/4 V/4. NAM. PJE.

HISTORY OF THE CORPS OF ENGINEERS
Anon (but attributed in the Foreword to Maj O N Karir and Maj D K Palit) * Palit & Palit, New Delhi, for the Engineer-in-Chief, AHQ, New Delhi, 1980. Blue, gold, 8.5 x 5.5, vii/510. 56 mono phots, 21 maps (bound in), Index. Apps: H&A (1948-1979).
* A worthy successor to Sandes (vide preceding page) to whom the authors pay tribute. Well written and authoritative, it picks up the story from where Sandes left it - the period of Partition - and carries it through to the organisation and events of 1975 (with awards listed through to 1979). Chapter I is a summary of the pre-1947 history of the Corps. A final chapter covers the organisation of the Corps and its involvement in sport, surveying and road construction. The bulk of the chapters are devoted to operations in the three Indo-Pakistan Wars, the Chinese incursion, operations in Hyderabad and Goa, and various United Nations commitments. The narrative includes a candid examination of the problems caused by 'Indianisation' of the Corps in the 1930s and 1940s. A most useful record in every way. R/2 V/5. CRLC. RBM.

BENGAL

HISTORY AND DIGEST OF SERVICE OF THE 1st KING GEORGE'S OWN SAPPERS & MINERS
Anon * 1st King George's Own Press, Roorkee, n.d. (c.1911). Marbled blue boards, brown leather spine and quarters, black, 13.0 x 8.5, -/75.
No ills, no maps, no appendixes, no Index.
* A brief summary of Stations, movements and campaigns, covering the period up to 1908. R/5 V/2. NAM. PJE.

A SHORT HISTORY OF THE CORPS OF KING GEORGE'S OWN BENGAL SAPPERS & MINERS DURING THE WAR, 1914-1918
Col A H Cunningham * Publication details not shown, 1930. Light blue boards, black spine and quarters, black, 13.0 x 8.5, -/85. No ills, no maps, no Index.
Apps: H&A, list of officers (with details of their services), notes on Corps strengths.
* A brief record of WWI services based upon official documents, with very little detail of any kind. R/4 V/2. NAM. PJE.

REGIMENTAL HISTORY OF THE KING GEORGE'S OWN BENGAL SAPPERS & MINERS
Anon * HQ Printing Press, KGO Bengal Sappers & Miners Press, Roorkee, 1937.
Stiff card, black with brown spine, black, 13.0 x 8.5, iii/76. No ills, no maps, no appendixes, no Index.
* Printed in English and in Urdu (38 pages of text for each language). It was used until 1939 for the instruction of Indian ORs, and covers all the campaigns in which the Corps was engaged between 1803 and 1930. It also deals with organisational matters up to 1933. Although very brief, the book does contain a surprising amount of detail (including instances of gallantry by named individuals during the Great War).R/5 V/2. PC. DCSD.

CALENDAR OF BATTLES, HONOURS AND AWARDS
King George V's Own Bengal Sappers & Miners from 1803 to 1939
Capt K S Rahmat Ullan Khan * Publication details not shown, n.d. (c.1944). Blue, gold lettering and embellishments, 13.0 x 8.5, -/63. No ills, no maps, no appendixes, no Index.
* As the title indicates, this is a compendium of information regarding all honours and awards gained by the Corps and by Corps personnel in all the campaigns in which its units took part during the stated period. It is unlikely that every single award winner appears in the book, but a great many individuals are named and it is clearly a useful source for medal collectors. An unusual and attractive little publication. R/4 V/3. NAM. PJE.

BRIEF HISTORY OF THE KING GEORGE V's OWN BENGAL SAPPERS & MINERS GROUP R.I.E. (AUGUST 1939 - JULY 1946)
Lieut Col G Pearson * Publication details not shown, Roorkee, 1947. Dark blue, gold, 9.5 x 6.5, vi/153. 11 mono phots, 7 maps (bound in at the rear), no Index.
Apps: H&A.
* A detailed account of the Corps' activities in the Western Desert, Malaya, Burma and Italy. This is the closest that the Bengal S&M ever came to producing a conventional record of their services. It was certainly a considerable improvement on its predecessors. R/4 V/3. NAM. PJE.

MADRAS

HISTORICAL RECORD OF THE 'QUEEN'S OWN' SAPPERS & MINERS
Containing an Account of the Establishment of Companies of Pioneers in 1770, the Formation of these Companies in Corps of Sappers & Miners in 1831, and the History of their Service from 1780 to 1876
Lieut Col W J Wilson * The Government Press, Madras, 1877. Grey, black, 9.25 x 6.5, -/104. No ills, no maps, no Index. Apps: list of former COs, extracts from Madras Army Regulations (relating to Sappers & Miners), rules for tasks in trade testing.
* A narrative account, arranged chronologically, covering the period 1780 to 1876, with details of Stations, movements and campaign services. Many individual officers are named in the text. R/5 V/3. IOL. AMM.

THE MILITARY HISTORY OF THE MADRAS ENGINEERS AND PIONEERS
From 1743 up to the Present Time
Maj H M Vibert * W H Allen & Co, London, 1881 and 1883. Two matching volumes, red, gold, 9.0 x 6.5.
Volume I : 1743-1829. xxiii/602. Fp, no other ills, 23 maps, Bibliography, no Index. Published in 1881.
Volume II : 1829-1879. xiv/627. Fp, no other ills, 26 maps, Index (for both vols). Published in 1883.
* This is a handsome and very well presented pair of books, with many individual officers mentioned in the narrative and with admirably full descriptions of battles and campaign services. Both volumes have appendixes which list casualties (officers only), honours and awards (British and Indian officers), former Chief Engineers and Commandants, and officers who served. R/4 V/5. IOL. AMM.
Note: this book is essentially the history of the Madras Engineers (officers) rather than a history of the Madras Sappers & Miners (other ranks). However, it has been thought appropriate to list it here (instead of in the 'Indian Engineers' section) because the services of the two Corps overlap at almost every point.

HISTORICAL RECORD OF THE 2nd 'QUEEN'S OWN' SAPPERS AND MINERS
From 1780 to 1909
Lieut Col C H Roe * 2nd 'QO' Sappers & Miners Press, Bangalore, 1909. Dark red, gold, 9.5 x 6.5, -/272. No ills, no maps, Index. Apps: Roll of Honour, list of former Commandants, idem former officers, notes on Stations and movements.
* The narrative is based upon Corps Orders and official records but, unusually for publications of this genre, is full of interesting detail. It covers almost all the campaigns fought during the stated period. R/4 V/4. IOL. AMM.

HISTORICAL RECORD OF THE 2nd 'QUEEN VICTORIA'S OWN' SAPPERS & MINERS FROM 1914 TO 1919
Lieut Col R L McClintock CMG DSO * 2nd 'QVO' Sappers & Miners Press, Bangalore, 1921. Stiff card, yellow, black, 10.0 x 6.5, -/39. No ills, no maps, no Index. Apps: Roll of Honour, H&A, list of officers who served.
* A brief account based upon official records, with few individuals named. Its main value are the references to active service in the Middle East.
R/4 V/2. NAM. PJE.
Note: it seems that this booklet was published as a provisional measure while the Corps was settling back at Bangalore after its wartime travels and pending the production of a more detailed history. It was not intended to be a 'Volume II' in the series commenced by Roe (vide preceding entry). However, at least one 'official' publication has been seen with a 'Volume II' imprint and which amalgamates McClintock's (1914-1919) text with Roe's (1780-1909) text, there being a short linking narrative to cover the gap (1910-1914). This publication, which is dated 1921, can be regarded as an 'early version Volume II'.

HISTORICAL RECORD OF THE 2nd 'QUEEN VICTORIA'S OWN' SAPPERS & MINERS
Lieut Col C H Roe and Lieut Col R L McClintock * 2nd 'QVO' Sappers & Miners Press, Bangalore. Two matching volumes, mauve, black, Corps crest, 10.0 x 6.5,
Volume I : From 1780 to 1910. Published in 1921, -/245. No ills, no maps, no Index. Apps: Roll of Honour, H&A, list of former officers.
Volume II : From 1910 to 1914, From 1914 to 1919, and From 1919 to 1923. Published in 1923, -/109 (arranged in three sections, the pages numbered through to 39, 39, and 31, respectively). No ills, no maps, no Index. Apps: Roll of Honour, H&A, list of officers.
* Volume I is an edited version of the history written by Roe which covered the period 1708-1909 (vide preceding page). Volume II is arranged in three sections, the first being new material written by Roe and covering the period 1910-1914 (39 pages). The second section is a reprint of McClintock's account of services between 1914 and 1919 as noted in the preceding entry (also having 39 pages). The third section deals with the post-war period, 1919-1923 (31 pages) and this section also was written by McClintock. By no means a complete Corps history, these two volumes do contain much interesting detail, presented in terse but readable form. R/4 V/4. PC. HLL.
Note: some copies of Volume II have been seen which do not contain Part II (1914 -1919). Then again, other copies of Volume II have been seen which additionally incorporate an 'Appendix J - Notes on Medals awarded to the Corps for its various Campaigns'. This material was compiled by McClintock. From the surviving evidence, it must be concluded that the printers at the 2nd 'QVO' Sappers & Miners Press produced at least two variant versions of Volume II, presumably to meet individual requests from serving and former officers of the Corps.

Q.V.O. MADRAS SAPPERS & MINERS IN FRANCE AND IRAQ, 1914-1920
Lieut Col R Hamilton and Maj A H Morin * Publication details not shown, Bangalore, n.d. (c.1922). Brown, black, 10.0 x 6.5, iv/78. 8 mono phots and 2 maps pasted in, plus 7 folding maps, bound in at the rear, no appendixes, no Index.
* Although brief, this is an informative account of the Corps' services on the Western Front, in the Mesopotamia campaign, and in the post-war Iraq operations. The narrative is based directly upon the War Diaries, other official sources, and the authors' own experiences. The result is authoritative. R/5 V/4. NAM. PJE.

DIGEST OF THE SERVICES OF QUEEN VICTORIA'S OWN SAPPERS & MINERS, 1923-1939
Brig Neville H L Chessyre * Produced at Bangalore, for the Regt, 1981. White, black, 9.0 x 7.0, iv/233. 20 mono phots, 2 diagrams and one map (folding, bound in), no Index. Apps: H&A (all ranks), list of Commandants, list of officers who served during the stated period.
* This substantial work is a facsimile reproduction of original typescript, and the print quality is correspondingly poor. The narrative content is mixed, being an amalgam of comments on inter-war frontier soldiering, routine exercises, social and sporting activities, all presented in the style of a Regtl journal. The roll of officers is reported to be incomplete. R/4 V/3. PC. HLL.

A SHORT HISTORY OF QUEEN VICTORIA'S OWN MADRAS SAPPERS & MINERS DURING DURING WORLD WAR II, 1939-1945
Lieut Col R A Lindsell * Publication details not shown, Bangalore, 1947. Hard case outer covers, folios stapled and poorly glued, blue, 8.5 x 5.5, -/148. Fp, 26 mono phots, 7 maps (stapled in at the rear), no Index. Apps: Roll of Honour (all ranks), H&A (all ranks), list of former Commandants.
* A good narrative account of services in Abyssinia, Egypt, the Western Desert, the Aegean, Italy, Greece, Malaya, Burma, and Indo-China. There are useful biographical notes on many officers who served. The number of copies printed is said to have been one thousand. The number still in existence is likely to be much reduced as a consequence of the original poor assembly and binding. The book was compiled at great speed, the author being given only two months in which to prepare his material (Partition was at the time imminent). R/5 V/4. RMAS. RP.

BOMBAY

SHORT HISTORY OF THE 3rd SAPPERS & MINERS

Anon * Publication details not shown, n.d. (c.1910). Black, gold, 8.0 x 5.5, -/18. No ills, no maps, no appendixes, no Index.
* A very brief record based upon Corps records. It covers the period 1820 to 1910, with some passing references to its services in Persia, the Mutiny, Second Afghan War, Third China War, and on the Frontier. R/4 V/1. NAM. PJE.

A BRIEF HISTORY OF THE ROYAL BOMBAY SAPPERS & MINERS

Anon * Royal Bombay Sappers & Miners Press, Kirkee, 1924. Red, black, 8.0 x 5.5, -/38. No ills, no maps, no appendixes, no Index.
* Another very brief account, this one produced for use in the Corps schools. The text is based upon official records. It includes a section devoted to honours and awards which might otherwise have appeared in the form of an appendix. R/5 V/1. IWM. PJE.

HISTORY OF THE 20th (FIELD) COMPANY, ROYAL BOMBAY SAPPERS & MINERS
Great War: 1914-1918

Maj H W R Hamilton DSO MC * Reprinted from an article first published in the Royal Engineers Journal, n.d. Stiff card, white boards with blue spine, black, 9.75 x 6.0, -/51. No ills, 6 maps (large flimsies, folding, bound in), no appendixes, no Index.
* To quote from the Introduction: 'Compiled mainly from the War Diary of the Company, supplemented by the memory of the writer'. An interesting narrative account, with many British officers mentioned in the text, of services in France and Flanders (1914-1915), Mesopotamia (1916-1917, including the Relief of Kut-al-Amara), and Palestine (1918). R/5 V/3. NAM. RP.

SHORT HISTORY OF THE 17th AND 22nd FIELD COMPANIES, THIRD SAPPERS & MINERS, IN MESOPOTAMIA, 1914-1918

Brig Gen U W Evans CB CMG, Col F A Wilson CB, Lieut Col E J Loring MC, Maj K B S Crawford, Maj K D Yearsley, and others * Publication details not shown, Kirkee, 1932. Calfskin, mid-blue boards with dark blue spine, gold, 8.5 x 5.5, vii/131. Fp, no other ills, 10 maps (bound in), Index. Apps: H&A (British and Indian, all ranks), statistics on casualties (KIA, WIA and POW), notes on the organisation of a Field Company.
* A very detailed account of two typical S&M Field Coys in WWI. Many British and Indian personnel of all ranks are mentioned in the narrative, and there is excellent coverage of several engagements barely mentioned (if at all) in other published sources. R/4 V/4. PC. EDS.

APPENDIX V

Designations of the Corps of Sappers & Miners

King George's Own Bengal Sappers & Miners (1923)
formerly
1st King George's Own Sappers & Miners (Great War period)
formerly
1st Sappers & Miners (1903)
formerly
Bengal Sappers & Miners

Queen Victoria's Own Madras Sappers & Miners (1923)
formerly
2nd Queen Victoria's Own Sappers & Miners (Great War period)
formerly
2nd Queen's Own Sappers & Miners (1903)
formerly
Madras Sappers & Miners

Royal Bombay Sappers & Miners (1923)
formerly
3rd Sappers & Miners (Great War period)
formerly
3rd Sappers & Miners (1903)
formerly
Bombay Sappers & Miners

Note: in 1922, the 4th Burma Sappers & Miners were formed. The title was changed in 1923 to, simply, Burma Sappers & Miners. No published record for this Corps has been traced.

THE PIONEERS

Sikh Pioneers

A SHORT HISTORY OF THE 23rd SIKH PIONEERS
Capt H M Pirouet * G F Amary, Finchley, London, 1927. Brown, dark brown, 5.0 x 4.5, -/68. 11 mono phots, no maps, no Index. Apps: Roll of Honour, list of former COs, idem former officers.
* The Preface states that this little book was intended to be 'accessible to all', but surviving copies are in fact very rarely seen. It is a condensed and fairly basic record - the only one dedicated exclusively to the 23rd Sikh Pioneers. It provides a handy overview of the Regt's forebears and their services between 1857 and 1923 - the Mutiny, China (1860), Umbeyla, Abyssinia, Second Afghan, Chitral, Tibet, Waziristan (1921-1923). Some gallantry awards and promotions are mentioned in the text (which is otherwise devoid of detail). R/5 V/3. USII/ASKBC. OSS/CB.

32nd SIKH PIONEERS
Volume I : Delhi 1857, Waziristan 1902
Lieut Col H R Brander * Thacker, Spink & Co, Calcutta, n.d. (c.1905). Red, black, 7.5 x 5.0, x/204. Fp, no other ills, no maps, no Index. Apps: notes on the Mahzbi (or Muzbee) Sikhs, idem the Delhi Pioneers/Punjab Pioneers, Army List extracts.
* Originally a scratch force of low-caste civilian canal-diggers, mobilised hurriedly in 1857 to assist in the siege operations at Delhi, the Muzbee Sikhs evolved into one of the Indian Army's most famous Regts. This account covers the period 1857 to 1902, and is informative and interesting. R/4 V/3. USII. OSS.

32nd SIKH PIONEERS
Volume II : Sikkim and Tibet, 1903-04
Lieut Col H R Brander * Edward Stanford, London, n.d. (c.1906). Red, black, 7.5 x 5.0, -/105. One topographical sketch, 4 maps (folding, bound in), no Index. Apps: Roll of Honour (British officers only, 1857-1904), list of former COs, Stations and movements (1857-1904), recipients of the Indian Order of Merit (1858-1904, with details).
* An excellent full account of the Regt's role in the Tibet campaign. Many individuals are mentioned in the narrative, with details of their actions and awards. R/4 V/4. RMAS/USII/NAM. RP.

THE HISTORY OF THE SIKH PIONEERS
(23nd, 32nd, 34th)
Lieut Gen Sir George MacMunn KCB KCSI DSO * Printed by Purnell & Son Ltd, for Sampson, Low, Marston & Co Ltd, n.d. (c.1936). Red, gold, 'Pioneer soldier and four Regtl crests' motif, 9.5 x 6.25, xvi/560. Fp, 45 mono phots, 4 maps (two bound in, two printed on the end-papers), Index. Apps: list of former COs, biographies of four famous members of the Corps.
* A magnificent work, beautifully printed and bound, a pleasure to handle. The narrative covers the evolution of the Corps and its component Regts over the period 1857 (formation) to 1933 (disbandment). For the 32nd Regt, it incorporates much of the material found in Brander (vide two preceding entries). This is a most desirable book. R/3 V/5. NAM/IOL. RP.

Madras Pioneers

RECORDS OF THE IV MADRAS PIONEERS (NOW THE 64th PIONEERS), 1759-1903
Maj H F Murland * Higginbothams Ltd, Bangalore, 1922. Dark blue, gold, 11.25 x 8.5, -/314. No ills, no maps, Bibliography, no Index. Apps: list of former COs, idem former officers.
* A history in expanded diary form. The author gives particular attention to the

origins and evolution of the Regt and to its earlier wars - Haidar Ali (the 1760s), Pondicherry (1778), and Tipu Sultan (1792-1799). There are good accounts of various Frontier campaigns and the Third China War. A very helpful source of reference. R/4 V/4. IOL. RGB.

REGIMENTAL RECORDS OF 2nd BATTALION, 1st MADRAS PIONEERS, 1903-1925
Anon ('Committee of the Regiment') * 2nd Bn 1st Madras Pioneers Press, Madras, 1926. Dark blue, gold, 10.5 x 8.25, -/235. No ills, no maps, no formal appendixes, no Index.
* A very detailed history in diary form, dedicated mainly to the WWI period. The Bn served in Mesopotamia and Palestine (1916-1919), Persia (1919-1921), and then in the suppression of the Moplah Rebellion (1921-1922). There are no appendixes, but Chapters IV and V contain comprehensive lists of British officers who served (1903-1925) with biographical notes for each. Lists of Indian officers are also included in the text. R/4 V/4. IOL/USII. RGB.

BAILLIE-KI-PALTAN
Being a History of the 2nd Battalion, Madras Pioneers (Formerly the IV Madras Pioneers), 1759-1930
Lieut Col H F Murland * Higginbothams, Madras, 1932. Blue, gold, Regtl crest, 10.0 x 8.5, viii/602. Fp, no other ills, 24 maps (20 printed in the text, 4 folding, bound in), Bibliography, Index (names of British officers only). Apps: list of former COs, idem other officers (British and Indian), a selected list of SNCOs.
* A major history, comprehensive and detailed. The contents are divided into five parts for ease of reference. The maps are particularly well executed. The Regt was disbanded in 1933. R/3 V/5. NAM/IOL. TA.

Bombay Pioneers

HISTORICAL RECORD OF THE 21st REGIMENT, BOMBAY NATIVE INFANTRY OR MARINE BATTALION
Anon ('A Committee of the Regiment') * The Education Society's Press, Bombay, 1875. Light blue, gold, 9.5 x 6.0, -/57. No ills, no maps, no appendixes, no Index.
* A simple compendium of official documents. The Regt was first raised, in 1777, by the HEIC's Bombay Marine for maritime service in the Arabian Sea and the Persian Gulf. There it was employed in actions against pirates and slavers. It also fought in the Mahratta War of 1817-1818 and was then converted into a Pioneer Regt. It was retitled 121st Pioneers in 1903, fought overseas in WWI, and became 10/2nd Bombay Pioneers in 1922. R/4 V/2. IOL. RGB.

BRIEF HISTORY OF THE 121st PIONEERS, 1915-1922
Anon * CMS Mission Press, Sikandra Agra, n.d. Purple boards, black spine, gold, 7.5 x 5.5, i/34. No ills, no maps, no appendixes, no Index.
* The Regt's movements during 1915 and 1916 are covered in the first ten lines of narrative. The rest of this little volume contains a sketchy account of the period February 1917 to March 1922 (Mesopotamia, Palestine, and Waziristan). In 1922, the Regt became the 10th (Training) Bn of the 2nd Bombay Pioneers. Almost all of information found here is repeated verbatim in Tugwell's history (vide the following entry), so it is possible that he compiled both books. R/5 V/2. PC. CJP.

HISTORY OF THE BOMBAY PIONEERS, 1777-1933
Lieut Col W B P Tugwell * The Sydney Press Ltd, Bedford, 1938. Half leather, half cloth, blue, gold, Regtl crest, 8.75 x 5.5, xix/439. Fp, 43 mono phots, 8 cld plates, 17 maps (14 printed in the text, 3 bound in), Bibliography, Index. Apps: thirteen in total, incl 'Genealogy of the Corps', notes on class compositions, the Colours, notes on dress and insignia, list of former Commandants, etc.
* One of the most comprehensive and handsomely produced of all Indian Army unit

histories. The narrative covers the period from 1790 through to the Waziristan campaign of 1920-1923, with good coverage of the First Afghan War, the Mutiny, Abyssinia, Second Afghan War, Frontier operations, and Somaliland in 1902-1904. The second half of the book is devoted entirely to WWI services on the Western Front, and in Mesopotamia, Palestine, and Persia. R/3 V/5. NAM/PCAL. RP.

HISTORY OF THE 121st PIONEERS
W B P Tugwell * The Regimental Printing Press, Meerut, 1918. Stiff card, olive, green, gold, 7.25 x 5.5, -/33. No ills, no maps, no appendixes, no Index.
* This little item was drafted while the war was still in progress, presumably for the instruction of newly joined officers. It is a very superficial list of all the major campaigns in which the Regt was engaged, with only the barest details shown for each. It is reasonable to assume that this was the seminal account from which the publications recorded in the two preceding entries later flowed. Interesting mainly for its rarity as a collector's item. R/5 V/1. NAM. PJE.

PIONEERS ON FOUR FRONTS
Being a Record of the Doings of the 107th Pioneers, now 1/2 Regiment of Pioneers, in the Great War
Edwin Haward * The Civil & Military Gazette Press, Lahore, 1923. Dark green, gold, 8.75 x 5.5, -/63. No ills, 4 maps (bound in at the rear), Index. Apps: Roll of Honour, H&A (1914-1920), list of COs, idem Adjutants, idem all officers, idem Subedar Majors (all from 1796 to 1923).
* A dry but quite detailed summary of WWI services on the Western Front, and in Mesopotamia, Waziristan, and East Persia (hence the title of the book). A useful source, especially the detailed appendixes of personnel. R/4 V/3. NAM/IOL. RGB.

Hazara Pioneers

A BRIEF HISTORY OF THE 106th HAZARA PIONEERS
Brig Gen N L S P Bunbury * Unpublished TS, no details shown, 1949. Seen in card covers, multi-coloured, MS ink lettering, 9.0 x 7.0, -/25.
* This Regt was raised in 1904. In 1922 it became 1/4th Hazara Pioneers, and this is the only known attempt at a formal history. Despite its brevity, it does contain some useful reference material - a list of COs, a list of Regtl officers, and so forth - with some mention of active services in WWI and operations in Siberia. The period covered is 1903 to 1933. R/5 V/2. IOL/NAM. PJE.
Note: it seems likely that Bunbury made several facsimile copies of his TS and presented them to a number of museums and libraries.

JAWAN TO GENERAL
Recollections of a Pakistani Soldier
Gen Mohammad Musa HJ MBE * ABC Publishing House, New Delhi, 1985. Green, white, 8.75 x 5.5, xv/240. Fp, 40 mono phots, 5 maps, no appendixes, Index.
* The author joined the Hazara Pioneers as a Jawan (private soldier) in 1926, was Commissioned ten years later, and then transferred to 6/13th Frontier Force Rifles. During WWII he served in East Africa and the Western Desert. Apart from being a very readable memoir by the first Pakistani soldier to rise from the ranks to full General, his account of his early years with the Hazara Pioneers provides continuity with the Bunbury notes (vide preceding entry). R/1 V/3. PC. JG.

Note:

Pioneers have been described as 'a superior kind of infantrymen who were as expert with the rifle as they were with the pick and shovel'. More formally, they were 'trained to carry out those military works requiring for their construction training less expert than Engineers but more skilled than infantry'.

By 1933, the role of the Pioneers and the Sappers & Miners had merged to the point at which they were almost identical. The Pioneers were then disbanded.

SIGNALS

HISTORY OF THE CORPS OF SIGNALS
Volume I : Early Times to the Outbreak of World War II, 1939
Anon ('The Corps of Signals Committee') * The Military College of Engineering Press, Mhow, 1975. Dark blue, gold, Corps crest, 9.5 x 6.5, ix/378. Fp, 30 mono phots, 3 sketches, 11 maps, no appendixes, Index.
* The book opens with a general history of signalling from the time of the Ancient Greeks onwards. It covers all the known methods of communication - drums, bells, flags, fires, smoke, mirrors, semaphore, electric telegraph and radio - and makes the point that the Mongols could despatch a message from Europe to Karakoram at an average speed of 250 miles per day. Like the later Pony Express in America, they employed a series of skilled horsemen. Military signalling was formalised in the 1870s and a School of Signalling was established at Kasauli in 1888. It was the responsibility of the Sappers & Miners. Army signallers were used in the field for the first time during the Abor Expedition of 1911-1912. The narrative then follows with five chapters on the various theatres of war between 1914 and 1919. The next chapter deals with the NWF operations of 1922-1927. Finally, the author covers the work of the Corps of Signals from 1927 to 1939. This book was the first in a projected 3-volume series. R/2 V/4. NAM. PJE.

A HISTORY OF THE CORPS OF SIGNALS
Col V A Subramanyam * Macmillan India Ltd, New Delhi, 1986. Dark blue, blind, 9.5 x 6.5, xii/303. 39 mono phots, 7 line drawings (cap badges), 22 maps, no Index. Apps: H&A (Indian recipients only, 1911-1986), list of Signal Officers in Chief (1901-1985, with biographical notes for those appointed after 1947), notes on equipment operated during WWII.
* The planned 3-volume series was abandoned some time after the publication of Volume I in 1975 (vide preceding entry). It was decided to instead produce a single-volume comprehensive Corps history. Volume I had covered the events of pre-1939 in great detail, so it is not surprising that Subramanyam's book contains only 23 pages devoted to that period. The next 63 pages cover the Corps' role and services in WWII, and the operations of 1945-1946 in the Dutch East Indies. Two chapters then explain the reorganisations leading up to Partition and the key function during that time of the Signals Directorate. The rest of the book deals with the work of the ISC from 1947 to 1985. A useful publication, but one which contains frustratingly little information concerning the Corps' valuable contribution during WWII. The 63 pages already mentioned barely do it justice. R/2 V/4. PC. CJP.

NOTES

INFANTRY REGIMENTS

1st PUNJAB REGIMENT

HISTORY OF THE 2nd MADRAS INFANTRY
Lieut Col R M Rainey-Robinson * Thacker Spink & Co, Calcutta. Two unmatched volumes, 9.0 x 6.0. No ills, no maps, no appendixes, no Indexes.
Volume I : dark green, gold, -/63, published in 1904.
Volume II : paper covers, olive, black, -/14, published in 1909.
* These two very slim volumes contain extracts from various Regtl records and official reports.The material is sparse and basically not very helpful. It deals mainly with movements and Stations, and with the comings and goings of officers. In 1903, the Regt was retitled as the 62nd Punjabis. R/4 V/1. NAM. PJE.

A BRIEF HISTORY OF THE 3rd BATTALION, 1st PUNJAB REGIMENT
Formerly 76th Punjabis, 16th Madras Infantry, 16th Regiment Madras Native Infantry, 2nd Battalion 5th Madras Native Infantry, 16th Madras Battalion, 16th Carnatic Battalion or Lane's Battalion
Anon * Gale & Polden Ltd, Aldershot, 1927. Green, gold, blind spine, Regtl crest on front cover, 7.5 x 5.0, v/56. Apps: Roll of Honour (officers only, KIA and WIA), H&A, list of former COs.
* A booklet published to commemorate the Regt's 150 years' existence (under the various designations shown in the sub-title). It contains a short summary of its services in the 19th Century, and then the WWI operations in which the Regt was awarded seven Battle Honours (mainly Mesopotamia). Subsequently it took part in the Third Afghan War and the Waziristan troubles of 1921-1923. R/4 V/4. NAM. RJW.

HISTORY OF THE 1st BATTALION, 1st PUNJAB REGIMENT
C W Sanders * The Civil & Military Gazette Press, Lahore, 1937. Dark green, gold, 6.5 x 5.0, ii/45. Fp, no other ills, no maps, no appendixes, no Index.
* A very brief history, based upon extracts from Regtl records and official papers, with some sketchy descriptions of battles. Collectable for its rarity value, but of little interest as a research source. R/4 V/1. NAM. PJE.
Note: a version having 61 pages has been noted but not seen.

AN OUTLINE HISTORY OF THE 1st PUNJAB REGIMENT, 1759-1944
Anon * Gouldsbury Press, Jhelum, n.d. (1944). Cloth-covered stiff boards with a 'bootlace' binding, green, black, Regtl crest, 9.25 x 5.25, vi/80. Fp, six line drawings (Bn crests), no maps, no Index. Apps: H&A (for all ranks, British and Indian, WWII only, up to 1944), notes on the evolution of the Bn titles.
* Almost certainly produced for the instruction of newly joined wartime officers, this handy book is based upon previously published histories of the six constituent Bns. For 'security reasons ... the present war', no individuals are named in the narrative. However, the H&A appendix is detailed and seemingly complete.
R/5 V/3. NAM. TK-C.

THE FIRST PUNJABIS
History of the First Punjab Regiment, 1759-1956
Maj Mohammad Ibrahim Qureshi * Gale & Polden Ltd, Aldershot, 1958. Green, gold, Regtl crest with red embellishment, 9.5 x 6.25, xix/484. Fp, 48 mono phots, 50 maps (43 printed in the text, 5 bound in, 2 printed on the end-papers), Index. Apps: H&A (WWII only, all ranks), list of former COs, idem Honorary Colonels, notes on past and present Bn titles.
* Published to commemorate the 200th anniversary of the founding of the Regt, this book was the first serious attempt to record its history in full. The author, an excellent historian, produced a tour de force. His narrative is informative and fluently written, and great care was taken with presentation, maps, and indexing. The printing and binding are equally good. R/3 V/5. NAM/IOL. RP.

VETERAN CAMPAIGNERS
A History of the Punjab Regiment, 1759-1981 (Pakistan Army)
Brig S Haider Abbas Rizvi * Printed by Wajidalis, Lahore, Pakistan, 1984. Green, gold, regtl crest, 9.0 x 6.0, xxxiii/585. Fp, 33 mono phots, 8 cld ills, 21 maps (19 printed in the text, 2 on the end-papers), Index. Apps: Roll of Honour (for officers only), H&A (statistics only), list of former officers, notes on uniforms, marching tunes, casualties, important events, Battle Honours.
* In its modern form, the Regt was raised in 1956 from 1st, 14th, 15th, and 16th Punjab Regts of the pre-1947 Indian Army. The author covers in brief terms the early histories (with war services) of those Regts. The period 1956 to 1981 saw the modern Regt expand to a strength of sixty-four Bns. Given the obvious difficulties of attempting to tell the story of each and every one of these Bns, in detail and within the confines of a single volume, this book must be regarded as a very good effort. It certainly provides most of the information which most researchers are likely to require. R/3 V/5. PC. RWH.

2nd PUNJAB REGIMENT

HISTORY OF THE 1st BATTALION, 2nd PUNJAB REGIMENT
Late 67th Punjabis, and Originally 7th Madras Infantry, 1761-1928
Col H Ogle and Lieut Col H W Johnston * Facsimile TS, no publisher's details shown, n.d. (c.1929). Green boards with dark green spine, blind, 10.5 x 8.5, ii/86. No ills, 3 maps, no Index. Apps: H&A, list of former COs, idem other officers, notes on Battle Honours, idem badges and insignia.
* This is a hybrid between the old-fashioned type of Indian Army unit history and the more informative style which later replaced it. The text is still rooted firmly in extracts from Regtl records and official reports, but the authors have expanded upon these with their own linking narrative. Although brief, the result is readable and informative. R/4 V/3. NAM. PJE/CJP.

REGIMENTAL HISTORY OF THE 3rd BATTALION, 2nd PUNJAB REGIMENT
Col H C Wylly CB * Gale & Polden Ltd, Aldershot, 1927. Green, gold, Regtl crest, 9.0 x 7.25, v/74. Fp, 3 mono phots, no maps, Index. Apps: list of Battle Honours.
* Col Wylly usually wrote substantial histories and provided plenty of detail. This booklet is an exception to his norm. It is based mainly upon official records and gives fairly superficial coverage of the services of the Bn's forebears between 1746 and 1923 (operations against Hyder and the French, the surrender of Cuddalore, the Second Mahratta War, First and Third Burma Wars, actions on the Frontier, and WWI service in Egypt and Palestine). Although there are no appendixes, the text does include numerous references to individuals and their awards. R/4 V/3. NAM/IOL. DM.

REGIMENTAL HISTORY, 4/2nd PUNJAB REGIMENT
Extract from the Regimental Records of the 74th Punjabis
Anon * Thacker & Co, Bombay, n.d. (c.1922). Dark green, gold, Regtl crest, 7.25 x 5.0, -/45. No ills, no maps, no appendixes, no Index.
* A very brief account based upon Regtl records. It covers the period from 1776 to 1922 and is useful only as a source for important dates. R/4 V/2. NAM. PJE.
Note: the 74th Punjabis were re-designated 4/2nd Punjab Regt in 1922, but then disbanded in 1939.

EXTRACTS FROM THE REGIMENTAL HISTORY OF 5th Bn, 2nd PUNJAB REGIMENT
Anon * G Narayam, Secunderabad, n.d. (c.1923). Paper covers, grey, black, 8.5 x 5.5, -/9. No ills, no maps, no Index. Apps: notes on casualties (WWI), H&A (WWI), notes on recruiting policy.
* A pamphlet which contains a few bits of information of possible reference value, but notable mainly for its rarity. R/5 V/1. NAM. PJE.

THE GOLDEN GALLEY
The Story of the Second Punjab Regiment, 1761–1947
Lieut Col Sir Geoffrey Betham KBE CIE MC and Maj H V R Geary MC * Printed by Charles Batey, at the Oxford University Press, for the 2nd Punjab Regt Officers' Association, 1956. Green, gold, Regtl crest, 8.75 x 5.75, xiii/330. Fp, 19 mono phots, 3 cld plates, 9 maps (folding, bound in), no appendixes, Index.
* This is a nicely presented book which traces the stories of all the Regts and Bns which, from 1761 onwards, evolved into the 2nd Punjab Regt. The early years are covered in informative style, but half of the pages are devoted to services in WWII and it is here that the greatest detail is found. The author does not focus entirely upon battles and skirmishes. He also paints a clear picture of other important matters such as recruiting policy, class/race compositions, the Regtl Centre, Stations, movements, and so forth. The lack of appendixes, in such an otherwise well-rounded book, is to be regretted. R/2 V/4. PCAL/NAM. SB/HIS.
Note: reprinted in Delhi in 1957. This version does not have the Regtl crest on the front cover and the general production quality is mediocre.

3rd MADRAS REGIMENT

HISTORICAL RECORDS OF THE XIII MADRAS INFANTRY
Lieut R P Jackson * W Thacker & Co, London and Calcutta, 1898. Red, gold, 'Crossed Colours' motif, 10.25 x 6.5, -/319/24 (the latter being commercial advertisements). Fp, 8 very fine cld plates (uniforms and badges), no maps, Bibliography, no Index. Apps: 11 in total, incl list of former COs, other former officers, Stations, notes on recruitment policy (with folding table of classes recruited), notes on Dress and accoutrements.
* A full history, full and informative, for the period 1776 to 1896. Many individuals, of all ranks, British and Indian, are named in the narrative. The appendixes are extensive and detailed. In 1903, the Regt became 73rd Carnatic Infantry, and then, in 1922, the 1/3rd Madras Regt.
R/5 V/4. NAM/RMAS. RP/CJP/BDM.

HISTORY OF THE 83rd WALLAJAHBAD LIGHT INFANTRY
Lieut Col J C W Erck * Printed at The Central Jail, Cannanore, 1910. Black, gold, 8.0 x 5.5, -/75. No ills, no maps, no Index. Apps: list of former officers (not complete), list of Stations.
* A brief history containing few details. The text is based upon Regtl and other records, and covers the period 1794 to 1910. The most useful parts refer to the campaigns against Tipu Sultan in 1799, the Mahratta War of 1817-1819, and the operations in the southern Maharatta country in 1844-1845. R/3 V/2. NAM. PJE.

MADRAS INFANTRY, 1748–1943
Lieut Col E G Phythian-Adams OBE * The Superintendent of the Government Printing Press, Madras, 1943. Stiff card, rifle green, white, embellished with the Regtl colours (stripes, red/white), 9.5 x 6.0, x/136. Fp, one mono phot (Assaye Day Parade, 23.9.1942), no maps, no appendixes, no Index.
* A very detailed and readable narrative history with liberal mention of personnel (British and Indian), and particularly good descriptions of many small-scale actions. There are helpful notes on Battle Honours, unit lineages, and unit war services.
R/3 V/4. PC. SDC.

THE MADRAS REGIMENT, 1758–1958
Lieut Col E G Phythian-Adams OBE * Printed by C D Dhody & Sons, Wellington, at the Defence Services Staff College Press, 1958. Green, gold, 9.0 x 6.0, viii/338. 8 mono phots, 5 cld plates, 6 maps (folding, bound in), Bibliography, Index.
Apps: 'Short History of the State Forces - Travancore, Cochin, Mysore'.
* The most comprehensive history of the Regt up to that time (mid 1950s). It is fluently written, with good supporting maps. The author provides short accounts of services in WWI and WWII, but the narrative is particularly detailed in its

coverage of the 18th and 19th Century conflicts - the French Wars (1746-1748, and 1757-1762), the four Mysore Wars, the two Maharatta Wars, the three Burma campaigns, the First and Second China Wars, the Second Afghan War, and the NWF campaigns between 1895 and 1898. Honours and awards are covered by a chapter within the main body of the narrative. R/3 V/5. NAM. PJE/BDM.

THE MADRAS SOLDIER

Lieut Col E G Phythian-Adams OBE * Government Press, Madras, 1948. Green spine, white/blue/red banding on front cover, blue lettering, 10.0 x 6.25, xii/215. Fp, no other ills, Bibliography, Index (limited). Apps: list of Madras units (WWII), H&A (WWII), notes on recruitment and Dress.

* Another broad-brush account, and one which seems to have provided the basis for the history described in the preceding entry by the same author. This one is notable for the WWII-period appendixes. R/3 V/3. PC. TA.

THE MADRAS REGIMENT FROM 1942-1946

Anon * Published by the Regt, India (no other details shown), 1946. Soft card, Regtl crest, white, gold/grey/black, 8.5 x 7.5, -/16. No ills, no maps, no Index. Apps: H&A.

* Although very slim, this little item does provide a useful synopsis for each Bn of the Regt - antecedents, date of formation or reformation, and war services. Included in the list is 1st Coorg Bn (embodied in August 1940 as 14th Coorg Bn of the Indian Territorial Force), and two Auxiliary Force (India) units - Southern Provinces Mounted Rifles and Madras Coast Bty RA. The H&A appendix is supplemented by a tipped-in Addendum of further awards (but excluding the Java campaign, awards for which were Gazetted too late for inclusion).
R/5 V/2. PC. CJP.

SHORT HISTORY OF THE MADRAS REGIMENT

Anon * Printed by 'MPH', Madras, n.d. (c.1951). Dark green, gold, Regtl crest, 9.0 x 6.0, -/30. No ills, no maps, no Index. Apps: H&A (WWII only), list of COs.

* No more than a thumb-nail sketch of the Regt during the period 1758 through to 1923 (when it was progressively disbanded), and then a condensed account of each Bn after the Regt was re-raised for war service in 1941. There is no evidence to suggest who sponsored this publication or what they hoped to achieve. R/5 V/1. NAM. PJE.

NOW OR NEVER

The Story of the 4th Bn The Madras Regiment in the Burma Campaign

Maj G D Garforth-Bles and Capt S D Clarke * Printed by E G Aylmer at Thacker's Press & Directories Ltd, Calcutta, October 1945. Rifle green, gold, Regtl crest, 10.0 x 7.5, vii/45. Fp, 11 mono phots, 3 cld plates, 2 maps, no Index. Apps: Roll of Honour, list of officers who served (British and Indian).

* A good fluent narrative account of the Bn's services between October 1943 (when it joined 20th Indian Div in Burma) and June 1945 (when it finally entered Rangoon). During those two years of hard fighting, the Bn took part in the Battle of Imphal, the capture of Ava Bridge, Mount Poppa, and the final destruction of the Japanese Army in Burma in mid-1945. R/4 V/4. PC. SDC.
Note: this Bn was the successor of the 83rd Wallajahbad Light Infantry noted on the preceding page.

THE BLACK POM-POMS

History of the Madras Regiment, 1941-1983

Story of the 'Thambis' in War and Peace

Lieut Col J R Daniel * Printed by Thomson Printing Press, Coonor, for the Madras Regtl Centre, Nilgiris, 1986. Red, gold, Regtl crest, 9.0 x 6.0, xxvii/600. Fp, more than 100 mono phots, 27 cld ills, 8 maps (bound in), Glossary, Bibliography, Index. Apps: H&A (1941-1983), list of COs (same period), list of Subedar Majors (same period), notes on Battle Honours (1767-1983), important Regtl dates, notes on the

Regtl March, Bn nicknames, etc.
* A useful and large scale work which neatly complements Phythian-Adams' books (vide preceding entries) and which brings the story forward by a further twenty-five years. It opens with a good summary of the WWII period, but the bulk of the narrative is then devoted to events at the time of and subsequent to the Partition of India - Kashmir (1947-1948), Congo (1962), Chinese Confrontation (1962), Indo-Pakistan Wars (1965 and 1971), and various counter-insurgency operations. The author, who served nearly twenty-nine years with the Regt, includes citations for post-1947 gallantry awards and much interesting detail regarding Regtl traditions, insignia, Bn lineages, and other aspects of the Regt's history. Sadly, for an otherwise exemplary book, the author was let down by the publisher. The text is poorly printed and the illustrations have been badly reproduced. R/2 V/5. PC. AN.
Note: referring to the book's second sub-title, 'thambi', or 'thumbi' is Tamil for 'younger brother'. The word is sometimes used in northern India, or in the Army, as an affectionate term for a man coming from southern India.

4th BOMBAY GRENADIERS

HISTORICAL RECORD OF THE SERVICES OF THE FIRST REGIMENT, BOMBAY INFANTRY GRENADIERS
Col H S Anderson * First Grenadiers Regt Association, Poona, 1885. Red, gold, 9.5 x 8.0, -/69. No ills, no maps, no Index. Apps: list of former COs, idem other officers (pre-1863), idem other officers (post-1863), idem Medical Officers.
* The text is based upon verbatim extracts from Regtl records and other official sources. It provides only the barest details. The Regt became 101st Grenadiers in 1903, then 1/4th Bombay Grenadiers in 1922. R/5 V/2. NAM/IOL. PJE.

THE 101st GRENADIERS
Historical Record of the Regiment, 1778-1923, Second Edition
Col H S Anderson ('Revised in 1927 by Capt A Frankland') * Gale & Polden Ltd, Aldershot, 1928. Dark blue, gold, Regtl crest, 10.0 x 7.5, vi/138. Fp, 7 mono phots, 2 cld plates (uniforms), 9 maps (folding, bound in), Index. Apps: list of former COs, idem other officers, idem Medical Officers, list of other units at times attached to the Regt, notes on the siege of Mangalore, notes on the return from Maiwand.
* This is essentially an updated and improved version of Anderson's 1885 history (vide the preceding entry). Again, it is based mainly upon official records, but Frankland manages to weave in some personal accounts and these help to enliven the text. It is lacking in fine detail, but is very accurate.
R/4 V/3. BM. PJE/BDM.

REGIMENTAL HISTORY OF THE 1st Bn, 4th BOMBAY GRENADIERS
Maj A Thompson * Shri Ramtatya Prakash Printing, Belgaum, n.d. Green, black, -/21. No ills, no maps, no appendixes, no Index.
* A very condensed account of no more than marginal interest. Probably compiled for the instruction of newly-joined officers. R/5 V/1. NAM. PJE.
Note: another version, printed in Roman Urdu, has been noted. It has a blue cloth binding and consists of 22 pages.

HISTORICAL RECORD OF THE SERVICES OF THE 2nd (THE PRINCE OF WALES'S OWN) GRENADIER REGIMENT, BOMBAY NATIVE INFANTRY
Anon (Col Stanley Edwardes) * Education Society's Press, Bombay, 1878. Stiff card, red, black, 9.5 x 7.5, -/124. No ills, no maps, no Index. Apps: alphabetical list of officers who served in the Regt (1796-1878), idem British Army and Staff Corps officers ('under the new organisation'), idem Medical Officers.
* A typical Regtl history of the period, with a brief year-by-year (1796-1877) summary of activities and the disposition of officers, based upon official records. In addition to duties in India, the Regt served in Egypt (1801-1802), Persia (1857), Abyssinia (1868), and Aden (1873-1875). Highlights of the book are a long account of the Battle of Koreygaum (1818), extracts from an officer's diary

of the fighting in Sind (1840), and an account of the loyalty of Subedar Gunga Singh (a veteran of fifty-one years of continuous service who was on home leave when, in 1857, the Mutiny erupted). The Regt served in WWI as 1st Bn, 102nd Grenadiers (King Edward's Own). In 1922, it became 2nd Bn, 4th Bombay Grenadiers (King Edward's Own). R/5 V/4. YUL. RBM.
Note: the NAM has a 'presentation' copy, in full blue Morocco, which incorporates a frontispiece (the Koreygaum Memorial) and twenty-eight original photographic prints pasted in. These do not appear in the 'standard' version recorded above. It is possible that several other examples of this 'de luxe' version were produced for presentation by the Regt to various senior officers and dignatories.

OUTLINE HISTORICAL RECORD OF THE PRINCE OF WALES'S OWN GRENADIER REGIMENT OF BOMBAY INFANTRY
Anon * The Education Society's Press, Bombay, 1887. Paper covers, pink, black, 8.5 x 5.5, -/9. No ills, no maps, no Index. Apps: notes on the general condition of the Regt, list of campaigns, battles and sieges.
* Only nine pages in length, this is indeed an 'outline'. Possibly written for the instruction of newly-joined young officers, but interesting only for its great rarity. R/5 V/1. NAM. PJE.

HISTORICAL RECORD OF THE SERVICES OF THE 2nd (PRINCE OF WALES'S OWN) GRENADIER REGIMENT, BOMBAY NATIVE INFANTRY
Anon * British India Press, Bombay, 1909. Morocco, dark green, gold, 10.5 x 8.5, ii/124. No ills, no maps, no Index. Apps: list of former officers, idem Medical Officers.
* This is another 'hybrid' history - part extracts from official documents, part quotations from officers' letters and anecdotes. A better-than-average effort for that period. R/4 V/3. NAM. PJE/BDM.

2nd BATTALION, 4th BOMBAY GRENADIERS (KING EDWARD'S OWN)
Formerly the 102nd King Edward's Own Grenadiers
Historical Record of the Regiment, 1796-1933, New Edition
Maj J T Gorman * Lawrence Brothers Ltd, Weston super Mare, Somerset, 1933. Dark blue, gold, Bn crest, 10.0 x 7.5, vi/173. Fp, 11 mono phots, 10 maps (bound in). Bibliography, no Index. Apps: list of former officers, notes on the Colours, idem the Regtl music, idem other units at times attached to the Bn.
* This is effectively the third edition of the history first produced by Anderson in 1885 and updated by Frankland in 1928 (vide the two entries on the preceding page). Gorman further updates the story, to 1933, and introduces even more reminiscences by former and serving officers, and quotations from their letters. This is a good quality production, with a detailed and informative narrative. R/4 V/4. NAM/IOL. PJE/CJP.

HISTORICAL RECORDS OF THE 8th REGIMENT, BOMBAY INFANTRY
Capt Sandwith (sic) * The Education Society's Steam Press, Bombay, 1894. Dark maroon, gold, -/85/iii/31 (see below). Measurements not recorded. Two large plates (folding, bound in) bearing sketches of soldiers, no maps, no Index. Apps: three pages (iii) listing Stations and movements, and thirty-one pages (31) devoted to extracts from Regtl Standing Orders (1896) and the music of the Regtl march.
* The bulk of the book (85 pages) is devoted to a fairly tedious narrative, which lacks detail and human interest, for the period 1768-1894. However, there is a a large fold-out page, bound in at the rear and compiled in 1891 by Capt J C Swann, which is very useful. The Regt later became the 108th Infantry and then the 3/4th Bombay Grenadiers. R/4 V/2. NAM. PJE.

5th BATTALION, 4th BOMBAY GRENADIERS (CXII INFANTRY) HISTORICAL RECORDS 1798-1923

Anon * Facsimile TS, publication details not shown, n.d. (c.1940). Seen rebound in pink and white patterned cloth, 163 pages (folios not numbered). Fp, 12 mono phots (original prints, pasted in), one line drawing, 8 maps, no Index. Apps: H&A, list of former COs, idem other officers, extracts from the Bombay Army Lists (1799 and 1800), Stations and movements, lists of Adjutants, Quartermasters, and Subedar Majors.

* This is a work which bears a strong resemblance to the work by Sandwith (vide preceding entry). It may have been an attempt to build on Sandwith's style of presentation and to apply it to the 112th Infantry (which became the 5/4th Bn Bombay Grenadiers after WWI). Unlike Sandwith, this anonymous author does not depend too heavily upon verbatim quotations from official documents but incorporates some fluent narrative descriptions of the Regt's war services in Mesopotamia and elsewhere during the period 1915-1918. It seems likely that more than one copy was made and distributed but, apart from the copy held by the NAM, no others have been sighted. R/5 V/4. NAM. PJE.

A SHORT HISTORY OF THE 113th INFANTRY, TOGETHER WITH AN ACCOUNT OF THE MESS PLATE OWNED BY THE REGIMENT

Lieut H W Bell * The Mission Press, Kolhapur, n.d. (c.1910). Green, gold, Regtl crest, 5.5 x 4.25, iv/23. 11 mono phots (one of a Colour Party, ten of the Mess silver), no maps, no appendixes, no Index.

* An unusual record which is devoted mainly to a description of the silver and only marginally to the Regt's history. The 113th Infantry became the 10/14th Bombay Grenadiers under the post-war reorganisations. R/5 V/1. PC. BDM.

THE GRENADIERS
A Regimental History

Brig Rajendra Singh * Army Educational Stores, New Delhi, 1962. Green, black, 'Grenade' motif, 10.0 x 7.5, xvi/328. Fp, 16 mono phots, one cld plate, 15 maps, Index. Apps: Roll of Honour, H&A, list of former COs, notes on the Colours, idem Dress, uniforms, and Regtl music.

* This was the first attempt to pull all the strands together and to compile a proper history of the Regt and its forebears. The author's task could not have been easy because his British predecessors had committed to print very few records of real merit (as can be seen from the preceding entries). His narrative contains errors, but the book is a good attempt at telling the story of all the Grenadier battalions in detailed readable style. R/3 V/4. NAM. PJE/RP.

THE GRENADIERS
A Tradition of Valour

Col R D Palsokar MC * Printed in Poona, for The Grenadiers Regtl Association, Jabalpur, n.d. (c.1980). Black, gold, 'Grenade' motif, xxiv/538. Fp, 120 mono phots, 5 cld plates, 49 maps, Bibliography, Index. Apps: H&A, list of former COs, idem Subedar Majors.

* The author is one of India's best known military historians and, in this book, he compiled a comprehensive account of all of the Grenadier battalions and their forebears between 1779 and 1980. The pictures are poorly printed, but the maps are helpful and it is pleasing to be able to acknowledge a book which, at last, gives proper recognition to this fine regiment. In 1945, the Bombay Grenadiers were re-titled The Indian Grenadiers. At Partition they became, simply, The Grenadiers (as an element of the Indian Army). Their post-Independence services are here described in detail. R/1 V/5. NAM. MCJ/RP.

5th MAHARATTA LIGHT INFANTRY

HISTORICAL RECORD OF THE 3rd BOMBAY LIGHT INFANTRY
Anon * Caxton Steam Printing Works, Bombay, 1892. Blue, gold, Regtl crest, 9.0 x 6.0, viii/109. No ills, no maps, no appendixes, Index (officers only).
* This is an amalgam of bits and pieces extracted from Regtl records and official reports. The result is dry, terse, and superficial, with no attempt at constructive analysis of what went right and what went wrong. There is some brief mention of operations in which the Regt was involved, but most of the text is taken up with Stations, movements, and officers' postings in and out. The Regt was retitled 103rd Mahratta Light Infantry in 1903, and then 1/5th Mahratta Light Infantry in 1922. R/5 V/2. NAM. PJE/BDM.

HISTORY OF THE 1st BATTALION, 5th MAHRATTA LIGHT INFANTRY (JANGI PALTAN)
Anon * Government of India Press, Calcutta, 1930. Dark green, gold, 10.0 x 8.0, viii/88. No ills, 14 maps (2 printed in the text, 12 folding, bound in), no Index. Apps: list of former officers, list of Stations.
* A short but readable history which covers the period 1768 to 1929 and which concentrates upon those engagements for which the Regt was awarded its Battle Honours - Mysore (1790), Seedaseer and Seringapatam (1799), Arabia (1821), Mooltan, Gujerat, and the Punjab (1848-1849), and then much later during WWI - Mesopotamia (1915-1916). R/5 V/3. IOL/NAM. PJE/CJP.
Note: referring to the title of this book, 'Jangi' translates as 'warlike' or 'warrior' in a positive or honorific way. 'Paltan' signifies 'Regiment', hence the soubriquet 'The Warrior Regiment'.

A FAMOUS INDIAN REGIMENT, THE KALI PANCHWIN
2/5th (Formerly the 105th) Mahratta Light Infantry, 1768-1923
Col Sir Reginald Hennell CVO DSO OBE * John Murray, London, 1927. Green, gold, Regtl crest, 8.75 x 5.5, xi/292. Fp, 11 mono phots, 2 maps, Index. Apps: H&A (1915-1921), list of former COs, idem other officers, notes on uniforms, Regtl ceremonies, the Colours, etc.
* This excellent history was written by Hennell, and then edited and prepared for publication by his sister-in-law, Mrs Mary Hennell. The narrative is informative and lucid, with plenty of good descriptions of campaigning in China (1860-1861), Burma (1886-1888), Aden (1901), and Mesopotamia and Palestine (1916-1918). The varied appendixes are useful. R/2 V/5. NAM/IOL. RP.
Note: a facsimile reprint was produced in 1985 by BR Publications, India (no other details known). Referring to the main title, 'Kali Panchwin' translates as 'the Black Fifth'.

EXTRACTS FROM THE DIGEST OF SERVICES OF THE 10th BOMBAY LIGHT INFANTRY
Compiled at Poona, October 1892
Lieut Col L F Heath and Lieut H C B Dann * G Claridge & Co Ltd, Bombay, 1938. Rifle green, Regtl crest, 9.75 x 6.75, i/51. No ills, no maps, no appendixes, no Index.
* Presented in the form of a diary and based upon the Annual Digest of Services, this history covers the period 1797 to 1887. It is not known why it remained unpublished until 1938. The Regt originated as 2nd Bn of the 5th (Travancore) Regt of Bombay Native Infantry. It became 10th Bombay Native Infantry in 1824. The main campaigns covered here are the Mutiny (when it served in Central India), and Abyssinia (1867-1868). To balance the absence of formal appendixes, there are lists of casualties (for both of those campaigns) within the narrative, plus a list of honours and awards (for Abyssinia only). A condensed but useful record. The Regt was retitled 110th Mahratta Light Infantry in 1903. It became the 3/5th Mahratta Light Infantry after WWI. R/5 V/3. RMAS. RP.

HISTORICAL RECORD, 110th MAHRATTA LIGHT INFANTRY (NOW 3rd BATTALION, 5th MAHRATTA LIGHT INFANTRY) DURING THE GREAT WAR, 1914 TO 1918
Anon ('Three officers who wish to remain anonymous') * Government of India Press, Calcutta, 1927. Green, gold, Regtl crest, 10.0 x 7.25, ix/109. 3 mono phots (incl a captioned group of officers, 1914), 12 maps (bound in), no Index. Apps: Roll of Honour (British officers and VCOs only), H&A, tables relating to the siege of Kut.
* The Regt was destroyed at Kut, but it was later reformed and saw action with the Egyptian Expeditionary Force in Palestine. The 3/5th MLI now forms part of the Indian Army's Order of Battle under the modern title of 2nd Parachute Regt, but it still retains many of the traditions of its forebear. R/5 V/4. NAM. CSM.
Note: it is understood that only 100 copies of this book were printed.

HISTORICAL RECORD OF THE 16th REGIMENT, BOMBAY INFANTRY
Anon * Publication details not shown, n.d. (c.1911). Red, gold, embellishments, 10.0 x 6.5, -/24. Fp, no other ills, one map (folding, bound in), no Index. Apps: list of Stations and summary of events at each, list of COs and Adjutants.
* The period covered is 1800 to 1910, and the contents are the customary (for that period) melange of extracts from 'official sources'. Brief, sparse, and apart from the references to the Second Afghan War, unlikely to be of much interest to the researcher. In 1903 the 16th Regt became the 116th Mahrattas. It 1922 it became the 4/5th Mahratta Light Infantry. R/5 V/1. NAM. PJE.

HISTORICAL RECORD OF THE 4/5th MAHRATTA LIGHT INFANTRY
Capt A R Solly * The Civil & Military Gazette Press, Lahore, 1924. Light green boards with dark green spine, black, 9.0 x 6.0, -/67. No ills, no maps, no Index. Apps: H&A, list of former COs, idem other officers (1914-1921), Mutiny-period orders and correspondence, list of former Adjutants, list of Stations and summary of events at each.
* A modest effort, based as usual upon verbatim extracts from official orders and reports (covering the period 1800 to 1924). The appendixes are probably the best feature, but the sections dealing with the Second Afghan War and the 1901 operations in East Africa (not widely recorded elsewhere) might prove useful also. R/4 V/3. NAM/IOL/USII. PJE.
Note: an edition dated 1932, and printed by Thacker & Co, has been noted.

CHRONOLOGY OF THE 114th MAHRATTAS
Parts I and II
Anon * Printed by The Times of India Press, Bombay, published privately, 1922. Royal blue, gold, 7.0 x 5.25, -/55. No ills, no maps, no Index. Apps: H&A (all ranks), list of former COs and other officers (1800-1922).
* A slim volume, of unknown provenance, which contains a great deal of useful information. The narrative is arranged in two sections. Part I covers the period 1800-1914 in condensed diary form and deals with 14th Bombay Infantry (1800 to 1903) and then the retitled 114th Mahrattas (1903 onwards). It contains brief references to the Pindari Wars, Sind, the Mutiny, and Abyssinia. Part II covers the period 1914-1922, with condensed descriptions of active services on the NWF around Tochi (1914-1915), Mesopotamia (1915-1918), and Iraq (1920). Stations and movements are noted in precise detail. The Regt became the 10/5th Mahratta Light Infantry in the post-war reorganisations. R/4 V/4. MODL. AMM.

A BRIEF HISTORY OF THE MAHRATTA LIGHT INFANTRY
Maj J S Barr * Printed by G Claridge & Co, Bombay, 1945. Green, gold, Regtl crest, 9.75 x 7.25, vi/65. Fp, no other ills, no maps, no appendixes, no Index.
* As the title suggests, this is indeed a very brief history. The first century and a half of the Regt's existence are dealt with in the opening eleven pages. The rest of the narrative then deals sketchily with the WWII services of each of the MLI battalions in North Africa, Italy, Assam, and Burma. Chapter VIII gives a numerical summary of honours and awards gained by officers and men of the Regt,

and very few of them are mentioned by name anywhere in the book. It was obviously compiled at speed, just as the war in South East Asia was ending. It would have provided the basis for an expanded history at a later date, but the upheavals of Independence may have prevented Maj Barr from proceeding with any such plan. R/4 V/2. PC. LDR.

VALOUR ENSHRINED
A History of the Mahratta Light Infantry, 1768–1947
Lieut Col M G Abhyankar * Orient Longman, New Delhi, 1971. Green, white, 9.5 x 6.5, xx/546. Fp, 35 mono phots, 13 cld plates, 70 maps, no Index. Apps: H&A, list of former COs, idem Subedar Majors, notes on the origins of the Regt, notes on archival sources.
* The author provides uniformly good coverage for all periods and for each of the modern Regt's forebears. He begins with the events of 1768 and brings to story through to the departure of the British in 1947. The numerous maps are helpful and the photographic illustrations are printed to a good standard. The overall quality of printing and binding, however, is disappointing, and it is hard to understand the lack of an Index in such an otherwise exemplary work.
R/2 V/4. NAM. MCJ/RP.
Note: the Regt's post-1947 services are covered in VALOUR ENSHRINED - A HISTORY OF THE MARATHA LIGHT INFANTRY, Volume II, by Lieut Col C L Proudfoot (published by the Regtl Centre, Belgaum, 1980).

6th RAJPUTANA RIFLES

HISTORY OF THE 1st BATTALION, 6th RAJPUTANA RIFLES (WELLESLEY'S)
Lieut Col F H James OBE MC * Gale & Polden Ltd, Aldershot, 1938. Dark green, silver, Regtl crest, 10.0 x 7.5, xx/277. Fp, 20 mono phots, 4 cld plates, 20 maps (4 printed in the text, 16 bound in), Index. Apps: H&A (WWI only), list of former COs, idem former Regtl officers, idem Honorary Colonels, idem Adjutants, idem Subedar Majors.
* One of the best Indian Army infantry histories. Very detailed, and a mine of information. It covers the period 1772 to 1937, with the first half of the book dealing objectively with the Regt's early history, and the second half devoted almost entirely to WWI services in Mesopotamia (and particularly to the debacle at Kut-al-Amara). R/3 V/5. NAM/IOL. RP.

THE HISTORY OF THE 2/6th RAJPUTANA RIFLES (PRINCE OF WALES'S OWN)
H G Rawlinson CIE * Oxford University Press, London, 1936. Green, gold, Regtl crest, 8.5 x 5.5, x/195. Fp, 8 mono phots, 10 maps (9 printed in the text, one bound in), Index. Apps: Roll of Honour (officers only), H&A (WWI only), list of former COs, idem other officers (WWI only), idem Honorary Colonels, idem Adjutants, idem Subedar Majors, idem Jemadar Adjutants, notes on Battle Honours, Stations and movements, synopsis of the war services and class compositions of the Regt.
* One of several excellent histories compiled by this author, and one of his best. It covers the period 1805 to 1922, and opens with a good summary of the early years (particularly the Mutiny period). The bulk of the book, and probably the pages of greatest interest to most readers, is devoted to the campaign in Mesopotamia (the Battle of Ctesiphon, the retreat to Kut-al-Amara, and the siege). Many officers are mentioned in the text, also summaries of casualties and citations for individual gallantry awards. R/3 V/5. NAM/IOL. MP.

HISTORICAL RECORDS OF THE 122nd RAJPUTANA RIFLES
From the Time it was First Raised in the Honourable East India Company's Service Under the Denomination of the 2nd Battalion, 11th Regiment, Native Infantry
Anon * The British India Press, Bombay, 1908. Green, gold, Regtl crest, 9.0 x 5.5, -/110. Fp, 6 mono phots, 9 sketches, no maps, no Index. Apps: list of former COs, idem other British officers, idem Indian officers, Stations and movements, notes on Dress, extracts from the Army Lists for 1805-1808, 1857, 1862, and 1900.
* A condensed history containing superficial material relating to various battles and campaigns. Typically of the period, the book is little more than a compilation of extracts from Regtl records and official reports, with some linking narrative. It is useful mainly for its appendixes. In 1922, the Regt became 3/6th Rajputana Rifles. R/4 V/2. RMAS/NAM. PJE/BDM.

HISTORICAL RECORDS OF THE 23rd REGIMENT (2nd RIFLE REGIMENT), BOMBAY INFANTRY, FORMERLY 1st Bn, 12th NATIVE INFANTRY
Capt W A M Wilson * Printed at The Education Society's Steam Press, Bombay, 1894. Green, gold, Regtl crest, 9.0 x 6.0, -/84. No ills, no maps, no Index. Apps: list of former COs, idem former officers, idem Adjutants, idem Medical Officers, notes on Stations and movements, etc.
* Although brief, this book does provide a useful summary of the Regt's evolution and various campaign services during the 19th Century. The material is neatly arranged and the appendixes are extensive. Reflecting its roots as a corps d'élite, the Regt was given the title 123rd Outram's Rifles under the reorganisations of 1903 (Capt James Outram having been the first Adjutant). In 1922 the title was changed to 4/6th Rajputana Rifles (Outram's). R/5 V/4. PC. RGH.

OUTRAM'S RIFLES
A History of the 4th Battalion, 6th Rajputana Rifles
H G Rawlinson CIE * Oxford University Press, London, 1933. Green, gold, Regtl crest, 8.5 x 5.5, viii/218. Fp, 11 mono phots, 7 maps (5 printed in the text, 2 bound in), chapter notes (bibliographies), Index. Apps: Roll of Honour (British and Indian officers, WWI only), H&A (all ranks, mainly WWI, with some entries for earlier years), list of former COs, Adjutants, and all officers serving (August 1914).
* Sound, well organised and readable, and therefore typical of Rawlinson's work. He covers the period 1817 to 1922 in brisk style, with good reporting of the war in Persia (1857), the Second Afghan War, Third Burmese War, Aden, the Persian Gulf, and WWI. In the latter, as 123rd Outram's Rifles, the Regt fought in Egypt and in the Palestine campaign. The coverage of the latter is good, with many individuals of all ranks mentioned by name. Chapter XIV is particularly important. It covers the services of 3/153rd Rifles, a unit to which Outram's Rifles sent a large draft (contributing 50.0% of its officers and men and its CO). These fourteen pages are a gem. They are crammed with war service details (Palestine and Arab Rebellion), list of officers, awards, etc, for this war-raised Bn between 1918 and 1922. R/3 V/5. NAM. RP/CJP.

BRIEF HISTORY OF NAPIER'S RIFLES
Lieut H J Huxford * DSO Press, Mhow, 1912. Stiff card, olive green boards with red cloth spine, 6.5 x 5.25, -/28. No ills, no maps, no Index. Apps: Stations and movements, list of notable events in the Regt's history.
* 'Brief' is the operative word in the title. A compilation of extracts from official records, it covers the period 1817 to 1912 in just twenty-eight pages. Collectable for its rarity, but almost useless as a source of reference. In 1922, the Regt became 5/6th Rajputana Rifles (Napier's). R/5 V/1. NAM. PJE/RP/BDM.

NAPIER'S RIFLES
The History of the 5th Battalion, 6th Rajputana Rifles
H G Rawlinson * Printed by The Wesleyan Mission Press, Mysore, for the Oxford University Press, London, 1929. Green, gold, Regtl crest, 8.5 x 5.5, xiii/200. Fp, 7 mono phots, 5 sketches, 13 maps (8 printed in the text, 5 folding, bound in), chapter notes (bibliographies), Index. Apps: H&A (WWI only), list of former COs, idem other former officers, list of notable events in the Regt's history, Stations and movements.
* Another good effort by this excellent historian. He provides good descriptions of the 3rd Mahratta War, the Sind campaign, the Mutiny, and services in WWI. His coverage of the latter, when Napier's Rifles fought in France and Flanders, and then later in Mesopotamia and Palestine, is detailed and well laced with incident.
R/4 V/5. NAM. PJE.

HISTORY OF THE 13th RAJPUTS (THE SHEKHAWATI REGIMENT)
From the Time of its Organisation as Part of the Shekhawati Brigade in A.D. 1835 TO A.D. 1907
Lieut Col W Prior * Traill & Co, Calcutta, 1908. Full calfskin, brown, gold, 10.0 x 6.5, ii/84. 7 mono phots, one sketch, one map, no Index. Apps: list of British officers, idem Indian officers (various years, post-1848), details of class compositions and recruitment policy, notes on the life and times of Col Harry Forster CB.
* A brief but readable history for the period stated in the title. Of particular interest is the description of the problems which existed in Rajputana in the 1830s and which led to the decision to raise the Regt at that time. The Battle of Aliwal (1846) also receives good coverage. In 1922, the Regt evolved into the 10/6th Rajputana Rifles (Shekhawati). R/4 V/4. NAM. PJE.

THE RAJPUTANA RIFLES
A History of the Regiment, 1775–1947
Maj M G Abhyankar * Printed by S C Ghose, at the Calcutta Press, for Orient Longman, 1961. Green, white, Regtl crest, 9.75 x 6.5, xxiv/468. Fp, 20 mono plates, 5 cld plates, 53 maps, Index. Apps: H&A, list of former COs, notes on Battle Honours, notes on Dress, idem Regtl customs.
* A large-scale comprehensive work which gives full details of the Regt's origins (the story of the early Bombay Regts which evolved into the Rajputana Rifles), and early services under Wellesley. The author includes good accounts of the Sikh Wars, the Sind campaign, the First and Second Afghan Wars, Persia, the Mutiny, Abyssinia, the Third Burma War, East Africa, and the two world wars.
R/4 V/5. USII. BDM/OSS.

TRADITIONS OF A REGIMENT
The Story of the Rajputana Rifles
Lieut Gen A M Sethna PVSM and Lieut Col Valmiki Katju * Lancer Publishers, New Delhi, 1983. Black, gold, 10.0 x 6.5, xiv/243. 44 mono phots, 25 maps, Bibliography, Index. Apps: H&A (full details for post-1947, with some pre-1947 awards noted in the narrative), lists of COs and Subedar Majors (post-1947), notes on Battle Honours.
* This is a generalised account of the Regt's history, but it is nevertheless quite useful as a research source. As a 'reading' source, it is very good indeed. The accounts of active service tend to lean mainly towards the post-1947 campaigns, However, the author provides a good explanation of the origins of the constituent battalions. His accounts of the raising of the war-time battalions – a subject barely covered in other WWII sources – are particularly helpful. He also covers all the actions for which the modern Regt inherited its Battle Honours – Bourbon (1809), Kirkee (1817), Meeanee (1843), Aliwal (1846), Bushire (1856), Keren (1941), and Djebel Garci (1943), each being accompanied by an explanatory map.
R/1 V/4. NAM. MCJ.

7th RAJPUT REGIMENT

SERVICES OF 2nd NATIVE LIGHT INFANTRY
Late 31st Native Light Infantry
Indian Mutiny 1857-8-9
Anon * P P Blaney, at the Kaiser Baugh Press, location not stated, n.d. (c.1863). Stiff card, grey, black, 8.0 x 5.5, -/39. No ills, no maps, no appendixes, no Index.
* A compendium of extracts from reports despatched during and just after the Mutiny and written by the Regt's Commandant to the Adjutant General (concerning operations in Central India). In its own way, an interesting and unusual item. After various changes of title, the Regt became 1/7th Rajput Regt.
R/5 V/3. NAM. PJE.
Note: the two following entries refer to the same Regt, but under its later titles.

HISTORY OF THE 2nd REGIMENT, BENGAL NATIVE INFANTRY
From its Formation in 1798
Lieut Col W B Shawe * Joseph D'Cruz, Cooch Behar Press, 1872. Marbled boards, leather spine, blind, 10.0 x 7.0, -/110 (plus several folios not numbered).
No ills, no maps, no Index. Apps: list of former officers (incl Medical Officers).
* The historical content is fairly sparse. It occupies just twenty-three pages, but the text is printed in small type and contains some useful information. The single appendix, on the other hand, is very useful. Occupying eighty-seven pages, it lists every officer who served between 1798 and 1870, with career and war service details shown for most of them. The book is self-evidently a good source for medal collectors and for genealogists. R/5 V/3. IOL/NAM. PJE/CJP.

HISTORICAL RECORDS OF THE SERVICES OF THE 2nd REGIMENT, NATIVE LIGHT INFANTRY
Anon ('Officers of the Regiment') * Central Government Press, Calcutta, 1877. Bound in with other fragments (as seen at the IOL), brown, gold, 9.75 x 7.0, -/11. No ills, no maps, no appendixes, no Index.
* A short and basically unhelpful pamphlet which deals with services between 1798 and 1877. Presumably it was intended to update the record from 1871 onwards (vide preceding entry), but it is remarkable only for its rarity.
R/5 V/1. NAM. PJE.

THE HISTORY OF THE 3rd BATTALION, 7th RAJPUT REGIMENT (DUKE OF CONNAUGHT'S OWN)
H G Rawlinson CIE * Printed by Headley Brothers Ltd, for Oxford University Press, London, 1941. Green, gold, Regtl crest, Regtl colours banding, black/yellow/red, 10.0 x 7.5, x/223. Fp, 30 mono phots, 15 maps (14 printed in the text, one bound in), Index. Apps: Roll of Honour (WWI), H&A (NWF, 1936-1937 only), list of former COs, idem Adjutants, idem Subedar Majors, notes on Stations and uniforms.
* This is another of Rawlinson's well researched and finely composed Indian Army unit histories. He covers the period from 1778 to 1940 in uniform detail, with many minor actions and individual acts of gallantry highlighted in the narrative. The principal campaigns described are - First Sikh War (1845-1847), Second China War (1860), Egypt (1882), Third China War (1900), and then Aden and Mesopotamia in WWI. The Index is accurate and the maps are well presented.
R/3 V/5. RMAS. RP/CJP.

HISTORICAL RECORDS OF THE XI RAJPUTS
Capt E D Roberts * The Pioneer Press, Allahabad, 1913. Red, black, 9.0 x 5.5, -/194. No ills, no maps, no appendixes, no Index.
* Although quite a substantial book, covering the period 1825 to 1913, it consists largely of extracts from annual Army Lists showing the names of British officers serving with the Regt at various dates. There are no equivalent listings of any of the Indian officers. The book's 'historical' content is minimal. In 1922, the Regt became the 5/7th Rajput Regt. R/5 V/1. NAM. PJE.

HISTORICAL RECORDS OF THE 5th Bn, 7th RAJPUT REGIMENT (LATE XI RAJPUTS)

Capt P C Scudamore MC * The Pioneer Press, Allahabad, 1925. Reversed calfskin, brown, gold, Regtl crest, 7.5 x 5.0, -/223. No ills, no maps, no Index. Apps: details of the General Order of the C-in-C, dated 29.5.1857, publishing a petition by loyal Indian officers to be allowed to serve against the mutineers.

* The first forty-five pages describe the role of the 5th Bn and its forebears from 1825 through to the Third Afghan War (1919), and including services during WWI. The coverage is therefore very superficial. The remainder of the book is composed of extracts from various Army Lists (British officers only). This author, Capt Scudamore, makes an acknowledgement of the previous work done by Capt E D Roberts (vide preceding entry) but, in the event, neither publication has any great merit. R/4 V/2. RMAS/NAM. PJE/CJP.

ARMY LISTS, 8th RAJPUTS

Anon * Publication details not shown, n.d. (c.1928). Black, gold, 11.0 x 8.0, -/220. No ills, no maps, no appendixes, no Index.

* This is a 'one off' compilation, held at the NAM, which consists of nothing more than extracts from various Army Lists dated between 1847 and 1927. In other words, it is basically an updated version of the listings produced by Roberts and Scudamore (vide the two preceding entries). Its only possible merit is that it demonstrates the continuity of service of the 7th Rajputs under many former titles - 59th Regt Native Infantry (1847-1861), 8th Regt Native Infantry (1861-1885), 8th Regt Bengal Infantry (1885-1897), 8th Rajput Regt Bengal Infantry (1897-1901), 8th Rajput Infantry (1901-1903), 8th Rajputs (1903-1922), and then 4/7th Rajput Regt (1922 onwards). R/5 V/2. NAM. PJE.

THE SEVENTH RAJPUT REGIMENT IN THE INDIAN MUTINY OF 1857

J W B T Tindall * SPG Mission Printing Press, Ahmednagar, 1936. Paper covers, green, black, 8.5 x 5.5, -/56. No ills, no maps, no Index. Apps: H&A, summary of caualties by rank, notes regarding the Regtl monument, Lucknow.

* An interesting retrospective which examines the work done during the time of the Mutiny by the various forebear Regts which, at the time of the 1922 reorganisations, were brought together (as Bns) to form the new 7th Rajput Regt. The coverage is fairly superficial, but the author has found in his book a novel way of recording part of the early roots of a 20th Century regiment. R/4 V/3. NAM. PJE.

HISTORY OF THE 1st Bn, 7th RAJPUT REGIMENT

Col A H McCleverty * Unpublished TS, n.d. (c.1964). A run of unnumbered TS folios, held loose in ten folders within five boxes, 14.0 x 8.0. No ills, no maps, no appendixes, no Index.

* It is a pity that McCleverty could not find a publisher. This is a full and useful history of the Bn, covering the period 1798 to 1918, with additional notes for the period up to 1964. It is a narrative account, with lists of awards for NWF operations (1889-1902) and for China (1900). Biographical details are given for some officers, and there is a record of the services of all officers who served between 1798 and 1948. Clearly, for medal collectors and for genealogists, this is a prime source. R/5 V/4. NAM. PJE.

HERITAGE
The History of the Rajput Regiment, 1778-1947

Lieut Col Mustasad Ahmad * Rakesh Press, New Delhi, for the Regt, Fategarh, 1989. Red, cream, 9.5 x 7.25, ix/382. Fp, 13 mono phots, 15 maps (bound in), Bibliography, no Index. Apps: H&A (statistics only), Bn designations, class compositions.

* A useful book, but not a comprehensive history. The narrative deals mainly with the services of the Regular battalions in WWI and WWII, with some reference to earlier campaigns. The war-raised battalions (1914-1918 and 1939-1945) receive little attention in this account, and much of the narrative seems to be based

exclusively upon the War Diaries. Perhaps the subject matter is too extensive for it to be successfully compressed within the covers of a single volume.
R/2 V/3. PC. RWH.

8th PUNJAB REGIMENT

HISTORY OF THE 1st BATTALION, 8th PUNJAB REGIMENT
Col N M Geoghegan DSO and Capt M H A Campbell OBE * Gale & Polden Ltd, Aldershot, 1928. Dark blue, gold, blind spine, Regtl crest, 10.0 x 7.5, xii/82. Fp, 9 mono phots, one line drawing (badge), 10 maps (9 printed in the text, one on the end-papers), no Index. Apps: Roll of Honour (British and Indian officers only), H&A.
* The author opens with a brief summary of the Bn's origins as a Madras Regt and its reorganisation in 1903 as the 89th Punjabis. The Bn had an exceptionally varied record during WWI, and the bulk of the book is devoted to that period. Between 1914 and 1920, it served in South West Arabia, Egypt, Gallipoli, France, Mesopotamia, back to India and the NWF, back again to Mesopotamia, then Salonika, the Caucasus and, finally, Constantinople. It then became 1/8th Punjab Regt.
R/4 V/4. IOL/NAM. CSM/CJP.

REGIMENTAL HISTORY, 3rd Bn, 8th PUNJAB REGIMENT, LATE 91st PUNJABIS
Anon * Publication details not shown, n.d. (c.1934). Mauve boards with brown spine and quarters, black on white label, 6.0 x 5.25, -/14. No ills, no maps, no appendixes, no Index.
* A very sketchy outline history for the entire period from 1800 (as the 16th Regt of Madras Native Infantry) through to 1934. A pretty little publication of no discernible reference value. R/4 V/1. NAM. PJE/CJP.
Note: it will be seen from the above two entries that there is no record of the 2/8th Punjab Regt (formerly 1st Bn, 90th Punjabis). That unit never published a history of its services. The only (tenuous) source which might be of interest is THE PUNJAB MAIL MURDER, by Roger Perkins (Picton Publishing, Chippenham, 1986). Essentially an account of the life and death of one of the Bn's junior officers - George Hext - it does have some reference to the Bn's role in suppressing the 'Red Shirt rebellion' on the NWF in 1930-1931.

REGIMENTAL HISTORY, 1914-1920, 93rd BURMA INFANTRY
Anon * Printed by William Lewis, Cardiff, n.d. (c.1921). Cream, gold, Regtl crest, 9.0 x 6.0, ii/138. No ills, 13 maps (folding, bound in at the rear), no Index. Apps: Roll of Honour.
* The 'Burma' element in the title is potentially misleading. It does not mean that the Regt recruited Burmans or aboriginal hill tribesmen in that country. Instead and in common with other post-1922 Bns of the 8th Punjab Regt, it could claim its roots in the regiments of the old Madras Army which, at one period, had been reformed as Punjab-recruited units and sent to Burma as a policing and security force. For various reasons, the 93rd retained 'Burma' in its title, but logically it should have been simply the 93rd Punjabis (in line with the 89th, 90th, 91st, and 92nd Punjabis, all of which had evolved from the same roots). This full and readable account covers the 93rd's services in India, Egypt, France, Mesopotamia (the attempted relief of Kut al Amara), and Palestine. In 1922, it became 5th (Burma) Bn, 8th Punjab Regt. R/4 V/4. NAM. PJE/CJP.

5th BURMA BATTALION, STANDING ORDERS
Anon * The Civil & Military Gazette Press, Lahore, 1928. Blue, gold, Regtl crest, 10.5 x 7.0, -/120. No ills, no maps, no Index. Apps: six in total, incl Duties, Dress, Promotion Examinations, etc.
* For the reasons explained in the preceding entry, the '5th Burma Battalion' in this case was the 5/8th Punjab Regt. The book consists mainly, and as might be expected, of the unit's rules and regulations. However, nineteen pages are given to narrative descriptions of the Bn's predecessors and their fighting services. This

material is arranged in three sections (1800-1890, 1890-1904, and 1904-1920), and is quite useful. R/5 V/2. NAM. PJE.
Note: the 8th Punjab Regt, as a complete entity, was one of those for which no complete history has ever been published. At Partition, it was allocated (less the Sikh Companies) to Pakistan.

9th JAT REGIMENT

HISTORICAL RECORD OF THE SIXTH REGIMENT OF BENGAL NATIVE INFANTRY
Compiled for Use in the Regimental School
Maj H C Westmorland * The Pioneer Press, Allahabad, 1896. Green, gold, Regtl crest, 5.25 x 4.5, -/40. No ills, no maps, no appendixes, no Index.
* As the title states, this is a basic summary prepared for use by the teaching staff in the regimental school. It covers the period 1803 to 1905. The text is very limited, but it might prove useful as a quick reference source for key dates. The 6th Regt BNI evolved into the 1st Royal Bn, 9th Jat Regt (Light Infantry). Between times, and following the abandonment of the old Presidential titles, it had been known as the 6th Jat Light Infantry. R/5 V/1. NAM. PJE.

19th REGIMENT, BOMBAY INFANTRY
Historical Records
Anon * Publication details not shown, n.d. (c.1892). Seen in library rebinding, 9.75 x 6.5, -/248. No ills, no maps, no Index. Apps: H&A ('Decorations specially awarded to individuals of the 19th Regt, Bombay Infantry, for service therewith'), list of former officers (with details of their ranks, promotions, appointments, etc), notes on 'medals received by the Regiment'.
* The first fifteen pages contain very short year-by-year descriptions of the Regt's activities. The period covered is 1817 to 1891 inclusive. Raised as 1st Bn, 10th Regt, BNI, it became the 19th Regt in 1824 and participated as such in the First and Second Afghan Wars, the First Sikh War, and in Central India during the period of the Mutiny. Apart from the appendixes listed above, the remainder of the 248 pages are entirely blank. Presumably this was the result of the person who rebound the original booklet having added extra folios in order to provide the volume with greater bulk and strength. In 1903, the Regt became the 119th Infantry (The Mooltan Regiment). R/5 V/2. NYPL. RBM.

119th REGIMENT, HISTORICAL RECORDS
Anon * Higginbothams & Co, Madras and Bangalore, n.d. (c.1909). Red, gold, 9.75 x 6.5, -/147 (but see below). No ills, no maps, no Index. Apps: H&A.
* A strange 'one off' volume held by the NAM. Pages 1-32 are a typeset printed history of the old 19th Bombay Infantry, renamed 119th Infantry (The Mooltan Regt) in 1903 (vide preceding entry). The period covered in these pages is 1817 to 1907. The following pages, 33-53, pasted in, are a TS history of the period 1907 to 1913. Pages 54-132 are totally blank, but pages 133-145 have more TS material pasted in. The latter are, effectively, two appendixes. The first lists all the officers who served with the 19th Regt of Bombay Infantry. The second (page 144) is a list of recipients of various awards. It seems likely that someone obtained a copy of Higginbothams' (1909) booklet, and then started to build on that to cover the next few years (up to 1913). They then combined the original printed pages with their own typescript within a single casing. The TS is thought to be unique, and the Higginbothams element - although formally printed and presumably distributed in numbers - seems to be rare. In 1922, the 119th Infantry became the 2nd Bn, 9th Jat Regt (Mooltan Bn). R/5 V/2. NAM. PJE.

WAR SERVICES OF THE 9th JAT REGIMENT

Lieut Col W L Hailes MC * Gale & Polden Ltd, Aldershot, 1938. Blue, gold, Regtl crest, 10.0 x 7.25, xii/185. Fp, 3 other cld plates, no mono phots, 6 maps (folding, bound in), no Index. Apps: H&A (WWI only, with London Gazette dates and theatres of war for which they were granted), notes on the Colours.

* A straight-forward well produced history, with good supporting maps. It is, in effect, Volume I of a pair (vide following entry). The period which it covers is unusually long - from 1803 (the Mahratta Wars) through to Waziristan (1937). The central third of the book deals with the services (particularly during WWI) of all the four Regts which, in 1922, were brought together to form the new 9th Jat Regt. This multiplies the value of the book considerably. Many individuals of all ranks are mentioned in the narrative, hence the lack of an Index is lamentable. R/4 V/4. RMAS/PCAL. RP/DBP-P.

HISTORY OF THE 9th JAT REGIMENT, 1937-1946

Maj J Ross * Unpublished TS, no details shown, n.d. (c.1948).

* This is the draft for a projected large-scale WWII history of all the Bns of the Regt. It was not published in toto, but it seems to have provided a large element in the compilation of the book recorded in the following entry. R/5 V/3. NAM. PJE.

WAR SERVICES OF THE JAT REGIMENT
Volume II : 1937-1948

Lieut Col W L Hailes MC and Maj J Ross * Sapphire Press Ltd, London, 1965. Dark blue, gold, Regtl crest, 10.0 x 7.5, v/227. Fp, 4 mono phots, 6 maps, no Index. Apps: H&A (WWII only), list of officers who served, summary of casualties, notes on recruiting, notes on the experiences of personnel taken POW.

* A full and informative history which details the services of each Bn between 1937 and 1948 - the Middle East, Malaya, Burma, and India (at the time of Partition). It seems likely that Hailes and Ross decided, sometime in the 1950s or early 1960s, to work together on a sequel to Hailes' earlier work (vide preceding entry at the top of this page) and to utilise the draft which Ross had already compiled (vide the immediately preceding entry). If so, this Volume II is a very successful outcome to their collaboration. R/4 V/4. IOL/NAM. MP.

THE JAT REGIMENT
A History of the Regiment, 1803-1947

Lieut Col W L Hailes MC and Maj J Ross * Published by the Commandant, The Jat Regtl Centre, Bareilly, 1967. Blue, gold, Regtl crest, 10.0 x 7.5, xxi/401. Fp, 19 mono phots, 6 cld plates, 13 maps, no Index. Apps: H&A, notes on the Colours.

* This book seems to have been the result of a decision by the post-Independence Jat Regt to fund the republication, in a single binding, of WAR SERVICES, by Hailes (1938), and WAR SERVICES, VOLUME II, by Hailes and Ross (1965). Those two books are here reproduced without amendment (and, unfortunately, still without an Index). The result is a very useful source of reference which, at least in theory, should be more accessible to most researchers than the earlier single volumes. R/3 V/4. IOL/NAM. PJE.

Note: the post-1947 period is covered in THE JAT REGIMENT, A HISTORY OF THE REGIMENT, 1947-1972, VOLUME III, by Lieut Col Gautam Sharma (Allied Publishers Ltd, New Delhi, 1979).This is a substantial, readable, and well produced book.

A BRIEF HISTORY OF THE MACHINE GUN BATTALION, THE JAT REGIMENT, 1941-1946

Lieut Col E Johnson * Printed by Higginbothams Ltd, Bangalore, for the Bn, 1947. Red, gold, Bn badge, 8.75 x 5.5, iv/86. 5 mono phots, 2 maps, no Index (but a good Contents page). Apps: H&A (all ranks), list of officers who served (with their home addresses at 1947).

* A very good account of the Bn's services from formation in 1941 through to disbandment in 1946. Along with several other Regts of the Indian Army, the 9th Jat Regt was ordered to raise a MG Bn from the Support Coys of its various (rifle) battalions. The new Bn was not allotted a number, being designated simply

'the Jat Regiment Machine Gun Battalion'. This book is based partly upon the War Diary and partly upon the personal recollections of officers who served with it in Burma. Their experiences were varied because its different companies were attached to a variety of other units and formations - British and Gurkha. The narrative follows the adventures of each Coy throughout each stage of the campaign - First Arakan, Imphal, the Irrawaddy crossing, the advance to Rangoon, and the final annihilation of Japanese troops attempting to escape from the Pegu Yomas. After VJ Day, the Bn was flown to Saigon where, for six months, it supported French anti-insurgency operations. A remarkable story of a remarkable Bn.
R/4 V/5. MODL. AMM.

STANDING ORDERS FOR WAR - MG Bn, 9th JAT REGIMENT
Anon * Printed at the Luckdist Press, Lucknow, for HQ Lucknow District, 1943. Stiff card, grey boards with blue cloth spine, black, 7.5 x 5.0, iv/64. No ills, no maps, no appendixes, no Index.
* An oddity, as very few Bn Standing Orders for that period have survived the passing years. It is of interest as an example of its genre, and also because it is one of the two only known printed records for this short-lived unit. Apart from the usual rules and regulations regarding the Bn's day-to-day functioning, it also makes revealing references to the battle tactics and methods practiced in the Indian Army in WWII. Former pilots and aircrew will savour the Standing Order which stated: '**All** low flying aircraft will be engaged by machine-gun fire'.
R/5 V/2. PC. RP.
Note: prior to 1939, there were no MG Bns in the Indian Army, but most Infantry Bns had an integral MG Platoon. No MG Bns were formed in WWII in the Gurkha Regts.

10th BALUCH REGIMENT

THE TENTH BALUCH REGIMENT
The First Battalion, Duchess of Connaught's Own (late 124th DCO Baluchistan Infantry) and the Tenth Battalion (late 2/124th Baluchistan Infantry)
O A Chaldecott * Printed at The Times of India Press, Bombay, n.d. (c.1935). Maroon, gold, Regtl crest, 8.75 x 5.5, xiii/250. Fp, 2 mono phots, 11 maps (loose in rear pocket), Index. Apps: ten in total, incl Roll of Honour (WWI), H&A (WWI), notes on lineages, idem class compositions, list of Stations (1820-1934), idem former COs (1820-1934).
* A well produced history of the 1st and 10th Bns of the 10th Baluch Regt and their antecedents prior to 1922. The narrative gives a perfunctory review of the early campaigns (mainly the Mutiny and the Second Afghan War) before then concentrating upon services in WWI - the Western Front, East Africa, Mesopotamia, Palestine, South Persia, and Afghanistan. R/3 V/5. NAM/IOL. RGB.

RECORDS OF THE 27th OR 1st BELOOCH REGIMENT, LIGHT INFANTRY
Lieut Col H Beville * Journal of the United Service Institution of India, Vol II, No 11.
* A ten-page article describing the Regt's early years (1844-1872). It is based upon extracts from Regtl records, but provides possibly useful detail regarding the postings in and out of officers. The 27th underwent various changes of title. It became the 127th Baluch Light Infantry in 1903, then the 3/10th Baluch Regt in 1922. R/5 V/1. NAM. PJE.

THE HISTORICAL RECORDS OF THE 127th BALUCH LIGHT INFANTRY
Compiled from the Official Records, from 1844 to 1905, by Officers of the Regiment
Anon * William Clowes & Sons Ltd, London, 1905. Dark green, silver, 8.5 x 5.5, ix/180. No ills, no maps, no appendixes, no Index.
* The text follows the usual style of the period, being based almost entirely upon Annual Digests and other official sources. However, the material was selected with

care and neatly arranged in the form of a yearly diary of events. All the actions in which the Regt was engaged during the stated period are covered in brief but useful detail, with lists of casualties and excerpts from despatches.
Particular actions are given extended additional narrative coverage. Much of the information which might otherwise have been presented in the form of a series of appendixes - the names of Commandants and Adjutants, officers' postings and appointments, their awards, wounds, and deaths - is to be found within the text. The book is more helpful - in terms of personnel and war services - than it might appear to be at first glance. R/5 V/4. NAM/IOL. PJE/RP.
Note: the copy held by the NAM was donated by the original owner, Col Sir Charles Edward Yates. It contains 21 mono phots and 6 cld ills, all of which seem to have been pasted in by him and not forming part of the original publication. They relate to several different Regts, and might be of interest to students of Dress and accoutrements.

A SHORT HISTORY OF THE 3rd BATTALION, 10th BALUCH REGIMENT (QUEEN MARY'S OWN), JULY 1941 - SEPTEMBER 1943
Anon (presumably one or more serving officers of the Regt) * Printed by Société Orientale de Publicité, Cairo, 1945. Stiff card, cream, black, Regtl crest, 8.0 x 6.0, -/54. 3 mono phots, one sketch, 2 maps, no appendixes, no Index.
* Although brief, this is an informative and quite detailed account of the Bn's services in Iran, Iraq, the Western Desert, and Syria. It is probable that no more than one or two hundred copies were printed. The booklet is of interest also as being one of the very few such WWII records to have been printed outside India. R/5 V/3. NAM. PJE.

CAPITAL CAMPAIGNERS
The History of the 3rd Battalion (Queen Mary's Own), The Baluch Regiment
Lieut Col W E Maxwell CIE * Gale & Polden Ltd, Aldershot, 1948. Dark green, gold, Regtl crest, 8.75 x 5.5, iv/167. Fp, 6 mono phots, 4 maps (2 printed in the text, 2 on the end-papers), Bibliography, Index. Apps: list of former COs.
* The Regt was raised in May 1844 from Baluchi and Scindi recruits as a local Corps. A second Bn was raised in May 1846. The Regt served in Persia (1856), at the siege of Delhi (1857), in Abyssinia (1867), in Afghanistan (1878-1880), in Burma (1886-1889), and in East Africa (1897-1899). It returned to East Africa in WWI for the campaign against von Lettow Vorbeck, then moved to Persia (1918-1919). After service on the NWF and in Burma between the wars, this much travelled unit fought in WWII in the Western Desert, Sicily, Italy, and Greece. The interesting narrative concludes with the return to India from Greece in 1946.
R/3 V/5. NAM/IOL. HIS.

THE FOURTH BATTALION, DUKE OF CONNAUGHT'S OWN, TENTH BALUCH REGIMENT IN THE GREAT WAR
W S Thatcher * University Press, Cambridge, 1932. Dark blue, gold, Regtl crest, 8.5 x 5.5, xix/290. Fp, 3 mono phots, 9 maps (3 printed in the text, 6 bound in), Index. Apps: H&A (for all ranks, with citations), list of former British and Indian officers, roll of personnel recommended for various awards, analysis of casualties.
* The Bn served with distinction on the Western Front and in East Africa, and this is an excellent record of its adventures during those two periods. The narrative is well written, with plenty of references to individual members and to their fighting actions. R/2 V/5. NAM/IOL. CSM/DBP-P.

THE TENTH BALUCH REGIMENT IN THE SECOND WORLD WAR
W S Thatcher (completed by his daughter, published posthumously) * The Baluch Regtl Centre, Abbottabad, Pakistan, 1980. Brown, gold, 10.0 x 7.5, ix/565. No ills, 6 maps, no Index. Apps: H&A, list of COs.
* Fifteen Bns wore the 10th Baluch Regt cap badge during WWII and several saw active service overseas. They went to four different theatres of war - 1st Bn (NWF, Iran, Iraq), 2nd Bn (Malaya), 3rd Bn (Iran, Western Desert, Sicily), 4th Bn

(Eritrea, Western Desert, Italy), 5th Bn (Burma), 6th Bn (NWF), 7th Bn (Burma), 8th Bn (Burma), 9th Bn (NWF), 14th Bn (Burma), 16th Bn (Burma), and 17th Bn (Middle East, Iraq, Greece). Two VCs were gained by members of the Regt - Sepoy Bhandari Ram and Naik Faizal Din. Although there are stated to be some minor inaccuracies in the narrative, this is a fine history. Presumably, if he had lived, Thatcher would have indexed his work (as he did with his WWI history recorded in the preceding entry). R/3 V/4. PC. JPR.

11th SIKH REGIMENT

A SHORT HISTORY OF THE 14th PRINCE OF WALES'S OWN SIKHS
Anon * The Khalsa Press, Kohat, 1908. Yellow, black, 8.0 x 6.0, -/43. No ills, no maps, no appendixes, no Index.
* A very superficial record, based upon Regtl Orders and summarising the period 1846 to 1907. The Regt went on to become 1st Bn, 11th Sikh Regt (King George's Own) (Ferozepore Sikhs) in 1922. R/5 V/1. NAM. PJE.

THE 14th KING GEORGE'S OWN SIKHS
The 1st Battalion (KGO) (Ferozepore Sikhs), The 11th Sikh Regiment, 1846-1933
Col F E G Talbot * Printed by Butler & Tanner, Frome and London, for the Royal United Service Institution, London, 1937. Maroon, gold, Regtl crest, 9.75 x 7.5, viii/164. Fp, no other ills, 8 maps, Index. Apps: list of former COs, idem British officers (at 29.10.1914), idem Subedar Majors, notes on casualties (1914-1919), notes on reinforcement drafts received (1914-1919).
* Although the book does cover the period through to 1933, the main title of this well written history refers to the Bn's pre-1922 designation. The sub-title is the post-1922 designation. The founder Regt was raised at the close of the First Sikh War as The Regiment of Ferozepore. It served with distinction at Lucknow during the Mutiny, and then on the NWF in many famous actions during the remainder of the 19th Century. It went to China in 1900 for the Third China War (the Boxer Rebellion), then returned to the NWF. In WWI, it saw action in Egypt, Gallipoli, and Palestine before returning once again to the NWF. One third of the book deals with the Regt's early history and evolution, most of the other pages then dealing with services in WWI. A good general record. R/3 V/4. IOL. RGH/HIS.

1st KING GEORGE V's OWN BATTALION, THE SIKH REGIMENT
The 14th King George's Own Ferozepore Sikhs, 1846-1946
Lieut Col P G Bamford DSO * Gale & Polden Ltd, Aldershot, 1948. Dark green, gold, Regtl crest, 9.75 x 7.75, -/174. Fp, 24 mono phots, 11 cld plates, 17 excellent maps, no Index. Apps: Roll of Honour (all officers KIA and WIA in all campaigns, 1846-1946), H&A (all ranks, 1846-1946, with some details of place and year), list of former COs, idem Subedar Majors, notes on Regtl titles, summary of casualties (all ranks, 1846-1946).
* A very handsome book, well presented, with a fluent and informative narrative. The author covers the story of the 1/11th Bn and its antecedents over the entire century in uniform style, with good coverage of its work in Burma in WWII.
R/3 V/4. RMAS. DBP-P.

REGIMENTAL LISTS, 15th SIKHS, 1846-1900
Anon * Northern Counties Printing & Publishing, Inverness, Scotland, 1902.
Red, gold, Regtl crest, 10.25 x 7.5, -/219. No ills, no maps, no formal appendixes, no Index.
* Largely a reprint of Bengal Army Lists from October 1846 (the Regt having been raised in July 1846 as The Regiment of Loodianah) through to October 1900. These Lists follow the standard pattern - the early editions state the names of British officers only. Senior Indian officers are included from 1861 onwards, with Indian officers of all ranks from July 1876 onwards. The last fifteen pages carry an alphabetical list of all British officers who served with the Regt but, apart from its quick reference value, it adds nothing to the preceding 214 pages. In 1903,

the Regt became the 15th Ludhiana Sikhs and, in 1922, the 2/11th Sikh Regt (Ludhiana Sikhs). R/4 V/2. PC. CJP.

MILESTONES
Sir John Smyth VC * Sidgewick & Jackson, London, 1979. Black, gold, 9.25 x 8.0, -/304. Fp, 35 mono phots, no maps, no appendixes, Index.
* An enjoyable autobiography by a practiced author (this was his 32nd book). He joined the Indian Army in 1913 and won his VC while serving with 15th Ludhiana Sikhs on the Western Front (Richebourg L'Aouve, 18.5.1915). Later in the war he was given command of the 47th Sikhs. During his career, he took part in seven separate Frontier campaigns and, in WWII, rose to command the 17th Indian Div in Burma. This was at the time of the Japanese invasion. His military career came to an end in the aftermath of the Sittang Bridge disaster and the chaotic British retreat to India. The book is noted here mainly for its descriptions of trench fighting with the 15th Ludhiana Sikhs. That Regt became 2/11th Sikh Regt in 1922. R/1 V/2. MODL. NH.

REGIMENTAL HISTORY OF THE 45th RATTRAY'S SIKHS
Volume I : 1856–1914
Col H StG M McRae * Robert Maclehose & Co Ltd, Glasgow, 1933. Dark blue, gold, Regtl crest, 9.0 x 6.0, xxiv/480. Fp, no other ills, 10 maps (folding, bound in), Bibliography, no appendixes, no Index.
* A full and readable history which would have been much improved by the addition of appendixes and an Index. The Regt traced its origins to 1855 when Capt Thomas Rattray was ordered to raise the Bengal Military Police Bn, in Lahore, for service in Bihar. Eighteen months later, the Mutiny erupted. The Bn found itself to be the only HEIC armed force anywhere between Calcutta and Benares. The men remained loyal and were a key element in stemming the tide of disorder in Bihar Province. The Bn later became part of the Indian Army as 45th Bengal Infantry, and then, when the 11th Sikh Regt was formed in 1922, as 3rd Bn (Rattray's Sikhs). R/3 V/3. NAM/IOL. PJE/RP/CJP.
Note: see footnote to following entry.

REGIMENTAL HISTORY OF THE 45th RATTRAY'S SIKHS DURING THE GREAT WAR AND AFTER, 1914–1921
Lieut Col R H Anderson * Sifton Praed & Co Ltd, London, 1925. Dark blue, gold, Regtl crest, 8.75 x 5.5, -/266. No ills, 19 maps (3 printed in the text, 16 bound in), no Index. Apps: Roll of Honour (in detailed tabular form, with details of KIA, WIA, and DOW, for British and Indian officers), H&A (with full citations for all awards of the DSO, MC, and IOM), list of British officers who served (with some biographical notes for each), idem Indian officers (with even more detailed notes regarding their services and promotions), table of reinforcement drafts (with much useful information regarding the British and Indian officers who accompanied each draft).
* An excellent history, packed with the names of officers and men, the names of places, details of events, and battles major and minor. Both the narrative and the appendixes are a goldmine for the genealogist and for the medal collector. The Regt spent the period 1914-1916 on the NWF of India, 1916-1918 fighting the Turks in Mesopotamia, and 1919-1921 in Kurdistan (being involved in the severe actions around Hillah). An exemplary book, and a pleasure to handle.
R/4 V/4. RMAS. RP.
Note: although Anderson makes no mention of him in his book, its opening pages (9 to 22) were written on his behalf by McRae (vide preceding entry). Under the title 'A Short Epitome of the Previous History of the 45th Rattray's Sikhs, 1856-1914', McRae's contribution was a short narrative with several valuable appendixes. Following the publication of Anderson's book in 1925, McRae evidently decided to expand his 'Short Epitome' into a full narrative history (but omitting the appendixes which he had produced for Anderson). Published as 'Volume I' in 1933, it in

effect made Anderson's book a 'Volume II'. Between them, these two officers covered the story of 45th Rattray's Sikhs very comprehensively. It is unfortunate that nobody has ever written a 'Volume III'.

SARAGARHI BATTALION
History of the 4th Battalion, The Sikh Regiment (XXXVI)
Col Kanwiljit Singh and Maj H S Ahluwalia * Lancer International, New Delhi, 1987. Black, gold, 8.75 x 5.5, -/300. 28 mono phots, 11 maps (8 printed in the text, 3 bound in), Bibliography, Index. Apps: Roll of Honour, H&A (statistics only, 1914-1928), list of former COs (1887-1986), idem Subedar Majors, notes on Battle Honours, an account (of 25 pages, by Maj E F Knox) of the siege of Tsing-Tao, North China, 1914.
* The Roman numerals in the sub-title - XXXVI - refer to one of the Bn's root designations, 36th Regt of Bengal Infantry. The book traces the story back to 1858 and the Bareilly Levy. It is a good readable history, with plenty of detail concerning most of the major events. The 36th was formed in 1861. It won fame when, at the tiny fort of Saragarhi, an attack by 7000 Orakzai tribesmen was held off for several hours by the defending force of nineteen Sepoys and two cookboys. They all died, and the Regt was awarded the Battle Honour shown in the title of this book. The narrative is based upon War Diaries, Regtl Orders, and eyewitness accounts, and appears to be an entirely reliable source. It covers the early decades in condensed style, has a useful but not detailed coverage of WWII, and then focuses on Jammu and Kashmir (1948), the Chinese aggression (1962), and the Indo-Pakistan Wars (1965 and 1971). R/1 V/5. NAM. PJE/CJP.

47th SIKHS, WAR RECORD
The Great War, 1914-1918
Anon * Carbon TS, compiled circa 1925, not formally published at that time, seen in various types of library binding, no details shown, 10.0 x 8.0, -/303. No ills, 2 maps (bound in), no Index. Apps: Roll of Honour, H&A, list of British and Indian officers who served, casualty statistics, note on establishments.
* The 47th Bengal Infantry was raised in 1901 as a class Regt, recruiting only Jat Sikhs. Two years later it was re-titled as 47th Sikhs and then, in 1922, it became the 5th Bn (Duke of Connaught's Own), 11th Sikh Regt. This is a narrative account of its time on the Western Front (where it suffered 1591 casualties, of whom 227 were fatal), and then its move to Egypt and Mesopotamia for the remainder of the war. R/5 (in this format) V/4. RMAS/IOL. VS/DBP-P.
Note: in 1992, an original TS copy was printed in facsimile and published in hardback by Picton Publishing Ltd, of Chippenham.

MY OWN WAR IN MALAYA
Denis Russell-Roberts * Published privately by the author, no details shown, n.d. (c.1946). Maroon, white, 7.75 x 6.25, vi/183. No ills, 6 maps (bound in), no Index. Apps: copy of Japanese C-in-C's letter to the British High Command demanding surrender, copy of Japanese leaflet dropped over Singapore encouraging Commonwealth soldiers to surrender, copy of Order issued to 11th Indian Div by its GOC on 15.2. 1942.
* A well written and candid account by an officer of 5/11th Sikh Regt who served from the time of the Japanese landing at Kuantan through to the capitulation on Singapore Island. The author has many words of praise for the courage, endurance and initiative shown by some of his men and some of his brother officers, but he writes bluntly when describing the performance of the Bn as a whole and the conduct of other units with which it had contact. The book was written soon after his release from captivity, when memories were still fresh. R/4 V/4. PC. CJP.

A DIARY OF THE 5th Bn (DCO), THE SIKH REGIMENT IN THE MALAYAN CAMPAIGN 8 December 1941 to 15 February 1942

Anon * Publication details not shown, n.d. Light blue, gold, 13.0 x 8.5, -/27. No ills, no maps, no Index. Apps: H&A.

* A strange little item of no discernible origin. Although sketchy, it does provide a useful day-by-day summary of events leading up to the surrender. Possibly based upon the Bn War Diary. R/5 V/2. NAM. PJE.

35th SIKHS REGIMENTAL RECORD, 1887-1900

Anon * Printed by H & J Pillans, Edinburgh, 1920. Olive green, gold, 10.0 x 7.5, -/70. No ills, no maps, no appendixes, no Index.

* The first fifteen pages carry a brief history of the 35th Bengal Infantry, raised in 1887, and the same Regt under its post-1903 title, the 35th Sikhs. The balance of the book's seventy pages are then given to extracts from Army Lists which show the postings in and out of the Regt's officers. R/5 V/1. NAM/RMAS. PJE.

35th SIKHS, REGIMENTAL RECORDS, 1887-1922

Col J C Freeland * Sham Lall & Sons, Peshawar, 1923. Green, gold, Regtl crest, 10.0 x 7.5, i/103. No ills, no maps, no Index. Apps: list of former COs, idem British and Indian officers of the Regt, idem Subedar Majors.

* This is basically an updated and slightly improved version of the item noted in the preceding entry. The Regt had seen some service in the 1897 Frontier campaign, but in WWI it remained in India as a training and draft-finding unit for the 47th Sikhs overseas. The first half of the book is a narrative account of these events, the second half being nothing more than extracts from Army Lists. R/3 V/3. NAM. MP.

Note: after 1922, the 35th continued in its training role, being restructured and re-designated as 10/11th Sikh Regt.

OPERATIONAL RECORD OF THE M.G. BATTALION, THE SIKH REGIMENT

Anon * Unpublished facsimile TS, disbound, 13.0 x 8.25, -/11. No ills, no maps, no Index. Apps: H&A, list of officers who served.

* The MG Bn (which like other such Bns did not carry a numerical designation) was raised in January 1942, served in the Burma campaign, and was disbanded in November 1947. This very short account contains all the basic facts concerning its formation and major deployments. It is possible that several copies were made and distributed. R/5 V/2. IWM. PJE.

Note: reference may be made also to EMERGENCY SAHIB, by Robin Schaefli (printed by R L Leach, location unknown, 1992). This is a personal memoir of the Bn.

A BRIEF HISTORY OF THE 11th SIKH REGIMENT

Anon * The Military Steam Press, Nowshera, n.d. (c.1943). Green, gold, Regtl crest, 9.5 x 6.5, -/60. No ills, no maps, no appendixes, no Index.

* A condensed record which attempts to tell the story of the 11th Sikh Regt battalions and their forbears from 1843 onwards. Presumably it was intended to mark the Centenary. Given the pressures of trying to compile and publish such a work in wartime, it was a valiant effort. R/4 V/2. IWM. PJE.

THE SIKH REGIMENT IN THE SECOND WORLD WAR

Col F T Birdwood OBE * Jarrold & Sons, Norwich, for the author, n.d. (c.1950). Red, gold, Regtl crest, 8.75 x 5.5, xviii/462. No ills, 18 maps, no Index. Apps: H&A (statistical summary only).

* The Regt had nine Infantry Bns and the MG Bn in the field, plus various training and administrative units. The task of recording their travels and battles in a coherent narrative manner could not have been easy. The author overcame most of the pitfalls by writing a strictly chronological history of the entire Regt but with numerous margin notes to clarify what each Bn was doing, where, and at what precise dates. The result is a massively factual compilation which is reasonably easy to follow and which deals with the Regt's services in almost every

theatre of war between 1939 and 1945. Having gone to so much trouble, it is surprising that Col Birdwood did not include an Index or more appendixes (other than the 'H&A' statistics which are not in themselves particularly helpful). R/3 V/4. NAM/PCAL. RP

12th FRONTIER FORCE REGIMENT

HISTORY OF THE 1st SIKH INFANTRY, 1846–1886
Anon * Thacker Spink & Co, Calcutta, 1887. Dark brown, gold, 10.0 x 6.5, –/184. No ills, no maps, no Index. Apps: Roll of Honour, H&A, list of former COs, idem other officers, idem Subedar Majors, list of Stations (cantonments).
* The text is based upon verbatim extracts from Regtl records, but it does also include some narrative references to service during the Mutiny period and on the NWF. In 1903, the Regt became the 51st Sikhs (Frontier Force). R/4 V/2. NAM. PJE.

HISTORY OF THE 1st SIKH INFANTRY 1846–1902 – 51st SIKHS (FRONTIER FORCE) 1903–1920 – 1st Bn, 12th FRONTIER FORCE REGIMENT (PRINCE OF WALES'S OWN) (SIKHS)
Anon * The Diocesan Press, Vepery, various dates (see below). Dark green, gold, three matching volumes, each having maps and appendixes but no ills or Indexes, 10.0 x 6.75.
Volume I : 1846–1886. Published in 1887, reprinted with amendments, 1903, –/171.
Volume II : 1887–1902. Published in 1903, –/101.
Volume III : 1902–1920. Published in 1929, –/229.
All three Volumes were produced separately on the dates shown. However, it is possible that a number of additional copies of Volumes I and II were produced in 1903 in a single (combined) binding. Certainly, when Volume III was produced in 1929, a number of additional copies were combined in a unified casing with reprints of Volumes I and II. This 'combined' history, consisting of 497 pages in total but not numbered consecutively, is the only one to have on its spine the full title as shown above (including the reference to 1/12th Frontier Force Rifles).
* A very full and complete history which contains all of the information which most researchers are likely to require. The eight maps (folding, bound in) are particularly helpful. R/4 V/4. NAM. RJW/CJP/PJE.

THE HISTORICAL RECORD OF THE 2nd (OR HILL) SIKH INFANTRY, PUNJAB FRONTIER FORCE
Anon ('By Authority') * The Punjab Government Press, Lahore, 1887. Red, gold, 10.5 x 7.0, ii/46. No ills, no maps, no appendixes, no Index (but two detailed 'Contents' pages).
* A short and superficial history based upon Regtl records and therefore typical of the series noted elsewhere in this bibliography which were official publications for the PFF. In 1903, the Regt was retitled 52nd Sikhs (Frontier Force). R/4 V/2. IOL/USII. PJE.

HISTORICAL RECORD OF THE 52nd SIKHS, FRONTIER FORCE
Late 2nd (or Hill) Sikh Infantry, Punjab Frontier Force
Anon * Rai Sahib M Gulab Singh & Sons, at the Mufid-i'-Am Press, Lahore, 1905. Half red cloth, hald red sides, gold, Regtl crest, 9.5 x 6.25, –/63. No ills, no maps, no appendixes, no Index.
* An account which commences with formation in 1846 as the 2nd Regt of Infantry, Frontier Brigade. The Regt was one of several raised at the instigation of Col Henry Lawrence at the time of the First Sikh War. It recruited mainly Kangra Hill Dogras and Gurkhas, thus earning the soubriquet 'The Hill Corps'. The author includes coverage of the Second Afghan War and the march to Kandahar (1878–1880), the Black Mountain Expedition (1888), the Kohat Moveable Column (1898), and service in Somaliland (1902–1903). The Regt became 2nd Bn (Sikhs), 12th Frontier Force Regt in 1922. R/5 V/2. PC. BDM.

HISTORY OF THE 2nd SIKHS, 12th FRONTIER FORCE REGIMENT, 1846-1933
Capt C W May * Printed by E C Davis at The Mission Press, Jubbulpore, for the Regt, 1933. Full Morocco in black, gold, Regtl crest, 10.0 x 7.25, -/153. 17 mono phots, 5 maps (loose in rear pocket), no Index. Apps: Roll of Honour (WWI), H&A (WWI), list of former COs, idem British and Indian officers, idem Adjutants, idem Quartermasters, idem Subedar Majors, notes on Dress, idem Battle Honours, idem Regtl organisation.
* A well written narrative history in an attractive binding. It provides good coverage of various Frontier campaigns, the Mutiny, the Second Afghan War, Somaliland, and services during WWI (when the 52nd Sikhs kept watch on the NWF and acted as a draft-finding unit for the 56th and 59th Rifles).
R/4 V/4. NAM. BDM/RP.

HISTORICAL RECORDS OF THE 3rd SIKH INFANTRY, PUNJAB FRONTIER FORCE
Anon ('By Authority') * The Punjab Government Press, Lahore, 1887. Red, gold, 10.5 x 7.0, v/75. No ills, no maps, no appendixes, no Index.
* Another in the PFF official series, but one of the better examples. It covers the period 1847 to 1887 in useful detail, the text being based, as usual, upon Regtl Orders and other formal sources. The material has been assembled in a diary format and shows Stations and movements, events, officers' postings, and so forth. Included are details of the Regt's role in operations during the Mutiny, Umbeyla (1863), Jowaki (1877-1878), and the Second Afghan War. The names of numerous individuals - their awards, wounds, and postings - are included in the text. In 1903, the Regt was retitled 53rd Sikhs (Frontier Force).
R/4 V/4. IOL/NAM. AMM/PJE.
Note: a corrected and much expanded version (-/165 pages) was published by the same source (undated, but either 1903 or early 1904). This edition is bound in black cloth with a leather spine, gold lettering, and Regtl crest embellishment.

HISTORICAL RECORDS OF THE 3rd SIKHS, 1847-1930
Lieut Col C I Shepherd * Pardy & Son, Bournemouth, UK, 1931. Black, gold, Regtl crest, 9.5 x 6.5, -/313. No ills, no maps, no Index. Apps: Roll of Honour (British and Indian officers, WWI only), H&A (with full citations for awards of the DSO, MC, and IOM), list of officers who served (1847-1930), idem battles in which the 53rd Sikhs took part (WWI).
* This is a record of dates rather than a full-blown narrative history. The author has copied the style of layout used in the 1887/1903 history (vide the preceding entry) and has extended the coverage forward into WWI and the inter-war years. It provides tedious reading for the general reader, but a very handy quick reference source for the researcher. The contents are arranged in three sections. Part I - 3rd Sikhs PFF, origins and Battle Honours (this being a reprint of the material published in 1903, vide preceding entry). Part II - 53rd Sikhs PFF, 1914-1918 (this deals mainly with Mesopotamia). Part III - 3rd Bn, 12th Frontier Force Regt, 1922-1930 (the amalgamations and post-war services). Apart from anything else, the book is a prime source for medal collectors and genealogists.
R/4 V/4. NAM/RMAS. HLL/RP.
Note: at least one copy of Part II (1914-1918) was produced in a 'de luxe' binding for the library of the Officers Mess. It contained maps and tipped-in photographs, and a few other copies may have been specially commissioned for individual officers.

THE HISTORICAL RECORD OF THE 4th SIKH INFANTRY, PUNJAB FRONTIER FORCE
Anon ('By Authority') * The Punjab Government Press, Lahore, 1887. Red, gold, Regtl crest, 10.5 x 7.25, v/89. No ills, no maps, no appendixes, no Index.
* A brief summary of services, based upon Regtl Orders and records. The period covered is 1847 to 1885 (during which time the Regt was engaged in operations on the NWF and in the suppression of the Mutiny). Some officers are named in the text. In 1903, the Regt became 54th Sikhs (Frontier Force).
R/4 V/2. USII/NAM. PJE.

HISTORY OF THE 54th SIKHS, FRONTIER FORCE
Previously Designated 4th Sikhs, Punjab Frontier Force, 1846-1914
Capt S R Shirley * Gale & Polden Ltd, Aldershot, 1915. Dark green, gold, 7.0 x 5.0, xvi/219. No ills, 9 maps (loose in rear pocket), no Index. Apps: ten in total, incl H&A, list of COs, idem former officers, idem campaigns.
* A narrative history which covers the stated period in considerable detail. The author included good descriptions of services during the Mutiny and on the NWF, and mentioned interesting incidents along the way. In 1922, the 54th Sikhs became 4th Bn (Sikhs), 12th Frontier Force Regt. R/4 V/4. NAM. PJE/CJP.
Note: the title as shown on the outer cover of this book is REGIMENTAL HISTORY OF THE 54th SIKHS.

THE FRONTIER FORCE REGIMENT
Brig W E H Condon OBE * Gale & Polden Ltd, Aldershot, 1962. Khaki, gold, Regtl crest, 9.75 x 7.25, xxii/592. Fp, 19 mono phots, 36 maps (26 printed in the text, 10 bound in), Bibliography, no Index. Apps: Roll of Honour (officers only, WWII), H&A (with citations for VCs, WWII only), notes on changes of title (1846-1956).
* An excellent book, by far the best on the Regt but marred by the lack of an Index. More than half of the narrative is devoted to the WWII services of the pre-war Regular Bns and the new Bns raised during the massive wartime expansion. Under the 1922 reorganisation, the FF Regt comprised six Bns - 1st Bn (Prince of Wales's Own) (Sikhs), formerly 51st Sikhs - 2nd Bn (Sikhs), formerly 52nd Sikhs - 3rd Bn (Sikhs), formerly 53rd Sikhs, and granted the 'Royal' prefix in 1935 - 4th Bn (Sikhs), formerly 54th Sikhs - 5th Bn (Queen Victoria's Own Corps of Guides), formerly 1st Bn Guides Infantry - 10th Bn (Queen Victoria's Own Corps of Guides), formerly 2nd Bn Guides Infantry. The near world-wide adventures of each Bn are described in detail, as is the way in which the Regt was allocated to the Pakistan Army at the time of Partition. R/2 V/4. IOL/NAM. PJE/CJP.
Note: the Frontier Force Regt derived in part from the Corps of Guides. Additional information regarding the origins and early history of the Corps will be found in LUMSDEN OF THE GUIDES, by Sir Peter Lumsden and George Elmslie (published in London, 1898). This is a substanial biography (333 pages) of the officer who raised the Corps in 1846, Sir Harry Lumsden. The post-1947 story of the Frontier Force Regt can be found in WARDENS OF THE MARCHES - A HISTORY OF THE PIFFERS, by Lieut Gen M Attiquir Rahman MC (Wajidalis, Lahore, 1980). For further information regarding the Guides, reference should be made to the Index - vide the Indian Cavalry section.

13th FRONTIER FORCE RIFLES

DIGEST OF SERVICES OF THE 1st (COKE'S) REGIMENT, PUNJAB INFANTRY
Col Theo Higginson * The Simla Chronicle Press, Simla, 1888. Brown, gold, 9.5 x 6.5, -/122. No ills, 5 maps (folding, bound in), no Index. Apps: notes on casualties, list of Stations and movements.
* A slightly better-than-average PFF publication for that period. The customary verbatim quotations from Regtl records are interspersed with verbatim quotations from campaign despatches. The period covered is 1849 to 1887. The Regt's title was changed in 1903 to 55th Coke's Rifles (Frontier Force).
R/4 V/3. USII/NAM. OSS/PJE.

HISTORY OF THE 55th COKE'S RIFLES, FRONTIER FORCE
Formerly Known as the 1st Panjab Infantry, Panjab Frontier Force
Capt J P Villiers-Stuart * Harvey & Co, Waterford, Ireland, 1908. Green boards, red spine, two Regtl crests, 10.5 x 6.5, ii/119. No ills, 6 maps (bound in), no Index. Apps: list of Indian officers 'who have served', with notes regarding their services and awards.
* Another assemblage of extracts from Regtl records with some linking narrative and with lists of Indian officers interspersed. The period covered is 1849 to 1908. It concentrates mainly upon the Mutiny and various Frontier operations. The 55th

Rifles became, in 1922, the 1st Bn (Coke's), 13th Frontier Force Rifles. R/4 V/3. NAM. PJE.

THE HISTORY OF COKE'S RIFLES

Col H C Wylly * Gale & Polden Ltd, Aldershot, 1930. Dark green, gold, Regtl crest, 10.0 x 7.5, iii/164. Fp, 11 mono phots, no maps, Index. Apps: list of former COs, idem Subedar Majors (with notes of their distinctions and awards).

* This is a good professionally written and nicely produced history which covers the period 1849 to 1928. In addition to the 19th Century conflicts, there is good coverage of the work done by the Regt during WWI - notably in East Africa and Persia. Many officers are mentioned in the narrative, with interesting quotations of their reminiscences. R/3 V/5. NAM. PJE/RP.

Note: seen also in a 'de luxe' binding, full Morocco, marbled end-papers, gold blocked all around.

HISTORY OF THE 2nd PUNJAB INFANTRY

Anon * Publication details not shown, n.d. (c.1903). Dark green, gold, 9.5 x 6.5, -/126. No ills, no maps, no Index. Apps: eight in total, incl H&A, list of officers (British and Indian), Stations and movements, notes on casualties.

* Based upon Regtl records and Orders, covering the period 1849-1902, and more useful than stimulating. As expected, the text deals mainly with the Mutiny and operations on the NWF. In 1903, the Regt became 52nd Sikhs (Frontier Force). R/4 V/3. IOL/NAM. PJE.

Note: an earlier edition, dated 1889 and covering events up to 1887, has been noted but not seen.

HISTORY OF THE 2nd BATTALION, 13th FRONTIER FORCE RIFLES, 1849-1931

Anon * Groom & Son Ltd, Bury St Edmunds, UK, 1933. Dark green, gold, 8.25 x 6.75, -/74. No ills, no maps, no appendixes, no Index.

* A very nicely printed and well bound book, but the contents are simply a diary of Stations and movements, plus a few explanatory notes and descriptions. There is little detail and no analysis. The Bn served in Egypt and Aden in 1914-1915, and in Syria and Palestine in 1918-1919. Possibly of value as a secondary source. R/4 V/3. RMAS/NAM. RP/PJE.

Note: the same item has been seen in dark blue cloth, with a leather spine, and without a leather spine. This suggests that the anonymous author was a former officer of the Regt who producd the book as a private venture and then gave or sold copies to other officers with bindings made according to their personal preferences (or perhaps according to the materials which the binder happened to have in stock at various times).

2nd BATTALION, 13th F.F, RIFLES
War History (Unofficial)

C J Weld * Facsimile TS, no publication details shown, seen in a yellow cloth library binding, black, 13.0 x 8.25, -/90. No ills, no maps, no Index. Apps: two lists of officers (at 30.10.1945 and in November 1946), list of arms and ammunition captured by the Bn during operations in Sumatra.

* This is a full and readable narrative account of the Bn's services in Burma and Sumatra between 1942 and 1946. Clearly a private initiative, it was presumably cyclostyled in limited numbers for presentation to officers who had served, as a memento. R/5 V/3. NAM. PJE.

THROUGH THE MUTINY WITH THE 4th PUNJAB INFANTRY, PUNJAB IRREGULAR FORCE

Surgeon-General J Fairweather * An unpublished TS (presumably copied from an original MS), n.d. Seen casebound in green, gold, 10.0 x 8.0, -/61. No ills, no maps, no appendixes, no Index.

* An autobiographical account of his experiencs with the Regt on the march to Delhi and the siege there. After the city fell, in September 1857, it fought its way, as an element of Greathed's column, to Lucknow. There it joined Sir Colin Campbell's force attempting to raise the siege. Great feats of bravery were

performed by individual officers and men at the storming of the Sikandarabagh. A useful secondary source. In 1903, the Regt became the 57th Wilde's Rifles (FF). R/5 V/2. NAM. PJE/CJP.

HISTORY OF THE 4th REGIMENT, PUNJAB INFANTRY
Anon * Thacker, Spink & Co, Calcutta, 1894. Mauve, gold, Regtl crest, 10.0 x 6.5, ii/66. No ills, no maps, no Index. Apps: list of British officers (with notes regarding their war services, awards, wounds, and deaths).
* Based upon Regtl records and Orders. The main events were the Mutiny and operations on the NWF, but these are covered in cursory style. However, many officers (British and Indian) and Other Ranks are mentioned by name in the text, with references to their awards. This aspect is probably the publication's best feature. R/4 V/3. NAM. PJE/CJP.

REGIMENTAL HISTORY OF THE 4th BATTALION, 13th FRONTIER FORCE RIFLES (WILDE'S)
Anon * Butler & Tanner, Frome and London, apparently for the Regt, n.d. (c.1932). Fawn boards with blue spine, gold, Regtl crest, 8.5 x 5.5, vii/235. Fp, 3 mono phots, one map (bound in at the rear), no Index. Apps: list of former COs, idem other officers (for the period 1849–1930, some with biographical details).
* A good narrative history, presented to Butler & Tanner's usual high standards. Many individual officers and men are mentioned in the text, also details of awards and casualties. After giving the expected summary of events in the 19th Century, the author devotes half of his pages to WWI (the Western Front, Egypt, and East Africa). There is also a complete chapter on the Third Afghan War (1919). An attractive book, readable, a good general account. R/3 V/4. RMAS/NAM. RP.

HISTORICAL RECORD OF THE 5th INFANTRY, PUNJAB FRONTIER FORCE
Anon ('By Authority') * The Punjab Government Press, Lahore, 1887. Red, gold, 10.5 x 7.0, v/79. No ills, no maps, no appendixes, no Index.
* Yet another example of the tedious books produced by the authorities in Lahore, circa 1887, to record the services of the constituent Regts and Btys of the Punjab Frontier Force. As usual, this is a catalogue of Stations, movements, and officers' postings and appointments. This one is remarkable only for the fact that it seems to have survived in even fewer numbers than others in the same series. In 1903, the 5th Punjab Infantry was retitled 58th Vaughan's Rifles (FF). R/5 V/2. USII. OSS.

A RECORD OF THE 58th RIFLES, F.F., IN THE GREAT WAR, 1914–1918
Col A G Lind DSO * The Commercial Steam Press, Dera Ismail Khan, 1933. Dark green, gold, 10.0 x 7.5, –/155. No ills, 7 maps (printed on two sheets, located loose in a rear pocket), no Index. Apps: H&A, notes on casualties, idem reinforcement drafts, Orders and verbatim correspondence.
* A good workmanlike narrative account of the Bn's services on the Western Front with the Indian Corps in 1914–1915, and then in Egypt. Replacements for the heavy losses in France were received from 55th Coke's Rifles. In 1922, the 58th became the 5/13th Frontier Force Rifles. R/4 V/4. IOL/NAM. PJE/BDM.

HISTORY OF THE 5th BATTALION, 13th FRONTIER FORCE RIFLES, 1849–1926
Col H C Wylly OBE * Gale & Polden Ltd, Aldershot, 1929. Green, gold, Regtl crest, 10.0 x 7.25, vii/135. Fp, 12 mono phots, 6 maps (loose in rear pocket), no Index. Apps: Roll of Honour (British and Indian officers, WWI only), H&A (WWI), list of former officers (with details of their services).
* A good professional narrative account of the entire period, with much helpful and interesting detail not recorded elsewhere. R/3 V/4. PC. CSM.

HISTORY OF THE VI PUNJAB INFANTRY, PUNJAB FRONTIER FORCE, FROM 1843 TO 1885
Lieut Col T Fraser Bruce * The Civil & Military Gazette Press, Lahore, 1886. Stiff card, sand, with red spine and quarters, black, 6.75 x 4.5, iv/30. No ills, no maps, no appendixes, no Index.
* A very slim volume, but handy as a quick source of reference. Presented in diary form, the material covers the story of the Scinde Camel Corps (1843–1853),

the Scinde Rifle Corps (1853-1856), then the Regt which evolved from the Scinde root - the 6th Punjab Infantry. The contents of the book consist mainly of notes regarding Stations, movements, and officers' postings, with only minimal mention of the principal campaigns (Sutlej, the Mutiny, Umbeyla, Jowaki). Bibliophiles who may have an interest in the PFF histories of that era might care to consider the possibility that this booklet was the prototype for the 'By Authority' series which started to emerge from the Punjab Government Press, in Lahore, in the following year. The binding is not the same, and the authorship is attributed, but the contents and internal layout are notably similar. R/4 V/2. MODL. AMM.

REGIMENTAL HISTORY OF THE 6th ROYAL BATTALION, 13th FRONTIER FORCE RIFLES (SCINDE), 1843-1923

Anon (Capt D M Lindsey) * Gale & Polden Ltd, Aldershot, 1926. Dark green, gold, 9.75 x 7.25, -/145. Fp, 30 mono phots, 8 maps (folding, bound in, very detailed), no Index. Apps: H&A (all ranks), list of former COs, idem other officers (with details of their services), notes regarding the 'Royal' designation.

* A well written narrative history from the time of the Scinde Camel Corps up to the formation of the 13th Frontier Force Rifles (when the 59th Royal Scinde Rifles became the 6th Royal Bn). The various reorganisations and their impact are clearly described, and there is good coverage of the WWI period - on the Western Front (1914-1915), in Mesopotamia (1916-1917), and under Allenby in Palestine (1918). Many individuals are mentioned by name in the text. R/4 V/4. RMAS/PCAL. RP.

Note: a copy has been seen in full Morocco, but it is not known if this was a 'de luxe' edition or a special commission. Confusingly, the title shown on the spine is HISTORY OF THE 59th RIFLES, 1843-1923. The contents are identical.

REGIMENTAL HISTORY OF THE 6th ROYAL BATTALION (SCINDE), 13th FRONTIER FORCE RIFLES, 1843-1934

Anon (probably Capt D M Lindsey, vide preceding entry) * Gale & Polden Ltd, Aldershot, 1935. Dark green, black, Regtl crest of the 59th Scinde Rifles, 9.75 x 7.25, xi/117. No mono phots, 9 line drawings (badges and buttons), no maps, no Index. Apps: H&A (WWI and post-war), list of COs, notes on the raising of the Scinde Camel Corps, notes on the granting (in 1921) of the 'Royal' distinction.

* The narrative is an updated version of that published in 1926 (vide preceding entry). The appendixes also are updated, to circa 1935. The author continues to cover the story in the same interesting style as previously but, unlike the 1926 history, this book has no illustrations, no maps, and no list of regimental officers. It was intended at that time to produce a 'de luxe' edition which would incorporate those features, with publication coinciding with the Centenary. This plan was shelved during the war and then overtaken by Partition. Instead, an entirely new history, covering the events of 1934 onwards, was published in 1951 (vide the following entry). The 'Lindsey' books are both good in their own way, but researchers working on the period 1914-1934 may need to consult both (rather than one or the other). R/3 V/4. NAM. CSM/RJW/HIS.

REGIMENTAL HISTORY OF THE 6th ROYAL BATTALION (SCINDE), 13th FRONTIER FORCE RIFLES, 1934-1947

Brig N L St P Bunbury DSO * Gale & Polden Ltd, Aldershot, 1951. Dark green, gold, Regtl crest, blind spine, 8.5 x 5.5, vii/116. Fp, no other ills, 5 maps (bound in), no Index. Apps: Roll of Honour (British officers only), H&A, idem officers who served.

* A useful and readable account, devoted mainly to WWII services in the Middle East, the Abyssinia campaign, then with Paiforce, in Palestine, and on the mainland of Italy. Pre-war operations on the NWF (1936-1937) are also well recorded in this book. A nice sensible history which would have been much improved if it had been indexed. R/3 V/4. NAM. CSM.

REGIMENTAL HISTORY, 13th FRONTIER FORCE RIFLES
W H H Young * Publisher's details not shown, Abbotobad, 1945. Green, black, 9.0 x 5.5, v/121. No ills, no maps, no Index. Apps: numerous and various, occupying eighty-three pages.
* This is a brief summary of the history of each Bn in the Regt, intended mainly for the instruction of newly joined officers. The narrative does include some short descriptions of actions fought during the Mutiny and in WWI, but the book's main value is the extensive run of appendixes which cover many aspects of the Regt's past, and which are handy as a quick reference source. R/4 V/2. NAM. PJE.

THE FRONTIER FORCES RIFLES
Brig W E H Condon OBE * Gale & Polden Ltd, Aldershot, 1953. Green, silver, Regtl crest, 10.0 x 7.0, xix/461. Fp, 21 mono phots, 26 maps (19 printed in the text, 7 bound in), no Index. Apps: Roll of Honour (officers only, WWII only), H&A (all ranks, incl Commendations, and full citations for six VCs, WWII), statistical summary of casualties.
* A highly detailed, extremely well written and well produced history. It covers the period 1849-1946, but concentrates mainly upon WWII. The author traces the travels and fighting services of the five Regular battalions, the nine war-raised Rifle and Garrison battalions, and the MG Bn. Those which went overseas were engaged in almost every theatre of war - Malaya, Syria, Eritrea, North Africa, Italy, and Burma. The book is comparable to Condon's other major work - THE FRONTIER FORCE REGIMENT - but in neither case did he provide an Index. In books of such scale and complexity, this omission creates a huge problem for anyone trying to consult them. R/2 V/4. IOL. RP.

13th FRONTIER FORCE RIFLES
A Summarised History of the 13th Frontier Force Rifles
During the Second World War
Lieut Col A D Fitzgerald MBE * Software Sciences Ltd, for the author, 1985. Soft card, green, black, 'Eight cap badges' motif, 12.0 x 8.0, ii/13. No ills, no maps, no appendixes, no Index.
* An 'economy' offset booklet having brief but concise details of the activities of each of the Frontier Force Rifles Bns and related units during WWII (seventeen in total). Based partly upon Condon's book (vide preceding entry) and partly upon information provided by former officers. Basically a disappointing effort, but possibly useful as a quick reference source. R/4 V/1. PC. RJW.
Note: this pamphlet has been seen bound also in plastic covers.

14th PUNJAB REGIMENT

HISTORY OF THE 1st BATTALION, 14th PUNJAB REGIMENT, SHERDIL-KI-PALTAN (LATE XIX PUNJABIS)
G Pigot * The Roxy Printing Press, New Delhi, 1946. Green, black, Regtl crest, 11.0 x 8.0, iv/243. No ills, 11 maps and 24 sketch plans (bound in), no Index. Apps: list of former COs, extracts from Bn Standing Orders, list of Stations and movements.
* Covers the period 1857 to 1946. For much of the 19th Century it was the 19th Bengal Infantry. In 1903 it became the 19th Punjabis, hence the (Roman) numerals in the title of the book. In 1922, it became 1/14th Punjab Regt. This is a sound and readable narrative history, with plenty of helpful detail. R/4 V/4. NAM. PJE.
Note: 'Sherdil-ki-Paltan' translates as 'Regiment of the Lion-hearted'.

HISTORY OF THE 20th (DUKE OF CAMBRIDGE'S OWN) INFANTRY, BROWNLOW'S PUNJABIS
From its Formation, in 1857, to 1907
Anon (presumably a Regtl Committee, formed to mark the 50th Anniversary) * Swiss & Co (Army & Navy Printer), Devonport, UK, n.d. (c.1910). Buff cloth boards, green leather spine, Regtl crest in gold, 9.5 x 6.0, -/147. Fp, 13 mono phots, one plan (bound in), no Index. Apps: expeditions in which the Regt (or units of) has taken part (with lists of participating British and Indian officers),

list of former COs, idem Subedar Majors, notes on Stations and movements, extracts from Indian Army Lists (at October 1909 and January 1910), list of former officers (British and Indian) at various dates between 1858 and 1901, notes on changes of Regtl title.
* A narrative history of the Regt from its formation in 1857 through to 1907, with detailed accounts of the sixteen campaigns in which it took part during that time. These include descriptions of specific actions, extracts from Despatches, casualty lists, medals and clasps awarded, and Battle Honours subsequently granted. There are interesting biographies of the Regt's founder, ultimately Field Marshal Sir Charles Brownlow GCB, and Subedar Major Mauladad Khan CIE, Sirdar Bahadur. The high quality photographs include several studio portraits of individual British and Indian officers (captioned) and group pictures of officers, NCOs, and ORs (not captioned). This is a book which covers a great deal of ground in its 147 pages. It might have been better if the narrative had been longer and less condensed, but it is neverthelss an excellent source of reference. The presentation and binding, as might be expected of Swiss & Co, is very good indeed. In 1903, the Regt was retitled the 20th Duke of Cambridge's Own Infantry (Brownlow's Punjabis). R/4 V/4. PC. BWR/RGH.

HISTORICAL RECORDS OF THE 20th (DUKE OF CAMBRIDGE'S OWN) INFANTRY, BROWNLOW'S PUNJABIS
Volume II : 1909–1922
Anon * Butler & Tanner, Frome and London, for the Regt, 1923. Khaki boards with green spine, gold, Regtl crest, 9.0 x 6.0, viii/86. Fp, 3 mono phots, 6 maps (all folding, bound in), no Index. Apps: Roll of Honour (all ranks, WWI), H&A (all ranks, WWI), list of COs (1908–1922), idem officers who served in WWI, idem former Subedar Majors, idem Indian personnel awarded the OBI and the IOM (1863–1922), list of Stations and movements.
* A detailed and very readable history devoted primarily to WWI. The Bn served in Mespotamia, Egypt, and Palestine. Although the narrative is quite short, it provides all the basic information in an attractive style. In 1922, the Regt became 2/14th Punjab Regt, still distinguished with the titles 'Duke of Cambridge's Own' and 'Brownlow's'. R/4 V/4. RMAS/NAM. RP/PJE.
Note: presumably the author(s) regarded this book as the natural successor to the preceding entry, hence the 'Volume II' sub-title.

REGIMENTAL HISTORY OF THE 3rd BATTALION, 14th PUNJAB REGIMENT, 1857–1922
Lieut Col W F R Webb * Facsimile TS, seen bound in green cloth and gold, 13.0 x 8.25, –/222. No ills, 8 maps, no Index. Apps: H&A, list of former COs, idem officers who served, notes on Dress.
* A full and detailed history which never found a publisher. The 3rd Bn was formerly the 22nd Punjabis (1903–1922), and the 22nd Regt of Bengal Infantry prior to that. In WWI, the 22nd Punjabis saw service in Mesopotamia and Persia. R/5 V/3. NAM. PJE.

STANDING ORDERS, 24th PUNJABIS
Third Edition, 1913
Anon * Printed at The Civil & Military Gazette Press, Lahore, for the Regt, 1913. Green cloth, blind, 9.0 x 5.5, iii/161. No ills, no maps, no formal appendixes, no Index (but detailed List of Contents).
* Organised by Lieut Col S H Climo, OC 24th Punjabis at Bannu in 1913, this otherwise typical volume of Standing Orders is noted here because it contains an interesting chapter (of 17 pages) headed – 'A Short History of the 24th Punjabis'. The 16th Punjab Infantry was raised at Peshawar during the Mutiny in August of 1857. It became 28th Bengal Native Infantry in 1861, then later in the same year, 24th (Punjab) Regt of Bengal Infantry. In 1903, the title was changed again, this time to 16th Punjabis. The ten pages of narrative are surprisingly detailed and include the names of numerous British and Indian officers and Other Ranks. Apart from action against the Mutineers in 1857–1859, the Regt served on the NWF, in Afghanistan (1878–1880), the Malakand (1897), and China (1900). There are tables

listing campaigns in which the Regt fought, awards to all ranks (with dates and locations), armaments used throughout the period, list of past Commandants (COs), British and Indian officers serving in 1913, and Regtl sporting achievements (incl the names of the winning Soccer team, China Expeditionary Force tournament, 1900). R/5 V/3. PC. CJP.

WAR RECORDS OF THE 24th PUNJABIS (4th BATTALION, 14th PUNJAB REGIMENT) 1914-20

Brig A B Haig * Gale & Polden Ltd, Aldershot, 1934. Dark green, gold, Regtl crest, 10.0 x 7.5, xi/84. Fp, one mono phot (named group of all officers, British and Indian, at October 1914), 9 maps (folding, bound in), no Index. Apps: Roll of Honour, H&A (all ranks), list of officers (British and Indian).

* The Regt fought in Mesopotamia from April 1915 onwards. It took part in the Battle of Shaiba, the advance to Ctesiphon, and the retreat to Kut-al-Amara. It was destroyed during the siege and the survivors were forced to surrender. A complete chapter deals with the terrible experiences of the personnel who were taken POW. The Regt was subsequently reformed with new personnel and served in Mesopotamia, Salonika, South Russia, and Anatolia between 1917 and 1920. In 1922, it was retitled 4/14th Punjab Regt. R/4 V/4. PCAL. CSM.

1857-1957 CENTENARY SOUVENIR, 8th BATTALION THE PUNJAB REGIMENT

Anon * Allied Press, Lahore, for the Bn, n.d. (1957). Illustrated paper covers, white, red, '28th Bengal Infantry soldiers' motif, Regtl crest in green. Outer covers bound with cord and tassels in Regtl colours, 6.5 x 8.0 (landscape), -/36. 19 mono phots, one cld ill (the Kandahar Star), no maps, no formal appendixes, no Index.

* Apart from one page devoted to the Bn's centenary agenda, this souvenir programme contains a condensed 16-page narrative of the Bn's history from 1857 to 1957, a number of interesting mono phots (incl Bn groups and individual award winners), and then several tables which fulfil the function of conventional appendixes, thus - Bn designations, Battle Honours, Stations, H&A (all ranks, incl MID up to 1956), and a list of officers serving in 1957. In 1947, the 4/14th Punjab Regt was allocated to Pakistan. In 1956, it became the 8th Bn, The Punjab Regt. R/4 V/1. PC. CJP.

THE 40th PATHANS IN THE GREAT WAR

Anon * The Civil & Military Gazette Press, Lahore, 1921. Paper covers, green, black, 9.0 x 6.0, -/73. Fp, 2 mono phots, 3 maps (folding, bound in), Index. Apps: H&A (WWI), notes on casualties.

* A sketchy history, based upon the War Diary and so at least reliable as far as it goes. Often known as 'the Forty Thieves', the Regt served in Hong Kong, France and Flanders, and in East Africa. A useful record which could have been much more fully developed. R/4 V/3. NAM. PJE.

HISTORY OF THE 5th BATTALION (PATHANS), 14th PUNJAB REGIMENT
Formerly 40th Pathans, 'The Forty Thieves'

Maj R S Waters OBE * James Bain Ltd, London, 1936. Green, gold, Regtl crest, 10.0 x 9.0, xxii/398. Two fps, 22 mono phots, 7 maps (folding, bound in), Index. Apps: a total of sixty pages, incl Roll of Honour (British and Indian officers only, WWI), H&A (all ranks, WWI), list of former COs, biographical notes for certain senior officers who formerly had served with the Bn, notes on Dress, idem war memorials, etc.

* A very thorough narrative, with excellent appendixes. The author covers the period from 1780 to 1935, but his account is particularly detailed when describing the Regt's work during WWI. His book is longer and contains more basic research material than is usually found in Indian Army unit histories of that period. It even has an Index. R/4 V/5. RMAS/IOL. VS/RP.

CONTINUATION OF THE HISTORY OF THE 5th BATTALION (PATHANS), 14th PUNJAB REGIMENT, 1937-1942

Maj R S Waters OBE * Lund Humphries, London, n.d. Paper covers, olive green, black, 7.0 x 4.5, -/81. No ills, one map (folding, bound in at the rear), no appendixes, Index.

* It seems likely that this booklet was written just after WWII when the survivors began to arrive back in India and England. The Bn had been unlucky. It was sent to Malaya in 1941 to bolster the defences there. It ended up being told to surrender when Singapore was handed over to the Japanese in February 1942. The narrative traces the route followed by the Bn down the length of the Peninsula, gives much detail on the blocking actions which it fought, and contains many references to casualties. All of this is covered in clear and interesting detail. There is also a chapter devoted to the experiences of the officers when obliged to work as slave labourers on the Burma-Siam railway. R/5 V/4. NAM. PJE.

7th Bn, 14th PUNJAB REGIMENT
Regimental History of Active Service during WWII

Anon * The Northern Army Press, Nowshera, n.d. (c.1947). Stiff card, light green, black, 10.0 x 6.0, -/63. No ills, no maps, no Index. Apps: Roll of Honour, H&A, notes on casualties.

* The Bn was raised at Mardan in November 1940 (as part of the Nowshera Bde) and disbanded in November 1946. It was trained specifically with frontier hill and jungle operations in mind, and served on the Manipur front and in the Lushai hills. This is a simple straightforward narrative history, from beginning to end of the Bn's existence. R/4 V/4. NAM. PJE/CJP.

NINTH BATTALION, FOURTEENTH PUNJAB REGIMENT
Raised 1st April 1941, Disbanded 8th July 1947

Lieut Col J R Booth and Lieut Col J B Hobbs * Western Mail & Echo Ltd, Cardiff, 1948. Green, gold, Regtl crest, 9.0 x 6.0, -/132. Fp, 9 mono phots, 2 maps (one printed on the end-papers, one folding and bound in), no Index. Apps: Roll of Honour, H&A, list of VCOs who served.

* Like the preceding entry, this is one of the few sad relics of those war-raised Bns which were formed at great speed, trained hard, fought valiantly in Burma, and were then brought back to India to be told that they had no future. Men who had served as comrades went home to villages which soon would be torn apart by the sectarian violence which accompanied Partition all over the Punjab. Many of the officers held wartime Commissions, so it was hard for them to keep in contact once they had resumed their civilian careers. No doubt Cols Booth and Hobbs were aware of the risk that the 9th Bn might soon be forgotten and took it upon themselves to produce this record while memories were still fresh. It is a well arranged narrative which incorporates numerous eyewitness accounts. R/5 V/4. NAM. PJE.

RECORDS OF THE I/XXI PUNJABIS

Maj P Murray * Gale & Polden Ltd, Aldershot, 1919. Green, gold, Regtl crest, 7.5 x 5.0, -/107. No ills, 3 maps (folding, bound in), no Index. Apps: list of former COs, notes on the war services of each Bn (1/21st Punjabis and 2/21st Punjabis).

* Previously (post-1885) the 21st (Punjab) Regt of Bengal Infantry, it became 21st Punjabis in 1903. During WWI it was expanded and formed into two Bns - 1/21st and 2/21st. This is the story of the 1/21st. The author begins by tracing its roots from 1857 onwards (the Mutiny, various NWF campaigns, the Dongola Expedition in the Sudan in 1896), and then through to 1919 (encompassing WWI actions in Egypt, Palestine, and South Russia). The wartime 2/21st Bn was disbanded at the end of the war, but the 1/21st Bn went on to become the 10/14th Punjab Regt (and so, like all 10th Bns under the 1922 arrangements, the Regt's Training Bn). R/4 V/3. NAM. PJE.

FOURTEENTH PUNJAB REGIMENT
A Short History, 1939-1945
Anon * Lund Humphries, London, n.d. (c.1947). Dark green, gold, Regtl crest, 9.0 x 6.0, ii/111. No ills, 3 maps (printed on the end-papers), no Index. Apps: H&A (numerical summary only), list of officers who served.
* This is a condensed history of each of the Bns - Regular and war-raised - during WWII, both in India and overseas. The narrative contains little in the way of fine detail, but it is a useful general record. R/4 V/3. NAM. PJE.

15th PUNJAB REGIMENT

A HISTORY OF THE 1st BATTALION, 15th PUNJAB REGIMENT, 1857-1937
Compiled from the Battalion's Digest of Services and Other Official Documents
Lieut Col J E Shearer MC * Gale & Polden Ltd, Aldershot, 1937. Dark blue, gold, Regtl crest, 8.5 x 5.25, xi/100. Fp, 17 mono phots (individual and group portraits, uniforms, etc), no maps, no Index. Apps: H&A, list of former COs, idem other former officers (extensive, some with details of service), notes on changes to the unit designation.
* Despite having a fairly short narrative, this is a very useful history, with all periods equally well covered. The photographs are a pleasing feature - they include several formal groups of identified officers. The 1/15th Punjab Regt was raised initially as The Lahore Punjab Bn (in 1857). It went through the periodic changes of title and internal organisation which were typical of Regts formed in the Punjab at around that time, being designated successively - 17th Punjab Infantry, 25th Bengal Native Infantry, 25th (Punjab) Regt of Bengal Infantry, and then (1903), the 25th Punjabis. As the latter, the Regt travelled widely during WWI. It served in Hong Kong, Salonika, Southern Russia, and Turkey.
R/3 V/4. NAM/IOL/PCAL. CSM/AMM.

A HISTORY OF THE 26th PUNJABIS, 1857-1907
Lieut P S Stoney * The Pioneer Press, Allahabad, 1908. Brown boards with red spine and quarters, red, 7.5 x 5.0, iv/51. No ills, no maps, no Index. Apps: list of former officers, idem Subedar Majors, records of Inspections, notes on musketry and signalling.
* Compiled from the annual Digests of Services and Regtl office records. Typically terse and dry, but certainly a good source for checking dates, Stations, officers' appointments, and so forth. In 1922, the Regt became the 2/15th Punjab Regt.
R/4 V/2. NAM. PJE.

A HISTORY OF THE 26th PUNJABIS, 1857-1923
Compiled from the Digest of Services and Other Official Records
Lieut Col P S Stoney * Gale & Polden Ltd, Aldershot, 1924. Red, gold, Regtl crest, 7.5 x 4.75, xii/144. Fp, 15 mono phots, 4 maps (folding, bound in), no Index. Apps: Roll of Honour (British and Indian officers only, WWI), H&A (WWI and Waziristan, 1921-1923), list of former officers (with useful biographical notes), Inspection Reports, notes on musketry and signalling, list of Subedar Majors, some extracts from Army Lists (1858, 1907, and 1922), notes on officers' final postings (at the time of reorganisation, 1922).
* Stoney was the author of the earlier edition (vide preceding entry), but this is a much more attractive and detailed book. It contains plenty of reference material, with numerous individuals mentioned in the text. The photographs have full captions and the maps are of better-than-average quality. In WWI, the Regt served in Hong Kong and Mesopotamia. R/4 V/4. RMAS/IOL. MGHW/RP.

NO GONGS FOR HEROES
Helene and John Scott * Unpublished facsimile TS, seen in library binding, yellow, 11.5 x 8.5, viii/149. 18 mono phots, 8 maps (bound in), Bibliography, no Index. Apps: H&A, list of officers (British and Indian).
* This is an excellent account of SARFOR (Sarawak Force), of which 2/15th Punjab

Regt formed the main element. Posted initially to Singapore in 1941, the Bn was moved to Sarawak (Borneo) as part of the local defence force. It was rapidly overrun when the island was invaded by the Japanese, and the survivors were taken POW. This is an account of the Bn's travels and travails during that period. In 1946, it was reformed (still as the 2/15th) by the redesignation of the war-raised 16th Bn. R/5 V/4. NAM. PJE.

A SHORT HISTORY OF THE 27th PUNJAB INFANTRY
Anon * Publication details not shown, n.d. (c.1903). Pale buff canvas on soft card, red, 8.5 x 6.0, -/25. No ills, no maps, no appendixes, no Index.
* A strange little book, apparently printed in India and presumably for the Regt. It contains a brief and not very helpful mention of some Frontier actions, Stations and movements. The quality of printing is poor, and the text generates far more questions than answers. The Regt was raised in 1857 to assist in the suppression of the Mutiny but saw little action. It went to China in 1860 but, again, had no opportunity to distinguish itself. As 27th (Punjab) Regt of Bengal Infantry, it became the 27th Punjabis in 1903. R/5 V/1. PC. RP/CJP.

THE 2/27th PUNJABIS
Being a Brief History of the Battalion from July 1918 to March 1919
Lieut J J Willoughby * The Pioneer Press, Allahabad, 1919. Khaki, black, Bn badge, 7.25 x 4.75, -/27. 2 mono phots, 19 line drawings (caricatures of officers, drawn by Lieut C S Barnes), no maps, no Index. Apps: list of British officers (two, at 4.8.1918 and 19.4.1919).
* This, as the sub-title suggests, is no more than a summary of events. However, it is of interest because it is one of the very few surviving records of any of the numerous 2nd Bns raised by Infantry Regts of the Indian Army during the second half of WWI. In 1918, while the 27th Punjabis were serving in Mesopotamia, a second full battalion was formed at home (thus making the pre-war unit the 1st Bn). Titled 2/27th Punjabis, the role of the new unit was recruitment, training, and draft-finding for the 1st Bn. It was disbanded in April 1921.
R/5 V/2. PC. BDM/CJP.

A SHORT HISTORY OF THE 4th BATTALION, 15th PUNJAB REGIMENT
Anon * Thacker & Co, Bombay, n.d. (c.1923). Black, gold, Regtl crest, 6.5 x 4.0, -/15. No ills, no maps, no Index. Apps: H&A (WWI), list of former COs (of the forebear Regts), list of Stations.
* This booklet was published only a year or so after the reorganisation of the 1/28th Punjabis as 4/15th Punjab Regt. Its purpose, therefore, was presumably that of marking the occasion and telling newly joined officers something about the unit of which they were now a part. The appendixes are possibly useful as a source of reference, but this item is interesting mainly because it must have been printed in very limited numbers and because relatively few such items were published in the immediate aftermath of the major 1922 reorganisations.
R/5 V/1. NAM. PJE.
Note: no collective history of the 15th Punjab Regt was published, nor is there a formal history for the 4th Bn in WWII. Reference may be made, however, to PRENDER'S PROGRESS - A SOLDIER IN INDIA, 1931-1947, by John Prendergast (Cassell, London, 1979). Amongst other periods in his military career, the author served with 4/15th Punjab Regt from 1932 to January 1943.

16th PUNJAB REGIMENT

30th PUNJABIS
James Lawford MC MA * Osprey Publishing Ltd, Reading, UK, 1972. Illustrated soft card, 'Perfect' bound, 9.75 x 7.25, -/40. 28 mono phots, 22 cld ills, no maps, no appendixes, no Index.
* This booklet is of interest mainly to students of Dress, insignia, and accoutrements. Typically of the Osprey series, it incorporates some excellent coloured

illustrations (drawn by Michael Youens). The author provides a condensed but useful account of the Bn's antecedents and its services, as 1/16th Punjab Regt, through to 1946 (in the Dutch East Indies). R/2 V/3. PCAL. RP.

REGIMENTAL HISTORY, VAN CORTLANDT'S LEVY
Afterwards called Bloomfield's Sikhs, 23rd Punjab Infantry, 35th Punjab Infantry, 31st Punjab Infantry, 2nd Bn 16th Punjab Regiment
Brig Gen A G Kemball * Thacker & Co Ltd, Bombay, 1926. Green, gold, 8.25 x 6.0, -/48 (last ten pages not numbered). Fp, 7 mono phots, no maps, no Index. Apps: H&A (all ranks, WWI only), list of former British and Indian officers (for the 31st Punjabis only).
* At Ferozepore, in May 1857, Deputy Commissioner van Cortlandt received orders to raise three Companies of Sikhs for service against the mutinied regiments of the Bengal Army. He gave the task to Capt C C Bloomfield, hence the Regt's early title. This little book is a condensed diary of events for the period from 1857 to 1918. It is handy as a quick reference source, and the tipped-in photographs are very good. The 31st Punjabis became, in 1922, the 2/16th Punjab Regt. R/5 V/3. RMAS. RP.

I AM READY
The Story of the 2nd and 3rd Battalions, 16th Punjab Regiment
Anon * Unpublished TS, no details shown, n.d. Seen in card covers, khaki, black, 13.0 x 8.25, -/42. No ills, 7 maps (bound in), no Index. Apps: Roll of Honour, H&A.
* A good descriptive account of the 2nd Bn in Malaya and its experiences in Japanese captivity. The 3rd Bn also was ordered to lay down its arms when the island of Singapore was surrendered, but this Bn does not receive the same coverage here. R/5 V/3. NAM. PJE.

THE STORY OF THE 33rd PUNJABIS, 1857-1925
Anon * Scottish Mission Industries, Poona, 1925. Black, gold, Regtl crest, 6.25 x 5.0, -/31. No ills, no maps, no appendixes, no Index.
* A brief summary of the Regt's origins, followed by a slightly more detailed account of its services in WWI (Egypt, Western Front, Aden, East Africa). The 33rd Punjabis became 3/16th Punjab Regt in 1922. R/4 V/1. NAM. PJE.

HISTORICAL RECORD OF THE 4th BATTALION, 16th PUNJAB REGIMENT
Anon (Maj C C Jackson, Lieut Col G D Martin MC, and Col H H Smith DSO) * Gale & Polden Ltd, Aldershot, 1931. Red, gold, 9.0 x 5.5, x/173. Line drawings of badges (on title page), no other ills, 8 maps (folding, bound in), Index. Apps: Roll of Honour (for 9th Bhopal Infantry, all ranks, with dates), H&A (all ranks, with full citations, incl VC award to Sepoy Chatta Singh), list of former COs, list of other officers (1818-1914 and 1922-1930, with service details), list of Honorary Colonels, notes on units which supplied reinforcement drafts to the Regt during WWI.
* This had been a local Corps - the Bhopal Levy (1859-1865) and the Bhopal Bn (1865-1903) - before gaining the title of 9th Bhopal Infantry (1903-1922). Its nick-name at that time was 'the Bo-peeps'. During WWI it raised three additional Bns, two of which served in Mesopotamia, but this book is concerned mainly with the original pre-war (Regular) 1st Bn. It served on the Western Front with the Indian Corps, in Egypt, and then in Mesopotamia. Its adventures are described here in good detail, with plenty of individuals being mentioned by name in the narrative. In 1922, the 1/9th Bhopal Infantry became the 4/16th Punjab Regt.
R/3 V/4. NAM. MCJ.

HISTORY OF THE 46th PUNJABIS
A Memoir
Brig A F F Thomas CIE * Unpublished facsimile TS, n.d. Seen casebound in green, black, 13.0 x 8.25, iii/17/11. No ills, no maps, no Index. Apps: list of officers serving in 1900, idem 1914, idem 1921.

* A very brief account arranged in two parts. The first, of seventeen pages, is a summary of WWI services in India and Egypt. The second, of eleven pages, is the listings of officers serving at various dates. The latter might be useful to medal collectors and genealogists. R/5 V/2. RMAS. MGHW.

SOLAH PUNJAB
The History of the 16th Punjab Regiment
Lieut Col J P Lawford MC and Maj W E Catto * Gale & Polden Ltd, Aldershot, 1967. Green, gold, Regtl crest, 8.75 x 5.5, xiii/302. 30 mono phots, 28 maps (26 printed in the text, two on the end-papers), no Index. Apps: H&A (WWI only), notes on Regtl titles, idem rank structures and titles, idem uniforms and equipment (1857-1922), list of British and Indian officers (at 1945).
* A good clear narrative account, and the only book which attempts to tell the story of the Regt in its entirety (pre-1947). The opening pages summarise the 19th Century campaigns but, from page 39 onwards, the author concentrates upon the WWI and WWII services of each of the component Bns (and their 1922 forebears). The book does the job expected of it, but it is in some ways a disappointing effort. It was presumably sponsored with too small a budget. There is no Index (sorely needed in a history of this complexity), and the paper and binding are well below Gale & Polden's traditional standards. R/1 V/4. NAM/IOL. RP/CJP.

17th DOGRA REGIMENT

A HISTORY OF THE 1st (P.W.O.) BATTALION, THE DOGRA REGIMENT, 1887-1947
37th Dogras 1887-1922, 1st (P.W.O.) Bn, 17th Dogra Regt, 1922-1945
C T Atkinson * Printed by the Camelot Press Ltd, Southampton, for the Regt, 1950. Blue, gold, Regtl crest, 8.0 x 5.5, xiii/210. Fp, 39 mono phots (indexed), 7 line drawings (insignia), 28 maps, Index. Apps: H&A, list of former COs and Regtl officers (with full career details for each), idem Subedar Majors.
* A good narrative account by an experienced military historian. He provides moderately detailed coverage of the period 1887 to 1914, a more detailed account of WWI services when the 37th Dogras served in Mesopotamia from 1915 onwards, and then a much more detailed account of services by 1/17th Dogra Regt during WWII. The illustrations are mainly individual studio portraits and groups, most of which are fully captioned with the names of those depicted. The Dogras are Hindus of Rajput origin and their home country is the hills of the Punjab and of Jammu and Kashmir. Hardy and courageous, they make first class soldiers.
R/3 V/5. IOL. MCJ.

HISTORY, 2nd Bn THE DOGRA REGIMENT (1861-1942)
Lieut Col W B Cunningham and Lieut Col J N Phelps * Krishan Sudama Press, Ferozepore, n.d. (c.1958). Blue, gold, 3 Regtl crests, 10.0 x 6.5, iii/334. No ills, no maps, no Index. Apps: H&A, list of former COs, idem officers, Stations and movements, notes on casualties (1891-1931).
* The 2nd Bn was originally a local Corps, raised during the Mutiny and entitled The Agra Levy. In 1861 it was established formally as the 38th Regt of Bengal Native Infantry. In 1890 it became the 38th (Dogra) Regt of Bengal Infantry and then, in 1903, was restyled as the 38th Dogras. In the 1922 reorganisations, it was assigned to the new 17th Dogra Regt as its 2nd Bn. This history begins with the induction of the Regt into the Bengal Army and continues through to February 1942 when it went into captivity at the fall of Singapore. The readable narrative deals with that disaster, but concentrates mainly upon campaigning on the NWF and WWI services in Aden and Egypt. R/4 V/4. NAM. PJE.

THE STORY OF THE 1st AND 2nd BATTALIONS, 41st DOGRAS
Volume I : October 1900 to December 1923, and October 1917 to March 1922
Anon ('Officers of the Regiment') * Thacker & Co, Bombay, for the Regt, n.d. (c.1923). Blue, gold, 'Regtl crest and Battle Honours' motif, 9.25 x 7.0, -/146. Fp, 14 mono phots, 5 maps (folding, bound in, 3 cld), Index. Apps: Roll of Honour (British and Indian officers only), H&A (all ranks), list of former COs, idem former officers (British and Indian).
* The 41st Dogras were raised in 1900 as the 41st (Dogra) Regt of Bengal Infantry. Renamed in 1903, the Regt went to China a year later as part of the international security force and remained there until 1908. In 1914, it served first on the Western Front, then in Mespotamia, and finally in Egypt and Palestine. In 1917, a 2nd Bn was formed (hence the sub-title of this book), but it saw no active service overseas. However, it did take part in the brief Third Afghan War of 1919. Under the 1922 reorganisations, the 1st Bn became the 3rd Bn of the new 17th Dogra Regt while the 2nd Bn became the 10th (Training) Bn. This is a handsome book, a pleasure to handle, and full of facts. The appendixes are exceptionally good. The 'H&A' appendix, for example, includes details of all IOM and IDSM awards, foreign awards, full citations where appropriate, and details of Recommendations. R/4 V/5. NAM. RP/CJP.
Note: seen also in full Morocco, black. No Volume II, as such, was ever published.

THE DOGRA QUARTERLY
The War Years
Col R C B Bristow and Lieut Col R W D Gloyne * The Civil & Military Gazette Press, Lahore, 1946. Paper covers, ivory, blue, Regtl crest, 8.5 x 5.5, iii/184. 7 mono phots, no maps, no Index. Apps: Roll of Honour, H&A.
* This is either a reprint of all the Regt's quarterly newsletters or a bound volume of back copies. It is, in any event, a superb source of reference. It consists of information of all kinds on the activities of all the Regular Bns (1st, 2nd, and 3rd), the war-raised Bns (4th, 5th, 6th, 7th MG, 25th, and 26th), and the Regtl Training Centre. As expected in this type of publication, it concentrates upon topics of interest to members who were serving at that time - promotions, awards, casualties, well known Regtl personalities, and so forth. R/5 V/4. PC. HRC.

THE DOGRA REGIMENT, A SAGA OF GALLANTRY AND VALOUR
A Historical Record, 1858-1981
Col R D Palsokar MC * The Dogra Regtl Centre, Faizabad, 1982. Black, gold, Regtl crest, 10.0 x 7.0, iv/590. Fp, 170 mono phots, 2 cld plates, one line drawing (of early uniform), 55 maps, Bibliography, Index. Apps: H&A, list of former COs, idem Subedar Majors, notes on the Regtl march.
* As its title and sub-title might suggest, this book is a comprehensive and detailed record of the Dogra Regt from its earliest roots through to 1982 (it remained in the Indian Army at Partition). Col Palsokar is a well known historian and it is reported that his excellent narrative contains only a few minor errors. As is often the case with books printed in India, the pictures have not reproduced well, but the quality of production as a whole is good. The maps are well drawn and clearly printed. The author does not concentrate upon post-1947 events but instead gives a balanced account of all the campaigns in which the Regt (and its forebears) took part in the 19th and 20th Centuries. R/2 V/5. IOL/NAM/RMAS. HRC.

18th ROYAL GARHWAL RIFLES

HISTORICAL RECORD OF THE 39th ROYAL GARHWAL RIFLES
Volume I : 1887-1922
Brig J Evatt DSO * Gale & Polden Ltd, Aldershot, for the Regt, 1922. Rifle green, gold, Regtl crest, page marker riband in Regtl colours, 10.0 x 7.25, xiv/215. Fp, 89 mono phots, 16 maps (11 bound in, 5 loose in rear pocket), Bibliography, no Index. Apps: Roll of Honour (British officers, with details of their war services, Indian officers named if KIA but no service details), H&A (with citations where available, 1887-1922), list of former officers (British and Indian), notes on the

1/50th Kumaon Rifles and the Tehri Imperial Service Sappers.
* A well written book, admirably produced. Despite the dates given in the sub-title, the bulk of the book is devoted to services in WWI. Garhwal is an area in the Himalaya, west of Nepal, where the people are very similar to the Gurkhas. Indeed, until 1887, many Garhwali men were recruited into Gurkha regiments and were almost indistinguishable from their Gurkha comrades. It was decided in that year to recruit only Garhwalis into 2/3rd Gurkha Rifles and then, in 1890, to give this Bn separate status as the 39th (The Garhwali) Regt of Bengal Infantry. In 1903, it was retitled as 39th Garhwal Rifles. At the outbreak of war, the Regt had two Bns - 1st and 2nd - and both sailed immediately for France with the Meerut Division, Indian Corps. They returned to India in 1915, refitted, and then moved to Mesopotamia. The 2nd Bn later served also in Salonika and Turkey. In August, a 3rd Bn was formed at Lansdowne (the Regtl Centre) to provide drafts for 1st and 2nd Bns. In October 1917, a 4th Bn was authorised, its men recruited mainly in the Kumaon District. This Bn was separated from the Garhwalis in April 1918 when it was given its own regimental establishment at the 1st Bn, 50th Kumaon Rifles. Another 4th Bn was formed at the end of 1918 and it served in the Third Afghan War. When the Army underwent its major reorganisations of 1922, the 39th did not need to be changed, only renumbered. With four Bns, it was self-sustaining. The 1st, 2nd, and 3rd Bns retained their numerals but, in line with the new practice, 4th Bn became 10th Bn (as training unit for the other three). The 'Royal' distinction was granted in 1921 in recognition of the Regt's war services. Like any such large-scale work, this book (as published) contains a number of errors. A package of 'Addenda and Corrigenda' slips was sent to all subscribers about one year after publication so that they might be tipped (glued) in. Today, a copy having these slips in place is obviously preferable to one which does not. Some copies of the book were sold with an additional page bound in, showing the name of an officer and headed 'In Honoured Memory of ...'. These may have been presentation copies (from the Regt) to the next-of-kin of officers who died.
R/3 V/4. NAM/IOL. RP.
Note: the original 1922 edition was reprinted at Lansdowne, Garhwal, sometime around 1975. It is a facsimile reprint, having 215 pages and the same contents including the bound in maps but not the loose maps in the rear pocket. This edition is bound in black cloth with gold lettering, and is produced to a good standard.

HISTORICAL RECORD OF THE ROYAL GARHWAL RIFLES
Volume II : 1923–1947
Lieut Gen Sir Ralph Deedes OBE MC * The Army Press, Dehra Dun, 1962. Black boards with green spine, gold, Regtl crest, 9.5 x 7.5, xxxv/276. Fp, 27 mono phots, 26 maps (bound in), no Index. Apps: H&A (all ranks, with citations), list of former British officers (1898–1947, with some details), notes on Battle Honours.
* This book continues the story commenced by Evatt (vide preceding entry), and the author sustains the high standards of fluent writing and factual research set by his predecessor. The Regt had nine Bns in WWII. The 2th and 5th Bns were lost in the fall of Singapore, a tremendous loss for a Regt which, pre-war, had only three active service Bns. Their comrades went on to give fine service in almost every theatre of war. It is not known how many copies of this book were printed but, even though it was published forty years after Volume I, it seems to surface in dealers' catalogues far less often. R/4 V/4. NAM. PJE/RP.

WITH THE ROYAL GARHWAL RIFLES IN THE GREAT WAR
From August 1914 to November 1917
Brig Gen D H Drake-Brockman CMG * Publication details not shown, n.d. (c.1934). Dark green, gold, 10.0 x 7.25, -/164. 33 mono phots, 14 maps (13 printed in the text, one bound in at the rear), no Index. Apps: H&A, list of British officers (with war services), copies of various Operational Orders, 'Notes on Trenches'.
* This interesting and informative memoir was written by an officer who went to France in 1914 with the 2nd Bn and who served throughout its time on the

Western Front. He commanded the Bn during the battles at Aubers, Festubert, and Loos, and his account bears the stamp of authority. At the outbreak of war, and leaving aside the Gurkha regiments, the 39th Garhwal Rifles were the only Regt of the Indian Army to have two Regular Bns. Both were swiftly committed to the early battles in France and Flanders and both suffered horrendous losses. Reduced by battle casualties to one-Bn strength, they were combined and then sent back to Lansdowne in 1915. After refit and reinforcement with new recruits, they were sent to Mesopotamia. Drake-Brockman's account does not cover later events, but it is a valuable adjunct to the official history by Evatt (vide first entry for this Regt). Unfortunately, like Evatt, Drake-Brockman neglected to index his work.
R/4 V/4. NAM/IOL. CSM/CJP.

STANDING ORDERS OF THE 18th ROYAL GARHWAL RIFLES
Anon * The Pioneer Press, Allahabad, 1928. Dark green boards with red spine, gold, 10.0 x 6.5, vi/104. No ills, no maps, no Index. Apps: notes on customs and traditions, idem sporting trophies, Hindu holidays, idem Dress (all ranks), idem common Garhwali Rajput names, idem clans and castes (showing their phonetic spellings, with equivalent Roman and Devanagri characters).
* This is a typical volume of Regtl Standing Orders and it covers all the expected aspects of the functioning of a rifle unit. However, the appendixes are unusually detailed and are very useful to researchers having an interest in the ethnic and social aspects of the Indian Army. R/5 V/3. PC. LBR.

19th HYDERABAD REGIMENT

HISTORY OF THE 1st BATTALION, 19th HYDERABAD REGIMENT
Anon * Gale & Polden Ltd, Aldershot, 1928. Dark green, gold, Regtl crest, 7.5 x 5.0, ii/31. No ills, no maps, no Index. Apps: list of Stations (1813-1928).
* For a book published in 1928, this is a curiously old-fashioned and inadequate effort. It is based upon Regtl records, makes passing reference to campaigns in the Deccan under the command of, first, the Nizam of Hyderabad, and later, under British leadership, and then leaves a lot of questions unanswered. The Bn served in WWI in Mesopotamia as the 94th Russell's Infantry, but those services are barely mentioned here. R/4 V/1. NAM/PCAL. PJE/RP.
Note: this book's descriptions of events up to 1905 are taken directly from A HISTORY OF THE HYDERABAD CONTINGENT, by Maj R G Burton (vide the 'Index of Authors').

REGIMENTAL HISTORY OF THE 2/19th HYDERABAD REGIMENT (BERAR)
Lieut Col J de L Conry * Gale & Polden Ltd, Aldershot, 1927. Dark green, gold, Regtl crest, 7.25 x 5.0, iv/32. No ills, no maps, no appendixes, no Index.
* Another very poor effort. The author presumes to cover the period 1780 to 1922 in just 32 pages, with passing mention of numerous wars, campaigns, and reorganisations along the way. Not surprisingly, the result is failure. As the 96th Berar Infantry, the Bn fought in WWI in Mesopotamia. R/4 V/1. NAM. PJE.
Note: a copy with the imprint 1928 has been seen (presumably a verbatim reprint).

STANDING ORDERS FOR THE 3/19th HYDERABAD REGIMENT, 19th INDIAN INFANTRY GROUP
Anon * The Commercial Press, Quetta, 1924. Red, black, 9.5 x 7.0, -/92. No ills, no maps, no appendixes, no Index.
* Simply a compilation of routine Standing Orders issued by the Commandant, with amendments issued thereafter. Noted here only because the Regt published so little about itself. R/5 V/1. USII. OSS.

THE STORY OF THE 97th DECCAN INFANTRY

Maj W C Kirkwood * The Government Central Press, Hyderabad, 1929. Dark green, gold, Regtl crest, 10.0 x 7.5, iii/165. Fp, 20 mono phots, one map (folding, bound in), no Index. Apps: eleven in total, incl Roll of Honour, H&A (WWI), list of former officers, lists of Regtl trophies and prizes.

* This is, and in contrast with the three preceding items, a readable history which contains much useful information. The coverage is fairly condensed, but it does deal helpfully with the early wars in Central and Southern India and with WWI services in Egypt and Palestine. In 1922, the 97th Deccan Infantry became the 3/19th Hyderabad Regt. R/4 V/3. NAM. PJE.

A HISTORY OF THE 4th BATTALION, 19th HYDERABAD REGT

G G C Bull * Gale & Polden Ltd, Aldershot, 1933. Rifle green, gold, Regtl crest, 7.5 x 5.0, iii/57. No ills, no maps, no Index. Apps: H&A (incl MSMs), list of COs (1804-1933), idem Adjutants (1819-1933), list of Stations (1788-1933).

* Under the framework of the 1922 reorganisations, the 4/19th Hyderabad Regt evolved from what had been, since 1903, the 98th Infantry. That Regt, in turn, traced its ancestry back to the earliest days of the Hyderabad Contingent. This booklet summarises the complex story (the various changes of title and status), gives an account of the early campaigns (the Mahratta and Pindari Wars, the Mutiny, the Boxer Rebellion in China), and describes the work of the 98th Infantry in WWI (East Africa and the East Persia Cordon). Many officers receive a mention by name in the text, especially those killed or wounded in WWI.
R/4 V/4. MODL/RMAS. AMM/CJP.

Note: the Preface states - 'This History replaces a previous edition printed in 1929'. The 1929 version has not been seen, but there is a report of a reprint of the 1933 edition (as recorded above) bearing the date 1939.

HISTORICAL RECORD OF THE KUMAON RIFLES

Maj J F A Overton * Facsimile TS, published privately, no details shown, 1983. Card covers, stapled, green, black, Regtl crest, 11.75 x 8.25, xiii/159. 44 mono phots (photo-copies), 23 maps (copied into the text), Bibliography, Index. Apps: H&A, list of former COs, idem Adjutants, idem Subedar Majors, idem all former officers (British and Indian, 1917-1947), nominal roll (all ranks, June 1941), nominal roll of the Mortar Platoon (1941), etc.

* The Regt was formed in October 1917 as a wartime expedient. Its roots were planted firmly in the 39th Garhwal Rifles (vide J Evatt in the 'Index of Authors'). There were several rapid changes of title but, by the end of the war, there were two Bns bearing the distinctive designations 1/50th and 2/50th Kumaon Rifles. The 2/50th was disbanded, but the 1/50th was allocated in 1923 to the Hyderabad Regt. Instead of becoming just another numbered Bn of that Regt, the 1/50th was permitted to retain its wartime title as The Kumaon Rifles, Hyderabad Regt. It performed garrison duties in Hong Kong during the 1930s and was part of Paiforce in Iraq and Iran from 1941 to 1945. After a brief spell in Malaya in 1946, it returned home for internal security duties during the period of Partition. In the meanwhile, in October 1945, the Hyderabad Regt was at last permitted to change its name. It had long ceased to have any connection with the State of Hyderabad. Its ranks were in fact comprised mainly of men recruited from the districts of Kumaon. It was retitled The Kumaon Regt (a title which endured after Partition when it was allocated to newly independent India as an all-Hindu establishment). This history was compiled by the son of a former officer, but never formally published. Fifty cyclostyled copies were made and presented to various archives and to officers who had served. It is a painstaking compilation and it contains all the information which any researcher is likely to require.
R/5 V/5. NAM/IOL/IWM. RP.

VALOUR TRIUMPHS
A History of the Kumaon Regiment
K C Praval * The Thomson Press (India), Faridabad, 1976. Green, gold, 10.0 x 6.5, xv/443. Fp, 49 mono phots, 26 maps (bound in), Bibliography, Index. Apps: H&A, list of former COs, idem Subedar Majors, notes on classes recruited, notes on Territorial and Garrison Bns.
* A readable and detailed history covering the period 1813-1972. The first 160 pages deal with the pre-1947 services of the Hyderabad Regt and its forebears. Praval is a first class historian and there are no apparent faults in his narrative. Apart from the story of the Kumaon Rifles (for which Overton is the best source - vide the preceding entry), Praval's book provides the most convenient single source for the Hyderabad Regt in toto. The rest of his book deals with the adventures of the Kumaon Regt after Partition. The photographic coverage is unusual and interesting. There are several good pictures of early Viceroy's Commissioned Officers, a picture of Lord Roberts's Orderly in South Africa (the war of 1899-1902), and illustrations of scarce badges. R/2 V/5. NAM. MCJ.

20th BURMA RIFLES

STANDING ORDERS OF THE SECOND BATTALION, THE BURMA RIFLES
With a Short Record of the Battalion
Anon * Gale & Polden Ltd, Aldershot, for the Regt, 1948. Green, gold, Regtl crest on front cover and spine, 9.25 x 6.5, ix/141. No ills, no maps, no appendixes, no Index.
* This publication is noted also under the 'Burma' section of this bibliography and the full details are noted there. Although the Burma Rifles originated in 1917 (as an element of the Indian Army), no author has yet compiled its formal history. The tale is complicated by the fact that Burma was separated from the Dominion of India in 1937 and became instead a Crown Colony. Many Indian Army officers continued to serve with the Burma Rifles after that date, but new officer recruitment came from regiments of the British Army (in accord with standard practice for all Colonial units whereby officers were seconded from their parent regiments for periods of two or three years, sometimes longer). There were at that time similar changes in the recruitment of the rank and file. Generally, they were gradually filled with men from the indigenous hill tribes - the Karens, Chins, and Kachins. There was no consistent policy towards the recruitment of Burmans, these being thought unlikely to make good soldiers (although, when the hammer fell, in WWII, some Burmans gave loyal and courageous service).
R/4 V/3. NAM. R/4 V/3. PJE/CJP.
Note: for further information, vide the 'Burma' section and refer to pages 347-370 of IMPERIAL SUNSET - FRONTIER SOLDIERING IN THE 20th CENTURY, by James Lunt (Macdonald, London, 1981).

DISBANDED INFANTRY REGIMENT

HISTORICAL RECORD OF THE 88th CARNATIC INFANTRY
Anon * Printed at The Edward Press, Cannanore, 1913. Soft card, grey, black, 8.0 x 5.0, -/139. No ills, no maps, no appendixes, no Index.
* This is a dry and somewhat terse summary of engagements between 1798 and 1909. The Regt was formerly the 28th Madras Infantry, becoming the 88th Carnatic in 1903. It had fought in many 19th Century campaigns - Travancore (1809), the Mahratta Wars (1815-1818), First Burma War (1825-1826), the Mutiny (1857-1859), and then the 1900 expedition to China - but by the turn of the century the recruitment of Madrassis was being reduced. In 1922, the Regt was disbanded. This book is its only known record. Although it has no formal appendixes, the final seven chapters fulfil the same purpose. They contain good reference material concerning uniforms and weaponry, badges and insignia, changes in unit title and organisation, Stations and movements, and lists of officers who distinguished themselves or who became casualties. R/5 V/4. BM/IOL. PJE/RGB.

INFANTRY REGIMENTS RAISED DURING WWII

THE HISTORY OF THE ASSAM REGIMENT
Volume I : 1941–1947
Capt Peter Steyn * Orient Longmans, Calcutta, 1959. Black, white, 'Regtl crest and Colours motif', 8.5 x 5.5, xvii/270. Fp, 6 mono phots, 14 maps (12 printed in the text, 2 on the end-papers), Index. Apps: Roll of Honour (all ranks), H&A (all ranks), list of COs, idem Subedar Majors.
* The Regt was raised in 1941 as part of the general expansion of the Indian Army. It was not at that stage anticipated that it would soon be expected to fight in one of the toughest campaigns of the war - the defeat of the Japanese in Burma. This pleasing book deals with the formation of the Regt and its major battles - Jessami, Kohima, Mawlaik, and the fighting advance to Rangoon. The narrative is packed with references to other lesser actions and skirmishes, and to individual members of the Regt's two Bns. R/2 V/5. IOL/NAM. AN/RP.
Note: Steyn never produced a Volume II. The Assam Regt must not be confused with the Assam Rifles (a Frontier Police unit).

THE BIHAR WARRIORS
A Historical Record of The Bihar Regiment, 1758–1986
Col R D Palsokar MC * Regtl Centre, Danapur, Bihar, 1986. Dark green, gold, 9.75 x 7.0, xx/410. Fp, more than 100 mono phots, 9 cld ills, 26 maps, Index. Apps: H&A, list of officers, idem SNCOs.
* The Regt was formed in December 1941 by converting to Regular Army status the pre-war 11/19th Hyderabad Regt (a Territorial Army unit). Four Bns were raised, but only the 1st Bn saw action (in Burma). At Partition, the Regt was allocated to India and it is still part of the Indian Army's Order of Battle. The author covers all campaign services, before and after Partition, in a fluent and interesting style. The otherwise confusing dates in the sub-title are explained in the opening chapters. They contain useful descriptions of Bihar Province, of its people and their culture, of various 19th Century units which recruited Biharis and, in particular, of their role during the Mutiny of 1857-1859. R/2 V/5. PC. RWH.

THE REGIMENTAL HISTORY OF THE MAHAR M.G. REGIMENT
Anon * The Army Press, Dehra Dun, 1954. Red, gold, Regtl crest, 9.75 x 7.0, iv/96. Fp, 7 mono phots, no maps, Glossary, Bibliography, no Index. Apps: Roll of Honour (for operations in Jammu and Kashmir), H&A (incl C-in-C's Commendations pre-1947 and MID for Jammu and Kashmir), list of COs, idem Subedar Majors, notes on Regtl history, cap badges, recruitment, Mahar marching song.
* The Regt was raised in 1941 but none of its Bns saw action overseas. In 1946, it was decided to convert it into a Machine-gun Regt, and the 'crossed Vickers' motif was incorporated in its cap badge. The Regt was allocated to the Indian Army at Partition, but it was converted back to its original infantry status in 1964. The author deals with the entire period in good detail. He also includes some interesting accounts of earlier wars and actions in which Mahar soldiers took part, notably the Battle of Koregaon on New Year's Day, 1818. R/4 V/4. PC. RWH.

HISTORY OF THE MAHAR REGIMENT
Maj B N Mittra * Printed by The Statesman Press, New Delhi, for the Regt, 1972. Brown, white, 9.5 x 6.5, vi/216. 97 mono phots, 5 cld plates, 6 sketches, 2 maps (printed on the end-papers), no Index. Apps: Roll of Honour, H&A, list of former COs, notes on the music of the Regt, list of old Regts in which Mahars had served prior to 1941, notes on cap badges and shoulder titles.
* Maj Mittra was serving with the Regt at the time when he compiled this book. His account is particularly good for the wartime years and the 1950s. It provided a basis for the definitive history by Col Longer (vide following entry).
R/2 V/4. PC. JWW.

FOREFRONT FOR EVER
History of the Mahar Regiment
Col V Longer * Printed by Allied Publishers Pte Ltd, New Delhi, for the Regt, 1981. Maroon, gold, 9.5 x 6.5, v/300. 130 mono phots, 19 cld plates, 5 sketches, 9 maps (one printed on the end-papers, 8 bound in), no Index. Apps: Roll of Honour (all ranks, for all post-1947 campaigns), list of former COs, notes on Regtl music, notes on earlier units in which Mahar men served (pre-1941), notes on badges and shoulder titles.
* A readable, accurate, and well documented narrative history which covers not only the services of the Regt from 1941 to 1980, but also its development in the broader context of the history of India and of the Indian Army. The Regt was formed at Belgaum on 1 October 1941 by Brig H J R Jackson. Recruitment was restricted initially to the Mahars, the indigenous low-caste Hindus of the former Bombay Presidency. Mahars had been recruited for their martial qualities by various regiments in the 19th Century, but the practice was discontinued in 1892. They were recruited again in 1917 to form the 111th Mahars, but this Regt was disbanded in 1922. The modern Mahar Regt is an important element of the Indian Army, with a strength of twenty battalions. R/2 V/4. PC. JWW.

APPENDIX III

The Designation of Indian Infantry Regiments
following the Re-organisations of 1921-1923

1st Punjab Regiment

2nd Punjab Regiment

3rd Madras Regiment

4th Bombay Grenadiers

5th Mahratta Light Infantry

6th Rajputana Rifles

7th Rajput Regiment

8th Punjab Regiment

9th Jat Regiment

10th Baluch Regiment

11th Sikh Regiment

12th Frontier Force Regiment

13th Frontier Force Rifles

14th Punjab Regiment

15th Punjab Regiment

16th Punjab Regiment

17th Dogra Regiment

18th Royal Garhwal Rifles

19th Hyderabad Regiment

20th Burma Rifles

Note:

Under the new system, each Regiment had an average of five active (field) Bns which were numbered consecutively 1st, 2nd, 3rd, etc. Some of the honour titles or titles of distinction awarded to their forebear regiments were perpetuated in the battalion titles [for example, 2nd Bn (Prince of Wales's Own), 6th Rajputana Rifles, and 4th Bn (Wilde's), 13th Frontier Force Rifles].

In addition, each Regiment had a 10th Battalion as a training unit for the active (field) battalions, and an 11th Battalion (Territorial Army).

Nine entirely new Regular regiments were raised between 1939 and 1946. Some were disbanded at the end of hostilities, others were retained as permanent elements in the post-Independence armies. Logically, their WWII services are less well recorded than those of regiments with a long tradition behind them (as listed above). However, all publications relating to the war-raised units are noted in the preceding pages of this bibliography.

NOTES

THE GURKHAS

'Gurkha' is the description given to all soldiers recruited in the Kingdom of Nepal. Historically, the term was confined to the warriors of the Army of Gorkha, a small principality in Western Nepal. In 1768, the local Rajah, Prithvi Narain Shah, overthrew the Malla dynasty and occupied its capital, Kathmandu. He and his successors pushed further eastwards through the Himalaya and, after clashing with the Chinese in Bhutan, established the modern State's eastern boundary. The Gurkhas next turned westwards, to Kumaon, Garhwal, the Doon Valley, Sirmoor, Simla and Kangra. Expansion brought conflict with the British. Between 1814 and 1816, the Gurkhas were gradually overcome by superior British fire-power until the opposing sides agreed an honourable peace. The mutual respect of the two races was born in the hard battles of those early encounters.

The tribes of the original Gurkha Army were the Thakurs and Chettris (the ruling and administrative classes) and the Magars and Gurungs (the yeoman farmers, of a lower order within the Hindu caste system, who formed the bulk of the fighting ranks). Strictly speaking, only these tribes qualify as Gurkhas. In practice, the term has long been applied also to the Kiranti tribes of Eastern Nepal - the Limbus, Rais and Sunwars.

The Gurkha Regiments listed on the following pages drew their recruits from all of these tribes over the years. In the first half of the 19th Century, and for some time after the Indian Mutiny, the older Gurkha Regiments recruited from the Magar, Gurung, Thakur and Chettri tribes. They recruited also in Garhwal. Towards the end of the century, a policy began to evolve whereby the 1st, 2nd, 3rd, 4th, 5th, 6th and 8th Gurkha Rifles recruited chiefly from the Magar and Gurung tribes in Western Nepal, while the 9th Gurkha Rifles began to select men from the higher caste Thakurs and Chettris and 7th and 10th Gurkha Rifles recruited from the Rai, Limbu and Sunwar tribes of Eastern Nepal.

The fighting men of Nepal have at one time or another served in a wide variety of other Empire units - the Assam Rifles, Baluch Light Infantry, Burma Frontier Force, Calcutta Armed Police, Corps of Guides, Punjab Frontier Force, and the Singapore Police. They have served also in a number of Princely State armies which, as Imperial Service Troops (Forces), fought for the British in the two world wars.

In WWI, when British and Indian Army formations were despatched for service overseas, nine Battalions of the Royal Nepalese Army took their place as a security force on the North West Frontier. In WWII, the King of Nepal again assisted the British Government by providing eight Battalions of his army for service in India and Burma. Two of these fought in the ferocious battle of Kohima.

Given the continuing popularity of the Gurkha soldier with the British public, it is not surprising that several dozens of 'general interest' books have been published over the past thirty years. This bibliography does not attempt to list them all but to instead concentrate upon the formal unit (regimental) histories with a supporting representative selection from the 'general' category.

The specialist researcher who needs to consult the full range of both 'general interest' and specialised Gurkha books (and indeed all of the recorded sources) should consult BIBLIOGRAPHY OF GURKHA REGIMENTS AND RELATED SUBJECTS, by Field Marshal Sir John Chapple and Colonel Denis Wood (vide following page).

GENERAL REFERENCE

BIBLIOGRAPHY OF GURKHA REGIMENTS AND RELATED SUBJECTS
Second Edition
FM Sir John Chapple GCB CBE and Col Denis Wood * The Trustees of the Gurkha Museum, Peninsula Barracks, Winchester, UK, 1993. Stiff card, cream, black, 'Crossed kukris' motif, 11.75 x 8.0, iv/135 (estimated). No ills, no appendixes, no Index (but highly detailed 'Contents' pages).
* Currently (1992) in course of preparation. Based upon many years of research by the authors and by the Gurkha Museum's advisors, this is a listing of all known books, documents, journals, magazine articles, newsletters and MS/TS papers relating to Gurkha Regiments and Corps. The lists are arranged under these headings - 1, 2, 3, 4, 5, 6, 7, 8, 9, 10 and 11 Gurkha Rifles, Queen's Gurkha Engineers, Queen's Gurkha Signals, Gurkha Army Service Corps/Transport Regt, Gurkha parachute units, Gurkha para-military units (Assam Rifles, etc), The Brigade of Gurkhas, and The Gorkha Brigade, the Gurkha Museum, General Works and Handbooks on Gurkhas, General Military History with Regard to Gurkhas, Nepal, and Nepali/Gurkhali language books. Each section is further divided into subjects - Regtl and unit histories, Standing Orders, Dress Regulations, Parades and Occasions, Biographies and Autobiographies, etc. With more than 2300 entries, this is a massive compilation and it will provide, therefore, an essential framework for the specialist researcher. R/2 V/5. GM. RP.

THE GURKHAS
Their Manners, Customs and Country
Maj W Brook-Northey and Capt S J Morris * John Lane, at the Bodley Head, London, 1928. Green, gold, 'Arms of the Maharajahs of Nepal' motif, 9.0 x 6.0, xxxvii/282. 68 mono phots, one map (bound in), Bibliography, Index. Apps: notes on Gurkha festivals, notes on the Kings and Hereditary Prime Ministers of Nepal.
* The authors were invited into Nepal by the then Maharajah (a great honour at the time) in order to write a comprehensive account of the country, its people and its customs. Although it does not deal specifically with Nepal's military tradition, and although the passage of time has overtaken the political aspect, this is stated to be the best general reference book. R/4 V/5. PC. AAM.

THE GURKHAS
H D James and D Sheil-Small * Macdonald, London, 1965. Light green, gold, 8.5 x 5.5, viii/283. 37 mono phots, 2 maps (printed on the end-papers), Bibliography, no appendixes, Index.
* An interesting record of Gurkha services in the pre-1947 Indian Army, the post-1947 Gurkha commitments in Malaya and Borneo, and the later operations in the Congo and during the Chinese incursion of 1962. R/2 V/3. PC. AMM.

GURKHAS
David Bolt * Weidenfeld & Nicolson, London, 1967. Pale green, gold, 8.75 x 5.5, -/128. 39 mono phots, one map, Bibliography, no appendixes, Index.
* Two chapters (pages 1 to 57) describe the history of Nepal and the evolution of the country's influence. The last chapter deals with political matters.The central section (pages 58 to 103) is a fairly superficial but pleasantly readable account of campaigns in which Gurkha soldiers fought. A useful introduction to the subject, especially if read in conjunction with Philip Mason's A MATTER OF HONOUR (vide the Index of Authors). R/2 V/3. NAM. AAM.

JOHNNY GURKHA
Friends in the Hills
E D Smith * Leo Cooper, in conjunction with Secker & Warburg, London, 1985. Black, gold, 9.5 x 6.0, xvi/176. 25 mono phots, one map (bound in), no Index. Apps: notes on the origins of the Gurkha Regts and Corps, the Gurkha Welfare Trusts, note on the kukri.
* A well-written summary of the Gurkha ethos. Few individuals are named in the narrative, and it contains only passing references to specific campaign services. It is instead a simple background briefing on the character of Nepal's warrior sons. R/1 V/3. NAM. AAM.

Notes:

Additionally, from the many other available sources, the following items are strongly recommended by those having knowledge of the subject.

GORKHA - THE STORY OF THE GURKHAS OF NEPAL, by Lieut Gen Sir Francis Tuker (Constable, London, 1957).

and

NOTES ON GURKHAS, by Capt Eden Vansittart (Government of India Press, Delhi, 1890), and the series of official handbooks which, over the following eight decades, have evolved from that first edition. They cover the geographical, religious and cultural aspects. They were intended for the instruction of young officers and as a wide-ranging authoritative source of reference.

The second edition appeared in 1896. The compiler was again Capt Vansittart, but he adopted a new title, **NOTES ON NEPAL.** Then came **HANDBOOK FOR THE INDIAN ARMY - GURKHAS.** This was an improved version, updated again by Capt Vansittart and published in 1906. It was produced within the framework of a series of official handbooks which dealt with various Indian racial/ethnic groups in excellent detail. This Gurkha handbook was revised by Col B U Nicolay and republished in 1915. It was reprinted without amendment in 1918.

The **HANDBOOK** title was retained for a new edition, updated by Maj C J Morris and published in 1933. Morris made further revisions for a 1936 edition which was reprinted without any further changes in 1942 and 1943. In 1965 a completely updated version, with different plates and a new text by Col R G Leonard, was published under a new title - **NEPAL AND THE GURKHAS.** This version is still in use for instructional purposes.

EARLY MERCENARIES

CHAR-EE-KAR AND SERVICE WITH THE SHAH SHOOJAH'S GOORKHA REGIMENT THERE
J C Haughton * The Baptist Mission Press, Calcutta, 1867. Soft card, cream, black, 8.5 x 5.25, vi/68. No ills, 3 maps (bound in), no appendixes, no Index.
* In 1839, in an ill-judged attempt to bring Afghanistan within their sphere of influence, the British mounted an invasion of that country. They deposed the ruling Amir and replaced him with their puppet, Shah Shoojah. The campaign was conducted by the British Army and HEIC Regiments advancing through the Bolan Pass, and a Sikh Army advancing through the Khyber. Additionally, there was a third force, a motley collection of mercenaries. Nominally the Shah Shoojah's own army, it was funded by the British and was intended to give the invasion a mantle of political respectability. The 4th Regt of this force was composed largely of Gurkha soldiers, commanded by British officers. The subsequent debacle and the almost total destruction of the British expeditionary force is a well-known story. The 4th Regt was destroyed as a fighting force (about 150 men scattered into the hills and were rescued six months later). Some of these survivors were later enlisted into Regular units of the HEIC. The title page of this well presented little book carries the imprint 'not published', suggesting thereby that it was intended only for a professional readership. R/5 V/3. PC. BDM.

GURKHA BRIGADES

A GURKHA BRIGADE IN ITALY
The Story of the 43rd Gurkha Lorried Infantry Brigade
Anon * The Times of India Press, Bombay, n.d. (c.1946). Illustrated paper covers, 'Kukris and Italian scene' motif, green/white, black, 6.0 x 3.5. Fp, 3 mono phots, one map, no appendixes, no Index.
* The Bde was formed in 1944 with a Bn each from 6th, 8th and 10th Gurkha Rifles. Its intended task was to take part in the planned breakout on the Adriatic coast as an element of 1st British Armoured Div. In the event, stubborn German resistance in the mountains and then the flooding of the plains north of Rimini led to a long hard series of battles in which the Gurkhas fought mainly in the conventional infantry role. Much of the action was fought at close quarters and the kukri was used to terrifying effect on several occasions. The Bde finished its war at Trieste. R/4 V/2. NAM. PJE.

The Gurkha Rifle Regiments

1st GURKHA RIFLES

REGIMENTAL HISTORY OF THE 1st BATTALION, 1st (PRINCE OF WALES'S OWN) GURKHA RIFLES (THE MALAUN REGIMENT), 1815–1910
H I Money * The Public Printing Press, Kangra, n.d. (c.1910).
* This booklet, of 39 pages, has been noted but not seen.

THE 1st KING GEORGE'S OWN GURKHA RIFLES, THE MALAUN REGIMENT, 1815–1921
F Loraine Petrie OBE * Printed by Butler & Tanner Ltd, Frome and London, for the Royal United Service Institution, 1925. Green, silver, Regtl crest on front cover and spine, 12.25 x 9.5, xii/260. Fp, one mono phot, 14 cld ills, 33 maps (15 printed in the text, 14 bound in, 4 loose in rear pocket), Index. Apps: list of former COs, idem officers (with service details), notes on Colours, uniforms and equipment.
* A big handsome book, typical of the high quality work of Butler & Tanner. The narrative is clear, informative and packed with useful detail. It covers the Sikh War, the Mutiny, numerous frontier campaigns and service during WWI (1st Bn in France, Mesopotamia and Palestine, 2nd Bn on the NWF, 3rd Bn on IS duties and the Third Afghan War). Approximately half of the narrative pages are devoted to the WWI period. The maps are excellent. The appendix listing former and serving officers has 345 individual entries. R/4 V/5. PCAL. RP.

THE HISTORY OF THE 1st KING GEORGE'S OWN GURKHA RIFLES (THE MALAUN REGIMENT) Volume II : 1920–1947
Brig E V R Bellers * Gale & Polden Ltd, Aldershot, for the Regtl History Committee, 1956. Rifle green, silver, Regtl crest, 8.75 x 5.5, xv/358. Fp, 21 mono phots, 37 maps, Index. Apps: Roll of Honour (WWII), H&A (WWII), list of former COs, idem former officers, summary of the events covered in 'Volume I', notes on actions behind Japanese lines in Malaya, summary of casualties during WWII.
* Although the Loraine Petrie book (vide preceding entry) was not published as Volume I of a series, this book by Bellers is, as it claims, effectively Volume II of a pair (even though the dimensions are totally different). The contents follow the same pattern and, again, the narrative includes plenty of action, with many individuals of all ranks mentioned by name. The main coverage is given to WWII (1st Bn in Egypt, Burma and Indo-China, 2nd Bn captured in Singapore, 3rd Bn in Burma and Indo-China, 4th in Burma and Siam, and 5th Bn in India). R/3 V/5. IOL. AMM.
Note: it is reported that Volume I (Loraine Petrie) was reprinted (without amendment) in 1965 by The Gondals Press, New Delhi. It is also reported that Volume II (Bellers) may also have been reprinted in recent years, possibly in India, but no such publication has been seen.

2nd GURKHA RIFLES

HISTORICAL RECORD OF THE SERVICES OF THE 2nd GOORKHA (THE SIRMOOR RIFLES) REGIMENT
Anon * The Government Central Press, Calcutta, 1870. Paper covers, pink, black, 9.5 x 7.5, –/15/iii. No ills, no maps, no appendixes, no Index.
*A modest little publication divided into two parts. The first 15 pages cover the period 1814-1869 in diary form and deal with matters such as changes of title, stations and movements, etc. The last 3 pages cover the years 1870-1876 and include some brief mention of acts of bravery in the Looshai campaign.
R/5 V/1. MODL. AMM.
Note: the Mutiny period is covered in EXTRACTS FROM LETTERS AND NOTES WRITTEN DURING THE SIEGE OF DELHI, by Maj Charles Reid (Henry S King, c.1890, 93 pages). An edited version of his account appeared in 2nd KING EDWARD VII's OWN GOORKHA RIFLES (THE SIRMOOR RIFLES), 1857-1957 - CENTENARY OF THE SIEGE OF DELHI, BASED UPON THE DIARIES OF MAJOR CHARLES REID (W G Kingham Printers Ltd, King's Langley, 1957, iii/61 pages).

HISTORY OF 2nd KING EDWARD'S OWN GOORKHA RIFLES, THE SIRMOOR RIFLES
Col L W Shakespear * Gale & Polden Ltd, Aldershot, 1912. Green boards, red leather spine and quarters, Regtl crest, 10.0 x 7.5, xiv/183. Fp, 22 mono phots, 4 maps (bound in), Bibliography, no Index. Apps: description of the Mahsud Waziri blockade, notes on the Coronation Contingent (1902), notes on officers' services outside India, description of the Officers' Mess, correspondence concerning the Nepal War, description of the Regtl Truncheon, etc.
* A good all-round narrative history for the period 1815-1899, with appendixes covering the period 1900-1910. Although not published as such, this work became effectively Volume I of a four-volume series (vide following entries).
R/4 V/4. RMAS. RP/RGH.
Note: it has been stated that this book was first published in 1910, and that the 1912 version recorded above was an identical reprint to satisfy popular demand. No examples of a 1910 imprint have been sighted, so this report cannot be confirmed. What is certain is that the book was reprinted in 1950. It had fewer pages (xv/150), with Fp, 18 mono phots, 4 maps (bound in), and still no Index. The casing of this version is rifle green cloth with gold Regtl crest on a broad red band.

HISTORY OF THE 2nd KING EDWARD'S OWN GOORKHAS, THE SIRMOOR RIFLE REGIMENT
Volume II : 1911-1921
Col L W Shakespear CB CIE * Gale & Polden Ltd, Aldershot, for the Regtl Committee, 1924. Rifle green, gold, Regtl crest on broad red band, 10.0 x 7.5, xix/246. Fp, 29 mono phots, 17 maps (bound in), Bibiography, no Index. Apps; 12 in total, incl H&A (WWI), list of officers (1911-1920, with service details), notes on the services of officers while ERE.
* Like the first volume, this book also is written in very great detail and regarding all three Bns (1st Bn in Mesopotamia, 2nd Bn on the Western Front, 3rd Bn in India). Individuals appear frequently throughout the narrative, with details of their gallantry awards which might otherwise have appeared in the appendixes. The maps are very good. A first-class history apart from the lamentable lack of an Index. R/4 V/4. MODL. AMM.

HISTORY OF THE 2nd KING EDWARD'S OWN GOORKHA RIFLES (THE SIRMOOR RIFLES)
Volume III : 1921-1948
Lieut Col G R Stevens OBE * Gale & Polden Ltd, Aldershot, 1952. Rifle green, gold, Regtl crest on broad red band, 10.0 x 7.25, xv/322. Fp, 88 mono phots, one cld ill, 2 line drawings, 18 maps, no Index. Apps: Roll of Honour (British and Gurkha officers only), H&A (statistical summary only), list of former COs (1921-1947).
* The author sustains the standards set in the two preceding volumes. The story of all five WWII Bns is told in detail (1st Bn with Paiforce and in North Africa, Italy and Greece, 2nd Bn captured at Singapore, 3rd Bn in Burma, Malaya and Siam, 4th Bn in Burma, Indo-China and Borneo, 5th Bn in India). There are numerous references to individuals and to minor actions. The maps and general layout are good but, once again, the lack of an Index is a serious omission in a book of such length and complexity. R/4 V/4. IOL/MODL. AMM.

Note: referring to the preceding three entries (Shakespear and Stevens), it was later established that each of these books contained a number of errors and omissions. In 1963, Maj Denis Wood produced a complete series of 'Addenda and Corrigenda' for all three volumes. These were printed in such a way that they could be easily tipped into the original books. They were distributed as a complete package, with 19 loose pre-gummed folios contained in an envelope (9.5 x 7.25) bearing, amongst other wording, the imprint 'With the Compliments of The 2nd King Edward's Own Goorkhas, Amendment No 1, 1963'. Approximately 250 of these envelopes were sent to holders of the books and to applicants. Second-hand copies of Shakespear's two books and of Stevens' book should be checked to see whether or not a previous owner ever tipped-in these important additional pages. They are no longer available from the Regiment.

THE STORY OF THE 4th BATTALION, 2nd KING EDWARD VII's OWN GURKHA RIFLES
Lieut Col J A Kitson * Gale & Polden Ltd, Aldershot, 1949. Rifle green, gold, Regtl crest, 8.75 x 5.5, xi/51. Fp, 6 mono phots, 3 maps, no Index. Apps: Roll of Honour (1941-1947), H&A (idem), copy of the recommendation for the award of the VC to Maj P R Collins (not conferred).
* A very readable narrative account of the Bn's services in Burma and the Far East in WWII. Numerous small actions are described in interesting detail, with frequent mention of named officers and ORs. The illustrations include three fully captioned groups of officers. R/4 V/4. IOL/MODL. AMM.

2nd KING EDWARD VII's OWN GOORKHA RIFLES (THE SIRMOOR RIFLES), 1857-1957
Centenary of the Siege of Delhi, Based upon the Diaries of Major Charles Reid
Anon * W G Kingham (Printers) Ltd, King's Langley, UK, 1957. Rifle green, gold, Regtl crest on red band, 8.75 x 5.5, iii/61. One mono phot, 2 cld ills, 2 sketches, 2 maps (bound in), Glossary, no appendixes, no Index.
* This slim volume was published to mark the 100th anniversary of the siege of Delhi at which The Sirmoor Rifles particularly distinguished themselves. The Regt was responsible for the defence of the Main Picquet at Hindoo Rao's house, on the Ridge. The narrative is based upon Maj Reid's earlier work EXTRACTS FROM LETTERS AND NOTES WRITTEN DURING THE SIEGE OF DELHI, published by Henry S King, c.1890 (93 pages, with an illustration of the house). R/2 V/3. MODL. AMM.

THE STORY OF THE SIRMOOR RIFLES
Lieut Col E D Smith DSO MBE * Jay-Birch & Co (Ltd), Singapore, 1969. Rifle green, gold, Regtl crest on red band, 9.5 x 7.0, -/58. Fp, 14 mono phots, 7 cld ills, no maps, no appendixes, no Index.
* A very condensed history which covers the period 1815 to 1967. The story is told in simple direct terms, and the booklet was probably intended for teaching purposes within the Regt. R/3 V/2. MODL. AMM.

A PRIDE OF GURKHAS
The 2nd King Edward's Own Goorkhas (The Sirmoor Rifles), 1948-1971
Harold D James and Denis Sheil-Small * Printed by Pitman Press, Bath, for Leo Cooper, London, 1975. Green, silver, Regtl crest, 8.75 x 5.5, xiv/274. 30 mono phots, 4 maps (2 printed in the text, 2 on the end-papers), Index. Apps: H&A, list of former COs.
* This is effectively Volume IV of the 2GR series. It is not as well provided with reference appendixes as the earlier books, but it does have an Index and is both readable and authoritative. R/1 V/3. PCAL. VS.
Note: at the present time (1992) it is planned that a full formal Volume IV will be published in 1995. The new book will incorporate some of the material found in A PRIDE OF GURKHAS for the period 1948-1971, but will then extend the history of 2GR through to the time when the Regt will be merged into a new one which will have the designation The Royal Gurkha Rifles. This book will be published by the Regtl Affairs Committee and the author will be Col Denis Wood.

2nd KING EDWARD VII's OWN GOORKHAS (THE SIRMOOR RIFLES)
2nd Battalion, 1886-1986
Anon (Maj J W Kaye and others) * Signland Ltd, Farnham, UK, 1986. Soft card, 'Perfect' bound, green, silver, 5 badges on the front cover, 8.0 x 6.0, vi/141. 121 mono phots, 2 cld ills, one map (Malaya), no Index. Apps: Roll of Honour, H&A (all ranks, 1948-1986), list of former COs (for both 1st and 2nd Bns), nominal rolls, copies of the two VC citations plus three gallantry citations for Borneo.

* An extremely detailed history, packed into a rather disappointing binding. The authors drew heavily upon archival and Regtl sources to compile the very helpful appendixes. The Roll of Honour, for example, lists all ranks KIA and WIA, for both 1st Bn and 2nd Bn, under the sub-headings 1824-1939, 1939-1947, Malaya, Brunei, Sabah, and Sarawak. The nominal roll appendix lists every officer and OR on the strength of 2nd Bn in February 1986, with his Service number, rank and name, and his Company, Platoon and Section, and a note of whether he was at that time on leave in Nepal. R/1 V/4. PC. TM.

3rd GURKHA RIFLES

A SHORT HISTORY OF THE 3rd (QUEEN'S OWN) GURKHA RIFLES
'H.D.H' (Maj Gen H D Hutchinson CSI) * Hugh Rees Ltd, London, 1907. Green, gold, 'Gurkha rifleman' motif, 9.5 x 7.0, -/51. Fp, 19 mono phots, no maps, no appendixes, no Index.
* A strange but attractive little book. There are some brief notes on the Regt's history, but most of the pages are devoted to photographic illustrations of various officers and men in uniform. A useful source, therefore, for researchers interested in Dress and insignia. R/5 V/3. IOL. RGH.
Note: the author was Director of Military Education (India). He wrote several books, including THE CAMPAIGN IN TIRAH, 1897-1898 (Macmillan, London, 1898).

STANDING ORDERS, 1st BATTALION, 3rd QUEEN ALEXANDRA'S OWN GURKHA RIFLES
Section XII, Historical
Compiled from the Regimental Records
Lieut Col W M Savage * C.O. Press, Calcutta, 1911. Green, gold, 7.5 x 5.0, viii/322/14. No ills, no maps, Index (the last 14 pages). Apps: list of Commandants, idem Subedar Majors, idem all British officers who served between 1815 and 1911.
* The bulk of the text covers all the usual topics found in any file of Standing Orders - the duties of officers, duties of NCOs, pay, Dress, leave, etc. However, pages 229 to 274 cover the Regt's history between 1815 and 1911 in a most useful style, hence the inclusion of the book in this bibliography.
R/5 V/3. PC. BDM.

THE REGIMENTAL HISTORY OF THE 3rd QUEEN ALEXANDRA'S OWN GURKHA RIFLES
From April 1815 to December 1927
Maj Gen Nigel G Woodyatt CB CIE * Philip Allan & Co, London, 1929. Dark green, gold, Regtl crest, 9.0 x 5.75, ix/441. Fp, 5 mono phots, 8 maps (bound in), Index. Apps: Roll of Honour (only for officers, 2nd Bn, Egypt), H&A (for 2nd, 3rd, and 4th Bns), list of former COs (1st and 2nd Bns), idem Subedar Majors, list of former officers, notes on weapons, idem Dress and establishments.
* A useful source, strongest in its coverage of the 19th Century campaigns. Services in WWI are surprisingly less well described. The appendixes are very good, and include details of each officer's career. R/5 V/4. IOL. MCJ.
Note: reprinted without amendment in 1951 by J Ray & Sons Ltd, Simla.

REGIMENTAL HISTORY OF THE 3rd QUEEN ALEXANDRA'S OWN GURKHA RIFLES
Volume II: 1927 to 1947
Brig C N Barclay CBE DSO * William Clowes & Sons Ltd, London, for the Regtl History Committee, 1953. Rifle green, gold, Regtl crest, xx/316. Fp, 43 mono phots, one sketch, 24 maps, Index. Apps: H&A (WWII only), list of former COs, idem officers, summary of the events described in Woodyatt's history (vide preceding entry), statistical summary of casualties, Roll of Honour (British and Gurkha officers, KIA and WIA).
* This is the best of the 3GR histories in terms of overall quality. The story-line is the activities of all four Bns in action on the NWF and in overseas campaigns during WWII. It also makes useful reference to 38th Gurkha Rifles. The appendixes are extensive, a primary source. R/3 V/5. MODL. AMM.

FLASH OF THE KUKRI
History of the 3rd Gurkha Rifles, 1947-1980
C L Proudfoot * Vision Books, New Delhi, 1984. Green, gold, 9.0 x 5.5, iv/222. 82 mono phots, 2 cld ills, 17 maps, Index. Apps: H&A, list of former COs, idem officers and Subedar Majors serving in 1947, notes on Dress, shoulder flashes, Battle Honours.
* Although the narrative relates primarily to the post-1947 period, three early chapters recapitulate the Regt's history from 1815 to 1947. Interesting and very readable. R/1 V/4. NAM. MCJ.

4th GURKHA RIFLES

A HISTORY OF THE 4th PRINCE OF WALES'S OWN GURKHA RIFLES, 1857-1937
Volumes I and II
Ranald MacDonnell and Marcus Macaulay * William Blackwood & Sons, Edinburgh, 1940. A matching pair, green, black, 10.0 x 7.5.
Volume I : xvi/433. Fp, 2 mono phots, 12 maps, no appendixes, no Index.
Volume II : viii/247. 10 mono phots, 17 maps, Index (for both volumes). Apps: Roll of Honour (WWI), H&A, list of former COs, idem former officers, numerous notes on Regtl badges, weapons, Dress, the Band and its music, recruiting, trophies.
* A lavish and satisfying pair of books which cover the stated period in very uniform and interesting detail. Although Volume I does not have any appendixes, there are lists of officers and their awards scattered throughout the narrative. R/4 V/5. MODL. AMM.

A HISTORY OF THE 4th PRINCE OF WALES'S OWN GURKHA RIFLES, 1938-1948
Volume III
Col J N Mackay DSO and Lieut Col C G Borrowman * William Blackwood & Sons Ltd, London, 1952. Green, black, Regtl crest, 10.0 x 7.5, xvii/620. Fp, 18 mono phots, numerous vignettes (by Borrowman), 44 maps (some folding, bound in), Index. Apps: Roll of Honour (WWII), H&A (WWII), list of COs, idem former officers, anecdotes of battles fought, note on Dress, trophies, and the Regtl memorial.
* This large and finely produced book maintains the same high standards as found in Volumes I and II. In addition to the information given in the appendixes, there are abundant references throughout the narrative to individual officers and their awards. All the WWII campaigns in which the four Bns took part are explained in splendid detail (1st Bn in Burma, 2nd Bn in Paiforce, Egypt and Italy, 3rd Bn in Burma and South East Asia, 4th Bn in Burma). There is also good coverage of 14th Gurkha Rifles (1943-1946). R/4 V/5. MODL. AMM.
Note: printed in a limited edition of 350 copies.

Reprints: it should be noted that each of the three 4GR volumes described above were subsequently reprinted without amendment to their narratives and with only minor changes to their format. The dates on which these reprints appeared were:

Volume I : 1959, 150 subscribed copies
Volume II : 1960, 150 subscribed copies
Volume III : 1963, 250 subscribed copies

They were produced to a good standard at The Army Press, Dehra Dun, on behalf of the Regt. EJG.

Note: for a personal view, reference should be made also to the autobiographical BUGLES AND A TIGER, by John Masters (Michael Joseph, London, 1956, and Viking Press, New York, 1956). This is an evocative account of soldiering with 4GR in the late 1930s. His later experiences, in the Burma campaign, are covered in THE ROAD PAST MANDALAY.

HISTORY OF THE 4th GORKHA RIFLES
Volume IV : 1947–1971

Brig H S Sodhi, Brig P K Gupta AVSM and Brig N K Gurung * Dhawan Printing Works, New Delhi, for Vanity Books, Delhi, 1985. Dark green, black, Regtl crest, viii/303. 9 mono phots, numerous line drawings in the margins (facsimiles of those used in Vol III, by Borrowman), 6 maps, Glossary, Index. Apps: Roll of Honour, H&A, list of the Colonels of the Regt, idem COs, idem officers, idem Subedar Majors, notes on the customs of the Regt.

* Although the book deals only with events following Partition, the Regt views itself as having the same spirit and traditions as the old 4th Gurkha Rifles of the Empire period, hence the sub-title. The authors regard their account as the fourth volume in the series initiated by Macdonnell and Macaulay in 1940 (vide preceding entries). It is indeed a worthy successor, being well written and packed with useful detail. The narrative covers the amalgamation of the Regtl Centre with the 1st Gorkha Rifles, the re-raising of the 4th Bn, the raising of the 5th Bn, and the numerous actions in which Bns of the Regt were engaged between 1947 and 1971. Many individuals (Indian officers, Gurkha officers and Gurkha ORs) are prominently mentioned in the text and whose names will be familiar to British officers who served with 4GR prior to Partition. R/3 V/5. PC. MKB.

CENTENARY OF THE FOURTH GURKHA RIFLES, 1857–1957

Anon * Billing & Sons Ltd, Guildford (UK), for the Regt, 1957. Stiff card, stapled, Regtl crest, rifle green, silver, 8.5 x 5.5, -/75. Fp, 20 mono phots, one line drawing, no maps, no appendixes, no Index.

* A potted history of the Regt from its origins as 'The Extra Goorkha Regiment', raised on 6 August 1957. A well-produced little book, published solely as a celebration of the Centenary. It incorporates a roll of former officers of the Regt who attended the festivities at Bakloh in 1957 and this might be useful to genealogists. R/4 V/1. RMAS. RP.

5th GURKHA RIFLES

THE HISTORICAL RECORD OF THE 5th GOORKHA BATTALION, OR THE HAZARA GOORKHA BATTALION, PUNJAB FRONTIER FORCE

Anon ('By Authority') * The Punjab Government Press, Lahore, 1886. Black, gold, Regtl crest, 10.5 x 7.0, iv/74. No ills, no maps, no appendixes, no Index.

* This is another of the familiar Punjab Frontier Force historical records published circa 1885–1887. The text is based upon official and Regtl records. It lacks any human interest, but it is a reliable source for checking dates and unit movements. R/5 V/4. USII. OSS.

HISTORY OF THE 5th GURKHA RIFLES (FRONTIER FORCE)
Volume I : 1858–1928

Anon * Gale & Polden Ltd, Aldershot, n.d. (c.1929). Rifle green/black, gold, Regtl crest, 10.0 x 7.25, xx/518. Fp, 65 mono phots, 22 maps (17 bound in, 5 loose in rear pocket), Index. Apps: Roll of Honour (British officers only), H&A, list of former officers.

* A superb unit history, produced to the best of the old Gale & Polden standards. The project was initiated by Col H E Weekes, but the final compilation and editing was carried through by several different officers of the Regt. They made an excellent job of it. They cover the early days at Abbottabad, the Second Afghan War (when Capt John Cook won the Regt's first VC at Peiwar Kotal), the Black Mountain expedition, the Hunza affair (when two more VCs were gained), and the services of the three Bns in WWI (1st Bn on Gallipoli, 2nd Bn in Mesopotamia, and 3rd Bn in India and Mesopotamia). R/4 V/5. IOL. CSM/VS.

HISTORY OF THE 5th ROYAL GURKHA RIFLES (FRONTIER FORCE)
Volume II : 1929-1947
Anon * Gale & Polden Ltd, Aldershot, for the Regtl Committee, 1956. Rifle green/black, gold, Regtl crest, 10.0 x 7.5, xvii/522. Fp, 38 mono phots, 22 maps (12 bound in, 10 printed in the text), Index. Apps: Roll of Honour (British and Gurkha officers), H&A, list of former officers.
* Like Volume I, this is another classic unit history, written and produced to the highest standards. The first-class narrative covers the stated period in uniform detail, with accounts of 1st Bn in Iraq, Syria and Italy, the 2nd Bn in Burma, the 3rd Bn in Burma and Java, and the 4th Bn in Burma and Siam. There is painstaking attention to the finer points, e.g. the Roll of Honour appendix gives full details of dates and locations of death of all officers who died between 1939 and 1945, with similar details for those wounded. The H&A appendix includes awards for Waziristan (1937-1939) and for WWII, with full citations for the VC winners. The appendix which lists all former officers has extensive biographical notes for each. R/4 V/5. PCAL. RP.

DESPERATE ENCOUNTERS
Stories of the 5th Royal Gurkha Rifles of the Punjab Frontier Force
Lieut Col R M Maxwell * Douglas Law, at The Pentland Press, Edinburgh, 1986. Green, gold, 8.5 x 6.0, xv/264. 9 mono phots, 27 maps (25 printed in the text, 2 on the end-papers), no Index. Apps: establishments, chronology.
* A useful history which covers the entire period from 1858 to 1947. It focuses upon active service on the NWF, in WWI (Gallipoli and Mesopotamia), and in WWII (Burma, the Middle East, and Italy). The author was presumably aiming to produce a simple narrative account rather than a full-blown source of reference. As such, it will serve for anyone who is unable to gain access to the formal accounts described in the two preceding entries. R/1 V/3. NAM. FWST.

HISTORY OF THE 5th GORKHA RIFLES (FRONTIER FORCE)
Col R D Palsokar * Printed in Bombay, for the Regt, 1991. Emerald green, gold, 10.0 x 7.0, xii/317. Fp, 117 mono phots, 3 cld ills, 3 line drawings, 48 maps, Index. Apps: H&A (with some details of pre-1947 VC, DSO and IOM awards, and full details of post-1947 awards, plus statistical summaries), list of Commandants (1858-1947, all Bns), list of Colonels (1947-1991), idem COs (post-1947), idem Subedar Majors, idem all officers.
* The first third of this book is devoted to events pre-1947. Although fairly superficial, these opening chapters present all the salient facts in accurate and digestible style. The bulk of the narrative then deals with the Regt's post-1947 services - the Indo-Pakistan wars, IS actions in Hyderabad and Sri Lanka, and the campaign in the Naga Hills. Here the detail is excellent, with much to interest the specialist and the general reader. R/2 V/5. PC. PJE.

6th GURKHA RIFLES

HISTORICAL RECORD OF THE 6th GURKHA RIFLES
Volume I : 1817-1919
Maj D G K Ryan DSO (for the 1st Bn), Maj G C Strachan OBE (for the 2nd Bn), and Capt J K Jones (for the 3rd Bn) * Gale & Polden Ltd, Aldershot, 1925. Olive green, silver, Regtl crest, 8.5 x 5.25, xix/320. Fp, 14 mono phots, 20 maps (bound in), no Index. Apps: 17 in total, incl H&A, lists of former officers, etc.
* The three Bns are dealt with separately - 1st Bn in full, for its entire span through to 1919, 2nd Bn from its formation in 1904 onwards, and 3rd Bn quite briefly because it was formed only in 1917. The narrative is based partly upon official records and partly upon the reminiscences of officers who served. The result is a book easy to read and full of useful information. R/4 V/4. NAM. VS.

HISTORICAL RECORD OF THE 6th GURKHA RIFLES
Lieut Col H R K Gibbs * Gale & Polden Ltd, Aldershot, 1955. Rifle green, silver, Regtl crest, 8.5 x 5.5, xix/320. Fp, 10 mono phots, 3 sketches, 5 maps (bound in), Index. Apps: Roll of Honour, H&A (1920-1945), list of former COs, idem former officers, notes on Dress and equipment from 1817 to 1939.
* Although not imprinted as such, this is effectively Volume II (in succession to the preceding entry). The period covered is 1919 to 1948. It is written in pleasant narrative style, with plenty of details and names woven into the main story. The events covered are NWF service during the inter-war years and then the activities of all four Bns in WWII (1st and 4th Bns in Burma, 2nd Bn in Paiforce, Egypt and Italy, 3rd Bn in Burma and Siam). The author also provides brief accounts of 26th and 56th Gurkha Rifles. R/3 V/5. MODL. AMM.

THE STEADFAST GURKHA
Volume III : 1948-1982
Charles Messenger * Leo Cooper Ltd, in conjunction with Secker & Warburg, London, 1985. Green, gold, 9.5 x 6.5, xii/147. 19 mono phots, 3 maps (printed on the end-papers), Glossary, Index. Apps: Rolls of Honour, H&A, list of former COs, idem Gurkha Majors, idem all former officers (incl those attached temporarily).
* A narrative account based mainly upon reminiscences by various officers who served in Malaya and Hong Kong. Easy reading, with plenty of detail.
R/1 V/4. MODL. MCJ/AMM.

THE HAPPY WARRIORS
The Gurkha Soldier in Malaya, 1948-1958
Brig A E C Bredin DSO MC * The Blackmore Press, Gillingham, Dorset, 1961. Green, gold, 8.5 x 6.0, -/356. 10 plates of mono phots, 2 maps, no appendixes, no Index.
* A highly detailed account of the Gurkha Brigade in the long campaign to eradicate the Communist gangs from the Malayan jungles, but with the main emphasis on the work of 6th Gurkha Rifles. R/2 V/3. PC. RJW.

7th GURKHA RIFLES

EXTRACTS FROM THE HISTORY OF THE SEVENTH GURKHA RIFLES
Anon * Gale & Polden Ltd, Aldershot, 1954. Stiff card, dark green with light green banding, silver, Regtl crest, 7.5 x 4.75, -/39. Fp, 8 mono phots, 2 maps (bound in at the rear), no Index. Apps: H&A (statistical summary only, for Malaya, 1948-1952).
* A very brief summary for the period 1902-1952, and presumably intended to mark the Regt's first fifty years and to have something in print pending the production of a first full-blown unit history. The general standard of presentation is superior to that usually found in booklets of this genre. R/4 V/2. RMAS. RP/BDM.
Note: another very brief record (28 pages) covering the early years is HISTORY OF THE 1st BATTALION, 7th GURKHA RIFLES, FROM 1902 TO 1914 (anon, Curzon Press, Quetta, n.d.).

HISTORY OF THE 7th DUKE OF EDINBURGH'S OWN GURKHA RIFLES
Col J N Mackay DSO * William Blackwood & Sons Ltd, Edinburgh and London, for the Regtl Committee, 1962. Green, silver, Regtl crest, 8.75 x 5.75, xxiii/383. Fp, 48 mono phots, 18 maps (folding, bound in), Index. Apps: Rolls of Honour (British and Gurkha officers, 1914-1920, 1939-1945 and 1946-1958, with a statistical summary for all ranks for the same periods), H&A (WWII only, all ranks, incl MID and foreign awards), list of former COs, idem Gurkha Majors, idem all former officers, notes on escapes and evasions, notes on the Regtl badge, Regtl commemoration dates, memorials, the band and the Regtl music.

* A complete account of the Regt's services from date of formation in 1902 through to 1959. The narrative is itself a good historical record, but the author's provision of extensive appendixes, and an Index, make this book a primary source. Three Bns served in WWI - the 1st and 2nd in Mesopotamia (the 2nd being forced to surrender at Kut-al-Amara) and the 3rd in India. Four served in WWII - the 1st in Burma, the 2nd in North Africa (captured at Tobruk but re-raised for Italy and Greece), the 3rd in Burma but then redesignated as 154 (Gurkha) Parachute Bn, and the 4th in India. R/2 V/5. PCAL. HLL/HIS.
Note: revised by Lieut Col I M Elliot OBE (from the notes made by the late Lieut Col A V A Mercer), printed by Blackwood Pillans & Wilson Ltd, Edinburgh, for the Regtl Trustees, 1987.

EAST OF KATMANDU
The Story of the 7th Duke of Edinburgh's Own Gurkha Rifles
Volume II : 1948-1973
Brig E D Smith DSO OBE * Leo Cooper Ltd, London, 1976. Green, silver, Regtl crest, 8.75 x 5.75, xviii/212. 14 mono phots, 2 line drawings, 3 maps, no Index. Apps: Roll of Honour, H&A, list of former COs, idem Honorary Colonels, idem Gurkha Majors, idem former officers, plus various notes.
* A good detailed history, devoted mainly to the Regt's services in Malaya, Borneo and Hong Kong. Plenty of individuals are mentioned but, sadly, the book has no Index. The sub-title presumably indicates that Mackay's book (vide preceding entry) was regarded as Volume I of a series. R/2 V/4. IOL. MCJ.

8th GURKHA RIFLES

HISTORY OF THE 8th GURKHA RIFLES
1st Battalion
Maj Alban Wilson (with translations by School Master Ganpati Jaisi) * Printed by Seeta Ram, at The Army Press, Cawnpore, 1906. Stiff card (blue), cloth spine (maroon), black, 8.0 x 5.0, v/39/39. No ills, no maps, no appendixes, no Index.
* The text is printed in both English and Gurkhali. Intended for instructional purposes within the Regt, it provides very superficial coverage of the period 1824 to 1906 and is stated to contain a number of errors. R/5 V/1. PC. BDM.
Note: the same author, Alban Wilson, wrote a personal memoir (of 320 pages) entitled SPORT AND SERVICE IN ASSAM AND ELSEWHERE (London, 1924).

HISTORY OF THE 8th GURKHA RIFLES
1st Battalion, Volume II
Lieut Col A L M Molesworth (with translations by Jemadar Bhawanidatt Joshi) * Printed by L Seeta Ram, at The Army Press, Cawnpore, 1926. Stiff card (blue), cloth spine (maroon), black lettering on white label, 8.25 x 5.25, i/32. No ills, no maps, no appendixes, no Index.
* As indicated in the sub-title, this is a continuation of the condensed history by Wilson (vide preceding entry). It covers the period 1907 to 1926 and, as with the earlier work, is printed in both English and Gurkhali. Again, because it was intended for use in the Regtl School, few copies have survived. R/5 V/1. PC. BDM.

A SHORT HISTORY OF THE 2nd BATTALION, 8th GURKHA RIFLES
Maj H J Huxford OBE and Capt H S Gordon * The Curzon Press, Quetta, 1928. Black, yellow, Regtl crest, 8.5 x 5.75, iii/112 (numbered 46 to 56 and 107 to 112). No ills, no maps, no Index. Apps: H&A, list of former officers (British and Gurkha), list of Subedar Majors, notes on Battle Honours.
* Compiled in diary form, this fairly sketchy account covers the period 1835 to 1927 and traces the evolution of the Bn over that time. Its forebears were the

Assam Sebundy Corps (1835-1844), 2nd Assam Native Infantry (1844-1891), 43rd Gurkha Rifle Regt of Bengal Native Infantry (1891-1903), 7th Gurkha Rifles (1903-1907), thereafter 2/8th Gurkha Rifles. In addition to the formal appendixes, there are references to officer casualties throughout the narrative. In WWI, the Bn served on the Western Front and in the Middle East. R/4 V/4. MODL. AMM.

A SHORT HISTORY OF 2nd BATTALION, 8th GURKHA RIFLES
Anon (Lieut Col H S Gordon) * The Commercial Steam Press, Dera Ismail Khan, 1939. Green/red, black, Regtl crest, 9.0 x 6.5, iv/71. No ills, no maps, no Index. Apps: H&A (all ranks), list of Colonels, idem COs, idem Subedar Majors.
* This condensed work was published to correct and enlarge the 1928 booklet (vide preceding entry) and as a stop-gap pending the production of a complete and comprehensive history of the Bn. In the event, the outbreak of war and the later Partition of India delayed any further progress until Col Huxford's major history appeared in 1952 (vide following entry). R/5 V/3. PC. BDM.

HISTORY OF THE 8th GURKHA RIFLES
Lieut Col H J Huxford OBE * Gale & Polden Ltd, Aldershot, 1952. Green, silver, Regtl crest, 8.75 x 5.5, xix/335. Fp, 15 mono phots, 17 maps (5 printed in the text, 12 bound in), Index. Apps: H&A (full citations for four VC winners, plus statistical summaries for other awards), list of former COs.
* A solid workmanlike narrative, with plenty of detail. The main coverage deals with 1st, 2nd and 3rd Bns in WWI (France, Mesopotamia and Palestine), and 1st, 2nd, 3rd and 4th Bns in WWII (Burma, Iraq, North Africa, Italy, Java and Borneo). The book was produced at the time when Gale & Polden were struggling to maintain their pre-war standards while faced with post-war shortages of good printing materials. The casing is satisfactory, but the paper is of mediocre grade. More reference appendixes would be have been helpful. R/3 V/4. IOL. VS/RP.

A BRIEF OUTLINE HISTORY OF THE 8th GURKHA RIFLES
Col F H Willasey-Wilsey MC * The Civil & Military Gazette Press, Quetta, 1945. Seen only in photo-copy form, details of original bindings not known, 6.75 x 4.5, iv/54. 17 mono phots, 13 line drawings, one map, no appendixes, no Index.
* As promised in the title, this is indeed an extremely brief summary of the period 1824 to 1939. Despite having been published in 1945, there is no mention of WWII. Given the fact that the booklet was intended for the instruction of young officers and officer cadets just joining the Regt at the end of the war, this omission seems very odd. Presumably the censors in AHQ Delhi were worried about 'security'. R/4 V/1. IWM. AMM/RP.

GREEN SHADOWS
Denis Sheil-Small MC * William Kimber, London, 1982. Green, gold, 9.5 x 5.75, -/198. 30 mono phots, 5 maps, no appendixes, Index.
* A very personal account, by an officer who was at the time a Coy Commander, of the services of 4/8th Gurkha Rifles in Burma (1943-1945) and in Java (1945-1946). Few of his brother officers are named in the text, but many of them appear in the photographs. Readable and interesting. R/1 V/3. MODL. AMM.

A CHILD AT ARMS
Echoes of War
Patrick Davis * Buchan & Enright, London, 1985. Illustrated stiff card, 'Gurkha soldier with Japanese bunker' motif, black, 8.5 x 5.25, iv/264. No ills, no appendixes, no Index.
* An eminently readable autobiography covering the author's time in the Army from February 1943 - Cadetship at Mhow, training at the 3GR Regtl Centre and with 38GR, then his service with 4/8GR in Burma, 1944-1945. His writing reflects an excellent 'feel' for the life of a Regtl officer (as IO, Coy officer and OC Rifle Coy). R/1 V/4. GM. DRW.

Note: A CHILD AT ARMS was first published in 1970 by Hutchinson & Co Ltd, London. It was followed a year later by an Arrow soft-back edition (258 pages). The version recorded here, the third edition, was published with an additional final chapter entitled 'Afterword 1985'.

A SHORT HISTORY OF THE 38th GURKHA RIFLES
Lieut Col C W Yeates DSO * The A.V. Press, Dehra Dun, n.d. (c.1946).
* 38th Gurkha Rifles was the training and draft-finding unit for 3GR and 8GR during WWII. The publication has been noted, but not seen. No other details are available, but it is presumably a pamphlet or booklet, produced in very limited numbers.

9th GURKHA RIFLES

THE 2nd BATTALION, 9th GURKHA RIFLES, 1904-1923
Anon * Trail & Co Ltd, Calcutta, 1924. Dark green, gold, Regtl crest, 7.5 x 5.0, iv/131. No ills, no maps, no Index. Apps: extracts from Indian Army Lists (1905 to 1923).
* This is an outline history, written in diary form and presumably based upon the Regtl records. It has no formal appendixes other than the one noted above, but there are numerous lists of officers, casualties, awards and other distinctions, relevant to various campaigns and wars, scattered throughout the text. An Index, therefore, would have been immensely helpful. In WWI, the Bn served in Mesopotamia. R/5 V/4. MODL. AMM.

THE NINTH GURKHA RIFLES
Volume I : 1817-1936
Lieut Col F S Poynder MVO OBE MC * Printed by Butler & Tanner Ltd, Frome and London, for the Royal United Service Institution, London, 1937. Green/black, silver, Regtl crest, 10.0 x 7.5, xx/275. Fp, 15 mono phots, 17 maps (bound in), Bibliography, Index. Apps: Roll of Honour (WWI only), H&A (1914-1923), officers' war services (1914-1923), Order of Battle for the Meerut Division (1914), Battle Honours.
* One of the rarest of all Gurkha unit histories, and produced to the finest standards of Butler & Tanner in their hey-day. The narrative is well-written and full of interest, with excellent supporting appendixes. The years which preceded conversion to a Gurkha Regiment (1817-1893) are dealt with in relatively superficial style, but the WWI coverage is superb. The 1st Bn served initially on the Western Front with the Indian Corps and then joined 2nd Bn in Mesopotamia. R/5 V/5. IOL. AMM.

THE 9th GURKHA RIFLES
Volume II : 1937-1947
Lieut Col G R Stevens OBE * Printed by Butler & Tanner, Frome and London, for the Regtl Assn, London, 1953. Green/black, silver, Regtl crest, 10.0 x 7.5, xviii/355. Fp, 5 mono phots, 12 maps (bound in), no appendixes, Index.
* An excellent narrative account which deals, in detail, with the approach of WWII, the Regt's services in various theatres of war, and then the trauma of the break-up of the old Indian Army. The bulk of the pages are devoted to WWII - 1st Bn in Paiforce, North Africa, Italy and Greece, 2nd Bn captured on Singapore Island, 3rd Bn in Burma, Malaya and Java, 4th Bn in Burma, and 5th Bn in India. The book's overall quality of production reflects the post-war difficulties of the printing industry, and the lack of appendixes was presumably prompted by a need to cut costs. R/3 V/3. PCAL. AAM.

9th GURKHA RIFLES
A Regimental History, 1817 to 1947
Lieut Col P Chaudhuri * Kay Kay Printers, Delhi, for Vision Books (Pvt) Ltd, New Delhi, for the Regt, 1984. Green, black, 8.5 x 5.5, v/260. 17 mono phots, no maps, no appendixes, Index.
* This is not a reprint but an amalgamation of information taken from the two earlier histories by Poynder and by Stevens. The Regt wished to produce a new book which could be easily studied by young officers who might not be able to gain access to the original works (particularly the rare Volume I). R/1 V/3. PC. AAM.

CHINESE CHINDITS
Being an Informal Account of Some of the Life of a Wartime Battalion
Anon * Gale & Polden Ltd, Aldershot, 1948. Dark green, black, 8.5 x 5.5, vii/53. No ills, one map (bound in), no appendixes, no Index.
* A personal memoir, written presumably by an officer who served, of the activities of 4/9th Gurkha Rifles on the NWF and in Burma. The Bn was raised in 1941 and disbanded in 1947. Names of officers appear frequently in the narrative, but often without their ranks. The story is readable, but lacks form and structure. This is a pity because the Bn served with Wingate's Chindits between 1943 and 1945. A more coordinated effort by the author, or some professional advice, could have produced an important historical record. R/4 V/3. MODL. AMM.
Note: another interesting personal record is A CHINDIT'S CHRONICLE, by Bill Towill (printed by Quack's Booklet Printers, York, for the author, Tadworth, Surrey, 1991). Towill served with 3/9th Gurkha Rifles at Broadway, 130 miles behind the Japanese main forward positions.

10th GURKHA RIFLES

BUGLE AND KUKRI
The Story of the 10th Princess Mary's Own Gurkha Rifles
Col B R Mullaly * William Blackwood & Sons Ltd, Edinburgh, for the Regt, 1957. Green, silver, Regtl crest, 10.0 x 7.5, xvii/492. Fps, 45 mono phots, one cld ill, 22 maps, Index. Apps: Roll of Honour (WWII only), H&A, notes on Regtl customs, notes on the 10th Madras Native Infantry (stated to be not entirely accurate).
* A good unit history, strongest in its coverage of WWI, WWII, and the post-1947 period. This is the book which is now regarded as Volume I of the Regt's history because it provides a detailed account of its two Bns in WWI and its four Bns in WWII. The Regt had the highest number of decorations of the Gurkha Bde in WWII and the second heaviest casualty list. The H&A appendix covers not only WWII but all such awards made between 1893 and 1945, this being a truly remarkable work of compilation. R/2 V/5. DH/MCJ/AS.

BUGLE AND KUKRI
The Story of the 10th Princess Mary's Own Gurkha Rifles
Volume II
Maj Gen R W L MacAlister CB OBE * Vectis Ltd, Newport, IOW, for the Regtl Trust, 1984. Glazed card covers, 'Perfect' bound, green, silver, 8.5 x 5.5, xii/506. Fp, 72 mono phots, 21 maps, Glossary, no Index. Apps: Roll of Honour, H&A, list of former COs, idem Gurkha Majors, notes on events at Lahore (1947), notes on the Hong Kong confrontation (1967).
* The book as described above was issued in an 'economy' binding, and with a limited print run of 350 copies, in order to establish what corrections or amendment it might provoke from qualified readers (a tactic which many other publishers of unit histories could have adopted with advantage). A full hard-back edition, of which 650 copies were printed, was published three years later, in 1987. For research purposes, the second edition is to be preferred. Apart from any other consideration, it contains 24 additional pages (at the rear). These carry an Index and a 'Digest of Services' which is useful for quick reference. The narrative

covers the period 1948 to 1975. It describes in detail the activities of the 1st and 2nd Bns in Malaya, Borneo and Sarawak, and then, following their amalgamation, in Penang. This is a painstaking record, well written and with excellent supporting illustrations and maps. R/2 V/5. PCAL. TM/DH.

HISTORY OF THE 10th GURKHA RIFLES
The First Battalion, 1890-1921
Capt B R Mullaly * Gale & Polden Ltd, Aldershot, for the Regtl Committee, 1924. Green, gold, Regtl crest, 10.0 x 7.5, vii/119. Fp, 30 mono phots, 7 maps (folding, cld, bound in), no Index. Apps: Roll of Honour (statistics only), H&A (1890-1921, complete for WWI but incomplete for 1890-1914), notes on other units affiliated to the Regtl Depot (1/70th Burma Rifles, 3/70th Kachin Rifles, and 4/70th Chin Rifles).
* A high quality production, with good paper and binding and having well-executed maps. The narrative covers operations in Burma (1891-1894), Mesopotamia (1916-1918), and Iraq/Kurdistan (1918-1921). The sub-title should be noted. This book deals only with the 1st Bn. It was therefore not regarded as having been a 'Volume I' when Mullaly's first full history of the Regt came to be published in 1957, followed by MacAlister's history in 1984 (vide the two preceding entries). R/4 V/4. IOL. DH.

NOTES FROM THE HISTORICAL RECORD OF THE 2nd Bn, 10th GURKHA RIFLES
Prepared by the Adjutant under the Direction of Lieut Col R E Coningham
Anon * The Curzon Press, Quetta, 1927. Stiff card (blue-grey), cloth spine (blue), 7.0 x 4.25, iv/46. No ills, no maps, no appendixes, no Index.
* A very brief summary of the Bn's history, written for educational purposes in the Regtl School and printed in both English and Gurkhali. Its research value is virtually nil but, given its original function, it is now only rarely encountered and is therefore a collector's item. R/5 V/1. PC. BDM.

ODTAA
Being Extracts from the Diary of an Officer who Served with the 4/10th Gurkha Rifles in Manipur and Burma
Anthony Charles Bickersteth * The Aberdeen University Press, 1953. Green, gold, Regtl crest, 8.75 x 5.5, xvi/258. Fp, no other ills, 18 maps (16 printed in the text, 2 bound in), Glossary, no Index. Apps: Diary of the Bn's movements (May 1942 to March 1946), author's own account of his being wounded in action and then later severely injured when run over by a Jeep, notes on the organisation of a Gurkha Battalion as authorised in August 1945.
* The author of the original diary served with the Bn throughout its WWII period of active service. This detailed record of his own experiences, as a Company Commander and as an eyewitness to the fighting in Burma, was used as a major source by Col Mullaly for his later formal history (vide BUGLE AND KUKRI, 1957). The maps are excellent and many individuals of all ranks are mentioned in the narrative. The author died prematurely in 1948. His diary was edited and prepared for publication by his father, Prof A C Bickersteth. The strange title of the book is an acronym for 'One Damned Thing After Another'. R/4 V/4. PC. CJP.

10th PRINCESS MARY'S OWN GURKHA RIFLES - A SHORT HISTORY
D F Harding * The Regtl Trust, 1990. Illustrated soft card, 'Cap badge and honorary arm badge' motif, 8.25 x 5.75, -/47. Fp, 8 mono phots, no maps, no Index. Apps: statistical tables of casualties and awards, lists of Colonels and COs (1766-1990), lists of Subedar Majors and Gurkha Majors (1766-1990), notes on the customs and traditions of the Regt, citation for the award of the VC to L/Cpl Rambahadur Limbu.
* The Regtl Trust first published a SHORT HISTORY in 1975. This new booklet doubled the historical coverage and corrected some minor inaccuracies found in that first edition. It included, for the first time, an account of the Regt's

period as a Madras infantry unit (1766-1890). The condensed narrative describes all war services during that time, and links campaigns and actions to the Regtl Battle Honours in a clear manner. The author explains also the restoration to the Regt by HM the Queen, in March 1988, of the pre-1890 Battle Honours, and, from May 1990, of the 'Elephant and Rock' honorary arm badges. A concise summary of the Regt's entire history. R/1 V/3. NAM. RP.

10th GURKHA RIFLES
One Hundred Years
Anon * Great Wall Graphics, Hong Kong, for the Regtl Trust, 1990. Rifle green, silver, 9.0 x 13.0 (landscape), -/208. More than 400 sepia and black/white mono phots, 7 maps, no appendixes, no Index.
* A commemorative work, published to celebrate the centenary of the Regt in its present form. As such, it is intended mainly to evoke the general spirit of the Regt rather than to record every episode in which it was engaged. The narrative, for this reason, is pleasantly readable but fairly generalised. The strength of the book, for military historians and genealogists, is its superb range of photographic illustrations. These include many captioned groups of personnel which coincidentally illustrate changing styles of uniform and details of insignia. Most of the pictures were selected from previously unpublished Mess Albums and private collections. The Regt had its roots in Burma, but became 10th Gurkha Rifles in 1903 with instructions to recruit entirely in Eastern Nepal. This is an opulent record which mirrors the Regt's proud history. R/1 V/4. NAM. RP.
Note: published with a limited print run of 1000 copies.

11th GURKHA RIFLES

BRIEF HISTORY OF THE XI GURKHA RIFLES, 1918-1921
Lieut Col H R K Gibbs * An article of 6 pages published in The Journal of the 6th Queen Elizabeth's Own Gurkha Rifles, No 69, Spring 1989.
* This wartime temporary Regt was raised in May 1918 at Kut-al-Amara and Baghdad with four Bns. The officers and ORs were mainly battle experienced personnel drawn from other Regts of Gurkha Rifles. They subsequently served in Palestine and Iraq and on the NWF. This brief account, anecdotal and written by a 6GR officer who served with 1st Bn XI GR, does contain all the basic details which a researcher is likely to require. R/2 V/3. NAM. RP.
Note: for lack of a formal published history of the Regt, reference should be made also to THE LEAST KNOWN HISTORY OF THE 11th GURKHA RIFLES, by Lieut Col V K Jain, this being an article of 3 pages published in THE GORKHA, 1978 (pages 37 to 40). It covers the same period as Gibbs' account. The Regt was disbanded in 1921, but the title was revived when the Indian Army formed a new 11th Gorkha Rifles shortly after Independence. This modern unit's services are recorded in THE PATH OF GLORY - EXPLOITS OF THE 11th GORKHA RIFLES, by Gautam Sharma (Allied Publishers, Ahmedabad, 1988).

OTHER GURKHA UNITS

GURKHA SAPPER
The Story of the Gurkha Engineers, 1948-1970
Maj Gen L E C M Perowne CB CBE * The Cathay Press Ltd, Hong Kong, for the Corps, 1973. Dark blue, gold, Corps crest, 9.25 x 5.75, x/390. 74 mono phots, 3 diagrams, 9 maps (bound in), Index. Apps: list of former COs, idem officers.
* An immensely detailed work, the narrative full of facts and with many lists of personnel inserted throughout. The pictures, although originally interesting and helpful, did not reproduce well at the printing stage. Otherwise, an excellent book. R/2 V/4. MODL. AMM.

THE STORY OF THE ROYAL ARMY SERVICE CORPS AND ROYAL CORPS OF TRANSPORT 1945-1982
Brig D J Sutton OBE * Leo Cooper, in conjunction with Secker & Warburg, London, 1983.
* This immense work deals primarily with the RASC and RCT of the British Army. However, it does contain a chapter (pages 579-604) in which the author covers in useful detail the structure and work of the Gurkha Army Service Corps and the Gurkha Transport Regiment. R/2 V/4. NAM. RP.

WITH PEGASUS IN INDIA
The Story of 153 (Gurkha) Parachute Battalion
Eric Neild * Jay Birch & Co (Pvt) Ltd, Singapore, n.d. (c.1970). Glazed card, cream, maroon, 'Pegasus' motif, 10.5 x 8.0, iv/110. Fp, 10 mono phots, 8 maps (bound in), no Index. Apps: Orders of Battle of 50th Indian Parachute Bde and 2nd Indian Airborne Div.
* This is a personal view of the formation and subsequent operations in Burma (1942-1945) of 153 (Gurkha) Parachute Bn. It was first authorised in October 1941. Although fully para-trained, it subsequently fought in the conventional infantry role. The personnel were volunteers from all Gurkha Regiments, the largest contingent coming from 2GR. The narrative flows along pleasantly and is full of interest, but few individuals are mentioned by name. This defect, combined with the lack of appendixes or an Index, limits the use of the book to certain categories of researcher. However, it is a worthwhile source of reference for an otherwise almost forgotten wartime unit. R/3 V/3. IOL/MODL. AMM/DH.
Note: reprinted in hard-back in 1990 by The Battery Press, USA, with the valuable addition of an Index.

Note: other aspects of Gurkha soldiering are recorded in a series of booklets published from time to time by the Gurkha Museum, Peninsula Barracks, Winchester, Hampshire. They deal with specialist aspects which may not receive such detailed coverage in the formal unit histories listed on the preceding pages of this bibliography, e.g. Battle Honours, badges, medals, uniforms, Regimental lineages.

APPENDIX IV

The designation of Gurkha Regiments
following the re-organisations of 1922

1st King George's Own Gurkha Rifles (The Malaun Regiment)
re-designated 1st King George V's Own Gurkha Rifles (The Malaun Regiment) in 1937

2nd King Edward's Own Gurkha Rifles (The Sirmoor Rifles)
re-designated 2nd King Edward VII's Own Gurkha Rifles (The Sirmoor Rifles) in 1936

3rd Queen Alexandra's Own Gurkha Rifles

4th Gurkha Rifles
re-designated 4th Prince of Wales's Own Gurkha Rifles in 1924

5th Royal Gurkha Rifles (Frontier Force)

6th Gurkha Rifles

7th Gurkha Rifles

8th Gurkha Rifles

9th Gurkha Rifles

10th Gurkha Rifles

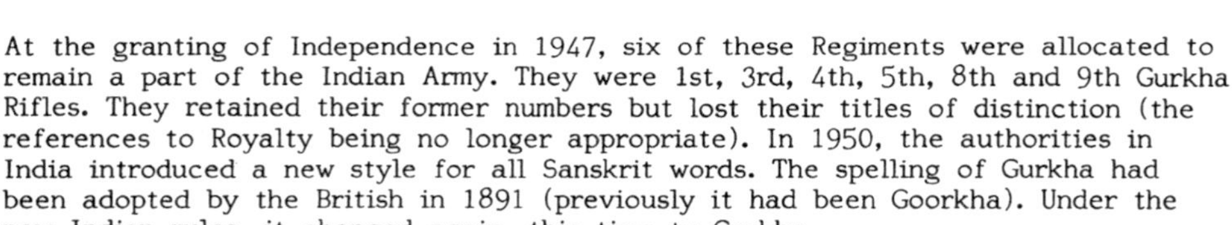
At the granting of Independence in 1947, six of these Regiments were allocated to remain a part of the Indian Army. They were 1st, 3rd, 4th, 5th, 8th and 9th Gurkha Rifles. They retained their former numbers but lost their titles of distinction (the references to Royalty being no longer appropriate). In 1950, the authorities in India introduced a new style for all Sanskrit words. The spelling of Gurkha had been adopted by the British in 1891 (previously it had been Goorkha). Under the new Indian rules, it changed again, this time to Gorkha.

The other four Regiments were transferred to the British Army as a newly created Brigade of Gurkhas. Again, they retained their pre-1947 numbers but, in the case of three of them, received new titles of distinction, thus:

2nd King Edward VII's Own Gurkha Rifles (The Sirmoor Rifles)

6th Gurkha Rifles
re-designated 6th Queen Elizabeth's Own Gurkha Rifles in 1959

7th Gurkha Rifles
re-designated 7th Duke of Edinburgh's Own Gurkha Rifles in 1959

10th Gurkha Rifles
re-designated 10th Princess Mary's Own Gurkha Rifles in 1950

Between 1968 and 1970, the number of battalions was reduced from eight to five, only 2nd Gurkha Rifles retaining its two battalions. In 1992, it was announced that all four regiments would be amalgamated in 1994-1995 with the title The Royal Gurkha Rifles, organised as two battalions.

SPECIAL AND IRREGULAR FORCES

The Punjab Frontier Force

The following diary of events explains the origins and evolution of the Force:

1849: at the conclusion of the Second Sikh War, and with the annexation of the Punjab, the **Trans-Frontier Brigade** was raised (19.5.1849) as a shield against incursions by the western tribes and to maintain control of all the Western Frontier areas from Hazara in the north to the confines of the Sind (Scinde) in the south. The Brigade had its own Commander and Staff, and it was controlled directly by the newly created Government of the Punjab.
1851: the Brigade was greatly expanded and reorganised as the **Punjab Irregular Force.** Apart from general service in the Punjab, it was given the additional task of stabilising the provinces to the west of the Indus River which came within the orbit of the Government of the Punjab. Its increased establishment consisted of - The Corps of Guides (with elements of Cavalry and Infantry), five Regiments of Cavalry, one Battery of Garrison Artillery, four Batteries of Mountain Artillery, four Regiments of Sikh Infantry, and six Regiments of Punjab Infantry. Some of these units were newly raised, others had been in existence from as early as 1843. The Force's units recruited mainly from the Sikh and Muslim population of the Punjab itself, some also accepted Gurkhas, Pathans, and Dogras.
1865: the designation was changed to **Punjab Frontier Force.**
1886: the PFF lost its autonomy. Its administration passed from the Government of the Punjab in Lahore to the Commander-in-Chief in Delhi.
1903: the entire structure and future role of the Indian Army was examined by Kitchener and a number of reforms were set in motion. One of these was the full integration of the PFF into the Indian Army. In effect, it was broken up. Released from PFF command, its component parts were retitled and renumbered in accordance with the new Kitchener system and were attached to various Indian Army District Commands. The effective date of the transition was 31 March 1903.

Although the PFF no longer existed as a single identifiable formation, its spirit and traditions were perpetuated in the new titles given to its (former) constituent units. Their officers continued to be known as 'Piffers', the men were still recruited from the Force's traditional classes, and the units themselves operated on familiar territory (being assigned to the District Commands of Rawalpindi, Peshawar, Kohat, and Derajat).

The 'Frontier Force' title survived the major reorganisations of 1922 and the dismemberment of the Indian Army in 1947. It is to be found in the Order of Battle of the present-day Pakistan Army, and the 'Piffer' soubriquet is still carried with pride by Pakistan officers who have inherited the traditions of their 19th Century predecessors.

Five 'general' histories of the PFF and its descendants are listed here. Publications in respect of individual units having connections with the Force are to be found in the Indexes under 'Cavalry', 'Mountain Artillery', 'Infantry', and 'Gurkhas'.

A BRIEF ACCOUNT OF THE PUNJAB FRONTIER FORCE FROM ORIGINATION IN 1849 TO REDISTRIBUTION ON 31.3.1903
Rai Sahib Boydo Nath Dey * W Newman & Co, at the Caxton Press, Abbottobad, 1903. Dark red, gold, 7.5 x 5.0, -/85. No ills, no maps, no Index. Apps: notes on Regts and Btys (where, when, and by whom raised), list of former COs, idem former Assistant Adjutants-General, Principal Medical Officers, and other senior officers.
* The author was a former Head Clerk to the Force. Although brief, this is an excellent history, full of facts, dates, and the names of individual officers (British and Indian). R/3 V/4. USII/IOL. RGB/LD.
Note: several examples of this book have been seen. The 1903 edition, as recorded

here, seems to have been published in two versions - one bound in cloth, the other in leather. A later (1905) edition has been reported, this having blue cloth covers and (apparently) identical contents.

THE PUNJAB FRONTIER FORCE
A Brief Record of their Services, 1846–1924
R North (known to have been R E F G North) * The Commercial Steam Press, Dera Ismail Khan, 1934. Dark green, gold, 10.5 x 7.5, xi/95. No ills, one map (loose in rear pocket), Bibliography, Index. Apps: H&A, list of former COs, notes on the Frontier Force War Memorial (1914–1918).
* A condensed history, arranged under headings for each component unit, presented in diary form with just one or two lines of text to record their activities during each year. Useful as a quick reference source, otherwise of only limited interest.
R/4 V/3. NAM. PJE.

ONE HUNDRED GLORIOUS YEARS
The History of the Punjab Frontier Force, 1849–1949
Maj Gen M Hayaud Din MBE MC * Civil & Military Gazette Ltd, Lahore, 1949. Red, black, green/gold quarter stripes, 9.25 x 6.0, -/36. No ills, no maps, Bibliography, no Index. Apps: H&A (VCs only, 26 in number), list of Colonels (to 15.8.1947), list of Commandants (1850–1903), notes on Battle Honours, notes regarding the raising of the constituent Regts.
* A nicely produced booklet with a text which summarises, briefly, the first one hundred years of the PFF and its descendants. Several individuals are named in the text, but there is little detail. Useful mainly for the appendixes.
R/3 V/2. RCSL/NAM. PJE/RP.

THE WARDENS OF THE MARCHES
A History of the Piffers, 1947–71
Lieut Gen M Attiqur Rahman MC * Wajidalis, Lahore, 1980. Dark green, gold, 9.0 x 6.0, xv/225. Fp, 19 mono phots, 12 maps (bound in), Index. Apps: Roll of Honour, H&A, list of former COs, Battle Honours, notes on changes of title.
* Only a small proportion of the narrative is devoted to pre-1947 services. The rest is a full account of involvements in the Indo-Pakistan and Bangladesh wars.
R/1 V/4. NAM. PJE.

Frontier Militias

THE FOUNDING OF THE NORTH WEST FRONTIER MILITIA
Thomas D Farrell * Journal of the Society for Asian Affairs, n.d. (c.1973). Offprint of an original Journal article, paper covers, stapled, 9.5 x 6.0, -/14. No ills, no maps, no appendixes, no Index.
* A short but useful account of the reasons for raising the NWF Scouts and Militias. R/4 V/2. NAM. PJE.

FRONTIER SCOUTS
Col H R C Pettigrew * Printer's details not shown, published privately by the author, Selsey, West Sussex, n.d. (c.1965). Illustrated stiff card, brown, 8.5 x 6.5, ii/122, Fp, 33 mono phots, 8 line drawings, one map (folding, bound in), no appendixes, no Index.
* An interesting account of this Irregular Corps. It consisted of the Pishin Scouts, Zhob Militia, South Waziristan Scouts, Tochi Scouts, Kurram Militia, Samana Rifles, Khyber Rifles, Chitral Scouts, and Gilgit Scouts. The period covered in this largely anecdotal book is from 1900 (year of formation) through to 1950.
R/4 V/3. JHG/JRS.

THE FRONTIER SCOUTS
Charles Chenevix Trench * Jonathan Cape, London, 1985. Blue, gold, 9.25 x 6.25, xxii/298. 38 mono phots, 13 maps, Glossary, Bibliography, no appendixes, Index.
* This is a formal history. It draws heavily upon the material compiled by Pettigrew (vide preceding entry), and this the author acknowledges, but his book includes a great deal of additional information which does not appear in Pettigrew and which is otherwise difficult to obtain. However, the material does overlap, so both books are recommended. R/1 V/4. PC. JHG/JRS.

THE FRONTIER
Maj Gen J G Elliott * Cassell, London, 1968. Yellow, black, 8.5 x 6.0, xii/306. 20 mono phots, 8 maps (bound in), Bibliography, no appendixes, Index.
* Not a formal history, but a full and readable description of police and military actions on the NWF over a period of 108 years. R/1 V/3. NAM. PJE.

DOSTAN (FRIENDS)
A Personal View of the North West Frontier
Maj Dick Corfield * Published by the author, no details shown, 1986. Soft card, plastic spiral spine, green, black, 11.5 x 8.25, ii/197. 21 mono phots, 3 line drawings, Bibliography, Glossary, no Index. Apps: notes on the major tribes.
* An autobiographical account by an officer who joined the Tochi Scouts from the Frontier Force Rifles in 1945, and who later served with the South Waziristan Scouts and the Khyber Rifles. Enjoyable background reading. R/3 V/3. PC. FWST.

HISTORY OF THE ASSAM RIFLES
Col L W Shakespear CB CIE * Macmillan & Co Ltd, London, 1929. Dark green, gold, Regtl crest, 9.0 x 6.0, xxiv/301. Fp, 84 mono phots, one cld plate, 6 maps (bound in), Bibliography, Index. Apps: list of former COs, notes on affiliations with Gurkha units, notes on Assam Rifles organisation changes from 1863 onwards.
* The Regt was raised in 1824 as Frontier Constabulary for border control duties between India and Burma. It consisted of specially recruited Gurkha rank and file commanded by British officers on secondment from the Indian Army. This is a comprehensive history, with good detail of operations in the Chin Hills, Naga Hills, Abor, Lushai, etc. In 1941, the Assam Rifles provided cadres for the newly-formed Assam Regiment. R/4 (for this 1929 edition) V/4. IOL/IWM. PJE/RP.
Note: copies of the first edition are seen only rarely. The book was reprinted by Firma KLM Pvt Ltd, for the Tribal Research Institute, Aizwal, Mizoram, in 1977, then by Spectrum Publications (date unknown), then again in India in 1983 (no other details available). Highly recommended as an additional or alternative source is SENTINELS OF THE NORTH EAST - THE ASSAM RIFLES, by Maj Gen D K Palit (Palit & Palit, New Delhi, 1984). This is another substantial history, with extensive appendixes, which updates Shakespear's account to 1982.

Bhil Corps

THE MEYWAR BHIL CORPS
Lieut H L Showers * Printed by Cotton & Morris, Simla, for the United Service Institution of India, 1891. Extract from the USII Journal, Volume XX, pages 87-97.
* Although not a free-standing book, this short article is the only known record of this militia-cum-police force (raised in 1841 for peace-keeping duties in Rajputana). It saw much hard action during the Mutiny period. R/4 V/2. NAM. PJE.

A SHORT HISTORY OF THE MALWA BHIL CORPS
Lieut Col A Poingdestre * Publisher's details not shown, Lucknow, 1905. Paper covers, cream, black, 8.0 x 5.0, -/5. No ills, no maps, no appendixes, no Index.
* A pamphlet which skims over the period 1840 to 1905. The Corps took part in the suppression of the Mutiny and was responsible for maintaining law and order in Bhopawar Agency, Central India. R/5 V/2. NAM. PJE.

A MEMOIR OF THE KHANDESH BHIL CORPS, 1825-1891
A H A Simcox * Thacker & Co, Bombay, 1912. Blue with green edgings, gold, 'Queen Victoria head' motif, 10.0 x 7.0, iv/281. Fp, 4 mono phots, one map (loose in rear pocket), no Index. Apps: list of former officers.
* An excellent full history for the period stated in the title. The Corps was raised in 1825, saw service during the Mutiny period, and was then converted into an armed police unit in 1862. The author provides good coverage not only of the unit's services but also some interesting observations on Khandesh and the life of its people. This book is the sole in-depth account of a Bhil Corps unit, of which there were several. R/4 V/4. IOL. PJE.

Jail Corps

SHORT HISTORY OF THE JAIL LABOUR CORPS
Anon * W B Lane, at the Government Press, Baghdad, 1920. Paper covers, beige, black, 13.0 x 8.25. No ills, no maps, no Index.
* This is a series of pamphlets which deal with a most unusual Corps. In order to augment the logistical manpower on the lines of supply in Mesopotamia, seven Jail Labour & Porter Corps units were recruited from the inmates of prisons in various regions of India. They were the 5th (United Provinces) Jail Porter Corps, the 6th (Punjab) Jail Labour Corps, the 8th (United Provinces) Jail Porter Corps, the 10th (Madras) Jail Porter Corps, the 11th (Bombay) Jail Corps, and the 12th (Burma) Jail Porter Corps. The pamphlets, all identical in format, describe the services of each unit, with separate appendixes for deaths, invalids, offences, desertions, work done, and bonuses paid. R/5 V/4. IWM. PJE.

Airborne Forces

INDIA'S PARATROOPERS
A History of the Parachute Regiment of India
K C Praval * Leo Cooper Ltd, London, 1975. Mauve, gold, 9.5 x 6.5, xiv/366. Fp, 52 mono phots (of indifferent quality), 30 maps (27 printed in the text, with three loose in rear pocket), Bibliography, Index. Apps: H&A (only for Jammu & Kashmir, 1947-1948), list of former COs (pre- and post-1947), Orders of Battle (1943, 1945, 1947, and post-1947).
* A good narrative account of the raising of the 50th Indian Para Bde in 1941, the subsequent expansion of Indian parachuting and air landing resources, the formation of 9th Indian Airborne Div in March 1944 (renumbered 44th Airborne Div in November 1944), and the Regt's evolution after Partition. The first 105 pages of this book are devoted to events during WWII. The fighting in Burma is well covered. R/2 V/4. PCAL. RP.
Note: first published in India in 1974 by Thomson Press (India) Ltd, Faridabad. This 1974 edition has blue covers with yellow lettering.

THE BATTLE AT SANGSHAK
Burma - March, 1944
Harry Seaman * Leo Cooper Ltd, London, 1989. Black, gold, 9.5 x 6.5, v/148. 11 mono phots, 4 maps, Bibliography, Index. Apps: Roll of Honour, list of officers, Orders of Battle (for IV Corps and for the Japanese 15th Army).
* A well written account of the formation of 50th Indian Para Bde and of its only battle - Sangshak, Burma. The author was a young Subaltern serving with 153 Gurkha Para Bn when it fought this dogged delaying action, the importance of which was not recognised until many years later. The Battle Honour 'Sangshak' was awarded to the Mahratta Light Infantry (the 4/5th MLI being under command at that time), but the same honour was never bestowed upon the pre-1947 or post-1947 Indian Parachute Regt. R/1 V/4. PC. JG.

Intelligence Services

FIELD SECURITY
Very Ordinary Intelligence
Lieut Col A A Mains * Picton Publishing (Chippenham) Ltd, Chippenham, Wiltshire, 1992. Illustrated soft card, 'Perfect' bound, white, black, 'Spider's web with Div flashes' motif, 8.5 x 5.5, vi/181. 8 mono phots, no maps, Glossary, no Index. Apps: notes on civil, military and police organisations in India (WWII).
* An autobiographical account by a pre-war 9th Gurkha Rifles officer who, in 1939, found himelf plunged into the secret world of Field Security almost by accident. This is a substantial record, full of detailed information and anecdotes, concerning the development of an Intelligence service which, at the outbreak of war, barely existed. The author pioneered intelligence-gathering and counter-espionage work in Iraq in 1941, moved to Burma in time to witness the debacle there, headed the Security section in Assam and with 14th Army, and was finally, in 1946, Chief Intelligence Officer, Cental Command India. A unique record of Field Security in that theatre of war. R/1 V/4. NAM. RP.
Note: by the same author, and from the same publisher, is SOLDIER WITH RAILWAYS. A companion volume to FIELD SECURITY, it concentrates upon the equipment, organisation and operations of the various railway networks in Iraq, India and Burma during WWII, and their vital contribution to the Allied war effort.

BEHIND ENEMY LINES
Dharmendra Guar * Sterling Publishers Pvt Ltd, New Delhi, 1975. Red, yellow, 8.75 x 5.75, viii/136. No ills, 2 maps (one printed in the text, one folding, bound in), no appendixes, no Index.
* A first-hand account of British intelligence operations behind Japanese lines in Burma and on the Andaman Islands in 1943. The author was seconded to Force 136 and he describes its various activities in a style which combines individual reminiscences with the wider picture. He devotes one long chapter to the Force's various headquarters, and its 'safe houses' in Calcutta, Bombay, Poona, and Kandy (Ceylon). An interesting and unusual record of Allied covert operations during WWII. R/3 V/3. PC. NH.

OTHER CORPS

Education Corps

HISTORY OF THE ARMY EDUCATION CORPS
Volume I : 1600–1947
Lieut Col (Dr) Pritam Singh * Imperial Press, for M/S Avtar Publishers, Dharamsala, 1983. Illustrated card, green, black/white, 8.75 x 6.5, vi/87. 8 mono phots, no maps, Index. Apps: list of Commandants of the School of Education (1921–1947).
* The period from 1600 to 1920 is covered in just the first eight pages because 'there was practically no education in the Army before 1921'. The book began life as a doctoral thesis which was later expanded. It makes dull reading for anyone not having a special interest in the subject. R/3 V/3. PC. NH.
Note: according to the dust-wrapper, the author wrote a follow-up Volume II (for the period 1947–1982). This has not been seen.

Postal Services

THE POST OFFICE IN INDIA IN THE GREAT WAR
Lieut Col H A Sams CIE ICS * The Times Press, Bombay, 1922. Part board, part cloth, red, black, 9.75 x 6.5, viii/430. Fp, 69 mono phots, one sketch map, Index. Apps: Roll of Honour (all ranks), H&A, list of officers, Sub-Conductors, Assistant Commissaries, Subedars, Jemadars and Havildars, nominal roll of 'followers' (with 74 pages of names).
* A strange and wonderful book, packed with names. The author (later Sir Hubert Sams) edited various officers' reminiscences and official records to compile this highly detailed narrative. The result is a readable mixture of colourful anecdotes and basic administrative material regarding a specialised but very important aspect of warfare. Between 1914 and 1920, the Indian military postal services operated in almost every theatre of war – France, Gallipoli, Egypt, Palestine, Mesopotamia, Arabia, East Africa and Persia. Many of the photographs are those of individual named officers. An excellent reference source for postal historians, philatelists and medal collectors. R/4 V/5. MODL/IOL. IAB.

INDIAN ARMY POST OFFICES IN THE SECOND WORLD WAR
Brig D S Virk * The Army Postal Service Association, New Delhi, 1982. Brick red, blind, 9.5 x 7.0, xi/362. No ills, 24 maps (printed in the text), Glossary, no Index. Apps: Roll of Honour, H&A, list of officers who served in principal IAPS HQs and postal installations, list of contributors.
* Written by one of its former Directors, this is a thorough and readable account of the IAPS from January 1942 through to Partition in 1947. All theatres of war are covered, chapter by chapter, with moving references to personnel taken POW in the Far East and in Europe. As happened in WWI, most members of the Service were 'civilians in uniform for the duration of the war'. R/4 V/5. MODL. AMM.
Note: the same author produced a companion history under the title INDIAN ARMY POST OFFICES – LOCATIONS AND MOVEMENTS, 1939–1947 (same publisher, 161 pages, n.d.). Compiled principally to meet the needs of philatelists, it contains complete details of the raising, deployment and disbandment of more than four hundred Army Post Offices. It contains also three hundred illustrations of their postmarks. MODL. AMM.

ARMY SERVICE CORPS

HISTORY OF THE ARMY SERVICE CORPS
Five authors (see below) * Sterling Publishers Pvt Ltd, New Delhi, various dates between 1976 and 1979. Five matching volumes, blue, gold, 8.75 x 5.5.
Volume I : 1760–1857. Brig Humphrey Bullock, published in 1976, xi/259. No ills, no maps, no appendixes, Bibliography, Index.
Volume II : 1858–1913. Lieut Col B N Mujamdar, published in 1976, xii/408. No ills, no maps, no appendixes, Bibliography, Index.
Volume III : 1914–1939. Lieut Col B N Mujamdar, published in 1976, xv/272. No ills, no maps, no appendixes, Bibliography, Index.
Volume IV : 1939–1946. Brig V J Moharir, published in 1979, xiii/444. No ills, 11 maps (bound in), Bibliography, Index. Apps: H&A (WWII only), lists of officers.
Volume V : 1947–1975. Brig V J Moharir, Maj Inder Luthra and Brig R I N Luthra, published in 1977, xvi/224. 16 pages of mono phots (56 pictures in total), 15 maps (bound in), no appendixes, Bibliography, Index.
* With a total spread of 1674 pages, these five volumes represent a tour de force by the officers who compiled them. Their work is not entirely free of fault. The fourth volume, for example, has three pages of 'Errata', with 107 corrections (of which some are themselves inaccurate). However, in such an ambitious work, some such errors are to be expected. The contents of the books are summarised below, but it is evident that they represent one of the most detailed and authoritative sources of reference ever published for any Corps of the Empire. The scale of the work reflects not only the long period of time covered but also the fact that the RIASC was the largest Corps, of any Army, to serve in WWII.
Vol I : describes the Commissariat Dept of the HEIC and its role in the Nepalese War (1814), First Burma War (1824-1826), First Afghan War (1838-1842), the two Sikh Wars, the Second Burma War (1852-1853), the Persian War (1856-1857), and the siege of Lucknow (1857).
Vol II : describes the role of military transport in the campaigns of Umbeyla (1863), Bhutan (1864), Abyssinia (1867-1868), Second Afghan War (1878-1880), Third Burmese War (1885), Sikkim (1888-1890), the Frontier Risings (1888-1898), Manipur (1891), Chitral (1895), Tibet (1904), and the Abor Expedition (1911-1912).
Vol III : describes the transport services on home duties and on active service overseas during WWI. It then continues with coverage of the Third Afghan War (1919), and the campaigns in Waziristan (1919-1920 and 1936-1937).
Vol IV : deals with the enormous expansion of the RIASC and its services in every theatre of war in which the Indian Army was engaged (but notably the Western Desert and Italy).
Vol V : covers the Indo-Pakistan conflicts (1947, 1965 and 1971), the seizure of Portugese Goa (1961), and the Chinese incursions (1962).
Much of the information is related directly to matters of organisation and reform, training, mechanisation, Indianisation, and the entire evolution and services of the Corps. However, as can be seen from the details given above, the books provide a collateral record of India's overall military history from 1760 to 1975.
R/3 V/5. IOL. GRB/BDM.

THE ROYAL INDIAN ARMY SERVICE CORPS, WORLD WAR II
Anon * Publication details not shown, n.d. (c.1948). Seen only in presentation leather binding, black, superimposed metal RIASC cap badge, 9.75 x 6.5, xx/35. Fp, 22 mono phots, 4 line drawings, one map (Chittagong), no appendixes, no Index.
* A curious little publication of no discernible origin. Well written and nicely printed, it summarises the activities of the RIASC in many theatres of war during WWII. The unknown author makes the point that nearly one sixth of the Indian Army's personnel 'was wearing the RIASC shoulder title by 1945'. The Corps had the task of transporting the fuels of war (food, munitions, clothing, stores) to the fighting formations wherever they were. R/5 V/2. PC. BDM.

FOOTPRINTS AND MILESTONES
The Story of the Army Service Corps

Maj Gen P K D Kapur VSM * Directorate of Supplies and Transport, AHQ New Delhi, 1990. Blue, gold/white, Corps crest, 11.25 x 9.0, xx/394. Fp, 725 mono phots, 72 cld ills, 29 line drawings, 27 maps, Glossary, no Index. Apps: Roll of Honour (by campaign, incl Korea and the Gaza Strip, for the period 1947 to 1990), H&A (incl MID, also for 1947-1990), list of Directors and Directors General, 'Who's Who' of leading Corps personalities (1947-1990, with portrait mono phots), list of Corps Colonels Commandant, idem officers who served on foreign assignments (1947-1990), idem officers who attended important courses.

* While the five-volume history by Bullock et al (vide preceding entry) remains unsurpassed for its quality of research and information, there was a clear need to make the 230 years' history of the Corps available in a single volume. This finely produced book meets that need. Aimed not only at the academic researcher but also at past and serving members of the Corps (for whom it must surely be an inspiration), the book is highly readable and packed with illustrations. Key events - both before and after Independence - are covered in uniform detail and the author is generous in his many references to former British personnel and the traditions and standards which they bequeathed to the modern ASC. He examines in detail the strengths and weaknesses of the Commissariat system operated by the HEIC, the crucial work of Lieut Thomas James during the siege of Lucknow, the impact on transport policy of the loss of 50,000 camels during the Second Afghan War, the development of the Mule Companies which did such fine work in WWI and WWII, the huge effort to move supplies by road through Persia into the USSR in 1942-1943, the key role of air supply in Burma in 1943-1945, the expansion of the RIASC from 20,000 to 354,000 all ranks, and much else of interest to students of the Empire period. R/1 V/5. NAM. PGM.

MEDICAL SERVICES

A HISTORY OF THE INDIAN MEDICAL SERVICE
Lieut Col D G Crawford * W Thacker & Co, London, and Thacker, Spink & Co, Calcutta, 1914. Two matching volumes, published simultaneously, dark blue, gold, 10.0 x 6.25
Volume I : xiv/529. Fp, one other mono plate, no maps, no appendixes, no Index.
Volume II : -/535. Fp, one other mono plate, Chapter Notes, Bibliography, Index (for both Volumes).
* This admirable pair of matching books is a very detailed and readable account of the evolution of the IMS over a period of three centuries. The work has much value for research on India's public health and social histories, but it is also of value to medal collectors and genealogists. The text incorporates many lists of IMS personnel, with details of their services, awards, wounds, deaths, dates and places of burial, and so forth. Numerous VC winners appear in the story. The Index is particularly helpful in tracing individual careers. R/4 V/5. PCAL. RP.

ROLL OF THE INDIAN MEDICAL SERVICE, 1615–1930
Lieut Col D G Crawford * W Thacker & Co, London, 1930. Black, gold, 9.75 x 7.0, Li/711. No ills, no maps, a very large number of appendixes, Index.
* An excellent research tool which lists 6586 former IMS personnel, giving details of their services, honours and awards, campaign medal entitlements, etc. This very large book also contains interesting information concerning Indian medical colleges and places of instruction. A primary source, by the same author who wrote the preceding entry, containing a huge amount of biographical detail which could be obtained from other sources only with great difficulty. R/4 V/5. PC. CSM.
Note: the book is reported to have been reprinted in 1986, in facsimile, and with a print run limited to 200 copies. No other details available.

SURGEONS TWOE (sic) AND A BARBER
Being an Account of the Life and Work of the Indian Medical Service, 1600–1947
Donald MacDonald * Heinemann, London, 1950. Dark blue, gold, 9.5 x 7.5, ixx/295. Fp, 11 mono phots, 10 sketches, no maps, Bibliography, listing of books written by serving or former IMS officers, Index. Apps: list of former Heads of the IMS.
* A readable and informative account of the IMS, covering most if not all of the campaigns in which the Indian Army took part. The author acknowledges Crawford's works (vide preceding entries) as being the definitive histories, but the story is here updated (to 1947) and condensed. R/3 V/4. NAM. PJE.
Note: reference should be made also to THE MORALE BUILDERS, by Lieut Gen D R Thapar (Asia Publishing House, Bombay, 1965). The period covered is WWI to 1947, but the book is particularly good for the final years (leading to the closure of the IMS, a time at which the author was commanding it).

HISTORY OF THE ARMED FORCES MEDICAL SERVICES: INDIA
Col A Ghosh * Orient Longman, New Delhi, 1988. Brown, yellow, AFMS crest, 8.75 x 5.75, xvi/333. 27 mono phots, no maps, no appendixes, reference notes, no Index.
* A sound general record, lacking in detail and human interest, but covering the entire period (1600–1971) of the Presidential Medical Services, the Indian Medical Service, and the Indian Army Medical Service. Probably best read in conjunction with the three books recorded above. R/1 V/3. PC. AN.

ELECTRICAL & MECHANICAL ENGINEERS

OFFICIAL HISTORY OF THE INDIAN ARMED FORCES IN THE SECOND WORLD WAR, 1939-1945
Technical Services: Ordnance and Electrical & Mechanical Engineers
P N Khara * Combined Inter-Services Historical Section (India and Pakistan), Delhi, 1962. Dark blue, gold, 9.5 x 6.5, xxii/479. 22 mono phots, 16 maps, Index. Apps: 24 in total (establishments, organisation, and statistics).
* As the title indicates, this is a detailed factual account of the IAOC and the IEME in WWII. Undoubtedly of great interest to the specialist researcher.
R/2 V/4. NAM. PJE.

HISTORY OF THE CORPS OF ELECTRICAL AND MECHANICAL ENGINEERS
Volume I : Their Formative Years
Lieut Col Rufus Simon * Vikas Publishing House PVT Ltd, New Delhi, 1977. Red, gold, Corps crest, 8.75 x 5.75, xxx/486. Fp, 13 mono phots, one cld ill, 3 maps, Bibliography, 47 appendixes, Index.
* Although well written and neatly presented, the narrative is fairly hard work for the non-specialist. The astonishing run of appendixes - forty-seven in total - deals with a wide range of technical and organisational subjects. This book was the first of a planned four-volume set, all to be published by the Director of the Corps of Electrical & Mechanical Engineers, AHQ New Delhi. It covers the evolution of the Corps, commencing with the appointment in 1895 of Capt W E Donohue as the first Inspector of Ordnance Machinery in the Indian Ordnance Department, and ending in 1945. The second volume in the set, to be entitled MANY SPLENDOURED ACTIVITY, was intended to describe the services of the IAOC Workshop Branch and IEME units during WWII, but plans for this publication seem to have been abandoned (vide following entry). R/2 V/5. IOL. RGB.

HISTORY OF THE CORPS OF ELECTRICAL AND MECHANICAL ENGINEERS, 1943-1971
Col Shushil Jagota VSM * Produced by the College of Electrical and Mechanical Engineering, for the Corps, 1981. Black, gold, 9.0 x 5.75, xxii/444. Fp, 13 pages of small mono phots, 5 cld plates, 7 charts, 19 maps (bound in), Bibliography, Index. Apps: three in total, organisational and technical.
* As the title indicates, this book covers the history of the Corps from the date of its formal inception in May, 1943, through to 1971. The contents are divided into four parts. The first is a condensed version of the material which appears in Lieut Col Simon's earlier work (vide preceding entry). The second is an account of services between 1943 and 1945, and then post-war services through to the time of Partition. The other two parts deal with events between 1947 and 1971. The result is a very comprehensive but digestible Corps history containing all the information which any researcher in this field is likely to require. Although it is no more than speculation to say so, it seems likely that the projected cost of the monumental four-volume history initiated when Lieut Col Simon's book was published (in 1977) led to a reappraisal by the Director of the Corps. This (1981) history by Col Shushil Jagota thereby became the complete official Corps history.
R/2 V/5. USII. OSS.

THE VOLUNTEER AND AUXILIARY FORCES

One consequence of the Mutiny was a sharply increased awareness of the great vulnerability of European communities living at a distance from the main garrison towns or cantonments. In the event of 'another Mutiny', they would be peculiarly dependent upon their own resources to defend themselves and their property. Several groups of armed Europeans had sprung up spontaneously while the events of 1857-1858 were in progress but, from the 1860s onwards, the Government of India gave active support to the raising of permanent part-time Volunteer units in many parts of Bengal, Madras, Bombay, Assam and Burma. The movement became increasingly formalised as the years went by. The authorities encouraged higher standards of training by providing the services of Regular officers (as Adjutants) and experienced BNCOs (as Permanent Instructors). There was further expansion when the railway operating companies promoted the formation of Railway Battalions and encouraged their employees to attest. Unlike the majority of Volunteer units, the Railway Battalions comprised a high proportion of Anglo-Indians (Eurasians).

India's tradition of part-time soldiering evolved from those early roots and it is still active today. The principal milestones along the way are summarised below.

1857–1917
Volunteer units were trained for local defence and to protect the vital railway and telegraph systems. As fears of a second major rebellion slowly subsided, so did the movement acquire a greater social and sporting ethos.

1916–1919
The Government agreed, after much hesitation, to the formation of the Anglo-Indian Force (AIF). This was in response to the Eurasian community's appeal to be permitted to serve their country - not just on a part-time basis, but on full-time service overseas. Some of the AIF's units did in fact succeed in reaching Mesopotamia and East Africa. The Force was disbanded after the war.

1917–1920
The easy-going ways of the pre-war Volunteer units changed abruptly with the introduction of the Indian Defence Force Act. It obliged all European males, between 18 and 41 years of age, to attend part-time military instruction. The old system was radically restructured and the 'Volunteer' title abandoned. The pre-war units were retitled as elements of this wartime Indian Defence Force (IDF).

1920–1947
The ending of hostilities signalled the need for further reform. The IDF was replaced by another new structure - the Auxiliary Force (India). Abbreviated as the AF(I), it had no connection with the recently defunct AIF (the Anglo-Indian Force). The new organisation was the natural successor to the old Volunteer movement - locally based, part-time, and predominantly white European in composition. It survived the financial constraints of the inter-war years (being from time to time called out in response to political and sectarian unrest) and then thrived during WWII (when some of its units generated a flow of experienced officer candidates for the Indian Army).

It was also in 1920 that the Government authorised the creation of the Indian Territorial Force (ITF). The ITF was based upon principles totally different to those of the AF(I). Comparable to the Territorial Army in Great Britain, its part-time membership was trained and equipped to reinforce the Indian Army in wartime. ITF units were an integral part of that Army. All ranks were attested for service overseas (or in India) - subject to the necessary Proclamation being issued. Apart from a handful of British European officers, seconded from the Regular Army, the personnel were entirely Indian. This organisation was retained by the Indian Army after Partition and is still extant (under an amended title, The Indian Territorial Army).

The surviving records of these various forces are sparse and not easy to trace. A handful of books have been written about the Anglo-Indian Force, the Indian Territorial Force (later Army), and some individual Volunteer/IDF/AF(I) units, and these are recorded on the following pages. In general terms, however, anyone wishing to research deeper into this field will need to consult the Annual Reports which the Volunteer/IDF/AF(I) units were obliged by order to produce. At first compiled for the information of the authorities in Delhi and London, they came to be a unique chronicle of the social, economic, sporting and military life of each community and district. As such, they are a most useful source of reference in a wide range of contexts.

The rate of attrition has been high, and copies of these Reports are today only rarely encountered. The following list gives details of those Annual Reports which have been traced by various contributors to this bibliography. The list shows the name of the unit, the years covered, the edition (year) where known or relevant, and the current location(s) of the copies in question.

Assam-Bengal Railway Battalion, 1940-1941 (40th), NAM.

Assam Valley Light Horse, 1914-1915, 1915-1916, 1916-1917, NAM.

Bangalore Rifle Volunteers, 1912-1913, NAM.

Bihar Light Horse, 1912-1913, PC.

Bombay Light Horse, 1915-1916, NAM.

Bombay Volunteer Rifles, 'J' (Scots) Company, 1915-1916 (1st), NAM.

Burma State Railway Volunteer Rifles, 1894-1895 (15th), BL. This unit was formerly the **Rangoon and Irrawaddy State Railway Volunteer Rifles**

Calcutta Light Horse, an almost continuous run of editions from 1887-1888 (1st) through to 1931-1932. NAM.

Calcutta Port Defence Corps, 1915-1916 (17th), NAM.

Calcutta & Presidency Battalion, 1934-1938 (1st), BL.

Chota Nagpur Light Horse, 1913-1914, 1915-1916, 1916-1917, AMOT. 1938-1939, PC.

East Indian Railway Volunteer Rifle Corps, 1880-1881 (12th), BL.

Punjab Light Horse, 1894-1895 (1st), AMOT.

Northern Bengal Mounted Rifles, 1910-1911 (30th), NAM.

Rangoon & Irrawaddy State Railway Volunteer Rifles, 1883-1884 (4th), 1884-1885, BL. This unit was later retitled the **Burma State Railway Volunteer Rifles.**

Rangoon Volunteer Rifle Corps, 1879-1880 (2nd), 1883-1884, 1884-1885, BL.

Southern Provinces Mounted Rifles, 1907-1908 (2nd), plus six other editions over the period 1921-1922 to 1938-1939, NAM.

Surma Valley Light Horse, 1894-1895, PC, and 1909-1910 (27th), 1912-1913, NAM.

United Provinces Light Horse, Northern Regiment, 1909-1910 (1st), AMOT.

Upper Burma Volunteer Rifles, a run of six editions from 1908-1909 (22nd) to 1913-1914 (27th), PC, plus a Report for 1918-1919 when the unit was carrying its wartime (numbered) designation, **34th Upper Burma Battalion IDF.**

A full listing of **all** AF(I) units, as they existed in 1945 but showing their former Volunteer and IDF designations, can be seen on pages 33 to 43 of SONS OF JOHN COMPANY - THE INDIAN AND PAKISTAN ARMIES, 1903-1991, by John Gaylor (vide Index of Authors).

The same book, on pages 44 and 45, shows in tabular form the complete list of Territorial Force units and the Regular Regiments of which they formed part.

All other known published sources of reference are shown in detail on the following pages.

NON-EUROPEAN UNITS

THE ANGLO-INDIAN FORCE, 1916

Capt J H Abbot VD ('and others') * Publisher's details not shown, Allahabad, 1919. Illustrated soft card, 'Historic military diorama' motif, grey, black, 10.0 x 7.25, -/47. 29 mono phots, no maps, no Index. Apps: lists of officers and SNCOs.

* On 5 August 1914, the senior representative of the Eurasian community in India offered to the Government the services of his people to assist the Empire war effort. It was not accepted until January 1916 when approval was given for the recruitment of Eurasians into some British Army units at that time stationed in India. Further representations won an agreement, two months later, for the raising of an Anglo-Indian Force with its own elements of cavalry, artillery and infantry. Due to the delay, 8000 men of the community - particularly the most competent and enthusiastic - had already volunteered for service with other Corps. Despite the difficulties, a Field Battery was despatched for service in Mesopotamia. At war's end, the Force was permitted to wither away. It is interesting to speculate upon the post-war social status of Eurasians if the AIF had been formed in 1914 or 1915, and its personnel thereby given the opportunity to show their mettle in combat. R/5 V/4. IOL. JG.

THE TERRITORIAL ARMY

H Bisham Pal * Tulsi Publishing House, New Delhi, 1983. Green, white, 8.5 x 5.5, xiv/94. 24 mono phots (all post-1947), no maps, no Index. Apps: Roll of Honour (pages 32-34), list of 'Honorary Commissioned Officers of the Territorial Army' (post-1947), idem 'Territorial Army Directors' (post-1947), roll of 'Best TA Units of the Year' (1957-1982).

* After WWI, many Indians expressed the desire to be more directly involved in the defence of their country but without becoming full-time professional soldiers. The Government responded by authorising, in 1920, the creation of the Indian Territorial Force (ITF). The members were part-timers, comparable with the 'Terriers' of the Territorial Army in Great Britain and therefore attested for full-time service, at home or overseas, in the event of war or national emergency. The units with which they trained were usually the 11th Bns of Regular Regiments of the Indian Army. Four or five Regular officers (British European) were attached to each such Bn. All other personnel were Indian. By 1935, the ITF had a strength of 15,000 all ranks. After Partition, the scheme was retained but with a change of title - Indian Territorial Army (ITA). This book deals mainly with post-1947 events, but it does include a brief resumé of the ITF of the Empire period (with short histories of several of those earlier Bns). R/3 V/3. UM. RBM.

AD HOC UNITS OF THE MUTINY PERIOD

SERVICE AND ADVENTURE WITH THE KHAKEE RESSALAH OR MEERUT VOLUNTEER HORSE DURING THE MUTINIES OF 1857-58
R H W Dunlop BCS * Richard Bentley, London, 1858. Red, gold, 'Winged Victory and vanquished foe' motif, 7.75 x 4.75, xi/168/xi (plus 32 pages of advertisements). Fp (attractive cld ill, 'A Volunteer of the Khakee Ressalah', mounted, in field dress), 6 mono plates, 2 cld plates, one line drawing ('The Wallace Guard', an arm protector for sabre fighting), no maps, no Index (but good Contents page).
Apps: 'A List of Corps which have Mutinied or been Disbanded' (5 pages).
* This was one of several bodies of mounted Militia, or vigilantes, which sprang into existence in the immediate aftermath of the outbreak at Meerut and the fall of Delhi. Despite the dates given in the book's title, the unit disbanded itself in October 1857. The term 'ressalah' loosely describes any formed body of horsemen. Such units, in this context, consisted of every man in the district willing and able to wield a sabre against the Mutineers - British and Indian officers whose HEIC regiments had mutinied or been disbanded, loyal Indian troopers, and European civilians. The story reflects a tragic and very violent period. R/5 V/4. PC. CJP.

MEMORANDUM OF THE BENGAL YEOMAN CAVALRY, 1857-58
Anon (known to have been John Tulloch Nash) * J F Bellamy, at The Englishman Press, Calcutta, n.d. (c.1859). Seen rebound, details of original binding not known, 9.75 x 7.0, i/28. No ills, no maps, no appendixes, no Index.
* A narrative account of a Volunteer unit raised in Calcutta. Recruited from local Europeans, it was sent to Amorah, on the Oudh/Behar border, in October 1857. It had several encounters with 'Pandis' - disaffected Sepoys. The text includes details of establishment, rates of pay, a unit nominal roll, and a list of KIA and WIA. R/5 V/4. NAM. TA.
Note: another book, entitled VOLUNTEERING IN INDIA, OR A NARRATIVE OF THE MILITARY SERVICE OF THE BENGAL YEOMAN CAVALRY DURING THE INDIAN MUTINY AND SEPOY WAR, has been noted but not seen. Published in London in 1893 (viii/136 pages), it is presumably an expanded version of the booklet described above.

HISTORY OF BEHAR INDIGO FACTORIES - REMINISCENCES OF BEHAR - TIRHOOT AND ITS INHABITANTS OF THE PAST - HISTORY OF BEHAR LIGHT HORSE VOLUNTEERS
Minden Wilson * Calcutta Printing Co, Calcutta, 1908. A book having 334 pages, of which just fifteen are devoted to Mutiny services and the post-Mutiny evolution of the Soubah Behar Mounted Rifles (renamed Behar Light Horse circa 1883). Although very brief, this charming and amusing account is full of interest. It is packed with the names of those who served during the early years. Full formal histories of the BLH are noted on the following two pages.
R/5 V/2. BM. JMAT.

THE VOLUNTEER FORCE OF INDIA - ITS PRESENT AND FUTURE
Maj E H H Collen * The United Services Institution of India, Delhi, 1883. Red, gold, 10.0 x 6.5, -/39. No ills, no maps, no Index. Apps: notes on the strength and organisation of the Volunteer Force.
* A prize-winning essay written in 1883 and then printed for wider circulation. The author presents a concise history of the evolution of the Volunteer movement and argues the case for its continuation. This seems to be the only general account ever published. R/5 V/3. USII. OSS.

VOLUNTEER AND AF(I) UNITS

COSSIPORE ARTILLERY VOLUNTEERS
A Brief History
Lieut Col D A Tyrie VD * Thacker Spink & Co, Calcutta, 1912. Brown, gold, 7.25 x 5.0, -/34. No ills, no maps, no Index. Apps: list of officers (1883-1910).
* This is not a free-standing book in its own right. It is instead an article of 34 pages bound within a volume entitled PAMPHLETS MILITARY AND NAVAL, held by IOL, London. It is listed here because it is the only known record of this particular unit (or of any Volunteer artillery unit in India). It is possible that copies of the original pamphlet may be seen in different (even individual) bindings. The CAV was a half-battery of gentlemen-volunteers who never saw any active service but who manned the guns on ceremonial occasions at the old Calcutta forts. R/5 V/3. IOL. RGB.

HISTORY OF THE BEHAR LIGHT HORSE
From Formation in 1862 to 1908 - The Oldest Volunteer Regiment in Bengal
Maj G W Disney * Edinburgh Press, Calcutta, 1908. Purple, silver, 'Musical notation' motif, 7.5 x 5.0, -/80. No ills, no maps, no Index. Apps: notes on Fort Pill Box (1857), nominal roll of the Soubah Behar Mounted Rifles (the original unit title, 1862), nominal rolls for various years through to 1906 (when the unit was transferred from the Government of Bengal to C-in-C India).
* Covers the period 1862-1907. This was a small Corps of gentlemen-volunteers (merchants, doctors, etc) which saw no action during the stated period (other than called out during the 'Basantapur Cattle Rescue Riots' of 1893.
R/4 V/3. IOL. RGB.

HISTORY OF THE BEHAR LIGHT HORSE
From Formation in 1862 to 1918
Maj G W Disney and Maj T R Filgate * Thacker Spink & Co, Calcutta, 1948. Ochre, gold, unit crest, 7.5 x 5.0, vi/180. Fp, one mono phot, no maps, no Index. Apps: list of former officers, extracts from the Indian Army Lists, result of competitions.
* As the title and sub-title suggest, this is a much enlarged and updated version by Filgate of Disney's earlier work (see preceding entry). R/4 V/4. NAM. PJE.

HISTORY OF THE BEHAR LIGHT HORSE
The Most Senior and Oldest Volunteer Cavalry Unit in India
Lieut Col W N R Kemp ED * Thacker's Press & Directories Ltd, Calcutta, 1948. Stiff card, light grey, gold, 7.5 x 5.0, xx/240. Fp, no other ills, no maps, no formal appendixes (but see below), no Index.
* This is an even larger and further updated history which is based in part upon the earlier accounts by Disney and Filgate (vide the two preceding entries), plus a great deal of additional research. The narrative is divided into three parts - 1857-1903, 1903-1919, and 1920-1947. Each section is supported by many notes and appendixes, all compiled in immense detail. The author's style of writing is tedious and uninspired, but the book is a first-class source of information regarding the unit and a great many of the individuals who were at one time or another associated with it. R/3 V/4. NAM/IOL. RJW.

A CONCISE HISTORY OF THE BIHAR LIGHT HORSE
Taken from Disney's, Filgate's and Kemp's Histories
F A C Munns * Cheriton Press, Folkestone (UK), n.d. (c.1958). Paper covers, dark blue, white, Regtl crest, 8.5 x 5.5, -/31. No ills, no maps, no Index. Apps: list of former COs, lists of officers, Adjutants, Chaplains.
* A very brief summary of limited value. The lists of officers might be useful to a genealogist. R/4 V/2. BM. PJE.

CALCUTTA LIGHT HORSE AF(I), 1759-1881-1947
Anon ('A Committee of the Regt') * Gale & Polden, Aldershot (UK), 1957. Dark blue, gold, Regtl crest, 8.75 x 5.5, xx/175. Fp, 40 mono phots, 4 line drawings, one cld ill, no maps, no Index. Apps: Roll of Honour (WWI and WWII), H&A (WWII only), list of former officers, notes on sporting trophies, nominal rolls (all ranks, 1914, 1939 and 1947).
* The Regt was essentially a social, sporting and military club for the British male community in Calcutta. However, it did take its military commitments seriously and many members were detached for full-time service with other Regts and Corps in both WWI and WWII. The CLH won popular fame for the clandestine attack on enemy shipping, by some of its members, in neutral Goa in 1943. This episode is not mentioned here ('for reasons of security'). Many individuals are mentioned in the narrative - an interesting and useful history. R/2 V/4. IOL/NAM. RGB/CSM.

BOARDING PARTY
Calcutta Light Horse
James Leasor * Heinemann, London, 1978. Blue, silver, 8.75 x 5.5, xv/204. Fp (map), 22 mono phots, one other map, no appendixes, Index.
* The CLH was formed in 1759 as the Calcutta Volunteer Cavalry and had several changes of title over the years. Apart from duties 'in aid to the civil power' in times of unrest, it never saw action as an integral unit. It is best remembered for the 'unofficial' raid into Portugese Goa which resulted in the sinking of German merchantmen, Ehrenfels, Drachenfels and Braunfels, and the Italian ship Anfora. The raiding party consisted of 15 members of the CLH and 4 of the Calcutta Scottish. James Leasor interviewed some of the participants and wrote this graphic version of a unique military operation. R/1 V/3. DLS. CLL/RGB.
Note: the book later formed the basis for a film, THE SEA WOLVES.

THE CALCUTTA AND PRESIDENCY BATTALION AF(I), 1857-1938
Anon * Wilson & Son, Calcutta, n.d. (c.1938). Green, gold, 9.0 x 5.5, i/30. Fp, 3 mono phots, no maps, no formal appendixes, no Index.
* A short readable account of one of the Volunteer units raised following the Mutiny and which later became part of the AF(I). R/5 V/2. NAM. PJE.
Note: there is mention in this volume of 'the original history of the Battalion written in 1934 by Lieut Col A H Bishop', but no book meeting that description has been traced. It may have been an unpublished draft.

A SHORT HISTORY OF THE MADRAS VOLUNTEER GUARDS FROM 1857, THE DATE OF FORMATION, TO 1907, THE JUBILEE YEAR OF THE CORPS
James Robert Coombes * The Lawrence Asylum Press, Madras, 1907. Stiff card, light grey/green, black, 8.5 x 5.5, xiv/223. 4 mono phots, no maps, no Index. Apps: list of former officers, notes on comparative strengths, 1857/1907.
* A very readable and detailed history, with plenty of names and incidents noted throughout. R/4 V/3. USII/IOL. OSS/PJE.
Note: this book has also been seen in a blue leather 'de luxe' binding with gold lettering. There is also reported to have been a similar history (xii/140 pages) published in 1883 to mark the unit's 25th anniversary.

THE KOLAR GOLD FIELDS BATTALION, MYSORE

Anon * Publication details not shown, n.d. Yellow, black, 7.5 x 6.0, -/4. No ills, no maps, no appendixes, no Index.

* With only four pages, this pamphlet barely qualifies as a unit history. However, it is the only record which has been traced. The period covered is 1847 to 1947. There is some mention of 'aid to the civil power' duties at various times, and particularly during the Moplah Rebellion of 1921-1922. R/5 V/1. NAM. PJE.

THE BOMBAY VOLUNTEER RIFLES

A History

Samuel T Sheppard * The Times Press, Bombay, 1919. Brown, gold, unit crest, 9.75 x 6.75, iii/199. Fp, 18 mono phots, no maps, Index. Apps: list of former COs, idem Adjutants, idem Sergeant Majors, idem officers serving in 1916, biographical notes on officers, roll of members who saw active service with other units in WWI.

* A comprehensive and interesting account of the unit's history between 1799 (then the Bombay Fencibles) through to the end of the Napoleonic Wars (when they were allowed to fade away). The story then resumes in 1860 when the unit was reactivated as the Bombay Volunteer Rifle Corps. Apart from occasional riot control duties, the Corps saw no active service until 1914 when a detachment sailed for East Africa to take part in that campaign. R/4 V/5. IOL/NAM. RGB.

THE BOMBAY LIGHT HORSE AND ITS SUCCESSOR, THE BOMBAY MOTOR PATROL AF(I)

Anon (known to have been Maj J S R Spelman)* Cranford Press (Croydon) Ltd, Croydon, UK, 1966. Dark blue, silver, unit crest, 9.75 x 6.25, -/47. Fp, 6 mono phots, no maps, no Index. Apps: Rolls of Honour (WWI and WWII), list of former COs, list of officers who served during the periods 1914-1918 and 1939-1945.

* Although very slim, the book contains much scarce information regarding equipment, uniforms, reorganisations, and individual services. The story begins with the formation of the Bombay Light Horse in 1887. In 1933 it was renamed the Bombay Light Patrol (Cavalry Group) and paired with a Light Motor Patrol of the Bombay Contingent. Jointly they became the Bombay Light Patrol. The author was the last CO of the Cavalry Group, but the title of his account is incorrect when it refers to 'the Bombay Motor Patrol'. No such unit designation was ever authorised. A tipped-in Erratum slip confirms that the casing and title page were wrongly printed. They should refer instead to the Bombay Light Patrol as the natural successor to the old Bombay Light Horse. R/4 V/4. NAM/IOL. WR.

THROUGH FIFTY YEARS

A History of the Surma Valley Light Horse

The Rev W H S Wood MC * The Assam Review Publishing Co, Calcutta, 1930. Black, gold, 10.0 x 6.5, xi/69. 31 mono phots, no maps, no Index (but a good Contents page). Apps: H&A, list of former COs, idem former officers, roll of permanent instructional staff (all ranks).

* Covers the period 1857-1930. Written in an easy style, with many names included in the text and in the picture captions. The unit served on the North East Frontier (Manipur) in 1891, and in South Africa (where it formed 'B' Coy of Lumsden's Horse). During WWI, many members volunteered for service with other Regts and Corps. R/5 V/5. MODL. AMM.

Researchers able to visit the National Army Museum, London, should consult an extract from a document compiled under the Chairmanship of Brig Enoch Powell and entitled REPORT OF THE COMMITTEE ON THE POST-WAR ARMY IN INDIA. Almost certainly printed by the Government of India Press, Delhi, it was never published because it was overtaken by the move to Independence. The extract, Appendix 'H' of the full Report, is headed UNITS OF THE AUXILIARY FORCE (INDIA) SO FAR AS EXISTING SINCE 1920. It gives details of their strengths at 3.9.1939 and 31.12.1944, their ethnic compositions at those dates, their 'call outs' and 'embodiments' since 1920, and the numbers of members from each unit who joined the Regular forces in WII as officers and Other Ranks.

WOMEN'S SERVICES

BENGAL JOURNEY
A Story of the Part Played by Women in the Province, 1939–1945
Rumer Godden * Longmans Green & Co Ltd, Calcutta, 1945. Light blue, red, 10.0 x 7.5, iv/132. Fp, 20 mono phots, several line drawings of Corps badges, one map (printed on the end-papers), no appendixes, no Index.
* Already an established author, Rumer Godden was given official backing to visit numerous units throughout Bengal in order to record, in general terms, the role of women in India's war effort. Although she did not attempt to compile a concise tally of formation dates, establishments, deployments, etc, she did succeed in producing an interesting description of many units and Corps which are today almost unknown or which have been neglected by post-war historians. Amongst there were - the Women's Auxiliary Service Burma (the 'Wasbies'), the Indian Military Nursing Service (IMNS), the Army Nursing Service (ANS), the Queen Alexandra's Imperial Military Nursing Reserve (QAIMNR), and the Women's Auxiliary Corps India (the 'Wac Eyes'). R/4 V/2. DCLS. CJP.
Note: refer to page 548 for details of the Women's Auxiliary Service Burma.

POLICE

THE INDIAN POLICE
J C Curry * Faber & Faber, London, 1932. Dark blue, gold, 8.5 x 5.5, -/353. No ills, one map, Index. Apps: tables of statistics and establishments.
* A useful general history, but particularly strong on matters relating to the structure and organisation of Indian Police departments. Certainly of interest to the specialist, less so to the general reader. R/3 V/3. IOL. JA.

TO GUARD MY PEOPLE
The History of the Indian Police
Sir Percival Griffiths KBE CIE * Ernest Benn Ltd, London, 1971. Brown, gold, 8.75 x 5.5, xii/431. 38 mono phots, 2 line drawings, one map (bound in), Index. Apps: Roll of Honour (Gazetted officers only), H&A, Index.
* A superb work, deeply researched and well written. The narrative covers more than 200 years of police work in India and Burma, and is full of incident with many individuals mentioned by name in the text. The evolution of the Indian Police reflected not only the changing patterns of criminality but also the emergence of nationalism. The book is therefore of interest to researchers of Indian history in general. The H&A section is a sound source for medal collectors. R/1 V/5. IOL. RP. Note: it is reported that the book was reprinted in 1972. Good additional sources are:

NO TEN COMMANDMENTS - Life in the Indian Police, by S T Hollins CIE (Hutchinson & Co, London, 1954)
POLICING THE RAJ, 1928-1947, by Leslie Robins (privately, 1954)
ON HONOURABLE TERMS - The Memoirs of Some Indian Police Officers, 1915-1918, by Martin Wynne (Indian Police UK Association, 1985)
DUTIES AND DIVERSIONS, anon (being a supplement to the preceding item)

POLICE AND CRIME IN INDIA
Sir Edmund C Cox * Stanley Paul & Co, London, n.d. (c.1910). Dark blue, gold, Force crest, 9.0 x 6.0, -/328. Fp, 21 mono phots, no maps, no appendixes, no Index.
* A long, detailed and very readable book devoted mainly to the Bombay Presidency Police, but with much information regarding the law, criminal activities, and police responsibilities in general. R/4 V/4. NAM. PJE.

THE BOMBAY CITY POLICE
A Historical Sketch, 1672-1916
S M Edwards * Printed at The Tutorial Press, Bombay, for the Oxford University Press, 1923. Blue, black, 9.0 x 6.0, viii/223. 10 mono phots, no maps, Index. Apps: report on the Moharram Riot of 1911.
* A history divided into nine chapters. The first three cover the formation by the HEIC of the Bhandari Militia of 1672 and events up to 1855. The rest of the book deals with the story of the Bombay Police, under seven different Commissioners, from 1855 to 1916. The author was the seventh of the Commissioners (1909-1916). R/4 V/4. SLV. PS.

THE POLICE IN BRITISH INDIA
Anandswarup Gupta * Concept Publishing Co, New Delhi, 1979. Blue, gold, 8.75 x 5.5, xxiv/579. No ills, no maps, no appendixes, Bibliography, Footnotes, Index.
* This large scale work was written by an officer who served in the Indian Police from 1939 to 1974. He quotes heavily from the original records of the Central and Provincial Governments, making much use of statistical returns and official statements regarding the moral and material progress of India. All of this is set against

the system of policing introduced with the Police Act of 1861 and which developed and operated with little change through to 1947. A book which is probably of interest mainly to the specialist rather than general reader. R/2 V/5. RCSL. TAB.

A BRIEF HISTORY OF THE OLD POLICE BATTALIONS IN THE PUNJAB
H L O Garrett * The Government Printing Press, Lahore, 1927. Yellow, black 10.0 x 7.5, iii/23. No ills, no maps, no appendixes, no Index.
* This is a very short account of the ten Police Battalions raised in the Punjab from 1849 onwards. With details of their services during the Mutiny and through to their disbandment in July 1861 (when they were replaced by the Frontier Militias). Lacking in detail, but a useful secondary source. R/5 V/3. NAM. PJE.

THE WHITE BELTS
History of the Corps of Military Police
Lieut Col R Ganapathi * Lancer Publishers, New Delhi, 1982. Black, gold, 8.5 x 5.75, xii/560. 56 mono phots, 8 pages of line drawings of badges and insignia, 11 maps, Bibliography, Index. Apps: Roll of Honour, H&A, list of former Commandants, notes on the evolution of the Corps badges.
* A comprehensive and readable account of the work and development of the Provost in India. It covers the entire period from the days of the HEIC through to the formation of the CMP(I) in 1939, and then its services in WWII. The story continues with post-1947 developments through to 1981. R/1 V/5. PC. AN.

Note: Before the Mutiny, civil policing was performed in part by units raised to meet specific regional needs. Examples were Gardner's Horse, formed in 1809 to collect revenues and keep the peace in the ceded areas between the Ganges and the Jumna, and the Khandesh Bhil Corps, formed in 1822 to control banditry in the Khandesh District. Likewise, in 1849, Military Preventative Police Battalions were raised with men from the former Sikh Army as the civil police arm of the new Government of the Punjab. In 1855-1856, Military Police Battalions were formed in Bengal and Oude for similar reasons. For the rest, civil police work was based upon traditional local methods, and these varied widely between one Presidency and another.

It was the Police Act of 1861 which authorised a permanent Indian Police force, trained and equipped solely for the prevention and detection of civil crime. The disparate former units were either disbanded or absorbed into the Indian Army. This clear division of responsibilities between the civil police and the military - which at times in the past had been obscure - remained fundamentally unchanged thereafter.

The North West Frontier required different and unique methods of policing. In 1878, when it became evident that the Punjab Frontier Force was being too often diverted from its primary role to deal with civil offences, the Border Military Police (BMP) were formed. Commanded by officers of the Indian Army, their highly mobile patrols covered the entire NWF border area. In 1913, they were reconstituted as the North West Frontier Constabulary (NWFC).

The BMP (later NWFC) were supplemented by local levies such as the Khyber Rifles (from 1878), the Zhob Levy Corps (from 1889), and the Kurram Militia (from 1893). Although commanded by officers of the Indian Army, these were units of armed police, not soldiers.

In the north east, the Assam border was policed by the Cachar Levy (from 1835) under civilian command. With other local levies, it became the Frontier Military Police in 1862. The FMP passed to Army command in 1882, and evolved as the Assam Rifles in 1917.

NOTES

PART 12

The Far East & Western Pacific

NOTES

THE FAR EAST and THE WESTERN PACIFIC A Military Chronology

1511: Portuguese traders explore the Malay Peninsula and establish a base on the west coast. The dominant local religion is Islam, introduced by Arab traders who have been frequenting these parts since the previous century.
1565: the Spanish occupy the Philippines and establish Manila as their administrative capital. The Portuguese and the Dutch fight for possession of Timor. Portugal wins the contest and administers the island from Portuguese India.
1557: Portugal establishes a base on Macao, off the coast of South China.
1599: the Honourable East India Company (HEIC) is formed in London.
1602: the Dutch East India Company (DEIC) is formed in Amsterdam. Over the next four decades, the Dutch will progressively eject the Portuguese and the HEIC from their various toeholds in the East Indies.
1644: in China, the Ming dynasty is overthrown by the Manchu (Ch'ing) dynasty. The new royal line will rule until 1912 when a republic is declared.
1762: a British expedition captures Manila but, a year later, it is returned to the Spanish under the terms of the Treaty of Paris.
1786: the Sultan of Kedah cedes the island of Penang (off the west coast of the Malay Peninsula) to the HEIC. The French have begun to establish their influence in Cochin-China.
1795: the British seize Malacca from the Dutch, but the DEIC continues to control most of the trade in the East Indies archipeligo. Its principal trading and administrative centre is Batavia (modern Jakarta) on the north coast of Java.
1811: the British forcibly occupy Java when Holland becomes part of Napoleon's empire. Sir Stamford Raffles is appointed Lieutenant Governor and carries out many basic reforms. The island is handed back to the Dutch in 1814.
1819: Raffles establishes a trading post on the island of Singapore.
1824-1826: the Dutch cede all trading rights on the Malay Peninsula to the HEIC. The Company creates the Straits Settlements - Singapore, Malacca, Penang (and its mainland province). The Settlements will be administered by the HEIC and the India Office until 1867.
1826: after two years of campaigning against the Kingdom of Ava, the HEIC creates a foothold in Burma, and Assam is ceded to Britain to become part of British India.
1839-1842: the First China War. The Chinese Government objects to the monopoly importation by British traders of huge quantities of opium. British warehouses are burned in Canton and the owners forced to flee. Three years of confused fighting and negotiations ensue. Royal Navy and HEIC warships play a prominent role, also units of the Army of the Madras Presidency. The Chinese are forced to submit. Under the terms of a peace treaty, the island of Hong Kong is ceded to Great Britain. Trade recommences in Canton, and four other ports (Foochow, Amoy, Ningpo and Shanghai) are opened to European commercial interests.
1840: James Brooke takes possession of Sarawak. He and his descendents will rule the territory under British protection until the Japanese invade in 1941. The family will cede it to the Crown in 1946.
1852-1853: the Second Burma War. The British annexe the Province of Pegu (Lower Burma). They will annexe Upper Burma in 1886 (the Third Burma War).
1853-1858: ships of the US Navy enter Tokyo Bay. Japan is persuaded to make a treaty which opens, initially, two ports (Shimoda and Hakodate) to American ships, diplomats, and commerce. Several European nations will follow the American lead.
1856-1863: the Second China War. Piracy at sea and local wars on the mainland are interrupting European trade. The British flag is insulted, but the Mutiny in India prevents a full-scale military response. The Royal Navy takes action at Canton in 1857. It is joined by a French fleet in 1858 for further actions at Fatshan and Taku. In 1860, a major Anglo-French expedition storms the Taku Forts and marches to Pekin. The Chinese submit, and are obliged to lease to Great Britain the mainland territory of Kowloon (opposite Hong Kong island).

1862–1867: France obtains possession of Cochin-China.
1863–1864: the Royal Navy and warships from other European nations bombard the Japanese ports of Kagoshima and Shimonoseki in reprisal for atrocities against Western envoys and traders.
1867: the Colonial Office takes over responsibility for the Straits Settlements.
1874: the chiefs on the island of Fiji agree a 'deed of unconditional cession' to Queen Victoria. It becomes a Crown Colony.
1875: a British punitive expedition invades Perak. Gurkha soldiers are part of the force. This is the first time they have been deployed overseas.
1875–1880: Russia annexes the Sakhalin Islands and Chinese Turkestan.
1876: Japan forces Korea to sign a treaty and opens diplomatic relations.
1880–1890: France annexes Tonkin and Annam.
1882: the USA is the first Western nation to conclude a treaty with Korea. The British North Borneo Company is founded by Royal Charter.
1883–1884: the Government of Queensland annexes eastern New Guinea in the name of the Crown. The British Government disallows the annexation but declares a temporary Protectorate over southeastern New Guinea (to be named Papua).
1884: the German Chancellor, Bismarck, annexes the northeastern coast of New Guinea and the islands of New Britain, New Ireland, the Admiralty Islands, and the North Solomon Islands. He names them, collectively, the Bismarck Archipeligo.
1885: Johore becomes a British Protectorate.
1886: Great Britain annexes Burma. It becomes a province of British India.
1894: hostilities erupt between Japan and China over their conflicting interests in Korea. The Japanese Army re-enters Korea and the Japanese Navy sinks much of the Chinese fleet.
1896: four Malay States (Perak, Selangor, Pahang and Negri Sembilan) unite to form the Federated Malay States under British protection.
1898: Russia forces China to grant a lease on the naval base at Port Arthur. Russia and Japan acknowledge the sovereignty of Korea. War breaks out between the USA and Spain. The US Navy sinks a Spanish fleet in Manila Bay. Spain cedes the Philippines and the island of Guam to the USA.
1898: Great Britain, Germany and the USA declare a tripartite Protectorate over the islands of Samoa.
1899: the British withdraw from the Samoa agreement. Germany takes over the Western Samoa islands, the USA takes over those in the east (subsequently named American Samoa).
1900: the Third China War (the Boxer Rising). Various secret societies organise attacks against the hated Europeans and their enclaves. The Legations in Peking are besieged. An international expeditionary force marches to the city, raises the siege, sacks the Summer Palace and systematically loots the city. The force includes troops from the armies of Austria, Germany, Great Britain, France, the USA, India, Italy, Japan, Russia and Australia. The latter contingent has been raised from various Australian Colonies and includes two naval vessels and a Naval Brigade of 500 bayonets. The French take the opportunity to unify their holdings in Cochin-China, Cambodia, Annam, and Tonkin, as part of the French Colonial Empire.
1904–1905: the Russo-Japanese War. Despite having recognised Korea's sovereignty, the Japanese invade that country. Korea is obliged to sign a 'treaty of alliance'. Russia raises objections, so the Japanese Navy attacks and destroys the Russian Baltic fleet when it arrives from the other side of the world. The Japanese triumph is completed when they annexe the entire Korean peninsula and the Sakhalin islands.
1911–1912: in China, the Manchu dynasty falls to the Kuomintang ('the nationalist people's party') headed by Sun Yat-sen.
1914: immediately war is declared, Australian troops occupy German New Guinea, New Britain, and New Ireland. New Zealand troops occupy German Samoa. In November, the first wave of the Australian Imperial Force (AIF) sails for Europe in convoy with the New Zealand Expeditionary Force (NZEF). Together, they will win immortal fame as the Australian and New Zealand Army Corps (ANZAC). The convoy is escorted by Japanese warships – one of the few contributions by Japan

to the Allied cause during the war. At the end of the year, the German cruiser Emden is destroyed by HMAS Sydney on the shores of the Cocos Islands.
1915–1918: with German bases in the Far East having been so swiftly neutralised, and with the Kaiser having no allies in the region, it has no strategic relevance to the war. Tens of thousands of Australian and New Zealand volunteers are thereby available to the British generals for their operations on Gallipoli, in Egypt, Gaza and Palestine, and on the Western Front.
1926–1931: Chiang Kai-shek takes control of the Kuomintang and its armies. The chaos which has prevailed in China since the brief presidency of Sun Yat-sen is gradually resolved as local warlords are brought to heel.
1932: Japan begins to infiltrate Chinese Manchuria. The Japanese Army will next invade China itself. In the coming years, it will attack and occupy such major cities as Nanking, Hankow and Canton. In each, it commits atrocities of the type which will typify its conduct in the coming world war.
1933: the first Malays are recruited for military service. Three years later, the Malay Regiment is formed and the first Commissions are granted to Malays.
1934: the people of the Philippines have for several years been asking for independence from the USA. In this year, the islands become a self-governing Commonwealth under an elected President. Full independence is promised for 1946. The Americans retain naval and military base rights on the islands. In China, Chiang Kai-shek's forces have overcome most of the Communist opposition and driven its survivors into the northern mountains.
1937: the US Navy river gunboat Panay is bombed and sunk by Japanese aircraft while evacuating American civilians down the Yangtse from Nanking. The Japanese Government offers apologies and reparations, but the incident marks a sharp deterioration in relations between the two countries.
1937–1939: after the initial stalemate, Japan commences full-scale (undeclared) war in China. The Kuomintang Government withdraws to Chungking. In occupied North China, Communist guerilla forces aid the Kuomintang by attacking the Japanese rear. The USA and Great Britain also aid the Kuomintang, sending supplies to South China via the Burma Road. Commenced in 1936 and completed in 1939, the road is closed briefly in mid-1940 at the demand of the Japanese, but then reopened in October as American attitudes towards Japan harden further.
1937–1942: the American aviator, Chennault, is asked by Chiang Kai-shek for advice on aerial warfare. Chennault forms an International Air Squadron with American, Dutch and British volunteer pilots. In August 1937, the USSR sends six of its air force squadrons to support the now allied Kuomintang/Communist ground troops. In 1939–1940, Chennault raises The Flying Tigers, with American aircraft and volunteer aircrew. In 1942, the Tigers will fight the Japanese Air Force over China proper, give aerial support to the British as they evacuate Burma, and attack Japanese shipping in Hong Kong harbour.
1940: with the compliance of the Vichy French administration, Japan declares a Protectorate over the whole of French Indo-China. This act permits the Japanese to establish forward bases for their planned invasion of Malaya. The USA responds to the Japanese 'co-prosperity sphere' by declaring an oil embargo. The reaction is a Japanese determination to seize the Dutch oilfields in the East Indies.
1941: in November, HMAS Sydney is sunk with all hands off north west Australia by the Kormoran, a German mercantile commerce raider. On 7 December, Japanese Navy aircraft and submarines attack the US Navy's base at Pearl Harbour, Honolulu. By this single act, Japan unwittingly ensures the eventual destruction of Nazi Germany and Fascist Italy. The war is now a world conflict. Roosevelt and Churchill will agree a strategy whereby the Pacific theatre of war will be mainly the domain of the US Navy and the US Marine Corps, while the Allied cause in Europe will be aided by the US Army and the US Army Air Force. Meantime, the Japanese overwhelm the British and Canadian defenders of Hong Kong, and invade Malaya at Singora, Kota Bharu, and Patani. The ill-prepared and poorly commanded British, Indian and Australian defending forces are driven down the Peninsula to Johore. At sea, the major units HMS Repulse and HMS Prince of Wales are sunk by Japanese aircraft.

1942: in February, the British sign a humiliating surrender in Singapore. Thousands of British, Australian and Indian soldiers will suffer the coming years as slave workers in Siam and elsewhere. The Japanese invade Java and, in the Battle of the Java Sea, destroy an Allied naval force sent to oppose them. On the Philippines, the Americans are defeated by superior Japanese tactics and surrender after brave last stands at Corregidor and Bataan. The Japanese press further southwards and land on the north coast of New Guinea at Lae and Salamaua. They attempt to land also on the south coast, at Port Moresby, but are thwarted by the US Navy in the Battle of the Coral Sea. A month later, in June, the US Navy inflicts a crucial defeat on the Japanese aircraft carriers in the Battle of Midway. At the same time, Japanese forces are landing in Papua, at Gona and at Milne Bay. They are ejected from Milne Bay by Australian forces - their first land defeat of the war. Other Japanese forces attempt to reach Port Moresby from Kokoda, but are halted a few miles short of their objective by a desperate Australian defence. In Burma, the last British, Indian and Chinese troops have been driven back into India and the invaders have reached Assam. In August, American marines open their counter-offensive by landing on Guadalcanal, in the Solomon Islands. At year's end, Australian forces are locked in bitter battle in New Guinea's Owen Stanley Mountains. Elsewhere during this momentous year, a Japanese carrier fleet has entered the Indian Ocean. Almost unopposed, it achieves extraordinary success. It sinks a Royal Navy aircraft carrier, two cruisers, seven destroyers, and numerous merchant ships. Its aircraft bomb Ceylon (Colombo and Trincomalee) and two Indian mainland bases.
1943: America is creating an enormous naval and amphibious warfare capability. Her strategy is to drive directly westwards across the Pacific, destroying some island garrisons, bypassing others. The first success, in February, is the removal of the Japanese from Guadalcanal after nearly six months of bloody fighting. This pivotal battle has absorbed men and supplies which the Japanese would otherwise have sent to New Guinea. They are still trying to reach Port Moresby. One of their convoys, headed for their base at Lae, is destroyed by the US Navy in the Battle of the Bismarck Sea. American forces attack and capture the Gilbert Islands (after severe fighting on Tarawa). Japanese aircraft repeatedly bomb Darwin, on the north coast of Australia, and Japanese submarines are active in Australia's main shipping lanes. By the end of the year, however, Australian forces have pushed the invaders back up the Kokoda Trail, broken through the Owen Stanley ranges, and captured Lae, Salamaua, and Finschafen. American forces land on Bougainville and New Britain.
1944: the Americans are preparing to reoccupy the Philippines. To distract Japanese attention and resources, and to create new forward air bases, they seize positions in the Marshall, Mariana and Palau island groups. The initial Philippines assault is made at Leyte. Japanese warships try to interrupt the landings and are crushingly defeated by the US Navy in the Battles of the Philippine Sea and Leyte Gulf. Australian forces take over operations in the Bismarck Archipeligo and the Solomon Islands. Elements of 3rd New Zealand Division have been providing garrisons on Fiji and other islands in the South Pacific. It also now takes over from the Americans the task of clearing the last pockets of Japanese resistance on the South West Pacific islands. In Burma, the Japanese have been beaten at Kohima and Imphal.
1945: the Americans continue to recoccupy the Philippines, assaulting in turn the many islands of the group. In February and March, they are locked into the fierce battle of Iwo Jima. American and Australian forces clear the last remaining Japanese from New Guinea's northern coastline. The Japanese home islands are being heavily bombarded by American long-range aircraft based in the Marianas. Japan's ability to wage war is being strangled by the big US Navy submarines ranging throughout her home waters. The fanatically defended island of Okinawa is the first Japanese home territory to fall. Australian forces reoccupy key locations in Borneo. In Burma, after three frustrating years, British and Empire forces finally destroy the starving Japanese Army in the Third Arakan campaign. They will move on to occupy French Indo-China. In August, following the destruction of Hiroshima and

Nagasaki, Japanese representatives sign an instrument of surrender aboard the USS Missouri in Tokyo Bay. US Army, US Marine Corps, and British Commonwealth forces arrive to form a standing army of occupation. In 1943, the US had promised full independence to Korea, once the war was won. Now that country is occupied by Soviet forces in the north and US forces in the south. They meet on the 38th Parallel and the peninsula is divided into two parts. Units of the US Marine Corps occupy parts of North China in order to supervise and repatriate the Japanese troops stranded there.

1945–1949: the British start to resume the administration of territories for which pre-war they had been responsible. They also try to assist the Dutch in quickly regaining the East Indies. By December, five British and Indian Divisions, with an Armoured Brigade and a Parachute Brigade, have landed in Java and Sumatra. The Indians are heavily engaged in fighting the Indonesian nationalist irregulars who oppose any return to colonial rule. An uneasy peace is achieved in Java in 1946 (February). Dutch troops arrive in large numbers to take over military control but, two years later, the Dutch will give up the political struggle. The United States of Indonesia are formally recognised in 1949.

1949–1950: civil war erupts in China. The opponents are the Kuomintang, still led by Chiang Kai-shek, and the forces of the Communist Party, led by Mao Tse-tung. In 1949, the Communists capture Nanking and Canton. The Chinese People's Republic is proclaimed and, in December, Chiang Kai-shek evacuates his nationalist government to Taipei, on the island of Formosa (Taiwan). The last US Marine Corps occupation units withdraw from North China.

1946–1954: France fights to retain her possessions in Indo-China and fails. Dien Bien Phu witnesses the culmination of a war with the Republic of Vietnam in which 3000 French soldiers have died, and 10,000 taken prisoner.

1949: in a near re-enactment of the Panay incident of 1937, HMS Amethyst is caught between two opposing armies (in this case, those of the Kuomintang and the Chinese Communists) when attempting to evacuate British civilian personnel from Nanking. Hit by Red Army gunfire while navigating the Yangtse River, she suffers fifty casualties and is immobilised. After three months of fruitless negotiation, she makes a heroic dash down river and breaks free.

1950–1953: North Korean forces invade South Korea and drive the small local and American defending units south to Pusan. America pours in major reinforcements. With 41 Commando, Royal Marines, under command, they force the invaders back to the Yalu River (the Chinese border). The Government of China intervenes, sending large formations of the Red Army to support the North Koreans. In response, various other governments send contingents to join what is now a major United Nations commitment. The British Commonwealth Brigade (later Division) is formed. Fighter aircraft of the South African Air Force join the air war. Two years of severe fighting, and fluctuating fortunes for the two sides, end with a truce which leaves them back where they started - on the 38th Parallel.

1960: peace finally returns to the Malay Peninsula. Since late 1941, it has been in constant turmoil. During their occupation, the Japanese never succeeded in entirely suppressing the various British, Malay, and Chinese special and irregular forces operating in the jungle and mountain areas. At war's end, when the British returned and made it clear that they intended to restore Crown administration, the Chinese Communist groups went back into the jungle and resumed their former style of warfare (but this time against the British). Their early successes led to a State of Emergency being declared in 1948. There then followed twelve years of conflict in which soldiers from the United Kingdom, Australia, New Zealand, East Africa, Southern Rhodesia, and Northern Rhodesia took part. The jungle 'gangs' were forced finally to give up, defeated more by exhaustion than firepower. Self-government was granted in 1955, and independence within the Commonwealth in 1957.

1958: guerilla units from North Vietnam invade South Vietnam. Fearful of yet another Communist takeover, the Americans decide to intervene. The conflict soon escalates, placing major strains upon American military resources and public opinion. In 1962, Australia deploys an Army Training Team under American command.

By 1966, the Australian contribution has increased to Task Force size (with New Zealand units serving alongside). The last Commonwealth troops will be withdrawn in 1973. The Americans will abandon Saigon in April 1975.
1962: three quarters of the island of Borneo form part of the Republic of Indonesia. The fourth quarter - the north west coastal regions - consists of Sabah, Brunei, and Sarawak. All are under British administration or protection. Sukarno, Indonesia's President, has ambitions to seize these territories and, ultimately, to take control of recently independent Malaya. In December, as a first step, he sponsors an armed revolt in the Sultanate of Brunei. This is swiftly put down by a scratch force of British and Gurkha troops, and by 42 Commando, Royal Marines.
1963: the Federation of Malaya is enlarged by the accession of Singapore, Sarawak, and Sabah. The name Malaysia is adopted. The British Army and Royal Navy provide protection from their bases at Singapore Island, but the resources are very limited.
1963-1966: undeterred by his reversal in Brunei, Sukarno orders an immediate infiltration by highly trained special forces and Indonesian Army units into Sarawak. They use 'Maoist' principles of war, attempting to subvert the local tribes and to establish 'liberated' areas. Over the next three years, along the one thousand miles of mountainous jungle border country separating the two sides, there is an almost secret war which is described by the diplomats as a 'confrontation'. The British apply the lessons learned in the Malayan Emergency of 1948-1960. They create a military and police infrastructure which includes British and Gurkha units, local irregular trackers, and units from Malaya, Australia, and New Zealand. Elsewhere, the Indonesians make feeble seaborne and airborne landings on the Malay peninsula. The invaders are rounded up with little difficulty. The campaign in Borneo gradually loses momentum and the conflict comes to an end in August 1960. The discredited President Sukarno is forced to resign from office a few months later.
1970: Fiji becomes an independent State within the Commonwealth but, in 1987, voluntarily leaves it after a series of internal coups by the military.
1975: Papua New Guinea, which since 1905 has been administered by Australia, becomes an independent State within the Commonwealth.
1992: having been established in the Philippines since 1898. the Americans break the last links by withdrawing from their naval and aviation bases in the islands.

CEYLON

THE MILITARY HISTORY OF CEYLON
An Outline
Anton Muttukumaru * Navrang, New Delhi, 1987. Black, gold, 9.75 x 6.25, -/227. 4 mono phots (of poor quality), 4 maps, list of Errata, Bibliography, no appendixes, Index.
* As the title suggests, this book covers the entire military history of Ceylon over many centuries. The author records the repeated invasions and occupations of the island by the peoples of Southern India. He then moves on to the arrival of the Portugese and the Dutch, and the island's later conquest by the British. Subsequent Chapters contain information regarding several locally-raised units - Ceylon Rifle Regt, Ceylon Mounted Rifles, Ceylon Light Infantry Volunteers, Ceylon Medical Corps, the Ceylon Defence Force. These passages are not intended as 'unit histories' but they do provide material useful to the researcher because some are barely mentioned elsewhere. The narrative is erudite and academic in tone, but is clear and easy to follow. The format is facsimile type-script, badly reproduced on flimsy paper and bound in a workmanlike casing. Not a thing of great beauty. R/2 V/4. RMAS. RP.

THE KANDYAN WARS
The British Army in Ceylon
Geoffrey Powell * Ebenezer Bayliss & Son Ltd, Worcester, for Leo Cooper Ltd, 1973. Purple, gold, 8.75 x 5.5, -/319. 29 mono phots, 3 maps (2 printed in the text, one on the front end-paper), Glossary, Bibliography, Chapter Notes & Sources, no appendixes, Index.
* This is the dramatic, often bloody, story of how Ceylon came to be one of the smaller but most dazzling jewels in the Crown of Empire. The author describes the arrival of the Portuguese in 1505, their expulsion by the Dutch in 1656, the first British attempt to gain possession of Trincomalee in 1782, and the defeat of the Dutch in 1795. The bulk of the narrative deals with the efforts of the British and Presidency Armies to subjugate the inhabitants of the island - a campaign not concluded until 1818. Useful background reading. R/1 V/4. RCSL. RP.

HIS MAJESTY'S REGIMENT DE MEURON
Julian James Cotton * Printed by The City Press, Calcutta, for the author, 1903. Red, gold, 9.0 x 5.5, -/43. No ills, no maps, no appendixes, no Index.
* A readable and informative history, doubtless the only one ever written, of this Swiss professional mercenary unit founded by Charles Daniel de Meuron, at Neufchatel, in 1781. The Regt was funded by the Dutch East Indies Company for service in defence of its interests in Ceylon. When the island was captured by the British in 1795, de Meuron negotiated successfully for the transfer of his entire Regt into Crown service. Four years later it took part, under the command of Col Arthur Wellesley, in the assault at Seringapatam. Subsequently it served in North America, but was then disbanded in 1817. The narrative refers to many named officers, and gives details of numerical strengths and national compositions at different dates. R/5 V/4. SSL. TA.

THE HISTORY OF THE CEYLON GARRISON ARTILLERY
Formerly Ceylon Artillery Volunteers
Sgt V Wijeyesekera and Sgt Ondapji * Times of Ceylon Press Ltd, Colombo, n.d. (c.1952). Soft card, light blue, black, Regtl crest, 12.0 x 9.0, -/101. Fp, 39 mono phots, no maps, Index. Apps: Roll of Honour, H&A, list of former officers, lists of SNCOs and ORs, note on the Instructions for War Service Mobilisation.
* A straightforward account of the unit's activities from inception in 1888 through to 1952. The text relies mainly upon Regtl Orders and the Regtl Diary, and is therefore somewhat dry and colourless. R/4 V/4. IWM/AMOT. PJE/JMAT.

REGIMENTAL ROLL OF THE CEYLON MOUNTED RIFLES
Raised as the Ceylon Mounted Infantry, a Mounted Company of the Ceylon Light Infantry, by the Late Colonel Evelyn Gordon Reeves VD, on the 12th July 1892, Disbanded 30th September 1938
Anon * Publication details not shown, n.d. (c.1939). Blue, silver, CMR crest, 7.5 x 5.5, iv/70. One mono phot, no maps, no appendixes, no Index.
* The first five pages provide a very condensed narrative history of the unit (for the period stated in the sub-title). The Regt was a part-time Volunteer force, with a European membership and trained for local defence and IS duties. Many of its officers and men attested for overseas service during the South African War (1899 -1902) and the Great War (1914-1918). On those occasions they served as contingents of Ceylon Mounted Infantry. The bulk of the book is devoted to a listing of every member of the CMR between 1898 and 1938. The information is arranged under two headings - a numerical roll (according to each man's Regtl service number), and alphabetically (by surname, irrespective of rank). It is frustrating that the lists do not give any details of those who served in the Boer War or in WWI. Similarly, the references to the CMI are very sparse. The book may be of use to a genealogist. Certainly, as a 'collectable', it is very rare. R/5 V/2. PC. NH.

THE HISTORY OF THE CEYLON LIGHT INFANTRY
Oscar Abey-Ratna * The Ceylon Daily News, Colombo, 1945. Grey, blue, CLI crest, 8.75 x 6.5, v/246. One cld ill (the Colours), 7 mono phots (portraits), no maps, no Index. Apps: unit nominal rolls (at raising in 1881 and at various dates thereafter), notes on the Regtl march, bugle calls and the Colours.
* A history of the Regt from 1881, when it was formed as the Ceylon Volunteers, through to its transformation as the CLI, then through to 1940. Compiled mainly from Regtl Records and Orders, it is a dry account of peacetime Volunteer soldiering, with all the main events neatly presented. Lists of personnel are scattered throughout the text and these would be useful to a genealogist. R/5 V/3. RCSL. PJE.

STANDING ORDERS OF THE CEYLON PLANTER'S RIFLE CORPS
Anon * Miller & Co Ltd, Kandy (presumably for the Corps), 1928. Green, gold, Regtl crest, 5.75 x 4.5, ii/109. No ills, no maps, no Index. Apps: H&A, lists of former COs and other officers, idem SNCOs, Dress Regulations, winners of shooting awards.
* Apart from the usual Regulations found in publications of this type, the book contains a complete nominal roll of members for the year 1928 and two rolls which would assist the researcher. These name all those members who volunteered for service in South Africa (1899-1902) and in the Great War (1914-1919), with details of casualties and decorations. An extremely rare item, and of great interest to any medal collector lucky enough to acquire a copy. R/5 V/3. PC. EGV.
Note: the example seen contains a pasted-in Errata slip, but the printing errors which it mentions are of a very minor nature.

THE HISTORY OF THE CEYLON ARMY MEDICAL CORPS
Sidney F Jayawardene * No publication details shown, Ceylon, n.d. (c.1953). Soft card, off-white, dark blue, 8.5 x 5.5, iv/67. 13 mono phots, no maps, no Index. Apps: 7 rolls of personnel - COs (1881-1950), officers (1881-1952), Adjutants (1881-1950), RSMs (1911-1951), all ORs (1881-1952), those who served with No 126 Ceylonese General Hospital (1942-1946), notes on authorised CAMC establishments, notes on 'Other Ranks who served in the Unit ... who have distinguished themselves in their civilian careers'.
* To quote from the Foreword by Andreas Nell: 'This brochure has been compiled to tell future generations of officers, non-commissioned officers and privates of the traditions and achievements that the Medical Corps looks to them to maintain'. The Corps was originally the Bearer Company of the Ceylon Light Infantry Volunteers. This is an unadorned record of facts and names, lacking either human interest or historical perspective. R/5 V/3. RCSL. TAB.

POLICE

THE HISTORY OF THE CEYLON POLICE
Volume I : 1795-1870
G K Pippet * The Times of Ceylon Co Ltd, Colombo, n.d. (c.1938). Buff, blue, Force badge, 8.5 x 5.5, xii/372. Fp, large number of portrait mono phots of police officers, no maps, Index. Apps: numerous, incl H&A, notes on Police Ordnances, Standing Instructions, etc.
* A very detailed coverage of the early history, packed with factual information, but deadly dull and lacking in colour. R/4 V/4. IOL. JA.

THE HISTORY OF THE CEYLON POLICE
Volume II : 1866-1913
A C Dep * The Times of Ceylon Co Ltd, Colombo, for the Police Amenities Fund, n.d. (c.1969). Light buff, blue, Force badge, 8.5 x 5.5, viii/527. Fp, large number of sketches and portraits of officers, no maps, Index. Apps: verbatim reproductions of various Police Ordnances, Standing Instructions, etc (of only limited interest).
* Like Volume I, this is a very detailed account of the development and work of the Force during the stated period. However, in contrast with the first volume, this book is written with verve and colour. Both the style and the content are much more stimulating, with abundant information regarding the services of individual named officers. R/4 V/5. IOL. JA.

BURMA

A great many books have been written about military operations in Burma. The Anglo-Burmese wars of the 19th Century and the long-range penetration operations pioneered by Brig Orde Wingate in 1943 are well recorded, but few of these books can be described as 'unit histories'. They do not, therefore, come within the scope of this bibliography.

The few publications which do relate directly to Burma-raised Corps or Regiments are noted below. Additionally, three generalised accounts have been listed as examples of their genre. For a historical overview, reference should be made to BRITISH RULE IN BURMA, 1824-1942, by G E Harvey (Faber & Faber, London, 1946). The period 1942-1946 is covered admirably in DEFEAT INTO VICTORY, by Field Marshal Sir William Slim (Cassell, London, 1956). The maps in Slim's book are particularly good. An even more detailed account is to be found in Volumes II and III of THE WAR AGAINST JAPAN, by Maj Gen S Woodburn Kirby CB CMG CIE (HMSO, London, 1958). Volume II deals with (amongst other subjects) the first Chindit campaign, and Volume III the second. Kirby's account underscores the fact that the 'forgotten war' in Burma was fought largely by non-European troops. About eighty percent were Indian Army, Indian States Forces, Royal Nepalese Army, Royal West African Frontier Force, King's African Rifles, Rhodesian African Rifles, Northern Rhodesia Regiment, Burma Rifles, and local levies.

Primary source documents are to be found in the Oriental & India Office Collections of the British Library (the former India Office Library) in the series L/MIL/17/7 'Burma Army'. Covering events from 1938 to 1946, they include various official documents relating to military affairs, and a run of the quarterly BURMA ARMY LIST for the period April 1938 to July 1941 (with a single volume for 1943).

To achieve a balanced interpretation of the 1942-1945 campaign, researchers are advised to consult American bibliographic sources. The 14th Army was at times heavily dependent upon the US Army Air Force for inward supply and outward casualty evacuation (techniques created and developed to a remarkable standard in Burma by the Americans and by the Royal Air Force). Due account must be taken also of the Chinese and US Army soldiers who fought an even more forgotten war in the north of Burma under the command of General Joseph 'Vinegar Joe' Stillwell.

HISTORY OF THE CHIN HILLS BATTALION, BURMA MILITARY POLICE

Capt A C Moore * Published in Falam, 1934, no other details shown. Green boards, brown spine, blind, 8.0 x 6.0, iii/47. Fp, one other mono phot, 8 cld ills, no maps, no Index. Apps: list of former COs.

* A readable but very condensed history covering the period 1894-1934. The unit was one of many which constituted the Burma Military Police until 1937 when the country was separated from India. The Chin Hills Bn then became part of the Burma Frontier Force. The rank and file were Gurkhas, recruited directly from Nepal. The author was at one time the Commandant. R/5 V/3. NAM. PJE.

STANDING ORDERS OF THE SECOND BATTALION, THE BURMA RIFLES
With a Short Record of the Battalion

Anon * Gale & Polden Ltd, Aldershot, for the Bn, 1948. Green, gold, Regtl device on the front cover and spine (Peacock and Burma Rifles motif), 9.25 x 6.5, ix/141. No ills, no maps, no appendixes, no Index.

* The book is arranged in three sections - Standing Orders (Peace), Standing Orders (War), and a Short Record of the Battalion. The latter consists of nine pages divided into seven parts - Bn history in diary form (1917-1948), class composition, Battle Honours, H&A (WWII, all ranks), and various lists of officers (1917-1948). Despite its brevity, the 'Short Record' element is useful because so little has ever been written about the Burma Rifles. The 2nd Bn was the only Bn not disbanded at the time of the Japanese invasion. R/4 V/3. NAM. PJE/CJP.

AMIABLE ASSASSINS
The Story of the Kachin Levies
I Fellowes-Gordon * Robert Hale Ltd, London, 1957. Green, gold, 9.0 x 6.0, -/159. 20 mono phots, no maps, no appendixes, no Index.
* Written almost in the form of a novel, this is a generalised account of the Kachin Levies in WWII. R/2 V/2. NAM. PJE.

THE BATTLE FOR NAW SENG'S KINGDOM
General Stillwell's North Burma Campaign and its Aftermath
Ian Fellowes-Gordon * Pitman Press, Bath, for Leo Cooper Ltd, London, 1971. Green, gold, 8.5 x 5.5, x/176. 20 mono phots, 2 maps (one printed in the text, one on the end-papers), no appendixes, no Index.
* Written by the same author as noted in the preceding entry, this book also fails to meet the needs of some specialist researchers. It contains too many digressions regarding the Burma campaign in general and the characters of Stillwell, Chiang Kai-Shek, Slim and Wingate in particular. Further, the lack of an Index and any appendixes or maps detract from what could have been an exemplary unit history (if the author had chosen to follow that route). However, as far as it goes, the book is an interesting account of the Kachin Levies, a small irregular force of 600 hill tribesmen raised in August 1942 by Lieut Col W M F Gamble MC and organised into five Companies. Some of its recruits had served previously with the Burma Rifles and the Burma Military Police, but the majority had no military experience. Motivated by a deep hatred of the Japanese invaders, they fought with immense ferocity and operated in a wide range of roles - supporting the Chinese-American forces as trackers, guides, interpreters, gatherers of intelligence and as clandestine raiders. Most of their officers - British and Anglo-Burman - had worked for years as forestry managers in North Burma, so all ranks were completely familiar with the operational environment. The levels of education amongst the Kachin were too low for them to serve as officers, but officer numbers were augmented by a number of Karen (from further south). They were equally loyal to the Crown and had served formerly with the Governor's Body Guard. The author himself served with the Levies, initially as a Company Commander and later in overall command. His coverage of operations is lucid and informative.
R/2 V/3. PC. JRStA.
Note: the Naw Seng named in the book's title was a Subedar who served with the Kachin Levies throughout the campaign and was twice decorated with the Burma Gallantry Medal. He survived the war and in 1971 was still fighting for independence for his people.

THE JUNGLE IN ARMS
Lieut Col Balfour Oatts DSO * William Kimber, London, 1962. Dark grey, gold, 8.75 x 5.5, -/207. No ills, one map, no appendixes, no Index.
* An excellent account of the author's experiences in WWII with the Chin Hills Bn of the Burma Frontier Force, then as CO of the Western (Chin) Levies and, lastly, with the newly-formed 1st and 2nd Chin Rifles. He also makes interesting references to the Burma Rifles, to 7/14th Punjab Regt, and to Za Hu's 'Forty Thieves' (a British-backed semi-autonomous irregular force led by a retired Chin bandit, Za Hu, whose one ambition was to kill every Japanese soldier he could find, preferably in hand-to-hand combat). Despite being an autobiography, and despite lacking an Index or any appendixes, the book is a prime source of reference. The author is no respecter of persons. He makes interesting references to many other officers and also to the Indian National Army. The period covered is 1940 to 1946. R/3 V/4. CFHT. SODW.

THE 'WASBIES'
The Story of the Women's Auxiliary Service (Burma)
Anon * War Facts Press, London, n.d. (c.1947). Soft card, red, black, 'Chinthe' badge, 8.75 x 5.75, -/80. Fp, 33 mono phots, 39 line drawings (formation and unit badges), 3 maps (one printed in the text, two on the end-papers), no Index. Apps: unit nominal roll (all ranks, c.1944).
* Eminently readable, and full of good reference material. Formed on 16 January 1942, from British (European) ladies then resident in Burma, it briefly provided the military with drivers, telephonists, office staff, etc. Following the retreat to India, the Service was restructured as a 'canteen and troops welfare' organisation. Some Eurasian (Anglo-Indian and Anglo-Burmese) ladies joined at that time. A number of detachments of the WAS(B) later followed the army back into Burma, working in base and forward areas alike. R/5 V/3. PC. TK-C.

General Accounts

A HELL OF A LICKING
The Retreat from Burma, 1941-1942
James Lunt (Major General) * Collins, London, 1986. Black, gold, 9.0 x 5.75, xxiii/318. 16 mono phots, 10 maps (8 printed in the text, 2 on the end-papers), Glossary, Bibliography, Chapter Notes, no appendixes, Index.
* The author was serving with the Burma Rifles at the time of the Japanese invasion. The book is primarily an account of his personal experiences during the ensuing chaos and the tragic exodus of military and civilian personnel, mainly on foot, from Burma to India. It includes much useful material on the subject of soldiering with the Burma Rifles both in peacetime and in wartime, and a sympathetic evaluation of the Rifles as a fighting force. R/2 V/4. NAM. RP.
Note: reprinted in soft covers by David & Charles, Newton Abbot, Devon, 1989. Several other books have been written about this unhappy episode in the Empire's history, one of the best known being THE LONG RETREAT, by Tim Carew (Hamish Hamilton, London, 1969, plus later reprints). Another is BEFORE THE DAWN, by Brig John Smyth VC (Cassell, London, 1957). Smyth was the officer blamed for the disaster at the Sittang Bridge. A third recommended source is MOUNTAIN BATTERY, by Pat Carmichael (Devin Books, Bournemouth, 1983 - vide the Index of Authors). In each case, the author begins with the Japanese invasion of southern Burma in mid-December, 1941. The Japanese intention was to seize the Irrawaddy oilfields, and to cut the Burma Road - the artery by which the Americans were supplying Chiang Kai-shek in southern China. General Iidas' 15th Army of 35,000 men proceeded to trounce the 17th Indian Division and the ill-equipped under-trained 1st Burma Division. By mid-April of 1942, the British position in Burma had become untenable, and the decision was made to pull back to the border with the Indian province of Assam. The retreat commenced on 26 April under conditions of great disorder. The monsoons, which would make any movement in the roadless jungle-covered hills extremely difficult, were expected only three weeks later, and this factor added to the desperation of the escaping civilians and fragmented military units.

THE CHINDIT WAR
The Campaign in Burma, 1944
Shelford Bidwell * Hodder & Stoughton, London, 1979. Brown, gold, 9.5 x 6.25, -/304. 33 mono phots, 11 maps, no appendixes, Bibliography, Chapter Notes, Index.
* One of the most comprehensive and analytical unofficial histories of the Chindits (the British, Gurkha, and Nigerian formations inspired by Wingate and which operated deep behind Japanese front lines). The author describes many specific actions and individual acts of gallantry, but he is concerned mainly with the entire concept and conduct of the two Chindit campaigns. Particularly helpful are his explanations of the troubled interface between the Chindits and their American and Chinese allies operating in North Burma. He is candid in his assessments and makes it clear that the troops engaged were asked to do too much for too long. R/1 V/4. DCLS/NAM. RP/PJE.

THE FORGOTTEN WAR
The British Army in the Far East, 1941-1945
David Smurthwaite (as editor) * National Army Museum, London, 1992. Illustrated stiff card, sepia, 'Indian and African troops in the jungle' motif, 11.5 x 8.0, iii/204. Many mono phots, 21 cld ills (medals, unit insignia, weapons, etc), 5 line drawings, 6 maps, Bibliography, Index. Apps: list of constributors, chronology.
* A wide-ranging superficial retrospective, published to commemorate the services of the Empire's soldiers in the east in WWII. The sub-title is to be ignored. The book is directed at Burma in particular rather than the Far East in general. Even more misleading is the reference to the British Army. The contents of the book do include, in fact, excellent accounts of the Indian and Colonial African troops who carried eighty percent of the burden in that theatre. Some of the picture captions are equally inaccurate. These careless aberrations aside, the book is a very useful quick guide, and the illustrations and maps are excellent.
R/1 V/3. NAM. RP.
Note: the chapter devoted to the role of the Colonial African troops in Burma was written by John Hamilton, a major contributor to this bibliography. His account is particularly good for its descriptions of the Royal West African Frontier Force.

MALAY STATES & SINGAPORE

BRITISH AND INDIAN ARMIES IN THE EAST INDIES (1685-1935)
Alan G Harfield * Picton Publishing (Chippenham) Ltd, Chippenham, UK, 1984. Dark green, gold, 8.5 x 6.0, xv/411. Fp, 102 mono phots, 8 cld ills, 13 maps (12 printed in the text, one on the end-papers), Glossary, Bibliography (extensive), Index. Apps: list of units which served as garrison troops in the Settlements of Penang, Malacca and Singapore (1805-1915), list of military graves and monuments in the Straits Settlements (1786-1899), various medal rolls and muster lists.
* A massively researched account of the British conquest, settlement and administration of the East Indies (comprising Singapore, Malaya, Java, Sumatra, Sarawak, etc). This is not a Regtl history but a goldmine for historians, genealogists, and medal collectors. The narrative is so stuffed with detail that it is difficult to follow. However, the style of presentation, backed by a good Index, enables the reader to find what he needs. An excellent production. R/1 V/5. PC. RP.

HISTORY OF THE MALAY STATES GUIDES, 1873-1919
Inder Singh s/o Sgt Ram Singh * Cathay Printers, Penang, n.d. (c.1965). Illustrated soft card, 'Sergeants with Colours' motif, 8.5 x 5.5, -/122. Fp, 14 mono phots, one map, Glossary, Bibliography, no Index. Apps: list of former COs, idem officers, idem Subedar Majors, idem Granthis (priests), notes on the Aden Field Force, notes on food, costumes, sport, Sikh history, etc.
* The only known record of this Indian-recruited Malay States unit from formation to disbandment. Strong on biographical information, but best read in conjunction with Harfield's work (vide preceding entry). R/4 V/3. PC. JLC.

THE MALAY REGIMENT
M C ff Sheppard * Dept of Public Relations Malay Peninsula, Kuala Lumpur, 1947. Illustrated stiff card, 'view of Port Dickson' motif, deep pink, 9.5 x 7.0, -/52. 28 mono phots, 2 line drawings, 3 maps (one of Malaya tipped in, one of Singapore tipped in, one printed in the text), no Index. Apps: Roll of Honour (KIA and WIA for all ranks, European and Malay, with details of where, when, how), H&A (all ranks), list of all British officers serving with the Regt in February 1942, idem all Malay officers holding High Commissioner's Commissions (with details of their post-war promotions if applicable).
* The Foreword is written by Maj Gen A E Percival who surrendered Singapore to the Japanese in 1942. This is a story of poor preparation, fierce resistance and ultimate captivity. The book is limited in its scope and produced to post-war 'utility' standards, but it is an invaluable source for its appendixes of personnel. Many founder members of the Regt (1933) appear in the group photographs and are named in the captions. R/4 V/4. RMAS. JRS/RP.

HISTORY OF THE MALAY REGIMENT, 1933-1942
Dol Ramli * Publisher's details not clear. Seemingly written by Dol Ramli in Singapore in 1955 as an academic exercise, subsequently printed by Life Printers of Kuala Lumpur in 1963. Green, gold, Regtl crest, 10.5 x 7.0, vi/150. 7 mono phots, 10 maps, Index. Apps: list of former COs (with biographical notes), list of former officers, H&A, nominal rolls, details of establishment and rates of pay.
* A condensed account from the original raising of the Regt through to the time of the Japanese invasion. This book contains more historical material than the book by Sheppard (vide preceding entry), but it has fewer illustrations and details of personnel. Excellent in its own way. R/4 V/4. AMOT. RP.

A HISTORY OF THE SINGAPORE VOLUNTEER CORPS, 1854-1937
Being also an Historical Account of Volunteering in Malaya
Capt T M Winsley * Govt Printing Office, Singapore, 1938. Soft card, light green, red, 9.5 x 7.5, xvii/205. Fp, 51 mono phots, one cld ill, 42 small line drawings (incl 32 of insignia), no maps, Index. Apps: H&A, list of former COs, list of casualties for the Singapore Mutiny, letters, Warrants, fortifications, Colours, etc.

* This is the only published history of the SVC. It contains much useful information also regarding the Volunteers of the Federated Malay States and the Straits Settlements. Having been published in 1938, it makes no reference to the role of the Volunteers when the Japanese invaded. R/4 V/4. PC. JLC.
Note: reprinted in 1978 without amendment to the text but with the addition of a 'Foreword to the Second Edition'.

THE SINGAPORE ARTILLERY - 100th YEAR COMMEMORATIVE BOOK
In Oriente Primus - First in the Orient
Anon * Stamford Press Pte Ltd, Singapore, for the Singapore Artillery Committee, 1988. Blue, gold, '155 mm field howitzer' motif, 11.75 x 8.5, xiii/184. 134 mono phots, 29 cld ills, 10 line drawings, 3 maps, no appendixes, no Index.
* Although intended mainly for those who had served with the post-Independence Singapore Armed Forces, the book does have five chapters devoted to the Empire period. Specifically, it traces the story of the Singapore Volunteer Corps Artillery, one of the earliest Volunteer units in the Far East. The narrative and supporting illustrations are arranged in chronological order for the period 1888-1988, but an Index and some appendixes would have enhanced the book's research value.
R/3 V/3. PC. AH.

BATTALION AT WAR - SINGAPORE 1942
Michael Moore * Gliddon Books, Norwich, UK, 1988. Dark blue, gold, Regtl crest, 9.5 x 6.75, xv/164. Fp, 48 mono phots, 9 maps (8 printed in the text, one on the end-papers), Bibliography, Index. Apps: Roll of Honour (KIA and WIA), 'Batttles and Honours' (from 1869), Orders of Battle (for 1st Cambridgeshire Regt, 18th British Division, Malaya Command, and for the Japanese Army).
* The Battalion of the book's title was 1st Bn Cambridgeshire Regt. The author, a Platoon Sergeant, tells the story of the Bn's departure from the UK, its arrival in Singapore, the conditions which it found there, the preparations for battle, and its fierce engagements with the enemy. He and other survivors later worked on the Burma-Siam railway. The book is one of the few accounts of the defence of Singapore as viewed by a front-line soldier. It includes interesting observations on the behaviour of Indian, Australian and other British troops in battle and in captivity. R/3 V/4. PC. JDB.

THE HEROES
Ronald McKie * Angus & Robertson, Sydney, 1960. Black, gold, 8.5 x 5.5, vi/235. No ills, 4 maps, no Index. Apps: muster rolls for Operations Jaywick and Rimau.
* 'Z' Special Unit was formed by Special Operations Australia in 1942. This is the story of its first major clandestine raid (Operation Jaywick), a sea-borne attack against Japanese shipping in Singapore harbour in September 1943. The raid was outstandingly successful. A second such attack, Operation Rimau, was mounted twelve months later and was a total disaster. Of the fifteen Australians and eight British servicemen who took part, not one survived. The gripping narrative is based upon the memories of Jaywick participants and contemporary secret records.
R/1 V/4. ANL. MCND'A.

THE HEROES OF RIMAU
Unravelling the Mystery of one of the World's most Daring Raids
Maj Tom Hall and Lynette Ramsay Silver * Sally Milner Publishing Pty Ltd, Birchgrove, NSW, 1990. Black, white, 9.5 x 7.5, vi/314. 50 mono phots, 8 maps, Bibliography, Index. Apps: 'The Case of Maj Gen H Gordon-Bennett', 'The Case of Maj Seymour Bingham'.
* Like the preceding entry (McKie), this book deals with the abortive second 'special forces' raid on Singapore harbour. However, having been written thirty years later, it contains many additional facts. In particular, it investigates the reasons behind the Australian Government's continuing refusal to grant any posthumous awards to those who died at the hands of the Japanese. Maj Hall also adds fresh detail to the story of Operation Jaywick (the first sortie). R/1 V/4. PC. PS.

THE LONG, LONG WAR
The Emergency in Malaya, 1948-1960
Richard Clutterbuck * Cassell & Co, London, 1967. Green, silver, 8.5 x 5.5, xiv/206. No ills, 7 maps and diagrams (indexed), no appendixes, Glossary, Bibliography, Index.
* A comprehensive account, written in a style which is blunt and always to the point. The narrative is arranged in three parts - 'Defensive' (1945-1951), 'Offensive' (1951-1955), and 'Victory' (1955-1960). Some readers will be frustrated by the fact that so few units or personnel are identified in the narrative, but the author does provide a good overview of the causes, progress and conclusion of a pioneering campaign. Many of the lessons learned in Malaya were later used with good effect in Kenya, Cyprus, Borneo, and Northern Ireland. R/2 V/4. DCLS. RP.

AUSTRALIA AND THE COMMONWEALTH IN THE MALAYA EMERGENCY, 1948-1960
Lieut Col C Smith AM * Publisher's details not shown, Melbourne, 1989. Soft card, green, black, 11.5 x 8.25, iv/125. 8 mono phots, one map, no Index. Apps: Roll of Australians who received the General Service Medal with the clasp 'Malaya', idem those with the clasp 'Brunei', locations of burials in Malaya.
* Seven thousand Australian servicemen were engaged in the Malaya Emergency. This book is essentially a list of their names, hence it is useful mainly to medal collectors. However, the brief narrative does include helpful references to some of the units engaged - 1st RAR, 2nd RAR, 3rd RAR, RAASC, RAA, and RAAF.
R/1 V/2. PC. PS.

Police

THE HISTORY OF THE MALAYAN POLICE
Patrick Morrah * Tien Wah Press, for the Malayan Branch of the Royal Asiatic Society, Singapore, 1968. Soft card, green, black, 9.5 x 6.25, -/172. Fp, 6 mono phots, no maps, Bibliography, footnotes, no appendixes, no Index.
* The material in this book was first published in quarterly instalments in THE MALAYAN POLICE JOURNAL, between 1954 and 1958. It was subsequently reprinted in its entirety in 1968 as No 202 of a series published under the generic heading THE JOURNAL OF THE MALAYAN BRANCH OF THE ROYAL ASIATIC SOCIETY. With 172 pages, it is in fact a substantial book-size work in its own right. The author traces the history of the police organisation in Malaya and Singapore from the earliest days (but with Singapore being touched upon only in those contexts when the island's history is inseparable from that of the peninsula). The early chapters are based upon various archival sources, the later chapters have the recollections of former and serving officers woven in. R/3 V/4. RCSL. TAB.

SPEARHEAD IN MALAYA
J W G Moran * Peter Davies, London, 1959. Green, 8.0 x 5.5, -/288. One mono phot (group of personnel), no maps, no Index. Apps: H&A.
* An autobiographical account of service with the Malayan Police during the years 1948 to 1956. It concentrates upon the work of the Jungle Companies and the way in which it was coordinated with that of the military and the civil administration.
R/2 V/3. DCLS. RP.
Note: the same author wrote a further account of his experiences with Police Jungle Companies under the title THE CAMP ACROSS THE RIVER (published in 1961, also by Peter Davies, London).

THE JUNGLE BEAT
Fighting Terrorists in Malaya, 1952-1961
Roy Follows ('with Hugh Popham') * Cassell, London, 1990. Grey, gold, 9.25 x 6.0, -/152. 11 mono phots, one map, Glossary, Bibliography, no appendixes, Index.
* Like the preceding entry, this is a personal account of five-and-a-half years of service with the Malayan Police. Vividly phrased, the narrative describes the role of the Jungle Companies and the reorganisation of his own 10th Coy, with two

other such Coys, to form the 4th Field Police. Jungle operations against the CT (Communist Terrorists) in the northern parts of the country (Kelentan and Perak), and later in the south (Johore), are described in clear and interesting detail. In 1958, the author transferred from this work to take up an appointment with the Malayan Maritime Police (which receives some mention here). His account ends in 1961. The illustrations are good, and they include one captioned group of Police personnel. R/2 V/3. ADFA. MCND'A.

Irregular Forces

RED STAR OVER MALAYA
Resistance and Social Conflict During and After the Japanese Occupation of Malaya 1941-1946
Cheeah Boon Kheng * Singapore University Press, National University of Singapore, 1983. Seen in library binding, 8.5 x 5.5, xviii/366. 18 mono phots, 2 sketches, 3 maps, Glossary, Chapter Notes, Bibliography, Index. Apps: verbatim extracts from Japanese memoranda and public statements, statement by the Selangor State Committee of the Communist Party of Malaya, Japanese statistics regarding their own casualties (as caused by the MPAJA).
* This is the only known authoritative account of what happened in Malaya during the Japanese occupation. Very lucidly written, it is massively researched. The author draws upon an awe-inspiring range of sources - British, Malayan, Australian, and Japanese - published, unpublished, and oral. He describes the origins, formation, organisation and operations of all eight Regts of the MPAJA (Malayan People's Anti-Japanese Army), the various bandit gangs, the Triads, and the British-formed Dalforce and Force 136. All of these were active from the earliest days. He then explores the emergence and role of the Malay Resistance (formed in December 1944) and the story of the Askar Melayu Setia and the Tentera Wataniah. From the invader's perspective, he covers the KMM (Kestuan Melayu Muda, the Fifth Column which helped the Japanese to overrun the peninsula in early 1942). Having established themselves, the Japanese raised various local forces - the Heiho, the Giyu Gun, the Giyu Tai, the Indian National Army, and the Special Police - to help them find and fight the guerilla units operating in the jungle. He concludes with the events following the Japanese surrender when the guerillas emerged into the light - 'men and women, gaunt, pale and deathly-looking from living in the jungle'. Apart from being an absorbing account of endurance and courage in the Allied cause, the book is an important counter to post-war British propaganda which suggested that the guerillas had done little more during the occupation than prepare themselves for their campaign of 1948-1960.
R/3 V/5. CFHT. SODW.

Note: additional sources for Malaya and Singapore are:

THE JUNGLE IS NEUTRAL, by F Spencer-Chapman (Chatto & Windus, London, 1953)
SHOOT TO KILL, by Richard Meirs (Faber & Faber, London, 1959)
MALAYA, THE COMMUNIST INSURGENT WAR, by Edgar O'Ballance (Faber & Faber, London, 1966)
THE WAR OF THE SPRINGING TIGERS, by Gerald Carr (Osprey, London, 1975)
TEMPLER, TIGER OF MALAYA, by J Cloake (Harrap, London, 1985)
FIGHTING FIT, THE SINGAPORE ARMED FORCES, by Mickey Chang (Times Editions Pte Ltd, Singapore, 1990). This substantial work (240 pages) is primarily a prestige and recruiting publication for the modern Singapore Armed Forces. However, one chapter is devoted to the history of the Singapore Volunteer Corps which existed in various forms from 1854 to 1957 (when the Singapore Infantry Regiment was formed).

BRUNEI AND BORNEO

SARAWAK LONG AGO
W J Chater * Borneo Literature Bureau, Kuching, 1969. Illustrated soft card, purple, white, 7.25 x 5.25, iii/120. 18 mono phots, 15 line drawings, 2 maps, no appendixes, no Index.
* This book covers all aspects of 'old' Sarawak, so the military content is no more than coincidental. However, it is the only known published record of The Sarawak Fortmen (1846–1879) and The Sarawak Rangers (1862–1932). The story of the two units is intermingled with the history of the Brooke family and the development of Kuching. Of additional interest are the references to Fort Margherita, Fort Alice, and the Sarawak Rangers Philippino Band. R/5 V/2. PC. AH.

THE ROYAL BRUNEI MALAY REGIMENT, 1961–1976
Maj A G Harfield * The Star Press, Bandar Seri Begawan, Brunei, 1977. Green, gold, RBMR badge, 10.25 x 7.25, xv/170. Fps (3, cld), 56 mono phots, no maps, no Index. Apps: list of senior officers (at 31.12.1976), nominal roll of the original sixty recruits.
* When the present State of Malaysia was formed in 1961, the Sultan of Brunei declined the invitation to become part of it. This led to the decision to raise an independent Brunein force, with responsibilities for IS and ceremonial duties. Trained and administered initially by the Malaysian Army, the RBMR had attained, by 1976, a number of assets which do not normally come within the compass of a 'regiment'. Additionally to the two Infantry Bns, an HQ Coy, and a pipe band, it had a flotilla of coastal patrol vessels and an Air Wing equipped with helicopters and fixed wing aircraft (the Sultan's Flight). The book contains much detail on the subjects of Dress, the Colours, and ceremonial duties. Other chapters describe active services against Indonesian infiltrators in 1966 and occasional combined exercises with the British Army in Hong Kong. R/2 V/4. NAM. RP.
Note: 2000 copies printed, 500 in English and 1500 in Brunei Malay.

'Z' SPECIAL UNIT'S SECRET WAR
Operation Semut 1 – Soldiering with the Head-hunters in Borneo
Bob Long * Australian Print Group, Maryborough, Victoria, 1989. Black, silver, 'Bayonet' motif, 9.5 x 6.0, –/608. 53 mono phots, 18 maps, Glossary, Index. Apps: 'History of Special Duties Flight 200', texts of operational orders and reports.
* An astonishing and excellently presented account of clandestine Australian units operating behind Japanese lines in various parts of the South West Pacific. The 'Z' Special Unit was engaged in sabotage, intelligence gathering, and the destruction of Japanese communications. Operation Semut 1 was a parachute-borne attack which, with the support of local irregular forces, killed more than one thousand Japanese soldiers in Borneo in the closing months of the war. A remarkable story, with well captioned photographs and good maps. R/1 V/5. ANL. MCND'A.
Note: a good additional source is AND TOMORROW FREEDOM, by Sheila Ross (Allen & Unwin, North Sydney, 1989). This book describes the adventures of a group of men of the 2/10th Australian Field Regt who, after 18 months of POW, escaped from Borneo to the Southern Philippines. There they operated against the Japanese with local guerrilla bands until early 1945. They then joined 'Z' Special Unit for the final elimination of the Japanese garrisons in Borneo.

SANDAKAN AFTER NIPPON
The Last March
Don Wall * William Brooks & Co, NSW, for the author, 1988. Green, gold, 9.75 x 6.5, x/193. More than 100 mono phots, 3 maps, Index. Apps: Roll of Honour.
* From July 1942, parties of Australian POW were sent to Sandakan, North Borneo, to build an airfield. Most of the officers were separated from the men and sent to Kuching. The soldiers, nearly 2000 of them, were deliberately worked and starved to death. Only six survived. This was the worst of the many atrocities committed against captured Australian servicemen by the Japanese Army. Their story is told

movingly and with restraint. Members of the 8th Aust Div, the prisoners came from 2/18th, 2/19th, 2/20th, 2/26th, 2/29th, and 2/30th Inf Bns, 2/4th MG Bn, 2/10th Field Ambulance, 2/10th and 2/15th Field Regts RAA, 2/10th and 2/12th Field Coys RAE, and 1st and 2nd Coys RAASC. The maps and photographs are of excellent quality, and the line drawings by Clem Seale are exceptional.
R/1 V/5. ANL. MCND'A.
Note: reference should be made also to: ABANDONED - AUSTRALIANS AT SANDAKAN, by the same author (published privately, Mona Vale, NSW, 1990), PRISONER OF WAR - AUSTRALIANS UNDER NIPPON, by Hank Nelson (Australian Broadcasting Corporation, Sydney, 1985), and IN JAPANESE HANDS - AUSTRALIAN NURSES AS PRISONERS OF WAR, by Jessie Elizabeth Simons (William Heinemann, Melbourne, 1985).

SAS - THE JUNGLE FRONTIER
22 Special Air Service Regiment in the Borneo Campaign, 1963-1966
Peter Dickens * Arms & Armour Press, London, 1983. Green, gold, 9.25 x 6.0, -/248. 39 mono phots, 5 maps, no appendixes, Glossary, Bibliography, Index.
* A highly detailed account based upon interviews with those who served. Indonesia made a determined attempt to destroy the new Federation of Malaysia (the constituent States being Malaya, Singapore, and North Borneo), and the issue was decided in the jungle border areas of the world's third largest island. This book deals not only with the work of the SAS, it also contains useful references to 3rd Royal Australian Regt, Gurkha Rifles (1/2nd, 1/6th, 2/7th, 1/10th and 2/10th), Gurkha Independent Parachute Coy, and The Cross-Border Scouts.
R/1 V/4. DCLS. RP.
Note: reference should be made also to THE UNDECLARED WAR - THE STORY OF THE INDONESIAN CONFRONTATION, 1962-1966, by H D James and D Sheil-Small (Leo Cooper, London, 1971), and KONFRONTASI, by J A Mackie (Oxford University Press, 1974).

HONG KONG

HONG KONG ECLIPSE
G B Endacott and Alan Birch * Oxford University Press, Hong Kong, 1978. Brown, gold, 8.75 x 5.75, xiv/428. Fp, 42 mono phots, 3 maps (bound in), Glossary, Index. Apps: 8 in total, all added by the Editor (Birch) to clarify the main narrative.
* A comprehensive study of Hong Kong during WWII. The chapters dealing with the Japanese assault provide a readable and straight-forward record, but with few details of individual combat experiences. The narrative covers the period from the late 1930s, when the Japanese Army was already active in South China, through to the reconstruction of Hong Kong in the late 1940s. The main theme is the Japanese occupation and its effects upon the local population, and upon the civilian internees and the military prisoners of war. R/2 V/4. PC. CGB.

CAPTIVE CHRISTMAS
The Battle for Hong Kong, December 1941
Alan Birch and Martin Cole * Po Fung Printing Co, for Heinemann Educational Books (Asia) Ltd, 1979. Illustrated soft card, 'Hong Kong under aerial attack' motif, black and white, 8.0 x 7.5, iv/179. Fp, 33 mono phots, line drawings (Regtl badges at chapter heads), one map (printed on both end-papers), Bibliography, Index. Apps: list of 'dramatis personae', list of other additional sources.
* The period covered is 8 to 25 December 1941. The narrative is a daily record of the Japanese assault and the final surrender of the Colony. It consists of an amalgam of official messages, extracts from private diaries, and eyewitness reminiscences. These are drawn from British and Japanese sources alike. Numerous individuals and their awards are mentioned in the text, and most of the units engaged receive a mention of one sort or another. There is good coverage of both major and minor incidents, many of the latter involving small isolated groups of defenders. R/3 V/4. PC. JDB.
Note: the same authors produced a sequel entitled CAPTIVE YEARS (Dah Hua Printing Press Co, for Heinemann Educational Books Asia Ltd, 1982).Of similar format to CAPTIVE CHRISTMAS, it covers the period from the surrender to the reoccupation by British forces on 30 August 1945. In addition to the many stories of individual experiences under the Japanese, CAPTIVE YEARS also has an account of the sinking of the SS Lisbon Maru in 1942 and the surrender ceremonies on 16 September 1945.

A RECORD OF THE ACTIONS OF THE HONG KONG VOLUNTEER DEFENCE CORPS IN THE BATTLE FOR HONG KONG, DECEMBER 1941
Anon ('An original member of the Corps') * Printrite, Hong Kong, 'printed and published privately as a record for those who served', 1953. Red, black, HKVDC badge, 8.25 x 5.5, ii/59. No ills, no maps, no Index. Apps: strength and casualties for each unit forming the garrison (incl sub-units of the HKVDC - artillery, infantry, transport, medical, etc, with details of KIA, WIA and MIA, all ranks), Order of Battle of the HKVDC.
* The narrative opens with a description of the defence plan and gives the name of each unit and sub-unit, its location and role, and the name of its CO. This is followed by an account of the assault on 7 December, a day-by-day coverage of the ensuing battle, and the final actions before the surrender on 25 December. Many individuals are named in the text - how they were killed, what weapons they used, the location and type of each strongpoint, and actions shared with neighbouring Regular units. At the start of the battle, the HKVDC's strength was 92 officers and 1665 ORs. Apart from the British Europeans, it comprised Chinese and Eurasians, and a variety of men of cosmopolitan origins. Although very condensed, this is said to be the most accurate record of the defence of Hong Kong and the sacrifices of HKVDC's valiant part-time soldiers. R/4 V/5. PC. JDB.
Note: a first edition was published in 1946. Two later editions, dated 1956 and 1970, have been noted. These were produced with the same text, but with soft card covers.They also contain two maps, bound in at the rear, which do not appear in the 1953 edition (as described above).

SECOND TO NONE
The Story of the Hong Kong Volunteers
Phillip Bruce * Oxford University Press, Hong Kong, 1991. Claret, gold, 8.75 x 5.75, iv/317. 54 mono phots, 2 maps (one printed in the text, one on the end-papers), no appendixes, Index.
* A broad account of the various Volunteer units which have existed intermittently from 1854 to the present day (disbandment will take place before the Chinese takeover in 1997). The Victorian period is covered in detail and the author speculates that Sun Yat-sen might have been a member in the 1890s. The troubled inter-war years are heavily illustrated with extracts from contemporary documents which give flavour to the period. The HKVDF's 'finest hour', December 1941, is described in detail, with vivid quotations from eye-witness testimony. The post-1945 period receives less attention. R/1 V/4. PC. CGB.

IN ORIENTE FIDELIS
The Army Medical Service in the Battle for Hong Kong, December 1941
P H Starling * F Bailey & Son Ltd, Gloucester, UK, for the RAMC Historical Museum, 1986. Soft card, white, black, RAMC crest, 9.5 x 7.0, i/31. Fp, 12 mono phots, 2 maps, Bibliography, Glossary, Index. Apps: Roll of Honour (with details of how died), H&A (all ranks, with biographical details), nominal roll at the time of the surrender, roll of staff (incl QAIMNS nurses) at BMH Bowen Road during captivity, nominal roll of the SS Lisbon Maru, register of graves at Stanley Military Cemetery, register of all personnel interred in the grounds of Bowen Road Hospital.
* The narrative covers the experiences of the Army's medical services during the battle and later in captivity. It describes the locations of each medical unit and its organisation. The account of the battle includes details of the massacre of RAMC personnel and others at the Salesian Mission and at St Stephen's College. There is graphic coverage also of the survivors' difficulties as POW. An essential reference source for that period. R/2 V/4. PC. JDB.

REPORT ON THE CANADIAN EXPEDITIONARY FORCE TO THE CROWN COLONY OF HONG KONG
The Rt Hon Sir Lyman P Duff GCMG * Edward Cloutier, Govt Printer, Ottawa, 1942. Paper cover, stapled, blue, black, National arms, 9.75 x 6.5, -/61. No ills, no maps, no appendixes, no Index.
* Following the effective destruction of Canadian units in the defence of Hong Kong, a Royal Commission was appointed to investigate the circumstances leading to the despatch of those troops and their deployment on the island by the British. The force sailed from Vancouver on 27 October 1941 and reached Hong Kong on 16 November. Its officers were given to understand that they would have ample time in which to catch up with the training in which their soldiers were deficient. They were also told that they would in due course receive mortars, anti-tank weapons and transport. In the event, the Canadians went into battle three weeks later without any vehicles and without any support weapons. R/4 V/3. PC. JRD.

THE ROYAL RIFLES OF CANADA IN HONG KONG, 1941-1945
Capt Grant S Garneau and Capt E L Hurd * Progressive Publications (1970) Inc, Quebec, for the Hong Kong Veterans' Assn of Canada, 1980. Rifle green, red, Regtl crest, 9.0 x 6.0, xxvii/443. 22 mono phots, one cld ill, 17 line drawings, 10 maps, Bibliography, no Index. Apps: Bn nominal roll (incl details of KIA, DOW, DOD and WIA, plus details of awards), separate rolls for those who died in various POW camps, Chapter summaries.
* The narrative is arranged in three sections. Part I describes the Colony, the battle, the period of captivity, and concludes with the appendixes (as above). Part II contains the illustrations. Part III is headed 'The Fight to Survive', and is based upon the recollections of individual soldiers. A precise record of the harrowing Canadian experience in the Far East. R/4 V/5. PC. JDB.

THE HIDDEN YEARS
Hong Kong, 1941-1945
John Luft * South China Morning Post Ltd, Hong Kong, 1967. Green, black, 10.25 x 7.0, iii/234. One mono phot, 5 maps, no Index. Apps: text of speech broadcast by Emperor Hirohito on 15.8.1945, remarks and statistics for British and Japanese forces (with strengths and casualties).
* A sound general account of the battle, the prison camps, and the underground resistance, between 1941 and 1945. All defending units are mentioned - British Army, Canadian Army, Hong Kong Volunteer Defence Force, and ancillary units. The HKVDF receives particularly good coverage, with many of its members named (and, as appropriate, with details of awards granted after the war for services rendered during the battle or during the occupation). R/4 V/4. PC. JDB.

BRITISH ARMY AID GROUP
(BAAG) - Hong Kong Resistance, 1942-1945
Edwin Ride * Oxford University Press, Hong Kong, 1981. Grey-brown, gold, 8.5 x 6.5, xv/347. 25 mono phots, 5 maps (3 printed in the text, 2 on the end-papers), Bibliography, Index. Apps: Roll of Honour (for all those who died), 5 nominal rolls (of agents and other personnel at various periods), summary of assistance rendered to escapers, notes on types of escape.
* A detailed account of a Resistance group established by the author's father, Col Lindsay Ride. Shortly after the surrender, Ride escaped to Free China. Once there, he set about creating the BAAG as an intelligence-gathering organisation and as a means of aiding others to escape. About 2000 people were assisted in this way. In addition, the BAAG smuggled food, medicines, and messages of hope, into those POW and internment camps from which escapes could not be arranged. Born in Australia, Lindsay Ride had been Professor of Physiology at Hong Kong University since 1928. The unusual story of an extraordinary man. R/3 V/5. RCSL. PJE.

THE GUNS AND GUNNERS OF HONG KONG
Denis Rollo * Corporate Cummunications Ltd, HK, for The Gunners' Roll of Hong Kong, n.d. (1992). Blue, gold, 12.0 x 8.0, ix/210. Fp, 77 mono phots, 9 line drawings (mainly technical, of artillery pieces and their mountings), 25 maps and plans, Glossary, Bibliography, no Index. Apps: list of Army Commanders (HK) who were officers of the Royal Artillery, list of Commanders RA/RAHK (1841-1963), list of all RA and associated units which ever served on Hong Kong (1840-1976), RA Orders of Battle (in 1914 and in 1941, with the names of officers then commanding each Regt and sub-unit), locations and movements of guns (between 8-25 December 1941), notes on 'The Gunners' Roll of Hong Kong' (as association of former and serving gunners), 'Gazeteer' of batteries.
* A book which tells the story of gunnery on Hong Kong and environs from the time of the First China War through to the departure of the last British Army gunner unit (20th Light Regt RA) in 1976. It is packed with information of all kinds regarding policy decisions, strategic and tactical considerations, weaponry, battery placements and construction, and the comings and goings of every artillery unit which ever served on the island. The maps are adequate, the photographs are technically interesting and have reproduced quite well, but it would have been helpful if both maps and illustrations had been indexed. Indeed, the lack of any kind of Index is an obstacle for anyone wishing to use this book as a quick source of reference. On the other hand, for those interested in defensive artillery in general, or the way in which the British presence evolved over the decades, it is a prime source and represents a great deal of specialised research. The location and technical specification of each of the fifty-four batteries is described in concise language. This is a book which fills an important niche in the overall history of the Colony. R/1 V/4. RAI. RP.

POLICE

THE ROYAL HONG KONG POLICE (1841–1945)
Colin Crisswell and Mike Watson * Macmillan Publishers (Hong Kong) Ltd, 1982. Slate blue, gold, 11.25 x 8.0, viii/208. 86 mono phots, no maps, Bibliography, Index. Apps: list of Commissioners, list of police stations (1841–1945).
* The authors trace the development of the Hong Kong Police force from its disreputable beginnings (when it was recruited partly from the infant Colony's local riff-raff) through to the eve of WWII (by which time it had become a relatively competent and respected organisation). There then follows a detailed account of its role during the Japanese invasion and occupation. A brief Epilogue deals with the post-war period of reconstruction. The narrative contains little information concerning organisation, command structures, equipment, or establishments. Instead, it concentrates upon Hong Kong's many legendary characters and the constant struggle against opium dealers, piracy, and corruption. The style is rather dry, being based largely upon verbatim documentary sources, but these provide many references to individuals and might be helpful to a genealogist. A good range of quality photographs is a feature of the book. R/2 V/4. PC. CGB.

ASIA'S FINEST
An Illustrated History of the Royal Hong Kong Police
Kevin Sinclair * Unicorn Books Ltd, Hong Kong, 1983. Dark blue, gold, 10.0 x 13.0, -/244. More than 200 mono phots and cld ills, 3 maps, no Index. Apps: Roll of Honour (officers killed while on duty, 1863–1983), list of Commissioners (with studio portraits of those appointed since 1946).
* The first part of this opulent book is a history of the Force from the 1840s to 1983. The pre-WWII coverage is superficial compared with the Criswell and Watson account (vide preceding entry), but the post-1946 narrative is detailed and, in places, dramatic. It focuses on the savage riots of 1956 and 1966, the Maoist-inspired disorders of 1967–1968, and the corruption scandals of the 1970s. The second part of the story is concerned with various facets of the Force as it existed in the 1970s and 1980s - recruitment and training, the work of the CID, Force traditions, disaster relief, the Triad societies, and so forth. The illustrations are well selected and finely presented. R/2 V/4. MODL. CGB.

SUI GENG
The Hong Kong Marine Police, 1841–1950
Iain Ward * Hong Kong University Press, Hong Kong, 1991. Soft card, 'Perfect' bound, blue, white, 9.5 x 6.5, xx/214. Fp, 45 mono phots, 4 line drawings, 2 maps, Bibliography, Index. Apps: Roll of Honour (Marine Police killed while on duty, 1945–1949), notes on manpower, idem marine offences, idem all the launches operated by the Force (with dates of purchase and disposal, technical specifications, etc).
* A history of the Hong Kong Water Police from formation in 1841 through to 1950 (its title was changed to Marine Police in 1948). It is reported that this is the first part of a planned two-volume history. The second part will cover events from 1950 onwards, and may be published in 1994. The narrative of the volume recorded here contains the expected stories of piracy, smuggling, natural disasters, and the colourful characters of the China Coast, but it is also a detailed record of the development of the Force in terms of its organisation, administration, and equipment. For readers interested in boats and their design, there are interesting notes regarding the introduction of different classes of vessel and their deployments and performance. All of this is presented against the background of the chaotic conditions which prevailed on the Chinese mainland throughout much of the relevant period. It is a good overall history, written in a readable and at times humorous style. R/1 V/5. PC. CGB.
Note: translated from the Cantonese dialect, SUI GENG means, simply, 'Water Police'.

CHINA

BRITISH AND INDIAN ARMIES ON THE CHINA COAST, 1785-1985
Alan Harfield * A&J Partnership, Surrey, UK, 1990. Blue, gold, 8.5 x 6.0, viii/524. 240 mono phots, 8 line drawings, 24 maps (23 printed in the text, one on the end-papers), Bibliography, Index. Apps: 13 in total, mainly extensive lists of personnel who received medals for various services in China and Hong Kong, with lists of Regts which served (1841-1940), Officers Commanding (1844-1985), and notes regarding military memorials and cemetery records.
* A deeply researched account of the role played by the British and Indian Armies on the China coast over the past two centuries. It covers the First and Second China Wars in some detail, the establishment of a garrison on Hong Kong in 1841, the many Regts stationed there at various times in later years, and the histories of the locally-raised units. Amonst these were - the Hong Kong Regt (1892-1905), 1st Chinese Regt (1898-1905), and part-time units such as the Shanghai Volunteer Corps, Tientsin Volunteer Corps, Hankow Volunteer Corps, and Newchwang Volunteer Corps. Lists of officers are inserted at many points in the text. Combined with the extensive appendixes, they represent a goldmine for the medal collector and genealogist. The book has in it a wealth of information brought together from a variety of original archival sources and thereby provides a unique and compact source of reference. R/2 V/5. NAM. RP.
Note: published in a limited (unnumbered) edition of 250 copies.

EIGHTY-FIVE YEARS OF THE SHANGHAI VOLUNTEER CORPS
Anon (I I Kounin) * The Cosmopolitan Press, Shanghai, n.d. (1938). Seen in fine alligator (or snake) skin, black, superb large gold and embroidered silk Corps crest on front cover, 6.0 x 12.0 (landscape), v/238. Profusely illustrated throughout (formal groups, ceremonial parades, personnel on exercises, plus many captioned studio portraits of officers), 2 maps, no appendixes, no Index.
* This was a cosmopolitan part-time Corps recruited from the international community residing in the city and district of Shanghai. The membership included Americans, Japanese, Portuguese, Philippinos, emigré Russians, Chinese, Austrians, Germans, Italians, stateless Jews, and the British. They were grouped under separate national and ethnic Company titles. The raison d'être of the Corps was to provide security for the Legations and to guard foreign commercial premises in the city during times of strife. It was mobilised on twenty-five different occasions for small wars and to deal with riots in Shanghai and the North China area. A truly splendid book, clearly arranged, with good coverage of the main events and the services of all the sub-units. R/4 V/5. NAM. PJE.
Note: in WWII, the SVC simply withered away. Some members left China in 1939 to join the armed forces of their home countries. Drills and parades continued until 8 December 1941 but were then suspended. Many members gave policing and administrative support to Shanghai Municipal Council in the early weeks of 1942, but all duties were then cancelled. In September of that year, the Council announced the disbandment of the Corps and ordered the surrender of weapons and uniforms. On 7 October the Colours were laid up in the Council Committee Room, the ceremony being witnessed by senior former members of the Corps. Many Europeans, including key British personnel, were allowed by the Japanese to remain at liberty following the occupation. Those between 20 and 55 years of age were conscripted to render part-time service with the Pao Chia, the Japanese-controlled civil defence and auxiliary police force. In January 1943, the International Settlement Agreement was terminated by the Allies, and this removed the original reason for the existence of the Corps. It was never reactivated. SODW.

'A' COMPANY, S.V.C. (SHANGHAI VOLUNTEER MIH-HO-LOONG RIFLES), 1870-1930
Lieut J Moffat * North China Daily News, Shanghai, n.d. (c.1932). Red boards, black spine, 10.5 x 8.0, i/40. 5 mono phots, no maps, no Index. Apps: Roll of Honour, list of former COs, idem former officers.
* A short history of the Coy, first formed as a part-time fire-fighting unit, then later converted to a military role following the Taiping Rebellion. Mih-ho-Loong (alternative spelling Meehouloung) means 'fire eating devil'. A useful source for names and details of individual services. R/5 V/4. NAM. PJE.

ON ACTIVE SERVICE WITH THE CHINESE REGIMENT
A Record of the Operations of the First Chinese Regiment in North China from March to October, 1900
Capt A A S Barnes * Grant Richards, London, 1902. Red, black, 7.25 x 4.75, xv/228. Fp, 11 mono phots, 3 diagrams, no Index. Apps: Roll of Honour (KIA and WIA, all ranks), verbatim newspaper reports, complimentary Orders issued in connection with the Relief of the Peking Legations, verbatim extracts from telegraphic and other despatches.
* The 1st Chinese Regt was raised in 1898 in the British concessionary territory of Wei-hai-Wei. It was, in fact, often referred to as the Wei-hai-Wei Regt. Its officers, and most SNCOs, were British. The rank and file were recruited in the locality from the Chinese population. This book is believed to be the only available history of the Regt and it deals solely with its role in the Third China War of 1900 (the Boxer Rebellion). Its total strength at that time was 14 British officers, 8 British SNCOs, and 363 Chinese NCOs and ORs. It took an active part in the fighting and two DCMs were earned by its members (as described in the text). One of the recipients was a Chinese Sergeant, and he was probably the only Chinese national ever to win such an award. The War Office ordered the disbandment of the Regt in 1906. R/5 V/4. MODL. JA.

AUSTRALIAN CONTINGENTS IN THE CHINA FIELD FORCE, 1900-1901
James J Atkinson * The Clarendon Press, Kensington, NSW, for the NSW Military History Society, 1976. Card, yellow, brown, 'Chinese dragon' motif in red, 8.5 x 5.75, -/69. Fp (map), 28 mono phots, 3 line drawings, Bibliography, no Index.
* Although the book does contain some information regarding the active services of Australian units, it is essentially a roll of the officers and men of the New South Wales and Victorian Contingents who received a campaign medal. Probably of interest only to medal collectors. R/2 V/2. PC. HEC.

BLUEJACKETS AND BOXERS
Australia's Naval Expedition to the Boxer Uprising
Bob Nicholls * Allen & Unwin Pty Ltd, North Sydney, 1986. Black, gold, 9.75 x 7.5, xi/161. More than 150 mono phots, 3 maps, Bibliography, Index. Apps: muster roll of HMAS Protector, idem the NSW Contingent, idem the Victorian Contingent, details of 'dead and sick', details of small arms and artillery used, medals awarded.
*A naval force, mounted by South Australia, New South Wales and Victoria, formed part of the international effort to suppress the Boxer Rebellion in 1900. Detachments from the ships' companies went ashore, equipped to fight as infantry, and it is for this reason that their services are noted here. The narrative is based upon newspaper reports, diaries, and participants' memories. R/1 V/3. PC. PS.

WAR, 1914-1919
Record of Services Given, and Honours Attained, by Members of the Chinese Customs Service
Anon * Produced by the Statistical Dept, The Inspectorate of Customs, Shanghai, 'Published by Order of the Inspector General of Customs', 1922. Dark red, gold, 9.75 x 7.5, ii/74. No ills, no maps, no Index. Apps: Roll of Honour (23 names), H&A, list of former officers, idem SNCOs.

* The Imperial Chinese Customs Service was created in 1843 by those European powers which had obtained trading concessions from the Emperors of China. Its task was to extract the agreed levels of tariff for the concessionary powers, to raise taxes for the Emperor, and to restrict the corruption which had always been a feature of the country's maritime trade. Staffed by officers from the various nations concerned, it was run on predominantly British lines. With the outbreak of war, many of these officers resigned or took indefinite leave in order to serve with their own nations' armed forces. This booklet is a record of those services. It contains biographical notes on sixty-seven men, mostly British but including some Russians, Italians, Frenchmen and Americans who survived. The appendix lists those who did not. The notes include details of awards, campaign medals, wounds, promotions, imprisonments, battles, etc. Little information is given regarding their peacetime careers with the Service, but this information is usually available from the archives of the Foreign & Commonwealth Office Library in London. R/5 V/5. PC. DM.
Note: the 'Imperial' prefix disappeared from the Service's title after the fall of the Manchu dynasty in 1911. The title seems to have continued as Chinese Customs Service until the 1920s. Records then refer to it as The Chinese Maritime Customs. Philatelists will note that the Imperial Chinese Post Office was started by the ICCS in 1896 and operated by it until 1910.

WITH THE CHINKS
Daryl Klein * The Bodley Head, London, 1919. Light brown, black, 'guns in action' motif, 7.75 x 5.25, xiii/258. Fp, 12 mono phots, no maps, no appendixes, no Index.
* A personal record by an officer who joined the Chinese Labour Corps, in China, in December 1917. After training his Coy of recruits for two months, he took it across the Pacific to the USA, crossed the Atlantic to France, and almost immediately saw his command split into small parties for attachment to other units. The narrative concentrates upon administration, locations, and the background and character of his men. A few European officers are mentioned by name, but the book is useful mainly as a description of those who volunteered for a cause which they only dimly comprehended on the other side of the world. The 'snapshot' pictures are evocative of the period. R/5 V/2. MODL. AMM.

SHANGHAI DEFENCE FORCES SOUVENIR
Volume I
Anon * North China Daily News, Shanghai, n.d. Orange, black, 'soldier, house and barbed wire' motif, 15.0 x 10.5, ii/24. 110 mono phots, no maps, no appendixes, no Index.
* A commemorative book relating to the British, US, French, Japanese and Indian units which constituted the Shanghai Defence Force (Shaiforce) in 1927. Primarily a pictorial history, with a condensed narrative. The main emphasis is upon British and Indian forces (military, naval and aviation). R/5 V/2. PC. GC.
Note: it seems that this was the only Vol published.

THE BUGLE
A Chronicle of the 2nd Bn The Durham Light Infantry, Sialkot to Shanghai
J F M Sumner * Shanghai Mercury, 1927. Stapled paper covers, light green, black, Regtl crest, 8.5 x 5.5, i/52. 27 mono phots, no maps, no appendixes, no Index.
* A useful little book which deals with the activities of 1 DLI when the Bn was part of 'Shaiforce'. R/5 V/3. PC. GC.

SHANGHAIED - A PICTORIAL RECORD OF THE 1st 16th FOOT
Volume II
Anon * The Willow Pattern Press Ltd, Shanghai, n.d. Stiff card, brown, gold, 9.75 x 7.25, -/33. 80 mono phots, one map, no appendixes, no Index.
* A booklet commemorating the services of 1st Bedfordshire & Hertfordshire Regt while part of 'Shaiforce' (1927). The Foreword states that Vols II and III

'deal with the Regt's experiences in China', while Vol I (of which 2400 copies are said to have been printed) 'deal for the greater part with the itinerary of the Battalion from Malta'. Vols I and III have not been seen, but presumably they have a format similar to this Vol II. R/4 V/2. PC. GC.

LOST LEGION
Mission 204 and the Reluctant Dragon
William Noonan * Printed in Singapore for Allen & Unwin, Sydney, 1987. Brown, silver, 9.75 x 6.25, xv/235. Fp, 44 mono phots, 5 maps, Bibliography, Index. Apps: notes on the composition of a mixed Chinese and British guerilla Bn, notes on the Mission's operational orders.
* In 1942 a small group of soldiers volunteered to undertake the longest overland deep penetration incursion behind enemy lines ever recorded in military history. 'Mission 204' was a secret cadre of demolition experts, despatched from Burma to China to cause mayhem along the Japanese lines of communication. The personnel were Chinese and Australian. Most of the latter came from the ranks of 2/19th and 2/20th Aust Inf Bns. They described themselves as 'the Marco Polo Diggers', and they spent two years operating under almost incredible conditions.
R/1 V/4. ANL. HEC.
Note: the author's personal experiences as a member of the Mission first appeared under the title THE SURPRISING BATTALION - AUSTRALIAN COMMANDOS IN CHINA (NSW Bookstall Co Pty Ltd, Sydney, 1945).

POLICE

SHANGHAI POLICEMAN
E W Peters (edited by Hugh Barnes) * Rich & Cowan Ltd, London, 1937. Dark green, white, 9.5 x 6.0, -/322. 18 mono phots, no maps, no appendixes, no Index.
* E W Peters joined the Shanghai Municipal Police Force in 1929 and departed in 1936 after being found not guilty of a charge of murder. This is a good solid autobiography by an author having personal experience of a unique Force, and is the only known published record of it. R/3 V/3. SLV. PS.

JAPAN

UNEASY LIES THE HEAD THAT WEARS THE CROWN
A History of the British Commonwealth Occupation Force, Japan
Arthur W John * The Gen Publishers, Cheltenham, Victoria (Australia), 1987. Illustrated soft card, 'Japanese scene' motif, buff, black, 9.75 x 6.5, vi/129. Fp, 36 mono phots, one line drawing, one map, Bibliography, no appendixes, no Index.
* The author, an Australian, served with the BCOFJ as an Education Officer. His book provides a personal view of the Force's work between 1946 and 1952. It is useful and informative, but fairly generalised. R/2 V/3. ANL. MCND'A.

THE ROYAL AUSTRALIAN ARMY SERVICE CORPS IN JAPAN, 1951
Maj W A Bunting * HQ Command, Kure, Japan, 1951. Soft card, RAASC badge, buff, blue, 10.25 x 7.5, ii/56. No ills, one sketch plan, no appendixes, no Index.
* A workmanlike description of every imaginable aspect of the RAASC element in the BCOFJ during the year of 1951. The text is packed with abundant facts and statistics, many of which would be impossible to find elsewhere. Useful for students of post-war Japan. R/4 V/5. AWM. MCND'A.

1st AUSTRALIAN ARMOURED CAR SQUADRON GROUP – BRITISH COMMONWEALTH OCCUPATION FORCE, JAPAN
Anon * Hiroshima Printing Co Ltd, Hiroshima, 1947. Red, gold, 'Armoured car and map of Japan' motif, 4.25 x 5.5, ii/56. No ills, one sketch plan, no appendixes, no Index.
* This was a unique unit, formed in February 1946 for security duties in the freshly conquered Japanese homeland. With 348 Australian Light Aid Detachment, it patrolled the countryside around devastated Hiroshima in its factory-new scout and armoured cars. It then moved to Tokyo where it performed guard duties at the Imperial Palace and at government buildings. In the event, there were no public disorders. The sole casualty was a soldier killed in an accident. This little book provides an interesting footnote to the BCOFJ story. R/5 V/4. AWM. MCND'A.

JAPAN AND THE BRITISH COMMONWEALTH OCCUPATION FORCE, 1946–1952
Peter Bates * BPCC Wheatons Ltd, Exeter, for Brassey's (UK), London, 1993. Blue, gold, 9.5 x 6.25, xviii/270. 16 mono phots, 3 maps (one printed in the text, one on each end-paper showing BCOFJ dispositions in 1946), Glossary, Bibliography, Chapter Notes, Index. Apps: BCOFJ strengths (1946–1949) broken down to show the numbers for each participating country.
* This is a deeply researched account of the entire BCOFJ episode, with important analyses of the political background and complete accounts of the work done by each of the four Commonwealth contingents. In order of their size, they were from Australia, the UK, India, and New Zealand. At their peak (June 1946), they amounted to more than 37,000 all ranks. The purpose of the Force was to assist the Americans – headed by General Douglas MacArthur – in maintaining a military government, liaising with the Japanese civil police, and securing conditions under which future democratic self-government could be formulated. Other WWII Allies – France and the Soviet Union – were invited to contribute, but declined to do so. The French were too involved in trying to recover their pre-war empire in South East Asia, and the Soviets refused to place their troops under American command. The Indians went home in 1946–1947, the British and New Zealanders in 1947. The Australians continued to serve under the BCOFJ command and the American control arrangements until 1952 (when the British Commonwealth Force Korea was formed). R/1 V/4. PC. PJE.
Note: additional sources are THE ALLIED OCCUPATION OF JAPAN, by E M Mark (Greenwood Press, Westpoint, Connecticut, USA, 1948), and TYPHOON IN TOKYO – THE OCCUPATION AND ITS AFTERMATH, by H E Wildes (Allen & Unwin, London, 1954).

KOREA

FIRST COMMONWEALTH DIVISION
The Story of the British Commonwealth Division, 1950-1953
Brig C N Barclay CBE DSO * Gale & Polden Ltd, Aldershot, 1954. Red, gold, 8.75 x 5.5, xviii/236. Fp, 29 mono phots (indexed), 20 maps (17 printed in the text, 3 folding, bound in), Index. Apps: statistical summary of awards, plus full citations for four VC winners (Maj K Muir, 1st Bn Argyll & Sutherland Highlanders, Lieut Col J P Carne, Gloucestershire Regt, Lieut P K E Curtis, Duke of Cornwall's Light Infantry, and Pte W Speakman, Black Watch), idem two George Cross winners (Fus D G Kinnie, Royal Northumberland Fusiliers, and Lieut T E Waters, West Yorkshire Regt), statistical summary of casualties, list of all HQs and major units which served with the Division (with the names of their Commanders), Div Order of Battle at October 1951 (Operation Commando).
* The author was not only a soldier but also a well established historian. Although compiled soon after the events which it describes, this account is admirably clear, accurate and detailed. Soldiers of many nations served under the command of the Commonwealth Division, particularly those of Great Britain, Canada, Australia and New Zealand. The narrative is well laced with minor detail, but is especially helpful to an understanding of the importance of a multi-national contribution to what otherwise would have been an exclusively USA/RoK war. R/2 V/5. RMAS. RP.
Note: another source which should be consulted is KOREA, THE COMMONWEALTH WAR, by Tim Carew (Cassell, London, 1967). This is a solid and graphic history (307 pages) based upon interviews with veterans of that war.

STRANGE BATTLEGROUND
Official History of the Canadian Army in Korea
Lieut Col Herbert Fairlie Wood * The Queen's Printer, Ottawa, for the Minister of National Defence, 1966. Red, gold, 10.0 x 6.5, x/317. Fp, 24 mono phots, 14 very good maps (drawn by Sgt E H Ellwand RCE, 12 bound in, several in colour, two printed on the end-papers), Chapter Notes and Sources, Index. Apps: H&A (1951-1953, all ranks, Canadian Army personnel in Korea, incl foreign awards), list of officers who served in Command and Staff appointments.
* The well-written narrative commences in 1951 when the Princess Patricia's Canadian Light Infantry fought its first engagement in Korea. It concludes in 1953 when 25th Cdn Inf Bde halted on the newly-agreed 'ceasefire' line. It tells the story of the Canadian soldiers who served with the Commonwealth Div, operating under UN control, but it also tells the broader story of the developing Canadian national policy during that period with regard to all international affairs. Readable, packed with interesting detail, and supported by a good Contents page, a fine Index, and outstandingly helpful maps. R/3 V/5. RCSL. RP.
Note: the Canadian Government had earlier (1956) sponsored the publication of a booklet entitled CANADA'S ARMY IN KOREA, but this was a poor effort and has negligible reference value.

AUSTRALIA IN THE KOREAN WAR
Dr Robert O'Neill * Griffin Press, Adelaide, for the Australian War Memorial, 1981-1985. Two matching volumes, black, gold, 10.0 x 7.0.
Volume I : STRATEGY AND DIPLOMACY. Published in 1981, xxi/548. 62 mono phots, 18 cartoons, 10 maps (cld, bound in), 9 appendixes.
Volume II : COMBAT OPERATIONS. Published in 1985, xxiii/782. 95 mono phots, 5 cartoons, 92 maps (cld, bound in), 17 appendixes.
* An infinitely readable tour de force by an author who devoted eleven years to his task. This, the official history of Australia's role in the war, contains every item of information any researcher is ever likely to require. Vol I describes the circumstances in which Australia committed herself to the war, sustained her contribution during the years of combat, and then finally withdrew her forces between 1954 and 1957. Vol II is divided into three sections. Part I (220 pages)

covers 'The War on Land', Parts II and III 'The War in the Air' and 'The War at Sea'. Each volume is provided with a Glossary, Chronology, Bibliography, and Index. Amongst the twenty-six appendixes are biographical notes on a great number of the persons involved (42 pages in Vol I, 63 pages in Vol II). An H&A appendix in Vol II lists all the recipients by unit, with details of both Commonwealth and foreign awards. Other appendixes list Battle Honours, Unit Citations, statistics on casualties and POW, etc. The photographs are adequate, the maps excellent, and the overall quality of production a model of its kind. R/2 V/5. ANL. MCND'A.
Note: reference may be made also to HOT WAR, COLD WAR - AN AUSTRALIAN PERSPECTIVE OF THE KOREAN WAR, by G McCormack (Hale & Iremonger, Sydney, 1983).

WITH THE AUSTRALIANS IN KOREA
Norman Bartlett * Australian War Memorial, Canberra, 1960. Blue, gold, 10.0 x 7.25, v/294. Fp, 123 mono phots, 6 maps, no formal appendixes, Index.
* The book is divided into two parts. The first 140 pages are a narrative account of the services of Australian troops in Korea as part of the UN force. Then follow 115 pages bearing eighteen personal impressions of the conflict, written mainly by official War Correspondents. Interesting, and well illustrated. Useful as a general background source. R/2 V/2. PC. SB.
Note: first published in 1954, reprinted without amendment in 1957 and 1960 (as recorded above).

HOME BY CHRISTMAS
The Australian Army in Korea, 1950-1956
Lieut Col Neil C Smith AM * Talkprint Pty Ltd, Melbourne, 1990. Navy blue, gold, 9.75 x 6.5, iv/279. 5 mono phots, 3 line drawings, 9 maps, Bibliography, Index. Apps: H&A (statistical summaries only), roll of all Australian military personnel who served (listed by unit, with notes on casualties), notes on medical services.
* Australia sent 16,000 men and women to Korea. Of these, 1500 became casualties. For any researcher unable to gain access to the accounts by O'Neill or Bartlett, this book provides a handy alternative source of reference. It has good coverage of the services of 1st, 2nd and 3rd RAR, particularly the latter's famous action at Kapyong in April 1951. The medical services also are well recorded. The extensive nominal rolls make the book a prime source for medal collectors and genealogists. R/1 V/5. ANL. MCND'A.

THE KAPYONG BATTALION
Medal Roll of the Third Battalion, The Royal Australian Regiment
Battle of Kapyong, 23-24 April 1951
James J Atkinson * New South Wales Military Historical Society, 1977. Green and white, 8.5 x 5.5, -/80. 11 mono phots, 3 maps, no Index. Apps: Roll of Honour, H&A (incl MID, with full citations where appropriate), nominal roll of all personnel who took part, Bn medal roll for Korea.
* A superb little book, with a clear narrative account of the battle followed by very good appendixes. It also has much useful detail regarding the Bn's movements and experiences in Korea generally. R/2 V/4. PACL. LM/CMF.

THE BATTLE OF MARYANG SAN
3rd Battalion, The Royal Australian Regiment, Korea, 2-8 October 1951
Lieut Col Bob Green (as editor) * HQ Training Command, Balmoral, NSW, 1991. Illustrated soft card, dark green, white, 8.75 x 5.75, viii/136. 20 mono phots, 7 maps (one printed in the text, 6 folding, bound in, all indexed), Glossary, Bibliography, no Index. Apps: H&A, photographic sources.
* 3 RAR had already distinguished itself six months earlier, at Kapyong, when, in October 1951, it was again plunged into a fierce action - the battle for control of four key features around Maryang San. The story is told by the then CO (later

promoted General) and sixteen other members of the Bn who took part. Their vivid recollections are skilfully edited and are supported by maps and diagrams of outstanding quality. Each phase of the battle is explained, as are the reasons for its loss and the aftermath. R/1 V/4. AWM. MCND'A.

16th FIELD REGIMENT, RNZA, 1950–1954

Lieut Col J A Pountney MBE * Facsimile TS, printed in Korea, no other details known, 1954. Stapled card covers, 10.75 x 7.0, -/29. No mono phots, 2 line drawings, 2 maps, no Index. Apps: Roll of Honour, H&A, list of COs.

* A very brief but interesting record of 16th Field Regt in Korea. The unit was raised in New Zealand from volunteers, then disbanded at the cessation of hostilities. It saw much action, firing more than three quarters of a million shells, suffering 89 casualties, and gaining 59 awards (incl 4 DSOs, 11 MCs, 1 DCM, and 7 MMs). It seems likely that this item was produced at RHQ in Korea as a memento for serving personnel just before they returned to New Zealand. R/5 V/3. PC. SB.

SOUTH VIETNAM

AUSTRALIA'S WAR IN VIETNAM
Frank Frost * Allen & Unwin, Sydney, 1987. Illustrated stiff card, grey/white, orange, 'Helicopter assault' motif, 8.5 x 5.5, xii/211. 12 mono phots, 6 maps, Glossary, Bibliography, Index. Apps: 'Australian Commanders in Vietnam, 1965-1972'.
* An erudite work which began as a PhD thesis but which then blossomed into a full-length analysis of the origins, development and progress of the Australian involvement in the Vietnam war. The narrative is scholarly and deeply analytical, and is supported by an extensive Bibliography. The author achieved a balance of opinions by interviewing many of those involved, including all of the former Commanders. He discusses the operational deployments of the Task Force in the field and the dilemmas which it faced, i.e. political controversy at home, American lack of command and control decisions, and the unreliability of the SVN ally. The Australians operated in Phoc Tuy Province. The maps and illustrations are helpful in setting the scene for readers unfamiliar with the environment in which the war was fought. R/1 V/5. ANL. MCND'A.
Note: a helpful adjunct to Frost's study is AUSTRALIA AND VIETNAM, by Kenneth Maddock and Barry Wright (Harper & Row, Artarmon, NSW, 1987). A collection of fifteen essays, it includes a Vietnamese historian's view of Australia's role in the war. A similar source is VIETNAM REMEMBERED, by Gregory Pemberton (Weldon Publishing, Willoughby, NSW, 1990). This is a collection of nine essays by various writers, with good analyses of the socio-political impact upon the Australian national ethos. Finally, reference may be made to CONTACT - AUSTRALIANS IN VIETNAM, by Lex McAulay (Hutchinson Australia, Sydney, 1989), this being another general account, with useful appendixes.

THE TEAM
Australian Army Advisers in Vietnam
Ian McNeill * University of Queensland Press, with the Australian War Memorial, Canberra, 1984. Green, gold, 9.5 x 7.0, xiv/534. More than 100 mono phots, 35 maps (33 printed in the text, one folding bound in at the rear, one printed on each end-paper), Glossary, Bibliography, Index. Apps: Roll of Honour, H&A (incl four VC awards), list of COs (1962-1972), unit nominal roll (incl personnel of New Zealand's RNZIR), chronology of events (1945-1975), notes on 'Unit Citations awarded to the AATTV'.
* The Australian Army Training Team Vietnam was formed in 1962 with a strength of thirty all ranks. This grew to more than two hundred. Despite its innocuous title, this elite force did much more than simply provide training for the SVN Army and Territorial Forces. Australian and New Zealand members of the AATTV came to be involved in a variety of clandestine operations sponsored by the US Special Forces and the CIA. In the process, four men gained the Victoria Cross - Maj P J Badcoe, WOII K Payne, WOII R S Simpson, and WOII K A Wheatley. The author of this handsome book was a Research Officer with the Defence Dept and was able to utilise previously unpublished material. He also interviewed many former member of the team and all of the former COs. R/1 V/5. ANL. MCND'A.

THE BATTLE OF CORAL
Fire Support Coral and Balmoral, May 1968
Lex McAulay * Century Hutchinson Pty Ltd, Hawthorn, Victoria, 1988. Red, white, 8.75 x 5.5, v/361. 46 mono phots, 7 maps, Index. Apps: Roll of Honour, after-action reports, notes on patrol actions, list of Viet Cong units engaged.
* This is a detailed account of a series of actions fought between 1st Australian Task Force and 7th North Vietnamese Army Division (plus local VC units) around the Coral and Balmoral fire support bases between 13 May and 6 June 1968. It was the largest unit-level battle involving Australian troops in the Vietnam war.
R/1 V/5. PC. PS.
Note: published also in paperback, 1989, by Arrow Books.

FIRST TO FIGHT
Australian Diggers, New Zealand Kiwis and US Paratroopers in Vietnam, 1965–1966
Col Bob Green * Allen & Unwin Australia Pty Ltd, Sydney, 1988. Maroon, gold, 9.25 x 6.0, xvi/316. 51 mono phots (indexed), 17 maps (indexed), Glossary, Bibliography, Index. Apps: H&A, unit nominal roll for 1 RAR Gp (incl Cavalry, Artillery, Engineer and Logistics personnel).
* Despite its misleading title, this is the meticulously researched story of Australia's entrance into an unwinnable war and that country's escalating commitment to it. In response to American appeals for more political and practical support, a force of 1600 Australian troops was sent to Vietnam in 1966 and placed under the command of the US 173rd Airborne Bde. The author is candid in detailing the problems which arose from the two Armies' differing tactical doctrines and operational philosophies. Labelled 1st Bn Royal Australian Regt Group, the force included specialists from both Australia and New Zealand: 105 Field Bty RAA, 161 Field Bty RNZA, 3 Field Engineer Tp RAE, 1 APC Tp (Prince of Wales's Light Horse), 161 Recce Flt AAC, and 1 Aust Logistical Support Coy. A very readable and compelling book, with excellent maps. R/1 V/5. ANL. MCND'A.

ARTILLERY

TWELVE IN FOCUS
12th Field Regiment, Royal Australian Artillery, in South Vietnam, 1971
A Memento for All Ranks of the Tour in South Vietnam
Maj G F B Rickards * Printcraft Press, Brookvale, NSW, for the Regt, 1971. Red boards with black spine, gold, 'two guns and map of Indo-China' motif, 11.0 x 8.25, -/144. 262 mono phots, 3 cld plates, 9 drawings and cartoons, 2 maps (one printed in the text, one on the end-papers), no Index. Apps: Roll of Honour, list of former officers, unit nominal roll.
* This is a pictorial record, produced mainly for the pleasure of those who served and for their families. It does not pretend to be a complete history. The mass of photographs is so great, however, that they coincidentally provide a very informative coverage of the Regt's active services. The book is divided into sections, each of which deals with a specific Bty or sub-unit, and this adds to the book's value as a reference source. An attractive production. R/2 V/3. RAI. AMM.

VIETNAM GUNNERS
161 Battery, Royal New Zealand Artillery, 1965–1971
Lieut S D Newman * Moana Press, Tauranga, NZ, 1988. Illustrated soft card, 9.75 x 8.25, -/152. 50 mono phots, 20 cld ills, 8 maps, Bibliography, no Index. Apps: Roll of Honour, H&A, nominal roll, notes on deployments.
* A sound workmanlike account of the services, at different times with the period stated in the sub-title, of various 161 Bty detachments in SVN. R/1 V/4. PC. HEC.

1st ROYAL AUSTRALIAN REGIMENT

THE FIGHTING FIRST
Combat Operations in Vietnam, 1968–1969, The First Battalion, The Royal Australian Regiment
Lex McAulay * Allen & Unwin Pty Ltd, North Sydney, 1991. Black, gold, 9.0 x 6.0, xiv/293. 79 mono phots, one sketch, 3 maps, Sources, Index. Apps: Roll of Honour (KIA and WIA, with dates), H&A (with citations), Battalion Prayer, 'Order of the Day on Departure'.
* This is the story of the Bn's second tour of duty (vide Col Green's combined history, head of this page, for the first tour). Combat with the North Vietnamese Army and the Viet Cong is described from the perspective of the soldiers who were there. The citations for awards speak volumes about the nature of their experiences. A highlight was the battle, in May 1968, around Fire Support Base 'Coral', the hardest action involving Australian forces in the Vietnam war (vide preceding page). The maps are adequate, but the photographs are not as good as those found in similar histories of the period. R/1 V/5. AWM. MCND'A.

2nd ROYAL AUSTRALIAN REGIMENT

THE ANZAC BATTALION
A Record of the Tour of 2nd Bn, The Royal Australian Regiment, and 1st Bn, The Royal New Zealand Infantry Regiment (the Anzac Bn), in South Vietnam
Maj K E Newman * Printcraft Press Pty, Brookvale, NSW, 1968. Two matching volumes in a single padded slip case, black, gold, two Regtl crests (RNZIR and RAR), 11.0 x 8.5.
Volume I : 209 mono phots, 48 cld ills, -/175.
Volume II : sixteen large folding maps (of excellent quality).
* A handsome and liberally illustrated pair of volumes which cover the Bn's work in Phoc Tuy Province, with generous mention of personnel attached from other arms - 108 Bty 4th Field Regt RAA, 1 Field Sqn RAE, and 104 Signals Sqn RA Sigs. The maps in Volume II assist the reader greatly in understanding the operations described in Volume I. R/3 V/5. NZMODL. HEC.

THE ANZAC BATTALION
Maj A R Roberts * Printcraft Press Pty, Brookvale, NSW, for the Bn, 1972. Black, gold, two Regtl crests (RNZIR and RAR), 11.0 x 8.5, -/176. More than 100 mono phots, 26 cld ills, 22 line drawings, 3 maps (2 bound in, one printed on the end-papers), no Index. Apps: Roll of Honour, H&A, unit nominal roll (29.4.1970 to 23.5.1971).
* This is an account of the Bn's second tour in SVN. The narrative is fairly superficial and light-hearted, but it does provide a useful record of the actions in which the Bn was engaged. The narrative is based mainly upon the experiences of named individuals within each Coy. The maps are good, and the pictures serve to capture the spirit of this famous bi-national unit. R/1 V/2. AWM. MCND'A.

3rd ROYAL AUSTRALIAN REGIMENT

3 RAR IN SOUTH VIETNAM, 1967-1968
A Record of the Operational Service of the Third Battalion, The Royal Australian Regiment, in South Vietnam, 12th December 1967 - 20th November 1968
Maj R F Stuart * Printcraft Press Pty, Brookvale, NSW, 1968. Light green boards, dark green spine, gold lettering on spine and dark green on front cover, 'Map of SVN and 3 RAR badge' motif, 11.0 x 8.5, -/104. 136 mono phots (incl two on the end-papers), 19 cld ills, one line drawing, 15 maps, no Index. Apps: unit nominal roll (incl details of KIA, WIA, DOW and DOD , by Coy), chronicle of events, notes on Bn operations.
* The Bn was engaged in countering the Tet offensive and took part in several other major operations. Each is described here in great detail and is explained with the aid of exceptionally good maps. The narrative also makes references to the units which supported it at various times - 'A' Sqn 3rd Cav Regt, 161st Field Bty RNZA, etc. Easy reading, workmanlike, but blighted by the lack of an Index for either the illustrations or the narrative. R/1 V/3. AWM. MCND'A.

YOURS FAITHFULLY
A Record of the Operational Service of the Third Battalion, The Royal Australian Regiment, in Australia and South Vietnam, 16 February 1969 - 16 October 1971
Capt Colin J Clarke * Printcraft Press Pty, Brookvale, NSW, for the Bn, 1972. Green, gold, 11.0 x 8.5, -/203. 392 mono phots, 38 line drawings, 11 maps, no Index. Apps: Roll of Honour, H&A, unit nominal roll.
* A pictorial record which concentrates mainly upon the personnel rather than the technical aspects of the campaign itself. The book will become increasingly useful, in future years, to family historians and to medal collectors. R/3 V/3. PC. JS.

4th ROYAL AUSTRALIAN REGIMENT

MISSION IN VIETNAM
The Tour in South Vietnam of 4 RAR/RNZIR (ANZAC) Battalion, and 104 Field Battery RAA, June 1968 to May 1969
Lieut J R Webb and Pte L A Drake * Times Printers, Singapore, 1969. White, black, 11.25 x 8.5, vi/130. More than 100 mono phots, 14 maps, Glossary, no Index. Apps: Roll of Honour, H&A, unit nominal roll.
* A mainly pictorial history of the Bn's initial tour in SVN. The narrative is pleasantly readable and is supported by good maps. R/2 V/4. NZMODL. HEC.
Note: available in later reprint by John Burridge.

THE FIGHTING FOURTH
A Pictorial Record of the Second Tour in South Vietnam by 4 RAR/RNZIR (ANZAC) Battalion, 1971-1972
Capt R L Sayce, Lieut M D O'Neill and Pte A Garton * Printcraft Press Pty, Brookvale, NSW, 1972. Red, gold, 11.0 x 8.5, -/208. 330 mono phots, 11 cld ills, 36 other ills, 9 maps, Index. Apps: Roll of Honour, H&A, unit nominal roll.
* This is another pictorial and anecdotal record, not a formal history. However, it is generally informative, and the only published account of the Bn during that period. The narrative deals mainly with operations around Nui Dat where the enemy was 274th Viet Cong Main Force Regt and 33rd North Vietnam Army Regt.
R/3 V/3. PC. HEC.
Note: available in later reprint by John Burridge. An additional source is IN GOOD COMPANY, by Lieut Gary McKay MC (Allen & Unwin, Sydney, 1987).

STASS STAR - B COMPANY, 4 RAR
South Vietnam, May-December, 1971
Capt T W Roderick ('and three others') * Printcraft Press Pty, Brookvale, NSW, for the 4th Bn RAR Assn, 1989. Soft card, green, blue, Coy logo, 10.75 x 8.0, -/32. Fp, 85 mono phots, 3 maps, no Index. Apps: Company nominal roll.
* An interesting but lightweight account of the second (last) tour in SVN served by B Coy, 4 RAR. It incorporates a chronology of events which may be useful to a researcher, but the work is essentially a souvenir for those who served. The meaning of 'Stass Star' is not revealed. R/4 V/2. AWM. MCND'A/PS.
Note: available in later reprint by John Burridge.

5th ROYAL AUSTRALIAN REGIMENT

VIETNAM TASK
5th Battalion, Royal Australian Regiment, 1966-1967
Maj Robert J O'Neill * Cassell Australia Ltd, Sydney, 1968. Black, gold, Regtl crest, 9.0 x 5.75, xvi/256. 30 mono phots, 22 maps (20 printed in the text, 2 on the end-papers), Index. Apps: Roll of Honour, H&A.
* Like other books of the genre, this is a graphic and interesting account of one Bn's tour of service in the SVN conflict. Unlike other publications recorded here, this one relies more upon a clear descriptive narrative and far less upon pictures. R/3 V/4. PC. HEC.

THE YEAR OF THE TIGER
The Second Tour of 5th Battalion, Royal Australian Regiment, in South Vietnam, 1969-1970
Capt M R Battle * Printcraft Press Pty, Brookvale, NSW, for the Regt, 1970. Brown, gold, 11.0 x 8.75, -/208. 280 mono phots, 41 cld ills, 16 maps (bound in), no Index. Apps: Roll of Honour, H&A (with full citations where applicable), unit nominal roll.
* Primarily a photographic record, many of the pictures being portraits and simple 'snapshots' of officer and NCOs of the Bn. R/3 V/2. PC. JBF.
Note: available in later reprint by John Burridge.

6th ROYAL AUSTRALIAN REGIMENT

VIETNAM
A Pictorial History of the Sixth Battalion, The Royal Australian Regiment, 1966–1967
Capt Ian Williams, Capt Brian Wickens, Lieut David Sabben and Sgt James McKenna * Printcraft Press Pty, Brookvale, NSW, 1967. Bright red, gold, Regtl crest, 11.0 x 8.5, -/136. Fp (map), 242 mono phots, 14 cld ills, 18 line drawings (by Sgt James McKenna), 11 maps, no Index. Apps: Roll of Honour (with dates), H&A (with full citations).
* Again, mainly a photographic record. It deals with the Bn's first tour of duty, making brief references to other units with which it was associated - 1st Aust Logistic Support Group, 9 Sqn RAAF, 161 Ind Recce Flight, RAE, RAA, etc. The main value of the book is its illustrations, these being very evocative of the period. The maps are good. R/2 V/3. AWM. HEC/MCND'A.

THE BATTLE OF LONG TAN
The Legend of ANZAC Upheld
Lex McAulay * Century Hutchinson Australia Ltd, Hawthorn, 1986. Black, white, 8.5 x 5.5, viii/187. 55 mono phots, 7 diagrams, one map, Glossary, Apps: H&A, notes on the artillery, the RAAF, the Viet Cong forces in Phoc Tuy Province, etc.
* The author tells the story from both sides, Australian and Vietnamese. In this fierce engagement, D Coy 6 RAR gained 2 DSOs, one MBE, 7 MID, and the United States Distinguished Unit Citation. The battle was claimed as an Australian victory. R/1 V/4. PC. PS.

THE SOLDIER'S STORY
The Battle for Xa Long Tan, Vietnam, 18 August 1966
Terry Burstall * University of Queensland Press, St Lucia, Queensland, 1986. Paper covers, white, red/black, 7.75 x 5.0, xv/188. 35 mono phots, 2 line drawings, 7 diagrams, 3 maps, Index. Apps: notes on Operation Long Tan, roll of personnel eligible to wear the US Distinguished Unit Citation.
* The author took part in the battle and subsequently interviewed others who were there. As the title suggests, this is a soldier's eyewitness account of 6 RAR's role, and as such is informative and graphic. Most useful when read in conjunction with McAulay's account (vide preceding entry). R/2 V/4. PC. PS.

6 RAR/NZ (ANZAC) BATTALION HISTORY, 1967–1970
Maj D L Johnson, Pte R J Dorizzi and Pte N S Howarth * Times Printers, Singapore, 1972. Orange, white, 11.5 x 8.5, viii/178. Very many mono phots, 8 cld plates, 19 maps (all loose in rear pocket), no Index. Apps: Roll of Honour, H&A, unit nominal roll, notes on pipe music.
* This publication follows the format described in respect of several of the preceding entries. It is largely pictorial, and seems to have been produced mainly as a memento for those who served. It is not a full formal history, but is certainly useful in its own way. R/3 V/3. PC. HEC.

A HISTORY OF THE SIXTH BATTALION, THE ROYAL AUSTRALIAN REGIMENT, 1965–1985
Including the History of 6 RAR–NZ (ANZAC) Battalion (1967–1970)
Capt Nick Welch * Cardinal Business Services, Enoggera, Queensland, 1986. Red, gold, 11.0 x 8.25, -/208. Fp, more than 100 mono phots, 2 line drawings, 36 maps (11 printed in the text, 25 loose in rear pocket), no Index. Apps: Roll of Honour (SVN, 1966-1967 and 1967-1970), H&A (with citations), unit nominal roll for 6 RAR-NZ Bn, plus 101st Field Battery RAA.
* An impressive publication arranged in three parts - 6 RAR pictorial history 1966/1967, 6 RAR-NZ Bn narrative history 1967/1970, and 6 RAR history 1970/1985. The first two parts are basically a reproduction of the two histories noted above, dated 1967 (Williams et al), and 1972 (Johnson et al). The third section updates the Bn's history to 1985 and, thereby, celebrates the 20th Anniversary of the Battle of Long Tan. Very comprehensive, excellent maps. R/1 V/4. ANL. MCND'A.

7th ROYAL AUSTRALIAN REGIMENT

SEVEN IN SEVENTY
A Pictorial Record of Seventh Battalion, The Royal Australian Regiment, 1970–1971
Anon * Printcraft Press Pty, Brookvale, NSW, for the Bn, 1971. Red, gold, Regtl crest, 10.75 x 8.5, -/208. Fp, more than 100 mono phots, one cld ill, 4 line drawings, 4 maps (3 printed in the text, one folding tipped-in at the rear), no appendixes, no Index.
* A lavishly produced book containing a great number of excellent photographs of members of the Bn and of the supporting arms. The story opens with a summary of the formation of the Bn in 1965, its training in Australia in 1966, and its first deployment in SVN in 1967. The rest of the book then covers the 1970-1971 tour, with much useful information regarding the various American and other Australian units with which 7th Bn operated in the field. R/1 V/3. ANL. MCND'A.

7th BATTALION, THE ROYAL AUSTRALIAN REGIMENT
Notes on Operations, Vietnam, 1970–1971
Anon (compiled jointly by fifteen former members) * Seen in facsimile TS only, no publication details shown, 1972. Privately bound, pages not numbered (approximately 200), one map, numerous diagrams, no other ills, no appendixes, no Index.
* A specialist work, intended to pass on the lessons learned to other professional soldiers. The contributors discuss all aspects of the Bn's work in SVN – Coy tactics, fire control, medical problems, field intelligence, fire support, air support, relations with indigenous populations, etc. R/3 V/4. ADFAL. MCND'A.

8th ROYAL AUSTRALIAN REGIMENT

THE GREY EIGHT IN VIETNAM
The History of Eighth Battalion, The Royal Australian Regiment, November 1969 – November 1970
Maj A Clunies-Ross * The Courier-Mail Printing Service, Brisbane, 1971. Grey, gold, 11.0 x 9.0, -/160. 155 mono phots, 19 cld plates, 4 line drawings, 10 maps, no Index. Apps: Roll of Honour, H&A (incl individual SVN awards), unit nominal roll.
* A helpful research source. The Bn saw much action, gaining one DSO, 2 MCs, and a unique SVN Government unit citation. R/3 V/4. PC. PS.

9th ROYAL AUSTRALIAN REGIMENT

9th BATTALION, ROYAL AUSTRALIAN REGIMENT – VIETNAM TOUR OF DUTY, 1968–1969
On Active Service
Anon * Globe Press, Melbourne, Victoria, for the University of Queensland Press, for 9th RAR Association, Brisbane, 1992. Brown, gold, 12.0 x 8.5, -/294. More than 100 mono phots, 15 maps (relating to each operation), 5 tables and plans, Glossary, no Index. Apps: Roll of Honour (with portrait photograph and details of each man), Bn nominal roll.
* The well produced history of a Bn raised in November 1967 specifically for service in SVN. The narrative is arranged in five parts and covers the twelve major actions in which the Bn was engaged. These were all set-piece assaults on fortified Viet Cong strongholds. The editor draws heavily upon personal reminiscences and eyewitness accounts. The experiences of each Rifle Coy and specialised Platoon are told in full, as are those of other units with which they operated in the field (including 161 Field Bty RNZA). Abundant and well captioned photographs appear throughout the book. R/1 V/4. AWM. MCND'A.

THE PACIFIC ISLANDS

HOW AUSTRALIA TOOK GERMAN NEW GUINEA
An Illustrated Record of the Australian Naval and Military Expeditionary Force
F S Burnell * W C Penfold & Co Ltd, Sydney, n.d. Soft card, red/green, 'Naval force and palm trees' motif, 9.0 x 7.0, -/34. Fp, 50 mono phots, no maps, no Index. Apps: complete roll of the Navy and Army personnel who participated.
* The seizure of German New Guinea in 1914 was the first occasion when Australian forces acted independently and not as part of a larger force from Great Britain. The Australian Expeditionary Force (as it was designated) sailed secretly on 19 August. After a brief campaign in which some casualties were incurred, the Germans on New Guinea and Rabaul (New Britain) were taken prisoner. The main strengths of this account are the interesting photographs and the roll of personnel (arranged by unit). R/4 V/3. AWM. MCND'A.
Note: the author produced a similar booklet entitled AUSTRALIA VERSUS GERMANY - THE STORY OF THE TAKING OF GERMAN NEW GUINEA.

AUSTRALIANS IN ACTION IN NEW GUINEA
L C Reeves * W C Penfold & Co Ltd, Sydney, 1915. Illustrated soft card, buff, red, 'Fighting scene with trophies' motif, 7.0 x 4.5, -/97. Fp, 37 mono phots, no maps, Glossary of native words, no Index. Apps: muster roll of all personnel (Navy and Army, by unit and rank) who participated.
* Another concise account of the first exclusively Australian overseas expedition of WWI. The author served in it as a Signalman, and his story is partly autobiographical. However, it is a useful source when read in conjunction with the one or both of the booklets by Burnell (vide preceding entry).
R/4 V/3. ANL. MCND'A.

OUR ISLAND CAPTURES
Being an Account of the Operations of the Australian Expeditionary Force in the South Pacific Ocean, 1914
Angus Hermon Worthington * G Hassell & Son, Adelaide, 1919. Soft card, grey-blue, black, 7.25 x 5.0, vi/92. Fp, 5 mono phots, no maps, no appendixes, no Index.
* Written in the form of a diary, this is an eyewitness account of the campaign to remove German forces from New Guinea and New Britain between August 1914 and January 1915. The land force consisted of one specially raised infantry Bn, two MG sections, and Signals and Medical elements. Useful as far as it goes, but best read in conjunction with Burnell and Reeves (vide preceding entries).
R/4 V/2. ANL. MCND'A.

THE SAMOA (NZ) EXPEDITIONARY FORCE, 1914-1915
An Account based upon Official Records of the Seizure and Occupation by New Zealand of the German Islands of Western Samoa
Stephen John Smith * Ferguson & Osborn Ltd, Wellington, NZ, 1924. Mottled blue-grey, black, 8.75 x 6.0, -/218. 234 mono phots (mainly small portraits of men who took part), 3 line drawings, 2 maps, no Index. Apps: Roll of Honour (with pictures and personal details of more than 100 individuals, most of whom died later in the war), embarkation rolls (5th Wellingtons, 3rd Aucklands, 4th Coy NZ Engineers).
* A very clear and handy record of this little known operation. The islands were (along with New Guinea and New Britain) the first enemy-held territory to be captured by Allied forces in WWI. The seizure was achieved with few casualties on either side. It was the first occasion when NZ forces served overseas under their own command. The islands remained in New Zealand trusteeship until 1961.
R/3 V/4. NZMOD. HEC.
Note: reference should be made also to NEW ZEALANDERS IN SAMOA, by Leonard P Leary (William Heinemann, London, 1918).

YESTERDAY AND TODAY
An Illustrated History of the Pacific Islands Regiment from its Formation on 19 June 1940 to the Present Day
Maj N E W Granter * South Pacific Post Pty Ltd, Port Moresby, 1970. Soft card, white, black, 10.75 x 8.25, -/60. More than 100 mono phots, one map, no Index. Apps: H&A (for the nine Bns, with citations, 1940-1968)
* An 'economy' publication, produced to modest standards and with numerous commercial advertisements throughout, this is nevertheless a handy source of reference. It provides brief accounts of each of the units which came to be known as the Pacific Islands Regt, i.e. Papua Inf Bn (PIB, 1940-1946), New Guinea Inf Bn (NGIB, 1944-1946), HQ Pacific Islands Regt (PIR, 1944-1946), the new PIR (1951 onwards), Papua New Guinea Training Depot (PNG, 1946 onwards), and 1st and 2nd Bns PIR (both 1965 onwards). The narrative, although brief, covers a wide spectrum of subjects - lists of officers, Regtl customs, the Colours, Regtl music, the Pipes and Drums, Dress and equipment, etc. The illustrations are excellent.
R/2 V/4. ANL. MCND'A.

TO FIND A PATH
The Life and Times of the Royal Pacific Islands Regiment
Volume I : Yesterday's Heroes, 1885-1950
James Sinclair * Boolarong Publications, Gold Coast, Queensland, 1990. Pale green, white, 11.5 x 8.5, viii/310. More than 100 mono phots, 19 maps (17 printed in the text, 2 on the end-papers), Bibliography, Index. Apps: H&A (with full citations), list of former COs, note on recruitment, notes on battle casualties, movements and locations.
* A splendidly produced book commemorating the 50th Anniversary of the founding of the PIR in 1940. It opens with an account of the Papuan Constabulary and the New Guinea Police Force during the Colonial period from 1885 to Independence in 1975. The Regt's first recruits came from these two armed Constabularies. They fought so well during the Japanese invasion that a Papuan Inf Bn was raised, followed by four New Guinea Inf Bns in 1944 and 1945. Other indigenous tribesmen served as trackers, irregular Scouts and raiding parties. The author makes the point that these fine fighting men were paid almost nothing, and received little in the way of post-war pensions or veterans' support services. R/1 V/5. ANL. MCND'A.
Note: reference should be made also to THE ROLE OF THE PAPUA NEW GUINEA DEFENCE FORCE, by Paul Mench (Australian National University, Canberra, 1975). This is an academic analysis of the socio-political factors influencing the creation of local armed forced in WWII and their subsequent effect upon the country's post-Independence development. Another useful source is VILLAGERS AT WAR - SOME PAPUA NEW GUINEA EXPERIENCES IN WWII, by N K Robinson (also published by the ANU, Canberra, in 1979).

GREEN SHADOWS
A War History of the Papuan Infantry Battalion, 1st New Guinea Infantry Battalion, 2nd New Guinea Infantry Battalion, 3rd New Guinea Infantry Battalion
G M Byrnes * Queensland Corrective Services Commission, Brisbane, for the author, 1989. Green, gold, 8.0 x 5.75, x/272. 43 mono phots, one cld ill (unit flash), 14 maps, Glossary, no Index. Apps: Roll of Honour (by unit), H&A (with citations and photographs), unit nominal rolls by Bn (Europeans and Papuans/New Guineans separately), note on 'First Recruits, 1940', notes on 'Battle Statistics', plus 24 other appendixes of varying type and utility.
* A first-class record of the units listed in the sub-title, all of which operated under the aegis of the Pacific Islands Regt. The Papuan Inf Bn was raised in 1940, the New Guinea Bns in 1944 and 1945. A total of 500 Australians and 3850 Papuans and New Guineans served in these units in every action of the campaign

(except Milne Bay) between July 1942 and July 1945. A captured Japanese document referred to them as 'green shadows', hence the title of the book. The initial formation and subsequent services of each unit are traced separately and in great detail, with frequent references to specific engagements and actions by named individuals. Apart from their contribution to the defeat of the Japanese invasion forces, the Bns had the indirect effect of bringing together the unsophisticated warriors of at least 700 different tribal cultures and languages, and welding them into a coherent whole. The crucible of war was thus the foundation of future nationhood. A very comprehensive history, with well captioned pictures, extensive appendixes, and maps which are helpful in following the narrative. The lack of an Index must be regretted. R/1 V/4. ANL. MCND'A.
Note: the Regt was redesignated The Royal Pacific Islands Regt following the Proclamation of Independence of Papua New Guinea in 1975.

HISTORY OF THE NEW GUINEA SURVEY SECTION
Later 8 Australian Survey Section
Jack S Viccars * Published privately by the author, Canberra, 1985. Illustrated soft card (map of New Guinea), 10.0 x 7.5, v/61. 18 mono phots, 2 maps (showing the 22 map areas covered, bound in), no Index. Apps: nominal roll (with biographical notes on each of the 82 members).
* When the Japanese invaded New Guinea, the only maps available to the defending forces were naval charts of the coastline. This small specialist unit was despatched from Australia in August 1942 with the task of preparing maps for those parts of the hinterland where fighting was taking place or was expected. Over the following sixteen months, it produced forty-seven maps to various scales, all sorely needed by the fighting units. This is a facsimile typescript account of the Section's work and is an interesting aspect of an extraordinary campaign. Many individuals are mentioned in the narrative and picture captions. R/1 V/3. AWM. MCND'A.

RING OF FIRE
Australian Guerilla Operations against the Japanese in World War II
D C Horton * Leo Cooper with Secker & Warburg, London, 1983. Blue, gold, 8.75 x 5.5, ix/164. 29 mono phots, one line drawing, 6 maps, Sources, Index. Apps: nominal rolls for Operations Jaywick and Rimau, details of parties launched from Colombo, idem parties which operated in Java, the Celebes, New Guinea and other islands.
* The sub-title is a fair summary of the contents. The author covers the wartime creation of Special Forces and their subsequent influence upon Allied operations throughout the SW Pacific. More than 6000 men were inserted into various Japanese-occupied territories at a loss to themselves of 112 lives. A total of eighty-one behind-the-lines operations were carried out, inflicting 1700 known casualties on the enemy. The physical and mental stress of such work is well described. Some of the more spectacular raids have been covered by other authors, but this book gathers them together with many other less publicised affairs. R/1 V/4. ANL. MCND'A.

THE PRIVATE WAR OF THE SPOTTERS
A History of the New Guinea Air Warning Wireless Company, February 1942/April 1945
Alex E Perrin * NGAWW Publication Committee, Foster, Victoria, 1990. Green, gold, 8.5 x 5.25, -/294. 24 mono phots, 14 sketches and diagrams. 10 maps, Glossary, Index. Apps: Roll of Honour, H&A, unit muster roll.
* Although published 45 years after its disbandment, this history of the NGAWWC is an important contribution to the record of WWII operations in the SW Pacific. Early in 1942, following the Japanese occupation of Rabaul, small detachments of Australian soldiers were deployed along isolated coastlines to keep watch for enemy air movements and report them by radio. Apart from providing this intelligence, the volunteer spotters rescued or buried more than 200 American and Australian aircrew between 1942 and 1945. Their lonely and dangerous way of life led to many acts

of great courage and sacrifice, and the NGAWWC became the most highly decorated Signals units in the Australian Army. A remarkable book about a remarkable unit. R/1 V/5. ANL. MCND'A.
Note: reference should be made also to A BRIEF HISTORY OF THE NEW GUINEA AIR WARNING WIRELESS, by Alan Mansfield (Kenneth James, Melbourne, 1961).

THE COAST WATCHERS
Eric Feldt (Commander, OBE, RAN) * Oxford University Press, Melbourne, 1946. Green, black, 8.75 x 5.5, xviii/425. Fp, 52 mono phots (indexed), 6 maps (5 printed in the text, one bound in), Glossary, Index. Apps: roll of all personnel (of all services) who participated, with details of casualties and awards.
* First conceived by Australian Naval Intelligence in 1919, the Coast Watching Organisation was activated in 1942. Its personnel comprised civilians and men from various American and Australian uniformed services. They were scattered throughout scores of islands to the north and north east of Australia. Equipped with tele-radio equipment, they reported Japanese air and shipping movements and gathered intelligence of all kinds. A large organisation of great value to the Allied cause, its work is well recorded in this absorbing book. R/1 V/5. ANL. MCND'A.
Note: the book was republished in 1967 by Angus Robertson Ltd, Sydney. A good additional source on the same subject is IF I DIE, by Malcolm Wright (Landsdowne Press, Melbourne, 1965), this being a lucid and informative account of the author's own experiences as a Coastwatcher.

HISTORY OF THE FIJI MILITARY FORCES, 1939-1945
Lieut R A Howlett * Published by the Crown Agents for the Colonies on behalf of the Government of Fiji, printed by Whitcombe & Tombs Ltd, Christchurch, 1948. Stiff card with cloth spine, red/green, black, crest of Fiji, 8.75 x 5.5, -/267. Fp, 52 mono phots, 2 line drawings, 3 maps (2 printed in the text, one large folding map of Bougainville Island bound in), no Index. Apps: Roll of Honour (all ranks), H&A (all ranks), lists of officers who served with Fiji's armed forces (incl Fiji Home Guard), plus other appendixes relating to Fiji Corps of Signals, Fiji Corps of Engineers, Fiji Artillery Regt, etc.
* A very comprehensive record of the Fijian military commitment to the SW Pacific campaign. Three Bns of infantry and supporting units saw much action against the Japanese. Training and administration, and some officers, were provided by New Zealand. On Bougainville Island, in June 1944, Cpl Sefanaia Sukanaivalu, of 3rd Bn Fijian Infantry Regt, won a posthumous VC for his self-sacrifice while rescuing wounded comrades under heavy fire. R/4 V/4. PCAL. RP.

AMONG THOSE PRESENT
The Official History of the Pacific Islands at War
Anon * Printed by the Whitefriars Press Ltd, for HMSO, London, 1946. Illustrated paper cover, grey-green, buff, 8.75 x 5.5, -/96. Fp, 58 mono phots, 4 maps, no appendixes, no Index.
* Not a Regtl history, but a splendid record of behind-the-lines operations by various ad hoc WWII native units on and around the Solomon Islands. They not only gathered intelligence and made clandestine raids, they also rescued many stranded Allied aircrew who had been shot down. R/2 V/3. PC. HEC.
Note: reference should be made also to THE WAR FROM COCONUT SQUARE - THE STORY OF THE DEFENCE OF THE PACIFIC ISLANDS, by H E L Priday (A H & A W Reed, Wellington, NZ, 1945).

PACIFIC COMMANDOS
New Zealanders and Fijians in Action
A History of Southern Independent Commando and First Commando Fiji Guerillas
Colin R Larsen * A H & A W Reed, Wellington, NZ, 1946. Yellow, black, 8.75 x 5.5, xiv/161. 12 mono phots, 5 maps, no Index. Apps: Roll of Honour, H&A, nominal rolls,

list of Commandos engaged on special raids.
* A useful and interesting account of a 'special forces' unit operating in an obscure off-shoot of the main Pacific campaign in WWII. R/4 V/3. PC. JS.

FIJIANS AT WAR
Aresula Ravuvu * Star Printery, Suva, for the Institute of Pacific Studies, 1988. Illustrated soft card, 'Soldier and Solomon Islands' motif, brown, red, 8.25 x 5.75, vii/69. 14 mono phots, one map, Bibliography, Chapter Notes, no appendixes, Index.
* A publication which seems to have started life as an academic exercise and which then developed into a nicely presented little book. The narrative lacks depth, but it neatly summarises Fijian early military experiences, initial responses to the Japanese threat, recruitment and training, and active services in the Solomons campaign (Kolombangara and Bougainville). There are useful references to 1st Fiji Regt and 1st Commando Fiji Guerrillas. R/3 V/3. NZMODL. HEC.
Note: reference should be made also to THE PACIFIC WAR - OFFICIAL HISTORY OF NEW ZEALAND IN THE SECOND WORLD WAR, 1939-1945, by Oliver A Gillespie (New Zealand Government, War History Branch, 1952). Gillespie helped to edit the unofficial histories of the 3rd NZ Division (vide the Index for New Zealand), but this is his major account of that theatre of war in toto. Chapter 10 deals with Fiji-raised units. These comprised mainly Fijian rank and file, with a small proportion of Tongans, all under the command of New Zealand officers and SNCOs. The chapter describes guerrilla warfare on the island of Guadalcanal in 1942-1943 (a party of twenty-three), the work of 1st Commando Fiji Guerrillas and 1st Fiji Regt on New Georgia and Vella Lavella in 1943, and 2nd Commando Fiji Guerrillas with 1st and 3rd Fiji Regt Brigade Group on Bougainville in 1943-1945. Fijians were trained also for service in Burma, but were never sent there. RH.

Note: several books relating to clandestine operations amongst the islands of the SW Pacific have been mentioned on this and the two previous pages, either as main entries or as footnotes. For those seeking further information, the following sources are recommended:

FIRE OVER THE ISLANDS, by D C Horton (Leo Cooper Ltd, London, 1975). Dick Horton was a coastwatcher in 1942-1943 on the island of New Georgia, and this is his personal memoir. As previously noted, he subsequently wrote a more comprehensive account - RING OF FIRE - for the same publisher.

LONELY VIGIL - COAST WATCHERS OF THE SOLOMONS, by Walter Lord (Viking Press, New York, USA, 1977). This book covers the Solomon Islands coastwatching services during the period 1942-1944.

AUSTRALIA IN THE WAR OF 1939-1945, Volume V, Series One (Army), by Dudley McCarthy (William Collins, for the Australian War Memorial, Canberra, 1959). This volume includes references to the Papua New Guinea Volunteer Rifles, a pre-war part-time unit consisting of Australians and Americans resident (employed) in that territory. Mobilised at the outbreak of war with Japan, they fulfilled subsequently a wide range of specialist roles in the New Guinea and Solomon Islands campaigns.

Police

A HISTORY OF THE FIJI POLICE
J B Collie * Available only in facsimile TS, reproduced in limited numbers from time to time for distribution to students at the Police Depot and Training School, n.d. No ills, no maps, no appendixes, no Index.
* A condensed account of police work in Fiji during roughly the first sixty years of the 20th Century. Packed with information regarding Stations, crimes, weapons, trials, etc. Few individuals are named other than those who received awards and decorations. The Fiji Police were a para-military force, responsible both for law enforcement and for local defence. The author gives local coverage for both WWI and for WWII (when the huge influx of Allied troops created exceptional policing problems). R/4 V/3. CFHT. PJE.

KNIGHTS ERRANT OF PAPUA
Lewis Letts * William Blackwood & Son, Edinburgh and London, 1935. Blue, gold, 8.75 x 5.5, xiv/284. Fp, one other mono phot, one map, Glossary, Bibliography, no appendixes, Index.
* The Papuan Armed Constabulary was formed by Sir William McGregor in 1890. This book, which includes numerous anecdotes and references to major trials, covers the period from formation through to 1927. R/4 V/2. SLV. PS.

PATROLLING IN PAPUA
W R Humphries * T Fisher Unwin Ltd, London, 1923. Red, gold, 8.75 x 5.5, -/287. Fp, 38 mono phots, one map, no appendixes, Index.
* A personal memoir by a man who was employed as a Patrol Officer with the Papuan Armed Constabulary in 1917. R/4 V/1. SLV. PS.
Note: similar memoirs are PAPUA EPIC, by Keith Bushell, and SAVAGES IN SERGE, by J G Hindes.

NOTES

PART 13

Australia

NOTES

INTRODUCTION

The writing of Australian unit histories does not conform with the pattern found in other former British Dominions. The majority of the three hundred and fifty titles listed in this section have been published in the last forty years. This tardiness in recording the nation's military history may perhaps be explained by its social history.

In the pre-Federation period, people came to settle in the Australian Colonies for different reasons at different times. The first arrivals, from 1788, were convicts and those who guarded them. The opening of the 19th Century marked the appearance of free settlers. They perceived the land as offering opportunities for profit and advancement in agriculture and trade, but within a less rigid class system than existed in Great Britain. This new society was saved from acquiring a class structure of its own by the wave of immigration which resulted from the development of the Victorian and New South Wales goldfields in the 1850s. The majority of these new settlers - who trebled the previous population of the Colonies - were of British stock. They brought with them British social values and mores but, as demonstrated by their decision to seek a new life, they were not hidebound by old conventions.

These Colonial societies began almost immediately, in the 1850s, to move towards responsible self-government, universal suffrage, trade unionism, and mass public education. Class differences existed, but they were less marked than in Great Britain, and social mobility was less constrained.

Even though they included a high proportion of men who had served in the British and Indian Armies, the early Australian Colonials were unlike their ancestors in that they had no particular tradition in the profession of arms. At the same time, they felt a profound loyalty to the Crown and actively supported a large number of militia units in the cities and also in the sparsely populated country areas.

The number and size of these units expanded greatly during the 1850s - the gold rush decade - and then again during the 1870s when the British Army garrison regiments had departed and there were fears of a Russian invasion. The enthusiasm of the volunteer militiamen, their willingness to provide their own horses and uniforms, might be partially explained by a need for the sort of social intercourse and companionship which these units provided in the more isolated districts. The military avocation also personified and strengthened the Australian spirit of 'mateship' which, in turn, implied and encouraged egalitarianism. Officers were primus inter pares. They earned the right to command by ability and character rather than quality of education or by inherited social standing.

These part-time volunteer soldiers were confident men, proud of themselves, their district, their Colony, and their association with the Empire. When the need arose - when called upon to assist 'the mother country' in New Zealand, the Sudan, China, and South Africa - they were more than willing to step forward. Sentiments of patriotism and loyalty were powerful factors, but each of those campaigns held the added attraction of travel to foreign parts and high adventure. They were almost irresistable to young men already sensing within themselves an emergent and distinctive national character.

Those early Colonial units, many of which are still today perpetuated in the Australian Army's Order of Battle, were raised at a time when horsemanship was an economic and social necessity, and when skilled horsemanship was a much admired attribute of manhood. It is not without significance that the earliest Australian unit history recorded in this bibliography, published in 1901, is that of the New South Lancers. The image of the dashing Lighthorseman is a potent icon in the national consciousness which has survived Australia's transition into a highly urbanised and sophisticated industrial nation.

As the events of 1914 and 1939 were to show, the economic and political changes which followed the coming together of the six Colonies in 1901 did nothing to diminish the willingness of young Australians to serve the Empire's military needs, or to reduce their yearning for travel and adventure. However, inevitable social change started to become evident after 1946. During the twenty years after the war, a fresh wave of migrants arrived from Continental Europe who had no ties of any kind with Great Britain. They have been succeeded, in turn, by more recent influxes of 'new Australians' from Asia. The effect has been a gradual dilution of the traditional bonds with Great Britain and the Crown. At the same time, most Australians are very aware of their country's roots. It may be a paradox, but public interest in the war services of those generations which fought on behalf of Great Britain and her allies is now greater than ever before. Australia's publishing industry has responded vigorously to a popular mood of enquiry and self-appraisal regarding the nation's military heritage. The publication dates recorded in many of the following entries are a reflection of this phenomenon.

In common with Canada, South Africa, and New Zealand, the expeditionary forces mounted by Australia to fight on various occasions outside their own natural frontiers have consisted, with rare exceptions, of volunteers. As citizen soldiers, attested for service only during a specific conflict, they did not belong to a military caste having an interest in perpetuating the traditions and ethos of that caste. When they came home from those conflicts, when they faced the difficulties of re-establishing themselves in civilian life after demobilisation, they were too busy and too dispersed to engage in the publication of a record of their individual and shared experiences. Only later, when they had settled into middle age, did they have time and opportunity to seek out former comrades and raise the funds needed for such enterprises. A substantial number of WWI unit histories was produced in the 1920s and 1930s, but many more were still appearing in the 1940s and 1950s. Following the same pattern, many of the Australian units raised for service in WWII have been publishing their histories in the 1980s - forty and more years after the events which they record. It is known that several more are in the course of preparation.

In general terms, the quality of authorship found in Australian unit histories is very good. A few are written in flippant 'digger' style, but the majority are subjective and authoritative. The quality of presentation is less consistent, varying widely between the professionally designed, printed and bound book, and the home-grown amateur 'economy' plastic-covered folder. Most of them share one common strength - they make plentiful mention of the invidual officers and men who served. As is the case in Canada, the authors have taken exceptional steps to record the name of everyone who joined, fought, died, was wounded or taken prisoner, was decorated, and who came safely home at the end of it all. These nominal roll appendixes are a prime source for genealogists and social historians.

Most Australian unit histories, certainly those published before the 1960s, can be classififed as rare or excessively rare. They were printed in relatively modest numbers, and copies were acquired mainly by those who had served and by their families. Only a few have reappeared subsequently on the open market. To meet the growing demand for such works of reference, John Burridge, a dealer resident in Swanbourne, Western Australia, decided in 1982 to sponsor the republication of the rarest titles. Since that date, he has produced sixty such reprints and more are planned for the future. They fall into two main categories - those reproduced in facsimile and without amendment, and those which John Burridge has expanded, corrected, and improved (by adding various important appendixes, for example). In this bibliography, an explanatory footnote has been added to those entries which refer to original works which have since been significantly modified. For the rest, with so many reprints having been produced, and with more to come, there is no such footnote.

ORDER OF PRECEDENCE
of the Regiments and Corps
as authorised, 1976

Regular Army

Australian Staff Corps
Royal Australian Armoured Corps
Royal Regiment of Australian Artillery
Royal Australian Engineers
Royal Australian Survey Corps
Royal Australian Corps of Signals
Royal Australian Infantry
Australian Army Aviation Corps
Australian Intelligence Corps
Royal Australian Army Chaplain's Department
Royal Australian Corps of Transport
Royal Australian Army Medical Corps
Royal Australian Army Dental Corps
Royal Australian Army Ordnance Corps
Royal Australian Electrical & Mechanical Engineers
Royal Australian Army Educational Corps
Australian Army Catering Corps
Royal Australian Army Pay Corps
Australian Army Legal Corps
Royal Australian Corps of Military Police
Australian Army Psychology Corps
Australian Army Band Corps
Royal Australian Army Nursing Corps
Women's Royal Australian Army Corps
The Royal Australian Regiment

Citizen Military Force (later Army Reserve)

The Royal Queensland Regiment
The Royal New South Wales Regiment
The Royal Victoria Regiment
The Royal South Australia Regiment
The Royal Western Australia Regiment
The Royal Tasmania Regiment
2nd/14th Queensland Mounted Infantry
12th/16th Hunter River Lancers
1st/15th Royal New South Wales Lancers
4th/19th Prince of Wales' Light Horse
8th/13th Victorian Mounted Rifles
3rd/9th South Australian Mounted Rifles
10th Light Horse
Queensland University Regiment
Sydney University Regiment
University of New South Wales Regiment
Melbourne University Regiment
Monash University Regiment
Adelaide University Regiment
Western Australian University Regiment

AUSTRALIA
A Military Chronology

1770: Capt James Cook RN claims Crown sovereignty at Botany Bay (the modern city of Sydney will evolve nearby).
1788: guarded by a detachment of Royal Marines, the first group of transported convicts arrives from England at Botany Bay in January. The practice of sending convicts to penal settlements on the eastern seaboard will continue for the next sixty-four years.
1789: the New South Wales Corps is recruited from ex-British Army soldiers and ex-Royal Marines for guard duties in the new settlements.
1803: an Englishman, Matthew Flinders, completes an eight years survey of the Continent's coastlines. He names it Terra Australis.
1852: the transportation of convicts to the eastern seaboard is discontinued.
1855: the war in the Crimea raises fears of a Russian invasion. Ports are fortified and local volunteer units are created to supplement the British Army garrisons. London grants 'responsible government' to New South Wales and Victoria (and later to the other Colonies, the last being Western Australia in 1890).
1860: the transportation of convicts is resumed, but only to the Swan River area (on the western seaboard, with the largest settlement later becoming the city of Fremantle). The Enrolled Pensioner Force, a unit composed of ex-British Army men, is formed in England and sent as guards aboard the transports and in the settlements after their arrival.
1863: most of the British Army garrison regiments depart for New Zealand to fight in the Maori (Land) Wars. With them are 1500 Australian Colonial volunteers (later to be described as 'the Waikato Militia').
1868: the transportation of convicts to the western seaboard is discontinued. The practice will never be resumed.
1870: twenty-nine British Army regiments have served at least one tour of duty in the Australian Colonies during the previous ninety years. The last of them now departs. New unpaid local Volunteer units are raised to replace them.
1884: the Colonies agree a scheme of mutual defence and the establishment of a Militia organisation. This consists of paid and partly-paid permanent and part-time units based in the more densely populated areas. The unpaid Volunteers, who provide their own uniforms and who have not contracted for a fixed term of service, are retained for service in the country districts.
1885: New South Wales sends a Contingent to join the Imperial Forces fighting in the Sudan. It is deployed briefly at Suakin. The unit sees little action, but the event is a milestone - this is the first occasion when troops from the Australian continent have fought for the Crown in another region of the world.
1900: volunteer Contingents from each of the six Colonies sail for South Africa to fight the Boers. They join the NSW Lancers who had landed at Cape Town some months earlier. More than 16,000 officers and men from the Australian Colonies will fight in this war before it is ended.
1901: the six Colonies federate. They form the Commonwealth of Australia under a Federal and State system of government. Defence becomes a national responsibility. The China Field Force, consisting of naval and military units from New South Wales, Victoria, and South Australia, returns home after serving in the international campaign against the Boxers.
1903-1904: the Commonwealth Defence Acts confirm the distinction between paid troops (Militia) and unpaid part-time troops (Volunteers). Collectively they are designated the CMF (Citizen Military Forces).
1909: the CMF is restructured as the Active Forces (encompassing the Militia and the Volunteers), and the Inactive Forces (reserves of officers, etc).
1911: compulsory part-time military training is introduced for all males between 12 and 18 years of age (as Cadets), and between 19 and 26 (as Militia). The Active Forces are radically overhauled, but they amount to only twelve battalions fit for service. This number will grow to fifty-two during the next three years. The Royal Military College, Duntroon, is established.

1914: an Australian Expeditionary Force captures German New Guinea and New Britain in the opening weeks of the war. By the terms of the Defence Acts, CMF units cannot be despatched for service in France. The call to aid 'the mother country' is met by creating an entirely new army - the AIF (Australian Imperial Force). An all-volunteer army, it takes its recruits from the trained and semi-trained ranks of the twelve Active Force battalions which had existed prior to 1912. The 1st Australian Division embarks for England. It is accompanied by the leading elements of the NZEF (New Zealand Expeditionary Force). Together they are designated ANZAC (Australian and New Zealand Army Corps).
1915: lack of accomodation in England has caused 1st Australian Division to disembark in Egypt. At this time, the assault on the Dardanelles is conceived. The Australian and New Zealand units in Egypt are assigned to it. The subsequent elan and gallantry of these men on Gallipoli gives birth to the ANZAC legend. After eight months of costly and bitter fighting, all Allied troops are evacuated from the Peninsula.
1916: after regrouping and reinforcement in Egypt, the AIF is divided into two elements. The Light Horse regiments revert to the mounted role and join the campaign to drive the Turks from Sinai, Gaza, Palestine, and Syria. The infantry element, now expanded to five Divisions, moves to France to fight on the Western Front. They are allocated to various Corps of the British Army.
1918: the British reluctantly agree that these Divisions be unified in an Australian Corps under their own commander, General Monash. The men respond magnificently. By war's end, 331,781 Australians have volunteered for military service. Of these, 63,163 have been killed and 152,422 wounded.
1919: there is a popular uprising in Egypt. Australian troops play a prominent role in suppressing it and thereby sustaining the British administration. Other Australian troops volunteer for service in North Russia against the Bolsheviks.
1921: the AIF is disbanded. Compulsory part-time training is scaled down and is applied only in urban areas. Total CMF strength declines to less than 40,000 all ranks.
1929: the Federal Government scraps compulsory training and introduces a part-time and partially-paid all-volunteer force to be known as the Volunteer Militia. Total strength falls to 27,000. The CMF title gradually falls into disuse. The Volunteer Militia, the Permanent Force, and the Reserves, have the collective title of AMF (Australian Military Forces).
1938: a national recruitment campaign boosts AMF membership to 80,000. All elements are attested for home service only.
1939: history repeats itself. Australia does not have an army enlisted and trained for service overseas. A new Australian Imperial Force (2nd AIF) is formed from men volunteering from all elements of the AMF. They are attested for service in any part of the world. The new units are distinguished by a 2/ prefix. They are authorised also to display an AIF suffix, but some choose not to do so.
1940: in January, the first elements of 6th Division embark for Egypt in company with ships carrying 4th New Zealand Brigade. In later months they are followed by 7th and 9th Divisions. The 6th will fight in Libya, Greece, Crete and Syria, the 7th and 9th in Syria, and the 9th will win fame and glory as 'Tobruk rats' and at El Alamein. On the south east coast of England, 18th Brigade is deployed briefly as part of the anti-invasion force.
1941: 8th Division joins units of the British and Indian Armies in Malaya. In November, the pride of the Royal Australian Navy, the cruiser HMAS Sydney, is sunk off north west Australia by a German commerce raider, the Kormoran. Three weeks later, Australia is at war not only with Germany and Italy but also her northern neighbour, Japan.
1942: the Japanese advance rapidly through Indo-China, the Philippines, and the Pacific islands. Singapore falls and 8th Australian Division is ordered to surrender. Serious disagreements develop between the governments of the United Kingdom and Australia. The former is concerned with defending the Suez Canal and the Iraqi oilfields, the latter is increasingly worried by the possibility that the Japanese

will invade its home territory. In May, Australian anxieties increase sharply when Japanese submarines penetrate Sydney harbour. Attempting to attack an American cruiser, the USS Chicago, they instead sink a floating barracks, the ferry ship Kuttabul. Australian perceptions of Great Britain as 'the mother country' begin to change fundamentally and permanently. Churchill and Premier Curtin resolve the immediate differences, and 6th and 7th Divisions are brought home from the Middle East and commence training for a campaign in New Guinea (where serious fighting started in March). En route, two Brigades of 6th Division are diverted to Ceylon to counter any possible invasion of the island. After six months, they too return to Australia. The northern coastlines are placed on a war footing.

1943: conscription for overseas service is introduced for the first time in the nation's history, but only for duties in the South West Pacific area (specifically, south of the Equator and including the Solomon Islands). Initially, units composed mainly of conscripts are granted neither the 2/ prefix nor the AIF suffix. Many of these conscripts subsequently re-attest as 'AIF volunteers'. Units having more than three-quarters of their strength composed of such men are then granted the AIF suffix (but not the 2/ prefix which remains the prized privilege of the pre-1943 units). This two-tier system of designation is not always helpful to good inter-unit cooperation. In this same year, the last Australian troops in the Middle East, 9th Division, return home and are reassigned to the Pacific campaign.

1944: there is a lull in the major and exhausting campaign, being fought alongside the Americans, to dislodge Japanese forces from the mountain jungles of New Guinea and from the islands of New Britain and Bougainville.

1945: the fighting in New Guinea reaches a new level of intensity and continues until August (when the island's northern coastline is finally cleared of invaders). Attention then turns to the island of Borneo where amphibious assaults are made at Tarakan, Brunei, Balikpapan, and Labuan.

1946: the 2nd AIF is disbanded. Compulsory service, in the part-time Volunteer Militia, is kept in force, but for home defence duties only. A small Regular Army (its all-volunteer personnel being attested for service worldwide) is established. It provides a Brigade Group to serve with the British Commonwealth Occupation Force in Japan.

1949: the AMF title falls into misuse. The term CMF is reinstated.

1950: Regular Army units serve with 1st British Commonwealth Division in Korea. The last of them are not withdrawn until 1957.

1951: a new National Service Act provides for compulsory full-time training of three months' duration in the CMF. It will be repealed seven years later.

1954: a Battalion Group commences ten years of continuous service in Malaya.

1960: following major changes in legislation and organisation, the Regular Army is expanded and the CMF becomes an all-volunteer Army Reserve with an overseas capability.

1962: Australia's involvement in the Vietnam war begins with the despatch of an Army Training Team. It is followed by a Battalion Group operating under US Army command. The Group later expands to Task Force size.

1965: the war does not enjoy popular support at home. Selective conscription is required to sustain the Task Force at full strength. In addition to the commitment in South Vietnam, the Australian Army is engaged in the 'confrontation' with Indonesia (in Borneo), and in the first of several UN peace-keeping missions in other parts of the world.

1972: reflecting public sentiment, a new government is elected with a mandate to end selective conscription and to withdraw all Australian forces from Vietnam. Both measures are put immediately into effect.

1975: the Department of Defence is reorganised. The three armed services retain their individual identity, but henceforth they are each answerable directly to a new Chief of Defence Force Staff. The armed forces are given the collective title The Australian Defence Force (ADF).

1984: the ADF moves further towards a unified command with the creation of a joint services headquarters.

1988–1989: the Active Army Reserve units are integrated into the Order of Battle of the Australian Regular Army.
1991: major reforms, to be spread over several years, are proposed. Some military bases will be closed, the number of Regular battalions reduced, administrative and support services increasingly 'civilianised', a Ready Reserve Brigade formed from volunteers enlisted on a short-service engagement, and the bulk of the Army's assets concentrated around Darwin and Townsville.
1992–1993: Australian units have participated, under US command, in the Gulf campaign. Others have served, or are serving, with UN peace-keeping missions in Namibia, Cambodia, the Western Sahara, Somalia, Cyprus, and the Middle East.

Reference sources:

The majority of published Australian unit histories are recorded in the following pages. For additional information regarding certain specific campaigns, reference should be made to other sections of this bibliography. Vide page 773, Index, 'Australians abroad'.

GENERAL REFERENCE

A SELECT BIBLIOGRAPHY OF AUSTRALIAN MILITARY HISTORY, 1891-1939
Jean Fielding and Robert O'Neill * Australian War Memorial, Canberra, ACT, 1978. Soft card, green, red, 'Digger' motif, 9.5 x 6.75, vi/351. No ills, no maps, no appendixes, Glossary, no Index.
* This important bibliographic source covers six distinct periods of military activity - pre-Federation (1891-1901), Anglo-Boer War (1899-1901), Boxer Rebellion (1900-1901), post-Federation (1901-1914), WWI (1914-1918), inter-war Defence and political themes (1919-1939), and general sources (1891-1939). Like most traditional bibliograpies, this one has entries which are extremely brief and which give little more than each item's title, sub-title, author, publisher, and date of publication. However, it does cover a very wide range of material and includes articles noted in newspapers and periodicals. The book is a good starting point for any military researcher. R/2 V/5. ANL. MCND'A.
Note: the weakness of the above-mentioned book is the fact that it does not cover WWII or post-WWII events. An additional source which does (at least partially) meet this need is AUSTRALIAN MILITARY BIBLIOGRAPHY, by C E Dornbusch (Hope Farm Press, Cornwallville, New York, 1963). Dornbusch was a professional librarian who created a fine collection of British and Commonwealth military records at the New York Public Library (where he worked for many years). He lists 544 items of all kinds. Their research value is patchy, and there are many gaps, but he does give useful details for many of his entries and his Index alone is a helpful source.

THE LINEAGES OF THE AUSTRALIAN ARMY
Alfred N Festberg * Allara Publishing Pty Ltd, Melbourne, 1972. Cloth-backed stiff card, red, gold, 10.25 x 7.5, x/118. No ills, no maps, no appendixes, Glossary, Indexes.
* This useful book explains the origins and complex evolution of all Australian mounted, mechanised, and infantry units, and gives details of their secondary titles, Battle Honours, Regtl marches, mottoes, etc. It includes an outline history of the military forces of the Australian Colonies prior to 1901, and the development of the Commonwealth's Army thereafter. Particularly helpful are the annotations which show the dates when the title of each unit was changed. R/2 V/5. PS/MCND'A.
Note: a first draft of this work was produced in 1966 under the auspices of The Military History Society of Australia (Victoria branch), with the title AUSTRALIAN ARMY LINEAGE BOOK. It was printed in facsimile typescript on flimsy paper and within an 'economy' binding. The 1972 edition (as described above) is to be preferred. However, there have been further changes in nomenclature and organisation, so even the second edition has been overtaken by events.

AUSTRALIA - TWO CENTURIES OF WAR AND PEACE
M McKernan and M Browne * Macarthur Press, Sydney, for Allen & Unwin, with the Australian War Memorial, 1988. Black, silver, 9.75 x 7.5, -/467. 43 mono phots, 14 cld ills, 4 sketches, no maps, no appendixes, Glossary, Bibliography, no Index.
* An important anthology of essays by several leading military historians. They take a fresh and often controversial look at the development of military activity on the Australian continent from the earliest days (the European conquest of the aboriginal tribes) through to the larger conflicts of the 20th Century (WWI, WWII, the post-war 'Empire' campaigns, Korea, and South Vietnam). References to the emergence of a national identity through the trials of war, and the creation of the ANZAC tradition, are particularly interesting. Recommended background reading. R/1 V/3. AWM. MCND'A.
Note: an additional source is SOLDIERING ON - THE AUSTRALIAN ARMY AT HOME AND OVERSEAS, compiled by the Australian War Memorial, Canberra, 1942, and based upon contributions from several anonymous soldiers who were then serving in various theatres of war. Well illustrated, and a useful mirror of the feelings and experiences of 1942.

ARMY AUSTRALIA – AN ILLUSTRATED HISTORY

George Odgers * The Griffin Press, Adelaide, for Child & Associates, 1988. Illustrated stiff card, red/yellow, 'Helicopter and troops' motif on front cover, 'Jungle patrol' on rear cover, 12.25 x 9.0, -/280. Fp, several hundred mono phots, 41 cld ills, 11 maps, Bibliography, Index. Apps: the ninety-six Australian VC winners, with individual picture of each.

* Although at first glance a 'coffee table' book, this splendid publication is in some ways the most complete record of military activity in Australia ever compiled. It covers the period 1788-1988, and is divided into six major parts - British Army units stationed in Australia, Australian Contingents which fought in the Maori (Land) Wars, in the Sudan and South Africa (1899-1902), the first AIF (1914-1919), the inter-war years, the second AIF and WWII, and then the post-war campaigns (Malaya, Korea, Borneo, and South Vietnam). The story-line concludes with a review of the Australian Army's role and status in the 1980s. The author is a professional historian. The quality of his research is reflected in the scale and quality of the information contained in this book. R/1 V/5. ANL. MCND'A.

THE COLONIAL VOLUNTEERS

The Defence Forces of the Australian Colonies, 1836–1901

Bob Nicholls * Allen & Unwin Pty Ltd, Sydney, 1988. Purple, gold, 9.25 x 6.0, xvii/215. 58 mono phots, 15 cld ills, no maps, Bibliography, Index. Apps: 'Tables of 1901 Stocktake of Ordnance', 'Text of the Colonial Naval Defence Act, 1865'.

* An excellent modern interpretation of the development of the Defence Forces raised by each of the six Colonies during the sixty years prior to Federation. Meticulously researched from original sources, but written in a style acceptable to both the specialist and the general reader. The narrative covers not only the land forces but also coastal defence and naval units. The actions of the Colonial Governments in sending forces to North China in 1900 (500 sailors from the NSW and Victorian Naval Brigades and a gunboat from South Australia) are described in interesting detail, as are the despatch of forces to South Africa during that same period. An intriguing and well illustrated book. R/1 V/5. ANL. MCND'A.

VICTORIAN LAND FORCES, 1853–1883

George F Ward * Talkprint Pty Ltd, Sunshine, Victoria, 1989. Illustrated soft card, buff, brown, 11.25 x 8.25, -/155. 49 mono phots, 3 maps, no appendixes, Bibliography, Glossary, Index of Persons, Index of Military Units.

* An informative account of all the military forces which served in Victoria during the stated period. Detailed information is given for more than eighty different local units (or unit designations), and also for the British Army units stationed in the Colony during that time. The text includes various rolls of officers, notes on medals, details of uniforms and administration, and much else of a specialist nature. R/1 V/5. ANL. MCND'A.

VOLUNTEERS AT HEART

The Queensland Defence Forces, 1860–1901

D H Johnson * University Press of Queensland, St Lucia, Queensland, 1975. Brown, white, 8.5 x 5.5, -/248. 20 mono phots, no maps, Bibliography, Glossary, Index. Apps: Volunteer Infantry Corps (1860-1879), The Queensland Defence Force (as constituted in 1884, 1893, and 1900).

* A formidably researched account of Queensland's early military history. The appendixes provide a mass of technical information for the specialist, but the main narrative is written in broader terms. It describes the problems facing the Colony in 1859 (when it became independent from New South Wales), and the subsequent tensions created by 'the Russian scare' of the 1870s and the arrival of the Germans in New Guinea in 1893. Queensland's contributions to the Sudan war, and the despatch of a Contingent to the South African war, are well covered.
R/1 V/5. ANL. MCND'A.

WITH THE VOLUNTEERS
A Historical Diary of the Volunteer Military Forces of the North West and West Coasts of Tasmania, 1886-1986
Maj D M Wyatt RFD * Richmond Printers, Devonport, Tasmania, for the author, 1987. Black, gold, 'Horse and bugle' motif, 11.5 x 8.0, xii/348. More than 100 mono phots, one line drawing, 2 maps, Bibliography, Glossary, Index. Apps: rolls of former officers (for each of the six units), 'Lineages of the NW Volunteer Defence Forces (of Tasmania), 1892-1898'.
* A well produced history of - the Tasmanian Rangers (1886-1945), Tasmanian Mounted Infantry (1899-1943), Volunteer Defence Corps (1940-1945), 12th Australian Bn (1948-1957), and 47th and 44th Coys of the RAASC/RACT. One chapter deals with the Tasmanian Contingent in the Boer War, another with services in WWI, and others with the various local Volunteer units raised in this area of Tasmania over nearly 100 years. R/1 V/5. ANL. MCND'A.
Note: published as a limited edition of 1000 copies.

A LION IN THE COLONY
An Historical Account of the Tasmanian Colonial Volunteer Military Forces 1859-1901
Maj D M Wyatt RFD * The Print Centre, Hobart, Tasmania, for the author, 1990. Illustrated soft card, red, 'Arms of Tasmania and Volunteers' motif, 9.75 x 6.75, x/62. 40 mono phots, 4 cld ills, one map, Bibliography, Index. Apps: list of British Army Regts which served in Tasmania (1803-1870), evolution of the Tasmanian Volunteer Force (1859-1901).
* Maj Wyatt's first book (vide preceding entry) was focussed upon a specific area of Tasmania from 1886 to 1986. This second (and much shorter) book examines the military history of Tasmania as a whole, but only in the second half of the 19th Century. Known as Van Diemen's Land until 1853, Tasmania was a British Colony until 1901. It then became part of the new Commonwealth of Australia. It was garrisoned by the British Army until 1870, twenty different Regts having been stationed there at various times from 1803 onwards. Local Volunteer units such as the Hobart Town Artillery were formed in the 1860s, but expansion in the 1870s and 1880s was rapid. Artillery units, and the Tasmanian Engineer Corps, were much preoccupied by the possibility of a Russian invasion, and the author provides good detail of their armaments, strengths and activities. Many local officers are named in the text. R/1 V/4. ANL. MCND'A.

THE VOLUNTEER MOVEMENT IN WESTERN AUSTRALIA, 1861-1903
George F Wieck * Paterson Brokenshaw Pty Ltd, Perth, WA, n.d. (c.1962). Illustrated stiff card, cream, red/blue, 7.25 x 4.74, -/88. Two line drawings (helmet plates), no maps, no Index. Apps: list of Commandants of WA Volunteer units, list of WA Volunteer Corps units (1862-1903), list of British Army garrison units (1829-1862).
* This little volume details the history of the various Volunteer units raised in WA from the time it accepted responsibility for its own defence (1861) through to the inauguration of the Federation of Australian Colonies (1901). The original threat to European settlers was from the Aborigines trying to protect their tribal lands, and then (1851-1868) from unruly transported convicts. Neither threat ever resulted in active service. The background is clearly explained, and Chapter 6 gives details of all thirty-nine units, large and small, long- and short-lived, which were formed during the stated period. Lists of officers and their dates of service are inserted in the text. Other chapters cover armament, defence works, finance, organisation, uniforms, badges, etc. R/4 V/4. RAI. AMM.

MUSKETS AND DRILLS
An Account of the Volunteer Corps raised in Western Australia in 1861
James Ritchie Grant * Grime's Dyke Publications, Perth, WA, 1983. Card, orange, blind, 11.5 x 8.25, iii/65. No ills, no maps, Bibliography, no appendixes, no Index.
* A survey of the seven most important Volunteer units raised in 1861 and their services over the next four decades - the Fremantle, Metropolitan and Sussex Volunteer Rifle Corps, the York Volunteers, the Pinjarrah Mounted Volunteer Corps, etc. Nominal rolls for each unit (as recorded in 1862-1863) appear at various points in the text. R/4 V/3. ANL. MCND'A.
Note: additional information regarding these units is to be found in OFFICERS OF THE WESTERN AUSTRALIA DEFENCE FORCE, 1861-1901, also by James Ritchie Grant (published by John Burridge Military Antiques, Swanbourne, WA, 1988). The author gives much biographical detail of officers Commissioned into the Force during that period, explains the lineages of local units, and includes details of the Western Australians who went to South Africa (1899-1902). A companion volume, from the same author and publisher, is FROM CAPTAINS TO COLONELS - A PHOTOGRAPHIC ACCOUNT OF THE DEVELOPMENT OF THE WESTERN AUSTRALIAN DEFENCE FORCE FROM 1861 TO 1901.

THE SHADOW'S EDGE
Australia's Northern War
Alan Powell * Melbourne University Press, Carlton, Victoria, 1988. Soft card, white, black, yellow, 8.5 x 5.5, xvi/346. 35 mono phots, 5 line drawings, 4 maps, Glossary, no appendixes, no Index.
* This is a history of the policies and deployments designed to defend Australia's northern coasts between 1876 and 1939. The author then shows how those arrangements were developed and altered during WWII when the possibility of a Japanese invasion was a cause for major concern. R/1 V/3. SLV. PS.

AUSTRALIAN MILITARY UNIFORMS, 1800-1982
Monty Wedd * Kangaroo Press, Kenthurst, NSW, 1982. Blue, gold, AIF badge, 11.5 x 8.5, -/144. Fp, 40 cld plates (indexed), more than 100 line drawings, no maps, Bibliography, Glossary, Index. Apps: 'Lists of Regts by Colony/State', 'List of Commonwealth Military Forces'.
* A meticulously researched book, well produced and finely illustrated. It covers the Volunteer units in all six Colonies, giving a brief history of the most important, with details of their uniforms, accoutrements and arms. It carries through to the changes resulting from Federation and the increasing standardisation of uniforms in the two world wars and after. R/1 V/5. AWM. MCND'A.

General Reference - Campaigns

ANZACS AT WAR
The Epic Story of the Battle Exploits that have made Australia and New Zealand a Fighting Legend since the Tragedy of Gallipoli
John Laffin * New Century Press Ltd, for Horwitz Grahame Books, Sydney, 1982. Illustrated paperback, full colour, 7.0 x 4.5, -/244. 16 mono phots, 5 maps, Index. Apps: list of 'gallant actions', VC awards (statistics only), explanatory notes.
* A well-known historian's account of Australian and New Zealand fighting men at war. Despite the wording of the sub-title, he commences with Elands River (South Africa, the Anglo-Boer War). Then follow a series of useful summaries of (seventy) actions or campaigns (mainly WWI and WWII) in which these troops distinguished themselves. Some the actions are well known, others much less so. R/1 V/3. PC. PS.
Note: reference may be made also to ANZACS - AUSTRALIANS AT WAR, A NARRATIVE HISTORY, by A K MacDougall (Reed Books, Sydney, 1991). This substantial work covers the same ground as the Laffin book, but it has additional references to Korea, Malaya, South Vietnam and the Gulf campaign.

THE AUSTRALIANS IN NINE WARS
Waikato to Long Tan
Peter Firkins * Robert Hale & Co, London, and Rigby Ltd, Adelaide, 1972. Green, gold, 9.5 x 6.5, -/448. 81 mono phots, 8 cld plates, 27 maps, no appendixes, Bibliography, 2 Indexes (General, Military Formations).
* A usefully detailed account of the wars in which Australian soldiers have taken part. Their major opponents have been, at one time or another, the Maori, the Dervishes, the Chinese Boxers, the Germans and Italians, the Japanese, the North Koreans and Chinese Communists, and the North Vietnamese. This is a background source which provides a good framework for the study of the formations and units named in the narrative. R/1 V/4. PC. RP.

THE OFFICIAL HISTORY OF AUSTRALIA'S INVOLVEMENT IN SOUTH EAST ASIAN CONFLICTS, 1948-1975
The Politics and Diplomacy of Australia's Involvement in South East Asian Conflicts, 1948-1965
Crises and Commitments
Peter Edwards and Gregory Pemberton * Allen & Unwin, North Sydney, in association with the Australian War Memorial, 1992. Black, gold, 9.75 x 7.5, xix/515. 36 mono phots, 33 line drawings (newspaper cartoons), 10 maps (8 printed in the text, indexed, two printed on the end-papers), Glossary, Bibliography, Chapter Notes. Apps: 'Major Office Bearers' (1945-1965), Biographical notes.
* This is the first in a major series of volumes which will be published from time to time in the coming years. It is a weighty and handsomely produced volume and the rest of the series, presumably, will be produced to the same high standard. Erudite and authoritative, the narrative describes the domestic and international politics of Australia's role in the Cold War (1945 onwards), the Malayan Emergency (1948-1960), the critical period of the Indonesian-Malaysian Conflict (1963-1966), and the crucial first decision to send Australian troops to South Vietnam in April 1965. This is a long awaited and much needed account of a tumultuous period in Australian history. The photographs are mainly of individuals. The line drawings are newspaper and magazine cartoons which reflected popular sentiment at various times. R/1 V/5. AWM. MCND'A.
Note: the second volume in the series was published in February 1993. Written by Ian McNeill and entitled TO LONG TAN - THE AUSTRALIAN ARMY AND THE VIETNAM WAR, 1950-1966, it is an account of Australian ground operations up to and including the Battle of Long Tan, August 1966. Like the first book in the series, it is a substantial work (522 pages), based upon a wide variety of sources. In due course, the publishers will be producing five more titles in the same format:
MEDICINE AT WAR, by Brendan O'Keefe and F B Smith
OPERATIONS IN BORNEO AND MALAYA, by Peter Dennis and Jeffrey Grey
POLITICS AND DIPLOMACY, 1965-1975, by Peter Edwards
GROUND OPERATIONS IN VIETNAM, by Jeffrey Grey and Chris Coulthard Clark
The seven books in the series are not serially numbered.

SOMETIMES FORGOTTEN
Being a Record of Australia's Military Forces who Died and those who were Decorated in Vietnam, Malaya, Borneo, Malay Peninsula, Korea, British Commonwealth Occupation Forces and with the United Nations
Frederick Kirkland OAM * Plaza Historical Service, Cremorne, NSW, 1990. Plastic, white, red, 9.75 x 6.75, -/238. No ills, no maps, Bibliography, Glossary, no Index. Apps: Rolls of Honour (one for each theatre), H&A (idem).
* This is a memorial designed primarily to assist medal collectors and family historians, but it has a wider research value. The author provides a remarkably detailed chronicle of all the conflicts in which Australian uniformed personnel (including those of the RAN and RAAF) were engaged between 1945 and 1970. The mass of historical and biographical information contained in this well arranged book is very helpful to several different categories of researcher.
R/1 V/4. ANL. MCND'A.

WORLD WAR I

THE OFFICIAL HISTORY OF AUSTRALIA IN THE WAR OF 1914-1918
Various authors (see below) * Angus & Robertson, Sydney, various dates in the 1920s and reprinted at numerous later dates in both hardback and softback covers. Red, gold, 8.5 x 5.5 (matching format), all volumes being heavily furnished with photographic illustrations, maps, appendixes, and Indexes.
* This official history fills twelve hefty volumes, only two of which (IX and XI) do not relate directly to the AIF. Each book is comprehensive, detailed, and easy to follow. Many individuals and their units are mentioned in the narrative, and the Indexes are excellent. The twelve volumes are:

Volume I, The Story of ANZAC from the Outbreak of War to the end of the First Phase of the Gallipoli Campaign, 4 May 1915
Volume II, The Story of ANZAC from 4 May 1915 onwards
Volume III, The Australian Imperial Force in France, 1916
Volume IV, The Australian Imperial Force in France, 1917
Volume V, The Australian Imperial Force in the Main German Offensive, 1918
Volume VI, The Australian Imperial Force during the Allied Offensive
Volume VII, The Australian Imperial Force in Sinai and Palestine, 1914-1918
Volume VIII, The Australian Flying Corps in the Western and Eastern Theatres of War, 1914-1918
Volume IX, The Royal Australian Navy
Volume X, The Australians at Rabaul, The Capture and Administration of the German Possessions in the Southern Pacific
Volume XI, Australia during the War
Volume XII, Photographic Record of the War, Pictures taken by Australian Official Photographers

The authors responsible for these volumes were - C E W Bean (I to VI inclusive), H S Gullett (VII), S S Mackenzie (X), and F M Cutlack, with Bean and Gullett (XII, this last volume containing 753 photographic illustrations).

ANZAC TO AMIENS
A Shorter History of the Australian Fighting Services in the First World War
C E W Bean * Halstead Press, Sydney, for the Australian War Memorial, Canberra, 1946. Maroon, gold, 8.5 x 6.0, xvi/567. 74 mono phots (indexed), 40 maps, Index (very detailed). Apps: notes on the 'Territorial Recruitment of the Australian Imperial Force', with all units comprehensively covered.
* This is a condensed version of the 12-volume Official History series described in the preceding entry. It is a handier format for those seeking information on the principal tribulations and successes of the AIF, but naturally it lacks most of the background detail to be found in the original major series. The excellent illustrations, maps and Index make the narrative easy to follow.
R/1 V/4. ANL. MCND'A.

AUSTRALIA IN ARMS
A Narrative of the Australian Imperial Force and their Achievement at ANZAC
Philip F E Schuler * T Fisher Unwin Ltd, London, 1916. Buff, black, AIF crest, 8.75 x 5.75, -/328. Fp, 51 mono phots, 9 maps (5 printed in the text, 4 bound in), Index. Apps: H&A (full citations for all awards, incl nine VCs, plus MIDs arranged by unit).
* The author was a War Correspondent who worked on Gallipoli. His remarkable record was published just four months after the evacuation, and his writing reflects the immediacy of its compilation. Arranged in three parts, his book describes the assembly of 1st Div AIF in Egypt, the ANZAC landing in April 1915 and the subsequent stalemate, and finally the fierce fighting around Lone Pine and Sari Bair. Helped by good illustrations and maps, the book serves to explain the birth of the ANZAC legend and is therefore of interest to Australian and New Zealand readers alike. R/3 V/4. ANL. MCND'A.

THE STORY OF THE FOURTH ARMY
In the Battle of the Hundred Days, August 8th to November 11th, 1918
Maj Gen Sir Archibald Montgomery KCMG CB * Hodder & Stoughton, London, n.d. (1920). Red, gold, 'Boar's head' motif, 11.5 x 8.75, xxiii/370. More than 100 mono phots, maps (case, separately, see below), Index. Apps: tables of casualties and drafts, statistics of POW and enemy equipment captured, Orders of Battle (for August, September, and November, 1918), notes on ammunition expenditure, idem MG unit organisation and tactics, full citations for all VCs awarded to Fourth Army personnel during that period.
* A massive compilation, and a primary source for a wide range of specialist researchers. The narrative opens with a summary of the Allied position on the Western Front as it existed in April 1918 and following the loss of Villers Bretonneux. It then describes the preparations for the major counter-offensive by the Allies which was to bring the war to an end in November. The book is inevitably concerned mainly with the larger events and the movements of the larger formations, but it provides a very good framework for an understanding of the actions of individual Australian and other Commonwealth units operating under Fourth Army's command. R/4 V/5. PC. RP.
Note: the book was published with an accompanying case of maps. These are very important if the research value of the narrative volume is to be exploited to the full.

THE AUSTRALIAN VICTORIES IN FRANCE IN 1918
Gen Sir John Monash GCMG KCB * Angus & Robertson Ltd, Sydney, 1936. Green, black, 7.75 x 5.0, xxvi/274. No ills, no maps, no Index. Apps: 'Grouping of Australian Divisions of Artillery, and Infantry Brigades, and the General Officers commanding them, May-October 1918'.
* This lucidly written book, by Australia's most famous commander and arguably the greatest tactician on the Allied side in WWI, is a classic account of the Australian Army Corps in the closing months of the war. The formation of an all-Australian fighting Corps was a development which had been too long delayed by the (British) senior commanders. Prior to 1918, Australian Divisions had been deployed piecemeal within British Army Corps. Australians at home and in the field resented the lack of confidence which these deployments implied. When eventually the Australian view prevailed, the Corps was brought together and was able to demonstrate its true worth. It had a marked influence upon the final Allied victory on the Western Front. Monash was the Corps Commander. He was a Jew of German descent. His parents had emigrated to Australia from Prussia and he had qualified as a civil engineer. He graduated also in Law and the Arts, and his wide-ranging intellect encompassed the theatre, music, literature, and the study of languages. None of this endeared him to the close-knit fraternity of the General Staff who found themselves outperformed by this Colonial amateur soldier. His book is essential reading for all students of the Western Front and 1918.
R/2 V/4. ANL. MCND'A.
Note: Monash is modest regarding his own achievements - he concentrates instead upon the courage and successes of his troops. The definitive account of his life is JOHN MONASH, A BIOGRAPHY, by Geoffrey Serle (Melbourne University Press, in conjunction with Monash University, 1982).

THE AUSTRALIANS - THEIR FINAL CAMPAIGN, 1918
An Account of the Concluding Operations of the Australian Divisions in France
F M Cutlack ('Official War Correspondent') * Sampson, Low, Marston & Co, London & Edinburgh, 1919. Red, gold lettering on spine, black on front cover, 7.5 x 5.25, viii/336. No ills, 15 maps and plans (8 printed in the text, 7 folding, bound in), Index. Apps: 'Composition of the Five Australian Divisions' (showing Order of Battle at Bde and Bn level).
* This book covers the same ground as that covered by Monash (vide preceding entry). Although written in lacklustre style, it does demonstrate that the aggressive

spirit of the Corps provided an important counter to the general war-weariness of many other Allied formations during the final year of the war. The excellent maps, and particularly the provision of an Index, make this book an easier source to consult than that written by Monash. R/2 V/4. ANL. MCND'A.

TASMANIA'S WAR RECORD, 1914–1918
L Broinowski * J Walch & Sons Ltd, for the Government of Tasmania, 1921. Red, gold, 10.0 x 6.25, xvi/370. Fp, 13 mono phots, one map, no Index. Apps: statistics on population/enlistments/deaths, nominal roll of all Tasmanians who served (with ranks, units, awards, casualties, length of service).
* This highly detailed book describes the services of every unit raised in Tasmania and is largely a narrative of places and events. Few names are mentioned in the main narrative, all such references appearing in the superb nominal roll appendix. Amongst the units mentioned are - 12th, 15th, 26th, 40th and 56th Bns AIF, and 3rd Light Horse. The author traces their respective services in Egypt, Gallipoli, Palestine, and on the Western Front. A goldmine for genealogists.
R/4 V/5. MODL. AMM.

A NOMINAL ROLL OF THE FIRST QUEENSLAND CONTINGENT, AIF, TO THE GREAT WAR
T A D Truswell * Ye Olde Curiosity Shoppe, Haberfield, NSW, 1983. Stiff card, yellow, black, 8.25 x 5.75, vi/53. No ills, no maps, no appendixes, no Index.
* This is simply a roll of every man who sailed for the Middle East in 1914 with the initial Queensland-raised units - 2nd Light Horse, 9th Inf Bn, and 3rd Field Ambulance. The names are arranged by unit, with a note of where and when each man embarked. R/2 V/2. PC. PS.
Note: while the above item was produced in 1983, an enterprising but unknown publisher produced a series of similar booklets in late 1914. The main title was FOR EMPIRE - AUSTRALIA'S RALLY TO THE DEAR OLD FLAG, followed by a 'State' sub-title, e.g. VICTORIA'S FIRST CONTINGENT TO THE MOTHERLAND.

THE POSTAL HISTORY OF THE AUSTRALIAN IMPERIAL FORCE DURING WORLD WAR ONE, 1914–1918
R C Emery * Hobbs the Printers, Southampton (UK), for the author, 1984. Green, gold, 10.0 x 8.0, viii/343. More than 200 ills and drawings, 18 maps, Glossary, Bibliography, Index. Apps: 17 in total, incl 'Composition and Record of Events' for each and every Div and Bde in the AIF, lists of Australian Transport and Hospital Ships, list of military hospitals and their movements and locations.
* The scale of this work is amazing. As the title might suggest, the author gives an exhaustive account of the role and operations of the postal services (Army, Navy, and Australian Flying Corps), from every aspect, in WWI. Postal activities, including the complex subject of censorship, are described for each theatre of war in interesting detail. In parallel, he covers the whole story of Australia's part in the war, and the appendixes are most helpful in this regard.
R/1 V/5. AWM. MCND'A.

DIVISIONS

AUSTRALIANS ON THE SOMME - POZIERES, 1916

Peter Charlton * Methuen Haynes, North Ryde, NSW, 1986. Grey, white, 9.0 x 6.0, xiv/317. 35 mono phots (indexed), 8 maps (7 printed in the text, one on the end-papers), no appendixes, Notes and Sources for each chapter, Index.

* This is the story of 1st Aust Div AIF in the Somme offensive which commenced on 1 July 1916. It concentrates upon the operations in the small area around the village of Pozieres. The author describes in a dispassionate way the conduct of the British and Australian general officers who wasted the lives of thousands of courageous but ill-prepared young Australian volunteer soldiers. The carnage of Pozieres had a deep impact upon the political climate in Australia, a repercussion which the author covers in detail. R/1 V/4. AWM. MCND'A.

OVER THE TOP WITH THE THIRD AUSTRALIAN DIVISION

G C Cuttriss * Charles H Kelly, London, n.d. (c.1919). Grey, red, 7.5 x 5.0, -/139. Fp, 2 mono phots, 18 sketches (by Neil McBeath), no maps, no appendixes, no Index.

* A book which is in no sense a serious attempt to describe the work done by this fine Division. Instead, it is a light-hearted and superficial look at the character and attitudes of the Australian soldier as perceived by the author. This subject is in fact covered by other authors in books of much greater substance. The Foreword was written by Gen John Monash, at one time Commander of 3 Div, and his succinct comments are the best feature of this otherwise disappointing publication. R/4 V/1. ANL. MCND'A.

THE STORY OF THE FIFTH AUSTRALIAN DIVISION
Being an Authoritative Account of the Division's Doings in Egypt, France and Belgium

Capt Alexander D Ellis MC * Hodder & Stoughton, London, n.d. (c.1920). Red, gold, 'Rising sun and figure 5' motif, 9.5 x 6.25, xix/468. Fp, 16 mono phots (indexed), 2 cld ills, 20 maps (17 printed in the text, 3 folding, bound in), no Index. Apps: Roll of Honour (every man KIA with the Div is listed, with details of his rank and unit), H&A (with names, ranks, and units, for every recipient in the Div, incl MID, with full citations for seven VCs), Divsl Order of Battle at 11.11.1918 (incl the names of the COs of every component unit).

* A very detailed and readable narrative which covers 5 Div's continuous service in France and Flanders between March 1916 and the end of 1918. All the main battles are well described, but there are many references also to minor actions and to individuals of all ranks. This is a large scale and very complete record of a famous fighting Divison. In such an otherwise excellent work, the lack of an Index is particularly frustrating. R/4 V/4. RMAS/RCSL/ANL. RP/MCND'A.

WORLD WAR II

AUSTRALIA IN THE WAR OF 1939-1945
Series 1 (Army)
Various authors (see below) * William Collins, in association with the Australian War Memorial, Canberra, published between 1952 and 1966. Red (but reprints seen also in sand and gold), black, 10.0 x 6.5. Numerous mono phots (up to 100 per volume), idem maps (up to 75 per volume),Glossaries, Indexes.
* The official history of Australia in WWII occupies twenty-two volumes. Of these, seven are devoted to the Army and are grouped under the collective title of 'Series 1'. Listed below, these books are all well written, authoritative, and easy to follow. They contain many references to individual officers and men, and to individual units and sub-units. Finding these people and their units is made easy by the provision of superbly arranged Indexes. The quality of the illustrations and maps is also very good. It should be noted that there are additional and more detailed references to military medical units in Series 5. The Series 1 titles are:

Volume I, To Benghazi, by Gavin Long, 1952
Volume II, Greece, Crete and Syria, by Gavin Long, 1953
Volume III, Tobruk to El Alamein, by Barton Maughan, 1966
Volume IV, The Japanese Thrust, by Lionel Wigmore, 1957
Volume V, South West Pacific Area, First Year, by Dudley McCarthy, 1959
Volume VI, The New Guinea Offensives, by David Dexter, 1961
Volume VII, The Final Campaigns, Gavin Long, 1963

All of these books have been frequently reprinted and are prime research sources. R/1 V/5. AWM. MCND'A.

THE SIX YEARS WAR
A Concise History of Australia in the 1939-45 War
Gavin Long * Australian Government Printing Service, for the Australian War Memorial, 1973. Black, silver, 9.5 x 6.0, xvii/517. 77 mono phots (indexed), 66 maps (indexed), Glossary, no appendixes, Index.
* This book, written by one of the co-authors of the series described in the preceding entry, was designed as a companion volume to ANZAC TO AMIENS, by C E W Bean (vide Index of Authors). The narrative covers all aspects of the nation's commitment to the business of war. It is a fascinating study of the strategic and tactical background to operations in the Middle East and the South West Pacific. The photographs and maps are first-class, and the Index is exemplary. R/1 V/5. ANL. MCND'A.

THE THIRTY-NINERS
Peter Charlton * The Macmillan Co of Australia, South Melbourne, 1981. Brown, white, 9.25 x 6.5, xix/279. 40 mono phots, 4 maps, Bibliography, Chapter Notes, no appendixes, Index.
* A high quality and well written account of the original units of the 2nd AIF which were raised in the closing months of 1939 and which sailed for the Middle East in 1940. Flamboyant and sometimes reckless, these first volunteers were determined to uphold the legend of the ANZAC of WWI fame. The narrative covers their early battles in the Western Desert, the move to Greece, the fight for Crete (when a third of them became POW), the occupation of Syria, the return home, and then the war in New Guinea. The only formation not covered is 9th Aust Div and its role at Tobruk and El Alamein. R/1 V/4. AWM. MCND'A.

THE CHOCOS
The Story of the Militia Infantry Battalions in the South West Pacific Area, 1941–1945
F M Budden * Colanco Publishing, NSW, 1987. Dark green, gold, 8.5 x 6.5, -/314. 29 mono phots, 37 maps, Bibliography, no appendixes, no Index.
* The book explains the differences between Militia and AIF soldiers, their terms of service, and financial status. The strength of the Militia units had grown to 173,000 all ranks by 1941, and the author recounts their services in the SW Pacific theatre. The lack of a Contents page, and the lack of chapter headings, an Index, or any appendixes, render the book very unhandy for reference purposes, but the narrative provides interesting general background reading. The title is taken from the derisory title 'Chocolate Soldiers' applied to Militia troops by men of the AIF. R/1 V/3. ANL. MCND'A.

FIRST FLEET AND EARLY COLONIAL REGIMENTS

THE FIRST FLEET MARINES, 1786–1792
John Moore * University of Queensland Press, St Lucia, Queensland, 1987. Red, white, 8.75 x 5.5, xii/345. 16 mono phots, one map, Glossary, Bibliography, Index. Apps: various tables, officers' biographies, notes on the children of Marines, nominal roll of the NSW Marines Corps Detachment (at July 1788).
* The story of the Royal Marines who escorted the earliest convict transports to Botany Bay and Norfolk Island. Men of the Chatham, Portsmouth and Plymouth Divisions volunteered for special three year detachments, accompanied by their families. The arrangement was not a success so, in 1789, the British Government decided to replace them with a new Colonial unit, the NSW Corps (recruited from ex-Army personnel and some former Marines). A short chapter describes the raising of this Corps, its despatch to Australia, and its work in guarding the penal settlements. The bulk of the book, however, is devoted to the services of the NSW Detachment of Marines during those first four years. Carefully researched and lucidly written, the book contains a mass of information on marriages and deaths, the ownership of livestock, land grants, pay, ration scales, and so forth. A prime source for an understanding of Australia's European colonisation.
R/1 V/5. ANL. MCND'A.
Note: in 1808, the NSW Corps mutinied. Known as 'the Rum Rebellion', this episode was effectively a coup d'état, and it had a profound effect upon the commercial life and administation of the Colony. Some collateral sources are:
THE RUM REBELLION – A Study of the Overthrow of Governor Bligh by John Macarthur and the New South Wales Corps, by H V Evatt (various editions between 1938 and 1984, latterly Times House Publishing, Kensington, NSW)
A SHORT HISTORY OF THE NEW SOUTH WALES CORPS, 1789–1818, by R Maurice Hill (Journal of the Society for Army Historical Research, Volume 13, Autumn, 1934)
CAPTAIN HENRY STEEL AND THE NEW SOUTH WALES CORPS, LATER 102nd REGIMENT, by Watson A Steel (Journal of the Royal Australian Historical Society, Volume 29, 1943)
A COLONIAL REGIMENT – New Sources Relating to the New South Wales Corps, 1789–1810, by Pamela Statham (Australian National University Printing Service, Canberra, for the author, 1992).

THE VETERANS
A History of the Enrolled Pensioner Force in Western Australia, 1850–1880
F H Broomhall * Hesperian Press, Carlisle, WA, 1983. Illustrated hard covers (photograph of Pensioner barracks), white, black, 8.75 x 5.5, vii/304. Fp, 19 mono phots, one map, Biographical Index (30 pages). Apps: 17 in total, incl various nominal rolls, Standing Orders, Rules of the Pensioner Benevolent Society (1863).
* The British practice of exporting convicted felons to the eastern seaboard of Australia commenced in 1787 and ceased in 1852. The transports were resumed in 1860, but no longer to the east. Instead, they sailed only to the Swan River Settlement in Western Australia. Over a period of eight years (1860–1868), ten thousand prisoners were landed at what is today the city of Fremantle. To escort these people during the voyage and to supervise them after their arrival, the British Government authorised the raising of The Enrolled Pensioner Force. Its ranks comprised former soldiers of the British Army who had completed at least twenty years of service and who were in receipt of out-pensions. Their terms of service with the Enrolled Pensioner Force were – free passage for themselves and their families, an initial six months engagement (after landing) on full military pay, a subsequent part-time training and 'call out' liability, and a land grant after their first seven years of residence. When the last of the British Army's garrison Regts departed from Australia in 1869–1870, the Pensioners were called upon to support the new locally-raised Volunteer units in defending the settlements against attack by Aboriginals or any possible foreign encroachment. At the crucial period of

settlement, the Pensioners and their families represented ten percent of the total European population on the western seaboard. This deeply researched book covers the entire Force story, and includes a chapter on a similar Pensioner Force in Van Diemen's Land (Tasmania). The biographical appendixes are a valuable source for genealogists, and the illustrations are excellent. R/1 V/5. ANL. MCND'A.

THE ARMY IN AUSTRALIA, 1840–1850
Prelude to the Golden Years
Brig M Austin DSO OBE * Australian Government Printing Service, Canberra, 1979. Red, gold, 10.25 x 7.0, xii/290. 4 mono phots, 8 cld ills, 9 sketches and charts, 12 maps, Glossary, Bibliography, Chapter Notes, 5 Indexes (Biographical, General, Geographical, Ships, and Corps & Regts). Apps: eleven in total, incl notes on Dress, distinctions, names of COs for the 11th, 28th, 50th, 51st, 58th, 65th, 80th, 96th and 99th Regts, names of troop transport ships (with dates), Standing Orders, unit strengths and locations (incl Tasmania, Norfolk Island, and New Zealand), mortality rates.
* A unique source for tracing the services of British Army units stationed in Australia in the mid-1800s, with details of their movements between the Colonies and to and from New Zealand. Coastal defence arrangements are also discussed in some detail. The appendixes contain an astonishing range and depth of reference material, and they make the book a prime source for genealogists in particular (many British soldiers becoming settlers, and joining local Volunteer units, upon the expiry of their Regular service). The indexes are very well arranged and helpful. R/2 V/5. ANL. MCND'A.

THE REMOTE GARRISON
The British Army in Australia, 1788–1870
Peter Stanley * Kangaroo Press, Kenthurst, NSW, 1986. Blue, gold, 11.5 x 8.5, -/96. Fp, 4 mono phots, 24 cld ills (all of uniforms, as worn by various British Army units), 44 line drawings (incl reproductions of old prints), 3 maps, Bibliography, Index. Apps: list of British Army units stationed in Australia, notes on genealogical research sources relating to those units.
* The author covers the First Fleet Marines (vide preceding page), the NSW Corps, the NSW Invalid & Veterans Company, the 73rd Regt of Foot and the 46th (South Devonshire) Regt of Foot (both described as 'General Macquarie's Regiments'), and the Regts which succeeded them during the first hundred years of settlement. He tells the story of how and why these various units first came to be despatched to Australia, the conditions under which they were required to serve, and actions in which they took part. In many ways, the troops were as much prisoners of circumstance as the transported convicts. Far from home, with little real work to do, they could not take 'tickets of leave' and could not purchase land while still in service. By 1870, however, when the British Army withdrew, several thousand time-expired soldiers had taken their discharge locally (rather than return home) and had become settlers. When read in conjunction with Austin (vide preceding entry), the book is a useful source for genealogists. However, this is essentially a military history, and it provides disturbing coverage of various 'aid to the civil power' operations in which the British Army was engaged. Amongst these was the attempt to capture all of the Tasmanian Aborigines in 1830 (the 40th Regt of Foot), and the suppression of the Eureka Stockade insurrection in 1854 (elements of the 12th and 40th Regts of Foot). R/1 V/5. ANL. MCND'A.
Note: in apparent conflict with the book's sub-title, the 'Contents' page and Appendix 1 both refer to the dates 1788-1913. This is not an error. The author makes the point that men of the Royal Marines - Britain's 'sea soldiers' - were serving on the Australia station through to 1913 (in which year the Royal Navy was succeeded by the Royal Australian Navy). The last Army units to depart, in 1870, were the 14th Foot (Buckinghamshire) and the 18th Foot (Royal Irish).

ABORIGINE SOLDIERS

FORGOTTEN HEROES
Aborigines at War from the Somme to Vietnam
Alick Jacomos and Derek Fowell * Victoria Press (The Government Printer, State of Victoria), for the authors, 1993. Plasticated illustrated soft card, 'Aborigine soldiers' motif, sepia/orange/black, 11.5 x 8.25, ii/88. More than 100 mono phots, 2 line drawings, no maps, list of sources, no Index. Apps: Roll of Honour (list of Aborigine soldiers known to have died in various campaigns, incomplete).
* To illustrate the services of Aborigine men and women who volunteered to fight in both world wars, and in Korea and South Vietnam, the authors compiled the personal stories of twenty-six of them. These accounts provide the bulk of the narrative of this moving book. The Aborigines - or 'Kooris', as they prefer to be known - suffered racial prejudice before they enlisted and again after they returned home, but remarkably little during their time in the armed forces. Indeed, the authors make the point that, in times of hardship and peril, when each man depends upon his comrades to see him through, the colour of their skin becomes irrelevant. R/1 V/3. ANL/AWM. MCND'A.

THE BLACK DIGGERS
Aborigines and Torres Strait Islanders in the Second World War
Robert A Hall * Allen & Unwin, North Sydney, NSW, 1989. Illustrated soft card, black/red, 9.0 x 6.0, xv/228. 35 mono phots, 7 maps/charts, Glossary, Bibliography, no appendixes, Index.
* Although 350 Aborigines had served in the 1st AIF of 1914-1918, officialdom was initially against their recruitment in WWII. Two chapters deal with the political arguments which preceded the eventual enlistment of 3000 of them. Most played an indispensable role in the potential invasion areas of the Northern Territory, and in the New Guinea campaign. Two hundred more were employed by the military as auxiliary scouts and trackers. By 1945, one in twenty Aborigines had been employed in war work of one kind or another, but it was not until 1991 that their services were fully acknowledged by the grant of their back pay and the issue of their medals. By then, only eleven of them were still alive. This is a very complete and in many ways disturbing story. It should be noted that Aborigines in uniform were granted the franchise in 1944, the entire race in 1962. R/1 V/4. AWM. MCND'A.

ABORIGINES IN THE SERVICES
Aboriginal History, Volume Sixteen, Parts 1 and 2
D J Mulvaney and P I Grimshaw (with others) * Aboriginal History Incorporated, Australian National University Central Printery, Canberra, 1992. Illustrated soft card, buff, black, 'Aborigine soldier' motif, 9.75 x 6.75, iv/156. 13 mono phots, 9 line drawings, 2 maps, Bibliography, no appendixes, no Index.
* A book based upon contributions by nine authors (including the two editors named above), with ten chapters dedicated to various aspects of Aboriginal service in the armed forces. Amongst the subjects covered are - the Northern Territory Coastal Patrol, two outstanding Aborigine personalities of WWII (Warrant Officer Leonard Waters, RAAF, fighter pilot, and Capt Reg Saunders MBE, infantry officer), and the work of Aborigine servicemen in Malaya and South Vietnam. The book contains much useful information regarding the ways in which researchers can locate Aboriginal archive material and service records. The line drawings are outstanding. R/2 V/4. AWM. MCND'A.
Note: Reg Saunders retired from the Army in 1954. Leonard Waters died in 1993.

TRAINING ESTABLISHMENTS

DUNTROON
The Royal Military College of Australia, 1911–1946
Col J E Lee DSO MC * Australian War Memorial, Canberra, 1946. Navy blue, red, RMC crest on the spine, 8.5 x 5.5, xviii/203. Fp, 30 mono phots (indexed), no maps, Index. Apps: 14 in total, incl Roll of Honour (for Australian graduates and New Zealander graduates, WWI and WWII), H&A (statistics only), nominal rolls of Staff Cadets (1911-1946), notes on ranks attained by graduates.
* This book lacks the flair of the following entry, and it covers much the same ground. However, it has a particularly fine run of appendixes which contain much biographical information and are easy to consult. It provides a good description of the College's staffing arrangements and internal organisation. The book is best read in conjunction with the history by Coulthard-Clark. R/2 V/5. ANL. MCND'A.

DUNTROON
The Royal Military College of Australia, 1911–1986
C D Coulthard-Clark * Allen & Unwin, Sydney (Aust), Wellington (NZ), Winchester (USA), and Hemel Hempsted (UK), 1986. Black, gold, RMS crest on the spine, 9.5 x 7.0, xvi/367. 97 mono phots, 15 cld ills (of which two are printed on the end-papers), 5 line drawings and diagrams, no maps, Glossary, Bibliography, Index. Apps: 10 in total, incl Roll of Cadets (1911-1985), roll of former Cadets who attained senior rank, list of Commandants, idem Professors on the staff, 'A Profile of the Corps of Staff Cadets'.
* A well researched and handsomely produced book, with good chapter notes and a helpful bibliography. Its publication marked the College's 75th Anniversary. There is a clear description of the circumstances which preceded the decision (1910-1911) to establish the RMC, and its subsequent role in producing a flow of Staff-trained officers for the armies and air forces of Australia and New Zealand in times of war and peace. An excellent narrative history, with good appendixes, but not quite as good as those found in the work by Lee. R/2 V/3. ANL. MCND'A.

OUR FIRST TWENTY-FIVE YEARS
The History of Adelaide University Regiment, 1948–1973
Lieut A L Graeme-Evans * Coudrey Offset Pty Ltd, Adelaide, 1973. Green, gold, 9.75 x 7.5, -/153. 118 mono phots, 6 drawings, 3 maps, no appendixes, no Index.
* A comprehensive history of the Regt from its formation in 1948. All aspects of its work are covered, and a roll of its first one hundred members is included. R/2 V/3. SLV. PS.

SYDNEY UNIVERSITY REGIMENT
A Description of the Insignia worn from 1900 to 1973 by Military Units of the University of Sydney, Together with Information on Honorary Colonels and Commanding Officers
Lieut Col A B Lilley CBE * Military History Society of Australia, 1970. Soft card, pale blue, UVRC crest, 7.5 x 6.25, viii/81. 2 fps, 20 mono phots, many line drawings of accoutrements, no maps, Bibliography, no Index. Apps: list of COs (with portraits and biographical notes), list of Honorary Colonels (idem), 'Brief Histories of Allied Regiments'.
* The Regt has its roots in the 'Russian scare' of 1885 when one hundred and twenty of the University's students and graduates volunteered for military service. This booklet covers the evolution of the University Volunteer Rifle Corps (1900-1903), the Sydney University Scouts (1903-1927), and the Sydney University Regt (1927-1970). The basic purpose of the publication was to record all of the badges, flashes and other insignia ever worn by their members. R/3 V/5. ANL. MCND'A.
Note: first printed in limited numbers in 1970, reprinted in 1974.

MOUNTED & MECHANISED

Mounted Units (General)

THE AUSTRALIAN LIGHT HORSE
Maj R J G Hall * W D Joynt & Co Ltd, Blackburn, Victoria, 1967. Black, gold, ALH crest, 8.5 x 5.5, viii/113. Fp, 14 mono phots, 2 diagrams (folding, bound in), no maps, no Index. Apps: 13 in total, notes on lineages.
* Although some errors have been detected in this first edition, it is a good source of reference for the complicated lineages of the Australian Light Horse in its entirety. R/2 V/4. PC. JLC.
Note: a second and revised edition was published in 1968.

AUSTRALIAN LIGHT HORSE
Ian Jones * Time-Life Books (Australia), Sydney, 1987. Illustrated hardback, full colour, 11.0 x 8.75, -/168. 122 mono phots, 9 cld plates, 13 sketches, 8 maps, Bibliography, no appendixes, Index.
* Like all books in the Time-Life series, this is a handsome production. Prepared with great care, it provides a superficial but very accurate account of ALH services in the Anglo-Boer War (1899-1902) and in Egypt and Palestine (WWI). The coloured plates are unusual and interesting, and the narrative represents a sound framework for more detailed research. R/1 V/4. PC. HEC.

LIGHT HORSE
The Story of Australia's Mounted Troops
Elyne Mitchell * The Macmillan Company of Australia, Sydney and Melbourne, 1978. Black, white, 9.75 x 10.0, viii/112. 27 mono phots, 30 drawings (some cld), 4 maps (all printed on the end-papers), Glossary, Bibliography, no appendixes, Index.
* Written by the daughter of Australia's greatest commander of horse-mounted troops, Gen Sir Harry Chauvel, the book traces their evolution from the 1880s through to the epic 1918 'race for Damascus'. Dismounted action in Gallipoli is covered in familiar detail, but the bulk of the WWI narrative deals with the brilliant Light Horse actions under Allenby in Palestine and Syria. Australia's horsemen had already come to world attention nearly twenty years earlier when, in South Africa, they had an impact greatly exceeding their numbers. A well produced book, with outstanding illustrations (many not seen elsewhere).
R/1 V/3. AWM. MCND'A.
Note: an attractive additional source for the Palestine period is NILE TO ALEPPO - WITH THE LIGHT HORSE IN THE MIDDLE EAST, by Hector Dinning (George Allen & Unwin, London, 1920). This is a substantial (287 pages) autobiography, with some delightful illustrations by James McBey.

Mounted Units (by States)

QUEENSLAND MOUNTED UNITS
Where and When Raised, 1860-1940
Maj I B Bates * Victoria Barracks Museum & Historical Society, 1988, Illustrated soft card, yellow, black, 'Mounted trooper' motif, 11.5 x 8.25, ii/62. No ills, no maps, Glossary, Bibliography, no Index. Apps: 10 in total, incl titles of units raised, locations, establishments and strengths, details of title changes at the time of Federation, Regulations for the QMR (at 1860).
* Unlike other Australian Colonies, Queensland raised its horsed units entirely as Mounted Infantry. There were no cavalry-titled units. The bulk of this 'economy' production is devoted to the clear and helpful appendixes, but the narrative does give a good summary of the evolution of the Militia and Volunteer movements, their contribution to the war in South Africa, the story of the 14th Light Horse, and so forth. A handy source of reference for a complicated subject.
R/3 V/3. ANL. MCND'A.

AUSTRALIAN CAVALRY
The NSW Lancer Regiment and First Australian Horse

Frank Wilkinson * Angus & Robertson, Sydney and Melbourne, 1901. Soft card, green, red, 10.0 x 7.5, v/64. Fp, 7 mono phots, no maps, no Index. Apps: Roll of Honour (South Africa, listed separately for NSW Lancers and 1st Australian Horse), list of COs and Majors (with dates, listed by unit), idem all other officers since inception, nominal rolls of all ranks who served in South Africa (listed under each unit title).

* This is an account of the first Volunteer Cavalry unit raised in NSW and the services of its component Squadrons and Half-Squadrons throughout the Colony. Entirely at its own expense, the NSW Lancer Regt made several 'expeditions' to Dublin and London to take part in Tournaments and Royal occasions. In 1899, while returning home after its latest visit to London, a detachment of NSW Lancers happened to be in Cape Town at the time when hostilisties broke out with the Boer Republics. The officers persuaded the authorities to grant permission for them to disembark their horses and weapons. The detachment was then able to join other Crown forces in some of the earliest actions of the war. In 1900 they were joined by the specially formed Contingents from each of the Australian Colonies. Collectively, they were known as The First Australian Commonwealth Horse (even though federation was not formalised until the following year). The main value of this booklet is to be found in the excellent nominal rolls. R/4 V/4. AWM. MCND'A. Note: reference should be made also to the South Africa section of this bibliography (vide Index of Authors - L M Field, Ralph Sutton, W T Reay, et al).

SWORD AND LANCE
The Story of the Richmond River Horsemen

Martin J Buckley * Northern Star Printers, Lismore, NSW, 1988. Red, gold, 11.0 x 8.25, xiii/258. More than 100 mono phots, 26 cld ills, 4 line drawings, 2 maps (on the end-papers), Bibliography, Glossary, Index. Apps: unit nominal rolls (for all five units at various dates between 1888 and 1902), biographical notes for some of these officers and men.

* An additional sub-title explains that the book deals with five Volunteer units which existed in the Richmond River area during the period 1885-1903 - the Upper Clarence Light Horse, Richmond River LH, 4th Sqn NSW Lancers, 'E' and 'G' Troops of the NSW Regt of Volunteer Cavalry. The narrative is based upon self-evidently meticulous research in contemporary records and local newspaper files. The result is a compelling picture of the military organisation and social structures of the late 19th Century in provincial New South Wales. There is good coverage also of the units' equipment and training, and their important role in South Africa (where the Light Horseman skills were unique amongst Crown forces in matching those of the Boers). R/1 V/5. ANL. MCND'A.

THE NSW NORTHERN RIVER LANCERS
Light Horse and Motor Regiments, 1903-1944

Martin J Buckley * Privately, Lismore, NSW, 1991. Green, silver, 11.0 x 8.25, xv/288. Fp, more than 100 mono phots, 3 cld plates, one map, Glossary, Bibliography, Chapter Notes, Index. Apps: nominal roll of all those who served (1903-1918, and 1919-1944, with some portrait photographs), list of subscribers, notes on Light Horse Training and Vehicle Establishments (1937 and 1942), table of Regtl locations (1903-1939).

* A handsome book, researched and produced to a high standard. It tells the story of the Northern Rivers men who were members of the 4th, 5th, and 15th LH Regts, and the 15th Australian Motor Regt (AIF). The period covered is 1903 to 1944. The book is therefore a continuation of the history described in the preceding entry and compiled by the same author. This is an amazingly detailed record, full of good reference material, and redolent with the spirit of the time and events which it describes. R/1 V/5. AWM. MCND'A.

HEROES AND GENTLEMEN
Colonel Tom Price and the Victorian Mounted Rifles
Winty Calder (Winifred Braithwaite Calder) * Jimaringle Publications, Melbourne, 1985. Plasticated illustrated covers, cream/red/grey, 11.5 x 8.25, x/189. Fp (lineage chart), 46 mono phots (indexed), 10 line drawings, 15 charts/tables, 10 maps, Bibliography, Index. Apps: list of officers (1886-1903, with service details), idem Permanent Staff Sergeant Majors, details of Coy strengths.
* A fine regtl history, with a good balance between readable narrative and well indexed reference material. Col Price had already served twenty-two years in India when he was asked to raise a Volunteer unit for the defence of Melbourne and its environs. The VMR was the result. This centennial publication covers the Regt's activities from foundation in 1903 (when it ceased to be a Colonial unit and was reorganised under the new Commonwealth of Australia scheme). Three of the highlights during this period were the Maritime Strike of 1890, the sending of a contingent to London for the Diamond Jubilee, and the despatch to South Africa of two contingents to serve in the Anglo-Boer War. The unit was perpetuated by the 8/13th VMR, Royal Australian Armoured Corps. R/1 V/5. ANL. MCND'A.
Note: a companion or supplementary source, having 59 pages and entitled GLIMPSES OF COLONEL TOM, was produced by the same author in 1985. This is a collection of extracts from Price's letters and public addresses during the period of his career in Australia, 1889 to 1909.

SADDLE AND SPUR
A Photographic Record of Gippsland's Mounted Regiments, 1885-1945
Allan Box * LV Printers Pty Ltd, for The Centre for Gippsland Studies, Churchill, 1989. Illustrated soft card, sepia/maroon, 11.75 x 8.0, x/110. 75 mono phots, no maps, no Index. Apps: roll of recipients of Long Service awards to members of Gippsland mounted regiments.
* Although it does not conform with any traditional format for a Regtl history, this attractive book contains plenty of useful information. The author made an in-depth study of the Volunteer movement in the Gippsland area of what was, originally, the Colony of Victoria. Commencing with 'the Russian scare' of the 1860s, he traces the development of the Victorian Mounted Rifles from 1885 to 1903, the Gippsland Light Horse in WWI, and various units carrying that designation in WWII. The photographs, all fully captioned, are of special interest to students of uniform and accoutrements, and various nominal rolls are scattered throughout the text. Sgt Maurice Buckley DCM was a Gippslander who volunteered in 1914, went overseas with the 13th Light Horse, was returned on medical grounds, then deserted, and re-enlisted in the Infantry under a false name. Three years later he won the highest award, the VC, while serving in France with 13th Aust Inf Bn AIF. The book contains many such items of interest. R/1 V/4. PC. RP.

Light Horse Brigades (World War I)

NARRATIVE OF OPERATIONS OF THE 3rd LIGHT HORSE BRIGADE, AUSTRALIAN MOUNTED DIVISION
From 27 October 1917 to 4 March 1919
Brig Gen L C Wilson CMG DSO * Oriental Advertising Company, Cairo, Egypt, 1919. Soft card, red, black, 9.5 x 6.5, -/64. No ills, no maps, no Index. Apps: H&A (listed by unit within the Bde, from 27.10.1917 onwards), list of officers (Bde Staff and unit COs), notes on casualties, idem veterinary problems.
* A brief but detailed day-to-day account of the Bde's services in Palestine, Syria, and Egypt. The Bde comprised 8th, 9th, and 10th Light Horse Regts.
R/4 V/3. ANL. MCND'A.

HISTORY OF THE FOURTH LIGHT HORSE BRIGADE, AIF
The War of 1914-1918, and the Egyptian Rebellion, 1919
Lieut G N Nutting and Mr E W Hammond * W R Smith & Paterson Pty Ltd, Brisbane, 1953. Maroon, gold, 8.75 x 5.5, -/69. No ills, no maps, no appendixes, no Index.
* An admirable little history, full of useful details - casualty statistics, awards, ration scales, equipment, POW captured, and so forth. The Bde was formed in May 1915 and consisted of 11th, 12th, and 13th Light Horse, with elements of 4th Light Horse. It was broken up when 11th and 12th LH went to Gallipoli, but was then reformed in February 1916. The Bde fought subsequently in the Palestine/Syria campaign as part of the ANZAC Mounted Div. The Egyptian uprising is mentioned only briefly. A very condensed record, but a model of its kind.
R/2 V/4. AWM. MCND'A.
Note: for details of the Egyptian civil unrest of 1919, and the 'aid to the civil power' work done by the Light Horse units in dealing with it, reference should be made to AUSTRALIANS AND EGYPT, 1914-1919, by Dr Suzanne Brugger (Melbourne University Press, Victoria, 1980). This deals with the subject in greater detail.

Light Horse Regiments

THE ROYAL NEW SOUTH WALES LANCERS, 1885-1960
Incorporating a Narrative of the 1st Light Horse Regiment, AIF, 1914-1919
P V Vernon * Halstead Press, Sydney, for the Regt, 1961. Pale blue, gold, Regtl crest on front cover and spine, 8.75 x 5.5, xii/380. Fp, 42 mono phots, one page of line drawings (shoulder patches), 9 maps (8 printed in the text, one on the end-papers), Glossary, Index. Apps: ten in total, incl Roll of Honour (WWII), H&A (WWII), nominal roll for South Africa (1899-1902), list of former COs, notes on Regtl title changes, locations of Troops and Detachments (1885-1941), notes on the 15th Northern River Lancers, uniforms, saddlery, weapons, etc.
* The NSW Lancers were raised as Volunteer Cavalry in 1885, being redesignated 1st Australian Light Horse Regt (NSW Lancers) from 1903 to 1912. In that year the title was changed again, to The Light Horse (New South Wales Lancers). This was retained through to 1918, but with some minor variations such as 1st Light Horse (Machine Gun) Regt (NSW Lancers). One Squadron was sent to South Africa for the Anglo-Boer War but, during WWI, the Lancers' role was restricted to finding drafts for 1st Light Horse Regt, AIF, which was serving in the Middle East. In WWII, the Regt saw active service, as an integral unit, in New Guinea and Borneo. A full and informative history. R/3 V/5. ANL. MCND'A.

THE ROYAL NEW SOUTH WALES LANCERS, 1885-1985
Incorporating a Narrative of 1st Light Horse Regiment, AIF, 1914-1919
P V Vernon OBE * Printed by Macarthur Press Ltd, Sydney, for the RNSWL Centenary Committee, 1986. Blue, gold, Regtl crest, 8.5 x 5.25, xiii/446. Fp, 71 mono phots (indexed), 9 maps (8 printed in the text, one on the end-papers), Glossary, Bibliography, Index. Apps: Roll of Honour (WWII), H&A (WWII), list of COs (with biographical details), unit nominal roll (for South Africa, 1899-1900 only), 'Designation of the Regiment, 1885-1956', 'Localities of Troops and Detachments, 1885-1941', notes on saddlery and uniforms.
* A well produced book, published to mark the Regt's centenary and updating the 75th Anniversary history (vide preceding entry). Written by the same author, this book also has good balanced coverage for each of the main periods, supported by first-class appendixes. R/1 V/5. ANL. MCND'A.

NULLI SECUNDUS
History of the Second Light Horse, Australian Imperial Force
August 1914 to April 1919
Lieut Col G H Bourne * The Northern Daily Leader Printers, Tamworth, NSW, 1926. Light brown boards, red spine, black, 10.0 x 7.0, -/84. 9 mono phots, 4 maps, no Index. Apps: Roll of Honour, H&A.
* This is the story of the 2nd Light Horse on Gallipoli and in Upper Egypt and

Palestine (the Jordan Valley and the Hills of Moab). It gained seventy awards for personal gallantry along the way. R/4 V/4. PC. PS.
Note: it is reported that this little book was first published in 1919, but it is not known by whom or where.

BIOGRAPHY OF THE 2nd LIGHT HORSE REGIMENT, AIF
Warrant Officer D R Needham Walker * Originally serialised in 'The Queensland Digger Magazine', 1926-1927, seen in soft card binding, green, 9.5 x 7.25, -/38. 5 mono phots, no maps, no appendixes, no Index.
* The author served with 2 LH throughout the war. His account was first published in eleven monthly parts in Queensland, then consolidated in the format of this free-standing booklet. In condensed language, he succeeds in describing the embarkation in September 1914, the landing and fighting on Gallipoli, and the campaign in Palestine, with verve and clarity. R/4 V/2. AWM. MCND'A.

3rd LIGHT HORSE REGIMENT, AIF, 1914-1919
Unit History
Sir George Bell (and 'other officers of the Regiment') * The Advocate Newspaper Press, Devonport, Tasmania, 1919. Soft card, green, black, 8.5 x 5.5, -/63. No ills, no maps, no Index. Apps: casualty statistics, H&A (with details of location and action for which each award was made).
* A summary of 3 LH activities taken directly from the War Diary, with little elaboration. The Regt followed the same path as most other LH units. It left Tasmania in 1914, fought on Gallipoli as dismounted infantry, reverted to the mounted role in Sinai, and drove the Turks north to Jerusalem and the Jordan Valley. Although presented in a basic and uninspired format, the text is packed with names and day-to-day incidents. R/4 V/4. AWM. MCND'A.
Note: reference may be made also to DIARY OF CORPORAL J M RANFORD, 3rd LIGHT HORSE (Howard College Printing Works, Adelaide, 1916).

THE STORY OF THE 3rd AUSTRALIAN LIGHT HORSE REGIMENT
3rd Light Horse (South Australia Mounted Rifles)
Frank M Blackwell, R H Douglas, and R A McFarlane * F Bowden & Sons Ltd, Adelaide, 1950. Soft card, buff, black, diagonal flash in black/white on front cover, 7.25 x 4.75, vi/142. Fp, 3 mono phots, 4 maps, no Index. Apps: H&A, 'Operations and Engagements, 3rd ALH' (located at front of book), 'Casualty Statistics' (by location).
* The Regt was raised in South Australia and Tasmania in August 1914 and spent the entire war in the Middle East (Gallipoli, Sinai, Palestine). More than 2000 horses passed through the Regt during that time. Much of the Sinai and Palestine material was written by R H Douglas, and there are several pages of useful comment by R A McFarlane as an Epilogue. R/3 V/4. ANL. MCND'A.

THE 4th AUSTRALIAN LIGHT HORSE REGIMENT
Some Aspects of its War Service, 1914-1918
Capt Cyril Smith OBE * Page & Bird Pty Ltd, Melbourne, 1954. Illustrated soft card, blue/red, 'Light horseman' motif, 7.0 x 4.75, -/16. One line drawing (4 LH Guidon), no maps, no appendixes, no Index.
* A pamphlet issued to commemorate the 40th Anniversary of the foundation and embarkation of 4 LH in 1914. The brief story is not always easy to follow because, after fighting as infantry on Gallipoli, the Regt was split into two parts. Two Squadrons went to France, where they fought in both the mounted and dismounted roles, while the remainder of the Regt joined the Australian Mounted Div in Sinai. Hence there were two quite separate units serving in different theatres of war but both having the same designation. The Regt's Battle Honours are thus a strange combination - 'Ypres/Messines 1917', 'Marne 1918', 'Gaza/Beersheba', 'Jerusalem', and 'Damascus'. R/4 V/2. AWM. MCND'A.
Note: refer also to MEN OF BEERSHEBA - A HISTORY OF THE 4th LIGHT HORSE REGIMENT, 1914-1919, by the same author, Melbourne University Press, 1993.

HOOVES, WHEELS AND TRACKS
A History of the 4/19th Prince of Wales's Light Horse Regiment and its Predecessors
David Holloway * Published by the Regtl Trustees, Fitzroy, Victoria, 1990. Black, silver, Regtl crest, 9.75 x 7.25, xiv/850. Fp, 87 mono phots, 15 cld ills, 8 line drawings (badges), 24 maps, Glossary, Index. Apps: 20 in total, incl lists of former COs (1870-1990), idem Adjutants, idem RSMs, nominal rolls for all the predecessor units, etc.
* This is a tremendous book. It traces the evolution of the Regt from its earliest roots in the country units of the 1850s through to the Victorian Mounted Rifles, their services in South Africa, and then, as the 4th Light Horse, on Gallipoli. The Regt was later split, serving under the same title on the Western Front and simultaneously in Palestine. Post-WWI, a variety of other units, all predecessors of the 4/19th, enter the story. Prominent amongst these was the WWII mechanised unit, 2/4th Armoured Regt. The 4/19th gained its present designation (as shown in the sub-title of the book) in 1948. The highly readable narrative is replete with explanatory notes and copious organisational diagrams to supplement the extensive appendixes. Some of the latter, particularly those relating to the history of Armour in Australia, have a wider interest than the purely regimental. The story ends with an account of a Troop of 'A' Squadron on active service in South Vietnam. It would have been better if the illustrations had been indexed, but the book is otherwise faultless. R/1 V/5. AWM. MCND'A.

THE REGIMENT
Being a Brief Account of the History, Customs and Traditions of the 4/19th Prince of Wales's Light Horse Regiment
Anon * Published by the Regt, Fitzroy, Victoria, 1977. Soft card, sandy orange, black, 11.5 x 8.25, -/24. Fp, 4 mono phots, 30 line drawings, 2 diagrams, no Index. Apps: list of COs (1948-1975).
* A collection of useful bits of information regarding the Regt's lineage, unit colour patches, vehicle signs, Guidons, Colours, Battle Honours, and so forth.
R/2 V/2. AWM. MCND'A.

HISTORY OF THE FIFTH LIGHT HORSE REGIMENT, AIF
From 1914 to October 1917, and from October 1917 to June 1919
Brig Gen L C Wilson CB CMG DSO and Capt J Wetherell * The Motor Press of Australia Ltd, Sydney, 1926. Brown, black, Regtl crest, 8.75 x 5.5, -/232. Fp, 3 mono phots, 7 maps (loose in rear pocket), no Index. Apps: full nominal roll (with details of casualties), statistical summary of casualties, H&A, list of officers, notes on ration scales, medical organisation.
* A history written in two parts by officers who served with the Regt. The first part covers formation in 1914, the move to Egypt, and dismounted service on Gallipoli. The bloody fighting there, and the casualty-free evacuation in December 1915, are described in great detail. The second part covers the return to the mounted role and service with the Mounted Div in Sinai and Palestine. There is good coverage of the Regt's role in blocking the Turkish advance into Egypt, the two famous Gaza battles in 1917, the raids on Amman and El Salt, and the final advance through the Jordan Valley to Armageddon. The difficulties of finding water and fodder for the horses in such arid country are made plain.
R/3 V/4. ANL. MCND'A.
Note: reference may be made also to THE DESERT HATH PEARLS, by R Hall (published in Melbourne, 1975, no other details known).

THE DESERT COLUMN
The Australian Light Horse in Action
Ion L Idriess * The Griffin Press, for Pacific Books, Adelaide, 1965. Illustrated soft card, 6.0 x 4.5, -/287. No ills, no maps, no Index. Apps: unit nominal roll for the 5th Light Horse Regt.
* A second sub-title states - 'Leaves from the Diary of an Australian Trooper in Gallipoli, Sinai and Palestine'. The author served with 5 LH in all three campaigns

and later became one of Australia's leading writers. He certainly enjoyed a very remarkable success with these memoirs of his days as a soldier (vide footnote). Like many accounts of this genre, it reflects the experiences of thousands of other young men who, for three or four years, travelled to unexpected destinations and went through a unique chapter in their lives. This author, however, struck a chord in the public's imagination, and his tale continues to enjoy popular interest. It is useful also as a research source, especially when read in conjuntion with the formal history compiled by Wilson and Wetherell (vide preceding entry).
R/1 V/3. DCLS. RP.
Note: first published by Angus & Robertson, Sydney, in 1932, reprinted in that same year. Thereafter, reprinted in 1933, 1934, 1935, 1936, 1939, 1941, 1944, 1951, 1965, and 1986. It is reported that the Pacific Books edition, as recorded here, is the only one to include the full 5 LH nominal roll.

UNDER FURRED HATS
6th Australian Light Horse
Lieut George L Berrie * W C Penfold & Co Ltd, Sydney, 1919. Buff, black, Regtl flash in green/red, 7.5 x 5.0, -/179. Fp, 48 mono phots, no maps, Index. Apps: Rolls of Honour (Gallipoli, and Sinai/Palestine),H&A.
* A well produced book covering the services of 6 LH from formation in September 1914 to its return to Australia in August 1919. Compiled by an officer who served with the Regt throughout, it is based partly upon the War Diary. His descriptions of the bitter fighting on Gallipoli are admirably clear, as are his accounts of the cavalry tactics and charges in the Sinai campaign (Battle of Romani). The advance into Palestine, the action at Beersheba, and the raids into the Jordan Valley, are similarly well covered. The lack of maps is a weakness in this book, and it is not always easy to know which year is under review. However, many officers and their appointments and promotions are noted in the narrative, and the book is a sound source for military and family historians alike. R/3 V/3. ANL. MCND'A.

THE HISTORY OF THE 7th LIGHT HORSE, 1914-1919
Lieut Col J D Richardson DSO * Radcliffe Press, Sydney, 1924. Red, gold, 9.5 x 7.0, -/122. Fp, 34 mono phots, 4 maps (bound in), Glossary, no Index. Apps: Roll of Honour (KIA, DOW, and WIA), H&A.
* The author was CO of the Regt. His narrative is presented in four parts - formation in NSW in 1914 through to the evacuation from Gallipoli, operations in Sinai, the operations around Gaza, Beersheba and Jaffa, and then finally the advance to Jerusalem and Amman. This is an authoritative work, written soon after the events which it describes. Lists of personnel and references to individuals appear throughout the text. The maps and illustrations are very good.
R/2 V/4. AWM. MCND'A.
Note: only 300 copies were printed. Subsequently, in the 1980s, the book has reappeared as a facsimile reprint.

WITH THE NINTH LIGHT HORSE IN THE GREAT WAR
Maj T H Darley OBE * The Hassell Press, Adelaide, 1924. Mauve, black, 8.75 x 5.75, viii/206. 2 fps, 28 mono phots, no maps, no Index. Apps: Roll of Honour (with ranks, dates and causes), H&A (two CMGs, six DSOs, one OBE, five MCs, eleven DCMs, fourteen MMs), notes on 'The Work of the Transport', 'The Egyptian Uprising', 'Guns Captured by the Regiment', etc.
* A workmanlike history. The Regt was raised in October 1914, fought in Egypt, Gallipoli, Sinai, Palestine, and Mesopotamia, and was then disbanded in Australia in August 1919. A total of 4000 officers and men passed through the Regt during the war. Of the original 500 who embarked, only 41 survived. Of unusual interest are the descriptions of the final advance into Syria (Homs and Tripoli), and the rebellion in Egypt in 1919. The Regt had the distinction of capturing the only Turkish unit Colour to be taken in the Middle East campaign.
R/3 V/4. ANL/NZMODL/NYPL. MCND'A/HEC.

WESTRALIAN CAVALRY IN THE WAR
The Story of the Tenth Light Horse Regiment, AIF, in the Great War, 1914–1918
Lieut Col A C N Olden DSO * Alexander McCubbin, Melbourne, 1921. Red, black, 8.5 x 5.5, x/333. Fp, 86 mono phots, 9 maps (3 bound in, 6 loose in rear pocket), no Index. Apps: Roll of Honour, H&A (basic facts only), Operational Order for the advance to Jerusalem, unit nominal roll.
* A well written and helpful Regtl history. The narrative is at its best when describing small-scale actions, especially in the section which deals with Gallipoli. The H&A appendix lists the recipients of one VC, three DSOs, one MBE, seventeen DCMs, fifteen MMS, six MSMs, and four foreign awards, but lacks detail. The unit nominal roll indicates whether a man was part of the original Regt or whether he joined later as a reinforcement. R/4 V/4. NYPL. BCC/PS.
Note: continuing interest in the story of 10 LH was such that the book was revised and reprinted in 1979. This second edition has at the rear a 45-page supplement, compiled by John Burridge, which extends the historical coverage from 1901 to 1979. It provides additional detail regarding honours and awards, quoting full citations where applicable. Burridge also added a roll of personnel killed or wounded on Gallipoli, a list of former COs (1900–1975), and notes concerning changes in the unit designation. The print run of this second edition is reported as having been 400 copies and, for research purposes, it is a great improvement on the original work by Olden.

HISTORY OF THE 11th LIGHT HORSE REGIMENT
Fourth Light Horse Brigade, 1914–1919
Ernest W Hammond * William Brooks & Co, Brisbane, 1942. Maroon, gold, 8.5 x 5.5, xii/186. Fp, 107 mono phots (indexed), 4 maps, no Index. Apps: Roll of Honour, H&A, unit nominal roll, notes on medical work, idem personnel taken POW by the Turks, idem certain operations behind enemy lines.
* The story covers formation in February 1915, the Regt's arrival in Egypt, its services on Gallipoli as dismounted infantry, and then the Palestine campaign. The author's descriptions of combat are particularly clear, and the Romani and Gaza battles are well covered. The maps and illustrations match the standard of the narrative, and individual casualties are noted throughout. R/3 V/4. ANL. MCND'A.

FORWARD
The History of the 2nd/14th Light Horse (Queensland Mounted Infantry)
Joan Starr and Christopher Sweeney * University of Queensland Press, Brisbane, 1989. Dark green, silver, 8.75 x 5.5, xvii/230. Fp, 54 mono phots, 2 cld ills, 12 maps, Glossary, Bibliography, Index. Apps: Rolls of Honour (one each for South Africa, WWI, and WWII), H&A (one each for South Africa, WWI, and WWII), list of COs (from 1860 to 1989, for each unit), explanatory notes on the main text, notes on Battle Honours, Orders of Battle (1860–1988).
* An exemplary unit history, written in clear, compact and sometimes brilliant style. The authors trace the evolution of the 2nd/14th (the title which it acquired in 1982) from its earliest roots amongst the skilled horsemen of Queensland. The 1st, 2nd, and 3rd QMI formed part of the Australian Contingents to South Africa, and their exploits against the Boers are well covered here. In WWI, the 2nd and 4th Light Horse Regts fought dismounted on Gallipoli, and then in Sinai and Palestine as part of the Desert Mounted Corps. Coverage of their various battles is very good, but the narrative also explains the development of Australian forces in general and makes useful references to 15th Light Horse, 27th North Queensland Light Horse, 2nd Moreton Light Horse, and 14th West Moreton Light Horse. The Regt did not serve overseas during WWII. Post-war events are covered briefly. In 1986, the Regt became the first unit of the Australian Army to be fully integrated – combining personnel from both the Regular Army and the Reserve Army.
R/1 V/5. ANL. MCND'A.

TWENTY-FIRST LIGHT HORSE REGIMENT
K H Hawkey * Riverina/Murray Institute of Higher Education, Wagga Wagga, NSW, 1987. Soft card, yellow, black, Regtl crest, 11.5 x 8.25, v/84. Fp, 19 mono phots, no maps, no Index. Apps: lists of COs, Adjutants, and Quartermasters.
* This short history covers the life of the Regt and its predecessors from 1903 onwards. It has a useful explanation of the evolution of all NSW Light Horse Regts from that date, through the 1921 reorganisations, the 1929 reductions, and the further reorganisations of 1936. The longest section of the book covers the WWII period, and there are some evocative photographs of the Riverina Horse (as it was then named), taken circa 1939-1940. The Regt changed its title and role several times, being a Reconnaissance Regt, a Cavalry Regt and, after disbandment, its constituent elements becoming Divisional Carrier Companies. It did not serve overseas. The difficulties of making the best use of Cavalry Regts of the Australian Army in the particular circumstances of WWII are well exemplified in this unit's history. R/1 V/3. ANL. MCND'A.

Armour

AUSTRALIAN ARMOUR
A History of the Royal Australian Armoured Corps, 1927-1972
Maj Gen R N L Hopkins CBE * Griffin Press, Netley, SA, for the AWM and the Australian Government Publication Service, Canberra, 1978. Khaki, red, 10.0 x 7.25, xvii/371. Fp, 62 mono phots, 11 drawings, 14 maps, Bibliography, Index. Apps: 8 in total, incl list of senior officers, unit locations, notes on armoured vehicles.
* The definitive account of the evolution of Australian armour over four decades. The author covers its modest origins in the 1930s, the rapid expansion of 1941-1942, the peak period of 1943 (when the Corps had three Armoured Divs and a Tank Bde), and active services in the SW Pacific area. There is some coverage of the Korean War, but the final seventy pages are a detailed account of the role of Australian armour in South Vietnam. R/2 V/5. PC. HEC/RH.

Divisional Regiments (WWII)

TO THE GREEN FIELDS BEYOND
The Story of 6th Australian Division Cavalry Commandos
Shawn O'Leary * Printed by Wilke Group, Zillmere, Queensland, presumably for the Regtl Association, 1975. Green, brown, Regtl flash in red/brown/green, 9.0 x 6.5, xii/398. 112 mono phots, 8 maps, Index. Apps: unified nominal roll (details of all who served, plus notes on those who became casualties and/or received an award).
* Originally formed in 1939 as 6th Australian Divisional Reconnaissance Regt, this unit was renamed (as in the book's sub-title) after returning home from service in the early Western Desert battles. The founding members came from a variety of Light Horse (Militia) units in NSW, Queensland, Victoria, South Australia, and Tasmania. The author, a professional writer, has compiled here a lucid and informative narrative, with generous references to a large number of the officers and men who served. After refitting in Australia, the unit fought in New Guinea (1944-1945) as dismounted 'Cavalry Commandos'. The maps, although not drawn to scale, are helpful to an understanding of the sequence of events.
R/3 V/5. ANL. MCND'A/RH.

THROUGH MUD AND BLOOD TO PASTURES GREEN
Report and Narrative of 2/7th Australian Divisional Cavalry Regiment
Anon * Burwood Press, Sydney, for 2/7th Div Cav Regt Welfare & Comforts Fund, 1941. Soft card, cream, AMF crest, Div flash, brown/red/green stripes, 8.5 x 5.5, -/24. 5 mono phots, no maps, no Index. Apps: unit nominal roll (all ranks, at embarkation, 26.12.1940).
* From its publication date, it is clear that this booklet is far from being a 'war history'. However, the brief narrative gives interesting coverage of the initial raising of the Regt (written by its CO), and its move to Cyprus, via Egypt, in May

1941. Some individuals are named in the picture captions. For the rest, the value of the work is to be found in the unit nominal roll. R/4 V/1. ANL/NYPL. MCND'A.

THE 2/7th AUSTRALIAN CAVALRY REGIMENT
A Pictorial History
N Grinyer and M R Birks * Produced by Daram Printing, Northmead, NSW, for the Regtl Association, 1974. Stiff card, brown/cream, Armoured Corps flash in green/red/brown, 8.5 x 6.5, -/77. 111 mono phots, 3 maps, no Index. Apps: 'Embarkation/Disembarkation Rolls for the Middle East, 1940/41'.
* Although sub-titled 'a pictorial history', the narrative line is sufficiently well developed for the reader to follow the Regt's active services in some detail. Raised in 1940, it sailed for the Middle East and was employed on guard and garrison duties on the Suez Canal, in Cyprus, and on the Syria/Turkey border. Returning to Australia in 1942, the Regt trained for jungle warfare and landed in New Guinea in September of that year. It was engaged in the heavy fighting at Sananada in late 1942, but ceased to exist as a front-line unit in February 1943. The pictures are interestingly evocative of the period but, overall, this is a fairly lightweight account. R/3 V/3. ANL. MCND'A.
Note: published with a reported print run of 250 copies.

BLACK BERETS
The History and the Battles of 9th Division Cavalry Regiment
Colin Pura * Dominion Press, Hedges & Bell, for the Regtl Association, Melbourne, 1983. Brown, gold, 11.0 x 8.5, xiv/113. Fp, 115 mono phots, one map, Glossary, no Index. Apps: H&A (with locations), unit nominal roll, diary of events (11.6.1940 to 13.2.1946, with some type-setting errors), notes on Battle Honours.
* This is basically a collection of reminiscences by some of those who served. The coverage is patchy. Operations in Syria, for example, are covered in interesting detail, while accounts of El Alamein are fairly brief. Later actions, in Labuan (Borneo), receive close attention (with details of casualties fully recorded). Because the book was published forty years after the events which it describes, and because the narrative seems to be based mainly upon the memories of those who served (a notoriously fallible source of reference), it is possible that some inaccuracies may have eluded the author (editor). The numerous photographs are good, and well captioned with dates and names. R/2 V/3. ANL. MCND'A/RH.

TANKS IN THE EAST
The Story of an Australian Cavalry Regiment
Colin Kerr * Oxford University Press, Melbourne, 1945. Sky blue, black, 8.5 x 5.5, -/199. 29 mono phots, 3 line drawings, 2 maps, no appendixes, no Index.
* An amusing but basically lightweight book. It covers the services of 9th Aust Div Cav from formation in 1940, through the Syrian campaign, through the two Alamein battles, and then the return to Australia in 1943. Although nicely written, and evocative of time and place, it is a disappointing effort. The lack of maps, appendixes and Index, are the main fault. R/2 V/2. ANL/NYPL. MCND'A.
Note: a helpful additional source for this Regt is BLOKES FROM THE CAV, by R J Martindale and R L Martindale, published privately by the authors in 1993 in an attempt to fill the gaps in Kerr's 1945 account. Their book contains rolls of casualties, rolls of recipients of awards, and a 'Register of Personnel', all of which is most helpful to the genealogist and other categories of researcher.

Other Armoured Units (WWII)

SPEED AND VIGILANCE
The Story of the 2nd Australian Tank Battalion, AIF, 1939–1944
Anon * New Century Press Ltd, Sydney, 1945. Soft card, fawn, Australian Army crest with Bn crest and flashes in green/brown/red, 9.0 x 6.75, -/105. Fp, 52 mono phots, no maps, no Index. Apps: Bn nominal roll (incl home addresses and date joined), 'List of nicknames and to whom they belonged' (over 300 such).

* Written in the style of a magazine rather than a book, this is the record of a Bn which did not itself go overseas but instead trained drafts for other tank units. In this context, the nominal roll is particularly useful. Covering forty-four pages, it includes details of the men who moved to those other units, the names and/or titles of the units in which they subsequently served, and if and when they were casualties. The list of nicknames is an amusing sidelight on this traditional Australian habit. R/3 V/3. ANL. MCND'A.

2/5 AUSTRALIAN ARMOURED REGIMENT
Anon * W R Smith & Paterson Pty Ltd, Brisbane, n.d. (c.1950). Blue, gold, Regtl crest, 4.5 x 5.5 (landscape), -/105 (not numbered). No ills, no maps, no Index. Apps: Roll of Honour, nominal roll (with ranks and home addresses).
* A modestly presented book containing little more than a roll of all those who were serving in the Regt (plus 2/91 Light Aid Detachment, AEME) at the end of the war, and incorporating some of those who had served with it earlier. The roll is the book's only possible reference value. R/3 V/1. AWM. MCND'A.

HISTORY OF THE 2/6 AUSTRALIAN ARMOURED REGIMENT
Anon * Bulletin Printery Pty Ltd, Southport, Queensland, 1945. Soft card, grey, blue, red/green striped quarter, 8.0 x 5.25, -/28. No ills, no maps, no Index. Apps:Roll of Honour, H&A, full nominal roll (at 13.10.1945, incl Signal Troop and LAD AEME).
* A very brief record compiled without access to the War Diary but based in part upon notes kept by the Regt's Intelligence Section. The Regt was formed in August 1941, fought in New Guinea mounted on American-supplied M3 tanks, and on foot as stretcher-bearers and porters on the Kokoda Trail, and lastly in their proper role at Buna and Sananadnda. The Regt returned to Australia in April 1943. The main value of this little publication - at least to genealogists - is the nominal roll. It does not show ranks, but it does give each man's home address, and this may be an aid to identification. R/4 V/1. AWM. MCND'A.

SANANANDA INTERLUDE
The 7th Aust Division Cavalry Regiment
F J Hartley * Printed by the Speciality Press Ltd, Melbourne, for The Book Depot, Melbourne, 1949. Illustrated stiff card, red/cream/black, 'Jungle scene' motif, 7.25 x 4.75, v/101. 16 mono phots (indexed), 9 maps, no Index. Apps: Roll of Honour (with dates and locations), 'Memorial church parade, 2 May 1943'.
* The author was the Regtl Chaplain. His eyewitness account of the fighting on the Sananada Track in December 1942 and January 1943 records the only battle in which this Regt was engaged during the entire war. He gives a detailed picture, aided by good sketch maps, of the Regt's position in relation to the American and Japanese units engaged in the struggle. R/2 V/4. ANL. MCND'A.

WALTZING MATILDAS
The Men and Machines of the 2/9th Australian Armoured Group in Australia and Borneo, 1941-1946
Peter Donovan * Published by 2/9th Aust Armd Regt Gp Assn, 1988. Green, yellow, 'Matilda tank' motif, 9.5 x 7.25, xv/257. Fp, more than 100 mono phots, one cld ill (Guidon of 9th Light Horse), 5 line drawings, 7 maps, Bibliography, Index. Apps: Roll of Honour, H&A, list of officers, idem WOs, idem SNCOs (all listed by Sqn), unit nominal roll, notes on "The Development of 'The Frog' Flame Thrower Tank".
* Australia raised seventeen Armoured Regts in WWII, but only four served in the role for which they were intended and trained. This excellent book describes in detail the amphibious assaults on Tarakan, Labuan Island, and Brunei Bay, when 2/9th took part in their Australian-designed variant of the Matilda tank. This very successful vehicle carried its flame fuel inboard, and was much superior to the equivalent British 'Crocodile' design. R/1 V/5. ANL. MCND'A.

ARTILLERY

GARRISON GUNNERS
Part I – The Legends of a Subaltern Part II – The Port-cullis
Anon ('Fronsac') * Tamworth Newspaper Co Ltd, Tamworth, NSW, 1929. Bright blue, black, 7.25 x 5.0, -/164. 2 mono phots, no maps, no appendixes, no Index.
* Of interest mainly because it includes a history of the Australian Garrison Artillery in New South Wales in WWI, and an account of the Volunteer Artillery Brigade from 1854 onwards. Many individuals are named in the text, so this basically lightweight book could be useful to genealogists. R/4 V/1. ANL. MCND'A.

A HISTORY OF 'A' BATTERY, NEW SOUTH WALES ARTILLERY (1871–1899), ROYAL AUSTRALIAN ARTILLERY (1899–1971)
Richmond Cubis * Elizabethan Press, Sydney, 1978. Black, gold, 8.75 x 5.75, -/335. 58 mono phots, 14 maps (all bound in at the rear), Glossary, Bibliography, Indexes (four – Persons, Places, Equipment, Formations). Apps: list of Bty Commanders, 'List of major Equipments held by the Battery, 1871-1971', notes on other Regular Btys (sixteen in total).
* An immaculately researched account of the oldest unit of the Australian Regular Army. The Bty served in every war in which Australian units were engaged, from the Sudan (1885) through to South Vietnam (1971). The author covers the entire period in uniform detail. He also describes the much broader history of the RAA and the Australian Army in general, and sets the facts against the background of Australia's development as a nation. R/2 V/5. AWM. MCND'A.

THE GALLOPING GUNS OF RUPERTSWOOD AND WERRIBEE PARK
A History of the Victorian Horse Artillery
Lindsay C Cox * Coonans Hill Press, Melbourne, 1986. Blue, gold, 11.0 x 8.5, viii/199. 54 mono phots, 4 cld plates, more than 100 line drawings, 3 maps and diagrams (2 printed in the text, one on the end-papers), Bibliography, Index. Apps: unit nominal rolls for the Victorian Nordenfeldt Battery (1885-1889), and the Victorian Horse Artillery (1889-1897), notes on unit strengths.
* Although it never saw active service, the VHA created for itself a magnificent reputation for excellence. Queen Victoria was so impressed by the bearing of the Regt that she commanded that it should lead her personal escort at the marriage of her grandson, the future King George V. This account is a labour of love by the author. The photographs are of outstanding quality, and the numerous line drawings illustrate all aspects of the Regt's insignia, accoutrements, weaponry, and uniforms. R/1 V/5. ANL. MCND'A.

ROUNDSHOT TO RAPIER
Artillery in South Australia, 1840–1984
David Brook * Investigator Press Pty Ltd, Hawthorndene, SA, for The Royal Artillery Association of South Australia, 1986. Blue, gold, 'Cannon' motif, 8.5 x 5.25, -/349. 42 mono phots, no maps, Glossary, Bibliography and Sources, Index. Apps: eight in total, incl 'Heavy Batteries in Rabaul and Timor, 1941-1942', 'Guns manned by South Australian gunners', 'Honorary Colonels and Colonels Commandant of Artillery', 'Aspects of Regimental History', and 'Artillery Designations and Organisations'.
* As its title suggests, this book is a comprehensive record of the development of gunnery in S Australia from the days of the smooth-bore muzzle-loader through to the Rapier surface-to-air missile. The narrative consists of numerous pieces contributed by various experts in their own fields, the whole then edited by David Brook. The State raised all manner of artillery unit in times of both war and peace, and each is recorded here with its full history. Individual officers are named throughout, and the pictures are well captioned. R/1 V/5. AWM. MCND'A.

THE WAR SERVICE RECORD OF THE FIRST AUSTRALIAN ARTILLERY BRIGADE 1914-1919

E T Dean * W H Thomas & Co, Adelaide, n.d. (1919). Dark green, gold, 8.5 x 5.5, -/247. Fp, 2 mono phots, 4 maps, no formal appendixes, no Index.

* Despite its unconventional layout, this book is a good record of the Bde's overseas travels and of those who served. It is arranged in four main sections. The first is a detailed diary of events from 19 August 1914 to 31 January 1919. The second is, in effect, a 'Roll of Honour' (KIA, WIA and DOW, with ranks and full forenames). The third is a list of honours and awards. The fourth, and largest, is the 'personnel lists'. These show the names of officers and men who served with the Bde - dates of joining and leaving, promotions, injuries, awards (with their citations), and so forth. The diary of events is helpful as a record of the Bde itself, but the great strength of the book is the mass of detail which it provides in respect of the Bde's personnel. R/4 V/4. AWM. MCND'A.

7th F.A.B. YANDOO
Containing Publications of the Organ of the 7th Field Artillery Brigade, Australian Imperial Forces, whilst on Active Service in France and its Return Journey ...

Anon ('The Yandoo Management', S E Rottu and E Harding for all three Volumes, plus B C Duckworth and S W Hodge for Volume II only) * Produced by the Regt, printed 'on the ship and in the field', 1916-1919. Soft card, 9.75 x 6.0, a large number of mono phots and line drawings in each Volume, no Indexes.

Volume I : brown, gold, no appendixes, -/36.
Volume II : green, gold/silver, 'Field gun' motif, no appendixes, -/52.
Volume III : blue, gold, 'Waratah flower' motif, 3 cld maps, -/200. Apps: Roll of Honour (KIA and WIA), H&A (for Bde HQ and each Bty, incl MID), Bde nominal rolls (arranged by Bde HQ and Btys), list of 7 FAB soldiers granted Commissions.

* The 7th Field Artillery Bde, AIF, succeeded in producing, every few weeks, a news magazine for its own personnel. The average print run was 1200 copies. They were subsequently bound and issued in three volumes which covered the Bde's major moves - May to June 1916 ('Troopship issue'), July to October 1916 ('Camp life in England'), and October 1916 to August 1919 ('Active Service issue'). The word 'Yandoo' signifies 'Messenger', hence the otherwise obscure title of the publication. It is followed by a very long sub-title which explains its purpose. The text consists of a mass of information which varies from the mundane (anecdotes and caricatures) to the historically important (movements, locations, fire tasks, and casualties).It is therefore a mirror of the experiences of many such units in WWI. The illustrations are good, the coloured maps are possibly unique, and the entire account is a goldmine for medal collectors, genealogists, and gunner researchers. The Bde's constituent elements were 25th, 26th, and 27th Btys.
R/4 V/4. ANL. MCND'A.

WITH THE 27th BATTERY IN FRANCE
7th Brigade, Australian Field Artillery

Anon (a committee of twenty members, Foreword signed by Bombardier T D Bridger) * St Clements Press Ltd, London, 1919. Buff, blue, 8.5 x 5.25, -/168. Fp, 9 mono phots, no maps, no appendixes, no Index.

* The author served as a Battery Observer with one of the 18-pounder Btys of 7th FAB on the Western Front. His story was written, for the most part, while the events he describes were unfolding. The prose is condensed, vivid, and highly descriptive. Many of his comrades, of all ranks, are named in the text, with some detail of their awards, wounds, and deaths. A useful source to supplement the YANDOO item noted in the preceding entry. R/4 V/3. ANL. MCND'A.

A ROUGH Y.M. BLOKE

Frank Grose * The Speciality Press Ltd, Melbourne, n.d.

* The author worked with the YMCA Canteen attached to 1st Divisional Artillery between 1915 and 1918. The only research value to be found in his 180 pages of memoirs is his Roll of Honour - a listing of all YMCA personnel killed or wounded while serving with the Canteen during that period. The names are arranged in order of event, not alphabetically. R/3 V/1. AWM. MCND'A.

World War II

SIX YEARS IN SUPPORT
Official History of 2/1st Australian Field Regiment

Brig A G Hanson DSO and Maj E V Haywood * Printed by Halstead Press Ltd, Sydney, for Angus & Robertson, 1959. Green, gold, 8.5 x 5.5, x/211. 35 mono phots (indexed), 5 maps, no Index. Apps: Roll of Honour, H&A.

* A very readable book, not too technical for the layman, and containing good maps and illustrations. The Regt was formed in October 1939, landed in Egypt in February 1940, took part in the advance to Benghazi, and then moved in April to Greece. Obliged to destroy their guns at the end of that disastrous campaign, most members of the Regt went into captivity. Reformed with new drafts, the Regt moved to New Guinea and fought in the Owen Stanley campaign (Kokoda Trail, Buna and Wau). After eighteen months back in Australia, it returned to New Guinea for the final destruction of Japanese forces at Wewak and Aitape. Casualty lists for each of the three main campaigns are included in the main narrative.
R/3. V/4. ANL/NYPL. MCND'A.

ACTION FRONT
The History of 2/2nd Australian Field Regiment, Royal Australian Artillery, AIF

Brig W Cremor ('and others') * Printed by G W Green & Sons, Melbourne, for 2/2nd Field Regt Association, 1961. Dark blue, gold, 8.5 x 5.5, viii/234. 28 mono phots, 3 maps, no Index. Apps: Roll of Honour, H&A, list of COs (with portrait photographs), 'Entries from a Diary of a POW'.

* The story of a Militia unit raised in November 1939 and which sailed for the Middle East five months later as part of 6 Aust Div. It took part in the capture of Bardia and Tobruk, embarked for Greece, fought fiercely in the Crete actions, refitted in Palestine, and then moved to Ceylon in 1942 to await the expected Japanese invasion of that island. It returned home for further training and then took part in the final actions in New Guinea in 1945 (Wewak and Aitape). This is a basic factual account, but it is often difficult to know which year is under review. Usually, only the days and months are stated. The pictures are all good quality, but they are not well captioned. R/2 V/3. AWM. MCND'A.

THE STORY OF THE 2/4th FIELD REGIMENT
A History of a Royal Australian Artillery Regiment during the Second World War

R L Henry * Printed by Rising Sun Press, Melbourne, for the Merrion Press, Melbourne, 1950. Blue, gold, 8.5 x 5.5, -/410. 111 mono phots, 8 maps, no Index. Apps: Roll of Honour, H&A, list of COs (with photographs), nominal roll (all ranks).

* The Regt was raised in Victoria and served with 7 Aust Div in Egypt and the Syria campaign before being moved back home to prepare for the New Guinea campaign. It fought at Lae and in the Ramu Valley before returning home a second time. Its final combat was the clearance of Japanese forces from Borneo. This is a clear and informative account by a former officer of the Regt. Various lists of officers, with photographs, are inserted in the main narrative.
R/3 V/4. ANL/NYPL. HEC/AMM.

Note: the 1950 edition (above) was printed in a limited edition of 300 copies. The book was republished in facsimile in 1987 by the 2/4th Field Regiment Association, at Burwood, Victoria.

GUNS AND GUNNERS
The Story of the 2/5th Australian Field Regiment in World War II
John W O'Brien * Halstead Press Pty Ltd, Sydney, for Angus & Robertson, Sydney, 1950. Navy blue, gold, 8.75 x 5.5, xviii/267. Fp, 36 mono phots, 13 maps (12 in the text, one on each of the end-papers), Glossary, Index. Apps: Roll of Honour, H&A (with citations).
* Raised in NSW in 1940, the Regt continued the traditions of 5th Field Artillery Bde of WWI vintage. This is a pleasantly readable account, by a former CO, of services in North Africa, Syria, New Guinea, and Borneo, with many individuals named in the text. The maps are helpful and the pictures well captioned. The reader may sometimes lose track of the date (year) under review, but the book is otherwise a very sound history. R/1 V/4. ANL/PCAL. MCND'A.

THE HISTORY OF THE 2/7th AUSTRALIAN FIELD REGIMENT
David Goodhart (with Brig T C Eastick and Maj R H Rungie) * Advertiser Printing Office, for Rigby Ltd, Adelaide, 1952. Pale green, gold, 9.5 x 6.0, xix/380. Fp, 20 mono phots, 5 line drawings, 17 maps (16 printed in the text, one on both end-papers), Glossary, Index. Apps: Roll of Honour, H&A (with citations, but incomplete).
* The Regt was formed in April 1940 from men volunteering in South Australia and Western Australia. It disembarked in Egypt at the end of that year and fought in Syria and in both of the El Alamein battles as part of 9th Aust Div. Returning to Australia in 1943, it did not see action again until the Tarakan operation in 1945. The narrative incorporates a great many references to individual personnel (with much detail on officers' postings in and out of each Bty). Of technical interest to gunners is the abundant information concerning ammunition expenditures, Counter Battery tasks, and technical subjects. The maps and illustrations are of a good standard. R/3 V/5. ANL. MCND'A/RH.

LAST STOP NAGASAKI
Hugh V Clarke * George Allen Unwin Pty Ltd, Sydney, 1984. Black, gold, 9.25 x 6.25, xvii/135. 41 mono phots, one sketch, 3 maps, no appendixes, no Index.
* A personal memoir. The author served with 2/10th Aust Field Regt in Malaya. He was captured there, and later was sent to Japan to work in a coalmine. In 1983 he made a pilgrimage to Nagasaki in tribute to those of his friends who did not survive. Evocative, and the only known source for this Regt. R/1 V/2. PC. PS.

OBSERVATION POST
Six Years of War with the 2/11th Australian Field Regiment
Bill Lewis * Brown Prior Anderson Pty Ltd, Victoria, for 2/11th Aust Field Regt Association, 1989. Royal blue, silver, 10.75 x 8.5, viii/215. Fp, approx 300 mono phots, 8 maps (6 printed in the text, 2 on the end-papers), Glossary, Index. Apps: Roll of Honour (with locations), H&A (some with full citations), list of former COs (with portraits and biographical notes), Regtl nominal roll.
* A handsomely produced history of a Militia unit raised in July 1940. Apart from recounting its purely military services, the book includes interesting comments on the places in which from time to time it found itself, the comings and goings of individual personnel, and sporting events. Each chapter is devoted to a specific year. After fighting the Vichy French in Syria (1941), the Regt returned home and formed part of the defence force at Darwin (the accounts of the Japanese air raids during that period are revealing). Moving then to New Guinea, the Regt fought in the Bougainville operations and remained in that area until the end of the war. Although published so many years later, the book conveys a true flavour of the period. R/1 V/4. ANL. MCND'A.

WE WERE THE 2/12th

Max Parsons * McKellar Renown Press, Carnegie, Victoria, 1984. Blue, gold, 11.0 x 8.5, -/56. Fp, 37 mono phots, 9 line drawings, 10 maps (one printed in the text, 9 loose in rear pocket), no Index. Apps: Roll of Honour.

* A brief account of one of Australia's most famous Artillery units. It is based upon six long articles published in the Regtl Assn magazine between 1980 and 1984 which, in turn, were based upon the War Diary and survivors' reminiscences. The coloured reproductions of contemporary maps are of particular interest to gunners. This history was largely replaced in 1991 by Max Parson's second and expanded account (vide following entry). R/3 V/3. ANL. MCND'A.

GUNFIRE

A History of the 2/12th Australian Field Regiment, 1940–1946

Max Parsons * Globe Press, Melbourne, for 2/12 Aust Field Regt Assn, Cheltenham, 1991. 67 mono phots, 6 line drawings, 10 maps (9 printed in the text, one on the end-papers), Glossary, Bibliography, Index. Apps: Roll of Honour (KIA and WIA, with locations and dates), H&A (with Gazette dates - full citations are quoted at the end of each of the appropriate chapters), unit nominal roll (with much detail, and incl attached personnel), list of personnel transferred in from 2/3 Aust LAA Regt, 2/3 Aust A/T Regt and 2/8 Aust Field Regt, notes on organisation and artillery equipment used.

* A nicely produced history of the only Australian gunner unit to serve in the Tobruk siege and which served longer in action than any other such Australian unit in WWII. Equipped initially with British and captured Italian pieces, it took part in both of the El Alamein battles as part of 9th Aust Div. Returning home in 1943, the Regt served subsequently in New Guinea (the Finschafen and Huon Peninsula operations). After another spell in Australia, its last actions were fought in Borneo. The book is finely illustrated and well written, with many personnel named in the text. The Index and appendixes are exemplary. R/1 V/5. AWM. MCND'A/RH.

GUNNERS IN THE JUNGLE

A Story of 2/15 Field Regiment, Royal Australian Artillery, 8th Division, AIF

Cliff Whitelocke and George O'Brien * Maxwell Printing Co Ltd, Eastwood, NSW, for 2/15 Field Regt Assn, 1983. Green, gold, 9.5 x 7.25, -/199. Fp, 88 mono phots, one line drawing, 8 maps (6 printed in the text, 2 on the end-papers), Glossary, no Index. Apps: H&A, unit nominal roll, summary of ammunition expenditure (Jan/Feb 1942), Regtl diary of events (November 1940 to February 1942).

* A thoughtfully presented history which tells the story of the first AIF Field Regt to engage the Japanese after their invasion of the Malay Peninsula. The task of the Regt was to provide support for 27th Aust Infantry Bde during its fighting retreat. Of particular interest is the coverage of the bloody engagement at Bukit Timah. An Epilogue of ten pages outlines the tribulations of the POWs after the surrender. At least 290 officers and men of the Regt died in captivity.
R/1 V/4. ANL. MCND'A.

100–ODD MATES

The Story of 2nd Mountain Battery AIF

Ron Slim * Canberra Bookbinders Ltd, Canberra, n.d. (c.1980). Buff, black, 11.5 x 8.25, v/83. 6 line drawings, 6 maps, no Index. Apps: list of unit 'characters' as mentioned in the narrative.

* Based upon the War Diary and the recollections of one hundred survivors, this is the story of an unusual element in the Royal Australian Artillery. Raised in 1943, it was air-lifted to Finschafen where it was in action between November 1943 and January 1944. There was no role for a Mountain Battery in the second stage of the New Guinea campaign, but it returned to active service for the Bougainville battles in November 1944. More than half of the text is devoted to this campaign. Only one other Mountain Battery was formed by the RAA in WWI, and this appears to be the sole published record for either of them. The author's comments regarding the use of the 75 mm pack howitzer in difficult terrain are of interest to all gunner researchers. R/3 V/4. AWM. MCND'A.

ON TARGET
With the American and Australian Ack-Ack Brigade in New Guinea
Anon ('Written and Illustrated by Men of the Front Line Forces') * Angus & Robertson Ltd, Sydney, 1943. Light grey, dark grey, 'American-Australian Brigade badge and bursting shells' motif, 9.75 x 7.5, -/171. Fp, 107 mono phots, 84 line drawings, no maps, no appendixes, no Index.
* A wartime publication which consists of numerous short essays written by various members of the Bde - American and Australian - recounting their experiences between 1939 and 1943. Censorship precluded any detail regarding dates, locations, or unit designations, but the Bde seems to have been an amalgam of several Australian Heavy A/A Btys and the American 40th Anti-aircraft Artillery Brigade, serving under unified American command. Several officers and ORs (enlisted men) are named in the text, and the varied photographic illustrations are evocative of the period. Limited though the narrative may be, it provides the basis for further research. The purpose of the book was presumably that of boosting public morale and demonstrating the value of Australian-American cooperation. R/4 V/2. PC. RH.
Note: the use of the same title for two totally different books should be kept in mind when consulting library catalogues and dealers' sales lists (vide following entry).

ON TARGET
The Story of 2/3rd Australian Light Anti-aircraft Regiment
C J Rae, A L Harris, R K Bryant * Enterprise Press Pty Ltd, Sale, Victoria, for the 2/3rd Aust Light A/A Regtl Assn, 1987. Dark blue, gold on red, 9.75 x 7.0, -/347. 67 mono phots, 4 other ills, 13 maps (11 printed in the text, 2 on the end-papers), Bibliography, Glossary, no Index. Apps: H&A, Regtl nominal roll, notes on the Regtl Association.
* This very good narrative account covers the services in WWII of 7th Bty (Crete, Palestine, and New Guinea), 8th Bty (as 'Desert Rats' in the Benghazi Handicap and the Tobruk siege, and later in New Guinea), and 9th Bty (Western Desert, defence of the Suez Canal, and later in the New Guinea and Borneo campaigns). The roll of personnel is detailed, giving particulars of deaths, wounds, and men taken prisoner. The only adverse features are the poor reproduction of some of the photographs and the lack of an Index. R/1 V/4. NLNZ. FC.

FROM ALAMEIN TO SCARLET BEACH
The History of 2/4th Light Anti-aircraft Regiment, Second AIF
Prof Francis West * Deakin University Press, Geelong, Victoria, 1989. Illustrated soft card, 'Bofors gun' motif, sky blue, white, 8.0 x 5.5, iii/160. 9 fps, 9 other ills, 3 maps, no Index. Apps: Roll of Honour (KIA and WIA), H&A (by Bty, with dates), unit nominal roll (incl attached personnel).
* The Regt was formed in Palestine in January 1942 from personnel who had earlier served with other A/A units attached to 6th and 7th Aust Divs. It moved to the Western Desert in time to take part in both of the El Alamein battles, then sailed some months later for Australia. It fought in the New Guinea campaign, taking a prominent role in the defence of Scarlet Beach during the battle for Lae. The Regt went home in August 1944 and saw no further action. A good history, with adequate maps and helpful appendixes. R/1 V/4. AWM. MCND'A.

THE LOG BOOK
Collected Record of 2/7th Australian Survey Battery, RAA, AIF, 1940-1945
Anon * D W Paterson Pty Ltd, location not shown, 1945. Soft card, buff, black, 9.5 x 7.0, -/76. One line drawing, 3 maps, no Index. Apps: Roll of Honour (KIA and WIA).
* Compiled by serving members, this is little more than a scrapbook of limericks, poems, and anecdotes. There is passing reference to the unit's map-making work in the Middle East and New Guinea between 1940 and 1945. R/4 V/1. AWM. MCND'A.

ON YOUR FEET

An Account of 2 Battery of the 2/1 Australian Tank Attack Regiment in the Wewak Campaign, New Guinea, 1945

R C Searle * William Brooks & Co Ltd, Brisbane, 1948. Brown, navy blue, gold, Artillery flash, 8.75 x 5.75, viii/74. 5 mono phots, one map (printed on the front end-paper), Glossary, no appendixes, no Index.

* This small book covers just three months of the Wewak campaign in early 1945 when the men of this Bty were deployed as infantrymen. They conducted a number of fighting patrols which inflicted heavy losses on the Japanese. The story sheds light on an unusual aspect of the campaign. R/4 V/2. AWM. MCND'A.

TARGET TANK

The History of the 2/3 Australian Anti-tank Regiment, 9th Division, AIF

Anon ('Silver John', otherwise Col J N L Argent OBE ED) * Cumberland Newspapers, Parramatta, NSW, for the Regtl History Committee, 1957. Royal blue, gold, 8.75 x 5.5, -/350. Fp, 45 mono phots (indexed), 13 maps (8 printed in the text, 5 bound in, all indexed), Glossary, Bibliography, Corrigenda, no Index. Apps: Rolls of Honour (separate for each specific action, ranks not shown), H&A, unit nominal roll (ranks not shown).

* A well written unit history, with excellent maps, fully captioned pictures, helpful appendixes, but no Index. The Regt was raised at Warwick Farm Racecourse, NSW, in July 1940, from a nucleus of 14 Bde RAA, CMF. It served with 6th and 9th Aust Divs in the Western Desert (Mechili, Tobruk, El Alamein) and with 7th and 9th Aust Divs in the Pacific (New Guinea and Labuan Island). It served in a wide diversity of roles at different periods of the war, but the author's descriptions of the Regt's part in defeating the German panzers at El Alamein are particularly absorbing. Lists of officers, WOs, and SNCOs, which might otherwise have appeared as appendixes, are inserted at key points in the narrative (at formation, at embarkation, in Egypt, and in Borneo). R/1 V/4. AWM/NYPL. MCND'A/RH.

Note: in 1975, the Regtl Association produced a pamphlet of five pages with the title THE STORY OF 2/3 ANTI-TANK REGIMENT RAA, AIF, NOW THE 23rd FIELD REGIMENT, RAA, ARMY RESERVE. This is a highly condensed precis of the 1957 publication described above. It also continues the Regt's history from disbandment in 1946 and its reformation as 23 Field Regt RAA in the Army Reserve in 1948.

TID-APA

The History of the 4th Anti-tank Regiment, 1940-1945

Lieut Col Neil C Smith AM * Produced by Mostly Unsung Military Research & Publications, Melbourne, 1992. Brown, gold, 8.5 x 6.0, xii/231. 23 mono phots (indexed), 11 maps, Glossary, Index of Persons. Apps: unit nominal roll (incorporating Roll of Honour details and notes on POW), H&A (with citations), technical data on the 2-pounder A/T gun and other weaponry, notes on the construction of the Death Railway (with dates, kilometre chart, etc).

* The Regt was raised in Victoria in late 1940 as part of 8th Aust Div. This is a high quality production, full of detail. It describes the despatch of the Regt's 13th Bty to Singapore/Malaya in February 1941, the arrival in June of the other Btys and HQ (less 14th Bty which went to Darwin for local defence duties), and the period of waiting up until the end of the year. The author then gives a vivid account of the fighting when the Japanese invaded the peninsula, the withdrawal southwards, and the Regt's part in the final battle on Singapore Island. The second half of the book deals with the three-and-a-half years of captivity in POW camps along the length of the Thailand/Burma railway. The outstanding range of appendixes, combined with the fluent narrative, make this a first class reference source. R/1 V/5. AWM. MCND'A/RH.

Note: 'Tid-apa' is Malay for 'never mind', or 'everything will be alright'. Men of the Regt started using the phrase in wry humour, and it became part of the Regt's tradition.

THE STORY OF 101 AUSTRALIAN TANK ATTACK REGIMENT (AIF)
1940 to 1943, and 1970 onwards
Compiled by nine named authors (R L Franklin, et al) * Published by the Reunion Committee, 1976. Illustrated stiff glossy card, grey, blue, 'Anti-tank gun' motif, 8.5 x 5.5, -/81. 4 mono phots, no maps, no Index. Apps: unit nominal roll.
* A collection of personal reminiscences by nine former members. Only one Bty saw service overseas (Milne Bay, 1942). R/3 V/1. ANL. MCND'A.

Coastal and Searchlight Units

THE HISTORY OF THE 'LETTER' BATTERIES IN WORLD WAR II
R J Kidd and R E Neal * Privately, no details shown, 1993. Facsimile TS, plastic covers on blue card, black, with ring binder, 11.75 x 8.25, -/52 (not numbered). 6 mono phots (photostats), 3 technical line drawings (155 mm guns), one map (folding), Bibliography, no appendixes, no Index.
* This is a condensed history of each of the 'Letter' Heavy Artillery Batteries, Royal Australian Artillery, raised in 1942 and 1943 for the defence of the Australian and American coastal bases against the possibility of seaborne attack. There were nineteen two-gun Btys, equipped from the USA with 155 mm mobile guns and 150 cm Sperry searchlights, and each having an establishment of 116 all ranks. Additionally, there were three mobile Fire Command units. The gun Btys were designated 'A' through to 'U', less 'I', plus 'X' (the latter going on to serve subsequently with 2/3rd Field Regt RAA in the Wewak campaign, 1945). In 1942, six Btys were deployed around Port Moresby and Milne Bay. In 1943, five other Btys were sent to the north coast of Papua and New Guinea. Another was located in the Torres Straits and two more at the large US Navy submarine base at Fremantle. In 1944, two more were deployed in the field at Lae and in Bougainville. The authors provide a chronology of movements and events for each Bty, and show their locations in Papua New Guinea. Although these 'Letter' Btys were never called upon to fire in anger in their primary coastal defence role, this publication is unique in recording a little known aspect of the evolution of gunnery in Australia. The 'economy' standard of production is disappointing, but the factual material is very good indeed. R/2 V/4. AWM. MCND'A.

THE LONG WHITE FINGER
A Narrative History of the 73rd Australian Mobile Searchlight Battery, AIF, during its Active Life, 1942–1945
Noel Hill and Bill Holder * Published by the 73rd A/SL Association, 1988. Illustrated soft card, green/black, white, 'Searchlight detachment' motif, 11.25 x 8.0, -/64. 89 mono phots, 2 maps (printed on the end-papers), Bibliography, Glossary, Index. Apps: unit nominal roll.
* The 73rd was the first such unit to be raised in Australia (1942) for overseas service. It formed part of the defences of Port Moresby, coming under the control of the Australian and American Ack-Ack Brigade. In late 1942, the unit moved to the northern coast of New Guinea where it was deployed around the base at Lae. By 1944, Japanese air attacks were no longer a threat, and the Bty was brought home. The authors give a clear account of its work, particularly during the night bombing attacks against Port Moresby at the most critical stage of the New Guinea campaign. The illustrations are excellent, and well captioned. A useful record of an otherwise little-known unit. R/2 V/5. AWM. MCND'A.

ENGINEERS

THE ROYAL AUSTRALIAN ENGINEERS
Maj Gen Ronald McNicoll * Griffin Press Ltd, Netley, SA, for the Corps Committee of the Royal Australian Engineers, various dates (see below). Three matching volumes, blue, gold, 9.25 x 5.75.
Volume I : THE COLONIAL ENGINEERS, 1835 TO 1902. Published in 1977, xviii/203. 39 mono phots (indexed), 4 maps (printed on the end-papers), Glossary, Chapter Notes, Bibliography, Index. Apps: 'Officers of the Royal Engineers who served in the Australian Colonies'.
* This is the first in a planned four-volume series. It describes, in a way which should interest both the general reader and the specialist, the activities of the officers of the British Army's Royal Corps of Engineers who worked in the Australian Colonies prior to their federation and the creation of the Commonwealth of Australia. The final chapter deals with the raising of the Corps of Australian Engineers in 1902.
Volume II : MAKING AND BREAKING, 1902 TO 1919. Published in 1979, xix/232. 49 mono phots (indexed), 11 maps (indexed, 9 folding, bound in at the rear, 2 printed on the end-papers), Chapter Notes, Bibliography, Index. Apps: Roll of Honour (statistical summary only), H&A (idem), biographical notes on many officers, list of Engineer units in the AIF, idem the Railway Coys, idem the Electrical, Mechanical, Mining and Boring Coys, idem the Wireless Sqns in Persia and Mesopotamia, notes on the Royal Australian Naval Bridging Train.
* Fifteen chapters which tell the story of the Australian Engineers from just after the Anglo-Boer War (1902) through to the end of WWI. There is good coverage of their work on Gallipoli and in Sinai, Palestine and Syria. The Western Front was a major commitment for the military engineers of every participating army, and this book describes in particular the work of the Australians at Bullecourt, Messines, Ypres, and the defence of Amiens.
Volume III : TEETH AND TAIL, 1919 TO 1945. Published in 1982, xix/432. 55 mono phots (indexed), 23 maps (indexed, 21 folding, bound in at the rear, 2 printed on the end-papers), Chapter Notes, Bibliography, Index. Apps: biographical notes on many officers, notes on coastal defence construction (1930s), idem A/A searchlight units (1939-1943), idem railway construction in the Levant, idem forestry units, idem camouflage, idem The Parachute Troop, idem chemical warfare.
* Twenty chapters written in greater detail than those found in the first two volumes. The author tackles not only the successes but also the failures of the campaigns in Cyrenaica, Greece, Crete and Syria in 1942. Other chapters cover Australian Engineer tasks in Malaya, New Guinea, Bougainville, New Britain and North Borneo. The varied appendixes reflect some of the more esoteric engineering tasks discussed in the main narrative.
Note: the word 'Volume' has been used here to describe these three books, but in fact it does not appear on the covers or on the title pages. The only time the author refers to Volume I, Volume II, or Volume III, is in small print on the verso of the title pages. It is reported that a fourth volume - to cover the period from 1945 to 1975 - is in course of preparation. If it is written with the same fluency and economy of words which characterise the first three books, it will complete a remarkable history. The maps and illustrations are excellent, and the entire work is exemplary in every way. R/2 V/5. ANL. MCND'A.

HISTORY OF THE NSW CORPS OF ENGINEERS, 1869-1901
Capt R J McKinnon * Seen only as a photo-copy, details of original binding not known, -/33. 6 mono phots, 2 line drawings, no maps, no appendixes, Bibliography, no Index.
* This is a short record of the beginnings of the Colony's military engineering organisation. Volunteer engineers were first accepted into military service in 1870. A list of the first members is included in the text. They were superceded in 1878 by the formation of the Torpedo & Signalling Corps (absorbed into a Corps of Engineers in 1893). In addition to two Field Coys, the Corps also comprised a

Submarine Miners Coy and an Electric Coy. The book offers an intriguing and unusual view of NSW's pre-Federation military history. R/5 V/2. ADFA. MCND'A. Note: the Mitchell Library (State Library of NSW) contains a copy of the equally rare publication compiled by Capt C Stuart-Cansdell - bearing the same title, but covering a slightly shorter period of time (1869-1899).

World War I

THE GALLIPOLI DIARY OF SERGEANT LAWRENCE OF THE AUSTRALIAN ENGINEERS 1st AIF, 1915

Cyril Lawrence and Sir Ronald East CBE * Melbourne University Press, Carlton, Victoria, 1981. Light brown, gold, 8.0 x 6.0, xi/167. 4 mono phots, 6 maps, Index. Apps: War Diary of the 2nd Field Coy, RAE, AIF, on Gallipoli.

* This edited diary records the activities and personal observations of a member of 2nd Field Coy from the time of his arrival at Suez through to the evacuation of Gallipoli. Although it does not pretend to be a comprehensive account, it does provide a valuable contemporary view of military engineering activities on the peninsula as recorded by one NCO and supported by the official War Diary. R/2 V/3. AWM. EDS.

Note: a similar and equally good personal memoir is PURPLE PATCHES - A TALE OF THE SAPPERS, by T H Prince (Jackson & Sullivan Ltd, Sydney, 1935). He describes, in 304 pages, his experiences on Gallipoli and the Western Front (1915-1917). The title of his book is very similar to that chosen for the WWII history of the 10th Field Coy RAE (vide Index of Authors - Jack Bourne and Jack Lavery).

THE SEVENTH FIELD COMPANY (FIELD ENGINEERS) AIF, 1915-1918

R H Chatto * Smith Newspapers Ltd, Sydney, 1936. Purple, gold, 'Diamond flash' motif, 8.5 x 5.5, -/214. Fp, 57 mono phots, numerous light-hearted pen-and-ink sketches reproduced from SMITH'S WEEKLY, one map (of poor quality), no Index. Apps: Roll of Honour (with ranks, locations, and dates), H&A.

* Despite its unhandy format (no 'Contents' page, no maps, no Index), this is a useful book. The period covered is October 1915 through to the Armistice, and the scene is predominantly the Western Front. The Coy suffered more casualties than any other AIF Field Coy, and the narrative includes abundant references to individual members who were killed or wounded. The author also provides much detail concerning personnel posted in and out (down to Section level). Likewise, he has given names to all those depicted in the photographs. A prime source for genealogists and medal collectors. R/4 V/3. ANL. MCND'A.

HISTORY OF THE 10th FIELD COMPANY OF ENGINEERS, AIF In the Field, 1916-1918

Anon * Gill & Hambly Printers, Melbourne, 1919. Soft card, buff, brown, AIF badge, 8.5 x 5.5, -/59. One mono phot, no maps, no Index. Apps: unit nominal roll (with details of casualties, dates of postings, honours and awards), statistics regarding casualties, idem drafts, etc.

* Produced as a souvenir when the unit returned home, this is a simple record of service. Although brief, it does provide a quite detailed description of the Coy's tasks which it was given in the build-up to operations at Messines, Ypres, Amiens, and the Somme. R/4 V/4. AWM. MCND'A.

HISTORY OF THE 11th FIELD COMPANY, AUSTRALIAN ENGINEERS, AIF

Anon ('Members of the Unit') * War Narratives Publishing Co, London, 1919. Soft card, grey, black, 8.5 x 5.5, -/75. No ills, no maps, no Index. Apps: Roll of Honour (with dates and locations), unit nominal roll (with dates of joining and departure, promotions, wounds and deaths), diary of locations.

* The Coy was raised in March 1916 and served on the Western Front from the end of that year through to the Armistice. This is a good contemporary account of the work of the sappers in support of 3rd Aust Div at Amiens, Villers Bretonneux, Hamel, and the Hindenburg Line. R/4 V/3. ANL. MCND'A.

NOTES ON THE WORK OF THE AUSTRALIAN TUNNELLING COMPANY IN FRANCE
Operations Carried Out by the First Australian Tunnelling Company
O H Woodward * Reprint from 'The Proceedings of the Australian Institute of Mining and Metallurgy' (Series 37), 1920. Soft card, dark green, black, 7.25 x 5.0, -/53. 22 diagrams, one map (bound in), no appendixes, no Index.
* Formed in 1915, the Coy's biggest project was the extensive mining system at Hill 60. The success of the assault at Messines was assured by the huge explosion which obliterated the German defences. The bulk of the text is devoted to a technical description of the mining methods employed and the difficulties overcome. These are of interest mainly to a qualified readership. R/4 V/4. AWM. MCND'A.

World War II

CORPS OF THE ROYAL AUSTRALIAN ENGINEERS IN THE SECOND WORLD WAR 1939-1945
Anon (a Committee, but principally Maj W Lennard) * The Speciality Press Pty Ltd, Melbourne, n.d. (c.1946). Stiff card, fawn, blue, Corps crest, 10.75 x 8.5, -/54 (plus 14 not numbered). 2 fps, 12 mono phots, 14 cld ills (see below), 6 line drawings (Darwin docks under repair, following the Japanese air raids), no maps, no Index. Apps: Roll of Honour (all ranks, for all RAE units), H&A (all ranks, all RAE units, incl Docks and Water Transport units, up to 30.9.1946), Order of Battle (all RAE units in WWII, down to Independent Platoon level, with their campaigns, locations, and dates), notes on Corps music, Blamey's 'VJ Order of the Day'.
* The Engineers grew to a maximum strength of 28,000 all ranks. They served in the Middle East and SW Pacific theatres of war, and this little book gives a useful summary of their work. However, its main value is the run of remarkably detailed appendixes, particularly the Order of Battle. It incorporates a great deal of useful information concerning the movements and locations of each unit and sub-unit, including those of the Docks, Forestry, Railway, and Water Transport elements. The fourteen coloured illustrations are reproductions of delightful water colours which were painted in 1945 by Sgt J A Salt in North Borneo. R/3 V/5. AWM. MCND'A/EJA. Note: a copy has been seen with a tipped-in 'supplement' of four pages which list additional 'honours and awards' recipients.

SAPPERS OF THE SILENT SEVENTH
Lindsay J Peck MBE * Published by the 7th Division Engineers Association, 1989. Illustrated soft card, purple, black, 'Purple diamond with caricature of soldier' motif, 11.5 x 8.0, iv/414. 24 mono phots, 26 sketches, 6 maps, Glossary, Index. Apps: Sources, 'History of the Corps of Engineers'.
* Sixteen narrative chapters, presented in large print, spaciously set out, with many places and persons named in the text, but without the customary run of appendixes. The 7 Aust Div Engineers were raised in April/May 1940 and consisted of 2/4th, 2/5th, 2/6th and 2/9th Field Coys, 2/25th Field Park Coy, and 7th Div Mobile Bath Unit. Written in a light-hearted style, the book covers in considerable detail the Div's services in the Middle East (to Benghazi in 1940, the Tobruk siege, Palestine and Syria), New Guinea (Milne Bay, the Kokoda Trail, Lae, Ramu Valley, Shaggy Ridge), and Borneo (Balikpapan). The accounts of combat, and in particular the desperate actions in New Guinea, are written with verve and in a way which can be clearly understood. While concentrating upon the work of the Engineers, the book is effectively a history of 7 Div. The exploits of this Division are less well known than those of 6 Div and 9 Div, hence it is a useful additional source in that larger context. R/1 V/4. ANL. MCND'A.

THE SAPPERS AT WAR WITH NINTH AUSTRALIAN DIVISION ENGINEERS
Volume I : 1939-1945
Ken Ward-Harvey * Sakoga Pty Ltd, Coffs Harbour, NSW, for 9th Div RAE Assn, 1989. Illustrated glazed soft card, spiral binding, purple, black, five 'Divsl patches' motif, 8.0 x 5.75, iv/167. No ills, 12 maps and diagrams (9 printed in the text, 3 folding, bound in), no appendixes, no Index.
* 9th Aust Div served in the Western Desert (1941-1942), New Guinea (1943-1944),

and North Borneo (1945). This is a record of the RAE units which served with it at various times during those three campaigns - 2/3rd, 2/7th, 2/13th, and 2/16th Field Coys, and 2/24th Field Park Coy. The narrative is heavily dependent upon eyewitness accounts and personal anecdotes contributed by officers and men who served. Many are named in the text, and there are several rolls of casualties and award winners. More a memoir than a history. R/1 V/3. ANL. MCND'A.

THE SAPPERS' WAR
With 9 Australian Division Engineers, 1939-1945
Ken Ward-Harvey * Sakoga Pty Ltd, Newcastle, NSW, for 9th Div RAE Assn, 1992. Illustrated soft card, olive, purple, 'Bailey bridge and Div patches' motif, 11.5 x 8.5, -/224. 112 mono phots, 13 line drawings, 22 maps, Bibliography, no Index. Apps: Roll of Honour (KIA and DOW, with dates and title of unit), H&A (with citations), unit nominal rolls (HQ RAE 9 Div, for 2/3, 2/7, 2/13, 2/16 Field Coys, 2/24 Field Park Coy, plus 72 Light Aid Detachment).
* Referring to the preceding entry, compiled by the same author, it will be seen that this (1992) publication is not Volume II of a series but a complete history in its own right. It is not known what happened to the Volume II work (which presumably had been planned), but the sponsors seem to have decided to make a fresh start with this new book. Its contents are arranged in two parts. The first covers events up to 1943 and the narrative is an expanded version of the first (1989) book. The second part covers events from 1943 to 1945. The general presentation is an improvement. There is a good range of illustrations (there were none in 'Volume I') and much of the reference material has this time been arranged in the form of easily-consulted appendixes. Unfortunately, there is still no Index. R/1 V/4. AWM. MCND'A.

THE BRIDGE IS GAPPED
Sappers at War with Nippon as Combatants and Captives
L J Robertson * K D Murray Productions, Grafton, NSW, 1980. Seen rebound in brown, gold, 10.5 x 8.25, -/337. Fp, 27 mono phots, 9 line drawings, 6 maps, no Index. Apps: Roll of Honour, H&A, 'Blackforce' nominal roll (1942), locations of prison camps, roll of those who died in captivitiy.
* This is the story of 2/6th Field Coy RAE. The lettering on the spine refers also to 'Seventh Division Engineers AIF', and the title page includes a form of sub-title, thus: 'Part I - Syria to Surrender, Part II - The Gap, or The Impossible takes a Little Longer'. Having penetrated the fog of the title and sub-titles, the reader will discover a story which is not generally known. In February 1942, after the fall of Singapore and Sumatra, the Australians landed a mixed force of 2500 all ranks on the island of Java. The aim was to maintain an Allied toehold there. Commanded by Lieut Col (acting Brigadier) A S Blackburn VC, and code-named 'Blackforce', it had a hopeless task and was obliged to surrender after only one month. All of this is covered in Part I of the book in full and interesting detail (with the emphasis on the role of 2/6 Field Coy). Part II, which occupies 200 of the book's 337 pages, recounts the travels and misfortunes of the sappers while in captivity in SE Asia and mainland Japan. An impressive production, and a worthy memorial to those who did not return. R/1 V/4. ANL. MCND'A.

WITH COURAGE HIGH
The History of the 2/8th Field Company, Royal Australian Engineers, 1940-1946
Reginald Davidson * G W Green & Sons, Melbourne, for 2/8 Field Coy RAE Assn, n.d. Grey/green, dark blue, 8.5 x 5.5, xvi/204. 42 mono phots, 4 maps, Glossary, no Index. Apps: Roll of Honour, various nominal rolls.
* A concise and well constructed history. The unit served in the early Western Desert battles, the disasters in Greece and Crete, and then returned to Australia in 1942. Almost immediately it was plunged into the desperate fighting on New Guinea (Milne Bay, Wau, and Tambu). After another brief spell at home, it returned to New Guinea for the operations around Aitape and Wewak. One entire chapter is given to the experiences of men taken prisoner in the Middle East and held in camps in Germany. R/3 V/4. AWM. MCND'A.

A PURPLE PATCH
A History of the 10th Field Company RAE (AIF), 1940-1945
Jack Bourne and Jack Lavery * Yarra Valley Press Pty Ltd, Victoria, for the 10th Field Coy Assn, 1991. Illustrated soft card, green/blue, white, 'Patch, Koala, and Cockatoo' motif, 8.25 x 5.75, xv/125. Fp, 38 mono phots (indexed), 4 maps, Index. Apps: Roll of Honour, H&A, unit nominal roll, schedule of unit movements (31.10.1941 to 14.12.1945).
* This Militia unit was formed in 1903, mobilised for service in 1914, then mobilised again in 1940. The book is written by two former members and is light-hearted but informative. The unit spent the first eighteen months of WWII in Australia, building bridges and water points on the lines of communication between Victoria and Queensland. The next two years were spent in New Guinea. There the unit was employed in constructing wharfs, roads and hospitals in the main base areas. It saw no front-line action, but it enabled the combat units to win the campaign. Individuals, of all ranks, are mentioned throughout the narrative.
R/2 V/5. ANL. MCND'A.

Engineer Amphibious Units

IN ALL RESPECTS READY
The Small Ships Companies of Water Transport, Royal Australian Engineers
Austin Stapleton * Pegasus Public Relations, Victoria, 1982. Facsimile TS in navy blue/gold covers, 8.25 x 6.75, -/188. 13 mono phots, some line drawings, one map, Glossary, no appendixes, no Index.
* Written by a former member, this is an account of the waterborne units of the Royal Australian Engineers which operated around the coastlines of New Guinea, Bougainville, and North Borneo. The material is presented in a cheerful rather than objective style, and no servicemen's real names are quoted. Combined with the lack of an Index or any appendixes which might have helped a researcher, these flaws tend to limit the book's historical worth. However, it sets the scene, and some readers may find it useful as a background source. R/2 V/2. ANL. MCND'A.

WATERMEN OF WAR
A History of No 43 Australian Water Transport Company (Landing Craft) AIF, of the Royal Australian Engineers
John Hemsley Pearn * Amphion Press, for the University of Queensland, Brisbane, 1993. Plasticated illustrated boards, 'Blue ensign and boat' motif, red/purple/white, 8.5 x 5.75, xvi/277. More than 100 mono phots, numerous sketches, 2 maps, Chapter Notes, Index. Apps: diary of events (December 1943 to February 1946), unit nominal roll (incl details of casualties and awards).
* A detailed record of a unit which carried out coastline transport and landing work around New Guinea and New Britain. Many of the vessels operated by the unit are shown in the photographs, and in line drawings and sketches. The Foreword was written by ex-Corporal Ninian Stephen, a beachmaster with this unit who later became Governor General of Australia. The clear factual narrative gives a good account of formation, training, and wartime operations, and then the task of evacuating Japanese troops from the surrendered islands. The book does not conform with the conventional 'unit history' layout, but it is full of useful detail and is certainly of value to everyone concerned with military logistics and the problems peculiar to amphibious warfare. R/1 V/5. AWM. MCND'A.

PIONEERS

World War I

WAR BOOK OF THE THIRD PIONEER BATTALION
Maj M B Keatinge MC * Speciality Press Pty Ltd, Melbourne, n.d. (1922). Purple, black, Bn flash, 8.5 x 5.5, -/192. Fp, 12 mono phots (indexed), 3 maps, no Index. Apps: unit nominal roll (incl dates of enlistment and casualties), H&A, notes on the VC action by L/Cpl Walter Peeler (Ypres Salient, 20.9.1917).
* Like the Pioneer units of the Indian Army, the Australian Pioneers were trained as both field engineers and combat troops. This is the story of one such Bn, raised in February 1916 and assigned to 3rd Aust Div. Its personnel were selected from all parts of Australia and according to each man's manual skills and personal character. They arrived in France in November 1916 and, for the next two years, were engaged primarily in constructing strongpoints in the forward areas. As the citation for Walter Peeler's VC demonstrates, this work often brought them into the closest proximity with their opponents. In 1918, the Bn was less involved in fortification work and served mainly in the conventional infantry role. This is a full and readable account of a unit which, apart from the VC award, won 4 DSOs, 10 DCMs, 69 MMs, 9 MSMs, one OBE, and one MBE. The narrative has good accounts of the battles for Messines, Villers Bretonneux, Hamel, and Second Amiens. Of the 1964 officers and men who served in the Bn, 960 became casualties.
R/3 V/4. AWM. MCND'A/PS.

THE STORY OF THE 5th PIONEER BATTALION, AIF
F H Stevens * Collotype Printers, Adelaide, 1937. Sky blue, dark blue, Bn patch, 9.75 x 7.25, -/116. Fp, 18 mono phots, 2 maps (folding, bound in), no Index. Apps: Roll of Honour, H&A (by HQ and Coys).
* Although lacking either a Contents page or an Index, this is an excellent account of a Pioneer Bn's services on the Western Front from July 1916 through to November 1918. The Bn was attached to 5th Aust Div for field engineering works. It drained the trenches at Fromelles, built defensive strongpoints around St Eloi and, becoming famous in the process, repaired the road through Villers Bretonneaux in less than four hours on 8 August 1918 (Germany's 'black day'). The illustrations are some of the best seen in any WWI history.
R/3 V/4. ADFA/NYPL. MCND'A.

World War II

THE PIONEERS
The Unit History of 2/1st Australian Pioneer Battalion, 2nd AIF, 1940-1946
Lieut Col Gordon Osborn * Macarthur Press, Parramatta, NSW, 1988. Blue, gold, 8.5 x 5.5, xiii/198. 54 mono phots, 10 maps (8 printed in the text, 2 on the end-papers), no Index. Apps: Roll of Honour (KIA, WIA, and POW), H&A, list of former COs (with portrait photographs), Bn nominal roll (names only, no ranks given), notes regarding the Bn's WWI and WWII flashes, idem Battle Honours.
* This stylish book opens with a brief history of the formation of Pioneer Bns in general. In WWI, one was assigned to each Australian Division from 1916 onwards 'for military works requiring for their construction training less expert than Engineers but more skilled than Infantry'. Five were raised in WWI, four (as Corps Troops) in WWII. The bulk of the narrative then covers the services of 2/1 Bn in the Western Desert (1940-1941), the New Guinea campaign (1942-1944), and the amphibious assault at Balikpapan (1945). The unit fought as infantry during the Tobruk siege, as infantry and track builders on the Kokoda Trail, and as porters of artillery pieces to 'impossible' positions in the Owen Stanley ranges. The maps are good, the photographs well captioned, and the text well spiced with the names of individual officers and men. An interestingly readable book about an unusual unit, diminished only by the lack of an Index. R/1 V/4. ANL. MCND'A.

THE STORY OF THE 2/2nd AUSTRALIAN PIONEER BATTALION
E F Aitken * 2/2nd Pioneer Bn Assn, Melbourne, 1953. Maroon, gold, 8.5 x 5.75, xiii/288. Fp, 90 mono phots (indexed), 14 maps (indexed), Glossary, Index. Apps: Roll of Honour, H&A, list of officers and WOs who embarked for the Middle East.
* The Bn was raised in 1940 and took part in the Syrian campaign in the following year. Early in 1942 it arrived in Java where, after fierce fighting, it was obliged to capitulate. Of the 860 personnel taken prisoner, 258 died in captivity. Reformed in Australia, a new 2/2nd Bn served on New Guinea in both the sapper and the infantry roles. Then, after amphibious training, it took part in the Tarakan and Balikpapan assaults of 1944-1945. A well written and detailed book, with frequent references to individual personnel, good maps, and good illustrations. R/2 V/5. ANL/NYPL. MCND'A,.

MUD AND SAND
The Official War History of the 2/3 Pioneer Battalion, AIF
J A Anderson and J G T Jackett * 2/3 Pioneer Bn Assn, Burwood, 1955. Seen rebound in hardback, brown, silver, 8.25 x 5.0, -/380. Fp, approx 80 mono phots, no maps, no Index. Apps: Roll of Honour, H&A.
* Published originally in seven parts, this history (as recorded here) consists of all those parts bound into a single case. The story covers the unit's formation in May 1940, its work in Syria and the Western Desert, regrouping in Palestine, and the return to Australia. Subsequently it served in the operations to reoccupy North Borneo where one of its NCOs - Cpl John Mackey - won a posthumous VC (12.5.1945, Tarakan Island). Typically of the Australian Pioneer units, it was employed in both the infantry and field engineering roles. At El Alamein, for example, it fought in the battle but also helped to construct defensive positions and clear mine fields. The story is written with verve, but it is sometimes difficult to follow. The layout is not well organised, and the book lacks both a Contents page and an Index. R/2 V/2. ANL. MCND'A.
Note: an edition dated 1963 has been reported.

CORPS OF SURVEY

The Corps of Survey was established as an independent surveying and map-making branch of the Australian Army in 1915. It made an important contribution to the Allied cause in both world wars.

LEBANON TO LABUAN
A Story of Mapping by the Australian Survey Corps, World War II
Brig Lawrence Fitzgerald OBE * J G Holmes Pty Ltd, Melbourne, for 2/1st Survey Association, 1980. White, blue, Corps crest, 11.5 x 8.75, xii/124. Fp, 79 mono phots, 5 other ills, 11 maps (9 printed in the text, 2 on the end-papers), Index.
Apps: list of officers, schedule of operations (June 1941 to January 1942), GHQ Mapping Directive.
* For both the layman and the specialist, this is an interesting book. For every professional cartographer, it must make absorbing reading. The narrative covers the work of various Corps units in Palestine, Jordan and Syria, and then in the SW Pacific theatre. R/3 V/4. NZMODL. HEC.

MEMORIES OF 2 AUSTRALIAN FIELD SURVEY COMPANY, 1940-1944
Lieut Col H P G Clews * Publication details not shown, 1966. Soft card, white, black, 'Survey triangle' motif in mauve, 9.5 x 7.25, -/48. Fp, 2 mono phots, 3 maps and diagrams, no Index. Apps: nominal roll, details of the maps produced by the Company.
* Written by its former Commanding Officer, this slim 'economy' booklet tells an important story. The author opens with a brief summary of the work of the Corps before the war, and then describes the tasks of the individual Sections of his 2nd Company in New Guinea, New Britain, and Bougainville (1943-1944). They produced thirty-one maps to varying scales, and the technical details of each are listed in the appendixes. During WWII in particular, Australia's armed forces often found themselves operating in areas where maps were non-existent, unreliable, or of a scale unsuitable to meet military needs. In the New Guinea campaign in particular, the troops were fighting in terrain which had never been surveyed and where very few Europeans had ever previously penetrated. This created great difficulties for all arms, but especially for the gunners (who needed to accurately compute the locations of their targets and their own positions), for the supply services (who needed to know where and how they could move their stores and equipment), and for the aviators (who needed to identify the features over which they were flying). The success of the Survey Corps in producing all manner of maps, at speed, and in quantity, was a campaign-winning factor.
R/4 V/4. AWM. MCND'A.

SIGNALS

SIGNALS
The Story of the Australian Corps of Signals
Anon ('Members of the Australian Corps of Signals') * Halstead Press Pty Ltd, Sydney, for the Corps, 1953. Dark green, black, Corps crest, 11.0 x 8.5, -/196. Fp, 127 mono phots, 3 maps, various line drawings, no Index. Apps: Roll of Honour.
* An interesting narrative, but not a definitive history. It is an anthology of sixty-one short pieces which include extracts from diaries and anecdotal items. The result is more akin to a regimental magazine than a structured story. Even so, the book does contain much meat. It has useful information regarding the role of the Corps in campaigns in which its units and sub-units were engaged (mainly WWII - the Middle East and the Pacific). R/3 V/3. PC. HEC.

World War I

WITH HORSE AND MORSE IN MESOPOTAMIA
The Story of ANZACS in Asia
Keast Burke * Arthur McQuitty & Co, Sydney, for the Australian & New Zealand Signal Sqn History Committee, 1927. Grey-green, blue on white, 'Mosque' motif, 11.0 x 8.25, viii/200. More than 100 mono phots, idem line drawings, 9 maps (7 printed in the text, 2 on the end-papers), Glossary, Index. Apps: Roll of Honour (by unit, with cause and date of death), nominal rolls for all Aust and NZ units as listed below (showing ranks and awards), movements and locations.
* To quote the additional sub-title - 'The Histories of 1st Australian Pack Wireless Signal Troop, the New Zealand Wireless Signal Squadron, the 1st Cavalry Divisional Signal Squadron, the Light Motor Wireless Sections, Australians in Dunsterforce, and Australian Nurses in India'. The narrative of this wide-ranging book is not easy to follow, but it covers a series of complex and always interesting operations in Mesopotamia, Southern Russia, and Kurdestan, between 1916 and 1919. A prime source for genealogists and for everyone having an interest in the early development of military radio communications. R/3 V/5. ANL. MCND'A.

World War II

GETTING THROUGH
The Unit War History of 3rd Australian Divisional Signals, 1939-1945
Anon ('Members of 3/66 Club Unit Association') * Produced by Kennalk Printing, Melbourne, for the Association, 1987. Soft card, buff, black, 'Signals' flash motif in white/blue, 8.25 x 5.75, vi/199. 27 mono phots, 19 line drawings and technical diagrams, 5 maps, Glossary, no Index. Apps: H&A, unit nominal roll.
* The story opens with a brief but useful account of the Australian Corps of Signals (founded in 1906), and of 3rd Div Signals between 1916 and 1939. The bulk of the narrative then deals with the unit's services in the Salamaua campaign (New Guinea, 1943) and the Solomon Islands and Bougainville operations (1945). Many former members contributed their reminiscences, they and their former comrades being named in the text. A book which is of interest mainly to the families of those who served. R/1 V/3. ANL. MCND'A.

THROUGH
The Story of Signals, 8th Australian Division, and Signals, AIF Malaya
J W Jacobs and R J Bridgeland * Halstead Press Pty Ltd, Sydney, for 8 Div Signals Assn, n.d. (c.1950). Grey, gold, 8.5 x 5.5, xviii/271. Fp, 18 mono phots, some line drawings, one map, six 'Signals locations' diagrams, no Index. Apps: Roll of Honour (KIA and died as POW), H&A (with citations), list of officers, idem SNCOs, unit nominal roll, diary of events.

* This is a well presented account of the AIF Signal Regt in the ill-fated attempt to defend Malaya and Singapore (1941-1942). It is an unusually helpful source because the Signal units and sub-units were widely spread and therefore witnessed all aspects of the fighting, the retreats, and the final surrender. The last one hundred pages of the book record the tribulations of those personnel (the majority) who were captured. A moving record. R/3 V/4. ANL/NYPL. MCND'A.

ON ULTRA ACTIVE SERVICE

The Story of Australia's Signals Intelligence Operations During World War II

Geoffrey Ballard * Spectrum Publications Pty Ltd, Richmond, Victoria, 1991. Brown, gold, 9.25 x 6.25, xvi/371. 118 mono phots, 22 cld ills, 8 maps, no appendixes, Glossary, Index.

* The author was one of the first Australians to be posted to crypto-graphic duties. He served with No 4 Australian Special Wireless Section in Greece, Crete and Syria, and later with No 51 Section at Darwin. In 1944 he was 'Sigint' Liaison Officer on McArthur's staff and, in 1945, held the same appointment on the staff of Mountbatten. This is a detailed and authoritative insight into a part of 'the secret war' of radio traffic interception and code-breaking. It is based not only upon the author's own experiences but also upon evidence which he collected by interviewing many former officers and operators. R/1 V/4. PC. PS.

INFANTRY

Brigades

THE WHITE GURKHAS
The 2nd Australian Infantry Brigade at Krithia, Gallipoli
Ronald J Austin * Globe Press Pty Ltd, McRae, Victoria, 1989. Red, gold, 8.75 x 5.5, xiii/156. 29 mono phots, 3 maps, Bibliography, Index. Apps: Order of Battle of the 5th Turkish Army (25 April 1915), Order of Battle of the Mediterranean Expeditionary Force (6 May 1915).
* Australian forces won fame and glory on Gallipoli for their courage at ANZAC Cove and Lone Pine. This book describes their less well-known services at the southern end of the Peninsula. After landing at Cape Helles, British and French forces had advanced five miles north to the village of Krithia. They launched a heavy attack but, despite severe losses, failed to dislodge the defenders. The 2nd Aust Inf Bde - consisting of 5th, 6th, and 7th Aust Inf Bns - was transported around from ANZAC Cove to take part in a second attack. Despite suffering 14,000 casualties in their second assault, the Allies failed to take their objective. The Australians showed such ferocity with the bayonet at Krithia that others who witnessed the battle dubbed them 'white Gurkhas'. The author rightly condemns the British senior command's mismanagement of what should have been the turning point in the campaign. A well researched book, with excellent footnotes, Bibliography, maps, and illustrations. R/1 V/5. ANL. MCND'A.

THE BLUE DIAMONDS
History of the 7th Brigade
Maj Peter J Denham * Publisher's details not shown, 1987. Soft card, pale green, black, 11.75 x 8.25, -/89 (plus 99 pages of appendixes), one line drawing (no other illustrations), 17 maps, no Index. Apps: Brigade Rolls of Honour (WWI and WWII), H&A (also in the narrative), 'Establishment and Officer Postings, 1915', list of COs (1915-1987), plus many other helpful appendixes which occupy half of the book.
* Very few histories cover the activities of a single Brigade over such a long period of time (1915-1987 inclusive). This is an 'economy' production printed in facsimile typecript and the maps, although complimentary to the storyline, are crudely executed. Presumbly the compilation was a labour of love and the publication a private venture. The Brigade's fighting services (the Western Front in WWI, New Guinea and Bougainville in WWII) are described in sufficient detail to provide interesting reading, but the work's main value is to be found in the numerous appendixes. R/3 V/3. ANL. MCND'A.

THE 17th AUSTRALIAN INFANTRY MAGAZINE
A Record of Four Years Campaigning
A R Ross * Publisher's details not shown, 1944. Stiff card, maroon, white, 17th Bde flash, 9.75 x 7.25, -/144. Fp, 92 mono phots, 15 line drawings, 7 maps, no Index. Apps: H&A (statistical summary only).
* An unusual compilation of extracts from PUCKAPUNYAL, the Brigade's own regular magazine. They record events in the life of the Bde and its constituent units between 1939 and 1944 (when its press was lost in action). The Bde served in the Middle East, Ceylon, and New Guinea. The text includes many references to individuals, and about one third of the illustrations are group photographs and personal portraits (captioned with the names of those depicted). Evocative of the period, but limited as a research source. R/3 V/2. ANL. MCND'A.

ONWARD BOY SOLDIERS
The Battle for Milne Bay, 1942
James Henderson * University of Western Australia Press, Perth, 1992. Illustrated soft card, multi-colour, cream, 9.0 x 5.75, ix/250. 33 mono phots (indexed), 7 maps (indexed), Glossary, Bibliography, no appendixes, Index.
* The book covers in considerable detail the initial Japanese landing at Milne Bay in August 1942 as part of the plan to capture Port Moresby. The defending 'Milne Force' blocked the Japanese advance after weeks of savage fighting (in which Cpl John A French of 2/9th Aust Inf Bn AIF won his posthumous VC). The defending Infantry Bns were under command of 7th and 18th Brigades, with supporting elements of 2/5th Field Regt RAA, 101 Anti-tank Regt RAA, and 2/9th Light A/A Bty RAA. Each unit receives good coverage, and many individuals are named in the text. The enemy lost over 750 dead in the assault, and the author received the cooperation of Japanese historians and participating Japanese Army former officers in seeking a balanced interpretation of the battle.
R/1 V/4. AWM. MCND'A.

TO THE BITTER END
The Japanese Defeat at Buna and Gona, 1942-43
Lex McAulay * Random House, Sydney, 1992. Black, white, 8.5 x 5.5, -/327. 33 mono phots, 2 line drawings, 9 maps, Bibliography, no appendixes, Index.
* A book which describes in detail the final destruction of Japanese forces in Papua in 1943, a defeat in which they lost 13,000 killed and died before the survivors were evacuated. Each of the participating Australian units receives comprehensive coverage. The infantry units came under command of 16th, 18th, 25th and 30th Bdes, with support from 2/6th Armd Regt, 7th Div Cavalry Regt, and 2/1st and 2/5th Field Regts RAA. The book also covers the actions of those United States forces which were involved, and upon which the author expresses some trenchant opinions. The author consulted many Japanese authorities and individuals before reaching his conclusions. The maps and illustrations are well presented.
R/1 V/4. AWM. MCND'A.

RED PLATYPUS
A Record of the Achievements of the 24th Australian Infantry Brigade, 9th Australian Division, 1940-1945
J D Yeates and W H Loh * Imperial Printing Co, Perth, WA, 1946. Soft card, red, black, 'Digger's head and Div symbol' motif, 10.5 x 8.5, -/85. 72 mono phots, 20 line drawings, 6 maps, no Index. Apps: H&A (with units and ranks).
* Written and presented in an informal style, this is a journal of the adventures of an Infantry Bde formed, literally under fire, during the siege of Tobruk. It consisted of 2/28th, 2/32nd, and 2/43rd Inf Bns AIF. They stayed together throughout the remainder of the war, fighting at El Alamein, in New Guinea, and in North Borneo, as an element of 9th Aust Div. The Platypus mentioned in the title was, with a boomerang, the Div flash. The illustrations are unique, few of them having been used in other publications, and the sketches were all drawn by men serving within the Brigade. A Western Australian, Pte L T Starcevich, won the VC while serving with 2/43rd Bn (at Beaufort, Borneo, 1945). Having been published so soon after the war, the book has an immediacy not always found in other formation histories. R/2 V/3. ANL. MCND'A.

Infantry Units (by States)

Queensland

MORETON REGIMENT, 1886
The 1st Regiment of Queensland Infantry
Peter Anderson * Watson Ferguson & Co, Queensland, for the author, 1986. Soft card, cream, red, Regtl crest, 9.75 x 6.75, x/48. 23 mono phots, one line drawing, no maps, Bibliography, no Index. Apps: notes on Queensland units at 24 February 1885, idem the Shearers' Strike of 1891.
* The last British Army (Imperial) troops left Australia in 1870. Fears of Russian expansionism in the Pacific region led, a few years later, to an awareness in Australia that the Colonies had no immediate means of self-defence. This fear led, in turn, to the formation of local volunteer military forces. In Queensland, these consisted (inter alia) of the 1st Queenslanders (Moreton Regt), the 2nd Queenslanders (Wide Bay and Burnett Regt), the 3rd Queenslanders (Darling Downs Regt), and various local Batteries of Artillery and a Company of Engineers. This little book provides a brief history of one of these units. The contemporary photographic illustrations are excellent. R/2 V/3. ANL. MCND'A.

CROSSED BOOMERANGS
Historical Journal of the Thirty-first
Capt R Burla ED * Facsimile TS, soft card, grey-green, black, 11.5 x 8.0, in excess of 1000 pages. Numerous mono phots, Bibliographies, no Indexes.
* This mammoth work consists of ten 'date' sections which the author produced in limited numbers over a four years period between 1971 and 1975. He then bound these ten sections into three volumes, copies of which he presented to ten selected libraries and archives in Queensland. A copy of each of these three volumes is held by the Library of the Australian War Memorial, Canberra. They are available via the Australian inter-library loan system. The story covers the period 1886 to 1974 and describes the complex evolution of the Royal Queensland Regt (formed in 1960 from a number of Queensland Militia units. Of the latter, those covered here are - Kennedy Infantry Regt, 31st Aust Inf Bn AIF, 2/31st Aust Inf Bn AIF, 31st/51st Aust Inf Bn AIF, and 2nd Bn The Queensland Regt. Each of the ten 'date volumes' covers a distinct period in time (such as) - the early years, the Anglo-Boer War (1886-1914), Egypt and the Western Front (1914-1918), 31/51 Bn in WWII (1943-1945), 2/31 Bn in WWII (1939-1945), 31st Inf Bn (The Kennedy Regt), and 31 RQR (1948-1974). The combined narrative provides an almost incredible amount of information of all kinds - officers' postings, actions, movements, casualties, awards (including the VC to Pte Patrick J Bugden in 1917), and much else besides. In sum, this source contains a great deal of information not readily available elsewhere. R/5 V/4. AWM. MCND'A.

SHORT HISTORY OF THE 47th BATTALION
And the 47th Battalion Memorial Trophy and Rugby League
E C 'Ted' Weber * Published privately, Maryborough, Queensland, 1990. Illustrated soft card, buff, black, 'Trophy' motif, 7.75 x 5.5, i/14. 2 mono phots, no maps, no appendixes, no Index.
* In 1860, at Maryborough and Bundaberg, local volunteers were organised as mounted infantry and became the Wide Bay Regiment of Militia. In February 1916, in Egypt, Queenslanders from those districts were brought together with other Gallipoli survivors to form the 47th Aust Inf Bn AIF. After refitting, the Bn moved to the Western Front where its members won 149 awards for gallantry during the next two years. Amongst them was the VC awarded to a Tasmanian member, Sgt S R McDougall. The Bn was mobilised again in 1941 and went on to serve in New Guinea and Bougainville. It was disbanded in January 1946, reactivated in 1952 as the 47th Inf Bn (The Wide Bay Regt), then absorbed in the 1st Royal Queensland Regt in 1960. R/3 V/1. AWM. MCND'A.

A NOMINAL ROLL OF THE FIRST QUEENSLAND CONTINGENT, AIF, TO THE GREAT WAR, 1914-1918

T A D Truswell * Ye Olde Curiosity Shoppe, Haberfield, NSW, 1983. Soft card, yellow, black, AMF 'Rising Sun' motif, 8.25 x 5.75, v/53. No ills, no maps, no formal appendixes, no Index.

* The entire book is devoted, as the title suggests, to a roll of all the officers and men who constituted the 1st Queensland Contingent. Included are details of the ships in which they sailed, the dates of embarkation, and subsequent deaths, wounds, and awards. Useful mainly to medal collectors and genealogists.
R/2 V/3. AWM. MCND'A.

ALWAYS FAITHFUL
A History of the 49th Australian Infantry Battalion, 1916-1982

Fred Cranston * Apple Printing Co Ltd, Brisbane, for Boolarong Publications, Brisbane, Qld, 1983. Illustrated laminated board, green, black, 'Historical montage' motif, 9.75 x 6.5, xxviii/243. 117 mono phots, 8 other ills, 13 maps, Bibliography, Glossary, Index. Apps: Rolls of Honour (WWI and WWII), list of former COs, notes on Battle Honours, nominal roll of officers and SNCOs at 1983, etc.

* A comprehensive coverage of this Militia unit in WWI (the Western Front) and in WWII (New Guinea, the major action at Sananada). Produced on good quality paper in a solid commercial binding. Some of the photographic illustrations are not of the highest quality, but are totally authentic in time and location. Without bitterness, the author explains how the Bn went to war in 1942 with inadequate training and equipment, and with the burden of being treated as second-rate troops by the men of the AIF units which had already seen action in the Middle East. The Bn was disbanded in 1943, most of the personnel then joining 2/1st Bn.
R/1 V/5. AWM. HEC/RH.

New South Wales

THE FIRST AUSTRALIAN INFANTRY REGIMENT (NSW)
Historical Record and Jubilee, 1854-1904

Anon * John Sands, Sydney, NSW, n.d. (c.1905). Blue, gold, Imperial crown, 9.5 x 4.75, -/36. Fp, 10 mono phots, no maps, no Index. Apps: unit nominal roll (for the South Africa contingent).

* This slim volume commemorates the foundation of the 1st NSW Rifle Volunteers in 1854 (and retitled in 1860). The Regt was remarkably active during the fifty years under review. It contributed officers and men to the Contingents sent to New Zealand in the 1860s (for the Maori Land Wars), to the Sudan in 1885, and to South Africa at the turn of the century. In 1903 it formed a Cyclist Section, being the only Australian unit to do so. Apart from describing these events, the booklet also contains information regarding the 'partial payment scheme' and other organisational matters of historical interest. R/4 V/4. AWM. MCND'A.

THE HISTORY AND REGIMENTAL STANDING ORDERS OF THE 30th INFANTRY BATTALION (THE NEW SOUTH WALES SCOTTISH REGIMENT)

Anon * Published by the Regt, Crow's Nest, NSW, 1959. Plastic binder, blue, gold, Regtl crest, 7.5 x 5.0, Lxviii/221. 16 mono phots, 6 cld ills, 6 diagrams, no maps, no appendixes, Index.

* The first 66 pages provide a condensed history of the Regt. It is divided into three sections - as the Sydney Scottish Rifles and NSW Scottish (1885-1960), as the 30th Aust Inf Bn AIF (1915-1919), and as the 2/30th Aust Inf Bn AIF (1939-1945). In its various guises, the Regt fought in South Africa, in France and Flanders, in Malaya and Singapore, and in Korea. The rest of the book is taken up with the Standing Orders (1959), and this section also is of interest. The illustrations of the Colours and the Regt's Highland uniforms are excellent. This is a useful source, especially when consulted in conjunction with one or more of the following publications. R/4 V/3. ANL. MCND'A.

IN ALL THINGS FAITHFUL
A History and Album of the 30th Battalion and New South Wales Scottish Regiment 1885–1985
T F Wade-Ferrell (as Editor) * Sam Ure Smith, at the Fine Arts Press Ltd, Killara, NSW, 1985. Blue, silver, Unit cap badge, 11.0 x 8.0, xviii/398. Fp, 508 mono phots, 2 cld plates, 6 maps (5 printed in the text, one on the end-papers), Glossary, Bibliography, no Index. Apps: Roll of Honour (WWII), H&A, list of COs, 7 separate nominal rolls, notes on 'Skill at Arms' (1938), notes on New Guinea operational orders.
* A handsome book, published to mark the centenary of the NSW Scottish. The first 50 pages cover the pre-1914 and 1918-1939 periods. Thereafter, the bulk of the book deals with WWII services (Madang and the Wewak battles, 1944-1945), and post-war developments (the Regt's reformation as a Citizen Military Force unit in 1948). There is little reference to WWI services because they are well covered in THE PURPLE AND GOLD, by Lieut Col H Sloan [recorded later in this bibliography under the 'Infantry Units (WWI)' section, vide the Index of Authors]. R/1 V/4. AWM. MCND'A/RH.

THE SCOTTISH RIFLES IN NORTHERN NEW SOUTH WALES
M J Buckley * Northern Star Ltd, Lismore, NSW, 1984. Illustrated soft card, green and white, 'Scottish Rifleman' motif, 8.25 x 6.0, -/68. Fp, 46 mono phots, no maps, Bibliography, Index. Apps: unit muster roll for 'E' Company, Lismore, idem The Maclean Scottish Rifles.
* An outline account of the raising of Volunteer units with Scottish associations in NSW. The first such was the short-lived Duke of Edinburgh's Highlanders, raised in Sydney in 1868. During 'the Russian scare' of 1885, the Scottish community tried again, this time forming the Sydney Reserve Corps of Scottish Rifles. Of Company strength, it first paraded in uniform in 1889. A second Company was formed in 1898. Following the example of Sydney, communities on the coast of Northern NSW raised 'E' Company (based at Lismore) and 'F' Company (at Maclean). This little book covers the story of these two units up until 1903. Despite its parochialism, the story is evocative of the period and indicates the circumstances under which the early Volunteer movement provided the basis for Australia's later military role in the two world wars. R/1 V/2. ANL. MCND'A.

SCARLET AND TARTAN
The Story of the Regiments and Regimental Bands of the NSW Scottish Rifles (Volunteers), The 30th Battalion (NSW Scottish Regiment), 'A' Company and Pipes and Drums, 17th Battalion, Royal New South Wales Regiment
Martin J Buckley * Published by The Red Hackle Association, Sydney, 1986. Green, gold, 11.0 x 8.25, xx/300. Approx 300 mono phots, 79 cld ills, 5 line drawings, no maps, Bibliography, Index. Apps: 50 pages of nominal rolls for the various units named in the sub-title (1868-1985), notes on Battle Honours, idem Regtl lineages.
* A magnificent volume commissioned to commemorate the Regt's centenary. The story is presented in eight parts, each of which covers a period or an aspect of the Regt's evolution and fighting services. The astonishing nominal roll appendixes name every officer and man who ever served in any of the units in the lineage. Of coincidental value is an appendix which describes all the other Australian Scottish units, raised in other Colonies before and after Federation. The illustrations are lavish and the entire work is of the highest quality.
R/1 V/5. ANL. MCND'A.

A HISTORY OF THE 41st BATTALION, THE ROYAL NEW SOUTH WALES REGIMENT, 1916–1984
J W Alcorn * Published privately, Lismore, NSW, 1984. Facsimile TS in stapled soft card covers, green, black, Regtl badges (four) on front cover, 11.5 x 8.0, -/24. No ills, no maps, no Index. Apps: Roll of Honour (WWI), H&A (WWI, with citation for the VC awarded to L/Cpl B S Gordon MM), list of former COs.
* A home-grown amateur production, of great interest. It covers the Bn's pedigree

(units raised between 1885 and 1912) and then its gallant services in France and Flanders (Ypres, Messines, and 'the last 100 days'). The inter-war years are dealt with briefly, as is the frustration of not being sent overseas in WWII. Instead, the Bn acted as a training and draft-finding unit for other Bns serving in the South West Pacific theatre. Included is an account of the post-war reorganisations of the Citizen Military Force and the unit's renaming as the 41st Royal New South Wales Regiment. This section is well supported with helpful bibliographic notes. R/2 V/3. AWM. MCND'A.
Note: two other editions of this booklet have been published.

TALES OF VALOUR FROM THE ROYAL NEW SOUTH WALES REGIMENT
Maj Gen G L Maitland * Playbill Pty Ltd, Pymble, NSW, 1992. Blue, gold, 10.0 x 6.5, x/245. 45 mono phots, 18 cld ills (the Colours and portraits), 5 line drawings, 11 maps, no appendixes, no Index.
* A quality production which describes the background to the campaigns, and the tactical circumstances pertaining, when each of the twenty-four members of the RNSW Regt performed the deed which resulted in the award of the Victoria Cross. This book has obvious value to all students of the VC, but the strategic and tactical descriptions provide a valuable adjunct to the history of the Regt in both world wars. Each recipient's background in described in detail, and the maps and illustrations are well presented. R/1 V/4. AWM. MCND'A.
Note: 2000 copies printed.

Victoria

MARCHING ON
The Bendigo Regiments and Companies, 1858–1988
William E Thomason * Bendigo Militaria Museum, Victoria, 1989. Brown, gold, 8.5 x 6.0, vi/194. Fp, 89 mono phots, no maps, Glossary, no Index. Apps: Rolls of Honour (for the Bendigo District - South Africa 1899-1902, WWI, WWII, Korea 1950-1954, Malaya and Borneo 1948-1965, and South Vietnam 1962-1972), H&A (WWII only, but incl local men who joined the RAAF and RAN).
* This is an account of the various military units originating in the Bendigo district of the State of Victoria during the period given in the title. The story commences with the Bendigo Volunteer Rifle Corps formed in 1861 and the Bendigo Cavalry formed in 1865. These evolved later into the 38th Aust Inf Bn AIF, the 67th Bn, and the 17th Light Horse. R/1 V/4. PS/MCND'A.
Note: a paper-back version of this title has been reported.

SOUVENIR OF 1st BATTALION, 5th AUSTRALIAN INFANTRY REGIMENT
C P Smith and Lieut Col J M Courtenay VD * Charles Steele & Co, Melbourne, 1912. Illustrated soft card, blue, gold, 'Regtl crest and drums' motif, 9.5 x 11.75 (landscape), –/24. 15 mono phots, no appendixes, no Index.
* Mainly a pictorial record, the photographs being of the officers, the SNCOs, each of the eight Rifle Coys, the Signallers, etc. Officers and SNCOs are identified in the captions. The accompanying narrative describes the raising of the Bn in 1903 (many of its founder personnel having served in the Contingents which went to South Africa), and its part-time services through to 1911 when, under the Kitchener system of universal training, it became the City of Melbourne Infantry. Brief but useful, and evocative of the period. R/5 V/3. AWM. MCND'A.

ESPRIT DE CORPS
The History of the Victorian Scottish Regiment and the 5th Infantry Battalion
Lieut Col F W Speed OBE * Allen & Unwin (Australia) Pty Ltd, North Sydney, 1988. Black, gold, 9.25 x 7.25, xviii/429. 178 mono phots, 22 cld ills, 47 maps, Bibliography, Index. Apps: Rolls of Honour (WWI and WWII, with locations), H&A, list of former COs, idem Honorary Colonels, notes on the Regt's lineage, Battle and Theatre Honours, etc.
* An attractive and lavishly produced book which covers the history of the

Victorian Scottish from inception in 1898 through to reorganisation as the Royal Victorian Regt in 1960, and then events through to 1985. Members of the Regt served with the Australian Contingents in South Africa, and as 5th Aust Inf Bn AIF in WWI (Gallipoli and the Western Front). Two chapters cover the inter-war years, and then three further chapters describe the WWII services of 2/5th Aust Inf Bn AIF in Libya, Greece, Syria, New Guinea, and Borneo. There is an account also of 5th Bn (Victorian Scottish Regt) which served on home defence duties from 1939 to 1944. The narrative is comprehensive and easy to follow, the illustrations are very good indeed, and the numerous maps excellent.
R/1 V/5. ANL/VSL. MCND'A/PS.

BOLD, STEADY, FAITHFUL
The History of the 6th Battalion, The Royal Melbourne Regiment, 1854-1993
Ronald J Austin RFD ED * Impact Printing Pty Ltd, for the 6th Bn Association, Melbourne, 1993. Blue, gold, Regtl crest, 10.0 x 7.0, x/322. Fp, 193 mono phots, 2 cld ills (cap badges), no maps, Bibliography, Chapter Notes, Index. Apps: 16 in total, incl H&A (Colonial Auxiliary Forces Long Service Medal, etc), list of COs, list of officers and men at various dates (1875-1993, and incld those who joined 64th Aust Inf Bn AIF), a lineage chart (well laid out), etc.
* A high quality book which tells the story of Melbourne's soldiers (and their comrades from other parts of Victoria) between 1854 and the present day. The Royal Melbourne Regt was raised in response to the unrest in the Victorian goldfields and against a feared Russian invasion. Nine chapters cover service thence through to 1914. Two chapters describe the Regt's services - as 64th Aust Inf Bn AIF - on Gallipoli (the ANZAC landings) and on the Western Front. Subsequent chapters deal with the inter-war years (Citizen Force), services in WWII (with a long account of 2/6th Aust Inf Bn AIF in North Africa, 1940-1941, the capture of Tobruk, the short campaign in Greece where 350 men were lost as POW,and then the war in New Guinea, 1942-1945), and finally the post-war period as 5/6th Royal Victorian Regt. The illustrations (which ideally should have been indexed) are of excellent quality and include many well captioned individual members and groups of personnel. An excellent source for genealogists. R/1 V/5. AWM. MCND'A.
Note: the WWII period is covered in much greater detail in NOTHING OVER US, a book devoted exclusively to the 2/6th Aust Inf Bn AIF (vide the Index of Authors - David Hay).

THE GIPPSLAND REGIMENT
A History of the 52nd Australian Infantry Battalion
Ron Blair * Drouin Commercial Printers, Drouin, Victoria, for the author, Warragul, n.d. (c.1989). Soft card, dark green, gold, Regtl crest, 9.5 x 7.0, ix/284. 136 mono phots (indexed), 2 maps, Glossary, Bibliography, Index. Apps: Roll of Honour (incl all former members who died after 1942 while serving with other units or other branches of the armed forces, with separate lists for 37/52 Bn in New Guinea and New Britain), H&A (incl those to men decorated later while serving with other arms/units), unit nominal roll (all those who were on the strength of 52 Bn at any time between 1.7.1936 and 11.9.1942), notes on the Bn Association.
* The same author wrote A HISTORY OF THE 37th/52nd AUSTRALIAN INFANTRY BATALION IN WORLD WAR II (vide the Index of Authors). That unit served from 1942 to 1946, having been formed by an amalgamation of those two pre-war Militia units. The book reviewed here is his account of the constituent 52nd Bn from 1936 (when it was reformed) through to 1942, hence it contains much interesting detail regarding Australia's response to the growing threat of conflict and the steps taken to support the Allied cause during the first two years of the war (as they applied to the Militia in the Gippsland area). The Prologue describes how men of the local Rifle Clubs formed the nucleus of the 52nd Bn of WWI vintage (for which no formal record has been traced). This is an unusual unit history, written mainly for the families of those who served, but it is also a mirror of an important period of transition in Australia's military history. R/1 V/5. AWM. MCND'A/RH.

HOLD HARD, COBBERS
The Story of the 57th and 60th, and 57/60th Australian Infantry Battalions, 1912–1990
Robin S Corfield * Brown Prior Anderson Pty Ltd, Burwood, Victoria, for the 57/60 Bn (AIF) Association, in two volumes, 10.0 x 7.0, 1991.
Volume I : 1912–1930. Brown, gold, -/288. Fp, more than 150 mono phots, 3 line drawings, 17 maps, Glossary, Indexes (for both Volumes). Apps: Rolls of Honour (for 57th and 60th Bns, separately, with dates), H&A (two listings, for 57th and 60th Bns separately), list of officers (with biographical details), nominal rolls for all three Bns (57th, 60th, and 57/60th).
Volume II: : 1930–1990. Dark green, gold, -/352. Fp, more than 250 mono phots, 15 line drawings, 8 maps, Glossary, no Index. Apps: Roll of Honour (1941-1945, with locations of burials), H&A (with locations of where gained, New Guinea and Bougainville), complete nominal roll (57/60th Bn, 1941-1945), notes on cemeteries.
* A meticulously researched history which draws heavily upon personal diaries, War Diaries, and personel reminiscences. The narrative is heavily supported with side-note extracts from official documents, and individual officers and men are named throughout. First raised as Volunteer Militia units in Victoria (57th Bn in 1915, 60th Bn in 1913), they were Brigaded together as elements of 5th Aust Div for service in defence of the Suez Canal (1915-1916) and on the Western Front (1916-1918). Volume I gives full coverage of those services and the post-war events which resulted in amalgamation in 1930. Volume II describes mobilisation in WWII and active services in New Guinea and Bougainville after 1943 (when the ban on deploying non-AIF units overseas was lifted). The illustrations are of fine quality and well captioned. Like the preceding entry, this too is a gold-mine for genealogists interested in Victorian families. R/1 V/5. AWM. MCND'A/RH.
Note: 1000 copies of Volume I were printed, 2000 copies of Volume II.

Tasmania

A HISTORY OF 'THE LAUNCESTON REGIMENT', 1860–1958
Thomas C T Cooley * G W Woolston & Sons, Launceston, Tasmania, 1958. Soft card, white, blue, Regtl badges (2), 8.5 x 6.0, -/16. No ills, no maps, no appendixes, no Index.
* The Regt was formed in Northern Tasmania in 1860 and this pamphlet is its only known record. It went through a bewildering series of redesignations during the century under review, serving in WWI as 12th Aust Inf Bn AIF, and in WWII as 12/50th and 12/40th Bns. The WWI period is covered in THE STORY OF THE TWELTH, by L M Newton (vide the Index of Authors). Cooley's work is useful only as a note of the unit's lineage and for the names of COs between 1860 and 1955. R/4 V/3. AWM. MCND'A.

INFANTRY

The Battalions of WWI

THE HISTORY OF THE FIRST BATTALION, AIF, 1914-1919
Lieut Col B V Stacy * James L Lee, for the Bn History Committee, 1931. Green, black, Bn badge and patch, 9.25 x 6.0, -/151. 21 mono phots, one map (folding, bound in at the rear), no Index. Apps: unit nominal roll (with details of H&A, KIA, DOW, and DOD), notes on Battle Honours, 'Diary of 1st Bn'.
* The Bn was formed in Sydney on 17 August 1914 and embarked for the Middle East just two months later. It landed at ANZAC Cove on 25 April 1915. The book has a good account of the fighting at Lone Pine where Capt A J Shout and Pte L Keysor each won the VC. After the evacuation, the Bn joined 1st Aust Div in France where, at Bullecourt, Cpl G J Howell won the Bn's third VC. This is a readable book, with helpful maps and pictures, but unfortunately it lacks either an Index or a Contents page. The Bn's total casualties during the war were 3328 officers and men, of which 1165 were fatal. R/4 V/3. AWM. MCND'A.

NULLI SECUNDUS
A History of the Second Battalion, AIF, 1914-1919
F W Taylor and T A Cusack * New Century Press Ltd, Sydney, 1942. Blue, gold, 8.5 x 5.5, -/357. Fp, 56 mono phots, no maps, no Index. Apps: H&A, notes on Battle Honours, diary of the Bn's movements.
* The Bn's services were identical to those of the other early-raised AIF units - rapid assembly in August 1914, embarkation with the first ANZAC convoy to the Middle East, training in Egypt, the Gallipoli campaign (ANZAC Cove and Lone Pine), and the Western Front (Pozieres, Bullecourt, Ypres, Passchendaele, the Hindenburg Line). The authors describe the bitter fighting, the heavy losses, and the horrors of chemical warfare, with sensitivity and great clarity. Many officers and SNCOs receive a mention in the narrative. A thoroughly workmanlike source of reference which would have been even better if it had been provided with some maps and an Index. R/3 V/3. ANL/NYPL. MCND'A.

IMPERISHABLE ANZACS
A Story of Australia's Famous First Brigade
Pte H W Cavill ('From the Diaries of ...') * William Brooks & Co Ltd, Sydney, 1916. Soft card, grey-blue, green/black, 'Digger' caricature motif, 9.0 x 6.5, -/112. Fp, 60 mono phots, 10 sketches, one map, no appendixes, no Index.
* The author served with 2nd Aust Inf Bn AIF and this book is based upon his day-by-day impressions of his early war service (August 1914 to late 1915). He records much detail regarding his initial training in Australia, the sea journey across the Indian Ocean to Egypt, and the fighting in Gallipoli. The illustrations are of a very good quality and are well captioned. A useful secondary source. R/3 V/3. ANL. MCND'A.

RANDWICK TO HARGICOURT
History of the 3rd Battalion, AIF
Eric Wren * Ronald G McDonald, Sydney, 1935. Navy blue, gold, 9.25 x 6.25, xxxii/401. Fp, more than 100 mono phots, 13 maps (12 printed in the text, one on the end-papers), no Index. Apps: unit nominal roll (with details of fatal casualties), H&A (with many entries accompanied by a photograph of the recipient), notes on Battle Honours.
* A stylishly written and well presented account of one of Australia's most celebrated 1st AIF units. It was raised at Randwick (NSW) in August 1914 and landed in Gallipoli on 25 April 1915. After the bitter fighting at Lone Pine and the subsequent evacuation, the Bn was moved to the Western Front in 1916. There it fought in several great battles of the period - Pozieres, Bullecourt, Ypres, Passchendaele, and the Hindenburg Line. Throughout the narrative there are notes and comments regarding Bn personalities, officers' postings in and out, and acts

of individual heroism. The maps complement the narrative well, and the pictures are clearly annotated. A prime source for the patient researcher.
R/3 V/4. ANL/NYPL. MCND'A.

FORWARD WITH THE FIFTH
The Story of Five Years' War Service, Fifth Infantry Bn, AIF
A W McKeown * Speciality Press Ltd, Melbourne, for the 5th Bn Regtl Association, 1921. Brown, black, 'Charging infantryman' motif, 7.25 x 5.0, -/326. Fp, 24 mono phots, no maps, no appendixes, no Index.
* The author served with the 5th Aust Inf Bn AIF as a private soldier. This is his memoir, and his book's thirty chapters are arranged in three parts - Australia/ Egypt (August 1914 to April 1915), Gallipoli/Egypt (April 1915 to January 1916), and France/Flanders (March 1916 to November 1918). His narrative is fluent and interesting, with good accounts of the many actions in which he was engaged. The absence of any maps, appendixes, or Indexes, preclude this work from being classified as full unit history, but it is the only known record of the Bn and is certainly a very helpful source. R/4 V/3. ANL/NYPL. MCND'A.

AS ROUGH AS RAGS
The History of the 6th Battalion, 1st AIF, 1914-1919
Ronald J Austin RFD ED * R J & S P Austin, McRae, Victoria, 1992. Maroon, gold, 10.0 x 7.0, xvi/394. Fp, more than 100 mono phots, 5 sketches, 12 maps, Bibliography, Chapter Notes, Index. Apps: Roll of Honour (with dates and locations), H&A, list of officers, unit nominal roll (extensive, with names of all those who served ab initio and then with the 25 replacement drafts, listed by Coy), Battle Honours, Operational Orders, Training Syllabus (1917).
* 6th Aust Inf Bn was raised in 1914 from volunteers who formerly were serving with various Militia units in the Melbourne area. Embarking in October, it moved to Egypt and then took part in the Gallipoli campaign (covered here in four chapters). Arriving in France in March 1916, it fought through all the major Australian battles through to the end of the war (covered here in six chapters). The Bn lost more than 1100 all ranks killed, with several thousand more wounded at least once. The VC was awarded to one member - 2nd Lieut Frederick Birks - for his valour in the Ypres Salient in September 1917. The format of the book depends heavily upon previously unpublished letters and diaries, and these are woven skilfully into a very readable narrative. The lack of indexes for the well drawn maps and numerous illustrations, and the obscure main title, are the only defects in this otherwise exemplary unit history. R/1 V/5. AWM. MCND'A.

THE SEVENTH BATTALION, AIF
Résumé of Activities of the Seventh Battalion in the Great War, 1914-1918
Arthur Dean and Eric W Gutteridge * W & K Purbrick Ltd, Melbourne, 1933. Brown, gold, Bn flash in brown/red, 8.75 x 5.5, -/191. 3 mono phots,6 maps, no Index. Apps: unit nominal roll (incl casualties and awards), notes on Battle Honours, H&A (statistical summary), notes on battle casualty statistics.
* This is the well produced history of a Bn raised in August 1914 which went on to become one of the most highly decorated in the 1st AIF (it gained four VCs at Lone Pine). Each chapter is dated to show the period being recorded, and at the end of most of them there is a summary of the casualties suffered. Many individuals are mentioned throughout. R/4 V/4. ANL. MCND'A.

SAVING THE CHANNEL PORTS, 1918
W D Joynt VC * Dominion Press, for Wren Publishing, North Blackburn, Victoria, 1975. Black, gold, xii/233. Fp, 34 mono phots (indexed), 12 maps (indexed), Bibliography and Acknowledgements, no appendixes, no Index.
* The author won his VC as a Lieutenant while serving with 8th Aust Inf Bn near Peronne in August 1918. His readable narrative is arranged in three parts. The first is a general summary of the work done by the Australian Divisions in stemming the great German offensive in March/April of that year. The second covers the

services of his own Bn between January and August. The third is devoted to the final weeks of the war and the Allied advance to the Rhine. The pictures are well annotated, and the maps are excellent. The only published source for the 8th Bn, the book is more than a memoir but less than a unit history. Some appendixes and an Index would have improved it. R/1 V/3. ADFA. MCND'A.

FROM ANZAC TO THE HINDENBURG LINE
The History of the 9th Battalion, AIF
Norman K Harvey * William Brooks & Co Pty Ltd, Brisbane, for the 9th Bn AIF Association, 1941. Brown, black, Bn flash, 8.5 x 5.5, -/300. Fp, 25 mono phots (indexed), 29 maps (indexed, 27 printed in the text, 2 folding, bound in), Glossary, Acknowledgements (extensive), Index. Apps: casualty statistics, H&A statistics, list of COs, note on 'Battles and Battle Honours'.
* A conventional history, covering the Bn's formation in Queensland in August 1914 and its subsequent services through to the end of the war. The Gallipoli fighting is described with verve and in good detail. The Western Front battles are covered in equally good detail. The Bn gained one VC, that awarded to Pte John Leak for his work at Pozieres on 23 July 1916. The maps are a great aid in following the narrative, and the pictures are evocative of the period. The Index and detailed Contents page are a 'plus' for the researcher. R/3 V/4. AWM. MCND'A.

CAMPAIGNING WITH THE FIGHTING NINTH
In and Out of the Line with the 9th Bn AIF, 1914-1919
C M Wrench MC * Boolarong Publications, Brisbane, for the 9th Bn Association, 1985. Sky blue, white, 9.0 x 6.0, xxvi/598. Many mono phots, 4 maps, Glossary, Bibliography, Chapter Notes (extensive), Index. Apps: 30 in total, but not including a Roll of Honour or a list of H&A.
* A history based upon personal accounts by those who served, plus extracts from the War Diary and extracts from Harvey's book (vide preceding entry). It begins with the Bn's formation in 1914 and then covers all its later battles. A great deal of useful information is to be found in the Bibliography, the Chapter Notes, and the numerous appendixes. An unusual book, readable and informative.
R/1 V/4. ANL. MCND'A.

HISTORY OF THE 10th BATTALION, AIF, 1914-1918
Egypt, Gallipoli, France, Belgium
Anon (Lieut A Limb) * Cassell & Company Ltd, Melbourne and London, 1919. Stiff card, buff, black, AMF badge in gold and Bn flash in purple/blue, 8.25 x 5.25, -/101. 44 mono phots (indexed), 4 maps (folding, bound in), no Index. Apps: Roll of Honour (with ranks and dates), H&A (with ranks and actions, incl 3 VCs), table of casualty statistics, 'Diary of Events, August 1914 - December 1918'.
* The Bn was formed in 1914 and fought in the Gallipoli and Western Front battles. The accounts of its fighting actions are written in a detached and impersonal style and are not always easy to follow. The poor quality of the maps does little to overcome this problem. However, the dates of all key events are shown in the page margins and these, when consulted in conjunction with the 'Diary of Events' appendix, are most useful in tracing the Bn's movements and deployments. In total, the Bn suffered 3509 casualties, of which 966 were fatal.
R/4 V/3. ANL/NYPL. MCND'A.

THE FIGHTING TENTH
A South Australian Centenary Souvenir of the 10th Bn AIF, 1914-1919
A Collection of Biographical, Historical and Statistical Records ...
C B L Lock * Webb & Son, Adelaide, 1936. Red, black, 8.0 x 5.0, vi/319. No ills, no maps, no Index. Apps: Roll of Honour, H&A, list of officers.
* This book contains a great deal of biographical information concerning officers and men who served. It is combined with numerous extracts from the Bn War Diary and from congratulatory messages received by the Bn from time to time. The style is unusual but certainly informative. The period covered is from 17.8.1914

(formation at Morphetville, South Australia) to 17.3.1919 (disbandment at Chatelet, Belgium). R/3 V/4. NYPL. PS/RP.

THE ANATOMY OF A RAID
Australia at Celtic Wood, October 9th, 1917
Tony Spagnoly and Ted Smith * Multidream Publications, London, 1991. Dark green, gold, 8.0 x 5.75, xxiv/158. 37 mono phots and 10 drawings (all indexed), 8 maps (cld, indexed), Glossary (very detailed), Bibliography, no Index. Apps: Raid Reports, German assessment of Passchendaele, notes on 'the Artillery debate'.
* The work of two Western Front historians, this is an absorbing study of just one of the hundreds of trench raids of WWI. In the early hours of 9 October, 1917, a party of eighty-five members of 10th Aust Inf Bn AIF left their position and moved towards the German front line. Their orders were to divert attention from an impending major attack at Passchendaele. An hour later, just sixteen survivors returned. Five bodies were found later, but the other forty-two soldiers had disappeared without trace. The book describes the incident in detail and attempts, without success, to explain what happened to the missing men. This is trench warfare in microcosm. R/1 V/5. AWM. MCND'A.

10th BATTALION AIF CLUB
1914-1935 Anniversary
Anon * Publisher's details not shown, 1935. Soft card, buff/yellow, Bn flash in purple/blue, 'Field gun' motif, 8.5 x 5.5, -/49. Fp, 6 mono phots, one map (folding, bound in), no Index. Apps: Roll of Honour (with dates and locations), H&A, casualty statistics, 'Chronicle of Events'.
* A souvenir booklet which gives a very brief account of the Bn's formation in South Australia, embarkation for Egypt in October 1914, participation in the Gallipoli campaign, and subsequent services on the Western Front with 1st Aust Div. Three VCs were awarded to members of the Bn - 2nd Lieut A S Blackburn, Cpl P Davey, and Pte R R Inwood. The 'Roll of Honour' and 'Chronicle of Events' appendixes are detailed and useful. R/4 V/4. AWM. MCND'A.

LEGS ELEVEN
Being the Story of the 11th Battalion (AIF) in the Great War of 1914-1918
Capt Walter C Belford * Imperial Printing Co Ltd, Perth, WA, 1940. Green, gold, 8.5 x 5.75, xi/667. Fp, 62 mono phots, 5 maps, no appendixes, no Index.
* This is one of the longest and best written 1st AIF unit histories. The narrative covers all aspects of the Bn's services in Gallipoli and on the Western Front. Officers and men are named liberally throughout the text. The lack of appendixes and Index make the book unhandy as a reference source. R/3 V/4. ANL. MCND'A.
Note: a modern reprint was produced in 1992 by John Burridge. He added an Index of Persons, so his version is much more useful than the original (1940) edition.

THE STORY OF THE TWELTH
A Record of the 12th Battalion AIF During the Great War of 1914-18
L M Newton * J Walch & Sons Pty Ltd, Hobart, Tasmania, for the 12th Bn Association, 1925. Grey/blue, blue/black, 6.5 x 4.0, xii/508. Fp, 20 mono phots, 6 maps (bound in at the rear), one diagram, no appendixes, no Index.
* A good narrative account, packed with names. The author was Adjutant of this Tasmanian-based unit and he covers its services from August 1914 through to the bitter end. It fought at Bullecourt in 1917, losing in one month 600 men and gaining two VCs (Capt J E Newland and Sgt J W Whittle). Many of the recipients of awards are named in the text. The final chapter is effectively an appendix of awards and casualties. R/4 V/4. ANL/NYPL. MCND'A/PS.

THE FIGHTING THIRTEENTH
The History of the 13th Battalion AIF
Capt Thomas A White * Tyrells Ltd, Sydney, 1924. Stiff card, Navy blue, Bn flash, 11.25 x 8.5, -/168. Fp, 9 mono phots (portraits of officers and SNCOs), 27 maps and diagrams, no Index. Apps: list of officers at Bn's formation, statistical summary of casualties.
* A very 'human' unit history. The Bn was raised in September 1914 as part of Monash's 4th Brigade. It took part in the bloody fighting at Suvla Bay and then, after a brief spell back in Egypt, moved to the Western Front. It served in the successful Australian actions at Pozieres and Bullecourt, and later at Messines and Passchendaele. The black days of the 1918 German offensive are well described, as are the final attacks against Hamel and the Hindenburg Line. Two members of the Bn were awarded the VC - Capt H W Murray and Sgt M V Buckley (alias Gerald Sexton). The horrors and monotony of life in the trenches are lightened by amusing dialogue and anecdotes, and lists of awards and casualties appear at frequent intervals throughout the fluent narrative. R/4 V/4. ANL/AWM. MCND'A.

THE HISTORY OF THE FOURTEENTH BATTALION AIF
Being the Story of the Vicissitudes of an Australian Unit during the Great War
Newton Wanliss * The Arrow Printery, Melbourne, for the Bn Association, 1929. Dark blue, gold, 8.5 x 5.5, xiv/416. Fp, 16 mono phots, 16 maps, Bibliography, Index. Apps: Rolls of Honour (one for Egypt/Gallipoli, one for France/Flanders), H&A, notes on Battle Honours, casualty statistics, list of brothers killed while serving with the Bn.
* A very thorough history, produced to the best standards of the 1920s. The Bn's principal battles are concisely described in forty-two chapters, with each page having extensive margin notes. Individual members are mentioned throughout, with lists of award winners listed for each action. One of these was the well-known L/Cpl Albert Jacka VC. A well produced book, full of interest, and easy to consult. R/4 V/5. ANL/NYPL. MCND'A/PS.
Note: printed as a limited edition of 200 copies.

HISTORY OF THE 15th BATTALION, AUSTRALIAN IMPERIAL FORCES, 1914-1918
Lieut T P Chataway (revised and edited by Lieut Col P Geldenstadt) * William Brooks & Co Pty Ltd, Brisbane, 1948. Brown, Navy blue, Bn flash in red/blue/gold, 8.5 x 5.75, xi/327. Fp, 48 mono phots, no maps, Bibliography, no Index. Apps: Roll of Honour (with dates, causes and locations, but no ranks), H&A, unit nominal roll (service numbers and forenames in full, but no ranks).
* The Bn was raised in September 1914 with volunteers from Queensland and Tasmania. It followed the familiar trail of so many other Australian units of that period - Egypt, Gallipoli, Egypt, France and Flanders. The 1915 actions at Quinn's Post, Hill 971, and Suvla Bay, are well described, as are the bitter actions of 1916-1918 on the Western Front. An excellent history of a Bn which suffered, in total, 1200 killed and 2500 wounded. It also gained an exceptional number of awards, including one VC. Many individuals are named in the narrative, and the pictures are fully captioned. R/2 V/4. ANL. MCND'A.
Note: for one man's view of the Bn's services, reference may be made to OVER THERE WITH THE AUSTRALIANS, by Capt R H Knyvett (Hodder & Stoughton, London, 1918). The author was the Bn's Intelligence Officer. His is a passionate account which redounds with a patriotic fervour not often found in such memoirs.

THE OLD SIXTEENTH
Being a Record of the 16th Battalion during the Great War, 1914-1918
Capt C Longmore * The Government Printer, for the History Committee, 16th Bn Association, Perth, WA, 1929. Brown, gold, 9.25 x 6.0, x/273. Fp, 48 mono phots (indexed), 5 maps, no Index. Apps: Roll of Honour (officers only), H&A, unit nominal roll (arranged by Coy, with forenames shown in full), notes on Battle Honours, casualty statistics, list of engagements in which the Bn took part, idem officers promoted from the ranks, idem officers taken POW.
* The Bn was raised in September 1914 from volunteers in Western Australia and

South Australia. It landed in Gallipoli on 25 April 1915 as part of the 4th Aust Inf Bde and took part in the desperate fighting around Sari Bair. Following the evacuation, it moved to the Western Front where three of its members gained the VC. The story is told with clarity and wry humour, each chapter having casualty statistics and details of awards for the period under review. The almost total lack of references to personnel other than Commissioned officers, and the lack of an Index, are the only weaknesses in this otherwise model unit history.
R/2 V/4. ANL. MCND'A.

THE STORY OF THE SEVENTEENTH BATTALION AIF IN THE GREAT WAR, 1914-1918
Lieut Col K W Mackenzie MC * Shipping Newspapers, Sydney, 1946. Green, black, 8.75 x 5.75, -/376. 67 mono phots, 8 maps and diagrams, no Index. Apps: Roll of Honour, H&A (with one full citation, Pte William Jackson VC), unit nominal roll, roll of men who served under assumed names, chronology of Bn moves and locations (30.3.1915 to 24.4.1919), notes on pay scales, etc.
* A conscientious and detailed history, each chapter having explanatory headings and each major action being accompanied by a clear explanatory map or diagram. The book covers the raising of the Bn in 1915, its services in Egypt and Gallipoli, at Suez, and then on the Western Front. A great many members are named in the narrative and in the picture captions. An excellent source for genealogists.
R/3 V/4. NYPL/ANL. MCND'A.

THE STORY OF THE TWENTY-FIRST
Being the Official History of the 21st Battalion AIF
Capt A R MacNeil MC * 21st Bn Association, Melbourne, 1971. Soft card, buff/ orange, black, 11.5 x 8.25, ii/25. No ills, 8 maps, no appendixes, no Index.
* A succinct summary of the Bn's formation in March 1915, its departure after just one month's training for the Mediterranean, its services in Gallipoli, and then two years on the Western Front. The maps are good, and some casualties are listed in the text. R/2 V/2. ADFA. MCND'A.
Note: first published in 1920.

TWENTY-FIRST BATTALION AIF
In Memoriam, 1915-1918
Anon * 21st Bn Association, Melbourne, n.d. Soft card, buff, purple, 9.5 x 6.75, -/20. No ills, no maps, no Index. Apps: Roll of Honour (rank, name, cause, and date for each fatal casualty), H&A.
* A booklet dedicated 'to the 47 officers and 827 NCOs and men of the 21st Australian Infantry Battalion who made the supreme sacrifice in the Great War'. The roll of those who died constitutes the bulk of the text but, of additional interest, there is a brief summary of the Bn's raising in Victoria in April 1915, its move to Egypt, its shipwreck while en route to Gallipoli (the ship was struck by a torpedo), and its work on the Western Front (where, at Mont St Quentin, Sgt A D Lowerson won the VC). The 21st claimed to have been the first Australian unit to enter the Western Front trenches (7.4.1916) and the last to leave them (6.10.1918). This item is probably of interest mainly to genealogists.
R/3 V/3. AWM. MCND'A.

WITH THE TWENTY SECOND
A History of the Twenty-Second Battalion, AIF
Capt Eugene Gorman MC * H H Champion, Australian Authors' Agency, Melbourne, 1919. Grey/green, purple, Bn flash in purple/red, 9.75 x 7.25, -/140. Fp, 35 mono phots, no maps, no Index. Apps: Roll of Honour (with names, service numbers, dates and causes of death), H&A (incl one VC, Sgt W Ruthven), notes on 'Transport to Salonika', casualty statistics.
* An unvarnished account of the Bn's services, compiled by the author in the field. It is not a diary but a full flowing narrative, and the circumstances under which it was written give the book an immediacy not often found in unit histories. The Bn was raised in March 1915, fought in Gallipoli (where it lost 616 men), then moved to France in March 1916. It suffered more appalling casualties at Pozieres,

then went on to take part in the battles around Bullecourt, Ypres, Villers-Bretonneux, and on the Hindenburg Line. The author's declared aim was 'to offer an acceptable memento to the thousands who passed through the Battalion and to their descendents'. The Bn had a total casualty list of 3305 all ranks, of which 844 were fatal. R/4 V/4. ANL. MCND'A.

THE 23rd BATTALION, AIF
Souvenir Issue of 'The Voice of the Battalion'
Col G H Knox and Col W Brazenor (and compiled and printed 'on the battlefield' by Cpl H H Ford) * Chandler & Lee, Melbourne, n.d. (c.1919). Soft card, buff, orange/brown, 'Bn Honours and patch' motif, 7.0 x 10.0 (landscape), -/32. 36 mono phots, no maps, no Index. Apps: H&A, music of the Bn march.
* The Bn fought in Gallipoli and on the Western Front. Throughout this time, it succeeded in producing a series of unit newsletters on its own mobile printing press. The booklet recorded here is a unified reprint of those newsletters. The text is understandably very condensed, but it is full of names, incidents, and Bn gossip. It also includes good summaries of the actions at Pozieres, Bullecourt, Villers-Bretonneux, and Hamel. The Bn's final battle was Mont St Quentin, an occasion when 300 soldiers of the US Army were attached to bolster numbers and when Pte Robert Mactier won his posthumous VC. These newsletters are the only known record of the 23rd Bn, 1st AIF. R/5 V/3. AWM/NYPL. MCND'A.

THE RED AND WHITE DIAMOND
Authorised History of the Twenty-Fourth Battalion AIF
Sgt W J Harvey MM * Printed by Alexander McCubbin, Melbourne, for the 24th Bn Association, 1920. Grey paper-covered boards, blue, 8.75 x 5.5, -/340. Fp, 24 mono phots (indexed), 4 maps, no Index. Apps: Roll of Honour (with dates), H&A (incl MID), list of officers, idem SNCOs, unit nominal rolls (arranged by drafts).
* The Bn was raised on 1 May 1915 and, amazingly, it embarked for the Middle East just one week later. By September it was fighting at Lone Pine, Gallipoli. After the evacuation and regrouping in Egypt, it moved to the Western Front where it first entered the trenches in April 1916 (at Pozieres). The narrative is clear and includes many references to individuals and to humorous moments, but the book suffers from the lack of an Index and the absence of a Contents page. R/4 V/4. ANL. MCND'A.
Note: the original print run (1920) was 200 copies. Reprinted in facsimile by John Burridge in 1984.

THE BLUE AND BROWN DIAMOND
A History of the 27th Battalion AIF, 1915-1919
Lieut Col Walter Dollman and Sgt H M Skinner MM * Lonnen & Cope, Adelaide, 1921. Seen rebound in brown/black, gold, 7.5 x 4.5, ix/213. 30 mono phots, 16 sketch plans, no Index. Apps: Roll of Honour, H&A, contributions from the Bn's three successive COs.
* The 'blue and brown' of the book's title were the colours of the Bn's cloth shoulder patch. The unit was raised in South Australia in early 1915 as part of 7th Inf Bde, 2nd Aust Div. This is a straightforward factual narrative of the Bn's services in Gallipoli and France/Flanders, with abundant mention of places, events, and individual members of all ranks. R/4 V/4. MODL. AMM.

THE 28th
A Record of War Service with the Australian Imperial Force, 1915-1919
Volume I : Egypt, Gallipoli, Lemnos Island, Sinai Peninsula
Col H B Collett CMG DSO * Published by the Public Library Museum and Art Gallery of Western Australia, Perth, 1922. Green, gold, Bn flash in white/blue/gold, 8.75 x 5.75, xv/220. Fp, 53 mono phots (indexed), 10 maps (7 printed in the text, 3 folding, bound in), Bibliography, no Index. Apps: Roll of Honour (with ranks, causes, and dates), H&A (of original members only), list of officers (at formation only), unit nominal roll (at embarkation only), list of reinforcement officers,

nominal roll of all ranks who joined as reinforcement drafts (up to March 1916).
* The Bn was raised in April 1915 and fought in Gallipoli and on the Western Front. This is a good old-fashioned production, with helpful Chapter summaries in the List of Contents, an interesting narrative, and first-class maps. A very good source for genealogists. R/4 V/4. ANL. MCND'A.
Note: the author never completed his planned Volume II (which would have dealt with the period from mid-1916 through to the Armistice).

THE 28th BATTALION, AUSTRALIAN IMPERIAL FORCE
A Record of War Service
Henry K Kahan * Printer's details not shown, published privately by the author, South Perth, 1968. Soft card, white, blue, Bn flash in white/blue, 10.0 x 7.5, vi/109. No ills, no maps, Bibliography, no Index.Apps: H&A (incl MID), list of officers, nominal roll for all Other Ranks, notes on Battle Honours, statistics for unit strength and casualties.
* This is not a sequel to Collett's book (vide preceding entry). It covers the same ground as Collett's Volume I, but then takes the story forward to the end of the war. The narrative is written without any great verve, but it contains plenty of factual material and appears to be authoritative. The appendixes are useful, being even more informative than Collett's compilations. The book itself is an 'economy' production. R/3 V/3. ANL. MCND'A.

IRON IN THE FIRE
Edgar Morrow * Angus & Robertson Ltd, Sydney, 1934. Seen rebound in red, gold, 7.25 x 4.75, viii/268. No ills, no maps, no appendixes, no Index.
* The author served as a Corporal with the 28th Aust Inf Bn from 1915 to 1918. Based upon his diaries and letters sent home, the book is a sensitive account of one man's war. A useful adjunct to the works by Collett and by Kahan (vide the two preceding entries). R/3 V/2. AWM. MCND'A.

THE PURPLE AND THE GOLD
A History of the 30th Battalion
Lieut Col H Sloan * Halstead Press Pty Ltd, Sydney, 1938. Blue, gold, 8.5 x 5.5, xx/399. Fp, 34 mono phots (indexed), no maps, no Index. Apps: unit nominal roll (incl details of KIA, DOW, and H&A), notes on Battle Honours.
* An unusual unit history, compiled by the former Adjutant. The first part of the book is a narrative account of the Bn's formation in NSW in August 1915, its arrival in Egypt (where it formed part of the Sinai Defence Force), and then its move to France in July 1916. Warfare on the Western Front is described fluently and without excessive detail. Amongst other notable battles, the Bn fought at Fromelles, Armentieres, Bapaume, Polygon Wood, Passchendaele, Amiens, and on the Hindenburg Line. Individual officers and men are mentioned liberally in the text and in some of the picture captions. The second part of the book consists of sixty-five contributions by former members of the Bn. These personal memoirs are of varying length and quality, but they make this history unusually vivid and absorbing. Apart from the lack of an Index, the main weakness is the lack of any maps. R/3 V/4. ANL/NYPL. MCND'A.

A SHORT HISTORY OF THE 34th BATTALION, AIF
Anon * Illwarra Press, Sydney, for the 34th Bn AIF Association, 1957. Soft card, red, black, Bn badge, 8.25 x 5.5, -/48. No ills, no maps, Glossary, no Index. Apps: Roll of Honour (officers only), list of officers who served (with notes of those who were wounded), notes on Battle Honours.
* Written forty years after the events which it describes, this brief record covers the services of the Bn from formation in 1916 through to the final stages of the war. In semi-diary form, it deals with the Bn's role in the battles of Messines, Ypres, Passchendaele, and the Hindenburg Line. Officers are mentioned throughout, but very few ORs. A useful little publication. R/3 V/2. ANL. MCND'A.

THE THIRTY-SEVENTH

History of the Thirty-Seventh Battalion, AIF

N G McNichol * Modern Printing Co Ltd, Melbourne, 1936. Navy blue, gold, 9.25 x 6.0, xiv/354. Fp, 10 mono phots (indexed), 12 maps (indexed), no main Index. Apps: Roll of Honour (with dates and causes), H&A, list of officers, unit nominal roll (with embarkation dates), Battle Honours, battle casualty statistics.

* A well produced history of a Bn raised in February 1916 as an element of the new 3rd Aust Div. The narrative is neatly balanced between accounts of fighting actions in the front lines and life behind the lines during periods of rest and reorganisation. The period covered is the last two years of the war on the Western Front. The illustrations are well annotated and the story is told with total competence. R/4 V/4. ANL/NYPL. MCND'A.

Note: reference may be made also to JIM'S STORY - WITH THE 37th BATTALION AIF, by Mary Reddrop (Spectrum Publications, Melbourne, 1982). Based upon his letters and diaries, this useful book records the experiences of James H Roberts, a former member of the Bn.

THE THIRTY-EIGHTH BATTALION, AIF

The Story and Official History of the 38th Battalion AIF, 1916-1918

Eric Fairey * Bendigo Advertiser Pty Ltd, Bendigo, Victoria, for the 38th Bn History Committee, 1920. Buff, red, 8.5 x 5.5, v/110. 17 mono phots, no maps, no Index. Apps: Roll of Honour, H&A, list of COs and other officers, nominal roll of all ranks.

* Raised on 1 March 1916, the Bn formed part of 10th Inf Bde, 3rd Aust Div. The book is basically a narrative account of where it went and what it did, without any frills. The narrative is interesting and entertaining, and it includes many references to individual members and their awards (some with the verbatim citations). R/3 V/4. NYPL/MODL. AMM.

THE THIRTY-NINTH

The History of the 39th Battalion, Australian Imperial Force

Anon (usually attributed to Lieut Col A T Paterson DSO MC VD, but in fact based upon research by Lieut P V Allan and other former members) * G W Green & Sons, Melbourne, 1934. Black, gold, 9.25 x 6.0, xxvii/371. Fp (portrait of Lieut Col A T Paterson), 29 mono phots, 6 line drawings, 12 maps (one printed in the text, 11 folding, bound in), Index. Apps: Roll of Honour, H&A (incl Recommendations), unit nominal roll.

* An exceptionally fine history. It covers the adventures of the Bn from its formation at Ballarat in early 1916 through to the Armistice. The narrative is fluent and full of detail, being based upon edited transcripts of interviews which Allan conducted after the war with former brother officers and with many of the other personnel. The result is reliable and authoritative in every way. The 39th fought as an element of 10th Inf Bde, 3rd Aust Div. Its Battle Honours speak for themselves - Messines, Ypres, Broodseinde, Passchendaele, Somme, Amiens, Mont St Quentin, Hindenburg Line, and St Quentin Canal. R/3 V/5. ANL/RCSL. TAB.

THE FORTIETH

A Record of the 40th Battalion AIF

Frank C Green * John Vail, Government Printer, for the 40th Bn Association, 1922. Maroon, white, 8.75 x 5.75, viii/248. Fp, no other ills, 12 maps (bound in at the rear), Index. Apps: unit nominal roll (with notes of KIA, DOW, and DOD), H&A, casualty statistics for all Inf Bns of the AIF.

* The 40th was a Tasmanian unit raised in March 1916 and which embarked for England as part of 10th Inf Bde, 3rd Aust Div. After three months training in the UK, it landed in France in November of that year. During the following twenty-four months on the Western Front, the Bn suffered 2167 casualties (of which 448 were fatal). Two of its members won the VC. A better-than-average unit history. R/3 V/5. AWM/NYPL. PS/RP.

Note: reference may be made also to ABROAD WITH THE FORTIETH, this being the experiences of Lieut Norman Meagher, as recorded by his parents and published by Davies Brothers, Hobart, 1918.

THE FORTY-FIRST
Being a Record of the 41st Bn AIF during the Great War, 1914-1918
Anon ('Members of the 41st Bn Intelligence Staff') * Tyrrell's, Sydney, 1920. Illustrated soft card, brown/black, grey, 11.0 x 8.75, -/157. No mono phots, 11 line drawings (by T Cross), no maps, no Index. Apps: Roll of Honour (ranks not stated), H&A, unit nominal roll (ranks not stated).
* Although lacking many of the attributes of a conventional unit history, this nicely presented book does have an informative style which holds the reader's attention. The Bn served in all the great Australian battles on the Western Front. It had the remarkable record of never losing a single man taken POW. The lack of a Contents page, and of an Index, are an obstacle to research, but there are plenty of references to individual members in the text for those with the patience to seek them. R/4 V/3. ANL/NYPL. MCND'A.

THE SPIRIT AND THE FORTY-SECOND
Narative of the 42nd Battalion, 11th Infantry Brigade, 3rd Division, Australian Imperial Forces, during the Great War, 1914-1918
Vivian Brahms * W R Smith & Paterson Pty Ltd, Brisbane, 1938. Dark blue, Bn badge, 8.75 x 6.0, -/186. 11 mono phots, 2 sketches, no maps, no Index. Apps: Roll of Honour, H&A (all ranks, arranged alphabetically, many with full citations), unit nominal roll, statistics for awards and casualties.
* This was a Queensland unit, first raised in late 1915 as the 36th Bn, but then redesignated as the 42nd Bn in early 1916. After three months' training in England, it landed in France on 26 November 1916 and fought on the Western Front for the remainder of the war. The Bn suffered 1674 casualties, of which 544 were fatal. The narrative gives good detail of places and events, but is almost entirely devoid of references to individual officers or men. Likewise, the picture captions do not identify the men portrayed. The overall effect is impersonal and distant. However, the book is a sound historical source. It includes an interesting account of the men's refusal to take orders for the end-of-war disbandment of their Bn. R/4 V/4. AMM/RP.

THE FORTY THIRD
The Story and Official History of the 43rd Battalion, AIF
Capt E J Colliver MC and Lieut B H Richardson * Rigby Ltd, Adelaide, 1920. Dark green, gold, 8.5 x 5.75, xiv/248. Fp, 22 mono phots, 17 maps, no Index. Apps: Roll of Honour (with details of date, engagement, and place of burial, for each), H&A (with date and location of each award gained), list of officers (with notes of Bn appointments), unit nominal roll (with ranks and joining dates), Diary of Events, various graphs recording casualties, prisoners taken, materiel captured, etc.
* A meticulous record of the Bn's formation in early 1916 and its subsequent services in France and Flanders. The Bn's time in the trenches is covered in great detail - Messines and Ypres (1917), the Somme (1917-1918), and the breaking of the Hindenburg Line (1918). The defence of Amiens and the bloody battles around Villers-Bretonneux and Hamel are particularly well described. Each chapter is accompanied by explanatory maps, and each concludes with a list of casualties and awards for the period under review. A punctilious work, containing an amazing mass of detail (including biogaphical notes on many of the officers and NCOs). R/4 V/4. ANL. MCND'A.

EGGS-A-COOK
The Story of the Forty-Fourth - War as the Digger saw it
Capt Cyril Longmore * The Colortype Press Ltd, Perth, WA, 1985. Green, gold, 8.25 x 5.5, vii/220. 48 mono phots, 4 line drawings, one map, Index. Apps: Roll of Honour, H&A (plus examples of original recommendations), unit nominal rolls (personnel who embarked for England on 6.6.1916, plus those who comprised the nine reinforcement drafts up to July 1917), notes on Battle Honours, unit diary of locations, notes on the death of Baron von Richthoven.
* The book's odd title derives from the nick-name given to this and other units of the 3rd Aust Div which wore the same 'fried egg' cloth arm flash. The 44th Bn was raised in February 1916 and moved to France eight months later. The author claims that one of the Bn's Lewis gunners did the damage which sealed the fate of the Red Baron, and an appendix is devoted to this episode. First published in 1920 as a straight narrative, the book had no appendixes. The 1985 edition, as recorded here, was produced by John Burridge. He arranged for the text to be completely re-typeset and he extended it with 100 pages of new material. His work greatly increases the book's reference value. R/1 V/5. ANL. MCND'A.
Note: the new (1985) edition was produced with a limited print run of 250 copies. The print run of the original (1920) edition is not known.

THE CHRONICLE OF THE 45th BATTALION AIF
Maj J E Lee DSO MC * Mortons Ltd, Sydney, for the 45th Bn Reunion Association, n.d. (c.1930). Blue, light blue, 7.5 x 5.0, -/132. Fp, 4 mono phots, 4 maps, no Index. Apps: H&A (with citations), unit nominal roll, tables of statistics.
* The Bn was formed in March 1916. It consisted of two Coys of the 13th Aust Inf Bn - survivors from Gallipoli - with the addition of fresh drafts from Australia. It moved to France in June and remained on the Western Front for the next two years. One of the appendixes - not specified above - is a list of two hundred engagements which resulted in at least one individual award for bravery. This is an unconventional and interesting way of presenting such information, and it reflects the intensity of the Bn's fighting services during those two years. A precisely compiled and impressive unit history. R/4 V/4. ANL. MCND'A.
Note: another source, by the same author, is A BRIEF HISTORY OF THE 45th BATTALION AIF, 1916-1919. A pamphlet of eleven pages, it was published in 1926 and then republished by the Bn Reunion Association in 1962. A condensed narrative account, it has no ills or maps but does list the Bn COs and Adjutants.

THE STORY OF A BATTALION
Being a Record of the 48th Battalion AIF
W Devine * Melville & Mullen Ltd, Melbourne, 1919. Seen rebound (originally case-bound in red cloth), 7.75 x 5.25, xi/179. 12 photographically reproduced paintings (from the originals by Daryl Lindsay, official AIF artist), 4 maps, no Index. Apps: Roll of Honour (casualties listed by date, and incl ranks and cause), H&A, verbatim quotation of 'General Birdwood's message to the Battalion'.
* An engaging book, written in fluent style. It was compiled in France in 1919 and therefore has the freshness and immediacy lacking in some unit histories. The Bn was formed in March 1916 in Egypt. It comprised a draft from 16th Aust Inf Bn (survivors from Gallipoli) and fresh drafts from Australia. Three months later the newly constituted Bn was in action at Pozieres as part of 12th Inf Bde, 4th Aust Div. It suffered heavy losses at Bullecourt, but went on to serve at Passchendaele and in the defence of Amiens in 1918. Its last action was Bapaume, in September 1918. In total, it suffered 2676 casualties, of which 840 were fatal. Only two individuals are mentioned in the entire narrative - the CO, Lieut Col R L Leane CMG DSO and bar, and one of the Company Commanders, Capt D G Cumming MC and bar. An old-fashioned production (in terms of presentation and assembly), but satisfying to read and helpful as a source of reference.
R/3 V/4. ANL. MCND'A.

50th BATTALION, AIF – A BRIEF HISTORY
Annual Reunion, 1935
R Fisher * OJD Printing, Adelaide, for the 50th Bn AIF Club, 1935. Soft card, cream, purple, Bn flash, 8.5 x 5.5, -/36. No ills, no maps, no Index. Apps: Roll of Honour, H&A (a statistical summary, with just one citation – the VC awarded to Pte Jensen), 'List of Important Battles of 50th Bn AIF, 1916-1918'.
* Little more than a pamphlet, but of some research merit. The Bn was raised in Egypt in March 1916. Its personnel were Gallipoli survivors from the 10th Aust Inf Bn, plus fresh drafts from Australia. Initially, it was involved in the defence of the Suez Canal. Following the removal of Turkish forces from the Sinai, the Bn moved to the Western Front and received its baptism of fire at Pozieres. The narrative is very condensed, but it contains a surprising amount of information on the Bn's work at Messines, Menin Ridge, Passchendaele, Villers Bretonneux, Amiens, and on the Hindenburg Line. The fight at Moreuil, where Danish-born Pte Jorgan Jensen won his VC, is given full coverage. R/4 V/3. AWM. MCND'A.

HURCOMBE'S HUNGRY HALF HUNDRED
A Memorial History of the 50th Battalion AIF, 1916-1919
R R Freeman * Peacock Publications, Norwood, SA, 1991. Green, gold, 12.0 x 9.0, x/350. Fp, more than 100 mono phots (indexed), one cld ill, no maps, Sources, Chapter Notes, Index. Apps: Roll of Honour (with dates), H&A (with recommendations and citations), list of officers (with war services, dates of joining, dates of promotion, etc), unit nominal roll (all ranks, showing casualties as appropriate), Diary of Events, Battle Honours.
* A handsome and complete record which tells the story of the 50th Aust Inf Bn from 1916 (when it was formed in Egypt) through to disbandment. The text is arranged in thirty chapters which deal mainly with the work of the Bn on the Western Front as an element of 4th Aust Div. Apart from its coverage of moves and battles, the book also provides useful informaton regarding the fate of Bn personnel taken POW by the Germans, the Australian soldiers' opinions of the Americans, their views on the general conduct of the war, and other matters of interest. The wealth of photographs is remarkable for its quality and range, and includes many captioned groups of officers and men. A prime source for family historians especially. R/1 V/5. AWM. MCND'A.
Note: the same author susequently (1993) produced a supplementary pamphlet of sixteen pages with a number of addenda and corrigenda to the 1991 text.

THE WHALE OIL GUARDS
J J Kennedy DSO * James Duffy & Co Ltd, Dublin, 1919. Dark green, gold, 7.25 x 5.0, -/143/16 (the latter being commerical advertisements). No ills, no maps, no Index. Apps: H&A only.
* An eccentric book by an eccentric author. Kennedy was Chaplain to the 53rd Aust Inf Bn between 1916 and 1918 (while it was serving in Egypt and in France and Flanders). His account is written in the style of a novel, about a unit which he does not specify but with characters who really existed and awards which really were made to some of them (all identifiable as members of 53rd Bn). The author's surname, and the publication details, suggest that the author was Irish. The strange title of his book is attributed to the fact that the CO ordered his men to polish their steel helmets with whale oil so that they would shine. Despite the strange behaviour of their CO and their Chaplain, the men of the 53rd were much respected for their fine services at Peronne, Le Catelet, Bullecourt, Polygon Wood, and the breaking of the Hindenburg Line. These battles are all covered in this very odd book. R/2 V/1. ANL. MCND'A.

THE GALLANT COMPANY
An Australian Soldier's Story of 1915-1918
H R Williams * Halstead Printing Co, for Angus & Robertson Ltd, Sydney, 1933. Orange, blue, vii/275. No ills, no maps, no appendixes, no Index.
* The author was formerly a Sergeant and then a Lieutenant serving with the 56th Aust Inf Bn AIF. The absence of an Index to his account is partly balanced by the useful summaries which head each of the twenty-one chapters. His well written narrative covers the Bn's active services in Egypt (1915), the move to France (mid-1916), the battles on the Somme under command of 5th Aust Div (late 1916), and the fierce defence of Amiens. Despite its obvious deficiencies (no ills, no maps, no appendixes, no Index), the book is useful as the sole published source of reference for this unit. R/4 V/3. ADFA. MCND'A.

HISTORY OF THE 59th BATTALION, 1st AIF
William E Pentreath * Printed by N K Gill, Belgrave, for the 59th Bn Association, 1968. Soft card, white, brown, 'Bn flag, Digger, map' motif, 8.5 x 5.5, -/32. No ills, no maps, no Index. Apps: Roll of Honour, H&A, list of COs.
* A belated and unsatisfying record of a fine unit and its sacrifices. Formed in 1915 in Egypt, it consisted initially of fresh drafts from Australia and drafts of officers and men who had survived their time in Gallipoli with various other units. Moving to the Western Front, the 59th was quickly plunged into the battle at Fromelles. Almost immediately, it lost 695 dead and wounded. Reinforced, it took part in most of the great actions during the following two years and more. The patchy narrative is written with little flair and is a meagre tribute to the men whom it commemorates. R/2 V/2. AWM. MCND'A.

INFANTRY

The Battalions of WWII

It will be noted that the titles of some of the following books incorporate a reference to the 2nd Australian Imperial Force (AIF) while others do not. The way in which Infantry Battalions were designated during WWII is explained in the 'Military Chronology'. It should be noted also that the Index has been compiled according to the designations shown in each book's main title or sub-title. In some instances, these do not correspond precisely with the designations which had been approved by authority. Any apparent anomalies in the bibliographic entries, or in the Index, will be resolved once the researcher has consulted the 'Military Chronology'.

THE FIRST AT WAR
The Story of the 2/1st Australian Infantry Battalion, 1939–1945
The City of Sydney Regiment
Anon ('Committee of the Association of First Infantry Battalions',with E C Givney as editor) * Macarthur Press Pty Ltd, Parramatta, NSW, for the Association, 1987. Dark green, gold, Regtl crest, 9.75 x 7.0, xi/558. 190 mono phots, 42 maps, Glossary, Bibliography, no Index. Apps: Rolls of Honour (KIA and WIA, listed by battle or campaign, with locations of burial for those who died), H&A, unit nominal roll (mentioning those taken POW but not stating ranks), roll of those personnel who were taken POW but who later escaped and rejoined the Bn.
* As the above technical description might suggest, this is a massively researched and superbly produced unit history. The narrative is arranged in seven parts, each dealing with a period in the Bn's travels and fighting services. The period covered is from mobilisation in October 1939 through to the end of hostilities. The 2/1st fought in the first Libya campaign (capture of Bardia and Tobruk), the operations in Greece and Crete, and the campaigns in New Guinea (Owen Stanley mountains and Kokoda Trail, 1942–1943, and Aitape and Wewak, 1944–1945). The narrative includes references to officers and ORs, the maps are very helpful, and each episode is carefully dated. In such a major work, it is unfortunate that the Contents section does not include an index of maps or illustrations, nor is there a main index for the narrative. As a 'reading' source, however, this is a remarkably comprehensive book. R/3 V/4. AWM. MCND'A/RH.

PURPLE OVER GREEN
The History of the 2/2nd Australian Infantry Battalion, 1939–1945
Stan Wick * Printcraft Press Pty Ltd, Guildford, NSW, for the Bn Association, 1977. Dark green, gold, Bn flash in purple/green, 8.5 x 6.0, x/454. 60 mono phots (all in one section), 20 maps, Index. Apps: Rolls of Honour (listed by campaign), H&A (with full citations), unit nominal roll (listing most of the 2851 personnel who served with the Bn during the war), 'Calendar of Events', Battle Honours, notes on the roles of the RSM and CSMs, notes on the OCTU, biographical notes on each of the successive COs, plus several other appendixes of a light-hearted variety.
* A very helpful book, finely bound and printed on good quality paper, but with crudely drawn maps. The fluent narrative covers the Bn's services in the Western Desert, Greece, Crete, Syria, Palestine, and New Guinea. One of the main eleven chapters deals with the experiences of men taken prisoner (160 of whom were captured in Greece and Crete). The bitter fighting on the Kokoda Trail is exceptionally well described. The author devotes much space to the adventures of each individual Company, and lists the names of all personnel posted in and out (with dates and locations). A fine source of reference for both the genealogist and the military researcher. R/2 V/5. ANL. MCND'A/RH.
Note: this book was reprinted in 1978. It has the same number of pages, but it includes (on page 369) some names of personnel who were mistakenly ommited from the nominal roll appendix in the first edition.

NULLI SECUNDUS LOG

Capt A J Marshall * Consolidated Press Ltd, Sydney, for 2/2 Aust Inf Bn AIF, 1946. Grey-green, dark green, 10.0 x 7.5, -/130. Fp, 41 mono phots, 2 line drawings, no maps, no Index. Apps: Roll of Honour (of KIA, DOW, and DOD, incl POW), Roll of Honour (separate list for WIA, MIA, and POW, this and the previous roll being arranged according to the two main campaigns, Middle East and New Guinea), H&A (likewise, by campaign, but incomplete for the final Aitape/Wewak battles), list of COs (with photographs and biographical details), list of other officers (likewise illustrated).

* An impressive production, based mainly upon personal recollections and stories gathered from various members of the Bn in late 1944. It is a record of their experiences in the Western Desert, Greece, Crete, and New Guinea, and has an immediacy and freshness which holds the reader's attention. The book is a 'good read', and the appendixes are most helpful. The 2/2nd was raised in New South Wales, mainly from local communities. The book itself, having been printed just after the end of the war, is printed on 'economy' paper which requires careful handling. R/4 V/4. AWM/NYPL. MCND'A/RH.

Note: a version has been seen in illustrated soft covers, with a 'Digger' motif, red on white ground.

WAR DANCE

A Story of the 2/3rd Aust Inf Battalion AIF

Ken Clift * Streamlined Press, Brookvale, NSW, for the 2/3rd Bn Association, 1980. Green, gold, 8.5 x 5.5, -/450. 123 mono phots, one cld ill, one sketch, 17 maps (15 printed in the text, 2 on the end-papers), no Index. Apps: Roll of Honour (with cause of death and location), H&A (names only), unit nominal roll (with home towns), notes on the services of the 3rd Royal Australian Regt in Korea, 1950.

* Raised in October 1939, in NSW, the Bn fought the Italians in 1941 at Bardia and Tobruk before being moved to Greece. Following the evacuation from that country, the bulk of the Bn sailed directly back to Egypt. However, the rear guard party - consisting of 100 all ranks - found itself in Crete and was involved in the short but violent defence of the island. After refitting, the Bn took part in the occupation of Vichy-controlled Syria before returning home to prepare for the New Guinea campaign (being diverted en route to bolster the defence force in Ceylon). Written in an informal style, the narrative has good accounts of those early days and then of the fighting in the Owen Stanleys, on the Kokoda Trail, and around Wewak and Aitape. It is not an easy book to consult. There are no page headings, and there are no indexes of any kind (for the pictures, maps, or narrative). Also, the illustrations are poorly reproduced. R/1 V/3. ANL. MCND'A/RH.

Note: the sub-title printed on the dust-wrapper is different to that which appears on the title page. The former has been ignored for the purposes of this bibliography. An additional source for this Bn is FROM INGLEBURN TO AITAPE - THE TRIALS AND TRIBULATIONS OF A FOUR FIGURE MAN, by Bob 'Hooker' Holt (Streamlined Press, Brookvale, NSW, 1981).

WHITE OVER GREEN

The 2/4th Battalion, and reference to the 4th Battalion

Anon ('Unit History Editorial Committee') * Angus & Robertson, Sydney, for 2/4th Aust Inf Bn Association, 1963. Pale grey-green, dark green, Bn flash in green and white, 9.5 x 6.25, xx/364. 78 mono phots, numerous sketches, 25 maps (19 printed in the text, 6 cld, bound in), 3 Indexes (maps, illustrations, narrative). Apps: Roll of Honour (KIA, DOW, DOD, and WIA), H&A (with citations, and incl MID), list of officers (with their appointments), unit nominal roll (with indication of those taken POW), notes on major actions in which the Bn took part.

* A well produced and competent history. It has particularly good maps, and the indexes are comprehensive. The narrative covers the WWI services of the 4th Aust Inf Bn AIF in Gallipoli and on the Western Front before dealing with the 4th's successor - 2/4th Bn - and its campaigns in the Middle East (Palestine 1940, Cyrenaica, Greece and Crete 1941) and in the Pacific theatre (New Guinea 1944-

1945). The actions at Aitape and Wewak are described in detail. It was at Wewak, on 15 May 1945, that Pte Edward Kenna won his VC. R/1 V/5. AWM. MCND'A/RH.

ALL THE KING'S ENEMIES
A History of the 2/5th Australian Infantry Battalion
S Trigellis-Smith * Griffin Press Ltd, South Australia, for the 2/5th Bn Association, 1988. Sand, gold, Bn Association badge, 9.5 x 7.0, -/423. Fp, 146 mono phots (indexed), numerous artistic pen and ink drawings throughout, 16 maps, Index. Apps: Roll of Honour (KIA and WIA), H&A (with citations), unit nominal roll (ranks not shown), notes on Japanese records.
* A model unit history. As with many Australian accounts of that period, the narrative deals with their common thread - moves and campaign services in the Middle East and then in the SW Pacific between 1940 and 1945. Each chapter deals with a specific event or major battle, and each has helpful introductory notes and concluding lists of casualties and awards. The latter are consolidated in the well presented appendixes. The author gives good accounts of the fighting in Greece and Crete, and in Syria where the Bn suffered heavy losses at the hands of the French. An interesting appendix is a translation from Japanese records of the actions at Wau/Salamaua and Aitape/Wewak. R/3 V/5. ANL. MCND'A.
Note: the print run was limited to 1000 copies.

ROUGH INFANTRY
Tales of 2/5th Australian Infantry Battalion in WWII
Cam Bennett * Globe Press Ltd, for Warrnambool Institute Press, Victoria, 1985. Red, gold, 9.5 x 6.0, ix/206. 14 mono phots, 7 maps, no appendixes, no Index.
* This autobiography was written by an officer who served with the Bn throughout the war, and is useful to any reader wishing to obtain a general impression of the Bn's experiences, good and bad. The narrative is well written, and the maps and pictures are excellent. R/1 V/2. ANL. MCND'A.

NOTHING OVER US
The Story of the 2/6th Australian Infantry Battalion
David Hay * Vega Press Pty Ltd, Blackburn, Victoria, for the Australian War Memorial, Canberra, 1984. Light brown, gold, 9.5 x 7.25, xii/604. Fp, 197 mono phots, 4 sketches, 22 maps, Glossary, no Index. Apps: Rolls of Honour (arranged by campaign), H&A, unit nominal roll (at date of embarkation), roll of personnel taken POW and escapees.
* A good workmanlike history, with much detail regarding individual services. The Bn was mobilised in Victoria in 1939, many of the later reinforcement drafts being men from Tasmania. An element of 6th Aust Div, it served in the Western Desert, Greece, Crete, Ceylon, and New Guinea. In total, its personnel were awarded 4 DSOs, 15 MCs, 5 DCMs, one MBE, one BEM, and 59 MID. The author, Sir David Hay, himself served with the Bn and was awarded the DSO and the MBE.
R/1 V/4. AWM. PS/FC/RH.
Note: the copies seen contained a tipped-in 'Errata' slip. Reference may be made also to BOLD, STEADY, FAITHFUL, by Ronald J Austin (vide the Index of Authors).

THE FIERY PHOENIX
The Story of the 2/7 Australian Infantry Battalion, 1939-1946
W P Bolger, J G Littlewood, and F C Folkland * Renwick Pride Pty Ltd, Collingwood, Victoria, for the 2/7 Bn Association, 1983. Brown, gold, 9.5 x 7.25, xxii/442. 11 mono phots (in a rear section), 3 sketches, 11 maps (also at the rear), no Index (but a good detailed Contents page). Apps: Rolls of Honour (KIA, DOW, DOD, and WIA, 216 names in total), H&A (incl detached personnel), list of personnel taken POW, unit nominal roll, Battle Honours.
* An excellent record of a gallant Bn which gained eighteen Battle Honours. It is arranged in three sections. Part I covers the unit's formation in Victoria and its early services in North Africa, Greece, and Crete in 1940-1941. Part II deals with with the return to Australia from Syria and actions in New Guinea (Buna, Wau and

Salamaua). Part III describes the final actions at Aitape and Wewak in 1945. The bn lost more than 200 men in WWII, and nearly 500 were lost as prisoners (mainly in Crete). Apart from the absence of an Index, this book is outstandingly good in every way. R/2 V/4. AWM. MCND'A/RH.

THE SECOND EIGHTH

A History of the 2/8th Australian Infantry Battalion

Arthur Bentley * Published by the 2/8th Bn Association, Melbourne, 1984. Maroon, gold, 8.75 x 6.0, xi/398. Fp, 132 mono phots, one cld ill, one sketch, 8 maps, Index. Apps: unit nominal roll (KIA, DOW, and POW), H&A.

* A very full and well produced book. The Bn was raised in October 1939, fought in the early Western Desert battles (Bardia, Tobruk, Derna, Benghazi), in the Greek and Crete campaigns, then returned home to refit and retrain. In 1944-1945 it took part in the final phase of the New Guinea campaign. Apart from the nominal roll presented as an appendix, similar rolls of personnel appear at various key points within the narrative. The numerous illustrations are well selected and well presented. R/1 V/4. ANL. MCND'A.

NOT A CONQUERING HERO

The Siege of Tobruk and the Battles of Milne Bay, Buna and Shaggy Ridge, with 2/9th Australian Infantry Battalion

Frank Rolleston * Hartfields Printers, Mackay, Queensland, 1984. Grey, white, 10.5 x 8.25, v/207. Fp, 94 mono phots, 11 maps, no appendixes, no Index.

* This book, printed on good quality paper and presented to a high standard, is the personal account of the author's experiences with 2/9th Bn from 1940 to 1945. It is a detailed work, with good accounts of the battles named in the sub-title. He includes his views regarding the political and strategic topics of the period, and these are interesting as a reflection of the thinking of his generation. R/1 V/4. ANL. MCND'A.

PURPLE AND BLUE

The History of the 2/10th Battalion, AIF (The Adelaide Rifles)

Lieut Col Frank Allchin MM * The Griffin Press, Adelaide, presumably for the Bn Association, n.d. (1958). Light blue, purple, Bn flash, 9.5 x 6.0, xxviii/454. Fp, 31 mono phots, 7 maps (6 printed in the text, one bound in at the rear), no Index. Apps: Roll of Honour (KIA, DOW, DOD, and WIA), H&A (listed by campaign, MID excluded), unit nominal roll (2/10th Bn AIF from May 1940 to December 1945, the latter date misprinted as 1955), notes on 10th Infantry Bn (The Adelaide Rifles), idem the Colours, operational orders for the Balikpapan assault.

* The Bn was mobilised in South Australia in October 1939. En route to the Middle East, it was diverted to England where it formed part of the anti-invasion force on the south coast. It later joined 7th Aust Div in Egypt (November 1940) and then 9th Aust Div as part of the Tobruk garrison (April-September 1941). After a spell in Syria, the Bn returned to prepare for action in New Guinea. It took part in the successful Milne Bay operation in August 1942, then the Buna, Gona, and Sananda battles at year's end. A refitting spell back in Australia was followed by the assaults on the Japanese bases around Lae. A third refitting period in Australia prepared the Bn for its final battle, the clearance of Borneo. This is a book written in an easy conversational style, packed with detail and periodic lists of officers and SNCOs, and well balanced between day-to-day events and the larger strategic and political background. R/4 V/4. NYPL. RH.

THE 2/11th (CITY OF PERTH) AUSTRALIAN INFANTRY BATTALION, 1939-1945

H M Binks (and others) * Publication details not shown, 1984. Soft card, brown, black, 11.5 x 8.25, -/220. Fp, 43 mono phots, 8 maps, no Index. Apps: Roll of Honour, notes on the Australian-Cretan War Memorial.

* This is not a formal history but a collection of reminiscences by many of those who served. It covers their early experiences in Cyrenaica (the capture of Tobruk and Derna), the campaign in Greece, the fighting in Crete (Retimo airfield), and

then the New Guinea campaign (Wewak in particular). Detailed references to the experiences of men taken prisoner in Crete are included. The book is a revealing insight into the ordinary soldier's impressions of war at first hand.
R/1 V/3. ANL. MCND'A.

OF STORMS AND RAINBOWS
The Story of the Men of the 2/12th Battalion, AIF
A L Graeme-Evans * Two matching volumes, Burgundy, gold, 11.5 x 8.5, published by the Bn Association.
Volume I : October 1939 to March 1942. Published in 1989, printed by Southern Holdings Pty Ltd, Hobart, v/258. 128 mono phots, 8 line drawings, 4 maps, Glossary, Sources, no Index. Apps: Roll of Honour (all causes, to March 1942), H&A (same period, with citations and portraits), unit nominal roll, battle casualty statistics.
Volume II : March 1942 to January 1946. Published in 1991, printed by Globe Press Pty Ltd, Hobart, ix/473. Fp, 114 mono phots, 6 line drawings, 9 maps, Glossary, Sources, no Index. Apps: Roll of Honour (detailed, all causes, March 1942 to August 1945), H&A (with citations), unit nominal roll, battle casualty statistics (by campaign).
* A superbly researched pair of books. The Bn, which regarded itself as the lineal descendant of 12th Bn AIF, was raised in Tasmania in October 1939 from local Militiamen and from volunteers drawn from all over Northern Queensland. Its early war services verged on the bizarre. Embarking in the Queen Mary as part of 18th Inf Bde, the Bn sailed for England where it arrived in May 1940. After a brief spell as part of the anti-invasion force, it re-embarked and sailed all the way back around the Cape of Good Hope, this time to Egypt. Having redisovered its land-legs, the Bn embarked once more, this time for Tobruk. It went ashore a few days before the town was encircled by Axis forces. Thereafter, until the relief on 25 August 1941, it fought on the perimeter as an element of 'the Tobruk rats'. Its actions during the siege are described in excellent detail. The final chapters of Volume I describe the move up through Palestine and Syria, to the Turkish border, and the return to Australia in March 1942. Volume II opens with coverage of the Bn's first battles in New Guinea - Milne Bay, Goodenough Island, Buna, and Sananandа. After a respite back home, the Bn returned to New Guinea for the thrust through the Finisterre Ranges in 1944. Following a further break at home, it returned to the fray in 1945 when it took part in the Borneo campaign and the assault at Balikpapan. The narrative is based upon extracts from the War Diary, from operational orders, and from personal reminiscences. The author at all times describes the work of the Bn against the larger background of campaign strategy. The atrocities committed by Japanese soldiers on their Australian captives at Milne Bay are recounted in brutal but impassionate detail. It is lamentable that such a magnificent unit history, comprising 747 pages and 231 illustrations, does not have an index of any kind. R/1 V/4. SLT. MCND'A/RH.

BAYONETS ABROAD
A History of the 2/13th Battalion AIF in the Second World War
Lieut G H Fearnside * Waite & Bull, Sydney, 1953. Red, gold, 8.75 x 5.75, xvi/434. 87 mono phots, 8 line drawings, 18 maps (17 printed in the text, one on the end-papers), Glossary, no Index. Apps: Roll of Honour (with dates and locations), H&A (arranged by campaign), diary of key dates, notes on troopships, Bn statistics, notes on the Colours, biographical notes on Brig F A Burrows (the Bn's first CO).
* The Bn was raised in NSW in May 1940. It embarked for the Middle East only four months later, took part in the advance to Benghazi, the subsequent retreat, and then the eight months' seige of Tobruk. The early Western Desert period is described with humour and clarity, many individuals being mentioned by name. The Bn returned to Australia in 1943, trained for jungle warfare, then took part in the landing at Lae, the capture of Finschafen, and the reoccupation of Brunei and Borneo. This is a good unit history, written by several former members and edited by Fearnside. It is well illustrated and easy to follow.
R/3 V/4. ANL/NYPL. MCND'A/RH. See following page for footnote.

Note: a 1993 edition, produced by John Burridge, has 508 pages and contains much useful additional material - a new short Foreword, a Bn nominal roll, a list of personnel taken POW in the Western Desert (1941-1942), details of officers' postings in and out, an explanation of the different cloth colour patches worn by the Bn, and numerous extra photographs. Ken Hall was the researcher responsible for these valuable improvements. The editor responsible for the original (1953) edition - G H Fearnside - had earlier written two other accounts of the Bn and of his time with it. They were SOJOURN IN TOBRUK (Ure Smith Pty Ltd, Sydney, 1944), this being a factual account but with the identity of personnel concealed by fictitious names, and HALF TO REMEMBER - THE REMINISCENCES OF AN AUSTRALIAN SOLDIER IN WORLD WAR II (Haldane Publishing Pty Co Ltd, Sydney, 1975), this being an informal but detailed personal memoir.

THE SECOND FOURTEENTH BATTALION
A History of an Australian Infantry Battalion in the Second World War
William B Russell * Halstead Press Pty Ltd, for Angus & Robertson, Sydney, 1948. Blue, gold, Bn flash, 8.75 x 5.75, xix/336. Fp, 92 mono phots, 14 sketches, 2 line drawings, 12 maps, Glossary, Index. Apps: Roll of Honour, H&A, casualty statistics.
* A well written history which covers the period from formation in Victoria in April 1940 through to the occupation of the Celebes following the Japanese surrender in August 1945. Between those dates, it served in Syria in the campaign of 1941, returned to Australia, retrained, moved north to New Guinea and helped to block the Japanese advance through the Owen Stanley Mountains and down the Kokoda Trail, fought in the actions at Gona and Lae, returned again to Australia for refit and reinforcement, and then took part in the assault at Balikpapan (Borneo). One member of the Bn was awarded the Victoria Cross. On 29 August 1942, at Isurava, Papua, Pte Bruce Kingsbury charged alone into a large party of advancing Japanese, firing a Bren gun from the hip and killing many of them before himself being shot dead. An attractive book, with good appendixes and maps. R/4 V/5. NYPL/AWM. HEC/MCND'A/RH.

MEN OF THE 2/14th BATTALION
J C McAllester * Griffin Press Ltd, Melbourne, for the 2/14th Bn Association, Ashburton, Victoria, 1990. Brown, white, Bn flash, 8.75 x 5.5, xiv/525. Fp, 226 mono phots, 6 line carcicatures, one map, Glossary, no Index. Apps: Roll of Honour, H&A (with dates and locations), list of officers (plus additional notations inserted in the narrative for posting dates of COs, 2 i/c, and Adjutants), unit nominal roll (166 pages in total, with details of highest ranks held, joining and leaving dates, service numbers, and Company and Platoon with which each man served).
* Russell's formal history of the Bn (vide preceding entry) is a dependable source for the military historian. McAllester's later and larger work was intended 'to give the Battalion a human face'. His narrative covers the same moves and battles, but as viewed from the perspective of each Platoon and sub-unit within the Bn - the Carrier Platoon, the Anti-tank Platoon, the MG Platoon, and so forth. The result is an astonishingly minuted record of the experiences of individual officers and men. The profusion of well captioned photographs is a delight. A remarkable book by any standard. R/1 V/4. AWM. MCND'A/RH.

A THOUSAND MEN AT WAR
The Story of the 2/16th Battalion, AIF
Malcolm Uren * The Griffin Press, Adelaide, for William Heinemann, Melbourne, 1959. Tan, gold, 8.75 x 5.5, xii/259. 38 mono phots (indexed, incl many captioned groups of personnel), 8 maps (indexed), no Index. Apps: unit nominal roll, notes on the 1940 Advance Party.
* A professionally researched and compiled history of high quality. Raised in 1940 in Western Australia, the Bn served in the first Libyan campaign with 7th Aust Div, fought the French in Syria (where it suffered 267 casualties), returned home to retrain for jungle warfare, then fought the Japanese on the Kokoda Trail and the Huon Peninsula. When relieved in February 1944, its effective strength was down

to just fifty men. Having rested and been reinforced, it fought its final actions in the Tarakan (Borneo) campaign in 1945. Many of the Bn's officers are named in the narrative, with biographical footnotes for each. A list of sources and acknowledgements would have added authority to the book, also an Index.
R/3 V/4. ANL/NYPL. MCND'A/RH.

17th BATTALION, THE NORTH SYDNEY REGIMENT
Souvenir Photograph Album, Inglebam, November 1940 to February 1941
Pte D Jacobson * A K Murray, Paddington, NSW, 1941. Soft card, green, black, Bn flash, 5.5 x 9.0 (landscape), -/26. Fp, 68 mono phots, no maps, no appendixes, no Index.
* An interesting item of ephemera, published to mark the Bn's ninety days of continuous initial training. Its main value is to be found in the fully captioned photographs of each Company (HQ, A, B, C, D, and MG), and the Band. Evocative of the period are the pictures of the ad hoc Motor Transport Section and the Horse Transport Section. R/5 V/1. AWM. MCND'A.

A HISTORY OF THE 2/17th AUSTRALIAN INFANTRY BATTALION, 1940-1945
Anon (Bn History Committee - Bruce Trebeck, Phil Pike, Maj Gen John R Broadbent, Ray Rudkin, and Dudley McCarthy) * Macarthur Press, Parramatta, NSW, n.d. (1990). Green, gold, Bn flash with Platypus motif, 10.0 x 7.0, xvi/463. Fp, more than 100 mono phots, 3 cld ills (incl the Colours), 19 maps (17 printed in the text, 2 on the end-papers), Glossary, Bibliography, no Index. Apps: H&A, nominal roll (with notes on casualties), 'Personal anecdotes' (72 pages).
* A comprehensive account of formation in February 1940, disbandment in 1945, and resurrection in 1948 (as part of The North Shore Regt, through to 1960). The narrative is arranged in four parts - through to the siege of Tobruk, then the relief and the Alamein battles, the New Guinea campaign through to Finschafen, then finally the Borneo/Brunei campaign. Coverage is uniformly good, with many lists of awards and casualties inserted in the text. Amongst the awards was the posthumous VC to Cpl John Edmondson, the first Australian VC winner of WWII (the night of 13/14 April, 1941, Tobruk). An admirable book, with excellent maps and well captioned illustrations. R/1 V/4. AWM. MCND'A.

'B' COMPANY, SECOND SEVENTEENTH INFANTRY
A Tribute to 'B' Company, 2/17th Infantry Battalion, AIF
H D Wells * Gosford Printing Co, Avoca Beach, NSW, 1984. Stiff card, green, black, AMF insignia, 8.25 x 5.5, -/175. 24 mono phots, 5 maps, no Index. Apps: Company nominal roll (with details of KIA, WIA, DOW, DOD, and POW).
* A factual account by a soldier who served with 'B' Coy throughout the war. He covers the embarkation for Egypt, the advance to Benghazi, the retreat to Tobruk, the second battle of El Alamein, then the return to Australia and the 1943-1944 campaign in New Guinea. The narrative is written in the first person, with many real or imagined passage of dialogue. This gives the book the flavour of a novel, but it is vivid and amusing and mirrors the emotions of the period. The illustrations include several unusual captured German, Italian, and Japanese photographs. R/1 V/3. ANL. MCND'A.

MEN MAY SMOKE
Being the Final Edition of the 2/18th Battalion AIF Magazine
Oswald L Ziegler * W E Smith Ltd, Sydney, 1948. Green, gold, 11.25 x 9.0, -/92. Fp, 46 mono phots, 5 maps, no Index. Apps: Roll of Honour (KIA, DOW, and died while POW), H&A (with photographs of the individuals so listed).
* This excellent and moving book has an immediacy and emotional impact not commonly found in unit histories. The clear chronology of events covers the Bn's arrival in Malaya in February 1941, the retreat down the Peninsula from Mersing following the first action in January 1942, the defence of Singapore Island, and the final action at Bukit Timah. All of this is covered in good detail. At the surrender, 359 officers and men were taken prisoner. Half of the book is devoted

to their ordeals at the hands of their Japanese captors. They were split into parties which were sent to work sites in Malaya, Thailand, and Japan. Although relatively brief, the book is a worthy record of gallantry in action and fortitude in captivity. R/4 V/4. AWM. MCND'A.

AGAINST ALL THE ODDS
The History of the 2/18th Battalion AIF
James Burfitt * Southwood Press, Sydney, for 2/18th Bn Association, 1991. Eucalyptus green, white, 10.0 x 6.5, -/296. Fp, 47 mono phots, 10 maps (indexed), Bibliography, chapter notes, no Index. Apps: Roll of Honour (incl POW and the location of their camps), H&A (incl MID), unit nominal roll.
* Raised in NSW in June 1940, the Bn moved to Malaya in February 1941 as an element of 8th Aust Div. The book gives a lucid account of its actions between 27 January and 15 February 1942, a period in which it lost 225 killed and 400 wounded. The survivors made their way to Singapore where they were obliged to lay down their arms. The second half of the book describes their tribulations as POW in Burma, Borneo, Sumatra, and Japan, a period during which another 200 men died of maltreatment. The maps and illustrations are very good.
R/1 V/4. AWM. MCND'A.

THE GRIM GLORY OF THE 2/19th BATTALION AIF
R W Newton ('and various other unit members') * Facsimile TS, produced by the 2/19th Bn Association, 1976. Green, gold, Bn crest, 10.75 x 8.75, xvi/837. Fp, 306 mono phots, 41 line drawings (mainly in Part II), 44 maps, no Index. Apps: Rolls of Honour, H&A, unit nominal rolls.
* A monumental and very fine history arranged in two sections. Part I covers the Bn's formation in NSW in July 1940, its move to Singapore in February 1941, and its unwilling surrender on 15 February 1942. This section has twenty-three sections and four appendixes. It describes in detail the organisation of the Bn by its sub-units, gives the names of their commanding officers, and paints the general strategic and political background against which they were required to operate. Coverage of the fighting withdrawal down the length of Malaya, and the final battle for Singapore, is excellent. Part II is devoted to the experiences of the Bn's personnel as POW. This material is presented in seventeen chapters, with eight further appendixes (casualties, nominal rolls, awards, including details of the VC won by Lieut Col C G W Anderson for his valour at the Muar River between 18 and 22 January 1942).The forty-five years old Anderson was one of many unconventional officers to be found in Australia's citizen Army. South African born, he had fought in the WWI campaign against von Lettow Vorbeck with the King's African Rifles. Having survived WWII, he became a Member of the House of Representatives for Hume, NSW. The book concludes with a short history of Mission 204, to which the Bn contributed a detachment. This is in every way an authoritative and satisfying record but, with 837 pages, it badly needs one day to be indexed.
R/3 V/4. AWM. HEC/MCND'A.
Note: first published in 1975, with three pages of 'Errata' tipped in.

SINGAPORE AND BEYOND
The Story of the Men of 2/20 Battalion, Told by the Survivors
Don Wall * Griffin Press Ltd, for the 2/20 Bn Association, South Australia, 1985. Green, gold, 9.75 x 7.25, -/377. Fp, 236 mono phots, 10 maps, 9 line drawings, Bibliography (sparse), no Index. Apps: Roll of Honour (KIA, and died while POW, with home towns), H&A, nominal rolls (extensive, and detailed for those taken POW).
* A well researched and sensitively written book which depends heavily upon interviews with (and statements made by) some of the personnel who survived. The opening section describes the Bn's formation in NSW in 1940, its fighting services in Malaya (Mersing, and the retreat southwards) and at Singapore (where the Bn took the brunt of the Japanese assault). The ten helpful maps refer mainly to that period. The final two-thirds of the narrative describe the captivity of the Bn's members in Changi Jail, on the Burma-Siam railway, in Borneo, and in Japan. Some

personnel had been despatched to Mission 204 (vide the Index of Special & Irregular Forces). A chapter is devoted to that subject. R/1 V/4. ANL. MCND'A/RH.

AMBON - ISLAND OF MIST
2/21st Battalion AIF (Gull Force) Prisoners of War, 1941-1945
Courtney T Harrison * Australian Print Group, Maryborough, Victoria, for the author, North Geelong, 1988. Red, gold, 8.75 x 5.5, -/262. 31 mono phots (some very moving, of near-dead survivors), 9 line drawings, 5 maps, no Index. Apps: unit nominal rolls (Ambon, 1942-1943, and Hainan Island, 1942-1945).
* The Bn was raised in Victoria in August 1940 as part of 23 Inf Bde, 8 Aust Div. The bulk of the Division went to Singapore and was lost there, but 23 Bde had been retained for a while at Darwin. It was then split up to provide outpost garrisons at Rabaul (2/22 Bn), in Portuguese Timor (2/40 Bn), and on the island of Ambon, Dutch East Indies (2/21 Bn). Code-named 'Gull Force', the 2/21st Bn landed on Ambon in December 1941. On 30 January 1942, a full Japanese Division invaded the island. The defending troops held out for four days but, with no hope of support, were then obliged to surrender. The 788 survivors from the battle were treated with appalling savagery. Only 302 of them were still alive at the end of the war. The author describes the Bn's origins and the Ambon battle in very readable style, and covers objectively the years of captivity. The appendixes give details of the fate of the men who did not come home, some of whom died of disease and exhaustion, some of whom were murdered by their guards, and some of whom escaped but did not survive. A moving account.
R/1 V/5. AWM. MCND'A/RH.
Note: the same story is told in GULL FORCE, by Dr Joan Beaumont (Allen & Unwin, 1990). Her account is based upon interviews and archival sources, and concludes with a report on the post-war medical aid programme for the people of Ambon organised by the Gull Force survivors.

ETCHED IN GREEN
The History of the 2/22nd Australian Infantry Battalion, 1939-1946
Graeme Macfarlan * Griffin Press, Adelaide, for 22 Aust Inf Bn Association, 1961. Green, gold, Bn flash in blue/red, 8.75 x 5.5, xiv/262. Fp, 38 mono phots, 8 maps (7 printed in the text, one on the end-papers), Glossary, Index. Apps: Roll of Honour.
* The author of this workmanlike history served with the Bn throughout the war, and it appears to be entirely authoritative. The Bn was formed in Victoria in August 1939 by splitting the pre-war 29th/22nd Militia Bn. In February 1943, it moved to Milne Bay as an element of 9th Div. Its actions on the north coast are clearly explained, and the maps are helpful to an understanding of a sometimes confusing campaign. The Bn took part in the final destruction of the Japanese in New Britain, and then the containment and occupation of Rabaul. A concise and well structured history, with plenty of references to individual members (including those posted out to other units). R/3 V/5. AWM/NYPL. MCND'A/RH.

MUD AND BLOOD
'Albury's Own Second Twenty-Third Australian Infantry Battalion, Ninth Australian Division'
Pat Share * Heritage Book Publications, Frankston, Victoria, in collaboration with the 2/23rd Aust Inf Bn Association, 1978. Red, white, 8.75 x 6.0, xvi/464. 134 mono phots (indexed), 4 cld plates, 8 maps, Glossary, Bibliography and Sources, Index. Apps: Roll of Honour, H&A.
* This very complete book covers the story of the Bn from raising in Victoria in 1940 through to the end of the war. It served with 9th Aust Div in North Africa (Tobruk and El Alamein) before returning to Australia to prepare for the jungles of Papua New Guinea (and, subsequently, Borneo). The Index is a valuable guide to finding the many individuals named in the narrative. Amongst them are the recipients of 4 DSOs, 11 MCs, 4 DCMs, one MBE, and 35 MID. R/3 V/5. PS/RH.
Note: Albury is the town where the Bn was first formed and trained. The town

adopted the unit, hence the unofficial title of 'Albury's Own'. The book was reprinted in 1991 by John Burridge. He made some corrections to errors identified in the original work, and made the valuable addition of a full unit nominal roll appendix. The Burridge version, naturally, is thicker. It has 490 pages.

MUD AND BLOOD IN THE FIELD
This Volume Contains a full Collection of Newsletters issued by 2/23 Australian Infantry Battalion from December 1941 to August 1945 and was Written and Composed by Officers and Men of the Battalion while on Active Service
Anon (compiled by Dick Franke) * John Sissons (Pty) Ltd, Hughesdale, Victoria, 1984. Red, white, 8.75 x 6.0, xvi/520. Fp, 6 mono phots, 83 sketches, no maps, no appendixes, Index.
* This volume is an essential complement to MUD AND BLOOD (vide the preceding entry). As the sub-title indicates, it is a reproduction of the internal newsletters produced by members of the Bn HQ staff at intervals throughout the war. Initially using a handpress (later lost in action at Benghazi), and then improvising with a typewriter and duplicating machine, they kept morale high with a flow of world news, messages from home, and Bn gossip. Production was maintained throughout the siege of Tobruk, the campaign in Syria, and the El Alamein period. Conditions in New Guinea made printing impossible, but production was resumed during the Borneo campaign of 1945. The Index is a vital aid in tracing the many personalities, casualties, and recipients of awards who are named. R/1 V/5. AWM. MCND'A.
Note: an earlier collection of editions, with the imprint Ramsay Ware, Victoria, has been noted. This book, of 168 pages, has the title MUD AND BLOOD, 1940-1942, ALBURY'S OWN. It would seem to have essentially the same contents as the 1984 edition as recorded above, but with the run of entries terminating soon after the second battle of Alamein (when the Bn was returning to Australia), and with no accompanying Index.

THAT'S THE WAY IT WAS
The History of the 24th Australian Infantry Battalion (AIF), 1939-1945
George Christensen * The Craftsman Press Ltd, Hawthorn, Victoria, for the 24th Bn (AIF) Association, 1982. Brown, gold, 9.25 x 5.5, xx/364. 73 mono phots (indexed), 3 line drawings, 11 maps, Glossary, Index. Apps: Roll of Honour (KIA and WIA, with locations), H&A, unit nominal roll, notes on Battle Honours (for the 24th Bn AIF in WWI, and for the 24th Bn AIF and the 2/24th Bn in WWII).
* The 24th Bn AIF of WWI vintage continued to exist under the Volunteer Militia system from 1929 to 1939. After a brief amalgamation with 39th Bn, it regained its status as 24th Bn in early 1942 and sailed for Port Moresby in February 1943. In September of that year it achieved a 75.0% 'overseas volunteer' composition and thereby qualified for the AIF suffix. Meanwhile, in 1940, an entirely unrelated and newly formed infantry unit was allocated the designation 2/24th Bn AIF, a fact to be kept in mind by future researchers. The subject of this book, 24th Bn (later 24th Bn AIF), was air-lifted north from Port Moresby and flown into the Wau Valley. It then fought in the Salamaua, Markham Valley, and Ramu Valley operations before returning to Australia for refit in June 1944. Six months later it moved to Bougainville and fought in that campaign until July 1945. It was disbanded in October. This is a full and effective unit history, the lucid narrative supported by good maps and illustrations. R/1 V/5. ANL. MCND'A.

24th AUSTRALIAN INFANTRY BATTALION AIF
Pictorial Battle History
Anon * Craftsman Press Pty, Melbourne, 1946. Soft card, khaki, red, Bn flash in red/silver, 8.25 x 11.25 (landscape), -/64. More than 100 mono phots, numerous line drawings, no maps, no Index. Apps: unit nominal roll (with details of awards and casualties up to 30.6.1945).
* As indicated in its sub-title, this is essentially an illustrated history. As such, although published thirty-six years before the major work by Christensen (vide the preceding entry), it should be regarded only as a secondary source. That said, it

should be noted that the brief narrative does include some unusual and interesting incidents - the rescue of twenty-nine Indian Army POW from a Japanese camp near the Sepik River in June 1944, the battles around Shaggy Ridge, and several amphibious operations aboard US Navy fast patrol boats against Japanese garrisons on offshore islands. The pictures, which relate mainly to the New Guinea period, are well captioned and are emotive of a unique campaign.
R/4 V/3. AWM/NYPL/LOC. MCND'A.

THE SECOND TWENTY-FOURTH AUSTRALIAN INFANTRY BATTALION OF THE NINTH DIVISION - A HISTORY

R P Serle * The Jacaranda Press, Brisbane, for the 2/24th Bn Association, 1963. Olive green, white, 9.75 x 6.75, ix/378. Fp, 23 mono phots (indexed), 10 maps (8 printed in the text, two on the end-papers), Glossary, Index. Apps: combined Roll of Honour (KIA only) with H&A recipients, notes on Battle Honours.
* The Bn was raised in Victoria in June 1940, sailed for the Middle East in November, joined 7th Aust Div in Palestine, transferred to 9th Aust Div in the Western Desert in February 1941, and then took part in the advance into Italian-held Cyrenaica. During the subsequent retreat, it withdrew into the fortified perimeter of Tobruk and remained there through the siege. An interesting chapter describes the experiences of Bn personnel taken POW during that period. After the raising of the siege, the Bn fought in the two Alamein battles before being returned to Australia via Palestine. The next deployment was New Guinea. The Bn fought at Lae and Finschafen, and then in the coast-hopping advance along the island's northern shoreline in 1943-1944. The Bn's final commitment, after a second refit in Australia, was the occupation of Tarakan (Borneo). This is an excellent account, a delight to read, and the narrative is well annotated. A model unit history. R/2 V/5. ANL. MCND'A.
Note: reprinted in 1986 by John Burridge, with some corrections to the text.

BOTH SIDES OF THE HILL
An Annexure to 'The Second Twenty-Fourth Australian Infantry Battalion', A History edited by R P Serle

Everard Baillieu * Printed by Burwood (Craftsman Press) Ltd, for the 2/24th Bn Association, 1985. Soft card, white, black, 'Rising sun and two Bn flashes' motif, 9.25 x 5.75, xi/32. 11 mono phots, 4 maps (printed in the text, two of these being captured German maps), Bibliography, Sources, no appendixes, Index.
* An additional sub-title states - 'The Capture of Company 621, a German Intercept and Intelligence Unit, by the sea near Tel El Aisa, Egypt, 10 July 1942'. As the author explains, Company 621 was a key element in Rommel's Intelligence network. It was captured intact by men of 2/24th Bn. This slim volume is based upon interviews with German and Australian participants. An unusual incident, and here interestingly described. R/1 V/4. ANL. MCND'A.

WAR IN THE SHADOWS
Bougainville, 1944-45

Peter Medcalf * William Collins Pty Ltd, Sydney, for the Australian War Memorial, Canberra, 1986. Green, gold, 8.75 x 5.5, -/115. One mono phot (the author), 2 maps, no appendixes, Glossary, no Index.
* The author, then nineteen years of age, served as an infantryman in the Bougainville campaign, and this autobiography is dedicated to the men of 29th Bde 'who did not return'. In his narrative, he does not specify exactly which Bn he was serving with. There is strong evidence to suggest that it was the 15th Bn, but it has also been reported as having been the 25th Bn. Whatever the answer, it is vividly written and is regarded as one of the very best junior rank's eye-witness records to emerge from WWII. It is the only published record to have been traced in respect of either 15th Bn or 25th Bn.
R/1 V/3. ANL. MCND'A/RH.

NEVER UNPREPARED
A History of the 26th Australian Infantry Battalion (AIF), 1939-1946
A N Turrell * Llenlees Press, Sandringham, Victoria, for the 26th Bn Association, 1992. Dark blue, gold, 8.5 x 6.0, xiv/194. 112 mono phots, 6 line drawings, 7 maps (5 printed in the text, 2 on the end-papers), Glossary, Bibliography, Index. Apps: Rolls of Honour (KIA, DOW, and 'Died on Active Service', with locations of the graves at Port Moresby), H&A (with citations), biographical notes on the Bn's first CO (Lieut Col H W Murray VC CMG DSO and bar DCM), unit nominal roll (all ranks, 1939-1946), summary of events, notes on reunions.
* This Militia Bn was raised in July 1939 in North Queensland. Recruited from local cattlemen and others accustomed to the outback and life in the bush, it was given the task of patrolling the territory which the men knew intimately. It was here that the prospect of a Japanese invasion was most likely. For the next five years, the Bn continued to serve in North Queensland and on the islands of the Torres Straits. In December 1944, it joined the Solomon Islands campaign and fought in the Bougainville battles. Disbandment came in August 1946 after a period as part of the post-war Rabaul garrison force. The narrative is full of references to individual members of all ranks, their postings, actions, and so forth, with many useful quotations from the Bn War Diary. An attractive record of a Bn which receives little mention elsewhere. R/1 V/5. AWM. MCND'A/RH.
Note: the title of the book was the motto of the 26th Bn (AIF) of WWI vintage.

THE BROWN AND BLUE DIAMOND AT WAR
The Story of 2/27th Battalion AIF
John Burns MM * Griffin Press, Adelaide, for 2/27th Bn Ex-Servicemen's Association, 1960. Creme, brown, Bn flash, 9.5 x 6.25, xvi/259. 65 mono phots, 7 maps (6 printed in the text, one on the rear end-paper), no Index. Apps: Roll of Honour (KIA and WIA), H&A, unit nominal roll (with corrigenda at rear of book).
* A well written and well produced work. The Bn was raised in South Australia in May 1940. Its baptism of fire was in the short but bitter campaign against the Vichy French in Syria. Having returned to Australia to refit and retrain, it was next committed to the even more ferocious fighting on the Kokoda Trail, in New Guinea (1942). After a short spell back in Australia, the Bn returned to New Guinea for the Markham Valley and Ramu Valley operations. A third return visit to Australia, for rest and reinforcement, was followed by the final campaign - the assault at Balikpapan (Borneo) in 1945. All of these operations are described in lucid language. The author mentions many individuals of all ranks, and also gives periodic lists of officers and NCOs at certain key dates. An Index would have been helpful in this context. The maps are well drawn, and the group photographs are clearly annotated with the names of the personnel depicted.
R/1 V/4. AWM/NYPL. MCND'A.

THE SECOND 28th
The Story of a Famous Battalion of the Ninth Australian Division
Brig Philip Masel OBE * The Griffin Press, Adelaide, for the 2/28th Bn and 24th Anti-tank Company Association, Perth, 1961. Dark green, gold, 8.5 x 5.5, -/196. Fp, 39 mono phots, 9 maps, Glossary, no Index. Apps: 'An Account of the 24th Anti-tank Company with which 2/28th Infantry Battalion was Closely Associated'.
* The Bn was raised in Western Australia. This is a well written book, with well drafted maps and easily understood accounts of the various actions in which the Bn was involved - Tobruk, the El Alamein battles, New Guinea, and Borneo. The illustrations are disappointing but are evocative of the period. Casualties, awards, and Bn personalities are mentioned throughout and in detail. Although the author did not provide a separate 'Honours & Awards' appendix, the relevant information is listed within the narrative and is arranged according to the campaign for which each was made. R/3 V/4. ANL/NYPL. MCND'A/RH.

A HISTORY OF THE 2/29th BATTALION, 8th AUSTRALIAN DIVISION AIF
Its Formative Years, Malaya and Singapore, and the Years as Prisoners of War of the Japanese

R W Christie (as Editor) * Enterprise Press, Sale, Victoria, for the 2/29 Bn AIF Association, 1983. Black, gold, 8.75 x 5.5, -/224. 24 mono phots, 3 maps, Glossary, no Index. Apps: H&A, unit nominal roll (incl details of casualties), casualty statistics.

* The Bn was raised in Victoria and sent to North Malaya in 1941. With 2/19th Bn, it resisted the advance of the Japanese 5th Division at Muar Road for six days before being forced to retreat southwards. After regrouping, it fought in the defence of Singapore Island, but was then ordered to surrender. A few men broke away and joined the guerilla and 'stay behind' forces in the Malayan jungles, but the rest of the Bn was scattered amongst working parties in Thailand, Borneo, Burma, and Japan. Their ordeals are movingly described, with clear evidence of the orders issued by the Japanese Army's high command regarding the manner in which Allied captives should be denied the most basic care. Each chapter of the book was written by a different former member of the Bn, and each draws upon his own memories and those of his comrades. Christie, as Editor, skillfully pulled their material together in coherent form, and the end result is both readable and informative. R/2 V/4. ANL. MCND'A/RH.

Note: one of the men who evaded capture was Arthur Shephard. For three and a half years, he lived with Chinese Communist guerilla bands in the Malayan jungle, working as their map maker. His story, based upon his diaries and anecdotes, is told by Iain Finlay in SAVAGE JUNGLE - AN EPIC STRUGGLE FOR SURVIVAL, published by Simon & Schuster, 1991.

THE UNOFFICIAL HISTORY OF THE 29/46th AUSTRALIAN INFANTRY BATTALION, AIF
September 1939 - September 1945

Rupert Charlott * Halstead Press Pty Ltd, Sydney and Melbourne, 1952. Sky blue, gold, Bn flash in yellow and black, 8.5 x 5.5, x/148. Fp, 56 mono phots, one cld ill, one map (printed on both end-papers), no Index. Apps: Roll of Honour.

* The unit was formed by an amalgamation of two Militia Bns (the 29th and the 46th), and the narrative is based mainly upon the edited personal recollections of officers and men who served. It fought in New Guinea in 1943-1944 (Milne Bay, Lae, Finschafen, Madang), and then in the occupation of New Britain (1944-1945). The narrative does not flow well, but it is a helpful source for dates, locations, and references to Bn personalities. The citations for various awards are woven into the text. The photographs are good, and they are well captioned with the names of the personnel portrayed in them. R/3 V/3. AWM. MCND'A.

GALLEGHAN'S GREYHOUNDS
The Story of the 2/30th Australian Infantry Battalion, 22 November 1940 to 10 October 1945.

A W Penfold, W C Bayliss, and K E Crispin * Halstead Press, Sydney, for 2/30th Bn AIF Association, 1949. Grey-blue, gold, Bn flash in blue/gold, 8.5 x 5.75, xvii/405. Fp, 25 mono phots (indexed), 7 maps, no Index. Apps: unit nominal roll (with details of KIA, DOW, and WIA), H&A (incl the names of those recommended but not rewarded), statistical summary of casualties, notes on POW working parties in Burma, Thailand, and Japan, table of Bn locations between December 1941 and February 1942.

* An impressive history with extraordinary origins. The Bn War Diary was buried in Johore in 1942. Subsequent events were recorded secretly on paper stolen from the Japanese and were buried at Selarang. After the war, these documents were retrieved and, combined with individual POW diaries, formed the basis for this book. The result is vivid and moving. The Bn was raised in October 1940 and commanded by Lieut Col F G Galleghan (hence the title). It served in the fighting retreat down the length of the Malay Peninsula, and in the defence of Singapore, before being ordered to surrender. The final third of the narrative deals with the experiences of the 800 officers and men taken prisoner (of whom fifteen were

later decorated for their services during the period of captivity). The illustrations are excellent, and the maps compliment the text admirably. Many individuals are mentioned throughout. R/4 V/4. ANL/NYPL. MCND'A.
Note: additional reference may be made to ONE MAN'S WAR, by S Arneil (published in Melbourne in 1982). The author was a member of the 2/30th Bn and his book is a memoir of his experiences in action and as a prisoner of war.

BRITAIN TO BORNEO
A History of the 2/32 Australian Infantry Battalion
S Trigellis-Smith * Impact Printing Pty Ltd, Brunswick, Victoria, for the 2/32 Aust Inf Bn Association, Sydney, 1993. Ochre, white, gold, Bn flash, 10.0 x 7.0, xviii/386. Fp, 95 mono phots (indexed), 10 line drawings (as chapter heads), 10 maps (indexed), Bibliography, Index. Apps: Roll of Honour (KIA and DOW, with dates and locations), H&A (with citations, plus MID), roll of POW (with dates and locations), list of Battle Honours, unit nominal roll (20 pages), officers' postings in and out and promotions.
* A high quality production, well written, and well laid out. The Bn was formed in the United Kingdom in June 1940 from various drafts which had been intended as reinforcements for other Bns of 6th Aust Div. Initially it was deployed on England's south coast as a counter-invasion force but, when the Germans failed to arrive, it embarked for the Middle East where it joined the 24th Inf Bde, 9th Aust Div. After going through the Tobruk siege it moved briefly to Palestine to refit and then fought in the two Alamein battles. Returning with the rest of 9th Div to Australia in 1943, the Bn retrained for jungle warfare and took part in the clearance of Japanese forces from the north coast of New Guinea (Lae, Huon, and Finschafen). Its final campaign was the reoccupation of North Borneo from May 1945 to January 1946. The maps and illustrations are very good, and a chapter devoted to the experiences of men taken prisoner (1941-1945) is of special interest. R/1 V/5. AWM. MCND'A/RH/PS.

THE FOOTSOLDIERS
The Story of the 2/33rd Australian Infantry Battalion, AIF, in the War of 1939-45
William Crooks * Printcraft Press, Brookvale, NSW, for the 2/33rd Aust Inf Bn AIF Association, 1971. Red, gold, 9.5 x 6.0, xxii/528. 212 mono phots, 8 sketches, 56 maps (54 printed in the text, 19 of which are cld, plus two on the end-papers), Glossary, Bibliography, Index. Apps: Rolls of Honour (all battle casualties and POW, plus a separate roll for the B24 disaster), notes on Battle Honours, idem the 33rd Bn AIF (of 1915-1918), diary of events, statistics regarding personnel (useful), notes on the B24 incident, Epilogue (the post-war Bn Association).
* The author was one of the thirty-four men who, having joined with Bn at formation, were still serving with it at the end of the war. This is fine history of its services. Raised in England in June 1940 as 72nd Bn, its original personnel comprised a variety of drafts which had been diverted from the Middle East to bolster the south coast's anti-invasion defences following the fall of France. Redesignated as 2/33rd Bn, it moved in 1941 to the Middle East where, in Syria, it fought the Vichy French as an element of 7th Aust Div. After returning home, to refit and retrain, it moved with 7th Div to New Guinea. On 7 September 1943, at Port Moresby, it began an air-lift to Tsili-Tsili so that it could take part in the offensive around Lae and the Ramu Valley. Several 'plane loads had already departed when a B24 Liberator bomber of the 5th US Army Air Force crashed on take-off. It came down in the Bn's nearby assembly area. Sixty men were killed or fatally injured, eighty-six others were hurt in varying degrees. Despite having lost a quarter of its strength, the Bn was still committed to the operation. Later, in 1945, it served in the Borneo campaign. For administrative purposes, the Bn was always treated as a NSW-based unit, but the men never thought of themselves in that light. They came from every part of Australia.
R/3 V/5. SLV. PS/RH.

THE 36th AUSTRALIAN INFANTRY BATTALION, 1939-1945
The Story of an Australian Infantry Battalion and its Part in the War against Japan
Stan Brigg and Les Brigg * Halstead Press Pty Ltd, Kingsgrove, NSW, for the 36th Bn (St George's English Rifle Regt) Association, Sydney, 1967. Green, gold, 'St George and Dragon' motif, 8.75 x 5.5, xvi/210. 46 mono phots (indexed), 9 maps (7 printed in the text, 2 on the end-papers), no Index. Apps: Roll of Honour (KIA and WIA), list of Battle Honours.
* A well produced account of this New South Wales unit and its services with the 6th Inf Bde in New Guinea and New Britain from May 1942 to June 1945. The first two pages summarise the WWI services of the 36th Bn AIF, but thereafter the book records in excellent detail the fighting on the Kokoda Trail, the Sananada Road, and in Papua. The maps are barely adequate, the illustrations are interesting, and the main story line is easy to follow. Part of the narrative is based upon captured Japanese documents and post-war sources, a feature which gives the work a sense of authority. R/1 V/4. ANL. MCND'A/RH.

A YOUNG MAN'S WAR
A History of the 37th/52nd Australian Infantry Battalion in World War Two
Ron Blair * Impact Printing (Victoria) Pty Ltd, Brunswick, Victoria, for the 37/52 Bn Association, Melbourne, 1992. Orange/brown, white, Bn flash, 10.0 x 7.0, xx/428. Fp, 111 mono phots, 13 maps (11 printed in the text, 2 on the end-papers), Glossary, Bibliography, Index. Apps: Rolls of Honour (KIA, DOW, and 'Died on Active Service', and WIA, both rolls with dates and locations), H&A (with full citations), unit nominal roll, notes on the Bn music, list of contributors.
* This Victoria Militia unit was formed in 1942 with personnel from the 37th East Gippsland Regt and the 52nd Gippsland Regt. The story opens with a summary of pre-war soldiering in Victoria and the services of the State's Militiamen with the 1st AIF. Thereafter, the narrative deals with early WWII training and local defence duties in Australia, the move to Milne Bay in February 1943 (as a local defence garrison), and the commitment to battle at Lae and Huon Gulf from September 1943 to August 1944. After six months back in Australia, the Bn was landed in New Britain to contain the inactive Japanese forces at Rabaul (which, after the end of the war, it occupied until June 1946). The Bn saw comparatively limited combat during the war. Much of the narrative is taken up with comments regarding Militia terms of service, command decisions affecting the deployment of Militia units in general, sporting activities, training exercises, and so forth. A well presented history, clear and easy to follow. R/1 V/5. PC. RH.

THOSE RAGGED BLOODY HEROES
From the Kokoda Trail to Gona Beach, 1942
Peter Brune * Allen & Unwin, Sydney, NSW, 1991. Black, gold, 9.0 x 6.25, xv/309. 62 mono phots, 6 sketches, 13 maps, Glossary, Bibliography, Chapter Notes, no appendixes, Index.
* The story of the desperate attempt to stop the Japanese thrust over the Owen Stanley Range after their initial landing at Gona in July 1942. The enemy objective was Port Moresby, a base from which an invasion of Australia might have been mounted. A scratch defence force, comprising 39th and 53rd Bns, had been sent to Port Moresby at the end of 1941 as a precautionary measure. When the crisis came, these two Bns were grouped with the 1st Papuan Infantry Bn and, with the designation Maroubra Force, were ordered north into the mountains. Outgunned, outnumbered, and poorly supplied, this small force, plus the newly arrived 21st Inf Bde, contested every ridge and every village as it was forced back down the Kokoda Trail to within sight of Port Moresby. The tide began to turn when the Japanese were brought to a halt and when their own bases at Gona and Sananada were directly assaulted. An air-lift took the depleted 39th Bn, and 21st Bde (consisting of 2/14th, 2/16th, and 2/27th Bns), over the Owen Stanley mountains to New Guinea's north coast in late 1942. Defence of the air-head was given to 39th Bn and it suffered heavy losses in the ensuing battle. The three Bns of 21st

Bde was reduced to 57, 56, and 70 all ranks respectively. Later rebuilt, they went on to win fresh laurels, but the 39th was withdrawn and disbanded in July 1943. The author of this book discusses what was felt to be the unfairness of this disbandment and the alleged clumsiness of Generals Blamey and MacArthur in their handling of this critical campaign. A well researched and impressive book. R/1 V/4. ANL. MCND'A.
Note: the other Australian component of Maroubra Force - 53rd Bn - suffered such severe losses on the Kokoda Trail and in the defence of Port Moresby that it was amalgamated (in fact, re-amalgamated) with the 55th Bn. The story of its services during the first phase of the war in New Guinea naturally overlaps and replicates that of the 39th Bn. Reference should be made, therefore, to another book noted hereafter in this bibliography - THAT MOB, by F M Budden. Further recommended reading is BLOODY BUNA - THE CAMPAIGN THAT HALTED THE JAPANESE INVASION OF AUSTRALIA, by Lida Mayo (Australian National Library Press, Canberra, 1975).

TO KOKODA AND BEYOND
The Story of the 39th Battalion, 1941-1943
Victor Austin * Brown Prior Anderson Pty Ltd, Carlton, Victoria, for Melbourne University Press, 1988. Red, black, 8.75 x 5.5, xviii/267. 24 mono phots (indexed), 10 maps (indexed), Glossary, Index. Apps: Roll of Honour (with locations), H&A (by area), unit nominal roll (1941-1943).
* The preceding entry (Peter Brune) describes the early Australian military effort to remove Japanese forces from New Guinea. This book deals specifically with the role of the 39th Bn, a Militia unit based in Victoria. Mobilised in November 1941 and embarked almost immediately in the SS Aquitania, it was transported to Port Moresby as part of a new garrison force. When the Japanese made their landings on New Guinea's northern coast and started to advance southwards through the mountains (June 1942), the 39th Bn was one of the units sent to stop them. The narrative gives a good account of the way in which the Japanese drive was doggedly resisted every yard of the way back from Kokoda village to the south coast. There is equally good coverage of the ferocious battles around Gona and Sananada. When the Bn was disbanded in July 1943 (along with the 3rd and 49th Bns), most of the men were posted to 36th Bn. This is a sound workmanlike history, with much detail of incidents, and with many personal reminiscences worked cleverly into the text. R/1 V/5. HEC/MCND'A.

THE STORY OF THE 42nd AUSTRALIAN INFANTRY BATTALION, 1940-46
S E Benson * Bridge Printery Pty Ltd, Sydney, for Dymock's Book Arcade Ltd, for the 42nd Aust Inf Bn Association, 1952. Purple, gold, Bn badge, 8.75 x 5.5, -/220. 20 mono phots, 5 maps, no Index. Apps: Rolls of Honour (KIA only, arranged separately for each of the three main campaigns), H&A (but not including awards announced after the disbandment).
* The story opens with a brief summary of the inter-war years, but then focuses upon WWII. The Bn landed at Milne Bay in January 1943 and took part in the Salamaua operation around Mount Tambu in August. After refitting in Australia, it fought in Bougainville in December 1944. The book is written in an informal style and is not always easy to follow. It was intended as a record to those who served, and many of them are mentioned in the text. There is some interesting detail of the periods of training, and comments upon military life in general, but more could have been made of the basic material. R/3 V/3. AWM. MCND'A/RH.

THE SECOND 43rd AUSTRALIAN INFANTRY BATTALION, 1940-1946
Gordon Combe MC, Frank Ligertwood ED, and Tom Gilchrist * Griffin Press Ltd, Adelaide, for 2/43rd Battalion AIF Club, 1972. Grey, red, Divsl flash, 9.5 x 6.25, xvii/283. Fp, 87 mono phots, 2 cld ills (one of Pte L Starcevich VC), 11 maps, 2 hand-drawn panoramas printed on the end-papers (Tobruk 1941, and Sattelberg, New Guinea, 1943), no Index. Apps: Rolls of Honour (KIA and WIA, listed by campaign, with dates), H&A (by campaign), full nominal roll (names only), statistics of casualties (by location), notes on Battle Honours, idem the 43rd Bn AIF (WWI),

idem lineages, chronology.
* A well produced book by two former members of the Bn who, sadly, decided not to index their meticulous work. Raised in South Australia in July 1940, the Bn was besieged at Tobruk, fought in the two Alamein battles, returned to Australia in 1943, and then fought in the New Guinea campaign (notably the capture of Lae and the operations on the Huon Peninsula). After another spell at home, the Bn took part in the assault and occupation of Labuan Island in June 1945. All of this is described in vivid detail, with a wealth of detail regarding the Bn's sub-units and numerous references to individual officers and men. A total of 2711 all ranks passed through the Bn, of whom 846 became casualties and of whom eighty-eight were decorated. The maps and illustrations are of a high quality. Apart from the omitted Index, an excellent unit history.
R/3 V/4. AWM. MCND'A/RH.
Note: reprinted by John Burridge in 1992, with numerous addenda and corrigenda.

DESERT SAND AND JUNGLE GREEN
A Pictorial History of the 2/43rd Australian Infantry Battalion (Ninth Division) in the Second World War, 1939-1945
Geoffrey Boss-Walker * Halstead Press Pty Ltd, Sydney, for Oldham Beddone & Meredith Pty Ltd, Hobart, Tasmania, 1948. Illustrated soft card, brown/buff/green, 11.0 x 8.25, vii/164. Fp, very many mono phots, 13 line drawings, 6 maps, no Index. Apps: one only, list of successive COs.
* Despite its 'pictorial' sub-title, this book does contain a succinct narrative which contains much useful reference material. The 1945 fighting in New Guinea and Borneo is well described, but the core of the story is that part which deals with the early Western Desert battles, the siege of Tobruk, and the El Alamein battles. The maps are of excellent quality, and the pictures are well selected and presented. R/3 V/3. ANL. MCND'A.
Note: a casebound version has been reported. The binding is cloth, orange/tan, gold, and the contents seemingly identical.

TOBRUK TO TARAKAN
The Story of the 2/48th Battalion, AIF
John G Glenn * The Griffin Press, Adelaide, for Rigsby Ltd, Adelaide, 1960. Grey-blue, bright blue, 'Rifleman' motif, 8.5 x 5.5, xiv/277. Fp, 18 mono phots, 11 maps, no Index. Apps: Roll of Honour, H&A (incl citations for four VC awards), list of officers and SNCOs at embarkation (17.11.1940).
* The Bn was raised in August 1940 and served in the early Cyrenaica battles as part of 9th Aust Div. After service in the defence of Tobruk, it fought in both of the El Alamein battles (July and October 1942), and these actions are very well described. After returning to Australia in 1943, the Bn served in the New Guinea campaign and the Tarakan assault. The award of four VCs was a unique record for any Australian unit in WWII. The narrative is comprehensive and lucid, the maps complement the text, and the chapter headings are explanatory and clearly dated. R/2 V/4. ANL. MCND'A/RH.
Note: the book was first published in two formats, both in 1960. The version recorded above was intended for former members of the Bn. The other version, with the sub-title 'The Story of a Fighting Unit', was aimed at a general readership and did not include the 'Roll of Honour' and 'Honours and Awards' appendixes. It is correspondingly slimmer (ix/269 pages). The larger (complete) version was reprinted in 1987 by John Burridge at the request of the Bn Association, with some corrections to the original text. It had a print run of 300 copies. Another source for this unit is DERRICK VC, by Murray Farquhar (Rigby Ltd, Adelaide, 1982). Sergeant (later Lieutenant) Tom Derrick won his VC at Sattelberg (New Guinea) on 23 November 1943. This detailed biography was compiled by an officer who had served with him. Derrick was killed in action on Tarakan Island in May 1945.

THAT MOB
The Story of the 55th/53rd Australian Infantry Battalion, AIF
F M Budden * John Sands Pty Ltd, Halstead Press, Sydney, 1973. Dark green, gold, 8.75 x 5.5, -/168. 46 mono phots, 8 maps (tipped in), Bibliography (sparse), no Index. Apps: Rolls of Honour (KIA and WIA, for 53rd Bn, 55th Bn, and 55th/53rd Bn), casualty statistics (by engagement).
* This is the story of three units - 53rd, 55th, and 55th/53rd Aust Inf Bns. In 1939, the 55th/53rd Bn was a composite Militia unit, but it was then split into its two component parts. In December 1941, the 53rd Bn was mobilised and rushed to Port Moresby (southern coast of New Guinea). The 55th Bn arrived five months later and was deployed for the defence of that port. Meanwhile, 53rd Bn had advanced into the Owen Stanley mountains and, grouped with the 39th Bn and the 1st Papuan Infantry Bn, had clashed with the advancing Japanese at the village of Kokoda. The Australians and Papuans were slowly driven back toward the coast in an epic series of battles on the Kokoda Trail. The 53rd was so weakened by its heavy battle losses that the order was given for it to re-amalgamate with the 55th Bn. This reconstituted composite Militia unit then fought with great bravery in the successful defence of Port Moresby and the subsequent operations at Sananada, Buna, and Gona Bay. In 1944-1945, after a period of rest and refit in Australia, it fought in the Bougainville battles. These actions are covered in detail and, unusually for such a short history, with good coverage of the political and general strategic background. There is particular emphasis upon the Bougainville period, and this may have been the author's reaction to the criticisms made by AIF men who had previously fought in the Middle East (Militia units often being described, disdainfully, as 'that mob'). The book is well printed and bound, but the maps and illustrations are disappointing. R/2 V/4. ANL. MCND'A/RH.
Note: reference should be made also to THOSE RAGGED BLOODY HEROES, by Peter Brune, and to TO KOKODA AND BEYOND, by Victor Austin, as noted on preceding pages of this bibliography.

MILITIA BATTALION AT WAR
The History of 58/59th Australian Infantry Battalion in the Second World War
Russell Mathews * Halstead Press, Sydney, for the Bn Association, 1961. Red, black, 8.75 x 5.75, xii/236. Fp, 43 mono phots, 7 maps, no Index. Apps: Rolls of Honour (KIA and WIA, separately for New Guinea and Bougainville), copy of operational order for the Hongorai River crossing).
* The Bn was an amalgam of the 58th and 59th Bns which, having fought in WWI, survived the inter-war years as Militia units in Victoria. Mobilised in August 1942, it went a year later to Port Moresby. The book has clear interesting coverage of the Wau and Salamaua actions (1943) and the operations in the Ramu Valley and the Finisterre Ranges (1944). After refitting and reinforcement in Australia, the Bn took part in the battle for Bougainville. The maps and illustrations are good, and the text includes plenty of references to individual members and their work.
R/3 V/4. ANL. MCND'A/RH.
Note: reprinted in Hong Kong in 1987 with soft card covers. The original 1961 edition has been reported with red/black covers, gold lettering, and with a slightly larger format (8.75 x 5.75).

Garrison Battalions

DIE LIKE THE CARP!
The Story of the Greatest Escape Ever
Harry Gordon * Hedges & Bell, Maryborough, Queensland, 1980. Illustrated paperback, 7.0 x 4.5, -/240. 27 mono phots, 2 diagrams, no appendixes, Index.
* A complete account of the attempted mass escape by 1100 Japanese POW from the camp at Cowra, NSW, on the night of 4/5 August 1944. During the breakout, 231 POW were killed, 107 wounded, and 334 achieved temporary freedom. The camp guard unit was the 22nd Aust Garrison Bn, and four of its men were killed. Two of these - Pte Benjamin Hardy and Pte Ralph Jones - were each awarded the

George Cross for having manned a machine-gun until overwhelmed by the rush of escapees. R/1 V/4. PC. PS.

Royal Australian Regiment

DUTY FIRST
The Royal Australian Regiment in War and Peace
D Horner * Allen & Unwin Australia Pty Ltd, Sydney, 1990. Black, gold, 9.25 x 6.25, xxviii/525. 66 mono phots, 9 maps (indexed), Glossary, Bibliography, Index. Apps: Roll of Honour (the names of 651 officers and men KIA since 1945), H&A, list of COs (by Bn, with dates), idem RSMs, Chapter Notes, list of actions which resulted in the award of a Battle Honour, Unit Citations.
* The Australian force nominated for duty with the British Commonwealth Occupation Force in Japan, in 1945, was the 34th Infantry Bde. It consisted of the 65th, 66th, and 67th Inf Bns. They sailed for Japan in February 1946. On 23 November 1948, these Bns were retitled 1st, 2nd, and 3rd Bns, The Australian Regt. On 10 March 1949, the Regt was granted the distinction of 'Royal'. In December 1948, 1st and 2nd Bns returned to Australia. The 3rd Bn continued to serve in the Hiroshima Prefecture until September 1950 when it moved to Korea as part of the UN response to the Communist invasion of that country. This large scale book - which is in many ways a complete history of Australia's military commitments and national defence policy from those early years onwards - is very good both as a reading source and as a handy quick reference source. The initial strength of three Bns later rose to nine, then reduced to six. The major periods covered are - BCOF Japan (1945-1952), Korea (1950-1956), the Malayan Emergency (1st, 2nd, and 3rd Bns, various dates), the Indonesian Confrontation, and garrisoning duties in Singapore and Malaya through to 1973. The RAR is Australia's only Regular infantry establishment, and this book is a high quality record of its first forty-five years of service. R/1 V/5. ANL. MCND'A.
Note: reference should be made to the South Vietnam section of this bibliography for other RAR sources. Further references will be found in the Japan and Korea sections.

MACHINE-GUN UNITS

World War I

IN GOOD COMPANY
An Account of the 6th Machine Gun Company AIF, in Search of Peace, 1915-1919
Lieut W A Carne * F J Hilton & Co Ltd, Melbourne, for the 6th MG Company Association, 1937. Blue, gold, 8.5 x 5.5, -/434. 11 mono phots (indexed), 12 maps, Acknowledgements, no Index. Apps: Roll of Honour (with dates), H&A (incl MID), list of officers, unit nominal roll (indicating founder members), list of serving brothers, notes on horses and mules, Company itinerary.
* The Coy was formed in Egypt in 1916 from the MG Sections of 21st, 22nd, 23rd, and 24th Aust Inf Bns. It moved to France and was an element of 2nd Aust Div until the end of the war. Equipped with the Vickers gun, it took part in numerous actions in the 'sustained fire' role. There is an interesting discussion in the book regarding the tactical deployment of such weapons in relation to contemporary trench warfare. Many members are named in the text, both as casualties and as award winnners. R/4 V/4. AWM. MCND'A.

World War II

AMATEUR SOLDIER
An Australian Machine Gunner's Memories of World War II
John Bellair * Spectrum Publications Ltd, Melbourne, 1984. Illustrated soft card, buff, red, 'MG Detachment in action' motif, 9.25 x 6.0, viii/165. Fp, 18 mono phots, no maps, Glossary, no appendixes, no Index.
* John Bellair served throughout the war as a machine-gun officer. From 1939 to 1942 he served with 2/1 Aust MG Bn in England, Egypt, Greece, Crete, Palestine, and Syria. From 1942 to 1945 he served with 2/3 Aust MG Bn in Australia and in the New Guinea campaign. Forty years later he wrote two books based upon those experiences. The first, AMATEUR SOLDIER, is basically a collection of reminiscences. It covers the entire period but is of interest mainly as the only published record of 2/1 Bn. His later FROM SNOW TO JUNGLE is a formal history of 2/3 Bn (vide later entry). R/2 V/3. AWM. MCND'A.

MUZZLE BLAST
Six Years of War with the 2/2 Australian Machine Gun Battalion, AIF
E E 'Bill' Oakes * Printed by Meulen Graphics Ltd, Sydney, for 2/2 Machine Gun Battalion War History Committee, 1980. White, green, Bn Assn 'Rising Sun' motif, 8.5 x 10.75 (landscape), -/301. Fp, 380 mono phots, one sketch, 10 maps (with 8 printed in the text and 2 on the end-papers), Index. Apps: Rolls of Honour (for the Middle East and the Pacific, KIA, DOW, and DOD), H&A, unit nominal roll (plus a loose Supplement dated August 1981), list of men granted Commissions in other units.
* This is a nicely presented book, with well captioned illustrations printed on high quality paper. The author served with the Bn, and his narrative carries the ring of authenticity. The chapters are headed 'Year One', 'Year Two', etc, and this is not helpful because it is often difficult to know from the text the year being discussed. The Bn fought in both of the El Alamein battles before returning to Australia to prepare for service in the New Guinea campaign. In 1944, it took part in the operations around Finschafen and, in 1945, in the Brunei/Labuan actions. Most of the Bn's personnel came from towns in New South Wales and Queensland. R/1 V/4. ANL. MCND'A/RH.

FROM SNOW TO JUNGLE
A History of the 2/3rd Australian Machine Gun Battalion
John Bellair * Kim Hup Lee Printing, Singapore, for Allen & Unwin (Australia) Pty Ltd, North Sydney, NSW, 1987. Grey, gold, 9.25 x 6.0, xxviii/298. 74 mono phots, 12 maps, Sources, Index. Apps: Roll of Honour, H&A, nominal roll (all ranks), Chronology, notes on the Vickers machine-gun, idem the organisation of a MG Bn in WWII, list of COs.
* The Bn was formed in 1940 and served in the Middle East before moving to Java (where many of its members were taken prisoner). It was reformed in Australia and subsequently took part in the New Guinea, Hollandia, and Aitape operations. This is a good working history, with better-than-average appendixes.
R/1 V/5. SLV. PS.

HISTORY OF THE 7th AUSTRALIAN MACHINE GUN BATTALION, AIF
Sgt D McGoldrick * The Committee of the 7th Aust MG Bn Assn, 1973. Soft card, pale blue, 'Sketch of a Vickers gun' motif, 8.0 x 5.25, -/40. Fp, 9 mono phots, no maps, no Index. Apps: Roll of Honour, H&A (with citations), biographical notes on Company Commanders and Bn HQ officers.
* The Bn was formed in November 1942 by amalgamating the MG Coys from the 3rd, 36th, 49th, 53rd, and 55th Aust Inf Bns. The book's brief chapters are arranged accordingly. The Bn served in New Guinea, but the coverage of its active services is fairly terse and condensed. It returned to Australia in August 1943 and was disbanded in March 1944. The main interest of this little book is to be found in the many references to individual officers and men. A good source for genealogists, less so for military historians. R/3 V/3. AWM. MCND'A.
Note: a full nominal roll for the Bn was published in Volume 13, No 2 (1992) of QUEENSLAND FAMILY HISTORIAN, Journal of the Queensland Family History Society, Indooroopilly, Queensland. It lists the name and Service number of each man, and specifies the Company in which he served.

SADDLE TO BOOTS
A History of the 19th (Australian) Machine Gun Battalion
Kathryn M Curkpatrick * Printed by B Jolley, Warracknabeal, for the author, 1990. Illustrated soft card, red/black/blue, 'Marching men' motif, 10.75 x 8.0, xvii/151. 47 mono phots (incl some named groups), 3 maps, Glossary, Bibliography, Chapter Notes, Index. Apps: list of officers (with portraits and war services), unit nominal roll (all those who served, 1941-1944).
* One of the few unit histories which deal with home defence duties only. The Bn was formed in 1940 from 1st Armoured Car Regt and 19th Light Horse MG Regt (hence the book's title and the reference to saddles). It was deployed in the Darwin area to repel any attempt by the Japanese to launch an invasion of the Australian mainland. It remained there until 1944 when it was disbanded. Darwin was raided many times by the Japanese Air Force, and an appendix to this book gives interesting details of sixty-four of those raids (dates, casualties, damage caused, and so forth). For the rest, the narrative is crammed with the daily incidents of a unit awaiting combat but never experiencing it. Individuals of all ranks are named throughout. R/1 V/5. AWM. MCND'A.

OTHER CORPS

THE CITIZEN GENERAL STAFF
The Australian Intelligence Corps, 1907–1914
C D Coulthard-Clark * Military History Society of Australia, Canberra, 1976. Blue, gold, 8.5 x 6.75, iv/95. Fp, 13 mono phots, no maps, Glossary, Bibliography, Index. Apps: H&A (statistics only), nominal roll of members who served with 1st AIF, 'Key Intelligence Appointments, 1907–1940'.
* Prior to WWI, Australia did not have a professional General Staff or Intelligence Corps. This book is the story of those Volunteers who dedicated themselves to creating such a structure even though the funding and politicial initiative were lacking. The author declared that this would be the first in a series of volumes concerning the AIC, but no further volumes have yet appeared. Despite the sub-title's cut-off date of 1914, he does include in this book some material relating to the inter-war years and to WWII. Ignoring these apparent ambiguities, the book is a valuable detailed source of information. The chapter notes are particularly helpful. R/2 V/5. ANL. MCND'A.

PADRE
Australian Chaplains in Gallipoli and France
Michael McKernan * Koon Wah Printing Co Ltd, Singapore, for Allen & Unwin Australia Pty Ltd, Sydney, 1986. Dark blue, gold, 9.25 x 6.25, xv/190. 32 mono phots (indexed), illustrated end-papers, no appendixes, Index.
* The Army Chaplains Department was formed in December 1913. More than four hundred Chaplains of diverse denominations served with the 1st AIF. This is an anthology of extracts from letters and diaries written by some of those who served on Gallipoli and the Western Front. Their graphic personal accounts give a unique insight into the work of this special band of men.
R/1 V/3. ANL. HEC/MCND'A.

THE ARMY THAT WENT WITH THE BOYS
A Record of Salvation Army Work with the Australian Imperial Force
Anon (Lieut Col John Bond) * Published by the Salvation Army, East Melbourne. Victoria, 1919. Sky blue, navy blue, 7.5 x 5.0, viii/190. Fp, 104 mono phots, no maps, no Index. Apps: statistics for 1918.
* The book contains many stories of individual Salvation Army Chaplains and nurses who gave close and courageous support to the men of the 1st AIF, both at home and overseas. Known to the troops as 'the Salvos', they suffered losses from natural causes and from enemy action. One chapter is in fact a roll of the names of those who died. R/3 V/3. ANL. MCND'A.

ARMY SERVICE CORPS

EQUAL TO THE TASK - PAR ONERI
The History of the Royal Australian Army Service Corps
Col H Fairclough ED * Halstead Press Pty Ltd, Sydney, for F W Cheshire Pty Ltd, 1962. Blue, gold, RAASC crest, 8.75 x 5.5, xxiii/310. Fp, 18 mono phots, 2 maps (printed on the end-papers), Index. Apps: list of senior officers (1912-1960), Command and Staff appointments at September 1944, notes on RAASC insignia, statistics (1939-1945).
* A detailed and informative account of the Corps as a whole. It does not try to record the history of every single unit within the Corps but, instead, to trace its evolution from inception in 1887 through to 1960. The contents are sensibly arranged in four main parts, each sub-divided into chapters devoted to specific aspects of organisation and active service. The author's description of the military supply difficulties peculiar to the WWII campaigns in New Guinea and the Pacific islands is exceptionally clear and informative. R/1 V/5. ANL. MCND'A.
Note: the experiences of one member of the Corps are to be found in THE DIARY OF A RAT, by F A Reeder (Roebuck Society Publications, 1977). The author served in the Western Desert (1940-1941) with 7th Aust Divsl Supply Column. His book is well illustrated, and written in a style which evokes the spirit of those times.

EQUAL TO THE TASK
Volume I : The Royal Australian Army Service Corps
Neville Lindsay * Historia Productions, Brisbane, 1992. Blue, gold, 9.5 x 7.0, xvi/511. More than 400 mono phots, 13 cld ills (uniforms and insignia), 17 maps (13 printed in the text, 4 folding, bound in), Bibliography, Chapter Notes, Glossary, four Indexes (Persons, Locations, Units, and General). Apps: Rolls of Honour (for the major conflicts - Maori Land Wars, Anglo-Boer War, WWI, WWII, Malaya, South Vietnam), H&A (idem, incl MID), list of units (with dates), notes on Tactical Signs, idem principal appointments.
* A monumental history, excellently produced, and arranged in four parts - general history from the early Colonial years, transport in each State prior to Federation, wartime services, and infrastructure. The story ends in 1973 when the RAASC was reformed as the Royal Australian Corps of Transport. The main theme is the story of how 'the galloping grocers' responded to the combat support role as a general transport and supply service. The narrative is stuffed with information of all kinds but remains digestible and informative throughout. R/1 V/5. AWM. MCND'A.
Note: the volume described above is the first of several yet to be published. Volume II will deal with railways, movements, transportation and the army postal services - tasks previously performed by the Royal Australian Engineers. The author of Volume I acknowledges the work of Fairclough (vide preceding entry) and refers to it in his Preface: 'It is perhaps unfortunate that the same title as Hugh Fairclough's earlier book should have to be used; but as it is the rendition of the motto of both the RAASC and the RACT, it is unavoidable that this long term multi-volume series must have available to it the most appropriate title'.

THE TWENTY-SECOND COMPANY
The Story of the Twenty-Second Headquarters Company, Third Division Train, Australian Army Service Corps, 1st AIF
E J Batten * Facsimile TS, produced privately for the author, 1948. Seen rebound, originally soft card, brown, black/gold, with unit patch in blue/white, 13.0 x 8.0, -/176. Fp, 36 mono phots, 4 cld ills, no maps, Acknowledgements, no Index. Apps: Roll of Honour, H&A, unit nominal roll.
* Based upon his own diary and those of his former comrades, this is a 'driver's-eye view of life, work and play in a horse-drawn transport unit'. The narrative covers the Company's activities as part of the 3rd Divsl Train from July 1915 (formation and training in Australia) to June 1916 (embarkation for the UK), then through to 1919 (active service on the Western Front). While this is a very

intimate account of the mud and stench of that war, it does provide an excellent record of a typical horse-drawn supply unit. Many individuals are mentioned, and there are good descriptions of now-vanished army trades - farriers, wheelers, saddlers, etc. The mounted photographs are direct prints from original negatives, of high quality and well captioned. It seems likely that only a dozen or so copies of this book were produced as presentation pieces.
R/5 V/4. AWM. MCND'A.

THE MICE OF MINGENEW
Unofficial History of 1st Australian Armoured Brigade Company, Army Service Corps 1941-1945
Neville Kidd * Meulen Graphics, Bankstown, NSW, for the Company Association, 1985. Stiff card, white, blue, Bde flash in red/green, 11.75 x 8.25, -/72. Fp, more than 100 mono phots, no maps, no Index. Apps: Coy nominal roll, list of officers and men's nicknames.
* A light-hearted account based upon reminiscences by former members. The Coy served in Australia throughout the war as part of the forces deployed to face a potential Japanese invasion. The pictures are of good quality, but the overall reference value of the book is limited. R/3 V/1. ANL. MCND'A.

CONVOYS UP THE TRACK
A History of 121st Australian General Transport Company (AIF), 1941-1946
Alan Carnegie Smith OAM * Printed by Griffin Press Ltd, Adelaide, 1991. Plasticated illustrated stiff card, full colour, 'Army convoy' motif, 10.0 x 6.75, xix/300. More than 100 mono phots, 14 tables and charts (indexed), 4 maps, Glossary, Bibliography, Chapter Notes, Index. Apps: 23 in total, incl nine nominal rolls.
* Even though the sub-title refers to only one Company-size unit, this scholarly and deeply researched book is an important record of a major military logistical campaign. When the Japanese first drove southwards through the South West Pacific, the authorities in Australia became quickly aware of their unpreparedness in the event of an invasion of their northern coastlines. To haul men and materiel up to the threatened area, a major road haulage programme was required. The nearest railheads were Alice Springs and Mount Isa. Between them and the key areas of Northern Queensland and the Northern Territory lay one thousand miles of rugged country, traversed only by a few rough roads. Along with other such units, 121 Coy was given the task of transporting thousands of tons of supplies and equipment over those roads. Even after the Japanese been driven out of New Guinea, the work went on. An absorbing book, even for the non-specialist.
R/1 V/5. AWM. MCND'A.

1st AUSTRALIAN PACK TRANSPORT COMPANY, AIF
The Unofficial and Incomplete Story, From 'Gee up', August 1942, to 'Whoa', May 1944
Jim Patterson * Publication details not shown, 1974. Illustrated soft card, pink, black, 'Pack horse' motif, 11.5 x 8.25, -/57. 20 mono phots, no maps, no appendixes, no Index.
* As indicated by its sub-title, this is a lightweight booklet of limited reference value. The unit served in New Guinea (1942-1944) with a strength of 113 all ranks, 177 horses, and 16 mules. Very little has been written about the use of pack transport in WWII - by any army - and it is unfortunate that this particular unit was not more seriously recorded. R/3 V/1. AWM. MCND'A.

MEDICAL

THE ORIGINS OF THE ROYAL AUSTRALIAN ARMY MEDICAL CORPS

Jacqueline Gurner * Hawthorn Press, Melbourne, 1970. Grey, maroon, 8.75 x 5.5, -/66. 13 mono phots (indexed), no maps, 3 diagrams, Glossary, Bibliography, no Index. Apps: General Orders (1902) establishing the AAMC, personnel establishments for 1912-1913, notes on the medical organisation of Expeditionary Forces.
* A thesis rather than a formal history, but useful in tracing the evolution of the NSW Medical Staff Corps (1891) into a complete Army medical service twenty years later. There is interesting reference to the NSW Corps' work in South Africa during the Anglo-Boer War, to post-Federation developments, and to some of the people involved. Of limited interest except to the specialist researcher.
R/3 V/3. AWM. MCND'A.

MEDICAL STORES

Rob Nash * Canberra Publishing & Printing Co, Canberra, 1980. Illustrated soft card, green, white, 9.75 x 6.75, ix/296. 51 mono phots, 6 maps/charts, Glossary, Bibliography & Sources, no appendixes, no Index.
* An extensive history of the Australian Medical Stores Services from 1901 to 1974. The thirty-nine chapters cover peacetime and wartime activities, with some of those chapters devoted directly to specific WWI and WWII units (2/1 Aust Base Depot Medical Store AIF, 2/4 Advanced Depot Medical Store, 1st Field Medical & Dental Depot, etc, etc). Many individuals are named throughout the text, but the lack of appendixes and an Index are an obstacle to the researcher. Of interest to the specialist medical historian. R/1 V/3. ANL. MCND'A.

HOSPITAL SHIPS
Manunda, Wanganella, Centaur, Oranje

Dr Rupert Goodman * Boolarong Publications, Brisbane, 1992. Glossy illustrated boards, pale blue, black, 'Aircraft attacking the Manunda' motif, 10.5 x 8.25, ix/170. 61 mono phots, one map, Glossary, Bibliography, Index. Apps: Roll of Honour (the names of ship's officers and personnel of 2/12 Field Ambulance and the AASC Detachment lost in the CENTAUR sinking, 1943), list of AMF personnel who served in the WANGANELLA (1941-1945), voyages of the ORANJE (1941-1946), idem the WANGANELLA (1941-1945).
* A book which covers in considerable detail the role of hospital ships in various conflicts from WWI to the Falklands conflict (1982). The four principal chapters describe the work of the four Australian hospital ships in WWII - the Manunda (bombed at Darwin in 1942), the Wanganella, the Centaur (torpedoed and sunk by a Japanese submarine off Queensland in 1943), and the Oranje. This is the only book devoted exclusively to all four ships and the medical personnel who served in them. The illustrations are good, and the Index most helpful.
R/1 V/5. ANL. MCND'A.
Note: further reference to hospital ships will be found in the New Zealand official history entitled MEDICAL SERVICES IN NEW ZEALAND AND THE PACIFIC, by T Duncan M Stout (vide the Index of Authors).

World War I

THE OFFICIAL HISTORY OF THE AUSTRALIAN ARMY MEDICAL SERVICES IN THE WAR OF 1914-1918

Col A G Butler DSO VD, Col R M Downes, Col F A Maguire, and Capt R W Cilento * Halstead Press Pty Ltd, for the Australian War Memorial, various dates (see below). Three matching volumes, dark blue, gold, 8.5 x 6.25.
Volume I : Gallipoli, Palestine and New Guinea. Published in 1938, xxvi/873.
Volume II : The Western Front. Published in 1940, xvi/1010.
Volume III : Special Problems and Services. Published in 1943, xx/1103.
All three books contain numerous illustrations, diagrams and charts, and each has its own separate Glossary and Index.

* It is not easy to understand the purpose of this truly huge work. The authors recorded every imaginable aspect of military medicine as experienced during a war which had ended twenty years earlier. Any lessons which might have been learned by the doctors and surgeons of WWII had since been overtaken by new techniques and new pharmaceutical products. The narrative records the minutiae of the work of the AAMS in stupefying detail, the text interrupted at frequent intervals by slabs of tabular statistics. The record is without question thorough, but only the most determined medical historian is likely to refer to it. The authors' purely technical approach to their task obscures the bravery and skill of the individuals who served in the AAMS. Amongst other decorations, they gained 140 MCs and 637 MMs. R/4 V/5. RCSL. RP.

THE AUSTRALIAN ARMY MEDICAL CORPS IN EGYPT
An Illustrated and Detailed Account of the Early Organisation and Work of the Australian Medical Units in Egypt in 1914-1915
Lieut Col James Barrett CMG and Lieut P E Deane * H K Lewis & Co Ltd, London, 1918. Maroon, gold, 8.75 x 5.5, xiv/259. Fp, 34 mono phots, 3 maps, Index. Apps: notes on the Geneva Conventions.
* A specialised but readable book containing many statistical tables demonstrating the work done by Australian medical units operating in Egypt during the first year of WWI. Highlighted are the problems specific to the arrival of large numbers of young soldiers in a country for which, by virtue of their origins, they were mentally and physically unprepared. The consequent disease problems - cholera, dysentery, eye and skin infections, venereal infections, etc - are discussed in some detail. There is also informative coverage of the arrangements made for the handling of battle casualties and their transportation back to Australia. The book concludes with various recommendations (dated 1918) for improving the management of military General Hospitals. A prime source for the medical historian.
R/3 V/5. ANL. MCND'A.

GALLIPOLI : THE MEDICAL WAR
The Australian Army Medical Services in the Dardanelles Campaign of 1915
Michael B Tyquin * New South Wales University Press, Kensington, NSW, 1993. Black, gold, 14.0 x 8.5, vii/277. 27 mono phots, 5 maps (indexed), 6 diagrams, 5 maps (indexed), Glossary, Bibliography, Chapter Notes, Index. Apps: 'Medical Chain of Control', chronology of events, biographical notes on medical/military personnel, notes on the medical arrangements for landings and evacuations, list of hospital ships engaged, casualty statistics, descriptions of field dressings and surgical panniers.
* A powerful appraisal, arranged in eight narrative chapters with solid supporting appendixes, of the medical side of the Gallipoli campaign. By dispassionate and easily read analysis, the author portrays the realities of the high casualty rates, the diseases, and the serious maladministration, of that conflict. He dispels some of the myths regarding ANZAC soldiers who were expected to be always bronzed, fit and cheerful, and examines the cultivated image of impeccable AAMC medical/nursing arrangements. A book of high quality, and a valuable source of reference.
R/1 V/5. AWM. MCND'A.

FOUR YEARS WITH THE FIRST
First Australian Field Ambulance
Anon * The Arden Press (W H Smith), London, 1919. Illustrated soft card, buff, red, 'Diggers with stretcher' motif, 9.75 x 7.0, -/35. 3 mono phots, 25 sketches, no maps, no Index. Apps: Roll of Honour, H&A (incl foreign awards).
* A souvenir booklet compiled by members of a unit raised in 1914 and which served on Gallipoli and the Western Front. Coverage of its activities is very sketchy, but the appendixes are useful. R/4 V/1. AWM. MCND'A.

FIVE MONTHS AT ANZAC
A Narrative of the Personal Experiences of the OC 4th Field Ambulance AIF
Joseph L Beeston * Angus & Robertson, Sydney, 1916. Maroon, red, gold, 7.25 x 5.0, -/68. Fp, 12 mono phots, no maps, no appendixes, no Index.
* The author commanded the unit from October 1914 until his evacuation from Gallipoli in September 1915. He tells, in general terms, the story of its travels from Australia to Egypt, and its services at ANZAC Cove and Sari Bair. A light-hearted record, but the only one available for this unit. R/3 V/1. AWM. MCND'A.

ABROAD WITH THE FIFTH
5th Australian Field Ambulance
Lieut Col W L Crowther * Published by the 5th Field Ambulance Committee, no other details shown, n.d. (c.1919). Illustrated soft card, khaki, black/blue, 'Stretcher-bearers' motif, 9.5 x 7.25, -/23. 15 line drawings, no maps, no Index. Apps: Roll of Honour, H&A.
* Little more than a souvenir, for friends and relatives. The narrative consists mainly of anecdotes and poems by those who served (Egypt, Gallipoli, and the Western Front). Its research value is limited to the two appendixes.
R/5 V/1. AWM. MCND'A.

THE 8th AUSTRALIAN FIELD AMBULANCE ON ACTIVE SERVICE
A Brief Account of its History and Services from 4th August 1914 to 5th March 1919
L W Colley-Priest * Printed by D S Ford, Sydney, 1919. Soft card, green, blue, unit flash in brown, 8.5 x 5.5, -/74. 2 sketches, no maps, Glossary, no Index. Apps: Roll of Honour.
* A thoughtful and well written account of services rendered between August 1915 (formation) through to March 1919 (amalgamation with 15th Field Ambulance). The material is presented in diary form and it covers the move to Egypt, then to France, and then (in detail) the battles in which it was involved. The names of its personnel who themselves became casualties are mentioned in the text. A moving story which brings out the awfulness of trench warfare. R/4 V/4. ANL. MCND'A.

THE HISTORY OF THE NINTH AUSTRALIAN FIELD AMBULANCE
March 1916 - March 1919
Staff Sergeant Mooney (sic) * Printed by John Sands, Sydney, 1920. Soft card, green, gold, Red Cross and unit flash, 11.0 x 8.5, -/100. 13 mono phots, 7 maps and diagrams, no Index. Apps: Roll of Honour, H&A, unit nominal roll (with details of joining and leaving dates, actions, awards, injuries and deaths), diary of events, notes on OR's civilian occupations, notes on crime in France, notes on detached personnel.
* Written in a colloquial style, this is a vivid account written while memory was still fresh but based upon a mass of factual information. The unit served for three years on the Western Front. The author describes every aspect of the handling and transportation of battle casualties during each of the great battles in which he and his comrades were involved. A separate chapter deals with the work of the 45th Dental Unit and the Motor Ambulance Companies. R/4 V/4. ANL. MCND'A.

SOUVENIR
Being an Unofficial Résumé of the History of 11th Australian Field Ambulance France 1916-1918
Anon * No publication details shown, 1919. Illustrated soft card, brown, 'Red Cross and ambulances' motif, 10.0 x 7.5, -/32. Fp, 9 mono phots, 2 line drawings, no maps, no appendixes, no Index.
* This slim magazine style publication is interesting only for its references to some members of the unit, and for its comments regarding the treatment of poison gas casualties. R/4 V/1. ANL. MCND'A.

World War II

THE WAR DIARIES OF WEARY DUNLOP
Java and the Burma-Thailand Railway, 1942-1945
Sir E E Dunlop CMG * Thomas Nelson, Melbourne, 1986. Maroon, gold, 10.0 x 6.75, xxiii/401. Fp, 68 mono phots, 70 line drawings (by various artists who were POW), 2 maps, Glossary, Sources, Index. Apps: 'New diet scheme, Chunkai, January 1944', 'Disease Returns, January 1944', 'Patients admitted to author's hospital, 1942-1943', 'Extracts from Chunkai Hospital Bulletin, January-March, 1944'.
* A remarkable book about captivity. The author was a surgeon who, at great personal risk, kept a diary from February 1942 to August 1945. From the technical viewpoint, his record of injuries, diseases and treatments is a prime source for researchers concerned with military and tropical medicine. For the general reader, the immediacy of his observations concerning Australian, British and Indian troops in Japanese hands are gripping. His notes are candid and largely unedited, hence their publication was deferred for forty-five years. He died in 1993. The illustrations are deeply moving. R/1 V/5. ANL. MCND'A.
Note: another intimate personal account, but relating to totally different circumstances, is ARMY DOCTOR - THE REMINISCENCES OF A WESTERN AUSTRALIAN ARMY MEDICAL OFFICER DURING THE WORLD WAR, 1939-1945, by Dr Philip Thomas (J Pilpel & Co Ltd), Perth, WA, 1981). It is the memoir of Lieut Col P Thomas, a doctor who saw a great deal of active service in Palestine, Egypt, Greece, Crete, and New Guinea.

A HOSPITAL AT WAR
The Story of 2/4 Australian General Hospital, 1940-1945
Rupert Goodman * Boolarong Publications, Brisbane, Queensland, 1983. Full colour, 'Div flash and medal ribbon' motif, 9.0 x 5.5, xvi/208. 64 mono phots (indexed), 2 line drawings, 2 maps, Glossary, Index. Apps: Roll of Honour, H&A, Sources and Contributors.
* The narrative opens with a description of the anatomy of an Australian General Hospital, its establishment and procedures. This and the later detailed accounts of surgery and nursing care under battle conditions are of interest to medical historians. The unit arrived in Egypt in February 1941, sailed for Benghazi but was shipwrecked near Bardia, was swept up in the retreat to Tobruk, and so became part of the 'Tobruk Rats' garrison. During the next seven months it dealt with 14,000 casualties. After being evacuated from Tobruk, it moved to Palestine and then to Colombo, Ceylon. Moving next to New Guinea via Australia, this well travelled hospital dealt with 19,000 more casualties between 1942 and 1944. Its final task was to accompany the initial landing force on Labuan Island. This is a fully referenced history of a General Hospital in wartime, and a fine tribute to all those who staffed it (including women of the Royal Australian Army Nursing Service). R/1 V/5. ANL. MCND'A.

PROUDLY WE SERVED
Stories of the 2/5 Australian General Hospital at War with Germany, behind German lines, and at War with Japan in the Pacific
Innes Brodziak * Regency Press Pty Ltd, North Parramatta, NSW, for the 2/5 AGH Association, 1988. Tan, gold, 8.0 x 6.0, -/279. 95 mono phots, no maps, no Index. Apps: Roll of Honour, nominal roll of all those who served (with their awards), roll of members taken POW in Greece (1941).
* 2/5 AGH was formed in 1940 at Greta, NSW. Moving to the Middle East, it was almost destroyed in Greece. Reformed from personnel of the disbanded 2/3 AGH, it served in Eritrea and Palestine before returning home in 1942. It then moved to New Guinea and remained there until its second return to Australia in 1944. In March 1945 it embarked again, this time for Morotai (one of the Molucca Islands). The intensity of its workload is reflected in the honours received by its personnel (two DSOs, one MC, two OBEs, one RRC, two ARRCs, two MMs, eight MID, and one US Bronze Star).Readable, and full of incident. R/2 V/4. PC. PS.

A SPECIAL KIND OF SERVICE
The Story of the 2/9th Australian General Hospital, 1940-1946
Joan Crouch * Alternative Publishing Cooperative, Chippendale, NSW, 1986. Red, gold, 8.75 x 5.5, xii/172. 52 mono phots, 3 maps, Glossary, Index. Apps: H&A, unit nominal roll (original members only).
* An interesting little book which recounts this hospital's services in the Middle East, and the New Guinea and Borneo campaigns. It reflects the role of other such units in the larger framework of the war, but the author makes specific references to the unusual health problems encountered during the fighting on the Kokoda Trail. The pictures are good, with many personnel named in the captions.
R/1 V/4. ANL. MCND'A.

2/5th AUTRALIAN FIELD AMBULANCE, AIF, 1940-1945
A Unit History
Lloyd Tann * Detail Printing, Richmond, Victoria, for the 2/5 Aust Field Ambulance Association, Melbourne, 1987. Illustrated stiff card, white, black, 'Diamond flash and military ambulance' motif, 11.5 x 8.25, ix/125. 48 mono phots (indexed), nine maps and diagrams, Glossary, Bibliography, no Index. Apps: Roll of Honour, H&A, unit embarkation rolls.
* Written by a soldier who served with the unit throughout the war, printed in facsimile typescript. It deals with the unit's services in the Middle East (Tobruk siege and Syria), New Guinea (Milne Bay, Buna, Sananada, and Ramu Valley), and the 1945 Borneo campaign (Balikpapan). This is a remarkably full account which includes tables of casualty/sickness rates and many references to individual officers and men. An easy-to-follow story. R/1 V/4. ANL. MCND'A.

HISTORY OF THE 2/6 AUSTRALIAN FIELD AMBULANCE, AIF
World War II, 1939-1945
Brian Wise ('With Members of the Committee') * 2/6 Aust Field Ambulance Social Club, 1989. Plastic spine and covers, 11.5 x 8.25, x/273. 5 line drawings, no maps, no Index. Apps: 3 nominal rolls (embarkation December 1940, disembarkation on the return to Australia, names of those who sailed in various ships, 1942-1943).
* Completed nearly fifty years after the events which it describes, this is a true labour of love by the surviving members. Consisting partly of facsimile reproductions of the original hand-written War Diary and partly of personal reminiscences, it describes the unit's travels in Australia, Egypt, Syria, New Guinea and Borneo. There is good coverage of the Markham Valley and Ramu Valley operations and the Balikpapan campaign of 1945, viewed from both the military and the medical perspectives. The 'economy' binding is the only disappointing feature.
R/3 V/4. AWM. MCND'A.

SOUVENIR TO COMMEMORATE THE 50th ANNIVERSARY OF THE FORMATION OF 7th FIELD AMBULANCE, 1915-1965
Frank R Symonds and Les J Smith * Privately for the authors, no details shown, 1965. Soft card, buff, black, 10.0 x 8.0, ii/28. No ills, no maps, no appendixes, no Index.
* The only known record of this unit. The contents consist mainly of lists of officers and men who served, with useful detail regarding their dates of joining, awards, dates of death, etc. The booklet also has some rather haphazard tables of casualties processed by all Australian Field Ambulances serving in France and Flanders at various periods of WWI. AWM. MCND'A.

MEDICAL SOLDIERS
2/10th Australian Field Ambulance, 8th Division, 1940-1945
Ray Connolly and Bob Wilson * Printed by Newey & Beath Pty Ltd, Kingsgrove, NSW, for 2/10th Aust Field Ambulance Assn, 1985. Illustrated soft card, red and black, 'Ambulance in jungle, with unit badge' motif, 7.25 x 4.75, -/304. 22 mono phots, 5 maps, Bibliography, no Index. Apps: Roll of Honour (incl portrait photograph of every man KIA, or who died while a POW, with details of locations of graves), unit

nominal roll.
* The Ambulance was formed in July 1940, was sent to Malaya with 8 Aust Div, and was then forced to surrender on Singapore Island. During this brief campaign, it dealt with more than 3000 casualties. A detachment had been sent to Rabaul (New Britain) to establish a field hospital there, but it too was engulfed in the Japanese conquests of early 1942. The second half of the book consists of neatly edited eyewitness accounts by survivors. More than half of the unit's 292 officers and men were either killed in action or died while prisoners of the Japanese.
R/1 V/4. ANL. MCND'A.

Women's Nursing Services

OUR WAR NURSES
The History of the Royal Australian Army Nursing Corps, 1902-1988
Rupert Goodman * Boolarong Publications, Brisbane, 1988. Illustrated boards, grey, red, 'AIF badge and army nurses' motif, 10.75 x 8.25, xv/294. 127 mono phots, 2 maps, Glossary, Index. Apps: Rolls of Honour (died as POW in WWII, DOD, and lost in the CENTAUR), H&A (statistical summaries only), nominal rolls by unit for the AANC in France in 1916, RRC Royal Warrant (1883), 'Provisions of the Florence Nightingale Medal'.
* The definitive history of the RAANC. It covers services in the Anglo-Boer War, WWI, WWII, Korea, Malaya (1948-1971), and South Vietnam (1962-1972). The narrattive is clear and informative, and is based upon meticulous research. The coverage is all-embracing, the appendixes and reference notes being exceptionally detailed. Every unit in which army nurses ever served is mentioned at some point in the text. The worst two disasters which befell the Corps were the sinking of the hospital ship CENTAUR (torpedoed off Brisbane in 1943, only one woman being rescued), and the ordeals of those captured by the Japanese at Singapore and on the islands of the Dutch East Indies. R/1 V/5. ANL. MCND'A.
Note: reference may be made also QUEENSLAND NURSES, by the same author, but published in 1985. This is a similar large-scale work, covering the wars of the 20th Century, but directed at the work done by nurses and nursing organisations having their origins in the State of Queensland. Other sources which deal specifically with the experiences of army nurses taken prisoner by the Japanese are:
CAPTIVES - AUSTRALIAN ARMY NURSES IN JAPANESE PRISON CAMPS, by Catherine Kenny (University of Queensland Press, St Lucia, Qld, 1986)
WOMEN BEYOND THE WIRE, by L Warner and J Sandilands (Hamlyn, reported as a reprint, 1983)
WHITE COOLIES, by B Jeffrey (Angus & Robertson, Sydney, 1958)
IN JAPANESE HANDS, by J E Simons (Heinemann, Melbourne, 1985, first published by the same house in 1954 as WHILE HISTORY PASSED).

GUNS AND BROOCHES
Australian Army Nursing from the Boer War to the Gulf War
Jan Bassett * Printed in Hong Kong, for Oxford University Press (Australia), South Melbourne, 1992. Maroon, gold, 10.25 x 7.5, x/261. 94 mono phots (indexed), no maps, Glossary, Bibliography, Chapter Notes, no appendixes, Index.
* A high quality production which covers every campaign in which Australian nurses have ever served. In total, 9000 nurses have been attached to the army, and the author deals in depth with the anomalies which have arisen from the fact that they were 'in but not of the army'. This paradox has created discrimination in matters such as pay and pensions. The main purpose of the book, however, is to trace their experiences in general terms. Many personal reminiscences are woven into the story. R/1 V/4. AWM. MCND'A.

NIGHTINGALES IN THE MUD
The Digger Sisters of the Great War, 1914-1918
Marianne Barker * Allen & Unwin Australia Pty Ltd, North Sydney, NSW, 1989. Blue, gold, 9.25 x 5.75, xvi/205. 58 mono phots (indexed), 5 sketches, one map, Glossary, Bibliography, Chapter Notes, Index. Apps: roll of nurses who served in WWI.
* A handsome and well written book, the clear narrative well supported with many chapter notes and first-class appendixes. Australia's military nurses served in every theatre of war during WWI, including some where no AIF fighting units were deployed. The story is presented in a logical format and describes, inter alia, the work of the nurses on hospital ships during the Gallipoli campaign, dealing with cholera outbreaks in India, and treating battle casualties in Macedonia, Salonika, on India's North West Frontier, on the Western Front, and in Vladivostock. This is a remarkable book, a model of its kind. R/1 V/5. ANL. MCND'A.

OUR KIND OF WAR
Mary Critch * Artlook Books Trust, Stirling, Western Australia, 1981. Red, gold, 8.75 x 5.75, -/211. 62 mono phots, no maps, Glossary, Bibliography, no Index. Apps: list of the titles and locations of medical units (by State and overseas) with which VAD/AAMWS personnel served, lists of AAMWS personnel and officers on the Active List.
* This is the story, told in considerable detail, of the VAD (Voluntary Aid Detachments) and the AAMWS (Australian Army Medical Women's Service) in WWII. It recounts, in nine clearly arranged chapters, their experiences while working in hospitals in Egypt, Ceylon, Palestine, New Guinea, Borneo, the Pacific islands, and the hospital ship ORANJE. Also covered is the work of those women who went to Singapore in 1945 to assist the newly liberated POW, to Japan with the British Commonwealth Occupation Force, and to Korea with No 130 Army General Hospital. The AAMWS was absorbed into the Royal Australian Army Nursing Corps in 1951. A well researched book, with plenty of source material for the researcher. Honours and awards are listed at the front of the book, not as an appendix at the rear. R/1 V/4. ANL. MCND'A.

VOLUNTARY AID DETACHMENTS IN PEACE AND WAR
Their History in Australia during the 20th Century
Dr Rupert Goodman * Boolarong Publications, Brisbane, 1991. Illustrated boards, pale blue, red/black, 'Nurse with VAD' motif, 10.5 x 8.0, -/231. Over 100 mono phots (indexed), 2 maps, Glossary, Bibliography, Index. Apps: Roll of Honour (with dates and locations, WWII), H&A (WWII only), list of names of VAD units in WWII (Brisbane and Melbourne) and in 1937, enlistment figures for WWII.
* An authoritative account of the role of the VAD and the AAMWS in times of peace and war. The author traces the origins of the VAD and their roots in the Order of St John and the British Red Cross Society. Their work in various theatres of war is described in fluent style, and the narrative is supported by a good Index and useful appendixes. R/1 V/5. ANL. MCND'A.
Note: a similar and equally helpful source is THEY WANTED TO BE NIGHTINGALES, by Enid Dalton Herring (Investigator Press Pty Ltd, Adelaide, 1982). This is another thorough account of services during WWII.

ARMY ORDNANCE CORPS

TO THE WARRIOR HIS ARMS
A History of the Ordnance Corps in the Australian Army
Maj John T Tilbrook * Macarthur Press Ltd, Parramatta, NSW, for the RAAOC Committee, 1989. Navy blue, gold, Corps crest, 9.75 x 7.25, x/702. More than 100 mono phots, 3 line drawings, 2 maps, Glossary, Acknowledgements, Index. Apps: Roll of Honour (WWI and WWII), list of serving Regular officers at November 1988, idem Army Reserve officers, similar lists for NCOs and ORs at that same date, notes on 'Ordnance Establishments, with Badge and Motto'.
* A mammoth work, written with skill and humour, which tells the story of the Australian ordnance services without excessive use of technical detail. It is a complete history, tracing each event from the early Colonial days through to the withdrawal from South Vietnam. Each period of war and peace receives equally full coverage, with the designations of each of the units concerned being identified in the narrative. The photographic content is very extensive and would have been even more useful if it had been indexed. R/2 V/5. AWM. MCND'A.

ELECTRICAL & MECHANICAL ENGINEERS

CRAFTSMEN OF THE AUSTRALIAN ARMY
The Story of the RAEME
Theo Barker * RAEME Corps Committee, Bathurst, NSW, 1992. Blue, gold, 11.5 x 8.5, xi/333. Fp, 167 mono phots, 23 cld plates, 4 maps, Glossary, no appendixes, three Indexes (Names, General, and Corps/formations/units).
* A splendidly presented formal history printed on glossy paper. It covers the evolution of Australia's military craftsmen throughout the 20th Century - the early Militia units, the AIF's workshops in WWI, the involvement with early aviation (1909-1919), and then the growth of mechanical engineering during the first half of WWII (leading up to the establishment of the AEME on 1 December of that year). Separate chapters are devoted to each of the principal theatres of war during WWII. The author then explains the changes of 1948, subsequent services in Korea, the atomic test programme, research in Antarctica, the campaigns in Malaya and Borneo, the South Vietnam and Gulf wars, service to the UN in Namibia, work done during the Olympic Games, Cyclone Tracy, the Tasman Bridge disaster, and so forth. There is full coverage of the Corps' traditions, the Colours, and leading personalities. The Indexes are most helpful, but it is curious that the book does not have the usual range of appendixes (Rolls of Honour, H&A, Order of Battle, etc). R/1 V/3. ANL. MCND'A.

THE A.E.M.E. IN THE FIELD
How the Corps of Australian Electrical & Mechanical Engineers Supports, Maintains, and Advises the Troops in the Field
Anon ('Staff of the Master General of Ordnance') * HQ AMF, Melbourne, 1945. Illustrated stapled soft card, full colour, 9.5 x 5.75, -/31. 54 mono phots, 4 cld sketches, one mono sketch, no appendixes, no Index.
* Produced some months before the end of the war, this is essentially a public relations item. AEME, it claimed, was the 'Aids Everyone, Mends Everything' Corps. Arranged in nine chapters and written in unadorned plain English, the narrative describes how this task was (then) currently being fulfilled throughout the SW Pacific theatre. The units described were - Light Aid Detachments, Bde Workshops, Base Workshops, Mechanical Equipment Workshops, Armoured Regt Workshops, Watercraft Workshops, Recovery units, and Generating units. Despite its slimness, it contains a great deal of useful material for the researcher, and helps to balance the record for the general reader of the history of WWII. The pictures are small but well annotated. R/4 V/4. AWM. MCND'A.

THE STORY OF 2/2 ARMY FIELD WORKSHOPS
Brig George Moran OBE * Outlook Press, Melbourne, 1964. Soft card, grey, blue, unit flash in red/blue, 5.5 x 4.0, -/48. No ills, no maps, no appendixes, no Index.
* Basically a personal memoir by the unit's first CO. His account is interesting only in the context that individual units of the AEME rarely receive the written tribute which they deserve. The narrative of this slim book deals with services in the Western Desert, the debacle in Greece, and the eventual return to Australia for reorganisation in 1942. R/4 V/2. AWM. MCND'A.

WOMEN'S SERVICES

WOMEN IN KHAKI
Australian Women's Army Service
Lorna Ollif * Southwood Press, Sydney, for the AWAS Association of NSW, 1981. Green, gold, 8.75 x 5.5, x/335. Fp, 77 mono phots (indexed), no maps, no appendixes, Bibliography, Chapter Notes, Index.
* The AWAS was formed in 1942 and disbanded in 1946. In this book, the author concentrates upon the major social and political factors, and the larger historical context. She describes the wartime strategic problems, and the difficulties on the home front, to set in context the original decision to raise a women's military force and then its value to the war effort. Her account concludes with the move, in 1951, to raise the Women's Royal Australian Army Corps. The writing style is slightly pedestrian, but the narrative is clearly well researched, authoritative, and packed with detailed information. R/1 V/4. ANL. MCND'A.

COLONEL BEST AND HER SOLDIERS
The Story of the 33 Years of the Women's Royal Australian Army Corps
Lorna Ollif * Ollif Publishing Co, Hornsby, NSW, 1985. Plasticated soft card, green, white, WRAAC crest, 8.5 x 5.5, xii/250. 30 mono phots, Bibliography, Index. Apps: Order of Battle, with the names of Commanders, Honorary Colonels, and Directors (with dates).
* This is the sequel to the author's WOMEN IN KHAKI (vide preceding entry) and is the story of the post-war WRAAC (natural successors to the wartime AWAS). It covers the period from 1951 onwards (when Lorna Ollif became its first Director), and it concludes with the events of 1984 (when it was disbanded and its members dispersed amongst the other Corps of the Australian Army). Like her first book, this one also is full of reliable information. Many former members are named in the text. R/1 V/5. ANL. MCND'A.

YOU'LL BE SORRY
Reflections on the Australian Women's Army Service, 1941-1945
Ann Howard * Tarka Publishing, Victoria, 1990. Green, gold, 10.0 x 7.0, -/193. More than 100 mono phots (indexed), 8 diagrams and line drawings, one map, Glossary, Bibliography & Sources, no appendixes, Index.
* Many thousands of young women volunteered for service in the AWAS in WWII. Of these, 3600 served with RAA coastal and anti-aircraft batteries and searchlight units. Others served in diverse roles - cypher clerks, drivers, vehicle mechanics, radio operators, and so forth. An informative and often amusing history, with many individuals named in the text. R/1 V/5. ANL. MCND'A.
Note: recommended additional sources are -
MEMOIRS OF AN AWAS DRIVER, by Lorna Staub Staude (Naracoorte Herald Pty Ltd, Naracoorte, SA, 1989)
AWAS - WOMEN MAKING HISTORY, by Jean Beveridge (Boolarong Publications Ltd, Chevron Island, Queensland, 1988). This book deals specifically with the AWAS contingent (12 officers and 332 ORs) which served at Lae and Hollandia in 1945-1946.

THANKS GIRLS AND GOODBYE
The Story of the Australian Women's Land Army, 1942-1945
Sue Hardisty * Penguin Books (Australia) Ltd, Ringwood, Victoria, 1990. Soft card, pink/grey, purple, 10.75 x 7.75, viii/231. 88 mono phots, 6 sketches, one map, no appendixes, Index.
* Formed in 1942, the AWLA recruited 3068 women to work on farms and thereby allowed more men to join the fighting forces. The author interviewed more than five hundred former members and based her book on their personal experiences and collections of snapshot photographs. R/1 V/4. SLV. PS.
Note: a similar source is GIRLS WITH GRIT - MEMORIES OF THE AUSTRALIAN WOMEN'S LAND ARMY, by Jean Scott (Allen & Unwin, North Sydney, NSW, 1986).

SPECIAL AND IRREGULAR FORCES

SAS - PHANTOMS OF THE JUNGLE
A History of the Australian Special Air Service
David Horner * Allen & Unwin, Sydney, 1989. Black, gold, Regtl crest, 9.25 x 6.25, xvii/527. 83 mono phots, 12 line drawings, 5 maps, Glossary, Bibliography, Index. Apps: Roll of Honour (with details of how and where killed), H&A (listed by campaign), nominal roll of all former members (with ranks and details of service).
* The author is a distinguished military historian and this book is a serious study of the evolution of the Australian SAS. Originally a Company-size unit, founded in 1957, it gained Regimental status in 1963. During the Indonesian Confrontation it served in Borneo and Brunei (1963-1965) and in Sarawak (1966). It then performed an 'eyes and ears' role for the Australian Task Force in South Vietnam (1966-1971) and has subsequently had a counter-terrorism role in Australia. All of this, and the Regt's value as a strategic asset, is described and analysed in good detail. R/1 V/5. AWM. MCND'A.

World War I

STALKY'S FORLORN HOPE
Capt S G Savige DSO MC * Alexander McCubbin, Melbourne, 1920. Brown, black, 7.25 x 5.0, -/176. Fp, 12 mono phots, one map, no appendixes, no Index.
* This book, which should be read in conjunction with WITH HORSE AND MORSE IN MESOPOTAMIA, by Keast Burke (vide the Index of Authors) is a classic account of unconventional warfare. The setting is North West Persia in 1919. The author was an Australian member of 'Dunsterforce' (code-named after Maj Gen L C Dunsterville, the model for Stalky, in Kipling's STALKY & CO). A volunteer force comprising officers and men from many parts of the Empire, it operated against the Turks and tried to assist the countless Armenian and Assyrian refugees in the region. The narrative includes many references to individual members and specifies their parent (British Army and Dominion) units. R/5 V/4. ANL. MCND'A.

World War II

CURTIN'S COWBOYS
Australia's Secret Bush Commandos
Richard and Helen Walker * Allen & Unwin, Sydney, 1986. Black, gold, 9.25 x 6.0, xviii/194. Fp, 39 mono phots, 3 sketch diagrams, 8 maps, no appendixes, Bibliography, Index.
* Between 1942 and 1945, the North Australia Observation Unit patrolled the coastlines between Normanton in Queensland and Wyndham in Western Australia. Operating in small groups of four or five men, 500 hand-picked volunteers kept watch for any unusual activity. Even after the threat of a Japanese invasion had evaporated, the Unit still had the task of looking for downed air crew and others who were lost in this vast and unpopulated region. Operating eight small vessels and working with local Aborigine tribesmen, their main problem was to survive in one of the world's loneliest and most hostile environments. The absorbing narrative is based upon interviews with men who served. R/1 V/4. ANL. MCND'A.
Note: John Curtin was Prime Minister throughout most of the war (1941 onwards).

BANDY'S BOYS
The Darwin Mobile Force
June Collins * Hi-Tone Offset, Melbourne, 1989. Soft card, pale green, black, RAA crest, 8.25 x 5.75, vii/82. 6 mono phots, no maps, no Index. Apps: H&A, unit nominal roll, current (1989) home addresses of seventy-five former members.
* In 1938, with remarkable foresight, the Army authorised the formation of a unit for the specific protection of Darwin and its environs. Under the command of Maj A B 'Bandy' MacDonald, it had an establishment of twelve officers and 245

volunteer ORs. Equipped with 18-pounders, 3" mortars and MMGs, they guarded the coastline and (after late 1941) kept watch for Japanese landings. The unit also endured the 380 air raids on Darwin in which 200 people were killed. Initially raised as a unit of the Royal Australian Artillery, it was redesignated 19th Aust Infantry Bn AIF in November 1941. Nearly half of the early members were later Commissioned. This well produced short history was written mainly to commemorate the unit's Jubilee, but it would be of value to genealogists and to everyone with an interest in the social climate in Australia as war approached.
R/4 V/4. ANL. MCND'A.
Note: it is stated that only 250 copies were printed.

TIMOR 1942
Australian Commandos at War with the Japanese
Christopher C H Wray * Hutchinson Australia, Hawthorn, Victoria, 1987. Blue, white, 8.5 x 5.5, x/190. 20 mono phots, 2 maps (printed on the end-papers), Bibliography, Index. Apps: H&A (to personnel of 2/2 Aust Ind Coy for services on Portuguese Timor, 16.2.1941 to 17.12,1942).
* An Australian garrison force, code-named 'Sparrow', was landed on Timor a few days before the Japanese invasion in February 1942. The main body was obliged to surrender two months later, but surviving members of 2/2 and 2/4 Independent Companies continued to conduct hit-and-run raids against Japanese installations for a full year before being evacuated. Their guerilla campaign would not have been possible without the courageous support of the indigenous Timorese in this former Portuguese colony (the natives of Dutch Timor, conversely, tended to side with the Japanese). A factual, exciting, and well written account.
R/1 V/4. ANL. MCND'A.
Note: a paperback edition was published by Mandarin Australia, in 1990.

A HISTORY OF THE 2/2nd INDEPENDENT COMPANY AND 2/2 COMMANDO SQUADRON
C D Doig * Valley Word Processing Service, Victoria, 1986. Illustrated soft card, grey/red, black, unit flash, 11.5 x 8.0, v/270. 46 mono phots, 6 sketch maps, Index. Apps: three full nominal rolls (2 Aust Ind Coy on Timor, 2 Cdo Sqn in New Guinea, 2 Cdo Sqn in New Britain), notes on Japanese work gangs, 1945.
* This sometimes confusingly written story is best read in conjunction with the those compiled by Wray and Callinan (vide preceding and following entries). The author traces the origins of Australia's Commando forces, their thrilling adventures on Timor, then 2 Cdo Sqn's operations in many part of New Guinea and the final campaign on New Britain. Two thirds of the narrative is devoted to the Timor period (1941-1942). The raid on Dili (the capital of East Timor) is well and amusingly described. The author was an original officer of 2 Cdo Sqn and he writes with authority, but it is sometimes difficult to know which year he is reviewing. R/1 V/4. AWM. MCND'A.

INDEPENDENT COMPANY
2/2 and 2/4 Australian Independent Companies in Portuguese Timor, 1941-1943
Bernard J Callinan DSO MC * Printed by Brown, Prior, Anderson Pty Ltd, Melbourne, for William Heinemann Ltd, Melbourne and London, 1953. Green, gold, 8.75 x 5.75, xxxiii/235. Fp, 37 mono phots, 8 maps (6 printed in the text, 2 on the end-papers), Index. Apps: list of officers who served.
* This book was the earliest in the series of three which have been written about 'Sparrow Force' and the extraordinary events on Portuguese Timor in 1942-1943. This author also does a fine job in capturing on paper the danger and fear created by the arrival of 6000 Japanese assault troops, the initial encounters, and the withdrawal into the mountains by the surviving Australians. Aided by local people, they lived off the land, carried their wounded with them, and kept up the fight. They were, at a crucial stage in the war, the only Allied force anywhere between India and New Guinea still in direct contact with the enemy. At their peak of activity, they were immobilising 30,000 Japanese troops (and inflicting considerable casualties and materiel losses upon them). R/3 V/5. AWM. HEC/JRS.

A STORY OF THE 2/5th AUSTRALIAN COMMANDO SQUADRON, AIF

Jack Boxall * Metropolitan Printers, Lakemba, n.d. Paper covers, pale blue, black, 7.5 x 5.5, -/35. No ills, no maps, no appendixes, no Index.

* This booklet, written by an original member of 2/5 Australian Independent Company (later renamed 2/5 Australian Commando Squadron AIF), describes its formation in 1942 and its arrival on New Guinea in April of that year. The names of the officers who embarked are listed in the text. Despite its lack of training, it was rushed into the desperate operations designed to halt the Japanese moves towards the key base of Port Morseby. It was given the task of infiltrating the Japanese dominated area around Lae and to cause as much disruption as possible. These actions, and the battle at Wau in January 1943, are described clearly and well. The unit returned home in mid-1943 and did not see action again until June 1945. It was then part of the assault force at Balikpapan, North Borneo. A very condensed history, but one which contains all the essential facts.
R/4 V/3. AWM. MCND'A.

THE PURPLE DEVILS

A History of the 2/6 Australian Commando Squadron, formerly the 2/6 Australian Independent Company, 1942-1946

S Trigellis-Smith * Valley Graphics, Pakenham, Victoria, for 2/6 Cdo Sqn Assn, 1992. Purple, silver/white, 8.5 x 5.5, xvii/305. Fp, 46 mono phots (indexed), 12 maps (indexed), Bibliography, Index. Apps: Roll of Honour (with dates and locations, plus separate list of WIA), H&A (with citations, plus MID), unit nominal roll (at July 1942), 'Intelligence Report, Markham Valley', 'Patrol Report, 2/6 Ind Coy Patrol, 1942'.

* The 2/6 Ind Coy was raised in May 1942 from all Corps and thereby having its own integral Signal, Engineer, and Medical elements. It commenced operations in August, giving flank protection and making deep-penetration patrols on each side of the Kokoda Trail. Some of these patrols lasted four months. Rolls of those who took part in them are included in the text. The Coy then fought in the Buna action in late 1942. It was redesignated a Commando Squadron in 1943, and was committed to the violent battles at Ramu and Markham Valley. Its final operation was the reoccupation of Balikpapan in 1945. This is a high quality production, with excellent illustrations, a clear narrative, and many individuals mentioned in the text. R/1 V/5. AWM. MCND'A.

Note: for further information regarding clandestine operations by Australian forces during WWII, reference should be made to SILENT FEET, by Lieut Col G B Courtney (R & S Austin, McRae, Victoria, 1993). Other important sources will be found in other sections of this bibliography - China (Mission 204), Brunei and Borneo ('Z' Special Unit), Malay States and Singapore (Operations Jaywick and Rimau), and The Pacific Islands (coast watching organisations).

THE FLYING FOOTSLOGGERS

Unofficial History of Australia's Paratroopers - A Saga of World War II

Norm Fuller * Publication details not shown, n.d. (c.1980). Illustrated soft card, green/white, red, 'Airborne troops' motif, 8.0 x 6.5, -/146. 58 mono phots, one line drawing, one map, no appendixes, no Index.

* 1st Australian Parachute Bn saw no active service and was disbanded in 1946. This strange book, which has no identifiable provenance, is based mainly upon anecdotes and barely qualifies as a 'unit history'. However, it is the only known record for the Bn, and its interest is sharpened by the inclusion of a detailed (though unrelated) account of the assault on Nadzab (New Guinea) in September 1943. A Battery of 2/24 Field Regt RAA was dropped into the Markham Valley with its 'short' 25-pounders. It was the first parachute descent ever made by the Battery, and seems to have been surprisingly successful and effective.
R/2 V/2. ANL. MCND'A.

Note: it is reported that an expanded edition, with 172 pages, was published in 1986. No other details known.

THE VOLUNTEER DEFENCE CORPS

ON GUARD
With the Volunteer Defence Corps
Anon * Halstead Press Pty Ltd, for the Australian War Memorial, 1944. Grey/buff, black, VDC crest, 11.0 x 8.5, -/172. Fp, 84 mono phots, 13 cld ills (indexed, all by VDC member artists), 78 line drawings, no maps, no appendixes, no Index.
* This is the only book which tells the story of the VDC as a whole. It is based upon contributions from fifty assorted members. The Corps was formed in 1939 by the RSL (a 'veterans' organisation similar to the Royal British Legion and having, at that time, the title 'Returned Sailors', Soldiers', and Airmens' Imperial League of Australia'). The VDC was the RSL's spontaneous response to the outbreak of war but, in June 1940, it was recognised by the Federal Government as the RSL VDC. A year later it was fully absorbed into the Australian Army's Order of Battle as, simply, the VDC. By dropping the RSL reference, the authorities were recognising the fact that the membership no longer consisted mainly of middle-aged RSL members (veterans of WWI). The ranks now included a high proportion of younger men - those in reserved occupations and those who were unfit for (or unwilling to volunteer for) service overseas. The role of the VDC was to guard the coastlines and key installations, to search for crashed aircraft, to man anti-aircraft and coastal batteries, and to generally relieve the burden on front-line units. In the event, the training and spirit of the VDC was never tested in action, but one VDC affiliated unit - the Papua New Guinea Volunteer Rifles - did go to war. As individuals, its Australian and American members operated in a variety of roles in the New Guinea, New Ireland, New Britain, and Bougainville campaigns. This is a lavishly illustrated book, a vintage record of the period. R/3 V/3. AWM. MCND'A.
Note: reprinted in 1953. For further information regarding the Papua New Guinea Volunteer Rifles, refer to Volume V, Series One (Army), by Dudley McCarthy, of the official AUSTRALIA IN THE WAR OF 1939-1945 series (vide Index of Authors).

4th BATTALION, VOLUNTEER DEFENCE CORPS, 1940-1945
Anon * Pilven & Stephens, Melbourne, 1946. Stiff card, red, black, 7.5 x 4.75, -/16. No ills, no maps, no Index. Apps: list of officers at disbandment, notes on sub-unit locations and strengths, Bn strength (by Company).
* A booklet which contains little more than verbatim quotations from Special Orders of the Day and messages from important persons at the time of disbandment, but which gives a useful picture of the work done by the VDC. The 4th Bn was located in New South Wales. R/4 V/1. AWM. MCND'A.

THE GREEN HORNETS
The Story of the 7th Battalion, Volunteer Defence Corps, New South Wales
Anon * Consolidated Press, Sydney, 1946. Illustrated soft card, pale green, white, 'VDC soldier' motif, 12.5 x 9.75, -/64. Fp, 66 mono phots, 10 pages of sketches, no maps, no Index. Apps: list of COs.
* An attractive little book, with a 'magazine' style of layout, and containing many poems, anecdotes, and caricatures. A mirror of popular sentiment on the home front. R/4 V/1. ANL. MCND'A.

WHEATBELT WARRIORS
The Story of the 15th (WA) Battalion, Volunteer Defence Corps
Paul de Pierres * Published privately by the author, no details shown, 1993. Illustrated soft card, red/white/khaki, 'Badges, medals, soldiers, map, VDC crest' motif, 9.75 x 6.25, vi/70. Fp, 71 mono phots, 11 line drawings, one sketch map, Glossary, no Index. Apps: unit nominal roll (with much detail).
* The 15th Bn was part of No 3 Group VDC. It was administered from Kalgoorlie, with its HQ at Merrindin. Consisting of 700 all ranks, recruited from all walks of

country life in Western Australia's central wheatbelt, it was formed in June 1940 and disbanded in October 1945. This short book, well illustrated with named and annotated photographs of groups and individuals, records the training and service of each of the four Coys as they prepared to defend their territory in the event of a Japanese invasion. It is a splendid story of five years' dedicated part-time service by one of the sixteen VDC Bns raised in Western Australia. The pictures include illustrations of the cap badge and shoulder flashes, and the nominal roll has self-evident value to the genealogist. R/1 V/4. ANL. MCND'A.

THAT 'B' COMPANY

E B Arney * Unpublished TS, no details shown, n.d. (c.1945), 68 octavo folios.
* A contemporary record of 'B' Coy, No 2 (Fremantle) Bn, VDC. It is strong on biographical detail, with lists of members, home addresses, previous war services, and so forth. Possibly a useful source for genealogists working in the Fremantle area. R/5 V/2. PC. PS.
Note: it seems likely that a few facsimile copies were presented by the author to various local libraries and other institutions.

JOLLY GOOD COMPANY

'B' Company, No 2 (Fremantle) Battalion, Volunteer Defence Corps, 1939–1945

A C Bellett * Publication details not shown, 1947. Soft card, buff/red, black, VDC crest, 8.5 x 5.5, iii/57. Fp, 2 mono phots, no maps, no Index. Apps: unit nominal roll.
* Surprisingly, this was the second attempt to produce something in writing about the same unit (vide preceding entry). In the event, it consists of little more than reminiscences by some of those who served. Of limited research value other than to descendent families. R/4 V/1. ANL/NYPL. MCND'A.

POLICE

General Reference

THE TROOPER POLICE OF AUSTRALIA
A Record of Mounted Police Work in the Commonwealth from the Earliest Days of Settlement to the Present Time
A L Haydon * A C McLurg & Co, Chicago and London, 1911. Dark green, gold, coat of arms of the Commonwealth of Australia, 9.0 x 6.0, xviii/431. Fp, 42 mono phots, 6 maps (5 printed in the text, one bound in), Index. Apps: list of Commissioners and Commandants, list of police officers killed or wounded by Bushrangers (1861-1879), notes on the Bushrangers Act (1830).
* This comprehensive book traces the evolution and services of the police forces of each of the six Colonies through to 1901-1902 (when the Colonies federated to form the Commonwealth of Australia). The first body of mounted police was formed in New South Wales to combat the lawlessness associated with the early gold rushes. Such units were recruited mainly from British Army regiments then stationed in the Colony, hence the police had a strongly military character. Their uniforms were similar to those of the 14th Light Dragoons and they were trained to fight the armed gangs of scavengers then infesting the rural areas. Police units were soon raised for similar purposes in the other Colonies, with their recruits coming from the ranks of the British police forces and the Royal Irish Constabulary. This is an entertaining and detailed history which coincidentally traces Australia's early settler days and the birth-pangs of nationhood. R/3 V/5. ANL. MCND'A.

THE AUSTRALIAN POLICE FORCES
G M O'Brien * Oxford University Press, Melbourne, 1960. Blue, gold, 8.75 x 5.5, xvi/268. 56 mono phots (indexed), no maps, Index. Apps: notes on the organisation of the Victoria and New South Wales police forces (at 1960).
* A wide-ranging overall history of the origins and growth of Australia's various police services - New South Wales (from 1789), Tasmania (from 1803), Western Australia (from 1830), Victoria (from 1836), South Australia (from 1837), Queensland (from 1842), Northern Territory (from 1865), and the Australian Capital Territory (from 1927). The narrative contains interesting descriptions of the operations of the mounted police against the Bushrangers and against those tribes of Aboriginals which resisted European encroachment. The story continues into the 20th Century, covering events up to the 1950s. R/1 V/4. ANL/MODL. MCND'A.
Note: reference may be made also to GOLD ESCORTS IN AUSTRALIA, by L J Blake (Rigby Ltd, Hong Kong, 1978). This booklet tells the story of the gold transport escorts between 1851, when gold was first discovered in Victoria, through to 1970. The gold-fields of South and Western Australia are also covered, with interesting mention of famous robberies, notorious Bushrangers, etc.

SIX AUSTRALIAN BATTLEFIELDS
The Black Resistance to Invasion and the White Struggle against Colonial Oppression
Al Grassby and Marji Hill * Angus & Robertson, North Ryde, NSW, 1988. Brown, white, 9.5 x 6.25, xii/324. 15 mono phots, 27 diagrams and line drawings, 7 maps, no appendixes, no Index.
* This book covers the activities of the British Army (1788-1870) and of the Australian Auxiliary and para-military forces (1800-1909) against the Aboriginal tribes. It includes the guerilla war fought by the Dharuk and Eora tribes against the settlers around Sydney (1788-1810), the destruction of the Wiradjuri tribe by the 40th Regiment of Foot at Bathurst (1824), the subjugation of the Nyungar tribe at Pinjarra, Western Australia (1834), and the last pitched battle between whites and blacks in North Queensland (1884). There are some good accounts also of the Battle of Vinegar Hill (1804), and the Eureka Stockade affair (1854).
R/2 V/4. SLV. PS.

BLOOD ON THE WATTLE
Massacres and Maltreatment of Australian Aboriginals since 1788
Bruce Elder * Child & Associates Publishing Pty Ltd, Frenchs Forest, NSW, 1988. Paperback, red, yellow/black, 9.0 x 5.75, -/208. 30 mono phots, 11 maps, 32 other ills, Bibliography, no appendixes, Index.
* A book which describes the destruction of the Aborigine tribes and their culture in every part of Australia by white gangs and, worse, by The Native Police. The latter were supposedly responsible for protecting and supervising the Aborigines. The officers were Europeans, the Troopers were a mixture of European adventurers, former convicts, free settlers, and full-blooded and mixed-race Aborigines (some of whom became Corporals and Sergeants). The first such unit was raised in Victoria in 1837. In the event, the Native Police Forces in each of the Colonies acquired, especially in the mid- and late-1800s, a reputation for brutality and undisguised genocide. The last major massacre, instigated by an officer of the Northern Territory Native Police, took place at Lander River in 1928. Seventy Aborigines were murdered on that occasion, but there had been many similar episodes during the previous decades. In 1861, for example, the Queensland Native Police killed three hundred Aborigines in a reprisal raid near Cullin-in-Ringo. The book recounts the darkest side of Australia's history. R/1 V/4. SLV. PS.

New South Wales

A CENTENARY HISTORY OF THE NEW SOUTH WALES POLICE, 1862-1962
Anon * NSW Government Printer, Sydney, 1962. Soft card, blue, gold, Force crest, 10.5 x 8.0, -/128. More than 100 mono phots, 7 cld ills, one map, no Index. Apps: Roll of Honour (WWI, WWII, and killed while on police duty), H&A (gallantry and distinguished service), list of Inspectors General and Commissioners (1862-1962, with portrait photographs and service details).
* Despite its 'economy' binding, this is an attractive book. It covers the entire history of police activities in NSW from 1788 through to the introduction of the Police Regulations Act of 1862, then the evolution of the modern police service as it existed in 1962. The narrative has no great substance, but it is comprehensive. R/1 V/4. ANL. MCND'A.

MOUNTED POLICE IN NEW SOUTH WALES
A History of Heroism and Duty since 1821
John O'Sullivan * Rigby Ltd, Hong Kong, 1979. Green, white, 9.0 x 5.75, ix/150. 30 mono phots, 14 line drawings, no maps, Index. Apps: notes on the Aboriginal Mounted Police.
* A fluent and informative account of the various horsed police units which maintained law and order in NSW from 1821 to 1963 (when the last active service horse was retired). The author provides vivid accounts of the services rendered by the Military Mounted Police, the Border Police, the Civil Mounted Police, the Gold Police, and the Mounted Road Patrols, during various periods before the final creation of the centralised NSW Mounted Police. R/1 V/4. VSL/ANL. PS/MCND'A.

THE BATTLE OF VINEGAR HILL
Australia's Irish Rebellion
Lynette Ramsay Silver * Doubleday Books, Moorebank, NSW, 1989. Soft card, off white, brown/black, 9.25 x 6.0, viii/168. 25 mono phots, 2 maps, Index. Apps: roll of the rebels, roll of Active Service Force members.
* The book tells the story of the ill-fated Irish revolt in New South Wales in 1804 which culminated in the Vinegar Hill battle on 4 March. Maj George Johnson, leading twenty-six men of the New South Wales Corps and sixty-seven men of the Active Defence Force, defeated a group of 233 rebels. Of these, fifteen were killed in the action and eight were later hanged. An interesting example of early Australian 'police' work. R/1 V/3. PC. PS.

THE POLICE OF SYDNEY, 1788-1862
Bruce Swanton * Australian Association of Criminology, with the NSW Police Historical Society, 1964. Soft card, yellow, black, 11.5 x 8.0, iv/76. One line drawing, no maps, Bibliography, Index. Apps: list of sovereigns and officers of the home government (1788-1862), idem Governors and administrators of NSW, police force strengths, Parliamentary papers (all for the same period).
* An informative research tool. Particularly useful for Police Regulations (1811), and for the chronology and for the lists of personnel (at 1833, 1834, 1839, etc). R/3 V/3. NSWPLS. PS.
Note: recommended additional sources are C.I.B. CENTENARY, 1879-1979, anon (NSW Police, Sydney, 1979), and DOCUMENTS ON POLICE IN NSW, 1789-1879, anon (NSW Police, Sydney, n.d. (c.1963). Both have solid contents of facts, figures, verbatim extracts from documents, and lists of personnel.

Victoria and Tasmania

COPS AND ROBBERS
A Guide to Researching 19th Century Police and Criminal Records in Victoria
Helen Doxford Harris and Gary Presland * Aristoc Press, Glen Waverley, Victoria, for Harriland Press, 1990. Soft card, light blue, dark blue, 8.25 x 6.25, xvi/130. 10 mono phots, 2 line drawings, Bibliography, Index. Apps: nominal rolls, extensive notes regarding original sources of reference for police and criminal subjects (1845-1900).
* A detailed guide to the police service and criminal justice records of the State of Victoria. The material is arranged in two parts - police personnel and station records, then criminal records, Court records, and prison records. R/2 V/5. SLV. PS.

RECOLLECTIONS OF A VICTORIAN POLICE OFFICER
John Sadleir * Seen as a paperback edition, by Penguin Books, of the first edition published in 1913 by George Robertson & Co, 7.75 x 5.0, -/312. 36 mono phots, 7 sketches, no maps, Index. Apps: list of VPF Cadets (1852-1854), list of senior VPF officers (1852-1907), notes on the Corps of Native Troopers.
* The author joined the Victoria Police Force as a Cadet in 1852. Later he rose to be Acting Chief Commissioner and retired in 1896. The high point of his career came in 1880 when, in the area around Glenrowan, he led the hunt for Ned Kelly and his gang. He also gives good coverage of the gold rush period of the 1850s. The appendixes are unusually helpful. R/1 V/3. PC. PS.

POLICE IN VICTORIA
Anon * Government Printer, Melbourne, for the VP Management Service Bureau, 1980. Blue, silver, 8.5 x 6.0, ix/126. 39 mono phots, 5 line drawings, no maps, Bibliography, Index. Apps: list of Chief Commissioners.
* A condensed but comprehensive history of the Victoria Police Force. The narrative deals with the early days, the Mounted Police, the Wireless Patrol, the Traffic Police, the 1923 police strike, the use of forensic science methods, and so forth. R/2 V/4. SLV. PS.
Note: published also in paperback.

THE PEOPLE'S POLICE
A History of the Victoria Police
Robert Haldane * Printed by Globe Press Ltd, Brunswick, for Melbourne University, 1986. Blue, silver, 9.5 x 6.25, xv/372. 48 mono phots, 12 line drawings, 2 maps, Glossary, Bibliography (14 pages), Chapter Notes (35 pages), no appendixes, Index.
* A nicely produced book which traces the application of law and order in Victoria from 1836 onwards. There were no police units in the Colony before 1852, hence public security was largely a matter for the British Army garrison forces. By virtue of the subject matter, the narrative is a mirror of the Colony's evolving social and political structures. The author works to scholarly standards, backing

his narrative with a wealth of reference sources and tables of facts and figures (for all periods through to 1986). The specialist will find here a wealth of helpful information. For the general reader, the accounts of the Eureka Stockade incident, the hunt for Ned Kelly, the impact of the gold rushes, and the squabbles amongst the great and famous, all make absorbing reading. R/1 V/5. SLV. PS/MCND'A.

GOOD MEN AND TRUE
The Aboriginal Police of the Port Phillip District, 1837-1853
Marie Hansen Fels * Brown Prior Anderson Pty Ltd, Burwood, Victoria, 1988. Dark red, gold, 9.75 x 5.5, xi/308. One mono phot, 14 sketches, 3 maps, Glossary, Bibliography, Index. Apps: Rules and Regulations (1842), Structure and Strength (1842), notes on recruitment, biographical details of some Corps members.
* The story of the Native Police Corps, formed by Supt Christiaan de Villiers in 1837 to guard Pentridge Prison and to police the Victorian goldfields. The Corps was restructured in 1842 by Capt Henry Dana, then disbanded in 1853.
R/1 V/5. SLV. PS.
Note: reference may be made also to CAPTAIN DANA AND THE NATIVE POLICE, by Les Blake (Neptune Press, Newtown, Victoria, 1982).

MOUNTED POLICE OF VICTORIA AND TASMANIA
A History of Heroism and Duty since 1837
John O'Sullivan * Rigby Publishers Ltd, Maryborough, Victoria, 1980. Tan, white, 8.0 x 5.5, -/211. 19 mono phots, 26 line drawings, no maps, Bibliography, no appendixes, Index.
* The book covers the military and civil mounted police units of Victoria and Tasmania and is arranged in three parts. Part I deals with the Military Mounted Police (1837-1849), Border Police (1839-1846), and Native Police (1837-1852). Part II deals with the Civil Mounted Police of Victoria (1851-1979). Part III deals with the Mounted Police of Tasmania (1827-1940). R/1 V/4. SLV. PS.

Queensland

POLICE OF THE PASTORAL FRONTIER
Native Police, 1849-1859
L E Skinner * University of Queensland Press, St Lucia, Queensland, 1975. Green, yellow, 8.75 x 5.5, x/455. 7 mono phots, 9 line drawings, 9 maps, Bibliography, Index. Apps: list of officers, list of NCOs, distribution of Native Police units at various dates, numerical strengths, notes on the 'habits and tempers of recruits'.
* A detailed history of the Native Police as it was constituted and as it operated in the Northern and Eastern Districts of New South Wales pending the creation of Queensland as an autonomous Colony in 1859. R/2 V/5. SLV. PS.

THE QUEENSLAND POLICE FORCE
100 Years, 1864-1963
A F Trueman * Courier Mail Printing, Brisbane, for the Brochure Committee, 1964. Illustrated soft card, maroon, white, 9.75 x 7.25, -/95. 55 mono phots, no maps, no Index. Apps: H&A (list of gallantry awards, idem distinguished service awards), list of former Commissioners (with portrait photographs and career details).
* This is not a well structured book, but the story is told with gusto and in interesting detail. It commences in 1833 with the convict settlement at Moreton Bay, then moves to the establishment of Queensland as a separate Colony in 1853. There are good references to the Native Mounted Police, fights with Bushrangers, the problem of the Gold Escorts, and more problems with miners' strikes, shearers' strikes, and race riots in the goldfields. Even though it grew into a truly modern force, the QPF has retained its traditional Mounted Unit. R/1 V/3. ANL. MCND'A.

THE LONG BLUE LINE
A History of the Queensland Police
W Ross Johnston * Boolarong Publications, Brisbane, 1992. Light grey, blue, 12.0 x 8.5, x/400. 217 mono phots, no maps, Chapter Notes, no appendixes, Index.
* The period covered is 1842 to 1992 and the narrative is arranged in four parts - the 1800s, the turn of the century and WWI, the inter-war years and WWII, and lastly the post-war period. Each part deals with a variety of subjects relevant to the period under review - Government policy, the work of the Commissioners, recruitment and training, conditions of service, discipline, equipment, and the work done in dealing with crime, strikes, social problems, traffic management, and much else besides. This is a very comprehensive work which should interest policemen and police researchers in other States and other countries. R/1 V/4. SLV. PS.

THE BLACK POLICE OF QUEENSLAND
Reminiscences of Official Work and Personal Adventures in the Early Days of the Colony
Edward B Kennedy * John Murray, London, 1902. Green, gold, additional wording on the front cover states: 'Murray's Imperial Library, Not to be Circulated in the British Isles', 8.0 x 5.25, xviii/273. Fp, 15 mono phots, 4 line drawings (two by Sir Frank Lockwood), no appendixes, Index.
* A book of reminiscences by a British police officer who served in the Native Mounted Police, Colony of Queensland, in the 1860s and 1870s. It describes a world so long past that it is difficult to comprehend in the 1990s. The author's views on the Aboriginal population, his descriptions of the hunting down of black murderers of white settlers, and the retaliatory actions taken against them, make the case argued by present-day Aboriginal activists more comprehensible and more justified. The contemporary photographs are evocative of this dark period in colonial history. Each of the twenty chapters is preceded by a summary of its contents. Combined with the good Index, these headings make the book an easily consulted source of reference. R/4 V/4. ANL. MCND'A.

Western Australia

POLICE REVIEW, 1829-1979
Since the Days of Stirling
Senior Inspector R M Lawrence * Government Printing Office, Perth, 1978. Soft card, blue/white, 9.5 x 6.0, -/86. 16 mono phots, 17 cld ills, no maps, no appendixes, no Index.
* A brief summary of the evolution of the Western Australian Police Force and its various Branches and Sections. Compiled primarily as a 'public relations' item, it is certainly a useful chronological summary of the first 150 years of European settlement and associated police work. The person referred to in the sub-title was Sir James Stirling (1791-1865) who founded the Swan River Colony in 1829 and was the first Governor of Western Australia. R/3 V/2. WAPL. SJH.
Note: the WAP have produced two other similar short general histories - TO THOSE WE SERVE, anon (1977), and IN STEP WITH THE LAW, anon, n.d. (c.1973).

ASPECTS OF THE WESTERN AUSTRALIAN POLICE FORCE, 1887-1905
A W Gill * Published privately by the author, Perth, 1975. Facsimile TS, seen in library binding, blue, gold, 13.25 x 8.5, vi/112. No ills, no maps, Glossary, Bibliography, no Index. Apps: 8 in total, incl Force strengths, locations of Police Stations, pay scales, deaths, dismissals, discharges and resignations (1887-1905).
* This is an in-depth examination of police work in Western Australia between 1887 (when the British Government withdrew its subsidy for the police and the magistrates) and 1905 (when an official report condemned the police for their persecution of the Aboriginals). This is the only serious published examination of the Western Australian Police during the Colony's (State's) greatest period of social and economic change. It was a challenge which the Force's senior officers did not entirely overcome. R/4 V/4. ANL. MCND'A.

South Australia

COLONIAL BLUE
A History of the South Australian Police, 1836-1916
Robert Clyne * Wakefield Press, Adelaide, 1987. Navy blue, silver, Force crest, 9.75 x 6.5, xxi/299. 93 mono phots (incl two on the end-papers), one map, Chapter Notes (extensive), Glossary, Bibliography, no appendixes, Index.
* Early South Australia had no penal settlements and was in many ways a model Colony. Even so, within two years of its foundation, it had established (in 1836) its own tiny police force with an establishment of just twenty Constables. Unlike other Australian Colonies, founded in earlier years, South Australia never had any British Army garrisons. These twenty men were therefore alone responsible for law and order in that vast region. Their numbers increased as the years went by, but their commitment also increased because, for several decades, they were responsible also for the Northern Territory. The author provides an impressive account of the evolution of the Force and its role in shaping the growth of South Australia as a whole. The illustrations are excellent. R/2 V/4. ANL. MCND'A.

TRACKS
Max Jones * J C Irving & Co, Berri, SA, 1990. Yellow, red/black, 9.25 x 6.5, vi/144. 36 mono phots, 16 line drawings, 2 maps, no appendixes, no Index.
* The author was a CIB officer who, between 1959 and 1990, was involved in many cases which required the skills of Aboriginal trackers employed by the SA Police. The narrative is based upon his personal diaries. An interesting collection of stories about manhunts for offenders and for people lost in the wilderness of the desert. R/1 V/3. PC. PS.

TO WALK A FAIR BEAT
A History of the South Australian Women Police, 1915-1987
Patricia Higg and Christine Bettess * Hyde Park Press Pty Ltd, Lockley, SA, for the Past & Present Women Police Association, 1987. Blue, silver, 9.5 x 7.0, xiii/234. 205 mono phots, no maps, Bibliography, Index. Apps: roll of personnel who have served in the SAWP (1915-1987, with dates of service).
* The introduction describes the relationship between women and the law from 1842 to 1915 when Kate Cocks, the first woman to join the SA Police, commenced her service. The bulk of the narrative then covers in detail the work of female officers through to 1987. R/1 V/4. SLV. PS.

Northern Territory

PATROL INDEFINITE
The Northern Territory Police
Sidney Downer * Rigby Ltd, Adelaide, 1963. Illustrated soft card, green, white/brown, 7.0 x 4.5, -/212. 33 mono phots (indexed), no maps, Bibliography, no appendixes, Index.
* This is the story of policing what was, and still is, a vast empty area of land sometimes called 'blackman's country'. Essentially a collection of stories of encounters and incidents, the book covers the period 1860 to 1960. Administered initially by South Australia, the Territory became a Federal responsibility in 1911. The lonely life of the NT policeman is well reflected in the accounts of Aboriginal 'troubles', while modern policing techniques are represented in the 1954 rescue of Mrs Petrov, at Darwin, from the Soviet KGB. The difficulties of reconciling Aboriginal custom with white man's law are discussed in considerable detail and sympathetically. R/1 V/5. MODL/ANL. MCND'A.
Note: a later and extended history has been compiled by a former Commissioner of the NT Police, W J McLaren. It exists in facsimile TS, but at the present time (1992) has not found a publisher. Interested researchers should contact NT Police Headquarters, Winnellie, NT 0821, for further details.

NOTES

PART 14

New Zealand

NOTES

INTRODUCTION

New Zealand's military bibliography differs markedly from those of the United Kingdom and of the other Dominions. When studying the following pages, certain facts should be kept in mind.

Until 1942, there was no provision within the governmental structure for the processing and publication of military historical records. Four official histories had been published immediately after WWI, but those were financed from army funds, not central funds. Although excellent in their own way, they were written by serving officers who were understandably constrained in what they could say about their superiors and their conduct of the war. When, early in WWII, the historian Dr E H McCormick began to lobby the authorities, he was proposing something quite new. He wanted to see a comprehensive range of volumes which would record 'a nation at war'. He made some progress when, in April 1942, he was appointed Archivist to the 2nd New Zealand Expeditionary Force, but he continued to press for a project of much larger scale. His ideas were accepted in April 1945 when the War Cabinet authorised the establishment of a War History Branch of the Department of Internal Affairs. By early 1946, it had more than one hundred persons on its staff, all working on separate aspects of the project in whatever office buildings could be found for them. Major General Sir Howard Kippenberger was appointed Editor-in-Chief so that order could be imposed upon what was proving to be a very large task. It was assumed that it would be completed within a period of seven to ten years.

The planned series of volumes - which were subsequently published over a period of twenty-two years - were arranged in four parts. They were described as 'departmental narratives', 'episodes and studies', 'unit histories', and 'campaign and general histories'. Seventy-one volumes were produced, and many of them - those which meet the parameters of REGIMENTS - are noted in detail on the following pages. The unique feature of the listings is the inclusion of the individual 'unit histories'. New Zealand is the only country which has ever assumed this responsibility (normally carried by old comrades associations, or by regimental committees, or by individual authors and publishers).

All these books have sub-titles which commence 'Official History of ...'. Most were printed on contract by Whitcombe & Tombs Ltd, of Wellington and Auckland, the others coming from the presses of J Wilkie & Co Ltd (later renamed Coulls, Somerville, Wilkie, Ltd), of Dunedin. The usual format is quarto (8.75 x 5.75), with red cloth covers. The title pages usually show the name of the publisher as being the 'War History Branch, Department of Internal Affairs', although in some books the wording is slightly different - 'Historical Publications Branch, New Zealand Internal Affairs'. To avoid unnecessary repetition, books forming part of the series are recorded in this bibliography without all these details. With two or three exceptions - where clarification is helpful - the sub-titles are not quoted in full and the provenance is shown simply as 'War History Branch'. The standards of printing, illustration, and binding, are consistently very good in all of these books.

The quality of authorship is less consistent. According to Ronald Walker, who worked for the Department and who wrote a retrospective account of the way in which the project had been managed, the peak period of activity was 1946-1947. The Branch was staffed at speed, under the pressures of post-war economy, with a variety of writers and administrative personnel each of whom were still coming to terms with peacetime conditions and the paradox of how to build a long-term career within what was then viewed as being a relatively short-term project. Much of the early material was written by former war correspondents, by former officers awaiting demobilisation, or by non-specialists with no military experience. Several professional historians were also successfully recruited but, in the early days, they could not always gain access to the source material which they required. There was also some pressure to start producing tangible results quickly, and this did not always contribute to the writing of sound history.

The 'departmental narratives' were accounts of the nation's wartime civil service administration. They were soon completed, reproduced in facsimile typescript, and circulated to interested parties within the government. They were not published for general consumption.

The 'episodes and studies' were slim booklets or pamphlets which dealt with particularly exciting incidents and emotive subjects, and were intended for a popular readership. Forty-eight were planned, twenty-four were produced. The authors, according to Walker, were mainly journalists, not historians. Their work was produced in haste, and he states that it contains numerous errors of fact. Only three such are recorded in this bibliography.

The 'unit histories' and 'campaign and general histories' were, by their nature, much more difficult to compile and took longer to produce. The majority were published in the 1950s and early 1960s. By then, the War History Branch was struggling with several inter-related difficulties. Popular enthusiasm for war stories had subsided, political backing for the project had diminished, funding had been reduced, and several key personnel had moved on to better paid appointments in permanent career structures. Those who remained were single-minded historians and researchers, determined to see the task through to its conclusion, even if to their personal disadvantage. This dedication, combined with the benefits which accrue when writers are no longer working against the clock, resulted in some of the finest printed records to emerge from any Commonwealth country after WWII. The quality of prose was not always inspired, but the factual content was beyond reproach and has withstood the test of time. One of their number, D O W Hall, who wrote several of the best 'episodes and studies', even found time to compile a record of the services of the New Zealand Contingents which had fought in the Anglo-Boer War of 1899-1902.

The following list names all the publications (less the 'episodes and studies' items) which have at various dates been published in New Zealand with support or sponsorship from official sources. Referring to the WWII series, with two exceptions the full sub-titles have been omitted. Further, because several authors were responsible for more than one book, their names are given priority here for the sake of condensation.

SOUTH AFRICAN WAR

The New Zealanders in South Africa, 1899-1902, by D O W Hall (1949)

FIRST WORLD WAR

The New Zealanders at Gallipoli, by Maj Fred Waite, DSO NZE (1919). Waite served as Divisional Staff Officer (Engineers).
The New Zealanders in France, by Col Hugh Stewart CMG DSO MC (1921). Stewart served with the NZ infantry in Gallipoli and on the Western Front.
The New Zealanders in Palestine, by Lieut Col Sir Guy Powles (1922). Powles served with the NZ Mounted Rifles in Gallipoli and Palestine. The material for this book was first prepared by Maj A Wilkie, Wellington Mounted Rifles.
The War Effort of New Zealand, by Lieut E H Drew (1923). Drew served with the Canterbury Infantry Regiment. The contents of this book include much of the information not mentioned in the first three volumes - the occupation of Samoa, the Senussi campaign, the work of HMS Philomel, NZ Army Nurses, NZ military hospitals, NZ hospital ships, NZ Dental Corps, NZ Veterinary Corps, etc.

The four titles listed at the foot of the preceding page are numbered as Volumes I to IV. A fifth volume, not numbered as such, was SOME RECORDS OF THE NEW ZEALAND EXPEDITIONARY FORCE. Published in 1928, it was compiled by Lieut Col J Studholme. It does not carry the formal 'official' accolade, but it is based upon official archives to which Studholme had free access. In practical terms, it can be regarded as Volume V in the series.

SECOND WORLD WAR

Anson, T V, NEW ZEALAND DENTAL SERVICES (1960)
Baker, J V T, WAR ECONOMY (1965)
Bates, P W, SUPPLY COMPANY (1960)
Borman, C A, DIVISIONAL SIGNALS (1954)
Burdon, R M, 24 BATTALION (1953)
Cody, J F, 21 BATTALION (1953), NEW ZEALAND ENGINEERS IN THE MIDDLE EAST (1961), and 28 (MAORI) BATTALION (1956)
Davin, D M, CRETE (1953)
Dawson, W D, 18 BATTALION AND ARMOURED REGIMENT (1961)
Gillespie, O A, THE PACIFIC (1952)
Henderson, J H, RMT - OFFICIAL HISTORY OF THE 4th AND 6th RESERVE MECHANICAL TRANSPORT COMPANIES (1954), and 22 BATTALION (1958)
Kay, R L, CHRONOLOGY OF NEW ZEALAND IN THE WAR, 1939-1946 (1968), 27 (MACHINE GUN) BATTALION (1958), and ITALY, VOLUME II, FROM CASSINO TO TRIESTE (1967).
Kidson, A L, PETROL COMPANY (1961)
Llewellyn, S P, JOURNEY TOWARDS CHRISTMAS - OFFICIAL HISTORY OF THE 1st AMMUNITION COMPANY, 2nd NZEF (1949)
Loughman, R J M, DIVISIONAL CAVALRY (1963)
McClymont, W G, TO GREECE (1959)
McKinney, J B, MEDICAL UNITS OF 2 NZEF IN THE MIDDLE EAST AND ITALY (1952)
Mason, W W, PRISONERS OF WAR (1954)
Murphy, W E, THE RELIEF OF TOBRUK (1961), and 2nd NEW ZEALAND DIVISIONAL ARTILLERY (1966)
Norton, F D, 26 BATTALION (1952)
Phillips, N C, ITALY, VOLUME I, SANGRO TO CASSINO (1957)
Pringle D J C and **Glue, W A,** 20 BATTALION AND ARMOURED REGIMENT (1957)
Puttick, Sir Edward, 25 BATTALION (1960)
Ross, A, 23 BATTALION (1959)
Ross, J M S, ROYAL NEW ZEALAND AIR FORCE (1955)
Scoullar, J L, BATTLE FOR EGYPT - THE SUMMER OF 1942 (1955)
Sinclair, D W, 19 BATTALION AND ARMOURED REGIMENT (1954)
Stevens, W G, PROBLEMS of 2 NZEF (1958), and BARDIA TO ENFIDAVILLE (1962)
Stout, T D M, NEW ZEALAND MEDICAL SERVICES IN NEW ZEALAND AND THE PACIFIC (1958), NEW ZEALAND MEDICAL SERVICES IN THE MIDDLE EAST AND ITALY (1956), and WAR SURGERY AND MEDICINE (1954)
Thompson, H L, NEW ZEALANDERS IN THE ROYAL AIR FORCE, VOLUME I (1953), VOLUME II (1956), and VOLUME III (1959)
Underhill, M L, with others, NEW ZEALAND CHAPLAINS IN THE SECOND WORLD WAR (1950)
Walker, R, ALAM HALFA AND ALAMEIN (1967)
Waters, S D, THE ROYAL NEW ZEALAND NAVY (1956)
Wood, F L W, THE NEW ZEALAND PEOPLE AT WAR - POLITICAL AND EXTERNAL AFFAIRS (1958)

Each former serviceman was given a free copy of the history of the unit with which he had served. Even though the balance of the stock was offered for sale at prices well below printing costs, inadequate marketing resulted in many copies remaining unsold for a long time. Today, all of these titles have become relatively rare and difficult to acquire, even in New Zealand.

NEW ZEALAND - ORDER OF PRECEDENCE OF CORPS
as authorised, 1990

Royal Regiment of New Zealand Artillery
Royal New Zealand Armoured Corps
Corps of Royal New Zealand Engineers
Royal New Zealand Corps of Signals
Royal New Zealand Infantry Regiment
New Zealand Army Air Corps
Royal New Zealand Corps of Transport
Royal New Zealand Army Medical Corps
Royal New Zealand Army Ordnance Corps
Royal New Zealand Electrical & Mechanical Engineers
Royal New Zealand Dental Corps
Royal New Zealand Chaplains' Department
New Zealand Army Pay Corps
New Zealand Army Legal Service
Corps of Royal New Zealand Military Police
Royal New Zealand Army Education Corps
New Zealand Army Physical Training Corps
New Zealand Women's Royal Army Corps

ORDER OF PRECEDENCE OF ARMOURED UNITS
Royal New Zealand Armoured Corps

Queen Alexandra's Squadron, RNZAC
Waikato/Wellington East Coast Squadron, RNZAC
1st Squadron, New Zealand Scottish, RNZAC
2nd Squadron, New Zealand Scottish, RNZAC

ORDER OF PRECEDENCE OF INFANTRY UNITS
Royal New Zealand Infantry Regiment

1st Battalion, RNZIR
2/1st Battalion, RNZIR
2nd Battalion (Canterbury and Nelson, Marlborough and West Coast), RNZIR
3rd Battalion [Auckland (Countess of Ranfurly's Own) and Northland], RNZIR
4th Battalion (Otago and Southland), RNZIR
5th Battalion (Wellington West Coast and Taranaki), RNZIR
6th Battalion (Hauraki), RNZIR
7th Battalion [Wellington (City of Wellington's Own) and Hawke's Bay], RNZIR

Units of the same Corps take precedence among themselves according to the dates of their formation. When a unit has been formed by the amalgamation of two or more units, it takes precedence according to the oldest of its component units.

The four Armoured Corps units listed above are elements of the Territorial Force. New Zealand does not have any Regular Army mechanised units.

Of the eight Infantry Battalions, only the first two - 1st Bn and 2/1st Bn - are Regular Army units. The six other Battalions are elements of the Territorial Force.

NEW ZEALAND
A Military Chronology

1769: Capt James Cook RN makes the first charts of the North and South Islands.
1827: the British Army's 57th Regiment lands at Kororareka.
1840: at Waitangi, British and Maori leaders sign a Treaty whereby the basis of European settlement on certain tracts of land is formalised. The first substantial British Army garrison is established at Auckland.
1843: disputes over the way in which the Waitangi Treaty is being observed lead to the outbreak of the First Maori War (1843-1847).
1845: the New Zealand Militia Act obliges all European males between 18 and 60 years of age to render military service when so ordered. In March, at Kororareka, Militia forces fight their first engagement.
1846: an Armed Constabulary is raised for civil law enforcement duties.
1855: the first full-time paid New Zealand Militia Infantry Battalion is formed at New Plymouth.
1858: a new Militia Act comes into force. The paid Militia is separated from the unpaid part-time Volunteers. In time, the latter will evolve into Rifle Volunteers (infantry) and Mounted Rifles (light cavalry).
1860: more disputes over land settlement mark the opening of the Second Maori War (1860-1872). The Taranaki Rifle Volunteers gain the battle honour 'Waireka', the first such distinction awarded to a New Zealand infantry unit.
1862: the Colonial Defence Act establishes the Defence Force Cavalry, a Regular force. It is disbanded five years later. Various short-lived Ranger units are raised to act as scouts for the British Army in the field.
1865: British Army units begin to leave the country.
1867: the Armed Constabulary Act replaces the Colonial Defence Act. The new Constabulary keeps the peace and does most of the fighting against the Maori.
1870: the last remaining British Army unit, the 18th Regiment, departs.
1872: the final battle of the Maori (Land) Wars is fought at Mangaone, in the North Island. The Volunteer movement is reorganised and passes through a long period of decline due to Government apathy and public indifference.
1886: the Armed Constabulary is divided into a purely police element and a Regular military element. The latter is entitled Permanent Militia. This separation marks the beginnings of the modern New Zealand Police and the New Zealand Army.
1897: the Permanent Militia is renamed the Permanent Force. Its main purpose is to maintain training and administrative cadres.
1899: the first Volunteer Contingent of Mounted Rifles embarks for service in South Africa. Nine more will follow later, gaining a fine reputation for bravery and discipline.
1902: the prefix 'Royal' is granted to the Artillery and Engineer branches of the Permanent Force.
1909: the Defence Act scraps the old part-time Militia and Volunteer system. It introduces compulsory part-time service in a new Territorial Force.
1911: the Royal Military College is opened at Duntroon, Australia. Cadets from New Zealand commence training there.
1914: German Samoa is seized by an ad hoc force of New Zealand troops. It is then decided to aid the British and Indian Armies in France. New Zealand does not have a standing army, ready for service overseas, so the Government orders that one shall be raised. Designated the New Zealand Expeditionary Force (NZEF), its ranks are filled with men from the Permanent Force and from the Territorial Force. The main body sails westward in convoy with a similar force from Australia (the AIF). Jointly they will be known as the Australian and New Zealand Army Corps (ANZAC). Lack of accommodation and training facilities in England, and the Turkish threat to Egypt, cause the ANZAC force to disembark, in December, in the latter country.
1915: in February, NZEF troops have their first encounter with Turkish forces on the Suez Canal. In April they land on Gallipoli and lose 2000 men in the first fortnight of fighting. By the time of the evacuation, in December, they have a casualty rate of 87.0%.

1916: the Military Conscription Act introduces conscription for Europeans for service overseas. The Maori are excluded from its terms, but many of them join as volunteers. In Egypt, the survivors from Gallipoli are reinforced and regrouped. The NZ Mounted Rifles Brigade joins an ANZAC Mounted Division for service in Sinai, Gaza and, ultimately, Palestine and Syria. The NZ Infantry Division moves to France where it suffers more appalling losses on the Western Front (particularly on the Somme in 1916, at Messines and Passchendaele in 1917, and again on the Somme in 1918). The Division gains a brilliant fighting reputation, at grievous cost for a new country with such a small population. By war's end, a total of 124,211 New Zealanders have served in uniform. Of these, 100,444 have gone overseas and 17,202 have died.

1921: the NZEF is officially disbanded. A national policy of retrenchment sharply reduces the strength of the Permanent Force.

1926: the total strength of the Permanent Force has shrivelled to 493 all ranks. The Territorial Force, in which service is still compulsory, has 21,218 all ranks.

1931: compulsory service in the Territorial Force, which has been in effect since 1909, is abandoned. Membership falls to 3644 all ranks.

1937: military aviation, until now administered by the Permanent Force, becomes the responsibility of the newly-formed Royal New Zealand Air Force. With war clouds gathering over Europe, the Government creates a Council of Defence.

1939: the country still has no Regular Army attested, trained and equipped for overseas service. The 2nd NZEF is formed from personnel of the Permanent Force and volunteers from the Territorial Force. The first echelon is 6600 officers and men. Advance elements embark for England and the Middle East.

1940: conscription of Europeans for full-time service at home and overseas is introduced again. As happened in 1916, the Maori are not subject to the Act, but many volunteer. The 28th (Maori) Battalion is formed. New Zealand troops are fighting in the first Libyan campaign, others are helping to guard England's 'invasion coast', and 8th Brigade lands at Suva, capital of Fiji.

1941: together with Australian and British troops from Egypt, New Zealand units land in Greece. After a fighting withdrawal, some return directly to Egypt while others move to Crete under General Bernard Freyberg VC. The Germans launch an aerial invasion of the island and there is bitter fighting lasting ten days. Some of the New Zealand survivors from the battle are evacuated to Egypt where they are reunited with those withdrawn directly from Greece. With reinforcements from home, 2nd NZ Division comes together for the first time as a complete formation.

1942: NZ Patrol, Long Range Desert Group, is formed. The 2nd Division moves to Syria for garrison duties. On its return to Egypt it is assigned to the war in the Western Desert and fights with outstanding determination at Ruweisat Ridge and in the second (October) battle at El Alamein. On the other side of the world, New Zealand forces on Fiji are expanded and designated 3rd NZ Division. Tonga, New Caledonia and Norfolk Island are garrisoned.

1943: 8th Army has triumphed at El Alamein and Rommel is withdrawing westward. 2nd NZ Division has made its famous 'left hook' at El Agheila, now it outflanks the Mareth Line and pushes into Tunisia. It returns to Egypt after the fall of Tunis in May. Five months later it moves to Italy for the fierce battles on the Sangro and at Orsogna. In the Pacific, elements of 3rd NZ Division arrive on Guadalcanal and the Treasury Islands.

1944: 3rd NZ Division is brought home from the Pacific Islands and disbanded in order to provide reinforcements for 2nd NZ Division in Italy, and to release manpower back into the economy.

1945: the Senio is crossed and 2nd NZ Division ends its war at Trieste.

1946: the 2nd NZEF is disbanded. A contingent of 4320 men, 'J' Force, joins the British Commonwealth Occupation Force (BCOF) in Japan and remains there until 1948.

1948: authorisation is given for a Permanent Force peacetime establishment of 333 officers and 2722 other ranks.

1949: after a national referendum, it is decided to reintroduce compulsory part-time training in the Territorial Force. Ten years later the scheme is again dropped.

1950: the New Zealand Army Act comes into effect. It replaces various earlier Acts and Regulations. The term 'the New Zealand Army' is introduced officially for the first time. A small Battle Group, 'K' Force, 1000 strong and built around the 16th Field Regiment RNZA, sails for Korea to join the 27th British Commonwealth Brigade under overall United Nations command.
1953: New Zealand officers and SNCOs are serving in Malaya with the Fiji Battalion.
1955: the New Zealand SAS Squadron is formed at Waiouru and commences operations in Malaya.
1957: 1st Bn New Zealand Regiment also moves to Malaya and replaces the NZ SAS. The remaining elements of 'K' Force return home from Korea. In Antarctica, military logistical personnel join New Zealand's research programme on that continent.
1962: yet another form of conscription is introduced, this time under the National Service Training Scheme. Each year, 3000 young men will be selected by ballot for part-time training, over three years,with the Territorial Force. This scheme also will be abandoned after ten years. Thereafter, all military service, in both the Regular and Territorial Forces, will be entirely voluntary.
1964: the first Contingent of New Zealand technical and instructional personnel, all volunteers, arrives in South Vietnam. Within a year, this commitment to assist American ground operations is augmented by combat troops.
1965: 1st Bn Royal New Zealand Infantry Regiment serves in Borneo during the Indonesian Confrontation. It returns for a second tour in the following year.
1971: a new Defence Act comes into force. The last remaining New Zealand combat troops serving in South Viet Nam are brought home (Army Training Team personnel follow them some months later).
1977: the Officer Cadet Training Company, first formed in Egypt in 1941, is located at Waiouru with the title Officer Cadet Training Unit (OCTU). In 1984, it will be upgraded to an Officer Cadet School.
1979: military personnel are sent to Southern Rhodesia/Zimbabwe to assist in supervising the handover to majority government (Operation Midford).
1982: New Zealand soldiers retrace their grandfathers' footsteps when they join the Multi-national and Observers Force in Sinai. Over the next decade, others will join United Nations missions to Lebanon, Israel, Iran, Namibia, Pakistan, Cambodia, Angola and Yugoslavia.
1984: the army is radically restructured to provide a 1200-man Ready Reaction Force backed by a Brigade Group containing both Regular and Territorial troops.
1989: the Ministry of Defence is divided into a policy-making MOD and an operational NZ Defence Force.
1990: New Zealand Army medical units join the Coalition Forces in the Arabian Gulf.

The majority of published New Zealand unit histories are recorded in the following pages. For additional information regarding New Zealand's role in certain specific wars and campaigns, reference should be made to other sections of this bibliography. Vide page 779, Index, 'New Zealanders abroad'.

GENERAL REFERENCE

There are several helpful general reference sources available for a study of New Zealand's military history, and some of them are noted below.

Researchers working on the New Zealand Contingents which served in the Anglo-Boer War of 1899-1902 should consult the 'South Africa' index of this bibliography.

New Zealand has a long tradition of part-time military service, at times voluntary, at others by conscription. For example, the ANNUAL RETURNS of 1905 show that there were 192 different Rifle Volunteers and Mounted Rifles Volunteers units in existence in that year. Some had a short life-span or had a very limited membership. A small population, scattered over two large islands which at that period had limited internal communications, made it difficult to organise and sustain a largely part-time military infrastructure. Few of the Volunteer units ever recorded their activities and services in formally published histories. However, a useful condensed summary of such units can be found in THE REGIMENTAL BADGES OF NEW ZEALAND, by D A Corbett (Pelorus Press, Remuera, Auckland, first published in the 1970s, reprinted in a slightly larger format in the 1980s). Although the work was compiled mainly as a reference source for collectors of military badges and insignia, it does have a wider application. It contains notes on individual units and Corps, on the Volunteer system (1845-1911), and on the Defence Act of 1911. Other useful sources are:

THE NEW ZEALAND ARMY
A Bibliography
Charles E Dornbusch * Hope Farm Press, Cornwallville, New York (USA), 1961. Facsimile TS, stiff card boards with cloth spine, blue, black, 9.0 x 6.0, -/116. Fp, 5 line drawings, no maps, no appendixes, Sources, Index.
* As noted elsewhere (vide the Index of Authors), Dornbusch was for many years Librarian at the New York Public Library. He had a special interest in the military history of the British Empire and was a pioneer in the field of unit history bibliography. His catalogue of New Zealand sources contains 400 entries. The majority refer, in fact, to items other than unit histories. However, it is a useful source for the specialist researcher because it mentions many items of ephemera which might otherwise be difficult to trace. R/4 V/3. PC. RP.
Note: apart from the version described above, Dornbusch produced a variant with soft card covers, sewn and glued. This also is dated 1961 and is in every other respect identical.

THE NEW ZEALAND ARMY
A History from the 1840s to the 1980s
Maj M R Wicksteed * P D Hasselberg, Government Printer, Wellington, 1982. Soft card, 'Perfect' bound, red, black, x/101. 103 mono phots, 7 maps, no appendixes, no Index.
* A superficial but useful overview of NZ military activity during the stated period. The illustrations are good, and will be unfamiliar to many readers in other countries. R/1 V/2. PC. HEC.

NEW ZEALANDERS AT WAR
Michael King * Heinneman Read, Auckland, 1988. Illustrated paperback, black, white, 11.0 x 8.5, viii/308. More than 400 mono phots, 68 line drawings, 7 maps, no appendixes, no Index.
* Although written for a general readership, this is 'the first and only book to compress into words and pictures the extent to which warfare has affected New Zealand life over two hundred years' (to quote the publisher). It is certainly a helpful background source. Lavishly illustrated, it covers everything from the

Maori (Land) Wars through to the South Vietnam commitment. An Index would have been helpful. R/1 V/3. SLV. PS.

FIFTY YEARS OF VOLUNTEERING
The Army of Regulations
Lieut Col H Slater VD * Whitcombe & Tombs, Wellington, 1910. Red, gold, 7.5 x 5.25, -/179. No ills, no maps, no appendixes, no Index.
* Although the author deals mainly with the story of all the Volunteer units which existed in and around Canterbury between 1859 and 1910, many of his observations and quotations relate to the Volunteer movement in New Zealand as a whole. He explains how the British Government first authorised the formation of Volunteer Rifle Corps in England in May 1859, and how the movement then spread quickly to the Dominions. Many of the units which he names and discusses are not recorded elsewhere (except in the New Zealand Gazettes and in occasional newspaper references). He also comments at useful length on the workings of the Militia Acts, the frequent changes of policy by the administration, and other matters of interest to more than one category of researcher.
R/4 V/4. NZMODL. HEC.

THE ARMY SCHOOLS, 1885-1985, CENTENNIAL JOURNAL
Anon * Government Printer, Wellington, 1985. Soft card, gold, black, Army Schools badge, 11.5 x 8.25, -/68. 31 mono phots, no maps, no Index. Apps: list of former officers and Chief Instructors.
* A very condensed account of the Army Schools of Instruction during the stated period. It is a less than satisfactory history because it ignores the Military Police School, the School of Military Engineering, the Royal New Zealand Army Ordnance School, and the Royal New Zealand Army Medical Corps School. More could have been made of this important subject. R/3 V/1. PC. HEC.

DIVISIONS

THE NEW ZEALAND DIVISION
A Popular History, Based on Official Records
Col H Stewart CMG DSO MC * Whitcombe & Tombs Ltd, Wellington, 1921. Brown, black, 'Koru pattern' embellishment, 8.75 x 6.25, xv/634. Fp, 142 mono phots, 22 maps (6 printed in the text, 16 bound in), Indexes. Apps: biographical notes on ten VC recipients (with portraits).
* A well produced solid history, printed on good quality paper. The narrative deals with the period from the formation of the Division in France (1916) through to disbandment (1919). For any student of New Zealand's role in WWI, this book is an essential source. The author covers all the larger events, many small scale engagements, and the work done by each component element within the Division. Some individual officers are mentioned by name, most of them in footnotes.
R/4 V/5. NZMODL. HEC.

MAORI MILITARY HISTORY

THE NEW ZEALAND WARS
A History of the Maori Campaign and the Pioneering Period
James Cowan * P D Hasselberg, Government Printer, Wellington, 1983. Pair of matching volumes, cypher on spine, red, gold, 9.0 x 5.5.
Volume I : 1845–1864. xxviii/466. Fp, 116 mono phots, 42 maps and plans, Index.
Volume II : THE HAUHAU WARS, 1864–1872. xx/633. Fp, 97 mono phots, 26 maps and plans, Index.
Apps: 20 various, incl a statistical summary of casualties (1845-1872), notes on the loss of HMS Orpheus, awards of the New Zealand Cross, list of engagements, supplementary notes on the narrative chapters.
* A classic comprehensive account of the several campaigns between the Maori and their enemies - the British Army and the local units raised under the New Zealand Militia Acts. The narrative is highly detailed, but always readable. It is based upon official records, private diaries, interviews with elderly survivors, and the author's personal visits to the ground over which many of the engagements were fought. Numerous individual participants - both Maori and European - are named and quoted. These two volumes are the recognised primary source for an understanding of all aspects of the Maori (Land) Wars. R/2 V/5. PC. HEC.
Note: the work was first published, with an inadequate Index, in 1922. It was republished, without amendment, in 1955. The third edition, as recorded above, was published with some amendments to the text and with a much improved Index in each volume. A valuable additional source, especially for genealogists, is THE DEFENDERS OF NEW ZEALAND ... MAORI HISTORY ... INCIDENTS OF THE WAR, by Thomas Gudgeon and Thomas McDonnell (published in Auckland in 1887). McDonnell covered the Maori view of the fighting while Gudgeon dealt with the European perspective. Of particular interest are the brief biographies of dozens of early European settlers (many accompanied by photographic portraits). An appendix lists winners of the New Zealand Cross.

AUSTRALIANS IN THE WAIKATO WAR, 1863–1864
Leonard L Barton * South Press, Marrickville, NSW, 1974. Dark red, gold, 8.75 x 5.5, -/119. 3 mono phots, 4 maps. Apps: nominal roll (Australians only) of the 1st, 2nd, 3rd, and 4th Waikato Regt (with details of service numbers, dates of enrolment and civilian trades), list of officers of the 3rd Waikato Regt who were awarded the New Zealand war medal for service with the Imperial Commissariat Transport Corps.
* A nicely researched account, of particular interest to medal collectors and genealogists. R/2 V/4. PC. PS.
Note: reference may be make also to FOR GLORY AND A FARM - THE STORY OF AUSTRALIA'S INVOLVEMENT IN THE NEW ZEALAND WARS OF 1860-1866, by Frank Glen (Whakatane & District Historical Society, NZ, 1984). This is a substantial work of 237 pages with a good Bibliography and Index.

THE MAORIS IN THE GREAT WAR
A History of the New Zealand Native Contingent and Pioneer Battalion - Gallipoli 1915, France and Flanders 1916–1918
James Cowan * Whitcombe & Tombs, Auckland, for the Maori Regtl Committee, 1926. Light brown, black, 'Te Hokowhitu a Tu' on front cover, 7.0 x 4.25, xii/180.
Fp, 52 mono phots, 8 maps (one printed in the text, 6 folding and bound in, one loose in rear pocket), Index. Apps: Roll of Honour, H&A, notes on the Maori recruiting song, notes on the services of Maori troops in the Gallipoli campaign.
* The Maori baptism into modern warfare was the landing at ANZAC Cove and the battle on Sari Bair. Following the evacuation, the survivors were sent to the Western Front where they took part in most of the major 'pushes' through to the end of the war. James Cowan had an affinity for the Maori and wrote warmly of their achievements as warriors. R/3 V/5. PC. HEC.
Note: see also 28th (Maori) Bn, 2nd NZEF, in the Index.

ARTILLERY

OFFICIAL HISTORY OF THE BAND OF THE ROYAL REGIMENT OF NEW ZEALAND ARTILLERY (NORTHERN MILITIA DISTRICT)
H F Batley * Auckland Artillery Band Association, 1964. Card, dark blue, gold, 8.75 x 5.5, -/164. 79 mono phots, no maps, no Index. Apps: list of former Directors of Music, idem Secretaries, idem Drum Majors.
* An attractive little book, particularly for those interested in military music. It was published in 1964 to mark the Band's centennary. R/2 V/2. PC. JS.

GUNNER'S STORY
A Short History of the Artillery Volunteers of Christchurch, 1867-1967
Guy C Bliss * Canterbury Artillery Officers' Mess, 1970. Illustrated stiff card, red, black, 9.25 x 7.0, -/80. 16 mono phots, no maps, no Index. Apps: Volunteer Regulations, 1840-1935.
* A review of Volunteer and Territorial Artillery units and their evolution in the Christchurch area during the stated period. The contents are of limited technical interest, but they are a worthwhile commentary upon the social history of the district and the evolution of the Volunteer movement in general. R/2 V/2. PC. JS.

'B' BATTERY, NEW ZEALAND FIELD ARTILLERY, 1863-1913
Anon * John McIndoe, Dunedin, 1913. Card, beige, red/black, 9.75 x 7.5, -/22. 13 mono phots, no maps, no Index. Apps: list of former officers, nominal roll (all ranks, 1913).
* A valuable little record of a Bty which is still in existence as a Territorial unit. The narrative is concerned mainly with events at the turn of the century. The photographs show good detail of uniforms and personal accoutrement.
R/5 V/3. PC. HEC.

NEW ZEALAND ARTILLERY IN THE FIELD
The History of the New Zealand Artillery, 1914-1918
Lieut J R Byrne NZFA * Whitcombe & Tombs Ltd, Wellington, 1922. Dark blue, gold, Regtl crest and red stripes, 8.5 x 5.75, xii/314. Fp, 30 mono phots, 10 maps, folding, bound in, one cld), no Index. Apps: H&A.
* This is a good attempt at describing a very large subject. The narrative lacks the finer details, but it is a sound broad description of New Zealand's gunners at work on Gallipoli and on the Western Front. R/3 V/3. NZMODL. HEC.
Note: seen with 'Errata' slip tipped in. 2000 copies printed.

WITH THE TRENCH MORTARS IN FRANCE
Capt W E L Napier MC * Alpe Brothers, Auckland, n.d. (c.1923). Stiff card, yellow/brown, black, 7.25 x 5.0, -/110. 25 mono phots, one line drawing, 3 diagrams, no maps, no appendixes, no Index.
* Mainly an autobiographical account, but it provides a useful explanation of the evolution of trench mortars and other equipment as used by New Zealanders on the Western Front. It covers the work of the 1st and 4th Light Trench Mortar Btys from 1916 to the end of the war. R/3 V/3. NYPL. JS/HEC.

2nd NEW ZEALAND DIVISIONAL ARTILLERY
W E Murphy * Historical Publications Branch, Department of Internal Affairs, Wellington, 1966. Red, gold, Regtl crest, 8.5 x 5.5, xx/796. Fp, 120 mono phots, one cld plate, 5 sketches, 88 maps (79 printed in the text, 9 bound in), Index. Apps: Roll of Honour (casualties listed by Regt), H&A (idem), verbatim Training Directive (dated 1.8.1943), statistical summary of casualties.
* An extremely detailed record of the Divisional Artillery Regts from the time of their formation in 1939-1940, through their services in Greece and Crete (1941) and North Africa (1941-1943), and finally in Italy (1943-1945). The maps are very clear and the photographs are well selected and printed. Many individuals are named throughout. Only the survivors of 4th and 5th Field Regts fought in the

battle for Crete (these two Regts having already lost some personnel in Greece). Of those who fought on Crete, no more than 30.0% succeeded in getting back to Egypt. In November 1941, during Operation Crusader (the action to relieve Tobruk), 6th Field Regt was overrun by German armour while giving support to the Infantry. Other NZ Artillery units had heavy losses during the same operation. Amongst those lost were the CRA (Commander Royal Artillery, of 2 NZ Div), and the COs of two Field Regts. At Mingar Qaim, in June 1942, losses were again heavy when part of 2 NZ Div was obliged to fight its way out of an encirclement. All of this, and the later actions in Tunisia and Italy, is described here with clarity and authority. R/3 V/5. RAI. AMM/RH.

THE DISTINGUISHED HISTORY OF 3rd FIELD REGIMENT, NEW ZEALAND ARTILLERY 1940–1990

Christine Rayward * Hilton Press, Christchurch, for the Education Section, Burnham Camp, 1990. Black, gold, 11.0 x 8.5, -/90. 48 mono phots, 4 line drawings (badges), no maps, no appendixes, no Index.

* A nicely produced book which gives a general overview of the Regt during the stated period. It has useful details of 'B' Bty and 'E' Bty, both of which had their origins in the Volunteer movement. A Territorial Force unit, the Regt is located at Burnham Camp, South Island. The illustrations are sharp and clear, but few of the people depicted are named in the captions. R/4 V/2. NLNZ. HEC.

FIFTY YEARS ON – A TIME TO REMEMBER
Historical Record of 14th New Zealand Anti-aircraft Regiment, 2nd New Zealand Divisional Artillery, 2 NZEF, Middle East Forces

Anon * The Regimental Association, Wellington, 1991. Stiff card, black, gold, Regtl crest, 11.0 x 8.0, vi/68. 3 mono phots, 3 maps (bound in), no Index. Apps: Roll of Honour, H&A.

* A useful short history which includes material not mentioned elsewhere. The 'economy' production format is photo-copied matrix print, and only barely adequate. The text is arranged in diary form and covers the period 1941-1945, with some mention of post-war events and the Regimental Association. R/3 V/3. NLNZ. HEC.

GUNS AGAINST TANKS
'L' Troop, 33 Battery, 7th New Zealand Anti-tank Regiment in Libya 23 November 1941

E H Smith * War History Branch, Wellington, 1948. Illustrated soft card, '2-pounder portee in action' motif, buff, black, 10.5 x 8.25, -/32. 24 mono phots, one map (printed on the end-papers), no Index. Apps: biographical notes on personnel mentioned in the text.

* This is an account of just one day's intense fighting in the desert. On the previous day, 22 November, the 5th South African Brigade had been overrun. The Germans tried to exploit their success by moving against the New Zealanders with a force of one hundred tanks. They were blocked by 'L' Troop with Field units in support. After several hours of combat, and having lost a quarter of their tanks, the Germans were beaten back. A readable narrative, with many individuals mentioned in the narrative. R/4 V/3. PC. HEC.

Note:

New Zealand gunners fought also in South Vietnam. For details, vide the Index of Authors – S D Newman.

MOUNTED AND MECHANISED

THE HISTORY OF THE CANTERBURY MOUNTED RIFLES, 1914-1919
Col C G Powles CMG DSO * Whitcombe & Tombs Ltd, Auckland, Christchurch, Dunedin and Wellington, 1928. Red, black, 'Kowhaiwhai' pattern around the title, 8.5 x 5.75, vii/267. 101 mono phots (incl badges worn by the three Sqns), 9 maps (2 printed in the text, 5 bound in, 2 printed on the end-papers), no Index. Apps: Roll of Honour, H&A, notes on thorough-bred horses, 'Regtl Diary - August 1914 to July 1919'.
* A well produced book printed on paper of good quality. The unit fought dismounted in the Gallipoli campaign and suffered horrendous losses. After the evacuation, the remnants were refitted in Egypt and then committed to the Sinai and Palestine campaigns (battles of Rafa, Romani and Gaza, and the advance to Jerusalem and Jericho). Throughout this time they fought in the mounted role for which they had previously trained. R/3 V/4. NYPL/NZMODL. HEC.

THE STORY OF TWO CAMPAIGNS
Official History of the Auckland Mounted Rifles, 1914-1919
Sgt C G Nichol * Wilson & Horton, Auckland, 1921. Red, black, 'Mounted rifleman' motif, 8.5 x 5.5, viii/265. 113 mono phots, one plate of line drawings of insignia, one cld ill, 4 maps (loose in rear pocket), Index. Apps: Roll of Honour, H&A.
* The narrative deals with the services of the AMR on Gallipoli and then in Sinai and Palestine (hence 'two campaigns'). The Regt was raised in August 1914 from three Territorial units (3rd Auckland Mounted Rifles, 4th Waikato Mounted Rifles, and 11th North Auckland Mounted Rifles). It finally returned to New Zealand for disbandment in 1919. R/4 V/4. NYPL. HEC/BCC.

KIWI TROOPER
The Story of Queen Alexandra's Own 2nd Wellington West Coast Mounted Rifles
Ted Andrews * Wanganui Chronicle Co Ltd, Wanganui, 1967. Yellow, 8.75 x 5.75, xiii/273. Fp, 33 mono phots, one map (bound in), no Index. Apps: four, but of limited local interest.
* The Regt was raised for service in the Maori (Land) Wars in 1860, and the narrative covers its history through to 1964. It provided drafts for all ten Contingents sent by New Zealand to fight in the South Africa war (1899-1902), but it then served as an integral unit in WWI (Gallipoli and Mesopotamia). In later years it converted to the mechanised role and became 1st Armoured Sqn, Royal NZ Armoured Corps. A most comprehensive account. R/2 V/4. PC. VS.

THE WAR HISTORY OF THE WELLINGTON MOUNTED RIFLES REGIMENT 1914-1919
Maj A H Wilkie * Whitcombe & Tombs Ltd, Auckland and Wellington, 1924. Buff, black, 3 Regtl crests, 8.25 x 5.5, xiv/259. 3 fps, 106 mono phots, one cld ill, 22 maps (bound in), no Index. Apps: Roll of Honour (KIA and WIA, Gallipoli and Palestine), H&A, list of COs.
* The Regt was established in 1911, but this book deals solely with its WWI services - Egypt, Gallipoli and Palestine (Gaza, Beersheba, Jerusalem, Jordan). The narrative is clear and informative, with plenty of detail and with many individuals mentioned by name (especially casualties). In a work of such quality, the lack of an Index is lamentable. R/3 V/4. NYPL. RP/HEC.

THE NEW ZEALAND CYCLIST CORPS IN THE GREAT WAR, 1914-1918
Anon ('By Officers of the Regiment') * Whitcombe & Tombs Ltd, Auckland, 1922. Brown, black, Corps crest, 8.75 x 5.75, -/139. Fp, 41 mono phots, one map, no Index. Apps: Roll of Honour, H&A, nominal roll (the original personnel of the Corps), notes on reinforcements.
* An interesting and complete account of this small Corps which never had more than 800 officers and men on its strength. Almost the entire narrative is devoted to their services in Egypt and on the Western Front. Detached from the NZEF, the

Corps was assigned to XXII Corps as Mounted Troops. In the event, they saw much hard service at Messines, Gravenstafel, Passchendaele, Kemmel, etc, in the infantry role and as cable layers. The appendixes are particularly helpful to genealogists and to medal collectors. R/4 V/4. NYPL/ATL. JS/HEC.

SECOND BATTALION, NEW ZEALAND SCOTTISH
Anon ('A Regimental Committee') * Printing Associates Ltd, Dunedin, for the ex-Members Association, 1981. Red, gold, Regtl crest, 8.75 x 6.0, xv/62. 157 mono phots, no maps, no Index. Apps: Roll of Honour, list of former COs, nominal rolls, notes on affiliated Regts, notes on the Scottish Volunteer units of Otago-Southland and Canterbury.
* The 'Battalion' prefix shown in the book's title may give the impression that this is an infantry history. The 2nd NZ Scottish did in fact start life, in 1939, as an infantry unit, but it was disbanded in 1942. The designation was then given an entirely new Territorial Force unit, raised in 1949 as an Armoured Reconnaissance Regt, and this publication refers to the post-1949 period. To assist the researcher unaware of the background, it has been recorded in this bibliography in both the 'Mounted & Mechanised' and 'Infantry' sections. The narrative - itself fluent and readable - covers events through to 1980 but is fairly superficial in content. R/2 V/3. NLNZ. JFS.
Note: 800 copies printed, of which 700 were bound as described above and 100 in a 'de luxe' binding.

2 NZEF

DIVISIONAL CAVALRY
R J M Loughman MBE * War History Branch, 1963. Red, gold, 8.75 x 5.75, xvi/446. Fp, 66 mono phots, 38 maps (31 printed in the text, 7 bound in, cld), Index. Apps: Roll of Honour, H&A, list of officers.
* Yet another volume in the official series, this one is written in exhilarating style and with a wealth of incidents and individuals mentioned in the narrative. Arranged in twenty-six chapters, it covers the Regt's departure for the Middle East with a strength of three fighting Squadrons (110 all ranks in each) and a HQ Sqn (140 all ranks). Equipped with Marmon-Herrington armoured cars, it fought in Greece before being evacuated to Crete. Losing all their vehicles there, the survivors were regrouped in Egypt and re-equipped with Bren Gun Carriers and Mark II tanks. They took part in the advance to Tripoli and beyond, fought in the Alam Halfa and El Alamein battles, and took part in the famous 'left hook' at El Agheila and the advance into Tunisia. Added to their inventory during this time were four Stuart (Honey) light tank originally the property of 4th Armoured Bde, captured and used by the Italians, and in turn recaptured from them. The Regt's final campaign was on mainland Italy where it operated in the reconnaissance role with Staghound armoured cars. The book has good descriptions of the River Sangro and Cassino battles, the pursuit to Florence, the forcing of the Rivers Savio and Adige, the advance to Padua, and then the final move to Trieste at war's end. Of added interest are the listings of officers and the appointments they were holding at the time of each of the unit's campaigns. A first class source, with excellent maps and well captioned illustrations. R/3 V/5. AWM. HEC/MCND'A.

ENGINEERS

OFFICIAL HISTORY OF THE NEW ZEALAND ENGINEERS DURING THE GREAT WAR 1914-1919

Maj Norman Annabell * Evans, Cobb & Sharpe Ltd, Wanganui, 1927. Chocolate brown, black, 8.5 x 5.5, viii/314. Fp, 30 mono phots, 9 maps (folding, in rear pocket), Index. Apps: Roll of Honour, H&A, list of officers.

* The narrative, which is sometimes hard to follow, covers the work of all NZ Field Coys, Field Troops, the Signal Troop, and the Wireless Troop. They served in Samoa (1914-1915), Egypt, Gallipoli, Sinai and Palestine (1916-1919), and Mesopotamia (1916-1918). This is not an attractive production, but the contents are accurate and informative. R/3 V/4. ATL/NLNZ. JS/HEC.

THE NEW ZEALAND TUNNELLING COMPANY, 1915-1919

James C Neill * Whitcombe & Tombs Ltd, Wellington, 1922. Chocolate brown, black, 8.5 x 5.5, iv/159. 31 mono phots, 6 diagrams, 4 maps (folding, bound in), no Index. Apps: Roll of Honour (KIA, DOW and WIA), H&A, nominal roll (all ranks).

* A readable narrative which describes the formation of the Company on 12.8.1915, its services on the Western Front, and its disbandment on 23.4.1919. The technical aspects are interesting, even to the non-specialist reader. The author explains the differences between the methods developed by the NZ Engineers and those of their British Army counterparts. The New Zealanders operated mainly in the chalk areas around Arras. They occupied some of the local natural caves which they extended until they were forty feet in height and several hundred feet across. The Company establishment was 19 officers and 500 ORs. Total awards gained were 4 DSOs, 4 MCs, 6 DCMs, 11 MMs, and 3 MSMs. R/3 V/5. NYPL/NLNZ. PS/HEC.

NEW ZEALAND ENGINEERS IN THE MIDDLE EAST

J F Cody * War History Branch, 1961. Red, gold, 8.75 x 5.75, xvi/774. Fp, 62 mono phots, 49 maps (42 printed in the text, 7 bound in), Index. Apps: Roll of Honour, H&A, list of OCs of all NZE units in the Middle East, Order of Battle.

* An excellent history, in the official series, of their WWII services in Greece, Crete, North Africa, and Italy, with a section devoted to the NZ Forestry Coys in the UK and elsewhere. Very readable, with a great many individuals named in the text (often with biographical notes for award winners). The appendixes include descriptions of the work of the NZ Army Postal Service and the Railway Survey Coys. The book is arranged in such a way that it is easy to find a particular unit or sub-unit and to then trace its movements. R/4 V/5. NLNZ. JFS/HEC/RH. Note: the original print run is reported to have been 5000 copies, but this was never enough to meet demand. Second-hand copies are now difficult to acquire. Other helpful sources are THE TURNING POINT - WITH THE NEW ZEALAND ENGINEERS AT EL ALAMEIN, by Lieut Col H Murray Reid (Collins, Auckland, 1944), and KALIMERA KIWI - TO OLYMPUS WITH THE NEW ZEALAND ENGINEERS, by Charles M Wheeler (A H & A W Reed, Wellington, n.d., c.1946).

14th FORESTRY COMPANY, 1940-1944, NEW ZEALAND ENGINEERS

Maj K O Tunnicliffe MBE * Published privately, Edgecumbe, no other details shown, 1990. Illustrated soft card, white, black, 11.75 x 8.25, circa 150 pages (folios not numbered), 31 mono phots (photo-copies, poor quality), no maps, no appendixes, no Index.

* Based upon the author's diary, this is the story of a Coy sent to Scotland in 1940 to operate saw-mills. In August 1943 it moved to Algiers and worked there during the next eighteen months. Its final move, for the closing months of the war, was to Italy. Many individuals are named in the text. As an unusual and otherwise unrecorded sapper unit, it deserved a better epitaph than this cheap and basically unattractive production. R/4 V/2. RNZECML. HEC.

SIGNALS

BY WIRES TO VICTORY
New Zealand Divisional Signals Company, 1914-1918
Roy F Ellis MM * Batley Printing Co Ltd, Auckland, 1968. Light blue, dark blue, 'Signaller reeling out cable' motif, 8.75 x 5.5, xiii/87. Fp, 5 mono phots, 3 line drawings, 2 maps (bound in), no Index. Apps: Roll of Honour (with much detail), H&A.
* A small book which covers the raising of the Company in 1914, its embarkation and services in Egypt/Sinai, and then its time on Gallipoli. The bulk of the narrative is devoted to its work on the Western Front (Armentieres, the Somme, Fleurbaix, Messines, Passchendaele, and Bapaume). The basic information was taken from the War Diary and then fleshed out with personal reminiscences and extracts from private diaries. A helpful record of an unusual early communications unit. R/3 V/4. NLNZ. HEC.

DIVISIONAL SIGNALS
C A Borman * War History Branch, 1954. Red, gold, 8.75 x 5.75, xvii/540. Fp, 66 mono phots, 18 maps (11 printed in the text, 7 bound in), Index. Apps: Roll of Honour, H&A, list of COs.
* The very readable narrative covers the NZ Signals involvement in all the Allied operations in the Middle East and Italy during WWII. This is a high quality production - another volume in the 2 NZEF series - with good detailed appendixes. Many officers and ORs are mentioned in the text, with numerous biographical footnotes. The author himself served with Div Signals for four years. In total, 398 of his comrades became casualties during the war - a third of them during the heavy summer fighting of 1942 (El Ruweisat Ridge, the El Mreir Depression, etc). R/3 V/5. NLNZ. HEC/RH.

Notes:

1. In WWI, a NZ Wireless Signal Squadron operated with Dunsterforce in Mesopotamia, South Russia, and Kurdistan. Vide the Index of Authors for Keast Burke. He wrote WITH HORSE AND MORSE IN MESOPOTAMIA, a book which also contains information on Australian signallers.

2. Reference should be made also to OFFICIAL HISTORY OF THE NEW ZEALAND ENGINEERS DURING THE GREAT WAR, 1914-1919, by Maj Norman Annabell (vide preceding page).

INFANTRY

MILITARY HISTORY OF WAVERLEY, 1866–1886
Maj C L Lovegrove * Patea Historical Society, Patea, 1969. Card, orange, black, 10.5 x 8.25, -/42. No ills, no maps, no Index. Apps: list of officers.
* A cyclo-styled production, with a poor presentation but useful contents. The narrative covers the later periods of the Maori (Land) Wars, including the affairs at Waitotara, Taurangaika Pa, Nukumara and Opotiki. Its main value is found in the references to units which later formed the Taranaki Regt (these being the Taranaki Military Settlers, the Patea Militia, the Wairoa Rifle Volunteers, and the Waverley Rifle Volunteers). There is mention also of the Wairoa Light Horse which later became a Squadron of Queen Alexandra's Mounted Rifles.
R/3 V/3. NLNZ. HEC.

CALL THE ROLL
The Unofficial History of the 11th Company of the National Military Reserve (Wanganui)
Anon ('Sandy', nom de plume of David G Strachan) * Wanganui Chronicle Print, Wanganui, 1946. Stiff card, maroon, gold, 8.75 x 5.75, viii/96. Fp, 2 mono phots, one line drawing, no maps, no appendixes, no Index. Apps: list of original officers and NCOs.
* The author uses a journalistic style to describe the activities of a local Volunteer unit during 1940–1942. It fulfilled home defence duties and provided trained men to reinforce the already mobilised Territorial Force. He provides some useful dates and statistics, with items of poetry woven in for good measure. The book is interesting mainly as a mirror of Wanganui society and its responses to wartime pressures. R/4 V/3. ATL. FC.

OFFICIAL HISTORY OF THE NEW ZEALAND RIFLE BRIGADE (THE EARL OF LIVERPOOL'S OWN)
Covering the Period of Service with the NZEF in the Great War from 1915 to 1919
Lieut Col W S Austin DSO * L T Watkins Ltd, Wellington, 1924. Olive green, black, Regtl crest, 8.5 x 5.5, xx/587. Fp, 97 mono phots, 11 maps (folding, bound in at the rear), Index. Apps: Roll of Honour, H&A, notes on the Training Bn, Dress Regulations, notes on Dunsterforce, diary of events, Orders of Battle (eleven).
* Despite its title, this Regt had no affiliation with the Rifle Brigade of the British Army. It was raised specifically for WWI service and its four Bns served in Egypt, the Senussi campaign, on the Western Front (the Somme, Messines, Ypres, Havrincourt, Cambrai and Le Quesnoy). The period covered is 1915–1919. In that time, the Regt gained 2 VCs, 2 CBs, 3 CGMs, 18 DSOs, 1 OBE, 2 MBEs, 93 MCs, 75 DCMs, 310 MMs, and 41 foreign awards. A well printed and handsomely bound book, one of the finest of all New Zealand unit histories.
R/3 V/5. NLNZ. PS/HEC.

SECOND BATTALION, NEW ZEALAND SCOTTISH
Anon ('A Regimental Committee') * Printing Associates Ltd, Dunedin, for the ex-Members Association, 1981. Red, gold, Regtl crest, 8.75 x 6.0, xv/62. 157 mono phots, no maps, no Index. Apps: Roll of Honour, list of former COs, nominal rolls, notes on affiliated Regts, notes on the Scottish Volunteer units of Otago-Southland and Canterbury.
* A pleasantly presented book, nicely printed and bound, but with a fairly sketchy and not very well written narrative. It covers the period from the foundation of the Regt shortly after WWII through to 1980. R/2 V/3. NLNZ. JFS.
Note: 800 copies printed (700 as above, 100 in 'de luxe' bindings). First raised as an infantry unit in 1939, the Bn was disbanded in 1942 and the title fell into disuse until 1949. It was then given to a new Territorial Force Armoured Reconnaissance Regt. This book refers almost entirely to the second period, but it is noted here (and also in the 'Mounted & Mechanised' section) for clarification.

FORWARD TOGETHER
A Short History of the Canterbury Regiment, The Nelson, Marlborough and West Coast Regiment, and the Second Battalion (Canterbury, Nelson, Marlborough, West Coast) Royal New Zealand Infantry Regiment, Short Title, 2 RNZIR, 1845-1970
Col E G Latter MBE * Produced by the Regt, Christchurch, 1970. Soft card, rifle green, white, 3 Regtl badges, 9.25 x 7.25, vi/96. 30 mono phots, no maps, no Index. Apps: list of officers (1946-1970, with dates and Bn appointments), list of historical relics.
* The narrative traces the beginnings of the NZ Army and Volunteer Corps from the Militia Act of 1858. There is useful detail regarding the many Coys raised and disbanded, Gazette authority dates, names of officers who served, etc, all in relation to the period 1865-1910. Active services in South Africa, WWI and WWII are covered adequately, with the VC citations for Sgt A C Hulme, Sgt J D Hinton, and Capt C H Upham. R/2 V/3. AWM. MCND'A.

MARCHING ONWARD
The History of the 2nd Battalion (Canterbury, Nelson, Marlborough, West Coast) Royal New Zealand Infantry Regiment
Brig Edward Latter MBE ED * Published by the Regt, Christchurch, 1992. Olive green, gold, 12.0 x 8.5, -/336. 425 mono phots, 7 cld ills (the Colours), one map, Bibliography, no Index. Apps: H&A (Efficiency Decorations and Efficiency Medals), list of former COs (1923-1992), idem Honorary Colonels, idem RSMs (1949-1992), idem Senior Weapons Instructors.
* A very fine modern assessment of the Battalion and its forebear units over the period 1845-1992. In his first book - vide preceding entry - the author took the story through to 1970 but, as that was a fairly slim volume, the coverage had no great depth to it. This is a much more substantial work. Not only does it bring the record forward by two more decades, it also has greatly improved coverage of all the earlier periods (with a complete chapter devoted to each significant series of events). Of the twenty-three chapters, five are given to matters which might otherwise have appeared in appendixes - the Band, the Colours and Battle Honours, Allied Regts, Dress Distinctions and Customs, and the Regtl Association. Nicely produced, heavily illustrated. R/1 V/4. NZMODL. HEC.

THE HISTORY OF THE CANTERBURY REGIMENT, NZEF, 1914-1919
Capt David Ferguson MC * Whitcombe & Tombs Ltd, Wellington, 1921. Reddish brown, black, red/blue stripes, 9.0 x 6.0, vii/364. Fp, 42 mono phots (all of personnel), 25 maps (one printed in the text, 24 bound in), no Index. Apps: Roll of Honour (incl two men shot for desertion), notes on officers' services, locations of the Canterbury Bns from April 1918 to the Armistice.
* An admirable history spoiled by the lack of an Index. It describes the formation, training, and active services, of the Regt's four Bns in Egypt, Gallipoli, France and Flanders (where Sgt H J Nicholas MM, of the 1st Bn, gained the VC at Polderhoek in 1917). In the later stages of the war, the 4th Bn became a reserve for the other three, and some personnel were transferred to the NZ Machine Gun Corps in which they formed the Canterbury Sections. The book contains especially good accounts of the Regt's battles on the Somme, at Messines, Passchendaele, Polygon Wood, Bapaume, Cambrai, and the assaults on the Hindenburg Line, all written in a clear and interesting style. R/4 V/4. NZMODL. HEC.

TALES OF THREE CAMPAIGNS
12th (Nelson) Company NZEF
Maj C B Brereton * Selwyn & Blount Ltd, London, 1926. Dark blue, gold, 8.75 x 6.0, ix/290. Fp, 8 mono phots, one line drawing, no maps, no appendixes, no Index.
* The Coy was part of the Canterbury Regt, but it retained its local title and character throughout WWI. It embarked in October 1914, served in Egypt and Sinai, fought in the Gallipoli battles (ANZAC Cove, Helles, and Krithia), and then went to the Western Front (Etaples, Armentieres, the Somme). The author commanded

the Company. He writes with deep feeling for Nelson, for his men, and for the cause which they sought to uphold. The book is not a blow-by-blow detailed record, but it does provide an evocative mirror of those times and events.
R/4 V/3. NZMODL. HEC.

THE AUCKLAND REGIMENT, 1914-1918
Being an Account of the Doings on Active Service of the First, Second and Third Battalions of the Auckland Regiment
Lieut O E Burton MM * Whitcombe & Tombs Ltd, Auckland, 1922. Olive green, black, 8.75 x 5.5, xiv/323. 12 mono phots, 14 maps (folding, bound in), no Index. Apps: Roll of Honour, H&A, Chronology of Events, notes on unit badges.
* A good general history, well-written and readable. Many individuals are named in the text, hence the lack of an Index is more than usually frustrating for the researcher. The quality of the paper also is a disappointment. The author, awarded the Military Medal for his WWI services with the Regt, subsequently became a cleric. In WWII he was imprisoned as a conscientious objector.
R/3 V/4. NZMODL. BCC/HEC.

2/AUCKLAND
Being a Partial Record of the War Service in France of the 2/Auckland Regiment during the Great War
Lieut Col S S Allen CMG DSO * Whitcombe & Tombs Ltd, Wellington, 1920. Buff, black, Regtl crest, 7.5 x 5.0, -/188. No ills, one map (bound in), no Index. Apps: Roll of Honour (KIA, DOW and MIA, all ranks).
* The unit was composed of drafts from various Territorial Bns amalgamated for service during the closing stages of the war. The narrative, therefore, covers only the last few months - the breakthrough and the final advance. A modest book, printed on paper of poor quality. R/3 V/2. NZMODL. HEC.

POUR DEVOIR
A History of the Northland Regiment and its Forebears
Harry Field * Unity Press, Auckland, 1960. Dark blue, black, 8.5 x 5.5, -/122. Fp, 20 mono phots, no maps, no Index. Apps: Battle Honours (WWII), list of former COs and other officers, unit nominal roll (at embarkation, 14.9.1914), notes on the affiliation with the Northamptonshire Regt.
* This Regt also has its roots in the Auckland area. The book is a lightweight but interesting account of the Regt from 1879 to 1911 ('the forebears'), and then from 1911 to 1960. All of the main events are covered, and the illustrations are helpful and well reproduced. Sadly, the author did not provide either an Index or a Table of Contents. Much more could have been made of the subject matter.
R/4 V/3. NZMODL. HEC.

OFFICIAL HISTORY OF THE OTAGO REGIMENT, NEW ZEALAND EXPEDITIONARY FORCE, IN THE GREAT WAR, 1914-1918
Lieut A E Byrne MC * J Wilkie & Co Ltd, Dunedin, 1921. Mauve, gold, 8.75 x 6.0, xvi/407. Fp, 55 mono phots, 11 maps (bound in), no Index. Apps: H&A, notes on the Reserve Bn.
* The story covers all of the Regt's WWI services in Egypt, Gallipoli, France and Flanders, with many small actions described in interesting detail. The author was one of the Regt's officers and his account is said to be very accurate. A famous member of the Regt was Sgt Dick Travis VC DCM MM. A good quality production.
R/3 V/4. NYPL. CSM/JFS.
Note: reprinted without amendment in 1922.

GALLIPOLI TO THE SOMME
Recollections of a New Zealand Infantryman
Alexander Aitken * Oxford University Press, London and Wellington, 1963. Deep pink, gold/black, 8.5 x 5.5, xi/177. No ills, one map (folding, bound in), no appendixes, no Index.

* A personal account by the author of his service with the Otago Bn from August 1915 to September 1916 (when he was severely wounded). The period encompasses the Bn's activities in Egypt, on Lemnos and Gallipoli, and then the defence of the Suez Canal, but the bulk of the narrative is devoted to the Western Front (Hazebrouk, Armentieres, Delville Wood, and Goose Alley). Fluently and helpfully written, and easy to follow. R/2 V/2. ANL. MCND'A.

THE WELLINGTON REGIMENT, NZEF, 1914-1919
W H Cunningham DSO, C A L Treadwell OBE, and J S Hanna * Ferguson & Osborne Ltd, Wellington, 1928. Brown, gold, 8.75 x 6.0, xii/399. Fp, 38 mono phots, 2 maps (folding, bound in), one fold-out page showing NZEF strengths at various dates, no Index. Apps: Roll of Honour, H&A, list of locations through which 1st and 2nd Bns of the Wellington Regt passed 'on the march from Beauvois to the German frontier'.
* A nicely produced book, well bound, printed on better-than-average paper for that period. The narrative is clear and informative. A substantial work, it is said to be one of the best unit histories not to have been sponsored by the New Zealand Government. R/3 V/4. NYPL. AGY/HEC.

SUNDAY SOLDIERS
A Brief History of the Wellington Regiment, City of Wellington's Own
Peter A Lea * Wellington Regt and 7 RNZIR Association, 1982. Beige, gold, 8.75 x 5.75, x/194. Fp, 23 mono phots, 2 cld ills, 2 sketches, no maps, Bibliography, no Index. Apps: notes on the RSM's cane, notes on the York & Lancaster Regt and the Wellington Plate, notes on a rifleman's experiences, etc.
* Written in informal style, and relying heavily upon anecdotes and reminiscences by and about former members. Readable, entertaining, and informative, but lacking the structure and cohesion expected in a conventional unit history.
R/1 V/3. NZMODL. JS/HEC.

THE TARANAKI RIFLE VOLUNTEERS
A Corps with a History, Being a Chronicle ... from 1859 to 1909
W J Penn * Thomas Avery, New Plymouth, 1909. Red, black, 8.5 x 5.5, vii/39. Fp, 11 mono phots, one cld ill, 3 maps, no Index. Apps: Roll of Honour, Capt Mace's account of Waireka, nominal roll of all ranks who served in South Africa.
* Although very brief, this is a pleasing early Volunteer history. The Roll of Honour is not a list of casualties but is instead a roll of recipients of the New Zealand War Medal. R/5 V/3. NYPL. HEC.

PRIMUS IN ARMIS
Journal of the Taranaki Regiment
Anon * Taranaki Daily News, New Plymouth, 1936. Soft card, red, black, Regtl crest, 10.75 x 8.5, -/94. 24 mono phots, one cld plate (the Colours), 6 other ills, no maps, no appendixes, no Index.
* A useful little book, published mainly to mark the presentation of new Colours, but containing a great deal of information helpful to the researcher. There is a short section recounting the Gallipoli experiences of the Taranaki Coy of the Wellington Regt, and various notes regarding members of the Regt serving during the 1930s period. In other words, much of the detail which might have appeared in appendixes is instead woven into the narrative. R/3 V/4. NZMODL. HEC.

WEEKEND WARRIORS
A Brief History of the Hawke's Bay Regiment
Peter A Lea * King Times Press, Hong Kong, 1991. Bronze, green, gold, 8.5 x 5.5, xii/186. 13 mono phots, no maps, Bibliography, no Index. Apps: citations for three VCs (Cpl L W Andrew, Sgt K Elliott, and Sgt J G Grant), rolls of recipients of the various Long Service awards, notes on Dress.
* A pleasant narrative covering 100 years of volunteer soldiering. Men from the Hawke's Bay area fought in the Maori (Land) Wars, in South Africa, in WWI (Gallipoli and the Western Front), and in WWII (the Mediterranean campaigns),

often as elements of the Wellington Regt. The story is based mainly upon newspaper files and personal interviews. There are some inconsistencies, and the lack of an Index further reduces the authority of the book, but it is a generally useful source of secondary reference. R/1 V/2. PC. HEC.

MACHINE-GUN UNITS

WITH THE MACHINE-GUNNERS IN FRANCE AND PALESTINE
The Official History of the New Zealand Machine-gun Corps in the Great World War, 1914-1918
Maj J H Luxford * Whitcombe & Tombs Ltd, Auckland, 1923. Red, black, Corps crest, 8.75 x 5.5, -/255. Fp, 51 mono phots (indexed), 9 maps, no Index. Apps: Roll of Honour (with dates and locations of burials), H&A (mostly with citations).
* The book is arranged in two parts. The first deals with 1st, 2nd, and 3rd Coys, from April 1916 when they left Egypt and subsequently fought in the battles of the Somme, the 1917 battles in Flanders, and the great offensives of 1918. The second part deals with the actions of the NZ Machine-gun Squadron in the NZ Mounted Bde in the Middle East from 1916 onwards. These were Romani and El Arish in 1916, Gaza and the advance to Jerusalem in 1917, and the final advance into Syria in 1918. A good detailed account of machine-gunner services in both theatres of WWI, with useful illustrations. R/3 V/4. AWM. MCND'A.
Note: vide Index for reference to 27 (MG) Bn of the 2nd NZEF.

2 NZEF - 1939-1945

The following entries relate to books of the category described in the introduction to the New Zealand section of this bibliography. All are very detailed, both as unit histories and as campaign histories. They are amongst the very best such Empire and Commonwealth records to be published after WWII. As a series, they serve as a history of the entire New Zealand military effort in the Mediterranean theatre of war.

In that theatre, the New Zealand Infantry Battalions were almost destroyed on a number of occasions. Their worst losses were suffered in the battles for Greece and Crete (April-May, 1941), the operation to raise the siege of Tobruk (Operation Crusader, November-December 1941), the defence of Egypt (El Ruweisat Ridge and El Mreir, July 1942), the Second Alamein battle (October-November 1942), and the long-running assault on Monte Cassino (January-May, 1944).

By the chances of war, not all Battalions took part in all of these operations. The 6th Brigade missed the Crete affair, having been evacuated directly from Greece to Egypt. The 4th Brigade was effectively destroyed at El Ruweisat and El Mreir, and withdrawn to rebuild and to convert to the armoured role (so missing Second Alamein and the pursuit to Tunisia). Monte Cassino involved the entire New Zealand Corps, incurring heavy losses, and the rest of the Italian campaign was a steady infantry slogging match which imposed a steady daily drain on effective manpower. The impact of these losses was even worse than the statistics might suggest because, after the disasters of 1941, the New Zealanders (like the Australians) adopted the 'left out of battle' (LOB) policy. Each unit left a nucleus of officers and men in the rear areas before going into action so that, in the event of heavy losses, that nucleus could be reinforced and expanded back to battleworthy size. From 1942, complete Companies were LOB. Therefore, the casualty statistics for the period after November 1941 are even worse than they might appear since the Battalions were not committed to battle in their entirety.

18 BATTALION AND ARMOURED REGIMENT
W D Dawson * War History Branch, 1961, xvi/676. Fp, 64 mono phots, 39 maps (32 printed in the text, 7 bound in), Index. Apps: Roll of Honour, H&A, list of COs.
* Initially deployed as infantry, 18 Bn fought in Greece and Crete, and suffered 67.0% casualties (KIA, WIA and POW). The survivors were evacuated to Egypt where they were reinforced and then committed to Operation Crusader. Losing a quarter of their men in the process, they broke through and joined the Tobruk garrison. After moving to Syria in early 1942 to refit and rebuild, the Bn returned to the Desert in time to help block Rommel's advance into Egypt at First Alamein. It was mauled in the fiascos at El Ruweisat and El Mreir, but remained in the Desert until September 1942 when it was pulled back into Egypt to become an armoured Regiment (hence the title of this book). By then, it had lost another 50.0% of its personnel. It moved to Italy, as part of 2 NZ Div, in November 1943 and remained there throughout the war. R/3 V/5. NZMODL. JFS/HEC/RH.

19 BATTALION AND ARMOURED REGIMENT
D W Sinclair * War History Branch, 1954, xvi/559. Fp, 70 mono phots, 30 maps (24 printed in the text, 6 bound in), Index. Apps: Roll of Honour, H&A, list of COs, notes on 'Lame Duck' (No 13 tank of 11 Troop, 'C' Squadron).
* The author served with the Bn from formation to July 1941 when he was invalided. His account is extremely detailed, with lists of officers inserted at many key points in the narrative. The Bn lost 23.0% of its strength in Greece, then 55.0% in Crete. After rest and reinforcement in Egypt, it had only thirty casualties during Operation Crusader but was then practically destroyed by German panzers on 15 July 1942 (the El Ruweisat Ridge disaster). Like the two other Bns in the 4th NZ Bde (18 and 20), it was pulled back to Egypt to refit and to retrain as an armoured Regiment. Until this time, each Company had carried a pre-war Territorial

title (Wellington, Wellington West Coast, Hawke's Bay, Taranaki), but they were redesignated 'A' Sqn, 'B' Sqn, etc, in conformity with Cavalry practice. Most of the men were posted away - to other (infantry) units - and replaced by trained drivers and gunners. The balance of the narrative covers the work of the re-titled 19 Armoured Regt in Italy. It played a prominent role in the Cassino battles, but Italy's poor tank country meant that the Regt was frequently dispersed and its tanks assigned to give close support to infantry units. R/3 V/5. NZMODL. HEC/RH.

20 BATTALION AND ARMOURED REGIMENT
D J C Pringle and W A Glue * War History Branch, 1957. -/631. Fp, 67 mono phots, 41 maps (34 printed in the text, 7 bound in), Index. Apps: Roll of Honour, H&A, list of COs.
* A well written account by two former members of the Bn. In Greece and Crete, it lost 149 and 297 men respectively. One of the Bn's officers was Charles Upham. In May 1941, in Crete, he won the Victoria Cross. In July 1942, on El Ruweisat Ridge, he won a bar to that award and thereby became one of only three men ever to be awarded the VC twice. As an infantry unit, 20 Bn was virtually destroyed on two occasions in the Western Desert - at Belhamed during Operation Crusader, and again at El Ruweisat Ridge. The latter battle was lost because the promised British armour and anti-tank support did not follow up the successful New Zealand night attack. The exposed infantrymen were almost defenceless when counter-attacked by German panzers. The fiasco led to the decision that the NZ infantry would in future have its own supporting armour. Like 18 Bn and 19 Bn, 20 Bn was withdrawn to Egypt and reorganised as a tank Regt. It fought as such in the Italian campaign with 2 NZ Div, seeing much action in the Cassino battles (February-May, 1944). The Bn's first CO was Howard Kippenberger, later elevated to Bde Commander, and then Deputy to Freyberg. R/3 V/5. NZMODL. JFS/HEC/RH.

21 BATTALION
J F Cody * War History Branch, 1953, xv/471. Fp, 64 mono phots, 22 maps (16 printed in the text, 6 bound in), Index. Apps: Roll of Honour, H&A, list of COs.
* Sent to England in the Spring of 1940, the Bn formed part of the anti-invasion force before joining 2 NZ Div in Egypt in March 1941. In the debacle in Greece, where it was much broken up, it lost 275 officers and men (most of them as POW). Some of the survivors were evacuated directly back to Egypt, others were shipped to Crete (where more than half were killed or captured). After refitting, the Bn took part in Operation Crusader and was heavily engaged in the fighting around Sidi Rezegh (losing the CO, all Coy Commanders, and 373 all ranks). Losses were much lighter in the El Ruweisat battle, and the Bn was able to take a full part in Second Alamein and the pursuit to Tunisia. Apart from having had the distinction of capturing General von Ravenstein in the Western Desert (29.11.1941), it could later claim, in Italy, to have captured 6000 German soldiers, several E-boats, a landing ship, a hospital ship, and nearly twenty other vessels. As with other books in the series, the supporting maps (some of which are multi-coloured) are well executed and very helpful. R/3 V/5. NZMODL. HEC/RH.

22 BATTALION
J H Henderson * War History Branch, 1958, xvi/487. Fp, 63 mono phots, 26 maps (19 printed in the text, 7 bound in), Index. Apps: Roll of Honour, H&A, list of COs.
* Jim Henderson, author of this book, is well known for his historical accuracy and easy style of writing. This is another excellent account of a New Zealand Bn at war in the Middle East and Italy. The Bn escaped from Greece with few casualties and landed on Crete with a strength of over 600 all ranks. It was given the task of defending Maleme airfield. This soon became the focus of the German airborne invasion, and the Bn lost 50.0% of its personnel in the subsequent fighting (62 KIA, 65 WIA, 175 POW). Those who managed to reach Egypt were reinforced and sent into the El Ruweisat battle where the Bn was almost wiped out. Rebuilt yet again, it fought in Second Alamein, on the long march to Tunisia, and in the Italian

campaign (as a motorised infantry unit with 4th Armoured Bde). This Bn also could claim a VC holder in its ranks - Sgt Keith Elliott. On El Ruweisat Ridge, although wounded, he captured 130 Germans after leading his much depleted Platoon in a bayonet charge. Many other individuals are mentioned in the narrative, often with biographical notes. R/3 V/5. NZMODL. JFS/HEC/RH.
Note: at the end of the war, 22 Bn was reorganised and served with the British Commonwealth Occupation Force in Japan (March 1946 to August 1947). It became an element of the Permanent Force (later Regular Army) as 2nd New Zealand Regt.

23 BATTALION
Angus Ross MC and bar ED * War History Branch, 1959, xvi/506. Fp, 66 mono phots, 37 maps (30 printed in the text, 7 bound in), Index. Apps: Roll of Honour, H&A, list of COs.
* The excellent narrative covers the entire WWII period, from arrival in Egypt through to the end of the war in Northern Italy. Very readable, with many individuals mentioned by name. The author served with the Bn from the beginning to the end, first as a Platoon Commander, then as Adjutant, finally as a Company Commander. R/3 V/5. NZMODL. JFS.

24 BATTALION
R M Burdon * War History Branch, 1953, xv/361. Fp, 62 mono phots, 31 maps (26 printed in the text, 5 folding, bound in), Index. Apps: Roll of Honour, H&A, list of COs.
* The Bn was in Greece as an element of 6th NZ Bde, but it came away with relatively light losses and was evacuated directly to Egypt. Its first serious set-back was the action at Sidi Rezegh on 30 November 1941 when it was overrun by German armour. Withdrawn to Syria with the rest of 2 NZ Div, it refitted and then returned to the Desert at speed to plug the gaps when Rommel made his last desperate push for Egypt in June 1942. The Bn was one of those caught up in the shambles at the El Mreir Depression when initial successes by the infantry were not supported by the British armour. Having 'left out of battle' one its Companies, the Bn had committed 440 officers and men to the attack. Of these, 280 were killed, wounded, or taken prisoner. After being reinforced in Egypt, the Bn took part in the Second Alamein battle (losing 111 all ranks), and then in the pursuit to Tunisia. Its next big battle was Cassino. After fighting steadily up the Italian peninsula to war's end, the Bn remained as part of the occupying force until disbanded in December 1946. A fine history. R/3 V/5. NZMODL. PS/JFS/HEC/RH.

THE TWENTY-FOURTH NEW ZEALAND INFANTRY BATTALION
A Pictorial History
F L Phillips and H R Gilmour * Richards Publishing, Auckland, 1980. Russet, gold, 11.5 x 8.5, iv/383. Many mono phots, 16 maps, no appendixes, no Index.
* This book does not form part of the Official History series, but it is noted here for the sake of continuity. The text is fairly limited, being facsimile typescript and very condensed. There are between one and six photographic illustrations on each of the 370 main pages, and they give an added and helpful dimension to the story as told by Burdon (vide preceding entry). R/1 V/4. PC. HEC.

25 BATTALION
Lieut Gen Sir Edward Puttick KCB DSO and bar MC (Greece) Legion of Merit (USA) * War History Branch, 1960, xvi/654. Fp, 65 mono phots, 43 maps (37 printed in the text, 6 bound in), Index. Apps: Roll of Honour, H&A, list of COs.
* The author was a veteran of WWI. He commanded 4th NZ Bde in Greece and he temporarily commanded 2 NZ Div on Crete before returning home to become Chief of Staff. This is his very comprehensive history of another of those NZ Infantry Bns which were sent to Greece, were then evacuated directly to Egypt, and

which were severely mauled at Sidi Rezegh during Operation Crusader (the attempt to relieve the garrison at Tobruk). Having lost half its personnel, the Bn was rebuilt but then suffered further heavy losses seven months later in the El Mreir affair. Again, it lost nearly half its strength but, because the threat to Egypt was so great, it was kept in the line. Its numbers had recovered sufficiently for it to take part in the Second Alamein battle and the pursuit to Tunisia (where it had 171 more casualties). Moving to Italy, the Bn fought at Cassino in February-April 1944 (with 223 battle casualties, plus many more evacuated through exposure to the Italian winter). Its other major actions were Orsogna, the Liri Valley, Rimini, and the Senio and Savio Rivers. All of this is clearly described.
R/3 V/5. NZMODL. JFS/HEC/RH.

26 BATTALION
Frazer D Norton * War History Branch, 1952, xvi/554. Fp, 67 mono phots, 47 maps (42 printed in the text, 5 folding, bound in), Index. Apps: Roll of Honour, H&A, list of COs.
* The author served with the Bn during the closing stages of the Italian campaign. He covers, in good interesting detail, the campaign in Greece (where casualties were light), the evacuation to Egypt, the Crusader operation (with heavy losses at Sidi Rezegh on 30 November 1941), the disaster at El Mreir (21 July 1942), the October battle at El Alamein, and the advance towards Tunisia. In Italy, the Bn was much involved in the battle for Cassino and the approaches to the Monastery (April-May 1944), and it saw hard action at several other key features during the long painful advance up the peninsula. As with other books in the series, this one has numerous lists of officers (serving with the Bn at certain important times) inserted at the appropriate points in the narrative. R/3 V/5. NZMODL. HEC/RH.

27 (MACHINE-GUN) BATTALION
Robin Kay * War History Branch, 1958, xiv/543. Fp, 68 mono phots, 48 maps (42 printed in the text, 6 bound in), Index. Apps: Roll of Honour, H&A, list of COs, notes on the Vickers machine-gun.
* The Bn had the distinction (shared with 2 NZ Divsl Cavalry) of completing the longest period of overseas service of any 2 NZEF unit (including its time as part of the post-war occupying forces in Italy and Japan). It served in all the Mediterannean theatre campaigns and areas - Greece, Crete, Egypt, Lebanon, Syria, the Western Desert, Tunisia, and Italy. As was normal with a MG Bn, its component sub-units were assigned to give supporting fire to Infantry Bns and were therefore widely dispersed. One fortunate effect of this policy was that the Bn in toto was never involved in a single disaster (such as Crete or El Mreir). Its casualties were therefore light compared with those of some Infantry Bns. Owing to the lack of reinforcement drafts arriving in Italy, the Bn converted to the infantry role in February 1945 and was grouped with 22 Bn and 2 NZ Divsl Cav to form the 9th NZ Bde for the final assault north into the Po Valley. R/3 V/5. NZMODL. HEC/RH.
Note: the Bn later formed part of the British Commonwealth Occupation Force in Japan. It was redesignated 3rd New Zealand Regt. For information regarding the NZ Machine-gun Corps, of WWI vintage, vide the Index of Authors - J H Luxford.

28 (MAORI) BATTALION
J F Cody * War History Branch, 1956, xvi/515. Fp, 60 mono phots, 32 maps (25 printed in the text, 7 bound in), Index. Apps: Roll of Honour, H&A (with details of the VC awarded to 2nd Lieut Moana-Nui-a-Kiwa Ngarimu (for an action in Tunis, 4.6.1943), list of COs.
* Although not legally obliged to do so, many men of the Maori people attested for service during both world wars. The personnel of 28 Bn were almost exclusively Maori. This official history is written and produced to the same high standard as the other books in the series, and the fine narrative describes in detail all the actions in which the Bn was engaged throughout the Middle East and Italy. Two of

its hardest fights were Orsogna and Cassino, but it had already distinguished itself in Greece, in Crete (Maleme airfield and 42nd Street), in Egypt and Syria, at El Alamein, and in Tunisia (Medenine and Takrouna). R/5 V/5. NZMODL. HEC. Note: today's Maori are very proud of their forebears' fighting services in the two world wars, and copies of this book held by Maori families are often handed down to the younger generations. As a result, they appear only rarely on the second-hand market.

28 MAORI BATTALION
He Tohu Aroha tenei, na tetahi Hoia Pakeha o te Whanga tuarua o nga Hoia o Aotearoa
Ray D Munro * Published privately, Wellington, 1991. Soft card, blue, black, facsimile TS, 11.5 x 8.25, vii/185. 78 mono phots (poorly reproduced), 8 line drawings, 11 maps, Glossary, Bibliography, Indexes. Apps: Rolls of Honour, H&A.
* This book supplements rather than replaces the official history described in the preceding entry. Instead of the 'shot by shot' approach, Munro takes a reflective look, with the benefit of forty-six years' hindsight, at the role of the Bn in the overall framework of the war. Useful notes concerning casualties and senior appointments appear at the end of each chapter. It is unfortunate that the author did not arrange for his important research to be commercially printed and casebound. R/3 V/4. PC. HEC.

THE MAORI BATTALION
Te Mura o Te Ahi
The Story of the Maori Battalion
Lieut Col Wira Gardiner * Printed in Singapore, for Reed Books, Birkenhead, Auckland, 1992. Black, white, 9.5 x 6.5, -/208. 37 mono phots, no maps, Chapter Notes, no appendixes, Index.
* Like the preceding entry (Munro), this book does not form part of the War History Branch series but is listed here for the sake of continuity. The narrative deals mainly with the adventures of 28 Bn in WWII and therefore covers the same ground as that covered by Cody and by Munro. However, the author of this book, himself a Maori, works on a broad canvas and places his people's contribution to the war in the larger context of their heritage and culture. Chapter 3 commences with the outbreak of WWII, and the bulk of the narrative then deals with the Bn's embarkation and subsequent services in the Middle East and Italy. This is a concise and very readable account, and it brings to the reader's attention some important aspects of Maori military tradition not recorded elsewhere.
R/1 V/4. NZMODL. HEC.

3rd DIVISION, 2 NZEF

In 1944, when it was disbanded, every unit which had served operationally with 3 NZ Div in the SW Pacific theatre was ordered to compile and submit to a coordinating committee an account of its wartime experiences. The publications listed below (with two identified exceptions) are the result of that instruction. Each was compiled by serving members, then edited and produced anonymously by the Third Division Historical Committee in matching volumes (casebound, orange, black, 8.5 x 5.5). The publisher, acting on behalf of the Committee, was A W & A H Reed, of Wellington. Some volumes were printed by Coulls, Somerville, Wilkie Ltd, of Dunedin, others by Hutcheson, Bowman & Stewart, of Wellington. They were published at various dates between 1945 and 1948. The volumes were numbered between one and thirteen but, for reasons unknown, two were given the number '4'. There was no Volume 6. For convenience, they are listed here in the conventional order of Corps precedence as followed throughout this bibliography. The quality of paper is not of the best, but the standards of production are otherwise good, and the illustrations are excellent. To avoid repetition, only part of this information is shown in the individual entries.

Initially, 3 NZ Div consisted of three Brigades - 8th and 14th (six Infantry Battalions and supporting arms), and the 15th (two Infantry Battalions, plus other units). The latter was sent to New Caledonia for further training but, after seven months and owing to manpower shortages in New Zealand, it was broken up. In July 1943, men from this Brigade were assigned to the understrength 8th and 14th Brigades as they prepared for service on the Solomon Islands. Nothing was published in respect of 15th Brigade, hence the following list of book titles is relatively brief.

HEADQUARTERS
A Brief Outline of the Activities of Headquarters of the 3rd Division and the 8th and 14th Brigades During their Service in the Pacific
Published in 1945, one of the two books bearing the imprint 'Volume 4'. Fp, 115 mono phots, one cartoon, 5 maps (3 printed in the text, two on the end-papers), no Index, -/278. Apps: H&A, 3 separate nominal rolls (8th Bde HQ and Defence Platoon, 14th Bde HQ and Defence Platoon, and 3 Div Signals).
* In effect, two short books combined - one for 'Headquarters', the other for 'Communications'. They cover the formation of 3 Div and its subsequent services, giving a useful insight into the 'command and control' aspect of a Div which had its component units spread over a wide geographical area. Many individuals are named, and the 'Communications' nominal roll includes details of those killed or wounded while serving with Divsl Signals. R/4 V/4. NZMODL. HEC/RH.

BASE WALLAHS
Story of the Units of the Base Organisations, NZEF IP
Published in 1946, Volume 3 in the series. Fp, 70 mono phots, 5 mono plates (being reproductions of paintings), 3 maps (one printed in the text, two on the end-papers), no appendixes, no Index, -/256.
* An interesting book, with information covering a number of 'rear area' units which formed part of the Divsl organisation. Some medical units are mentioned, and there are brief references to 1st Bn New Zealand Scottish Regt and 1st Bn Ruahine Regt (the latter being a Territorial unit formed from 2nd Hawke's Bay Regt in 1941 and not recorded elsewhere). R/4 V/3. NZMODL. HEC/RH.
Note: the 'IP' in the sub-title signifies 'in the Pacific'.

THE TANKS
An Unofficial History of the Activities of the Third New Zealand Division Tank Squadron in the Pacific
Published in 1945, Volume 12 in the series. Fp, 88 mono phots, 6 maps (4 printed in the text, 2 on the end-papers), Index, -/227. Apps: H&A (Ordnance personnel only).

* This volume consists of three books in one, each having its own 'Contents' page and each dealing with a separate topic - the tanks, the medium machine-guns, and the Ordnance services. The overall result is scrappy, and the lack of appendixes is an obstacle to research, but there is plenty of useful material (including nominal rolls) scattered throughout the narrative. The Div's tanks saw limited combat on the Solomon Islands in 1943-1944. R/4 V/3. NLNZ. HEC/RH.

THE GUNNERS

An Intimate Record of Units of the 3rd New Zealand Divisional Artillery in the Pacific - From 1940 to 1945

Published in 1948, Volume 11 in the series. Fp, 85 mono phots, 10 drawings, 8 maps (6 printed in the text, 2 on the end-papers), no Index, -/290. Apps: Roll of Honour & H&A combined.

* A lively interesting account which incorporates poems, personal anecdotes, and many references to named individuals. The Divsl Artillery units recorded in the book are - 33 Heavy Regt, 17 and 38 Field Regts, 144 Independent Field Bty, 28 HAA Regt, 29 LAA Regt, 53 and 54 A/T Btys, and 4 Survey Troop. R/4 V/4. NZMODL. HEC/RH.

PACIFIC PIONEERS

The Story of the Engineers of the New Zealand Expeditionary Force in the Pacific

Published in 1945, Volume 2 in the series. Fp, 54 mono phots, 8 maps (6 printed in the text, 2 on the end-papers), no appendixes, no Index, -/168.

* The narrative tells a similar story to that described in the preceding entries, but makes specific references to the operations on Nissan and Mono Islands. Although there are no 'Roll of Honour' and 'Honours & Awards' appendixes, several such lists are inserted in the main text, plus an extensive nominal roll and a table of locations and movements. R/4 V/4. NZMODL. HEC/RH.

STEPPING STONES TO THE SOLOMONS

The Unofficial History of the 29th Battalion with the Second New Zealand Expeditionary Force in the Pacific

Published in 1947, this being the other book in the series numbered as 'Volume 4'. Fp, 43 mono phots, 13 line drawings and sketches, 8 maps (5 printed in the text, one bound in, two on the end-papers), no Index, -/121. Apps: Roll of Honour, H&A (with citations), songs and poems, biographical notes on some officers, nominal roll of all those who served with the Bn (16 pages, incl notes on where and when they served).

* The Bn was formed in September 1940 and served on Fiji, New Caledonia and the Solomon Islands. It saw little fighting and was fortunate to lose only six men killed. A pleasantly readable story, with good illustrations.
R/4 V/4. NZMODL. HEC/RH.

PACIFIC KIWIS

Being the Story of the Service in the Pacific of the 30th Battalion, Third Division, Second New Zealand Expeditionary Force

Published in 1947, Volume 9 in the series. Fp, 58 mono phots, 3 drawings, 6 maps (4 printed in the text, 2 on the end-papers), no Index, -/150. Apps: Roll of Honour, H&A, four unit nominal rolls (at 11.11.1940, 3.7.1942, 3.12.1942, and those who joined later), brief biographies of COs (with mono portraits).

* A book having twenty-two chapters which cover embarkation for Fiji in November 1940, the move to Guadalcanal to replace American forces there in August 1943, then the move to Vella Lavella (Solomon Islands) in October 1943 for mopping-up operations. The final move was to Green Island (Bougainville) in February 1944. The Bn saw little action on any of these islands, suffering only eight dead, but the story is well told, with many individuals named.
R/4 V/4. AWM. MCND'A/RH.

THE STORY OF THE 34th
The Unofficial History of a New Zealand Infantry Battalion with the Third Division in the Pacific
Published in 1947, Volume 7 in the series. Fp, 68 mono phots, 5 line drawings, 6 maps (4 printed in the text, 2 on the end-papers), no Index, -/159. Apps: Roll of Honour (KIA, WIA, DOW, and DOD), H&A (with citations for the Treasury Islands), unit nominal roll (with illustrated biographical notes on the COs).
* The story deals mainly with the period 1940-1944 and includes some poems written by members of the Bn. The 'appendix' material described above is not gathered at the end of the book but is inserted at various points within the main narrative. However, it is easy to find and to consult. Like all other books in this series, it is full of information which should interest both the general reader and the specialist researcher. R/4 V/4. NLNZ. FC/RH.

THE 35th BATTALION
A Record of Service of the 35th Battalion with the 3rd Division in the Pacific
Published in 1947, Volume 5 in the series. Fp, 38 mono phots, 10 line drawings, 7 maps (5 printed in the text, 2 on the end-papers), no Index, -/143. Apps: Roll of Honour (KIA, WIA, DOW, and DOD), H&A (with 14 citations), unit nominal roll (all ranks, with notes on their services and incl attached personnel).
* Conforming with the general pattern of the series, this book covers the work of 35th Bn from December 1941 to November 1944 - Fiji, New Caledonia, New Hebrides, Guadalcanal, and Vella Lavella. For much of the time its duties were as a defensive garrison force, but it did see limited combat on Vella Lavella and on Nissan Island (the Solomons). R/4 V/4. NZMODL. HEC/RH.

THE 36th BATTALION
A Record of Service of the 36th Battalion with the Third Division in the Pacific
Published in 1948, Volume 13 in the series. Fp, 54 mono phots (incl 20 of casualties), 11 line drawings and sketches, 5 maps (3 printed in the text, 2 on the end-papers), no Index. Apps: Roll of Honour (for the 36th Bn and for ex-members who died later while serving in Italy with other units), H&A (with portraits), unit nominal roll (with names of those who landed on Mono Island), list of original officers, brief biographical notes on COs and SNCOs, six songs and poems.
* The period covered is December 1941 (formation at Papakura Camp) through to 1944 (disbandment in New Zealand, when many of the Bn's personnel volunteered for service in Italy as drafts for other units). Like other books in this series, it has numerous passages devoted to sporting and off-duty activities.
R/4 V/4. NZMODL. HEC/RH.

THE 36th IN THE PACIFIC
The History of a New Zealand Battalion, 1941-1944
Privates G Watson and D H Leigh * Whitcombe & Tombs Ltd, Wellington, n.d. (1945). 'Soldier and Pacific map' motif, ochre, yellow/black, 9.5 x 7.25, -/98. Fp, 51 mono phots, one cld ill, 19 line drawings, one map, no Index. Apps: Roll of Honour, H&A (with citations for one MC and two MMs), brief biographies of COs and SNCOs, list of original key officers.
* This book is not part of the authorised 'unofficial' 3 NZ Div histories, but it does seem to have been the prototype for the item described in the preceding entry. It is listed here for the sake of continuity. The authors, who were backed by an editorial committee and the Bn's last CO, commence with formation in Papakura Camp, early training, and embarkation. They then describe the Bn's time in Fiji, Norfolk Island, New Caledonia, Guadalcanal, and the Treasury Islands, with good coverage of actions in which it took part. There are interesting descriptions also of rest periods, 'unit characters', and sporting activities. The text of the Foreword and of the first chapter is identical to that found in the preceding entry and, with only minor changes, the rest of the narrative is the same. The illustrations likewise are the same, but the 1948 version has more of them. The (1945) version has no Contents page. R/4 V/3. CPL/NZMODL. JFS/HEC/RH.

PACIFIC SAGA

The Personal Chronicle of the 37th Battalion and its Part in the Third Division's Campaign

Published in 1947, Volume 10 in the series. Fp, 71 mono phots, 6 maps (4 printed in the text, 2 on the end-papers), no Index, -/114. Apps: Roll of Honour (eleven men, with portraits), H&A (with citations and portraits), unit nominal roll.

* A book having eleven chapters which cover the Bn's embarkation for Fiji in January 1942, its return to New Zealand in August, re-embarkation for New Caledonia in December, and then the move to Vella Lavella (Solomon Islands) to mop up the Japanese remnants in August 1943. This slow and dangerous task is described in some detail. The Bn returned home for disbandment in June 1944. In addition to the full nominal roll noted above, the book also contains a list of officers, WOs and SNCOs at the time of formation (December 1941).
R/4 V/4. AWM. MCND'A/RH.

PACIFIC SERVICE

The Story of the New Zealand Army Service Corps Units with the 3rd Division in the Pacific

Published in 1948, Volume 8 in the series. Fp, 75 mono phots, 14 line drawings, 7 maps (5 printed in the text, 2 on the end-papers), no Index, -/140. Apps: organisational chart.

* The period covered is November 1940 to April 1945. The comprehensive narrative describes the vital if sometimes unglamorous work done by the Division's various NZASC units and sub-units (motor transport, butchery, bakery, etc) on Fiji, New Caledonia, and the Solomon Islands. R/4 V/4. NZMODL. HEC/RH.

SHOVEL, SWORD AND SCALPEL

A Record of Service of Medical Units of the Second New Zealand Expeditionary Force in the Pacific

Published in 1945, Volume 1 in the series. Fp, 65 mono phots, 8 maps (6 printed in the text, 2 on the end-papers), no appendixes, no Index, -/171.

* All of 3 NZ Div's medical units are listed here - 7th, 22nd and 24th Field Ambulances, 4th General Hospital, 6th Field Hygiene Section, 2nd Casualty Clearing Station, 2nd Convalescent Depot, and 4th Motor Ambulance Company. Individual medical personnel (mainly officers) are mentioned freely throughout. The lack of an Index or any of the expected appendixes in a book which deals with so many units, sub-units, and people, is a major flaw in an otherwise very good book.
R/4 V/3. NZMODL. HEC/RH.
Note: 3 NZ Div medical units receive some mention also in BASE WALLAHS (vide the opening page of this section).

OFFICERS BOOK: 14th BRIGADE, NEW ZEALAND EXPEDITIONARY FORCE IN THE PACIFIC

Anon (presumably compiled by the Bde Staff) * Clarke Matheson Printers, Auckland, n.d. (c.1948). Light card, blue-grey, black, 9.75 x 6.75, -/126. Fp, 202 mono phots, no maps, no appendixes, no Index.

* A strange but absorbing book. These is no clue to indicate who sponsored its publication. It does not conform with the 3 NZ Div Historical Committee format, but the Committee may have had some part in it. The book is listed here because 14th Bde was a major element in the Division. It opens with a brief summary of the Bde's services in the Pacific, but the bulk of the pages is devoted to personal biographies of each of the 204 officers who served within it. The entries are listed alphabetically, hence no Index was needed. Almost every entry is accompanied by a photographic portrait of the officer concerned. The book is, of course, a goldmine for genealogists. R/4 V/4. NZMODL. HEC.

ROYAL NEW ZEALAND INFANTRY REGIMENT

FIRST BATTALION, ROYAL NEW ZEALAND INFANTRY REGIMENT
25th Anniversary Commemorative Edition
Maj P J Fry * Singapore National Printers (Pte) Ltd, Singapore, 1983. Green, gold, Regtl crest, 9.5 x 7.0, -/203. Fp, more than 100 mono phots, 4 cld ills, one map (printed on the end-papers), no Index. Apps: Roll of Honour (KIA, DOW and DOD), H&A (3 rolls, Malaya 1957-1961, Indonesia Confrontation 1964-1966, and South Vietnam 1965-1972), list of all officers (with captioned group photographs, 1958-1983), idem WOs and SNCOs, unit nominal roll (with captioned group photographs, arranged by Pl, Coy, and Bn HQ).
* A magazine style of production which deals with 1st New Zealand Regt (1957-1959 and 1961-1963), 2nd New Zealand Regt (1959-1961), and then 1st RNZIR (1963 onwards, under the new designation). The book is an amalgam of information based upon reports written by each CO during the period 1957-1982, with some additional chapters on allied Regts, the Colours, Battle Honours in WWI and WWII, and so forth. The appendixes listed above are incorporated in the main narrative. This is not an easy book to consult, and the lack of an Index is a hindrance, but it is a good reflection of the NZ Army's activities during that period.
R/2 V/3. ADFA. MCND'A.

THE JOURNAL OF THE FIRST BATTALION, ROYAL NEW ZEALAND INFANTRY REGIMENT 1957-1989
Capt D G Close * Nep Printer, Singapore, 1989. Bottle green, gold, RNZIR crest, 12.0 x 8.5, -/218. Fp, more than 400 mono phots, 78 cld ills, 2 maps, no Index. Apps: Roll of Honour (KIA, accidental deaths, Malaya, Indonesian Confrontation, South Vietnam), list of officers (1957-1989), Platoon nominal rolls (at 1989).
* The story continues that described in the preceding entry. It is better edited, but, again, there is no Index, and the almost complete lack of captions to the photographic illustrations severely limits their interest. The Bn's services are pursued through to 1989 when it finally returned home from Singapore. A good general narrative account. R/1 V/3. PC. HEC.

KIA KAHA, A HISTORY OF THE HAURAKIS
Official History, 6th Battalion (Hauraki), RNZIR, 1898-1978
L H Barber * Published by the Regt, Tauranga, 1978. White, black, 7.5 x 5.25, -/63. Fp, 10 mono phots, 2 cld ills, no maps, no Index. Apps: Roll of Honour (WWI only), list of former COs, chronology of the Regt's evolution, notes on the Colours, Battle Honours, trophies.
* The Haurakis were formed in 1898 by the amalgamation of several small local Volunteer units, e.g. Ohinemuri Rifles, Te Aroha Rifles Volunteers, Hauraki Rifle Volunteers, Coromandel Volunteers, etc. Men from the unit volunteered for service in the Anglo-Boer War (1899-1902), and the first casualty of that conflict was RSM George Bradford, formerly a Colour Sergeant with the Coldstream Guards.
In WWI, as part of the Auckland Regt, the unit served in Suez, on Gallipoli (Cape Helles and Suvla) before moving to the Western Front. The narrative next gives good coverage of 'the years of discouragement' (1929-1938) and of services in WWII and Korea. The narrative lacks depth and detail, but in general terms this is a nicely produced booklet which offers a general guide to events.
R/3 V/3. ATL. JS/HEC.
Note: the title - KIA KAHA - can be loosely translated from the Maori tongue as 'Be brave', 'Be valiant', or 'Be a worthy warrior'.

SPECIAL FORCES

LONG RANGE DESERT GROUP, 1940-1941
R L Kay * War History Branch, 1949. Illustrated soft card, 'LRDG' motif, buff, black, 10.5 x 8.5, -/32. 33 mono phots, 3 maps, no Index. Apps: biographical notes (with H&A included, as appropriate).
* A booklet which describes the work of New Zealanders who served with the LRDG in North Africa. Initially they kept watch on the Italian garrisons on the Gialo-Kufra axis, then served in the Libyan Desert as 'R', 'T', and 'W' Patrols. The author gives a brief account of the various raids conducted in the Fezzan area - 1000 miles from Cairo and 350 miles from the nearest (Free French) supporting unit. He gives just enough detail to whet the appetite for more information on the LRDG in general and the New Zealand contribution in particular. R/4 V/3. PC. HEC.
Note: subsequently the LRDG operated in the Aegean. That period is covered in LONG RANGE DESERT GROUP IN THE MEDITERRANEAN, another booklet of 32 pages, also published by the War History Branch, and likewise written by R L Kay. For a more comprehensive account of the LRDG, vide Maj Gen D L Lloyd-Owen in the Index of Authors.

DARE TO WIN
The Story of the New Zealand Special Air Service
W D Baker * Lothian Publishing Co, Melbourne, Australia, 1987. Dark brown, gold, 11.5 x 8.5, vii/107. 111 mono phots, 16 cld plates, 3 maps, no appendixes, no Index.
* It was the author's stated intention to cover the entire evolution and active services of the NZSAS from its earliest roots (as the NZ Patrols of the LRDG in the Western Desert and the Aegean in WWII) through to 1986. The result is a very generalised account, the best feature being the illustrations.
R/1 V/2. NLNZ/SLV. HEC/PS.

MEDICAL

THE FIRST FIFTY YEARS
A Commentary on the Development of the Royal New Zealand Army Medical Corps From its Inception
Anon * Medical Section, Army HQ, Wellington, 1958. Soft card, maroon, white, Corps crest, dimensions not recorded, vi/24. 20 mono phots, 2 line drawings, no maps, no appendixes, no Index.
* A very limited summary of the evolution of New Zealand's military medical services up to 1958. Presumably intended for 'public relations' purposes, it has limited value as a research source. R/3 V/1. ATL. JS.

RNZAMC - 75 YEARS OF HISTORY, 1908-1983
Capt K R Treanor * Government Printing Office, Christchurch, 1983. Soft card, pink, Corps crest, 8.25 x 5.75, -/96. 30 mono phots, 4 maps, Bibliography, Index. Apps: H&A (for the entire period, all campaigns, incl South Africa, 1899-1902).
* Although printed by the Govt Printer, this is only a facsimile reproduction of original typescript. The illustrations are photo-copies, of poor quality. The style and format suggest a lack of official commitment to what is otherwise a first-class source of reference. Of special interest are the author's coverage of the medical aspects of four deployments which are not much recorded elsewhere - 'J' Force (the post-war occupation force in Japan), the Malay Peninsula, Korea, and South Vietnam. The appendix is, of course, a prime source for medal collectors.
R/3 V/4. NZMODL. HEC.

THE NEW ZEALAND MEDICAL SERVICES IN THE GREAT WAR, 1914-1919
Based on Official Documents
Lieut Col A D Carbery CBE * Whitcombe & Tombs Ltd, Auckland, 1924. Maroon, black, 9.5 x 6.75, xix/567. Fp, 14 mono phots, 2 maps (loose in rear pocket), Bibliography, Index. Apps: nominal roll of Colonial Medical Officers (1845-1860), Roll of Honour (KIA and WIA, WWI only), H&A (WWI only), specifications for the fitment of hospital ships, etc (20 appendix sections and sub-sections in total).
* A fine example of how the job ought to be done. Apart from being a detailed analysis of New Zealand's medical services on Gallipoli and the Western Front, it is also a mirror of the progress of the Great War in general and its attendant medical and surgical problems and techniques. Of interest to both the general and the specialist reader. The appendixes alone make the book a desirable possession.
R/4 V/5. NYPL. HEC.

MEDICAL UNITS OF 2 NZEF IN THE MIDDLE EAST AND ITALY
J B McKinney * War History Branch, 1952. Red, gold, 8.75 x 5.75, xv/462. Fp, 62 mono phots, 14 maps (12 printed in the text, 2 bound in), 2 Indexes (People and Places, Medical Units). Apps: Roll of Honour, H&A, list of COs and Matrons.
* Another fine official history. It covers the raising of the various (2 NZEF) medical units in 1939-1940 and all their subsequent services in the Mediterranean region. Very readable, with references to the hospital ship MAUNGANUI and with plenty to interest the general reader. R/3 V/4. NZMODL. HEC/RH.

NEW ZEALAND MEDICAL SERVICES IN THE MIDDLE EAST AND ITALY
T Duncan M Stout * War History Branch, 1956. Red, gold, 9.75 x 6.0, xv/721. Fp, 57 mono phots, 37 maps (32 printed in the text, 5 bound in), Glossary, no Index. Apps: various, all being tabular and statistical summaries concerning casualties, sickness rates, incidence of disease, etc.
* By contrast with the preceding entry, this is a technical account. It deals less with the services of individual medical units and much more with the medical and surgical problems which they encountered and overcame. As the title might suggest, the contents are not restricted to the military medical units but cover all branches of NZ medical services in that theatre of war. R/3 V/4. RMAS. RP.

MEDICAL SERVICES IN NEW ZEALAND AND THE PACIFIC
In Royal New Zealand Navy, Royal New Zealand Air Force, and with Prisoners of War
T Duncan M Stout * War History Branch, 1958. Red, gold, 9.75 x 6.75, xiv/450. Fp, 61 mono phots, 10 maps (5 printed in the text, 5 bound in), Glossary, no appendixes, two Indexes (Names, and General).
* Despite the limitations implied by its title, this book in fact covers the full spectrum of NZ medical work (army, navy, aviation) in all theatres of war in WWII - the SW Pacific, the Middle East and Italy, and Germany (post-war). The book has no formal appendixes, but some references to honours and awards appear at various points in the narrative. There is some over-lapping of information as found in the other official history by the same author (vide preceding page), but the two volumes compliment each other well (particularly with regard to the SW Pacific). The final section has a few pages dedicated to the hospital ships ORANJE and MAUNGANUI. R/3 V/5. NZMODL. HEC.

KIA KAHA
Life at 3 New Zealand General Hospital, 1940-1946
E M Somers-Cocks * Caxton Press, Christchurch, 1958. Grey green red, 8.5 x 5.5, -/283. Fp, 113 mono phots, no maps, no Index. Apps: Roll of Honour, H&A, Diary of Events (29.10.1943 and 9.1.1946).
* The narrative is arranged in five parts, each covering a distinct region at a different period in time - 1940-1941 (at home and at sea), 1941-1942 (Egypt), 1942-1943 (Syria), 1943 (Tripolitania), and 1943-1946 (Bari, Italy). A well illustrated book, readable and full of interest. R/4 V/4. NLNZ. HEC.
Note: the main title - KIA KAHA - can be freely translated from the Maori tongue as signifying 'Be brave', or 'Be valiant', or 'Be a worthy warrior'. The words have been adopted by several different units over the years, either as a motto or as a rallying cry.

NEW ZEALAND MILITARY NURSING
A History of the RNZNC, Boer War to Present Day
Sherayl Kendall and David Corbett * Alpine North Print Ltd, Auckland, 1990. Illustrated plasticated boards, grey, red/black, 'Beret and badge' motif on front board and six cap badges on rear, 11.75 x 8.5, viii/240. Fp, 190 mono phots, no maps, Glossary, Bibliography, Index. Apps: Roll of Honour, H&A, list of former officers, list of ORs, notes on the Florence Nightingale Medal, idem uniforms, etc.
* Published to mark the 75th Anniversary of the founding of the NZ Army Nursing Service, this book is a comprehensive record of devoted service. Full recognition by senior command of the need for female nurses was not achieved until 1915 (when the service was established). Male chauvinism then blocked the granting of Commissions to nursing personnel for a further forty years. The New Zealand Army Nursing Service (NZANS) was retitled in 1953 when it became The Royal New Zealand Nursing Corps (RNZNC). This is a useful and interesting book. Some of the illustrations are of indifferent quality, but the well written narrative is supported by excellent appendixes. R/1 V/4. NZMODL. HEC.
Note: highly commended as an additional source for the early years is NURSING IN NEW ZEALAND - HISTORY AND REMINISCENCES, by Hester Maclean RRC (Tolan Printing Co, Wellington, 1932). A substantial work (-/227 pages), it deals inter alia with military nursing prior to, during, and just after WWI. The writer was Matron-in-Chief of the NZANS.

THE NEW ZEALAND DENTAL SERVICES (NEW ZEALAND DENTAL CORPS)
T V Anson * War History Branch, 1960. Green, gold, 9.75 x 6.75, xi/422. 30 mono phots, 7 maps, Index. Apps: H&A.
* An official history which covers the services of the military dental service during WWII. Of prime interest to the dental care specialist. R/3 V/4. SLV. PS.

CLOUD OVER MARQUETTE

John Meredith Smith * Caxton Press, Christchurch, 1990. Maroon, gold, 8.5 x 6.25, -/223. 51 mono phots, 3 cld ills (incl nurses' memorials in Christchurch), 3 maps, Glossary, Bibliography, Index. Apps: Roll of Honour, H&A, list of personnel.

* An attractively presented book which tells the story of No 1 New Zealand Stationary Hospital and its services in Salonika and on the Western Front (at Wisques), but with the main emphasis on the Marquette episode. On 19 October 1915, this 7000 ton steamer departed Egypt for Salonika with a mixed passenger list of 610 military personnel and 541 transport animals. Most of the soldiers were members of the Royal Field Artillery, being the Ammunition Column of the 29th Division. The rest were New Zealand medical staff, of whom thirty-six were nurses. On 23 October, south of Salonika harbour, the ship was torpedoed by U-35. The total loss of life was 128, of whom eleven were nurses. R/1 V/5. PC. HEC.

OTHER ARMS AND CORPS

RMT

4th and 6th Reserve Mechanical Transport Companies

J H Henderson * War History Branch, 1954. Red, gold, 8.75 x 5.75, xv/378. Fp, 67 mono phots, 18 maps (12 printed in the text, 6 bound in), Index. Apps: Roll of Honour, H&A, list of COs, notes on the first New Zealander POW to escape from Germany.

* A good narrative account which traces the operations of the RMT Coys through all the major events in the Middle East and in Italy. Many officers and men are mentioned, usually with biographical notes. R/4 V/5. NZMODL. HEC/RH.

SUPPLY COMPANY

P W Bates * War History Branch, 1955. Red, gold, 8.75 x 5.75, xv/371. Fp, 66 mono phots, 14 maps (8 printed in the text, 6 bound in), Index. Apps: Roll of Honour, H&A, list of COs.

* This was one of 2 NZEF's logistical units in the Mediterranean theatre. Despite its apparently unglamorous role, it is revealed in this book to have seen its fair share of incident and action. R/4 V/5. NZMODL. HEC.

PETROL COMPANY

A L Kidson * War History Branch, 1961. Red, gold, 8.75 x 5.75, xv/363. Fp, 68 mono phots, 18 maps (11 printed in the text, 7 bound in), Index. Apps: Roll of Honour, H&A, list of COs.

* This is another extensive account of the logistical effort which kept 2 NZEF in action in the Middle East and Italy. R/4 V/5. NZMODL. HEC.

JOURNEY TOWARDS CHRISTMAS

S P Llewellyn * War History Branch, 1949. Red, gold, 8.75 x 5.75, xix/457/4 (the latter being the appendixes and not numbered). Fp, 66 mono phots, 9 maps (bound in), Index. Apps: Roll of Honour, H&A, list of COs.

* The story is that of 1st Ammunition Company, 2 NZEF, and the title derives from the hope of every soldier - to be 'home by Christmas'. The Company was organised into specialist sections. They worked in almost every area of Europe and the Middle East (including the United Kingdom during the Battle of Britain).
R/4 V/4. NLNZ. HEC/RH.

Note: the four books noted above all form part of the excellent 2 NZEF series published by authority of the New Zealand Government. In common with other volumes described elsewhere in this bibliography, they each carry a sub-title which commences 'Official History of ...' and they were produced to a very high standard. Even for the non-specialist reader, they provide a vivid 'feel' for the experiences of New Zealand's soldiers in WWII.

DESERT WHEELS

S H Betts MBE * Publication details not shown, 1987. Illustrated soft card, white, black, -/91. Fp, 33 mono phots, 3 maps, no Index. Apps: unit nominal roll.

* A slim volume, of no known provenance, which attempts to convey to the reader the enormous effort extended by the Light Aid Detachments (later renamed Infantry Brigade Workshops) during their time in North Africa. The story relates mainly to 17 LAD, 5th (NZ) Inf Bde, during the period 15.1.1942 to 1.9.1943. The text is facsimile typescript of indifferent quality, but the illustrations are reproduced to a high standard. Readable, with interesting details not found in the official campaign histories. R/5 V/4. NLNZ. HEC.

A HISTORY OF THE ROYAL NEW ZEALAND ARMY ORDNANCE CORPS
J S Bolton * Wright & Carmen, Wellington, 1992. Soft card, dark blue, burnt orange (the Corps colours), white, Corps crest, 9.5 x 6.25, -/267. Fp, 86 mono phots, 16 line drawings, no maps, Glossary, Bibliography, no Index. Apps: list of RNZAOC personnel (officers, WOs and SNCOs).
* A good well researched Corps history. The text covers the period 1842 to 1992 in uniform detail and with helpful references to the traditions and practices inherited from the British Army. The pictures have reproduced well and the book is generally a pleasure to handle. R/1 V/3. NZMODL. HEC.

CRAFTSMEN IN UNIFORM
The Corps of Royal New Zealand Electrical & Mechanical Engineers - An Account
Peter Cape * MGV Printers, Wellington, for the Corps, 1976. Blue, gold, Corps crest, 8.25 x 6.0, xi/198. Fp, 55 mono phots, one cld ill, 4 maps (all folding, bound in), list of sources, no Index. Apps: Roll of Honour (WWII, for NZOC and NZEME, with H&As included), H&A (1901-1972, for both Corps, incl the VC to Farrier Major W J Hardham), list of Directors (1946-1972), idem Colonels Commandant.
* The NZEME was formed in the Middle East in 1942 by hiving off men having certain trades and skills from the NZ Ordnance Corps. The author covers the Ordnance story from the 1880s through to 1942, then the NZEME's services in the Western Desert, Tunisia, Italy, and the Pacific. He concludes with post-war events such as the further transfer of personnel and responsibilities from the Ordnance Corps in 1946. Technical subjects are discussed in the narrative, but in a way which the layman can understand. R/2 V/4. ANL. MCND'A.

MEN OF FAITH AND COURAGE
The Official History of the New Zealand Army Chaplains
J Bryant Haigh * The World Publishers Ltd, Auckland, 1983. Red, gold, 8.75 x 5.75, -/216. 134 mono phots, 3 line drawings, no maps, Bibliography, Index. Apps: eight in total, incl notes on Dress, badges, medal rolls (the VD and ED), list of former Chaplains Commandant.
* A book which covers the entire 130 years of New Zealand's military history from the time of the Maori (Land) Wars through to the conflict in South Vietnam. Many NZ chaplains have been killed or wounded in action, and many have been granted decorations for their gallantry under fire during the period under review. The author has brought together an impressive selection of anecdotes and reports of their exploits, with plenty of action and human interest. R/2 V/4. NZMODL. HEC.

NEW ZEALAND CHAPLAINS IN THE SECOND WORLD WAR
M L Underhill, S D Waters, J M S Ross and N E Winhall * War History Branch, 1950. Red, gold, 8.75 x 5.75, xvii/188. Fp, 37 mono phots, 3 maps (bound in), Index. Apps: Roll of Honour, H&A.
* As the title and provenance suggest, this is the official history of the work done by NZ chaplains (Army, Navy and Air Force) in all theatres of war during WWII. Interesting and informative. R/2 V/4. NZMODL. HEC.

THE WAAC STORY
The Story of the New Zealand Women's Army Corps
Iris Latham * Published privately by the authoress, Wellington, 1986. Green and brown, white, 8.25 x 5.75, vii/214. 52 mono phots, 2 cartoons, no maps, no Index. Apps: Roll of Honour.
* A pleasing book, full of anecdotes and personal reminiscences. The photographs cover a wide range of subject matter, from formal parades to coal shovelling duties. The authoress acknowledges that the 'Roll of Honour' is incomplete, but this is nevertheless a useful source for social researchers and for a study of the impact of WWII on New Zealand women. R/2 V/3. ATL. JS.

POLICE

THE HISTORY OF POLICING IN NEW ZEALAND
Policing the Colonial Frontier
Richard S Hill * The Government Printer, Wellington, 1986. Produced in two parts, each with separate bindings, dark blue, gold, 9.5 x 6.5.
Part I : xxi/409. 21 mono phots, no maps, no appendixes, no Index.
Part II : folios numbered -/414 to 1142. 54 mono phots, 16 maps, no appendixes, Bibliography and Sources (138 pages), Index (42 pages, for both Parts).
* As the above details might suggest, this is the first volume (albeit arranged in two parts) of a monumental and deeply researched examination of the origins and development of New Zealand's national police force. The academic tone is emphasised by a further sub-title - THE THEORY AND PRACTICE OF COERCIVE SOCIAL AND RACIAL CONTROL IN NEW ZEALAND. Despite this daunting terminology, the narrative, which commences with events in 1867, is well presented and readable. This pair of books, together with their sister volume (vide following entry), is the definitive work on the subject. R/2 V/5. PPL. HEC.

THE HISTORY OF POLICING IN NEW ZEALAND
The Colonial Frontier Tamed
Richard S Hill * The Government Printer, Wellington, 1989. Effectively Volume II, although not marked as such, and bound in different colours (light brown, silver). The same format as Volume I (9.5 x 6.5), xiv/386. 38 mono phots, one line drawing, one map, Bibliography and Sources, no other appendixes, Index (very extensive).
* This book takes up the story from the period when the Maori were moving from a state of turbulence to one of relative quiescence and integration with the people whom they called the Pakeha - the European settlers. The earlier need for Armed Constabularies, which were para-military units committed mainly to the subjugation of the Maori tribes, gave way to the requirement for a modern police force trained to prevent and detect crime per se. While describing the broader perspectives, the author includes interesting details regarding specific events such as strikes, riots, murders and public scandals. The narrative is arranged in three main elements - The Armed Constabularies (1867-1877, a period of semi-war), The Provincial Forces (1868-1877, when separate police forces started to develop), and The Constabulary Force (1877-1886, a period which marked the demise of the 'soldier-policeman'). Like the first volume, this book is deeply researched and heavily supported with source references. The work was compiled under the authority of the Historical Branch, Dept of Internal Affairs. R/2 V/5. PPL. HEC.
Note: reference should be made also to IN THE LINE OF DUTY - 100 YEARS OF THE NEW ZEALAND POLICE, by M Hill (Endeavour, Auckland, 1986), and SOLDIERING IN NEW ZEALAND - BEING THE REMINISCENCES OF A VETERAN, MAJOR F J W GASCOIGNE, by Capt G A Preece (T J S Guildford Ltd, London, 1916). The latter is useful for a study of the final stages of the Maori (Land) Wars.

SHARING THE CHALLENGE
A Social and Pictorial History of the Christchurch Police District
Barry Thomson and Robert Neilson * Printed by Kyodo-Shing Loong, Singapore, for Caxton Press, Christchurch, 1989, Dark blue, gold, Force crest, 12.0 x 8.5, -/360. 555 mono phots, 16 cld ills, 74 line drawings, 5 maps, Bibliography, Index. Apps: Roll of Honour, H&A.
* Probably the best of the Provincial Police histories - an exemplary work. It is full of interest, even for the general reader, with plenty of personnel lists inserted in the text and comments on equipment, buildings and vehicles. A section is devoted to the Mount Erebus DC10 disaster. A pleasure to handle. R/1 V/5. PPL. HEC.

POLICING IN THE RIVER DISTRICT, 1886–1986
The First Hundred Years of the Wanganui Police
Charles E Spicer * Wanganui Newspapers Ltd, Wanganui, 1988. Dark blue, gold, 9.75 x 7.0, –/320. 103 mono phots, 14 line drawings, 6 maps, Bibliography, no Index. Apps: Roll of Honour, H&A, notes on Wanganui Policewomen, notes on police dogs.
* An entertaining and informative account of local policing, with many thumbnail descriptions of individual members of the force. The illustrations are poor, but the narrative is a helpful source for genealogists. R/1 V/4. PPL. HEC.
Note: published as a limited edition of 1000 numbered copies.

POLICING IN THE MOUNTAIN SHADOW
A History of the Taranaki Police
Margaret Carr * TNL Print, New Plymouth, 1989. Dark blue, gold, 10.0 x 7.5, x/163. Fp, 84 mono phots, 3 line drawings, one map, Bibliography, no Index. Apps: list of former District Commanders, roll of Station Staffs.
* This is one of a series of books describing the history of policing in various Districts. It covers the period 1842 to 1989 and contains a wealth of local anecdotes and legends. The utility of the book is spoiled by the lack of an Index. R/1 V/3. NZPCL. HEC.

CAPITAL COPPERS
An Illustrated Review of the Wellington Police District, 1840–1986
R T Hermans * Colonial Associates, Whitcoulls, Wellington, 1985. Illustrated soft card, dark/light blue, yellow/white, 10.0 x 8.0, –/56. 93 mono phots, 20 line drawings, no maps, no appendixes, no Index.
* A very brief account of the Wellington Police which covers, superficially, a wide range of topics. The photographs are interesting, and some details of dress and equipment are well illustrated. R/1 V/2. PPL. HEC.

NOTES

Key to Indexes of Regiments and Corps

Refer to page 783 for details of additional indexes.

Part I – GENERAL REFERENCE SOURCES and Multi-national Units

Part 2 – THE SOUTHERN & CENTRAL AMERICAS

Prominent Loyalist Commanders

Part 4 – CANADA, with NEWFOUNDLAND

General Reference Sources

Canadians abroad

British Regiments with a Canadian connection

French (Imperial) Regiments

Arms, Formations, and Corps

Named Mounted & Mechanised Units

Numbered Mounted & Mechanised Units

Artillery Units

Named Infantry Units

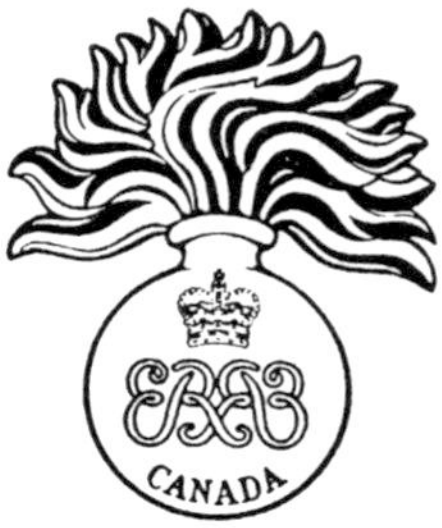
CANADA

Battalions of the Canadian Expeditionary Force (WWI)

Special & Irregular Forces

Police Forces

Part 5 - EUROPE

Part 6 – THE MIDDLE EAST

Part 7 – BRITISH COLONIAL AFRICA, with WEST AFRICA

Part 8 - EAST AFRICA, with ANGLO-EGYPTIAN SUDAN

KING'S AFRICAN RIFLES

Part 9 – CENTRAL SOUTHERN AFRICA

PRO LEGE
PRO REGE
PRO PATRIA
BRITISH
POLICE
- SOUTH AFRICA -

Part 10 - SOUTH AFRICA

General Reference Sources

South Africans abroad

Non-European Units

Arms, Formations, and Corps

Artillery

Named Infantry Units

Named Mounted & Mechanised Units

Police Forces

(*) Translated from Afrikaans, 'Koevoet' signifies crowbar, lever, or jemmy.

Units of the Anglo-Boer War, 1899-1902

Part 11 – INDIA, with NEPAL

General Reference Sources

British Regiments with an Indian Connection

Arms, Formations, and Corps

Named Mounted Units

Cavalry Units under their final pre-Partition designations

Numbered Mounted Units (under the successive systems of designation)

Artillery Units

Engineers, Sappers & Miners, and Pioneers

Named Infantry Units

Numbered Infantry Units (under the successive systems of designation)

Infantry Units under their final pre-Partition designations

India, with Nepal

The Princely States

Volunteer and Auxiliary Forces

Gurkha Regiments, Corps, Formations, and Connections

Note:

Additional and general background information regarding Gurkha units and military traditions will be found on pages 493, 494, 495, and 512.

Part 12 – THE FAR EAST, and WESTERN PACIFIC

Note:

For information regarding British Army, Indian Army, Canadian, Australian, and New Zealand units which have served at various times in the Far East and the Western Pacific, refer to the appropriate national sections of the Indexes.

Part 13 - AUSTRALIA

General Reference Sources

Australians abroad

Arms, Formations, and Corps

Named Mounted & Mechanised Units

Numbered Mounted & Mechanised Units

Artillery (Militia)

Artillery (WWI and WWII)

Engineers

Named Infantry Units

Numbered Infantry Units (WWI and WWII combined)
with unit designations as shown in their published histories

Medical Units

Special & Irregular Forces

Police Forces

Part 14 - NEW ZEALAND

General Reference Sources

New Zealanders abroad

Arms, Formations, and Corps

Divisions

Brigades

Named Mounted & Mechanised Units

Artillery Units

Named Infantry Units

Numbered Infantry Units (2 NZEF)

Special & Irregular Forces

Police Forces

Key to Indexes of Subjects

Index of British Army and Royal Marines Units

Regiments of the Line

Index of Operational Codenames

Index of Illustrators and Map Draughtsmen

Index of Ships Mentioned

Index of Scottish Regiments

Index of Irish Regiments

Index of Ethnic Minority Soldiers

Note:

Men of numerous racial and cultural groups (often referred to as 'classes') served in the Indian Army, its forebears, and related Corps. Four such are noted in the above list, but detailed information will be found in many of the entries on pages 371 and 372, and thereafter.

Referring to the forces of West Africa and East Africa (the RWAFF and the KAR in particular), no published research has been traced with regard to the wide diversity of racial groups, tribes, and sub-tribes, from which their personnel were recruited.

Index of Special & Irregular Forces

Index of Women's Units and Services

Index of Medical Units and Services

Index of Police Forces

Pipes and Pipers

Note:

The rank of each individual, as shown here, is that which he was holding at the time of his highest award.